Sweet & Maxwell's Statutes Series

Public Law and Human Rights 2002–2003

AUSTRALIA
Law Book Co.
Sydney

CANADA and USA
Carswell
Toronto

HONG KONG
Sweet & Maxwell Asia

NEW ZEALAND
Brookers
Auckland

SINGAPORE and MALAYSIA
Sweet & Maxwell Asia
Singapore and Kuala Lumpur

Sweet & Maxwell's Statutes Series

Public Law and Human Rights 2002–2003

Edited by

Claire de Than, B.A. (Hons), LL.M.

Senior Lecturer in Law, City University

and

Edwin Shorts, M.A.

Barrister-at-Law

First Edition

London
Sweet & Maxwell
2002

*Published in 2002 by Sweet & Maxwell Limited of
100 Avenue Road, Swiss Cottage
London NW3 3PF
www.sweetandmaxwell.co.uk
Typeset by Wyvern 21 Ltd
Bristol
Printed and bound in Great Britain by
Ashford Colour Press, Gosport, Hants.*

No natural forests were destroyed to make this product;
only farmed timber was used and replanted

**A CIP Catalogue record for this book is available from the
British Library**

ISBN 0421 786 809

PUBLISHERS' NOTE

Please note due to the publishers' wish to consolidate the legislation all footnotes have been removed from the text. Square brackets signifying a change to the text have been left in for your convenience.

CONTENTS

OTHER MATERIALS

Magna Carta 1297

(25 Edw. 1)

THE GREAT CHARTER OF THE LIBERTIES OF ENGLAND, AND OF THE LIBERTIES OF THE FOREST; CONFIRMED BY KING EDWARD, IN THE TWENTY-FIFTH YEAR OF HIS REIGN. EDWARD by the Grace of God King of England, Lord of Ireland, and Duke of Guyan, [to all Archbishops, Bishops, etc.] We have seen the Great Charter of the Lord Henry sometimes King of England, our Father, of the Liberties of England in these words:

HENRY by the Grace of God King of England, Lord of Ireland, Duke of Normandy and Guyan, and Earl of Anjou, to all Archbishops, Bishops, Abbots, Priors, Earls, Barons, Sheriffs, Provosts, Officers, and to all Bailiffs, and other our faithful Subjects, which shall see this present Charter, Greeting: Know Ye, that We, unto the honour of Almighty God, and for the salvation of the souls of our Progenitors and Successors [Kings of England,] to the advancement of Holy Church and amendment of our Realm, of our meer and free will, have given and granted to all Archbishops, Bishops, Abbots, Priors, Earls, Barons, and to all [Freemen] of this our Realm, these Liberties following, to be kept in our Kingdom of England for ever.

1–001

Confirmation of Liberties

I. FIRST, We have granted to God, and by this our present Charter have confirmed, for Us and our Heirs for ever, that the Church of England shall be free, and shall have all her whole Rights and Liberties inviolable. We have granted also, and given to all the Freemen of our Realm, for Us and our Heirs for ever, these Liberties under-written, to have and to hold to them and their Heirs, of Us and our Heirs for ever.

1–002

. . . . . .

Imprisonment, etc. contrary to Law. Administration of Justice

XXIX. NO Freeman shall be taken or imprisoned, or be disseised of his Freehold, or Liberties, or free Customs, or be outlawed, or exiled, or any other wise destroyed; nor will We not pass upon him, nor [condemn him][1] but by lawful judgment of his Peers, or by the Law of the Land. We will sell to no man, we will not deny or defer to any man either Justice or Right.

1–003

[1] deal with him

Treason Act 1351

(1351 c. 2)

In the Parliament holden in the Feast of Saint Hilary; In the Twenty-fifth Year of the Reign of K. EDWARD the Third.

2–001

. . . . . .

Declaration what Offences shall be adjudged Treason

2–002   **II.** Statute the Fifth.

ITEM, Whereas divers Opinions have been before this Time in what Case Treason shall be said, and in what not; the King, at the Request of the Lords and of the Commons, hath made a Declaration in the Manner as hereafter followeth, that is to say; When a Man doth Compassing the Death of the King, Queen, or their eldest Son; violating the Queen, or the King's eldest Daughter unmarried, or his eldest Son's Wife; levying War; adhering to the King's Enemies; compass or imagine the Death of our Lord the King, or of our Lady his Queen or of their eldest Son and Heir; or if a Man do violate the King's Companion, or the King's eldest Daughter unmarried, or the Wife[1] the King's eldest Son and Heir; or if a Man do levy War against our Lord the King in his Realm, or be adherent to the King's Enemies in his Realm, giving to them Aid and Comfort in the Realm, or else-where, and thereof be probably attainted of open Deed by the People of their Condition: and if a Man slea the Chancellor, Treasurer, or killing the Chancellor, Treasurer, or Judges in Execution of their Duty, the King's Justices of the one Bench or the other, Justices in Eyre, or Justices of Assise, and all other Justices assigned to hear and determine, being in their Places, doing their Offices: And it is to be understood, that in the Cases above rehearsed, that ought to be judged Treason which extends to our Lord the King, and his Royal Majesty.

[1] Read as if "of" inserted here.

Justices of the Peace Act 1361

(1361 c. 1)

3–001   *A STATUTE made in the Parliament holden at Westminster; In the Thirty-fourth Year. These be the Things which our Lord the King, the Prelates, Lords, and the Commons have ordained in this present Parliament, holden at Westminster, the Sunday next before the Feast of the Conversion of St. Paul, to be holden and published openly through the Realm*

3–002   **I.** Who shall be Justices of the Peace. First, that in every County of England shall be assigned for the keeping of the Peace, one Lord, and with him three or four of the most worthy in the County, with some learned in the Law, and they shall have Power to restrain Their Jurisdiction over Offenders; Rioters; Barrators; the Offenders, Rioters, and all other Barators, and to pursue, arrest, take, and chastise them according their Trespass or Offence; and to cause them to be imprisoned and duly punished according to the Law and Customs of the Realm, and according to that which to them shall seem best to do by their Discretions and good Advisement; They may take Surety for good Behaviour. and to take and arrest all those that they may find by Indictment, or by Suspicion, and to put them in Prison; and to take of all them that be [not] of good Fame, where they shall be found, sufficient Surety and Mainprise of their good Behaviour towards the King and his People, and the other duly to punish; to the Intent that the People be not by such Rioters or Rebels troubled nor endamaged, nor the

Peace blemished, nor Merchants nor other passing by the Highways of the Realm disturbed, nor put in the Peril which may happen of such Offenders.

Habeas Corpus Act 1679

(1679 c. 2)

An Act for the better secureing the Liberty of the Subject and for Prevention of Imprisonments beyond the Seas. Recital that Delays had been used by Sheriffs in making Returns of Writs of Habeas Corpus, etc.   **4–001**

WHEREAS great Delayes have beene used by Sheriffes Goalers and other Officers to whose Custody any of the Kings Subjects have beene committed for criminall or supposed criminall Matters in makeing Returnes of Writts of Habeas Corpus to them directed by standing out an Alias and Pluries Habeas Corpus and sometimes more and by other shifts to avoid their yeilding Obedience to such Writts contrary to their Duty and the knowne Lawes of the Land whereby many of the Kings Subjects have beene and hereafter may be long detained in Prison in such Cases where by Law they are baylable to their great charge and vexation.

Sheriff, etc. within Three Days after Service of Habeas Corpus, with the Exception of Treason and Felony, as and under the Regulations herein mentioned, to bring up the Body before the Court to which the Writ is returnable;

[I.] For the prevention whereof and the more speedy Releife of all persons imprisoned for any such criminall or supposed criminall Matters whensoever any person or persons shall bring any Habeas Corpus directed unto any Sheriffe or Sheriffes Goaler Minister or other Person whatsoever for any person in his or their Custody and the said Writt shall be served upon the said Officer or left at the Goale or Prison with any of the Under Officers Underkeepers or Deputy of the said Officers or Keepers that the said Officer or Officers his or their Under Officers Under-Keepers or Deputyes shall within Three dayes after the Service thereof as aforesaid (unlesse the Committment aforesaid were for Treason [. . .]¹ plainely and specially expressed in the Warrant of Committment) [upon Payment or Tender of the Charges of bringing the said Prissoner to be ascertained by the Judge or Court that awarded the same and endorsed upon the said Writt not exceeding [5p]² per Mile and upon Security given by his owne Bond to pay the Charges of carrying backe the Prisoner if he shall bee remanded by the Court or Judge to which he shall be brought according to the true intent of this present Act and that he will not make any escape by the way make Returne of such Writt [or] bring or cause to be brought the Body of the Partie soe committed or restrained unto or before the Lord Chauncellor or Lord Keeper of the Great Seale of England for the time being or the Judges or Barons of the said Court from whence the said Writt shall issue or unto and before such other person [and] persons before whome the said Writt is made returnable according to the Command thereof, and shall [likewise then] and certify the true Causes of Imprisonment. certifie the true causes of his Detainer or Imprisonment unlesse the Committment of the said Partie be in any place beyond the distance of Exceptions in respect of Distance. Twenty miles from the place or places where such Court or Person is or shall be resideing and if beyond the distance of   **4–002**

Twenty miles and not above One hundred miles then within the space of Ten
dayes and if beyond the distance of One hundred miles then within the space of
Twenty dayes after such delivery aforesaid and not longer.

[1] Words repealed by Criminal Law Act 1967 (c. 58), Sched. 3, Pt III.
[2] Word substituted by Decimal Currency Act 1969 (c. 19), s. 10(1).

Bill of Rights 1688

(1 Wm. M. 2, c. 2)

5–001   *An Act declareing the Rights and Liberties of the Subject and Setleing the
Succession of the Crowne.*

Whereas the Lords Spirituall and Temporall and Comons assembled at
Westminster lawfully fully and freely representing all the Estates of the People
of this Realme did upon the thirteenth day of February in the yeare of our Lord
one thousand six hundred eighty eight present unto their Majesties then called
and known by the Names and Stile of William and Mary Prince and Princesse
of Orange being present in their proper Persons a certaine Declaration in
Writeing made by the said Lords and Comons in the Words following *viz*.

The Heads of Declaration of Lords and Commons, recited

5–002   **I.** Whereas the late King James the Second by the Assistance of diverse evill
Councellors Judges and Ministers imployed by him did endeavour to subvert and
extirpate the Protestant Religion and the Lawes and Liberties of this Kingdome.
Dispensing and Suspending Power. By Assumeing and Exerciseing a Power
of Dispensing with and Suspending of Lawes and the Execution of Lawes without Consent of Parlyament.
Committing Prelates. By Committing and Prosecuting diverse Worthy Prelates for humbly Petitioning to be excused from Concurring to the said Assumed
Power.
Ecclesiastical Commission. By issueing and causeing to be executed a Commission under the Great Seale for Erecting a Court called The Court of Commissioners for Ecclesiasticall Causes.
Levying Money. By Levying Money for and to the Use of the Crowne by
ptence of Prerogative for other time and in other manner then the same was
granted by Parlyament.
Standing Army. By raising and keeping a Standing Army within this Kingdome in time of Peace without Consent of Parlyament and Quartering Soldiers
contrary to Law.
Disarming Protestants, etc. By causing severall good Subjects being Protestants to be disarmed at the same time when Papists were both Armed and
Imployed contrary to Law.
Violating Elections. By Violating the Freedome of Election of Members to
serve in Parlyament.
Illegal Prosecutions. By Prosecutions in the Court of Kings Bench for Matters
and Causes cognizable onely in Parlyament and by diverse other Arbitrary and
Illegall Courses.
Juries. And whereas of late yeares Partiall Corrupt and Unqualifyed Persons
have beene returned and served on Juryes in Tryalls and particularly diverse
Jurors in Tryalls for High Treason which were not Freeholders,

Excessive Bail. And excessive Baile hath beene required of Persons committed in Criminall Cases to elude the Benefitt of the Lawes made for the Liberty of the Subjects.

Fines. And excessive Fines have beene imposed.

Punishments. And illegall and cruell Punishments inflicted.

Grants of Fines, etc. before Conviction, etc. And severall Grants and Promises made of Fines and Forfeitures before any Conviction or Judgment against the Persons upon whome the same were to be levyed.

All which are utterly directly contrary to the knowne Lawes and Statutes and Freedome of this Realme.

Recital that the late King James II. had abdicated the Government, and that the Throne was vacant, and that the Prince of Orange had written Letters to the Lords and Commons for the choosing Representatives in Parliament. And whereas the said late King James the Second haveing Abdicated the Government and the Throne being thereby Vacant His [Hignesse] the Prince of Orange (whome it hath pleased Almighty God to make the glorious Instrument of Delivering this Kingdome from Popery and Arbitary Power) did (by the Advice of the Lords Spirituall and Temporall and diverse principall Persons of the Commons) cause Letters to be written to the Lords Spirituall and Temporall being Protestants and other Letters to the severall Countyes Cityes Universities Burroughs and Cinque Ports for the Choosing of such Persons to represent them as were of right to be sent to Parlyament to meete and sitt at Westminster upon the two and twentyeth day of January in this Yeare one thousand six hundred eighty and eight in order to such an Establishment as that their Religion Lawes and Liberties might not againe be in danger of being Subverted, Upon which Letters Elections haveing beene accordingly made.

The Subject's Rights. And thereupon the said Lords Spirituall and Temporall and Commons pursuant to their respective Letters and Elections being now assembled in a full and free Representative of this Nation takeing into their most serious Consideration the best means for attaining the Ends aforesaid Doe in the first place (as their Auncestors in like Case have usually done) for the Vindicating and Asserting their auntient Rights and Liberties, Declare

Dispensing Power. That the pretended Power of Suspending of Laws or the Execution of Laws by Regall Authority without Consent of Parlyament is illegall.

Late dispensing Power. That the pretended Power of Dispensing with Laws or the Execution of Laws by Regall Authorities as it hath beene assumed and exercised of late is illegall.

Ecclesiastical Courts illegal. That the Commission for erecting the late Court of Commissioners for Ecclesiasticall Causes and all other Commissions and Courts of like nature are Illegall and Pernicious.

Levying Money. That levying Money for or to the Use of the Crowne by ptence of Prerogative without Grant of Parlyament for longer time or in other manner then the same is or shall be granted is Illegall.

Right to petition. That it is the Right of the Subjects to petition the King and all Commitments and Prosecutions for such Petitioning are Illegall.

Standing Army. That the raising or keeping a standing Army within the Kingdome in time of Peace unlesse it be with Consent of Parlyament is against Law.

Subjects' Arms. That the Subjects which are Protestants may have Arms for their Defence suitable to their Conditions and as allowed by Law.

Freedom of Election. That Election of Members of Parlyament ought to be free.

Freedom of Speech. That the Freedome of Speech and Debates or Proceedings in Parlyament ought not to be impeached or questioned in any Court or Place out of Parlyament.

Excessive Bail. That excessive Baile ought not to be required nor excessive Fines imposed nor cruell and unusuall Punishments inflicted.

Juries. That Jurors ought to be duely impannelled and returned.

Grants of Forfeitures. That all Grants and Promises of Fines and Forfeitures of particular persons before Conviction are illegall and void.

Frequent Parliaments. And that for Redresse of all Grievances and for the amending strengthening and preserveing of the Lawes Parlyaments ought to be held frequently.

The said Rights claimed. And they doe Claime Demand and Insist upon all and singular the Premises as their undoubted Rights and Liberties and that noe Declarations Judgements Doeings or Proceedings to the Prejudice of the People in any of the said Premisses ought in any wise to be drawne hereafter into Consequence or Example. To which Demand of their Rights they are particularly encouraged by the Declaration of this Highnesse the Prince of Orange as being the onely meanes for obtaining a full Redresse and Remedy therein. Haveing therefore an intire Confidence That his said Highnesse the Prince of Orange will perfect the Deliverance soe farr advanced by him and will still preserve them from the Violation of their Rights which they have here asserted and from all other Attempts upon their Religion Rights and Liberties.

Tender of the Crown. The said Lords Spirituall and Temporall and Commons assembled at Westminster doe Resolve That William and Mary Prince and Princesse of Orange be and be declared King and Queene of England France and Ireland and the Dominions thereunto belonging to hold the Crowne and Royall Dignity of the said Kingdomes and Dominions to them the said Prince and Princesse during their Lives and the Life of the Survivour of them And that Regal Power exercised. the sole and full Exercise of the Regall Power be onely in and executed by the said Prince of Orange in the Names of the said Prince and Princesse dureing their joynt Lives And after their Deceases the said Crowne and Royall Dignitie of the said Kingdoms and Dominions to be to the Heires of the Body of the said Princesse And for default of such Issue to the Princesse Anne of Denmarke and the Heires of her Body And for default of such Issue to the Limitation of the Crown. Heires of the Body of the said Prince of Orange. And the Lords Spirituall and Temporall and Commons doe pray the said Prince and Princesse to accept the same accordingly.

New Oaths of Allegiance, etc. And that the Oathes hereafter mentioned be taken by all Persons of whome the Oathes of Allegiance and Supremacy might be required by Law instead of them And that the said Oathes of Allegiance and Supremacy be abrogated.

Allegiance. I A B doe sincerely promise and sweare That I will be faithfull and beare true Allegiance to their Majestyes King William and Queene Mary Soe helpe me God.

Supremacy. I A B doe sweare That I doe from my Heart Abhorr, Detest and Abjure as Impious and Hereticall this damnable Doctrine and Position That Princes Excommunicated or Deprived by the Pope or any Authority of the See of Rome may be deposed or murdered by their Subjects or any other whatsoever. And I doe declare That noe Forreigne Prince Person Prelate, State or Potentate hath or ought to have any Jurisdiction Power Superiority Preeminence or Authoritie Ecclesiasticall or Spirituall within this Realme Soe helpe me God.

Acceptance of the Crown. Upon which their said Majestyes did accept the Crowne and Royall Dignitie of the Kingdoms of England France and Ireland and the Dominions thereunto belonging according to the Resolution and Desire of the said Lords and Commons contained in the said Declaration. And thereupon their Majestyes were pleased That the said Lords Spirituall and Temporall and Commons being The Two Houses to sit, the two Houses of Parlyament should continue to sitt and with their Majesties Royall Concurrence make effectuall Provision for the Setlement of the Religion Lawes and Liberties of this Kingdome soe that the same for the future might not be in danger againe of being subverted, To which the said Lords Spirituall and Temporall and Commons did agree and proceede to act accordingly.

Subjects' Liberties to be allowed. Now in pursuance of the Premisses the said Lords Spirituall and Temporall and Commons in Parlyament assembled for the ratifying confirming and establishing the said Declaration and the Articles Clauses Matters and Things therein contained by the Force of a Law made in due Forme by Authority of Parlyament doe pray that it may be declared and enacted That all and singular the Rights and Liberties asserted and claimed in the said Declaration are the true auntient and indubitable Rights and Liberties of the People of this Kingdome and soe shall be esteemed allowed adjudged deemed and taken to be and that all and every the particulars aforesaid shall be firmly and strictly holden and observed as they are expressed in the said Declaration And all Officers and Ministers hereafter to serve according to the same. and Ministers whatsoever shall serve their Majestyes and their Successors according to the same in all times to come. And the said Lords Spirituall and Temporall and Commons seriously considering how it hath pleased Almighty God in his marvellous Providence and mercifull Goodness to this Nation to provide and preserve their said William and Mary declared King and Queen. Majestyes Royall Persons most happily to Raigne over us upon the Throne of their Auncestors for which they render unto him from the bottome of their Hearts their humblest Thanks and Praises doe truely firmely assuredly and in the Sincerity of their Hearts thinke and doe hereby recognize acknowledge and declare That King James the Second haveing abdicated the Government and their Majestyes haveing accepted the Crowne and Royall Dignity [as] aforesaid Their said Majestyes did become were are and of rights ought to be by the Lawes of this Realme our Soveraigne Liege Lord and Lady King and Queen of England France and Ireland and the Dominions thereunto belonging in and to whose Princely Persons the Royall State Crowne and Dignity of the said Realmes with all Honours Stiles Titles Regalities Prerogatives Powers Jurisdictions and Authorities to the same belonging and appertaining are most fully rightfully and intirely invested and incorporated united and annexed.

Limitation of the Crown. And for preventing all Questions and Divisions in this Realme by reason of any pretended Titles to the Crowne and for preserveing a Certainty in the Succession thereof in and upon which the Unity Peace Tranquillity and Safety of this Nation doth under God wholly consist and depend The said Lords Spirituall and Temporall and Commons doe beseech their Majestyes That it may be enacted established and declared That the Crowne and Regall Government of the said Kingdoms and Dominions with all and singular the Premises thereunto belonging and appertaining shall be and continue to their said Majestyes and the Survivour of them dureing their Lives and the Life of the Survivour of them And that the entire perfect and full Exercise of the Regall Power and Government be onely in and executed by his Majestie in the Names of both their Majestyes dureing their joynt Lives And after their deceases the said Crowne and Premisses shall be and remaine to the Heires of the Body of her Majestie and for default of such Issue to her Royall Highnesse the Princess Anne of Denmarke and the Heires of her Body and for default of such Issue to the Heires of the Body of his said Majestie And thereunto the said Lords Spiritual and Temporall and Commons doe in the Name of all the People aforesaid most humbly and faithfully submitt themselves their Heires and Posterities for ever and doe faithfully promise That they will stand to maintaine and defend their said Majesties and alsoe the Limitation and Succession of the Crowne herein specified and contained to the utmost of their Powers with their Lives and Estates against all Persons whatsoever that shall attempt any thing to the contrary.

Papists debarred the Crown. And whereas it hath beene found by Experience that it is inconsistent with the Safety and Welfaire of this Protestant Kingdome to be governed by a Popish Prince or by any King or Queene marrying a Papist the said Lords Spirituall and Temporall and Commons doe further pray that it may be enacted That all and every person and persons that is are or shall be reconciled to or shall hold Communion with the See or Church of Rome or shall professe the Popish Religion or shall marry a Papist shall be excluded and be for ever uncapeable to inherit possesse or enjoy the Crowne and Government of this Realme and Ireland and the Dominions there-unto belonging or any part of the same or to have use or exercise any Regall Power Authoritie or Jurisdiction within the same [And in all and every such Case or Cases the People of these Realmes shall be and are hereby absolved of their Allegiance] And the said Crowne and Government shall from time to time descend to and be enjoyed by such person or persons being Protestants as should have inherited and enjoyed the same in case the said person or persons soe reconciled holding Communion or Professing or Marrying as aforesaid were naturally dead.

Every King, etc. shall make the Declaration of 30 Car. II. [And that every King and Queene of this Realme who at any time hereafter shall come to and succeede in the Imperiall Crowne of this Kingdome shall on the first day of the meeting of the first Parlyament next after his or her comeing to the Crowne sitting in his or her Throne in the House of Peeres in the presence of the Lords and Commons therein assembled or at his or her Coronation before such person or persons who shall administer the Coronation Oath to him or her at the time of his or her takeing the said Oath (which shall first happen) make subscribe and audibly repeate the Declaration mentioned in the Statute made in the thirtyeth yeare of the Raigne of King Charles the Second Entituled An Act for the more effectuall Preserveing the Kings Person and Government by disableing Papists from sitting in either House of Parlyament.

If under 12 Years old, to be done after Attainment thereof. King's and Queen's Assent. But if it shall happen that such King or Queene upon his or her Succession to the Crowne of this Realme shall be under the Age of twelve yeares then every such King or Queene shall make subscribe and audibly repeate the said Declaration at his or her Coronation or the first day of the meeting of the first Parlyament as aforesaid which shall first happen after such King or Queene shall have attained the said Age of twelve yeares.] All which Their Majestyes are contented and pleased shall be declared enacted and established by Authoritie of this present Parliament and shall stand remaine and be the Law of this Realme for ever And the same are by their said Majesties by and with the advice and consent of the Lords Spirituall and Temporall and Commons in Parlyament assembled and by the authoritie of the same declared enacted and established accordingly.

Non obstantes made void

5–003   **II.** Noe Dispensation by Non obstante of or to any Statute or any part thereof shall be allowed but the same shall be held void and of noe effect Except a Dispensation be allowed of in such Statute [. . .]¹

---

¹ Words repealed by Statute Law Revision Act 1948 (c. 62), Sched. 1.

Crown and Parliament Recognition Act 1689

(1689 c. 1)

6–001   *An Act for Recognizing King William and Queene Mary and for avoiding all Questions touching the Acts made in the Parliament assembled at Westminster the thirteenth day of February one thousand six hundred eighty eight.*

King and Queen recognized

1. Wee your Majestyes most humble and loyall Subjects the Lords Spirituall **6–002** and Temporall and Commons in this present Parlyament assembled doe beseech your most excellent Majestyes that it may be published and declared in this High Court of Parlyament and enacted by authoritie of the same That we doe recognize and acknowledge your Majestyes were are and of Right ought to be by the Laws of this Realme our Soveraigne Liege Lord and Lady King and Queene of England France and Ireland and the Dominions thereunto belonging in and to whose Princely Persons the Royall State Crowne and Dignity of the said Realms with all Honours Stiles Titles Regalities Prerogatives Powers Jurisdictions and Authorities to the same belonging and appertaining are most fully rightfully and intireley invested and incorporated united and annexed. And for the avoiding of all Disputes and Questions concerning the Being and Authority of the late Parliament assembled at Westminister the thirteenth day of February one thousand six hundred eighty [eight] Wee doe most humbly beseech your Majestyes that it may be enacted And bee it enacted by the King and Queenes most excellent Majestyes by and with the advice and consent of the Lords Spirituall and Temporall and Commons in this present Parlyament assembled and by authoritie of the same The Acts of the said Parliament were and are Laws and Statutes, and to be obeyed. That all and singular the Acts made and enacted in the said Parlyament were and are Laws and Statutes of this Kingdome and as such ought to be reputed taken and obeyed by all the People of this Kingdome.

Act of Settlement 1700

(12 & 13 WM. 3, c. 2)

An Act for the further Limitation of the Crown and better securing the Rights   **7–001**
   and Liberties of the Subject

Whereas in the First Year of the Reign of Your Majesty and of our late most gracious Sovereign Lady Queen Mary (of blessed Memory) An Act of Parliament was made intituled [An Act for declaring the Rights and Liberties of the Subject and for setling the Succession of the Crown] wherein it was (amongst other things) enacted established and declared That the Crown and Regall Government of the Kingdoms of England France and Ireland and the Dominions thereunto belonging should be and continue to Your Majestie and the said late Queen during the joynt Lives of Your Majesty and the said Queen and to the Survivor And that after the Decease of Your Majesty and of the said Queen the said Crown and Regall Government should be and remain to the Heirs of the Body of the said late Queen And for Default of such Issue to Her Royall Highness the Princess Ann of Denmark and the Heirs of Her Body And for Default of such Issue to the Heirs of the Body of Your Majesty And it was thereby further enacted That all and every Person and Persons that then were or afterwards should be reconciled to or shall hold Communion with the See or Church of Rome or should professe the Popish Religion or marry a Papist should be excluded and are by that Act made for ever [incapable] to inherit possess or enjoy the Crown and Government of this Realm and Ireland and the Dominions thereunto belonging or any part of the same or to have use or exercise any regall Power Authority or Jurisdiction within the same And in all and every such Case and Cases the People of these Realms shall be and are thereby absolved of their

Allegiance And that the said Crown and Government shall from time to time descend to and be enjoyed by such Person or Persons being Protestants as should have inherited and enjoyed the same in case the said Person or Persons so reconciled holding Communion professing or marrying as aforesaid were naturally dead After the making of which Statute and the Settlement therein contained Your Majesties good Subjects who were restored to the full and free Possession and Enjoyment of their [Religion] Rights and Liberties by the Providence of God giving Success to Your Majesties just Undertakings and unwearied Endeavours for that Purpose had no greater temporall Felicity to hope or wish for then to see a Royall Progeny descending from Your Majesty to whom (under God) they owe their Tranquility and whose Ancestors have for many Years been principall Assertors of the reformed Religion and the Liberties of [Europe] and from our said most gracious Sovereign Lady whose Memory will always be precious to the Subjects of these Realms And it having since pleased and that the late Queen and Duke of Gloucester are dead; Almighty God to take away our said Sovereign Lady and also the most hopefull Prince William Duke of Gloucester (the only surviving Issue of Her Royall Highness the Princess Ann of Denmark) to the unspeakable Grief and Sorrow of Your Majesty and Your said good Subjects who under such Losses being sensibly put in mind that it standeth wholly in the Pleasure of Almighty God to prolong the Lives of Your Majesty and of Her Royall Highness and to grant to Your Majesty or to Her Royall Highness such Issue as may be inheritable to the Crown and Regall Government aforesaid by the respective Limitations in the said recited Act contained doe constantly implore the Divine Mercy for those Blessings And Your Majesties said and that His Majesty had recommended from the Throne a further Provision for the Succession of the Crown in the Protestant Line. Subjects having Daily Experience of Your Royall Care and Concern for the present and future Wellfare of these Kingdoms and particularly recommending from Your Throne a further Provision to be made for the Succession of the Crown in the Protestant Line for the Happiness of the Nation and the Security of our Religion And it being absolutely necessary for the Safety Peace and Quiet of this [Realm] to obviate all Doubts and Contentions in the same by reason of any pretended Titles to the [Crown] and to maintain a Certainty in the Succession thereof to which Your Subjects may safely have Recourse for their Protection in case the Limitations in the said recited [Act] should determine Therefore for a further Provision of the Succession of the Crown in the Protestant Line We Your Majesties most dutifull and Loyall Subjects the Lords Spirituall and Temporall and Commons in this present Parliament assembled do beseech Your Majesty that it may be enacted and declared and be it enacted and declared by the Kings most Excellent Majesty by and with the Advice and Consent of the Lords Spirituall and Temporall and Commons in this present Parliament assembled and by the Authority of the same.

The Princess Sophia, Electress and Duchess Dowager of Hanover, Daughter of the late Queen of Bohemia, Daughter of King James the First, to inherit after the King and the Princess Anne, in Default of Issue of the said Princess and His Majesty, respectively; and the Heirs of her Body, being Protestants

7–002   **I.** That the most Excellent Princess Sophia Electress and Dutchess Dowager of Hannover Daughter of the most Excellent Princess Elizabeth late Queen of Bohemia Daughter of our late Sovereign Lord King James the First of happy Memory be and is hereby declared to be the next in Succession in the Protestant Line to the Imperiall Crown and Dignity of the [said] Realms of England France and Ireland with the Dominions and Territories thereunto belonging after His Majesty and the Princess Ann of Denmark and in Default of Issue of the said Princess Ann and of His Majesty respectively and that from and after the

Deceases of His said Majesty our now Sovereign Lord and of Her Royall Highness the Princess Ann of Denmark and for Default of Issue of the said Princess Ann and of His Majesty respectively the Crown and Regall Government of the said Kingdoms of England France and Ireland and of the Dominions thereunto belonging with the Royall State and Dignity of the said Realms and all Honours Stiles Titles Regalities Prerogatives Powers Jurisdictions and Authorities to the same belonging and appertaining shall be remain and continue to the said most Excellent Princess Sophia and the Heirs of Her Body being Protestants And thereunto the said Lords Spirituall and Temporall and Commons shall and will in the Name of all the People of this Realm most humbly and faithfully submitt themselves their Heirs and Posterities and do faithfully promise That after the Deceases of His Majesty and Her Royall Highness and the failure of the Heirs of their respective Bodies to stand to maintain and defend the said Princess Sophia and the Heirs of Her Body being [Protestants] according to the Limitation and Succession of the Crown in this Act specified and contained to the utmost of their Powers with their Lives and Estates against all Persons whatsoever that shall attempt any thing to the contrary.

The Persons inheritable by this Act, holding Communion with the Church of Rome, incapacitated as by the former Act; to take the Oath at their Coronation, according to Stat. 1 W. & M. c.6

II. Provided always and it is hereby enacted That all and every Person and Persons who shall or may take or inherit the said Crown by vertue of the Limitation of this present Act and is are or shall be reconciled to or shall hold Communion with the See or Church of Rome or shall profess the Popish Religion or shall marry a Papist shall be subject to such Incapacities as in such Case or Cases are by the said recited Act provided enacted and established And that every King and Queen of this Realm who shall come to and succeed in the Imperiall Crown of this Kingdom by vertue of this Act shall have the Coronation Oath administred to him her or them at their respective Coronations according to the Act of Parliament made in the First Year of the Reign of His Majesty and the said late Queen Mary intituled An Act for establishing the Coronation Oath and shall make subscribe and repeat the Declaration in the Act first above recited mentioned or referred to in the Manner and Form thereby prescribed.

7–003

Further Provisions for securing the Religion, Laws, and Liberties of these Realms

III. And whereas it is requisite and necessary that some further Provision be made for securing our Religion Laws and Liberties from and after the Death of His Majesty and the Princess Ann of Denmark and in default of Issue of the Body of the said Princess and of His Majesty respectively Be it enacted by the Kings most Excellent Majesty by and with the Advice and Consent of the Lords Spirituall and Temporall and Commons in Parliament assembled and by the Authority of the same.

7–004

That whosoever shall hereafter come to the Possession of this Crown shall joyn in Communion with the Church of England as by Law established.

That in case the Crown and Imperiall Dignity of this Realm shall hereafter come to any Person not being a Native of this Kingdom of England this Nation be not obliged to ingage in any Warr for the Defence of any Dominions or Territories which do not belong to the Crown of England without the Consent of Parliament.

[. . .]¹ [That after the said Limitation shall take Effect as aforesaid no Person born out of the Kingdoms of England Scotland or Ireland or the Dominions thereunto belonging (although he be [. . .]² made a Denizen (except such as [are] born of English Parents) shall be capable to be of the Privy Council or a Member of either House of Parliament or to enjoy any Office or Place of Trust either Civill or Military or to have any Grant of Lands Tenements or Hereditaments from the Crown to himself or to any other or others in Trust for him][3][. . .][4]

That no Pardon under the Great Seal of England be pleadable to an Impeachment by the Commons in Parliament.

[1] Words repealed by the Act 4 & 5 Anne (c. 20), s. 27 and the Act 1 Geo. 1 St. 2 (c.51).
[2] Words repealed by British Nationality and Status of Aliens Act 1914 (c.17), Sched. 3.
[3] Words repealed, so far as they relate to British subjects and citizens of Eire, by British Nationality Act 1948 (c. 56), Sched. 4, Pt I.
[4] Words repealed by the Act 4 & 5 Anne (c. 20), s. 28, by Statute Law Revision and Civil Procedure Act 1881 (c. 59), Sched. and by Statute Law Revision Act 1950 (c. 6), Sched. 1.

The Laws and Statutes of the Realm confirmed

7–005   **IV.** And whereas the Laws of England are the Birthright of the People thereof and all the Kings and Queens who shall ascend the Throne of this Realm ought to administer the Government of the same according to the said Laws and all their Officers and Ministers ought to serve them respectively according to the same The said Lords Spirituall and Temporall and Commons do therefore further humbly pray That all the Laws and Statutes of this Realm for securing the established Religion and the Rights and Liberties of the People thereof and all other Laws and Statutes of the same now in Force may be ratified and confirmed And the same are by His Majesty by and with the Advice and Consent of the said Lords Spirituall and Temporall and Commons and by Authority of the same ratified and confirmed accordingly.

Union with Scotland Act 1706

(6 ANNE, c. 11)

8–001   *An Act for an Union of the Two Kingdoms of England and Scotland*

Most Gracious Sovereign
Recital of Articles of Union, dated 22nd July, 5 Ann.;
Whereas Articles of Union were agreed on the Twenty Second day of July in the Fifth year of Your Majesties reign by the Commissioners nominated on behalf of the Kingdom of England under Your Majesties Great Seal of England bearing date at Westminster the Tenth day of April then last past in pursuance of an Act of Parliament made in England in the Third year of Your Majesties reign and the Commissioners nominated on the behalf of the Kingdom of Scotland under Your Majesties Great Seal of Scotland bearing date the Twenty Seventh day of February in the Fourth year of Your Majesties Reign in pursuance of the Fourth Act of the Third Session of the present Parliament of Scotland to treat of and concerning an Union of the said Kingdoms and of an Act of Parliament passed in Scotland, 16th January, 5 Ann. And Whereas an Act hath passed in the Parliament of Scotland at Edinburgh the Sixteenth day of January in the Fifth year of Your Majesties reign wherein 'tis mentioned that the Estates of Parliament considering the said Articles of Union of the two Kingdoms had agreed to and approved of the said Articles of Union with some Additions and Explanations And that Your Majesty with Advice and Consent of the Estates of Parliament for establishing the Protestant Religion and Presbyterian Church Government within the Kingdom of Scotland had passed in the same Session

of Parliament an Act intituled Act for securing of the Protestant Religion and Presbyterian Church Government which by the Tenor thereof was appointed to be inserted in any Act for ratifying the Treaty and expressly declared to be a fundamental and essential Condition of the said Treaty or Union in all times coming the Tenor of which Articles as ratified and approved of with Additions and Explanations by the said Act of Parliament of Scotland follows.

ARTICLE I

The Kingdoms United

Ensigns Armorial, That the two Kingdoms of England and Scotland shall upon the First day of May which shall be in the year One thousand seven hundred and seven and for ever after be united into one Kingdom by the name of Great Britain And that the Ensigns Armorial of the said United Kingdom be such as Her Majesty shall appoint and the Crosses of St. George and St. Andrew be conjoyned in such manner as Her Majesty shall think fit and used in all Flags Banners Standards and Ensigns both at Sea and Land.

8–002

ARTICLE II

Succession to the Monarchy

That the Succession to the Monarchy of the United Kingdom of Great Britain and of the Dominions thereto belonging after Her most Sacred Majesty and in default of Issue of Her Majesty be remain and continue to the most Excellent Princess Sophia Electoress and Dutchess Dowager of Hanover and the Heirs of her body being Protestants upon whom the Crown of England is settled by an Act of Parliament made in England in the Twelfth year of the reign of His late Majesty King William the Third intituled an Act for the further Limitation of the Crown and better securing the rights and Liberties of the Subject And that all Papists and persons marrying Papists shall be excluded from and for ever incapable to inherit possess or enjoy the Imperial Crown of Great Britain and the Dominions thereunto belonging or any part thereof and in every such Case the Crown and Government shall from time to time descend to and be enjoyed by such person being a Protestant as should have inherited and enjoyed the same in case such Papist or person marrying a Papist was naturally dead according to the Provision for the descent of the Crown of England made by another Act of Parliament in England in the first year of the reign of Their late Majesties King William and Queen Mary intituled an Act declaring the Rights and Liberties of the Subject and settling the Succession of the Crown.

8–003

ARTICLE III

Parliament

That the United Kingdom of Great Britain be represented by one and the same Parliament to be stiled The Parliament of Great Britain.

8–004

ARTICLE IIII

Trade and Navigation and other Rights

That all the Subjects of the United Kingdom of Great Britain shall from and after the Union have full freedom and Intercourse of Trade and Navigation to and from any port or place within the said United Kingdom and the Dominions and Plantations thereunto belonging And that there be a Communication of all

8–005

other Rights Privileges and Advantages which do or may belong to the Subjects of either Kingdom except where it is otherwise expressly agreed in these Articles.

. . . . . .

ARTICLE VI

Regulations of Trade, Duties, etc.

8–006   That all parts of the United Kingdom for ever from and after the Union shall have the same Allowances Encouragements and Drawbacks and be under the same prohibitions restrictions and regulations of Trade and liable to the same Customs and Duties on Import and Export And that the Allowances Encouragements and Drawbacks prohibitions restrictions and regulations of Trade and the Customs and Duties on Import and Export settled in England when the Union commences shall from and after the Union take place throughout the whole United Kingdom [. . .][1]

[1] Words repealed by Statute Law Revision Act 1948 (c. 62), Sched. 1 and Statute Law (Repeals) Act 1973 (c. 39), Sched. 1, Pt XIII.

. . . . . .

ARTICLE XVIII

Laws concerning public rights

8–007   Private rights, That the Laws concerning regulation of Trade Customs and such Excises to which Scotland is by virtue of this Treaty to be liable be the same in Scotland from and after the Union as in England and that all other Laws in use within the Kingdom of Scotland do after the Union and notwithstanding thereof remain in the same force as before (except such as are contrary to or inconsistent with this Treaty) but alterable by the Parliament of Great Britain with this difference betwixt the Laws concerning publick right Policy and Civil Government and those which concern private right that the Laws which concern publick right Policy and Civil Government may be made the same throughout the whole United Kingdom But that no alteration be made in Laws which concern private right Except for evident Utility of the Subjects within Scotland.

. . . . . .

ARTICLE XIX

Court of session

8–008   Writers to the signet lords of session; Court of Justiciary; Other Courts; Causes in Scotland not cognizable in courts in Westminster Hall
    That the Court of Session or colledge of justice do after the union and notwithstanding thereof remain in all time coming within Scotland as it is now constituted by the laws of that kingdom and with the same authority and privileges as before the union subject nevertheless to such regulations for the better administration of justice as shall be made by the Parliament of Great Britain

and that hereafter none shall be named by Her Majesty or her royal successors to be ordinary lords of session but such who have served in the colledge of justice as advocates or principal clerks of session for the space of five years or as writers to the signet for the space of ten years with this provision that no writer to the signet be capable to be admitted a lord of the session unless he undergo a private and publick tryal on the civil law before the faculty of advocates and be found by them qualified for the said office two years before he be named to be a lord of the session yet so as the qualifications made or to be made for capacitating persons to be named ordinary lords of session may be alterd by the Parliament of Great Britain And that the Court of Justiciary do also after the Union and notwithstanding thereof remain in all time coming within Scotland as it is now constituted by the Laws of that Kingdom and with the same authority and privileges as before the Union Subject nevertheless to such regulations as shall be made by the Parliament of Great Britain and without prejudice of other rights of Justiciary [. . .][1] And that the heretable rights of Admiralty and Vice Admiralties in Scotland be reserved to the respective proprietors as rights of property Subject nevertheless as to the manner of exercising such heretable rights to such regulations and alterations as shall be thought proper to be made Other Courts. by the Parliament of Great Britain And that all other Courts now in being within the Kingdom of Scotland do remain but Subject to alterations by the Parliament of Great Britain And that all inferior Courts within the said limits do remain Subordinate as they are now to the supreme Courts of Justice within the same in all time coming Causes in Scotland not cognizable in Courts in Westminster Hall. And that no Causes in Scotland be cognoscible by the Courts of Chancery Queen's Bench Common Pleas or any other Court in Westminster Hall and that the said Courts or any other of the like nature after the Union shall have no Power to cognosce review or alter the Acts or Sentences of the Judicatures within Scotland or stop the Execution of the same [. . .][2]

[1] Words repealed by Statute Law (Repeals) Act 1973 (c. 39), Sched. 1, Pt XIII.
[2] Words repealed by Statute Law Revision Act 1948 (c. 62), Sched. 1 and Statute Law (Repeals) Act 1973 (c. 39), Sched. 1, Pt XIII.

. . . . . .

ARTICLE XXV

Laws inconsistent with the Articles, void

I. That all Laws and Statutes in either Kingdom so far as they are contrary to or inconsistent with the Terms of these Articles or any of them shall from and after the Union cease and become void and shall be so declared to be by the respective Parliaments of the said Kingdoms.

   As by the said Articles of Union ratified and approved by the said Act of Parliament of Scotland relation thereunto being had may appear

8–009

Acts of Scotland herein mentioned, confirmed

II. And the Tenor of the aforesaid Act for securing the Protestant Religion and Presbyterian Church Government within the Kingdom of Scotland is as follows.

   Our Sovereign Lady and the Estates of Parliament considering that by the late Act of Parliament for a Treaty with England for an Union of both Kingdoms it is provided that the Commissioners for that Treaty should not treat of or concerning any Alteration of the Worship Discipline and Government of the Church of this Kingdom as now by Law established which Treaty being now reported

8–010

to the Parliament and it being reasonable and necessary that the true Protestant Religion as presently professed within this Kingdom with the Worship Discipline and Government of this Church should be effectually and unalterably secured Therefore Her Majesty with Advice and Consent of the said Estates of Parliament doth hereby establish and confirm the said true Protestant Religion and the Worship Discipline and Government of this Church to continue without any Alteration to the People of this Land in all succeeding Generations And more especially Her Majesty with Advice and Consent aforesaid ratifies approves and for ever confirms the Fifth Act of the First Parliament of King William and Queen Mary instituted Act ratifying the Confession of Faith and settling Presbyterian Church Government with all other Acts of Parliament relating thereto in Prosecution of the Declaration of the Estates of this Kingdom, containing the Claim of Right bearing date the Eleventh of April One thousand six hundred and eighty nine And Her Majesty with Advice and Consent aforesaid expressly provides and declares that the foresaid true Protestant Religion contained in the above mentioned Confession of Faith with the Form and Purity of Worship presently in use within this Church and its Presbyterian Church Government and Discipline (that is to say) the Government of the Church by Kirk Sessions Presbyteries Provincial Synods and General Assemblies all established by the foresaid Acts of Parliament pursuant to the Claim of Right shall remain and continue unalterable And that the said Presbyterian Government shall be the only Government of the Church within the Kingdom of Scotland.

Universities and Colleges of Saint Andrew, Glasgow, Aberdeen and Edinburgh, to continue. And further for the Greater Security of the foresaid Protestant Religion and of the Worship Discipline and Government of this Church as above established Her Majesty with Advice and Consent foresaid statutes and ordains that the Universities and Colledges of Saint Andrew's Glasgow Aberdeen and Edinburgh as now established by Law shall continue within this Kingdom for ever [. . .]¹

Subjects not liable to Oath, Test, or Subscription, inconsistent with the Presbyterian Church Government; And further Her Majesty with Advice aforesaid expressly declares and statutes that none of the Subjects of this Kingdom shall be liable to but all and every one of them for ever free of any Oath Test or Subscription within this Kingdom contrary to or inconsistent with the foresaid true Protestant Religion and Presbyterian Church Government Worship and Discipline as above established and that the same within the Bounds of this Church and Kingdom shall never be imposed upon or required of them in any sort And lastly that after the decease of Her present Majesty (whom God long preserve) the Successor to swear to maintain the said Settlement of Religion. Sovereign succeeding to Her in the Royal Government of the Kingdom of Great Britain shall in all time coming at His or Her Accession to the Crown swear and subscribe that they shall inviolably maintain and preserve the foresaid Settlement of the true Protestant Religion with the Government Worship Discipline right and Privileges of this Church as above established by the Laws of this Kingdom in Prosecution of the Claim of Right.

This Act to be held a fundamental Condition of Union, and to be inserted in any Act of Parliament for concluding the said Union; And it is hereby statute and ordained that this Act of Parliament with the Establishment therein contained shall be held and observed in all time coming as a Fundamental and Essential Condition of any Treaty or Union to be concluded betwixt the two Kingdoms without any Alteration thereof or Derogation thereto in any sort for ever As also that this Act of Parliament and Settlement therein contained shall be insert and repeated in any Act of Parliament that shall pass for agreeing and concluding the foresaid Treaty or Union betwixt the two Kingdoms and that the same shall be therein expressly declared to be a Fundamental and Essential Condition of the said Treaty or Union in all time coming which Articles of Union and Act immediately above written Her Majesty with Advice and Consent aforesaid statutes enacts and ordains to be and continue in all time coming the Sure and perpetual Foundation of a complete and entire Union of the two Kingdoms of Scotland and England under the This Ratification of the said Articles not binding until they are ratified by Parliament of England, etc. express Conditions and provision that this approbation and ratification of the foresaid Articles and Act shall be no ways binding on this Kingdom until the said Articles and Act be ratified approved and confirmed by Her Majesty with and by the Authority of the Parliament of England as they are now agreed to approved and confirmed by Her Majesty with and by the Authority of the Parliament of Scotland declaring nevertheless that the Parliament of England may provide for the Security of the Church of England as they think expedient to take place within the Bounds of the said Kingdom of England and not derogating from the Security above provided for establishing of the Church of Scotland within the Bounds of this Kingdom As also the said Parliament of England may extend the Additions and other Provisions contained in the Articles of Union as above insert in favours of the Subjects of Scotland to and in favours of the Subjects of England which shall not suspend or derogate from the force and effect of this present Ratification but shall be understood as herein included without the necessity of any new ratification in the Parliament of Scotland.

Laws contrary to Articles, void. And lastly Her Majesty enacts and declares that all Laws and Statutes in this Kingdom so far they are contrary to or inconsistent with the Terms of these Articles as above mentioned shall from and after the Union cease and become void.

c. 8. ante

III. And Whereas an Act hath passed in this present Session of Parliament **8–011** intituled An Act for securing the Church of England as by Law established the Tenor whereof follows Whereas by an Act made in the Session of Parliament held in the third and fourth year of Her Majesties reign whereby Her Majesty was impowered to appoint Commissioners under the Great Seal of England to treat with Commissioners to be authorized by the Parliament of Scotland concerning an Union of the Kingdoms of England and Scotland It is Provided and enacted that the Commissioners to be named in pursuance of the said Act should not treat of or concerning any Alteration of the Liturgy Rites Ceremonies Discipline or Government of the Church as by Law established within this Realm And whereas certain Commissioners appointed by Her Majesty in pursuance of the said Act and also other Commissioners nominated by Her Majesty by the Authority of the Parliament of Scotland have met and agreed upon a Treaty of Union of the said Kingdoms which Treaty is now under the Consideration of this present Parliament And whereas the said Treaty (with some Alterations therein made) is ratified and approved by Act of Parliament in Scotland and the said Act of Ratification is by Her Majesties Royal Command laid before the Parliament of this Kingdom And whereas it is reasonable and necessary that the true Protestant Religion Professed and established by Law in the Church of England and the Doctrine Worship Discipline and Government thereof should be effectually and unalterably secured Be it enacted by the Queens most Excellent Majesty by and with the Advice and Consent of the Lords Spiritual and Temporal and the Commons in this present Parliament assembled and by Authority of the same That an [. . .]² Act made in the thirteenth year of the reign of the late King Charles the Second intituled an Act for the Uniformity of the publick Prayers and Administration of Sacraments and other rites and ceremonies and for establishing the form of making ordaining and consecrating Bishops Priests and Deacons in the Church of England (other than such Clauses in the said Acts or either of them as have been repealed or altered by any subsequent Act or Acts of Parliament) and all and singular other Acts of Parliament now in force for the Establishment and Preservation of the Church of England and the

Doctrine Worship Discipline and Government thereof shall remain and be in full force for ever And be it further enacted by the Authority aforesaid That after the Demise of Her Majesty (whom God long preserve) the Sovereign next succeeding to Her Majesty in the Royal Government of the Kingdom of Great Britain and so for ever hereafter every King or Queen succeeding and coming to the Royal Government of the Kingdom of Great Britain at His or Her Coronation shall in the presence of all persons who shall be attending assisting or otherwise then and there present take and subscribe an Oath to maintain and preserve inviolably the said Settlement of the Church of England and the Doctrine Worship Discipline and Government thereof as by Law established within the Kingdoms of England and Ireland the Dominion of Wales and Town of Berwick upon Tweed and the Territories thereunto belonging.

And be it further enacted by the Authority aforesaid That this Act and all and every the matters and things therein contained be and shall for ever be holden and adjudged to be a Fundamental and Essential part of any Treaty of Union to be concluded between the said two Kingdoms and also that this Act shall be inserted in express Terms in any Act of Parliament which shall be made for settling and ratifying any such Treaty of Union and shall be therein declared to be an Essential and Fundamental part thereof.

The said Articles and Act of Parliament of Scotland confirmed

8–012   **IV.** May It therefore please Your most Excellent Majesty that it may be enacted and be it enacted by the Queen's most Excellent Majesty by and with the Advice and Consent of the Lords Spiritual and Temporal and Commons in this present Parliament assembled and by Authority of the same That all and every the said Articles of Union as ratified and approved by the said Act of Parliament of Scotland as aforesaid and herein before particularly mentioned and inserted and also the said Act of Parliament of Scotland for establishing the Protestant Religion and Presbyterian Church Government within that Kingdom intituled Act for Securing the Protestant Religion and Presbyterian Church Government and every Clause matter and thing in the said Articles and Act contained shall be and the said Articles and Act are hereby for ever ratified approved and confirmed.

Cap. 8. ante, and the said Act of Parliament of Scotland to be observed as fundamental Conditions of the said Union

8–013   **V.** And it is hereby further enacted by the Authority aforesaid That the said Act passed in this present Session of Parliament intituled An Act for securing the Church of England as by Law established and all and every the matters and things therein contained And also the said Act of Parliament of Scotland intituled Act for securing the Protestant Religion and Presbyterian Church Government with the Establishment in the said Act contained be and shall for ever be held and adjudged to be and observed as Fundamental and Essential Conditions of the said Union And shall in all times coming be taken to be and are hereby declared to be essential and fundamental parts of and the said Articles and Acts of Parliament to continue the Union. the said Articles and Union And the said Articles of Union so as aforesaid ratified approved and confirmed by Act of Parliament of Scotland and by this present Act And the said Act passed in this present Session of Parliament intituled An Act for securing the Church of England as by Law established And also the said Act passed in the Parliament of Scotland intituled Act for securing the Protestant Religion and Presbyterian Church Government are hereby enacted and ordained to be and continue in all times coming the complete and intire Union of the two Kingdoms of England and Scotland

Recital of Act of Parliament of Scotland for settling Election of the Sixteen Peers and Forty-five Members for Scotland

VI. And whereas since the passing the said Act in the Parliament of Scotland for ratifying the said Articles of Union one other Act intituled Act settling the manner of electing the Sixteen Peers and Forty Five Members to represent Scotland in the Parliament of Great Britain hath likewise passed in the said Parliament of Scotland at Edinburgh the Fifth day of February One thousand seven hundred and seven the Tenor whereof follows

8–014

Our Sovereign Lady considering that by the Twenty Second Article of the Treaty of Union as the same is ratified by an Act passed in this Session of Parliament upon the Sixteenth of January last It is provided That by virtue of the said Treaty of the Peers of Scotland at the time of the Union Sixteen shall be the number to sit and vote in the House of Lords and Forty Five the number of the Representatives of Scotland in the House of Commons of the Parliament of Great Britain and that the said Sixteen Peers and Forty Five Members in the House of Commons be named and chosen in such manner as by a subsequent Act in this present Session of Parliament in Scotland should be settled which Act is thereby declared to be as valid as if it were a part of and ingrossed in the said Treaty Therefore Her Majesty with Advice and Consent of the Estates of Parliament statutes enacts and ordains that the said Sixteen Peers who shall have right to sit in the House of Peers in the Parliament of Great Britain on the part of Scotland by virtue of this Treaty shall be named by the said Peers of Scotland whom they represent their Heirs or Successors to their Dignities and Honours out of their own number and that by open Election and Plurality of Voices of the Peers present and of the Proxies for such as shall be absent the said Proxies being Peers and producing a Mandate in Writing duly signed before Witnesses and both the Constituent and Proxy being qualified according to Law declaring also that such Peers as are absent being qualified as aforesaid may send to all such meetings Lists of the Peers whom they judge fittest validly signed by the said absent Peers which shall be reckoned in the same manner as if the parties had been present and given in the said List And in case of the Death or legal incapacity of any of the said Sixteen Peers that the aforesaid Peers of Scotland shall nominate another of their own Number in place of the said Peer or Peers in manner before and after mentioned [. . .][3] It is always hereby expressly provided and declared that none shall be capable to elect or be elected for any of the said Estates but such as are twenty one years of Age complete [. . .][4]

The said Act declared valid, as if it had been Part of the said Articles of Union

VII. As by the said Act passed in Scotland for settling the manner of electing the Sixteen Peers and Forty Five Members to represent Scotland in the Parliament of Great Britain may appear Be it therefore further enacted and declared by the Authority aforesaid That the said last mentioned Act Passed in Scotland for settling the manner of electing the Sixteen Peers and Forty Five Members to represent Scotland in the Parliament of Great Britain as aforesaid shall be and the same is hereby declared to be as valid as if the same had been part of and engrossed in the said Articles of Union ratified and approved by the said Act of Parliament of Scotland and by this Act as aforesaid.

8–015

---

[1] Words repealed by Statute Law Revision Act 1948 (c. 62), Sched. 1.
[2] Words repealed by Statute Law (Repeals) Act 1973 (c. 39), Sched. 1 Pt. XIII.
[3] Words repealed by Statute Law Revision Act 1948 (c.62), Sched. 1.
[4] *ibid.*

Metropolitan Police Act 1839

(1839 c. 47)

9–001   *An Act for further improving the Police in and near the Metropolis.*
[17th August 1839]

. . . . . .

Regulations for preventing obstruction in the streets during public processions, etc.

9–002   **52.** It shall be lawful for the commissioners of police from time to time, and as occasion shall require, to make regulations for the route to be observed by all carts, carriages, horses, and persons, and for preventing obstruction of the streets and thoroughfares within the metropolitan police district, in all times of public processions, public rejoicings, or illuminations, and also to give directions to the constables for keeping order and for preventing any obstruction of the thoroughfares in the immediate neighbourhood of her Majesty's palaces and the public offices, the High Court of Parliament, the courts of law and equity, the [magistrates' courts][1], the theatres, and other places of public resort, and in any case when the streets or thoroughfares may be thronged or may be liable to be obstructed.

[1] words substituted by Access to Justice Act 1999 (c.22), Sched. 11, para. 2.

. . . . . .

Prohibition of nuisances by persons in the thoroughfares

9–003   **54.** Every person shall be liable to a penalty not more than level 2 on the standard scale, who, within the limits of the metropolitan police district, shall in any thoroughfare or public place, commit any of the following offences; (that is to say,)

12. Every person who shall sell or distribute or offer for sale or distribution, or exhibit to public view, any profane, [. . .][1] book, paper, print, drawing, painting or representation, or sing any profane, indecent, or obscene song or ballad, [. . .][2] or use any profane, indecent or obscene language to the annoyance of the inhabitants or passengers:

[. . .][3]

[1] Words repealed by Indecent Displays Control Act 1981 (c. 42), s. 5(2), Sched.
[2] Words repealed by Indecent Displays Control Act 1981 (c. 42), s. 5(2), Sched.
[3] Words repealed by Police and Criminal Evidence Act 1984 (c.60), s. 121(1), Sched. 7, Pt I.

Parliamentary Papers Act 1840

(3 & 4 Vict., c. 9)

An Act to give summary Protection to Persons employed in the Publication of **10–001**
Parliamentary Papers. [14th April 1840]

Proceedings, criminal or civil, against persons for publication of papers printed by order of Parliament, to be stayed upon delivery of a certificate and affidavit to the effect that such publication is by order of either House of Parliament

1. It shall and may be lawful for any person or persons who now is or are, or **10–002** hereafter shall be, a defendant or defendants in any civil or criminal proceeding commenced or prosecuted in any manner soever, for or on account or in respect of the publication of any such report, paper, votes, or proceedings by such person or persons, or by his, her, or their servant or servants, by or under the authority of either House of Parliament, to bring before the court in which such proceeding shall have been or shall be so commenced or prosecuted, or before any judge of the same (if one of the superior courts at [the Royal Courts of Justice]¹), first giving twenty-four hours' notice of his intention so to do to the prosecutor or plaintiff in such proceeding, a certificate under the hand of the lord high chancellor of Great Britain, or the lord keeper of the great seal, or of the speaker of the House of Lords, for the time being, or of the clerk of the Parliaments, or of the speaker of the House of Commons, or of the clerk of the same house, stating that the report, paper, votes, or proceedings, as the case may be, in respect whereof such civil or criminal proceeding shall have been commenced or prosecuted, was published by such person or persons, or by his, her, or their servant or servants, by order or under the authority of the House of Lords or of the House of Commons, as the case may be, together with an affidavit verifying such certificate; and such court or judge shall thereupon immediately stay such civil or criminal proceeding; and the same, and every writ or process issued therein, shall be and shall be deemed and taken to be finally put an end to, determined, and superseded by virtue of this Act.

¹ Words substituted by virtue of Supreme Court of Judicature (Consolidation) Act 1925 (c.49), s. 224(1).

. . . . . .

Proceedings to be stayed when commenced in respect of a copy of an authenticated report, etc.

2. In case of any civil or criminal proceeding hereafter to be commenced or **10–003** prosecuted for or on account or in respect of the publication of any copy of such report, paper, votes, or proceedings, it shall be lawful for the defendant or defendants at any stage of the proceedings to lay before the court or judge such report, paper, votes or proceedings, and such copy, with an affidavit verifying such report, paper, votes, or proceedings, and the correctness of such copy, and the court or judge shall immediately stay such civil or criminal proceeding; and the same, and every writ or process issued therein, shall be and shall be deemed and taken to be finally put an end to, determined, and superseded by virtue of this Act.

In proceedings for printing any extract or abstract of a paper, it may be shewn that such extract was bonâ fide made

10–004   **3.** It shall be lawful in any civil or criminal proceeding to be commenced or prosecuted for printing any extract from or abstract of such report, paper, votes, or proceedings, to give in evidence [. . .][1] such report, paper, votes, or proceedings, and to show that such extract or abstract was published bonâ fide and without malice; and if such shall be the opinion of the jury, a verdict of not guilty shall be entered for the defendant or defendants.

[1] Words repealed by Statute Law Revision Act 1958 (c.46), Sched. 3.

. . . . . .

Act not to affect the privileges of Parliament

10–005   **4.** Provided always, that nothing herein contained shall be deemed or taken, or held or construed, directly or indirectly, by implication or otherwise, to affect the privileges of Parliament in any manner whatsoever.

Riot (Damages) Act 1886

(1886 c. 38)

11–001   *An Act to provide Compensation for Losses by Riots.*   [25th June 1886]

Short title

11–002   **1.** This Act may be cited for all purposes as the Riot (Damages) Act 1886.

Compensation to persons for damage by riot

11–003   **2.**—(1) Where a house, shop, or building in [a police area][1] has been injured or destroyed, or the property therein has been injured, stolen, or destroyed, by any persons riotously and tumultuously assembled together, such compensation as hereinafter mentioned shall be paid out of [the police fund][2] of [the area][3] to any person who has sustained loss by such injury, stealing, or destruction; but in fixing the amount of such compensation regard shall be had to the conduct of the said person, whether as respects the precautions taken by him or as respects his being a party or accessory to such riotous or tumultuous assembly, or as regards any provocation offered to the persons assembled or otherwise.

(2) Where any person having sustained such loss as aforesaid has received, by way of insurance or otherwise, any sum to recoup him, in whole or in part, for such loss, the compensation otherwise payable to him under this Act shall, if exceeding such sum, be reduced by the amount thereof, and in any other case shall not be paid to him, and the payer of such sum shall be entitled to compensation under this Act in respect of the sum so paid in like manner as if he had sustained the said loss, and any policy of insurance given by such payer shall continue in force as if he had made no such payment, and where such person was recouped as aforesaid otherwise than by payment of a sum, this enactment shall apply as if the value of such recoupment were a sum paid.

[1] Words substituted by Police Act 1996 (c.16), Sched. 7 (II), para. 9(a).
[2] Words substituted by Police Act 1964 (c. 48), Sched. 9.
[3] Words substituted by Police Act 1996 (c.16), Sched. 7 (II), para. 9(b).

Public Meeting Act 1908

(8 Edw. 7, c. 66)

An Act to prevent disturbance of Public Meetings.   [21st December 1908]   **12–001**

Penalty on endeavour to break up public meeting

1.—(1) Any person who at a lawful public meeting acts in a disorderly   **12–002**
manner for the purpose of preventing the transaction of the business for which
the meeting was called together shall be guilty of an offence, [. . .][1] and shall
on summary conviction be liable to imprisonment for a term not exceeding six
months or to a fine not exceeding [level 5 on the standard scale] or to both.

(2) Any person who incites others to commit an offence under this section
shall be guilty of a like offence.

[(3) If any constable reasonably suspects any person of committing an offence
under the foregoing provisions of this section, he may if requested so to do by
the chairman of the meeting require that person to declare to him immediately
his name and address and, if that person refuses or fails so to declare his name
and address or gives a false name and address he shall be guilty of an offence
under this subsection and liable on summary conviction thereof to a fine not
exceeding [level 1 on the standard scale].]

[(4) This section does not apply as respects meetings to which section 97 of
the Representation of the People Act 1983 applies.]

[1] Words repealed by Representation of the People Act 1949 (c. 68), s. 175(2)–(7), Sched. 9 and
Public Order Act 1963 (c. 52), s. 1(2).

Official Secrets Act 1911

(1 & 2 Geo. 5, c. 28)

An Act to re-enact the Official Secrets Act 1889 with Amendments.   **13–001**
                                                    [22nd August 1911]

Penalties for spying

1.—(1) If any person for any purpose prejudicial to the safety or interests of   **13–002**
the State—

   (a) approaches, [inspects, passes over][1] or is in the neighbourhood of, or
       enters any prohibited place within the meaning of this Act; or
   (b) makes any sketch, plan, model, or note which is calculated to be or
       might be or is intended to be directly or indirectly useful to an
       enemy; or

(c) obtains, [collects, records, or publishers,][2] or communicates to any other person [any secret official code word, or pass word, or][3] any sketch, plan, model, article, or note, or other document or information which is calculated to be or might be or is intended to be directly or indirectly useful to an enemy;

he shall be guilty of felony [. . .][4]

(2) On a prosecution under this section, it shall not be necessary to show that the accused person was guilty of any particular act tending to show a purpose prejudicial to the safety or interests of the State, and, notwithstanding that no such act is proved against him, he may be convicted if, from the circumstances of the case, or his conduct, or his known character as proved, it appears that his purpose was a purpose prejudicial to the safety or interests of the State; and if any sketch, plan, model, article, note, document, or information relating to or used in any prohibited place within the meaning of this Act, or anything in such a place [or any secret official code word or pass word][5], is made, obtained, [collected, recorded, published][6], or communicated by any person other than a person acting under lawful authority, it shall be deemed to have been made, obtained, [collected, recorded, published][7] or communicated for a purpose prejudicial to the safety or interests of the State unless the contrary is proved.

[1] Words inserted by Official Secrets Act 1920 (c. 75), Sched. 1.
[2] *ibid.*
[3] *ibid.*
[4] Words inserted by Official Secrets Act 1920 (c. 75), Sched. 2.
[5] Words inserted by Official Secrets Act 1920 (c. 75), Sched. 1.
[6] *ibid.*
[7] *ibid.*

. . . . . .

Definition of prohibited place

13–003   3. For the purposes of this Act, the expression "prohibited place" means—

[(a) any work of defence, arsenal, naval or air force establishment or station, factory, dockyard, mine, minefield, camp, ship, or aircraft belonging to or occupied by or on behalf of His Majesty, or any telegraph, telephone, wireless or signal station, or office so belonging or occupied, and any place belonging to or occupied by or on behalf of His Majesty and used for the purpose of building, repairing, making, or storing any munitions of war, or any sketches, plans, models or documents relating thereto, or for the purpose of getting any metals, oil, or minerals of use in time of war][1];

(b) any place not belonging to His Majesty where any [munitions of war][2], or any [sketches, models, plans][3]; or documents relating thereto, are being made, repaired, [gotten,][4] or stored under contract with, or with any person on behalf of, His Majesty, or otherwise on behalf of His Majesty; and

(c) any place belonging to [or used for the purposes of][5] His Majesty which is for the time being declared [by order of a Secretary of State][6] to be a prohibited place for the purposes of this section on the ground that information with respect thereto, or damage thereto, would by useful to an enemy; and

(d) any railway, road, way, or channel, or other means of communication by land or water (including any works or structures being part thereof or connected (therewith), or any place used for gas, water, or electricity works or other works for purposes of a public character, or any place where any [munitions of war][7], or any [sketches, models, plans][8] or documents relating thereto, are being made, repaired, or stored otherwise than on behalf of His Majesty, which is for the time being declared [by order of a Secretary of State][9] to be a prohibited place for the purposes of this section, on the ground that information with respect thereto, or the destruction or obstruction thereof, or interference therewith, would be useful to an enemy.

[1] s.3(a) substituted by Official Secrets Act 1920 (c.75), Sched. 1.
[2] Words substituted by Official Secrets Act 1920 (c. 75), Sched. 1.
[3] *ibid.*
[4] Words inserted by Official Secrets Act 1920 (c. 75), Sched. 1.
[5] *ibid.*
[6] Words substituted by Official Secrets Act 1920 (c. 75), Sched. 1.
[7] *ibid.*
[8] *ibid.*
[9] *ibid.*

. . . . . .

Power to arrest

6. Any person who is found committing an offence under this Act, or who is reasonably suspected of having committed, or having attempted to commit, or being about to commit, such an offence, may be apprehended and detained   **13–004**

. . . . . .

Restriction on prosecution

8. A prosecution for an offence under this Act shall not be instituted except by or with the consent of the Attorney-General.   **13–005**

Search Warrants

9.—(1) If a justice of the peace is satisfied by information on oath that there is reasonable ground for suspecting that an offence under this Act has been or is about to be committed, he may grant a search warrant authorising any constable to enter at any time any premises or place named in the warrant, if necessary, by force, and to search the premises or place and every person found therein, and to seize any sketch, plan, model, article, note, or document, or anything of a like nature or anything which is evidence of an offence under this Act having been or being about to be committed, which he may find on the premises or place or on any such person, and with regard to or in connexion with which he has reasonable ground for suspecting that an offence under this Act has been or is about to be committed.   **13–006**

(2) Where it appears to a superintendent of police that the case is one of great emergency and that in the interest of the State immediate action is necessary, he may by a written order under his hand give to any constable the like authority as may be given by the warrant of a justice under this section.

Extent of Act and place of trial of offence

10.—(1) This Act shall apply to all acts which are offences under this Act when committed in any part of His Majesty's dominions, or when committed by British Officers or subjects elsewhere.   **13–007**

(2) An offence under this Act, if alleged to have been committed out of the United Kingdom, may be inquired of, heard, and determined, in any competent British court in the place where the offence was committed, or in England.

(3) An offence under this Act shall not be tried by the sheriff court in Scotland, nor by any court out of the United Kingdom which has not jurisdiction to try crimes which involve the greatest punishment allowed by law.

Parliament Act 1911

(1911 c. 13)

14–001 *An Act to make provision with respect to the powers of the House of Lords in relation to those of the House of Commons, and to limit the duration of Parliament.* [18th August 1911]

Whereas it is expedient that provision should be made for regulating the relations between the two Houses of Parliament:

And whereas it is intended to substitute for the House of Lords as it at present exists a Second Chamber constituted on a popular instead of hereditary basis, but such substitution cannot be immediately brought into operation:

And whereas provision will require hereafter to be made by Parliament in a measure effecting such substitution for limiting and defining the powers of the new Second Chamber, but it is expedient to make such provision as in this Act appears for restricting the existing powers of the House of Lords:

Powers of House of Lords as to Money Bills

14–002 1.—(1) If a Money Bill, having been passed by the House of Commons, and sent up to the House of Lords at least one month before the end of the session, is not passed by the House of Lords without amendment within one month after it is so sent up to that House, the Bill shall, unless the House of Commons direct to the contrary, be presented to His Majesty and become an Act of Parliament on the Royal Assent being signified, notwithstanding that the House of Lords have not consented to the Bill.

(2) A Money Bill means a Public Bill which in the opinion of the Speaker of the House of Commons contains only provisions dealing with all or any of the following subjects, namely, the imposition, repeal, remission, alteration, or regulation of taxation; the imposition for the payment of debt or other financial purposes of charges on the Consolidated Fund, the National Loans Fund or on money provided by Parliament, or the variation or repeal of any such charges; supply; the appropriation, receipt, custody, issue or audit of accounts of public money; the raising or guarantee of any loan or the repayment thereof; or subordinate matters incidental to those subjects or any of them. In this subsection the expressions "taxation," "public money," and "loan" respectively do not include any taxation, money, or loan raised by local authorities or bodies for local purposes.

(3) There shall be endorsed on every Money Bill when it is sent up to the House of Lords and when it is presented to His Majesty for assent the certificate of the Speaker of the House of Commons signed by him that it is a Money Bill. Before giving his certificate the Speaker shall consult, if practicable, two members to be appointed from the Chairmen's Panel at the beginning of each Session by the Committee of Selection.

Restriction of the powers of the House of Lords as to Bills other than Money Bills

2.—(1) If any Public Bill (other than a Money Bill or a Bill containing any provision to extend the maximum duration of Parliament beyond five years) is passed by the House of Commons [in two successive sessions] (whether of the same Parliament or not), and, having been sent up to the House of Lords at least one month before the end of the session, is rejected by the House of Lords in each of those sessions, that Bill shall, on its rejection [for the second time] by the House of Lords, unless the House of Commons direct to the contrary, be presented to His Majesty and become an Act of Parliament on the Royal Assent being signified thereto, notwithstanding that the House of Lords have not consented to the Bill:

14–003

Provided that this provision shall not take effect unless [one year has elapsed] between the date of the second reading in the first of those sessions of the Bill in the House of Commons and the date on which it passes the House of Commons [in the second of these sessions.]

(2) When a Bill is presented to His Majesty for assent in pursuance of the provisions of this section, there shall be endorsed on the Bill the certificate of the Speaker of the House of Commons signed by him that the provisions of this section have been duly complied with.

(3) A Bill shall be deemed to be rejected by the House of Lords if it is not passed by the House of Lords either without amendment or with such amendments only as may be agreed to by both Houses.

(4) A Bill shall be deemed to be the same Bill as a former Bill sent up to the House of Lords in the preceding session if, when it is sent up to the House of Lords, it is identical with the former Bill or contains only such alterations as are certified by the Speaker of the House of Commons to be necessary owing to the time which has elapsed since the date of the former Bill, or to represent any amendments which have been made by the House of Lords in the former Bill in the preceding session, and any amendments which are certified by the Speaker to have been made by the House of Lords [in the second session] and agreed to by the House of Commons shall be inserted in the Bill as presented for Royal Assent in pursuance of this section:

Provided that the House of Commons may, if they think fit, on the passage of such a Bill through the House [in the second session,] suggest any further amendments without inserting the amendments in the Bill, and any such suggested amendments shall be considered by the House of Lords, and, if agreed to by that House, shall be treated as amendments made by the House of Lords and agreed to by the House of Commons; but the exercise of this power by the House of Commons shall not affect the operation of this section in the event of the Bill being rejected by the House of Lords.

Certificate of Speaker

3. Any certificate of the Speaker of the House of Commons given under this Act shall be conclusive for all purposes, and shall not be questioned in any court of law.

14–004

Enacting words

4.—(1) In every Bill presented to His Majesty under the preceding provisions of this Act, the words of enactment shall be as follows, that is to say:—

14–005

"Be it enacted by the King's most Excellent Majesty, by and with the advice and consent of the Commons in this present Parliament assembled, in accordance with the provisions of [the Parliament Acts 1911 and 1949] and by authority of the same, as follows."

(2) Any alteration of a Bill necessary to give effect to this section shall not be deemed to be an amendment of the Bill.

Provisional Order Bills excluded

14–006   **5.** In this Act the expression "Public Bill" does not include any Bill for confirming a Provisional Order.

Saving for existing rights and privileges of the House of Commons

14–007   **6.** Nothing in this Act shall diminish or qualify the existing rights and privileges of the House of Commons.

Duration of Parliament

14–008   **7.** Five years shall be substituted for seven years as the time fixed for the maximum duration of Parliament under the Septennial Act 1715.

Official Secrets Act 1920

(10 & 11 GEO. 5, c. 75)

15–001   *An Act to amend the Official Secrets Act 1911.*   [23rd December 1920]

Unauthorised use of uniforms; falsification of reports, forgery, personation, and false documents

15–002   **1.** (1) If any person for the purpose of gaining admission, or of assisting any other person to gain admission, to a prohibited place, within the meaning of the Official Secrets Act 1911 (hereinafter referred to as "the principal Act"), or for any other purpose prejudicial to the safety or interests of the State within the meaning of the said Act—

(a) uses or wears, without lawful authority, any naval, military, air-force, police, or other official uniform, or any uniform so nearly resembling the same as to be calculated to deceive, or falsely represents himself to be a person who is or has been entitled to use or wear any such uniform; or

(b) orally, or in writing in any declaration or application, or in any document signed by him or on his behalf, knowingly makes or connives at the making of any false statement or any omission; or

(c) tampers with any passport or any naval, military, air-force, police, or official pass, permit, certificate, licence, or other document of a similar character (hereinafter in this section referred to as an official document), or has in his possession any forged, altered, or irregular official document; or

(d) personates, or falsely represents himself to be a person holding, or in the employment of a person holding, office under His Majesty, or to be or not to be a person to whom an official document or secret official codeword or password has been duly issued or communicated, or with intent to obtain an official document, secret official codeword or password, whether for himself or any other person, knowingly makes any false statement; or

(e) uses, or has in his possession or under his control, without the authority of the Government Department or the authority concerned, any die, seal, or stamp of or belonging to, or used, made or provided by any Government Department, or by any diplomatic, naval, military, or air-force authority appointed by or acting under the authority of His Majesty, or any die, seal or stamp so nearly resembling any such die, seal or stamp as to be calculated to deceive, or counterfeits any such die, seal or stamp, or uses, or has in his possession, or under his control, any such counterfeited die, seal or stamp;

he shall be guilty of a misdemeanour.

(2) If any person—

(a) retains for any purpose prejudicial to the safety or interests of the State any official document, whether or not completed or issued for use, when he has no right to retain it, or when it is contrary to his duty to retain it, or fails to comply with any directions issued by any Government Department or any person authorised by such department with regard to the return or disposed thereof; or

(b) allows any other person to have possession of any official document issued for his use alone, or communicates any secret official code word or pass word so issued, or, without lawful authority or excuse, has in his possession any official document or secret official code word or pass word issued for the use of some person other than himself, or on obtaining possession of any official document by finding or otherwise, neglects or fails to restore it to the person or authority by whom or for whose use it was issued, or to a police constable; or

(c) without lawful authority or excuse, manufactures or sells, or has in his possession for sale any such die, seal or stamp as aforesaid;

he shall be guilty of a misdemeanour.

(3) In the case of any prosecution under this section involving the proof of a purpose prejudicial to the safety or interests of the State, subsection (2) of section one of the principal Act shall apply in like manner as it applies to prosecutions under that section.

. . . . . .

Duty of giving information as to commission of offences

6.—(1) Where a chief officer of police is satisfied that there is reasonable ground for suspecting that an offence under section one of the principal Act has been committed and for believing that any Person is able to furnish information as to the offence or suspected offence, he may apply to the Secretary of State for permission to exercise the powers conferred by this subsection and, if such permission is granted, he may authorise a superintendent of police, or any police officer not below the rank of inspector, to require the person believed to be able to furnish information to give any information in his power relating to the offence or suspected offence, and, if so required and on tender of his reasonable expenses, to attend at such reasonable time and place as may be specified by the superintendent or other officer; and if a person required insurance of pursuance of such an authorisation to give information, or to attend as aforesaid, fails

15–003

to comply with any such requirement or knowingly gives false information, he shall be guilty of a misdemeanour.

(2) Where a chief officer of police has reasonable grounds to believe that the case is one of great emergency and that in the interest of the State immediate action is necessary, he may exercise the powers conferred by the last foregoing subsection without applying for or being granted the permission of a Secretary of State, but if he does so shall forthwith report the circumstances to the Secretary of State.

(3) References in this section to a chief officer of police shall be construed as including references to any officer of police expressly authorised by a chief officer of police to act on his behalf for the purposes of this section when by reason of illness, absence, or other cause he is unable to do so.[1]

[1] s. 6 substituted by Official Secrets Act 1939 (c. 121), ss. 1, 2(2).

. . . . . .

Attempts, incitements, etc.

15–004   **7.**—Any person who attempts to commit any offence under the principal Act or this Act, or solicits or incites or endeavours to persuade another person to commit an offence, or aids or abets and does any act preparatory to the commission of an offence under the principal Act or this Act, shall be guilty of a felony or a misdemeanour or a summary offence according as the offence in question is a felony, a misdemeanour or a summary offence, and on conviction shall be liable to the same punishment, and to the proceeded against in the same manner, as if he had committed the offence.

Provisions as to trial and punishment of offences

15–005   **8.**—(1) Any person who is guilty of a felony under the principal Act or this Act shall be liable to penal servitude for a term of not less than three years and not exceeding fourteen years.

(2) Any person who is guilty of a misdemeanour under the principal Act or this Act shall be liable on conviction on indictment to imprisonment, for a term not exceeding two years, or, on conviction under the Summary Jurisdiction Acts, to imprisonment, for a term not exceeding three months or to a fine not exceeding fifty pounds, or both such imprisonment and fine:

Provided that no misdemeanour under the principal Act or this Act shall be dealt with summarily except with the consent of the Attorney General.

(3) For the purposes of the trial of a person for an offence under the principal Act or this Act, the offence shall be deemed to have been committed either at the place in which the same actually was committed, or at any place in the United Kingdom in which the offender may be found.

(4) In addition and without prejudice to any powers which a court may possess to order the exclusion of the public from any proceedings if, in the course of proceedings before a court against any person for an offence under the principal Act or this Act or the proceedings on appeal, or in the course of the trial of a person for felony or misdemeanour under the principal Act or this Act, application is made by the prosecution, on the ground that the publication of any evidence to be given or of any statement to be made in the course of the proceedings would be prejudicial to the national safety, that all or any portion of the public shall be excluded during any part of the hearing, the court may make an order to that effect, but the passing of sentence shall in any case take place in public.

(5) Where the person guilty of an offence under this principal Act or this Act is a company or corporation, every director and officer of the company

or corporation shall be guilty of the like offence unless he proves that the act or omission constituting the offence took place without his knowledge or consent.

Statute of Westminster 1931

(22 & 23 GEO. 5, c. 4)

An Act to give effect to certain resolutions passed by Imperial Conferences held in the years 1926 and 1930.   [11th December 1931]

16–001

Whereas the delegates of His Majesty's Governments in the United Kingdom, the Dominion of Canada, the Commonwealth of Australia, the Dominion of New Zealand, the Union of South Africa, the Irish Free State and Newfoundland, at Imperial Conferences holden at Westminster in the years of our Lord nineteen hundred and twenty-six and nineteen hundred and thirty did concur in making the declarations and resolutions set forth in the Reports of the said Conferences:

And whereas it is meet and proper to set out by way of preamble to this Act that, inasmuch as the Crown is the symbol of the free association of the members of the British Commonwealth of Nations, and as they are united by a common allegiance to the Crown, it would be in accord with the established constitutional position of all the members of the Commonwealth in relation to one another that any alteration in the law touching the Succession to the Throne or the Royal Style and Titles shall hereafter require the assent as well of the Parliaments of all the Dominions as of the Parliament of the United Kingdom:

And whereas it is in accord with the established constitutional position that no law hereafter made by the Parliament of the United Kingdom shall extend to any of the said Dominions as part of the law of that Dominion otherwise than at the request and with the consent of that Dominion:

And whereas it is necessary for the ratifying, confirming and establishing of certain of the said declarations and resolutions of the said Conferences that a law be made and enacted in due form by authority of the Parliament of the United Kingdom:

And whereas the Dominion of Canada, the Commonwealth of Australia, the Dominion of New Zealand, the Union of South Africa, the Irish Free State and Newfoundland have severally requested and consented to the submission of a measure to the Parliament of the United Kingdom for making such provision with regard to the matters aforesaid as is hereafter in this Act contained:

Meaning of "Dominion" in this Act

1. In this Act the expression "Dominion" means any of the following Dominions, that is to say, the Dominion of Canada, the Commonwealth of Australia, the Dominion of New Zealand, the Irish Free State and Newfoundland.

16–002

Validity of laws made by Parliament of a Dominion

2.—(1) The Colonial Laws Validity Act 1865 shall not apply to any law made after the commencement of this Act by the Parliament of a Dominion.

16–003

(2) No law and no provision of any law made after the commencement of this Act by the Parliament of a Dominion shall be void or inoperative on the ground that it is repugnant to the law of England, or to the provisions of any

existing or future Act of Parliament of the United Kingdom, or to any order, rule or regulation made under any such Act, and the powers of the Parliament of a Dominion shall include the power to repeal or amend any such Act, order, rule or regulation in so far as the same is part of the law of the Dominion.

Power of Parliament of Dominion to legislate extra-territorially

16–004   **3.** It is hereby declared and enacted that the Parliament of a Dominion has full power to make laws having extra-territorial operation.

Parliament of United Kingdom not to legislate for Dominion except by consent

16–005   **4.** No Act of Parliament of the United Kingdom passed after the commencement of this Act shall extend, or be deemed to extend, to a Dominion as part of the law of that Dominion, unless it is expressly declared in that Act that that Dominion has requested, and consented to, the enactment thereof.

Public Order Act 1936

(1 EDW. 8 & 1 GEO. 6, c. 6)

17–001   *An Act to prohibit the wearing of uniforms in connection with political objects and the maintenance by private persons of associations of military or similar character; and to make further provision for the preservation of public order on the occasion of public processions and meetings and in public places.*   [18th December 1936]

Prohibition of uniforms in connection with political objects

17–002   **1.**— (1) Subject as hereinafter provided, any person who in any public place or at any public meeting wears uniform signifying his association with any political organisation or with the promotion of any political object shall be guilty of an offence:

Provided that, if the chief officer of police is satisfied that the wearing of any such uniform as aforesaid on any ceremonial, anniversary, or other special occasion will not be likely to involve risk of public disorder, he may, with the consent of a Secretary of State, by order permit the wearing of such uniform on that occasion either absolutely or subject to such conditions as may be specified in the order.

(2) Where any person is charged before any court with an offence under this section, no further proceedings in respect thereof shall be taken against him without the consent of the Attorney-General [except such as are authorised by [section 6 of the Prosecution of Offences 1979] so, however, that if that person is remanded in custody he shall, after the expiration of a period of eight days from the date on which he was so remanded, be entitled to be [released on bail] without sureties unless within that period the Attorney-General has consented to such further proceedings as aforesaid.

Prohibition of quasimilitary organisations

17–003   **2.**—(1) If the members or adherents of any association of persons, whether incorporated or not, are—

(a) organised or trained or equipped for the purposes of enabling them to be employed in usurping the functions of the police or of the armed forces of the Crown; or

(b) organised and trained or organised and equipped either for the purpose of enabling them to be employed for the use or display of physical force in promoting any political object, or in such manner as to arouse reasonable apprehension that they are organised and either trained or equipped for that purpose;

then any person who takes part in the control or management of the association, or in so organising or training as aforesaid any members or adherents thereof, shall be guilty of an offence under this section:

Provided that in any proceedings against a person charged with the offence of taking part in the control or management of such an association as aforesaid it shall be a defence to that charge to prove that he neither consented to nor connived at the organisation, training, or equipment of members or adherents of the association in contravention of the provisions of this section.

(2) No prosecution shall be instituted under this section without the consent of the Attorney-General.

(3) If upon application being made by the Attorney-General it appears to the High Court that any association is an association of which members or adherents are organised, trained, or equipped in contravention of the provisions of this section, the Court may make such order as appears necessary to prevent any disposition without the leave of the Court of property held by or for the association and in accordance with rules of court may direct an inquiry and report to be made as to any such property as aforesaid and as to the affairs of the association and make such further orders as appear to the Court to be just and equitable for the application of such property in or towards the discharge of the liabilities of the association lawfully incurred before the date of the application or since that date with the approval of the Court, in or towards the repayment of moneys to persons who became subscribers or contributors to the association in good faith and without knowledge of any such contravention as aforesaid, and in or towards any costs incurred in connection with any such inquiry and report as aforesaid or in winding-up or dissolving the association, and may order that any property which is not directed by the Court to be so applied as aforesaid shall be forfeited to the Crown.

(4) In any criminal or civil proceedings under this section proof of things done or of words written, spoken or published (whether or not in the presence of any party to the proceedings) by any person taking part in the control or management of an association or in organising, training or equipping members or adherents of an association shall be admissible as evidence of the purposes for which, or the manner in which, members or adherents of the association (whether those persons or others) were organised, or trained, or equipped.

(5) If a judge of the High Court is satisfied by information on oath that there is reasonable ground for suspecting that an offence under this section has been committed, and that evidence of the commission thereof is to be found at any premises or place specified in the information, he may, on an application made by an officer of police of a rank not lower than that of inspector, grant a search warrant authorising any such officer as aforesaid named in the warrant together with any other persons named in the warrant and any other officers of police to enter the premises or place at any time within one month from the date of the warrant, if necessary by force, and to search the premises or place and every person found therein, and to seize anything found on the premises or place or on any such person which the officer has reasonable ground for suspecting to be evidence of the commission of such an offence as aforesaid:

Provided that no woman shall, in pursuance of a warrant issued under this subsection, be searched except by a woman.

(6) Nothing in this section shall be construed as prohibiting the employment of a reasonable number of persons as stewards to assist in the preservation of order at any public meeting held upon private premises, or the making of arrangements for that purpose or the instruction of the persons to be so employed in their lawful duties as such stewards, or their being furnished with badges or other distinguishing signs.

. . . . . .

Enforcement

17–004   **7.**— (1) Any person who commits an offence under section two of this Act shall be liable on summary conviction to imprisonment for a term not exceeding six months or to a fine not exceeding one hundred pounds, or to both such imprisonment and fine, or, on conviction on indictment, to imprisonment for a term not exceeding two years or to a fine not exceeding five hundred pounds, or to both such imprisonment and fine.

(2) Any person guilty of [any offence under this Act other than an offence under section two] shall be liable on summary conviction to imprisonment for a term not exceeding three months or to a fine not exceeding [level 4 on the standard scale] or to both such imprisonment and fine.

(3) A constable may without warrant arrest any person reasonably suspected by him to be committing an offence under section one of this Act.

Application to Scotland

17–005   **8.** This Act shall apply to Scotland subject to the following modifications:—

(1) Subsection (2) of section one and subsection (2) of section two of this Act shall not apply.

(2) In subsection (3) of section two the Lord Advocate shall be substituted for the Attorney-General and the Court of Session shall be substituted for the High Court.

(3) Subsection (5) of section two shall have effect as if for any reference to a judge of the High Court there were substituted a reference to the sheriff and any application for a search warrant under the said subsection shall be made by the procurator fiscal instead of such officer as is therein mentioned.

(4) The power conferred on the sheriff by subsection (5) of section two, as modified by the last foregoing paragraph, shall not be exercisable by an [honorary sheriff]

(5) [. . .][1]

(6) [. . .][2]

---

[1] Repealed by District Courts (Scotland) Act 1975 (c. 20), Sched. 2.
[2] Repealed by Public Order Act 1986 (c. 64), s. 40(3), Sched. 3.

. . . . . .

Interpretation, etc.

17–006   **9.**— (1) In this Act the following expressions have the meanings hereby respectively assigned to them, that is to say:—

"Meeting" means a meeting held for the purpose of the discussion of matters of public interest or for the purpose of the expression of views on such matters;

"Private premises" means premises to which the public have access (whether on payment or otherwise) only by permission of the owner, occupier, or lessee of the premises;

"Public meeting" includes any meeting in a public place and any meeting which the public or any section thereof are permitted to attend, whether on payment or otherwise;

"Public place" includes any highway, [or in Scotland any road within the meaning of the Roads (Scotland) Act 1984] and any other premises or place to which at the material time the public have or are permitted to have access, whether on payment or otherwise.

(2) [. . .][1]

(3) Any order made under this Act by a chief officer of police may be revoked or varied by a subsequent order made in like manner.

(4) The powers conferred by this Act on any chief officer of police may, in the event of a vacancy in the office or in the event of the chief officer of police being unable to act owing to illness or absence, be exercised by the person duly authorised in accordance with directions given by a Secretary of State to exercise those powers on behalf of the chief officer of police.

[1] Repealed by Law Officers Act 1997 (c.60), Sched. 1, para. 1.

Bank of England Act 1946

(9 & 10 GEO. 6, c. 27)

An Act to bring the capital stock of the Bank of England into public ownership   **18–001**
and bring the Bank under public control, to make provision with respect to the relations between the Treasury, the Bank of England and other banks and for purposes connected with the matters aforesaid.

[14th February 1946]

. . . . . .

Treasury directions to the Bank and relations of the Bank with other banks

4.— (1) The Treasury may from time to time give such directions to the Bank   **18–002**
as, after consultation with the Governor of the Bank, they think necessary in the public interest [except in relation to monetary policy][1].

(2) [. . .][2]

(3) The Bank, if they think it necessary in the public interest, may request information from and make recommendations to bankers, and may, if so authorised by the Treasury, issue directions to any banker for the purpose of securing that effect is given to any such request or recommendation:

Provided that:—

(a) no such request or recommendations shall be made with respect to the affairs of any particular customer of a banker; and

(b) before authorising the issue of any such directions the Treasury shall give the banker concerned, or such person as appears to them to represent him, an opportunity of making representations with respect thereto.

(4) [. . .]³
(5) [. . .]⁴
(6) In this section the expression "banker" means any such person carrying on a banking undertaking as may be declared by order of the Treasury to be a banker for the purposes of this section.

(7) Any order made under the last foregoing subsection may be varied or revoked by a subsequent order.

(8) [. . .]⁵

¹ Words inserted by Bank of England Act 1998 (c.11), Pt II, s. 10.
² Repealed by Bank of England Act 1998 (c.11), Sched. 9 (I), para. 1.
³ Repealed by Official Secrets Act 1989 (c.6), s. 16(4), Sched. 2.
⁴ *ibid.*
⁵ Repealed by Statute Law Revision Act 1950 (c. 6), Sched. 1.

Statutory Instruments Act 1946

(9 & 10 Geo. 6, c. 36)

19–001 *An Act to repeal the Rules Publication Act 1893, and to make further provision as to the instruments by which statutory powers to make orders, rules, regulations and other subordinate legislation are exercised.*

[26th March 1946]

Definition of "Statutory Instrument"

19–002　　**1.**—(1) Where by this Act or any Act passed after the commencement of this Act power to make, confirm or approve orders, rules, regulations or other subordinate legislation is conferred on His Majesty in Council or on any Minister of the Crown then, if the power is expressed—

(a) in the case of a power conferred on His Majesty, to be exercisable by Order in Council;
(b) in the case of a power conferred on a Minister of the Crown, to be exercisable by statutory instrument,

any document by which that power is exercised shall be known as a "statutory instrument" and the provisions of this Act shall apply thereto accordingly.

[(1A) The references in subsection (1) to a Minister of the Crown shall be construed as including references to the National Assembly for Wales.]¹

(2) Where by any Act passed before the commencement of this Act power to make statutory rules within the meaning of the Rules Publication Act 1893, was conferred on any rule-making authority within the meaning of that Act, any document by which that power is exercised after the commencement of this Act shall, save as is otherwise provided by regulations made under this Act, be known as a "statutory instrument" and the provisions of this Act shall apply thereto accordingly.

¹ Added by Government of Wales Act 1998 (c.38), Sched. 12, para. 2.

Numbering, printing, publication and citation

19–003　　**2.**— (1) Immediately after the making of any statutory instrument, it shall be sent to the King's printer of Acts of Parliament and numbered in accordance with regulations made under this Act, and except in such cases as may be provided by any Act passed after the commencement of this Act or prescribed by regulations made under this Act, copies thereof shall as soon as possible be printed and sold by the King's printer of Acts of Parliament.

(2) Any statutory instrument may, without prejudice to any other mode of citation, be cited by the number given to it in accordance with the provisions of this section, and the calendar year.

Supplementary provisions as to publication

3.—(1) Regulations made for the purposes of this Act shall make provision   **19–004**
for the publication by His Majesty's Stationery Office of lists showing the date upon which every statutory instrument printed and sold by the King's printer of Acts of Parliament was first issued by [or under the authority of][1] that office; and in any legal proceedings a copy of any list so published [. . .][2] shall be received in evidence as a true copy, and an entry therein shall be conclusive evidence of the date on which any statutory instrument was first issued by [or under the authority of][3] His Majesty's Stationery Office.

(2) In any proceedings against any person for an offence consisting of a contravention of any such statutory instrument, it shall be a defence to prove that the instrument had not been issued by [or under the authority of][4] His Majesty's Stationery Office at the date of the alleged contravention unless it is proved that at that date reasonable steps had been taken for the purpose of bringing the purport of the instrument to the notice of the public, or of persons likely to be affected by it, or of the person charged.

(3) Save as therein otherwise expressly provided, nothing in this section shall affect any enactment or rule of law relating to the time at which any statutory instrument comes into operation.

[1] Words added by Statutory Instruments (Production and Sale) Act 1996 (c. 54), s. 1(1)(a).
[2] Words repealed by Statutory Instruments (Production and Sale) Act 1996 (c. 54), s. 1(1)(b).
[3] Words added by Statutory Instruments (Production and Sale) Act 1996 (c. 54), s. 1(1)(a).
[4] *ibid.*

Statutory Instruments which are required to be laid before Parliament

4.—(1) Where by this Act or any Act passed after the commencement of this   **19–005**
Act any statutory instrument is required to be laid before Parliament after being made, a copy of the instrument shall be laid before each House of Parliament and, subject as hereinafter provided, shall be so laid before the instrument comes into operation:

Provided that if it is essential that any such instrument should come into operation before copies thereof can be so laid as aforesaid, the instrument may be made so as to come into operation before it has been so laid; and where any statutory instrument comes into operation before it is laid before Parliament, notification shall forthwith be sent to the Lord Chancellor and to the Speaker of the House of Commons drawing attention to the fact that copies of the instrument have yet to be laid before Parliament and explaining why such copies were not so laid before the instrument came into operation.

(2) Every copy of any such statutory instrument sold by [or under the authority of][1] the King's printer of Acts of Parliament shall bear on the face thereof:

(a) a statement showing the date on which the statutory instrument came or will come into operation; and
(b) either a statement showing the date on which copies thereof were laid before Parliament or a statement that such copies are to be laid before Parliament.

(3) Where any Act passed before the date of the commencement of this Act contains provisions requiring that any Order in Council or other document made in exercise of any power conferred by that or any other Act be laid before Parliament after being made, any statutory instrument made in exercise of that power shall by virtue of this Act be laid before Parliament and the foregoing provisions of this section shall apply thereto accordingly in substitution for any such provisions as aforesaid contained in the Act passed before the said date.

[1] Words added by Statutory Instruments (Production and Sale) Act 1996 (c.54), s. 1(1)(a).

Statutory Instruments which are subject to annulment by resolution of either House of Parliament

19–006   5.— (1) Where by this Act or any Act passed after the commencement of this Act, it is provided that any statutory instrument shall be subject to annulment in pursuance of resolution of either House of Parliament, the instrument shall be laid before Parliament after being made and the provisions of the last foregoing section shall apply thereto accordingly, and if either House within the period of forty days beginning with the day on which a copy thereof is laid before it, resolves that an Address be presented to His Majesty praying that the instrument be annulled, no further proceedings shall be taken thereunder after the date of the resolution, and His Majesty may by Order in Council revoke the instrument, so, however, that any such resolution and revocation shall be without prejudice to the validity of anything previously done under the instrument or to the making of a new statutory instrument.

(2) Where any Act passed before the date of the commencement of this Act contains provisions requiring that any Order in Council or other document made in exercise of any power conferred by that or any other Act shall be laid before Parliament after being made and shall cease to be in force or may be annulled, as the case may be, if within a specified period either House presents an address to His Majesty or passes a resolution to that effect, then, subject to the provisions of any Order in Council made under this Act, any statutory instrument made in exercise of the said power shall by virtue of this Act be subject to annulment in pursuance of a resolution of either House of Parliament and the provisions of the last foregoing subsection shall apply thereto accordingly in substitution for any such provisions as aforesaid contained in the Act passed before the said date.

Statutory Instruments of which drafts are to be laid before Parliament

19–007   6.— (1) Where by this Act or any Act passed after the commencement of this Act it is provided that a draft of any statutory instrument shall be laid before Parliament, but the Act does not prohibit the making of the instrument without the approval of Parliament, then, in the case of an Order in Council the draft shall not be submitted to His Majesty in Council, and in any other case the statutory instrument shall not be made, until after the expiration of a period of forty days beginning with the day on which a copy of the draft is laid before each House of Parliament, or, if such copies are laid on different days, with the later of the two days, and if within that period either House resolves that the draft be not submitted to His Majesty or that the statutory instrument be not made, as the case may be, no further proceedings shall be taken thereon, but without prejudice to the laying before Parliament of a new draft.

(2) Where any Act passed before the date of the commencement of this Act contains provisions requiring that a draft of any Order in Council or other document to be made in exercise of any power conferred by that or any other Act shall be laid before Parliament before being submitted to His Majesty, or before being made, as the case may be, and that it shall not be so submitted or made

if within a specified period either House presents an address to His Majesty or passes a resolution to that effect, then, subject to the provisions of any Order in Council made under this Act, a draft of any statutory instrument made in exercise of the said power shall by virtue of this Act be laid before Parliament and the provisions of the last foregoing subsection shall apply thereto accordingly in substitution for any such provisions as aforesaid contained in the Act passed before the said date.

Crown Proceedings Act 1947

(10 & 11 GEO. 6, c. 44)

An Act to amend the law relating to the civil liabilities and rights of the Crown   **20–001**
and to civil proceedings by and against the Crown, to amend the law relating to the civil liabilities of persons other than the Crown in certain cases involving the affairs or property of the Crown, and for purposes connected with the matters aforesaid.   [31st July 1947]

PART I

SUBSTANTIVE LAW

Right to sue the Crown

1. Where any person has a claim against the Crown after the commencement   **20–002**
of this Act, and, if this Act had not been passed, the claim might have been enforced, subject to the grant of His Majesty's fiat, by petition of right, or might have been enforced by a proceeding provided by any statutory provision repealed by this Act, then, subject to the provisions of this Act, the claim may be enforced as of right, and without the fiat of His Majesty, by proceedings taken against the Crown for that purpose in accordance with the provisions of this Act.

Liability of the Crown in tort

2.—(1) Subject to the provisions of this Act, the Crown shall be subject to   **20–003**
all those liabilities in tort to which, if it were a private person of full age and capacity, it would be subject:—

  (a) in respect of torts committed by its servants or agents;
  (b) in respect of any breach of those duties which a person owes to his servants or agents at common law by reason of being their employer; and
  (c) in respect of any breach of the duties attaching at common law to the ownership, occupation, possession or control of property:
    Provided that no proceedings shall lie against the Crown by virtue of paragraph (a) of this subsection in respect of any act or omission of a servant or agent of the Crown unless the act or omission would apart from the provisions of this Act have given rise to a cause of action in tort against that servant or agent or his estate.

(2) Where the Crown is bound by a statutory duty which is binding also upon persons other than the Crown and its officers, then, subject to the provisions of this Act, the Crown shall, in respect of a failure to comply with that duty, be subject to all those liabilities in tort (if any) to which it would be so subject if it were a private person of full age and capacity.

(3) Where any functions are conferred or imposed upon an officer of the Crown as such either by any rule of the common law or by statute, and that officer commits a tort while performing or purporting to perform those functions, the liabilities of the Crown in respect of the tort shall be such as they would have been if those functions had been conferred or imposed solely by virtue of instructions lawfully given by the Crown.

(4) Any enactment which negatives or limits the amount of the liability of any Government department, [part of the Scottish Administration] or officer of the Crown in respect of any tort committed by that department, [part] or officer shall, in the case of proceedings against the Crown under this section in respect of a tort committed by that department, [part] or officer, apply in relation to the Crown as it would have applied in relation to that department, [part] or officer if the proceedings against the Crown had been proceedings against that department [, part] or officer.

(5) No proceedings shall lie against the Crown by virtue of this section in respect of anything done or omitted to be done by any person while discharging or purporting to discharge any responsibilities of a judicial nature vested in him, or any responsibilities which he has in connection with the execution of judicial process.

(6) No proceedings shall lie against the Crown by virtue of this section in respect of any act, neglect or default of any officer of the Crown, unless that officer has been directly or indirectly appointed by the Crown and was at the material time paid in respect of his duties as an officer of the Crown wholly out of the Consolidated Fund of the United Kingdom, moneys provided by Parliament, [the Scottish Consolidated Fund] [. . .]¹ or any other Fund certified by the Treasury for the purposes of this subsection or was at the material time holding an office in respect of which the Treasury certify that the holder thereof would normally be so paid.

¹ Words repealed by Statute Law (Repeals) Act 1981 (c.19), Sched. 1, Pt I.

Infringement of intellectual property rights

20–004   **3.**— (1) Civil proceedings lie against the Crown for an infringement committed by a servant or agent of the Crown, with the authority of the Crown, of—

    (a) a patent,
    (b) a registered trade mark,
    (c) the right in a registered design,
    (d) design right, or
    (e) copyright;

but save as provided by this subsection no proceedings lie against the Crown by virtue of this Act in respect of an infringement of any of those rights.

[(2) Nothing in this section, or in any other provision of this Act, shall be construed as affecting—

    (a) the rights of a government department [or any part of the Scottish Administration] under section 55 of the Patents Act 1977, Schedule 1 to the Registered Designs Act 1949or section 240 of the Copyright, Designs and Patents Act 1988 (Crown use of patents and designs) or,

(b) the rights of the Secretary of State under section 22 of the Patents Act 1977 or section 5 of the Registered Designs Act 1949 (security of information prejudicial to defence or public safety.]¹

¹ s. 3 substituted by Copyright, Designs and Patents Act 1988 (c.48), s.303(1), Sched. 7, para. 4(1).

Application of law as to indemnity, contribution, joint and several tortfeasors, and contributory negligence

4.— (1) Where the Crown is subject to any liability by virtue of this Part of this Act, the law relating to indemnity and contribution shall be enforceable by or against the Crown in respect of the liability to which it is so subject as if the Crown were a private person of full age and capacity.   **20–005**

(2) [. . .]¹

(2) Without prejudice to the effect of the preceding subsection, Part II of the Law Reform (Married Women and Tortfeasors) Act 1935 (which relates to proceedings against, and contribution between, joint and several tortfeasors) shall bind the Crown.

(3) Without prejudice to the general effect of section one of this Act, the Law Reform (Contributory Negligence) Act 1945 (which amends the law relating to contributory negligence) shall bind the Crown.

¹ Repealed by Civil Liability (Contribution) Act 1978 (c.47), s.9(2), Sched. 2.

Saving in respect of acts done under prerogative and statutory powers

11.— (1) Nothing in Part I of this Act shall extinguish or abridge any powers or authorities which, if this Act had not been passed, would have been exercisable by virtue of the prerogative of the Crown, or any powers or authorities conferred on the Crown by any statute, and, in particular, nothing in the said Part I shall extinguish or abridge any powers or authorities exercisable by the Crown, whether in time of peace or of war, for the purpose of the defence of the realm or of training, or maintaining the efficiency of, any of the armed forces of the Crown.   **20–006**

(2) Where in any proceedings under this Act it is material to determine whether anything was properly done or omitted to be done in the exercise of the prerogative of the Crown, [. . .]¹ a Secretary of State may, if satisfied that the act or omission was necessary for any such purpose as is mentioned in the last preceding subsection, issue a certificate to the effect that the act or omission was necessary for that purpose; and the certificate shall, in those proceedings, be conclusive as to the matter so certified.

¹ Words repealed except as regards certificates issued before April 1, 1964 by S.I. 1964 No. 488, Sched. 1, Pt II.

. . . . . .

PART II

JURISDICTION AND PROCEDURE

Parties to proceedings

17.— (1) The [Minister for the Civil Service] shall publish a list specifying the several Government departments which are authorised departments for the purposes of this Act, and the name and address for service of the person who is, or is acting for the purposes of this Act as, the solicitor for each such   **20–007**

department, and may from time to time amend or vary the said list. Any document purporting to be a copy of a list published under this section and purporting to be printed under the superintendence or the authority of His Majesty's Stationery Office shall in any legal proceedings be received as evidence for the purpose of establishing what departments are authorised departments for the purposes of this Act, and what person is, or is acting for the purposes of this Act as, the solicitor for any such department.

(2) Civil proceedings by the Crown may be instituted either by an authorised Government department in its own name, whether that department was or was not at the commencement of this Act authorised to sue, or by the Attorney General.

(3) Civil proceedings against the Crown shall be instituted against the appropriate authorised Government department, or, if none of the authorised Government departments is appropriate or the person instituting the proceedings has any reasonable doubt whether any and if so which of those departments is appropriate, against the Attorney General.

(4) Where any civil proceedings against the Crown are instituted against the Attorney General, an application may at any stage of the proceedings be made to the court by or on behalf of the Attorney General to have such of the authorised Government departments as may be specified in the application substituted for him as defendant to the proceedings; and where any such proceedings are brought against an authorised Government department, an application may at any stage of the proceedings be made to the court on behalf of that department to have the Attorney General or such of the authorised Government departments as may be specified in the application substituted for the applicant as the defendant to the proceedings.

Upon any such application the court may if it thinks fit make an order granting the application on such terms as the court thinks just; and on such an order being made the proceedings shall continue as if they had been commenced against the department specified in that behalf in the order, or, as the case may require, against the Attorney General.

(5) No proceedings instituted in accordance with this Part of this Act by or against the Attorney General or an authorised Government department shall abate or be affected by any change in the person holding the office of Attorney General or in the person or body of persons constituting the department.

Service of documents

20–008   **18.** All documents required to be served on the Crown for the purpose of or in connection with any civil proceedings by or against the Crown shall, if those proceedings are by or against an authorised Government department, be served on the solicitor, if any, for that department, or the person, if any, acting for the purposes of this Act as solicitor for that department, or if there is no such solicitor and no person so acting, or if the proceedings are brought by or against the Attorney General, on the Solicitor for the affairs of His Majesty's Treasury.

Venue and related matters

20–009   **19.—** (1) In any case in which civil proceedings against the Crown in the High Court are instituted by the issue of a writ out of a district registry the Crown may enter an appearance either in the district registry or in the central office of the High Court, and if an appearance is entered in the central office all steps in relation to the proceedings up to trial shall be taken at the Royal Courts of Justice.

(2) The trial of any civil proceedings by or against the Crown in the High Court shall be held at the Royal Courts of Justice unless the court, with the consent of the Crown, otherwise directs.

Where the Crown refuses its consent to a direction under this subsection the court may take account of the refusal in exercising its powers in regard to the award of costs.

(3) Nothing in this section shall prejudice the right of the Crown to demand a local venue for the trial of any proceedings in which the Attorney General has waived his right to a trial at bar.

Removal and transfer of proceedings

20.— (1) If in a case where proceedings are instituted against the Crown in a county court an application in that behalf is made by the Crown to the High Court, and there is produced to the court a certificate of the Attorney General to the effect that the proceedings may involve an important question of law, or may be decisive of other cases arising out of the same matter, or are for other reasons more fit to be tried in the High Court, the proceedings shall be removed into the High Court.

20–010

Where any proceedings have been removed into the High Court on the production of such a certificate as aforesaid, and it appears to the court by whom the proceedings are tried that the removal has occasioned additional expense to the person by whom the proceedings are brought, the court may take account of the additional expense so occasioned in exercising its powers in regard to the award of costs.

(2) Without prejudice to the rights of the Crown under the preceding provisions of this section, all rules of law and enactments relating to the removal or transfer of proceedings from a county court to the High Court, or the transfer of proceedings from the High Court to a county court, shall apply in relation to proceedings against the Crown:

[. . .]¹
Provided that:—

    (a) an order for the transfer to a county court of any proceedings against the Crown in the High Court shall not be made without the consent of the Crown; and

    (b) the duty of a judge to make an order [under section forty-four of the County Courts Act 1959], for the transfer to the High Court of proceedings commenced against the Crown in a county court shall not be conditional upon the giving of security by the Crown.

¹ Proviso repealed by Supreme Court Act 1981 (c.54), s.152(4), Sched. 7.

Nature of relief

21.— (1) In any civil proceedings by or against the Crown the court shall, subject to the provisions of this Act, have power to make all such orders as it has power to make in proceedings between subjects, and otherwise to give such appropriate relief as the case may require:
Provided that:—

20–011

    (a) where in any proceedings against the Crown any such relief is sought as might in proceedings between subjects be granted by way of injunction or specific performance, the court shall not grant an injunction or make an order for specific performance, but may in lieu thereof make an order declaratory of the rights of the parties; and

    (b) in any proceedings against the Crown for the recovery of land or other property the court shall not make an order for the recovery of the land or the delivery of the property, but may in lieu thereof make an order declaring that the plaintiff is entitled as against the Crown to the land or property or to the possession thereof.

(2) The court shall not in any civil proceedings grant any injunction or make any order against an officer of the Crown if the effect of granting the injunction or making the order would be to give any relief against the Crown which could not have been obtained in proceedings against the Crown.

Children and Young Persons (Harmful Publications) Act 1955

(1955 c. 28)

21–001 *An Act to prevent the dissemination of certain pictorial publications harmful to children and young persons.* [6th May 1955]

Works to which this Act applies

21–002 **1.** This Act applies to any book, magazine or other like work which is of a kind likely to fall into the hands of children or young persons and consists wholly or mainly of stories told in pictures (with or without the addition of written matter), being stories portraying—

(a) the commission of crimes; or
(b) acts of violence or cruelty; or
(c) incidents of a repulsive or horrible nature;

in such a way that the work as a whole would tend to corrupt a child or young person into whose hands it might fall.

Penalty for printing, publishing, selling, etc., works to which this Act applies

21–003 **2.**— (1) A person who prints, publishes, sells or lets on hire a work to which this Act applies, or has any such work in his possession for the purpose of selling it or letting it on hire, shall be guilty of an offence and liable, on summary conviction, to imprisonment for a term not exceeding four months or to a fine not exceeding one hundred pounds or to both:

Provided that, in any proceedings taken under this subsection against a person in respect of selling or letting on hire a work or of having it in his possession for the purpose of selling it or letting it on hire, it shall be a defence for him to prove that he had not examined the contents of the work and had no reasonable cause to suspect that it was one to which this Act applies.

(2) A prosecution for an offence under this section shall not, in England or Wales, be instituted except by, or with the consent, of the Attorney General.

. . . . . .

Prohibition of importation of works to which this Act applies and articles for printing them.

4. The importation of—   **21–004**

(a) any work to which this Act applies; and
(b) any plate prepared for the purpose of printing copies of any such work and any photographic film prepared for that purpose;

is hereby prohibited.

Life Peerages Act 1958

(1958 c. 21)

An Act to make provision for the creation of life peerages carrying the right to   **22–001**
sit and vote in the House of Lords.   [30th April 1958]

Power to create life peerages carrying right to sit in the House of Lords

1.— (1) Without prejudice to Her Majesty's powers as to the appointment of   **22–002**
Lords of Appeal in Ordinary, Her Majesty shall have power by letters patent to confer on any person a peerage for life having the incidents specified in subsection (2) of this section.

(2) A peerage conferred under this section shall, during the life of the person on whom it is conferred, entitle him—

(a) to rank as a baron under such style as may be appointed by the letters patent; and
(b) subject to subsection (4) of this section, to receive writs of summons to attend the House of Lords and sit and vote therein accordingly,

and shall expire on his death.

(3) A life peerage may be conferred under this section on a woman.

(4) Nothing in this section shall enable any person to receive a writ of summons to attend the House of Lords, or to sit and vote in that House, at any time when disqualified therefor by law.

Public Records Act 1958

(1958 c. 51)

An Act to make new provision with respect to public records and the Public   **23–001**
Record Office, and for connected purposes.   [23rd July 1958]

General responsibility of the Lord Chancellor for public records

23–002   **1.**—(1) The direction of the Public Record Office shall be transferred from the Master of the Rolls to the Lord Chancellor, and the Lord Chancellor shall be generally responsible for the execution of this Act and shall supervise the care and preservation of public records.

(2) There shall be an Advisory Council on Public Records to advise the Lord Chancellor on matters concerning public records in general and, in particular, on those aspects of the work of the Public Record Office which affect members of the public who make use of the facilities provided by the Public Record Office.

The Master of the Rolls shall be chairman of the said Council and the remaining members of the Council shall be appointed by the Lord Chancellor on such terms as he may specify.

(3) The Lord Chancellor shall in every year lay before both Houses of Parliament a report on the work of the Public Record Office, which shall include any report made to him by the Advisory Council on Public Records.

The Public Record Office

23–003   **2.**—(1) The Lord Chancellor may appoint a Keeper of Public Records to take charge under his direction of the Public Record Office and of the records therein and may, with the concurrence of the Treasury as to numbers and conditions of service, appoint such other persons to serve in the Public Record Office as he may think fit.

(2) The Keeper of Public Records and other persons appointed under this Act shall receive such salaries and remuneration as the Treasury may from time to time direct.

(3) It shall be the duty of the Keeper of Public Records to take all practicable steps for the preservation of records under his charge.

(4) The Keeper of Public Records shall have power to do all such things as appear to him necessary or expedient for maintaining the utility of the Public Record Office and may in particular—

    (a) compile and make available indexes and guides to, and calendars and texts of, the records in the Public Record Office;

    (b) prepare publications concerning the activities of and facilities provided by the Public Record Office;

    (c) regulate the conditions under which members of the public may inspect public and other records or use the other facilities of the Public Record Office;

    (d) provide for the making and authentication of copies of and extracts from records required as evidence in legal proceedings or for other purposes;

    (e) accept responsibility for the safe keeping of records other than public records;

    (f) make arrangements for the separate housing of films and other records which have to be kept under special conditions;

    (g) lend records, in a case where the Lord Chancellor gives his approval, for display at commemorative exhibitions or for other special purposes;

    (h) acquire records and accept gifts and loans.

(5) The Lord Chancellor may by regulations made with the concurrence of the Treasury and contained in a statutory instrument prescribe the fees which

may be charged for the inspection of records under the charge of the Keeper of Public Records, for authenticated copies or extracts from such records and for other services afforded by officers of the Public Record Office and authorise the remission of the fees in prescribed cases.

(6) Fees received under the last foregoing subsection shall be paid into the Exchequer.

Selection and preservation of public records

3.—(1) It shall be the duty of every person responsible for public records of any description which are not in the Public Record Office or a place of deposit appointed by the Lord Chancellor under this Act to make arrangements for the selection of those records which ought to be permanently preserved and for their safe-keeping.   **23–004**

(2) Every person shall perform his duties under this section under the guidance of the Keeper of Public Records and the said Keeper shall be responsible for co-ordinating and supervising all action taken under this section.

(3) All public records created before the year sixteen hundred and sixty shall be included among those selected for permanent preservation.

(4) Public records selected for permanent preservation under this section shall be transferred not later than thirty years after their creation either to the Public Record Office or to such other place of deposit appointed by the Lord Chancellor under this Act as the Lord Chancellor may direct:

Provided that any records may be retained after the said period if, in the opinion of the person who is responsible for them, they are required for administrative purposes or ought to be retained for any other special reason and, where that person is not the Lord Chancellor, the Lord Chancellor has been informed of the facts and given his approval.

(5) The Lord Chancellor may, if it appears to him in the interests of the proper administration of the Public Record Office, direct that the transfer of any class of records under this section shall be suspended until arrangements for their reception have been completed.

(6) Public records which, following the arrangements made in pursuance of this section, have been rejected as not required for permanent preservation shall be destroyed or, subject in the case of records for which some person other than the Lord Chancellor is responsible, to the approval of the Lord Chancellor, disposed of in any other way.

(7) Any question as to the person whose duty it is to make arrangements under this section with respect to any class of public records shall be referred to the Lord Chancellor for his decision.

(8) The provisions of this section shall not make it unlawful for the person responsible for any public record to transmit it to the Keeper of the Records of Scotland or to the Public Record Office of Northern Ireland.

. . . . . .

Access to public records

5.—(1) Public records in the Public Record Office, other than those to which members of the public had access before their transfer to the Public Record Office, shall not be available for public inspection [until the expiration of the period of thirty years beginning with the first day of January in the year next after that in which they were created, or of such other period], either longer or shorter, as the Lord Chancellor may, with the approval, or at the request, of the Minister or other person, if any, who appears to him to be primarily concerned, for the time being prescribe as respects any particular class of public records.   **23–005**

(2) Without prejudice to the generality of the foregoing subsection, if it appears to the person responsible for any public records which have been selected by him under section three of this Act for permanent preservation that they contain information which was obtained from members of the public under such conditions that the opening of those records to the public after the period determined under the foregoing subsection would or might constitute a breach of good faith on the part of the Government or on the part of the persons who obtained the information, he shall inform the Lord Chancellor accordingly and those records shall not be available in the Public Record Office for public inspection even after the expiration of the said period except in such circumstances and subject to such conditions, if any, as the Lord Chancellor and that person may approve, or, if the Lord Chancellor and that person think fit, after the expiration of such further period as they may approve.

(3) Subject to the foregoing provisions of this section, subject to the enactments set out in the Second Schedule to this Act (which prohibit the disclosure of certain information obtained from the public except for certain limited purposes) and subject to any other Act or instrument whether passed or made before or after this Act which contains a similar prohibition, it shall be the duty of the Keeper of Public Records to arrange that reasonable facilities are available to the public for inspecting and obtaining copies of public records in the Public Record Office.

(4) Subsection (1) of this section shall not make it unlawful for the Keeper of Public Records to permit a person to inspect any records if he has obtained special authority in that behalf given by an officer of a government department or other body, being an officer accepted by the Lord Chancellor as qualified to give such an authority.

(5) The Lord Chancellor shall, as respects all public records in places of deposit appointed by him under this Act outside the Public Record Office, require arrangements to be made for their inspection by the public comparable to those made for public records in the Public Record Office and subject to restrictions corresponding with those contained in the foregoing provisions of this section.

. . . . . .

Section 10   SCHEDULE 1

DEFINITION OF PUBLIC RECORDS

23–006   **1.** The provisions of this Schedule shall have effect for determining what are public records for the purposes of this Act.

23–007   **2.** —(1) Subject to the provisions of this paragraph, administrative and departmental records belonging to Her Majesty, whether in the United Kingdom or elsewhere, in right of Her Majesty's Government in the United Kingdom and, in particular,—

    (a) records of, or held in, any department of Her Majesty's Government in the United Kingdom, or

    (b) records of any office, commission or other body or establishment whatsoever under Her Majesty's Government in the United Kingdom,

shall be public records.

(2) Sub-paragraph (1) of this paragraph shall not apply—

    (a) to records of any government department or body which is wholly or mainly concerned with Scottish affairs, or which carries on its activities wholly or mainly in Scotland, or

    (b) to registers or certified copies of entries in registers being registers or certified copies kept or deposited in the General Register Office under or in pursuance of any enactment, whether past or future, which provides for the registration of births, deaths, marriages or adoptions, or

    (c) except so far as provided by paragraph 4 of this Schedule, to records of the Duchy of Lancaster, or

(d) to records of the office of the Public Trustee relating to individual trusts[; or]

[(e) to Welsh public records (as defined in the Government of Wales Act 1998).][1]

[1] Sched. 1, para. 2(2)(e) and the word "or" immediately preceding it by Government of Wales Act 1998 (c.38), Sched. 12, para. 3(2).

Obscene Publications Act 1959

(1959 c. 66)

An Act to amend the law relating to the publication of obscene matter; to pro- **24–001**
vide for the protection of literature; and to strengthen the law concerning
pornography.   [29th July 1959]

Test of obscenity

1.—(1) For the purposes of this Act an article shall be deemed to be obscene   **24–002**
if its effect or (where the article comprises two or more distinct items) the effect
of any one of its items is, if taken as a whole, such as to tend to deprave and
corrupt persons who are likely, having regard to all relevant circumstances, to
read, see or hear the matter contained or embodied in it.

(2) In this Act "article" means any description of article containing or
embodying matter to be read or looked at or both, any sound record, and any
film or other record of a picture or pictures.

(3) For the purposes of this Act a person publishes an article who—

(a) distributes, circulates, sells, lets on hire, gives, or lends it, or who offers
it for sale or for letting on hire; or

(b) in the case of an article containing or embodying matter to be looked
at or a record, shows, plays or projects it[, or, where the matter is
data stored electronically, transmits that data][1]:

[(4) For the purposes of this Act a person also publishes an article to the
extent that any matter recorded on it is included by him in a programme included
in a programme service.

(5) Where the inclusion of any matter in a programme so included would, if
that matter were recorded matter, constitute the publication of an obscene article
for the purposes of this Act by virtue of subsection (4) above, this Act shall
have effect in relation to the inclusion of that matter in that programme as if it
were recorded matter.

(6) In this section "programme" and "programme service" have the same
meaning as in the Broadcasting Act 1990.][2]

[1] Words inserted by Criminal Justice and Public Order Act 1994 (c.33), Sched. 9, para. 3.
[2] s. 1(4)(5) and (6) inserted by Broadcasting Act 1990 (c.42), s. 162(1)(b).

Prohibition of publication of obscene matter

2.—(1) Subject as hereinafter provided, any person who, whether for gain or   **24–003**
not, publishes an obscene article [or who has an obscene article for publication
for gain (whether gain to himself or gain to another)][1] shall be liable—

(a) on summary conviction to a fine not exceeding one hundred pounds or
to imprisonment for a term not exceeding six months;

(b) on conviction on indictment to a fine or to imprisonment for a term not exceeding three years or both.

(3) A prosecution for an offence against this section shall not be commenced more than two years after the commission of the offence.

[(3A) Proceedings for an offence under this section shall not be instituted except by or with the consent of the Director of Public Prosecutions in any case where the article in question is a moving picture film of a width of not less than sixteen millimetres and the relevant publication or the only other publication which followed or could reasonably have been expected to follow from the relevant publication took place or (as the case may be) was to take place in the course of a [film exhibition]; and in this subsection "the relevant publication" means —

(a) in the case of any proceedings under this section for publishing an obscene article, the publication in respect of which the defendant would be charged if the proceedings were brought; and
(b) in the case of any proceedings under this section for having an obscene article for publication for gain, the publication which, if the proceedings were brought, the defendant would be alleged to have had in contemplation.][2]

(4) A person publishing an article shall not be proceeded against for an offence at common law consisting of the publication of any matter contained or embodied in the article where it is of the essence of the offence that the matter is obscene.

[(4A) Without prejudice to subsection (4) above, a person shall not be proceeded against for an offence at common law—

(a) in respect of a [film exhibition] or anything said or done in the course of a [film exhibition], where it is of the essence of the common law offence that the exhibition or, as the case may be, what was said or done was obscene, indecent, offensive, disgusting or injurious to morality; or
(b) in respect of an agreement to give a [film exhibition] or to cause anything to be said or done in the course of such an exhibition where the common law offence consists of conspiring to corrupt public morals or to do any act contrary to public morals or decency.][3]

(5) A person shall not be convicted of an offence against this section if he proves that he had not examined the article in respect of which he is charged and had no reasonable cause to suspect that it was such that his publication of it would make him liable to be convicted of an offence against this section.

(6) In any proceedings against a person under this section the question whether an article is obscene shall be determined without regard to any publication by another person unless it could reasonably have been expected that the publication by the other person would follow from publication by the person charged.

[(7) In this section "film exhibition" has the same meaning as in the Cinemas Act 1985.][4]

[1] Words inserted by Obscene Publications Act 1964 (c. 74), s. 1(1).
[2] s. 2(3A) inserted by Criminal Law Act 1977 (c. 45), s. 53(2).
[3] s. 2(4A) inserted by Criminal Law Act 1977 (c. 45), s. 53(3).
[4] s. 2(7) substituted by Cinemas Act 1985 (c.13), s. 24(1), Sched. 2, para. 6(3).

Powers of search and seizure

3.—(1) If a justice of the peace is satisfied by information on oath that there **24–004**
is reasonable ground for suspecting that, in any premises in the petty sessions
area for which he acts, or on any stall or vehicle in that area, being premises or
a stall or vehicle specified in the information, obscene articles are, or are from
time to time, kept for publication for gain, the justice may issue a warrant under
his hand empowering any constable to enter (if need be by force) and search
the premises, or to search the stall or vehicle and to seize and remove any
articles found therein or thereon which the constable has reason to believe to be
obscene articles and to be kept for publication for gain.

(2) A warrant under the foregoing subsection shall, if any obscene articles are
seized under the warrant, also empower the seizure and removal of any documents found in the premises or, as the case may be, on the stall or vehicle which
relate to a trade or business carried on at the premises or from the stall or
vehicle.

(3) [Subject to subsection (3A) of this section][1] any articles seized under
subsection (1) of this section shall be brought before a justice of the peace acting
for the same petty sessions area as the justice who issued the warrant, and the
justice before whom the articles are brought may thereupon issue a summons to
the occupier of the premises or, as the case may be, the user of the stall or
vehicle to appear on a day specified in the summons before a magistrates' court
for that petty sessions area to show cause why the articles or any of them should
not be forfeited; and if the court is satisfied, as respects any of the articles, that
at the time when they were seized they were obscene articles kept for publication
for gain, the court shall order those articles to be forfeited:

Provided that if the person summoned does not appear, the court shall not
make an order unless service of the summons is proved. [Provided also that this
subsection does not apply in relation to any article seized under subsection (1)
of this section which is returned to the occupier of the premises or, as the case
may be, to the user of the stall or vehicle in or on which it was found][2]

[(3A) Without prejudice to the duty of a court to make an order for the
forfeiture of an article where section 1(4) of the Obscene Publications Act 1964
applies (orders made on conviction), in a case where by virtue of subsection
(3A) of section 2 of this Act proceedings under the said section 2 for having an
article for publication for gain could not be instituted except by or with the
consent of the Director of Public Prosecutions, no order for the forfeiture of the
article shall be made under this section unless the warrant under which the
article was seized was issued on an information laid by or on behalf of the
Director of Public Prosecutions][3]

(4) In addition to the person summoned, any other person being the owner,
author or maker of any of the articles brought before the court, or any other
person through whose hands they had passed before being seized, shall be
entitled to appear before the court on the day specified in the summons to show
cause why they should not be forfeited.

(5) Where an order is made under this section for the forfeiture of any articles,
any person who appeared, or was entitled to appear, to show cause against the
making of the order may appeal to [the Crown Court], and no such order shall
take effect until the expiration of [the period within which notice of appeal to
the Crown Court may be given against the order,] or, if before the expiration
thereof notice of appeal is duly given or application is made for the statement
of a case for the opinion of the High Court, until the final determination or
abandonment of the proceedings on the appeal or case.

(6) If as respects any articles brought before it the court does not order forfeiture, the court may if it thinks fit order the person on whose information the
warrant for the seizure of the articles was issued to pay such costs as the court
thinks reasonable to any person who has appeared before the court to show

cause why those articles should not be forfeited; and costs ordered to be paid under this subsection shall be enforceable as a civil debt.

(7) For the purposes of this section the question whether an article is obscene shall be determined on the assumption that copies of it would be published in any manner likely having regard to the circumstances in which it was found, but in no other manner.

[1] Words inserted by Criminal Law Act 1977 (c. 45), s. 53(5).
[2] Proviso added by Criminal Law Act 1977 (c. 45), Sched. 12.
[3] s. 3(3A) inserted by Criminal Law Act 1977 (c. 45), s. 53(5).

Defence of public good

24–005   **4.**—(1) [Subject to subsection (1A) of this section][1] a person shall not be convicted of an offence against section two of this Act, and an order for forfeiture shall not be made under the foregoing section, if it is proved that publication of the article in question is justified as being for the public good on the ground that it is in the interests of science, literature, art or learning, or of other objects of general concern.

[(1A) Subsection (1) of this section shall not apply where the article in question is a moving picture film or soundtrack, but—

(a) a person shall not be convicted of an offence against section 2 of this Act in relation to any such film or soundtrack; and
(b) an order for forfeiture of any such film or soundtrack shall not be made under section 3 of this Act;

if it is proved that publication of the film or soundtrack is justified as being for the public good on the ground that it is in the interests of drama, opera, ballet or any other art, or of literature or learning.][2]

(2) It is hereby declared that the opinion of experts as to the literary, artistic, scientific or other merits of an article may be admitted in any proceedings under this Act either to establish or to negative the said ground.

[(3) In this section "moving picture soundtrack" means any sound record designed for playing with a moving picture film, whether incorporated with the film or not.][3]

[1] Words inserted by Criminal Law Act 1977 (c. 45), s. 53(6).
[2] s. 4(1A) inserted by Criminal Law Act 1977 (c. 45), s. 53(6).
[3] s. 4(3) added by Criminal Law Act 1977 (c. 45), s. 53(7).

Obscene Publications Act 1964

(1964 c. 74)

25–001   *An Act to strengthen the law for preventing the publication for gain of obscene matter and the publication of things intended for the production of obscene matter.*   *[July 31, 1964]*

25–002   **1.**—(2) For the purpose of any proceedings for an offence against the said section 2 a person shall be deemed to have an article for publication for gain if with a view to such publication he has the article in his ownership, possession or control.

(3) In proceedings brought against a person under the said section 2 for having an obscene article for publication for gain the following provisions shall apply in place of subsections (5) and (6) of that section, that is to say,—

(a) he shall not be convicted of that offence if he proves that he had not examined the article and had no reasonable cause to suspect that it was such that his having it would make him liable to be convicted of an offence against that section; and

(b) the question whether the article is obscene shall be determined by reference to such publication for gain of the article as in the circumstances it may reasonably be inferred he had in contemplation and to any further publication that could reasonably be expected to follow from it, but not to any other publication.

(4) Where articles are seized under section 3 of the Obscene Publications Act 1959 (which provides for the seizure and forfeiture of obscene articles kept for publication for gain), and a person is convicted under section 2 of that Act of having them for publication for gain, the court on his conviction shall order the forfeiture of those articles:

Provided that an order made by virtue of this subsection (including an order so made on appeal) shall not take effect until the expiration of the ordinary time within which an appeal in the matter of the proceedings in which the order was made may be instituted or, where such an appeal is duly instituted, until the appeal is finally decided or abandoned; and for this purpose—

(a) an application for a case to be stated or for leave to appeal shall be treated as the institution of an appeal; and

(b) where a decision on appeal is subject to a further appeal, the appeal shall not be deemed to be finally decided until the expiration of the ordinary time within which a further appeal may be instituted or, where a further appeal is duly instituted, until the further appeal is finally decided or abandoned.

(5) References in section 3 of the Obscene Publications Act 1959 and this section to publication for gain shall apply to any publication with a view to gain, whether the gain is to accrue by way of consideration for the publication or in any other way.

2.—(1) The Obscene Publications Act 1959 (as amended by this Act) shall **25–003** apply in relation to anything which is intended to be used, either alone or as one of a set, for the reproduction or manufacture therefrom of articles containing or embodying matter to be read, looked at or listened to, as if it were an article containing or embodying that matter so far as that matter is to be derived from it or from the set.

(2) For the purposes of the Obscene Publications Act 1959 (as so amended) an article shall be deemed to be had or kept for publication if it is had or been kept for the reproduction or manufacture therefrom of articles for publication; and the question whether an article so had or kept is obscene shall—

(a) for purposes of section 2 of the Act be determined in accordance with section 1(3)(b) above as if any reference there to publication of the article were a reference to publication of articles reproduced or manufactured from it; and

(b) for purposes of section 3 of the Act be determined on the assumption that articles reproduced or manufactured from it would be published in any manner likely having regard to the circumstances in which it was found, but in no other manner.

War Damage Act 1965

(1965, c. 18)

26–001 *An Act to abolish rights at common law to compensation in respect of damage to, or destruction of, property effected by, or on the authority of, the Crown during, or in contemplation of the outbreak of, war.* [2nd June 1965]

Abolition of rights at common law to compensation for certain damage to, or, destruction of, property

26–002 **1.**—(1) No person shall be entitled at common law to receive from the Crown compensation in respect of damage to, or destruction of, property caused (whether before or after the passing of this Act, within or outside the United Kingdom) by acts lawfully done by, or on the authority of, the Crown during, or in comtemplation of the outbreak of, a war in which the Sovereign was, or is, engaged.

(2) [. . .]¹

¹ Repealed by Statute Law (Repeals) Act 1995 (c.44), Sched. 1 (VI), para. 1.

Criminal Law Act 1967

(1967, c. 58)

27–001 *An Act to amend the law of England and Wales by abolishing the division of crimes into felonies and misdemeanours and to amend and simplify the law in respect of matters arising from or related to that division or the abolition of it; to do away (within or without England and Wales) with certain obsolete crimes together with the torts of maintenance and champerty; and for purposes connected therewith.* [21st July 1967]

PART I

FELONY AND MISDEMEANOUR

. . . . . .

Use of force in making arrest, etc.

27–002 **3.**—(1) A person may use such force as is reasonable in the circumstances in the prevention of crime, or in effecting or assisting in the lawful arrest of offenders or suspected offenders or of persons unlawfully at large.

(2) Subsection (1) above shall replace the rules of the common law on the question when force used for a purpose mentioned in the subsection is justified by that purpose.

Parliamentary Commissioner Act 1967

(1967 c. 13)

An Act to make provision for the appointment and functions of a Parliamentary Commissioner for the investigation of administrative action taken on behalf of the Crown, and for purposes connected therewith.   [22nd March 1967]   **28–001**

The Parliamentary Commissioner for Administration

Appointment and tenure of office

1.—(1) For the purpose of conducting investigations in accordance with the following provisions of this Act there shall be appointed a Commissioner, to be known as the Parliamentary Commissioner for Administration.   **28–002**

(2) Her Majesty may by Letters Patent from time to time appoint a person to be the Commissioner, and any person so appointed shall (subject to [Subsections (3) and (3A)][1] of this section) hold office during good behaviour.

(3) A person appointed to be the Commissioner may be relieved of office by Her Majesty at his own request, or may be removed from office by Her Majesty in consequence of Addresses from both Houses of Parliament, and shall in any case vacate office on completing the year of service in which he attains the age of sixty-five years.

[(3A) Her Majesty may declare the office of Commissioner to have been vacated if satisfied that the person appointed to be the Commissioner is incapable for medical reasons—

    (a) of performing the duties of his office; and
    (b) of requesting to be relieved of it.][2]

[1] Words substituted by Parliamentary and Health Service Commissioners Act 1987 (c. 39), s. 2(1)(a).
[2] s. 1(3A) inserted by Parliamentary and Health Service Commissioners Act 1987 (c. 39), s. 2(1)(b).

Administrative provisions

3.—(1) The Commissioner may appoint such officers as he may determine with the approval of the Treasury as to numbers and conditions of service.   **28–003**

[(2) Any function of the Commissioner under this Act may be performed by any officer of the Commissioner authorised for that purpose by the Commissioner, by any member of the staff so authorised of the Welsh Administration Ombudsman or of the Health Service Commissioner for Wales or by any officer so authorised of the Health Service Commissioner for England or of the Health Service Commissioner for Scotland.][1]

(3) The expenses of the Commissioner under this Act, to such amount as may be sanctioned by the Treasury, shall be defrayed out of moneys provided by Parliament.

[1] Words substituted by Government of Wales Act 1998 (c.38) Sched. 12, para. 5.

Appointment of acting Commissioner

28–004   [**3A.**—(1) Where the office of Commissioner becomes vacant, Her Majesty may, pending the appointment of a new Commissioner, appoint a person under this section to act as the Commissioner at any time during the period of twelve months beginning with the date on which the vacancy arose.

(2) A person appointed under this section shall hold office during Her Majesty's pleasure and, subject to that, shall hold office—

(a) until the appointment of a new Commissioner or the expiry of the period of twelve months beginning with the date on which the vacancy arose, whichever occurs first; and

(b) in other respects, in accordance with the terms and conditions of his appointment which shall be such as the Treasury may determine.

(3) A person appointed under this section shall, while he holds office, be treated for all purposes, except those of section 2 of this Act, as the Commissioner.

(4) Any salary, pension or other benefit payable by virtue of this section shall be charged on and issued out of the Consolidated Fund.][1]

[1] s. 3(3A) inserted by Parliamentary and Health Service Commissioners Act 1987 (c. 39), s. 6(1).

Investigation by the Commissioner

Departments etc. subject to investigation

28–005   [**4.**—(1) Subject to the provisions of this section and to the notes contained in Schedule 2 to this Act, this Act applies to the government departments, corporations and unincorporated bodies listed in that Schedule; and references in this Act to an authority to which this Act applies are references to any such corporation or body.

(2) Her Majesty may by Order in Council amend Schedule 2 to this Act by the alteration of any entry or note, the removal of any entry or note or the insertion of any additional entry or note.

(3) An Order in Council may only insert an entry if—

(a) it relates—

(i) to a government department; or

(ii) to a corporation or body whose functions are exercised on behalf of the Crown; or

(b) it relates to a corporation or body—

(i) which is established by virtue of Her Majesty's prerogative or by an Act of Parliament or an Order in Council or order made under an Act of Parliament or which is established in any other way by a Minister of the Crown in his capacity as a Minister or by a government department;

(ii) at least half of whose revenues derive directly from money provided by Parliament, a levy authorised by an enactment, a fee or charge of any other description so authorised or more than one of those sources; and

(iii) which is wholly or partly constituted by appointment made by Her Majesty or a Minister of the Crown or government department.

[[(3A) No entry shall be made if the result of making it would be that the Parliamentary Commissioner could investigate action which can be investigated by the Welsh Administration Ombudsman under Schedule 9 to the Government of Wales Act 1998.][1]]

[(3B) No entry shall be made in respect of–

   (a) the Scottish Administration of any part of it;
   (b) any Scottish public authority with mixed functions or no reserved functions within the meaning of the Scotland Act 1998; or
   (c) the Scottish Parliamentary Corporate Body.]

(4) No entry shall be made in respect of a corporation or body whose sole activity is, or whose main activities are, included among the activities specified in subsection (5) below.

(5) The activities mentioned in subsection (4) above are—

   (a) the provision of education, or the provision of training otherwise than under the Industrial Training Act 1982;
   (b) the development of curricula, the conduct of examinations or the validation of educational courses;
   (c) the control of entry to any profession or the regulation of the conduct of members of any profession;
   (d) the investigation of complaints by members of the public regarding the actions of any person or body, or the supervision or review of such investigations or of steps taken following them.

(6) No entry shall be made in respect of a corporation or body operating in an exclusively or predominantly commercial manner or a corporation carrying on under national ownership an industry or undertaking or part of an industry or undertaking.

(7) Any statutory instrument made by virtue of this section shall be subject to annulment in pursuance of a resolution of either House of Parliament.

(8) In this Act—

   (a) any reference to a government department to which this Act applies includes a reference to any of the Ministers or officers of such a department; and
   (b) any reference to an authority to which this Act applies includes a reference to any members or officers of such an authority.][2]

---

[1] Added by Government of Wales Act 1998 (c.38), Sched. 12, para. 6.
[2] s. 4 substituted by Parliamentary and Health Service Commissioners Act 1987 (c. 39), s. 1(1).

Matters subject to investigation

5.—(1) Subject to the provisions of this section, the Commissioner may   **28–006** investigate any action taken by or on behalf of a government department or other authority to which this Act applies, being action taken in the exercise of administrative functions of that department or authority, in any case where—

   (a) a written complaint is duly made to a member of the House of Commons by a member of the public who claims to have sustained injustice in consequence of maladministration in connection with the action so taken; and
   (b) the complaint is referred to the Commissioner, with the consent of the person who made it, by a member of that House with a request to conduct an investigation thereon.

(2) Except as hereinafter provided, the Commissioner shall not conduct an investigation under this Act in respect of any of the following matters, that is to say—

>   (a) any action in respect of which the person aggrieved has or had a right of appeal, reference or review to or before a tribunal constituted by or under any enactment or by virtue of Her Majesty's prerogative;
>   (b) any action in respect of which the person aggrieved has or had a remedy by way of proceedings in any court of law:

Provided that the Commissioner may conduct an investigation notwithstanding that the person aggrieved has or had such a right or remedy if satisfied that in the particular circumstances it is not reasonable to expect him to resort or have resorted to it.

(3) Without prejudice to subsection (2) of this section, the Commissioner shall not conduct an investigation under this Act in respect of any such action or matter as is described in Schedule 3 to this Act.

(4) Her Majesty may by Order in Council amend the said Schedule 3 so as to exclude from the provisions of that Schedule such actions or matters as may be described in the Order; and any statutory instrument made by virtue of this subsection shall be subject to annulment in pursuance of a resolution of either House of Parliament.

(5) In determining whether to initiate, continue or discontinue an investigation under this Act, the Commissioner shall, subject to the foregoing provisions of this section, act in accordance with his own discretion; and any question whether a complaint is duly made under this Act shall be determined by the Commissioner.

[[(5A) For the purposes of this section, administrative functions of a government department to which this Act applies include functions exercised by the department on behalf of the Scottish Ministers by virtue of section 93 of the Scotland Act 1998.

(5B) The Commissioner shall not conduct an investigation under this Act in respect of any action concerning Scotland and not relating to reserved matters which is taken by or on behalf of a cross-border public authority within the meaning of the Scotland Act 1998.]

(6) For the purposes of this section, administrative functions exercisable by any person appointed by the Lord Chancellor as a member of the administrative staff of any court or tribunal shall be taken to be administrative functions of the Lord Chancellor's Department or, in Northern Ireland, of the Northern Ireland Court Service.][1]

[(7) For the purposes of this section, administrative functions exercisable by any person appointed as a member of the administrative staff of a relevant tribunal—

>   (a) by a government department or authority to which this Act applies; or
>   (b) with the consent (whether as to remuneration and other terms and conditions of service or otherwise) of such a department or authority;

shall be taken to be administrative functions of that department or authority.

(8) In subsection (7) of this section, 'relevant tribunal' means a tribunal listed in Schedule 4 to this Act.

(9) Her Majesty may by Order in Council amend the said Schedule 4 by the alteration or removal of any entry or the insertion of any additional entry; and any statutory instrument made by virtue of this subsection shall be subject to annulment in pursuance of a resolution of either House of Parliament.][2]

[(9A) No entry shall be made in the said Schedule 4 in respect of the holder of any office in the Scottish Administration which is not a ministerial office or in respect of any Scottish public authority with mixed functions or no reserved functions within the meaning of the Scotland Act 1998.]

¹ s. 5(6) inserted by Courts and Legal Services Act 1990 (c.41), s. 110(1).
² Added by Parliamentary Commissioner Act 1994 (c.14), s. 1(1).

Provisions relating to complaints

6.—(1) A complaint under this Act may be made by any individual, or by   **28–007** any body of persons whether incorporated or not, not being—

(a) a local authority or other authority or body constituted for purpose of the public service or of local government or for the purposes of carrying on under national ownership any industry or undertaking or part of an industry or undertaking;

[(b) any other authority or body within subsection (1A) below.]

[(1A) An authority or body is within this subsection if–

(a) its members are appointed by–

(i) Her Majesty;
(ii) any Minister of the Crown;
(iii) any government department;
(iv) the Scottish Ministers;
(v) the First Minister; or
(vi) the Lord Advocate; or

(b) its revenues consist wholly or mainly of–

(i) money provided by Parliament; or
(ii) sums payable out of the Scottish Consolidated Fund (directly or indirectly).]

(2) Where the person by whom a complaint might have been made under the foregoing provisions of this Act had died or is for any reason unable to act for himself, the complaint may be made by his personal representative or by a member of his family or other individual suitable to represent him; but except as aforesaid a complaint shall not be entertained under this Act unless made by the person aggrieved himself.

(3) A complaint shall not be entertained under this Act unless it is made to a member of the House of Commons not later than twelve months from the day on which the person aggrieved first had notice of the matters alleged in the complaint; but the Commissioner may conduct an investigation pursuant to a complaint not made within that period if he considers that there are special circumstances which make it proper to do so.

(4) [Except as provided in subsection (5) below]¹ a complaint shall not be entertained under this Act unless the person aggrieved is resident in the United Kingdom (or, if he is dead, was so resident at the time of his death) or the complaint relates to action taken in relation to him while he was present in the United Kingdom or on an installation in a designated area within the meaning of the Continental Shelf Act 1964 or on a ship registered in the United Kingdom or an aircraft so registered, or in relation to rights or obligations which accrued or arose in the United Kingdom or on such an installation, ship or aircraft.

[(5) A complaint may be entertained under this Act in circumstances not falling within subsection (4) above where—

(a) the complaint relates to action taken in any country or territory outside the United Kingdom by an officer (not being an honorary consular officer) in the exercise of a consular function on behalf of the Government of the United Kingdom; and

(b) the person aggrieved is a citizen of the United Kingdom and Colonies who, under section 2 of the Immigration Act 1971, has the right of abode in the United Kingdom.]²

¹ Words inserted by Parliamentary Commissioner (Consular Complaints) Act 1981 (c. 11), s. 1.
² s. 6(5) inserted by Parliamentary Commissioner (Consular Complaints) Act 1981 (c. 11), s. 1.

Procedure in respect of investigations

28–008   **7.**—(1) Where the Commissioner proposes to conduct an investigation pursuant to a complaint under this Act, he shall afford to the principal officer of the department or authority concerned, and to any other person who is alleged in the complaint to have taken or authorised the action complained of, an opportunity to comment on any allegations contained in the complaint.

(2) Every such investigation shall be conducted in private, but except as aforesaid the procedure for conducting an investigation shall be such as the Commissioner considers appropriate in the circumstances of the case; and without prejudice to the generality of the foregoing provision the Commissioner may obtain information from such persons and in such manner, and make such inquiries, as he thinks fit, and may determine whether any person may be represented, by counsel or solicitor or otherwise, in the investigation.

(3) The Commissioner may, if he thinks fit, pay to the person by whom the complaint was made and to any other person who attends or furnishes information for the purposes of an investigation under this Act—

(a) sums in respect of expenses properly incurred by them;
(b) allowances by way of compensation for the loss of their time;

in accordance with such scales and subject to such conditions as may be determined by the Treasury.

(4) The conduct of an investigation under this Act shall not affect any action taken by the department or authority concerned, or any power or duty of that department or authority to take further action with respect to any matters subject to the investigation; but where the person aggrieved has been removed from the United Kingdom under any Order in force under the Aliens Restriction Acts 1914 and 1919 or under [the Immigration Act 1971]¹, he shall, if the Commissioner so directs, be permitted to re-enter and remain in the United Kingdom, subject to such conditions as the Secretary of State may direct, for the purposes of the investigation.

¹ Words substituted by virtue of Interpretation Act 1978 (c. 30), s. 17(2)(a).

Evidence

28–009   **8.**—(1) For the purposes of an investigation under this Act the Commissioner may require any Minister, officer or member of the department or authority concerned or any other person who in his opinion is able to furnish information or produce documents relevant to the investigation to furnish any such information or produce any such document.

(2) For the purposes of any such investigation the Commissioner shall have the same powers as the Court in respect of the attendance and examination of witnesses (including the administration of oaths or affirmations and the examination of witnesses abroad) and in respect of the production of documents.

(3) No obligation to maintain secrecy or other restriction upon the disclosure

of information obtained by or furnished to persons in Her Majesty's service, whether imposed by any enactment or by any rule of law, shall apply to the disclosure of information for the purposes of an investigation under this Act; and the Crown shall not be entitled in relation to any such investigation to any such privilege in respect of the production of documents or the giving of evidence as is allowed by law in legal proceedings.

(4) No person shall be required or authorised by virtue of this Act to furnish any information or answer any question relating to proceedings of the Cabinet or of any committee of the Cabinet or to produce so much of any document as relates to such proceedings; and for the purposes of this subsection a certificate issued by the Secretary of the Cabinet with the approval of the Prime Minister and certifying that any information, question, document or part of a document so relates shall be conclusive.

(5) Subject to subsection (3) of this section, no person shall be compelled for the purposes of an investigation under this Act to give any evidence or produce any document which he could not be compelled to give or produce in civil proceedings before the Court.

Obstruction and contempt

9.—(1) If any person without lawful excuse obstructs the Commissioner or any officer of the Commissioner in the performance of his functions under this Act, or is guilty of any act or omission in relation to an investigation under this Act which, if that investigation were a proceeding in the Court, would constitute contempt of court, the Commissioner may certify the offence to the Court.

28–010

(2) Where an offence is certified under this section, the Court may inquire into the matter and, after hearing any witnesses who may be produced against or on behalf of the person charged with the offence, and after hearing any statement that may be offered in defence, deal with him in any manner in which the Court could deal with him if he had committed the like offence in relation to the Court.

(3) Nothing in this section shall be construed as applying to the taking of any such action as is mentioned in subsection (4) of section 7 of this Act.

Reports by Commissioner

10.—(1) In any case where the Commissioner conducts an investigation under this Act or decides not to conduct such an investigation, he shall send to the member of the House of Commons by whom the request for investigation was made (or if he is no longer a member of that House, to such member of that House as the Commissioner thinks appropriate) a report of the results of the investigation or, as the case may be, a statement of his reasons for not conducting an investigation.

28–011

(2) In any case where the Commissioner conducts an investigation under this Act, he shall also send a report of the results of the investigation to the principal officer of the department or authority concerned and to any other person who is alleged in the relevant complaint to have taken or authorised the action complained of.

(3) If, after conducting an investigation under this Act, it appears to the Commissioner that injustice has been caused to the person aggrieved in consequence of maladministration and that the injustice has not been, or will not be, remedied, he may, if he thinks fit, lay before each House of Parliament a special report upon the case.

(4) The Commissioner shall annually lay before each House of Parliament a general report on the performance of his functions under this Act and may from time to time lay before each House of Parliament such other reports with respect to those functions as he thinks fit.

(5) For the purposes of the law of defamation, any such publication as is hereinafter mentioned shall be absolutely privileged, that is to say—

    (a) the publication of any matter by the Commissioner in making a report to either House of Parliament for the purposes of this Act;

    (b) the publication of any matter by a member of the House of Commons in communicating with the Commissioner or his officers for those purposes or by the Commissioner or his officers in communicating with such a member for those purposes;

    (c) the publication by such a member to the person by whom a complaint was made under this Act of a report or statement sent to the member in respect of the complaint in pursuance of subsection (1) of this section;

    (d) the publication by the Commissioner to such a person as is mentioned in subsection (2) of this section of a report sent to that person in pursuance of that subsection.

Provision for secrecy of information

28–012   **11.**—(1) [. . .]¹

(2) Information obtained by the Commissioner or his officers in the course of or for the purposes of an investigation under this Act shall not be disclosed except—

    (a) for the purposes of the investigation and of any report to be made thereon under this Act;

    (b) 1920 c. 75 for the purposes of any proceedings for an offence under [the Official Secrets Acts 1911 to 1989]² alleged to have been committed in respect of information obtained by the Commissioner or any of his officers by virtue of this Act or for an offence of perjury alleged to have been committed in the course of an investigation under this Act or for the purposes of an inquiry with a view to the taking of such proceedings; or

    (c) for the purposes of any proceedings under section 9 of this Act;

and the Commissioner and his officers shall not be called upon to give evidence in any proceedings (other than such proceedings as aforesaid) of matters coming to his or their knowledge in the course of an investigation under this Act.

[(2A) Where the Commissioner also holds office as [Welsh Administration Ombudsman]³ or a Health Service Commissioner and a person initiates a complaint to him in his capacity as [Welsh Administration Ombudsman or a Health Service Commissioner]⁴ which relates partly to a matter with respect to which that person has previously initiated a complaint under this Act, or subsequently initiates such a complaint, information obtained by the Commissioner or his officers in the course of or for the purposes of investigating the complaint under this Act may be disclosed for the purposes of his carrying out his functions in relation to the other complaint.]⁵

(3) A Minister of the Crown may give notice in writing to the Commissioner, with respect to any document or information specified in the notice, or any class of documents or information so specified, that in the opinion of the Minister the disclosure of that document or information, or of documents or information of that class, would be prejudicial to the safety of the State or otherwise contrary to the public interest; and where such a notice is given nothing in this Act shall be construed as authorising or requiring the Commissioner or any officer of the Commissioner to communicate to any person or for any purpose any document or information specified in the notice, or any document or information of a class so specified.

(4) The references in this section to a Minister of the Crown include refer-

ences to the Commissioners of Customs and Excise and the Commissioners of Inland Revenue.

[(5) Information obtained from the Information Commissioner by virtue of section 76(1) of the Freedom of Information Act 2000 shall be treated for the purposes of subsection (2) of this section as obtained for the purposes of an investigation under this Act and, in relation to such information, the reference in paragraph (a) of that subsection to the investigation shall have effect as a reference to any investigation.][6]

[1] Repealed by Official Secrets Act 1989 (c.6), s. 16(4), Sched. 2.
[2] Words substituted by Official Secrets Act 1989 (c.6), s. 16(3), Sched. 1, para. 1.
[3] Words inserted by Government of Wales Act 1998 (c.38), Sched. 12, para. 7 (a).
[4] Words substituted by Government of Wales Act 1998 (c.38), Sched. 12, para. 7 (b).
[5] s. 11(2A) inserted by Parliamentary and Health Service Commissioners Act 1987 (c. 39), s. 4(1).
[6] Added by Freedom of Information Act 2000 (c.36), Sched. 7, para. 1.

[Consultations between Parliamentary Commissioner and [Welsh Administration Ombudsman or][1] Health Service Commissioners

11A.—(1) Where, at any stage in the course of conducting an investigation under this Act, the Commissioner forms the opinion that the complaint relates partly to a matter within the jurisdiction of [the Welsh Administration Ombudsman][2] or of the Health Service Commissioner for England, Wales or Scotland, he shall—   **28–013**

(a) unless he also holds [the office concerned][3], consult about the complaint with him; and

(b) if he considers it necessary, inform the person initiating the complaint under this Act of the steps necessary to initiate a complaint under [the Government of Wales Act 1998 or][4] [the Health Service Commissioners Act 1993.][5]

(2) Where by virtue of subsection (1) above the Commissioner consults with the [Welsh Administration Ombudsman][6] or a Health Service Commissioner in relation to a complaint under this Act, he may consult him about any matter relating to the complaint, including—

(a) the conduct of any investigation into the complaint; and

(b) the form, content and publication of any report of the results of such an investigation.

(3) Nothing in section 11(2) of this Act shall apply in relation to the disclosure of information by the Commissioner or any of his officers in the course of consultations held in accordance with this section.][7]

[1] Word inserted by Government of Wales Act 1998 (c.38), Sched. 12, para. 8(4).
[2] Words inserted by Government of Wales Act 1998 (c.38), Sched. 12, para. 8(2)(a).
[3] Words substituted by Government of Wales Act 1998 (c.38), Sched. 12, para. 8(2)(b).
[4] Words inserted by Government of Wales Act 1998 (c.38), Sched. 12, para. 8(2)(c).
[5] Words substituted by Health Service Commissioners Act 1993 (c.46), Sched. 2, para. 1.
[6] Words inserted by Government of Wales Act 1998 (c.38), Sched. 12, para. 8(3).
[7] s. 11A added by Parliamentary and Health Service Commissioners Act 1987 (c. 39), s. 4(2).

[Disclosure of information by Parliamentary Commissioner to Information Commissioner

11AA.—(1) The Commissioner may disclose to the Information Commissioner any information obtained by, or furnished to, the Commissioner under or for the purposes of this Act if the information appears to the Commissioner to relate to—   **28–014**

    (a) a matter in respect of which the Information Commissioner could exercise any power conferred by—

        (i) Part V of the Data Protection Act 1998 (enforcement);

        (ii) section 48 of the Freedom of Information Act 2000 (practice recommendations); or

        (iii) Part IV of that Act (enforcement); or

    (b) the commission of an offence under—

        (i) any provision of the Data Protection Act 1998 other than paragraph 12 of Schedule 9 (obstruction of execution of warrant), or

        (ii) section 77 of the Freedom of Information Act 2000 (offence of altering, etc. records with intent to prevent disclosure).

    (2) Nothing in section 11(2) of this Act shall apply in relation to the disclosure of information in accordance with this section.][1]

[1] Added by Freedom of Information Act 2000 (c.36), Sched. 7, para. 2.

[The Criminal Injuries Compensation Scheme

28–015   **11B.**—(1) For the purposes of this Act, administrative functions exercisable by an administrator of the Criminal Injuries Compensation Scheme ("Scheme functions") shall be taken to be administrative functions of a government department to which this Act applies.

    (2) For the purposes of this section, the following are administrators of the Scheme—

    (a) a claims officer appointed under section 3(4)(b) of the Criminal Injuries Compensation Act 1995;

    (b) a person appointed under section 5(3)(c) of that Act;

    (c) the Scheme manager, as defined by section 1(4) of that Act, and any person assigned by him to exercise functions in relation to the Scheme.

    (3) The principal officer in relation to any complaint made in respect of any action taken in respect of Scheme functions is—

    (a) in the case of action taken by a claims officer, such person as may from time to time be designated by the Secretary of State for the purposes of this paragraph;

    (b) in the case of action taken by a person appointed under section 5(3)(c) of the Act of 1995, the chairman appointed by the Secretary of State under section 5(3)(b) of that Act; or

    (c) in the case of action taken by the Scheme manager or by any other person mentioned in subsection (2)(c) of this section, the Scheme manager.

    (4) The conduct of an investigation under this Act in respect of any action taken in respect of Scheme functions shall not affect—

    (a) any action so taken; or

    (b) any power or duty of any person to take further action with respect to any matters subject to investigation.][1]

[1] Added by Criminal Injuries Compensation Act 1995 (c.53), s. 10(1).

Supplemental

Interpretation

12.—(1) In this Act the following expressions have the meanings hereby respectively assigned to them, that is to say—   **28–016**

"action" includes failure to act, and other expressions connoting action shall be construed accordingly;

"the Commissioner" means the Parliamentary Commissioner for Administration;

"the Court" means, in relation to England and Wales the High Court, in relation to Scotland the Court of Session, and in relation to Northern Ireland the High Court of Northern Ireland;

"enactment" includes an enactment of the Parliament of Northern Ireland, and any instrument made by virtue of an enactment;

"officer" includes employee;

"person aggrieved" means the person who claims or is alleged to have sustained such injustice as is mentioned in section 5(1)(a) of this Act;

"tribunal" includes the person constituting a tribunal consisting of one person.

(2) References in this Act to any enactment are references to that enactment as amended or extended by or under any other enactment.

(3) It is hereby declared that nothing in this Act authorises or requires the Commissioner to question the merits of a decision taken without maladministration by a government department or other authority in the exercise of a discretion vested in that department or authority.

. . . . . .

Section 5   SCHEDULE 3

MATTERS NOT SUBJECT TO INVESTIGATION

1. Action taken in matters certified by a Secretary of State or other Minister of the Crown to affect relations or dealings between the Government of the United Kingdom and any other Government or any international organisation of States or Governments.   **28–017**

2. Action taken, in any country or territory outside the United Kingdom, by or on behalf of any officer representing or acting under the authority of Her Majesty in respect of the United Kingdom, or any other officer of the Government of the United Kingdom [other than action which is taken by an officer (not being an honorary consular officer) in the exercise of a consular function on behalf of the government of the United Kingdom.]   **28–018**

3. Action taken in connection with the administration of the government of any country or territory outside the United Kingdom which forms part of Her Majesty's dominions or in which Her Majesty has jurisdiction.   **28–019**

4. Action taken by the Secretary of State under the Extradition Act 1870 the Fugitive Offenders Act 1967 or the Extradition Act 1989.   **28–020**

5. Action taken by or with the authority of the Secretary of State for the purposes of investigating crime or of protecting the security of the State, including action so taken with respect to passports.   **28–021**

6. The commencement or conduct of civil or criminal proceedings before any court of law in the United Kingdom, of proceedings at any place under the Naval Discipline Act 1957, the Army Act 1955 or the Air Force Act 1955, or of proceedings before any international court or tribunal.   **28–022**

[**6A.** Action taken by any person appointed by the Lord Chancellor as a member of the administrative staff of any court or tribunal, so far as that action is taken at the direction, or on the authority   **28–023** (whether express or implied), of any person acting in a judicial capacity or in his capacity as a member of the tribunal.]¹

¹ Sched. 3, para. 6A inserted by Courts and Legal Services Act 1990 (c.41), s. 110(2).

28–024

[**6B.**—(1) Action taken by any member of the administrative staff of a relevant tribunal, so far as that action is taken at the direction, or on the authority (whether express or implied), of any person acting in his capacity as a member of the tribunal.

(2) In this paragraph, 'relevant tribunal' has the meaning given by section 5(8) of this Act.]¹

¹ Added by Parliamentary Commissioner Act 1994 (c.14), s. 1(2).

28–025

[**6C.** Action taken by any person appointed under section 5(3)(c) of the Criminal Injuries Compensation Act 1995, so far as that action is taken at the direction, or on the authority (whether express or implied), of any person acting in his capacity as an adjudicator appointed under section 5 of that Act to determine appeals.]¹

¹ para. 6C inserted after para. 6B by Criminal Injuries Compensation Act 1995 (c.53), s. 10(2).

28–026

7. Any exercise of the prerogative of mercy or of the power of a Secretary of State to make a reference in respect of any person to the High Court of Justiciary or the Courts-Martial Appeal Court.

28–027

[**8.** (1) Action taken on behalf of the Minister of Health or the Secretary of State by a Health Authority, a Primary Care Trust, a Special Health Authority except the Rampton Hospital Review Board ... the Rampton Hospital Board, the Broadmoor Hospital Board or the Moss Side and Park Lane Hospitals Board, a Health Board or the Common Services Agency for the Scottish Health Service, by the Dental Practice Board or the Scottish Dental Practice Board or by the Public Health Laboratory Service Board.

(2) For the purposes of this paragraph, action taken by a Health Authority, Special Health Authority or Primary Care Trust in the exercise of functions of the Secretary of State shall be regarded as action taken on his behalf.]

28–028

9. Action taken in matters relating to contractual or other commercial transactions, whether within the United Kingdom or elsewhere, being transactions of a government department or authority to which this Act applies or of any such authority or body as is mentioned in paragraph (a) or (b) of subsection (1) of section 6 of this Act and not being transactions for or relating to—

(a) the acquisition of land compulsorily or in circumstances in which it could be acquired compulsorily;

(b) the disposal as surplus of land acquired compulsorily or in such circumstances as aforesaid.

28–029

10. [(1)] Action taken in respect of appointments or removals, pay, discipline, superannuation or other personnel matters, in relation to—

(a) service in any of the armed forces of the Crown, including reserve and auxiliary and cadet forces;

(b) service in any office or employment under the Crown or under any authority [to which this Act applies]¹; or

(c) service in any office or employment, or under any contract for services, in respect of which power to take action, or to determine or approve the action to be taken, in such matters is vested in Her Majesty, any Minister of the Crown or any such authority as aforesaid.

[(2) Sub-paragraph (1)(c) above shall not apply to any action (not otherwise excluded from investigation by this Schedule) which is taken by the Secretary of State in connection with:—

(a) the provision of information relating to the terms and conditions of any employment covered by an agreement entered into by him under section 12(1) of the Overseas Development and Co-operation Act 1980 or

(b) the provision of any allowance, grant or supplement or any benefit (other than those relating to superannuation) arising from the designation of any person in accordance with such an agreement.]

¹ Words substituted by Parliamentary and Health Service Commissioners Act 1987 (c. 39), s. 1(3)(c).

28–030

11. The grant of honours, awards or privileges within the gift of the Crown, including the grant of Royal Charters.

Theatres Act 1968

(1968, c. 54)

An Act to abolish censorship of the theatre and to amend the law in respect of **29–001**
theatres and theatrical performances.   [26th July 1968]

Abolition of censorship of the theatre

Abolition of censorship of the theatre

1.—(1) The Theatres Act 1843 is hereby repealed; and none of the powers **29–002**
which were exercisable thereunder by the Lord Chamberlain of Her Majesty's
Household shall be exercisable by or on behalf of Her Majesty by virtue of Her
royal prerogative.

(2) In granting, renewing or transferring any licence under this Act for the
use of any premises for the public performance of plays or in varying any of
the terms, conditions or restrictions on or subject to which any such licence is
held, the licensing authority shall not have power to impose any term, condition
or restriction as to the nature of the plays which may be performed under the
licence or as to the manner of performing plays thereunder:

Provided that nothing in this subsection shall prevent a licensing authority
from imposing any term, condition or restriction which they consider necessary
in the interests of physical safety or health or any condition regulating or prohibiting the giving of an exhibition, demonstration or performance of hypnotism
within the meaning of the Hypnotism Act 1952.

Provisions with respect to performances of plays

Prohibition of presentation of obscene performances of plays

2.—(1) For the purposes of this section a performance of a play shall be **29–003**
deemed to be obscene if, taken as a whole, its effect was such as to tend to
deprave and corrupt persons who were likely, having regard to all relevant circumstances, to attend it.

(2) Subject to sections 3 and 7 of this Act, if an obscene performance of a
play is given, whether in public or private, any person who (whether for gain or
not) presented or directed that performance shall be liable—

  (a) on summary conviction, to a fine not exceeding £400 or to imprison-
      ment for a term not exceeding six months;
  (b) on conviction on indictment, to a fine or to imprisonment for a term
      not exceeding three years, or both.

(3) A prosecution on indictment for an offence under this section shall not be
commenced more than two years after the commission of the offence.

(4) No person shall be proceeded against in respect of a performance of a
play or anything said or done in the course of such a performance—

  (a) for an offence at common law where it is of the essence of the offence
      that the performance or, as the case may be, what was said or done
      was obscene, indecent, offensive, disgusting or injurious to morality; or
  (b) [. . .]^1
  (c) [. . .]^2

and no person shall be proceeded against for an offence at common law of
conspiring to corrupt public morals, or to do any act contrary to public morals

or decency, in respect of an agreement to present or give a performance of a play, or to cause anything to be said or done in the course of such a performance.

[1] Repealed by Indecent Displays (Control) Act 1981 (c.42), s. 5(2), Sched.
[2] Repealed by Civic Government (Scotland) Act 1982 (c.45), s. 137(2), Sched. 4.

Defence of public good

29–004   **3.**—(1) A person shall not be convicted of an offence under section 2 of this Act if it is proved that the giving of the performance in question was justified as being for the public good on the ground that it was in the interest of drama, opera, ballet or any other art, or of literature or learning.

(2) It is hereby declared that the opinion of experts as to the artistic, literary or other merits of a performance of a play may be admitted in any proceedings for an offence under section 2 of this Act either to establish or negative the said ground.

Amendment of law of defamation

29–005   **4.**—(1) For the purposes of the law of libel and slander (including the law of criminal libel so far as it relates to the publication of defamatory matter) the publication of words in the course of a performance of a play shall, subject to section 7 of this Act, be treated as publication in permanent form.

(2) The foregoing subsection shall apply for the purposes of section 3 (slander of title, etc.) of the Defamation Act 1952 as it applies for the purposes of the law of libel and slander.

(3) In this section "words" includes pictures, visual images, gestures and other methods of signifying meaning.

(4) This section shall not apply to Scotland.

. . . . . .

Exceptions for performances given in certain circumstances

29–006   **7.**—(1) Nothing in sections 2 to 4 of this Act shall apply in relation to a performance of a play given on a domestic occasion in a private dwelling.

(2) Nothing in sections 2 to 6 of this Act shall apply in relation to a performance of a play given solely or primarily for one or more of the following purposes, that is to say—

(a) rehearsal; or
(b) to enable—

(i) a record or cinematograph film to be made from or by means of the performance; or
(ii) the performance to be broadcast; or
[(iii) the performance to be included in a programme service (within the meaning of the Broadcasting Act 1990) other than a sound or television broadcasting service;][1]

but in any proceedings for an offence under section 2 or 6 of this Act alleged to have been committed in respect of a performance of a play or an offence at common law alleged to have been committed in England and Wales by the publication of defamatory matter in the course of a performance of a play, if it is proved that the performance was attended by persons other than persons directly connected with the giving of the performance or the doing in relation thereto of any of the things mentioned in paragraph (b) above, the performance shall be taken not to have been given solely or primarily for one or more of the said purposes unless the contrary is shown.

(3) In this section—

"broadcast" means broadcast by wireless telegraphy (within the meaning of the Wireless Telegraphy Act 1949), whether by way of sound broadcasting or television;

"cinematograph film" means any print, negative, tape or other article on which a performance of a play or any part of such a performance is recorded for the purposes of visual reproduction;

"record" means any record or similar contrivance for reproducing sound, including the sound-track of a cinematograph film.

¹ s. 7(2)(b)(iii) substituted by Broadcasting Act 1990 (c.42), s. 203(1), Sched. 20, para. 13.

Restriction on institution of proceedings

8. Proceedings for an offence under section 2 or 6 of this Act or an offence at common law committed by the publication of defamatory matter in the course of a performance of a play shall not be instituted in England and Wales except by or with the consent of the Attorney-General.   **29–007**

. . . . . .

Interpretation

18.—(1) In this Act—   **29–008**

"licensing authority" means—

[(a) as respects premises in a London borough or the City of London, the council of that borough or the Common Council, as the case may be;]

(b) [as respect premises in a district in England, the council of that district];

[(bb) as respects premises in a county or county borough in Wales, the council of that area;]¹

(c) in relation to Scotland, [a council constituted under section 2 of the Local Government etc. (Scotland) Act 1994]²;

"play" means—

(a) any dramatic piece, whether involving improvisation or not, which is given wholly or in part by one or more persons actually present and performing and in which the whole or a major proportion of what is done by the person or persons performing, whether by way of speech, singing or action, involves the playing of a role; and

(b) any ballet given wholly or in part by one or more persons actually present and performing, whether or not it falls within paragraph (a) of this definition;

"police officer" means a member, or in Scotland a constable, of a police force;

"premises" includes any place;

"public performance" includes any performance in a public place within the meaning of the Public Order Act 1936 and any performance which the public or any section thereof are permitted to attend, whether on payment or otherwise;

"script" has the meaning assigned by section 9(2) of this Act.

(2) For the purposes of this Act—

(a) a person shall not be treated as presenting a performance of a play by reason only of his taking part therein as a performer;

(b) a person taking part as a performer in a performance of a play directed by another person shall be treated as a person who directed the performance if without reasonable excuse he performs otherwise than in accordance with that person's direction; and

(c) a person shall be taken to have directed a performance of a play given under his direction notwithstanding that he was not present during the performance;

and a person shall not be treated as aiding or abetting the commission of an offence under section 2 or 6 of this Act in respect of a performance of a play by reason only of his taking part in that performance as a performer.

¹ Added by Local Government (Wales) Act 1994 (c.19), Sched. 16, para. 32.
² Words substituted by Local Government etc. (Scotland) Act 1994 (c.39), Sched. 13, para. 77.

Foreign Compensation Act 1969

(1969, c. 20)

30–001   *An Act to make provision with respect to certain property (including the proceeds thereof and any income or other property accruing therefrom) of persons formerly resident or carrying on business in Estonia, Latvia, Lithuania or a part of Czechoslovakia, Finland, Poland or Rumania which has been ceded to the Union of Soviet Socialist Republics, and to amend the Foreign Compensation Act 1950.*   [16th May 1969]

. . . . . .

Determinations of the Foreign Compensation Commission and appeals against such determinations

30–002   **3.**—(1) The Foreign Compensation Commission shall have power to determine any question as to the construction or interpretation of any provision of an Order in Council under section 3 of the Foreign Compensation Act 1950 with respect to claims falling to be determined by them.

(2) Subject to subsection (4) below, the Commission shall, if so required by a person mentioned in subsection (6) below who is aggrieved by any determination of the Commission on any question of law relating to the jurisdiction of the Commission or on any question mentioned in subsection (1) above, state and sign a case for the decision of the Court of Appeal.

(3) In this section "determination" includes a determination which under rules under section 4(2) of the Foreign Compensation Act 1950 (rules of procedure) is a provisional determination, and anything which purports to be a determination.

(4) Where the Court of Appeal decide a question on a case stated and signed by the Commission on a provisional determination in any proceedings, subsection (2) above shall not require the Commission to state and sign a case on a final determination by them of that question in those proceedings.

(5) Any person mentioned in subsection (6) below may, with a view to requiring the Commission to state and sign a case under this section, request the Commission to furnish a written statement of the reasons for any determination of theirs, but the Commission shall not be obliged to state the reasons for any determination unless it is given on a claim in which a question mentioned in subsection (2) above arises.

(6) The persons who may make a request under subsection (5) above or a requirement under subsection (2) above in relation to any claim are the claimant and any person appointed by the Commission to represent the interests of any fund out of which the claim would, if owed be met.

(7) Any such request or requirement must be in writing, and—

(a) any such request may be disregarded unless it is received by the Commission within the period of four weeks beginning with the date on which the Commission send notice of the determination in question or such other period as may be provided for by or under rules under section 4(2) of the Foreign Compensation Act 1950; and

(b) any such requirement may be disregarded unless it is received by the Commission within the period of eight weeks beginning with that date or the period of four weeks beginning with the date on which the Commission send a statement of reasons for the determination in question, whichever expires last, or within such other period as may be provided for by or under rules of court.

(8) Notwithstanding anything in section 3 of the Appellate Jurisdiction Act 1876 (right of appeal to the House of Lords from decisions of the Court of Appeal), no appeal shall lie to the House of Lords from a decision of the Court of Appeal on an appeal under this section.

(9) Except as provided by subsection (2) above and subsection (10) below, no determination by the Commission on any claim made to them under the Foreign Compensation Act 1950 shall be called in question in any court of law.

(10) Subsection (9) above shall not affect any right of any person to bring proceedings questioning any determination of the Commission on the ground that it is contrary to natural justice.

(11) [. . .]¹

(12) [. . .]²

---

¹ Repealed by Statute Law (Repeals) Act 1989 (c.43), s. 1(1), Sched. 1, Pt. II, Gp. 2.
² *ibid.*

Courts Act 1971

(1971, c. 23)

31–001 *An Act to make further provision as respects the Supreme Court and county courts, judges and juries, to establish a Crown Court as part of the Supreme Court to try indictments and exercise certain other jurisdiction, to abolish courts of assize and certain other courts and to deal with their jurisdiction and other consequential matters, and to amend in other respects the law about courts and court proceedings.*   [12th May 1971]

. . . . . .

PART III

JUDGES

Appointment of Circuit Judges

31–002   **16.**—(1) Her Majesty may from time to time appoint as Circuit judges, to serve in the Crown Court and county courts and to carry out such other judicial functions as may be conferred on them under this or any other enactment, such qualified persons as may be recommended to Her by the Lord Chancellor.

(2) The maximum number of Circuit judges shall be such as may be determined from time to time by the Lord Chancellor with the concurrence of the Minister for the Civil Service.

(3) No person shall be qualified to be appointed a Circuit judge [unless—

  (a) he has a 10 year Crown Court or 10 year County Court qualification within the meaning of section 71of the Courts and Legal Services Act 1990;
  (b) he is a Recorder; or
  (c) he has held as a full-time appointment for at least 3 years one of the offices listed in Part IA of Schedule 2.][1]

(4) Before recommending any person to Her Majesty for appointment as a Circuit judge, the Lord Chancellor shall take steps to satisfy himself that that person's health is satisfactory.

(5) The provisions of Part I of Schedule 2 to this Act shall have effect with respect to the appointment as Circuit judges of the holders of certain judicial offices, and the supplementary provisions in Part II of that Schedule shall have effect.

[1] Words substituted by Courts and Legal Services Act 1990 (c.41), s. 71(2), Sched. 10, para. 31(1).

Retirement, removal and disqualifications of Circuit judge

31–003   **17.**— [(1) Subject to subsection (4) below and to subsections (4) to (6) of section 26 of the Judicial Pensions and Retirement Act 1993 (power to authorise continuance in office up to the age of 75), a Circuit judge shall vacate his office on the day on which he attains the age of 70.][1]

(2) The Lord Chancellor may, if he thinks fit, remove a Circuit judge from office on the ground of incapacity or misbehaviour.

[1] Substituted by Judicial Pensions and Retirement Act 1993 (c.8), Sched. 6, para. 8(2).

Immigration Act 1971

(1971, c. 77)

An Act to amend and replace the present immigration laws, to make certain related changes in the citizenship law and enable help to be given to those wishing to return abroad, and for purposes connected therewith.

[28th October 1971]

32–001

PART I

REGULATION OF ENTRY INTO AND STAY IN UNITED KINGDOM

General principles

1.—(1) All those who are in this Act expressed to have the right of abode in the United Kingdom shall be free to live in, and to come and go into and from, the United Kingdom without let or hindrance except such as may be required under and in accordance with this Act to enable their right to be established or as may be otherwise lawfully imposed on any person.

32–002

(2) Those not having that right may live, work and settle in the United Kingdom by permission and subject to such regulation and control of their entry into, stay in and departure from the United Kingdom as is imposed by this Act; and indefinite leave to enter or remain in the United Kingdom shall, by virtue of this provision, be treated as having been given under this Act to those in the United Kingdom at its coming into force, if they are then settled there (and not exempt under this Act from the provisions relating to leave to enter or remain).

(3) Arrival in and departure from the United Kingdom on a local journey from or to any of the Islands (that is to say, the Channel Islands and Isle of Man) or the Republic of Ireland shall not be subject to control under this Act, nor shall a person require leave to enter the United Kingdom on so arriving, except in so far as any of those places is for any purpose excluded from this subsection under the powers conferred by this Act; and in this Act the United Kingdom and those places, or such of them as are not so excluded, are collectively referred to as "the common travel area".

(4) The rules laid down by the Secretary of State as to the practice to be followed in the administration of this Act for regulating the entry into and stay in the United Kingdom of persons not having the right of abode shall include provision for admitting (in such cases and subject to such restrictions as may be provided by the rules, and subject or not to conditions as to length of stay or otherwise) persons coming for the purpose of taking employment, or for purposes of study, or as visitors, or as dependants of persons lawfully in or entering the United Kingdom.[1]

[1] Separate provisions apply in relation to the Isle of Man, Jersey and Guernsey.

Statement of right of abode in United Kingdom

2.—(1) A person is under this Act to have the right of abode in the United Kingdom if—

32–003

(a) he is a British citizen; or
(b) he is a Commonwealth citizen who—

    (i) immediately before the commencement of the British Nationality Act 1981 was a Commonwealth citizen having the right of abode in the British Kingdom by virtue of section 2(1)(d) or section 2(2) of this Act as then in force; and

(ii) has not ceased to be a Commonwealth citizen in the meanwhile.

(2) In relation to Commonwealth citizens who have the right of abode in the United Kingdom by virtue of subsection (1)(b) above, this Act, except this section and [section 5(2)]¹, shall apply as if they were British citizens; and in this Act (except as aforesaid) "British citizen" shall be construed accordingly.

¹ Words substituted by Immigration Act 1988 (c. 14), s. 3(3).

General provisions for regulation and control

32–004   **3.**—(1) Except as otherwise provided by or under this Act, where a person is not [a British citizen]

- (a) he shall not enter the United Kingdom unless given leave to do so in accordance with [the provisions of, or made under,]¹ this Act;
- (b) he may be given leave to enter the United Kingdom (or, when already there, leave to remain in the United Kingdom) either for a limited or for an indefinite period;
- (c) if he is given a limited leave to enter or remain in the United Kingdom, it may be given subject to conditions restricting his employment or occupation in the United Kingdom, or requiring him to register with the police, or both.

(2) The Secretary of State shall from time to time (and as soon as may be) lay before Parliament statements of the rules, or of any changes in the rules, laid down by him as to the practice to be followed in the administration of this Act for regulating the entry into and stay in the United Kingdom of persons required by this Act to have leave to enter, including any rules as to the period for which leave is to be given and the conditions to be attached in different circumstances; and section 1(4) above shall not be taken to require uniform provision to be made by the rules as regards admission of persons for a purpose or in a capacity specified in section 1(4) (and in particular, for this as well as other purposes of this Act, account may be taken of citizenship or nationality).

If a statement laid before either House of Parliament under this subsection is disapproved by a resolution of that House passed within the period of forty days beginning with the date of laying (and exclusive of any period during which Parliament is dissolved or prorogued or during which both Houses are adjourned for more than four days), then the Secretary of State shall as soon as may be make such changes or further changes in the rules as appear to him to be required in the circumstances, so that the statement of those changes be laid before Parliament at latest by the end of the period of forty days beginning with the date of the resolution (but exclusive as aforesaid).

(3) In the case of a limited leave to enter or remain in the United Kingdom,—

- (a) a person's leave may be varied, whether by restricting, enlarging or removing the limit on its duration, or by adding, varying or revoking conditions, but if the limit on its duration is removed, any conditions attached to the leave shall cease to apply; and
- (b) the limitation on and any conditions attached to a person's leave [(whether imposed originally or on a variation) shall], if not superseded, apply also to any subsequent leave he may obtain after an absence from the United Kingdom within the period limited for the duration of the earlier leave.

(4) A person's leave to enter or remain in the United Kingdom shall lapse on his going to a country or territory outside the common travel area (whether or

not he lands there), unless within the period for which he had leave he returns to the United Kingdom in circumstances in which he is not required to obtain leave to enter; but, if he does so return, his previous leave (and any limitation on it or conditions attached to it) shall continue to apply.

[(4A) For the purposes of subsection (4) above a person seeking to leave the United Kingdom through the tunnel system who is refused admission to France shall be treated as having gone to a country outside the common travel area.]

(5) A person who is not [a British citizen]² shall be liable to deportation from the United Kingdom—

(a) if, having only a limited leave to enter or remain, he does not observe a condition attached to the leave or remains beyond the time limited by the leave; or

[(aa) if he has obtained leave to remain by deception; or]³

(b) if the Secretary of State deems his deportation to be conducive to the public good; or

(c) if another person to whose family he belongs is or has been ordered to be deported.

(6) Without prejudice to the operation of subsection (5) above, a person who is not [a British citizen] shall also be liable to deportation from the United Kingdom if, after he has attained the age of seventeen, he is convicted of an offence for which he is punishable with imprisonment and on his conviction is recommended for deportation by a court empowered by this Act to do so.

(7) Where it appears to Her Majesty proper so to do by reason of restrictions or conditions imposed on [British citizens, [British overseas territories citizens] or British Overseas citizens] when leaving or seeking to leave any country or the territory subject to the government of any country, Her Majesty may by Order in Council make provision for prohibiting persons who are nationals or citizens of that country and are not [British citizens] from embarking in the United Kingdom, or from doing so elsewhere than at a port of exit, or for imposing restrictions or conditions on them when embarking or about to embark in the United Kingdom; and Her Majesty may also make provision by Order in Council to enable those who are not [British citizens]⁴ to be, in such cases as may be prescribed by the Order, prohibited in the interests of safety from so embarking on a ship or aircraft specified or indicated in the prohibition.

Any Order in Council under this subsection shall be subject to annulment in pursuance of a resolution of either House of Parliament.

(8) When any question arises under this Act whether or not a person is [a British citizen]⁵ or is entitled to any exemption under this Act, it shall lie on the person asserting it to prove that he is.

[(9) A person seeking to enter the United Kingdom and claiming to have the right of abode there shall prove that he has that right by means of either—

(a) a United Kingdom passport describing him as a British citizen or as a citizen of the United Kingdom and Colonies having the right of abode in the United Kingdom; or

(b) a certificate of entitlement issued by or on behalf of the Government of the United Kingdom certifying that he has such a right of abode.]

¹ Words added by Immigration and Asylum Act 1999 (c. 33), Sched. 14, para. 44(1).
² *ibid.*
³ Added by Asylum and Immigration Act 1996 (c. 49).
⁴ Words added by Immigration and Asylum Act 1999 (c. 33), Sched. 14, para. 44(1).
⁵ *ibid.*

Further provision as to leave to enter

32–005   **3A.**—(1) The Secretary of State may by order make further provision with respect to the giving, refusing or varying of leave to enter the United Kingdom.
(2) An order under subsection (1) may, in particular, provide for—

(a) leave to be given or refused before the person concerned arrives in the United Kingdom;
(b) the form or manner in which leave may be given, refused or varied;
(c) the imposition of conditions;
(d) a person's leave to enter not to lapse on his leaving the common travel area.

(3) The Secretary of State may by order provide that, in such circumstances as may be prescribed—

(a) an entry visa, or
(b) such other form of entry clearance as may be prescribed,

is to have effect as leave to enter the United Kingdom.
(4) An order under subsection (3) may, in particular—

(a) provide for a clearance to have effect as leave to enter—

(i) on a prescribed number of occasions during the period for which the clearance has effect;
(ii) on an unlimited number of occasions during that period;
(iii) subject to prescribed conditions; and

(b) provide for a clearance which has the effect referred to in paragraph (a)(i) or (ii) to be varied by the Secretary of State or an immigration officer so that it ceases to have that effect.

(5) Only conditions of a kind that could be imposed on leave to enter given under section 3 may be prescribed.
(6) In subsections (3), (4) and (5) "prescribed" means prescribed in an order made under subsection (3).
(7) The Secretary of State may, in such circumstances as may be prescribed in an order made by him, give or refuse leave to enter the United Kingdom.
(8) An order under subsection (7) may provide that, in such circumstances as may be prescribed by the order, paragraphs 2, 4, 6, 7, 8, 9 and 21 of Part I of Schedule 2 to this Act are to be read, in relation to the exercise by the Secretary of State of functions which he has as a result of the order, as if references to an immigration officer included references to the Secretary of State.
(9) Subsection (8) is not to be read as affecting any power conferred by subsection (10).
(10) An order under this section may—

(a) contain such incidental, supplemental, consequential and transitional provision as the Secretary of State considers appropriate; and
(b) make different provision for different cases.

(11) This Act and any provision made under it has effect subject to any order made under this section.
(12) An order under this section must be made by statutory instrument.
(13) But no such order is to be made unless a draft of the order has been laid before Parliament and approved by a resolution of each House.][1]

[1] Added by Immigration and Asylum Act 1999 (c.33), Pt I, s. 1.

Further provision as to leave to remain

[3B.—(1) The Secretary of State may by order make further provision with 32–006
respect to the giving, refusing or varying of leave to remain in the United Kingdom.

(2) An order under subsection (1) may, in particular, provide for—

    (a) the form or manner in which leave may be given, refused or varied;
    (b) the imposition of conditions;
    (c) a person's leave to remain in the United Kingdom not to lapse on his
        leaving the common travel area.

(3) An order under this section may—

    (a) contain such incidental, supplemental, consequential and transitional
        provision as the Secretary of State considers appropriate; and
    (b) make different provision for different cases.

(4) This Act and any provision made under it has effect subject to any order
made under this section.

(5) An order under this section must be made by statutory instrument.

(6) But no such order is to be made unless a draft of the order has been laid
before Parliament and approved by a resolution of each House.]¹

¹ Added by Immigration and Asylum Act 1999 (c.33), Pt I, s. 2.

. . . . . .

Recommendations by court for deportation

6.—(1) Where under section 3(6) above a person convicted of an offence is 32–007
liable to deportation on the recommendation of a court, he may be recommended
for deportation by any court having power to sentence him for the offence unless
the court commits him to be sentenced or further dealt with for that offence by
another court:

Provided that in Scotland the power to recommend a person for deportation
shall be exercisable only by the sheriff or the High Court of Justiciary, and shall
not be exercisable by the latter on an appeal unless the appeal is against a
conviction on indictment or against a sentence upon such a conviction.

(2) A court shall not recommend a person for deportation unless he has been
given not less than seven days notice in writing stating that a person is not liable
to deportation if he is [a British citizen], describing the persons who are [British
citizens] and stating (so far as material) the effect of section 3(8) above and
section 7 below; but the powers of adjournment conferred by [section 10(3) of
the Magistrates' Courts Act 1980], [section 179 or 380 of the Criminal Procedure (Scotland) Act 1975] or any corresponding enactment for the time being in
force in Northern Ireland shall include power to adjourn, after convicting an
offender, for the purpose of enabling a notice to be given to him under this
subsection or, if a notice was so given to him less than seven days previously,
for the purpose of enabling the necessary seven days to elapse.

(3) For purposes of section 3(6) above—

    (a) a person shall be deemed to have attained the age of seventeen at the
        time of his conviction if, on consideration of any available evidence,
        he appears to have done so to the court making or considering a recom-
        mendation for deportation; and

(b) the question whether an offence is one for which a person is punishable with imprisonment shall be determined without regard to any enactment restricting the imprisonment of young offenders or [persons who have not previously been sentenced to imprisonment];

and for purposes of deportation a person who on being charged with an offence is found to have committed it shall, notwithstanding any enactment to the contrary and notwithstanding that the court does not proceed to conviction, be regarded as a person convicted of the offence, and references to conviction shall be construed accordingly.

(4) Notwithstanding any rule of practice restricting the matters which ought to be taken into account in dealing with an offender who is sentenced to imprisonment, a recommendation for deportation may be made in respect of an offender who is sentenced to imprisonment for life.

(5) Where a court recommends or purports to recommend a person for deportation, the validity of the recommendation shall not be called in question except on an appeal against the recommendation or against the conviction on which it is made; but—

(a) [. . .]¹ the recommendation shall be treated as a sentence for the purpose of any enactment providing an appeal against sentence [. . .]²
(b) [. . .]³

(6) A deportation order shall not be made on the recommendation of a court so long as an appeal or further appeal is pending against the recommendation or against the conviction on which it was made; and for this purpose an appeal or further appeal shall be treated as pending (where one is competent but has not been brought) until the expiration of the time for bringing that appeal or, in Scotland, until the expiration of twenty-eight days from the date of the recommendation.

(7) For the purpose of giving effect to any of the provisions of this section in its application to Scotland, the High Court of Justiciary shall have power to make rules by act of adjournal.

¹ Words repealed by Criminal Justice Act 1982 (c. 48), ss. 77, 78, Sched. 15, para. 15(b), Sched. 16.
² Words repealed by Criminal Justice Act 1982 (c. 48), ss. 77, 78, Sched. 15, para. 15(b), Sched. 16.
³ s. 6(5)(b) repealed by Criminal Justice Act 1982 (c. 48), ss. 77, 78, Sched. 15, para. 15(b), Sched. 16.

Exemption from deportation for certain existing residents

32–008   7.—(1) Notwithstanding anything in section 3(5) or (6) above but subject to the provisions of this section, a Commonwealth citizen or citizen of the Republic of Ireland who was such a citizen at the coming into force of this Act and was then ordinarily resident in the United Kingdom—

(a) shall not be liable to deportation under section 3(5)(b) if at the time of the Secretary of State's decision he had at all times since the coming into force of this Act been ordinarily resident in the United Kingdom and Islands; and
(b) shall not be liable to deportation under section 3(5)(a), (b) or (c) if at the time of the Secretary of State's decision he had for the last five years been ordinarily resident in the United Kingdom and Islands; and
(c) shall not on conviction of an offence be recommended for deportation under section 3(6) if at the time of the conviction he had for the last five years been ordinarily resident in the United Kingdom and Islands.

(2) A person who has at any time become ordinarily resident in the United

Kingdom or in any of the Islands shall not be treated for the purposes of this section as having ceased to be so by reason only of his having remained there in breach of the immigration laws.

(3) The "last five years" before the material time under subsection (1)(b) or (c) above is to be taken as a period amounting in total to five years exclusive of any time during which the person claiming exemption under this section was undergoing imprisonment or detention by virtue of a sentence passed for an offence on a conviction in the United Kingdom and Islands, and the period for which he was imprisoned or detained by virtue of the sentence amounted to six months or more.

(4) For purposes of subsection (3) above—

(a) "sentence" includes any order made on conviction of an offence; and
(b) two or more sentences for consecutive (or partly consecutive) terms shall be treated as a single sentence; and
(c) a person shall be deemed to be detained by virtue of a sentence—

(i) at any time when he is liable to imprisonment or detention by virtue of the sentence, but is unlawfully at large; and
(ii) (unless the sentence is passed after the material time) during any period of custody by which under any relevant enactment the term to be served under the sentence is reduced.

In paragraph (c)(ii) above "relative enactment" means section 67 of the Criminal Justice Act 1967 (or, before that section operated, section 17(2) of the Criminal Justice Administration Act 1962) and any similar enactment which is for the time being or has (before or after the passing of this Act) been in force in any part of the United Kingdom and Islands.

(5) Nothing in this section shall be taken to exclude the operation of section 3(8) above in relation to an exemption under this section.

· · · · · ·

Part III

Criminal Proceedings

Illegal entry and similar offences

24.—(1) A person who is not [a British citizen] shall be guilty of an offence   **32–009**
punishable on summary conviction with a fine of not more than [[level 5] on the standard scale] or with imprisonment for not more than six months, or with both, in any of the following cases:—

(a) if contrary to this Act he knowingly enters the United Kingdom in breach of a deportation order or without leave;
(aa) [. . .]¹
(b) if, having only a limited leave to enter or remain in the United Kingdom, he knowingly either—

(i) remains beyond the time limited by the leave; or
(ii) fails to observe a condition of the leave;

(c) if, having lawfully entered the United Kingdom without leave by virtue of section 8(1) above, he remains without leave beyond the time allowed by section 8(1);
(d) if, without reasonable excuse, he fails to comply with any requirement

imposed on him under Schedule 2 to this Act to report to a medical officer of health, or to attend, or submit to a test or examination, as required by such an officer;

(e) if, without reasonable excuse, he fails to observe any restriction imposed on him under Schedule 2 or 3 to this Act as to residence [, as to his employment or occupation]² or as to reporting to the police or to an immigration officer;

(f) if he [leaves a train in the United Kingdom] after being placed on board under Schedule 2 or 3 to this Act with a view to his removal from the United Kingdom;

(g) if he [leaves or seeks to leave the United Kingdom through the tunnel system] in contravention of a restriction imposed by or under an Order in Council under section 3(7) of this Act.

[(1A) A person commits an offence under subsection (1)(b)(i) above on the day when he first knows that the time limited by his leave has expired and continues to commit it throughout any period during which he is in the United Kingdom thereafter; but a person shall not be prosecuted under that provision more than once in respect of the same limited leave.]³

(2) [. . .]⁴

(3) The extended time limit for prosecutions which is provided for by section 28 below shall apply to offences under [subsection (1)(a) and (c)] above.

(4) In proceedings for an offence against subsection (1)(a) above of entering the United Kingdom without leave,—

(a) any stamp purporting to have been imprinted on a passport or other travel document by an immigration officer on a particular date for the purpose of giving leave shall be presumed to have been duly so imprinted, unless the contrary is proved;

(b) proof that a person had leave to enter the United Kingdom shall lie on the defence if, but only if, he is shown to have entered within six months before the date when the proceedings were commenced.

¹ Repealed by Immigration and Asylum Act 1999 (c.33), Sched. 16, para. 1.
² Words inserted by Immigration Act 1988 (c. 14), s. 10 Sched. 1, para. 10(3)(4).
³ s. 24(1A) inserted by Immigration Act 1988 (c. 14), s. 6(1)(3).
⁴ Repealed by Immigration and Asylum Act 1999 (c. 33), Sched. 16, para. 1.

Deception

32–010   [24A.—(1) A person who is not a British citizen is guilty of an offence if, by means which include deception by him—

(a) he obtains or seeks to obtain leave to enter or remain in the United Kingdom; or

(b) he secures or seeks to secure the avoidance, postponement or revocation of enforcement action against him.

(2) "Enforcement action", in relation to a person, means—

(a) the giving of directions for his removal from the United Kingdom ("directions") under Schedule 2 to this Act or section 10 of the Immigration and Asylum Act 1999;

(b) the making of a deportation order against him under section 5 of this Act; or

(c) his removal from the United Kingdom in consequence of directions or a deportation order.

(3) A person guilty of an offence under this section is liable—

(a) on summary conviction, to imprisonment for a term not exceeding six months or to a fine not exceeding the statutory maximum, or to both; or

(b) on conviction on indictment, to imprisonment for a term not exceeding two years or to a fine, or to both.

(4) The extended time limit for prosecutions which is provided for by section 28 applies to an offence under this section.][1]

[1] Added by Immigration and Asylum Act 1999 (c.33), Pt I, s. 28.

Assisting illegal entry, and harbouring

25.— [(1) Any person knowingly concerned in making or carrying out **32–011** arrangements for securing or facilitating—

(a) the entry into the Bailiwick of Guernsey of anyone whom he knows or has reasonable cause for believing to be an illegal entrant;

(b) the entry into the Bailiwick of Guernsey of anyone whom he knows or has reasonable cause for believing to be an asylum claimant; or

(c) the obtaining by anyone of leave to remain in the Bailiwick of Guernsey by means which he knows or has reasonable cause for believing to include deception;

shall be guilty of an offence, punishable on summary conviction with a fine of not more than £400 or with imprisonment for not more than six months, or with both, or on conviction on indictment with a fine or with imprisonment for not more than [ten] years, or with both.]

[(1A) Nothing in subsection (1)(b) applies to anything done in relation to a person who—

(a) has been detained under paragraph 16 of Schedule 2 to this Act; or

(b) has been granted temporary admission under paragraph 21 of that Schedule.

(1B) Nothing in subsection (1)(b) applies to anything done by a person otherwise than for gain.

(1C) Nothing in subsection (1)(b) applies to anything done to assist an asylum claimant by a person in the course of his employment by a bona fide organisation, if the purposes of that organisation include assistance to persons in the position of the asylum claimant.

(1D) "Asylum claimant" means a person who intends to make a claim that it would be contrary to the United Kingdom's obligations under the Refugee Convention or the Human Rights Convention for him to be removed from, or required to leave, the United Kingdom.

(1E) "Refugee Convention" and "Human Rights Convention" have the meaning given in the Immigration and Asylum Act 1999.][1]

(2) Without prejudice to subsection (1) above a person knowingly harbouring anyone whom he knows or has reasonable cause for believing to be either an illegal entrant or a person who has committed an offence under section 24(1)(b) or (c) above, shall be guilty of an offence, punishable on summary conviction with a fine of not more than [level 5 on the standard scale] or with imprisonment for not more than six months, or with both.

(3) [. . .][2]

(4) The extended time limit for prosecutions which is provided for by section 28 below shall apply to offences under this section.

(5) [Paragraphs (a) and (b) of subsection (1)][3] above shall apply to things done outside as well as to things done in the United Kingdom where they are done—

[(a) by a British citizen, a [British overseas territories citizen][4], or a British Overseas citizen;
  (b) by a person who under the British Nationality Act 1981 is a British subject; or
  (c) by a British protected person (within the meaning of that Act).]

[(6) Where a person convicted on indictment of an offence under [subsection (1)(a) or (b)][5] above is at the time of the offence–

(a) the owner or one of the owners of a through train, shuttle train or vehicle used or intended to be used in carrying out the arrangements in respect of which the offence is committed; or
(b) a director or manager of a company which is the owner or one of the owners of any such train or vehicle; or
[(c) the train manager of any such train; or][6]
[(d) the driver of any such vehicle;][7]

then subject to subsections (7) and (8) below the court before which he is convicted may order the forfeiture of the train or vehicle.
In this subsection (but not in subsection (7) below)–

"owner" in relation to a train or vehicle which is the subject of a hire-purchase agreement includes the person in possession of it under that agreement, and in relation to a train, includes a charterer; and
"vehicle" includes a railway vehicle capable of being uncoupled from a train and a road vehicle carried on a train.]

(7) A court shall not order a [train] to be forfeited under subsection (6) above on a person's conviction, unless—

(b) the person convicted is at the time of the offence the owner or one of the owners, or a director or manager of a company which is the owner or one of the owners, of the [train]; or
(c) the [train], under the arrangements in respect of which the offence is committed, has been used for bringing more than 20 persons at one time to the United Kingdom as illegal entrants, and the intention to use the [train] in bringing persons to the United Kingdom as illegal entrants was known to, or could by the exercise of reasonable diligence, have been discovered by, some person on whose conviction the [train] would have been liable to forfeiture in accordance with paragraph (b) above. [. . .]

(8) A court shall not order a [train] or vehicle to be forfeited under subsection (6) above, where a person claiming to be the owner of the [train] or vehicle or otherwise interested in it applies to be heard by the court, unless an opportunity has been given to him to show cause why the order should not be made.

[1] subs. (1A) substituted for a new subs. (1A) to (1E) by Immigration and Asylum Act 1999 (c.33), Pt I, s. 29(3).
[2] Repealed by Immigration and Asylum Act 1999 (c.33), Sched. 16, para. 1.
[3] Words substituted by Immigration and Asylum Act 1999 (c.33), Pt I, s. 29(4).
[4] Words substituted by British Overseas Territories Act 2002 (c.8), s. 2(3).
[5] Words substituted by Asylum and Immigration Act 1996 (c.49), s. 5(4).

[6] para. (d) and word "or" immediately preceding it added by Immigration and Asylum Act 1999 (c.33), Pt II, s. 38(1).
[7] *ibid.*

......

Interpretation

33.—(1) For purposes of this Act, except in so far as the context otherwise **32–012** requires—

"aircraft" includes hovercraft,

"captain" means master (of a ship) or commander (of an aircraft);

"certificate of entitlement" means such a certificate as is referred to in section 3(9) above;

"crew", in relation to a ship or aircraft, means all persons actually employed in the working or service of the ship or aircraft, including the captain, [and in relation to a through train or a shuttle train, means all persons on the train who are actually employed in its service or working, including the train manager,] and "member of the crew" shall be construed accordingly;

["entrant" means a person entering or seeking to enter the Bailiwick of Guernsey and "illegal entrant" means a person—

(a) unlawfully entering or seeking to enter in breach of a deportation order or of the immigration laws; or

(b) entering or seeking to enter by means which include deception by another person;

and includes also a person who has entered as mentioned in paragraph (a) or (b) above;][1]

"entry clearance" means a visa, entry certificate or other document which, in accordance with the immigration rules, is to be taken as evidence [or the requisite evidence] of a person's eligibility, though not [a British citizen], for entry into the United Kingdom (but does not include a work permit);

"immigration laws" means this Act and any law for purposes similar to this Act which is for the time being or has (before or after the passing of this Act) been in force in any part of the United Kingdom and Islands;

"immigration rules" means the rules for the time being laid down as mentioned in section 3(2) above;

"the Islands" means the Channel Islands and the Isle of Man, and "the United Kingdom and Islands" means the United Kingdom and the Islands taken together;

"legally adopted" means adopted in pursuance of an order made by any court in the United Kingdom and Islands or by any adoption specified as an overseas adoption by order of the Secretary of State under section 72(2) of the Adoption Act 1976;

"limited leave" and "indefinite leave" means respectively leave under this Act to enter or remain in the United Kingdom which is, and one which is not, limited as to duration;

"settled"shall be construed in accordance [with subsection (2A) below;]

"ship"includes every description of vessel used in navigation;

["United Kingdom passport" means a current passport issued by the Government of the United Kingdom, or by the Lieutenant-Governor of any of the Islands, or by the Government of any territory which is for the time being a dependent territory within the meaning of the British Nationality Act 1981;]

"work permit" means a permit indicating, in accordance with the immigration rules, that a person named in it is eligible, though not [a British citizen], for entry into the United Kingdom for the purpose of taking employment.

(2) It is hereby declared that, except as otherwise provided in this Act, a person is not to be treated for the purposes of any provision of this Act as ordinarily resident in the United Kingdom or in any of the Islands at a time when he is there in breach of the immigration laws.

[(2A) Subject to section 8(5) above, references to a person being settled in the United Kingdom are references to his being ordinarily resident there without being subject under the immigration laws to any restriction on the period for which he may remain.]

(3) The [international stations for purposes of this Act shall be such railway stations as may from time to time be designated by order of the Secretary of State], and the ports of exit for purposes of any Order in Council under section 3(7) above, shall be such ports as may from time to time be designated for the purpose by order of the Secretary of State made by statutory instrument.

(4) For purposes of this Act an appeal under Part II shall, subject to any express provision to the contrary, be treated as pending during the period beginning when notice of appeal is duly given and ending when the appeal is finally determined or withdrawn [or is abandoned by reason of the appellant leaving the United Kingdom][2]; and [an] appeal shall not be treated as finally determined so long as a further appeal can be brought by virtue of section 20 [or section 9 of the Asylum and Immigration Appeals Act 1993] [or section 7 of the Special Immigration Appeals Commission Act 1997] nor, if such an appeal is duly brought, until it is determined or withdrawn.

(5) This Act shall not be taken to supersede or impair any power exercisable by Her Majesty in relation to aliens by virtue of Her prerogative.[3]

[1] Definitions substituted by Asylum and Immigration Act 1996 (c.49), Sched 2, para. 4(1).
[2] Words inserted by Asylum and Immigration Act 1996 (c.49), Sched. 2, para. 4(2).
[3] Modified by S.I. 1993 No. 1796, Sched. 1, Pt I, para. 18.

Misuse of Drugs Act 1971

(1971, c. 38)

33–001	*An Act to make new provision with respect to dangerous or otherwise harmful drugs and related matters, and for purposes connected therewith.*
[27th May 1971]

. . . . . .

Restrictions relating to controlled drugs etc.

Restriction of production and supply of controlled drugs

33–002	**4.**—(1) Subject to any regulations under section 7 of this Act for the time being in force, it shall not be lawful for a person—

(a) to produce a controlled drug; or

(b) to supply or offer to supply a controlled drug to another.

(2) Subject to section 28 of this Act, it is an offence for a person—

(a) to produce a controlled drug in contravention of subsection (1) above; or

(b) to be concerned in the production of such a drug in contravention of that subsection by another.

(3) Subject to section 28 of this Act, it is an offence for a person—

(a) to supply or offer to supply a controlled drug to another in contravention of subsection (1) above; or

(b) to be concerned in the supplying of such a drug to another in contravention of that subsection; or

(c) to be concerned in the making to another in contravention of that subsection of an offer to supply such a drug.

Restriction of possession of controlled drugs

5.—(1) Subject to any regulations under section 7 of this Act for the time being in force, it shall not be lawful for a person to have a controlled drug in his possession.   **33–003**

(2) Subject to section 28 of this Act and to subsection (4) below, it is an offence for a person to have a controlled drug in his possession in contravention of subsection (1) above.

(3) Subject to section 28 of this Act, it is an offence for a person to have a controlled drug in his possession, whether lawfully or not, with intent to supply it to another in contravention of section 4(1) of this Act.[1]

(4) In any proceedings for an offence under subsection (2) above in which it is proved that the accused had a controlled drug in his possession, it shall be a defence for him to prove—

(a) that, knowing or suspecting it to be a controlled drug, he took possession of it for the purpose of preventing another from committing or continuing to commit an offence in connection with that drug and that as soon as possible after taking possession of it he took all such steps as were reasonably open to him to destroy the drug or to deliver it into the custody of a person lawfully entitled to take custody of it; or

(b) that, knowing or suspecting it to be a controlled drug, he took possession of it for the purpose of delivering it into the custody of a person lawfully entitled to take custody of it and that as soon as possible after taking possession of it he took all such steps as were reasonably open to him to deliver it into the custody of such a person.

(6) Nothing in subsection (4) above shall prejudice any defence which it is open to a person charged with an offence under this section to raise apart from that subsection.

[1] S. 5(2)(3) saved by Criminal Law Act 1977 (c. 45), Sch. 5 para. 1(2)(a)(b)(iii) and Criminal Procedure (Scotland) Act 1975 (c. 21), Sch. 7B, para. 1(2)(a)(b)(iii)

. . . . . .

Law enforcement and punishment of offences

Powers to search and obtain evidence

33–004   **23.**—(1) A constable or other person authorised in that behalf by a general or special order of the Secretary of State (or in Northern Ireland either of the Secretary of State or the Ministry of Home Affairs for Northern Ireland) shall, for the purposes of the execution of this Act, have power to enter the premises of a person carrying on business as a producer or supplier of any controlled drugs and to demand the production of, and to inspect, any books or documents relating to dealings in any such drugs and to inspect any stocks of any such drugs.

(2) If a constable has reasonable grounds to suspect that any person is in possession of a controlled drug in contravention of this Act or of any regulations made thereunder, the constable may—

(a) search that person, and detain him for the purpose of searching him;

(b) search any vehicle or vessel in which the constable suspects that the drug may be found, and for that purpose require the person in control of the vehicle or vessel to stop it;

(c) seize and detain, for the purposes of proceedings under this Act, anything found in the course of the search which appears to the constable to be evidence of an offence under this Act.

In this subsection "vessel" includes a hovercraft within the meaning of the Hovercraft Act 1968; and nothing in this subsection shall prejudice any power of search or any power to seize or detain property which is exercisable by a constable apart from this subsection.

(3) If a justice of the peace (or in Scotland a justice of the peace, a magistrate or a sheriff) is satisfied by information on oath that there is reasonable ground for suspecting—

(a) that any controlled drugs are, in contravention of this Act or of any regulations made thereunder, in the possession of a person on any premises; or

(b) that a document directly or indirectly relating to, or connected with, a transaction or dealing which was, or an intended transaction or dealing which would if carried out be, an offence under this Act, or in the case of a transaction or dealing carried out or intended to be carried out in a place outside the United Kingdom, an offence against the provisions of a corresponding law in force in that place, is in the possession of a person on any premises;

he may grant a warrant authorising any constable acting for the police area in which the premises are situated at any time or times within one month from the date of the warrant, to enter, if need be by force, the premises named in the warrant, and to search the premises and any persons found therein and, if there is reasonable ground for suspecting that an offence under this Act has been committed in relation to any controlled drugs found on the premises or in the possession of any such persons, or that a document so found is such a document as is mentioned in paragraph (b) above, to seize and detain those drugs or that document, as the case may be.

[(3A) The powers conferred by subsection (1) above shall be exercisable also for the purposes of the execution of Part II of the Criminal Justice (International Co-operation) Act 1990 [or section 49 of the Drug Trafficking Act 1994][1] and subsection (3) above (excluding paragraph (a)) shall apply also to offences under section 12 or 13 of that Act [of 1990][2], taking references in those provisions to controlled drugs as references to scheduled substances within the meaning of that Part.][3]

(4) A person commits an offence if he—

(a) intentionally obstructs a person in the exercise of his powers under this section; or

(b) conceals from a person acting in the exercise of his powers under subsection (1) above any such books, documents, stocks or drugs as are mentioned in that subsection; or

(c) without reasonable excuse (proof of which shall lie on him) fails to produce any such books or documents as are so mentioned where their production is demanded by a person in the exercise of his powers under that subsection.

(5) In its application to Northern Ireland subsection (3) above shall have effect as if the words "acting for the police area in which the premises are situated" were omitted.

[1] Words inserted by Drug Trafficking Act 1994 (c.37), Sched. 1, para. 4(a).
[2] Words inserted by Drug Trafficking Act 1994 (c.37), Sched. 1, para. 4(b).
[3] Added by Criminal Justice (International Co-operation) Act 1990 (c.5), Pt II, s. 23(4).

. . . . . .

Miscellaneous and supplementary provisions

Proof of lack of knowledge etc. to be a defence in proceedings for certain offences

28.—(1) This section applies to offences under any of the following provisions of this Act, that is to say section 4(2) and (3), section 5(2) and (3), section 6(2) and section 9.   **33–005**

(2) Subject to subsection (3) below, in any proceedings for an offence to which this section applies it shall be a defence for the accused to prove that he neither knew of nor suspected nor had reason to suspect the existence of some fact alleged by the prosecution which it is necessary for the prosecution to prove if he is to be convicted of the offence charged.

(3) Where in any proceedings for an offence to which this section applies it is necessary, if the accused is to be convicted of the offence charged, for the prosecution to prove that some substance or product involved in the alleged offence was the controlled drug which the prosecution alleges it to have been, and it is proved that the substance or product in question was that controlled drug, the accused—

(a) shall not be acquitted of the offence charged by reason only of proving that he neither knew nor suspected nor had reason to suspect that the substance or product in question was the particular controlled drug alleged; but

(b) shall be acquitted thereof—

(i) if he proves that he neither believed nor suspected nor had reasons to suspect that the substance or product in question was a controlled drug; or

(ii) if he proves that he believed the substance or product in question to be a controlled drug, or a controlled drug of a description, such that, if it had in fact been that controlled drug or a controlled drug of that description, he would not at the material time have been committing any offence to which this section applies.

(4) Nothing in this section shall prejudice any defence which it is open to a person charged with an offence to which this section applies to raise apart from this section.

European Communities Act 1972

(1972, c. 68)

34–001 *An Act to make provision in connection with the enlargement of the European Communities to include the United Kingdom, together with (for certain purposes) the Channel Islands, the Isle of Man and Gibraltar.*

[17th October 1972]

PART I

GENERAL PROVISIONS

Short title and interpretation

34–002 1.—(1) This Act may be cited as the European Communities Act 1972.
(2) In this Act—

"the Communities" means the European Economic Community, the European Coal and Steel Community and the European Atomic Energy Community;
"the Treaties" or "the Community Treaties" means, subject to subsection (3) below, the pre-accession treaties, that is to say, those described in Part I of Schedule 1 to this Act, taken with—

(a) the treaty relating to the accession of the United Kingdom to the European Economic Community and to the European Atomic Energy Community, signed at Brussels on the 22nd January 1972; and

(b) the decision, of the same date, of the Council of the European Communities relating to the accession of the United Kingdom to the European Coal and Steel Community; [and]

[(c) the treaty relating to the accession of the Hellenic Republic to the European Economic Community and to the European Atomic Energy Community, signed at Athens on 28th May 1979; and

(d) the decision, of 24th May 1979, of the Council relating to the accession of the Hellenic Republic to the European Coal and Steel Community; [and]]

[[(e) the decisions of the Council of 7th May 1985, 24th June 1988, 31st October 1994 and 29th September 2000, on the Communities' system of own resources; and]

(g) the treaty relating to the accession of the Kingdom of Spain and the Portuguese Republic to the European Economic Community and to the European Atomic Energy Community, signed at Lisbon and Madrid on 12th June 1985; and

(h) the decision, of 11th June 1985, of the Council relating to the accession of the Kingdom of Spain and the Portuguese Republic to the European Coal and Steel Community; [and]]

[(j) the following provisions of the Single European Act signed at Luxembourg and The Hague on 17th and 28th February 1986, namely Title II (amendment of the treaties establishing the Communities) and, so far as they relate to any of the Communities or any Community institution, the preamble and Titles I (common provisions) and IV (general and final provisions); [and]¹]²

[(k) Titles II, III and IV of the Treaty on European Union signed at Maastricht on 7th February 1992, together with the other provisions of the Treaty so far as they relate to those Titles, and the Protocols adopted at Maastricht on that date and annexed to the Treaty establishing the European Community with the exception of the Protocol on Social Policy on page 117 of Cm 1934; [and]³]⁴

[(l) the decision, of 1st February 1993, of the Council amending the Act concerning the election of the representatives of the European Parliament by direct universal suffrage annexed to Council Decision 76/787/ECSC, EEC, Euratom of 20th September 1976; [and]]⁵

[(m) the Agreement on the European Economic Area signed at Oporto on 2nd May 1992 together with the Protocol adjusting that Agreement signed at Brussels on 17th March 1993; [and]⁶]

[(n) the treaty concerning the accession of the Kingdom of Norway, the Republic of Austria, the Republic of Finland and the Kingdom of Sweden to the European Union, signed at Corfu on 24th June 1994; [and]⁷]⁸

[(o) the following provisions of the Treaty signed at Amsterdam on 2nd October 1997 amending the Treaty on European Union, the Treaties establishing the European Communities and certain related Acts—

(i) Articles 2 to 9,
(ii) Article 12, and
(iii) the other provisions of the Treaty so far as they relate to those Articles,

and the Protocols adopted on that occasion other than the Protocol on Article J.7 of the Treaty on European Union [and]⁹]¹⁰

[(p) the following provisions of the Treaty signed at Nice on 26th February 2001 amending the Treaty on European Union, the Treaties establishing the European Communities and certain related Acts—

(i) Articles 2 to 10, and
(ii) the other provisions of the Treaty so far as they relate to those Articles,

and the Protocol adopted on that occasion.]¹¹

and any other treaty entered into by any of the Communities, with or without any of the member States, or entered into, as a treaty ancillary to any of the Treaties, by the United Kingdom;
and any expression defined in Schedule 1 to this Act has the meaning there given to it.

(3) If Her Majesty by Order in Council declares that a treaty specified in the Order is to be regarded as one of the Community Treaties as herein defined, the Order shall be conclusive that it is to be so regarded; but a treaty entered into by the United Kingdom after the 22nd January 1972, other than a pre-accession treaty to which the United Kingdom accedes on terms settled on or before that date, shall not be so regarded unless it is so specified, nor be so specified unless

a draft of the Order in Council has been approved by resolution of each House of Parliament.

(4) For purposes of subsections (2) and (3) above, "treaty" includes any international agreement, and any protocol or annex to a treaty or international agreement.

1 para. added by European Communities (Amendment) Act 1993 (c. 32), s.1(1).
2 s.1(2)(j) inserted by European Communities (Amendment) Act 1986 (c. 58), s.1.
3 para. (1) and the word "and" immediately preceding it added by European Parliamentary Elections Act 1993 (c. 41), s.3(2).
4 para. added by European Communities (Amendment) Act 1993 (c. 32), s.1(1).
5 para. (1) and the word "and" immediately preceding it added by European Parliamentary Elections Act 1993 (c. 41), s.3(2).
6 para. (n) and the word "and" preceding it are inserted by European Union (Accessions) Act 1994 (c. 38), s.1.
7 Added by European Communities (Amendment) Act 1998 (c. 21), s.1).
8 para. (n) and the word "and" preceding it are inserted by European Union (Accessions) Act 1994 (c. 38), s.1.
9 subs. (p) and the word "and" immediately preceding it inserted by European Communities (Amendment) Act 2002 (c. 3), s.1(1).
10 Added by European Communities (Amendment) Act 1998 (c. 21), s.1).
11 subs. (p) and the word "and" immediately preceding it inserted by European Communities (Amendment) Act 2002 (c. 3), s.1(1).

General implementation of Treaties

34–003   **2.**—(1) All such rights, powers, liabilities, obligations and restrictions from time to time created or arising by or under the Treaties, and all such remedies and procedures from time to time provided for by or under the Treaties, as in accordance with the Treaties are without further enactment to be given legal effect or used in the United Kingdom shall be recognised and available in law, and be enforced, allowed and followed accordingly; and the expression "enforceable Community right" and similar expressions shall be read as referring to one to which this subsection applies.

(2) Subject to Schedule 2 to this Act, at any time after its passing Her Majesty may by Order in Council, and any designated Minister or department may by regulations, make provision—

    (a) for the purpose of implementing any Community obligation of the United Kingdom, or enabling any such obligation to be implemented, or of enabling any rights enjoyed or to be enjoyed by the United Kingdom under or by virtue of the Treaties to be exercised; or

    (b) for the purpose of dealing with matters arising out of or related to any such obligation or rights or the coming into force, or the operation from time to time, of subsection (1) above;

and in the exercise of any statutory power or duty, including any power to give directions or to legislate by means of orders, rules, regulations or other subordinate instrument, the person entrusted with the power or duty may have regard to the objects of the Communities and to any such obligation or rights as aforesaid.

In this subsection "designated Minister or department" means such Minister of the Crown or government department as may from time to time be designated by Order in Council in relation to any matter or for any purpose, but subject to such restrictions or conditions (if any) as may be specified by the Order in Council.

(3) There shall be charged on and issued out of the Consolidated Fund or, if so determined by the Treasury, the National Loans Fund the amounts required to meet any Community obligation to make payments to any of the Communities or member States, or any Community obligation in respect of contributions to the capital or reserves of the European Investment Bank or in respect of loans

to the Bank, or to redeem any notes or obligations issued or created in respect of any such Community obligation; and, except as otherwise provided by or under any enactment,—

    (a) any other expenses incurred under or by virtue of the Treaties or this Act by any Minister of the Crown or government department may be paid out of moneys provided by Parliament; and

    (b) any sums received under or by virtue of the Treaties or this Act by any Minister of the Crown or government department, save for such sums as may be required for disbursements permitted by any other enactment, shall be paid into the Consolidated Fund or, if so determined by the Treasury, the National Loans Fund.

(4) The provision that may be made under subsection (2) above includes, subject to Schedule 2 to this Act, any such provision (of any such extent) as might be made by Act of Parliament, and any enactment passed or to be passed, other than one contained in this part of this Act, shall be construed and have effect subject to the foregoing provisions of this section; but, except as may be provided by any Act passed after this Act, Schedule 2 shall have effect in connection with the powers conferred by this and the following sections of this Act to make Orders in Council and regulations.

(5) [. . .][1] and the references in that subsection to a Minister of the Crown or government department and to a statutory power or duty shall include a Minister or department of the Government of Northern Ireland and a power or duty arising under or by virtue of an Act of the Parliament of Northern Ireland.

(6) A law passed by the legislature of any of the Channel Islands or of the Isle of Man, or a colonial Law (within the meaning of the Colonial Laws Validity Act 1865) passed or made for Gibraltar, if expressed to be passed or made in the implementation of the Treaties and of the obligations of the United Kingdom thereunder, shall not be void or inoperative by reason of any inconsistency with or repugnancy to an Act of Parliament, passed or to be passed, that extends to the Island or Gibraltar or any provision having the force and effect of an Act there (but not including this section), nor by reason of its having some operation outside the Island or Gibraltar; and any such Act or provision that extends to the Island or Gibraltar shall be construed and have effect subject to the provisions of any such law.

[1] Words repealed by Northern Ireland Constitution Act 1973 (c. 36), Sched. 6, Pt. I.

Decisions on, and proof of, Treaties and Community instruments etc.

3.—(1) For the purposes of all legal proceedings any question as to the meaning or effect of any of the Treaties, or as to the validity, meaning or effect of any Community instrument, shall be treated as a question of law (and, if not referred to the European Court, be for determination as such in accordance with the principles laid down by and any relevant [decision of the European Court or any court attached thereto)][1].   **34–004**

(2) Judicial notice shall be taken of the Treaties, of the Official Journal of the Communities and of any decision of, or expression of opinion by, the European Court [or any court attached thereto][2] on any such question as aforesaid; and the Official Journal shall be admissible as evidence of any instrument or other act thereby communicated of any of the Communities or of any Community institution.

(3) Evidence of any instrument issued by a Community institution, including any judgment or order of the European Court [or any court attached thereto][3], or of any document in the custody of a Community institution, or any entry in or extract from such a document, may be given in any legal proceedings by

production of a copy certified as a true copy by an official of that institution; and any document purporting to be such a copy shall be received in evidence without proof of the official position or handwriting of the person signing the certificate.

(4) Evidence of any Community instrument may also be given in any legal proceedings—

    (a) by production of a copy purporting to be printed by the Queen's Printer;

    (b) where the instrument is in the custody of a government department (including a department of the Government of Northern Ireland), by production of a copy certified on behalf of the department to be a true copy by an officer of the department generally or specially authorised so to do;

and any document purporting to be such a copy as is mentioned in paragraph (b) above of an instrument in the custody of a department shall be received in evidence without proof of the official position or handwriting of the person signing the certificate, or of his authority to do so, or of the document being in the custody of the department.

(5) In any legal proceedings in Scotland evidence of any matter given in a manner authorised by this section shall be sufficient evidence of it.

[1] Words substituted by European Communities (Amendment) Act 1986 (c. 58), s. 2(a).
[2] Words inserted by European Communities (Amendment) Act 1986 (c. 58), s. 2(b).
[3] *ibid.*

. . . . . .

Section 2   SCHEDULE 2

PROVISIONS AS TO SUBORDINATE LEGISLATION

34–005

1.—(1) The powers conferred by section 2(2) of this Act to make provision for the purposes mentioned in section 2(2) (a) and (b) shall not include power—

    (a) to make any provision imposing or increasing taxation; or
    (b) to make any provision taking effect from a date earlier than that of the making of the instrument containing the provision; or
    (c) to confer any power to legislate by means of orders, rules, regulations or other subordinate instrument, other than rules of procedure for any court or tribunal; or
    (d) to create any new criminal offence punishable with imprisonment for more than two years or punishable on summary conviction with imprisonment for more than three months or with a fine of more than [level 5 on the standard scale] (if not calculated on a daily basis) or with a fine of more than [£100 a day].

(2) Sub-paragraph (1)(c) above shall not be taken to preclude the modification of a power to legislate conferred otherwise than under section 2(2), or the extension of any such power to purposes of the like nature as those for which it was conferred; and a power to give directions as to matters of administration is not to be regarded as a power to legislate within the meaning of sub-paragraph (1)(c).

34–006

2.—(1) Subject to paragraph 3 below, where a provision contained in any section of this Act confers power to make regulations (otherwise than by modification or extension of an existing power), the power shall be exercisable by statutory instrument.

(2) Any statutory instrument containing an Order in Council or regulations made in the exercise of a power so conferred, if made without a draft having been approved by resolution of each House of Parliament, shall be subject to annulment in pursuance of a resolution of either House.

34–007

3. Nothing in paragraph 2 above shall apply to any Order in Council made by the Governor of Northern Ireland or to any regulation made by a Minister or department of the Government of Northern Ireland; but where a provision contained in any section of this Act confers power to make such an Order in Council or regulations, then any Order in Council or regulations made in the

exercise of that power, if made without a draft having been approved by resolution of each House of the Parliament of Northern Ireland, shall be subject to negative resolution within the meaning of section 41(6) of the Interpretation Act (Northern Ireland) 1954 as if the Order or regulations were a statutory instrument within the meaning of that Act.

[**4.**—(1) The power to make orders under section 5(1) or (2) of this Act shall be exercisable in accordance with the following provisions of this paragraph.   **34–008**

(2) The power to make such orders shall be exercisable by statutory instrument and includes power to amend or revoke any such order made in the exercise of that power.

(3) Any statutory instrument containing any such order shall be subject to annulment in pursuance of a resolution of the House of Commons except in a case falling within sub-paragraph (4) below.

(4) Subject to sub-paragraph (6) below, where an order imposes or increases any customs duty, or restricts any relief from customs duty under the said section 5, the statutory instrument containing the order shall be laid before the House of Commons after being made and, unless the order is approved by that House before the end of the period of 28 days beginning with the day on which it was made, it shall cease to have effect at the end of that period, but without prejudice to anything previously done under the order or to the making of a new order.

In reckoning the said period of 28 days no account shall be taken of any time during which Parliament is dissolved or prorogued or during which the House of Commons is adjourned for more than 4 days.

(5) Where an order has the effect of altering the rate of duty on any goods in such a way that the new rate is not directly comparable with the old, it shall not be treated for the purposes of sub-paragraph (4) above as increasing the duty on those goods if it declares the opinion of the Treasury to be that, in the circumstances existing at the date of the order, the alteration is not calculated to raise the general level of duty on the goods.

(6) Sub-paragraph (4) above does not apply in the case of an instrument containing an order which states that it does not impose or increase any customs duty or restrict any relief from customs duty otherwise than in pursuance of a Community obligation.]

[**5.** As soon as may be after the end of each financial year the Secretary of State shall lay before each House of Parliament a report on the exercise during that year of the powers conferred by section 5(1) and (2) of this Act with respect to the imposition of customs duties and the allowance of exemptions and reliefs from duties so imposed (including the power to amend or revoke orders imposing customs duties or providing for any exemption or relief from duties so imposed).]   **34–009**

Local Government Act 1972

(1972, c. 70)

An Act to make provision with respect to local government and the functions of local authorities in England and Wales; to amend Part II of the Transport Act 1968; to confer rights of appeal in respect of decisions relating to licences under the Home Counties (Music and Dancing) Licensing Act 1926; to make further provision with respect to magistrates' courts committees; to abolish certain inferior courts of record; and for connected purposes.   [26th October 1972]   **35–001**

. . . . . .

Part VA

Access to Meetings and Documents of Certain Authorities, Committees and Sub-Committees

Admission of public and press to local authority committee meetings

100.—(1) For the purpose of securing the admission, so far as practicable, of the public (including the press) to all meetings of committees of local authorities   **35–002**

as well as to meetings of local authorities themselves, the Public Bodies (Admission to Meetings) Act 1960 (in this section referred to as "the 1960 Act") shall have effect subject to the following provisions of this section.

(2) Without prejudice to section 2(1) of the 1960 Act (application of section 1 of that Act to any committee of a body whose membership consists of or includes all members of that body) section 1 of the 1960 Act shall apply to any committee appointed by one or more local authorities under section 102 below, not being a committee falling within section 2(1) of the 1960 Act[or section 100E(3)(a) or (b) below (whether or not by virtue of section 100J below)].

(3) Where section 1 of the 1960 Act applies to a committee by virtue of subsection (2) above, then, for the purposes of subsection (4)(c) of that section, premises belonging to the local authority or one or more of the local authorities which appointed the committee shall be treated as belonging to the committee.

PART VA

ACCESS TO MEETINGS AND DOCUMENTS OF CERTAIN AUTHORITIES, COMMITTEES AND SUB-COMMITTEES

Admission to meetings of principal councils

35–003   [**100A.**—(1) A meeting of a principal council shall be open to the public except to the extent that they are excluded (whether during the whole or part of the proceedings) under subsection (2) below or by resolution under subsection (4) below.

(2) The public shall be excluded from a meeting of a principal council during an item of business whenever it is likely, in view of the nature of the business to be transacted or the nature of the proceedings, that, if members of the public were present during that item, confidential information would be disclosed to them in breach of the obligation of confidence; and nothing in this Part shall be taken to authorise or require the disclosure of confidential information in breach of the obligation of confidence.

(3) For the purposes of subsection (2) above, "confidential information" means—

(a) information furnished to the council by a Government department upon terms (however expressed) which forbid the disclosure of the information to the public; and

(b) information the disclosure of which to the public is prohibited by or under any enactment or by the order of a court;

and, in either case, the reference to the obligation of confidence is to be construed accordingly.

(4) A principal council may by resolution exclude the public from a meeting during an item of business whenever it is likely, in view of the nature of the business to be transacted or the nature of the proceedings, that if members of the public were present during that item there would be disclosure to them of exempt information, as defined in section 100I below.

(5) A resolution under subsection (4) above shall—

(a) identify the proceedings, or the part of the proceedings, to which it applies, and

(b) state the description, in terms of Schedule 12A to this Act, of the exempt information giving rise to the exclusion of the public,

and where such a resolution is passed this section does not require the meeting to be open to the public during proceedings to which the resolution applies.

(6) The following provisions shall apply in relation to a meeting of a principal council, that is to say—

(a) public notice of the time and place of the meeting shall be given by posting it at the offices of the council three [1] clear days at least before the meeting or, if the meeting is convened at shorter notice, then at the time it is convened;

(b) while the meeting is open to the public, the council shall not have power to exclude members of the public from the meeting; and

(c) while the meeting is open to the public, duly accredited representatives of newspapers attending the meeting for the purpose of reporting the proceedings for those newspapers shall, so far as practicable, be afforded reasonable facilities for taking their report and, unless the meeting is held in premises not belonging to the council or not on the telephone, for telephoning the report at their own expense.

(7) Nothing in this section shall require a principal council to permit the taking of photographs of any proceedings, or the use of any means to enable persons not present to see or hear any proceedings (whether at the time or later), or the making of any oral report on any proceedings as they take place.

(8) This section is without prejudice to any power of exclusion to suppress or prevent disorderly conduct or other misbehaviour at a meeting.][2]

[1] In relation to the Service Authority for the National Crime Squad:
    (6) The following provisions shall apply in relation to a meeting of a principal council, that is to say—

(a) public notice of the time and place of the meeting shall be given by posting it at the offices of the council seven clear days at least before the meeting or, if the meeting is convened at shorter notice, then at the time it is convened;

(b) while the meeting is open to the public, the council shall not have power to exclude members of the public from the meeting; and

(c) while the meeting is open to the public, duly accredited representatives of newspapers attending the meeting for the purpose of reporting the proceedings for those newspapers shall, so far as practicable, be afforded reasonable facilities for taking their report and, unless the meeting is held in premises not belonging to the council or not on the telephone, for telephoning the report at their own expense.

[2] Pt VA inserted by Local Government (Access to Information) Act 1985 (c. 43), s. 1(1).

Access to agenda and connected reports

[**100B.**—(1) Copies of the agenda for a meeting of a principal council and, subject to subsection (2) below, copies of any report for the meeting shall be open to inspection by members of the public at the offices of the council in accordance with subsection (3) below.   **35–004**

(2) If the proper officer thinks fit, there may be excluded from the copies of reports provided in pursuance of subsection (1) above the whole of any report which, or any part which, relates only to items during which, in his opinion, the meeting is likely not to be open to the public.

(3) Any document which is required by subsection (1) above to be open to inspection shall be so open at least three clear days before the meeting, except that—

(a) where the meeting is convened at shorter notice, the copies of the agenda and reports shall be open to inspection from the time the meeting is convened; and

(b) where an item is added to an agenda copies of which are open to inspection by the public, copies of the item (or of the revised agenda),

and the copies of any report for the meeting relating to the item, shall
be open to inspection from the time the item is added to the agenda;

but nothing in this subsection requires copies of any agenda, item or report to
be open to inspection by the public until copies are available to members of the
council.

(4) An item of business may not be considered at a meeting of a principal
council unless either—

> (a) a copy of the agenda including the item (or a copy of the item) is open
> to inspection by members of the public in pursuance of subsection (1)
> above for at least three clear days before the meeting or, where the
> meeting is convened at shorter notice, from the time the meeting is
> convened; or
> (b) by reason of special circumstances, which shall be specified in the
> minutes, the chairman of the meeting is of the opinion that the item
> should be considered at the meeting as a matter of urgency.

(5) Where by virtue of subsection (2) above the whole or any part of a report
for a meeting is not open to inspection by the public under subsection (1)
above—

> (a) every copy of the report or of the part shall be marked "Not for pub-
> lication"; and
> (b) there shall be stated on every copy of the whole or any part of the
> report the description, in terms of Schedule 12A to this Act, of the
> exempt information by virtue of which the council are likely to exclude
> the public during the item to which the report relates.

(6) Where a meeting of a principal council is required by section 100A above
to be open to the public during the proceedings or any part of them, there shall
be made available for the use of members of the public present at the meeting
a reasonable number of copies of the agenda and, subject to subsection (8)
below, of the reports for the meeting.

(7) There shall, on request and on payment of postage or other necessary
charge for transmission, be supplied for the benefit of any newspaper—

> (a) a copy of the agenda for a meeting of a principal council and, subject
> to subsection (8) below, a copy of each of the reports for the meeting;
> (b) such further statements or particulars, if any, as are necessary to indic-
> ate the nature of the items included in the agenda; and
> (c) if the proper officer thinks fit in the case of any item, copies of any
> other documents supplied to members of the council in connection with
> the item.

(8) Subsection (2) above applies in relation to copies of reports provided in
pursuance of subsection (6) or (7) above as it applies in relation to copies of
reports provided in pursuance of subsection (1) above.]¹

¹ Pt VA inserted by Local Government (Access to Information) Act 1985 (c. 43), s. 1(1).

Inspection of minutes and other documents after meetings

35–005   [**100C.**—(1) After a meeting of a principal council the following documents
shall be open to inspection by members of the public at the offices of the council
until the expiration of the period of six years beginning with the date of the
meeting, namely—

(a) the minutes, or a copy of the minutes, of the meeting, excluding so much of the minutes of proceedings during which the meeting was not open to the public as discloses exempt information;

(b) where applicable, a summary under subsection (2) below;

(c) a copy of the agenda for the meeting; and

(d) a copy of so much of any report for the meeting as relates to any item during which the meeting was open to the public.

(2) Where, in consequence of the exclusion of parts of the minutes which disclose exempt information, the document open to inspection under subsection (1)(a) above does not provide members of the public with a reasonably fair and coherent record of the whole or part of the proceedings, the proper officer shall make a written summary of the proceedings or the part, as the case may be, which provides such a record without disclosing the exempt information.]¹

¹ Pt VA inserted by Local Government (Access to Information) Act 1985 (c. 43), s. 1(1).

Inspection of background papers

[**100D.**—(1) Subject, in the case of section 100C(1), to subsection (2) below, if and so long as copies of the whole or part of a report for a meeting of a principal council are required by section 100B(1) or 100C(1) above to be open to inspection by members of the public–   **35–006**

(a) those copies shall each include a copy of a list, compiled by the proper officer, of the background papers for the report or the part of the report, and

(b) at least one copy of each of the documents included in that list shall also be open to inspection at the offices of the council.

(2) Subsection (1) above does not require a copy of any document included in the list, to be open to inspection after the expiration of the period of four years beginning with the date of the meeting.

(3) Where a copy of any of the background papers for a report is required by subsection (1) above to be open to inspection by members of the public, the copy shall be taken for the purposes of this Part to be so open if arrangement sexist for its production to members of the public as soon as is reasonably practicable after the making of a request to inspect the copy.

(4) Nothing in this section—

(a) requires any document which discloses exempt information to be included in the list referred to in subsection (1) above; or

(b) without prejudice to the generality of subsection (2) of section 100A above, requires or authorises the inclusion in the list of any document which, if open to inspection by the public, would disclose confidential information in breach of the obligation of confidence, within the meaning of that subsection.

(5) For the purposes of this section the background papers for a report are those documents relating to the subject matter of the report which—

(a) disclose any facts or which, matters on which, in the opinion of the proper officer, the report or an important part of the report is based, and

(b) have, in his opinion, been relied on to a material extent in preparing the report,

but do not include any published works.]¹

¹ Substituted by Local Government Act 2000 (c.22), Pt V, s. 97.

Application to committees and sub-committees

35–007 [**100E.**—(1) Sections 100A to 100D above shall apply in relation to a committee or sub-committee of a principle council as they apply in relation to a principal council.

(2) In the application by virtue of this section of sections 100A to 100D above in relation to a committee or sub-committee—

(a) section 100A(6)(a) shall be taken to have been complied with if the notice is given by posting it at the time there mentioned at the offices of every constituent principal council and, if the meeting of the committee or sub-committee to which that section so applies is to be held at premises other than the offices of such a council, at those premises;
(b) for the purposes of section 100A(6)(c), premises belonging to a constituent principal council shall be treated as belonging to the committee or sub-committee; and
(c) for the purposes of sections 100B(1), 100C(1) and 100D(1), offices of any constituent principal council shall be treated as offices of the committee or sub-committee.

(3) Any reference in this Part to a committee or sub-committee of a principle council is a reference to—

(a) a committee which is constituted under an enactment specified in section 101(9) below or which is appointed by one or more principal councils under section 102 below; or
(b) a joint committee not falling within paragraph (a) above which is appointed or established under any enactment by two or more principal councils and is not a body corporate; or
[(bb) the Navigation Committee of the Broads Authority; or]¹
(c) a sub-committee appointed or established under any enactment by one or more committees falling within [paragraphs(a) to (bb)] above.

(4) Any reference in this Part to a constituent principal council, in relation to a committee or sub-committee, is a reference—

(a) in the case of a committee, to the principal council, or any of the principal councils, of which it is a committee; and
(b) in the case of a sub-committee, to any principal council which, by virtue of paragraph (a) above, is a constituent principal council in relation to the committee, or any of the committees, which established or appointed the sub-committee.]²

¹ s.100E(3)(bb) inserted by Norfolk and Suffolk Broads Act 1988 (c.4), ss. 21, 23(2), 27(2), Sched. 6, para. 10(4).
² Pt VA inserted by Local Government (Access to Information) Act 1985 (c. 43), s. 1(1).

Principal councils to publish additional information

[**100G.**—(1) A principal council shall maintain a register stating— **35–008**

    (a) the name and address of every member of the council for the time being and the ward or division which he represents; and

(2) A principal council shall maintain a list—

    (a) specifying those powers of the council which, for the time being, are exercisable from time to time by officers of the council in pursuance of arrangements made under this Act or any other enactment for their discharge by those officers; and

    (b) stating the title of the officer by whom each of the powers so specified is for the time being so exercisable;

but this subsection does not require a power to be specified in the list if the arrangements for its discharge by the officer are made for a specified period not exceeding six months.

(3) There shall be kept at the offices of every principal council a written summary of the rights—

    (a) to attend meetings of a principal council and of committees and sub-committees of a principal council, and

    (b) to inspect and copy documents and to be furnished with documents,

which are for the time being conferred by this Part, Part XI below and such other enactments as the Secretary of State by order specifies.

(4) The register maintained under subsection (1) above, the list maintained under subsection (2) above and the summary kept under subsection (3) above shall be open to inspection by the public at the offices of the council.][1]

[1] Pt VA inserted by Local Government (Access to Information) Act 1985 (c. 43), s. 1(1).

PART VI

DISCHARGE OF FUNCTIONS

Arrangements for discharge of functions by local authorities

101.—(1) Subject to any express provision contained in this Act or any Act **35–009**
passed after this Act, a local authority may arrange for the discharge of any of their functions—

    (a) by a committee, a sub-committee or an officer of the authority; or

    (b) by any other local authority.

(1A) A local authority may not under subsection (1)(b) above arrange for the discharge of any of their functions by another local authority if, or to the extent that, that function is also a function of the other local authority and is the responsibility of the other authority's executive.

(1B) Arrangements made under subsection (1)(b) above by a local authority ("the first authority") with respect to the discharge of any of their functions shall cease to have effect with respect to that function if, or to the extent that,—

(a) the first authority are operating or begin to operate executive arrangements, and that function becomes the responsibility of the executive of that authority; or

(b) the authority with whom the arrangements are made ("the second authority") are operating or begin to operate executive arrangements, that function is also a function of the second authority and that function becomes the responsibility of the second authority's executive.

(1C) Subsections (1A) and (1B) above do not affect arrangements made by virtue of section 19 of the Local Government Act 2000 (discharge of functions of and by another authority).

(2) Where by virtue of this section any functions of a local authority may be discharged by a committee of theirs, then, unless the local authority otherwise direct, the committee may arrange for the discharge of any of those functions by a sub-committee or an officer of the authority and where by virtue of this section any functions of a local authority may be discharged by a sub-committee of the authority, then, unless the local authority or [¹] the committee otherwise direct, the sub-committee may arrange for the discharge of any of those functions by an officer of the authority.

(3) Where arrangements are in force under this section for the discharge of any functions of a local authority by another local authority, then, subject to the terms of the arrangements, that other authority may arrange for the discharge of those functions by a committee, sub-committee or officer of theirs and subsection (2) above shall apply in relation to those functions as it applies in relation to the functions of that other authority.

(4) Any arrangements made by a local authority or committee under this section for the discharge of any functions by a committee, sub-committee, officer or local authority shall not prevent the authority or committee by whom the arrangements are made from exercising those functions.

(5) Two or more local authorities may discharge any of their functions jointly and, where arrangements are in force for them to do so,—

(a) they may also arrange for the discharge of those functions by a joint committee of their or by an officer of one of them and subsection (2) above shall apply in relation to those functions as it applies in relation to the functions of the individual authorities; and

(b) any enactment relating to those functions or the authorities by whom or the areas in respect of which they are to be discharged shall have effect subject to all necessary modifications in its application in relation to those functions and the authorities by whom and the areas in respect of which (whether in pursuance of the arrangements or otherwise) they are to be discharged.

(5A) Arrangements made under subsection (5) above by two or more local authorities with respect to the discharge of any of their functions shall cease to have effect with respect to that function if, or to the extent that, the function becomes the responsibility of an executive of any of the authorities.

(5B) Subsection (5A) above does not affect arrangements made by virtue of section 20 of the Local Government Act 2000 (joint exercise of functions).

(6) A local authority's functions with respect to levying, or issuing a precept for, a rate shall be discharged only by the authority.

(7) A local authority shall not make arrangements under this section for the discharge of any of their functions under the Diseases of Animals Act 1950 by any other local authority.

[(7A) Subsection (7) above does not apply to arrangements as between principal councils in Wales.]²

(8) Any enactment, except one mentioned in subsection (9) below, which contains any provision—

    (a) which empowers or requires local authorities or any class of local authorities to establish committees (including joint committees) for any purpose or enables a Minister to make an instrument establishing committees of local authorities for any purpose or empowering or requiring a local authority or any class of local authorities to establish committees for any purpose; or

    (b) which empowers or requires local authorities or any class of local authorities to arrange or to join with other authorities in arranging for the exercise by committees so established or by officers of theirs of any of their functions, or provides that any specified functions of their shall be discharged by such committees or officers, or enables any Minister to make an instrument conferring such a power, imposing such a requirement or containing such a provision;

shall, to the extent that it makes any such provision, cease to have effect.

(9) The following enactments, that is to say—

    (d) section 1 of the Sea Fisheries Regulation Act 1966;

    (f) section 2 of the Local Authority Social Services Act 1970 (social services committees);

are exempted from subsection (8) above.

(10) This section shall not authorise a local authority to arrange for the discharge by any committee, sub-committee or local authority of any functions which by any enactment mentioned in subsection (9) above are required or authorised to be discharged by a specified committee, but the foregoing provision shall not prevent a local authority who are required by or under any such enactment to establish, or delegate functions to, a committee established by or under any such enactment from arranging under this section for the discharge of their functions by an officer of the local authority or committee, as the case may be.

[(10A) In determining what arrangements to make for the discharge of any functions, a principal council in Wales may act as if paragraph (f) were omitted from subsection (9) above.]

(12) References in this section and section 102 below to the discharge of any of the functions of a local authority include references to the doing of anything which is calculated to facilitate, or is conducive or incidental to, the discharge of any of those functions.

(13) In this Part of this Act "local authority" includes the Common Council, the Sub-Treasurer of the Inner Temple, the Under Treasurer of the Middle Temple, [[the London Fire and Emergency Planning Authority,] any joint authority except a police authority,] a joint board on which a local authority within the meaning of this Act or any of the foregoing authorities are represented and, without prejudice to the foregoing, any port health authority.

(14) Nothing in this section affects the operation of section 5 of the 1963 Act or the Local Authorities (Goods and Services) Act 1970.

---

[1] In its application to an area committee that is established by a council in accordance with a decentralisation scheme:

(2) Where by virtue of this section any functions of a local authority may be discharged by a committee of theirs, then, the committee may arrange for the discharge of any of those functions by a sub-committee or an officer of the authority and where by virtue of this section any functions of a local authority may be discharged by a sub-committee of the authority, then, unless the committee otherwise direct, the sub-committee may arrange for the discharge of any of those functions by an officer of the authority.

[2] Added by Local Government (Wales) Act 1994 (c.19), Sched. 15, para. 26(2).

PART VII

MISCELLANEOUS POWERS OF LOCAL AUTHORITIES

Subsidiary powers

Subsidiary powers of local authorities

35–010 **111.**—(1) Without prejudice to any powers exercisable apart from this section but subject to the provisions of this Act and any other enactment passed before or after this Act, a local authority shall have power to do any thing (whether or not involving the expenditure, borrowing or lending of money or the acquisition or disposal of any property or rights) which is calculated to facilitate, or is conductive or incidental to, the discharge of any of their functions.

(2) For the purposes of this section, transacting the business of a parish or community meeting or any other parish or community business shall be treated as a function of the parish or community council.

(3) A local authority shall not by virtue of this section raise money, whether by means of rates, precepts or borrowing, or lend money except in accordance with the enactments relating to those matters respectively.

(4) In this section "local authority" includes the Common Council.

Staff

Appointment of staff

35–011 **112.**—(1) Without prejudice to section 111 above but subject to the provisions of this Act, a local authority shall appoint such officers as they think necessary for the proper discharge by the authority of such of their or another authority's functions as fall to be discharged by them and the carrying out of any obligations incurred by them in connection with an agreement made by them in pursuance of section 113 below.

(2) An officer appointed under subsection (1) above shall hold office on such reasonable terms and conditions, including conditions as to remuneration, as the authority appointing him think fit.

(3) Subject to subsection (4) below, any enactment or instrument made under an enactment which requires or empowers all local authorities or local authorities of any description or committees of local authorities to appoint a specified officer shall, to the extent that it makes any such provisions, cease to have effect.

The reference in this section to committees of local authorities does not include a reference to any committee of which some members are required to be appointed by a body or person other than a local authority.

(4) Subsection (3) above does not apply to the following officers, that is to say—

   (b) chief education officers appointed under [section 532 of the Education Act 1996];
   (c) chief officers and other members of fire brigades maintained under the Fire Services Act 1947;
   (f) agricultural analysts and deputy agricultural analysts appointed under section 67(3) of the Agriculture Act 1970; and
   (g) directors of social services appointed under section 6 of the Local Authority Social Services Act 1970;

and it is hereby declared that subsection (3) above does not apply to any other person appointed by a local authority to perform a specified function.

(5) Without prejudice to the provisions of subsection (1) above, a parish or

community council may appoint one or more persons from among their numbers to be officers of the council, without remuneration.

(6) Nothing in this section affects the operation of section 5 of the 1963 Act or the Local Authorities (Goods and Services) Act 1970.

. . . . . .

Part XI

General Provisions as to Local Authorities

Legal proceedings

Power of local authorities to prosecute or defend legal proceedings

222.—(1) Where a local authority consider it expedient for the promotion or protection of the interests of the inhabitants of their area—   **35–012**

(a) they may prosecute or defend or appear in any legal proceedings and, in the case of civil proceedings, may institute them in their own name; and

(b) they may, in their own name, make representations in the interests of the inhabitants at any public inquiry held by or on behalf of any Minister or public body under any enactment.

(2) In this section "local authority" includes the Common Council [and the London Fire and Emergency Planning Authority].[1]

[1] Words added by Greater London Authority Act 1999 (c.29), Sched. 29, Part I, para. 20.

. . . . . .

Byelaws

Power of councils to make byelaws for good rule and government and suppression of nuisances

235.—(1) The council of a district [the council of a principal area in Wales][1] and the council of a London borough may make byelaws for the good rule and government of the whole or any part of the district [principal area][2] or borough, as the case may be, and for the prevention and suppression of nuisances therein.   **35–013**

(2) The confirming authority in relation to byelaws made under this section shall be the Secretary of State.

(3) Byelaws shall not be made under this section for any purpose as respects any area if provision for that purpose as respects that area is made by, or is or may be made under, any other enactment.

[1] Words inserted by Local Government (Wales) Act 1994 (c.19), Sched. 15, para. 49.
[2] *ibid.*

. . . . . .

MEETINGS AND PROCEEDINGS OF LOCAL AUTHORITIES

PART I

PRINCIPAL COUNCILS

35–014

1.—(1) A principal council shall in every year hold an annual meeting.

(2) The annual meeting of a principal council shall be held—

 (a) in a year of ordinary elections of councillors to the council, on the eighth day after the day of retirement of councillors or such other day within the twenty-one days immediately following the day of retirements as the council may fix;

 (b) in any other year, on such day in the month of [March, April, May or June] as the council may fix.

(4) An annual meeting of a principal council shall be held at such hour as the council may fix, or if no hour is so fixed at twelve noon.

35–015

2.—(1) A principal council may in every year hold, in addition to the annual meeting, such other meetings as they may determine.

(2) Those other meetings shall be held at such hour and on such days as the council may determine.

35–016

3.—(1) An extraordinary meeting of a principal council may be called at any time by the chairman of the council.

(2) If the chairman refuses to call an extraordinary meeting of a principal council after a requisition for that purpose, signed, by five members of the council, has been presented to him, or if, without so refusing, the chairman does not call an extraordinary meeting within seven days after the requisition has been presented to him, then, any five members of the council, on that refusal or on the expiration of those seven days, as the case may be, may forthwith call an extraordinary meeting of the council.

35–017

4.—(1) Meetings of a principal council shall be held at such place, either within or without their area, as they may direct.

(2) Three clear days at least before a meeting of a principal council—

 (a) notice of the time and place of the intended meeting shall be published at the council's offices, and where the meeting is called by members of the council the notice shall be signed by those members and shall specify the business proposed to be transacted thereat; and

 (b) a summons to attend the meeting, specifying the business proposed to be transacted thereat, and signed by the proper officer of the council, shall, subject to sub-paragraph (3) below, be left at or sent by post to the usual place of residence of every member of the council.

(3) If a member of a principal council gives notice in writing to the proper officer of the council that he desires summonses to attend meetings of the council to be sent to him at some address specified in the notice other than his place of residence, any summons addressed to him and left at or sent by post to that address shall be deemed sufficient service of the summons.

(4) Want of service of a summons on any member of a principal council shall not affect the validity of a meeting of the council.

(5) Except in the case of business required by or under this or any other Act to be transacted at the annual meeting of a principal council and other business brought before that meeting as a matter of urgency in accordance with the council's standing orders, no business shall be transacted at a meeting of the council other than that specified in the summons relating thereto.

35–018

[4A.—(1) The Secretary of State may by order amend paragraph 4(2) above so as to substitute for the reference to three clear days such greater number of days as may be specified in the order.

(2) Any statutory instrument containing an order under sub-paragraph (1) above shall be subject to annulment in pursuance of a resolution of either House of Parliament.][1]

[1] Added by Local Government Act 2000 (c.22), Pt V, s. 98(2).

35–019

[5.—(1) At a meeting of a principal council the chairman, if present, shall preside.

(2) If the chairman is absent from a meeting of a principal council, then—

 (a) the vice-chairman of the council, if present, shall preside;

(c) in the case of a London borough council, the deputy mayor, if at that time he remains a councillor and is chosen for that purpose by the members of the council then present, shall preside.

(3) If—

(a) in the case of a principal council, both the chairman and vice-chairman of the council are absent from a meeting of the council;
(c) in the case of a London borough council, the mayor and deputy mayor are so absent or the deputy may or being present is not chosen;

another member of the council chosen by the members of the council present shall preside.

(4) A member of an executive of a principal council may not be chosen to preside under sub-paragraph (3) above.

(5) Sub-paragraphs (2)(c) and (3)(c) above do not apply where a London borough council are operating executive arrangements which involve a mayor and cabinet executive or a mayor and council manager executive.][1]

[1] Added by Local Government Act 2000 (c.22), Sched. 3, para. 14(2).

6. Subject to paragraph 45 below, no business shall be transacted at a meeting of a principal council unless at least one quarter of the whole number of members of the council are present.　　**35–020**

Local Government Act 1974

(1974, c. 7)

An Act to make further provision, in relation to England and Wales, with respect　　**36–001**
to the payment of grants to local authorities, rating and valuation, bor-
rowing and lending by local authorities and the classification of highways;
to extend the powers of the Countryside Commission to give financial
assistance; to provide for the establishment of Commissions for the investi-
gation of administrative action taken by or on behalf of local and other
authorities; to restrict certain grants under the Transport Act 1968; to
provide for the removal or relaxation of certain statutory controls affecting
local government activities; to make provision in relation to the collection
of sums by local authorities on behalf of water authorities; to amend sec-
tion 259(3) of the Local Government Act 1972 and to make certain minor
amendments of or consequential on that Act; and for connected purposes.
[8th February 1974]

. . . . . .

PART III

LOCAL GOVERNMENT ADMINISTRATION

The Commissions for Local Administration

23.—(1) For the purpose of conducting investigations in accordance with this　　**36–002**
Part of this Act, there shall be—

(a) a body of commissioners to be known as the Commission for Local Administration in England, and

(b) a body consisting of two or more commissioners to be known as the Commission for Local Administration in Wales.

[but each of the Commissions may include persons appointed to act as advisers, not exceeding the number appointed to conduct investigations.][1]

(2) The Parliamentary Commissioner shall be a member of each of the Commissions.

[(2A) The Welsh Administration Ombudsman shall be a member of the Commission for Local Administration in Wales (so that, where the offices of Parliamentary Commissioner and Welsh Administration Ombudsman are held by different persons, the Commission for Local Administration in Wales shall consist of at least three commissioners).][2]

(3) In the following provisions of this Part of this Act the expression "Local Commissioner" means a person, other than the Parliamentary Commissioner [[, the Welsh Administration Ombudsman][3] or an advisory member][4], who is a member of one of the Commissions.

(4) Appointments to the office of Commissioner shall be made by Her Majesty on the recommendation of the Secretary of State after consultation with the [such persons as appear to the Secretary of State to represent authorities in England or, as the case may be, authorities in Wales to which this Part of this Act applies], and a person so appointed shall, subject to subsection (6) below, hold office during good behaviour.

(5) Commissioners may be appointed to serve either as full-time commissioners or as part-time commissioners.

(6) A Commissioner may be relieved of office by Her Majesty at his own request or may be removed from office by Her Majesty on grounds of incapacity or misbehaviour, and shall in any case vacate office on completing the year of service in which he attains the age of sixty-five years.

(7) The Secretary of State shall designate two of the Local Commissioners for England as chairman and vice-chairman respectively of the Commission for Local Administration in England and, in the event of there being more than one Local Commissioner for Wales, shall designate one of them as chairman of the Commission for Local Administration in Wales.

(8) The Commission for Local Administration in England shall divide England into areas and shall provide, in relation to each area, for one or more of the Local Commissioners to be responsible for the area; and where the Commission for Local Administration in Wales consist of more than one Local Commissioner they may, if they think fit, act in a similar way in Wales.

A Local Commissioner may, by virtue of this subsection, be made responsible for more than one area.

(9) It shall be the duty of the Commission for Local Administration in England to ensure that any Local Commissioner made responsible for an area which includes the county of Cornwall is made responsible for an area which also includes the Isles of Scilly.

(10) Each of the Commissions—

(a) shall make arrangements for Local Commissioners to accept cases for which they are not responsible including, where the other Commission so request, a case arising in the country of that other Commission, and
(b) shall publish information about the procedures for making complaints under this Part of this Act.

(11) For the year ending on 31st March 1975, and for each subsequent financial year, every Local Commissioner shall prepare a general report on the discharge of his functions and shall submit it to his Commission; and where he has discharged functions at the request of the other Commission he shall prepare a

general report on the discharge of those functions and shall submit it to the other Commission.

Any such report shall be submitted to the appropriate Commission not later than two months after the end of the year to which it relates.

(12) [In the financial year beginning on 1st April 1990, and in every third financial year afterwards, the Commissions shall review the operation (since the last review was made under this subsection) of the provisions of this Part of this Act about the investigation of complaints, and shall have power to convey to authorities to which this Part of this Act applies], or to government departments [or the National Assembly for Wales]⁵, any recommendations or conclusions reached in the course of their reviews [and shall send copies of those recommendations or conclusions to the representative persons and authorities concerned]⁶.

[(12A) Each of the Commissions may, after consultation with the representative persons and authorities concerned, provide to the authorities or any of the authorities to which this Part of this Act applies such advice and guidance about good administrative practice as appears to the Commission to be appropriate and may arrange for it to be published for the information of the public.

(12B) The representative persons and authorities concerned are—

(a) for the purposes of subsection (12) above, such persons appearing to the Commission to represent authorities in England or, as the case may be, authorities in Wales to which this Part of this Act applies, and in the case of such authorities as are not so represented, those authorities; and

(b) for the purposes of subsection (12A) above, such of those persons and authorities as the Commission think appropriate.]⁷

(13) Schedule 4 to this Act shall have effect as respects the Commissions.

¹ Words inserted by Local Government and Housing Act 1989 (c.42), s. 22(2).
² Added by Government of Wales Act 1998 (c.38), Sched. 12, para. 12(2).
³ Words inserted by Government of Wales Act 1998 (c.38), Sched. 12, para. 12(3).
⁴ Words inserted by Local Government and Housing Act 1989 (c.42), s. 22(3).
⁵ Words inserted by Government of Wales Act 1998 (c.38), Sched. 12, para. 12(4).
⁶ Words inserted by Local Government and Housing Act 1989 (c.42), s. 194(1), Sched. 11, para. 38.
⁷ ss. (12A)(12B) inserted by Local Government and Housing Act 1989 (c.42), s. 23(1).

Authorities subject to investigation

25.—(1) This Part of this Act applies to [the following authorities]¹— **36–003**

(a) any local authority,
[[(b) the Greater London Authority;.]
(c) a National Park authority;]
(d) any joint board the constituent authorities of which are all local authorities,
[(e) the Commission for the New Towns,
(f) any development corporation established for the purposes of a new town,
[(g) the London Development Agency;]
(h) any urban development corporation established by an order under section 135 of the Local Government, Planning and Land Act 1980,]²
[(i) any housing action trust established under Part III of the Housing Act 1988]³
[[(j) the Urban Regeneration Agency;]
[(k) a fire authority constituted by a combination scheme under the Fire Services Act 1947;]

    (l) any joint authority established by Part IV of the Local Government Act 1985;

  [(m) the London Fire and Emergency Planning Authority;]

  [(n) any police authority established under [section 3 of the Police Act 1996]]

  [(o) the Metropolitan Police Authority;]⁴

  [(p) Transport for London;]]⁵

  [(q) in relation to the flood defence functions of the Environment Agency, within the meaning of the Water Resources Act 1991, the Environment Agency and any regional flood defence committee[; and]⁶]

  [(r) the London Transport Users' Committee.]⁷

(2) Her Majesty may by Order in Council provide that this Part of this Act shall also apply, subject to any modifications or exceptions specified in the Order, to any authority specified in the Order, being an authority which is established by or under an Act of Parliament, and which has power to levy a rate, or to issue a precept.

(3) An Order made by virtue of subsection (2) above may be varied or revoked by a subsequent Order so made and shall be subject to annulment in pursuance of a resolution of either House of Parliament.

(4) Any reference to an authority to which this Part of this Act applies includes a reference—

  (a) to the members and officers of that authority, and

  (b) to any person or body of persons acting for the authority under section 101), or

  (c) any committee mentioned in section 101(9) of the said Act.

[[(4A) Any reference to an authority to which this Part of this Act applies also includes, in the case of the Greater London Authority, a reference to each of the following—

  (a) the London Assembly;

  (b) any committee of the London Assembly;

  (c) any body or person exercising functions on behalf of the Greater London Authority.]

[(4B) Any reference to an authority to which this Part of this Act applies also includes, in the case of the London Transport Users' Committee, a reference to a sub-committee of that Committee.]

(5) Any reference to an authority to which this Part of this Act applies also includes a reference to—

  (a) a school organisation committee constituted in accordance with section 24 of the School Standards and Framework Act 1998;

  (b) an exclusion appeals panel constituted in accordance with Schedule 18 to that Act;

  (c) an admission appeals panel constituted in accordance with Schedule 24 or paragraph 3 of Schedule 25 to that Act; and

  (d) the governing body of any community, foundation or voluntary school so far as acting in connection with the admission of pupils to the school or otherwise performing any of their functions under Chapter I of Part III of that Act.]

[(8) Where the authority concerned is the Greater London Authority, any functions exercisable under this section by or in relation to the Authority (other than functions exercisable by or in relation to the proper officer of the Authority) shall be exercisable by or in relation to the Mayor and the Assembly acting jointly on behalf of the Authority, and references to the authority concerned (other than references to the proper officer or a member of the authority concerned) shall be construed accordingly.]

[1] Words inserted by Local Government Act 1988 (c.9), s. 29, Sched. 3, para. 4.
[2] Subs. 25(ba)(bb)(bc)(bd) inserted by Local Government Act 1988 (c.9), s. 29, Sched. 3, para. 4.
[3] Subs. 25(be) inserted by Housing Act 1988 (c.50), s. 140(1), Sched. 17, para. 19.
[4] Added by Greater London Authority Act 1999 (c.29), Pt XI, s. 394 (4).
[5] s. 25(1)(c)(ca)(cb) substituted for s. 25(1)(c) by Local Government Act 1985 (c.51), s. 84, Sched. 14, Pt. II, para. 51(a).
[6] Added by Greater London Authority Act 1999 (c.29), Sched. 18, para. 16(2)(b).

Matters subject to investigation

26.—(1) Subject to the provisions of this Part of this Act where a written **36–004** complaint is made by or on behalf of a member of the public who claims to have sustained injustice in consequence of maladministration in connection with action taken by or on behalf of an authority to which this Part of this Act applies, being action taken in the exercise of administrative functions of that authority, a Local Commissioner may investigate that complaint.

(2) A complaint shall not be entertained under this Part of this Act unless [it is made in writing to the Local Commissioner specifying the action alleged to constitute maladministration or]—

    (a) it is made in writing to a member of the authority, or of any other authority concerned, specifying the action alleged to constitute maladministration, and

    (b) it is referred to the Local Commissioner, with the consent of the person aggrieved, or of a person acting on his behalf, by that member, or by any other person who is a member of any authority concerned, with a request to investigate the complaint.

(3) If the Local Commissioner is satisfied that any member of any authority concerned has been requested to refer the complaint to a Local Commissioner, and has not done so, the Local Commissioner may, if he thinks fit, dispense with the requirements in subsection (2)(b) above.

(4) A complaint shall not be entertained unless it was made to [the Local Commissioner or] a member of any authority concerned within twelve months from the day on which the person aggrieved first had notice of the matters alleged in the complaint, but a Local Commissioner may conduct an investigation pursuant to a complaint not made within that period if he considers that [it is reasonable] to do so.

(5) Before proceeding to investigate a complaint, a Local Commissioner shall satisfy himself that the complaint has been brought, by or on behalf of the person aggrieved, to the notice of the authority to which the complaint relates and that that authority has been afforded a reasonable opportunity to investigate, and reply to, the complaint.

(6) A Local Commissioner shall not conduct an investigation under this Part of this Act in respect of any of the following matters, that is to say,—

    (a) any action in respect of which the person aggrieved has or had a right of appeal, reference or review to or before a tribunal constituted by or under any enactment;

    (b) any action in respect of which the person aggrieved has or had a right of appeal to a Minister of the Crown [or the National Assembly for Wales]; or

    (c) any action in respect of which the person aggrieved has or had a remedy by way of proceedings in any court of law:

Provided that a Local Commissioner may conduct an investigation notwithstanding the existence of such a right or remedy if satisfied that in the particular circumstances it is not reasonable to expect the person aggrieved to resort or have resorted to it.

(7) A Local Commissioner shall not conduct an investigation in respect of any action which in his opinion affects all or most of the inhabitants of the [following area—]

> [[(a) where the complaint relates to a National Park authority, the area of the Park for which it is such an authority;.]
> (b) where the complaint relates to the Commission for the New Towns, the area of the new town or towns to which the complaint relates;
> [(c) where the complaint relates to the Urban Regeneration Agency, any designated area within the meaning of Part III of the Leasehold Reform, Housing and Urban Development Act 1993;.]
> (d) in any other case, the area of the authority concerned.]

(8) Without prejudice to the preceding provisions of this section, a Local Commissioner shall not conduct an investigation under this Part of this Act in respect of any such action or matter as is described in Schedule 5 to this Act.

(9) Her Majesty may by Order in Council amend the said Schedule 5 so as to [add to or exclude from the provisions of that Schedule (as it has effect for the time being)] such actions or matters as may be described in the Order; and any Order made by virtue of this subsection shall be subject to annulment in pursuance of a resolution of either House of Parliament.

(10) In determining whether to initiate, continue or discontinue an investigation, a Local Commissioner shall, subject to the preceding provisions of this section, act at discretion; and any question whether a complaint is duly made under this Part of this Act shall be determined by the Local Commissioner.

[(11) In this section—

> (a) references to a person aggrieved include references to his personal representatives; and
> (b) references to a member of an authority concerned include, in the case of a complaint relating to a joint authority established by Part IV of the Local Government Act 1985, references to a member of a constituent council of that authority.]

(12) A complaint shall not be entertained under this Part of this Act if and so far as it is in respect of anything done before 1st April 1974, or in respect of any default or alleged default first arising before that date.

[(13) A complaint as regards an authority mentioned in section 25(1)(ba), (bb), or (bd) above shall not be entertained under this Part of this Act if and so far as it is in respect of anything done before the coming into force of Schedule 3 to the Local Government Act 1988, or in respect of any default or alleged default first arising before its coming into force; and subsection (12) above shall have effect subject to this.]

Provisions relating to complaints

36–005   27.—(1) A complaint under this Part of this Act may be made by any individual, or by any body of persons whether incorporated or not, not being—

> (a) a local authority or other authority or body constituted for purposes of the public service or of local government [(including the National Assembly for Wales)], or for the purposes of carrying on under national

ownership any industry or undertaking or part of an industry or under-taking;

(b) any other authority or body whose members are appointed by Her Maj-esty or any Minister of the Crown or government department [or by the National Assembly for Wales], or whose revenues consist wholly or mainly of moneys provided by Parliament [or the National Assembly for Wales].

(2) Where the person by whom a complaint might have been made under the preceding provisions of this Part of this Act has died or is for any reason unable to act for himself, the complaint may be made by his personal representative or by a member of his family or by some body or individual suitable to represent him; but except as aforesaid a complaint shall not be entertained under this Part of this Act unless made by the person aggrieved himself.

Procedure in respect of investigations

28.—(1) Where a Local Commissioner proposes to conduct an investigation pursuant to a complaint, he shall afford to the authority concerned, and to any person who is alleged in the complaint to have taken or authorised the action complained of, an opportunity to comment on any allegations contained in the complaint.

36–006

(2) Every such investigation shall be conducted in private, but except as the procedure for conducting an investigation shall be such as the Local Commis-sioner considers appropriate in the circumstances of the case; and without preju-dice to the generality of the preceding provision the Local Commissioner may obtain information from such persons and in such manner, and make such inquir-ies, as he thinks fit, and may determine whether any person may be represented (by counsel or solicitor or otherwise) in the investigation.

(3) The Local Commissioner may, if he thinks fit, pay to the person by whom the complaint was made, and to any other person who attends or furnishes information for the purposes of an investigation under this Part of this Act—

(a) sums in respect of the expenses properly incurred by them;
(b) allowances by way of compensation for the loss of their time,

in accordance with such scales and subject to such conditions as may be deter-mined by [the Treasury].

(4) The conduct of an investigation under this Part of this Act shall not affect any action taken by the authority concerned, or any power or duty of that author-ity to take further action with respect to any matters subject to the investigation.

Investigations: further provisions

29.—(1) For the purposes of an investigation under this Part of this Act a Local Commissioner may require any member or officer of the authority con-cerned, or any other person who in his opinion is able to furnish information or produce documents relevant to the investigation, to furnish any such information or produce any such documents.

36–007

(2) For the purposes of any such investigation a Local Commissioner shall have the same powers as the High Court in respect of the attendance and exam-ination of witnesses, and in respect of the production of documents.

(3) A Local Commissioner may, under subsection (1) above, require any person to furnish information concerning communications between the authority concerned and any Government department [or the National Assembly for Wales], or to produce any correspondence or other documents forming part of any such written communications.

(4) No obligation to maintain secrecy or other restriction upon the disclosure of information obtained by or furnished to persons in Her Majesty's service, whether imposed by any enactment or by any rule of law, shall apply to the disclosure of information in accordance with subsection (3) above; and where that subsection applies the Crown shall not be entitled to any such privilege in respect of the production of documents or the giving of evidence as is allowed by law in legal proceedings.

(5) Nothing in subsection (1) or subsection (3) above affects—

    (a) the restriction, imposed by section 11(2) of the Parliamentary Commissioner Act 1967, on the disclosure of information by the Parliamentary Commissioner or his officers; or

    [(b) the restriction, imposed by paragraph 25(1) of Schedule 9 to the Government of Wales Act 1998, on the disclosure of information by the Welsh Administration Ombudsman or members of his staff;.]

    (c) the restriction, imposed by [section 15 of the Health Service Commissioners Act 1993], on the disclosure of information by the Health Service Commissioner for England or the Health Service Commissioner for Wales, or by their officers.

(6) To assist him in any investigation, a Local Commissioner may obtain advice from any person who in his opinion is qualified to give it and may pay to any such person such fees or allowances as he may determine with the approval of [the Treasury].

(7) Subject to subsection (4) above, no person shall be compelled for the purposes of an investigation under this Part of this Act to give any evidence or produce any document which he could not be compelled to give or produce in civil proceedings before the High Court.

(8) If any person without lawful excuse obstructs a Local Commissioner in the performance of his functions under this Part of this Act, or any officer of the Commission assisting in the performance of those functions, or is guilty of any act or omission in relation to an investigation under this Part of this Act which, if that investigation were a proceeding in the High Court, would constitute contempt of court, the Local Commissioner may certify the offence to the High Court.

(9) Where an offence is so certified, the High Court may inquire into the matter and, after hearing any witnesses who may be produced against or on behalf of the person charged with the offence, and after hearing any statement that may be offered in defence, deal with him in any manner in which the High Court could deal with him if he had committed the like offence in relation to the High Court.

(10) Nothing in subsection (8) above shall be construed as applying to the taking of any such action as is mentioned in section 28(4) above.

Reports on investigations

36–008   **30.**—(1) In any case where a Local Commissioner conducts an investigation, or decides not to conduct an investigation, he shall send a report of the results of the investigation, or as the case may be a statement of his reasons for not conducting an investigation—

    (a) to the person, if any, who referred the complaint to the Local Commissioner in accordance with section 26(2) above, and

    (b) to the complainant, and

    (c) to the authority concerned, and to any other authority or person who is alleged in the complaint to have taken or authorised the action complained of.

(2) Where the complaint was referred by a person who was a member of an authority but who has since ceased to be a member of that authority, the report or statement shall be sent to the chairman, or, as the case may be, mayor of that authority.

[(2AA) If the authority concerned is the Greater London Authority—

(a) the duty imposed by subsection (1)(c) above shall be discharged by sending the report or statement to both the Mayor of London and the London Assembly; and

(b) in a case falling within subsection (2) above, the duty imposed by that subsection shall be discharged by sending the report or statement to both the Mayor of London and the London Assembly.]

(3) Apart from identifying the authority or authorities concerned, the report shall not—

(a) mention the name of any person, or

(b) contain any particulars which, in the opinion of the Local Commissioner, are likely to identify any person and can be omitted without impairing the effectiveness of the report,

unless, after taking into account the public interest as well as the interests of the complainant and of persons other than the complainant, the Local Commissioner considers it necessary to mention the name of that person or to include in the report any such particulars.

[[(3AA) Nothing in subsection (3) above prevents a report—

(a) mentioning the name of, or

(b) containing particulars likely to identify,

the Mayor of London or any member of the London Assembly.]

(3A) Where the Local Commissioner is of the opinion—

(a) that action constituting maladministration was taken which involved a member of the authority concerned, and

(b) that the member's conduct constituted a breach of the National Code of Local Government Conduct,

then, unless the Local Commissioner is satisfied that it would be unjust to do so, the report shall name the member and give particulars of the breach.]¹

(4) Subject to the provisions of subsection (7) below, the authority concerned shall for a period of three weeks make copies of the report available for inspection by the public without charge at all reasonable hours at one or more of their offices; and any person shall be entitled to take copies of, or extracts from, the report when so made available.

[(4A) Subject to subsection (7) below, the authority concerned shall supply a copy of the report to any person on request if he pays such charge as the authority may reasonably require.]²

(5) Not later than [two weeks] after the report is received by the authority concerned, the proper officer of the authority shall give public notice, by advertisement in newspapers and such other ways as appear to him appropriate, that the [copies of the report will be available as provided by subsections (4) and (4A)] subsection (4) above, and shall specify the date, being a date after the giving of the public notice, from which the period of three weeks will begin.

(6) If a person having the custody of a report made available for inspection as provided by subsection (4) above obstructs any person seeking to inspect the

report, or to make a copy of, or extract from, the report, he shall be liable on summary conviction to a fine not exceeding [level 3 on the standard scale].

(7) The Local Commissioner may, if he thinks fit after taking into account the public interest as well as the interests of the complainant and of persons other than the complainant, direct that a report specified in the direction shall not be subject to the provisions of subsections (4)[, (4A) (5) above].

¹ s.30(3A) inserted by Local Government and Housing Act 1989 (c.42), s.32(1)(b).
² subs. 30(4A) inserted by Local Government Act 1988 (c.9), Sched. 3, para. 6(2)(5).

Reports on investigations: further provisions

36–009   **31.**—[(1) This section applies where a Local Commissioner reports that injustice has been caused to a person aggrieved in consequence of maladministration.

(2) The report shall be laid before the authority concerned and it shall be the duty of that authority to consider the report and, within the period of three months beginning with the date on which they received the report, or such longer period as the Local Commissioner may agree in writing, to notify the Local Commissioner of the action which the authority have taken or propose to take.

(2A) If the Local Commissioner—

  (a) does not receive the notification required by subsection (2) above within the period allowed by or under that subsection, or
  (b) is not satisfied with the action which the authority concerned have taken or propose to take, or
  (c) does not within a period of three months beginning with the end of the period so allowed, or such longer period as the Local Commissioner may agree in writing, receive confirmation from the authority concerned that they have taken action, as proposed, to the satisfaction of the Local Commissioner,

he shall make a further report setting out those facts and making recommendations.

(2B) Those recommendations are such recommendations as the Local Commissioner thinks fit to make with respect to action which, in his opinion, the authority concerned should take to remedy the injustice to the person aggrieved and to prevent similar injustice being caused inthe future.

(2C) Section 30 above, with any necessary modifications, and subsection (2) above shall apply to a report under subsection (2A) above as they apply to a report under that section.

(2D) If the Local Commissioner—

  (a) does not receive the notification required by subsection (2) above as applied by subsection (2C) above within the period allowed by or under that subsection or is satisfied before the period allowed by that subsection has expired that the authority concerned have decided to take no action, or
  (b) is not satisfied with the action which the authority concerned have taken or propose to take, or
  (c) does not within a period of three months beginning with the end of the period allowed by or under subsection (2) above as applied by subsection (2C) above, or such longer period as the Local Commissioner may agree in writing, receive confirmation from the authority concerned that they have taken action, as proposed, to the satisfaction of the Local Commissioner,

he may, by notice to the authority, require them to arrange for a statement to be published in accordance with subsections (2E) and (2F) below.

(2E) The statement referred to in subsection (2D) above is a statement, in such form as the authority concerned and the Local Commissioner may agree, consisting of—

    (a) details of any action recommended by the Local Commissioner in his further report which the authority have not taken;

    (b) such supporting material as the Local Commissioner may require; and

    (c) if the authority so require, a statement of the reasons for their having taken no action on, or not the action recommended in, the report.

(2F) The requirements for the publication of the statement are that—

    (a) publication shall be in any two editions within a fortnight of a newspaper circulating in the area of the authority agreed with the Local Commissioner or, in default of agreement, nominated by him; and

    (b) publication in the first such edition shall be arranged for the earliest practicable date.

(2G) If the authority concerned—

    (a) fail to arrange for the publication of the statement in accordance with subsections (2E) and (2F) above, or

    (b) are unable, within the period of one month beginning with the date on which they received the notice under subsection (2D) above, or such longer period as the Local Commissioner may agree in writing, to agree with the Local Commissioner the form of the statement to be published,

the Local Commissioner shall arrange for such a statement as is mentioned in subsection (2E) above to be published in any two editions within a fortnight of a newspaper circulating within the authority's area.

(2H) The authority concerned shall reimburse the Commission on demand any reasonable expenses incurred by the Local Commissioner in performing his duty under subsection (2G) above.]

[(3) In any case where—

    (a) a report is laid before an authority under subsection [(2) or (2C)] above, and

    (b) on consideration of the report, it appears to the authority that a payment should be made to, or some other benefit should be provided for, a person who has suffered injustice in consequence of maladministration [to which the report relates],

the authority may incur such expenditure as appears to them to be appropriate in making such a payment or providing such a benefit.][1]

[(4) Where the authority concerned is the Greater London Authority, any functions exercisable under this section by or in relation to the Authority shall be exercisable by or in relation to the Mayor and the Assembly acting jointly on behalf of the Authority, and references to the authority concerned (other than references to a member of the authority concerned) shall be construed accordingly.]

[1] s.31(3) added by Local Government Act 1978 (c. 39), s.1.

......

Interpretation of Part III

36–010   [34.—(1) In this Part of this Act, unless the context otherwise requires—

"action" includes failure to act, and other expressions connoting action shall be construed accordingly,

"the Commissions" means the Commission for Local Administration in England and the Commission for Local Administration in Wales,

"executive" and "executive arrangements" have the same meaning as in Part II of the Local Government Act 2000;

"local authority" means a county council, a district council, [the Broads Authority] [a Welsh county council, a county borough council], a London borough council, the Common Council of the City of London, or the Council of the Isles of Scilly,

"member"—

[(a) in relation to the Greater London Authority, means—

(i) the Mayor of London,
(ii) the Deputy Mayor, or
(iii) a member of the London Assembly;

(b)]¹ in relation to a joint board [and]

[(c) in relation to a National Park authority, includes a member of any of the councils by whom a local authority member of the authority is appointed, includes a member of any of the constituent authorities of the joint board,]²

"person aggrieved" means the person who claims or is alleged to have sustained any such injustice as is mentioned in section 26(1) above,

"Parliamentary Commissioner" means the Parliamentary Commissioner for Administration,

"tribunal" includes the person constituting a tribunal consisting of one person."]

¹ para. (c) inserted before the words "in relation to a National Park Authority" by Greater London Authority Act 1999 (c.29), Pt II, s. 74(10).
² *ibid.*

. . . . . .

Section 26   SCHEDULE 5

MATTERS NOT SUBJECT TO INVESTIGATION

36–011   1. The commencement or conduct of civil or criminal proceedings before any court of law.

36–012   2. Action taken by any [police] authority in connection with the investigation or prevention of crime.

36–013   3.—(1) Action taken in matters relating to contractual or other commercial transactions of any authority to which Part III of this Act applies, including transactions falling within sub-paragraph (2) below but excluding transactions falling within sub-paragraph (3) below.

(2) The transactions mentioned in sub-paragraph (1) above as included in the matters which, by virtue of that sub-paragraph, are not subject to investigation are all transactions of an authority to which Part III of this Act applies relating to the operation of public passenger transport, the carrying on of a dock or harbour undertaking, the provision of entertainment, or the provision and operation of industrial establishments and of markets [other than transactions relating to the grant, renewal or revocation of a licence to occupy a pitch or stall in a fair or market, or the attachment of any condition to such a licence].

(3) The transactions mentioned in sub-paragraph (1) above as not included in those matters are—

(a) transactions for or relating to the acquisition or disposal of land [or the provision of moor-

ings (not being moorings provided in connection with a dock or harbour undertaking)]; and
(b) all transactions (not being transactions falling within sub-paragraph (2) above) in the discharge of functions exercisable under any public general Act, other than those required for the procurement of the goods and services necessary to discharge those functions.

4. Action taken in respect of appointments or removals, pay, discipline, superannuation or other personnel matters.   **36–014**

5.—(1) [. . .]¹   **36–015**
(2) Any action concerning—

(a) the giving of instruction, whether secular or religious, or
(b) conduct, curriculum, internal organisation, management or discipline,

[in any school or other educational establishment maintained by the authority]² —

(i) in any school maintained by the authority, or
(ii) in any college of education or establishment of further education maintained by the authority.

¹ Repealed by School Standards and Framework Act 1998 (c.31), Sched. 31, para. 1.
² Words substituted by Education Reform Act 1988 (c. 40), ss. 231(7), 235(6), 237(1), Sched. 12, para. 71.

[**6.** Action taken by an authority mentioned in [section 25(1)(ba) or (bb)] of this Act which is not action in connection with functions in relation to housing.]   **36–016**

[**7.** Action taken by an authority mentioned in section 25(1)(bd) of this Act which is not action in connection with functions in relation to town and country planning.]   **36–017**

[**8.** Action taken by the Urban Regeneration Agency which is not action in connection with functions in relation to town and country planning.]   **36–018**

House of Commons Disqualification Act 1975

(1975, c. 24)

An Act to consolidate certain enactments relating to disqualification for membership of the House of Commons.   [8th May 1975]   **37–001**

Disqualification of holders of certain offices and places

1.—(1) Subject to the provisions of this Act, a person is disqualified for membership of the House of Commons who for the time being—   **37–002**

[a) is a Lord Spiritual;]
(b) holds any of the judicial offices specified in Part I of Schedule 1 to this Act;
(c) is employed in the civil service of the Crown, whether in an established capacity or not, and whether for the whole or part of his time;
(d) is a member of any of the regular armed forces of the Crown or the Ulster Defence Regiment;
(e) is a member of any police force maintained by a police authority;
[(f) is a member of the National Criminal Intelligence Service or the National Crime Squad;]
(g) is a member of the legislature of any country or territory outside the Commonwealth [(other than Ireland)]; or
(h) holds any office described in Part II or Part III of Schedule 1.

(2) A person who for the time being holds any office described in Part IV of Schedule 1 is disqualified for membership of the House of Commons for any constituency specified in relation to that office in the second column of Part IV.

(3) In this section—

"civil service of the Crown" includes the civil service of Northern Ireland, the Northern Ireland Court Service, Her Majesty's Diplomatic Service and Her Majesty's Overseas Civil Service;

"police authority" means any police authority within the meaning of [the Police Act 1996] or the Police (Scotland) Act 1967, or the Police Authority for Northern Ireland; and "member" in relation to a police force means a person employed as a full-time constable;

"regular armed forces of the Crown" means the Royal Navy, the regular forces as defined by section 225 of the Army Act 1955 [or the regular air force as defined by section 223 of the Air Force Act 1955]

(4) Except as provided by this Act, a person shall not be disqualified for membership of the House of Commons by reason of his holding an office or place of profit under the Crown or any other office or place; and a person shall not be disqualified for appointment to or for holding any office or place by reason of his being a member of that House.

Ministerial offices

37–003   **2.**—(1) Not more than ninety-five persons being the holders of offices specified in Schedule 2 to this Act (in this section referred to as Ministerial offices) shall be entitled to sit and vote in the House of Commons at any one time.

(2) If at any time the number of members of the House of Commons who are holders of Ministerial offices exceeds the number entitled to sit and vote in that House under subsection (1) above, none except any who were both members of that House and holders of Ministerial offices before the excess occurred shall sit or vote therein until the number has been reduced, by death, resignation or otherwise, to the number entitled to sit and vote as aforesaid.

(3) A person holding a Ministerial office is not disqualified by this Act by reason of any office held by him ex officio as the holder of that Ministerial office.

Reserve and auxiliary forces, etc.

37–004   **3.**—(1) Notwithstanding section 1(1)(c) above—

(a) a person who is an officer on the retired or emergency list of any of the regular armed forces of the Crown, or who holds an emergency commission in any of those forces, or belongs to any reserve of officers of any of those forces, is not disqualified as a member of those forces; and

(b) a naval, army, marine or air force pensioner [, or former soldier,] who is recalled for service for which he is liable as such is not disqualified as a member of the regular armed forces of the Crown.

(2) A person is not disqualified under section 1(1)(c) above by reason of his being an Admiral of the Fleet, a Field Marshal or a Marshal of the Royal Air Force, if he does not for the time being hold an appointment in the naval, military or air force service of the Crown.

(3) A person is not disqualified under section 1(1)(b) above by reason of his being a member of the Royal Observer Corps unless he is employed as such for the whole of his time.

Stewardship of Chiltern Hundreds, etc.

4. For the purposes of the provisions of this Act relating to the vacation of the seat of a member of the House of Commons who becomes disqualified by this Act for membership of that House, the office of steward or bailiff of Her Majesty's three Chiltern Hundreds of Stoke, Desborough and Burnham, or of the Manor of Northstead, shall be treated as included among the offices described in Part III of Schedule 1 to this Act.   **37–005**

Power to amend Schedule 1

5.—(1) If at any time it is resolved by the House of Commons that Schedule 1 to this Act be amended, whether by the addition or omission of any office or the removal of any office from one Part of the Schedule to another, or by altering the description of any office specified therein, Her Majesty may by Order in Council amend that Schedule accordingly.   **37–006**

(2) A copy of this Act as from time to time amended by Order in Council under this section or by or under any other enactment shall be prepared and certified by the Clerk of the Parliaments and deposited with the rolls of Parliament; and all copies of this Act thereafter to be printed by Her Majesty's printer shall be printed in accordance with the copy so certified.

Effects of disqualification and provision for relief

6.—(1) Subject to any order made by the House of Commons under this section—   **37–007**

    (a) if any person disqualified by this Act for membership of that House, or for membership for a particular constituency, is elected as a member of that House, or as a member for that constituency, as the case may be, his election shall be void; and

    (b) if any person being a member of that House becomes disqualified by this Act for membership, or for membership for the constituency for which he is sitting, his seat shall be vacated.

(2) If, in a case falling or alleged to fall within subsection (1) above, it appears to the House of Commons that the grounds of disqualification or alleged disqualification under this Act which subsisted or arose at the material time have been removed, and that it is otherwise proper so to do, that House may by order direct that any such disqualification incurred on those grounds at that time shall be disregarded for the purposes of this section.

(3) No order under subsection (2) above shall affect the proceedings on any election petition or any determination of an election court, and this subsection shall have effect subject to the provisions of section 144(7) of the Representation of the People Act 1983 (making of an order by the House of Commons when informed of a certificate and any report of an election court).

(4) In any case where, by virtue of the Recess Elections Act 1975, the Speaker of the House of Commons would be required to issue during a recess of that House a warrant for a new writ for election of a member, in the room of a member becoming disqualified by this Act, he may, if it appears to him that an opportunity should be given to that House to consider the making of an order under subsection (2) above, defer the issue of his warrant pending the determination of that House.

Jurisdiction of Privy Council as to disqualification

37–008   7.—(1) Any person who claims that a person purporting to be a member of the House of Commons is disqualified by this Act, or has been so disqualified at any time since his election, may apply to Her Majesty in Council, in accordance with such rules as Her Majesty in Council may prescribe, for a declaration to that effect.

(2) Section 3 of the Judicial Committee Act 1833 (reference to the Judicial Committee of the Privy Council of appeals to Her Majesty in Council) shall apply to any application under this section as it applies to an appeal to Her Majesty in Council from a court.

(3) Upon any such application the person in respect of whom the application is made shall be the respondent; and the applicant shall give such security for the costs of the proceedings, not exceeding £200, as the Judicial Committee may direct.

(4) For the purpose of determining any issue of fact arising on an application under this section the Judicial Committee may direct the issue to be tried—

(a) if the constituency for which the respondent purports to be a member is in England or Wales, in the High Court;

(b) if that constituency is in Scotland, in the Court of Session;

(c) if that constituency is in Northern Ireland, in the High Court in Northern Ireland;

and the decision of that Court shall be final.

(5) A declaration under this section may be made in respect of any person whether the grounds of the alleged disqualification subsisted at the time of his election or arose subsequently; but no such declaration shall be made—

(a) in the case of disqualification incurred by any person on grounds which subsisted at the time of his election, if an election petition is pending or has been tried in which his disqualification on those grounds is or was in issue;

(b) in the case of disqualification incurred by any person on any grounds, if an order has been made by the House of Commons under section 6(2) above directing that any disqualification incurred by him on those grounds shall be disregarded for the purposes of that section.

. . . . . .

Section 2   SCHEDULE 2

MINISTERIAL OFFICES

37–009   Prime Minister and First Lord of the Treasury.
Lord President of the Council.
Lord Privy Seal.
Chancellor of the Duchy of Lancaster.
Paymaster General.
Secretary of State.
Chancellor of the Exchequer.
Minister of Agriculture, Fisheries and Food.
President of the Board of Trade.
Minister of State.
Chief Secretary to the Treasury.
Minister in charge of a public department of Her Majesty's Government in the United Kingdom (if not within the other provisions of this Schedule).
Attorney General.
Solicitor General.
[Advocate General for Scotland]

Parliamentary Secretary to the Treasury.
Financial Secretary to the Treasury.
Parliamentary Secretary in a Government Department other than the Treasury, or not in a department.
Junior Lord of the Treasury.
Treasurer of Her Majesty's Household.
Comptroller of Her Majesty's Household.
Vice-Chamberlain of Her Majesty's Household.
Assistant Government Whip.

Ministerial and other Salaries Act 1975

(1975, c. 27)

An Act to consolidate the enactments relating to the salaries of Ministers and Opposition Leaders and Chief Whips and to other matters connected therewith. [8th May 1975]   **38–001**

Salaries

1.—(1) Subject to the provisions of this Act—   **38–002**

    (a) there shall be paid to the holder of any Ministerial office specified in Schedule 1 to this Act such salary as is provided for by that Schedule; and

    (b) there shall be paid to the Leaders and Whips of the Opposition such salaries as are provided for by Schedule 2 to this Act.

(2) There shall be paid to the Lord Chancellor a salary (which shall be charged on and paid out of the Consolidated Fund of the United Kingdom) at such rate as together with the salary payable to him as Speaker of the House of Lords will amount to [[£2,500] a year more than the salary for the time being payable to the Lord Chief Justice].

(3) There shall be paid to the Speaker of the House of Commons a salary (which shall be charged on and paid out of the Consolidated Fund of the United Kingdom) of [£60,000] a year; and on a dissolution of Parliament the Speaker of the House of Commons at the time of the dissolution shall for this purpose be deemed to remain Speaker until a Speaker is chosen by the New Parliament.

(5) A person to whom any salary is payable under subsection (1) above shall be entitled to receive only one such salary, but if he is the holder of two or more offices in respect of which a salary is so payable and there is a difference between the salaries payable in respect of those offices, the office in respect of which a salary is payable to him shall be that in respect of which the highest salary is payable.

Alteration of salaries

[1A.—(1) For each year starting with 1st April, from 1998 onwards, the   **38–003**
annual amount, or maximum or minimum annual amount, of any salary payable under section 1(1) or (3) of this Act shall be increased by the relevant percentage.

(2) The relevant percentage is the average percentage by which the mid-points of the Senior Civil Service pay bands having effect from 1st April of the year concerned have increased compared with the previous 1st April.

(3) The mid-point of a Senior Civil Service pay band is the point half way between the maximum and the minimum.]

Power to make further alterations

38–004 [**1B.**—(1) Her Majesty may from time to time by Order in Council make provision for changing the annual amount, or maximum or minimum annual amount, of any salary payable under section 1 of this Act.

(2) An Order in Council under subsection (1) above may—

(a) specify a new amount, or
(b) provide for an amount to be determined, or to change from time to time, by reference to another amount or a specified formula.

(3) An Order in Council under subsection (1) above may—

(a) make different provision for different circumstances, and
(b) make amendments to this Act.

(4) No recommendation shall be made to Her Majesty to make an Order in Council under subsection (1) above unless a draft of the Order has been approved—

(a) by resolution of each House of Parliament, or
(b) in the case of a draft which relates only to the salary of the Speaker of the House of Commons, by resolution of that House.]

Opposition Leaders and Whips

38–005 **2.**—(1) In this Act "Leader of the Opposition" means, in relation to either House of Parliament, that Member of that House who is for the time being the Leader in that House of the party in opposition to Her Majesty's Government having the greatest numerical strength in the House of Commons; and "Chief Opposition Whip" means, in relation to either House of Parliament, the person for the time being nominated as such by the Leader of the Opposition in that House; and "Assistant Opposition Whip", in relation to the House of Commons, means a person for the time being nominated as such, and to be paid as such, by the Leader of the Opposition in the House of Commons.

(2) If any doubt arises as to which is or was at any material time the party in opposition to Her Majesty's Government having the greatest numerical strength in the House of Commons, or as to who is or was at any material time the leader in that House of such a party, the question shall be decided for the purposes of this Act by the Speaker of the House of Commons, and his decision, certified in writing under his hand, shall be final and conclusive.

(3) If any doubt arises as to who is or was at any material time the Leader in the House of Lords of the said party, the question shall be decided for the purposes of this Act by the Lord Chancellor, and his decision, certified in writing under his hand, shall be final and conclusive.

. . . . . .

Interpretation

4.—(1) In this Act—   **38–006**

> "Junior Lord of the Treasury" means any Lord Commissioner of the Treasury other than the First Lord and the Chancellor of the Exchequer;
> "Minister of State" and "Parliamentary Secretary" have the same meanings as in the House of Commons Disqualification Act 1975.

[(2) The amount provided for by or under this Act as the amount of any salary payable out of money provided by Parliament shall be taken to be the maximum amount so payable; and accordingly the salary so payable in any year may be of a less amount than that provided for.][1]

[1] Substituted by Ministerial and other Salaries Act 1997 (c.62), s. 2(1).

Sex Discrimination Act 1975

(1975, c. 65)

An Act to render unlawful certain kinds of sex discrimination and discrimination   **39–001**
on the ground of marriage, and establish a Commission with the function of working towards the elimination of such discrimination and promoting equality of opportunity between men and women generally; and for related purposes.   [12th November 1975]

PART I

DISCRIMINATION TO WHICH ACT APPLIES

Direct and indirect discrimination against women

[**1.** (1) In any circumstances relevant for the purposes of any provision of this   **39–002**
Act, other than a provision to which subsection (2) applies, a person discriminates against a woman if—

(a) on the ground of her sex he treats her less favourably than he treats or would treat a man, or
(b) he applies to her a requirement or condition which he applies or would apply equally to a man but—

    (i) which is such that the proportion of women who can comply with it is considerably smaller than the proportion of men who can comply with it, and
    (ii) which he cannot show to be justifiable irrespective of the sex of the person to whom it is applied, and
    (iii) which is to her detriment because she cannot comply with it.

(2) In any circumstances relevant for the purposes of a provision to which this subsection applies, a person discriminates against a woman if—

(a) on the ground of her sex, he treats her less favourably than he treats or would treat a man, or

(b) he applies to her a provision, criterion or practice which he applies or would apply equally to a man, but—

    (i) which is such that it would be to the detriment of a considerably larger proportion of women than of men, and

    (ii) which he cannot show to be justifiable irrespective of the sex of the person to whom it is applied, and

    (iii) which is to her detriment.

(3) Subsection (2) applies to—

(a) any provision of Part 2,
(b) sections 35A and 35B, and
(c) any other provision of Part 3, so far as it applies to vocational training.

(4) If a person treats or would treat a man differently according to the man's marital status, his treatment of a woman is for the purposes of subsection (1)(a) or (2)(a) to be compared to his treatment of a man having the like marital status.]

Sex discrimination against men

39–003   **2.**—(1) Section 1, and the provisions of Parts II and III relating to sex discrimination against women, are to be read as applying equally to the treatment of men, and for that purpose shall have effect with such modifications as are requisite.

(2) In the application of subsection (1) no account shall be taken of special treatment afforded to women in connection with pregnancy or childbirth.

Discrimination on the grounds of gender reassignment

39–004   [**2A.**—(1) A person ("A") discriminates against another person ("B") in any circumstances relevant for the purposes of–

(a) any provision of Part II,
(b) section 35A or 35B, or
(c) any other provision of Part III, so far as it applies to vocational training,

if he treats B less favourably than he treats or would treat other persons, and does so on the ground that B intends to undergo, is undergoing or has undergone gender reassignment.

(2) Subsection (3) applies to arrangements made by any person in relation to another's absence from work or from vocational training.

(3) For the purposes of subsection (1), B is treated less favourably than others under such arrangements if, in the application of the arrangements to any absence due to B undergoing gender reassignment–

(a) he is treated less favourably than he would be if the absence was due to sickness or injury, or

(b) he is treated less favourably than he would be if the absence was due to some other cause and, having regard to the circumstances of the case, it is reasonable for him to be treated no less favourably.

(4) In subsections (2) and (3) "arrangements" includes terms, conditions or arrangements on which employment, a pupillage or tenancy or vocational training is offered.

(5) For the purposes of subsection (1), a provision mentioned in that subsection framed with reference to discrimination against women shall be treated

as applying equally to the treatment of men with such modifications as are requisite.]

Direct and indirect discrimination against married persons in employment field

[**3.**—(1) In any circumstances relevant for the purposes of any provision of Part 2, a person discriminates against a married person of either sex if—

39–005

    (a) on the ground of his or her marital status he treats that person less favourably than he treats or would treat an unmarried person of the same sex, or

    (b) he applies to that person a provision, criterion or practice which he applies or would apply equally to an unmarried person, but—

        (i) which is such that it would be to the detriment of a considerably larger proportion of married persons than of unmarried persons of the same sex, and

        (ii) which he cannot show to be justifiable irrespective of the marital status of the person to whom it is applied, and

        (iii) which is to that person's detriment.

(2) For the purposes of subsection (1), a provision of Part 2 framed with reference to discrimination against women shall be treated as applying equally to the treatment of men, and for that purpose shall have effect with such modifications as are requisite.]

Discrimination by way of victimisation

4.—(1) A person ("the discriminator") discriminates against another person ("the person victimised") in any circumstances relevant for the purposes of any provision of this Act if he treats the person victimised less favourably than in those circumstances he treats or would treat other persons, and do so by reason that the person victimised has—

39–006

    (a) brought proceedings against the discriminator or any other person under this Act or the Equal Pay Act 1970 [or sections 62 to 65 of the Pensions Act 1995]; or

    (b) given evidence or information in connection with proceedings brought by any person against the discriminator or any other person under this Act or the Equal Pay Act 1970 [or sections 62 to 65 of the Pensions Act 1995]; or

    (c) otherwise done anything under or by reference to this Act or the Equal Pay Act 1970 [or sections 62 to 65 of the Pensions Act 1995] in relation to the discriminator or any other person; or

    (d) alleged that the discriminator or any other person has committed an act which (whether or not the allegation so states) would amount to a contravention of this Act or give rise to a claim under the Equal Pay Act 1970 [or under sections 62 to 65 of the Pensions Act 1995];

or by reason that the discriminator knows the person victimised intends to do any of those things, or suspects the person victimised has done, or intends to do, any of them.

(2) Subsection (1) does not apply to treatment of a person by reason of any allegation made by him if the allegation was false and not made in good faith.

(3) For the purposes of subsection (1), a provision of Part II or III framed with reference to discrimination against women shall be treated as applying

equally to the treatment of men and for that purpose shall have effect with such modifications as are requisite.

Interpretation

39–007 **5.**—(1) In this Act—

(a) references to discrimination refer to any discrimination falling within sections 1 to 4; and
(b) references to sex discrimination refer to any discrimination falling within section 1 or 2;

and related expressions shall be construed accordingly.

(2) In this Act—

"woman" includes a female of any age, and
"man" includes a male of any age.

(3) A comparison of the cases of persons of different sex or marital status under [[section 1(1) or (2) or 3(1)], or a comparison of the cases of persons required for the purposes of section 2A,] must be such that the relevant circumstances in the one case are the same, or not materially different, in the other.

PART II

DISCRIMINATION IN THE EMPLOYMENT FIELD

Discrimination by employers

Discrimination against applicants and employees

39–008 **6.**—(1) It is unlawful for a person, in relation to employment by him at an establishment in Great Britain, to discriminate against a woman—

(a) in the arrangements he makes for the purpose of determining who should be offered that employment, or
(b) in the terms on which he offers her that employment, or
(c) by refusing or deliberately omitting to offer her that employment.

(2) It is unlawful for a person, in the case of a woman employed by him at an establishment in Great Britain, to discriminate against her—

(a) in the way he affords her access to opportunities for promotion, transfer or training, or to any other benefits, facilities or services, or by refusing or deliberately omitting to afford her access to them, or
(b) by dismissing her, or subjecting her to any other detriment.

[(4) Subsections (1)(b) and (2) do not render it unlawful for a person to discriminate against a woman in relation to her membership of, or rights under, an occupational pension scheme in such a way that, were any term of the scheme to provide for discrimination in that way, then, by reason only of any provision made by or under sections 62 to 64 of the Pensions Act 1995 (equal treatment), an equal treatment rule would not operate in relation to that term.

(4A) In subsection (4), "occupational pension scheme" has the same meaning as in the Pension Schemes Act 1993 and "equal treatment rule" has the meaning given by section 62 of the Pensions Act 1995.]

(5) Subject to section 8(3), subsection (1)(b) does not apply to any provision

for the payment of money which, if the woman in question were given the employment, would be included (directly [. . .] or otherwise) in the contract under which she was employed.

(6) Subsection (2) does not apply to benefits consisting of the payment of money when the provision of those benefits is regulated by the woman's contract of employment.

(7) Subsection (2) does not apply to benefits, facilities or services of any description if the employer is concerned with the provision (for payment or not) of benefits, facilities or services of that description to the public, or to a section of the public comprising the woman in question, unless—

(a) that provision differs in a material respect from the provision of the benefits, facilities or services by the employer to his employees; or

(b) the provision of the benefits, facilities or services to the woman in question is regulated by her contract of employment; or

(c) the benefits, facilities or services relate to training.

[(8) In its application to any discrimination falling within section 2A, this section shall have effect with the omission of subsections (4) to (6).]

Exception where sex is a genuine occupational qualification

7.—(1) In relation to sex discrimination—   **39–009**

(a) section 6(1)(a) or (c) does not apply to any employment where being a man is a genuine occupational qualification for the job; and

(b) section 6(2)(a) does not apply to opportunities for promotion or transfer to, or training for, such employment.

(2) Being a man is a genuine occupational qualification for a job only where—

(a) the essential nature of the job calls for a man for reasons of physiology (excluding physical strength or stamina) or, in dramatic performances or other entertainment, for reasons of authenticity, so that the essential nature of the job would be materially different if carried out by a woman; or

(b) the job needs to be held by a man to preserve decency or privacy because—

(i) it is likely to involve physical contact with men in circumstances where they might reasonably object to its being carried out by a woman; or

(ii) the holder of the job is likely to do his work in circumstances where men might reasonably object to the presence of a woman because they are in a state of undress or are using sanitary facilities; or

[(ba) the job is likely to involve the holder of the job doing his work, or living, in a private home and needs to be held by a man because objection might reasonably be taken to allowing to a woman–

(i) the degree of physical or social contact with a person living in the home, or

(ii) the knowledge of intimate details of such a person's life,

which is likely, because of the nature or circumstances of the job or of the home, to be allowed to, or available to, the holder of the job; or][1]

(c) the nature or location of the establishment makes it impracticable for the holder of the job to live elsewhere than in premises provided by the employer, and—

    (i) the only such premises which are available for persons holding that kind of job are lived in, or normally lived in, by men and are not equipped with separate sleeping accommodation for women and sanitary facilities which could be used by women in privacy from men, and

    (ii) it is not reasonable to expect the employer either to equip those premises with such accommodation and facilities or to provide other premises for women; or

(d) the nature of the establishment, or of the part of it within which the work is done, requires the job to be held by a man because—

    (i) it is, or is part of, a hospital, prison or other establishment for persons requiring special care, supervision or attention, and

    (ii) those persons are all men (disregarding any woman whose presence is exceptional), and

    (iii) it is reasonable, having regard to the essential character of the establishment or that part, that the job should not be held by a woman; or

(e) the holder of the job provides individuals with personal services promoting their welfare or education, or similar personal services, and those services can most effectively be provided by a man, or

(f) [. . .]²

(g) the job needs to be held by a man because it is likely to involve the performance of duties outside the United Kingdom in a country whose laws or customs are such that the duties could not, or could not effectively, be performed by a woman, or

(h) the job is one of two to be held by a married couple.

(3) Subsection (2) applies where some only of the duties of the job fall within paragraphs (a) to (g) as well as where all of them do.

(4) Paragraph (a), (b), (c), (d), (e) or (g) of subsection (2) does not apply in relation to the filling of a vacancy at a time when the employer already has male employees—

(a) who are capable of carrying out the duties falling within that paragraph, and

(b) whom it would be reasonable to employ on those duties, and

(c) whose numbers are sufficient to meet the employer's likely requirements in respect of those duties without undue inconvenience.

¹ s. 7(2)(ba) inserted by Sex Discrimination Act 1986 (c.59), s. 1(2).
² Repealed by Employment Act 1989 (c.38), ss. 3(2), 29(4), Sched. 7, Pt. II (subject to a saving in Sched. 9 para. 1).

Corresponding exception relating to gender reassignment

39–010   [7A.—(1) In their application to discrimination falling within section 2A, subsections (1) and (2) of section 6 do not make unlawful an employer's treatment of another person if–

(a) in relation to the employment in question–

    (i) being a man is a genuine occupational qualification for the job, or

    (ii) being a woman is a genuine occupational qualification for the job, and

(b) the employer can show that the treatment is reasonable in view of the circumstances described in the relevant paragraph of section 7(2) and any other relevant circumstances.

(2) In subsection (1) the reference to the employment in question is a reference–

(a) in relation to any paragraph of section 6(1), to the employment mentioned in that paragraph;
(b) in relation to section 6(2)–

    (i) in its application to opportunities for promotion or transfer to any employment or for training for any employment, to that employment;
    (ii) otherwise, to the employment in which the person discriminated against is employed or from which that person is dismissed.

(3) In determining for the purposes of subsection (1) whether being a man or being a woman is a genuine occupational qualification for a job, section 7(4) applies in relation to dismissal from employment as it applies in relation to the filling of a vacancy.]

Supplementary exceptions relating to gender reassignment

[**7B.**—(1) In relation to discrimination falling within section 2A–   **39–011**

(a) section 6(1)(a) or (c) does not apply to any employment where there is a supplementary genuine occupational qualification for the job,
(b) section 6(2)(a) does not apply to a refusal or deliberate omission to afford access to opportunities for promotion or transfer to or training for such employment, and
(c) section 6(2)(b) does not apply to dismissing an employee from, or otherwise not allowing him to continue in, such employment.

(2) Subject to subsection (3), there is a supplementary genuine occupational qualification for a job only if–

(a) the job involves the holder of the job being liable to be called upon to perform intimate physical searches pursuant to statutory powers;
(b) the job is likely to involve the holder of the job doing his work, or living, in a private home and needs to be held otherwise than by a person who is undergoing or has undergone gender reassignment, because objection might reasonably be taken to allowing to such a person–

    (i) the degree of physical or social contact with a person living in the home, or
    (ii) the knowledge of intimate details of such a person's life,

    which is likely, because of the nature or circumstances of the job or of the home, to be allowed to, or available to, the holder of the job;
(c) the nature or location of the establishment makes it impracticable for the holder of the job to live elsewhere than in premises provided by the employer, and–

    (i) the only such premises which are available for persons holding that kind of job are such that reasonable objection could be taken, for the purpose of preserving decency and privacy, to the holder of the job sharing accommodation and facilities with either sex whilst undergoing gender reassignment, and

(ii) it is not reasonable to expect the employer either to equip those premises with suitable accommodation or to make alternative arrangements; or

(d) the holder of the job provides vulnerable individuals with personal services promoting their welfare, or similar personal services, and in the reasonable view of the employer those services cannot be effectively provided by a person whilst that person is undergoing gender reassignment.

(3) Paragraphs (c) and (d) of subsection (2) apply only in relation to discrimination against a person who—

(a) intends to undergo gender reassignment, or
(b) is undergoing gender reassignment.]

Equal Pay Act 1970

39–012   **8.**—(2) Section 1(1) of the Equal Pay Act 1970 (as set out in subsection (1) above) does not apply in determining for the purposes of section 6(1)(b) of this Act the terms on which employment is offered.

(3) Where a person offers a woman employment on certain terms, and if she accepted the offer then, by virtue of an equality clause, any of those terms would fall to be modified, or any additional term would fall to be included, the offer shall be taken to contravene section 6(1)(b).

(4) Where a person offers a woman employment on certain terms, and subsection (3) would apply but for the fact that, on her acceptance of the offer, section 1(3) of the Equal Pay Act 1970 (as set out in subsection (1) above) would prevent the equality clause from operating, the offer shall be taken not to contravene section 6(1)(b).

(5) An act does not contravene section 6(2) if—

(a) it contravenes a term modified or included by virtue of an equality clause, or
(b) it would contravene such a term but for the fact that the equality clause is prevented from operating by section 1(3) of the Equal Pay Act 1970.

(6) The Equal Pay Act 1970 is further amended as specified in Part I of Schedule 1, and accordingly has effect as set out in Part II of Schedule 1.

[(7) In its application to any discrimination falling within section 2A, this section shall have effect with the omission of subsections (3), (4) and (5)(b).]

Discrimination against contract workers

39–013   **9.**—(1) This section applies to any work for a person ("the principal") which is available for doing by individuals ("contract workers") who are employed not by the principal himself but by another person, who supplies them under a contract made with the principal.

(2) It is unlawful for the principal, in relation to work to which this section applies, to discriminate against a woman who is a contract worker—

(a) in the terms on which he allows her to do that work, or
(b) by not allowing her to do it or continue to do it, or
(c) in the way he affords her access to any benefits, facilities or services

or by refusing or deliberately omitting to afford her access to them, or

(d) by subjecting her to any other detriment.

(3) [Subject to subsection (3A), t] he principal does not contravene subsection (2)(b) by doing any act in relation to a woman at a time when if the work were to be done by a person taken into his employment being a man would be a genuine occupational qualification for the job.

[(3A) Subsection (3) does not apply in relation to discrimination falling within section 2A.

(3B) In relation to discrimination falling within section 2A, the principal does not contravene subsection (2)(a), (b), (c) or (d) by doing any act in relation to a woman if—

(a) he does it at a time when, if the work were to be done by a person taken into his employment–

  (i) being a man would be a genuine occupational qualification for the job, or
  (ii) being a woman would be a genuine occupational qualification for the job, and

(b) he can show that the act is reasonable in view of the circumstances relevant for the purposes of paragraph (a) and any other relevant circumstances.

(3C) In relation to discrimination falling within section 2A, the principal does not contravene subsection (2)(b) by doing any act in relation to a woman at a time when, if the work were to be done by a person taken into his employment, there would be a supplementary genuine occupational qualification for the job.]

(4) Subsection (2)(c) does not apply to benefits, facilities or services of any description if the principal is concerned with the provision (for payment or not) of benefits, facilities or services of that description to the public, or to a section of the public to which the woman belongs, unless that provision differs in a material respect from the provision of the benefits, facilities or services by the principal to his contract workers.

Meaning of employment at establishment in Great Britain

10.—(1) For the purposes of this Part and section 1 of the Equal Pay Act **39–014** 1970 ("the relevant purposes"), employment is to be regarded as being at an establishment in Great Britain unless the employee does his work wholly.

[(2) The reference to "employment" in subsection (1) includes—

(a) employment on board a ship registered at a port of registry in Great Britain, and
(b) employment on aircraft or hovercraft registered in the United Kingdom and operated by a person who has his principal place of business, or is ordinarily resident, in Great Britain.]

(3) In the case of employment on board a ship registered at a port of registry in Great Britain (except where the employee does his work wholly outside Great Britain, and outside any area added under subsection (5)) the ship shall for the relevant purposes be deemed to be the establishment.

(4) Where work is not done at an establishment it shall be treated for the relevant purposes as done at the establishment from which it is done or (where it is not done from any establishment) at the establishment with which it has the closest connection.

(5) In relation to employment concerned with exploration of the sea bed or

subsoil or the exploitation of their natural resources, Her Majesty may by Order in Council provide that subsections (1) and (2) shall each have effect as if the last reference to Great Britain included any area for the time being designated under section 1(7) of the Continental Shelf Act 1964, except an area or part of an area in which the law of Northern Ireland applies.

(6) An Order in Council under subsection (5) may provide that, in relation to employment to which the Order applies, this Part and section 1 of the Equal Pay Act 1970 are to have effect with such modifications as are specified in the Order.

(7) An Order in Council under subsection (5) shall be of no effect unless a draft of the Order was laid before and approved by each House of Parliament.

Discrimination by other bodies

Partnerships

39–015   **11.**—(1) It is unlawful for a firm, in relation to a position as partner in the firm, to discriminate against a woman—

(a) in the arrangements they make for the purpose of determining who should be offered that position, or
(b) in the terms on which they offer her that position, or
(c) by refusing or deliberately omitting to offer her that position, or
(d) in a case where the woman already holds that position—

(i) in the way they afford her access to any benefits, facilities or services, or by refusing or deliberately omitting to afford her access to them, or
(ii) by expelling her from that position, or subjecting her to any other detriment.

(2) Subsection (1) shall apply in relation to persons proposing to form themselves into a partnership as it applies in relation to a firm.

(3) [Subject to subsection (3A), s]ubsection (1)(a) and (c) do not apply to a position as partner where, if it were employment, being a man would be a genuine occupational qualification for the job.

[(3A) Subsection (3) does not apply in relation to discrimination falling within section 2A.

(3B) In relation to discrimination falling within section 2A, subsection (1) does not make unlawful a firm's treatment of a person in relation to a position as partner where–

(a) if it were employment–

(i) being a man would be a genuine occupational qualification for the job, or
(ii) being a woman would be a genuine occupational qualification for the job, and

(b) the firm can show that the treatment is reasonable in view of the circumstances relevant for the purposes of paragraph (a) and any other relevant circumstances.

(3C) In relation to discrimination falling within section 2A, subsection (1)(a), (c) and, so far as it relates to expulsion, (d)(ii) do not apply to a position as partner where, if it were employment, there would be a supplementary genuine occupational qualification for the job.]

(4) Subsection (1)(b) and (d) do not apply to provision made in relation to

death or retirement [except in so far as, in their application to provision made in relation to retirement, they render it unlawful for a firm to discriminate against a woman—]

[(a) in such of the terms on which they offer her a position as partner as provide for her expulsion from that position; or
(b) by expelling her from a position as partner or subjecting her to any detriment which results in her expulsion from such a position.]

(5) In the case of a limited partnership references in subsection (1) to a partner shall be construed as references to a general partner as defined in section 3 of the Limited Partnerships Act 1907.

[(6) This section applies to a limited liability partnership as it applies to a firm; and, in its application to a limited liability partnership, references to a partner in a firm are references to a member of the limited liability partnership.]

Trade unions, etc.

12.—(1) This section applies to an organisation of workers, an organisation of employers, or any other organisation whose members carry on a particular profession or trade for the purposes of which the organisation exists.

39–016

(2) It is unlawful for an organisation to which this section applies, in the case of a woman who is not a member of the organisation, to discriminate against her—

(a) in the terms on which it is prepared to admit her to membership, or
(b) by refusing, or deliberately omitting to accept, her application for membership.

(3) It is unlawful for an organisation to which this section applies, in the case of a woman who is a member of the organisation, to discriminate against her—

(a) in the way it affords her access to any benefits, facilities or services, or by refusing or deliberately omitting to afford her access to them, or
(b) by depriving her of membership, or varying the terms on which she is a member, or
(c) by subjecting her to any other detriment.

(4) This section does not apply to provision made in relation to the death or retirement from work of a member.

Qualifying bodies

13.—(1) It is unlawful for an authority or body which can confer an authorisation or qualification which is needed for, or facilitates, engagement in a particular profession or trade to discriminate against a woman—

39–017

(a) in the terms on which it is prepared to confer on her that authorisation or qualification, or
(b) by refusing or deliberately omitting to grant her application for it, or
(c) by withdrawing it from her or varying the terms on which she holds it.

(2) Where an authority or body is required by law to satisfy itself as to his good character before conferring on a person an authorisation or qualification which is needed for, or facilitates, his engagement in any profession or trade then, without prejudice to any other duty to which it is subject, that requirement shall be taken to impose on the authority or body a duty to have regard to any

evidence tending to show that he, or any of his employees, or agents (whether past or present), has practised unlawful discrimination in, or in connection with, the carrying on of any profession or trade.

(3) In this section—

    (a) "authorisation or qualification" includes recognition, registration, enrolment, approval and certification,

    (b) "confer" includes renew or extend.

(4) Subsection (1) does not apply to discrimination which is rendered unlawful by section 22 or 23.

Persons concerned with provision of vocational training

39–018   [**14.**—(1) It is unlawful, in the case of a woman seeking or undergoing training which would help fit her for any employment, for any person who provides, or makes arrangements for the provision of, facilities for such training to discriminate against her—

    (a) in the terms on which that person affords her access to any training course or other facilities concerned with such training, or

    (b) by refusing or deliberately omitting to afford her such access, or

    (c) by terminating her training, or

    (d) by subjecting her to any detriment during the course of her training.

(2) Subsection (1) does not apply to—

    [(a) the Secretary of State,

    (b) discrimination which is rendered unlawful by section 6(1) or (2) or section 22 or 23, or]

    (c) discrimination which would be rendered unlawful by any of those provisions but for the operation of any other provision of this Act.]

Employment agencies

39–019   **15.**—(1) It is unlawful for an employment agency to discriminate against a woman—

    (a) in the terms on which the agency offers to provide any of its services, or

    (b) by refusing or deliberately omitting to provide any of its services, or

    (c) in the way it provides any of its services.

[(2) It is unlawful for a local education authority or education authority or any other person to do any act in providing services in pursuance of arrangements made, or a direction given, under section 10 of the Employment and Training Act 1973 which constitutes discrimination.]

(3) References in subsection (1) to the services of an employment agency include guidance on careers and any other services related to employment.

(4) This section does not apply if the discrimination only concerns employment which the employer could lawfully refuse to offer the woman.

(5) An employment agency or local education authority [, education authority or other person] shall not be subject to any liability under this section if it proves—

    (a) that it acted in reliance on a statement made to it by the employer to the effect that, by reason of the operation of subsection (4), its action would not be unlawful, and

(b) that it was reasonable for it to rely on the statement.

(6) A person who knowingly or recklessly makes a statement such as is referred to in subsection (5)(a) which in a material respect is false or misleading commits an offence, and shall be liable on summary conviction to a fine not exceeding [level 5 on the standard scale].

Manpower Services Commission, etc.

[**16.**—(1) It is unlawful for the [Secretary of State] to discriminate in the provision of facilities or services under section 2 of the Employment and Training Act 1973.]   **39–020**

[(1A) It is unlawful for Scottish Enterprise or Highlands and Islands Enterprise to discriminate in the provision of facilities or services under such arrangements as are mentioned in section 2(3) of the Enterprise and New Towns (Scotland) Act 1990 (arrangements analogous to arrangements in pursuance of section 2 of the said Act of 1973).]

(2) This section does not apply in a case where—

(a) section 14 applies, or
(b) the [Secretary of State] is acting as an employment agency.

Special cases

Police

17.—(1) For the purposes of this Part, the holding of the office of constable shall be treated as employment—   **39–021**

(a) by the chief officer of police as respects any act done by him in relation to a constable or that office;
(b) by the police authority as respects any act done by them in relation to a constable or that office.

(2) Regulations made under [section 50, 51 or 52 of the Police Act 1996] shall not treat men and women differently except—

(a) as to requirements relating to height, uniform or equipment, or allowances in lieu of uniform or equipment, or
(b) so far as special treatment is accorded to women in connection with pregnancy or childbirth, or
(c) in relation to pensions to or in respect of special constables or police cadets.

(3) Nothing in this Part renders unlawful any discrimination between male and female constables as to matters such as are mentioned in subsection (2)(a).

(4) There shall be paid out of the police fund—

(a) any compensation, costs or expenses awarded against a chief officer of police in any proceedings brought against him under this Act, and any costs or expenses incurred by him in any such proceedings so far as not recovered by him in the proceedings; and
(b) any sum required by a chief officer of police for the settlement of any claim made against him under this Act if the settlement is approved by the police authority.

(5) Any proceedings under this Act which, by virtue of subsection (1), would lie against a chief officer of police shall be brought against the chief officer of police for the time being or, in the case of a vacancy in that office, against the person for the time being performing the functions of that office; and references in subsection (4) to the chief officer of police shall be construed accordingly.

(6) Subsections (1) and (3) apply to a police cadet and appointment as a police cadet as they apply to a constable and the office of constable.

(7) In this section—

"chief officer of police"—

(a) in relation to a person appointed, or an appointment falling to be made, under a specified Act, has the same meaning as in [the Police Act 1996],

[(b) in relation to a person appointed, or an appointment falling to be made, under section 9(1)(b) or 55(1)(b) of the Police Act 1997 (police members of the National Criminal Intelligence Service and the National Crime Squad) means the Director General of the National Criminal Intelligence Service or, as the case may be, the Director General of the National Crime Squad,]

(c) in relation to any other person or appointment means the officer who has the direction and control of the body of constables or cadets in question;

"police authority"—
(a) in relation to a person appointed, or an appointment falling to be made, under a specified Act, has the same meaning as in [the Police Act 1996],

(b) in relation to any other person or appointment, means the authority by whom the person in question is or on appointment would be paid;

"police cadet" means any person appointed to undergo training with a view to becoming a constable;
"police fund" in relation to a chief officer of police within paragraph (a) of the above definition of that term has the same meaning as in [the Police Act 1996], [in relation to a chief officer of police within paragraph (aa) of that definition means the service fund established under section 16 or, as the case may be, 61 of the Police Act 1997,] and in any other case means money provided by the police authority;
"specified Act" means the Metropolitan Police Act 1829, the City of London Police Act 1839 or [the Police Act 1996].

(8) In the application of this section to Scotland, in subsection (7) for any reference to [the Police Act 1996] there shall be substituted a reference to the Police (Scotland) Act 1967, and for the reference to [sections 50, 51 and 52] of the former Act in subsection (2) there shall be substituted a reference to sections 26 and 27 of the latter Act.

Prison officers

39–022   **18.**—(1) Nothing in this Part renders unlawful any discrimination between male and female prison officers as to requirements relating to height.

Ministers of religion etc.

19.—(1) Nothing in this Part applies to employment for purposes of an
organised religion where the employment is limited to one sex so as to comply
with the doctrines of the religion or avoid offending the religious susceptibilities
of a significant number of its followers.

(2) Nothing in section 13 applies to an authorisation or qualification (as
defined in that section) for purposes of an organised religion where the authorisation or qualification is limited to one sex so as to comply with the doctrines of
the religion or avoid offending the religious susceptibilities of a significant
number of its followers.

[(3) In relation to discrimination falling within section 2A, this Part does not
apply to employment for purposes of an organised religion where the employment is limited to persons who are not undergoing and have not undergone
gender reassignment, if the limitation is imposed to comply with the doctrines
of the religion or avoid offending the religious susceptibilities of a significant
number of its followers.

(4) In relation to discrimination falling within section 2A, section 13 does not
apply to an authorisation or qualification (as defined in that section) for purposes
of an organised religion where the authorisation or qualification is limited to
persons who are not undergoing and have not undergone gender reassignment,
if the limitation is imposed to comply with the doctrines of the religion or avoid
offending the religious susceptibilities of a significant number of its followers.]

39–023

Midwives

20.—(1) [Until 1st September 1983] section 6(1) does not apply to employment as a midwife.

(2) [Until 1st September 1983] section 6(2)(a) does not apply to promotion,
transfer or training as a midwife.

(3) [Until 1st September 1983] section 14 does not apply to training as a
midwife.

39–024

PART III

DISCRIMINATION IN OTHER FIELDS

Education

Discrimination by bodies in charge of educational establishments

22. It is unlawful in relation to an educational establishment falling within
column 1 of the following table, for a person indicated in relation to the establishment in column 2 (the "responsible body") to discriminate against a
woman—

39–025

(a) in the terms on which it offers to admit her to the establishment as a
pupil, or

(b) by refusing or deliberately omitting to accept an application for her
admission to the establishment as a pupil, or

(c) where she is a pupil of the establishment—

(i) in the way it affords her access to any benefits, facilities or services, or by refusing or deliberately omitting to afford her access
to them, or

(ii) by excluding her from the establishment or subjecting her to any
other detriment.

Meaning of pupil in section 22

39–026   [**22A.** For the purposes of section 22, "pupil" includes, in England and Wales, any person who receives education at a school or institution to which that section applies.]

Other discrimination by local education authorities

39–027   **23.**—(1) It is unlawful for a local education authority, in carrying out such of its functions under the Education Acts 1944 to 1975[the Education Acts] as do not fall under section 22, to do any act which constitutes sex discrimination.

(2) It is unlawful for an education authority, in carrying out such of its functions under [the Education (Scotland) Acts 1939 to 1980 [Act 1980]] as do not fall under section 22, to do any act which constitutes sex discrimination.

Discrimination by Further Education and Higher Education Funding Councils

39–028   [**23A.** It is unlawful for [the Learning and Skills Council for England, the National Council for Education and Training for Wales,] the Higher Education Funding Council for England or the Higher Education Funding Council for Wales in carrying out their functions under [the Education Acts] [and the Learning and Skills Act 2000], to do any act which constitutes sex discrimination.][1]

[1] Added by Further and Higher Education Act 1992 (c.13), Sched. 8 Part II, para. 78.

Discrimination by Scottish Further and Higher Education Funding Councils

39–029   [**23B.** It is unlawful for the Scottish Further Education Funding Council or the Scottish Higher Education Funding Council in carrying out any of their functions to do any act which constitutes sex discrimination.]

39–030   **23C.** [. . .][1]

[1] Repealed by School Standards and Framework Act 1998 (c.31), Sched. 31, para. 1.

Discrimination by Teacher Training Agency

39–031   [**23D.** It is unlawful for the Teacher Training Agency in carrying out their functions under Part I of the Education Act 1994 to do any act which constitutes sex discrimination.][1]

[1] Added by Education Act 1994 (c.30), Sched. 2, para. 5(3).

Designated establishments

39–032   **24.**—(1) The Secretary of State may by order designate for the purposes of paragraph 5 of the table in section 22 such establishments of the description mentioned in that paragraph as he thinks fit.

(2) An establishment shall not be designated under subsection (1) unless—

(b) it is an establishment in respect of which grants are payable out of money provided by Parliament, or

(c) it is assisted by a local education authority [for the purposes] of the [the Education Act 1996], or

(d) it provides full-time education for persons who have attained the upper limit of compulsory school age [(construed in accordance with section 8 of the Education Act 1996)] but not the age of nineteen.

(3) A designation under subsection (1) shall remain in force until revoked notwithstanding that the establishment ceases to be within subsection (2).

General duty in public sector of education

25.—(1) Without prejudice to its obligation to comply with any other provi-   **39–033**
sion of this Act, a body to which this subsection applies shall be under a general duty to secure that facilities for education provided by it, and any ancillary benefits or services, are provided without sex discrimination.

(2) The following provisions of [the Education Act 1996], namely—

(a) [section 496] (power of Secretary of State to require duties under that Act to be exercised reasonably), and
(b) [section 497] (powers of Secretary of State where local education authorities etc. are in default),

shall apply to the performance by a body to which subsection (1) applies of the duties imposed by [sections 22, 23, 23A and 23D] and shall also apply to the performance of the general duty imposed by subsection (1), as they apply to the performance by a local education authority of a duty imposed by that Act.

(3) Section [70 of the Education (Scotland) Act 1980] (power of the Secretary of State to require duties in that Act to be exercised) shall apply to the performance by a body to which subsection (1) applies of the duties imposed by sections 22 and 23 and shall also apply to the performance of the general duty imposed by subsection (1), as the [said section 70] applies to the performance by an education authority of a duty imposed by that Act.

(4) The sanctions in subsections (2) and (3) shall be the only sanctions for breach of the general duty in subsection (1), but without prejudice to the enforcement of sections 22 and 23 [, 23, 23A] [and 23D] under section 66 or otherwise (where the breach is also a contravention of [any] of those sections).

(5) The Secretary of State shall have the power to cause a local inquiry to be held into any matter arising from subsection (3) under [67 of the Education (Scotland) Act 1980].

(6) Subsection (1) applies to—

(a) local education authorities in England and Wales;
(b) education authorities in Scotland;
(c) any other body which is a responsible body in relation to—

(i) an establishment falling within paragraph 1, 3 [[, 3B,] or 7[,] [7, 7A, 7B or 7C] of the table in section 22;
(ii) an establishment designated under section 24(1) as falling within paragraph (c) of section 24(2);
(iii) an establishment designated under section 24(1) as falling within paragraph (b) of section 24(2) where the grants in question are payable under [section 485 of the Education Act 1996]

[(f) the Teacher Training Agency.]

General duty: post-16 education and training etc.

[**25A.**—(1) The Learning and Skills Council for England and the National   **39–034**
Council for Education and Training for Wales shall be under a general duty to

secure that the facilities falling within subsection (2) and any ancillary benefits or services are provided without sex discrimination.

(2) Facilities falling within this subsection are facilities for—

    (a) education,

    (b) training, and

    (c) organised leisure-time occupation connected with such education or training,

the provision of which is secured by the Learning and Skills Council for England or the National Council for Education and Training for Wales.

(3) The provisions of sections 25 and 47 of the Learning and Skills Act 2000 shall be the only sanction for breach of the general duty in subsection (1), but without prejudice to the enforcement of section 23A under section 66 or otherwise (where the breach is also a contravention of that section).]

Exception for single-sex establishments

39–035 **26.**—(1) [Sections 22(a) and (b), 25 and 25A] do not apply to the admission of pupils to any establishment (a "single-sex establishment") which admits pupils of one sex only, or which would be taken to admit pupils of one sex only if there were disregarded pupils of the opposite sex—

    (a) whose admission is exceptional, or

    (b) whose numbers are comparatively small and whose admission is confined to particular courses of instruction or teaching classes.

(2) Where a school which is not a single-sex establishment has some pupils as boarders and others as non-boarders, and admits as boarders pupils of one sex only (or would be taken to admit as boarders pupils of one sex only if there were disregarded boarders of the opposite sex whose numbers are comparatively small), sections 22(a) and (b) [, 25 and 25A] do not apply to the admission of boarders and [sections 22(c)(i), 25 and 25A] do not apply to boarding facilities.

(3) Where an establishment is a single-sex establishment by reason of its inclusion in subsection (1)(b), the fact that pupils of one sex are confined to particular courses of instruction or teaching classes shall not be taken to contravene section 22(c)(i) or the duty in section 25 [or 25A].

[(4) In this section, as it applies to an establishment in England and Wales, "pupil" includes any person who receives education at that establishment.]

Exception for single-sex establishments turning co-educational

39–036 **27.**—(1) Where at any time—

    (a) the responsible body for single-sex establishment falling within column 1 of the table in section 22 determines to alter its admissions arrangements so that the establishment will cease to be a single-sex establishment; or

    (b) section 26(2) applies to the admission of boarders to a school falling within column 1 of that table but the responsible body determines to alter its admissions arrangements so that section 26(2) will cease so to apply;

the responsible body may apply in accordance with Schedule 2 for an order (a "transitional exemption order") authorising discriminatory admissions during the transitional period specified in the order.

[(1A) Without prejudice to subsection (1), a transitional exemption order may be made in accordance with paragraph 21 or 22 of Schedule 6 or paragraph 16 or 17 of Schedule 7 to the School Standards and Framework Act 1998 (transitional exemption orders for purposes of the Sex Discrimination Act 1975: England and Wales).]

(2) Where during the transitional period specified in a transitional exemption order applying to an establishment the responsible body refuses or deliberately omits to accept an application for the admission of a person to the establishment as a pupil the refusal or omission shall not be taken to contravene any provision of this Act.

(3) Subsection (2) does not apply if the refusal or omission contravenes any condition of the transitional exemption order.

(4) Except as mentioned in subsection (2), a transitional exemption order shall not afford any exemption from liability under this Act.

(5) Where, during the period between the making of an application for a transitional exemption order in relation to an establishment and the determination of the application, the responsible body refuses or deliberately omits to accept an application for the admission of a person to the establishment as a pupil the refusal or omission shall not be taken to contravene any provision of this Act.

[(6) In this section, as it applies to an establishment in England and Wales, "pupil" includes any person who receives education at that establishment.]

Exception for physical training

28. [Sections 22, 23, 25 and 25A] do not apply to any [course in physical education which is a further education course or, in England and Wales, a higher education course within the meaning of the Education Reform Act 1988.] **39–037**

Goods, facilities, services and premises

Discrimination in provision of goods, facilities or services

29.—(1) It is unlawful for any person concerned with the provision (for payment or not) of goods, facilities or services to the public or a section of the public to discriminate against a woman who seeks to obtain or use those goods, facilities or services— **39–038**

(a) by refusing or deliberately omitting to provide her with any of them, or
(b) by refusing or deliberately omitting to provide her with goods, facilities or services of the like quality, in the like manner and on the like terms as are normal in his case in relation to male members of the public or (where she belongs to a section of the public) to male members of that section.

(2) The following are examples of the facilities and services mentioned in subsection (1)—

(a) access to and use of any place which members of the public or a section of the public are permitted to enter;
(b) accommodation in a hotel, boarding house or other similar establishment;
(c) facilities by way of banking or insurance or for grants, loans, credit or finance;
(d) facilities for education;
(e) facilities for entertainment, recreation or refreshment;
(f) facilities for transport or travel;

(g) the services of any profession or trade, or any local or other public authority.

(3) For the avoidance of doubt it is hereby declared that where a particular skill is commonly exercised in a different way for men and for women it does not contravene subsection (1) for a person who does not normally exercise it for women to insist on exercising it for a woman only in accordance with his normal practice or, if he reasonably considers it impracticable to do that in her case, to refuse or deliberately omit to exercise it.

[(4) In its application in relation to vocational training to discrimination falling within section 2A, subsection (1)(b) shall have effect as if references to male members of the public, or of a section of the public, were references to members of the public, or of a section of the public, who do not intend to undergo, are not undergoing and have not undergone gender reassignment.]

Discrimination in disposal or management of premises

39–039   **30.**—(1) It is unlawful for a person, in relation to premises in Great Britain of which he has power to dispose, to discriminate against a woman—

(a) in the terms on which he offers her those premises, or
(b) by refusing her application for those premises, or
(c) in his treatment of her in relation to any list of persons in need of premises of that description.

(2) It is unlawful for a person, in relation to premises managed by him, to discriminate against a woman occupying the premises—

(a) in the way he affords her access to any benefits or facilities, or by refusing or deliberately omitting to afford her access to them, or
(b) by evicting her, or subjecting her to any other detriment.

(3) Subsection (1) does not apply to a person who owns an estate or interest in the premises and wholly occupies them unless he uses the services of an estate agent for the purposes of the disposal of the premises, or publishes or causes to be published an advertisement in connection with the disposal.

Discrimination: consent for assignment or sub-letting

39–040   **31.**—(1) Where the licence or consent of the landlord or of any other person is required for the disposal to any person of premises in Great Britain comprised in a tenancy, it is unlawful for the landlord or other person to discriminate against a woman by withholding the licence or consent for disposal of the premises to her.

(2) Subsection (1) does not apply if—

(a) the person withholding a licence or consent, or a near relative of his ("the relevant occupier") resides, and intends to continue to reside, on the premises, and
(b) there is on the premises, in addition to the accommodation occupied by the relevant occupier, accommodation (not being storage accommodation or means of access) shared by the relevant occupier with other persons residing on the premises who are not members of his household, and
(c) the premises are small premises as defined in section 32(2).

(3) In this section "tenancy" means a tenancy created by a lease or sub-lease,

by an agreement for a lease or sub-lease or by a tenancy agreement or in pursuance of any enactment; and "disposal" , in relation to premises comprised in a tenancy, includes assignment or assignation of the tenancy and sub-letting or parting with possession of the premises or any part of the premises.

(4) This section applies to tenancies created before the passing of this Act, as well as to others.

Exception for small dwellings

32.—(1) Sections 29(1) and 30 do not apply to the provision by a person of accommodation in any premises, or the disposal of premises by him, if—   **39–041**

    (a) that person or a near relative of his ("the relevant occupier") resides, and intends to continue to reside, on the premises, and

    (b) there is on the premises, in addition to the accommodation occupied by the relevant occupier, accommodation (not being storage accommodation or means of access) shared by the relevant occupier with other persons residing on the premises who are not members of his household, and

    (c) the premises are small premises.

(2) Premises shall be treated for the purposes of subsection (1) as small premises if—

    (a) in the case of premises comprising residential accommodation for one or more households (under separate letting or similar agreements) in addition to the accommodation occupied by the relevant occupier, there is not normally residential accommodation for more than two such households and only the relevant occupier and any member of his household reside in the accommodation occupied by him;

    (b) in the case of premises not falling within paragraph (a), there is not normally residential accommodation on the premises for more than six persons in addition to the relevant occupier and any members of his household.

Exception for political parties

33.—(1) This section applies to a political party if—   **39–042**

    (a) it has as its main object, or one of its main objects, the promotion of parliamentary candidatures for the Parliament of the United Kingdom, or

    (b) it is an affiliate of, or has as an affiliate, or has similar formal links with, a political party within paragraph (a).

(2) Nothing in section 29(1) shall be construed as affecting any special provision for persons of one sex only in the constitution, organisation or administration of the political party.

(3) Nothing in section 29(1) shall render unlawful an act done in order to give effect to such a special provision.

Exception for voluntary bodies

34.—(1) This section applies to a body—   **39–043**

    (a) the activities of which are carried on otherwise than for profit, and

    (b) which was not set up by any enactment.

(2) Sections 29(1) and 30 shall not be construed as rendering unlawful—

    (a) the restriction of membership of any such body to persons of one sex (disregarding any minor exceptions), or

    (b) the provision of benefits, facilities or services to members of any such body where the membership is so restricted,

even though membership of the body is open to the public, or to a section of the public.

(3) Nothing in section 29 or 30 shall—

    (a) be construed as affecting a provision to which this subsection applies, or

    (b) render unlawful an act which is done in order to give effect to such a provision.

(4) Subsection (3) applies to a provision for conferring benefits on persons of one sex only (disregarding any benefits to persons of the opposite sex which are exceptional or are relatively insignificant), being a provision which constitutes the main object of a body within subsection (1).

Further exceptions from ss. 29(1) and 30

39–044   **35.**—(1) A person who provides at any place facilities or services restricted to men does not for that reason contravene section 29(1) if—

    (a) the place is, or is part of, a hospital, [resettlement unit provided under Schedule 5 to the Supplementary Benefits Act 1976][1] or other establishment for persons requiring special care, supervision or attention; or

    (b) the place is (permanently or for the time being) occupied or used for the purposes of an organised religion, and the facilities or services are restricted to men so as to comply with the doctrines of that religion or avoid offending the religious susceptibilities of a significant number of its followers; or

    (c) the facilities or services are provided for, or are likely to be used by, two or more persons at the same time; and

        (i) the facilities or services are such, or those persons are such, that male users are likely to suffer serious embarrassment at the presence of a woman, or

        (ii) the facilities or services are such that a user is likely to be in a state of undress and a male user might reasonably object to the presence of a female user.

(2) A person who provides facilities or services restricted to men does not for that reason contravene section 29(1) if the services or facilities are such that physical contact between the user and any other person is likely, and that other person might reasonably object if the user were a woman.

(3) Sections 29(1) and 30 do not apply—

    (a) to discrimination which is rendered unlawful by any provision in column 1 of the table below, or

    (b) to discrimination which would be so unlawful but for any provision in column 2 of that table, or

    (c) to discrimination which contravenes a term modified or included by virtue of an equality clause.

---

[1] Words substituted by Social Security Act 1980 (c.30), Sched. 4, para. 11.

Barristers

Discrimination by, or in relation to, barristers

[**35A.**—(1) It is unlawful for a barrister or barrister's clerk, in relation to any **39–045** offer of a pupillage or tenancy, to discriminate against a woman—

(a) in the arrangements which are made for the purpose of determining to whom it should be offered;

(b) in respect of any terms on which it is offered; or

(c) by refusing, or deliberately omitting, to offer it to her.

(2) It is unlawful for a barrister or barrister's clerk, in relation to a woman who is a pupil or tenant in the chambers in question, to discriminate against her—

(a) in respect of any terms applicable to her as a pupil or tenant;

(b) in the opportunities for training, or gaining experience, which are afforded or denied to her;

(c) in the benefits, facilities or services which are afforded or denied to her; or

(d) by terminating her pupillage or by subjecting her to any pressure to leave the chambers or other detriment.

(3) It is unlawful for any person, in relation to the giving, withholding or acceptance of instructions to a barrister, to discriminate against a woman.

(4) In this section—

"barrister's clerk" includes any person carrying out any of the functions of a barrister's clerk; and

"pupil", "pupillage", "tenancy" and "tenant" have the meanings commonly associated with their use in the context of a set of barristers' chambers.

(5) Section 3 applies for the purposes of this section as it applies for the purposes of any provision of Part II.

(6) This section does not apply to Scotland.][1]

[1] ss. 35A and 35B inserted by Courts and Legal Services Act 1990 (c.41), ss. 64(1), 65(1), Sched. 19, para. 1.

Advocates

Discrimination by, or in relation to, advocates

[**35B.**—(1) It is unlawful for an advocate, in relation to taking any person as **39–046** his pupil, to discriminate against a woman—

(a) in the arrangements which he makes for the purpose of determining whom he will take as his pupil;

(b) in respect of any terms on which he offers to take her as his pupil; or

(c) by refusing, or deliberately omitting, to take her as his pupil.

(2) It is unlawful for an advocate, in relation to a woman who is a pupil, to discriminate against her—

(a) in respect of any terms applicable to her as a pupil;

(b) in the opportunities for training, or gaining experience, which are afforded or denied to her;

(c) in the benefits, facilities or services which are afforded or denied to her; or

(d) by terminating the relationship or by subjecting her to any pressure to terminate the relationship or other detriment.

(3) It is unlawful for any person, in relation to the giving, withholding or acceptance of instructions to an advocate, to discriminate against a woman.

(4) In this section—

"advocate" means a member of the Faculty of Advocates practising as such; and

"pupil" has the meaning commonly associated with its use in the context of a person training to be an advocate.

(5) Section 3 applies for the purposes of this section as it applies for the purposes of any provision of Part II.

(6) This section does not apply to England and Wales.]¹

¹ ss. 35A and 35B inserted by Courts and Legal Services Act 1990 (c.41), ss. 64(1), 65(1), Sched. 19, para. 1.

Extent

Extent of Part III

39–047   **36.**—(1) Section 29(1)—

(a) does not apply to goods, facilities or services outside Great Britain except as provided in subsections (2) and (3), and

(b) does not apply to facilities by way of banking or insurance or for grants, loans, credit or finance, where the facilities are for a purpose to be carried out, or in connection with risks wholly or mainly arising, outside Great Britain.

(2) Section 29(1) applies to the provision of facilities for travel outside Great Britain where the refusal or omission occurs in Great Britain or on a ship, aircraft or hovercraft within subsection (3).

(3) Section 29(1) applies on and in relation to—

(a) any ship registered at a port of registry in Great Britain, and

(b) any aircraft or hovercraft registered in the United Kingdom and operated by a person who has his principal place of business, or is ordinarily resident, in Great Britain,

(c) any ship, aircraft or hovercraft belonging to or possessed by Her Majesty in right of the Government of the United Kingdom,

even if the ship, aircraft or hovercraft is outside Great Britain.

(4) This section shall not render unlawful an act done in or over a country outside the United Kingdom, or in or over that country's territorial waters, for the purpose of complying with the laws of that country.

(5) Sections 22, 23 and 25 do not apply to benefits, facilities or services outside Great Britain except—

(a) travel on a ship registered at a port of registry in Great Britain, and

(b) benefits, facilities or services provided on a ship so registered.

PART IV

OTHER UNLAWFUL ACTS

Discriminatory practices

37.—[(1) In this section "discriminatory practice" means—   **39–048**

(a) the application of a provision, criterion or practice which results in an act of discrimination which is unlawful by virtue of any provision of Part 2 or 3 taken with section 1(2)(b) or 3(1)(b) or which would be likely to result in such an act of discrimination if the persons to whom it is applied were not all of one sex, or

(b) the application of a requirement or condition which results in an act of discrimination which is unlawful by virtue of any provision of Part 3 taken with section 1(1)(b) or which would be likely to result in such an act of discrimination if the persons to whom it is applied were not all of one sex.]

(2) A person acts in contravention of this section if and so long as—

(a) he applies a discriminatory practice, or

(b) he operates practices or other arrangements which in any circumstances would call for the application by him of a discriminatory practice.

(3) Proceedings in respect of a contravention of this section shall be brought only by the Commission in accordance with sections 67 to 71.

Discriminatory advertisements

38.—(1) It is unlawful to publish or cause to be published an advertisement   **39–049** which indicates, or might reasonably be understood as indicating, an intention by a person to do any act which is or might be unlawful by virtue of Part II or III.

(2) Subsection (1) does not apply to an advertisement if the intended act would not in fact be unlawful.

(3) For the purposes of subsection (1), use of a job description with a sexual connotation (such as "waiter", "salesgirl", "postman" or "stewardess") shall be taken to indicate an intention to discriminate, unless the advertisement contains an indication to the contrary.

(4) The publisher of an advertisement made unlawful by subsection (1) shall not be subject to any liability under that subsection in respect of the publication of the advertisement if he proves—

(a) that the advertisement was published in reliance on a statement made to him by the person who caused it to be published to the effect that, by reason of the operation of subsection (2), the publication would not be unlawful, and

(b) that it was reasonable for him to rely on the statement.

(5) A person who knowingly or recklessly makes a statement such as is referred to in subsection (4) which in a material respect is false or misleading commits an offence, and shall be liable on summary conviction to a fine not exceeding [level 5 on the standard scale].

Instructions to discriminate

39–050   **39.** It is unlawful for a person—

(a) who has authority over another person, or
(b) in accordance with whose wishes that other person is accustomed to act,

to instruct him to do any act which is unlawful by virtue of Part II or III, or procure or attempt to procure the doing by him of any such act.

Pressure to discriminate

39–051   **40.**—(1) It is unlawful to induce, or attempt to induce, a person to do any act which contravenes Part II or III by—

(a) providing or offering to provide him with any benefit, or
(b) subjecting or threatening to subject him to any detriment.

(2) An offer or threat is not prevented from falling within subsection (1) because it is not made directly to the person in question, if it is made in such a way that he is likely to hear of it.

Liability of employers and principals

39–052   **41.**—(1) Anything done by a person in the course of his employment shall be treated for the purposes of this Act as done by his employer as well as by him, whether or not it was done with the employer's knowledge or approval.

(2) Anything done by a person as agent for another person with the authority (whether express or implied, and whether precedent or subsequent) of that other person shall be treated for the purposes of this Act as done by that other person as well as by him.

(3) In proceedings brought under this Act against any person in respect of an act alleged to have been done by an employee of his it shall be a defence for that person to prove that he took such steps as were reasonably practicable to prevent the employee from doing that act, or from doing in the course of his employment acts of that description.

Aiding unlawful acts

39–053   **42.**—(1) A person who knowingly aids another person to do an act made unlawful by this Act shall be treated for the purposes of this Act as himself doing an unlawful act of the like description.

(2) For the purposes of subsection (1) an employee or agent for whose act the employer or principal is liable under section 41 (or would be so liable but for section 41(3)) shall be deemed to aid the doing of the act by the employer or principal.

(3) A person does not under this section knowingly aid another to do an unlawful act if—

(a) he acts in reliance on a statement made to him by that other person that, by reason of any provision of this Act, the act which he aids would not be unlawful, and
(b) it is reasonable for him to rely on the statement.

(4) A person who knowingly or recklessly makes a statement such as is referred to in subsection (3)(a) which in a material respect is false or misleading

commits an offence, and shall be liable on summary conviction to a fine not exceeding [level 5 on the standard scale].

PART V

GENERAL EXCEPTIONS FROM PARTS II TO IV

Selection of candidates

[**42A.** (1) Nothing in Parts 2 to 4 shall—   **39–054**

(a) be construed as affecting arrangements to which this section applies, or
(b) render unlawful anything done in accordance with such arrangements.

(2) This section applies to arrangements made by a registered political party which—

(a) regulate the selection of the party's candidates in a relevant election, and
(b) are adopted for the purpose of reducing inequality in the numbers of men and women elected, as candidates of the party, to be members of the body concerned.

(3) The following elections are relevant elections for the purposes of this section—

(a) parliamentary elections;
(b) elections to the European Parliament;
(c) elections to the Scottish Parliament;
(d) elections to the National Assembly for Wales;
(e) local government elections within the meaning of section 191, 203 or 204 of the Representation of the People Act 1983 (c. 2) (excluding any election of the Mayor of London).

(4) In this section "registered political party" means a party registered in the Great Britain register under Part 2 of the Political Parties, Elections and Referendums Act 2000 (c. 41).]¹

¹ Added by Sex Discrimination (Election Candidates) Act 2002 (c.2), s. 1.

Charities

43.—(1) Nothing in Parts II to IV shall—   **39–055**

(a) be construed as affecting a provision to which this subsection applies, or
(b) render unlawful an act which is done in order to give effect to such a provision.

(2) Subsection (1) applies to a provision for conferring benefits on persons of one sex only (disregarding any benefits to persons of the opposite sex which are exceptional or are relatively insignificant), being a provision which is contained in a charitable instrument.
[(3) In this section "charitable instrument" means an enactment or other instrument passed or made for charitable purposes, or an enactment or other instrument so far as it relates to charitable purposes, and in Scotland includes the governing instrument of an endowment or of an educational endowment as

those expressions are defined in section 135(1) of the Education (Scotland) Act 1962.

In the application of this section to England and Wales, "charitable purposes" means purposes which are exclusively charitable according to the law of England and Wales.]

Sport, etc.

39–056   **44.** Nothing in Parts II to IV shall, in relation to any sport, game or other activity of a competitive nature where the physical strength, stamina or physique of the average woman puts her at a disadvantage to the average man, render unlawful any act related to the participation of a person as a competitor in events involving that activity which are confined to competitors of one sex.

Insurance, etc.

39–057   **45.** Nothing in Parts II to IV shall render unlawful the treatment of a person in relation to an annuity, life assurance policy, accident insurance policy, or similar matter involving the assessment of risk, where the treatment—

(a) was effected by reference to actuarial or other data from a source on which it was reasonable to rely, and
(b) was reasonable having regard to the data and any other relevant factors.

Communal accommodation

39–058   **46.**—(1) In this section "communal accommodation" means residential accommodation which includes dormitories or other shared sleeping accommodation which for reasons of privacy or decency should be used by men only, or by women only (but which may include some shared sleeping accommodation for men, and some for women, or some ordinary sleeping accommodation).

(2) In this section "communal accommodation" also includes residential accommodation all or part of which should be used by men only, or by women only, because of the nature of the sanitary facilities serving the accommodation.

(3) Nothing in Part II or III shall render unlawful sex discrimination in the admission of persons to communal accommodation if the accommodation is managed in a way which, given the exigencies of the situation, comes as near as may be to fair and equitable treatment of men and women.

(4) In applying subsection (3) account shall be taken of—

(a) whether and how far it is reasonable to expect that the accommodation should be altered or extended, or that further alternative accommodation should be provided; and
(b) the frequency of the demand or need for use of the accommodation by men as compared with women.

(5) Nothing in Part II or III shall render unlawful sex discrimination against a woman, or against a man, as respects the provision of any benefit, facility or service if—

(a) the benefit, facility or service cannot properly and effectively be provided except for those using communal accommodation, and
(b) in the relevant circumstances the woman or, as the case may be, the man could lawfully be refused the use of the accommodation by virtue of subsection (3).

(6) Neither subsection (3) nor subsection (5) is a defence to an act of sex discrimination under Part II unless such arrangements as are reasonably practicable are made to compensate for the detriment caused by the discrimination; but in considering under subsection (5)(b) whether the use of communal accommodation could lawfully be refused (in a case based on Part II), it shall be assumed that the requirements of this subsection have been complied with as respects subsection (3).

(7) Section 25 shall not apply to sex discrimination within subsection (3) or (5).

(8) This section is without prejudice to the generality of section 35(1)(c).

Discriminatory training by certain bodies

47.—(1) Nothing in Parts II to IV shall render unlawful any act done in relation to particular work by [any person] in, or in connection with— **39–059**

(a) affording women only, or men only, access to facilities for training which would help to fit them for that work, or
(b) encouraging women only, or men only, to take advantage of opportunities for doing that work,

where [it reasonably appears to that person] that at any time within the 12 months immediately preceding the doing of the act there were no persons of the sex in question doing that work in Great Britain, or the number of persons of that sex doing the work in Great Britain was comparatively small.

(2) Where in relation to particular work [it reasonably appears to any person] that although the condition for the operation of subsection (1) is not met for the whole of Great Britain it is met for an area within Great Britain, nothing in Parts II to IV shall render unlawful any act done by [that person] in, or in connection with—

(a) affording persons who are of the sex in question, and who appear likely to take up that work in that area, access to facilities for training which would help to fit them for that work, or
(b) encouraging persons of that sex to take advantage of opportunities in the area for doing that work.

(3) Nothing in Parts II to IV shall render unlawful any act done by [any person] in, or in connection with, affording persons access to facilities for training which would help to fit them for employment, where [it reasonably appears to that person] that those persons are in special need of training by reason of the period for which they have been discharging domestic or family responsibilities to the exclusion of regular full time employment. The discrimination in relation to which this subsection applies may result from confining the training to persons who have been discharging domestic or family responsibilities, or from the way persons are selected for training, or both.

[(4) The preceding provisions of this section shall not apply in relation to any discrimination which is rendered unlawful by section 6.]

Other discriminatory training etc.

48.—(1) Nothing in Parts II to IV shall render unlawful any act done by an employer in relation to particular work in his employment, being an act done in, or in connection with,— **39–060**

(a) affording his female employees only, or his male employees only, access to facilities for training which would help to fit them for that work, or

(b) encouraging women only, or men only, to take advantage of opportunities for doing that work,

where at any time within the twelve months immediately preceding the doing of the act there were no persons of the sex in question among those doing that work or the number of persons of that sex doing the work was comparatively small.

(2) Nothing in section 12 shall render unlawful any act done by an organisation to which that section applies in, or in connection with,—

(a) affording female members of the organisation only, or male members of the organisation only, access to facilities for training which would help to fit them for holding a post of any kind in the organisation, or

(b) encouraging female members only, or male members only, to take advantage of opportunities for holding such posts in the organisation,

where at any time within the twelve months immediately preceding the doing of the act there were no persons of the sex in question among persons holding such posts in the organisation or the number of persons of that sex holding such posts was comparatively small.

(3) Nothing in Parts II to IV shall render unlawful any act done by an organisation to which section 12 applies in, or in connection with, encouraging women only, or men only, to become members of the organisation where at any time within the twelve months immediately preceding the doing of the act there were no persons of the sex in question among those members or the number of persons of that sex among the members was comparatively small.

Trade unions, etc.: elective bodies

39–061

49.—(1) If an organisation to which section 12 applies comprises a body the membership of which is wholly or mainly elected, nothing in section 12 shall render unlawful provision which ensures that a minimum number of persons of one sex are members of the body—

(a) by reserving seats on the body for persons of that sex, or

(b) by making extra seats on the body available (by election or co-option or otherwise) for persons of that sex on occasions when the number of persons of that sex in the other seats is below the minimum,

where in the opinion of the organisation the provision is in the circumstances needed to secure a reasonable lower limit to the number of members of that sex serving on the body; and nothing in Parts II to IV shall render unlawful any act done in order to give effect to such a provision.

(2) This section shall not be taken as making lawful—

(a) discrimination in the arrangements for determining the persons entitled to vote in an election of members of the body, or otherwise to choose the persons to serve on the body, or

(b) discrimination in any arrangements concerning membership of the organisation itself.

Indirect access to benefits, etc.

39–062

50.—(1) References in this Act to the affording by any person of access to benefits, facilities or services are not limited to benefits, facilities or services provided by that person himself, but include any means by which it is in that person's power to facilitate access to benefits, facilities or services provided by any other person (the "actual provider").

(2) Where by any provision of this Act the affording by any person of access to benefits, facilities or services in a discriminatory way is in certain circumstances prevented from being unlawful, the effect of the provision shall extend also to the liability under this Act of any actual provider.

Acts done for purposes of protection of women

[**51.**—(1) Nothing in the following provisions, namely—   **39–063**

(a) Part II,
(b) Part III so far as it applies to vocational training, or
(c) Part IV so far as it has effect in relation to the provisions mentioned in paragraphs (a) and (b),

shall render unlawful any act done by a person in relation to a woman if—

(i) it was necessary for that person to do it in order to comply with a requirement of an existing statutory provision concerning the protection of women, or
(ii) it was necessary for that person to do it in order to comply with a requirement of a relevant statutory provision (within the meaning of Part I of the Health and Safety at Work, etc. Act 1974) and it was done by that person for the purpose of the protection of the woman in question (or of any class of women that included that woman).

(2) In subsection (1)—

(a) the reference in paragraph (i) of that subsection to an existing statutory provision concerning the protection of women is a reference to any such provision having effect for the purpose of protecting women as regards—

(i) pregnancy or maternity, or
(ii) other circumstances giving rise to risks specifically affecting women,

whether the provision relates only to such protection or to the protection of any other class of persons as well; and

(b) the reference in paragraph (ii) of that subsection to the protection of a particular woman or class of women is a reference to the protection of that woman or class of women as regards any circumstances falling within paragraphs (a)(i) or (ii) above.

(3) In this section "existing statutory provision" means (subject to subsection (4)) any provision of—

(a) an Act passed before this Act, or
(b) an instrument approved or made by or under such an Act (including one approved or made after the passing of this Act).

(4) Where an Act passed after this Act re-enacts (with or without modification) a provision of an Act passed before this Act, that provision as

re-enacted shall be treated for the purposes of subsection (3) as if it continued to be contained in an Act passed before this Act.][1]

[1] s. 51 substituted by Employment Act 1989 (c.38), ss. 3(3), 4 (subject to a (temp.) saving in Sched. 9, para. 1.

Acts done under statutory authority to be exempt from certain provisions of Part III

39–064 [51A.—(1) Nothing in—

(a) the relevant provisions of Part III, or
(b) Part IV so far as it has effect in relation to those provisions,

shall render unlawful any act done by a person if it was necessary for that person to do it in order to comply with a requirement of an existing statutory provision within the meaning of section 51.

(2) In subsection (1) "the relevant provisions of Part III" means the provisions of that Part except so far as they apply to vocational training.][1]

[1] s. 51 substituted by Employment Act 1989 (c.38), ss. 3(3), 4 (subject to a (temp.) saving in Sched. 9, para. 1.

Acts safeguarding national security

39–065 52.—(1) Nothing in Parts II to IV shall render unlawful an act done for the purpose of safeguarding national security.

(2) A certificate purporting to be signed by or on behalf of a Minister of the Crown and certifying that an act specified in the certificate was done for the purpose of safeguarding national security shall be conclusive evidence that it was done for that purpose.

(3) A document purporting to be a certificate such as is mentioned in subsection (2) shall be received in evidence and, unless the contrary is proved, shall be deemed to be such a certificate.

Construction of references to vocational training

39–066 [52A. In the following provisions, namely—

(a) sections 51 and 51A, and
(b) the provisions of any Order in Council modifying the effect of section 52,

"vocational training" includes advanced vocational training and retraining; and any reference to vocational training in those provisions shall be construed as including a reference to vocational guidance.][1]

[1] s. 52A inserted by Employment Act 1989 (c.38), s. 3(4).

PART VI

EQUAL OPPORTUNITIES COMMISSION

Establishment and duties of Commission

39–067 53.—(1) There shall be a body of Commissioners named the Equal Opportunities Commission, consisting of at least eight but not more than fifteen individuals each appointed by the Secretary of State on a full-time or part-time basis, which shall have the following duties—

    (a) to work towards the elimination of discrimination,
    (b) to promote equality of opportunity between men and women generally,
  [(ba) to promote equality of opportunity, in the field of employment and of vocational training, for persons who intend to undergo, are undergoing or have undergone gender reassignment, and]
    (c) to keep under review the working of this Act and the Equal Pay Act 1970 and, when they are so required by the Secretary of State or otherwise think it necessary, draw up and submit to the Secretary of State proposals for amending them.

[(1A) One of the Commissioners shall be a person who appears to the Secretary of State to have special knowledge of Scotland.]
(2) The Secretary of State shall appoint—

    (a) one of the Commissioners to be chairman of the Commission, and
    (b) either one or two of the Commissioners (as the Secretary of State thinks fit) to be deputy chairman or deputy chairmen of the Commission.

(3) The Secretary of State may by order amend subsection (1) so far as it regulates the number of Commissioners.
(4) Schedule 3 shall have effect with respect to the Commission.

Research and education

54.—(1) The Commission may undertake or assist (financially or otherwise) the undertaking by other persons of any research, and any educational activities, which appear to the Commission necessary or expedient for the purposes of section 53(1).   **39–068**

(2) The Commission may make charges for educational or other facilities or services made available by them.

Review of discriminatory provisions in health and safety legislation

55.—(1) Without prejudice to the generality of section 53(1), the Commission, in pursuance of the duties imposed by paragraphs (a) and (b) of that subsection—   **39–069**

    (a) shall keep under review the relevant statutory provisions in so far as they require men and women to be treated differently, and
    (b) if so required by the Secretary of State, make to him a report on any matter specified by him which is connected with those duties and concerns the relevant statutory provisions.

Any such report shall be made within the time specified by the Secretary of State, and the Secretary of State shall cause the report to be published.
(2) Whenever the Commission think it necessary, they shall draw up and submit to the Secretary of State proposals for amending the relevant statutory provisions.
(3) The Commission shall carry out their duties in relation to the relevant statutory provisions in consultation with the Health and Safety Commission.
(4) In this section "the relevant statutory provisions" has the meaning given by section 53 of the Health and Safety at Work, etc. Act 1974

56.—(1) As soon as practicable after the end of each calendar year the Com-   **39–070**

mission shall make to the Secretary of State a report on their activities during the year (an "annual report").

(2) Each annual report shall include a general survey of developments, during the period to which it relates, in respect of matters falling within the scope of the Commission's duties.

(3) The Secretary of State shall lay a copy of every annual report before each House of Parliament, and shall cause the report to be published.

Codes of practice

Codes of practice.

39–071　　[**56A.**—(1) The Commission may issue codes of practice containing such practical guidance as the Commission think fit for [one or more] of the following purposes, namely—

  (a) the elimination of discrimination in the field of employment;
  (b) the promotion of equality of opportunity in that field between men and women;
  [(c) the promotion of equality of opportunity in that field for persons who intend to undergo, are undergoing or have undergone gender reassignment.]

(2) When the Commission propose to issue a code of practice, they shall prepare and publish a draft of that code, shall consider any representations made to them about the draft and may modify the draft accordingly.

(3) In the course of preparing any draft code of practice for eventual publication under subsection (2) the Commission shall consult with—

  (a) such organisations or associations of organisations representative of employers or of workers; and
  (b) such other organisations, or bodies,

as appear to the Commission to be appropriate.

(4) If the Commission determine to proceed with the draft, they shall transmit the draft to the Secretary of State who shall—

  (a) if he approves of it, lay it before both Houses of Parliament; and
  (b) if he does not approve of it, publish details of his reasons for withholding approval.

(5) If, within the period of forty days beginning with the day on which a copy of a draft code of practice is laid before each House of Parliament, or, if such copies are laid on different days, with the later of the two days, either House so resolves, no further proceedings shall be taken thereon, but without prejudice to the laying before Parliament of a new draft.

(6) In reckoning the period of forty days referred to in subsection (5), no account shall be taken of any period during which Parliament is dissolved or prorogued or during which both Houses are adjourned for more than four days.

(7) If no such resolution is passed as is referred to in subsection (5), the Commission shall issue the code in the form of the draft and the code shall come into effect on such day as the Secretary of State may by order appoint.

(8) Without prejudice to section 81(4), an order under subsection (7) may contain such transitional provisions or savings as appear to the Secretary of State to be necessary or expedient in connection with the code of practice thereby brought into operation.

(9) The Commission may from time to time revise the whole or any part of

a code of practice issued under this section and issue that revised code, and subsections (2) to (8) shall apply (with appropriate modifications) to such a revised code as they apply to the first issue of a code.

(10) A failure on the part of any person to observe any provision of a code of practice shall not of itself render him liable to any proceedings; but in any proceedings under this Act [or the Equal Pay Act 1970] before an [employment tribunal] any code of practice issued under this section shall be admissible in evidence, and if any provision of such a code appears to the tribunal to be relevant to any question arising in the proceedings it shall be taken into account in determining that question.

(11) Without prejudice to subsection (1), a code of practice issued under this section may include such practical guidance as the Commission think fit as to what steps it is reasonably practicable for employers to take for the purpose of preventing their employees from doing in the course of their employment acts made unlawful by this Act.]¹

¹ Cross-heading and s. 56A inserted by Race Relations Act 1976 (c. 74), Sched. 4, para. 1.

Investigations

Power to conduct formal investigations

57.—(1) Without prejudice to their general power to do anything requisite for the performance of their duties under section 53(1), the Commission may if they think fit, and shall if required by the Secretary of State, conduct a formal investigation for any purpose connected with the carrying out of those duties. **39–072**

(2) The Commission may, with the approval of the Secretary of State, appoint, on a full-time or part-time basis, one or more individuals as additional Commissioners for the purposes of a formal investigation.

(3) The Commission may nominate one or more Commissioners, with or without one or more additional Commissioners, to conduct a formal investigation on their behalf, and may delegate any of their functions in relation to the investigation to the persons so nominated.

Terms of reference

58.—(1) The Commission shall not embark on a formal investigation unless the requirements of this section have been complied with. **39–073**

(2) Terms of reference for the investigation shall be drawn up by the Commission or, if the Commission were required by the Secretary of State to conduct the investigation, by the Secretary of State after consulting the Commission.

(3) It shall be the duty of the Commission to give general notice of the holding of the investigation unless the terms of reference confine it to activities of persons named in them, but in such a case the Commission shall in the prescribed manner give those persons notice of the holding of the investigation.

[(3A) Where the terms of reference of the investigation confine it to activities of persons named in them and the Commission in the course of it propose to investigate any act made unlawful by this Act which they believe that a person so named may have done, the Commission shall—

(a) inform that person of their belief and of their proposal to investigate the act in question; and

(b) offer him an opportunity of making oral or written representations with regard to it (or both oral and written representations if he thinks fit);

and a person so named who avails himself of an opportunity under this subsection of making oral representations may be represented—

    (i) by counsel or a solicitor; or

    (ii) by some other person of his choice, not being a person to whom the Commission object on the ground that he is unsuitable.]¹

(4) The Commission or, if the Commission were required by the Secretary of State to conduct the investigation, the Secretary of State after consulting the Commission may from time to time revise the terms of reference; and subsections (1) [(3) and (3A)]² shall apply to the revised investigation and terms of reference as they applied to the original.

¹ s. 58(3A) inserted by Race Relations Act 1976 (c. 74), Sched. 4, para. 2(1).
² Words substituted by Race Relations Act 1976 (c. 74), Sched. 4, para. 2(2).

Power to obtain information

39–074   **59.**—(1) For the purposes of a formal investigation the Commission, by a notice in the prescribed form served on him in the prescribed manner,—

    (a) may require any person to furnish such written information as may be described in the notice, and may specify the time at which, and the manner and form in which, the information is to be furnished;

    (b) may require any person to attend at such time and place as is specified in the notice and give oral information about, and produce all documents in his possession or control relating to, any matter specified in the notice.

(2) Except as provided by section 69, a notice shall be served under subsection (1) only where—

    (a) service of the notice was authorised by an order made by or on behalf of the Secretary of State, or

    (b) the terms of reference of the investigation state that the Commission believe that a person named in them may have done or may be doing acts of all or any of the following descriptions—

        (i) unlawful discriminatory acts,

        (ii) contraventions of section 37,

        (iii) contraventions of sections 38, 39 or 40, and

        (iv) acts in breach of a term modified or included by virtue of an equality clause,

and confine the investigation to those acts.

(3) A notice under subsection (1) shall not require a person—

    (a) to give information, or produce any documents, which he could not be compelled to give in evidence, or produce, in civil proceedings before the High Court or the Court of Session, or

    (b) to attend at any place unless the necessary expenses of his journey to and from that place are paid or tendered to him.

(4) If a person fails to comply with a notice served on him under subsection (1) or the Commission has reasonable cause to believe that he intends not to comply with it, the Commission may apply to a county court for an order requiring him to comply with it or with such directions for the like purpose as may be contained in the order; and [section 55 (penalty for neglecting or refusing to give evidence) of the County Courts Act 1984] shall apply to failure without reasonable excuse to comply with any such order as it applies in the cases there provided.

(5) In the application of subsection (4) to Scotland—

(a) for the reference to a county court there shall be substituted a reference to a sheriff court, and
(b) for the words after "order; and" to the end of the subsection there shall be substituted the words "paragraph 73 of the First Schedule to the Sheriff Courts (Scotland) Act 1907 (power of sheriff to grant second diligence for compelling the attendances of witnesses or havers) shall apply to any such order as it applies in proceedings in the sheriff court".

(6) A person commits an offence if he—

(a) wilfully alters, suppresses, conceals or destroys a document which he has been required by a notice or order under this section to produce, or
(b) in complying with such a notice or order, knowingly or recklessly makes any statement which is false in a material particular,

and shall be liable on summary conviction to a fine not exceeding [level 5 on the standard scale].

(7) Proceedings for an offence under subsection (6) may (without prejudice to any jurisdiction exercisable apart from this subsection) be instituted—

(a) against any person at any place at which he has an office or other place of business;
(b) against an individual at any place where he resides, or at which he is for the time being.

Recommendations and reports on formal investigations

60.—(1) If in the light of any of their findings in a formal investigation it appears to the Commission necessary or expedient, whether during the course of the investigation or after its conclusion,— **39–075**

(a) to make to any persons, with a view to promoting equality of opportunity between men and women who are affected by any of their activities, recommendations for changes in their policies or procedures, or as to any other matters, or
(b) to make to the Secretary of State any recommendations, whether for changes in the law or otherwise,

the Commission shall make those recommendations accordingly.

(2) The Commission shall prepare a report of their findings in any formal investigation conducted by them.

(3) If the formal investigation is one required by the Secretary of State—

(a) the Commission shall deliver the report to the Secretary of State, and
(b) the Secretary of State shall cause the report to be published,

and unless required by the Secretary of State the Commission shall not publish the report.

(4) If the formal investigation is not one required by the Secretary of State, the Commission shall either publish the report, or make it available for inspection in accordance with subsection (5).

(5) Where under subsection (4) a report is to be made available for inspection,

any person shall be entitled, on payment of such fee (if any) as may be determined by the Commission—

(a) to inspect the report during ordinary office hours and take copies of all or any part of the report, or
(b) to obtain from the Commission a copy, certified by the Commission to be correct, of the report.

(6) The Commission may if they think fit determine that the right conferred by subsection (5)(a) shall be exercisable in relation to a copy of the report instead of, or in addition to, the original.

(7) The Commission shall give general notice of the place or places where, and the times when, reports may be inspected under subsection (5).

Restriction on disclosure of information

39–076   **61.**—(1) No information given to the Commission by any person ("the informant") in connection with a formal investigation shall be disclosed by the Commission, or by any person who is or has been a Commissioner, additional Commissioner or employee of the Commission, except—

(a) on the order of any court, or
(b) with the informant's consent, or
(c) in the form of a summary or other general statement published by the Commission which does not identify the informant or any other person to whom the information relates, or
(d) in a report of the investigation published by the Commission or made available for inspection under section 60(5), or
(e) to the Commissioners, additional Commissioners or employees of the Commission, or, so far as may be necessary for the proper performance of the functions of the Commission, to other persons, or
(f) for the purpose of any civil proceedings under this Act to which the Commission are a party, or any criminal proceedings.

(2) Any person who discloses information in contravention of subsection (1) commits an offence and shall be liable on summary conviction to a fine not exceeding [level 5 on the standard scale].

(3) In preparing any report for publication or for inspection the Commission shall exclude, so far as is consistent with their duties and the object of the report, any matter which relates to the private affairs of any individual or business interests of any person where the publication of that matter might, in the opinion of the Commission, prejudicially affect that individual or person.

Part VII

Enforcement

General

Restriction of proceedings for breach of Act

39–077   [**62.**—(1) Except as provided by this Act no proceedings, whether civil or criminal, shall lie against any person in respect of an act by reason that the act is unlawful by virtue of a provision of this Act.

(2) Subsection (1) does not preclude the making of an order of certiorari, mandamus or prohibition.

(3) In Scotland, subsection (1) does not preclude the exercise of the jurisdic-

tion of the Court of Session to entertain an application for reduction or suspension of any order or determination, or otherwise to consider the validity of any order or determination, or to require reasons for any order or determination to be stated.]¹

¹ s. 62 substituted by Race Relations Act 1976 (c. 74), Sched. 4, para. 3.

Enforcement in employment field

Jurisdiction of [employment tribunals]¹

63.—(1) A complaint by any person ("the complainant") that another person ("the respondent")—   **39–078**

(a) has committed an act of discrimination against the complainant which is unlawful by virtue of Part II, or
(b) is by virtue of section 41 or 42 to be treated as having committed such an act of discrimination against the complainant,

may be presented to an [employment tribunal]².

(2) Subsection (1) does not apply to a complaint under section 13(1) of an act in respect of which an appeal, or proceedings in the nature of an appeal, may be brought under any enactment.

¹ Words substituted by Employment Rights (Dispute Resolution) Act 1998 (c.8), Pt I, s. 1(2).

Burden of proof: employment tribunals

[**63A.**—(1) This section applies to any complaint presented under section 63 to an employment tribunal.   **39–079**

(2) Where, on the hearing of the complaint, the complainant proves facts from which the tribunal could, apart from this section, conclude in the absence of an adequate explanation that the respondent—

(a) has committed an act of discrimination against the complainant which is unlawful by virtue of Part 2, or
(b) is by virtue of section 41 or 42 to be treated as having committed such an act of discrimination against the complainant,

the tribunal shall uphold the complaint unless the respondent proves that he did not commit, or, as the case may be, is not to be treated as having committed, that act.]¹

¹ Added by S.I. 2001 No. 2660, reg 5.

Remedies on complaint under section 63

65.—(1) Where an [employment tribunal] finds that a complaint presented to it under section 63 is well-founded the tribunal shall make such of the following as it considers just and equitable—   **39–080**

(a) an order declaring the rights of the complainant and the respondent in relation to the act to which the complaint relates;
(b) an order requiring the respondent to pay to the complainant compensation of an amount corresponding to any damages he could have been ordered by a county court or by a sheriff court to pay to the complainant if the complaint had fallen to be dealt with under section 66;

(c) a recommendation that the respondent take within a specified period action appearing to the tribunal to be practicable for the purpose of obviating or reducing the adverse effect on the complainant of any act of discrimination to which the complaint relates.

[(1A) In applying section 66 for the purposes of subsection (1)(b), no account shall be taken of subsection (3) of that section.

(1B) As respects an unlawful act of discrimination falling within [section 1(2)(b) or section 3(1)(b)], if the respondent proves that the [provision, criterion or practice] in question was not applied with the intention of treating the complainant unfavourably on the ground of his sex or marital status as the case may be, an order may be made under subsection (1)(b) only if the [employment tribunal]—

(a) makes such order under subsection (1)(a) and such recommendation under subsection (1)(c) (if any) as it would have made if it had no power to make an order under subsection (1)(b); and
(b) (where it makes an order under subsection (1)(a) or a recommendation under subsection (1)(c) or both) considers that it is just and equitable to make an order under subsection (1)(b) as well.]

(3) If without reasonable justification the respondent to a complaint fails to comply with a recommendation made by an [employment tribunal] under subsection (1)(c), then, if they think it just and equitable to do so—

(a) the tribunal may [(subject to the limit in subsection (2))] increase the amount of compensation required to be paid to the complainant in respect of the complaint by an order made under subsection (1)(b), or
(b) if an order under subsection (1)(b) [was not made], the tribunal may make such an order.

Enforcement of Part III

Claims under Part III

39–081   66.—(1) A claim by any person ("the claimant") that another person ("the respondent")—

(a) has committed an act of discrimination against the claimant which is unlawful by virtue of Part III, or
(b) is by virtue of section 41 or 42 to be treated as having committed such an act of discrimination against the claimant,

may be made the subject of civil proceedings in like manner as any other claim in tort or (in Scotland) in reparation for breach of statutory duty.

(2) Proceedings under subsection (1)—

(a) shall be brought in England and Wales only in a county court, and
(b) shall be brought in Scotland only in a sheriff court,

but all such remedies shall be obtainable in such proceedings as, apart from this subsection [and section 62(1)], would be obtainable in the High Court or the Court of Session, as the case may be.

(3) As respects an unlawful act of discrimination falling within section 1(1)(b) [...] no award of damages shall be made if the respondent proves that the

requirement or condition in question was not applied with the intention of treating the claimant unfavourably on the ground of his sex [. . .].

[(3A) Subsection (3) does not affect the award of damages in respect of an unlawful act of discrimination falling within section 1(2)(b).]

(4) For the avoidance of doubt it is hereby declared that damages in respect of an unlawful act of discrimination may include compensation for injury to feelings whether or not they include compensation under any other head.

(5) Civil proceedings in respect of a claim by any person that he has been discriminated against in contravention of section 22 or 23 by a body to which section 25(1) applies shall not be instituted unless the claimant has given notice of the claim to the Secretary of State and either the Secretary of State has by notice informed the claimant that the Secretary of State does not require further time to consider the matter, or the period of two months has elapsed since the claimant gave notice to the Secretary of State; but nothing in this subsection applies to a counterclaim.

[(5A) In Scotland, when any proceedings are brought under this section, in addition to the service on the defender of a copy of the summons or initial writ initiating the action a copy thereof shall be sent as soon as practicable to the Commission in a manner to be prescribed by Act of Sederunt.]

(6) For the purposes of proceedings under subsection (1)—

(a) [section 63(1) (assessors) of the County Courts Act 1984] shall apply with the omission of the words "on the application of any party", and

(b) the remuneration of assessors appointed under the said section [63(1)] shall be at such rate as may be determined by the Lord Chancellor with the approval of the Minister for the Civil Service.

(7) For the purpose of proceedings before the sheriff, provision may be made by act of sederunt for the appointment of assessors by him, and the remuneration of any assessors so appointed shall be at such rate as the Lord President of the Court of Session with the approval of [the Treasury] may determine.

(8) A county court or sheriff court shall have jurisdiction to entertain proceedings under subsection (1) with respect to an act done on a ship, aircraft or hovercraft outside its district, including such an act done outside Great Britain.

Burden of proof: county and sheriff courts

[66A.—(1) This section applies to any claim brought under section 66(1) in **39–082** a county court in England and Wales or a sheriff court in Scotland.

(2) Where, on the hearing of the claim, the claimant proves facts from which the court could, apart from this section, conclude in the absence of an adequate explanation that the respondent—

(a) has committed an act of discrimination against the claimant which is unlawful by virtue of—

(i) section 35A or 35B, or

(ii) any other provision of Part 3 so far as it applies to vocational training, or

(b) is by virtue of section 41 or 42 to be treated as having committed such an act of discrimination against the claimant,

the court shall uphold the claim unless the respondent proves that he did not commit, or, as the case may be, is not to be treated as having committed, that act.]

Non-discrimination notices

Issue of non-discrimination notice

39–083 67.—(1) This section applies to—

(a) an unlawful discriminatory act, and
(b) a contravention of section 37, and
(c) a contravention of section 38, 39 or 40, and
(d) an act in breach of a term modified or included by virtue of an equality clause,

and so applies whether or not proceedings have been brought in respect of the act.

(2) If in the course of a formal investigation the Commission become satisfied that a person is committing, or has committed, any such acts, the Commission may in the prescribed manner serve on him a notice in the prescribed form ("a non-discrimination notice") requiring him—

(a) not to commit any such acts, and
(b) where compliance with paragraph (a) involves changes in any of his practices or other arrangements—

   (i) to inform the Commission that he has effected those changes and what those changes are, and
   (ii) to take such steps as may be reasonably required by the notice for the purpose of affording that information to other persons concerned.

(3) A non-discrimination notice may also require the person on whom it is served to furnish the Commission with such other information as may be reasonably required by the notice in order to verify that the notice has been complied with.

(4) The notice may specify the time at which, and the manner and form in which, any information is to be furnished to the Commission, but the time at which any information is to be furnished in compliance with the notice shall not be later than five years after the notice has become final.

(5) The Commission shall not serve a non-discrimination notice in respect of any person unless they have first—

(a) given him notice that they are minded to issue a non-discrimination notice in his case, specifying the grounds on which they contemplate doing so, and
(b) offered him an opportunity of making oral or written representations in the matter (or both oral and written representations if he thinks fit) within a period of not less than 28 days specified in the notice, and
(c) taken account of any representations so made by him.

(6) Subsection (2) does not apply to any acts in respect of which the Secretary of State could exercise the powers conferred on him by section 25(2) and (3); but if the Commission become aware of any such acts they shall give notice of them to the Secretary of State.

(7) Section 59(4) shall apply to requirements under subsection (2)(b), (3) and (4) contained in a non-discrimination notice which has become final as it applies to requirements in a notice served under section 59(1).

Appeal against non-discrimination notice

68.—(1) Not later than six weeks after a non-discrimination notice is served   **39–084**
on any person he may appeal against any requirement of the notice—

  (a) to an [employment tribunal][1], so far as the requirement relates to acts
      which are within the jurisdiction of the tribunal;
  (b) to a county court or to a sheriff court so far as the requirement relates
      to acts which are within the jurisdiction of the court and are not within
      the jurisdiction of an [employment tribunal][2].

(2) Where the court or tribunal considers a requirement in respect of which
an appeal is brought under subsection (1) to be unreasonable because it is based
on an incorrect finding of fact or for any other reason, the court or tribunal shall
quash the requirement.

(3) On quashing a requirement under subsection (2) the court or tribunal may
direct that the non-discrimination notice shall be treated as if, in place of the
requirement quashed, it had contained a requirement in terms specified in the
direction.

(4) Subsection (1) does not apply to a requirement treated as included in a
non-discrimination notice by virtue of a direction under subsection (3).

[1] Words substituted by Employment Rights (Dispute Resolution) Act 1998 (c.8), Pt I, s. 1(2).
[2] *ibid.*

Investigation as to compliance with non-discrimination notice

69.—(1) If—   **39–085**

  (a) the terms of reference of a formal investigation state that its purpose
      is to determine whether any requirements of a non-discrimination
      notice are being or have been carried out, but section 59(2)(b) does not
      apply, and
  (b) section 58(3) is complied with in relation to the investigation on a date
      ("the commencement date") not later than the expiration of the period
      of five years beginning when the non-discrimination notice became
      final,

the Commission may within the period referred to in subsection (2) serve notices
under section 59(1) for the purposes of the investigation without needing to
obtain the consent of the Secretary of State.

(2) The said period begins on the commencement date and ends on the later
of the following dates—

  (a) the date on which the period of five years mentioned in subsection
      (1)(b) expires;
  (b) the date two years after the commencement date.

Register of non-discrimination notices

70.—(1) The Commission shall establish and maintain a register ("the   **39–086**
register") of non-discrimination notices which have become final.

(2) Any person shall be entitled, on payment of such fee (if any) as may be
determined by the Commission,—

  (a) to inspect the register during ordinary office hours and take copies of
      any entry, or

(b) to obtain from the Commission a copy, certified by the Commission to be correct, of any entry in the register.

(3) The Commission may, if they think fit, determine that the right conferred by subsection (2)(a) shall be exercisable in relation to a copy of the register instead of, or in addition to, the original.

(4) The Commission shall give general notice of the place or places where, and the times when, the register or a copy of it may be inspected.

Other enforcement by Commission

Persistent discrimination

39–087   **71.**—(1) If, during the period of five years beginning on the date on which either of the following became final in the case of any person, namely,—

(a) a non-discrimination notice served on him,
(b) a finding by a court or tribunal undersection 63 or 66, or section 2 of the Equal Pay Act 1970that he has done an unlawful discriminatory act or an act in breach of a term modified or included by virtue of an equality clause,

it appears to the Commission that unless restrained he is likely to do one or more acts falling within paragraph (b), or contravening section 37, the Commission may apply to a county court for an injunction, or to the sheriff court for an order, restraining him from doing so; and the court, if satisfied that the application is well-founded, may grant the injunction or order in the terms applied for or in more limited terms.

(2) In proceedings under this section the Commission shall not allege that the person to whom the proceedings relate has done an act which is within the jurisdiction of an [employment tribunal] unless a finding by an [employment tribunal] that he did that act has become final.

Enforcement of ss. 38 to 40

39–088   **72.**—(1) Proceedings in respect of a contravention of section 38, 39 or 40 shall be brought only by the Commission in accordance with the following provisions of this section.

(2) The proceedings shall be—

(a) an application for a decision whether the alleged contravention occurred, or
(b) an application under subsection (4) below,

or both.

(3) An application under subsection (2)(a) shall be made—

(a) in a case based on any provision of Part II, to an [employment tribunal], and
(b) in any other case to a county court or sheriff court.

(4) If it appears to the Commission—

(a) that a person has done an act which by virtue of section 38, 39 or 40 was unlawful, and
(b) that unless restrained he is likely to do further acts which by virtue of that section are unlawful,

the Commission may apply to a county court for an injunction; or to a sheriff court for an order, restraining him from doing such acts; and the court, if satisfied that the application is well-founded, may grant the injunction or [. . .]¹ order in the terms applied for or more limited terms.

(5) In proceedings under subsection (4) the Commission shall not allege that the person to whom the proceedings relate has done an act which is unlawful under this Act and within the jurisdiction of an [employment tribunal] unless a finding by an [employment tribunal] that he did that act has become final.

¹ Words repealed by Race Relations Act 1976 (c. 74), Sched. 5.

Preliminary action in employment cases

73.—(1) With a view to making an application under section 71(1) or 72(4) in relation to a person the Commission may present to an [employment tribunal] a complaint that he has done an act within the jurisdiction of an [employment tribunal], and if the tribunal considers that the complaint is well-founded they shall make a finding to that effect and, if they think it just and equitable to do so in the case of an act contravening any provision of Part II may also (as if the complaint had been presented by the person discriminated against) make an order such as is referred to in section 65(1)(a), or a recommendation such as is referred to in section 65(1)(c), or both.

39–089

(2) Subsection (1) is without prejudice to the jurisdiction conferred by section 72(2).

(3) Any finding of an [employment tribunal] under—

(a) this Act, or
(b) the Equal Pay Act 1970,

in respect of any act shall, if it has become final, be treated as conclusive—

(i) by the county court or sheriff court on an application under section 71(1) or 72(4) or in proceedings on an equality clause,
(ii) by an [employment tribunal] on a complaint made by the person affected by the act under section 63 or in relation to an equality clause.

(4) In sections 71 and 72 and this section, the acts "within the jurisdiction of an [employment tribunal]" are those in respect of which such jurisdiction is conferred by sections 63 and 72 and by section 2 of the Equal Pay Act 1970.

Help for persons suffering discrimination

Help for aggrieved persons in obtaining information etc.

74.—(1) With a view to helping a person ("the person aggrieved") who considers he may have been discriminated against in contravention of this Act to decide whether to institute proceedings and, if he does so, to formulate and present his case in the most effective manner, the Secretary of State shall by order prescribe—

39–090

(a) forms by which the person aggrieved may question the respondent on his reasons for doing any relevant act, or on any other matter which is or may be relevant;
(b) forms by which the respondent may if he so wishes reply to any questions.

(2) Where the person aggrieved questions the respondent (whether in accordance with an order under subsection (1) or not)—

(a) the question, and any reply by the respondent (whether in accordance with such an order or not) shall, subject to the following provisions of this section, be admissible as evidence in the proceedings;

(b) if it appears to the court or tribunal that the respondent deliberately, and without reasonable excuse, omitted to reply within a reasonable period or that his reply is evasive or equivocal, the court or tribunal may draw any inference from that fact that it considers it just and equitable to draw, including an inference that he committed an unlawful act.

(3) The Secretary of State may by order—

(a) prescribe the period within which questions must be duly served in order to be admissible under subsection (2)(a), and

(b) prescribe the manner in which a question, and any reply by the respondent, may be duly served.

(4) Rules may enable the court entertaining a claim under section 66 to determine, before the date fixed for the hearing of the claim, whether a question or reply is admissible under this section or not.

(5) This section is without prejudice to any other enactment or rule of law regulating interlocutory and preliminary matters in proceedings before a county court, sheriff court or industrial tribunal, and has effect subject to any enactment or rule of law regulating the admissibility of evidence in such proceedings.

(6) In this section "respondent" includes a prospective respondent and "rules"—

(a) in relation to county court proceedings, means county court rules;

(b) in relation to sheriff court proceedings, means sheriff court rules.

Assistance by Commission

39–091   75.—(1) Where, in relation to proceedings or prospective proceedings either under this Act or in respect of an equality clause, an individual who is an actual or prospective complainant or claimant applies to the Commission for assistance under this section, the Commission shall consider the application and may grant it if they think fit to do so on the ground that—

(a) the case raises a question of principle, or

(b) it is unreasonable, having regard to the complexity of the case or the applicant's position in relation to the respondent or another person involved or any other matter, to expect the applicant to deal with the case unaided,

or by reason of any other special consideration.

(2) Assistance by the Commission under this section may include—

(a) giving advice;

(b) procuring or attempting to procure the settlement of any matter in dispute;

(c) arranging for the giving of advice or assistance by a solicitor or counsel;

(d) arranging for representation by any person including all such assistance as is usually given by a solicitor or counsel in the steps preliminary or incidental to any proceedings, or in arriving at or giving effect to a compromise to avoid or bring to an end any proceedings, [(e) any other form of assistance which the Commission may consider appropriate][1]

but paragraph (d) shall not affect the law and practice regulating the descriptions of persons who may appear in, conduct, defend and address the court in, any proceedings.

(3) In so far as expenses are incurred by the Commission in providing the applicant with assistance under this section the recovery of those expenses (as taxed or assessed in such manner as may be prescribed by rules or regulations) shall constitute a first charge for the benefit of the Commission—

(a) on any costs or expenses which (whether by virtue of a judgment or order of a court or tribunal or an agreement or otherwise) are payable to the applicant by any other person in respect of the matter in connection with which the assistance is given, and

(b) so far as relates to any costs or expenses, on his rights under any compromise or settlement arrived at in connection with that matter to avoid or bring to an end any proceedings.

(4) The charge conferred by subsection (3) is subject to any charge [imposed by section 10(7) of the Access to Justice Act 1999], or any charge or obligation for payment in priority to other debts under the Legal Aid and Advice (Scotland) Acts 1967 and 1972 [the Legal Aid (Scotland) Act 1986], and is subject to any provision in [[, or made under,] either of those Acts for payment of any sum to the [Legal Services Commission] or into the Scottish Legal Aid Fund].

(5) In this section "respondent" includes a prospective respondent and "rules or regulations"—

(a) in relation to county court proceedings, means county court rules;

(b) in relation to sheriff court proceedings, means sheriff court rules;

(c) in relation to [employment tribunal] proceedings, means [industrial tribunal procedure regulations under] [Part I of the Employment Tribunals Act 1996]

[1] s. 75(2)(e) inserted by Race Relations Act 1976 (c. 74), Sched. 4, para. 7.

Period within which proceedings to be brought

Period within which proceedings to be brought

76.—(1) An [employment tribunal] shall not consider a complaint under section 63 unless it is presented to the tribunal before the end of [—]   **39–092**

[(a) the period of three months beginning when the act complained of was done; or

(b) in a case to which section 85(9A) applies, the period of six months so beginning.]

(2) A county court or a sheriff court shall not consider a claim under section 66 unless proceedings in respect of the claim are instituted before the end of—

[(a) the period of six months beginning when the act complained of was done; or

(b) in a case to which section 66(5) applies, the period of eight months so beginning.]

[(3) An [employment tribunal], county court or sheriff court shall not consider an application under section 72(2)(a) unless it is made before the end of the period of six months beginning when the act to which it relates was done; and a county court or sheriff court shall not consider an application under section 72(4) unless it is made before the end of the period of five years so beginning.]

(4) An [employment tribunal] shall not consider a complaint under section 73(1) unless it is presented to the tribunal before the end of the period of six months beginning when the act complained of was done.

(5) A court or tribunal may nevertheless consider any such complaint, claim or application which is out of time if, in all the circumstances of the case, it considers that it is just and equitable to do so.

(6) For the purposes of this section—

(a) where the inclusion of any term in a contract renders the making of the contract an unlawful act that act shall be treated as extending throughout the duration of the contract, and

(b) any act extending over a period shall be treated as done at the end of that period, and

(c) a deliberate omission shall be treated as done when the person in question decided upon it,

and in the absence of evidence establishing the contrary a person shall be taken for the purposes of this section to decide upon an omission when he does an act inconsistent with doing the omitted act or, if he has done no such inconsistent act, when the period expires within which he might reasonably have been expected to do the omitted act if it was to be done.

Part VIII

Supplemental

Validity and revision of contracts

39–093   77.—(1) A term of a contract is void where—

(a) its inclusion renders the making of the contract unlawful by virtue of this Act, or

(b) it is included in furtherance of an act rendered unlawful by this Act, or

(c) it provides for the doing of an act which would be rendered unlawful by this Act.

(2) Subsection (1) does not apply to a term the inclusion of which constitutes, or is in furtherance of, or provides for, unlawful discrimination against a party to the contract, but the term shall be unenforceable against that party.

(3) A term in a contract which purports to exclude or limit any provision of this Act or the Equal Pay Act 1970 is unenforceable by any person in whose favour the term would operate apart from this subsection.

(4) Subsection (3) does not apply—

(a) to a contract settling a complaint to which section 63(1) of this Act or section 2 of the Equal Pay Act 1970 applies where the contract is made with the assistance of a conciliation officer;

[(b) to a contract settling a complaint to which section 63(1) of this Act or section 2 of the Equal Pay Act 1970 applies if the conditions regulating compromise contracts under this Act are satisfied in relation to the contract;]

(c) to a contract settling a claim to which section 66 applies.

[(4A) The conditions regulating compromise contracts under this Act are that—

    (a) the contract must be in writing;

    (b) the contract must relate to the particular complaint;

    (c) the complainant must have received [advice from a relevant independent adviser] as to the terms and effect of the proposed contract and in particular its effect on his ability to pursue his complaint before an [employment tribunal];

    (d) there must be in force, when the adviser gives the advice, a [contract of insurance, or an indemnity provided for members of a profession or professional body,] covering the risk of a claim by the complainant in respect of loss arising in consequence of the advice;

    (e) the contract must identify the adviser; and

    (f) the contract must state that the conditions regulating compromise contracts under this Act are satisfied.]

[(4B) A person is a relevant independent adviser for the purposes of subsection (4A)(c)—

    (a) if he is a qualified lawyer,

    (b) if he is an officer, official, employee or member of an independent trade union who has been certified in writing by the trade union as competent to give advice and as authorised to do so on behalf of the trade union,

    (c) if he works at an advice centre (whether as an employee or a volunteer) and has been certified in writing by the centre as competent to give advice and as authorised to do so on behalf of the centre, or

    (d) if he is a person of a description specified in an order made by the Secretary of State.

(4BA) But a person is not a relevant independent adviser for the purposes of subsection (4A)(c) in relation to the complainant—

    (a) if he is, is employed by or is acting in the matter for the other party or a person who is connected with the other party,

    (b) in the case of a person within subsection (4B)(b) or (c), if the trade union or advice centre is the other party or a person who is connected with the other party,

    (c) in the case of a person within subsection (4B)(c), if the complainant makes a payment for the advice received from him, or

    (d) in the case of a person of a description specified in an order under subsection (4B)(d), if any condition specified in the order in relation to the giving of advice by persons of that description is not satisfied.

(4BB) In subsection (4B)(a), "qualified lawyer" means—

    (a) as respects England and Wales, a barrister (whether in practice as such or employed to give legal advice), a solicitor who holds a practising certificate, or a person other than a barrister or solicitor who is an authorised advocate or authorised litigator (within the meaning of the Courts and Legal Services Act 1990), and

    (b) as respects Scotland, an advocate (whether in practice as such or employed to give legal advice), or a solicitor who holds a practising certificate.

(4BC) In subsection (4B)(b) "independent trade union" has the same meaning as in the Trade Union and Labour Relations (Consolidation) Act 1992.

(4C) For the purposes of subsection (4BA) any two persons are to be treated as connected—

(a) if one is a company of which the other (directly or indirectly) has control, or

(b) if both are companies of which a third person (directly or indirectly) has control.]

[(4D) An agreement under which the parties agree to submit a dispute to arbitration—

(a) shall be regarded for the purposes of subsection (4)(a) and (aa) as being a contract settling a complaint if—

  (i) the dispute is covered by a scheme having effect by virtue of an order under section 212A of the Trade Union and Labour Relations (Consolidation) Act 1992, and

  (ii) the agreement is to submit it to arbitration in accordance with the scheme, but

(b) shall be regarded for those purposes as neither being nor including such a contract in any other case.]

(5) On the application of any person interested in a contract to which subsection (2) applies, a county court or sheriff court may make such order as it thinks just for removing or modifying any term made unenforceable by that subsection; but such an order shall not be made unless all persons affected have been given notice of the application (except where under rules of court notice may be dispensed with) and have been afforded an opportunity to make representations to the court.

(6) An order under subsection (5) may include provision as respects any period before the making of the order.

Educational charities in England and Wales

39–094   78.—(1) This section applies to any trust deed or other instrument—

(a) which concerns property applicable for or in connection with the provision of education in any establishment in paragraphs 1 to 5 of the Table in section 22, and

(b) which in any way restricts the benefits available under the instrument to persons of one sex.

(2) If on the application of the trustees, or of the responsible body (as defined in section 22), the Secretary of State is satisfied that the removal or modification of the restriction would conduce to the advancement of education without sex discrimination, he may by order make such modifications of the instrument as appear to him expedient for removing or modifying the restrictions, and for any supplemental or incidental purposes.

(3) If the trust was created by gift or bequest, no order shall be made until 25 years after the date on which the gift or bequest took effect, unless the donor or his personal representatives, or the personal representatives of the testator, have consented in writing to the making of the application for the order.

(4) The Secretary of State shall require the applicant to publish notice—

(a) containing particulars of the proposed order, and

(b) stating that representations may be made to the Secretary of State within a period specified in the notice.

(5) The period specified in the notice shall not be less than one month from the date of the notice.

(6) The applicants shall publish the notice in such manner as may be specified by the Secretary of State, and the cost of any publication of the notice may be defrayed out of the property of the trust.

(7) Before making the order the Secretary of State shall take into account any representations duly made in accordance with the notice.

(8) This section does not apply in Scotland.

Educational endowments, etc. to which [Part VI of the Education (Scotland) Act 1980] applies

79.—(1) This section applies to any educational endowment to which [Part VI of the Education (Scotland) Act 1980] applies and which in any way restricts the benefit of the endowment to persons of one sex, and any reference to an educational endowment in this section includes a reference to— **39–095**

    (a) a scheme made or approved for that endowment under that Part of the Education (Scotland) Act 1962;

    (b) any endowment which is, by virtue of [section 108(1) of the Education (Scotland) Act 1980], dealt with as if it were an educational endowment; and

    (c) a university endowment, the Carnegie Trust, a theological endowment and a new endowment.

(2) If, on the application of the governing body of an educational endowment, the Secretary of State is satisfied that the removal or modification of the provision which restricts the benefit of the endowment to persons of one sex would conduce to the advancement of education without sex discrimination, he may, by order, make such modifications to the endowment as appear to him expedient for removing or modifying the restriction and for any supplemental or incidental purposes.

(3) Where the Secretary of State proposes to make an order under this section, he shall publish a notice, in such manner as he thinks sufficient for giving information to persons whom he considers may be interested in the endowment—

    (a) containing particulars of the proposed order; and

    (b) stating that representations may be made with respect thereto within such period as may be specified in the notice, not being less than one month from the date of publication of the notice,

and the cost of publication of any such notice shall be paid out of the funds of the endowment to which the notice relates.

(4) Before making any order under this section, the Secretary of State shall consider any representations duly made in accordance with the said notice and he may cause a local inquiry to be held into such representations under [section 67 of the Education (Scotland) Act 1980].

(5) Without prejudice to section 81(5) of this Act, any order made under this section may be varied or revoked in a scheme made or approved under [Part VI of the Education (Scotland) Act 1980].

(7) This section shall be construed as one with [Part VI of the Education (Scotland) Act 1980].

Power to amend certain provisions of Act

39–096 **80.**—(1) The Secretary of State may by an order the draft of which has been approved by each House of Parliament—

(a) amend any of the following provisions, namely, sections 6(3), 7, 19, 20(1), (2) and (3), 31(2), 32, 34, 35 and 43 to 48 (including any such provision as amended by a previous order under this subsection);

(b) amend or repeal any of the following provisions, namely, sections 11(4), 12(4), 33 and 49 (including any such provision as amended by a previous order under this subsection);

(c) amend Part II, III or IV so as to render lawful an act which, apart from the amendment, would be unlawful by reason of section 6(1) or (2), 29(1), 30 or 31;

(2) The Secretary of State shall not lay before Parliament the draft of an order under subsection (1) unless he has consulted the Commission about the contents of the draft.

(3) An order under subsection (1)(c) may make such amendments to the list of provisions given in subsection (1)(a) as in the opinion of the Secretary of State are expedient having regard to the contents of the order.

Orders

39–097 **81.**—(1) Any power of the Secretary of State to make orders under the provisions of this Act (except sections 27, and 59(2)) shall be exercisable by statutory instrument.

(2) An order made by the Secretary of State under the preceding provisions of this Act (except sections 27, 59(2) and 80(1)) shall be subject to annulment in pursuance of a resolution of either House of Parliament.

(3) Subsections (1) and (2) do not apply to an order under section 78 or 79, but—

(a) an order under section 78 which modifies an enactment, and

(b) any order under section 79 other than one which relates to an endowment to which section [115 of the Education (Scotland) Act 1980][3] (small endowments) applies,

shall be made by statutory instrument subject to annulment in pursuance of a resolution of either House of Parliament.

(4) An order under this Act may make different provision in relation to different cases or classes of case, may exclude certain cases or classes of case, and may contain transitional provisions and savings.

(5) Any power conferred by this Act to make orders includes power (exercisable in the like manner and subject to the like conditions) to vary or revoke any order so made.

Application to Crown

39–098 **85.**— (1) This Act applies—

(a) to an act done by or for purposes of a Minister of the Crown or government department, or

(b) to an act done on behalf of the Crown by a statutory body, or a person holding a statutory office,

as it applies to an act done by a private person.

(2) Parts II and IV apply to—

(a) service for purposes of a Minister of the Crown or government department, other than service of a person holding a statutory office, or

(b) service on behalf of the Crown for purposes of a person holding a statutory office or purposes of a statutory body, [or]¹

[(c) service in the armed forces,]²

as they apply to employment by a private person, and shall so apply as if references to a contract of employment included references to the terms of service.

(3) Subsections (1) and (2) have effect subject to section 17.

[(4) Nothing in this Act shall render unlawful an act done for the purpose of ensuring the combat effectiveness of the [armed forces.]]

(5) Nothing in this Act shall render unlawful discrimination in admission to the Army Cadet Force, Air Training Corps, Sea Cadet Corps or Combined Cadet Force, or any other cadet training corps for the time being administered by the Ministry of Defence.

(7) Subsection (2) of section 10 shall have effect in relation to any ship, aircraft or hovercraft belonging to or possessed by Her Majesty in right of the Government of the United Kingdom as it has effect in relation to a ship, aircraft or hovercraft mentioned in paragraph (a) or (b) of that subsection, and section 10(5) shall apply accordingly.

(8) The provisions of Parts II to IV of the Crown Proceedings Act 1947 shall apply to proceedings against the Crown under this Act as they apply to proceedings in England and Wales which by virtue of section 23 of that Act are treated for the purposes of Part II of that Act as civil proceedings by or against the Crown, except that in their application to proceedings under this Act section 20 of that Act (removal of proceedings from county court to High Court) shall not apply.

(9) The provisions of Part V of the Crown Proceedings Act 1947 shall apply to proceedings against the Crown under this Act as they apply to proceedings in Scotland which by virtue of the said Part are treated as civil proceedings by or against the Crown, except that in their application to proceedings under this Act the proviso to section 44 of that Act (removal of proceedings from the sheriff court to the Court of Session) shall not apply.

[(9A) This subsection applies to any complaint by a person ("the complainant") that another person—

(a) has committed an act of discrimination against the complainant which is unlawful by virtue of section 6, or

(b) is by virtue of section 41 or 42 to be treated as having committed such an act of discrimination against the complainant,

if at the time when the act complained of was done the complainant was serving in the armed forces and the discrimination in question relates to his service in those forces.

(9B) No complaint to which subsection (9A) applies shall be presented to an [employment tribunal]³ under section 63 unless—

(a) the complainant has made a complaint to an officer under the service redress procedures applicable to him and has submitted that complaint to the Defence Council under those procedures; and

(b) the Defence Council have made a determination with respect to the complaint.

(9C) Regulations may make provision enabling a complaint to which subsection (9A) applies to be presented to an [employment tribunal]⁴ under section 63 in such circumstances as may be specified by the regulations, notwithstanding that subsection (9B) would otherwise preclude the presentation of the complaint to an [employment tribunal][5].

(9D) Where a complaint is presented to an [employment tribunal][6] under section 63 by virtue of regulations under subsection (9C), the service redress procedures may continue after the complaint is so presented.

(9E) Regulations under subsection (9C) shall be made by the Secretary of State by statutory instrument and shall be subject to annulment in pursuance of a resolution of either House of Parliament.][7]

[(10) In this section—

"armed forces" means any of the naval, military or air forces of the Crown;
"service for purposes of a Minister of the Crown or government department" does not include service in any office for the time being mentioned in Schedule 2 (Ministerial offices) to the House of Commons Disqualification Act 1975;
"the service redress procedures" means the procedures, excluding those which relate to the making of a report on a complaint to Her Majesty; referred to in section 180 of the Army Act 1955, section 180 of the Air Force Act 1955 and section 130 of the Naval Discipline Act 1957; and
"statutory body" means a body set up by or in pursuance of an enactment and "statutory office" means an office so set up.]

[1] Added by Armed Forces Act 1996 (c.46), s. 21(2).
[2] *ibid.*
[3] Words substituted by Employment Rights (Dispute Resolution) Act 1998 (c.8), Pt I, s. 1(2).
[4] *ibid.*
[5] *ibid.*
[6] *ibid.*
[7] Added by Armed Forces Act 1996 (c.46), s. 21(4).

Application to House of Commons staff

39–099   [85A.— (1) Parts II and IV apply to an act done by an employer of a relevant member of the House of Commons staff, and to service as such a member, as they apply to an act done by and to service for the purposes of a Minister of the Crown or government department, and accordingly apply as if references to a contract of employment included references to the terms of service of such a member.

(2) In this section "relevant member of the House of Commons staff" has the same meaning as in [section 195 of the Employment Rights Act 1996]; and [subsections (6) to (12)] of that section (person to be treated as employer of House of Commons staff) apply, with any necessary modifications, for the purposes of Parts II and IV as they apply by virtue of this section.]

Application to House of Lords staff

39–100   [85B.— (1) Parts II and IV apply in relation to employment as a relevant member of the House of Lords staff as they apply in relation to other employment.

(2) In this section "relevant member of the House of Lords staff" has the same meaning as in [section 194 of the Employment Rights Act 1996; and subsection (7)] of that section applies for the purposes of this section..]

Government appointments outside section 6

86.— (1) This section applies to any appointment by a Minister of the Crown **39–101**
or government department to an office or post where section 6 does not apply
in relation to the appointment.

(2) In making the appointment, and in making the arrangements for determining who should be offered the office or post, the Minister of the Crown or
government department shall not do an act which would be unlawful under
section 6 if the Crown were the employer for the purposes of this Act.

Short title and extent

87.— (1) This act may be cited as the Sex Discrimination Act 1975.   **39–102**
(2) This Act (except paragraph 16 of Schedule 3) does not extend to Northern
Ireland.

Race Relations Act 1976

(1976, c. 74)

An Act to make fresh provision with respect to discrimination on racial grounds **40–001**
and relations between people of different racial groups; and to make in the
Sex Discrimination Act 1975 amendments for bringing provisions in that
Act relating to its administration and enforcement into conformity with the
corresponding provisions in this Act.   [22nd November 1976]

PART I

DISCRIMINATION TO WHICH ACT APPLIES

Racial discrimination

1.— (1) A person discriminates against another in any circumstances relevant **40–002**
for the purposes of any provision of this Act if—

(a) on racial grounds he treats that other less favourably than he treats or
would treat other persons; or
(b) he applies to that other a requirement or condition which he applies or
would apply equally to persons not of the same racial group as that
other but—

(i) which is such that the proportion of persons of the same racial
group as that other who can comply with it is considerably smaller
than the proportion of persons not of that racial group who can
comply with it; and
(ii) which he cannot show to be justifiable irrespective of the colour,
race, nationality or ethnic or national origins of the person to
whom it is applied; and
(iii) which is to the detriment of that other because he cannot comply
with it.

(2) It is hereby declared that, for the purposes of this Act, segregating a person

from other persons on racial grounds is treating him less favourably than they are treated.

Discrimination by way of victimisation

40–003   2.— (1) A person ("the discriminator") discriminates against another person ("the person victimised") in any circumstances relevant for the purposes of any provision of this Act if he treats the person victimised less favourably than in those circumstances he treats or would treat other persons, and does so by reason that the person victimised has—

(a) brought proceedings against the discriminator or any other person under this Act; or
(b) given evidence or information in connection with proceedings brought by any person against the discriminator or any other person under this Act; or
(c) otherwise done anything under or by reference to this Act in relation to the discriminator or any other person; or
(d) alleged that the discriminator or any other person has committed an act which (whether or not the allegation so states) would amount to a contravention of this Act,

or by reason that the discriminator knows that the person victimised intends to do any of those things, or suspects that the person victimised has done, or intends to do, any of them.

(2) Subsection (1) does not apply to treatment of a person by reason of any allegation made by him if the allegation was false and not made in good faith.

Meaning of "racial grounds", "racial group", etc.

40–004   3.— (1) In this Act, unless the context otherwise requires—

"racial grounds" means any of the following grounds, namely colour, race, nationality or ethnic or national origins;
"racial group" means a group of persons defined by reference to colour, race, nationality or ethnic or national origins, and references to a person's racial group refer to any racial group into which he falls.

(2) The fact that a racial group comprises two or more distinct racial groups does not prevent it from constituting a particular racial group for the purposes of this Act.

(3) In this Act—

(a) references to discrimination refer to any discrimination falling within section 1 or 2; and
(b) references to racial discrimination refer to any discrimination falling within section 1;

and related expressions shall be construed accordingly.

(4) A comparison of the case of a person of a particular racial group with that of a person not of that group under section 1(1) must be such that the relevant circumstances in the one case are the same, or not materially different, in the other.

PART II

DISCRIMINATION IN THE EMPLOYMENT FIELD

Discrimination by employers

Discrimination against applicants and employees

4.— (1) It is unlawful for a person, in relation to employment by him at an establishment in Great Britain, to discriminate against another—   **40–005**

(a) in the arrangements he makes for the purpose of determining who should be offered that employment; or
(b) in the terms on which he offers him that employment; or
(c) by refusing or deliberately omitting to offer him that employment.

(2) It is unlawful for a person, in the case of a person employed by him at an establishment in Great Britain, to discriminate against that employee—

(a) in the terms of employment which he affords him; or
(b) in the way he affords him access to opportunities for promotion, transfer or training, or to any other benefits, facilities or services, or by refusing or deliberately omitting to afford him access to them; or
(c) by dismissing him, or subjecting him to any other detriment.

(3) Except in relation to discrimination falling within section 2, subsections (1) and (2) do not apply to employment for the purposes of a private household.
(4) Subsection (2) does not apply to benefits, facilities or services of any description if the employer is concerned with the provision (for payment or not) of benefits, facilities or services of that description to the public, or to a section of the public comprising the employee in question, unless—

(a) that provision differs in a material respect from the provision of the benefits, facilities or services by the employer to his employees; or
(b) the provision of the benefits, facilities or services to the employee in question is regulated by his contract of employment; or
(c) the benefits, facilities or services relate to training.

Exceptions for genuine occupational qualifications

5.— (1) In relation to racial discrimination—   **40–006**

(a) section 4(1)(a) or (c) does not apply to any employment where being of a particular racial group is a genuine occupational qualification for the job; and
(b) section 4(2)(b) does not apply to opportunities for promotion or transfer to, or training for, such employment.

(2) Being of a particular racial group is a genuine occupational qualification for a job only where—

(a) the job involves participation in a dramatic performance or other entertainment in a capacity for which a person of that racial group is required for reasons of authenticity; or
(b) the job involves participation as an artist's or photographic model in the production of a work of art, visual image or sequence of visual

images for which a person of that racial group is required for reasons of authenticity; or

    (c) the job involves working in a place where food or drink is (for payment or not) provided to and consumed by members of the public or a section of the public in a particular setting for which, in that job, a person of that racial group is required for reasons of authenticity; or

    (d) the holder of the job provides persons of that racial group with personal services promoting their welfare, and those services can most effectively be provided by a person of that racial group.

(3) Subsection (2) applies where some only of the duties of the job fall within paragraph (a), (b), (c) or (d) as well as where all of them do.

(4) Paragraph (a), (b), (c) or (d) of subsection (2) does not apply in relation to the filling of a vacancy at a time when the employer already has employees of the racial group in question—

    (a) who are capable of carrying out the duties falling within that paragraph; and

    (b) whom it would be reasonable to employ on those duties; and

    (c) whose numbers are sufficient to meet the employer's likely requirements in respect of those duties without undue inconvenience.

Exception for employment intended to provide training in skills to be exercised outside Great Britain

40–007   **6.**— Nothing in section 4 shall render unlawful any act done by an employer for the benefit of a person not ordinarily resident in Great Britain in or in connection with employing him at an establishment in Great Britain, where the purpose of that employment is to provide him with training in skills which he appears to the employer to intend to exercise wholly outside Great Britain.

Discrimination against contract workers

40–008   **7.**— (1) This section applies to any work for a person ("the principal") which is available for doing by individuals ("contract workers") who are employed not by the principal himself but by another person, who supplies, them under a contract made with the principal.

(2) It is unlawful for the principal, in relation to work to which this section applies, to discriminate against a contract worker—

    (a) in the terms on which he allows him to do that work; or

    (b) by not allowing him to do it or continue to do it; or

    (c) in the way he affords him access to any benefits, facilities or services or by refusing or deliberately omitting to afford him access to them; or

    (d) by subjecting him to any other detriment.

(3) The principal does not contravene subsection (2)(b) by doing any act in relation to a person not of a particular racial group at a time when, if the work were to be done by a person taken into the principal's employment, being of that racial group would be a genuine occupational qualification for the job.

(4) Nothing in this section shall render unlawful any act done by the principal for the benefit of a contract worker not ordinarily resident in Great Britain in or in connection with allowing him to do work to which this section applies, where the purpose of his being allowed to do that work is to provide him with training in skills which he appears to the principal to intend to exercise wholly outside Great Britain.

(5) Subsection (2)(c) does not apply to benefits, facilities or services of any

description if the principal is concerned with the provision (for payment or not) of benefits, facilities or services of that description to the public, or to a section of the public to which the contract worker in question belongs, unless that provision differs in a material respect from the provision of the benefits, facilities or services by the principal to his contract workers.

Meaning of employment at establishment in Great Britain

8.— (1) For the purposes of this Part ("the relevant purposes"), employment is to be regarded as being at an establishment in Great Britain unless the employee does his work wholly [. . .] outside Great Britain.

40–009

(3) In the case of employment on board a ship registered at a port of registry in Great Britain (except where the employee does his work wholly outside Great Britain) the ship shall for the relevant purposes be deemed to be the establishment.

(4) Where work is not done at an establishment it shall be treated for the relevant purposes as done at the establishment from which it is done or (where it is not done from any establishment) at the establishment with which it has the closest connection.

(5) In relation to employment concerned with exploration of the sea bed or subsoil or the exploitation of their natural resources, Her Majesty may by Order in Council provide that subsections (1) to (3) shall have effect as if in both subsection (1) and subsection (3) the last reference to Great Britain included any area for the time being designated under section 1(7) of the Continental Shelf Act 1964, except an area or part of an area in which the law of Northern Ireland applies.

(6) An Order in Council under subsection (5) may provide that, in relation to employment to which the Order applies, this Part is to have effect with such modifications as are specified in the Order.

(7) An Order in Council under subsection (5) shall be of no effect unless a draft of the Order has been laid before and approved by resolution of each House of Parliament.

Exception for seamen recruited abroad

9.— (1) Nothing in section 4 shall render unlawful any act done by an employer in or in connection with employment by him on any ship in the case of a person who applied or was engaged for that employment outside Great Britain.

40–010

(2) Nothing in section 7 shall, as regards work to which that section applies, render unlawful any act done by the principal in or in connection with such work on any ship in the case of a contract worker who was engaged outside Great Britain by the person by whom he is supplied.

(3) Subsections (1) and (2) do not apply to employment or work concerned with exploration of the sea bed or subsoil or the exploitation of their natural resources in any area for the time being designated under section 1(7) of the Continental Shelf Act 1964, not being an area or part of an area in which the law of Northern Ireland applies.

(4) For the purposes of subsection (1) a person brought to Great Britain with a view to his entering into an agreement in Great Britain to be employed on any ship shall be treated as having applied for the employment outside Great Britain.

Discrimination by other bodies

Partnerships

10.— (1) It is unlawful for a firm consisting of six or more partners, in relation to a position as partner in the firm, to discriminate against a person—

40–011

(a) in the arrangements they make for the purpose of determining who should be offered that position; or

(b) in the terms on which they offer him that position; or

(c) by refusing or deliberately omitting to offer him that position; or

(d) in a case where the person already holds that position—

    (i) in the way they afford him access to any benefits, facilities or services, or by refusing or deliberately omitting to afford him access to them; or

    (ii) by expelling him from that position, or subjecting him to any other detriment.

(2) Subsection (1) shall apply in relation to persons proposing to form themselves into a partnership as it applies in relation to a firm.

(3) Subsection (1)(a) and (c) do not apply to a position as partner where, if it were employment, being of a particular racial group would be a genuine occupational qualification for the job.

(4) In the case of a limited partnership references in this section to a partner shall be construed as references to a general partner as defined in section 3 of the Limited Partnerships Act 1907.

[(5) This section applies to a limited liability partnership as it applies to a firm; and, in its application to a limited liability partnership, references to a partner in a firm are references to a member of the limited liability partnership.]

Trade unions, etc.

40–012   11.— (1) This section applies to an organisation of workers, an organisation of employers, or any other organisation whose members carry on a particular profession or trade for the purposes of which the organisation exists.

(2) It is unlawful for an organisation to which this section applies, in the case of a person who is not a member of the organisation, to discriminate against him—

(a) in the terms on which it is prepared to admit him to membership; or

(b) by refusing or deliberately omitting to accept, his application for membership.

(3) It is unlawful for an organisation to which this section applies, in the case of a person who is a member of the organisation, to discriminate against him—

(a) in the way it affords him access to any benefits, facilities or services, or by refusing or deliberately omitting to afford him access to them; or

(b) by depriving him of membership, or varying the terms on which he is a member; or

(c) by subjecting him to any other detriment.

Qualifying bodies

40–013   12.— (1) It is unlawful for an authority or body which can confer an authorisation or qualification which is needed for, or facilitates, engagement in a particular profession or trade to discriminate against a person—

(a) in the terms on which it is prepared to confer on him that authorisation or qualification; or

(b) by refusing, or deliberately omitting to grant, his application for it; or

(c) by withdrawing it from him or varying the terms on which he holds it.

(2) In this section—

(a) "authorisation or qualification" includes recognition, registration, enrolment, approval and certification;

(b) "confer" includes renew or extend.

(3) Subsection (1) does not apply to discrimination which is rendered unlawful by section 17 or 18.

Persons concerned with provision of vocational training

[13.— (1) It is unlawful, in the case of an individual seeking or undergoing   **40–014**
training which would help fit him for any employment, for any person who provides, or makes arrangements for the provision of, facilities for such training to discriminate against him–

(a) in the terms on which that person affords him access to any training course or other facilities concerned with such training; or

(b) by refusing or deliberately omitting to afford him such access; or

(c) by terminating his training; or

(d) by subjecting him to any detriment during the course of his training.

(2) Subsection (1) does not apply to—

(a) discrimination which is rendered unlawful by section 4(1) or (2) or section 17 or 18; or

(b) discrimination which would be rendered unlawful by any of those provisions but for the operation of any other provision of this Act.]

Employment agencies

14.— (1) It is unlawful for an employment agency to discriminate against a   **40–015**
person—

(a) in the terms on which the agency offers to provide any of its services; or

(b) by refusing or deliberately omitting to provide any of its services; or

(c) in the way it provides any of its services.

[(2) It is unlawful for a local education authority or education authority or any other person to do any act in providing services in pursuance of arrangements made, or a direction given, under section 10 of the Employment and Training Act 1973 which constitutes discrimination.]

(3) References in subsection (1) to the services of an employment agency include guidance on careers and any other services related to employment.

(4) This section does not apply if the discrimination only concerns employment which the employer could lawfully refuse to offer the person in question.

(5) An employment agency or local education authority [, education authority or other person] shall not be subject to any liability under this section if it proves—

(a) that it acted in reliance on a statement made to it by the employer to the effect that, by reason of the operation of subsection (4), its action would not be unlawful; and

(b) that it was reasonable for it to rely on the statement.

(6) A person who knowingly or recklessly makes a statement such as is referred to in subsection (5)(a) which in a material respect is false or misleading

commits an offence, and shall be liable on summary conviction to a fine not exceeding [level 5 on the standard scale].

Manpower Services Commission, etc.

40–016   [**15.**— (1) It is unlawful for the [Secretary of State] to discriminate in the provision of facilities or services under section 2 of the Employment and Training Act 1973]

[(1A) It is unlawful for Scottish Enterprise or Highlands and Islands Enterprise to discriminate in the provision of facilities or services under such arrangements as are mentioned in section 2(3) of the Enterprise and New Towns (Scotland) Act 1990 (arrangements analogous to arrangements in pursuance of section 2 of the said Act of 1973).]

(2) This section does not apply in a case where—

(a) section 13 applies; or
(b) the [Secretary of State] is acting as an employment agency.

Police

40–017   **16.** [. . .]¹

¹ Repealed by Race Relations (Amendment) Act 2000 (c.34), Sched. 3, para. 1.

PART III

DISCRIMINATION IN OTHER FIELDS

Education

Discrimination by bodies in charge of educational establishments

40–018   **17.** It is unlawful, in relation to an educational establishment falling within column 1 of the following table, for a person indicated in relation to the establishment in column 2 (the "responsible body") to discriminate against a person—

(a) in the terms on which it offers to admit him to the establishment as a pupil; or
(b) by refusing or deliberately omitting to accept an application for his admission to the establishment as a pupil; or
(c) where he is a pupil of the establishment—

(i) in the way it affords him access to any benefits, facilities or services, or by refusing or deliberately omitting to afford him access to them; or
(ii) by excluding him from the establishment or subjecting him to any other detriment.

Meaning of pupil in section 17

40–019   [**17A.** For the purposes of section 17, "pupil" includes, in England and Wales, any person who receives education at a school or institution to which that section applies.]¹

¹ Added by Further and Higher Education Act 1992 (c.13), Sched. 8, Pt II, para. 86.

Other discrimination by local education authorities

18.— (1) It is unlawful for a local education authority, in carrying out such   **40–020**
of its functions under the Education Acts 1944 to 1975 [the Education Acts] as
do not fall under section 17, to do any act which constitutes racial discrimination.

(2) It is unlawful for an education authority, in carrying out such of its functions under the Education (Scotland) Acts 1939 to 1974 [the Education
(Scotland) [Act 1980]] as do not fall under section 17, to do any act which
constitutes racial discrimination.

Discrimination by Further Education and Higher Education Funding
     Councils

[**18A.** It is unlawful for [the Learning and Skills Council for England, the   **40–021**
National Council for Education and Training for Wales,] the Higher Education
Funding Council for England or the Higher Education Funding Council for
Wales in carrying out their functions under [the Education Acts] [and the Learn-
ing and Skills Act 2000], to do any act which constitutes racial discrimination.]

Discrimination by Scottish Further and Higher Education Funding
     Councils

[**18B.** It is unlawful for the Scottish Further Education Funding Council or   **40–022**
the Scottish Higher Education Funding Council in carrying out any of their
functions to do any act which constitutes racial discrimination.]

Discrimination by Teacher Training Agency

[**18D.** It is unlawful for the Teacher Training Agency in carrying out their   **40–023**
functions under Part I of the Education Act 1994 to do any act which constitutes
racial discrimination.]

Planning

Discrimination by planning authorities

[**19A.**— (1) It is unlawful for a planning authority to discriminate against a   **40–024**
person in carrying out their planning functions.

(2) In this section "planning authority" means —

  (a) in England and Wales, a county, [county borough,] district or London
      borough council [the Broads Authority], [a National Park authority or]
      a joint planning board, and
  (b) in Scotland, a planning authority or regional planning authority,

and includes an urban development corporation and a body having functions
(whether as an enterprise zone authority or a body invited to prepare a scheme)
under Schedule 32 to the Local Government, Planning and Land Act 1980.

(3) In this section "planning functions" means —

  (a) in England and Wales, functions under [the Town and Country Plan-
      ning Act 1990, the Planning (Listed Buildings and Conservation Areas)
      Act 1990 and the Planning (Hazardous Substances) Act 1990] and such
      other functions as may be prescribed, and
  (b) in Scotland, functions under the [Town and Country Planning
      (Scotland) Act 1997, the Planning (Listed Buildings and Conservation

Areas) (Scotland) Act 1997 and the Planning (Hazardous Substances) (Scotland) Act 1997] or Part IX of the Local Government (Scotland) Act 1973, and such other functions as may be prescribed,

and includes, in relation to an urban development corporation, planning functions under Part XVI of the Local Government, Planning and Land Act 1980 and, in relation to an enterprise zone authority or body invited to prepare an enterprise zone scheme, functions under Part XVIII of that Act.]

Public authorities

Discrimination by public authorities

40–025   [**19B.**— (1) It is unlawful for a public authority in carrying out any functions of the authority to do any act which constitutes discrimination.
(2) In this section "public authority"—

    (a) includes any person certain of whose functions are functions of a public nature; but
    (b) does not include any person mentioned in subsection (3).

(3) The persons mentioned in this subsection are—

    (a) either House of Parliament;
    (b) a person exercising functions in connection with proceedings in Parliament;
    (c) the Security Service;
    (d) the Secret Intelligence Service;
    (e) the Government Communications Headquarters; and
    (f) any unit or part of a unit of any of the naval, military or air forces of the Crown which is for the time being required by the Secretary of State to assist the Government Communications Headquarters in carrying out its functions.

(4) In relation to a particular act, a person is not a public authority by virtue only of subsection (2)(a) if the nature of the act is private.
(5) This section is subject to sections 19C to 19F.
(6) Nothing in this section makes unlawful any act of discrimination which—

    (a) is made unlawful by virtue of any other provision of this Act; or
    (b) would be so made but for any provision made by or under this Act.]¹

¹ Added by Race Relations (Amendment) Act 2000 (c.34), s. 1.

Exceptions or further exceptions from section 19B for judicial and legislative acts etc.

40–026   [**19C.**— (1) Section 19B does not apply to—

    (a) any judicial act (whether done by a court, tribunal or other person); or
    (b) any act done on the instructions, or on behalf, of a person acting in a judicial capacity.

(2) Section 19B does not apply to any act of, or relating to, making, confirming or approving any enactment or Order in Council or any instrument made by a Minister of the Crown under an enactment.
(3) Section 19B does not apply to any act of, or relating to, making or approv-

ing arrangements, or imposing requirements or conditions, of a kind falling within section 41.

(4) Section 19B does not apply to any act of, or relating to, imposing a requirement, or giving an express authorisation, of a kind mentioned in section 19D(3) in relation to the carrying out of immigration and nationality functions.

(5) In this section—

"immigration and nationality functions" has the meaning given in section 19D; and

"Minister of the Crown" includes the National Assembly for Wales and a member of the Scottish Executive.]¹

¹ Added by Race Relations (Amendment) Act 2000 (c.34), s. 1.

Exception from section 19B for certain acts in immigration and nationality cases

[**19D.**— (1) Section 19B does not make it unlawful for a relevant person to discriminate against another person on grounds of nationality or ethnic or national origins in carrying out immigration and nationality functions.   **40–027**

(2) For the purposes of subsection (1), "relevant person" means—

(a) a Minister of the Crown acting personally; or
(b) any other person acting in accordance with a relevant authorisation.

(3) In subsection (2), "relevant authorisation" means a requirement imposed or express authorisation given—

(a) with respect to a particular case or class of case, by a Minister of the Crown acting personally;
(b) with respect to a particular class of case—

(i) by any of the enactments mentioned in subsection (5); or

(ii) by any instrument made under or by virtue of any of those enactments.

(4) For the purposes of subsection (1), "immigration and nationality functions" means functions exercisable by virtue of any of the enactments mentioned in subsection (5).

(5) Those enactments are—

(a) the Immigration Acts (within the meaning of the Immigration and Asylum Act 1999 but excluding sections 28A to 28K of the Immigration Act 1971 so far as they relate to offences under Part III of that Act);
(b) the British Nationality Act 1981;
(c) the British Nationality (Falkland Islands) Act 1983;
(d) the British Nationality (Hong Kong) Act 1990;
(e) the Hong Kong (War Wives and Widows) Act 1996;
(f) the British Nationality (Hong Kong) Act 1997; and
(g) the Special Immigration Appeals Commission Act 1997;

and include any provision made under section 2(2) of the European Communities Act 1972, or any provision of Community law, which relates to the subject-matter of any of the enactments mentioned above.]¹

¹ Added by Race Relations (Amendment) Act 2000 (c.34), s. 1.

Monitoring of exception in relation to immigration and nationality cases

40–028   [**19E.**— (1) The Secretary of State shall appoint a person who is not a member of his staff to act as a monitor.

(2) Before appointing any such person, the Secretary of State shall consult the Commission.

(3) The person so appointed shall monitor, in such manner as the Secretary of State may determine—

> (a) the likely effect on the operation of the exception in section 19D of any relevant authorisation relating to the carrying out of immigration and nationality functions which has been given by a Minister of the Crown acting personally; and
>
> (b) the operation of that exception in relation to acts which have been done by a person acting in accordance with such an authorisation.

(4) The monitor shall make an annual report on the discharge of his functions to the Secretary of State.

(5) The Secretary of State shall lay a copy of any report made to him under subsection (4) before each House of Parliament.

(6) The Secretary of State shall pay to the monitor such fees and allowances (if any) as he may determine.

(7) In this section "immigration and nationality functions" and "relevant authorisation" have the meanings given to them in section 19D.][1]

[1] Added by Race Relations (Amendment) Act 2000 (c.34), s. 1.

Exceptions from section 19B for decisions not to prosecute etc.

40–029   [**19F.** Section 19B does not apply to—

> (a) a decision not to institute criminal proceedings and, where such a decision has been made, any act done for the purpose of enabling the decision whether to institute criminal proceedings to be made;
>
> (b) where criminal proceedings are not continued as a result of a decision not to continue them, the decision and, where such a decision has been made—
>
>> (i) any act done for the purpose of enabling the decision whether to continue the proceedings to be made; and
>>
>> (ii) any act done for the purpose of securing that the proceedings are not continued.][1]

[1] Added by Race Relations (Amendment) Act 2000 (c.34), s. 1.

Goods, facilities, services and premises

Discrimination in provision of goods, facilities or services

40–030   **20.**— (1) It is unlawful for any person concerned with the provision (for payment or not) of goods, facilities or services to the public or a section of the public to discriminate against a person who seeks to obtain or use those goods, facilities or services—

> (a) by refusing or deliberately omitting to provide him with any of them; or
>
> (b) by refusing or deliberately omitting to provide him with goods, facilit- ies or services of the like quality, in the like manner and on the like

terms as are normal in the first-mentioned person's case in relation to other members of the public or (where the person so seeking belongs to a section of the public) to other members of that section.

(2) The following are examples of the facilities and services mentioned in subsection (1)—

(a) access to and use of any place which members of the public are permitted to enter;
(b) accommodation in a hotel, boarding house or other similar establishment;
(c) facilities by way of banking or insurance or for grants, loans, credit or finance;
(d) facilities for education;
(e) facilities for entertainment, recreation or refreshment;
(f) facilities for transport or travel;
(g) the services of any profession or trade, or any local or other public authority.

Discrimination in disposal or management of premises

21.— (1) It is unlawful for a person, in relation to premises in Great Britain of which he has power to dispose, to discriminate against another—   **40–031**

(a) in the terms on which he offers him those premises; or
(b) by refusing his application for those premises; or
(c) in his treatment of him in relation to any list of persons in need of premises of that description.

(2) It is unlawful for a person, in relation to premises managed by him, to discriminate against a person occupying the premises—

(a) in the way he affords him access to any benefits or facilities, or by refusing or deliberately omitting to afford him access to them; or
(b) by evicting him, or subjecting him to any other detriment.

(3) Subsection (1) does not apply to a person who owns an estate or interest in the premises and wholly occupies them unless he uses the services of an estate agent for the purposes of the disposal of the premises, or publishes or causes to be published an advertisement in connection with the disposal.

Exception from ss. 20(1) and 21: small dwellings

22.— (1) Sections 20(1) and 21 do not apply to the provision by a person of accommodation in any premises, or the disposal of premises by him, if—   **40–032**

(a) that person or a near relative of his ("the relevant occupier") resides, and intends to continue to reside, on the premises; and
(b) there is on the premises, in addition to the accommodation occupied by the relevant occupier, accommodation (not being storage accommodation or means of access) shared by the relevant occupier with other persons residing on the premises who are not members of his household; and
(c) the premises are small premises.

(2) Premises shall be treated for the purposes of this section as small premises if—

(a) in the case of premises comprising residential accommodation for one or more households (under separate letting or similar agreements) in addition to the accommodation occupied by the relevant occupier, there is not normally residential accommodation for more than two such households and only the relevant occupier and any member of his household reside in the accommodation occupied by him;

(b) in the case of premises not falling within paragraph (a), there is not normally residential accommodation on the premises for more than six persons in addition to the relevant occupier and any members of his household.

Further exceptions from ss. 20(1) and 21

40–033 23.— (1) Sections 20(1) and 21 do not apply—

(a) to discrimination which is rendered unlawful by any provision of Part II or section 17 or 18; or

(b) to discrimination which would be rendered unlawful by any provision of Part II but for any of the following provisions, namely sections 4(3), 5(1)(b), 6, 7(4), 9 and 14(4).

(2) Section 20(1) does not apply to anything done by a person as a participant in arrangements under which he (for reward or not) takes into his home, and treats as if they were members of his family, children, elderly persons, or persons requiring a special degree of care and attention.

Discrimination: consent for assignment or sub-letting

40–034 24.— (1) Where the licence or consent of the landlord or of any other person is required for the disposal to any person of premises in Great Britain comprised in a tenancy, it is unlawful for the landlord or other person to discriminate against a person by withholding the licence or consent for disposal of the premises to him.

(2) Subsection (1) does not apply if—

(a) the person withholding a licence of consent, or a near relative of his ("the relevant occupier") resides, and intends to continue to reside, on the premises; and

(b) there is on the premises, in addition to the accommodation occupied by the relevant occupier, accommodation (not being storage accommodation or means of access) shared by the relevant occupier with other persons residing on the premises who are not members of his household; and

(c) the premises are small premises.

(3) Section 22(2) (meaning of "small premises") shall apply for the purposes of this as well as of that section.

(4) In this section "tenancy" means a tenancy created by a lease or sub-lease, by an agreement for a lease or sub-lease or by a tenancy agreement or in pursuance of any enactment; and "disposal", in relation to premises comprised in a tenancy, includes assignment or assignation of the tenancy and sub-letting or parting with possession of the premises or any part of the premises.

(5) This section applies to tenancies created before the passing of this Act, as well as to others.

Discrimination: associations not within s. 11

25.— (1) This section applies to any association of persons (however described, whether corporate or unincorporate, and whether or not its activities are carried on for profit) if—

    (a) it has twenty-five or more members; and

    (b) admission to membership is regulated by its constitution and is so conducted that the members do not constitute a section of the public within the meaning of section 20(1); and

    (c) it is not an organisation to which section 11 applies.

(2) It is unlawful for an association to which this section applies, in the case of a person who is not a member of the association, to discriminate against him—

    (a) in the terms on which it is prepared to admit him to membership; or

    (b) by refusing or deliberately omitting to accept his application for membership.

(3) It is unlawful for an association to which this section applies, in the case of a person who is a member or associate of the association, to discriminate against him—

    (a) in the way it affords him access to any benefits, facilities or services, or by refusing or deliberately omitting to afford him access to them; or

    (b) in the case of a member, by depriving him of membership, or varying the terms on which he is a member; or

    (c) in the case of an associate, by depriving him of his rights as an associate, or varying those rights; or

    (d) in either case, by subjecting him to any other detriment.

(4) For the purposes of this section—

    (a) a person is a member of an association if he belongs to it by virtue of his admission to any sort of membership provided for by its constitution (and is not merely a person with certain rights under its constitution by virtue of his membership of some other association), and references to membership of an association shall be construed accordingly;

    (b) a person is an associate of an association to which this section applies if, not being a member of it, he has under its constitution some or all of the rights enjoyed by members (or would have apart from any provision in its constitution authorising the refusal of those rights in particular cases).

Exception from s. 25 for certain associations

26.— (1) An association to which section 25 applies is within this subsection if the main object of the association is to enable the benefits of membership (whatever they may be) to be enjoyed by persons of a particular racial group defined otherwise than by reference to colour; and in determining whether that is the main object of an association regard shall be had to the essential character of the association and to all relevant circumstances including, in particular, the extent to which the affairs of the association are so conducted that the persons primarily enjoying the benefits of membership are of the racial group in question.

(2) In the case of an association within subsection (1), nothing in section 25

40–035

40–036

shall render unlawful any act not involving discrimination on the ground of colour.

Barristers

Discrimination by, or in relation to, barristers

40–037   [26A.— (1) It is unlawful for a barrister or barrister's clerk, in relation to any offer of a pupillage or tenancy, to discriminate against a person—

    (a) in the arrangements which are made for the purpose of determining to whom it should be offered;
    (b) in respect of any terms on which it is offered; or
    (c) by refusing, or deliberately omitting, to offer it to him.

(2) It is unlawful for a barrister or barrister's clerk, in relation to a pupil or tenant in the chambers in question, to discriminate against him—

    (a) in respect of any terms applicable to him as a pupil or tenant;
    (b) in the opportunities for training, or gaining experience which are afforded or denied to him;
    (c) in the benefits, facilities or services which are afforded or denied to him; or
    (d) by terminating his pupillage or by subjecting him to any pressure to leave the chambers or other detriment.

(3) It is unlawful for any person, in relation to the giving, withholding or acceptance of instructions to a barrister, to discriminate against any person.
(4) In this section—

    "barrister's clerk" includes any person carrying out any of the functions of a barrister's clerk; and
    "pupil", "pupillage", "tenancy" and "tenant" have the meanings commonly associated with their use in the context of a set of barristers' chambers.

(5) This section does not apply to Scotland.][1]

[1] ss. 26A and 26B inserted by Courts and Legal Services Act 1990 (c.41), ss. 64(2), 65(2) Sched. 19, para. 1.

Advocates

Discrimination by, or in relation to, advocates

40–038   [26B.— (1) It is unlawful for an advocate, in relation to taking any person as his pupil, to discriminate against a person—

    (a) in the arrangements which he makes for the purpose of determining whom he will take as his pupil;
    (b) in respect of any terms on which he offers to take any person as his pupil; or
    (c) by refusing, or deliberately omitting, to take a person as his pupil.

(2) It is unlawful for an advocate, in relation to a person who is a pupil, to discriminate against him—

(a) in respect of any terms applicable to him as a pupil;
(b) in the opportunities for training, or gaining experience, which are afforded or denied to him;
(c) in the benefits, facilities or services which are afforded or denied to him; or
(d) by terminating the relationship or by subjecting him to any pressure to terminate the relationship or other detriment.

(3) It is unlawful for any person, in relation to the giving, withholding or acceptance of instructions to an advocate, to discriminate against any person.
  (4) In this section—

  "advocate" means a member of the Faculty of Advocates practising as such;and
  "pupil" has the meaning commonly associated with its use in the context of a person training to be an advocate.

(5) This section does not apply to England and Wales.][1]

[1] ss. 26A and 26B inserted by Courts and Legal Services Act 1990 (c.41), ss. 64(2), 65(2) Sched. 19, para. 1.

Extent

Extent of Part III

27.— (1) [Sections 17 to 18D][1] do not apply to benefits, facilities or services outside Great Britain except—   **40–039**

  (a) travel in a ship registered at a port of registry in Great Britain; and
  (b) benefits, facilities or services provided on a ship so registered.

[(1A) In its application in relation to granting entry clearance (within the meaning of the Immigration Act 1971) section 19B applies in relation to acts done outside the United Kingdom, as well as those done within Great Britain.][2]
  (2) Section 20(1)—

  (a) does not apply to goods, facilities or services outside Great Britain except as provided in subsections (3) and (4); and
  (b) does not apply to facilities by way of banking or insurance or for grants, loans, credit or finance, where the facilities are for a purpose to be carried out, or in connection with risks wholly or mainly arising, outside Great Britain.

(3) Section 20(1) applies to the provision of facilities for travel outside Great Britain where the refusal or omission occurs in Great Britain or on a ship, aircraft or hovercraft within subsection (4).
  (4) Section 20(1) applies on and in relation to—

  (a) any ship registered at a port of registry in Great Britain; and
  (b) any aircraft or hovercraft registered in the United Kingdom and operated by a person who has his principal place of business, or is ordinarily resident, in Great Britain,

even if the ship, aircraft or hovercraft is outside Great Britain.
  (5) This section shall not render unlawful an act done in or over a country outside the United Kingdom, or in or over that country's territorial waters, for the purpose of complying with the laws of that country.

¹ Word substituted by Race Relations (Amendment) Act 2000 (c.34), Sched. 2, para. 2.
² Added by Race Relations (Amendment) Act 2000 (c.34), Sched. 2, para. 3.

PART IV

OTHER UNLAWFUL ACTS

Discriminatory practices

40–040   **28.**— (1) In this section "discriminatory practice" means the application of a requirement or condition which results in an act of discrimination which is unlawful by virtue of any provision of Part II or III taken with section 1(1)(b), or which would be likely to result in such an act of discrimination if the persons to whom it is applied included persons of any particular racial group as regards which there has been no occasion for applying it.

(2) A person acts in contravention of this section if and so long as—

    (a) he applies a discriminatory practice; or

    (b) he operates practices or other arrangements which in any circumstances would call for the application by him of a discriminatory practice.

(3) Proceedings in respect of a contravention of this section shall be brought only by the Commission in accordance with sections 58 to 62.

Discriminatory advertisements

40–041   **29.**— (1) It is unlawful to publish or to cause to be published an advertisement which indicates, or might reasonably be understood as indicating, an intention by a person to do an act of discrimination, whether the doing of that act by him would be lawful or, by virtue of Part II or III, unlawful.

(2) Subsection (1) does not apply to an advertisement—

    (a) if the intended act would be lawful by virtue of any of sections 5, 6, 7(3) and (4), 10(3), 26, 34(2)(b), 35 to 39 and 41; or

    (b) if the advertisement relates to the services of an employment agency (within the meaning of section 14(1)) and the intended act only concerns employment which the employer could by virtue of section 5, 6 or 7(3) or (4) lawfully refuse to offer to persons against whom the advertisement indicates an intention to discriminate.

(3) Subsection (1) does not apply to an advertisement which indicates that persons of any class defined otherwise than by reference to colour, race or ethnic or national origins are required for employment outside Great Britain.

(4) The publisher of an advertisement made unlawful by subsection (1) shall not be subject to any liability under that subsection in respect of the publication of the advertisement if he proves—

    (a) that the advertisement was published in reliance on a statement made to him by the person who caused it to be published to the effect that, by reason of the operation of subsection (2) or (3), the publication would not be unlawful; and

    (b) that it was reasonable for him to rely on the statement.

(5) A person who knowingly or recklessly makes a statement such as is mentioned in subsection (4)(a) which in a material respect is false or misleading commits an offence, and shall be liable on summary conviction to a fine not exceeding [level 5 on the standard scale]¹.

¹ Words substituted by Criminal Justice Act 1982 (c.48), ss. 38, 46 and Criminal Procedure (Scotland) Act 1975 (c.21), ss. 289F, 289G.

Instructions to discriminate

30. It is unlawful for a person—   **40–042**

(a) who has authority over another person; or

(b) in accordance with whose wishes that other person is accustomed to act,

to instruct him to do any act which is unlawful by virtue of Part II or III, or procure or attempt to procure the doing by him of any such act.

Pressure to discriminate

31.— (1) It is unlawful to induce, or attempt to induce, a person to do any   **40–043**
act which contravenes Part II or III.

(2) An attempted inducement is not prevented from falling within subsection (1) because it is not made directly to the person in question, if it is made in such a way that he is likely to hear of it.

Liability of employers and principals

32.— (1) Anything done by a person in the course of his employment shall   **40–044**
be treated for the purposes of this Act (except as regards offences thereunder) as done by his employer as well as by him, whether or not it was done with the employer's knowledge or approval.

(2) Anything done by a person as agent for another person with the authority (whether express or implied, and whether precedent or subsequent) of that other person shall be treated for the purposes of this Act (except as regards offences thereunder) as done by that other person as well as by him.

(3) In proceedings brought under this Act against any person in respect of an act alleged to have been done by an employee of his it shall be a defence for that person to prove that he took such steps as were reasonably practicable to prevent the employee from doing that act, or from doing in the course of his employment acts of that description.

Aiding unlawful acts

33.— (1) A person who knowingly aids another person to do an act made   **40–045**
unlawful by this Act shall be treated for the purposes of this Act as himself doing an unlawful act of the like description.

(2) For the purposes of subsection (1) an employee or agent for whose act the employer or principal is liable under section 32 (or would be so liable but for section 32(3)) shall be deemed to aid the doing of the act by the employer or principal.

(3) A person does not under this section knowingly aid another to do an unlawful act if—

(a) he acts in reliance on a statement made to him by that other person that, by reason of any provision of this Act, the act which he aids would not be unlawful; and

(b) it is reasonable for him to rely on the statement.

(4) A person who knowingly or recklessly makes a statement such as is mentioned in subsection (3)(a) which in a material respect is false or misleading

commits an offence, and shall be liable on summary conviction to a fine not exceeding [level 5 on the standard scale][1].

[1] Words substituted by Criminal Justice Act 1982 (c.48), ss. 38, 46 and Criminal Procedure (Scotland) Act 1975 (c.21), ss. 289F, 289G.

PART V

CHARITIES

Charities

40–046   **34.**— (1) A provision which is contained in a charitable instrument (whenever that instrument took or takes effect) and which provides for conferring benefits on persons of a class defined by reference to colour shall have effect for all purposes as if it provided for conferring the like benefits—

(a) on persons of the class which results if the restriction by reference to colour is disregarded; or
(b) where the original class is defined by reference to colour only, on persons generally;

but nothing in this subsection shall be taken to alter the effect of any provision as regards any time before the coming into operation of this subsection.

(2) Nothing in Parts II to IV shall—

(a) be construed as affecting a provision to which this subsection applies; or
(b) render unlawful an act which is done in order to give effect to such a provision.

(3) Subsection (2) applies to any provision which is contained in a charitable instrument (whenever that instrument took or takes effect) and which provides for conferring benefits on persons of a class defined otherwise than by reference to colour (including a class resulting from the operation of subsection (1)).

(4) In this section "charitable instrument" means an enactment or other instrument passed or made for charitable purposes, or an enactment or other instrument so far as it relates to charitable purposes, and in Scotland includes the governing instrument of an endowment or of an educational endowment as those expressions are defined in section 135(1) of the Education (Scotland) Act 1962.

In the application of this section to England and Wales, "charitable purposes" means purposes which are exclusively charitable according to the law of England and Wales.

PART VI

GENERAL EXCEPTIONS FROM PARTS II TO IV

Special needs of racial groups in regard to education, training or welfare

40–047   **35.**— Nothing in Parts II to IV shall render unlawful any act done in affording persons of a particular racial group access to facilities or services to meet the special needs of persons of that group in regard to their education, training or welfare, or any ancillary benefits.

Provision of education or training for persons not ordinarily resident in Great Britain

36.— Nothing in Parts II to IV shall render unlawful any act done by a person **40–048** for the benefit of persons not ordinarily resident in Great Britain in affording them access to facilities for education or training or any ancillary benefits, where it appears to him that the persons in question do not intend to remain in Great Britain after their period of education or training there.

Discriminatory training by certain bodies

37.— (1) Nothing in Parts II to IV shall render unlawful any act done in **40–049** relation to particular work by [any person] in or in connection with—

(a) affording only persons of a particular racial group access to facilities for training which would help to fit them for that work; or
(b) encouraging only persons of a particular racial group to take advantage of opportunities for doing that work, where [it reasonably appears to that person] that at any time within the twelve months immediately preceding the doing of the act—

   (i) there were no persons of that group among those doing that work in Great Britain; or
   (ii) the proportion of persons of that group among those doing that work in Great Britain was small in comparison with the proportion of persons of that group among the population of Great Britain.

(2) Where in relation to particular work [it reasonably appears to any person] that although the condition for the operation of subsection (1) is not met for the whole of Great Britain it is met for an area within Great Britain, nothing in Parts II to IV shall render unlawful any act done by [that person] in or in connection with—

(a) affording persons who are of the racial group in question, and who appear likely to take up that work in that area, access to facilities for training which would help to fit them for that work; or
(b) encouraging persons of that group to take advantage of opportunities in the area for doing that work.

[(3) The preceding provisions of this section shall not apply to any discrimination which is rendered unlawful by section 4(1) or (2).]

Other discriminatory training etc.

38.— (1) Nothing in Parts II to IV shall render unlawful any act done by **40–050** an employer in relation to particular work in his employment at a particular establishment in Great Britain, being an act done in or in connection with—

(a) affording only those of his employees working at that establishment who are of a particular racial group access to facilities for training which would help to fit them for that work; or
(b) encouraging only persons of a particular racial group to take advantage of opportunities for doing that work at that establishment,

where any of the conditions in subsection (2) was satisfied at any time within the twelve months immediately preceding the doing of the act.
(2) Those conditions are—

   (a) that there are no persons of the racial group in question among those doing that work at that establishment; or

   (b) that the proportion of persons of that group among those doing that work at that establishment is small in comparison with the proportion of persons of that group—

      (i) among all those employed by that employer there; or

      (ii) among the population of the area from which that employer normally recruits persons for work in his employment at that establishment.

(3) Nothing in section 11 shall render unlawful any act done by an organisation to which that section applies in or in connection with—

   (a) affording only members of the organisation who are of a particular racial group access to facilities for training which would help to fit them for holding a post of any kind in the organisation; or

   (b) encouraging only members of the organisation who are of a particular racial group to take advantage of opportunities for holding such posts in the organisation,

where either of the conditions in subsection (4) was satisfied at any time within the twelve months immediately preceding the doing of the act.

(4) Those conditions are—

   (a) that there are no persons of the racial group in question among persons holding such posts in that organisation; or

   (b) that the proportion of persons of that group among those holding such posts in that organisation is small in comparison with the proportion of persons of that group among the members of the organisation.

(5) Nothing in Parts II to IV shall render unlawful any act done by an organisation to which section 11 applies in or in connection with encouraging only persons of a particular racial group to become members of the organisation where at any time within the twelve months immediately preceding the doing of the act—

   (a) no persons of that group were members of the organisation; or

   (b) the proportion of persons of that group among members of the organisation was small in comparison with the proportion of persons of that group among those eligible for membership of the organisation.

(6) Section 8 (meaning of employment at establishment in Great Britain) shall apply for the purposes of this section as if this section were contained in Part II.

Sports and competitions

40–051   **39.**— Nothing in Parts II to IV shall render unlawful any act whereby a person discriminates against another on the basis of that other's nationality or place of birth or the length of time for which he has been resident in a particular area or place, if the act is done—

   (a) in selecting one or more persons to represent a country, place or area, or any related association, in any sport or game; or

   (b) in pursuance of the rules of any competition so far as they relate to eligibility to compete in any sport or game.

Indirect access to benefits, etc.

40.— (1) References in this Act to the affording by any person of access to benefits, facilities or services are not limited to benefits, facilities or services provided by that person himself, but include any means by which it is in that person's power to facilitate access to benefits, facilities or services provided by any other person (the "actual provider").

(2) Where by any provision of this Act the affording by any person of access to benefits, facilities or services in a discriminatory way is in certain circumstances prevented from being unlawful, the effect of the provision shall extend also to the liability under this Act of any actual provider.

40–052

Acts done under statutory authority, etc.

41.— (1) Nothing in Parts II to IV shall render unlawful any act of discrimination done—

(a) in pursuance of any enactment or Order in Council; or
(b) in pursuance of any instrument made under any enactment by a Minister of the Crown; or
(c) in order to comply with any condition or requirement imposed by a Minister of the Crown (whether before or after the passing of this Act) by virtue of any enactment.

40–053

References in this subsection to an enactment, Order in Council or instrument include an enactment, Order in Council or instrument passed or made after the passing of this Act.

(2) Nothing in Parts II to IV shall render unlawful any act whereby a person discriminates against another on the basis of that other's nationality or place of ordinary residence or the length of time for which he has been present or resident in or outside the United Kingdom or an area within the United Kingdom, if that act is done—

(a) in pursuance of any arrangements made (whether before or after the passing of this Act) by or with the approval of, or for the time being approved by, a Minister of the Crown; or
(b) in order to comply with any condition imposed (whether before or after the passing of this Act) by a Minister of the Crown.

Acts safeguarding national security

42. Nothing in Parts II to IV shall render unlawful an act done for the purpose of safeguarding national security [if the doing of the act was justified by that purpose][1].

40–054

[1] Words inserted by Race Relations (Amendment) Act 2000 (c.34), s. 7(1).

PART VII

THE COMMISSION FOR RACIAL EQUALITY

General

Establishment and duties of Commission

43.— (1) There shall be a body of Commissioners named the Commission for Racial Equality consisting of at least eight but not more than fifteen indi-

40–055

viduals each appointed by the Secretary of State on a full-time or part-time basis, which shall have the following duties—

    (a) to work towards the elimination of discrimination;

    (b) to promote equality of opportunity, and good relations, between persons of different racial groups generally; and

    (c) to keep under review the working of this Act and, when they are so required by the Secretary of State or otherwise think it necessary, draw up and submit to the Secretary of State proposals for amending it.

[(1A) One of the Commissioners shall be a person who appears to the Secretary of State to have special knowledge of Scotland.]

(2) The Secretary of State shall appoint—

    (a) one of the Commissioners to be chairman of the Commission; and

    (b) either one or more of the Commissioners (as the Secretary of State thinks fit) to be deputy chairman or deputy chairmen of the Commission.

(3) The Secretary of State may by order amend subsection (1) so far as it regulates the number of Commissioners.

(4) Schedule 1 shall have effect with respect to the Commission.

(5) The Race Relations Board and the Community Relations Commission are hereby abolished.

Assistance to organisations

40–056   **44.**— (1) The Commission may give financial or other assistance to any organisation appearing to the Commission to be concerned with the promotion of equality of opportunity, and good relations, between persons of different racial groups, but shall not give any such financial assistance out of money provided (through the Secretary of State) by Parliament except with the approval of the Secretary of State given with the consent of the Treasury.

(2) Except in so far as other arrangements for their discharge are made and approved under paragraph 13 of Schedule 1—

    (a) the Commission's functions under subsection (1); and

    (b) other functions of the Commission in relation to matters connected with the giving of such financial or other assistance as is mentioned in that subsection,

shall be discharged under the general direction of the Commission by a committee of the Commission consisting of at least three but not more than five Commissioners, of whom one shall be the deputy chairman or one of the deputy chairmen of the Commission.

Research and education

40–057   **45.**— (1) The Commission may undertake or assist (financially or otherwise) the undertaking by other persons of any research, and any educational activities, which appear to the Commission necessary or expedient for the purposes of section 43(1).

(2) The Commission may make charges for educational or other facilities or services made available by them.

Annual reports

46.— (1) As soon as practicable after the end of each calendar year the Com-   **40–058**
mission shall make to the Secretary of State a report on their activities during
the year (an "annual report").

(2) Each annual report shall include a general survey of developments, during
the period to which it relates, in respect of matters falling within the scope of
the Commission's functions.

(3) The Secretary of State shall lay a copy of every annual report before each
House of Parliament, and shall cause the report to be published.

Codes of practice

Codes of practice

47.— (1) The Commission may issue codes of practice containing such prac-   **40–059**
tical guidance as the Commission think fit for [all or any] of the following
purposes, namely—

    (a) the elimination of discrimination in the field of employment;
    (b) the promotion of equality of opportunity in that field between persons
        of different racial groups;
   [(c) the elimination of discrimination in the field of housing;
    (d) the promotion of equality of opportunity in the field of housing between
        persons of different racial groups]

(2) When the Commission propose to issue a code of practice, they shall
prepare and publish a draft of that code, shall consider any representations made
to them about the draft and may modify the draft accordingly.

(3) In the course of preparing any draft code of practice [relating to the field
of employment] for eventual publication under subsection (2) the Commission
shall consult with—

    (a) such organisations or associations of organisations representative of
        employers or of workers; and
    (b) such other organisations, or bodies,

as appear to the Commission to be appropriate.

[(3A) In the course of preparing any draft code of practice relating to the field
of housing for eventual publication under subsection (2) the Commission shall
consult with such organisations or bodies as appear to the Commission to be
appropriate having regard to the content of the draft code.]

(4) If the Commission determine to proceed with [a draft code of practice],
they shall transmit the draft to the Secretary of State who shall—

    (a) if he approves of it, lay it before both Houses of Parliament; and
    (b) if he does not approve of it, publish details of his reasons for with-
        holding approval.

(5) If, within the period of forty days beginning with the day on which a copy
of a draft code of practice is laid before each House of Parliament, or, if such
copies are laid on different days, with the later of the two days, either House so
resolves, no further proceedings shall be taken thereon, but without prejudice to
the laying before Parliament of a new draft.

(6) In reckoning the period of forty days referred to in subsection (5), no
account shall be taken of any period during which Parliament is dissolved or
prorogued or during which both Houses are adjourned for more than four days.

(7) If no such resolution is passed as is referred to in subsection (5), the Commission shall issue the code in the form of the draft and the code shall come into effect on such day as the Secretary of State may by order appoint.

(8) Without prejudice to section 74(3), an order under subsection (7) may contain such transitional provisions or savings as appear to the Secretary of State to be necessary or expedient in connection with the code of practice thereby brought into operation.

(9) The Commission may from time to time revise the whole or any part of a code of practice issued under this section and issue that revised code, and subsections (2) to (8) shall apply (with appropriate modifications) to such a revised code as they apply to the first issue of a code.

(10) A failure on the part of any person to observe any provision of a code of practice shall not of itself render him liable to any proceedings; but in any proceedings under this Act before an [[employment tribunal] a county court or, in Scotland, a sheriff court] any code of practice issued under this section shall be admissible in evidence, and if any provision of such a code appears to the tribunal [or the court] to be relevant to any question arising in the proceedings it shall be taken into account in determining that question.

(11) Without prejudice to subsection (1), a code of practice issued under this section may include such practical guidance as the Commission think fit as to what steps it is reasonably practicable for employers to take for the purpose of preventing their employees from doing in the course of their employment acts made unlawful by this Act.

Investigations

Power to conduct formal investigations

40–060　　**48.**— (1) Without prejudice to their general power to do anything requisite for the performance of their duties under section 43(1), the Commission may if they think fit, and shall if required by the Secretary of State, conduct a formal investigation for any purpose connected with the carrying out of those duties.

(2) The Commission may, with the approval of the Secretary of State, appoint, on a full-time or part-time basis, one or more individuals as additional Commissioners for the purposes of a formal investigation.

(3) The Commission may nominate one or more Commissioners, with or without one or more additional Commissioners, to conduct a formal investigation on their behalf, and may delegate any of their functions in relation to the investigation to the persons so nominated.

Terms of reference

40–061　　**49.**— (1) The Commission shall not embark on a formal investigation unless the requirements of this section have been complied with.

(2) Terms of reference for the investigation shall be drawn up by the Commission or, if the Commission were required by the Secretary of State to conduct the investigation, by the Secretary of State after consulting the Commission.

(3) It shall be the duty of the Commission to give general notice of the holding of the investigation unless the terms of reference confine it to activities of persons named in them, but in such a case the Commission shall in the prescribed manner give those persons notice of the holding of the investigation.

(4) Where the terms of reference of the investigation confine it to activities of persons named in them and the Commission in the course of it propose to investigate any act made unlawful by this Act which they believe that a person so named may have done, the Commission shall—

(a) inform that person of their belief and of their proposal to investigate the act in question; and

(b) offer him an opportunity of making oral or written representations with regard to it (or both oral and written representations if he thinks fit);

and a person so named who avails himself of an opportunity under this subsection of making oral representations may be represented—

(i) by counsel or a solicitor; or

(ii) by some other person of his choice, not being a person to whom the Commission object on the ground that he is unsuitable.

(5) The Commission or, if the Commission were required by the Secretary of State to conduct the investigation, the Secretary of State after consulting the Commission may from time to time revise the terms of reference; and subsections (1), (3) and (4) shall apply to the revised investigation and terms of reference as they applied to the original.

Power to obtain information

[50.— (1) For the purposes of a formal investigation the Commission, by a **40–062** notice in the prescribed form served on him in the prescribed manner—

(a) may require any person to furnish such written information as may be described in the notice, and may specify the time at which, and the manner and form in which, the information is to be furnished;

(b) may require any person to attend at such time and place as is specified in the notice and give oral information about, and produce all documents in his possession or control relating to, any matter specified in the notice.

(2) Except as provided by section 60, a notice shall be served under subsection (1) only where—

(a) service of the notice was authorised by an order made by the Secretary of State; or

(b) the terms of reference of the investigation state that the Commission believe that a person named in them may have done or may be doing acts of all or any of the following descriptions—

(i) unlawful discriminatory acts;

(ii) contraventions of section 28; and

(iii) contraventions of sections 29, 30 or 31,

and confine the investigation to those acts.

(3) A notice under subsection (1) shall not require a person—

(a) to give information, or produce any documents, which he could not be compelled to give in evidence, or produce, in civil proceedings before the High Court or the Court of Session; or

(b) to attend at any place unless the necessary expenses of his journey to and from that place are paid or tendered to him.

(4) If a person fails to comply with a notice served on him under subsection (1) or the Commission have reasonable cause to believe that he intends not to comply with it, the Commission may apply to a county court or, in Scotland, a sheriff court for an order requiring him to comply with it or with such directions for the like purpose as may be contained in the order.

(5) [Section 55 of the County Courts Act 1984] (penalty for neglecting witness summons) shall apply to failure without reasonable excuse to comply with an order of a county court under subsection (4) as it applies in the cases provided in the [said section 55]; and paragraph 73 of Schedule 1 to the Sheriff Courts (Scotland) Act 1907 (power of sheriff to grant second diligence for compelling the attendance of witnesses or havers) shall apply to an order of a sheriff court under subsection (4) as it applies in proceedings in the sheriff court.

(6) A person commits an offence if he—

> (a) wilfully alters, suppresses, conceals or destroys a document which he has been required by a notice or order under this section to produce; or
> (b) in complying with such a notice or order, knowingly or recklessly makes any statement which is false in a material particular,

and shall be liable on summary conviction to a fine not exceeding [level 5 on the standard scale].

(7) Proceedings for an offence under subsection (6) may (without prejudice to any jurisdiction exercisable apart from this subsection) be instituted—

> (a) against any person at any place at which he has an office or other place of business;
> (b) against an individual at any place where he resides, or at which he is for the time being.

Recommendations and reports on formal investigations

40–063   51.— (1) If in the light of any of their findings in a formal investigation it appears to the Commission necessary or expedient, whether during the course of the investigation or after its conclusion—

> (a) to make to any person, with a view to promoting equality of opportunity between persons of different racial groups who are affected by any of his activities, recommendations for changes in his policies or procedures, or as to any other matters; or
> (b) to make to the Secretary of State any recommendations, whether for changes in the law or otherwise,

the Commission shall make those recommendations accordingly.

(2) The Commission shall prepare a report of their findings in any formal investigation conducted by them.

(3) If the formal investigation is one required by the Secretary of State—

> (a) the Commission shall deliver the report to the Secretary of State; and
> (b) the Secretary of State shall cause the report to be published,

and, unless required by the Secretary of State, the Commission shall not publish the report.

(4) If the formal investigation is not one required by the Secretary of State, the Commission shall either publish the report, or make it available for inspection in accordance with subsection (5).

(5) Where under subsection (4) a report is to be made available for inspection, any person shall be entitled, on payment of such fee (if any) as may be determined by the Commission—

> (a) to inspect the report during ordinary office hours and take copies of all or any part of the report; or

(b) to obtain from the Commission a copy, certified by the Commission to be correct, of the report.

(6) The Commission may, if they think fit, determine that the right conferred by subsection (5)(a) shall be exercisable in relation to a copy of the report instead of, or in addition to, the original.

(7) The Commission shall give general notice of the place or places where, and the times when, reports may be inspected under subsection (5).

Restriction on disclosure of information

52.—(1) No information given to the Commission by any person ("the informant") in connection with a formal investigation shall be disclosed by the Commission, or by any person who is or has been a Commissioner, additional Commissioner or employee of the Commission, except—

    40–064

(a) on the order of any court; or

(b) with the informant's consent; or

(c) in the form of a summary or other general statement published by the Commission which does not identify the informant or any other person to whom the information relates; or

(d) in a report of the investigation published by the Commission or made available for inspection under section 51(5); or

(e) to the Commissioners, additional Commissioners or employees of the Commission, or, so far as may be necessary for the proper performance of the functions of the Commission, to other persons; or

(f) for the purpose of any civil proceedings under this Act to which the Commission are a party, or any criminal proceedings.

(2) Any person who discloses information in contravention of subsection (1) commits an offence and shall be liable on summary conviction to a fine not exceeding [level 5 on the standard scale].

(3) In preparing any report for publication or for inspection the Commission shall exclude, so far as is consistent with their duties and the object of the report, any matter which relates to the private affairs of any individual or the business interests of any person where the publication of that matter might, in the opinion of the Commission, prejudicially affect that individual or person.

Part VIII

Enforcement

General

Restriction of proceedings for breach of Act

53.—(1) Except as provided by this Act [or the Special Immigration Appeals Commission Act 1997 or Part IV of the Immigration and Asylum Act 1999][1] no proceedings, whether civil or criminal, shall lie against any person in respect of an act by reason that the act is unlawful by virtue of a provision of this Act.

    40–065

(2) Subsection (1) does not preclude the making of an order of certiorari, mandamus or prohibition.

(3) In Scotland, subsection (1) does not preclude the exercise of the jurisdiction of the Court of Session to entertain an application for reduction or suspension of any order or determination or otherwise to consider the validity of any order or determination, or to require reasons for any order or determination to be stated.

[(4) Subsections (2) and (3) do not, except so far as provided by section 76, apply to any act which is unlawful by virtue of section 76(5) or (9) or by virtue of section 76(10)(b) and (11).]²

¹ Words inserted by Race Relations (Amendment) Act 2000 (c.34), Sched. 2, para. 4.
² Added by Race Relations (Amendment) Act 2000 (c.34) Sched. 2, para. 5.

Enforcement in employment field

Jurisdiction of [employment tribunals]

40–066   **54.**—(1) A complaint by any person ("the complainant") that another person ("the respondent")—

(a) has committed an act of discrimination against the complainant which is unlawful by virtue of Part II; or
(b) is by virtue of section 32 or 33 to be treated as having committed such an act of discrimination against the complainant,

may be presented to an [employment tribunal].

(2) Subsection (1) does not apply to a complaint under section 12(1) of an act in respect of which an appeal, or proceedings in the nature of an appeal, may be brought under any enactment.

Remedies on complaint under s. 54

40–067   **56.**—(1) Where an [employment tribunal] finds that a complaint presented to it under section 54 is well-founded, the tribunal shall make such of the following as it considers just and equitable—

(a) an order declaring the rights of the complainant and the respondent in relation to the act to which the complaint relates;
(b) an order requiring the respondent to pay to the complainant compensation of an amount corresponding to any damages he could have been ordered by a county court or by a sheriff court to pay to the complainant if the complaint had fallen to be dealt with under section 57;
(c) a recommendation that the respondent take within a specified period action appearing to the tribunal to be practicable for the purpose of obviating or reducing the adverse effect on the complainant of any act of discrimination to which the complaint relates.

(4) If without reasonable justification the respondent to a complaint fails to comply with a recommendation made by an [employment tribunal] under subsection (1)(c), then, if it thinks it just and equitable to do so—

(a) the tribunal may increase the amount of compensation required to be paid to the complainant in respect of the complaint by an order made under subsection (1)(b); or
(b) if an order under subsection (1)(b) could have been made but was not, the tribunal may make such an order.

[(5) The Secretary of State may by regulations make provision—

(a) for enabling a tribunal, where an amount of compensation falls to be awarded under subsection (1)(b), to include in the award interest on that amount; and
(b) specifying, for cases where a tribunal decides that an award is to

include an amount in respect of interest, the manner in which and the periods and rate by reference to which the interest is to be determined;

and the regulations may contain such incidental and supplementary provisions as the Secretary of State considers appropriate.

(6) The Secretary of State may by regulations modify the operation of any order made under [section 14 of the Employment Tribunals Act 1996] (power to make provision as to interest on sums payable in pursuance of industrial tribunal decisions) to the extent that it relates to an award of compensation under subsection (1)(b).]

Enforcement of Part III

Claims under Part III

[**57.**—(1) A claim by any person ("the claimant") that another person ("the respondent")— **40–068**

(a) has committed an act of discrimination against the claimant which is unlawful by virtue of Part III; or

(b) is by virtue of section 32 or 33 to be treated as having committed such an act of discrimination against the claimant,

may be made the subject of civil proceedings in like manner as any other claim in tort or (in Scotland) in reparation for breach of statutory duty.

(2) Proceedings under subsection (1)—

(a) shall, in England and Wales, be brought only in a designated county court; and

(b) shall, in Scotland, be brought only in a sheriff court;

but all such remedies shall be obtainable in such proceedings as, apart from this subsection and section 53(1), would be obtainable in the High Court or the Court of Session, as the case may be.

(3) As respects an unlawful act of discrimination falling within section 1(1)(b), no award of damages shall be made if the respondent proves that the requirement or condition in question was not applied with the intention of treating the claimant unfavourably on racial grounds.

(4) For the avoidance of doubt it is hereby declared that damages in respect of an unlawful act of discrimination may include compensation for injury to feelings whether or not they include compensation under any other head.

[(4A) As respects an act which is done, or by virtue of section 32 or 33 is treated as done, by a person in carrying out public investigator functions or functions as a public prosecutor and which is unlawful by virtue of section 19B, no remedy other than—

(a) damages; or

(b) a declaration or, in Scotland, a declarator;

shall be obtainable unless the court is satisfied that the remedy concerned would not prejudice a criminal investigation, a decision to institute criminal proceedings or any criminal proceedings.

(4B) In this section—

"criminal investigation" means—

(a) any investigation which a person in carrying out functions to which section 19B applies has a duty to conduct with a view to it being ascertained whether a person should be charged with, or in Scotland prosecuted for, an offence, or whether a person charged with or prosecuted for an offence is guilty of it;

(b) any investigation which is conducted by a person in carrying out functions to which section 19B applies and which in the circumstances may lead to a decision by that person to institute criminal proceedings which the person has power to conduct; or

(c) any investigation which is conducted by a person in carrying out functions to which section 19B applies and which in the circumstances may lead to a decision by that person to make a report to the procurator fiscal for the purpose of enabling him to determine whether criminal proceedings should be instituted; and

"public investigator functions" means functions of conducting criminal investigations or charging offenders;

and in this subsection "offence" includes any offence under the Army Act 1955, the Air Force Act 1955 or the Naval Discipline Act 1957 (and "offender" shall be construed accordingly).

(4C) Subsection (4D) applies where a party to proceedings under subsection (1) which have arisen by virtue of section 19B has applied for a stay or sist of those proceedings on the grounds of prejudice to—

(a) particular criminal proceedings;
(b) a criminal investigation; or
(c) a decision to institute criminal proceedings.

(4D) The court shall grant the stay or sist unless it is satisfied that the continuance of the proceedings under subsection (1) would not result in the prejudice alleged.][1]

(5) Civil proceedings in respect of a claim by any person that he has been discriminated against in contravention of section 17 or 18 by a body to which [subsection (5A)][2] applies shall not be instituted unless the claimant has given notice of the claim to the Secretary of State [. . .][3].

[(5A) This subsection applies to—

(a) local education authorities in England and Wales;
(b) education authorities in Scotland; and
(c) any body which is a responsible body in relation to an establishment falling within paragraph 3, 3B or 7B of the table in section 17.][4]

(6) In Scotland, when any proceedings are brought under this section, in addition to the service on the defender of a copy of the summons or initial writ initiating the action a copy thereof shall be sent as soon as practicable to the Commission in a manner to be prescribed by Act of Sederunt.

[(7) This section has effect subject to section 57A.][5]

[1] Added by Race Relations (Amendment) Act 2000 (c.34), s. 5(1).
[2] Words substituted by Race Relations (Amendment) Act 2000 (c.34), Sched. 2, para. 6(a).
[3] Words repealed by Race Relations (Amendment) Act 2000 (c.34), Sched. 3, para. 1.
[4] Added by Race Relations (Amendment) Act 2000 (c.34), Sched. 2, para. 7.
[5] Added by Race Relations (Amendment) Act 2000 (c.34), s. 6(1).

Claims under section 19B in immigration cases

40–069   [57A.—(1) No proceedings may be brought by a claimant under section 57(1) in respect of an immigration claim if—

(a) the act to which the claim relates was done in the taking by an immigration authority of a relevant decision and the question whether that act was unlawful by virtue of section 19B has been or could be raised in proceedings on an appeal which is pending, or could be brought, under the 1997 Act or Part IV of the 1999 Act; or

(b) it has been decided in relevant immigration proceedings that that act was not unlawful by virtue of that section.

(2) For the purposes of this section an immigration claim is a claim that a person—

(a) has committed a relevant act of discrimination against the claimant which is unlawful by virtue of section 19B; or

(b) is by virtue of section 32 or 33 to be treated as having committed such an act of discrimination against the claimant.

(3) Where it has been decided in relevant immigration proceedings that an act to which an immigration claim relates was unlawful by virtue of section 19B, any court hearing that claim under section 57 shall treat that act as an act which is unlawful by virtue of section 19B for the purposes of the proceedings before it.

(4) No relevant decision of an immigration authority involving an act to which an immigration claim relates and no relevant decision of an immigration appellate body in relation to such a decision shall be subject to challenge or otherwise affected by virtue of a decision of a court hearing the immigration claim under section 57.

(5) In this section—

"the Immigration Acts" has the same meaning as in the 1999 Act;

"immigration appellate body" means an adjudicator appointed for the purposes of the 1999 Act, the Immigration Appeal Tribunal, the Special Immigration Appeals Commission, the Court of Appeal, the Court of Session or the House of Lords;

"immigration authority" means an authority within the meaning of section 65 of the 1999 Act (human rights and racial discrimination cases);

"immigration claim" has the meaning given by subsection (2) above;

"pending" has the same meaning as in the 1997 Act or, as the case may be, Part IV of the 1999 Act;

"relevant act of discrimination" means an act of discrimination done by an immigration authority in taking any relevant decision;

"relevant decision" means—

(a) in relation to an immigration authority, any decision under the Immigration Acts relating to the entitlement of the claimant to enter or remain in the United Kingdom; and

(b) in relation to an immigration appellate body, any decision on an appeal under the 1997 Act or Part IV of the 1999 Act in relation to a decision falling within paragraph (a);

"relevant immigration proceedings" means proceedings on an appeal under the 1997 Act or Part IV of the 1999 Act;

"the 1997 Act" means the Special Immigration Appeals Commission Act 1997;

"the 1999 Act" means the Immigration and Asylum Act 1999;

and, for the purposes of subsection (1)(a), any power to grant leave to appeal out of time shall be disregarded.][1]

[1] Added by Race Relations (Amendment) Act 2000 (c.34), s. 6(2).

Non-discrimination notices

Issue of non-discrimination notice

40–070 **58.**—(1) This section applies to—

(a) an unlawful discriminatory act; and
(b) an act contravening section 28; and
(c) an act contravening section 29, 30 or 31,

and so applies whether or not proceedings have been brought in respect of the act.

(2) If in the course of a formal investigation the Commission become satisfied that a person is committing, or has committed, any such acts, the Commission may in the prescribed manner serve on him a notice in the prescribed form ("a non-discrimination notice") requiring him—

(a) not to commit any such acts; and
(b) where compliance with paragraph (a) involves changes in any of his practices or other arrangements—

(i) to inform the Commission that he has effected those changes and what those changes are; and
(ii) to take such steps as may be reasonably required by the notice for the purpose of affording that information to other persons concerned.

(3) A non-discrimination notice may also require the person on whom it is served to furnish the Commission with such other information as may be reasonably required by the notice in order to verify that the notice has been complied with.

(4) The notice may specify the time at which, and the manner and form in which, any information is to be furnished to the Commission, but the time at which any information is to be furnished in compliance with the notice shall not be later than five years after the notice has become final.

(5) The Commission shall not serve a non-discrimination notice in respect of any person unless they have first—

(a) given him notice that they are minded to issue a non-discrimination notice in his case, specifying the grounds on which they contemplate doing so; and
(b) offered him an opportunity of making oral or written representations in the matter (or both oral and written representations if he thinks fit) within a period of not less than 28 days specified in the notice; and
(c) taken account of any representations so made by him.

(6) [. . .][1]
(7) Section 50(4) shall apply to requirements under subsection (2)(b), (3) and (4) contained in a non-discrimination notice which has become final as it applies to requirements in a notice served under section 50(1).

[1] Repealed by Race Relations (Amendment) Act 2000 (c.34) Sched. 3, para. 1.

Appeal against non-discrimination notice

59.—(1) Not later than six weeks after a non-discrimination notice is served on any person he may appeal against any requirement of the notice— **40–071**

(a) to an [employment tribunal][1], so far as the requirement relates to acts which are within the jurisdiction of the tribunal;

(b) to a designated county court or a sheriff court, so far as the requirement relates to acts which are within the jurisdiction of the court [(ignoring section 57A)][2] and are not within the jurisdiction of an [employment tribunal][3].

(2) Where the tribunal or court considers a requirement in respect of which an appeal is brought under subsection (1) to be unreasonable because it is based on an incorrect finding of fact or for any other reason, the tribunal or court shall quash the requirement.

(3) On quashing a requirement under subsection (2) the tribunal or court may direct that the non-discrimination notice shall be treated as if, in place of the requirement quashed, it had contained a requirement in terms specified in the direction.

(4) Subsection (1) does not apply to a requirement treated as included in a non-discrimination notice by virtue of a direction under subsection (3).

[1] Words substituted by Employment Rights (Dispute Resolution) Act 1998 (c.8), Pt I, s.1(2).
[2] Words inserted by Race Relations (Amendment) Act 2000 (c.34), Sched. 2, para. 8.
[3] Words substituted by Employment Rights (Dispute Resolution) Act 1998 (c.8), Pt I, s.1(2).

Investigation as to compliance with non-discrimination notice

60.—(1) If— **40–072**

(a) the terms of reference of a formal investigation state that its purpose is to determine whether any requirements of a non-discrimination notice are being or have been carried out, but section 50(2)(b) does not apply; and

(b) section 49(3) is complied with in relation to the investigation on a date ("the commencement date") not later than the expiration of the period of five years beginning when the non-discrimination notice became final,

the Commission may within the period referred to in subsection (2) serve notices under section 50(1) for the purposes of the investigation without needing to obtain the consent of the Secretary of State.

(2) The said period begins on the commencement date and ends on the later of the following dates—

(a) the date on which the period of five years mentioned in subsection (1)(b) expires;

(b) the date two years after the commencement date.

Register of non-discrimination notices

61.— (1) The Commission shall establish and maintain a register ("the register") of non-discrimination notices which have become final. **40–073**

(2) Any person shall be entitled, on payment of such fee (if any) as may be determined by the Commission—

(a) to inspect the register during ordinary office hours and take copies of any entry; or

(b) to obtain from the Commission a copy, certified by the Commission to be correct, of any entry in the register.

(3) The Commission may, if they think fit, determine that the right conferred by subsection (2)(a) shall be exercisable in relation to a copy of the register instead of, or in addition to, the original.

(4) The Commission shall give general notice of the place or places where, and the times when, the register or a copy of it may be inspected.

Other enforcement by Commission

Persistent discrimination

40–074　　　　62.— (1) If, during the period of five years beginning on the date on which any of the following became final in the case of any person, namely—

(a) a non-discrimination notice served on him; or

(b) a finding by a tribunal or court under section 54 or 57; that he has done an unlawful discriminatory act; or

[(ba) a finding under the Special Immigration Appeals Commission Act 1997 or Part IV of the Immigration and Asylum Act 1999 that he has done an act which was unlawful by virtue of section 19B; or][1]

(c) a finding by a court in proceedings under section 19 or 20 of the Race Relations Act 1968 that he has done an act which was unlawful by virtue of any provision of Part I of that Act,

it appears to the Commission that unless restrained he is likely to do one or more acts falling within paragraph (b), or contravening section 28, the Commission may apply to a designated county court for an injunction, or to a sheriff court for an order, restraining him from doing so; and the court, if satisfied that the application is well-founded, may grant the injunction or order in the terms applied for or in more limited terms.

(2) In proceedings under this section the Commission shall not allege that the person to whom the proceedings relate has done an act falling within subsection (1)(b) or contravening section 28 which is within the jurisdiction of an [employment tribunal][2] unless a finding by an [employment tribunal][3] that he did that act has become final.

[1] Added by Race Relations (Amendment) Act 2000 (c.34), Sched. 2, para. 9.
[2] Words substituted by Employment Rights (Dispute Resolution) Act 1998 (c.8), Pt I, s. 1(2).
[3] *ibid.*

Enforcement of ss. 29 to 31

40–075　　　　63.— (1) Proceedings in respect of a contravention of section 29, 30 or 31 shall be brought only by the Commission in accordance with the following provisions of this section.

(2) The proceedings shall be—

(a) an application for a decision whether the alleged contravention occurred; or

(b) an application under subsection (4),

or both.

(3) An application under subsection (2)(a) shall be made—

(a) in a case based on any provision of Part II, to an [employment tribunal][1]; and

(b) in any other case, to a designated county court or a sheriff court.

(4) If it appears to the Commission—

(a) that a person has done an act which by virtue of section 29, 30 or 31 was unlawful; and

(b) that unless restrained he is likely to do further acts which by virtue of that section are unlawful,

the Commission may apply to a designated county court for an injunction, or to a sheriff court for an order, restraining him from doing such acts; and the court, if satisfied that the application is well-founded, may grant the injunction or order in the terms applies for or more limited terms.

(5) In proceedings under subsection (4) the Commission shall not allege that the person to whom the proceedings relate has done an act which is unlawful under this Act and within the jurisdiction of an [employment tribunal][2] unless a finding by an [employment tribunal][3] that he did that act has become final.

[1] Words substituted by Employment Rights (Dispute Resolution) Act 1998 (c.8), Pt I, s. 1(2).
[2] *ibid.*
[3] *ibid.*

Preliminary action in employment cases

64.— (1) With a view to making an application under section 62(1) or 63(4) in relation to a person the Commission may present to an an [employment tribunal][1] a complaint that he has done an act within the jurisdiction of an [employment tribunal][2], and if the tribunal considers that the complaint is well-founded it shall make a finding to that effect and, if it thinks it just and equitable to do so in the case of an act contravening any provision of Part II may also (as if the complaint had been presented by the person discriminated against) make an order such as is referred to in section 56(1)(a), or a recommendation such as is referred to in section 56(1)(c), or both.

(2) Subsection (1) is without prejudice to the jurisdiction conferred by section 63(2).

(3) In sections 62 and 63 and this section, the acts "within the jurisdiction of an [employment tribunal][3]" are those in respect of which such jurisdiction is conferred by sections 54 and 63.

40–076

[1] Words substituted by Employment Rights (Dispute Resolution) Act 1998 (c.8), Pt I, s. 1(2).
[2] *ibid.*
[3] *ibid.*

Help for persons suffering discrimination

Help for aggrieved persons in obtaining information etc.

65.— (1) With a view to helping a person ("the person aggrieved") who considers he may have been discriminated against in contravention of this Act to decide whether to institute proceedings and, if he does so, to formulate and present his case in the most effective manner, the Secretary of State shall by order prescribe—

40–077

(a) forms by which the person aggrieved may question the respondent on his reasons for doing any relevant act, or on any other matter which is or may be relevant; and

(b) forms by which the respondent may if he so wishes reply to any questions.

(2) Where the person aggrieved questions the respondent (whether in accordance with an order under subsection (1) or not)—

(a) the question, and any reply by the respondent (whether in accordance with such an order or not) shall, subject to the following provisions of this section, be admissible as evidence in the proceedings;
(b) if it appears to the court or tribunal that the respondent deliberately, and without reasonable excuse, omitted to reply within a reasonable period or that his reply is evasive or equivocal, the court or tribunal may draw any inference from that fact that it considers it just and equitable to draw, including an inference that he committed an unlawful act.

(3) The Secretary of State may by order—

(a) prescribe the period within which questions must be duly served in order to be admissible under subsection (2)(a); and
(b) prescribe the manner in which a question, and any reply by the respondent, may be duly served.

(4) Rules may enable the court entertaining a claim under section 57 to determine, before the date fixed for the hearing of the claim, whether a question or reply is admissible under this section or not.

[(4A) In section 19B proceedings, subsection (2)(b) does not apply in relation to a failure to reply, or a particular reply, if the conditions specified in subsection (4B) are satisfied.

(4B) Those conditions are that—

(a) at the time of doing any relevant act, the respondent was carrying out public investigator functions or was a public prosecutor; and
(b) he reasonably believes that a reply or (as the case may be) a different reply would be likely to prejudice any criminal investigation, any decision to institute criminal proceedings or any criminal proceedings or would reveal the reasons behind a decision not to institute, or a decision not to continue, criminal proceedings.

(4C) For the purposes of subsections (4A) and (4B)—

"public investigator functions" has the same meaning as in section 57;
"section 19B proceedings" means proceedings in respect of a claim under section 57 which has arisen by virtue of section 19B.]¹

(5) This section is without prejudice to any other enactment or rule of law regulating interlocutory and preliminary matters in proceedings before a county court, sheriff court or industrial tribunal, and has effect subject to any enactment or rule of law regulating the admissibility of evidence in such proceedings.

(6) In this section "respondent" includes a prospective respondent and "rules"—

(a) in relation to county court proceedings, means county court rules;
(b) in relation to sheriff court proceedings, means sheriff court rules.

[(7) This section does not apply in relation to any proceedings under—

(a) the Special Immigration Appeals Commission Act 1997; or

(b) Part IV of the Immigration and Asylum Act 1999.][2]

[1] Added by Race Relations (Amendment) Act 2000 (c.34), s. 5(2).
[2] Added by Race Relations (Amendment) Act 2000 (c.34), Sched. 2, para. 10.

Assistance by Commission

66.— (1) Where, in relation to proceedings or prospective proceedings under **40–078**
this Act, an individual who is an actual or prospective complainant or claimant
applies to the Commission for assistance under this section, the Commission
shall consider the application and may grant it if they think fit to do so—

(a) on the ground that the case raises a question of principle; or

(b) on the ground that it is unreasonable, having regard to the complexity
of the case, or to the applicant's position in relation to the respondent
or another person involved, or to any other matter, to expect the applicant to deal with the case unaided; or

(c) by reason of any other special consideration.

(2) Assistance by the Commission under this section may include—

(a) giving advice;

(b) procuring or attempting to procure the settlement of any matter in dispute;

(c) arranging for the giving of advice or assistance by a solicitor or counsel;

(d) arranging for representation by any person, including all such assistance as is usually given by a solicitor or counsel in the steps preliminary or incidental to any proceedings, or in arriving at or giving effect
to a compromise to avoid or bring to an end any proceedings;

(e) any other form of assistance which the Commission may consider
appropriate,

but paragraph (d) shall not affect the law and practice regulating the descriptions
of persons who may appear in, conduct, defend, and address the court in, any
proceedings.

(3) Where under subsection (1) an application for assistance under this section
is made in writing, the Commission shall, within the period of two months
beginning when the application is received—

(a) consider the application after making such enquiries as they think fit;
and

(b) decide whether or not to grant it; and

(c) inform the applicant of their decision, stating whether or not assistance
under this section is to be provided by the Commission and, if so, what
form it will take.

(4) If, in a case where subsection (3) applies, the Commission within the
period of two months there mentioned give notice to the applicant that, in relation to his application—

(a) the period of two months allowed them by that subsection is by virtue
of the notice extended to three months; and

(b) the reference to two months in section 68(3) is by virtue of the notice
to be read as a reference to three months,

subsection (3) and section 68(3) shall have effect accordingly.

(5) In so far as expenses are incurred by the Commission in providing the applicant with assistance under this section, the recovery of those expenses (as taxed or assessed in such manner as may be prescribed by rules or regulations) shall constitute a first charge for the benefit of the Commission—

(a) on any costs or expenses which (whether by virtue of a judgment or order of a court or tribunal or an agreement or otherwise) are payable to the applicant by any other person in respect of the matter in connection with which the assistance is given; and

(b) so far as relates to any costs or expenses, on his rights under any compromise or settlement arrived at in connection with that matter to avoid or bring to an end any proceedings.

(6) The charge conferred by subsection (5) is subject to any charge [imposed by section 10(7) of the Access to Justice Act 1999], or any charge or obligation for payment in priority to other debts under the Legal Aid and Advice (Scotland) Acts 1967 and 1972[the Legal Aid (Scotland) Act 1986], and is subject to any provision in [[, or made under,] either of those Acts for payment of any sum to the [Legal Services Commission] or into the Scottish Legal Aid Fund].

(7) In this section "respondent" includes a prospective respondent and "rules or regulations"—

(a) in relation to county court proceedings, means county court rules;
(b) in relation to sheriff court proceedings, means sheriff court rules;
(c) in relation to [employment tribunal] proceedings, means [industrial tribunal procedure regulations under Part I of the Industrial Tribunals Act 1996].

[(8) This section (except for subsection (4)) applies to proceedings or prospective proceedings under the Special Immigration Appeals Commission Act 1997 or Part IV of the Immigration and Asylum Act 1999 so far as they relate to acts which may be unlawful by virtue of section 19B as it applies to proceedings or prospective proceedings under this Act.

(9) In this section as it applies by virtue of subsection (8) "rules and regulations" means—

(a) in relation to proceedings under the Act of 1997, rules under section 5 or 8 of that Act;
(b) in relation to proceedings under Part IV of the Act of 1999, rules under paragraph 3 or 4 of Schedule 4 to that Act.][1]

[1] Added by Race Relations (Amendment) Act 2000 (c.34), Sched. 2, para. 11.

Sheriff courts and designated county courts

Sheriff courts and designated county courts

40–079   67.— (1) For the purposes of this Act a "designated" county court is one designated for the time being for those purposes by an order made by the Lord Chancellor.

(2) An order under subsection (1) designating any county court for the purposes of this Act shall assign to that court as its district for those purposes any county court district or two or more county court districts.

(3) A designated county court or a sheriff court shall have jurisdiction to entertain proceedings under this Act with respect to an act done on a ship, aircraft or hovercraft outside its district, including such an act done outside Great Britain.

[(3A) A designated county court or a sheriff court shall have jurisdiction to entertain proceedings under this Act with respect to an act done outside the United Kingdom where section 19B applies in relation to such an act by virtue of section 27(1A).][1]

(4) In any proceedings under this Act in a designated county court or a sheriff court the judge or sheriff shall, unless with the consent of the parties he sits without assessors, be assisted by two assessors appointed from a list of persons prepared and maintained by the Secretary of State, being persons appearing to the Secretary of State to have special knowledge and experience of problems connected with relations between persons of different racial groups.

(5) The remuneration of assessors appointed under subsection (4) shall be at such rate as may, with the approval of [the Treasury], be determined by the Lord Chancellor (for proceedings in England and Wales) or the Lord President of the Court of Session (for proceedings in Scotland).

(6) Without prejudice to section 74(3), an order for the discontinuance of the jurisdiction of any county court under this Act, whether wholly or within a part of the district assigned to it for the purposes of this Act, may include provision with respect to any proceedings under this Act commenced in that court before the order comes into operation.

[1] Added by Race Relations (Amendment) Act 2000 (c.34), Sched. 2, para. 12.

National security: procedure

[67A.— (1) Rules may make provision for enabling a court in which relevant proceedings have been brought, where it considers it expedient in the interests of national security—   **40–080**

   (a) to exclude from all or part of the proceedings—

      (i) the claimant;
      (ii) the claimant's representatives; or
      (iii) the assessors (if any) appointed by virtue of section 67(4);

   (b) to permit a claimant or representative who has been excluded to make a statement to the court before the commencement of the proceedings, or the part of the proceedings, from which he is excluded;
   (c) to take steps to keep secret all or part of the reasons for its decision in the proceedings.

(2) The Attorney General or, in Scotland, the Advocate General for Scotland, may appoint a person to represent the interests of a claimant in, or in any part of, any proceedings from which the claimant and his representatives are excluded by virtue of subsection (1).

(3) A person appointed under subsection (2)—

   (a) if appointed for the purposes of proceedings in England and Wales, must have a general qualification (within the meaning of section 71 of the Courts and Legal Services Act 1990); and
   (b) if appointed for the purposes of proceedings in Scotland, must be—

      (i) an advocate; or
      (ii) a solicitor who has by virtue of section 25A of the Solicitors (Scotland) Act 1980 rights of audience in the Court of Session or the High Court of Justiciary.

(4) A person appointed under subsection (2) shall not be responsible to the person whose interests he is appointed to represent.

(5) In this section—

"relevant proceedings" means proceedings brought under this Act—

    (a) in England and Wales, in a designated county court; or
    (b) in Scotland, in a sheriff court; and

"rules" has the same meaning as in section 65.]¹

¹ Added by Race Relations (Amendment) Act 2000 (c.34), s. 8.

Period within which proceedings to be brought

Period within which proceedings to be brought

40–081   **68.**— (1) An [employment tribunal] shall not consider a complaint under section 54 unless it is presented to the tribunal before the end of [—]

    [(a) the period of three months beginning when the act complained of was done; or
    (b) in a case to which section 75(8) applies, the period of six months so beginning.]

(2) [Subject to subsection (2A) a]¹ county court or a sheriff court shall not consider a claim under section 57 unless proceedings in respect of the claim are instituted before the end of—

    (a) the period of six months beginning when the act complained of was done; [. . .]²
    (b) [. . .]³

[(2A) In relation to an immigration claim within the meaning of section 57A, the period of six months mentioned in subsection (2)(a) begins on the expiry of the period during which, by virtue of section 57A(1)(a), no proceedings may be brought under section 57(1) in respect of the claim.]⁴

(3) Where, in relation to proceedings or prospective proceedings by way of a claim under section 57, an application for assistance under section 66 is made to the Commission before the end of the period of six [. . .]⁵ months mentioned in paragraph (a) [. . .]⁶ of subsection (2), the period allowed by that paragraph for instituting proceedings in respect of the claim shall be extended by two months.

(4) An [employment tribunal], county court or sheriff court shall not consider an application under section 63(2)(a) unless it is made before the end of the period of six months beginning when the act to which it relates was done; and a county court or sheriff court shall not consider an application under section 63(4) unless it is made before the end of the period of five years so beginning.

(5) An [employment tribunal] shall not consider a complaint under section 64(1) unless it is presented to the tribunal before the end of the period of six months beginning when the act complained of was done.

(6) A court or tribunal may nevertheless consider any such complaint, claim or application which is out of time if, in all the circumstances of the case, it considers that it is just and equitable to do so.

(7) For the purposes of this section—

    (a) when the inclusion of any term in a contract renders the making of the contract an unlawful act, that act shall be treated as extending throughout the duration of the contract; and
    (b) any act extending over a period shall be treated as done at the end of that period; and

(c) a deliberate omission shall be treated as done when the person in question decided upon it;

and in the absence of evidence establishing the contrary a person shall be taken for the purposes of this section to decide upon an omission when he does an act inconsistent with doing the omitted act or, if he has done no such inconsistent act, when the period expires within which he might reasonably have been expected to do the omitted act if it was to be done.

[1] Words inserted by Race Relations (Amendment) Act 2000 (c.34), Sched. 2, para. 13.
[2] Repealed by Race Relations (Amendment) Act 2000 (c.34), Sched. 3, para. 1.
[3] *ibid.*
[4] Added by Race Relations (Amendment) Act 2000 (c.34), Sched. 2, para. 14.
[5] Words repealed by Race Relations (Amendment) Act 2000 (c.34), Sched. 3, para. 1.
[6] *ibid.*

Evidence

Evidence

69.— (1) Any finding by a court under section 19 or 20 of the Race Relations Act 1968, or by a court or [employment tribunal] under this Act, in respect of any act shall, if it has become final, be treated as conclusive in any proceedings under this Act.   **40–082**

(2) In any proceedings under this Act [or any enactment mentioned in section 19D(5)][1] a certificate signed by or on behalf of a Minister of the Crown and certifying—

(a) that any arrangements or conditions specified in the certificate were made, approved or imposed by a Minister of the Crown and were in operation at a time or throughout a period so specified; [. . .][2]

[. . .][3]shall be conclusive evidence of the matters certified.

(3) A document purporting to be a certificate such as is mentioned in subsection (2) shall be received in evidence and, unless the contrary is proved, shall be deemed to be such a certificate.

[1] Words inserted by Race Relations (Amendment) Act 2000 (c.34), Sched. 2, para. 15.
[2] Repealed by Race Relations (Amendment) Act 2000 (c.34), Sched. 3, para. 1.
[3] *ibid.*

Part X

Supplemental

Specified authorities: general statutory duty

[**71.**— (1) Every body or other person specified in Schedule 1A or of a description falling within that Schedule shall, in carrying out its functions, have due regard to the need—   **40–083**

(a) to eliminate unlawful racial discrimination; and
(b) to promote equality of opportunity and good relations between persons of different racial groups.[[1]][2]

(2) The Secretary of State may by order impose, on such persons falling within Schedule 1A as he considers appropriate, such duties as he considers appropriate for the purpose of ensuring the better performance by those persons of their duties under subsection (1).

(3) An order under subsection (2)—

    (a) may be made in relation to a particular person falling within Schedule 1A, any description of persons falling within that Schedule or every person falling within that Schedule;

    (b) may make different provision for different purposes.

(4) Before making an order under subsection (2), the Secretary of State shall consult the Commission.

(5) The Secretary of State may by order amend Schedule 1A; but no such order may extend the application of this section unless the Secretary of State considers that the extension relates to a person who exercises functions of a public nature.

(6) An order under subsection (2) or (5) may contain such incidental, supplementary or consequential provision as the Secretary of State considers appropriate (including provision amending or repealing provision made by or under this Act or any other enactment).

(7) This section is subject to section 71A and 71B and is without prejudice to the obligation of any person to comply with any other provision of this Act.][3]

[1] In relation to the carrying out of immigration and nationality functions:

    (1) Every body or other person specified in Schedule 1A or of a description falling within that Schedule shall, in carrying out its functions, have due regard to the need—

        (a) to eliminate unlawful racial discrimination; and

        (b) to promote good relations between persons of different racial groups.

[2] Words repealed by Race Relations Act 1976 (c.74), Pt X s. 71A(1).
[3] Substituted by Race Relations (Amendment) Act 2000 (c.34), s. 2(1).

General statutory duty: special cases

40–084   **[71A.**— (1) In relation to the carrying out of immigration and nationality functions (within the meaning of section 19D(1)), section 71(1)(b) has effect with the omission of the words "equality of opportunity and".

(2) Where an entry in Schedule 1A is limited to a person in a particular capacity, section 71(1) does not apply to that person in any other capacity.

(3) Where an entry in Schedule 1A is limited to particular functions of a person, section 71(1) does not apply to that person in relation to any other functions.][1]

[1] Substituted by Race Relations (Amendment) Act 2000 (c.34), s. 2(1).

General statutory duty: Scotland and Wales

40–085   **[71B.**— (1) For the purposes of the Scotland Act 1998, subsections (2) to (4) of section 71 (and sections 71(6) and 74 so far as they apply to the power conferred by subsection (2) of section 71) shall be taken to be pre-commencement enactments within the meaning of that Act.

(2) Before making an order under section 71(2) in relation to functions exercisable in relation to Wales by a person who is not a Welsh public authority, the Secretary of State shall consult the National Assembly for Wales.

(3) The Secretary of State shall not make an order under section 71(2) in relation to functions of a Welsh public authority except with the consent of the National Assembly for Wales.

(4) In this section "Welsh public authority" means any person whose functions are exercisable only in relation to Wales and includes the National Assembly for Wales.][1]

[1] Substituted by Race Relations (Amendment) Act 2000 (c.34), s. 2(1).

General statutory duty: codes of practice

[**71C.**— (1) The Commission may issue codes of practice containing such **40–086** practical guidance as the Commission think fit in relation to the performance by persons of duties imposed on them by virtue of subsections (1) and (2) of section 71.

(2) When the Commission propose to issue a code of practice under this section, they—

(a) shall prepare and publish a draft of the code;
(b) shall consider any representations made to them about the draft; and
(c) may modify the draft accordingly.

(3) In the course of preparing any draft code of practice under this section the Commission shall consult such organisations or bodies as appear to the Commission to be appropriate having regard to the content of the draft code.

(4) If the Commission determine to proceed with a draft code of practice, they shall transmit the draft to the Secretary of State who shall consult the Scottish Ministers and the National Assembly for Wales.

(5) After consulting the Scottish Ministers and the National Assembly for Wales, the Secretary of State shall—

(a) if he approves of the draft code, lay it before both Houses of Parliament; and
(b) if he does not approve of it, publish details of his reasons for withholding approval.

(6) If, within the period of forty days beginning with the day on which a copy of a draft code of practice is laid before each House of Parliament, or, if such copies are laid on different days, with the later of the two days, either House so resolves, no further proceedings shall be taken on the draft code of practice, but without prejudice to the laying before Parliament of a new draft.

(7) In reckoning the period of forty days referred to in subsection (6), no account shall be taken of any period during which Parliament is dissolved or prorogued or during which both Houses are adjourned for more than four days.

(8) If no such resolution is passed as is referred to in subsection (6), the Commission shall issue the code in the form of the draft and the code shall come into effect on such day as the Secretary of State may, after consulting the Scottish Ministers and the National Assembly for Wales, by order appoint.

(9) Without prejudice to section 74(3), an order under subsection (8) may contain such transitional provisions or savings as appear to the Secretary of State to be necessary or expedient in connection with the code of practice thereby brought into operation.

(10) The Commission may revoke, or from time to time revise, the whole or any part of a code of practice issued under this section; and, where they revise the whole or any part of such a code, they shall issue the revised code, and subsections (2) to (9) shall apply (with appropriate modifications) to such a revised code as they apply to the first issue of a code.

(11) A failure on the part of any person to observe any provision of a code of practice shall not of itself render that person liable to any proceedings; but any code of practice issued under this section shall be admissible in evidence in any legal proceedings, and if any provision of such a code appears to the court or tribunal concerned to be relevant to any question arising in the proceedings it shall be taken into account in determining that question.

(12) Without prejudice to subsection (1), a code of practice issued under this section may include such practical guidance as the Commission think fit as to

what steps it is reasonably practicable for persons to take for the purpose of preventing their staff from doing in the course of their duties acts made unlawful by this Act.][1]

[1] Substituted by Race Relations (Amendment) Act 2000 (c.34), s. 2(1).

General statutory duty: compliance notices

40–087   [**71D.**— (1) If the Commission are satisfied that a person has failed to comply with, or is failing to comply with, any duty imposed by an order under section 71(2), the Commission may serve on that person a notice ("a compliance notice").

(2) A compliance notice shall require the person concerned—

    (a) to comply with the duty concerned; and
    (b) to inform the Commission, within 28 days of the date on which the notice is served, of the steps that the person has taken, or is taking, to comply with the duty.

(3) A compliance notice may also require the person concerned to furnish the Commission with such other written information as may be reasonably required by the notice in order to verify that the duty has been complied with.
(4) The notice may specify—

    (a) the time (no later than three months from the date on which the notice is served) at which any information is to be furnished to the Commission;
    (b) the manner and form in which any such information is to be so furnished.

(5) A compliance notice shall not require a person to furnish information which the person could not be compelled to furnish in evidence in civil proceedings before the High Court or the Court of Session.][1]

[1] Substituted by Race Relations (Amendment) Act 2000 (c.34), s. 2(1).

Enforcement of compliance notices

40–088   [**71E.**— (1) The Commission may apply to a designated county court or, in Scotland, a sheriff court for an order requiring a person falling within Schedule 1A to furnish any information required by a compliance notice if—

    (a) the person fails to furnish the information to the Commission in accordance with the notice; or
    (b) the Commission have reasonable cause to believe that the person does not intend to furnish the information.

(2) If the Commission consider that a person has not, within three months of the date on which a compliance notice was served on that person, complied with any requirement of the notice for that person to comply with a duty imposed by an order under section 71(2), the Commission may apply to a designated county court or, in Scotland, a sheriff court for an order requiring the person to comply with the requirement of the notice.
(3) If the court is satisfied that the application is well-founded, it may grant the order in the terms applied for or in more limited terms.

(4) The sanctions in section 71D and this section shall be the only sanctions for breach of any duty imposed by an order under section 71(2), but without prejudice to the enforcement under section 57 or otherwise of any other provision of this Act (where the breach is also a contravention of that provision).]¹

¹ Substituted by Race Relations (Amendment) Act 2000 (c.34), s. 2(1).

Validity and revision of contracts

72.— (1) A term of a contract is void where—   **40–089**

(a) its inclusion renders the making of the contract unlawful by virtue of this Act; or

(b) it is included in furtherance of an act rendered unlawful by this Act; or

(c) it provides for the doing of an act which would be rendered unlawful by this Act.

(2) Subsection (1) does not apply to a term the inclusion of which constitutes, or is in furtherance of, or provides for, unlawful discrimination against a party to the contract, but the term shall be unenforceable against that party.

(3) A term in a contract which purports to exclude or limit any provision of this Act is unenforceable by any person in whose favour the term would operate apart from this subsection.

(4) Subsection (3) does not apply—

(a) to a contract settling a complaint to which section 54(1) applies where the contract is made with the assistance of a conciliation officer; or

[(b) to a contract settling a complaint to which section 54(1) applies if the conditions regulating compromise contracts under this Act are satisfied in relation to the contract;]

(c) to a contract settling a claim to which section 57 applies.

[(4A) The conditions regulating compromise contracts under this Act are that—

(a) the contract must be in writing;

(b) the contract must relate to the particular complaint;

(c) the complainant must have received [advice from a relevant independent adviser] as to the terms and effect of the proposed contract and in particular its effect on his ability to pursue his complaint before an [employment tribunal];

(d) there must be in force, when the adviser gives the advice, a [contract of insurance, or an indemnity provided for members of a profession or professional body,] covering the risk of a claim by the complainant in respect of loss arising in consequence of the advice;

(e) the contract must identify the adviser; and

(f) the contract must state that the conditions regulating compromise contracts under this Act are satisfied.]

[(4B) A person is a relevant independent adviser for the purposes of subsection (4A)(c)—

(a) if he is a qualified lawyer;

(b) if he is an officer, official, employee or member of an independent trade union who has been certified in writing by the trade union as competent to give advice and as authorised to do so on behalf of the trade union;

(c) if he works at an advice centre (whether as an employee or a volunteer) and has been certified in writing by the centre as competent to give advice and as authorised to do so on behalf of the centre; or

(d) if he is a person of a description specified in an order made by the Secretary of State.

(4BA) But a person is not a relevant independent, adviser for the purposes of subsection (4A)(c) in relation to the complainant—

(a) if he is, is employed by or is acting in the matter for the other party or a person who is connected with the other party;

(b) in the case of a person within subsection (4B)(b) or (c), if the trade union or advice centre is the other party or a person who is connected with the other party;

(c) in the case of a person within subsection (4B)(c), if the complainant makes a payment for the advice received from him; or

(d) in the case of a person of a description specified in an order under subsection (4B)(d), if any condition specified in the order in relation to the giving of advice by persons of that description is not satisfied.

(4BB) In subsection (4B)(a) "qualified lawyer" means—

(a) as respects England and Wales, a barrister (whether in practice as such or employed to give legal advice), a solicitor who holds a practising certificate, or a person other than a barrister or solicitor who is an authorised advocate or authorised litigator (within the meaning of the Courts and Legal Services Act 1990), and

(b) as respects Scotland, an advocate (whether in practice as such or employed to give legal advice), or a solicitor who holds a practising certificate.

(4BC) In subsection (4B)(b) "independent trade union" has the same meaning as in the Trade Union and Labour Relations (Consolidation) Act 1992.

(4C) For the purposes of subsection (4BA) any two persons are to be treated as connected—

(a) if one is a company of which the other (directly or indirectly) has control, or

(b) if both are companies of which a third person (directly or indirectly) has control.][1]

[(4D) An agreement under which the parties agree to submit a dispute to arbitration—

(a) shall be regarded for the purposes of subsection (4)(a) and (aa) as being a contract settling a complaint if—

(i) the dispute is covered by a scheme having effect by virtue of an order under section 212A of the Trade Union and Labour Relations (Consolidation) Act 1992, and

(ii) the agreement is to submit it to arbitration in accordance with the scheme, but

(b) shall be regarded for those purposes as neither being nor including such a contract in any other case.][2]

(5) On the application of any person interested in a contract to which subsection (2) applies, a designated county court or a sheriff court may make such

order as it thinks just for removing or modifying any term made unenforceable by that subsection; but such an order shall not be made unless all persons affected have been given notice of the application (except where under rules of court notice may be dispensed with) and have been afforded an opportunity to make representations to the court.

(6) An order under subsection (5) may include provision as respects any period before the making of the order.

---

¹ Subsections (4B) and (4C) substituted by (4B), (4BA), (4BB), (4BC) and (4C) by Employment Rights (Dispute Resolution) Act 1998 (c.8), Sched. 1, para. 3.
² Added by Employment Rights (Dispute Resolution) Act 1998 (c.8), Pt II, s. 8(2).

Power to amend certain provisions of Act

73.— (1) The Secretary of State may by an order the draft of which has been approved by each House of Parliament—   **40–090**

- (a) amend or repeal section 9 (including that section as amended by a previous order under this subsection);
- (b) amend Part II, III or IV so as to render lawful an act which, apart from the amendment, would be unlawful by reason of [section 4(1) or (2), 19B, 20(1), 21, 24 or 25]¹,
- (c) amend section 10(1) or 25(1)(a) so as to alter the number of partners or members specified in that provision.

(2) The Secretary of State shall not lay before Parliament the draft of an order under subsection (1) unless he has consulted the Commission about the contents of the draft.

---

¹ Words inserted by Race Relations (Amendment) Act 2000 (c.34), Sched. 2, para. 16.

Orders and regulations

74.— (1) Any power of a Minister of the Crown to make orders or regulations under the provisions of this Act (except [section] 50(2)(a)) shall be exercisable by statutory instrument.   **40–091**

(2) An order made by a Minister of the Crown under the preceding provisions of this Act (except sections 50(2)(a) and 73(1)), and any regulations made under [section 56(5), (6) or 75(5)(a)]¹ [or (9A)], shall be subject to annulment in pursuance of a resolution of either House of Parliament.

(3) An order under this Act may make different provision in relation to different cases or classes of case, may exclude certain cases or classes of case, and may contain transitional provisions and savings.

(4) Any power conferred by this Act to make orders include power (exercisable in the like manner and subject to the like conditions) to vary or revoke any order so made.

(5) Any document purporting to be an order made by the Secretary of State under section 50(2)(a) and to be signed by him or on his behalf shall be received in evidence, and shall, unless the contrary is proved, be deemed to be made by him.

---

¹ Words added by Race Relations (Remedies) Act 1994 (c.10), s. 2(2).

Application to Crown, etc.

75.— (1) This Act applies—   **40–092**

- (a) to an act done by or for purposes of a Minister of the Crown or government department; or

(b) to an act done on behalf of the Crown by a statutory body, or a person holding a statutory office,

as it applies to an act done by a private person.

(2) Parts II and IV apply to—

(a) service for purposes of a Minister of the Crown or government department, other than service of a person holding a statutory office; or
(b) service on behalf of the Crown for purposes of a person holding a statutory office or purposes of a statutory body; or
(c) service in the armed forces,

as they apply to employment by a private person, and shall so apply as if references to a contract of employment included references to the terms of service.

[(2A) Subsections (1) and (2) do not apply in relation to the provisions mentioned in subsection (2B).

(2B) Sections 19B to 19F, sections 71 to 71E (including Schedule 1A) and section 76 bind the Crown; and the other provisions of this Act so far as they relate to those provisions shall be construed accordingly (including, in particular, references to employment in Part IV).][1]

(3) Subsections (1) [to (2B)][2] have effect subject to [sections 76A and 76B][3].

(4) Subsection (2) of section 8 and subsection (4) of section 27 shall have effect in relation to any ship, aircraft or hovercraft belonging to or possessed by Her Majesty in right of the Government of the United Kingdom as it has effect in relation to a ship, aircraft or hovercraft such as is mentioned in paragraph (a) or (b) of the subsection in question; and section 8(3) shall apply accordingly.

(5) Nothing in this Act shall—

(a) invalidate any rules (whether made before or after the passing of this Act) restricting employment in the service of the Crown or by any public body prescribed for the purposes of this subsection by regulations made by the Minister for the Civil Service to persons of particular birth, nationality, descent or residence; or
(b) render unlawful the publication, display or implementation of any such rules, or the publication of advertisements stating the gist of any such rules.

In this subsection "employment" includes service of any kind, and "public body" means a body of persons, whether corporate or unincorporate, carrying on a service or undertaking of a public nature.

(6) The provisions of Parts II to IV of the Crown Proceedings Act 1947 shall apply to proceedings against the Crown under this Act as they apply to proceedings in England and Wales which by virtue of section 23 of that Act are treated for the purposes of Part II of that Act as civil proceedings by or against the Crown, except that in their application to proceedings under this Act section 20 of that Act (removal of proceedings from county court to High Court) shall not apply.

(7) The provisions of Part V of the Crown Proceedings Act 1947 shall apply to proceedings against the Crown under this Act as they apply to proceedings in Scotland which by virtue of the said Part are treated as civil proceedings by or against the Crown, except that in their application to proceedings under this Act the proviso to section 44 of that Act (removal of proceedings from the sheriff court to the Court of Session) shall not apply.

(8) This subsection applies to any complaint by a person ("the complainant") that another person—

(a) has committed an act of discrimination against the complainant which is unlawful by virtue of section 4; or

(b) is by virtue of section 32 or 33 to be treated as having committed such an act of discrimination against the complainant;

if at the time when the act complained of was done the complainant was serving in the armed forces and the discrimination in question relates to his service in those forces.

[(9) No complaint to which subsection (8) applies shall be presented to an [employment tribunal] under section 54 unless—

(a) the complainant has made a complaint to an officer under the service redress procedures applicable to him and has submitted that complaint to the Defence Council under those procedures; and

(b) the Defence Council have made a determination with respect to the complaint.

(9A) Regulations may make provision enabling a complaint to which subsection (8) applies to be presented to an [employment tribunal] under section 54 in such circumstances as may be specified by the regulations, notwithstanding that subsection (9) would otherwise preclude the presentation of the complaint to an [employment tribunal].

(9B) Where a complaint is presented to an [employment tribunal] under section 54 by virtue of regulations under subsection (9A), the service redress procedures may continue after the complaint is so presented.]

(10) In this section—

(a) "the armed forces" means any of the naval, military or air forces of the Crown [. . .]⁴;

[(aa) "regulations" means regulations made by the Secretary of State;

(ab) "the service redress procedures" means the procedures, excluding those which relate to the making of a report on a complaint to Her Majesty, referred to in section 180 of the Army Act 1955, section 180 of the Air Force Act 1955 and section 130 of the Naval Discipline Act 1957;]⁵

(b) "statutory body" means a body set up by or in pursuance of an enactment, and "statutory office" means an office so set up; and

(c) "service" for purposes of a Minister of the Crown or government department does not include service in any office in Schedule 2 (Ministerial offices) to the House of Commons Disqualification Act 1975 as for the time being in force.

¹ Added by Race Relations (Amendment) Act 2000 (c.34), Sched. 2, para. 17.
² Words substituted by Race Relations (Amendment) Act 2000 (c.34), Sched. 2, para. 18(a).
³ Words substituted by Race Relations (Amendment) Act 2000 (c.34), Sched. 2, para. 18(b).
⁴ Words repealed with saving by Armed Forces Act 1981 (c.55), s. 28(2), Sched. 5, Pt. I, note.
⁵ Added by Armed Forces Act 1996 (c.46), s. 23(3).

Application to House of Commons staff

[75A.— (1) Parts II and IV apply to an act done by an employer of a relevant member of the House of Commons staff, and to service as such a member, as they apply to an act done by and to service for the purposes of a Minister of the Crown or government department, and accordingly apply as if references to a contract of employment included references to the terms of service of such a member.   **40–093**

(2) In this section "relevant member of the House of Commons staff" has the same meaning as in [section 195 of the Employment Rights Act 1996]; and

[subsections (6) to (12)] of that section (person to be treated as employer of House of Commons staff) apply, with any necessary modifications, for the purposes of Parts II and IV as they apply by virtue of this section.]

Application to House of Lords staff

40–094 [**75B.**— (1) Parts II and IV apply in relation to employment as a relevant member of the House of Lords staff as they apply in relation to other employment.

(2) In this section "relevant member of the House of Lords staff" has the same meaning as in [section 194 of the Employment Rights Act 1996] and [subsection (7)] of that section applies for the purposes of this section.]

Government appointments outside s. 4

40–095 **76.**— (1) [Subsection (2)]¹ applies to any appointment by a Minister of the Crown or government department to an office or post where section 4 does not apply in relation to the appointment.

(2) In making the appointment, and in making the arrangements for determining who should be offered the office or post, the Minister of the Crown or government department shall not do an act which would be unlawful under section 4 if the Crown were the employer for the purposes of this Act.

[(3) Subsection (5) applies to—

    (a) any recommendation made by a Minister of the Crown or government department in relation to an appointment to an office or post where section 4 does not apply in relation to the appointment; and

    (b) any approval given by such a Minister or department in relation to any such appointment.

(4) Subsection (5) also applies to—

    (a) any recommendation made by a Minister of the Crown or government department in relation to a conferment by the Crown of a dignity or honour; and

    (b) any approval given by such a Minister or department in relation to any such conferment.

(5) In making the recommendation, or giving the approval, and in making the arrangements for determining who should be recommended or approved, the Minister of the Crown or government department shall not do an act which would be unlawful under section 4 if the recommendation or approval were an offer of employment and the Crown were the employer for the purposes of this Act.

(6) Subsections (3) to (5) do not apply in relation to the making of negative recommendations.

(7) Subsection (9) applies to—

    (a) any negative recommendation made by a Minister of the Crown or government department, or any refusal to make a recommendation by such a Minister or department, in relation to an appointment to an office or post where section 4 does not apply in relation to the appointment; and

    (b) any approval refused by such a Minister or department in relation to any such appointment.

(8) Subsection (9) also applies to—

(a) any negative recommendation made by a Minister of the Crown or government department, or any refusal to make a recommendation by such a Minister or department, in relation to a conferment by the Crown of a dignity or honour; and
(b) any approval refused by such a Minister or department in relation to any such conferment.

(9) In making a negative recommendation or in refusing to make a recommendation or give an approval, and in making the arrangements for determining whether to make such a recommendation or refusal, the Minister of the Crown or government department shall not do an act which would be unlawful under section 4 if the recommendation or refusal were a refusal to offer the person concerned employment and the Crown were the employer for the purposes of this Act.

(10) Subsection (11) applies in relation to any appointment to an office or post where section 4 does not apply and—

(a) the appointment is made by a Minister of the Crown or government department; or
(b) the office or post is an office or post in relation to which a Minister of the Crown or government department has made a recommendation (other than a negative recommendation) or given an approval.

(11) A Minister of the Crown or government department shall not do an act in connection with—

(a) the terms of the appointment;
(b) access for the person appointed to opportunities for promotion, transfer or training, or to any other benefits, facilities or services; or
(c) the termination of the appointment, or subjecting the person appointed to any other detriment;

which would be unlawful under section 4 if the Crown were the employer for the purposes of this Act.

(12) The High Court may, on an application for judicial review, make a declaration to the effect that a Minister of the Crown or government department has contravened subsection (5), subsection (9) or, in relation to an appointment falling within subsection (10)(b), subsection (11), and may award damages in respect of the contravention.

(13) In Scotland, the Court of Session may, in a petition for judicial review, grant declarator to the like effect and may award damages in respect of the contravention.

(14) The sanctions provided by virtue of the operation of section 53(2) to (4) in relation to this section shall be the only sanctions under this Act in relation to appointments, conferments and other acts to which this section applies.

(15) In this section—

(a) references to refusal include references to deliberate omission;
(b) references to Ministers of the Crown and government departments include references to the National Assembly for Wales and any part of the Scottish Administration; and
(c) references to Ministers of the Crown and government departments so far as they relate to the making of a recommendation or a refusal to make a recommendation, or the giving or refusal of an approval, in relation to a conferment of a peerage for life under section 1 of the

Life Peerages Act 1958 include references to any body established by a Minister of the Crown to make such a recommendation to the Prime Minister or to determine whether to give such an approval.][2]

[1] Words substituted by Race Relations (Amendment) Act 2000 (c.34), s. 3(2).
[2] Added by Race Relations (Amendment) Act 2000 (c.34), s. 3(3).

Police

Police forces

40–096   [**76A.**— (1) In this section, "relevant police office" means—

(a) the office of constable held—

  (i) as a member of a police force; or
  (ii) on appointment as a special constable for a police area; or

(b) an appointment as police cadet to undergo training with a view to becoming a member of a police force.

(2) For the purposes of Part II, the holding of a relevant police office shall be treated as employment—

(a) by the chief officer of police as respects any act done by him in relation to that office or a holder of it;
(b) by the police authority as respects any act done by it in relation to that office or a holder of it.

(3) For the purposes of section 32—

(a) the holding of a relevant police office shall be treated as employment by the chief officer of police (and as not being employment by any other person); and
(b) anything done by a person holding such an office in the performance, or purported performance, of his functions shall be treated as done in the course of that employment.

(4) There shall be paid out of the police fund—

(a) any compensation, costs or expenses awarded against a chief officer of police in any proceedings brought against him under this Act, and any costs or expenses incurred by him in any such proceedings so far as not recovered by him in the proceedings; and
(b) any sum required by a chief officer of police for the settlement of any claim made against him under this Act if the settlement is approved by the police authority.

(5) Any proceedings under this Act which, by virtue of this section, would lie against a chief officer of police shall be brought against—

(a) the chief officer of police for the time being; or
(b) in the case of a vacancy in that office, against the person for the time being performing the functions of that office;

and references in subsection (4) to the chief officer of police shall be construed accordingly.

(6) A police authority may, in such cases and to such extent as appear to it to be appropriate, pay out of the police fund—

    (a) any damages or costs awarded in proceedings under this Act against a person under the direction and control of the chief officer of police;

    (b) any costs incurred and not recovered by such a person in such proceedings; and

    (c) any sum required in connection with the settlement of a claim that has or might have given rise to such proceedings.][1]

[1] Added by Race Relations (Amendment) Act 2000 (c.34), s. 4.

Other police bodies, etc.

[**76B.**— (1) Section 76A applies in relation to the National Criminal Intelligence Service ("NCIS") and the National Crime Squad ("the NCS") as it applies in relation to a police force but as if any reference—   **40–097**

    (a) to the chief officer of police were to the Director General of NCIS or of the NCS, as the case may be;

    (b) to the police authority were to the Service Authority for the National Criminal Intelligence Service or the Service Authority for the National Crime Squad, as the case may be;

    (c) to the police fund were to the service fund established under section 16 of the Police Act 1997 (NCIS service fund) or section 61 of that Act (the NCS service fund), as the case may be.

(2) Section 76A also applies in relation to any other body of constables or cadets as it applies in relation to a police force, but as if any reference—

    (a) to the chief officer of police were to the officer or other person who has the direction and control of the body in question;

    (b) to the police authority were to the authority by whom the members of the body are paid;

    (c) to the police fund were to money provided by that authority.

(3) In relation to a member of a police force or a special constable who is not under the direction and control of the chief officer of police for that police force or, as the case may be, for the police area to which he is appointed, references in section 76A to the chief officer of police are references to the chief officer under whose direction and control he is.][1]

[1] Added by Race Relations (Amendment) Act 2000 (c.34), s. 4.

Financial provisions

77. There shall be defrayed out of money provided by Parliament—   **40–098**

    (a) sums required by the Secretary of State for making payments under paragraph 5 or 16 of Schedule 1 or paragraph 12 of Schedule 2, and for defraying any other expenditure falling to be made by him under or by virtue of this Act;

    (b) any expenses incurred by the Secretary of State with the consent of the Treasury in undertaking, or financially assisting the undertaking by other persons of, research into any matter connected with relations between persons of different racial groups;

    (c) payments falling to be made under section 67(5) in respect of the remuneration of assessors; and

(d) any increase attributable to the provisions of this Act in the sums payable out of money provided by Parliament under any other Act.

[European Parliamentary Elections Act 1978][1]

(1978, c. 10)

41–001 *An Act to make provision for and in connection with the election of representatives to the [European Parliament], and to prevent any treaty providing for any increase in the powers of the [European Parliament] from being ratified by the United Kingdom unless approved by Act of Parliament.*

[5th May 1978]

[1] Short-title substituted by reason of the retrospective amendment of s. 9(1) of this Act by European Communities (Amendment) Act 1986 (c.58), s. 3(1)(b), (2)(b), (3).

Election of MEPs

41–002 [**1.** This Act makes provision for the election in the United Kingdom of Members of the European Parliament ("MEPs").][1]

[1] s.1 to s.3D substituted for ss.1 to 3 by European Parliamentary Elections Act 1999 (c.1), s. 1.

Electoral regions and number of MEPs

41–003 [**2.**—(1) The United Kingdom shall be divided into electoral regions.

(2) England shall be divided into nine electoral regions.

(3) Scotland, Wales and Northern Ireland shall each constitute a single electoral region.

(4) The number of MEPs elected in the United Kingdom shall be 87, of whom—

(a) 71 shall be elected for electoral regions in England;
(b) 8 shall be elected for Scotland;
(c) 5 shall be elected for Wales; and
(d) 3 shall be elected for Northern Ireland.

(5) Schedule 2 (which sets out the electoral regions in England and makes provision for the number of MEPs to be elected for each region) shall have effect.]

Electoral system in Great Britain

41–004 [**3.**—(1) The system of election in an electoral region in Great Britain shall be a regional list system complying with the following conditions.

(2) A vote may be cast for a registered party, or an individual candidate, named on the ballot paper.

(3) The first seat shall be allocated to the party or individual candidate with the greatest number of votes.

(4) The second and subsequent seats shall be allocated in the same way, except that the number of votes given to a party to which one or more seats have already been allocated shall be divided by the number of seats allocated plus one.

(5) In allocating the second or any subsequent seat there shall be disregarded any votes given to—

(a) a party to which there has already been allocated a number of seats equal to the number of names on the party's list of candidates, and
(b) an individual candidate to whom a seat has already been allocated.

(6) Seats allocated to a party shall be filed by the persons named on the party's list of candidates in the order in which they appear on that list.

(7) For the purposes of subsections (3) and (4) fractions shall be taken into account.

(8) In this section—

(a) "registered party" means [a party registered under Part II of the Political Parties, Elections and Referendums Act 2000][1];
(b) a reference to a party's "list of candidates" is a reference to the list submitted in accordance with regulations made as required by paragraph 2(3B) of Schedule 1.]

---

[1] Words substituted by Political Parties, Elections and Referendums Act 2000 (c.41), Sched. 21, para. 5(2).

Electoral system in Northern Ireland

[**3A.** The system of election in Northern Ireland shall be a single transferable vote system under which—   **41–005**

(a) a vote is capable of being given so as to indicate the voter's order of preference for the candidates, and
(b) a vote is capable of being transferred to the next choice—

(i) when the vote is not required to give a prior choice the necessary quota of votes, or
(ii) when, owing to the deficiency in the number of votes given for a prior choice, that choice is eliminated from the list of candidates.]

Electoral system supplementary

[**3B.** Schedule 1 (which makes supplementary provision about the holding of elections, the filling of vacancies, and disqualification) shall have effect.]   **41–006**

. . . . . .

Parliamentary approval of treaties increasing Assembly's powers

6.—(1) No treaty which provides for any increase in the powers of the [European Parliament] shall be ratified by the United Kingdom unless it has been approved by an Act of Parliament.   **41–007**

(2) In this section "treaty" includes any international agreement, and any protocol or annex to a treaty or international agreement.

Expenses

41–008   **7.**—(1) There shall be charged on, and paid out of, the Consolidated Fund—

[(a) charges to which persons on whom functions are conferred by regulations made by virtue of paragraph 4(2) of Schedule 1 are entitled by virtue of regulations under this Act, and

(aa) any sums required by the Secretary of State for expenditure on the provision of training relating to functions conferred by regulations made by virtue of paragraph 4(2) of Schedule 1;][1]

(b) any increase attributable to this Act in the sums charged on and payable out of that Fund under any other enactment.

(2) There shall be paid out of money provided by Parliament—

(a) any additional sums payable by way of rate support grant because of an increase attributable to this Act in the registration expenses of registration officers in Great Britain;

(b) any increase so attributable in the sums payable out of money so provided under [section 54(2) of the Representation of the People Act 1983] on account of the registration expenses of registration officers in Northern Ireland; and

(c) any increase so attributable in the sums payable out of money so provided under the House of Commons (Redistribution of Seats) Act 1949.

[1] subss. (a) and (aa) substituted for s.7(1)(a) by European Parliamentary Elections Act 1999 (c.1), s. 4.

Customs and Excise Management Act 1979

(1971, c. 2)

42–001   *An Act to consolidate the enactments relating to the collection and management of the revenues of customs and excise and in some cases to other matters in relation to which the Commissioners of Customs and Excise for the time being perform functions, with amendments to give effect to recommendations of the Law Commission and the Scottish Law Commission.*

[22nd February 1979]

. . . . . .

Power to search persons

42–002   **164.**—(1) Where there are reasonable grounds to suspect that any person to whom this section applies [(referred to in this section as "the suspect")] is carrying any article—

(a) which is chargeable with any duty which has not been paid or secured; or

(b) with respect to the importation or exportation of which any prohibition or restriction is for the time being in force under or by virtue of any enactment.

[an officer may exercise the powers conferred by subsection (2) below and, if the suspect is not under arrest, may detain him for so long as may be necessary for the exercise of those powers and (where applicable) the exercise of the rights conferred by subsection (3) below].

[(2) The officer may require the suspect—

(a) to permit such a search of any article which he has with him; and
(b) subject to subsection (3) below, to submit to such searches of his person, whether rub-down, strip or intimate,

as the officer may consider necessary or expedient; but no such requirement may be imposed under paragraph (b) above without the officer informing the suspect of the effect of subsection (3) below.

(3) If the suspect is required to submit to a search of his person, he may require to be taken—

(a) except in the case of a rub-down search, before a justice of the peace or a superior of the officer concerned; and
(b) in the excepted case, before such a superior;

and the justice or superior shall consider the grounds for suspicion and direct accordingly whether the suspect is to submit to the search.

(3A) A rub-down or strip search shall not be carried out except by a person of the same sex as the suspect; and an intimate search shall not be carried out except by a suitably qualified person.]

(4) This section applies to the following persons, namely—

(a) any person who is on board or has landed from any ship or aircraft;
(b) any person entering or about to leave the United Kingdom;
(c) any person within the dock area of a port;
(d) any person at a customs and excise airport;
(e) any person in, entering or leaving any approved wharf or transit shed which is not in a port;
[(f) any person in, entering or leaving a free zone;]
(g) in Northern Ireland, any person travelling from or to any place which is on or beyond the boundary.

[(5) In this section—

"intimate search" means any search which involves a physical examination (that is, an examination which is more than simply a visual examination) of a person's body orifices;

"rub-down search" means any search which is neither an intimate search nor a strip search;

"strip search" means any search which is not an intimate search but which involves the removal of an article of clothing which—

(a) is being worn (wholly or partly) on the trunk; and
(b) is being so worn either next to the skin or next to an article of underwear;
"suitably qualified person" means a registered medical practitioner or a registered nurse.

(6) Notwithstanding anything in subsection (4) of section 48 of the Criminal Justice (Scotland) Act 1987 (detention and questioning by customs officers),

detention of the suspect under subsection (1) above shall not prevent his subsequent detention under subsection (1) of that section.]

Highways Act 1980

(1980, c. 66)

43–001 *An Act to consolidate the Highways Acts 1959 to 1971 and related enactments, with amendments to give effect to recommendations of the Law Commission.* [13th November 1980]

. . . . . .

PART IX

LAWFUL AND UNLAWFUL INTERFERENCE WITH HIGHWAYS AND STREETS

Obstruction of highways and streets

Penalty for wilful obstruction

43–002   137.—(1) If a person, without lawful authority or excuse, in any way wilfully obstructs the free passage along a highway he is guilty of an offence and liable to a fine not exceeding [level 3 on the standard scale][1].

[1] Words substituted by Criminal Justice Act 1982 (c.48), ss. 38, 46.

Magistrates' Courts Act 1980

(1980, c. 43)

44–001 *An Act to consolidate certain enactments relating to the jurisdiction of, and the practice and procedure before, magistrates' courts and the functions of justices' clerks, and to matters connected therewith, with amendments to give effect to recommendations of the Law Commission.* [1st August 1980]

PART I

CRIMINAL JURISDICTION AND PROCEDURE

Jurisdiction to issue process and deal with charges

Issue of summons to accused or warrant for his arrest

44–002   1.—(1) Upon an information being laid before a justice of the peace for an area to which this section applies that any person has, or is suspected of having, committed an offence, the justice may, in any of the events mentioned in subsection (2) below, but subject to subsections (3) to (5) below—

(a) issue a summons directed to that person requiring him to appear before a magistrates' court for the area to answer to the information, or

(b) issue a warrant to arrest that person and bring him before a magistrates' court for the area or such magistrates' court as is provided in subsection (5) below.

(2) A justice of the peace for an area to which this section applies may issue a summons or warrant under this section—

(a) if the offence was committed or is suspected to have been committed within the area; or

(b) if it appears to the justice necessary or expedient, with a view to the better administration of justice, that the person charged should be tried jointly with, or in the same place as, some other person who is charged with an offence, and who is in custody, or is being or is to be proceeded against, within the area; or

(c) if the person charged resides or is, or is believed to reside or be, within the area; or

(d) if under any enactment a magistrates' court for the area has jurisdiction to try the offence; or

(e) if the offence was committed outside England and Wales and, where it is an offence exclusively punishable on summary conviction, if a magistrates' court for the area would have jurisdiction to try the offence if the offender were before it.

(3) No warrant shall be issued under this section unless the information is in writing and substantiated on oath.

(4) No warrant shall be issued under this section for the arrest of any person who has attained [the age of 18 years] unless—

(a) the offence to which the warrant relates is an indictable offence or is punishable with imprisonment, or

(b) the person's address is not sufficiently established for a summons to be served on him.

(5) Where the offence charged is not an indictable offence—

(a) no summons shall be issued by virtue only of paragraph (c) of subsection (2) above, and

(b) any warrant issued by virtue only of that paragraph shall require the person charged to be brought before a magistrates' court having jurisdiction to try the offence.

(6) Where the offence charged is an indictable offence, a warrant under this section may be issued at any time notwithstanding that a summons has previously been issued.

(7) A justice of the peace may issue a summons or warrant under this section upon an information being laid before him notwithstanding any enactment requiring the information to be laid before two or more justices.

(8) The areas to which this section applies are [commission areas].

. . . . . .

Discharge or committal for trial

44–003   **6.**—[(1) A magistrates' court inquiring into an offence as examining justices shall on consideration of the evidence—

    (a) commit the accused for trial if it is of opinion that there is sufficient evidence to put him on trial by jury for any indictable offence;

    (b) discharge him if it is not of that opinion and he is in custody for no other cause than the offence under inquiry;

but the preceding provisions of this subsection have effect subject to the provisions of this and any other Act relating to the summary trial of indictable offences.

(2) If a magistrates' court inquiring into an offence as examining justices is satisfied that all the evidence tendered by or on behalf of the prosecutor falls within section 5A(3) above, it may commit the accused for trial for the offence without consideration of the contents of any statements, depositions or other documents, and without consideration of any exhibits which are not documents, unless—

    (a) the accused or one of the accused has no legal representative acting for him in the case, or

    (b) a legal representative for the accused or one of the accused, as the case may be, has requested the court to consider a submission that there is insufficient evidence to put that accused on trial by jury for the offence;

and subsection (1) above shall not apply to a committal for trial under this subsection.]

(3) Subject to section 4 of the Bail Act 1976 and section 41 below, the court may commit a person for trial—

    (a) in custody, that is to say, by committing him to custody there to be safety kept until delivered in due course of law, or

    (b) on bail in accordance with the Bail Act 1976, that is to say, by directing him to appear before the Crown Court for trial;

and where his release on bail is conditional on his providing one or more surety or sureties and, in accordance with section 8(3) of the Bail Act 1976, the court fixes the amount in which the surety is to be bound with a view to his entering into his recognizance subsequently in accordance with subsections (4) and (5) or (6) of that section the court shall in the meantime commit the accused to custody in accordance with paragraph (a) of this subsection.

(4) Where the court has committed a person to custody in accordance with paragraph (a) of subsection (3) above, then, if that person is in custody for no other cause, the court may, at any time before his first appearance before the Crown Court, grant him bail in accordance with the Bail Act 1976 subject to a duty to appear before the Crown Court for trial.

(5) Where a magistrates' court acting as examining justices commits any person for trial or determines to discharge him, the [justices' chief executive for] the court shall, on the day on which the committal proceedings are concluded or the next day, cause to be displayed in a part of the court house to which the public have access a notice—

    (a) in either case giving that person's name, address, and age (if known);

    (b) in a case where the court so commits him, stating the charge or charges on which he is committed and the court to which he is committed;

(c) in a case where the court determines to discharge him, describing the offence charged and stating that it has so determined;

but this subsection shall have effect subject to [section 4 of the Sexual Offences (Amendment) Act 1976 (anonymity of complainant in rape etc. cases)].

(6) A notice displayed in pursuance of subsection (5) above shall not contain the name or address of any person under [the age of 18 years] unless the justices in question have stated that in their opinion he would be mentioned in the notice apart from the preceding provisions of this subsection and should be mentioned in it for the purpose of avoiding injustice to him.

. . . . . .

Bail on arrest

[**43.**—(1) Where a person has been granted bail under [Part IV of] the Police and Criminal Evidence Act 1984 subject to a duty to appear before a magistrates' court, the court before which he is to appear may appoint a later time as the time at which he is to appear and may enlarge the recognizances of any sureties for him at that time.

(2) The recognizance of any surety for any person granted bail subject to a duty to attend at a police station may be enforced as if it were conditioned for his appearance before a magistrates' court for the petty sessions area in which the police station named in the recognizance is situated.]

44–004

. . . . . .

PART VI

RECOGNIZANCES

Recognizances to keep the peace or be of good behaviour

Binding over to keep the peace or be of good behaviour

115.—(1) The power of a magistrates' court on the complaint of any person to adjudge any other person to enter into a recognizance, with or without sureties, to keep the peace or to be of good behaviour towards the complainant shall be exercised by order on complaint.

(2) Where a complaint is made under this section, the power of the court to remand the defendant under subsection (5) of section 55 above shall not be subject to the restrictions imposed by subsection (6) of that section.

(3) If any person ordered by a magistrates' court under subsection (1) above to enter into a recognizance, with or without sureties, to keep the peace or to be of good behaviour fails to comply with the order, the court may commit him to custody for a period not exceeding 6 months or until he sooner complies with the order.

44–005

. . . . . .

Remand

Remand in custody or on bail

44–006   128.—(1) Where a magistrates' court has power to remand any person, then, subject to section 4 of the Bail Act 1976 and to any other enactment modifying that power, the court may—

> (a) remand him in custody, that is to say, commit him to custody to be brought before the court, [subject to subsection (3A) below,] at the end of the period of remand or at such earlier time as the court may require; or
>
> (b) where it is inquiring into or trying an offence alleged to have been committed by that person or has convicted him of an offence, remand him on bail in accordance with the Bail Act 1976, that is to say, by directing him to appear as provided in subsection (4) below; or
>
> (c) except in a case falling within paragraph (b) above, remand him on bail by taking from him a recognizance (with or without sureties) conditioned as provided in that subsection;

and may, in a case falling within paragraph (c) above, instead of taking recognizances in accordance with that paragraph, fix the amount of the recognizances with a view to their being taken subsequently in accordance with section 119 above.

[(1A) Where—

> (a) on adjourning a case under [section 5, 10(1), 17C, or 18(4)]¹ above the court proposes to remand or further remand a person in custody; and
>
> (b) he is before the court; and
>
> (c) [. . .]²
>
> (d) he is legally represented in that court,

it shall be the duty of the court—

> (i) to explain the effect of subsections (3A) and (3B) below to him in ordinary language; and
>
> (ii) to inform him in ordinary language that, notwithstanding the procedure for a remand without his being brought before a court, he would be brought before a court for the hearing and determination of at least every fourth application for his remand, and of every application for his remand heard at a time when it appeared to the court that he had no [legal representative] acting for him in the case.

(1B) For the purposes of subsection (1A) above a person is to be treated as legally represented in a court if, but only if, he has the assistance of [a legal representative] to represent him in the proceedings in that court.

(1C) After explaining to an accused as provided by subsection (1A) above the court shall ask him whether he consents to hearing and determination of such applications in his absence.]³

(2) Where the court fixes the amount of a recognizance under subsection (1) above or section 8(3) of the Bail Act 1976 with a view to its being taken subsequently the court shall in the meantime commit the person so remanded to custody in accordance with paragraph (a) of the said subsection (1).

(3) Where a person is brought before the court after remand, the court may further remand him.

[(3A) Subject to subsection (3B) below, where a person has been remanded in custody [and the remand was not a remand under section 128A below for a period exceeding 8 clear days,], the court may further remand him [(otherwise than in the exercise of the power conferred by that section)] on an adjournment under [section 5, 10(1), 17C or 18(4)]⁴ above without his being brought before it, if it is satisfied—

(a) that he gave his consent, either in response to a question under subsection (1C) above or otherwise, to the hearing and determination in his absence of any application for his remand on an adjournment of the case under any of those provisions; and

(b) that he has not by virtue of this subsection been remanded without being brought before the court on more than two such applications immediately preceding the application which the court is hearing; and

(c) [. . .]⁵

(d) that he has not withdrawn his consent to their being so heard and determined.

(3B) The court may not exercise the power conferred by subsection (3A) above if it appears to the court, on an application for a further remand being made to it, that the person to whom the application relates has no [legal representative] acting for him in the case (whether present in court or not).

(3C) Where—

(a) a person has been remanded in custody on an adjournment of a case under [section 5, 10(1), 17C or 18(4)]⁶ above; and

(b) an application is subsequently made for his further remand on such an adjournment; and

(c) he is not brought before the court which hears and determines the application; and

(d) that court is not satisfied as mentioned in subsection (3A) above, the court shall adjourn the case and remand him in custody for the period for which it stands adjourned.

(3D) An adjournment under subsection (3C) above shall be for the shortest period that appears to the court to make it possible for the accused to be brought before it.

(3E) Where—

(a) on an adjournment of a case under section 5, 10(1) [, 17C]⁷ or 18(4) above a person has been remanded in custody without being brought before the court; and

(b) it subsequently appears—

(i) to the court which remanded him in custody; or

(ii) to an alternate magistrates' court to which he is remanded under section 130 below,

that he ought not to have been remanded in custody in his absence, the court shall require him to be brought before it at the earliest time that appears to the court to be possible.]⁸

(4) Where a person is remanded on bail under subsection (1) above the court may, where it remands him on bail in accordance with the Bail Act 1976 direct him to appear or, in any other case, direct that his recognizance be conditioned for his appearance—

(a) before that court at the end of the period of remand; or

(b) at every time and place to which during the course of the proceedings the hearing may be from time to time adjourned;

and, where it remands him on bail conditionally on his providing a surety during an inquiry into an offence alleged to have been committed by him, may direct that the recognizance of the surety be conditioned to secure that the person so bailed appears—

  (c) at every time and place to which during the course of the proceedings the hearing may be from time to time adjourned and also before the Crown Court in the event of the person so bailed being committed for trial there.

   (5) Where a person is directed to appear or a recognizance is conditioned for a person's appearance in accordance with paragraph (b) or (c) of subsection (4) above, the fixing at any time of the time for him next to appear shall be deemed to be a remand; but nothing in this subsection or subsection (4) above shall deprive the court of power at any subsequent hearing to remand him afresh.

   (6) Subject to the provisions of [sections 128A and] 129 below, a magistrates' court shall not remand a person for a period exceeding 8 clear days, except that—

  (a) if the court remands him on bail, it may remand him for a longer period if he and the other party consent;
  (b) where the court adjourns a trial under [section 10(3) above or section 11 of the Powers of Criminal Courts (Sentencing) Act 2000], the court may remand him for the period of the adjournment;
  (c) where a person is charged with an offence triable either way, then, if it falls to the court to try the case summarily but the court is not at the time so constituted, and sitting in such a place, as will enable it to proceed with the trial, the court may remand him until the next occasion on which it will be practicable for the court to be so constituted, and to sit in such a place, as aforesaid, notwithstanding that the remand is for a period exceeding 8 clear days.

   (7) A magistrates' court having power to remand a person in custody may, if the remand is for a period not exceeding 3 clear days, commit him to [detention at a police station].

   [(8) Where a person is committed to detention at a police station under subsection (7) above—

  (a) he shall not be kept in such detention unless there is a need for him to be so detained for the purposes of inquiries into other offences;
  (b) if kept in such detention, he shall be brought back before the magistrates' court which committed him as soon as that need ceases;
  (c) he shall be treated as a person in police detention to whom the duties under section 39 of the Police and Criminal Evidence Act 1984 (responsibilities in relation to persons detained) relate;
  (d) his detention shall be subject to periodic review at the times set out in section 40 of that Act (review of police detention).][9]

---

[1] Words added; s. 49 applies where a person appears or is brought before a magistrates' court on or after the appointed day, unless he has appeared or been brought before such a court in respect of by Criminal Procedure and Investigations Act 1996 (c.26), Pt VI, s.49(5)(a).

[2] s.52(1) applies where the offence with which the person concerned is charged is alleged to be committed on or after the appointed day by Criminal Procedure and Investigations Act 1996 (c.25), Pt VI, s.52(1).

[3] s.128(1A)-(1C) inserted by Criminal Justice Act 1982 (c.48), s.59(1), Sched. 9, para. 3.

[4] Words added; s. 49 applies where a person appears or is brought before a magistrates' court on or after the appointed day, unless he has appeared or been brought before such a court in respect of by Criminal Procedure and Investigations Act 1996 (c.26), Pt VI, s.49(5)(a).

[5] s.52(1) applies where the offence with which the person concerned is charged is alleged to be

committed on or after the appointed day by Criminal Procedure and Investigations Act 1996 (c.25), Pt VI, s.52(1).

[6] Words added; s. 49 applies where a person appears or is brought before a magistrates' court on or after the appointed day, unless he has appeared or been brought before such a court in respect of by Criminal Procedure and Investigations Act 1996 (c.26), Pt VI, s.49(5)(a).

[7] *ibid.*

[8] s. 128(3A)-(3E) inserted by Criminal Justice Act 1982 (c.48), s. 59(1), Sched. 9, para. 4.

[9] s. 128(8) inserted by Police and Criminal Evidence Act 1984 (c.60), ss. 48(b), 51, 52.

British Nationality Act 1981

(1981, c. 61)

An Act to make fresh provision about citizenship and nationality, and to amend the Immigration Act 1971 as regards the right of abode in the United Kingdom.   [30th October 1981]   **45–001**

PART I

BRITISH CITIZENSHIP

Acquisition after commencement

Acquisition by birth or adoption

1.—(1) A person born in the United Kingdom after commencement shall be a British citizen if at the time of the birth his father or mother is—   **45–002**

   (a) a British citizen; or
   (b) settled in the United Kingdom.

(2) A new-born infant who, after commencement, is found abandoned in the United Kingdom shall, unless the contrary is shown, be deemed for the purposes of subsection (1)—

   (a) to have been born in the United Kingdom after commencement; and
   (b) to have been born to a parent who at the time of the birth was a British citizen or settled in the United Kingdom.

(3) A person born in the United Kingdom after commencement who is not a British citizen by virtue of subsection (1) or (2) shall be entitled to be registered as a British citizen if, while he is a minor—

   (a) his father or mother becomes a British citizen or becomes settled in the United Kingdom; and
   (b) an application is made for his registration as a British citizen.

(4) A person born in the United Kingdom after commencement who is not a British citizen by virtue of subsection (1) or (2) shall be entitled, on an application for his registration as a British citizen made at any time after he has attained the age of ten years, to be registered as such a citizen if, as regards each of the first ten years of that person's life, the number of days on which he was absent from the United Kingdom in that year does not exceed 90.

(5) Where after commencement an order authorising the adoption of a minor who is not a British citizen is made by any court in the United Kingdom, he shall be a British citizen as from the date on which the order is made if the adopter or, in the case of a joint adoption, one of the adopters is a British citizen on that date.

(6) Where an order in consequence of which any person became a British citizen by virtue of subsection (5) ceases to have effect, whether on annulment or otherwise, the cesser shall not affect the status of that person as a British citizen.

(7) If in the special circumstances of any particular case the Secretary of State thinks fit, he may for the purposes of subsection (4) treat the person to whom the application relates as fulfilling the requirement specified in that subsection although, as regards any one or more of the first ten years of that person's life, the number of days on which he was absent from the United Kingdom in that year or each of the years in question exceeds 90.

(8) In this section and elsewhere in this Act "settled" has the meaning given by section 50.

Acquisition by descent

45–003   **2.**—(1) A person born outside the United Kingdom after commencement shall be a British citizen if at the time of the birth his father or mother—

(a) is a British citizen otherwise than by descent; or
(b) is a British citizen and is serving outside the United Kingdom in service to which this paragraph applies, his or her recruitment for that service having taken place in the United Kingdom; or
(c) is a British citizen and is serving outside the United Kingdom in service under a Community institution, his or her recruitment for that service having taken place in a country which at the time of the recruitment was a member of the Communities.

(2) Paragraph (b) of subsection (1) applies to—

(a) Crown service under the government of the United Kingdom; and
(b) service of any description for the time being designated under subsection (3).

(3) For the purposes of this section the Secretary of State may by order made by statutory instrument designate any description of service which he considers to be closely associated with the activities outside the United Kingdom of Her Majesty's government in the United Kingdom.

(4) Any order made under subsection (3) shall be subject to annulment in pursuance of a resolution of either House of Parliament.

Acquisition by registration: minors

45–004   **3.**—(1) If while a person is a minor an application is made for his registration as a British citizen, the Secretary of State may, if he thinks fit, cause him to be registered as such a citizen.

(2) A person born outside the United Kingdom shall be entitled, on an application for his registration as a British citizen made within the period of twelve months from the date of birth, to be registered as such a citizen if the requirements specified in subsection (3) or, in the case of a person born stateless, the requirements specified in paragraphs (a) and (b) of that subsection, are fulfilled in the case of either that person's father or his mother ("the parent in question").

(3) The requirements referred to in subsection (2) are—

(a) that the parent in question was a British citizen by descent at the time of the birth; and

(b) that the father or mother of the parent in question—

(i) was a British citizen otherwise than by descent at the time of the birth of the parent in question; or

(ii) became a British citizen otherwise than by descent at commencement, or would have become such a citizen otherwise than by descent at commencement but for his or her death; and

(c) that, as regards some period of three years ending with a date not later than the date of the birth—

(i) the parent in question was in the United Kingdom at the beginning of that period; and

(ii) the number of days on which the parent in question was absent from the United Kingdom in that period does not exceed 270.

(4) If in the special circumstances of any particular case the Secretary of State thinks fit, he may treat subsection (2) as if the reference to twelve months were a reference to six years.

(5) A person born outside the United Kingdom shall be entitled, on an application for his registration as a British citizen made while he is a minor, to be registered as such a citizen if the following requirements are satisfied, namely—

(a) that at the time of that person's birth his father or mother was a British citizen by descent; and

(b) subject to subsection (6), that that person and his father and mother were in the United Kingdom at the beginning of the period of three years ending with the date of the application and that, in the case of each of them, the number of days on which the person in question was absent from the United Kingdom in that period does not exceed 270; and

(c) subject to subsection (6), that the consent of his father and mother to the registration has been signified in the prescribed manner.

(6) In the case of an application under subsection (5) for the registration of a person as a British citizen—

(a) if his father or mother died, or their marriage was terminated, on or before the date of the application, or his father and mother were legally separated on that date, the references to his father and mother in paragraph (b) of that subsection shall be read either as references to his father or as references to his mother;

(b) if his father or mother died on or before that date, the reference to his father and mother in paragraph (c) of that subsection shall be read as a reference to either of them; and

(c) if he was born illegitimate, all those references shall be read as references to his mother.

Acquisition by registration: [British Overseas Territories Citizens][1] etc.

4.—(1) This section applies to any person who is a [British overseas territories citizen][2], [a British National (Overseas),] a British Overseas citizen, a British subject under this Act or a British protected person.   **45–005**

(2) A person to whom this section applies shall be entitled, on an application for his registration as a British citizen, to be registered as such a citizen if the following requirements are satisfied in the case of that person, namely—

(a) subject to subsection (3), that he was in the United Kingdom at the beginning of the period of five years ending with the date of the application and that the number of days on which he was absent from the United Kingdom in that period does not exceed 450; and

(b) that the number of days on which he was absent from the United Kingdom in the period of twelve months so ending does not exceed 90; and

(c) that he was not at any time in the period of twelve months so ending subject under the immigration laws to any restriction on the period for which he might remain in the United Kingdom; and

(d) that he was not at any time in the period of five years so ending in the United Kingdom in breach of the immigration laws.

(3) So much of subsection (2)(a) as requires the person in question to have been in the United Kingdom at the beginning of the period there mentioned shall not apply in relation to a person who was settled in the United Kingdom immediately before commencement.

(4) If in the special circumstances of any particular case the Secretary of State thinks fit, he may for the purposes of subsection (2) do all or any of the following things, namely—

(a) treat the person to whom the application relates as fulfilling the requirement specified in subsection (2)(a) or subsection (2)(b), or both, although the number of days on which he was absent from the United Kingdom in the period there mentioned exceeds the number there mentioned;

(b) disregard any such restriction as is mentioned in subsection (2)(c), not being a restriction to which that person was subject on the date of the application;

(c) treat that person as fulfilling the requirement specified in subsection (2)(d) although he was in the United Kingdom in breach of the immigration laws in the period there mentioned.

(5) If, on an application for registration as a British citizen made by a person to whom this section applies, the Secretary of State is satisfied that the applicant has at any time served in service to which this subsection applies, he may, if he thinks fit in the special circumstances of the applicant's case, cause him to be registered as such a citizen.

(6) Subsection (5) applies to—

(a) Crown service under the government of a [British overseas territory][3]; and

(b) paid or unpaid service (not falling within paragraph (a)) as a member of any body established by law in a [British overseas territory][4] members of which are appointed by or on behalf of the Crown.

---

[1] Words substituted by British Overseas Territories Act 2002 (c.8), s. 2(2).
[2] *ibid.*
[3] Words substituted by British Overseas Territories Act 2002 (c.8), s. 1(1)(b).
[4] *ibid.*

Acquisition by registration: nationals for purposes of the Community Treaties

45–006   5. A [British overseas territories citizen][1] who falls to be treated as a national of the United Kingdom for the purposes of the Community Treaties shall be entitled to be registered as a British citizen if an application is made for his registration as such a citizen.

¹ Words substituted by British Overseas Territories Act 2002 (c.8), s. 2(2).

Acquisition by naturalisation

6.—(1) If, on an application for naturalisation as a British citizen made by a person of full age and capacity, the Secretary of State is satisfied that the applicant fulfils the requirements of Schedule 1 for naturalisation as such a citizen under this subsection, he may, if he thinks fit, grant to him a certificate of naturalisation as such a citizen.

45–007

(2) If, on an application for naturalisation as a British citizen made by a person of full age and capacity who on the date of the application is married to a British citizen, the Secretary of State is satisfied that the applicant fulfils the requirements of Schedule 1 for naturalisation as such a citizen under this subsection, he may, if he thinks fit, grant to him a certificate of naturalisation as such a citizen.

Acquisition after commencement: special cases

Right to registration by virtue of residence in U.K. or relevant employment

7.—(1) A person shall be entitled, on an application for his registration as a British citizen made (subject to subsections (6) and (7)) within five years after commencement, to be registered as such a citizen if either of the following requirements is satisfied in his case, namely—

45–008

(a) that, if paragraphs 2 and 3 (but not paragraph 4 or 5) of Schedule 1 to the Immigration Act 1971 had remained in force, he would (had he applied for it) have been, on the date of the application under this subsection, entitled under the said paragraph 2 to be registered in the United Kingdom as a citizen of the United Kingdom and Colonies; or

(b) that, if section 5A of the 1948 Act (and section 2 of the Immigration Act 1971 as in force immediately before commencement) had remained in force, he would (had he applied for it) have been, both at commencement and on the date of the application under this subsection, entitled under section 5A(1) of the 1948 Act to be registered as a citizen of the United Kingdom and Colonies.

(2) A person shall be entitled, on an application for his registration as a British citizen made (subject to subsection (8)) within six years after commencement, to be registered as such a citizen if he—

(a) was ordinarily resident in the United Kingdom throughout a period ending at commencement but not amounting to five years; and

(b) throughout the period from commencement to the date of the application—

(i) remained ordinarily resident in the United Kingdom; and

(ii) had the right of abode in the United Kingdom under the Immigration Act 1971; and

(c) had on the date of the application been ordinarily resident in the United Kingdom for the last five years or more.

(3) Subject to subsection (5), if, in the case of an application for the registra-

tion of a person under subsection (2) as a British citizen, that person has been engaged in relevant service throughout any period (of whatever length), that period shall for the purposes of subsection (2) be treated as a period throughout which he was ordinarily resident in the United Kingdom.

(4) For the purposes of subsection (3) "relevant service" means —

(a) Crown service under the government of the United Kingdom; or
(b) service under any international organisation of which the United Kingdom or Her Majesty's government therein is a member; or
(c) service in the employment of any company or association established in the United Kingdom.

(5) A person shall not be registered under subsection (2) wholly or partly by reason of service within subsection (4)(b) or (c) unless it seems to the Secretary of State fitting that he should be so registered by reason of his close connection with the United Kingdom.

(6) If in the special circumstances of any particular case the Secretary of State thinks fit, he may treat subsection (1) as if—

(a) the reference to five years after commencement were a reference to eight years after commencement; or
(b) where subsection (7) applies, as if the reference to five years from the date on which the person to whom the application relates attains full age were a reference to eight years from that date,

but shall not do so in the case of an application based on paragraph (b) of subsection (1) unless the person to whom the application relates would have been entitled to be registered under that subsection on an application so based made immediately before the end of the five years after commencement.

(7) In the case of any person who is a minor at commencement, the reference to five years after commencement in subsection (1) above shall be treated as a reference to five years from the date on which he attains full age.

(8) If in the special circumstances of any particular case the Secretary of State thinks fit, he may treat subsection (2) as if the reference to six years after commencement were a reference to eight years after commencement.

Registration by virtue of marriage

45–009   **8.**—(1) A woman who immediately before commencement was the wife of a citizen of the United Kingdom and Colonies shall be entitled, on an application for her registration as a British citizen made within five years after commencement, to be registered as a British citizen if—

(a) immediately before commencement she would (if she had applied for it) have been entitled under section 6(2) of the 1948 Act to be registered as a citizen of the United Kingdom and Colonies by virtue of her marriage to the man who was then her husband; and
(b) that man became a British citizen at commencement and did not at any time in the period from commencement to the date of the application under this subsection cease to be such a citizen as a result of a declaration of renunciation; and
(c) she remained married to him throughout that period.

(2) On an application for her registration as a British citizen made within five years after commencement, the Secretary of State may, if he thinks fit, cause a woman to be registered as such a citizen if—

(a) immediately before commencement she would (if she had applied for it) have been entitled under section 6(2) of the 1948 Act to be registered as a citizen of the United Kingdom and Colonies by virtue of having been married to a man to whom she is no longer married on the date of the application under this subsection; and

(b) that man became a British citizen at commencement or would have done so but for his death.

(3) On an application for her registration as a British citizen made within five years after commencement by a woman who at the time of the application is married, the Secretary of State may, if he thinks fit, cause her to be registered as such a citizen if—

(a) immediately before commencement she would (if she had applied for it) have been entitled under section 6(2) of the 1948 Act to be registered as a citizen of the United Kingdom and Colonies by virtue of her being or having been married to the man who is her husband on the date of the application under this subsection; and

(b) that man either—

  (i) became a British citizen at commencement but has ceased to be such a citizen as a result of a declaration of renunciation; or

  (ii) would have become a British citizen at commencement but for his having ceased to be a citizen of the United Kingdom and Colonies as a result of a declaration of renunciation.

Right to registration by virtue of father's citizenship, etc.

9.—(1) A person born in a foreign country within five years after commencement shall be entitled, on an application for his registration as a British citizen made within the period of twelve months from the date of the birth, to be registered as such a citizen if—   **45–010**

(a) the requirements specified in subsection (2) are fulfilled in the case of that person's father; and

(b) had that person been born before commencement and become a citizen of the United Kingdom and Colonies by virtue of section 5 of the 1948 Act (citizenship by descent) as a result of the registration of his birth at a United Kingdom consulate under paragraph (b) of the proviso to section 5(1) of that Act, he would immediately before commencement have had the right of abode in the United Kingdom by virtue of section 2(1)(b) of the Immigration Act 1971 as then in force (connection with United Kingdom through parent or grandparent).

(2) The requirements referred to in subsection (1)(a) are that the father of the person to whom the application relates—

(a) immediately before commencement or at his death (whichever was earlier)—

  (i) was a citizen of the United Kingdom and Colonies by virtue of section 5 of the 1948 Act (citizenship by descent) or was a person who, under any provision of the British Nationality Acts 1948 to 1965, was deemed for the purposes of the proviso to section 5(1) of the 1948 Act to be a citizen of the United Kingdom and Colonies by descent only; and

  (ii) was married to that person's mother; and

(iii) was ordinarily resident in a foreign country (no matter which) within the meaning of the 1948 Act; and

(b) either—

(i) became a British citizen at commencement and remained such a citizen throughout the period from commencement to the date of the application or, if he died during that period, throughout the period from commencement to his death; or

(ii) would have become a British citizen at commencement but for his death.

Registration following renunciation of citizenship of U.K. and Colonies

45–011   **10.**—(1) Subject to subsection (3), a person shall be entitled, on an application for his registration as a British citizen, to be registered as such a citizen if immediately before commencement he would (had he applied for it) have been entitled under section 1(1) of the British Nationality Act 1964 (resumption of citizenship) to be registered as a citizen of the United Kingdom and Colonies by virtue of having an appropriate qualifying connection with the United Kingdom or, if a woman, by virtue of having been married before commencement to a person who has, or would if living have, such a connection.

(2) On an application for his registration as a British citizen made by a person of full capacity who had before commencement ceased to be a citizen of the United Kingdom and Colonies as a result of a declaration of renunciation, the Secretary of State may, if he thinks fit, cause that person to be registered as a British citizen if that person—

(a) has an appropriate qualifying connection with the United Kingdom; or

(b) if a woman, has been married to a person who has, or would if living have, such a connection.

(3) A person shall not be entitled to registration under subsection (1) on more than one occasion.

(4) For the purposes of this section a person shall be taken to have an appropriate qualifying connection with the United Kingdom if he, his father or his father's father—

(a) was born in the United Kingdom; or

(b) is or was a person naturalised in the United Kingdom; or

(c) was registered as a citizen of the United Kingdom and Colonies in the United Kingdom or in a country which at the time was mentioned in section 1(3) of the 1948 Act.

Acquisition at commencement

Citizens of U.K. and Colonies who are to become British citizens at commencement

45–012   **11.**—(1) Subject to subsection (2), a person who immediately before commencement—

(a) was a citizen of the United Kingdom and Colonies; and

(b) had the right of abode in the United Kingdom under the Immigration Act 1971 as then in force,

shall at commencement become a British citizen.

(2) A person who was registered as a citizen of the United Kingdom and Colonies under section 1 of the British Nationality (No. 2) Act 1964 (stateless persons) on the ground mentioned in subsection (1)(a) of that section (namely that his mother was a citizen of the United Kingdom and Colonies at the time when he was born) shall not become a British citizen under subsection (1) unless—

(a) his mother becomes a British citizen under subsection (1) or would have done so but for her death; or

(b) immediately before commencement he had the right of abode in the United Kingdom by virtue of section 2(1)(c) of the Immigration Act 1971 as then in force (settlement in United Kingdom, combined with five or more years' ordinary residence there as a citizen of the United Kingdom and Colonies).

(3) A person who—

(a) immediately before commencement was a citizen of the United Kingdom and Colonies by virtue of having been registered under subsection (6) of section 12 of the 1948 Act (British subjects before commencement of 1948 Act becoming citizens of United Kingdom and Colonies) under arrangements made by virtue of subsection (7) of that section (registration in independent Commonwealth country by United Kingdom High Commissioner); and

(b) was so registered on an application under the said subsection (6) based on the applicant's descent in the male line from a person ("the relevant person") possessing one of the qualifications specified in subsection (1)(a) and (b) of that section (birth or naturalisation in the United Kingdom and Colonies),

shall at commencement become a British citizen if the relevant person was born or naturalised in the United Kingdom.

Renunciation and resumption

Renunciation

12.—(1) If any British citizen of full age and capacity makes in the prescribed manner a declaration of renunciation of British citizenship, then, subject to subsections (3) and (4), the Secretary of State shall cause the declaration to be registered.

45–013

(2) On the registration of a declaration made in pursuance of this section the person who made it shall cease to be a British citizen.

(3) A declaration made by a person in pursuance of this section shall not be registered unless the Secretary of State is satisfied that the person who made it will after the registration have or acquire some citizenship or nationality other than British citizenship; and if that person does not have any such citizenship or nationality on the date of registration and does not acquire some such citizenship or nationality within six months from that date, he shall be, and be deemed to have remained, a British citizen notwithstanding the registration.

(4) The Secretary of State may withhold registration of any declaration made in pursuance of this section if it is made during any war in which Her Majesty may be engaged in right of Her Majesty's government in the United Kingdom.

(5) For the purposes of this section any person who has been married shall be deemed to be of full age.

......

Part II

British Overseas Territories Citizenship

Acquisition after commencement

Acquisition by birth or adoption

45–014   **15.**—(1) A person born in a [British overseas territory][1] after commencement shall be a [British overseas territories citizen][2] if at the time of the birth his father or mother is—

    (a)   a [British overseas territories citizen][3]; or
    (b)   settled in a [British overseas territory][4].

(2) A new-born infant who, after commencement, is found abandoned in a [British overseas territory][5] shall, unless the contrary is shown, be deemed for the purposes of subsection (1)—

    (a)   to have been born in that territory after commencement; and
    (b)   to have been born to a parent who at the time of the birth was a [British overseas territories citizen][6] or settled in a [British overseas territory][7].

(3) A person born in a [British overseas territory][8] after commencement who is not a [British overseas territories citizen][9] by virtue of subsection (1) or (2) shall be entitled to be registered as such a citizen if, while he is a minor—

    (a)   his father or mother becomes such a citizen or becomes settled in a [British overseas territory][10]; and
    (b)   an application is made for his registration as such a citizen.

(4) A person born in a [British overseas territory][11] after commencement who is not a [British overseas territories citizen][12] by virtue of subsection (1) or (2) shall be entitled, on an application for his registration as a [British overseas territories citizen][13] made at any time after he has attained the age of ten years, to be registered as such a citizen if, as regards each of the first ten years of that person's life, the number of days on which he was absent from that territory in that year does not exceed 90.

(5) Where after commencement an order authorising the adoption of a minor who is not a [British overseas territories citizen][14] is made by a court in any [British overseas territory][15], he shall be a [British overseas territories citizen][16] as from the date on which the order is made if the adopter or, in the case of a joint adoption, one of the adopters, is a [British overseas territories citizen][17] on that date.

(6) Where an order in consequence of which any person became a [British overseas territories citizen][18] by virtue of subsection (5) ceases to have effect, whether on annulment or otherwise, the cesser shall not affect the status of that person as such a citizen.

(7) If in the special circumstances of any particular case the Secretary of State thinks fit, he may for the purposes of subsection (4) treat the person to whom the application relates as fulfilling the requirements specified in that subsection although, as regards any one or more of the first ten years of that person's life, the number of days on which he was absent from the [British overseas territory][19] there mentioned in that year or each of the years in question exceeds 90.

---

[1]   Words substituted by British Overseas Territories Act 2002 (c.8), s.1(1)(b).
[2]   Words substituted by British Overseas Territories Act 2002 (c.8), s.2(2).

[3] *ibid.*
[4] Words substituted by British Overseas Territories Act 2002 (c.8), s.1(1)(b).
[5] *ibid.*
[6] Words substituted by British Overseas Territories Act 2002 (c.8), s.2(2).
[7] Words substituted by British Overseas Territories Act 2002 (c.8), s.1(1)(b).
[8] *ibid.*
[9] Words substituted by British Overseas Territories Act 2002 (c.8), s.2(2).
[10] Words substituted by British Overseas Territories Act 2002 (c.8), s.1(1)(b).
[11] *ibid.*
[12] Words substituted by British Overseas Territories Act 2002 (c.8), s.2(2).
[13] *ibid.*
[14] *ibid.*
[15] Words substituted by British Overseas Territories Act 2002 (c.8), s.1(1)(b).
[16] Words substituted by British Overseas Territories Act 2002 (c.8), s.2(2).
[17] *ibid.*
[18] *ibid.*
[19] Words substituted by British Overseas Territories Act 2002 (c.8), s.1(1)(b).

Acquisition by descent

16.—(1) A person born outside the [British overseas territories][1] after commencement shall be a [British overseas territories citizen][2] if at the time of the birth his father or mother—   **45–015**

(a) is such a citizen otherwise than by descent; or

(b) is such a citizen and is serving outside the [British overseas territories][3] in service to which this paragraph applies, his or her recruitment for that service having taken place in a [British overseas territory][4].

(2) Paragraph (b) of subsection (1) applies to—

(a) Crown service under the government of a [British overseas territory][5]; and

(b) service of any description for the time being designated under subsection (3).

(3) For the purposes of this section the Secretary of State may by order made by statutory instrument designate any description of service which he considers to be closely associated with the activities outside the [British overseas territories][6] of the government of any [British overseas territory][7].

(4) Any order made under subsection (3) shall be subject to annulment in pursuance of a resolution of either House of Parliament.

[1] Words substituted by British Overseas Territories Act 2002 (c.8), s.1(1)(b).
[2] Words substituted by British Overseas Territories Act 2002 (c.8), s.2(2).
[3] Words substituted by British Overseas Territories Act 2002 (c.8), s.1(1)(b).
[4] *ibid.*
[5] *ibid.*
[6] *ibid.*
[7] *ibid.*

. . . . . .

PART III

BRITISH OVERSEAS CITIZENSHIP

Citizens of U.K. and Colonies who are to become British Overseas citizens at commencement

26. Any person who was a citizen of the United Kingdom and Colonies immediately before commencement and who does not at commencement become   **45–016**

either a British citizen or a [British overseas territories citizen][1] shall at commencement become a British Overseas citizen.

[1] Words substituted by British Overseas Territories Act 2002 (c.8), s.2(2).

. . . . . .

PART V

MISCELLANEOUS AND SUPPLEMENTARY

Commonwealth citizenship

45–017   **37.**—(1) Every person who—

(a) under [the British Nationality Acts 1981 and 1983][1] is a British citizen, a [British overseas territories citizen][2], [a British National (Overseas),] a British Overseas citizen or a British subject; or
(b) under any enactment for the time being in force in any country mentioned in Schedule 3 is a citizen of that country,

shall have the status of a Commonwealth citizen.

(2) Her Majesty may by Order in Council amend Schedule 3 by the alteration of any entry, the removal of any entry, or the insertion of any additional entry.

(3) Any Order in Council made under this section shall be subject to annulment in pursuance of a resolution of either House of Parliament.

(4) After commencement no person shall have the status of a Commonwealth citizen or the status of a British subject otherwise than under this Act.

[1] Words substituted by British Nationality (Falkland Islands) Act 1983 (c.6), s.4(3).
[2] Words substituted by British Overseas Territories Act 2002 (c.8), s. 2(2).

. . . . . .

Deprivation of citizenship

45–018   **40.**—(1) Subject to the provisions of this section, the Secretary of State may by order deprive any British citizen to whom this subsection applies of his British citizenship if the Secretary of State is satisfied that the registration or certificate of naturalisation by virtue of which he is such a citizen was obtained by means of fraud, false representation or the concealment of any material fact.

(2) Subsection (1) applies to any British citizen who—

(a) became a British citizen after commencement by virtue of—

(i) his registration as a British citizen under any provision of [the British Nationality Acts 1981 and 1983][1]; or
(ii) a certificate of naturalisation granted to him under section 6; or

(b) being immediately before commencement a citizen of the United Kingdom and Colonies by virtue of registration as such a citizen under any provision of the British Nationality Acts 1948 to 1964, became at commencement a British citizen; or

(c) at any time before commencement became a British subject (within the meaning of that expression at that time), or a citizen of Eire or of the Republic of Ireland, by virtue of a certificate of naturalisation granted to him or in which his name was included.

(3) Subject to the provisions of this section, the Secretary of State may by order deprive any British citizen to whom this subsection applies of his British citizenship if the Secretary of State is satisfied that that citizen—

(a) has shown himself by act or speech to be disloyal or disaffected towards Her Majesty; or

(b) has, during any war in which Her Majesty was engaged, unlawfully traded or communicated with an enemy or been engaged in or associated with any business that was to his knowledge carried on in such a manner as to assist an enemy in that war; or

(c) has, within the period of five years from the relevant date, been sentenced in any country to imprisonment for a term of not less than twelve months.

(4) Subsection (3) applies to any British citizen who falls within paragraph (a) or (c) of subsection (2); and in subsection (3) "the relevant date", in relation to a British citizen to whom subsection (3) applies, means the date of the registration by virtue of which he is such a citizen or, as the case may be, the date of the grant of the certificate of naturalisation by virtue of which he is such a citizen.

(5) The Secretary of State—

(a) shall not deprive a person of British citizenship under this section unless he is satisfied that it is not conducive to the public good that that person should continue to be a British citizen; and

(b) shall not deprive a person of British citizenship under subsection (3) on the ground mentioned in paragraph (c) of that subsection if it appears to him that that person would thereupon become stateless.

(6) Before making an order under this section the Secretary of State shall give the person against whom the order is proposed to be made notice in writing informing him of the ground or grounds on which it is proposed to be made and of his right to an inquiry under this section.

(7) If the person against whom the order is proposed to be made applies in the prescribed manner for an inquiry, the Secretary of State shall, and in any other case the Secretary of State may, refer the case to a committee of inquiry consisting of a chairman, being a person possessing judicial experience, appointed by the Secretary of State and of such other members appointed by the Secretary of State as he thinks proper.

(8) The Secretary of State may make rules for the practice and procedure to be followed in connection with references under subsection (7) to a committee of inquiry; and such rules may, in particular, provide for conferring on any such committee any powers, rights or privileges of any court, and for enabling any powers so conferred to be exercised by one or more members of the committee.

(9) The power of the Secretary of State to make rules under subsection (8) shall be exercisable by statutory instrument subject to annulment in pursuance of a resolution of either House of Parliament.

(10) The preceding provisions of this section shall apply in relation to [British overseas territories citizens][2] and [British overseas territories citizenship][3] as they apply in relation to British citizens and British citizenship, but as if in subsection (2)(a)(ii) the reference to section 6 were a reference to section 18.

[1] Words substituted by British Nationality (Falkland Islands) Act 1983 (c.6), s.4(3).
[2] Words substituted by British Overseas Territories Act 2002 (c.8), s.2(2).
[3] *ibid.*

. . . . . .

Registration and naturalisation: general provisions

45–019   42.—(1) Subject to subsection (2)—

(a) a person shall not be registered under any provision of this Act as a citizen of any description or as a British subject; and

(b) a certificate of naturalisation shall not be granted to a person under any provision of this Act,

unless—

(i) any fee payable by virtue of this Act in connection with the registration or, as the case may be, the grant of the certificate has been paid; and

(ii) the person concerned has within the prescribed time taken an oath of allegiance in the form indicated in Schedule 5.

(2) So much of subsection (1) as requires the taking of an oath of allegiance shall not apply to a person who—

(a) is not of full age; or

(b) is already a British citizen, a [British overseas territories citizen][1], [a British National (Overseas)] a British Overseas citizen, a British subject, or a citizen of any country of which Her Majesty is Queen.

(3) Any provision of this Act which provides for a person to be entitled to registration as a citizen of any description or as a British subject shall have effect subject to the preceding provisions of this section.

(4) A person registered under any provision of this Act as a British citizen, or as a [British overseas territories citizen][2] or as a British Overseas citizen [, or as a British National (Overseas),] or as a British subject, shall be a citizen of that description or, as the case may be, [a British National (Overseas) or] a British subject as from the date on which he is so registered.

(5) A person to whom a certificate of naturalisation as a British citizen or as a [British overseas territories citizen][3] is granted under any provision of this Act shall be a citizen of that description as from the date on which the certificate is granted.

[(6) A person who applies for registration or naturalisation as a [British overseas territories citizen][4] under any provision of this Act by virtue (wholly or partly) of his having a connection with Hong Kong, may not be naturalised or registered, as the case may be, unless he makes his application on or before 31st March 1996.]

[1] Words substituted by British Overseas Territories Act 2002 (c.8), s.2(2).
[2] *ibid.*
[3] *ibid.*
[4] *ibid.*

. . . . . .

Decisions involving exercise of discretion

45–020   44.—(1) Any discretion vested by or under this Act in the Secretary of State, a Governor or a Lieutenant-Governor shall be exercised without regard to the race, colour or religion of any person who may be affected by its exercise.

(2) The Secretary of State, a Governor or a Lieutenant-Governor, as the case may be, shall not be required to assign any reason for the grant or refusal of any application under this Act the decision on which is at his discretion; and

the decision of the Secretary of State or a Governor or Lieutenant-Governor on any such application shall not be subject to appeal to, or review in, any court.

(3) Nothing in this section affects the jurisdiction of any court to entertain proceedings of any description concerning the rights of any person under any provision of this Act.

. . . . . .

Legitimated children

47.—(1) A person born out of wedlock and legitimated by the subsequent marriage of his parents shall, as from the date of the marriage, be treated for the purposes of this Act as if he had been born legitimate.

(2) A person shall be deemed for the purposes of this section to have been legitimated by the subsequent marriage of his parents if by the law of the place in which his father was domiciled at the time of the marriage the marriage operated immediately or subsequently to legitimate him, and not otherwise.

45–021

Posthumous children

48. Any reference in this Act to the status or description of the father or mother of a person at the time of that person's birth shall, in relation to a person born after the death of his father or mother, be construed as a reference to the status or description of the parent in question at the time of that parent's death; and where that death occurred before, and the birth occurs after, commencement, the status or description which would have been applicable to the father or mother had he or she died after commencement shall be deemed to be the status or description applicable to him or her at the time of his or her death.

45–022

. . . . . .

Interpretation

50.—(1) In this Act, unless the context otherwise requires—

45–023

"the 1948 Act" means the British Nationality Act 1948;

"alien" means a person who is neither a Commonwealth citizen nor a British protected person nor a citizen of the Republic of Ireland;

"association" means an unincorporated body of persons;

["British National (Overseas)" means a person who is a British National (Overseas) under the Hong Kong (British Nationality) Order 1986, and "status of a British National (Overseas)" shall be construed accordingly;

"British Overseas citizen" includes a person who is a British Overseas citizen under the Hong Kong (British Nationality) Order 1986[;]][1]

["British overseas territory" means a territory mentioned in Schedule 6;][2]

"British protected person" means a person who is a member of any class of persons declared to be British protected persons by an Order in Council for the time being in force under section 38 or is a British protected person by virtue of the Solomon Islands Act 1978;

"Crown service" means the service of the Crown, whether within Her Majesty's dominions or elsewhere;

"Crown service under the government of the United Kingdom" means Crown service under Her Majesty's government in the United Kingdom or under Her Majesty's government in Northern Ireland [or under the Scottish Administration];

[. . .]³

"enactment" includes an enactment comprised in Northern Ireland legislation;

"foreign country" means a country other than the United Kingdom, a [British overseas territory]⁴, a country mentioned in Schedule 3 and the Republic of Ireland;

"the former nationality Acts" means—

(a) the British Nationality Acts 1948 to 1965;

(b) the British Nationality and Status of Aliens Acts 1914 to 1943; and

(c) any Act repealed by the said Acts of 1914 to 1943 or by the Naturalization Act 1870;

"Governor", in relation to a [British overseas territory]⁵, includes the officer for the time being administering the government of that territory;

"High Commissioner" includes an acting High Commissioner;

"immigration laws"—

(a) in relation to the United Kingdom, means the Immigration Act 1971 and any law for purposes similar to that Act which is for the time being or has at any time been in force in any part of the United Kingdom;

(b) in relation to a [British overseas territory]⁶, means any law for purposes similar to the Immigration Act 1971 which is for the time being or has at any time been in force in that territory;

"the Islands" means the Channel Islands and the Isle of Man;

"prescribed" means prescribed by regulations made under section 41;

"settled" shall be construed in accordance with subsections (2) to (4);

"ship" includes a hovercraft;

"United Kingdom consulate" means the office of a consular officer of Her Majesty's government in the United Kingdom where a register of births is kept or, where there is no such office, such office as may be prescribed.

(2) Subject to subsection (3), references in this Act to a person being settled in the United Kingdom or in a [British overseas territory]⁷ are references to his being ordinarily resident in the United Kingdom or, as the case may be, in that territory without being subject under the immigration laws to any restriction on the period for which he may remain.

(3) Subject to subsection (4), a person is not to be regarded for the purposes of this Act—

(a) as having been settled in the United Kingdom at any time when he was entitled to an exemption under section 8(3) or (4)(b) or (c) of the Immigration Act 1971 or, unless the order under section 8(2) of that Act conferring the exemption in question provides otherwise, to an exemption under the said section 8(2), or to any corresponding exemption under the former immigration laws; or

(b) as having been settled in a [British overseas territory]⁸ at any time when he was under the immigration laws entitled to any exemption corresponding to any such exemption as is mentioned in paragraph (a) (that paragraph being for the purposes of this paragraph read as if the words from "unless" to "otherwise" were omitted).

(4) A person to whom a child is born in the United Kingdom after commencement is to be regarded for the purposes of section 1(1) as being settled in the United Kingdom at the time of the birth if—

(a) he would fall to be so regarded but for his being at that time entitled to an exemption under section 8(3) of the Immigration Act 1971; and
(b) immediately before he became entitled to that exemption he was settled in the United Kingdom; and
(c) he was ordinarily resident in the United Kingdom from the time when he became entitled to that exemption to the time of the birth;

but this subsection shall not apply if at the time of the birth the child's father or mother is a person on whom any immunity from jurisdiction is conferred by or under the Diplomatic Privileges Act 1964.

(5) It is hereby declared that a person is not to be treated for the purpose of any provision of this Act as ordinarily resident in the United Kingdom or in a [British overseas territory][9] at a time when he is in the United Kingdom or, as the case may be, in that territory in breach of the immigration laws.

[1] Definition inserted by British Overseas Territories Act 2002 (c.8), s.1(1)(a).
[2] *ibid.*
[3] Definition repealed by British Overseas Territories Act 2002 (c.8), Sched. 2, para. 1.
[4] Words substituted by British Overseas Territories Act 2002 (c.8), s.1(1)(b).
[5] *ibid.*
[6] *ibid.*
[7] *ibid.*
[8] *ibid.*
[9] *ibid.*

. . . . . .

Sections 6 and 18   SCHEDULE 1

REQUIREMENTS FOR NATURALISATION

NATURALISATION AS A BRITISH CITIZEN UNDER SECTION 6(1)

1.—(1) Subject to paragraph 2, the requirements for naturalisation as a British citizen under section 6(1) are, in the case of any person who applies for it—   **45–024**

(a) the requirements specified in sub-paragraph (2) of this paragraph, or the alternative requirement specified in sub-paragraph (3) of this paragraph; and
(b) that he is of good character; and
(c) that he has a sufficient knowledge of the English, Welsh or Scottish Gaelic language; and
(d) that either—

   (i) his intentions are such that, in the event of a certificate of naturalisation as a British citizen being granted to him, his home or (if he has more than one) his principal home will be in the United Kingdom; or
   (ii) he intends, in the event of such a certificate being granted to him, to enter into, or continue in, Crown service under the government of the United Kingdom, or service under an international organisation of which the United Kingdom or Her Majesty's government therein is a member, or service in the employment of a company or association established in the United Kingdom.

(2) The requirements referred to in sub-paragraph (1)(a) of this paragraph are—

(a) that the applicant was in the United Kingdom at the beginning of the period of five years ending with the date of the application, and that the number of days on which he was absent from the United Kingdom in that period does not exceed 450; and

(b) that the number of days on which he was absent from the United Kingdom in the period of twelve months so ending does not exceed 90; and

(c) that he was not at any time in the period of twelve months so ending subject under the immigration laws to any restriction on the period for which he might remain in the United Kingdom; and

(d) that he was not at any time in the period of five years so ending in the United Kingdom in breach of the immigration laws.

(3) The alternative requirement referred to in sub-paragraph (1)(a) of this paragraph is that on the date of the application he is serving outside the United Kingdom in Crown service under the government of the United Kingdom.

45–025   2. If in the special circumstances of any particular case the Secretary of State thinks fit, he may for the purposes of paragraph 1 do all or any of the following things, namely—

(a) treat the applicant as fulfilling the requirement specified in paragraph 1(2)(a) or paragraph 1(2)(b), or both, although the number of days on which he was absent from the United Kingdom in the period there mentioned exceeds the number there mentioned;

(b) treat the applicant as having been in the United Kingdom for the whole or any part of any period during which he would otherwise fall to be treated under paragraph 9(1) as having been absent;

(c) disregard any such restriction as is mentioned in paragraph 1(2)(c), not being a restriction to which the applicant was subject on the date of the application;

(d) treat the applicant as fulfilling the requirement specified in paragraph 1(2)(d) although he was in the United Kingdom in breach of the immigration laws in the period there mentioned;

(e) waive the need to fulfil the requirement specified in paragraph 1(1)(c) if he considers that because of the applicant's age or physical or mental condition it would be unreasonable to expect him to fulfil it.

NATURALISATION AS A BRITISH CITIZEN UNDER SECTION 6(2)

45–026   3. Subject to paragraph 4, the requirements for naturalisation as a British citizen under section 6(2) are, in the case of any person who applies for it—

(a) that he was in the United Kingdom at the beginning of the period of three years ending with the date of the application, and that the number of days on which he was absent from the United Kingdom in that period does not exceed 270; and

(b) that the number of days on which he was absent from the United Kingdom in the period of twelve months so ending does not exceed 90; and

(c) that on the date of the application he was not subject under the immigration laws to any restriction on the period for which he might remain in the United Kingdom; and

(d) that he was not at any time in the period of three years ending with the date of the application in the United Kingdom in breach of the immigration laws; and

(e) the requirement specified in paragraph 1(1)(b).

45–027   4. Paragraph 2 shall apply in relation to paragraph 3 with the following modifications, namely—

(a) the reference to the purposes of paragraph 1 shall be read as a reference to the purposes of paragraph 3;

(b) the references to paragraphs 1(2)(a), 1(2)(b) and 1(2)(d) shall be read as references to paragraphs 3(a), 3(b) and 3(d) respectively;

(c) paragraph 2(c) and (e) shall be omitted; and

(d) after paragraph (e) there shall be added—

"(f) waive the need to fulfil all or any of the requirements specified in paragraph 3(a) and (b) if on the date of the application the person to whom the applicant is married is serving in service to which section 2(1)(b) applies, that person's recruitment for that service having taken place in the United Kingdom".

NATURALISATION AS A BRITISH OVERSEAS TERRITORIES CITIZEN UNDER SECTION 18(1)

45–028   5.—(1) Subject to paragraph 6, the requirements for naturalisation as a [British overseas territories citizen][1] under section 18(1) are, in the case of any person who applies for it—

(a) the requirements specified in sub-paragraph (2) of this paragraph, or the alternative requirement specified in sub-paragraph (3) of this paragraph; and

(b) that he is of good character; and

(c) that he has a sufficient knowledge of the English language or any other language recognised for official purposes in the relevant territory; and

(d) that either—

(i) his intentions are such that, in the event of a certificate of naturalisation as a [British overseas territories citizen][2] being granted to him, his home or (if he has more than one) his principal home will be in the relevant territory; or

(ii) he intends, in the event of such a certificate being granted to him, to enter into, or continue in, Crown service under the government of that territory, or service under an international organisation of which that territory or the government of that territory is a member, or service in the employment of a company or association established in that territory.

(2) The requirements referred to in sub-paragraph (1)(a) of this paragraph are—

(a) that he was in the relevant territory at the beginning of the period of five years ending with the date of the application, and that the number of days on which he was absent from that territory in that period does not exceed 450; and

(b) that the number of days on which he was absent from that territory in the period of twelve months so ending does not exceed 90; and

(c) that he was not at any time in the period of twelve months so ending subject under the immigration laws to any restriction on the period for which he might remain in that territory; and

(d) that he was not at any time in the period of five years so ending in that territory in breach of the immigration laws.

(3) The alternative requirement referred to in sub-paragraph (1)(a) of this paragraph is that on the date of the application he is serving outside the relevant territory in Crown service under the government of that territory.

[1] Words substituted by British Overseas Territories Act 2002 (c.8), s. 2(2).
[2] *ibid.*

6. If in the special circumstances of any particular case the Secretary of State thinks fit, he may for the purposes of paragraph 5 do all or any of the following things, namely—   **45–029**

(a) treat the applicant as fulfilling the requirement specified in paragraph 5(2)(a) or paragraph 5(2)(b), or both, although the number of days on which he was absent from the relevant territory in the period there mentioned exceeds the number there mentioned;

(b) treat the applicant as having been in the relevant territory for the whole or any part of any period during which he would otherwise fall to be treated under paragraph 9(2) as having been absent;

(c) disregard any such restriction as is mentioned in paragraph 5(2)(c), not being a restriction to which the applicant was subject on the date of the application;

(d) treat the applicant as fulfilling the requirement specified in paragraph 5(2)(d) although he was in the relevant territory in breach of the immigration laws in the period there mentioned;

(e) waive the need to fulfil the requirement specified in paragraph 5(1)(c) if he considers that because of the applicant's age or physical or mental condition it would be unreasonable to expect him to fulfil it.

NATURALISATION AS A BRITISH OVERSEAS TERRITORIES CITIZEN UNDER SECTION 18(2)

7. Subject to paragraph 8, the requirements for naturalisation as a [British overseas territories citizen][1] under section 18(2) are, in the case of any person who applies for it—   **45–030**

(a) that he was in the relevant territory at the beginning of the period of three years ending with the date of the application, and that the number of days on which he was absent from that territory in that period does not exceed 270; and

(b) that the number of days on which he was absent from that territory in the period of twelve months so ending does not exceed 90; and

(c) that on the date of the application he was not subject under the immigration laws to any restriction on the period for which he might remain in that territory; and

(d) that he was not at any time in the period of three years ending with the date of the application in that territory in breach of the immigration laws; and

(e) the requirement specified in paragraph 5(1)(b).

[1] Words substituted by British Overseas Territories Act 2002 (c.8), s. 2(2).

8. Paragraph 6 shall apply in relation to paragraph 7 with the following modifications, namely—   **45–031**

(a) the reference to the purposes of paragraph 5 shall be read as a reference to the purposes of paragraph 7;

(b) the references to paragraphs 5(2)(a), 5(2)(b) and 5(2)(d) shall be read as references to paragraphs 7(a), 7(b) and 7(d) respectively;

(c) paragraph 6(c) and (e) shall be omitted; and
(d) after paragraph (e) there shall be added—
"(f) waive the need to fulfil all or any of the requirements specified in paragraph 7(a) and (b) if on the date of the application the person to whom the applicant is married is serving in service to which section 16(1)(b) applies, that person's recruitment for that service having taken place in a [British overseas territory]¹."

¹ Words substituted by British Overseas Territories Act 2002 (c.8), s. 1(1)(b).

PERIODS TO BE TREATED AS PERIODS OF ABSENCE FROM U.K. OR A BRITISH OVERSEAS TERRITORY

45–032 9.—(1) For the purposes of this Schedule a person shall (subject to paragraph 2(b)) be treated as having been absent from the United Kingdom during any of the following periods, that is to say—

(a) any period when he was in the United Kingdom and either was entitled to an exemption under section 8(3) or (4) of the Immigration Act 1971 (exemptions for diplomatic agents etc. and members of the forces) or was a member of the family and formed part of the household of a person so entitled;
(b) any period when he was detained—

    (i) in any place of detention in the United Kingdom in pursuance of a sentence passed on him by a court in the United Kingdom or elsewhere for any offence;
    (ii) in any hospital in the United Kingdom under a hospital order made under [Part III of the Mental Health Act 1983]¹ or section 175 or 376 of the Criminal Procedure (Scotland) Act 1975 or Part III of the Mental Health [(Northern Ireland) Order 1986], being an order made in connection with his conviction of an offence; or
    (iii) under any power of detention conferred by the immigration laws of the United Kingdom;
(c) any period when, being liable to be detained as mentioned in paragraph (b)(i) or (ii) of this sub-paragraph, he was unlawfully at large or absent without leave and for that reason liable to be arrested or taken into custody;
(d) any period when, his actual detention under any such power as is mentioned in paragraph (b)(iii) of this sub-paragraph being required or specifically authorised, he was unlawfully at large and for that reason liable to be arrested.

(2) For the purposes of this Schedule a person shall (subject to paragraph 6(b)) be treated as having been absent from any particular [British overseas territory]² during any of the following periods, that is to say—

(a) any period when he was in that territory and either was entitled to an exemption under the immigration laws of that territory corresponding to any such exemption as is mentioned in sub-paragraph (1)(a) or was a member of the family and formed part of the household of a person so entitled;
(b) any period when he was detained—

    (i) in any place of detention in the relevant territory in pursuance of a sentence passed on him by a court in that territory or elsewhere for any offence;
    (ii) in any hospital in that territory under a direction (however described) made under any law for purposes similar to [Part III of the Mental Health Act 1983]³ which was for the time being in force in that territory, being a direction made in connection with his conviction of an offence and corresponding to a hospital order under that Part; or
    (iii) under any power of detention conferred by the immigration laws of that territory;
(c) any period when, being liable to be detained as mentioned in paragraph (b)(i) or (ii) of this sub-paragraph, he was unlawfully at large or absent without leave and for that reason liable to be arrested or taken into custody;
(d) any period when, his actual detention under any such power as is mentioned in paragraph (b)(iii) of this sub-paragraph being required or specifically authorised, he was unlawfully at large and for that reason liable to be arrested.

¹ Words substituted by Mental Health Act 1983 (c.20), s.148, Sched. 4, para. 60(a).
² Words substituted by British Overseas Territories Act 2002 (c.8), s. 1(1)(b).
³ Words substituted by Mental Health Act 1983 (c.20), s.148, Sched. 4, para. 60(b).

INTERPRETATION

45–033 10. In this Schedule "the relevant territory" has the meaning given by section 18(3).

Contempt of Court Act 1981

(1981, c. 49)

An Act to amend the law relating to contempt of court and related matters.   **46–001**
[27th July 1981]

Strict liability

The strict liability rule

1. In this Act "the strict liability rule" means the rule of law whereby conduct   **46–002**
may be treated as a contempt of court as tending to interfere with the course of
justice in particular legal proceedings regardless of intent to do so.

Limitation of scope of strict liability

2.—(1) The strict liability rule applies only in relation to publications, and   **46–003**
for this purpose "publication" includes any speech, writing, [programme
included in a cable programme service] or other communication in whatever
form, which is addressed to the public at large or any section of the public.

(2) The strict liability rule applies only to a publication which creates a substantial risk that the course of justice in the proceedings in question will be
seriously impeded or prejudiced.

(3) The strict liability rule applies to a publication only if the proceedings
in question are active within the meaning of this section at the time of the
publication.

(4) Schedule 1 applies for determining the times at which proceedings are to
be treated as active within the meaning of this section.

[(5) In this section "programme service" has the same meaning as in the
Broadcasting Act 1990.][1]

[1] s. 2(5) inserted by Broadcasting Act 1990 (c.42), s.203(1), Sched. 20, para. 31(1)(b).

Defence of innocent publication or distribution

3.—(1) A person is not guilty of contempt of court under the strict liability   **46–004**
rule as the publisher of any matter to which that rule applies if at the time of
publication (having taken all reasonable care) he does not know and has no
reason to suspect that relevant proceedings are active.

(2) A person is not guilty of contempt of court under the strict liability rule
as the distributor of a publication containing any such matter if at the time of
distribution (having taken all reasonable care) he does not know that it contains
such matter and has no reason to suspect that it is likely to do so.

(3) The burden of proof of any fact tending to establish a defence afforded
by this section to any person lies upon that person.

Contemporary reports of proceedings

4.—(1) Subject to this section a person is not guilty of contempt of court   **46–005**
under the strict liability rule in respect of a fair and accurate report of legal
proceedings held in public, published contemporaneously and in good faith.

(2) In any such proceedings the court may, where it appears to be necessary
for avoiding a substantial risk of prejudice to the administration of justice in
those proceedings, or in any other proceedings pending or imminent, order that
the publication of any report of the proceedings, or any part of the proceedings,
be postponed for such period as the court thinks necessary for that purpose.

(3) For the purposes of subsection (1) of this section [. . .]¹ a report of proceedings shall be treated as published contemporaneously—

(a) in the case of a report of which publication is postponed pursuant to an order under subsection (2) of this section, if published as soon as practicable after that order expires;

(b) in the case of a report of committal proceedings of which publication is permitted by virtue only of subsection (3) of section 8 of the Magistrates' Courts Act 1980, if published as soon as practicable after publication is so permitted.²

¹ Words repealed by Defamation Act 1996 (c.31), Sched. 2, para. 1.
² Added by Criminal Procedure and Investigations Act 1996 (c.25), Pt VII, s. 57(3).

Discussion of public affairs

46–006   **5.** A publication made as or as part of a discussion in good faith of public affairs or other matters of general public interest is not to be treated as a contempt of court under the strict liability rule if the risk of impediment or prejudice to particular legal proceedings is merely incidental to the discussion.

Savings

46–007   **6.** Nothing in the foregoing provisions of this Act—

(a) prejudices any defence available at common law to a charge of contempt of court under the strict liability rule;

(b) implies that any publication is punishable as contempt of court under that rule which would not be so punishable apart from those provisions;

(c) restricts liability for contempt of court in respect of conduct intended to impede or prejudice the administration of justice.

Consent required for institution of proceedings

46–008   **7.** Proceedings for a contempt of court under the strict liability rule (other than Scottish proceedings) shall not be instituted except by or with the consent of the Attorney General or on the motion of a court having jurisdiction to deal with it.

Other aspects of law and procedure

Confidentiality of jury's deliberations

46–009   **8.**—(1) Subject to subsection (2) below, it is a contempt of court to obtain, disclose or solicit any particulars of statements made, opinions expressed, arguments advanced or votes cast by members of a jury in the course of their deliberations in any legal proceedings.

(2) This section does not apply to any disclosure of any particulars—

(a) in the proceedings in question for the purpose of enabling the jury to arrive at their verdict, or in connection with the delivery of that verdict, or

(b) in evidence in any subsequent proceedings for an offence alleged to have been committed in relation to the jury in the first mentioned proceedings,

or to the publication of any particulars so disclosed.

(3) Proceedings for a contempt of court under this section (other than Scottish proceedings) shall not be instituted except by or with the consent of the Attorney General or on the motion of a court having jurisdiction to deal with it.

Use of tape recorders

9.—(1) Subject to subsection (4) below, it is a contempt of court—   **46–010**

   (a) to use in court, or bring into court for use, any tape recorder or other instrument for recording sound, except with the leave of the court;

   (b) to publish a recording of legal proceedings made by means of any such instrument, or any recording derived directly or indirectly from it, by playing it in the hearing of the public or any section of the public, or to dispose of it or any recording so derived, with a view to such publication;

   (c) to use any such recording in contravention of any conditions of leave granted under paragraph (a).

(2) Leave under paragraph (a) of subsection (1) may be granted or refused at the discretion of the court, and if granted may be granted subject to such conditions as the court thinks proper with respect to the use of any recording made pursuant to the leave; and where leave has been granted the court may at the like discretion withdraw or amend it either generally or in relation to any particular part of the proceedings.

(3) Without prejudice to any other power to deal with an act of contempt under paragraph (a) of subsection (1), the court may order the instrument, or any recording made with it, or both, to be forfeited; and any object so forfeited shall (unless the court otherwise determines on application by a person appearing to be the owner) be sold or otherwise disposed of in such manner as the court may direct.

(4) This section does not apply to the making or use of sound recordings for purposes of official transcripts of proceedings.

Sources of information

10. No court may require a person to disclose, nor is any person guilty of   **46–011** contempt of court for refusing to disclose, the source of information contained in a publication for which he is responsible, unless it be established to the satisfaction of the court that disclosure is necessary in the interests of justice or national security or for the prevention of disorder or crime.

Publication of matters exempted from disclosure in court

11. In any case where a court (having power to do so) allows a name or other   **46–012** matter to be withheld from the public in proceedings before the court, the court may give such directions prohibiting the publication of that name or matter in connection with the proceedings as appear to the court to be necessary for the purpose for which it was so withheld.

Offences of contempt of magistrates' courts

12.—(1) [Section 135 of the Powers of Criminal Courts (Sentencing) Act   **46–013** 2000 (limit on fines in respect of young persons) and a] magistrates' court has jurisdiction under this section to deal with any person who—

   (a) wilfully insults the justice or justices, any witness before or officer of the court or any solicitor or counsel having business in the court, during his or their sitting or attendance in court or in going to or returning from the court; or

(b) wilfully interrupts the proceedings of the court or otherwise misbehaves in court.

(2) In any such case the court may order any officer of the court, or any constable, to take the offender into custody and detain him until the rising of the court; and the court may, if it thinks fit, commit the offender to custody for a specified period not exceeding one month or impose on him a fine not exceeding [£2,500], or both.

[(2A) A fine imposed under subsection (2) above shall be deemed, for the purposes of any enactment, to be a sum adjudged to be paid by a conviction.]

(4) A magistrates' court may at any time revoke an order of committal made under subsection (2) and, if the offender is in custody, order his discharge.

(5) The following provisions of the Magistrates' Courts Act 1980 apply in relation to an order under this section as they apply in relation to a sentence on conviction or finding of guilty of an offence[; and those provisions of the Magistrates' Court Act 1980 are sections 75 to 91 (enforcement); section 108 (appeal to Crown Court); section 136 (overnight detention in default of payment); and section 142(1)(power to rectify mistakes)].

. . . . . .

Penalties for contempt and kindred offences

Proceedings in England and Wales

46–014 14.—(1) In any case where a court has power to commit a person to prison for contempt of court and (apart from this provision) no limitation applies to the period of committal, the committal shall (without prejudice to the power of the court to order his earlier discharge) be for a fixed term, and that term shall not on any occasion exceed two years in the case of committal by a superior court, or one month in the case of committal by an inferior court.

(2) In any case where an inferior court has power to fine a person for contempt of court and (apart from this provision) no limit applies to the amount of the fine, the fine shall not on any occasion exceed [£2,500].

[(2A) A fine imposed under subsection (2) above shall be deemed, for the purposes of any enactment, to be a sum adjudged to be paid by a conviction.]

(4) Each of the superior courts shall have the like power to make a hospital order or guardianship order under [section 37 of the Mental Health Act 1983] [or an interim hospital order under] [section 38 of that Act] in the case of a person suffering from mental illness or [severe mental impairment] who could otherwise be committed to prison for contempt of court as the Crown Court has under that section in the case of a person convicted of an offence.

Penalties for contempt of court in Scottish proceedings

46–015 15.—(1) In Scottish proceedings, when a person is committed to prison for contempt of court the committal shall (without prejudice to the power of the court to order his earlier discharge) be for a fixed term.

(2) The maximum penalty which may be imposed by way of imprisonment or fine for contempt of court in Scottish proceedings shall be two years' imprisonment or a fine or both, except that—

(a) where the contempt is dealt with by the sheriff in the course of or in connection with proceedings other than criminal proceedings on indict-

ment, such penalty shall not exceed three months' imprisonment or a
fine of [level 4 on the standard scale] or both; and

(b) where the contempt is dealt with by the district court, such penalty
     shall not exceed sixty days' imprisonment or a fine of [level 4 on the
     standard scale] or both.

[(3) The following provisions of the Criminal Procedure (Scotland) Act 1995
shall apply in relation to persons found guilty of contempt of court in Scottish
proceedings as they apply in relation to persons convicted of offences—

(a) in every case, section 207 (restrictions on detention of young
     offenders);
(b) in any case to which paragraph (b) of subsection (2) above does not
     apply, sections 58, 59 and 61 (persons suffering from mental disorder);

and in any case to which the said paragraph (b) does apply, subsection (5) below
shall have effect.]

(5) Where a person is found guilty by a district court of contempt of court
and it appears to the court that he may be suffering from mental disorder, it
shall remit him to the sheriff in the manner provided by [section 7(9) and (10)
of the Criminal Procedure (Scotland) Act 1995] and the sheriff shall, on such
remit being made, have the like power to make an order under [section 58(1)]
of the said Act in respect of him as if he had been convicted by the sheriff of
an offence, or in dealing with him may exercise the like powers as the court
making the remit.

. . . . . .

Interpretation

19. In this Act—   **46–016**

"court" includes any tribunal or body exercising the judicial power of the
    State, and "legal proceedings" shall be construed accordingly;
"publication" has the meaning assigned by subsection (1) of section 2, and
    "publish" (except in section 9) shall be construed accordingly;
"Scottish proceedings" means proceedings before any court, including the
    Courts-Martial Appeal Court, the Restrictive Practices Court and the
    Employment Appeal Tribunal, sitting in Scotland, and includes pro-
    ceedings before the House of Lords in the exercise of any appellate
    jurisdiction over proceedings in such a court;
"the strict liability rule" has the meaning assigned by section 1;
"superior court" means the Court of Appeal, the High Court, the Crown
    Court, the Courts-Martial Appeal Court, the Restrictive Practices
    Court, the Employment Appeal Tribunal and any other court exercis-
    ing in relation to its proceedings powers equivalent to those of the
    High Court, and includes the House of Lords in the exercise of its
    appellate jurisdiction.

. . . . . .

SCHEDULE 1

TIMES WHEN PROCEEDINGS ARE ACTIVE FOR PURPOSES OF SECTION 2

PRELIMINARY

46–017 **1.** In this Schedule "criminal proceedings" means proceedings against a person in respect of an offence, not being appellate proceedings or proceedings commenced by motion for committal or attachment in England and Wales or Northern Ireland; and "appellate proceedings" means proceedings on appeal from or for the review of the decision of a court in any proceedings.

46–018 **2.** Criminal, appellate and other proceedings are active within the meaning of section 2 at the times respectively prescribed by the following paragraphs of this Schedule; and in relation to proceedings in which more than one of the steps described in any of those paragraphs is taken, the reference in that paragraph is a reference to the first of those steps.

CRIMINAL PROCEEDINGS

46–019 **3.** Subject to the following provisions of this Schedule, criminal proceedings are active from the relevant initial step specified in paragraph 4 until concluded as described in paragraph 5.

46–020 **4.** The initial steps of criminal proceedings are:—

    (a) arrest without warrant;
    (b) the issue, or in Scotland the grant, of a warrant for arrest;
    (c) the issue of a summons to appear, or in Scotland the grant of a warrant to cite;
    (d) the service of an indictment or other document specifying the charge;
    (e) except in Scotland, oral charge.

46–021 [**4A.** Where as a result of an order under section 54 of the Criminal Procedure and Investigations Act 1996 (acquittal tainted by an administration of justice offence) proceedings are brought against a person for an offence of which he has previously been acquitted, the initial step of the proceedings is a certification under subsection (2) of that section; and paragraph 4 has effect subject to this.[1]][2]

    [1] Except in relation to Scotland: para. 4A is inserted.
    [2] Added by Criminal Procedure and Investigations Act 1996 (c.25), Pt VII, s. 57(4).

46–022 **5.** Criminal proceedings are concluded—

    (a) by acquittal or, as the case may be, by sentence;
    (b) by any other verdict, finding, order or decision which puts an end to the proceedings;
    (c) by discontinuance or by operation of law.

46–023 **6.** The reference in paragraph 5(a) to sentence includes any order or decision consequent on conviction or finding of guilt which disposes of the case, either absolutely or subject to future events, and a deferment of sentence under [section 1 of the Powers of Criminal Courts (Sentencing) Act 2000][1], section 219 or 432 of the Criminal Procedure (Scotland) Act 1975 or Article 14 of the Treatment of Offenders (Northern Ireland) Order 1976.

    [1] Words substituted by Powers of Criminal Courts (Sentencing) Act 2000 (c.6), Sched. 9, para. 86.

46–024 **7.** Proceedings are discontinued within the meaning of paragraph 5(c)—

    (a) in England and Wales or Northern Ireland, if the charge or summons is withdrawn or a nolle prosequi entered;
    [(aa) in England and Wales, if they are discontinued by Virtue of section 23 of the Prosecution of Offences Act 1985;][1]
    (b) in Scotland, if the proceedings are expressly abandoned by the prosecutor or are deserted *simpliciter*;
    (c) in the case of proceedings in England and Wales or Northern Ireland commenced by arrest without warrant, if the person arrested is released, otherwise than on bail, without having been charged.

    [1] para. 7(aa) inserted by Prosecution of Offences Act 1985 (c.23), s.31(5), Sched. 1, Pt I, para. 4.

46–025 **8.** Criminal proceedings before a court-martial or standing civilian court are not concluded until the completion of any review of finding or sentence.

9. Criminal proceedings in England and Wales or Northern Ireland cease to be active if an order is made for the charge to lie on the file, but become active again if leave is later given for the proceedings to continue.

46–026

[**9A.** Where proceedings in England and Wales have been discontinued by virtue of section 23 of the Prosecution of Offences Act 1985, but notice is given by the accused under subsection (7) of that section to the effect that he wants the proceedings to continue, they become active again with the giving of that notice.]¹

46–027

¹ para. 9A inserted by Prosecution of Offences Act 1985 (c.23), s.31(5), Sched. 1, Pt I, para. 5.

10. Without prejudice to paragraph 5(b) above, criminal proceedings against a person cease to be active—

46–028

   (a) if the accused is found to be under a disability such as to render him unfit to be tried or unfit to plead or, in Scotland, is found to be insane in bar of trial; or
   (b) if a hospital order is made in his case under [section 51(5) of the Mental Health Act 1983] or paragraph (b) of subsection (2) of section 62 of the Mental Health Act (Northern Ireland) 1961 or, in Scotland, where a transfer order ceases to have effect by virtue of [section 73(1) of the Mental Health (Scotland) Act 1984],

but become active again if they are later resumed.

11. Criminal proceedings against a person which become active on the issue or the grant of a warrant for his arrest cease to be active at the end of the period of twelve months beginning with the date of the warrant unless he has been arrested within that period, but become active again if he is subsequently arrested.

46–029

OTHER PROCEEDINGS AT FIRST INSTANCE

12. Proceedings other than criminal proceedings and appellate proceedings are active from the time when arrangements for the hearing are made or, if no such arrangements are previously made, from the time the hearing begins, until the proceedings are disposed of or discontinued or withdrawn; and for the purposes of this paragraph any motion or application made in or for the purposes of any proceedings, and any pre-trial review in the county court, is to be treated as a distinct proceeding.

46–030

13. In England and Wales or Northern Ireland arrangements for the hearing of proceedings to which paragraph 12 applies are made within the meaning of that paragraph—

46–031

   (a) in the case of proceedings in the High Court for which provision is made by rules of court for setting down for trial, when the case is set down;
   (b) in the case of any proceedings, when a date for the trial or hearing is fixed.

14. In Scotland arrangements for the hearing of proceedings to which paragraph 12 applies are made within the meaning of that paragraph—

46–032

   (a) in the case of an ordinary action in the Court of Session or in the sheriff court, when the Record is closed;
   (b) in the case of a motion or application, when it is enrolled or made;
   (c) in any other case, when the date for a hearing is fixed or a hearing is allowed.

APPELLATE PROCEEDINGS

15. Appellate proceedings are active from the time when they are commenced—

46–033

   (a) by application for leave to appeal or apply for review, or by notice of such an application;
   (b) by notice of appeal or of application for review;
   (c) by other originating process,

until disposed of or abandoned, discontinued or withdrawn.

16. Where, in appellate proceedings relating to criminal proceedings, the court—

46–034

   (a) remits the case to the court below; or
   (b) orders a new trial or a venire de novo, or in Scotland grants authority to bring a new prosecution,

any further or new proceedings which result shall be treated as active from the conclusion of the appellate proceedings.

Indecent Displays (Control) Act 1981

(1981, c. 42)

47–001 *An Act to make fresh provision with respect to the public display of indecent matter; and for purposes connected therewith.* [27th July 1981]

Indecent displays

47–002 **1.**—(1) If any indecent matter is publicly displayed the person making the display and any person causing or permitting the display to be made shall be guilty of an offence.

(2) Any matter which is displayed in or so as to be visible from any public place shall, for the purposes of this section, be deemed to be publicly displayed.

(3) In subsection (2) above, "public place", in relation to the display of any matter, means any place to which the public have or are permitted to have access (whether on payment or otherwise) while that matter is displayed except—

    (a) a place to which the public are permitted to have access only on payment which is or includes payment for that display; or

    (b) a shop or any part of a shop to which the public can only gain access by passing beyond an adequate warning notice;

but the exclusions contained in paragraphs (a) and (b) above shall only apply where persons under the age of 18 years are not permitted to enter while the display in question is continuing.

(4) Nothing in this section applies in relation to any matter—

    [(a) included by any person in a television broadcasting service or other television programme service (within the meaning of Part I of the Broadcasting Act 1990);][1]

    (b) included in the display of an art gallery or museum and visible only from within the gallery or museum; or

    (c) displayed by or with the authority of, and visible only from within a building occupied by, the Crown or any local authority; or

    (d) included in a performance of a play (within the meaning of the Theatres Act 1968); or

    [(e) included in a film exhibition as defined in the Cinemas Act 1985—

        (i) given in a place which as regards that exhibition is required to be licensed under section 1 of that Act or by virtue only of section 5, 7 or 8 of that Act is not required to be so licensed; or

        (ii) which is an exhibition to which section 6 of that Act applies given by an exempted organisation as defined in subsection (6) of that section.][2]

(5) In this section "matter" includes anything capable of being displayed, except that it does not include an actual human body or any part thereof; and in determining for the purpose of this section whether any displayed matter is indecent—

(a) there shall be disregarded any part of that matter which is not exposed to view; and

(b) account may be taken of the effect of juxtaposing one thing with another.

(6) A warning notice shall not be adequate for the purposes of this section unless it complies with the following requirements—

(a) The warning notice must contain the following words, and no others—

"WARNING

Persons passing beyond this notice will find material on display which they may consider indecent. No admittance to persons under 18 years of age."

(b) The word "WARNING" must appear as a heading.

(c) No pictures or other matter shall appear on the notice.

(d) The notice must be so situated that no one could reasonably gain access to the shop or part of the shop in question without being aware of the notice and it must be easily legible by any person gaining such access.

---

[1] Substituted by Broadcasting Act 1990 (c.42), Sched. 20, para. 30.
[2] s.1(4)(e) substituted by Cinemas Act 1985 (c.13), s.24(1), Sched. 2, para. 13.

Supreme Court Act 1981

(1981, c. 54)

An Act to consolidate with amendments the Supreme Court of Judicature (Consolidation) Act 1925 and other enactments relating to the Supreme Court in England and Wales and the administration of justice therein; to repeal certain obsolete or unnecessary enactments so relating; to amend Part VIII of the Mental Health Act 1959, the Courts-Martial (Appeals) Act 1968, the Arbitration Act 1979 and the law relating to county courts; and for connected purposes.   [28th July 1981]   **48–001**

PART I

CONSTITUTION OF SUPREME COURT

The Supreme Court

The Supreme Court

1.—(1) The Supreme Court of England and Wales shall consist of the Court   **48–002** of Appeal, the High Court of Justice and the Crown Court, each having such jurisdiction as is conferred on it by or under this or any other Act.

(2) The Lord Chancellor shall be president of the Supreme Court.

The Court of Appeal

The Court of Appeal

2.—(1) The Court of Appeal shall consist of ex-officio judges and not more   **48–003** than eighteen ordinary judges.

(2) The following shall be ex-officio judges of the Court of Appeal—

    (a) the Lord Chancellor;
    (b) any person who has been Lord Chancellor;
    (c) any Lord of Appeal in Ordinary who at the date of his appointment was, or was qualified for appointment as, an ordinary judge of the Court of Appeal or held an office within paragraphs (d) to (g);
    (d) the Lord Chief Justice;
    (e) the Master of the Rolls;
    (f) the President of the Family Division; and
    (g) the Vice-Chancellor;

but a person within paragraph (b) or (c) shall not be required to sit and act as a judge of the Court of Appeal unless at the Lord Chancellor's request he consents to do so.

(3) The ordinary judges of the Court of Appeal (including the vice-president, if any, of either division) shall be styled "Lords Justices of Appeal".

(4) Her Majesty may by Order in Council from time to time amend subsection (1) so as to increase or further increase the maximum number of ordinary judges of the Court of Appeal.

(5) No recommendation shall be made to Her Majesty in Council to make an Order under subsection (4) unless a draft of the Order has been laid before Parliament and approved by resolution of each House of Parliament.

(6) The Court of Appeal shall be taken to be duly constituted notwithstanding any vacancy in the office of Lord Chancellor, Lord Chief Justice, Master of the Rolls, President of the Family Division or Vice-Chancellor.

Divisions of Court of Appeal

48–004   3.—(1) There shall be two divisions of the Court of Appeal, namely the criminal division and the civil division.

(2) The Lord Chief Justice shall be president of the criminal division of the Court of Appeal, and the Master of the Rolls shall be president of the civil division of that court.

(3) The Lord Chancellor may appoint one of the ordinary judges of the Court of Appeal as vice-president of both divisions of that court, or one of those judges as vice-president of the criminal division and another of them as vice- president of the civil division.

(4) When sitting in a court of either division of the Court of Appeal in which no ex-officio judge of the Court of Appeal is sitting, the vice-president (if any) of that division shall preside.

(5) Any number of courts of either division of the Court of Appeal may sit at the same time.

The High Court

48–005   4.—(1) The High Court shall consist of—

    (a) the Lord Chancellor;
    (b) the Lord Chief Justice;
    (c) the President of the Family Division;
    (d) the Vice-Chancellor; and
    [(e) the Senior Presiding Judge]
    [(f) the vice-president of the Queen's Bench Division;]
    (g) not more than eighty puisne judges of that court.

(2) The puisne judges of the High Court shall be styled "Justices of the High Court".

(3) All the judges of the High Court shall, except where this Act expressly provides otherwise, have in all respects equal power, authority and jurisdiction.

(4) Her Majesty may by Order in Council from time to time amend subsection (1) so as to increase or further increase the maximum number of puisne judges of the High Court.

(5) No recommendation shall be made to Her Majesty in Council to make an Order under subsection (4) unless a draft of the Order has been laid before Parliament and approved by resolution of each House of Parliament.

(6) The High Court shall be taken to be duly constituted notwithstanding any vacancy in the office of Lord Chancellor, Lord Chief Justice, President of the Family Division [or Vice-Chancellor or Senior Presiding Judge] [and whether or not an appointment has been made to the office of vice-president of the Queen's Bench Division].

......

Other provisions

Appointment of judges of Supreme Court

10.—(1) Whenever the office of Lord Chief Justice, Master of the Rolls, **48–006** President of the Family Division or Vice-Chancellor is vacant, Her Majesty may by letters patent appoint a qualified person to that office.

(2) Subject to the limits on numbers for the time being imposed by sections 2(1) and 4(1), Her Majesty may from time to time by letters patent appoint qualified persons as Lords Justices of Appeal or as puisne judges of the High Court.

(3) No person shall be qualified for appointment—

(a) as Lord Chief Justice, Master of the Rolls, President of the Family Division or Vice-Chancellor, unless he is qualified for appointment as a Lord Justice of Appeal or is a judge of the Court of Appeal;

(b) as a Lord Justice of Appeal, [unless—

(i) he has a 10 year High Court qualification within the meaning of section 71 of the Courts and Legal Services Act 1990; or
(ii) he is a judge of the High Court;]; or

(c) as a puisne judge of the High Court, [unless—

(i) he has a 10 year High Court qualification, within the meaning of section 71 of the Courts and Legal Services Act 1990; or
(ii) he is a Circuit judge who has held that office for at least 2 years.].

(4) Every person appointed to an office mentioned in subsection (1) or as a Lord Justice of Appeal or puisne judge of the High Court shall, as soon as may be after his acceptance of office, take the oath of allegiance and the judicial oath, as set out in the Promissory Oaths Act 1868, in the presence of the Lord Chancellor.

Tenure of office of judges of Supreme Court

11.—(1) This section applies to the office of any judge of the Supreme Court **48–007** except the Lord Chancellor.

(2) A person appointed to an office to which this section applies shall vacate

it on the day on which he attains the age of [seventy] years unless by virtue of this section he has ceased to hold it before then.

(3) A person appointed to an office to which this section applies shall hold that office during good behaviour, subject to a power of removal by Her Majesty on an address presented to Her by both Houses of Parliament.

(4) A person holding an office within section 2(2)(d) to (g) shall vacate that office on becoming Lord Chancellor or a Lord of Appeal in Ordinary.

(5) A Lord Justice of Appeal shall vacate that office on becoming an ex-officio judge of the Court of Appeal.

(6) A puisne judge of the High Court shall vacate that office on becoming a judge of the Court of Appeal.

(7) A person who holds an office to which this section applies may at any time resign it by giving the Lord Chancellor notice in writing to that effect.

(8) The Lord Chancellor, if satisfied by means of a medical certificate that a person holding an office to which this section applies—

> (a) is disabled by permanent infirmity from the performance of the duties of his office; and
>
> (b) is for the time being incapacitated from resigning his office,

may, subject to subsection (9), by instrument under his hand declare that person's office to have been vacated; and the instrument shall have the like effect for all purposes as if that person had on the date of the instrument resigned his office.

(9) A declaration under subsection (8) with respect to a person shall be of no effect unless it is made—

> (a) in the case of any of the Lord Chief Justice, the Master of the Rolls, the President of the Family Division and the Vice-Chancellor, with the concurrence of two others of them;
>
> (b) in the case of a Lord Justice of Appeal, with the concurrence of the Master of the Rolls;
>
> (c) in the case of a puisne judge of any Division of the High Court, with the concurrence of the senior judge of that Division.

(10) [. . .]¹

¹ s. 11(10) repealed by Statute Law (Repeals) Act 1989 (c.43), s.1(1), Sched. 1, Pt I.

. . . . . .

THE HIGH COURT

General jurisdiction

General jurisdiction of High Court

48–008   19.—(1) The High Court shall be a superior court of record.

(2) Subject to the provisions of this Act, there shall be exercisable by the High Court—

> (a) all such jurisdiction (whether civil or criminal) as is conferred on it by this or any other Act; and
>
> (b) all such other jurisdiction (whether civil or criminal) as was exercisable by it immediately before the commencement of this Act (including jurisdiction conferred on a judge of the High Court by any statutory provision).

(3) Any jurisdiction of the High Court shall be exercised only by a single judge of that court, except in so far as it is—

(a) by or by virtue of rules of court or any other statutory provision required to be exercised by a divisional court; or
(b) by rules of court made exercisable by a master, registrar or other officer of the court, or by any other person.

(4) The specific mention elsewhere in this Act of any jurisdiction covered by subsection (2) shall not derogate from the generality of that subsection.

. . . . . .

Other particular fields of jurisdiction

Orders of mandamus, prohibition and certiorari

29.—(1) [Subject to subsection (3A),]¹[t]²he High Court shall have jurisdiction to make orders of mandamus, prohibition and certiorari in those classes of cases in which it had power to do so immediately before the commencement of this Act.   **48–009**

(2) Every such order shall be final, subject to any right of appeal therefrom.

(3) In relation to the jurisdiction of the Crown Court, other than its jurisdiction in matters relating to trial on indictment, the High Court shall have all such jurisdiction to make orders of mandamus, prohibition or certiorari as the High Court possesses in relation to the jurisdiction of an inferior court.

[(3A) The High Court shall have no jurisdiction to make orders of mandamus, prohibition or certiorari in relation to the jurisdiction of a court-martial in matters relating to—

(a) trial by court-martial for an offence, or
(b) appeals from a Standing Civilian Court;

and in this subsection "court-martial" means a court-martial under the Army Act 1955, the Air Force Act 1955 or the Naval Discipline Act 1957.]³

(4) The power of the High Court under any enactment to require justices of the peace or a judge or officer of a county court to do any act relating to the duties of their respective offices, or to require a magistrates' court to state a case for the opinion of the High Court, in any case where the High Court formerly had by virtue of any enactment jurisdiction to make a rule absolute, or an order, for any of those purposes, shall be exercisable by order of mandamus.

(5) In any enactment—

(a) references to a writ of mandamus, of prohibition or of certiorari shall be read as references to the corresponding order; and
(b) references to the issue or award of any such writ shall be read as references to the making of the corresponding order.

[(6) In subsection (3) the reference to the Crown Court's jurisdiction in matters relating to trial on indictment does not include its jurisdiction relating to orders under section 17 of the Access to Justice Act 1999.]⁴

---

¹ Words inserted by Armed Forces Act 2001 (c.19), Pt 3, s.23(2).
² *ibid.*
³ Added by Armed Forces Act 2001 (c.19), Pt 3, s.23(3).
⁴ Added by Access to Justice Act 1999 (c.22), Sched. 4, para. 23.

. . . . . .

Application for judicial review

48–010   31.—(1) An application to the High Court for one or more of the following forms of relief, namely—

    (a) an order of mandamus, prohibition or certiorari;

    (b) a declaration or injunction under subsection (2); or

    (c) an injunction under section 30 restraining a person not entitled to do so from acting in an office to which that section applies,

shall be made in accordance with rules of court by a procedure to be known as an application for judicial review.

(2) A declaration may be made or an injunction granted under this subsection in any case where an application for judicial review, seeking that relief, has been made and the High Court considers that, having regard to—

    (a) the nature of the matters in respect of which relief may be granted by orders of mandamus, prohibition or certiorari;

    (b) the nature of the persons and bodies against whom relief may be granted by such orders; and

    (c) all the circumstances of the case,

it would be just and convenient for the declaration to be made or the injunction to be granted, as the case may be.

(3) No application for judicial review shall be made unless the leave of the High Court has been obtained in accordance with rules of court; and the court shall not grant leave to make such an application unless it considers that the applicant has a sufficient interest in the matter to which the application relates.

(4) On an application for judicial review the High Court may award damages to the applicant if—

    (a) he has joined with his application a claim for damages arising from any matter to which the application relates; and

    (b) the court is satisfied that, if the claim had been made in an action begun by the applicant at the time of making his application, he would have been awarded damages.

(5) If, on an application for judicial review seeking an order of certiorari, the High Court quashes the decision to which the application relates, the High Court may remit the matter to the court, tribunal or authority concerned, with a direction to reconsider it and reach a decision in accordance with the findings of the High Court.

(6) Where the High Court considers that there has been undue delay in making an application for judicial review, the court may refuse to grant—

    (a) leave for the making of the application; or

    (b) any relief sought on the application,

if it considers that the granting of the relief sought would be likely to cause substantial hardship to, or substantially prejudice the rights of, any person or would be detrimental to good administration.

(7) Subsection (6) is without prejudice to any enactment or rule of court which has the effect of limiting the time within which an application for judicial review may be made.

Canada Act 1982

(1982, c. 11)

An Act to give effect to a request by the Senate and House of Commons of   **49–001**
Canada.   [29th March 1982]

Whereas Canada has requested and consented to the enactment of an Act of the Parliament of the United Kingdom to give effect to the provisions hereinafter set forth and the Senate and the House of Commons of Canada in Parliament assembled have submitted an address to Her Majesty requesting that Her Majesty may graciously be pleased to cause a Bill to be laid before the Parliament of the United Kingdom for that purpose:

Constitution Act, 1982 enacted

1. The Constitution Act, 1982 set out in Schedule B to this Act is hereby   **49–002**
enacted for and shall have the force of law in Canada and shall come into force as provided in that Act.

Termination of power to legislate for Canada

2. No Act of the Parliament of the United Kingdom passed after the Constitu-   **49–003**
tion Act, 1982 comes into force shall extend to Canada as part of its law.

French version

3. So far as it is not contained in Schedule B, the French version of this Act   **49–004**
is set out in Schedule A to this Act and has the same authority in Canada as the English version thereof.

Short title

4. This Act may be cited as the Canada Act 1982.   **49–005**

. . . . . .

SCHEDULE B

CONSTITUTION ACT, 1982

PART I

CANADIAN CHARTER OF RIGHTS AND FREEDOMS
   Whereas Canada is founded upon principles that recognize the supremacy of God and the rule of law:

Guarantee of Rights and Freedoms

Rights and freedoms in Canada
   1. The Canadian Charter of Rights and Freedoms guarantees the rights and freedoms set out in it   **49–006**
subject only to such reasonable limits prescribed by law as can be demonstrably justified in a free and democratic society.

Fundamental Freedoms

Fundamental Freedoms
   2. Everyone has the following fundamental freedoms: **49–007**

   (a) freedom of conscience and religion;

(b) freedom of thought, belief, opinion and expression, including freedom of the press and other media of communication;

(c) freedom of peaceful assembly; and

(d) freedom of association.

Democratic Rights

Democratic rights of citizens

49–008 3. Every citizen of Canada has the right to vote in an election of members of the House of Commons or of a legislative assembly and to be qualified for membership therein.

Maximum duration of legislative bodies

49–009 **4.**—(1) No House of Commons and no legislative assembly shall continue for longer than five years from the date fixed for the return of the writs at a general election of its members.

(2) Continuation in special circumstances In time of real or apprehended war, invasion or insurrection, a House of Commons may be continued by Parliament and a legislative assembly may be continued by the legislature beyond five years if such continuation is not opposed by the votes of more than one-third of the members of the House of Commons or the legislative assembly, as the case may be.

Annual sitting of legislative bodies

49–010 5. There shall be a sitting of Parliament and of each legislature at least once every twelve months.

Mobility Rights

Mobility of citizens

49–011 **6.**—(1) Every citizen of Canada has the right to enter, remain in and leave Canada.

(2) *Rights to move and gain livelihood* Every citizen of Canada and every person who has the status of a permanent resident of Canada has the right—

(a) to move to and take up residence in any province; and

(b) to pursue the gaining of a livelihood in any province.

(3) *Limitation* The rights specified in subsection (2) are subject to

(a) any laws or practices of general application in force in a province other than those that discriminate among persons primarily on the basis of province of present or previous residence; and

(b) any laws providing for reasonable residency requirements as a qualification for the receipt of publicly provided social services.

(4) *Affirmative action programs* Subsections (2) and (3) do not preclude any law, program or activity that has as its object the amelioration in a province of conditions of individuals in that province who are socially or economically disadvantaged if the rate of employment in that province is below the rate of employment in Canada.

Legal Rights

Life, liberty and security of person

49–012 7. Everyone has the right to life, liberty and security of the person and the right not to be deprived thereof except in accordance with the principles of fundamental justice.

Search or seizure

49–013 8. Everyone has the right to be secure against unreasonable search or seizure.

Detention or imprisonment

49–014 9. Everyone has the right not to be arbitrarily detained or imprisoned.

Arrest or detention

49–015 10. Everyone has the right on arrest or detention

(a) to be informed promptly of the reasons therefor;

(b) to retain and instruct counsel without delay and to be informed of that right; and

(c) to have the validity of the detention determined by way of **habeas corpus** and to be released if the detention is not lawful.

Proceedings in criminal and penal matters

49–016 11. Any person charged with an offence has the right—

(a) to be informed without unreasonable delay of the specific offence;

(b) to be tried within a reasonable time;

(c) not to be compelled to be a witness in proceedings against that person in respect of the offence:

(d) to be presumed innocent until proven guilty according to law in a fair and public hearing by an independent and impartial tribunal;

(e) not to be denied reasonable bail without just cause;

(f) except in the case of an offence under military law tried before a military tribunal, to the benefit of trial by jury where the maximum punishment for the offence is imprisonment for five years or a more severe punishment;

(g) not to be found guilty on account of any act or omission unless, at the time of the act or omission, it constituted an offence under Canadian or international law or was criminal according to the general principles of law recognized by the community of nations;

(h) if finally acquitted of the offence, not to be tried for it again and, if finally found guilty and punished for the offence, not to be tried or punished for it again; and

(i) if found guilty of the offence and if the punishment for the offence has been varied between the time of commission and the time of sentencing, to the benefit of the lesser punishment.

Treatment or punishment

12. Everyone has the right not to be subjected to any cruel and unusual treatment or punishment. **49–017**

Self-crimination

13. A witness who testifies in any proceedings has the right not to have any incriminating evidence so given used to incriminate that witness in any other proceedings, except in a prosecution for perjury or for the giving of contradictory evidence. **49–018**

Interpreter

14. A party or witness in any proceedings who does not understand or speak the language in which the proceedings are conducted or who is deaf has the right to the assistance of an interpreter. **49–019**

Equality Rights

Equality before and under law and equal protection and benefit of law

15.—(1) Every individual is equal before and under the law and has the right to the equal protection and equal benefit of the law without discrimination and, in particular, without discrimination based on race, national or ethnic origin, colour, religion, sex, age or mental or physical disability. **49–020**

(2) *Affirmative action programs* Subsection (1) does not preclude any law, program or activity that has as its object the amelioration of conditions of disadvantaged individuals or groups including those that are disadvantaged because of race, national or ethnic origin, colour, religion, sex, age or mental or physical disability.

Official Languages of Canada

Official languages of Canada

16.—(1) English and French are the official languages of Canada and have equality of status and equal rights and privileges as to their use in all institutions of the Parliament and government of Canada. **49–021**

(2) *Official languages of New Brunswick* English and French are the official languages of New Brunswick and have equality of status and equal rights and privileges as to their use in all institutions of the legislature and government of New Brunswick.

(3) *Advancement of status and use* Nothing in this Charter limits the authority of Parliament or a legislature to advance the equality of status or use of English and French.

Proceedings of Parliament

17.—(1) Everyone has the right to use English or French in any debates and other proceedings of Parliament. **49–022**

(2) *Proceedings of New Brunswick legislature* Everyone has the right to use English or French in any debates and other proceedings of the legislature of New Brunswick.

Parliamentary statutes and records

18.—(1) The statutes, records and journals of Parliament shall be printed and published in English and French and both language versions are equally authoritative. **49–023**

(2) *New Brunswick statutes and records* The statutes, records and journals of the legislature of New Brunswick shall be printed and published in English and French and both language versions are equally authoritative.

Proceedings in courts established by Parliament

19.—(1) Either English or French may be used by any person in, or in any pleading in or process issuing from, any court established by Parliament. **49–024**

(2) *Proceedings in New Brunswick courts* Either English or French may be used by any person in, or in any pleading in or process issuing from, any court of New Brunswick.

Communications by public with federal institutions

49–025   20.—(1) Any member of the public in Canada has the right to communicate with, and to receive available services from, any head or central office of an institution of the Parliament or government of Canada in English or French, and has the same right with respect to any other office of any such institution where—

(a) there is a significant demand for communications with and services from that office in such language; or

(b) due to the nature of the office, it is reasonable that communications with and services from that office be available in both English and French.

(2) Communications by public with New Brunswick institutions Any member of the public in New Brunswick has the right to communicate with, and to receive available services from, any office of an institution of the legislature or government of New Brunswick in English or French.

Continuation of existing constitutional provisions

49–026   21. Nothing in sections 16 to 20 abrogates or derogates from any right, privilege or obligation with respect to the English and French languages, or either of them, that exists or is continued by virtue of any other provision of the Constitution of Canada.

Rights and privileges preserved

49–027   22. Nothing in sections 16 to 20 abrogates or derogates from any legal or customary right or privilege acquired or enjoyed either before or after the coming into force of this Charter with respect to any language that is not English or French.

Minority Language Educational Rights

Language of instruction

49–028   23.—(1) Citizens of Canada—

(a) whose first language learned and still understood is that of the English or French linguistic minority population of the province in which they reside, or

(b) who have received their primary school instruction in Canada in English or French and reside in a province where the language in which they received that instruction is the language of the English or French linguistic minority population of the province,

have the right to have their children receive primary and secondary school instruction in that language in that province.

(2) Continuity of language instruction Citizens of Canada of whom any child has received or is receiving primary or secondary school instruction in English or French in Canada, have the right to have all their children receive primary and secondary school instruction in the same language.

(3) Application where numbers warrant The right of citizens of Canada under subsections (1) and (2) to have their children receive primary and secondary school instruction in the language of the English or French linguistic minority population of a province—

(a) applies wherever in the province the number of children of citizens who have such a right is sufficient to warrant the provision to them out of public funds of minority language instruction; and

(b) includes, where the number of those children so warrants, the right to have them receive that instruction in minority language educational facilities provided out of public funds.

Enforcement

Enforcement of guaranteed rights and freedoms

49–029   24.—(1) Anyone whose rights or freedoms, as guaranteed by this Charter, have been infringed or denied may apply to a court of competent jurisdiction to obtain such remedy as the court considers appropriate and just in the circumstances.

(2) *Exclusion of evidence bringing administration of justice into disrepute* Where, in proceedings under subsection (1), a court concludes that evidence was obtained in a manner that infringed or denied any rights or freedoms guaranteed by this Charter, the evidence shall be excluded if it is established that, having regard to all the circumstances, the admission of it in the proceedings would bring the administration of justice into disrepute.

General

Aboriginal rights and freedoms not affected by Charter

49–030   25. The guarantee in this Charter of certain rights and freedoms shall not be construed so as to abrogate or derogate from any aboriginal, treaty or other rights or freedoms that pertain to the aboriginal peoples of Canada including—

(a) any rights or freedoms that have been recognized by the Royal Proclamation of October 7, 1763; and

(b) any rights or freedoms that may be acquired by the aboriginal peoples of Canada by way of land claims settlement.

Other rights and freedoms not affected by Charter

26. The guarantee in this Charter of certain rights and freedoms shall not be construed as denying the existence of any other rights or freedoms that exist in Canada.

49–031

Multicultural heritage

27. This Charter shall be interpreted in a manner consistent with the preservation and enhancement of the multicultural heritage of Canadians.

49–032

Rights guaranteed equally to both sexes

28. Notwithstanding anything in this Charter, the rights and freedoms referred to in it are guaranteed equally to male and female persons.

49–033

Rights respecting certain schools preserved

29. Nothing in this Charter abrogates or derogates from any rights or privileges guaranteed by or under the Constitution of Canada in respect of denominational, separate or dissentient schools.

49–034

Application to territories and territorial authorities

30. A reference in this Charter to a province or to the legislative assembly or legislature of a province shall be deemed to include a reference to the Yukon Territory and the Northwest Territories, or to the appropriate legislative authority thereof, as the case may be.

49–035

Legislative powers not extended

31. Nothing in this Charter extends the legislative powers of any body or authority.

49–036

Application of Charter

Application of Charter

32(1) This Charter applies—

49–037

(a) to the Parliament and government of Canada in respect of all matters within the authority of Parliament including all matters relating to the Yukon Territory and Northwest Territories; and

(b) to the legislature and government of each province in respect of all matters within the authority of the legislature of each province.

(2) Exception Notwithstanding subsection (1), section 15 shall not have effect until three years after this section comes into force.

Exception where express declaration

33.—(1) Parliament or the legislature of a province may expressly declare in an Act of Parliament or of the legislature, as the case may be, that the Act or a provision thereof shall operate notwithstanding a provision included in section 2 or sections 7 to 15 of this Charter.

49–038

(2) *Operation of exception* An Act or a provision of an Act in respect of which a declaration made under this section is in effect shall have such operation as it would have but for the provision of this Charter referred to in the declaration.

(3) *Five year limitation* A declaration made under subsection (1) shall cease to have effect five years after it comes into force or on such earlier date as may be specified in the declaration.

(4) *Re-enactment* Parliament or the legislature of a province may re-enact a declaration made under subsection (1).

(5) *Five year limitation* Subsection (3) applies in respect of a re-enactment made under subsection (4).

Citation

Citation

34. This Part may be cited as the **Canadian Charter of Rights and Freedoms.**

49–039

Part II

Rights of the Aboriginal Peoples of Canada

Recognition of existing aboriginal and treaty rights

35.—(1) The existing aboriginal and treaty rights of the aboriginal peoples of Canada are hereby recognized and affirmed.

49–040

(2) Definition of "aboriginal peoples of Canada" In this Act, "aboriginal peoples of Canada"includes the Indian, Inuit and Métis peoples of Canada.

PART III

EQUALIZATION AND REGIONAL DISPARITIES

Commitment to promote equal opportunities

49–041   **36.**—(1) Without altering the legislative authority of Parliament or of the provincial legislatures, or the rights of any of them with respect to the exercise of their legislative authority, Parliament and the legislatures, together with the government of Canada and the provincial governments, are committed to—

(a) promoting equal opportunities for the well-being of Canadians;
(b) furthering economic development to reduce disparity in opportunities; and
(c) providing essential public services of reasonable quality to all Canadians.

(2) Commitment respecting public services Parliament and the government of Canada are committed to the principle of making equalization payments to ensure that provincial governments have sufficient revenues to provide reasonably comparable levels of public services at reasonably comparable levels of taxation.

PART IV

CONSTITUTIONAL CONFERENCE

Constitutional conference

49–042   **37.**—(1) A constitutional conference composed of the Prime Minister of Canada and the first ministers of the provinces shall be convened by the Prime Minister of Canada within one year after this Part comes into force.

(2) *Participation of aboriginal peoples* The conference convened under subsection (1) shall have included in its agenda an item respecting constitutional matters that directly affect the aboriginal peoples of Canada, including the identification and definition of the rights of those peoples to be included in the Constitution of Canada, and the Prime Minister of Canada shall invite representatives of those peoples to participate in the discussions on that item.

(3) *Participation of territories* The Prime Minister of Canada shall invite elected representatives of the governments of the Yukon Territory and the Northwest Territories to participate in the discussions on any item on the agenda of the conference convened under subsection (1) that, in the opinion of the Prime Minister, directly affects the Yukon Territory and the Northwest Territories.

PART V

PROCEDURE FOR AMENDING CONSTITUTION OF CANADA

General procedure for amending Constitution of Canada

49–043   **38.**—(1) An amendment to the Constitution of Canada may be made by proclamation issued by the Governor General under the Great Seal of Canada where so authorized by—

(a) resolutions of the State and House of Commons; and
(b) resolutions of the legislative assemblies of at least two-thirds of the provinces that have, in the aggregate, according to the then latest general census, at least fifty per cent. of the population of all the provinces.

(2) *Majority of members* An amendment made under subsection (1) that derogates from the legislative powers, the proprietary rights or any other rights or privileges of the legislature or government of a province shall require a resolution supported by a majority of the members of each of the Senate, the House of Commons and the legislative assemblies required under subsection (1).

(3) *Expression of dissent* An amendment referred to in subsection (2) shall not have effect in a province the legislative assembly of which has expressed its dissent thereto by resolution supported by a majority of its members prior to the issue of the proclamation to which the amendment relates unless that legislative assembly, subsequently, by resolution supported by a majority of its members, revokes its dissent and authorizes the amendment.

(4) *Revocation of dissent* A resolution of dissent made for the purposes of subsection (3) may be revoked at any time before or after the issue of the proclamation to which it relates.

Restriction on proclamation

49–044   **39.**—(1) A proclamation shall not be issued under subsection 38(1) before the expiration of one year from the adoption of the resolution initiating the amendment procedure thereunder, unless the legislative assembly of each province has previously adopted a resolution of assent or dissent.

(2) *Idem* A proclamation shall not be issued under subsection 38(1) after the expiration of three years from the adoption of the resolution initiating the amendment procedure thereunder.

Compensation

40. Where an amendment is made under subsection 38(1) that transfers provincial legislative powers relating to education or other cultural matters from provincial legislatures to Parliament, Canada shall provide reasonable compensation to any province to which the amendment does not apply.

49–045

Amendment by unanimous consent

41. An amendment to the Constitution of Canada in relation to the following matters may be made by proclamation issued by the Governor General under the Great Seal of Canada only where authorized by resolutions of the Senate and House of Commons and of the legislative assembly of each province:

49–046

    (a) the office of the Queen, the Governor General and the Lieutenant Governor of a province;
    (b) the right of a province to a number of members in the House of Commons not less than the number of Senators by which the province is entitled to be represented at the time this Part comes into force;
    (c) subject to section 43, the use of the English or the French language;
    (d) the composition of the Supreme Court of Canada; and
    (e) an amendment to this Part.

Amendment by general procedure

42.—(1) An amendment to the Constitution of Canada in relation to the following matters may be made only in accordance with subsection 38(1):

49–047

    (a) the principle of proportionate representation of the provinces in the House of Commons prescribed by the Constitution of Canada;
    (b) the powers of the Senate and the method of selecting Senators;
    (c) the number of members by which a province is entitled to be represented in the Senate and the residence qualifications of Senators;
    (d) subject to paragraph 41(d), the Supreme Court of Canada;
    (e) the extension of existing provinces into the territories; and
    (f) notwithstanding any other law or practice, the establishment of new provinces.

(2) Exception Subsections 38(2) to (4) do not apply in respect of amendments in relation to matters referred to in subsection (1).

Amendment of provisions relating to some but not all provinces

43. An amendment to the Constitution of Canada in relation to any provision that applies to one or more, but not all, provinces, including—

49–048

    (a) any alteration to boundaries between provinces, and
    (b) any amendment to any provision that relates to the use of the English or the French language within a province,

may be made by proclamation issued by the Governor General under the Great Seal of Canada only where so authorized by resolution of the Senate and House of Commons and of the legislative assembly of each province to which the amendment applies.

Amendments by Parliament

44. Subject to sections 41 and 42, Parliament may exclusively make laws amending the Constitution of Canada in relation to the executive government of Canada or the Senate and House of Commons.

49–049

Amendments by provincial legislatures

45. Subject to section 41, the legislature of each province may exclusively make laws amending the constitution of the province.

49–050

Initiation of amendment procedures

46.—(1) The procedures for amendment under sections 38, 41, 42 and 43 may be initiated either by the Senate or the House of Commons or by the legislative assembly of a province.

49–051

(2) *Revocation of authorization* A resolution of assent made for the purposes of this Part may be revoked at any time before the issue of a proclamation authorized by it.

Amendments without Senate resolution

47.—(1) An amendment to the Constitution of Canada made by proclamation under section 38, 41, 42 or 43 may be made without a resolution of the Senate authorizing the issue of the proclamation if, within one hundred and eighty days after the adoption by the House of Commons of a resolution authorizing its issue, the Senate has not adopted such a resolution and if, at any time after the expiration of that period, the House of Commons again adopts the resolution.

49–052

(2) Computation of period Any period when Parliament is prorogued or dissolved shall not be counted in computing the one hundred and eighty day period referred to in subsection (1).

Advice to issue proclamation

49–053   **48.** The Queen's Privy Council for Canada shall advise the Governor General to issue a proclamation under this Part forthwith on the adoption of the resolutions required for an amendment made by proclamation under this Part.

Constitutional conference

49–054   **49.** A constitutional conference composed of the Prime Minister of Canada and the first ministers of the provinces shall be convened by the Prime Minister of Canada within fifteen years after this Part comes into force to review the provisions of this Part.

. . . . . .

PART VII

GENERAL

Primacy of Constitution of Canada

49–055   **52.**—(1) The Constitution of Canada is the supreme law of Canada, and any law that is inconsistent with the provisions of the Constitution is, to the extent of the inconsistency, of no force or effect.

(2) *Constitution of Canada* The Constitution of Canada includes—

(a) the Canada Act 1982, including this Act;
(b) the Acts and orders referred to in the schedule; and
(c) any amendment to any Act or order referred to in paragraph (a) or (b).

(3) *Amendments to Constitution of Canada* Amendments to the Constitution of Canada shall be made only in accordance with the authority contained in the Constitution of Canada.

Repeals and new names

49–056   **53.**—(1) The enactments referred to in Column I of the schedule are hereby repealed or amended to the extent indicated in Column II thereof and, unless repealed, shall continue as law in Canada under the names set out in Column III thereof.

(2) *Consequential amendments* Every enactment, except the Canada Act 1982, that refers to an enactment referred to in the schedule by the name in Column I thereof is hereby amended by substituting for that name the corresponding name in Column III thereof, and any British North America Act not referred to in the Schedule may be cited as the **Constitution Act** followed by the year and number, if any, of its enactment.

Repeal and consequential amendments

49–057   **54.** Part IV is repealed on the day that is one year after this Part comes into force and this section may be repealed and this Act renumbered, consequentially upon the repeal of Part IV and this section, by proclamation issued by the Governor General under the Great Seal of Canada.

French version of Constitution of Canada

49–058   **55.** A French version of the portions of the Constitution of Canada referred to in the schedule shall be prepared by the Minister of Justice of Canada as expeditiously as possible and, when any portion thereof sufficient to warrant action being taken has been so prepared, it shall be put forward for enactment by proclamation issued by the Governor General under the Great Seal of Canada pursuant to the procedure then applicable to an amendment of the same provisions of the Constitution of Canada.

English and French versions of certain constitutional texts

49–059   **56.** Where any portion of the Constitution of Canada has been or is enacted in English and French or where a French version of any portion of the Constitution is enacted pursuant to section 55, the English and French versions of that portion of the Constitution are equally authoritative.

English and French versions of this Act

49–060   **57.** The English and French versions of this Act are equally authoritative.

Commencement

49–061   **58.** Subject to section 59, this Act shall come into force on a day to be fixed by proclamation issued by the Queen or the Governor General under the Great Seal of Canada.

Commencement of paragraph 23(1)(a) in respect of Quebec

49–062   **59.**—(1) Paragraph 23(1)(a) shall come into force in respect of Quebec on a day to be fixed by proclamation issued by the Queen or the Governor General under the Great Seal of Canada.

(2) *Authorization of Quebec* A proclamation under subsection (1) shall be issued only where authorized by the legislative assembly or government of Quebec.

(3) *Repeal of this Section* This section may be repealed on the day paragraph 23(1)(a) comes into force in respect of Quebec and this Act amended and renumbered, consequentially upon the repeal of this section, by proclamation issued by the Queen or the Governor General under the Great Seal of Canada.

Short title and citations

60. This Act may be cited as the Constitution Act 1982, and the Constitution Acts 1867 to 1975 (No. 2) and this Act may be cited together as the **Constitution Acts 1867 to 1982.**   **49–063**

Representation of the People Act 1983

(1983, c. 2)

An Act to consolidate the Representation of the People Acts of 1949, 1969, 1977,   **50–001**
1978 and 1980, the Electoral Registers Acts of 1949 and 1953, the Elec-
tions (Welsh Forms) Act 1964, Part III of the Local Government Act 1972,
sections 6 to 10 of the Local Government (Scotland) Act 1973, the Repres-
entation of the People (Armed Forces) Act 1976, the Returning Officers
(Scotland) Act 1977, section 3 of the Representation of the People Act
1981, section 62 of and Schedule 2 to the Mental Health (Amendment) Act
1982, and connected provisions; and to repeal as obsolete the Representa-
tion of the People Act 1979 and other enactments related to the Representa-
tion of the People Acts.   [8th February 1983]

PART I

PARLIAMENTARY AND LOCAL GOVERNMENT FRANCHISE AND ITS EXERCISE

Parliamentary and local government franchise

Parliamentary electors

[**1.**—(1) A person is entitled to vote as an elector at a parliamentary election   **50–002**
in any constituency if on the date of the poll he—

(a) is registered in the register of parliamentary electors for that constituency;
(b) is not subject to any legal incapacity to vote (age apart);
(c) is either a Commonwealth citizen or a citizen of the Republic of Ireland; and
(d) is of voting age (that is, 18 years or over).

(2) A person is not entitled to vote as an elector—

(a) more than once in the same constituency at any parliamentary election; or
(b) in more than one constituency at a general election.]¹

---

¹ Substituted by Representation of the People Act 2000 (c.2), Pt I, s.1(1).

Local government electors

50–003   2.—(1) A person is entitled to vote as an elector at a local government election in any electoral area if on the date of the poll he—

(a) is registered in the register of local government electors for that area;
(b) is not subject to any legal incapacity to vote (age apart);
(c) is a Commonwealth citizen, a citizen of the Republic of Ireland or a relevant citizen of the Union; and
(d) is of voting age (that is, 18 years or over).

(2) A person is not entitled to vote as an elector—

(a) more than once in the same electoral area at any local government election; or
(b) in more than one electoral area at an ordinary election for a local government area which is not a single electoral area.][¹]

¹ Substituted by Representation of the People Act 2000 (c.2), Pt I, s.1(1).

. . . . . .

PART II

THE ELECTION CAMPAIGN

Election expenses

Prohibition of expenses not authorised by election agent

50–004   75.—(1) No expenses shall, with a view to promoting or procuring the election of a candidate (or, in the case of an election of the London members of the London Assembly at an ordinary election, a registered political party or candidates of that party) at an election, be incurred by any person other than the candidate, his election agent and persons authorised in writing by the election agent on account—

(a) of holding public meetings or organising any public display; or
(b) of issuing advertisements, circulars or publications; or
(c) of otherwise presenting to the electors the candidate or his views or the extent or nature of his backing or disparaging another candidate, or
(d) in the case of an election of the London members of the London Assembly at an ordinary election, of otherwise presenting to the electors the candidate's registered political party (if any) or the views of that party or the extent or nature of that party's backing or disparaging any other registered political party,

but paragraph (c) or (d) of this subsection shall not—

(i) restrict the publication of any matter relating to the election in a newspaper or other periodical or in a broadcast made by the British Broadcasting Corporation or or by Sianel Pedwar Cymru or in a programme included in any service licensed under Part I or III of the Broadcasting Act 1990 or Part I or II of the Broadcasting Act 1996;
(ii) apply to any expenses incurred by any person which do not exceed in the aggregate the permitted sum (and are not incurred by that person

as part of a concerted plan of action), or to expenses incurred by any person in travelling or in living away from home or similar personal expenses.[1]

[(1ZA) For the purposes of subsection (1)(ii) above, "the permitted sum" means—

(a) in respect of a candidate at a parliamentary election, £500;
(b) in respect of a candidate at a local government election, £50 together with an additional 0.5p for every entry in the register of local government electors for the electoral area in question as it has effect on the last day for publication of notice of the election;

and expenses shall be regarded as incurred by a person "as part of a concerted plan of action" if they are incurred by that person in pursuance of any plan or other arrangement whereby that person and one or more other persons are to incur, with a view to promoting or procuring the election of the same candidate, expenses which (disregarding subsection (1)(ii)) fall within subsection (1) above.] [2]

(1A) In the application of subsection (1) above in relation to an election of the London members of the London Assembly at an ordinary election, any reference to the candidate includes a reference to all or any of the candidates of a registered political party; and in the application of subsection (1ZA) above in relation to such an election the reference to the same candidate includes a reference to all or any of the candidates of the same registered political party.

(2) Where a person incurs any expenses required by this section to be authorised by the election agent—

(a) that person shall within 21 days after the day on which the result of the election is declared deliver to the appropriate officer a return of the amount of those expenses, stating the election at which and the candidate in whose support they were incurred; and
(b) the return shall be accompanied by a declaration made by that person (or in the case of an association or body of persons, by a director, general manager, secretary or other similar officer of the association or body) verifying the return and giving particulars of the matters for which the expenses were incurred;

but this subsection does not apply to any person engaged or employed for payment or promise of payment by the candidate or his election agent.

(3) The return and declaration under the foregoing provisions of this section shall be in the prescribed form, and the authority received from the election agent shall be annexed to and deemed to form part of the return.

(4) A copy of every return and declaration made under subsection (2) above in relation to a parliamentary election in England, Wales or Northern Ireland shall be sent to the Clerk of the Crown within 21 days after the day on which the result of the election is declared by the person making the return or declaration, and rule 57 of the parliamentary elections rules applies to any documents sent to the Clerk of the Crown under this subsection.

In this subsection references to the Clerk of the Crown in relation to an election in Northern Ireland are references to the Clerk of the Crown for Northern Ireland.[3]

(5) If a person—

(a) incurs, or aids, abets, counsels or procures any other person to incur, any expenses in contravention of this section, or
(b) knowingly makes the declaration required by subsection (2) falsely,

he shall be guilty of a corrupt practice; and if a person fails to deliver or send any declaration or return or a copy of it as required by this section he shall be guilty of an illegal practice, but—

(i) the court before whom a person is convicted under this subsection may, if they think it just in the special circumstances of the case, mitigate or entirely remit any incapacity imposed by virtue of section 173 below; and

(ii) a candidate shall not be liable, nor shall his election be avoided, for a corrupt or illegal practice under this subsection committed by an agent without his consent or connivance.

(6) Where any act or omission of an association or body of persons, corporate or unincorporate, is an offence declared to be a corrupt or illegal practice by this section, any person who at the time of the act or omission was a director, general manager, secretary or other similar officer of the association or body, or was purporting to act in any such capacity, shall be deemed to be guilty of that offence, unless he proves—

(a) that the act or omission took place without his consent or connivance; and

(b) that he exercised all such diligence to prevent the commission of the offence as he ought to have exercised having regard to the nature of his functions in that capacity and to all the circumstances.

[1] In relation to the election for the New Northern Ireland Assembly held by virtue of Art. 3(1) of The New Northern Ireland Assembly (Elections) Order 1998:

(ii) apply to any expenses not exceeding in the aggregate the sum of £100 which may be incurred by an individual and are not incurred in pursuance of a plan suggested by or concerted with others, or to expenses incurred by any person in travelling or in living away from home or similar personal expenses.

[2] Added by Political Parties, Elections and Referendums Act 2000 (c.41), Pt VIII, s.131(3).

[3] Subsection (4) shall be omitted in relation to the election for the New Northern Ireland Assembly held by virtue of Art. 3(1) of the New Northern Ireland Assembly (Elections) Order 1998.

. . . . . .

Publicity at parliamentary elections

Broadcasting from outside United Kingdom

50–005   **92.**—[(1) No person shall, with intent to influence persons to give or refrain from giving their votes at a parliamentary or local government election, include, or aid, abet, counsel or procure the inclusion of, any matter relating to the election in any programme service (within the meaning of the Broadcasting Act 1990) provided from a place outside the United Kingdom otherwise than in pursuance of arrangements made with—

(a) the British Broadcasting Corporation;

(b) Sianel Pedwar Cymru; or

(c) the holder of any licence granted by the Independent Television Commission or the Radio Authority,

for the reception and re-transmission of that matter by that body or the holder of that licence, [or in pursuance of arrangements made with—

(i) the Independent Television Commission or the Radio Authority, or

(ii) any programme contractor whose contract continues in force by virtue of Part II or IV of Schedule 11 to the Broadcasting Act 1990, for the matter to be received by that body or contractor and re-transmitted by that body in the provision of any broadcasting service in accordance with the said Schedule 11.]¹]²

(2) An offence under this section shall be an illegal practice, but the court before whom a person is convicted of an offence under this section may, if they think it just in the special circumstances of the case, mitigate or entirely remit any incapacity imposed by virtue of section 173 below.

(3) Where any act or omission of an association or body of persons, corporate or unincorporate, is an illegal practice under this section, any person who at the time of the act or omission was a director, general manager, secretary or other similar officer of the association or body, or was purporting to act in any such capacity, shall be deemed to be guilty of the illegal practice, unless he proves—

(a) that the act or omission took place without his consent or connivance; and

(b) that he exercised all such diligence to prevent the commission of the illegal practice as he ought to have exercised having regard to the nature of his functions in that capacity and to all the circumstances.

¹ Words inserted by Broadcasting Act 1990 (c.42), s.203(4), Sched. 22, para. 6(b).
² s.92(1) substituted by Broadcasting Act 1990 (c.42), s.203(1), Sched. 20, para. 35(3)(5).

Broadcasting of local items during election period

93.—(1) Each broadcasting authority shall adopt a code of practice with **50–006** respect to the participation of candidates at a parliamentary or local government election in items about the constituency or electoral area in question which are included in relevant services during the election period.

(2) The code for the time being adopted by a broadcasting authority under this section shall be either—

(a) a code drawn up by that authority, whether on their own or jointly with one or more other broadcasting authorities, or

(b) a code drawn up by one or more other such authorities;

and a broadcasting authority shall from time to time consider whether the code for the time being so adopted by them should be replaced by a further code falling within paragraph (a) or (b).

(3) Before drawing up a code under this section a broadcasting authority shall have regard to any views expressed by the Electoral Commission for the purposes of this subsection; and any such code may make different provision for different cases.

(4) The Independent Television Commission and the Radio Authority shall each do all that they can to secure that the code for the time being adopted by them under this section is observed in the provision of relevant services; and the British Broadcasting Corporation and Sianel Pedwar Cymru shall each observe in the provision of relevant services the code so adopted by them.

(5) For the purposes of subsection (1) "the election period", in relation to an election, means the period beginning—

(a) (if a parliamentary general election) with the date of the dissolution of Parliament or any earlier time at which Her Majesty's intention to dissolve Parliament is announced,

(b) (if a parliamentary by-election) with the date of the issue of the writ for the election or any earlier date on which a certificate of the vacancy is notified in the London Gazette in accordance with the Recess Elections Act 1975, or

(c) (if a local government election) with the last date for publication of notice of the election,

and ending with the close of the poll.

(6) In this section—

"broadcasting authority" means the British Broadcasting Corporation, the Independent Television Commission, the Radio Authority or Sianel Pedwar Cymru;

"candidate", in relation to an election, means a candidate standing nominated at the election or included in a list of candidates submitted in connection with it;

"relevant services"—

(a) in relation to the British Broadcasting Corporation or Sianel Pedwar Cymru, means services broadcast by that body;

(b) in relation to the Independent Television Commission, means services licensed under Part I of the Broadcasting Act 1990 or Part I of the Broadcasting Act 1996; and

(c) in relation to the Radio Authority, means services licensed under Part III of the Broadcasting Act 1990 or Part II of the Broadcasting Act 1996.]¹

¹ Substituted by Political Parties, Elections and Referendums Act 2000 (c.41) Pt X, s.144.

. . . . . .

Election meetings

Disturbances at election meetings

50–007   **97.**—(1) A person who at a lawful public meeting to which this section applies acts, or incites others to act, in a disorderly manner for the purpose of preventing the transaction of the business for which the meeting was called together shall be guilty of an illegal practice.

(2) This section applies to—

(a) a political meeting held in any constituency between the date of the issue of a writ for the return of a member of Parliament for the constituency and the date at which a return to the writ is made;

(b) a meeting held with reference to a local government, election in the electoral area for that election [in the period beginning with the last date on which notice of the election may be published in accordance with rules made under section 36 or, in Scotland, section 42 above and ending with]¹, the day of election.

(3) If a constable reasonably suspects any person of committing an offence under subsection (1) above, he may if requested so to do by the chairman of the meeting require that person to declare to him immediately his name and address and, if that person refuses or fails so to declare his name and address or gives a false name and address, he shall be liable on summary conviction to a fine not exceeding level 1 on the standard scale, and—

(a) if he refuses or fails so to declare his name and address, or

(b) if the constable reasonably suspects him of giving a false name and address,

the constable may without warrant arrest him.
    This subsection does not apply in Northern Ireland.

¹ Words substituted by Representation of the People Act 1985 (c.50), s.24, Sched. 4 para. 39.

. . . . . .

Agency by election officials and canvassing by police officers

Illegal canvassing by police officers

100.—(1) No member of a police force shall by word, message, writing or in **50–008**
any other manner, endeavour to persuade any person to give, or dissuade any
person from giving, his vote, whether as an elector or as proxy—

(a) at any parliamentary election for a constituency, or
(b) at any local government election for any electoral area,

wholly or partly within the police area.¹
    (2) A person acting in contravention of subsection (1) above shall be liable
[on summary conviction to a fine not exceeding level 3 on the standard scale,
but] nothing in that subsection shall subject a member of a police force to any
penalty for anything done in the discharge of his duty as a member of the force.
    (3) In this section references to a member of a police force and to a police
area are to be taken in relation to Northern Ireland as references to a member
of the Royal Ulster Constabulary and to Northern Ireland.

Police and Criminal Evidence Act 1984

(1984, c. 60)

An Act to make further provision in relation to the powers and duties of the **51–001**
police, persons in police detention, criminal evidence, police discipline and
complaints against the police; to provide for arrangements for obtaining
the views of the community on policing and for a rank of deputy chief
constable; to amend the law relating to the Police Federations and Police
Forces and Police Cadets in Scotland; and for connected purposes.
[31st October 1984]

PART I

POWERS TO STOP AND SEARCH

Power of constable to stop and search persons, vehicles, etc.

1.—(1) A constable may exercise any power conferred by this section— **51–002**

(a) in any place to which at the time when he proposes to exercise the
power the public or any section of the public has access, on payment or
otherwise, as of right or by virtue of express or implied permission; or
(b) in any other place to which people have ready access at the time when
he proposes to exercise the power but which is not a dwelling.

(2) Subject to subsection (3) to (5) below, a constable—

   (a) may search—

      (i) any person or vehicle;

      (ii) anything which is in or on a vehicle,

for stolen or prohibited articles [or any article to which subsection (8A) below applies]; and

   (b) may detain a person or vehicle for the purpose of such a search.

(3) This section does not give a constable power to search a person or vehicle or anything in or on a vehicle unless he has reasonable grounds for suspecting that he will find stolen or prohibited articles [or any article to which subsection (8A) below applies].

(4) If a person is in a garden or yard occupied with and used for the purposes of a dwelling or on other land so occupied and used, a constable may not search him in the exercise of the power conferred by this section unless the constable has reasonable grounds for believing—

   (a) that he does not reside in the dwelling; and

   (b) that he is not in the place in question with the express or implied permission of a person who resides in the dwelling.

(5) If a vehicle is in a garden or yard occupied with and used for the purposes of a dwelling or on other land so occupied and used, a constable may not search the vehicle or anything in or on it in the exercise of the power conferred by this section unless he has reasonable grounds for believing—

   (a) that the person in charge of the vehicle does not reside in the dwelling; and

   (b) that the vehicle is not in the place in question with the express or implied permission of a person who resides in the dwelling.

(6) If in the course of such a search a constable discovers an article which he has reasonable grounds for suspecting to be a stolen or prohibited article [or an article to which subsection (8A) below applies], he may seize it.

(7) An article is prohibited for the purposes of this Part of this Act if it is—

   (a) an offensive weapon; or

   (b) an article—

      (i) made or adapted for use in the course of or in connection with an offence to which this sub-paragraph applies; or

      (ii) intended by the person having it with him for such use by him or by some other person.

(8) The offences to which subsection (7)(b)(i) above applies are—

   (a) burglary;

   (b) theft;

   (c) offences under section 12 of the Theft Act 1968 (taking motor vehicle or other conveyance without authority); and

   (d) offences under section 15 of that Act (obtaining property by deception).

[(8A) This subsection applies to any article in relation to which a person has committed, or is committing or is going to commit an offence under section 139 of the Criminal Justice Act 1988.]

(9) In this Part of this Act "offensive weapon" means any article—

(a) made or adapted for use for causing injury to persons; or
(b) intended by the person having it with him for such use by him or by some other person.

Provisions relating to search under section 1 and other powers

2.—(1) A constable who detains a person or vehicle in the exercise—   **51–003**

(a) of the power conferred by section 1 above; or
(b) of any other power—

(i) to search a person without first arresting him; or
(ii) to search a vehicle without making an arrest,

need not conduct a search if it appears to him subsequently—

(i) that no search is required; or
(ii) that a search is impracticable.

(2) If a constable contemplates a search, other than a search of an unattended vehicle, in the exercise—

(a) of the power conferred by section 1 above; or
(b) of any other power, except the power conferred by section 6 below and the power conferred by section 27(2) of the Aviation Security Act 1982—

(i) to search a person without first arresting him; or
(ii) to search a vehicle without making an arrest,

it shall be his duty, subject to subsection (4) below, to take reasonable steps before he commences the search to bring to the attention of the appropriate person—

(i) if the constable is not in uniform, documentary evidence that he is a constable; and
(ii) whether he is in uniform or not, the matters specified in subsection (3) below;

and the constable shall not commence the search until he has performed that duty.

(3) The matters referred to in subsection (2)(ii) above are—

(a) the constable's name and the name of the police station to which he is attached;
(b) the object of the proposed search;
(c) the constable's grounds for proposing to make it; and
(d) the effect of section 3(7) or (8) below, as may be appropriate.

(4) A constable need not bring the effect of section 3(7) or (8) below to the attention of the appropriate person if it appears to the constable that it will not be practicable to make the record in section 3(1) below.

(5) In this section "the appropriate person" means—

(a) if the constable proposes to search a person, that person; and
(b) if he proposes to search a vehicle, or anything in or on a vehicle, the person in charge of the vehicle.

(6) On completing a search of an unattended vehicle or anything in or on such a vehicle in the exercise of any such power as is mentioned in subsection (2) above a constable shall leave a notice—

(a) stating that he has searched it;
(b) giving the name of the police station to which he is attached;
(c) stating that an application for compensation for any damage caused by the search may be made to that police station; and
(d) stating the effect of section 3(8) below.

(7) The constable shall leave the notice inside the vehicle unless it is not reasonably practicable to do so without damaging the vehicle.

(8) The time for which a person or vehicle may be detained for the purposes of such a search is such time as is reasonably required to permit a search to be carried out either at the place where the person or vehicle was first detained or nearby.

(9) Neither the power conferred by section 1 above nor any other power to detain and search a person without first arresting him or to detain and search a vehicle without making an arrest is to be construed—

(a) as authorising a constable to require a person to remove any of his clothing in public other than an outer coat, jacket or gloves; or
(b) as authorising a constable not in uniform to stop a vehicle.

(10) This section and section 1 above apply to vessels, aircraft and hovercraft as they apply to vehicles.

Duty to make records concerning searches

51–004 3.—(1) Where a constable has carried out a search in the exercise of any such power as is mentioned in section 2(1) above, other than a search—

(a) under section 6 below; or
(b) under section 27(2) of the Aviation Security Act 1982,

he shall make a record of it in writing unless it is not practicable to do so.
(2) If—

(a) a constable is required by subsection (1) above to make a record of a search; but
(b) it is not practicable to make the record on the spot,

he shall make it as soon as practicable after the completion of the search.

(3) The record of a search of a person shall include a note of his name, if the constable knows it, but a constable may not detain a person to find out his name.

(4) If a constable does not know the name of a person whom he has searched, the record of the search shall include a note otherwise describing that person.

(5) The record of a search of a vehicle shall include a note describing the vehicle.

(6) The record of a search of a person or a vehicle—

(a) shall state—

(i) the object of the search;

(ii) the grounds for making it;

(iii) the date and time when it was made;

(iv) the place where it was made;

(v) whether anything, and if so what, was found;

(vi) whether any, and if so what, injury to a person or damage to property appears to the constable to have resulted from the search; and

(b) shall identify the constable making it.

(7) If a constable who conducted a search of a person made a record of it, the person who was searched shall be entitled to a copy of the record if he asks for one before the end of the period specified in subsection (9) below.

(8) If—

(a) the owner of a vehicle which has been searched or the person who was in charge of the vehicle at the time when it was searched asks for a copy of the record of the search before the end of the period specified in subsection (9) below; and

(b) the constable who conducted the search made a record of it;

the person who made the request shall be entitled to a copy.

(9) The period mentioned in subsections (7) and (8) above is the period of 12 months beginning with the date on which the search was made.

(10) The requirements imposed by this section with regard to records of searches of vehicles shall apply also to records of searches of vessels, aircraft and hovercraft.

Road checks

4.—(1) This section shall have effect in relation to the conduct of road checks   **51–005** by police officers for the purpose of ascertaining whether a vehicle is carrying—

(a) a person who has committed an offence other than a road traffic offence or a [vehicle] excise offence;

(b) a person who is a witness to such an offence;

(c) a person intending to commit such an offence; or

(d) a person who is unlawfully at large.

(2) For the purposes of this section a road check consists of the exercise in a locality of the power conferred by [section 163 of the Road Traffic Act 1988] in such a way as to stop during the period for which its exercise in that way in that locality continues all vehicles or vehicles selected by any criterion.

(3) Subject to subsection (5) below, there may only be such a road check if a police officer of the rank of superintendent or above authorises it in writing.

(4) An officer may only authorise a road check under subsection (3) above—

(a) for the purpose specified in subsection (1)(a) above, if he has reasonable grounds—

(i) for believing that the offence is a serious arrestable offence; and

(ii) for suspecting that the person is, or is about to be, in the locality in which vehicles would be stopped if the road check were authorised;

(b) for the purpose specified in subsection (1)(b) above, if he has reasonable grounds for believing that the offence is a serious arrestable offence;

(c) for the purpose specified in subsection (1)(c) above, if he has reasonable grounds—

　(i) for believing that the offence would be a serious arrestable offence; and

　(ii) for suspecting that the person is, or is about to be, in the locality in which vehicles would be stopped if the road check were authorised;

(d) for the purpose specified in subsection (1)(d) above, if he has reasonable grounds for suspecting that the person is, or is about to be, in that locality.

(5) An officer below the rank of superintendent may authorise such a road check if it appears to him that it is required as a matter of urgency for one of the purposes specified in subsection (1) above.

(6) If an authorisation is given under subsection (5) above, it shall be the duty of the officer who gives it—

(a) to make a written record of the time at which he gives it; and

(b) to cause an officer of the rank of superintendent or above to be informed that it has been given.

(7) The duties imposed by subsection (6) above shall be performed as soon as it is practicable to do so.

(8) An officer to whom a report is made under subsection (6) above may, in writing, authorise the road check to continue.

(9) If such an officer considers that the road check should not continue, he shall record in writing—

(a) the fact that it took place; and

(b) the purpose for which it took place.

(10) An officer giving an authorisation under this section shall specify the locality in which vehicles are to be stopped.

(11) An officer giving an authorisation under this section, other than an authorisation under subsection (5) above—

(a) shall specify a period, not exceeding seven days, during which the road check may continue; and

(b) may direct that the road check—

　(i) shall be continuous; or

　(ii) shall be conducted at specified times,

during that period.

(12) If it appears to an officer of the rank of superintendent or above that a road check ought to continue beyond the period for which it has been authorised he may, from time to time, in writing specify a further period, not exceeding seven days, during which it may continue.

(13) Every written authorisation shall specify—

(a) the name of the officer giving it;

(b) the purpose of the road check; and

(c) the locality in which vehicles are to be stopped.

(14) The duties to specify the purposes of a road check imposed by subsections (9) and (13) above include duties to specify any relevant serious arrestable offence.

(15) Where a vehicle is stopped in a road check, the person in charge of the vehicle at the time when it is stopped shall be entitled to obtain a written statement of the purpose of the road check if he applies for such a statement not later than the end of the period of twelve months from the day on which the vehicle was stopped.

(16) Nothing in this section affects the exercise by police officers of any power to stop vehicles for purposes other than those specified in subsection (1) above.

Reports of recorded searches and of road checks

5.—(1) Every annual report—   **51–006**

   [(a) under section 22 of the Police Act 1996; or]
   (b) made by the Commissioner of Police of the Metropolis,

shall contain information—

   (i) about searches recorded under section 3 above which have been carried out in the area to which the report relates during the period to which it relates; and
   (ii) about road checks authorised in that area during that period under section 4 above.

[(1A) Every annual report under section 57 of the Police Act 1997 (reports by Director General of the National Crime Squad) shall contain information—

   (a) about searches recorded under section 3 above which have been carried out by members of the National Crime Squad during the period to which the report relates; and
   (b) about road checks authorised by members of the National Crime Squad during that period under section 4 above.]

(2) The information about searches shall not include information about specific searches but shall include—

   (a) the total numbers of searches in each month during the period to which the report relates—

     (i) for stolen articles;
     (ii) for offensive weapons [or articles to which section 1(8A) above applies]; and
     (iii) for other prohibited articles;

   (b) the total number of persons arrested in each such month in consequence of searches of each of the descriptions specified in paragraph (a)(i) to (iii) above.

(3) The information about road checks shall include information—

   (a) about the reason for authorising each road check; and
   (b) about the result of each of them.

Statutory undertakers, etc.

51–007   **6.**—(1) A constable employed by statutory undertakers may stop, detain and search any vehicle before it leaves a goods area included in the premises of the statutory undertakers.

[(1A) Without prejudice to any powers under subsection (1) above, a constable employed [by the Strategic Rail Authority] may stop, detain and search any vehicle before it leaves a goods area which is included in the premises of any successor of the British Railways Board and is used wholly or mainly for the purposes of a relevant undertaking.]

(2) In this section "goods area" means any area used wholly or mainly for the storage or handling of goods[, and "successor of the British Railways Board" and "relevant undertaking" have the same meaning as in the Railways Act 1993 (Consequential Modifications) Order 1999].

(3) For the purposes of section 6 of the Public Stores Act 1875, any person appointed under the Special Constables Act 1923 to be a special constable within any premises which are in the possession or under the control of British Nuclear Fuels Limited shall be deemed to be a constable deputed by a public department and any goods and chattels belonging to or in the possession of British Nuclear Fuels Limited shall be deemed to be Her Majesty's Stores.

(4) In the application of subsection (3) above to Northern Ireland, for the reference to the Special Constables Act 1923 there shall be substituted a reference to paragraph 1(2) of Schedule 2 to the Emergency Laws (Miscellaneous Provisions) Act 1947.

Part I—supplementary

51–008   **7.**—(1) The following enactments shall cease to have effect—

(a) section 8 of the Vagrancy Act 1824;
(b) section 66 of the Metropolitan Police Act 1839;
(c) section 11 of the Canals (Offences) Act 1840;
(d) section 19 of the Pedlars Act 1871;
(e) section 33 of the County of Merseyside Act 1980; and
(f) section 42 of the West Midlands County Council Act 1980.

(2) There shall also cease to have effect—

(a) so much of any enactment contained in an Act passed before 1974, other than—

(i) an enactment contained in a public general Act; or
(ii) an enactment relating to statutory undertakers,

as confers power on a constable to search for stolen or unlawfully obtained goods; and

(b) so much of any enactment relating to statutory undertakers as provides that such a power shall not be exercisable after the end of a specified period.

(3) In this Part of this Act "statutory undertakers" means persons authorised by any enactment to carry on any railway, light railway, road transport, water transport, canal, inland navigation, dock or harbour undertaking.

PART II

POWERS OF ENTRY, SEARCH AND SEIZURE

Search warrants

Power of justice of the peace to authorise entry and search of premises

8.—(1) If on an application made by a constable a justice of the peace is satisfied that there are reasonable grounds for believing— **51–009**

(a) that a serious arrestable offence has been committed; and

(b) that there is material on premises specified in the application which is likely to be of substantial value (whether by itself or together with other material) to the investigation of the offence; and

(c) that the material is likely to be relevant evidence; and

(d) that it does not consist of or include items subject to legal privilege, excluded material or special procedure material; and

(e) that any of the conditions specified in subsection (3) below applies,

he may issue a warrant authorising a constable to enter and search the premises.

(2) A constable may seize and retain anything for which a search has been authorised under subsection (1) above.

(3) The conditions mentioned in subsection (1)(e) above are—

(a) that it is not practicable to communicate with any person entitled to grant entry to the premises;

(b) that it is practicable to communicate with a person entitled to grant entry to the premises but it is not practicable to communicate with any person entitled to grant access to the evidence;

(c) that entry to the premises will not be granted unless a warrant is produced;

(d) that the purpose of a search may be frustrated or seriously prejudiced unless a constable arriving at the premises can secure immediate entry to them.

(4) In this Act "relevant evidence", in relation to an offence, means anything that would be admissible in evidence at a trial for the offence.

(5) The power to issue a warrant conferred by this section is in addition to any such power otherwise conferred.

[(6) This section applies in relation to a relevant offence (as defined in section 28D(4) of the Immigration Act 1971) as it applies in relation to a serious arrestable offence.][1]

[1] Added by Immigration and Asylum Act 1999 (c.33), Sched. 14, para. 80(2).

Special provisions as to access

9.—(1) A constable may obtain access to excluded material or special procedure material for the purposes of a criminal investigation by making an application under Schedule 1 below and in accordance with that Schedule. **51–010**

(2) Any Act (including a local Act) passed before this Act under which a search of premises for the purposes of a criminal investigation could be authorised by the issue of a warrant to a constable shall cease to have effect so far as it relates to the authorisation of searches—

(a) for items subject to legal privilege; or

(b) for excluded material; or

(c) for special procedure material consisting of documents or records other than documents.

[(2A) Section 4 of the Summary Jurisdiction (Process) Act 1881 (c. 24) (which includes provision for the execution of process of English courts in Scotland) and section 29 of the Petty Sessions (Ireland) Act 1851 (c. 93) (which makes equivalent provision for execution in Northern Ireland) shall each apply to any process issued by a circuit judge under Schedule 1 to this Act as it applies to process issued by a magistrates' court under the Magistrates' Courts Act 1980 (c. 43).][1]

[1] Added by Criminal Justice and Police Act 2001 (c.16), Pt 3, s. 86(1).

Meaning of "items subject to legal privilege"

51–011 **10.**—(1) Subject to subsection (2) below, in this Act "items subject to legal privilege" means—

(a) communications between a professional legal adviser and his client or any person representing his client made in connection with the giving of legal advice to the client;

(b) communications between a professional legal adviser and his client or any person representing his client or between such an adviser or his client or any such representative and any other person made in connection with or in contemplation of legal proceedings and for the purposes of such proceedings; and

(c) items enclosed with or referred to in such communications and made—

(i) in connection with the giving of legal advice; or

(ii) in connection with or in contemplation of legal proceedings and for the purposes of such proceedings,

when they are in the possession of a person who is entitled to possession of them.

(2) Items held with the intention of furthering a criminal purpose are not items subject to legal privilege.

Meaning of "excluded material"

51–012 **11.**—(1) Subject to the following provisions of this section, in this Act "excluded material" means—

(a) personal records which a person has acquired or created in the course of any trade, business, profession or other occupation or for the purposes of any paid or unpaid office and which he holds in confidence;

(b) human tissue or tissue fluid which has been taken for the purposes of diagnosis or medical treatment and which a person holds in confidence;

(c) journalistic material which a person holds in confidence and which consists—

(i) of documents; or

(ii) of records other than documents.

(2) A person holds material other than journalistic material in confidence for the purposes of this section if he holds it subject—

(a) to an express or implied undertaking to hold it in confidence; or

(b) to a restriction on disclosure or an obligation of secrecy contained in any enactment, including an enactment contained in an Act passed after this Act.

(3) A person holds journalistic material in confidence for the purposes of this section if—

(a) he holds it subject to such an undertaking, restriction or obligation; and
(b) it has been continuously held (by one or more persons) subject to such an undertaking, restriction or obligation since it was first acquired or created for the purposes of journalism.

Meaning of "personal records"

12. In this Part of this Act "personal records" means documentary and other records concerning an individual (whether living or dead) who can be identified from them and relating—   **51–013**

(a) to his physical or mental health;
(b) to spiritual counselling or assistance given or to be given to him; or
(c) to counselling or assistance given or to be given to him, for the purposes of his personal welfare, by any voluntary organisation or by any individual who—

    (i) by reason of his office or occupation has responsibilities for his personal welfare; or

    (ii) by reason of an order of a court has responsibilities for his supervision.

Meaning of "journalistic material"

13.—(1) Subject to subsection (2) below, in this Act "journalistic material" means material acquired or created for the purposes of journalism.   **51–014**

(2) Material is only journalistic material for the purposes of this Act if it is in the possession of a person who acquired or created it for the purposes of journalism.

(3) A person who receives material from someone who intends that the recipient shall use it for the purposes of journalism is to be taken to have acquired it for those purposes.

Meaning of "special procedure material"

14.—(1) In this Act "special procedure material" means —   **51–015**

(a) material to which subsection (2) below applies; and
(b) journalistic material, other than excluded material.

(2) Subject to the following provisions of this section, this subsection applies to material, other than items subject to legal privilege and excluded material, in the possession of a person who—

(a) acquired or created it in the course of any trade, business, profession or other occupation or for the purpose of any paid or unpaid office; and
(b) holds it subject—

    (i) to an express or implied undertaking to hold it in confidence; or

(ii) to a restriction or obligation such as is mentioned in section 11(2)(b) above.

(3) Where material is acquired—

   (a) by an employee from his employer and in the course of his employment; or

   (b) by a company from an associated company;

it is only special procedure material if it was special procedure material immediately before the acquisition.

(4) Where material is created by an employee in the course of his employment, it is only special procedure material if it would have been special procedure material had his employer created it.

(5) Where material is created by a company on behalf of an associated company, it is only special procedure material if it would have been special procedure material had the associated company created it.

(6) A company is to be treated as another's associated company for the purposes of this section if it would be so treated under section 302 of the Income and Corporation Taxes Act 1970.

Search warrants—safeguards

51–016   15.—(1) This section and section 16 below have effect in relation to the issue to constables under any enactment, including an enactment contained in an Act passed after this Act, of warrants to enter and search premises; and an entry on or search of premises under a warrant is unlawful unless it complies with this section and section 16 below.

(2) Where a constable applies for any such warrant, it shall be his duty—

   (a) to state—

      (i) the ground on which he makes the application; and

      (ii) the enactment under which the warrant would be issued;

   (b) to specify the premises which it is desired to enter and search; and

   (c) to identify, so far as is practicable, the articles or persons to be sought.

(3) An application for such a warrant shall be made ex parte and supported by an information in writing.

(4) The constable shall answer on oath any question that the justice of the peace or judge hearing the application asks him.

(5) A warrant shall authorise an entry on one occasion only.

(6) A warrant—

   (a) shall specify—

      (i) the name of the person who applies for it;

      (ii) the date on which it is issued;

      (iii) the enactment under which it is issued; and

      (iv) the premises to be searched; and

   (b) shall identify, so far as is practicable, the articles or persons to be sought.

(7) Two copies shall be made of a warrant.

(8) The copies shall be clearly certified as copies.

Execution of warrants

16.—(1) A warrant to enter and search premises may be executed by any **51–017**
constable.

(2) Such a warrant may authorise persons to accompany any constable who
is executing it.

(3) Entry and search under a warrant must be within one month from the date
of its issue.

(4) Entry and search under a warrant must be at a reasonable hour unless it
appears to the constable executing it that the purpose of a search may be frustrated on an entry at a reasonable hour.

(5) Where the occupier of premises which are to be entered and searched is
present at the time when a constable seeks to execute a warrant to enter and
search them, the constable—

(a) shall identify himself to the occupier and, if not in uniform, shall produce to him documentary evidence that he is a constable;
(b) shall produce the warrant to him; and
(c) shall supply him with a copy of it.

(6) Where—

(a) the occupier of such premises is not present at the time when a constable seeks to execute such a warrant; but
(b) some other person who appears to the constable to be in charge of the
premises is present,

subsection (5) above shall have effect as if any reference to the occupier were
a reference to that other person.

(7) If there is no person present who appears to the constable to be in charge
of the premises, he shall leave a copy of the warrant in a prominent place on
the premises.

(8) A search under a warrant may only be a search to the extent required for
the purpose for which the warrant was issued.

(9) A constable executing a warrant shall make an endorsement on it stating—

(a) whether the articles or persons sought were found; and
(b) whether any articles were seized, other than articles which were sought.

(10) A warrant which—

(a) has been executed; or
(b) has not been executed within the time authorised for its execution, shall
be returned—

(i) if it was issued by a justice of the peace, to the [chief executive]¹
to the justices for the petty sessions area for which he acts; and
(ii) if it was issued by a judge, to the appropriate officer of the court
from which he issued it.

(11) A warrant which is returned under subsection (10) above shall be retained
for 12 months from its return—

(a) by the [chief executive]¹ to the justices, if it was returned under paragraph (i) of that subsection; and
(b) by the appropriate officer, if it was returned under paragraph (ii).

(12) If during the period for which a warrant is to be retained the occupier of

the premises to which it relates asks to inspect it, he shall be allowed to do so.

¹ Words substituted by Access to Justice Act 1999 (c.22), Sched. 13, para. 126.

Entry and search without search warrant

Entry for purpose of arrest etc.

51–018   **17.**—(1) Subject to the following provisions of this section, and without, pre-judice to any other enactment, a constable may enter and search any premises for the purpose—

> (a) of executing—
>
> > (i) a warrant of arrest issued in connection with or arising out of criminal proceedings; or
> > (ii) a warrant of commitment issued under section 76 of the Magistrates' Courts Act 1980;
>
> (b) of arresting a person for an arrestable offence;
> (c) of arresting a person for an offence under—
>
> > (i) section 1 (prohibition of uniforms in connection with political objects) of the Public Order Act 1936;
> > (ii) any enactment contained in sections 6 to 8 or 10 of the Criminal Law Act 1977 (offences relating to entering and remaining on property);
> > [(iii) section 4 of the Public Order Act 1986 (fear or provocation of violence);]¹
> > [(iv) section 76 of the Criminal Justice and Public Order Act 1994 (failure to comply with interim possession order);]
>
> [(d) of arresting, in pursuance of section 32(1A) of the Children and Young Persons Act 1969, any child or young person who has been remanded or committed to local authority accommodation under section 23(1) of that Act;
> (e) of recapturing any person who is, or is deemed for any purpose to be, unlawfully at large while liable to be detained—
>
> > (i) in a prison, remand centre, young offender institution or secure training centre, or
> > (ii) in pursuance of [section 92 of the Powers of Criminal Courts (Sentencing) Act 2000] (dealing with children and young persons guilty of grave crimes), in any other place;]
>
> (f) of recapturing [any person whatever] who is unlawfully at large and whom he is pursuing; or
> (g) of saving life or limb or preventing serious damage to property.

(2) Except for the purpose specified in paragraph (e) of subsection (1) above, the powers of entry and search conferred by this section—

> (a) are only exercisable if the constable has reasonable grounds for believing that the person whom he is seeking is on the premises; and
> (b) are limited, in relation to premises consisting of two or more separate dwellings, to powers to enter and search—
>
> > (i) any parts of the premises which the occupiers of any dwelling comprised in the premises use in common with the occupiers of any other such dwelling; and

      (ii) any such dwelling in which the constable has reasonable grounds
          for believing that the person whom he is seeking may be.

(3) The powers of entry and search conferred by this section are only exercisable for the purposes specified in subsection (1)(c)(ii) [or (iv)] above by a constable in uniform.

(4) The power of search conferred by this section is only a power to search to the extent that is reasonably required for the purpose for which the power of entry is exercised.

(5) Subject to subsection (6) below, all the rules of common law under which a constable has power to enter premises without a warrant are hereby abolished.

(6) Nothing in subsection (5) above affects any power of entry to deal with or prevent a breach of the peace.

¹ s.17(1)(c)(iii) inserted by Public Order Act 1986 (c.64), s.40(2), Sched. 2, para. 7.

Entry and search after arrest

18.—(1) Subject to the following provisions of this section, a constable may   **51–019**
enter and search any premises occupied or controlled by a person who is under
arrest for an arrestable offence, if he has reasonable grounds for suspecting that
there is on the premises evidence, other than items subject to legal privilege,
that relates—

    (a) to that offence; or
    (b) to some other arrestable offence which is connected with or similar to
        that offence.

(2) A constable may seize and retain anything for which he may search under subsection (1) above.

(3) The power to search conferred by subsection (1) above is only a power to search to the extent that is reasonably required for the purpose of discovering such evidence.

(4) Subject to subsection (5) below, the powers conferred by this section may not be exercised unless an officer of the rank of inspector or above has authorised them in writing.

(5) A constable may conduct a search under subsection (1) above—

    (a) before taking the person to a police station; and
    (b) without obtaining an authorisation under subsection (4) above,

if the presence of that person at a place other than a police station is necessary for the effective investigation of the offence.

(6) If a constable conducts a search by virtue of subsection (5) above, he shall inform an officer of the rank of inspector or above that he has made the search as soon as practicable after he has made it.

(7) An officer who—

    (a) authorises a search; or
    (b) is informed of a search under subsection (6) above, shall make a record
        in writing—

        (i) of the grounds for the search; and
        (ii) of the nature of the evidence that was sought.

(8) If the person who was in occupation or control of the premises at the time of the search is in police detention at the time the record is to be made, the officer shall make the record as part of his custody record.

Seizure, etc.

General power of seizure, etc.

51–020   **19.**—(1) The powers conferred by subsections (2), (3) and (4) below are exercisable by a constable who is lawfully on any premises.

(2) The constable may seize anything which is on the premises if he has reasonable grounds for believing—

(a) that it has been obtained in consequence of the commission of an offence; and

(b) that it is necessary to seize it in order to prevent it being concealed, lost, damaged, altered or destroyed.

(3) The constable may seize anything which is on the premises if he has reasonable grounds for believing—

(a) that it is evidence in relation to an offence which he is investigating or any other offence; and

(b) that it is necessary to seize it in order to prevent the evidence being concealed, lost, altered or destroyed.

(4) The constable may require any information which is contained in a computer and is accessible from the premises to be produced in a form in which it can be taken away and in which it is visible and legible if he has reasonable grounds for believing—

(a) that—

(i) it is evidence in relation to an offence which he is investigating or any other offence; or

(ii) it has been obtained in consequence of the commission of an offence; and

(b) that it is necessary to do so in order to prevent it being concealed, lost, tampered with or destroyed.

(5) The powers conferred by this section are in addition to any power otherwise conferred.

(6) No power of seizure conferred on a constable under any enactment (including an enactment contained in an Act passed after this Act) is to be taken to authorise the seizure of an item which the constable exercising the power has reasonable grounds for believing to be subject to legal privilege.

Extension of powers of seizure to computerised information

51–021   **20.**—(1) Every power of seizure which is conferred by an enactment to which this section applies on a constable who has entered premises in the exercise of a power conferred by an enactment shall be construed as including a power to require any information contained in a computer and accessible from the premises to be produced in a form in which it can be taken away and in which it is visible and legible.

(2) This section applies—

(a) to any enactment contained in an Act passed before this Act;

(b) to sections 8 and 18 above;

(c) to paragraph 13 of Schedule 1 to this Act; and

(d) to any enactment contained in an Act passed after this Act.

Access and copying

21.—(1) A constable who seizes anything in the exercise of a power conferred **51–022** by any enactment, including an enactment contained in an Act passed after this Act, shall, if so requested by a person showing himself—

(a) to be the occupier of premises on which it was seized; or
(b) to have had custody or control of it immediately before the seizure;

provide that person with a record of what he seized.

(2) The officer shall provide the record within a reasonable time from the making of the request for it.

(3) Subject to subsection (8) below, if a request for permission to be granted access to anything which—

(a) has been seized by a constable; and
(b) is retained by the police for the purpose of investigating an offence,

is made to the officer in charge of the investigation by a person who had custody or control of the thing immediately before it was so seized or by someone acting on behalf of such a person, the officer shall allow the person who made the request access to it under the supervision of a constable.

(4) Subject to subsection (8) below, if a request for a photograph or copy of any such thing is made to the officer in charge of the investigation by a person who had custody or control of the thing immediately before it was so seized, or by someone acting on behalf of such a person, the officer shall—

(a) allow the person who made the request access to it under the supervision of a constable for the purpose of photographing or copying it; or
(b) photograph or copy it, or cause it to be photographed or copied.

(5) A constable may also photograph or copy, or have photographed or copied, anything which he has power to seize, without a request being made under subsection (4) above.

(6) Where anything is photographed or copied under subsection (4)(b) above, the photograph or copy shall be supplied to the person who made the request.

(7) The photograph or copy shall be so supplied within a reasonable time from the making of the request.

(8) There is no duty under this section to grant access to, or to supply a photograph or copy of, anything if the officer in charge of the investigation for the purposes of which it was seized has reasonable grounds for believing that to do so would prejudice—

(a) that investigation;
(b) the investigation of an offence other than the offence for the purposes of investigating which the thing was seized; or
(c) any criminal proceedings which may be brought as a result of—

(i) the investigation of which he is in charge; or
(ii) any such investigation as is mentioned in paragraph (b) above.

Retention

22.—(1) Subject to subsection (4) below, anything which has been seized by **51–023** a constable or taken away by a constable following a requirement made by virtue of section 19 or 20 above may be retained so long as is necessary in all the circumstances.

(2) Without prejudice to the generality of subsection (1) above—

(a) anything seized for the purposes of a criminal investigation may be retained, except as provided by subsection (4) below—

(i) for use as evidence at a trial for an offence; or
(ii) for forensic examination or for investigation in connection with an offence; and

(b) anything may be retained in order to establish its lawful owner, where there are reasonable grounds for believing that it has been obtained in consequence of the commission of an offence.

(3) Nothing seized on the ground that it may be used—

(a) to cause physical injury to any person;
(b) to damage property;
(c) to interfere with evidence; or
(d) to assist in escape from police detention or lawful custody,

may be retained when the person from whom it was seized is no longer in police detention or the custody of a court or is in the custody of a court but has been released on bail.

(4) Nothing may be retained for either of the purposes mentioned in subsection (2)(a) above if a photograph or copy would be sufficient for that purpose.

(5) Nothing in this section affects any power of a court to make an order under section 1 of the Police (Property) Act 1897.

[(6) This section also applies to anything retained by the police under section 28H(5) of the Immigration Act 1971.][1]

[1] Added by Immigration and Asylum Act 1999 (c.33), Sched. 14, para. 80(3).

Meaning of "premises" etc.

51–024   23. In this Act—

"premises" includes any place and, in particular, includes—

(a) any vehicle, vessel, aircraft or hovercraft;

(b) any offshore installation; and

(c) any tent or movable structure; and

"offshore installation" has the meaning given to it by section 1 of the Mineral Workings (Offshore Installations) Act 1971.

PART III

ARREST

Arrest without warrant for arrestable offences

51–025   24.—(1) The powers of summary arrest conferred by the following subsections shall apply—

(a) to offences for which the sentence is fixed by law;
(b) to offences for which a person of 21 years of age or over (not previously convicted) may be sentenced to imprisonment for a term of five

years (or might be so sentenced but for the restrictions imposed by section 33 of the Magistrates' Courts Act 1980); and

(c) to the offences to which subsection (2) below applies,

and in this Act "arrestable offence" means any such offence.

(2) The offences to which this subsection applies are—

(a) offences for which a person may be arrested under the customs and excise Acts, as defined in section 1(1) of the Customs and Excise Management Act 1979;

(b) offences under the [the Official Secrets Act 1920] that are not arrestable offences by virtue of the term of imprisonment for which a person may be sentenced in respect of them;

[(c) offences under any provision of the Official Secrets Act 1989 except section 8(1), (4) or (5);]

(d) offences under 22 (causing prostitution of women) or 23 (procuration of girl under 21) of the Sexual Offences Act 1956;

[(e) an offence under section 46 of the Criminal Justice and Police Act 2001;]

(f) offences under section 12(1) (taking motor vehicle or other conveyance without authority etc.) or 25(1) (going equipped for stealing, etc.) of the Theft Act 1968; and

[[(g) any offence under the Football (Offences) Act 1991.

(h) an offence under section 2 of the Obscene Publications Act 1959 (publication of obscene matter);

(i) an offence under section 1 of the Protection of Children Act 1978 (indecent photographs and pseudo-photographs of children);]

[(j) an offence under section 1 of the Sexual Offences Act 1985 (c.44) (kerb-crawling);

(k) an offence under subsection (4) of section 170 of the Road Traffic Act 1988 (c.52) (failure to stop and report an accident) in respect of an accident to which that section applies by virtue of subsection (1)(a) of that section (accidents causing personal injury);.]

(l) an offence under section 166 of the Criminal Justice and Public Order Act 1994 (sale of tickets by unauthorised persons);]

[[(m) an offence under section 19 of the Public Order Act 1986 (publishing, etc. material intended or likely to stir up racial hatred);]

(n) an offence under section 167 of the Criminal Justice and Public Order Act 1994 (touting for hire car services).]

[(o) an offence under section 1(1) of the Prevention of Crime Act 1953 (prohibition of the carrying of offensive weapons without lawful authority or reasonable excuse);

(p) an offence under section 139(1) of the Criminal Justice Act 1988 (offence of having article with blade or point in public place);

(q) an offence under section 139A(1) or (2) of the Criminal Justice Act 1988 (offence of having article with blade or point (or offensive weapon) on school premises).]

[(r) an offence under section 2 of the Protection from Harassment Act 1997 (harassment).]

[[[(s) an offence under [section 60AA(7) of the Criminal Justice and Public Order Act 1994] (failing to comply with requirement to remove mask etc.);]

(t) an offence falling within section 32(1)(a) of the Crime and Disorder Act 1998 ([racially or religiously aggravated]);]]

[[(u) an offence under section 14J or 21C of the Football Spectators Act 1989 (failure to comply with requirements imposed by or under a banning order or a notice under section 21B);]

[[(v) an offence under section 12(4) of the Criminal Justice and Police Act 2001.]

(w) an offence under section 1(1) or (2) or 6 of the Wildlife and Countryside Act 1981 (taking, possessing, selling etc. of wild birds) in respect of a bird included in Schedule 1 to that Act or any part of, or anything derived from, such a bird;

(x) an offence under any of the following provisions of the Wildlife and Countryside Act 1981—

   (i) section 1(5) (disturbance of wild birds),
   (ii) section 9 or 13(1)(a) or (2) (taking, possessing, selling etc. of wild animals or plants),
   (iii) section 14 (introduction of new species, etc.).]

[(y) an offence under section 21C(1) or 21D(1) of the Aviation Security Act 1982 (c.36) (unauthorised presence in restricted zone or on aircraft);

(z) an offence under section 39(1) of the Civil Aviation Act 1982 (c.16) (trespass on aerodrome).]]

(3) Without prejudice to section 2 of the Criminal Attempts Act 1981, the powers of summary arrest conferred by the following subsections shall also apply to the offences of—

(a) conspiring to commit any of the offences mentioned in subsection (2) above;

(b) attempting to commit any such offence [other than an offence under section 12(1) of the Theft Act 1968];

(c) inciting, aiding, abetting, counselling or procuring the commission of any such offence;

and such offences are also arrestable offences for the purposes of this Act.

(4) Any person may arrest without a warrant—

(a) anyone who is in the act of committing an arrestable offence;

(b) anyone whom he has reasonable grounds for suspecting to be committing such an offence.

(5) Where an arrestable offence has been committed, any person may arrest without a warrant—

(a) anyone who is guilty of the offence;

(b) anyone whom he has reasonable grounds for suspecting to be guilty of it.

(6) Where a constable has reasonable grounds for suspecting that an arrestable offence has been committed, he may arrest without a warrant anyone whom he has reasonable grounds for suspecting to be guilty of the offence.

(7) A constable may arrest without a warrant—

(a) anyone who is about to commit an arrestable offence;

(b) anyone whom he has reasonable grounds for suspecting to be about to commit an arrestable offence.

General arrest conditions

51–026   25.—(1) Where a constable has reasonable grounds for suspecting that any offence which is not an arrestable offence has been committed or attempted, or is being committed or attempted, he may arrest the relevant person if it appears to him that service of a summons is impracticable or inappropriate because any of the general arrest conditions is satisfied.

(2) In this section "the relevant person" means any person whom the constable has reasonable grounds to suspect of having committed or having attempted to commit the offence or of being in the course of committing or attempting to commit it.

(3) The general arrest conditions are—

  (a) that the name of the relevant person is unknown to, and cannot be readily ascertained by, the constable;
  (b) that the constable has reasonable grounds for doubting whether a name furnished by the relevant person as his name is his real name;
  (c) that—

   (i) the relevant person has failed to furnish a satisfactory address for service; or
   (ii) the constable has reasonable grounds for doubting whether an address furnished by the relevant person is a satisfactory address for service;

  (d) that the constable has reasonable grounds for believing that arrest is necessary to prevent the relevant person—

   (i) causing physical injury to himself or any other person;
   (ii) suffering physical injury;
   (iii) causing loss of or damage to property;
   (iv) committing an offence against public decency; or
   (v) causing an unlawful obstruction of the highway;

  (e) that the constable has reasonable grounds for believing that arrest is necessary to protect a child or other vulnerable person from the relevant person.

(4) For the purposes of subsection (3) above an address is a satisfactory address for service if it appears to the constable—

  (a) that the relevant person will be at it for a sufficiently long period for it to be possible to serve him with a summons; or
  (b) that some other person specified by the relevant person will accept service of a summons for the relevant person at it.

(5) Nothing in subsection (3)(d) above authorises the arrest of a person under sub-paragraph (iv) of that paragraph except where members of the public going about their normal business cannot reasonably be expected to avoid the person to be arrested.

(6) This section shall not prejudice any power of arrest conferred apart from this section.

Repeal of statutory powers of arrest without warrant or order

26.—(1) Subject to subsection (2) below, so much of any Act (including a **51–027** local Act) passed before this Act as enables a constable—

  (a) to arrest a person for an offence without a warrant; or
  (b) to arrest a person otherwise than for an offence without a warrant or an order of a court;

shall cease to have effect.

(2) Nothing in subsection (1) above affects the enactments specified in Schedule 2 to this Act.

Fingerprinting of certain offenders

51–028   27.—(1) If a person—

    (a) has been convicted of a recordable offence;
    (b) has not at any time been in police detention for the offence; and
    (c) has not had his fingerprints taken—

        (i) in the course of the investigation of the offence by the police; or
        (ii) since the conviction;

any constable may at any time not later than one month after the date of the conviction require him to attend a police station in order that his fingerprints may be taken.

(2) A requirement under subsection (1) above—

    (a) shall give the person a period of at least 7 days within which he must so attend; and
    (b) may direct him to so attend at a specified time of day or between specified times of day.

(3) Any constable may arrest without warrant a person who has failed to comply with a requirement under subsection (1) above.

(4) The Secretary of State may by regulations make provision for recording in national police records convictions for such offences as are specified in the regulations.

[(4A) In subsection (4) above "conviction" includes—

    (a) a caution within the meaning of Part V of the Police Act 1997; and
    (b) a reprimand or warning given under section 65 of the Crime and Disorder Act 1998.]

(5) Regulations under this section shall be made by statutory instrument and shall be subject to annulment in pursuance of a resolution of either House of Parliament.

Information to be given on arrest

51–029   28.—(1) Subject to subsection (5) below, where a person is arrested, otherwise than by being informed that he is under arrest, the arrest is not lawful unless the person arrested is informed that he is under arrest as soon as is practicable after his arrest.

(2) Where a person is arrested by a constable, subsection (1) above applies regardless of whether the fact of the arrest is obvious.

(3) Subject to subsection (5) below, no arrest is lawful unless the person arrested is informed of the ground for the arrest at the time of, or as soon as is practicable after, the arrest.

(4) Where a person is arrested by a constable, subsection (3) above applies regardless of whether the ground for the arrest is obvious.

(5) Nothing in this section is to be taken to require a person to be informed—

    (a) that he is under arrest; or
    (b) of the ground for the arrest,

if it was not reasonably practicable for him to be so informed by reason of his having escaped from arrest before the information could be given.

Voluntary attendance at police station, etc.

29. Where for the purpose of assisting with an investigation a person attends voluntarily at a police station or at any other place where a constable is present or accompanies a constable to a police station or any such other place without having been arrested—   **51–030**

(a) he shall be entitled to leave at will unless he is placed under arrest;
(b) he shall be informed at once that he is under arrest if a decision is taken by a constable to prevent him from leaving at will.

Arrest elsewhere than at police station

30.—(1) Subject to the following provisions of this section, where a person—   **51–031**

(a) is arrested by a constable for an offence; or
(b) is taken into custody by a constable after being arrested for an offence by a person other than a constable,

at any place other than a police station, he shall be taken to a police station by a constable as soon as practicable after the arrest.

(2) Subject to subsections (3) and (5) below, the police station to which an arrested person is taken under subsection (1) above shall be a designated police station.

(3) A constable to whom this subsection applies may take an arrested person to any police station unless it appears to the constable that it may be necessary to keep the arrested person in police detention for more than six hours.

(4) Subsection (3) above applies—

(a) to a constable who is working in a locality covered by a police station which is not a designated police station; and
(b) to a constable belonging to a body of constables maintained by an authority other than a police authority.

(5) Any constable may take an arrested person to any police station if—

(a) either of the following conditions is satisfied—

(i) the constable has arrested him without the assistance of any other constable and no other constable is available to assist him;
(ii) the constable has taken him into custody from a person other than a constable without the assistance of any other constable and no other constable is available to assist him; and

(b) it appears to the constable that he will be unable to take the arrested person to a designated police station without the arrested person injuring himself, the constable or some other person.

(6) If the first police station to which an arrested person is taken after his arrest is not a designated police station, he shall be taken to a designated police station not more than six hours after his arrival at the first police station unless he is released previously.

(7) A person arrested by a constable at a place other than a police station shall be released if a constable is satisfied, before the person arrested reaches a police station, that there are no grounds for keeping him under arrest.

(8) A constable who releases a person under subsection (7) above shall record the fact that he has done so.

(9) The constable shall make the record as soon as is practicable after the release.

(10) Nothing in subsection (1) above shall prevent a constable delaying taking a person who has been arrested to a police station if the presence of that person elsewhere is necessary in order to carry out such investigations as it is reasonable to carry out immediately.

(11) Where there is delay in taking a person who has been arrested to a police station after his arrest, the reasons for the delay shall be recorded when he first arrives at a police station.

(12) Nothing in subsection (1) above shall be taken to affect—

   (a) paragraphs 16(3) or 18(1) of Schedule 2 to the Immigration Act 1971;
   (b) section 34(1) of the Criminal Justice Act 1972; or
   [(c) any provision of the Terrorism Act 2000.]¹

(13) Nothing in subsection (10) above shall be taken to affect paragraph 18(3) of Schedule 2 to the Immigration Act 1971.

¹ Substituted by Terrorism Act 2000 (c.11), Sched. 15, para. 5(2).

Arrest for further offence

51–032   31. Where—

   (a) a person—

        (i) has been arrested for an offence; and
        (ii) is at a police station in consequence of that arrest; and

   (b) it appears to a constable that, if he were released from that arrest, he would be liable to arrest for some other offence,

he shall be arrested for that other offence.

Search upon arrest

51–033   32.—(1) A constable may search an arrested person, in any case where the person to be searched has been arrested at a place other than a police station, if the constable has reasonable grounds for believing that the arrested person may present a danger to himself or others.

(2) Subject to subsections (3) to (5) below, a constable shall also have power in any such case—

   (a) to search the arrested person for anything—

        (i) which he might use to assist him to escape from lawful custody; or
        (ii) which might be evidence relating to an offence; and

   (b) to enter and search any premises in which he was when arrested or immediately before he was arrested for evidence relating to the offence for which he has been arrested.

(3) The power to search conferred by subsection (2) above is only a power to search to the extent that is reasonably required for the purpose of discovering any such thing or any such evidence.

(4) The powers conferred by this section to search a person are not to be construed as authorising a constable to require a person to remove any of his

clothing in public other than an outer coat, jacket or gloves [but they do authorise a search of a person's mouth].

(5) A constable may not search a person in the exercise of the power conferred by subsection (2)(a) above unless he has reasonable grounds for believing that the person to be searched may have concealed on him anything for which a search is permitted under that paragraph.

(6) A constable may not search premises in the exercise of the power conferred by subsection (2)(b) above unless he has reasonable grounds for believing that there is evidence for which a search is permitted under that paragraph on the premises.

(7) In so far as the power of search conferred by subsection (2)(b) above relates to premises consisting of two or more separate dwellings, it is limited to a power to search—

(a) any dwelling in which the arrest took place or in which the person arrested was immediately before his arrest; and

(b) any parts of the premises which the occupier of any such dwelling uses in common with the occupiers of any other dwellings comprised in the premises.

(8) A constable searching a person in the exercise of the power conferred by subsection (1) above may seize and retain anything he finds, if he has reasonable grounds for believing that the person searched might use it to cause physical injury to himself or to any other person.

(9) A constable searching a person in the exercise of the power conferred by subsection (2)(a) above may seize and retain anything he finds, other than an item subject to legal privilege, if he has reasonable grounds for believing—

(a) that he might use it to assist him to escape from lawful custody; or

(b) that it is evidence of an offence or has been obtained in consequence of the commission of an offence.

(10) Nothing in this section shall be taken to affect the power conferred by [section 43 of the Terrorism Act 2000].

. . . . . .

PART IV

DETENTION

Detention—conditions and duration

Limitations on police detention

34.—(1) A person arrested for an offence shall not be kept in police detention   **51–034** except in accordance with the provisions of this Part of this Act.

(2) Subject to subsection (3) below, if at any time a custody officer—

(a) becomes aware, in relation to any person in police detention, that the grounds for the detention of that person have ceased to apply; and

(b) is not aware of any other grounds on which the continued detention of that person could be justified under the provisions of this Part of this Act;

it shall be the duty of the custody officer, subject to subsection (4) below, to order his immediate release from custody.

(3) No person in police detention shall be released except on the authority of a custody officer at the police station where his detention was authorised or, if it was authorised at more than one station, a custody officer at the station where it was last authorised.

(4) A person who appears to the custody officer to have been unlawfully at large when he was arrested is not to be released under subsection (2) above.

(5) A person whose release is ordered under subsection (2) above shall be released without bail unless it appears to the custody officer—

> (a) that there is need for further investigation of any matter in connection with which he was detained at any time during the period of his detention; or
>
> [(b) that, in respect of any such matter, proceedings may be taken against him or he may be reprimanded or warned under section 65 of the Crime and Disorder Act 1998]

and, if it so appears, he shall be released on bail.

(6) For the purposes of this Part of this Act a person arrested under [section 6(5) of the Road Traffic Act 1988] is arrested for an offence.

[(7) For the purposes of this Part of this Act a person who returns to a police station to answer to bail or is arrested under section 46A below shall be treated as arrested for an offence and the offence in connection with which he was granted bail shall be deemed to be that offence.][1]

[1] Added by Criminal Justice and Public Order Act 1994 (c.33), Pt II, s.29(3).

Designated police stations

51–035   **35.**—(1) The chief officer of police for each police area shall designate the police stations in his area which, subject to section 30(3) and (5) above, are to be the stations in that area to be used for the purpose of detaining arrested persons.

(2) A chief officer's duty under subsection (1) above is to designate police stations appearing to him to provide enough accommodation for that purpose.

[(2A) The Chief Constable of the British Transport Police Force may designate police stations which (in addition to those designated under subsection (1) above) may be used for the purpose of detaining arrested persons.][1]

(3) Without prejudice to section 12 of the Interpretation Act 1978 (continuity of duties) a chief officer—

> (a) may designate a station which was not previously designated; and
>
> (b) may direct that a designation of a station previously made shall cease to operate.

(4) In this Act "designated police station" means a police station for the time being designated under this section.

[1] Added by Anti-terrorism, Crime and Security Act 2001 (c.24), Sched. 7, para. 12.

Custody officers at police stations

51–036   **36.**—(1) One or more custody officers shall be appointed for each designated police station.

(2) A custody officer for [a police station designated under section 35(1) above][1] shall be appointed—

> (a) by the chief officer of police for the area in which the designated police station is situated; or

(b) by such other police officer as the chief officer of police for that area may direct.

[(2A) A custody officer for a police station designated under section 35(2A) above shall be appointed—

(a) by the Chief Constable of the British Transport Police Force; or
(b) by such other member of that Force as that Chief Constable may direct.][2]

(3) No officer may be appointed a custody officer unless he is of at least the rank of sergeant.

(4) An officer of any rank may perform the functions of a custody officer at a designated police station if a custody officer is not readily available to perform them.

(5) Subject to the following provisions of this section and to section 39(2) below, none of the functions of a custody officer in relation to a person shall be performed by an officer who at the time when the function falls to be performed is involved in the investigation of an offence for which that person is in police detention at that time.

(6) Nothing in subsection (5) above is to be taken to prevent a custody officer—

(a) performing any function assigned to custody officers—

(i) by this Act; or
(ii) by a code of practice issued under this Act;

(b) carrying out the duty imposed on custody officers by section 39 below;
(c) doing anything in connection with the identification of a suspect; or
(d) doing anything under [sections 7 and 8 of the Road Traffic Act 1988].

(7) Where an arrested person is taken to a police station which is not a designated police station, the functions in relation to him which at a designated police station would be the functions of a custody officer shall be performed—

(a) by an officer who is not involved in the investigation of an offence for which he is in police detention, if such an officer is readily available; and
(b) if no such officer is readily available, by the officer who took him to the station or any other officer.

(8) References to a custody officer in the following provisions of this Act include references to an officer other than a custody officer who is performing the functions of a custody officer by virtue of subsection (4) or (7) above.

(9) Where by virtue of subsection (7) above an officer of a force maintained by a police authority who took an arrested person to a police station is to perform the functions of a custody officer in relation to him, the officer shall inform an officer who—

(a) is attached to a designated police station; and
(b) is of at least the rank of inspector,

that he is to do so.

(10) The duty imposed by subsection (9) above shall be performed as soon as it is practicable to perform it.

---

[1] Words substituted by Anti-terrorism, Crime and Security Act 2001 (c.24), Sched. 7, para. 13(2).
[2] Added by Anti-terrorism, Crime and Security Act 2001 (c.24), Sched. 7, para. 13(3).

Duties of custody officer before charge

51–037   37.—(1) Where—

  (a) a person is arrested for an offence—

    (i) without a warrant; or
    (ii) under a warrant not endorsed for bail, [. . .]¹

[. . .]² the custody officer at each police station where he is detained after his arrest shall determine whether he has before him sufficient evidence to charge that person with the offence for which he was arrested and may detain him at the police station for such period as is necessary to enable him to do so.

 (2) If the custody officer determines that he does not have such evidence before him, the person arrested shall be released either on bail or without bail, unless the custody officer has reasonable grounds for believing that his detention without being charged is necessary to secure or preserve evidence relating to an offence for which he is under arrest or to obtain such evidence by questioning him.

 (3) If the custody officer has reasonable grounds for so believing, he may authorise the person arrested to be kept in police detention.

 (4) Where a custody officer authorises a person who has not been charged to be kept in police detention, he shall, as soon as is practicable, make a written record of the grounds for the detention.

 (5) Subject to subsection (6) below, the written record shall be made in the presence of the person arrested who shall at that time be informed by the custody officer of the grounds for his detention.

 (6) Subsection (5) above shall not apply where the person arrested is, at the time when the written record is made—

  (a) incapable of understanding what is said to him;
  (b) violent or likely to become violent; or
  (c) in urgent need of medical attention.

 (7) Subject to section 41(7) below, if the custody officer determines that he has before him sufficient evidence to charge the person arrested with the offence for which he was arrested, the person arrested—

  (a) shall be charged; or
  (b) shall be released without charge, either on bail or without bail.

 (8) Where—

  (a) a person is released under subsection (7)(b) above; and
  (b) at the time of his release a decision whether he should be prosecuted for the offence for which he was arrested has not been taken,

it shall be the duty of the custody officer so to inform him.

 (9) If the person arrested is not in a fit state to be dealt with under subsection (7) above, he may be kept in police detention until he is.

 (10) The duty imposed on the custody officer under subsection (1) above shall be carried out by him as soon as practicable after the person arrested arrives at the police station or, in the case of a person arrested at the police station, as soon as practicable after the arrest.

 (11) [. . .]³
 (12) [. . .]⁴
 (13) [. . .]⁵

(14) [. . .]⁶
(15) In this Part of this Act—

"arrested juvenile" means a person arrested with or without a warrant who
   appears to be under the age of 17 [. . .]⁷;
"endorsed for bail" means endorsed with a direction for bail in accordance
   with section 117(2) of the Magistrates' Courts Act 1980.

¹ para. (b) and the word "or" immediately preceding it repealed by Criminal Justice and Public
  Order Act 1994 (c.33), Sched. 11, para. 1.
² *ibid.*
³ Repealed by Criminal Justice Act 1991 (c.53), Sched. 13, para. 1.
⁴ *ibid.*
⁵ *ibid.*
⁶ *ibid.*
⁷ Words repealed by Children Act 1989 (c.41), Sched. 15, para. 1.

Duties of custody officer after charge

38.—(1) Where a person arrested for an offence otherwise than under a war-   **51–038**
rant endorsed for bail is charged with an offence, the custody officer shall,
[subject to section 25 of the Criminal Justice and Public Order Act 1994,] order
his release from police detention, either on bail or without bail, unless—

(a) if the person arrested is not an arrested juvenile—

   (i) his name or address cannot be ascertained or the custody officer
      has reasonable grounds for doubting whether a name or address
      furnished by him as his name or address is his real name or
      address;

   [(ii) the custody officer has reasonable grounds for believing that the
      person arrested will fail to appear in court to answer to bail;

   (iii) in the case of a person arrested for an imprisonable offence, the
      custody officer has reasonable grounds for believing that the
      detention of the person arrested is necessary to prevent him from
      committing an offence;

   [(iiia) in the case of a person who has attained the age of 18, the custody
      officer has reasonable grounds for believing that the detention of
      the person is necessary to enable a sample to be taken from him
      under section 63B below,]¹

   (iv) in the case of a person arrested for an offence which is not an
      imprisonable offence, the custody officer has reasonable grounds
      for believing that the detention of the person arrested is necessary
      to prevent him from causing physical injury to any other person
      or from causing loss of or damage to property;

   (v) the custody officer has reasonable grounds for believing that the
      detention of the person arrested is necessary to prevent him from
      interfering with the administration of justice or with the investi-
      gation of offences or of a particular offence; or

   (vi) the custody officer has reasonable grounds for believing that the
      detention of the person arrested is necessary for his own protec-
      tion;]

(b) if he is an arrested juvenile—

   (i) any of the requirements of paragraph (a) above is satisfied; or

   (ii) the custody officer has reasonable grounds for believing that he
      ought to be detained in his own interests.

(2) If the release of a person arrested is not required by subsection (1) above,

the custody officer may authorise him to be kept in police detention [but may not authorise a person to be kept in police detention by virtue of subsection (1)(a)(iiia) after the end of the period of six hours beginning when he was charged with the offence].

[(2A) The custody officer, in taking the decisions required by subsection (1)(a) and (b) above (except (a)(i) and (vi) and (b)(ii)), shall have regard to the same considerations as those which a court is required to have regard to in taking the corresponding decisions under paragraph 2 of Part I of Schedule 1 to the Bail Act 1976.]²

(3) Where a custody officer authorises a person who has been charged to be kept in police detention, he shall, as soon as practicable, make a written record of the grounds for the detention.

(4) Subject to subsection (5) below, the written record shall be made in the presence of the person charged who shall at that time be informed by the custody officer of the grounds for his detention.

(5) Subsection (4) above shall not apply where the person charged is, at the time when the written record is made—

    (a) incapable of understanding what is said to him;
    (b) violent or likely to become violent; or
    (c) in urgent need of medical attention.

[[(6) Where a custody officer authorises an arrested juvenile to be kept in police detention under subsection (1) above, the custody officer shall, unless he certifies—

    (a) that, by reason of such circumstances as are specified in the certificate, it is impracticable for him to do so; or
    (b) in the case of an arrested juvenile who has attained the [age of 12 years], that no secure accommodation is available and that keeping him in other local authority accommodation would not be adequate to protect the public from serious harm from him,

secure that the arrested juvenile is moved to local authority accommodation.

(6A) In this section—

    "local authority accommodation" means accommodation provided by or on behalf of a local authority (within the meaning of the Children Act 1989);
    "secure accommodation" means accommodation provided for the purpose of restricting liberty;
    "sexual offence" and "violent offence" have the same meanings as in [the Powers of Criminal Courts (Sentencing) Act 2000];

and any reference, in relation to an arrested juvenile charged with a violent or sexual offence, to protecting the public from serious harm from him shall be construed as a reference to protecting members of the public from death or serious personal injury, whether physical or psychological, occasioned by further such offences committed by him.]

(6B) Where an arrested juvenile is moved to local authority accommodation under subsection (6) above, it shall be lawful for any person acting on behalf of the authority to detain him.]

(7) A certificate made under subsection (6) above in respect of an arrested juvenile shall be produced to the court before which he is first brought thereafter.

[(7A) In this section "imprisonable offence" has the same meaning as in Schedule 1 to the Bail Act 1976.]

(8) In this Part of this Act "local authority" has the same meaning as in the Children and Young Persons Act 1969.

¹ Added by Criminal Justice and Court Services Act 2000 (c.43), Pt III, c.II, s.57(3)(a).
² Added by Criminal Justice and Public Order Act 1994 (c.33), Pt II, s.28(3).

Responsibilities in relation to persons detained

39.—(1) Subject to subsections (2) and (4) below, it shall be the duty of the   **51–039**
custody officer at a police station to ensure—

  (a) that all persons in police detention at that station are treated in accord-
      ance with this Act and any code of practice issued under it and relating
      to the treatment of persons in police detention; and
  (b) that all matters relating to such persons which are required by this Act
      or by such codes of practice to be recorded are recorded in the custody
      records relating to such persons.

(2) If the custody officer, in accordance with any code of practice issued
under this Act, transfers or permits the transfer of a person in police detention—

  (a) to the custody of a police officer investigating an offence for which
      that person is in police detention; or
  (b) to the custody of an officer who has charge of that person outside the
      police station,

the custody officer shall cease in relation to that person to be subject to the duty
imposed on him by subsection (1)(a) above; and it shall be the duty of the officer
to whom the transfer is made to ensure that he is treated in accordance with the
provisions of this Act and of any such codes of practice as are mentioned in
subsection (1) above.

(3) If the person detained is subsequently returned to the custody of the custody officer, it shall be the duty of the officer investigating the offence to report
to the custody officer as to the manner in which this section and the codes of
practice have been complied with while that person was in his custody.

(4) If an arrested juvenile is transferred to the care of a local authority in
pursuance of arrangements made under section 38(6) above, the custody officer
shall cease in relation to that person to be subject to the duty imposed on him
by subsection (1) above.

  (5) [. . .]¹
  (6) Where—

  (a) an officer of higher rank than the custody officer gives directions relat-
      ing to a person in police detention; and
  (b) the directions are at variance—

      (i) with any decision made or action taken by the custody officer in
          the performance of a duty imposed on him under this Part of this
          Act; or
      (ii) with any decision or action which would but for the directions
           have been made or taken by him in the performance of such a
           duty,

the custody officer shall refer the matter at once to an officer of the rank of
superintendent or above who is responsible for the police station for which the
custody officer is acting as custody officer.

¹ Repealed by Children Act 1989 (c.41), Sched. 15, para. 1.

Review of police detention

51–040   **40.**—(1) Reviews of the detention of each person in police detention in connection with the investigation of an offence shall be carried out periodically in accordance with the following provisions of this section—

(a) in the case of a person who has been arrested and charged, by the custody officer; and

(b) in the case of a person who has been arrested but not charged, by an officer of at least the rank of inspector who has not been directly involved in the investigation.

(2) The officer to whom it falls to carry out a review is referred to in this section as a "review officer".

(3) Subject to subsection (4) below—

(a) the first review shall be not later than six hours after the detention was first authorised;

(b) the second review shall be not later than nine hours after the first;

(c) subsequent reviews shall be at intervals of not more than nine hours.

(4) A review may be postponed—

(a) if, having regard to all the circumstances prevailing at the latest time for it specified in subsection (3) above, it is not practicable to carry out the review at that time;

(b) without prejudice to the generality of paragraph (a) above—

(i) if at that time the person in detention is being questioned by a police officer and the review officer is satisfied that an interruption of the questioning for the purpose of carrying out the review would prejudice the investigation in connection with which he is being questioned; or

(ii) if at that time no review officer is readily available.

(5) If a review is postponed under subsection (4) above it shall be carried out as soon as practicable after the latest time specified for it in subsection (3) above.

(6) If a review is carried out after postponement under subsection (4) above, the fact that it was so carried out shall not affect any requirement of this section as to the time at which any subsequent review is to be carried out.

(7) The review officer shall record the reasons for any postponement of a review in the custody record.

(8) Subject to subsection (9) below, where the person whose detention is under review has not been charged before the time of the review, section 37(1) to (6) above shall have effect in relation to him, but with the substitution—

(a) of references to the person whose detention is under review for references to the person arrested; and

(b) of references to the review officer for references to the custody officer.

(9) Where a person has been kept in police detention by virtue of section 37(9) above, section 37(1) to (6) shall not have effect in relation to him but it shall be the duty of the review officer to determine whether he is yet in a fit state.

(10) Where the person whose detention is under review has been charged before the time of the review, section 38(1) to (6) above shall have effect in

relation to him, but with the substitution of references to the person whose detention is under review for references to the person arrested.

(11) Where—

(a) an officer of higher rank than the review officer gives directions relating to a person in police detention; and

(b) the directions are at variance—

(i) with any decision made or action taken by the review officer in the performance of a duty imposed on him under this Part of this Act; or

(ii) with any decision or action which would but for the directions have been made or taken by him in the performance of such a duty;

the review officer shall refer the matter at once to an officer of the rank of superintendent or above who is responsible for the police station for which the review officer is acting as review officer in connection with the detention.

(12) Before determining whether to authorise a person's continued detention the review officer shall give—

(a) that person (unless he is asleep); or

(b) any solicitor representing him who is available at the time of the review,

an opportunity to make representations to him about the detention.

(13) Subject to subsection (14) below, the person whose detention is under review or his solicitor may make representations under subsection (12) above either orally or in writing.

(14) The review officer may refuse to hear oral representations from the person whose detention is under review if he considers that he is unfit to make such representations by reason of his condition or behaviour.

Limits on period of detention without charge

41.—(1) Subject to the following provisions of this section and to sections 42 and 43 below, a person shall not be kept in police detention for more than 24 hours without being charged.   **51–041**

(2) The time from which the period of detention of a person is to be calculated (in this Act referred to as "the relevant time")—

(a) in the case of a person to whom this paragraph applies, shall be—

(i) the time at which that person arrives at the relevant police station; or

(ii) the time 24 hours after the time of that person's arrest,

whichever is the earlier;

(b) in the case of a person arrested outside England and Wales, shall be—

(i) the time at which that person arrives at the first police station to which he is taken in the police area in England or Wales in which the offence for which he was arrested is being investigated; or

(ii) the time 24 hours after the time of that person's entry into England and Wales,

whichever is the earlier;

(c) in the case of a person who—

    (i) attends voluntarily at a police station; or

    (ii) accompanies a constable to a police station without having been arrested,

and is arrested at the police station, the time of his arrest;

(d) in any other case, except where subsection (5) below applies, shall be the time at which the person arrested arrives at the first police station to which he is taken after his arrest.

(3) Subsection (2)(a) above applies to a person if—

(a) his arrest is sought in one police area in England and Wales;

(b) he is arrested in another police area; and

(c) he is not questioned in the area in which he is arrested in order to obtain evidence in relation to an offence for which he is arrested;

and in sub-paragraph (i) of that paragraph "the relevant police station" means the first police station to which he is taken in the police area in which his arrest was sought.

(4) Subsection (2) above shall have effect in relation to a person arrested under section 31 above as if every reference in it to his arrest or his being arrested were a reference to his arrest or his being arrested for the offence for which he was originally arrested.

(5) If—

(a) a person is in police detention in a police area in England and Wales ("the first area"); and

(b) his arrest for an offence is sought in some other police area in England and Wales ("the second area"); and

(c) he is taken to the second area for the purposes of investigating that offence, without being questioned in the first area in order to obtain evidence in relation to it,

the relevant time shall be—

    (i) the time 24 hours after he leaves the place where he is detained in the first area; or

    (ii) the time at which he arrives at the first police station to which he is taken in the second area,

whichever is the earlier.

(6) When a person who is in police detention is removed to hospital because he is in need of medical treatment, any time during which he is being questioned in hospital or on the way there or back by a police officer for the purpose of obtaining evidence relating to an offence shall be included in any period which falls to be calculated for the purposes of this Part of this Act, but any other time while he is in hospital or on his way there or back shall not be so included.

(7) Subject to subsection (8) below, a person who at the expiry of 24 hours after the relevant time is in police detention and has not been charged shall be released at that time either on bail or without bail.

(8) Subsection (7) above does not apply to a person whose detention for more than 24 hours after the relevant time has been authorised or is otherwise permitted in accordance with section 42 or 43 below.

(9) A person released under subsection (7) above shall not be re-arrested without a warrant for the offence for which he was previously arrested unless

new evidence justifying a further arrest has come to light since his release; [but this subsection does not prevent an arrest under section 46A below].

Authorisation of continued detention

42.—(1) Where a police officer of the rank of superintendent or above who **51–042** is responsible for the police station at which a person is detained has reasonable grounds for believing that—

(a) the detention of that person without charge is necessary to secure or preserve evidence relating to an offence for which he is under arrest or to obtain such evidence by questioning him;

(b) an offence for which he is under arrest is a serious arrestable offence; and

(c) the investigation is being conducted diligently and expeditiously.

he may authorise the keeping of that person in police detention for a period expiring at or before 36 hours after the relevant time.

(2) Where an officer such as is mentioned in subsection (1) above has authorised the keeping of a person in police detention for a period expiring less than 36 hours after the relevant time, such an officer may authorise the keeping of that person in police detention for a further period expiring not more than 36 hours after that time if the conditions specified in subsection (1) above are still satisfied when he gives the authorisation.

(3) If it is proposed to transfer a person in police detention to another police area, the officer determining whether or not to authorise keeping him in detention under subsection (1) above shall have regard to the distance and the time the journey would take.

(4) No authorisation under subsection (1) above shall be given in respect of any person—

(a) more than 24 hours after the relevant time; or

(b) before the second review of his detention under section 40 above has been carried out.

(5) Where an officer authorises the keeping of a person in police detention under subsection (1) above, it shall be his duty—

(a) to inform that person of the grounds for his continued detention; and

(b) to record the grounds in that person's custody record.

(6) Before determining whether to authorise the keeping of a person in detention under subsection (1) or (2) above, an officer shall give—

(a) that person; or

(b) any solicitor representing him who is available at the time when it falls to the officer to determine whether to give the authorisation,

an opportunity to make representations to him about the detention.

(7) Subject to subsection (8) below, the person in detention or his solicitor may make representations under subsection (6) above either orally or in writing.

(8) The officer to whom it falls to determine whether to give the authorisation may refuse to hear oral representations from the person in detention if he considers that he is unfit to make such representations by reason of his condition or behaviour.

(9) Where—

(a) an officer authorises the keeping of a person in detention under subsection (1) above; and

(b) at the time of the authorisation he has not yet exercised a right conferred on him by section 56 or 58 below,

the officer—

(i) shall inform him of that right;

(ii) shall decide whether he should be permitted to exercise it;

(iii) shall record the decision in his custody record; and

(iv) if the decision is to refuse to permit the exercise of the right, shall also record the grounds for the decision in that record.

(10) Where an officer has authorised the keeping of a person who has not been charged in detention under subsection (1) or (2) above, he shall be released from detention, either on bail or without bail, not later than 36 hours after the relevant time, unless—

(a) he has been charged with an offence; or

(b) his continued detention is authorised or otherwise permitted in accordance with section 43 below.

(11) A person released under subsection (10) above shall not be re-arrested without a warrant for the offence for which he was previously arrested unless new evidence justifying a further arrest has come to light since his release[; but this subsection does not prevent an arrest under section 46A below].

Warrants of further detention

51–043   43.—(1) Where, on an application on oath made by a constable and supported by an information, a magistrates' court is satisfied that there are reasonable grounds for believing that the further detention of the person to whom the application relates is justified, it may issue a warrant of further detention authorising the keeping of that person in police detention.

(2) A court may not hear an application for a warrant of further detention unless the person to whom the application relates—

(a) has been furnished with a copy of the information; and

(b) has been brought before the court for the hearing.

(3) The person to whom the application relates shall be entitled to be legally represented at the hearing and, if he is not so represented but wishes to be so represented—

(a) the court shall adjourn the hearing to enable him to obtain representation; and

(b) he may be kept in police detention during the adjournment.

(4) A person's further detention is only justified for the purposes of this section or section 44 below if—

(a) his detention without charge is necessary to secure or preserve evidence relating to an offence for which he is under arrest or to obtain such evidence by questioning him;

(b) an offence for which he is under arrest is a serious arrestable offence; and

(c) the investigation is being conducted diligently and expeditiously.

(5) Subject to subsection (7) below, an application for a warrant of further detention may be made—

    (a) at any time before the expiry of 36 hours after the relevant time; or

    (b) in a case where—

        (i) it is not practicable for the magistrates' court to which the application will be made to sit at the expiry of 36 hours after the relevant time; but

       (ii) the court will sit during the 6 hours following the end of that period,

at any time before the expiry of the said 6 hours.

(6) In a case to which subsection (5)(b) above applies—

    (a) the person to whom the application relates may be kept in police detention until the application is heard; and

    (b) the custody officer shall make a note in that person's custody record—

        (i) of the fact that he was kept in police detention for more than 36 hours after the relevant time; and

       (ii) of the reason why he was so kept.

(7) If—

    (a) an application for a warrant of further detention is made after the expiry of 36 hours after the relevant time; and

    (b) it appears to the magistrates' court that it would have been reasonable for the police to make it before the expiry of that period,

the court shall dismiss the application.

(8) Where on an application such as is mentioned in subsection (1) above a magistrates' court is not satisfied that there are reasonable grounds for believing that the further detention of the person to whom the application relates is justified, it shall be its duty—

    (a) to refuse the application; or

    (b) to adjourn the hearing of it until a time not later than 36 hours after the relevant time.

(9) The person to whom the application relates may be kept in police detention during the adjournment.

(10) A warrant of further detention shall—

    (a) state the time at which it is issued;

    (b) authorise the keeping in police detention of the person to whom it relates for the period stated in it.

(11) Subject to subsection (12) below, the period stated in a warrant of further detention shall be such period as the magistrates' court thinks fit, having regard to the evidence before it.

(12) The period shall not be longer than 36 hours.

(13) If it is proposed to transfer a person in police detention to a police area other than that in which he is detained when the application for a warrant of further detention is made, the court hearing the application shall have regard to the distance and the time the journey would take.

(14) Any information submitted in support of an application under this section shall state—

(a) the nature of the offence for which the person to whom the application relates has been arrested;
(b) the general nature of the evidence on which that person was arrested;
(c) what inquiries relating to the offence have been made by the police and what further inquiries are proposed by them;
(d) the reasons for believing the continued detention of that person to be necessary for the purposes of such further inquiries.

(15) Where an application under this section is refused, the person to whom the application relates shall forthwith be charged or, subject to subsection (16) below, released, either on bail or without bail.

(16) A person need not be released under subsection (15) above—

(a) before the expiry of 24 hours after the relevant time; or
(b) before the expiry of any longer period for which his continued detention is or has been authorised under section 42 above.

(17) Where an application under this section is refused, no further application shall be made under this section in respect of the person to whom the refusal relates, unless supported by evidence which has come to light since the refusal.

(18) Where a warrant of further detention is issued, the person to whom it relates shall be released from police detention, either on bail or without bail, upon or before the expiry of the warrant unless he is charged.

(19) A person released under subsection (18) above shall not be re-arrested without a warrant for the offence for which he was previously arrested unless new evidence justifying a further arrest has come to light since his release[; but this subsection does not prevent an arrest under section 46A below].

Extension of warrants of further detention

51–044

44.—(1) On an application on oath made by a constable and supported by an information a magistrates' court may extend a warrant of further detention issued under section 43 above if it is satisfied that there are reasonable grounds for believing that the further detention of the person to whom the application relates is justified.

(2) Subject to subsection (3) below, the period for which a warrant of further detention may be extended shall be such period as the court thinks fit, having regard to the evidence before it.

(3) The period shall not—

(a) be longer than 36 hours; or
(b) end later than 96 hours after the relevant time.

(4) Where a warrant of further detention has been extended under subsection (1) above, or further extended under this subsection, for a period ending before 96 hours after the relevant time, on an application such as is mentioned in that subsection a magistrates' court may further extend the warrant if it is satisfied as there mentioned; and subsections (2) and (3) above apply to such further extensions as they apply to extensions under subsection (1) above.

(5) A warrant of further detention shall, if extended or further extended under this section, be endorsed with a note of the period of the extension.

(6) Subsections (2), (3) and (14) of section 43 above shall apply to an application made under this section as they apply to an application made under that section.

(7) Where an application under this section is refused, the person to whom the application relates shall forthwith be charged or, subject to subsection (8) below, released, either on bail or without bail.

(8) A person need not be released under subsection (7) above before the expiry of any period for which a warrant of further detention issued in relation to him has been extended or further extended on an earlier application made under this section.

Detention before charge—supplementary

45.—(1) In sections 43 and 44 of this Act "magistrates' court" means a court consisting of two or more justices of the peace sitting otherwise than in open court.   **51–045**

(2) Any reference in this Part of this Act to a period of time or a time of day is to be treated as approximate only.

Detention—miscellaneous

Detention after charge

46.—(1) Where a person—   **51–046**

(a) is charged with an offence; and
(b) after being charged—

    (i) is kept in police detention; or
    (ii) is detained by a local authority in pursuance of arrangements made under section 38(6) above,

he shall be brought before a magistrates' court in accordance with the provisions of this section.

(2) If he is to be brought before a magistrates' court for the petty sessions area in which the police station at which he was charged is situated, he shall be brought before such a court as soon as is practicable and in any event not later than the first sitting after he is charged with the offence.

(3) If no magistrates' court for that area is due to sit either on the day on which he is charged or on the next day, the custody officer for the police station at which he was charged shall inform the [justices' chief executive] for the area that there is a person in the area to whom subsection (2) above applies.

(4) If the person charged is to be brought before a magistrates' court for a petty sessions area other than that in which the police station at which he was charged is situated, he shall be removed to that area as soon as is practicable and brought before such a court as soon as is practicable after his arrival in the area and in any event not later than the first sitting of a magistrates' court for that area after his arrival in the area.

(5) If no magistrates' court for that area is due to sit either on the day on which he arrives in the area or on the next day—

(a) he shall be taken to a police station in the area; and
(b) the custody officer at that station shall inform the [justices' chief executive] for the area that there is a person in the area to whom subsection (4) applies.

(6) Subject to subsection (8) below, where [the justices' chief executive] for a petty sessions area has been informed—

(a) under subsection (3) above that there is a person in the area to whom subsection (2) above applies; or
(b) under subsection (5) above that there is a person in the area to whom subsection (4) above applies,

[the justices' chief executive] shall arrange for a magistrates' court to sit not later than the day next following the relevant day.

(7) In this section "the relevant day"—

(a) in relation to a person who is to be brought before a magistrates' court for the petty sessions area in which the police station at which he was charged is situated, means the day on which he was charged; and

(b) in relation to a person who is to be brought before a magistrates' court for any other petty sessions area, means the day on which he arrives in the area.

(8) Where the day next following the relevant day is Christmas Day, Good Friday or a Sunday, the duty of the [justices' chief executive] under subsection (6) above is a duty to arrange for a magistrates' court to sit not later than the first day after the relevant day which is not one of those days.

(9) Nothing in this section requires a person who is in hospital to be brought before a court if he is not well enough.

Power of arrest for failure to answer to police bail

51–047 [46A.—(1) A constable may arrest without a warrant any person who, having been released on bail under this Part of this Act subject to a duty to attend at a police station, fails to attend at that police station at the time appointed for him to do so.

(2) A person who is arrested under this section shall be taken to the police station appointed as the place at which he is to surrender to custody as soon as practicable after the arrest.

(3) For the purposes of—

(a) section 30 above (subject to the obligation in subsection (2) above), and

(b) section 31 above,

an arrest under this section shall be treated as an arrest for an offence.]

Bail after arrest

51–048 47.—(1) Subject to subsection (2) below, a release on bail of a person under this Part of this Act shall be a release on bail granted in accordance with [sections 3, 3A, 5 and 5A of the Bail Act 1976 as they apply to bail granted by a constable].

[(1A) The normal powers to impose conditions of bail shall be available to him where a custody officer releases a person on bail under section 38(1) above (including that subsection as applied by section 40(10) above) but not in any other cases.

In this subsection, "the normal powers to impose conditions of bail" has the meaning given in section 3(6) of the Bail Act 1976.]

(2) Nothing in the Bail Act 1976 shall prevent the re-arrest without warrant of a person released on bail subject to a duty to attend at a police station if new evidence justifying a further arrest has come to light since his release.

(3) Subject to [subsections (3A) and (4)] below, in this Part of this Act references to "bail" are references to bail subject to a duty—

(a) to appear before a magistrates' court at such time and such place; or

(b) to attend at such police station at such time,

as the custody officer may appoint.

[(3A) Where a custody officer grants bail to a person subject to a duty to appear before a magistrates' court, he shall appoint for the appearance—

    (a) a date which is not later than the first sitting of the court after the person is charged with the offence; or

    (b) where he is informed by the [justices' chief executive.] for the relevant petty sessions area that the appearance cannot be accommodated until a later date, that later date.]

(4) Where a custody officer has granted bail to a person subject to a duty to appear at a police station, the custody officer may give notice in writing to that person that his attendance at the police station is not required.

(5) [. . .][1]

(6) Where a person [who has been granted bail and either has attended at the police station in accordance with the grant of bail or has been arrested under section 46A above is detained at a police station][2], any time during which he was in police detention prior to being granted bail shall be included as part of any period which falls to be calculated under this Part of this Act.

(7) Where a person who was released on bail subject to a duty to attend at a police station is re-arrested, the provisions of this Part of this Act shall apply to him as they apply to a person arrested for the first time; [but this subsection does not apply to a person who is arrested under section 46A above or has attended a police station in accordance with the grant of bail (and who accordingly is deemed by section 34(7) above to have been arrested for an offence)][3].

(8) In the Magistrates' Courts Act 1980—

    (a) the following section shall be substituted for section 43—

        Bail on arrest

        43.—"(1) Where a person has been granted bail under the Police and Criminal Evidence Act 1984 subject to a duty to appear before a magistrates' court, the court before which he is to appear may appoint a later time as the time at which he is to appear and may enlarge the recognizances of any sureties for him at that time.

        (2) The recognizance of any surety for any person granted bail subject to a duty to attend at a police station may be enforced as if it were conditioned for his appearance before a magistrates' court for the petty sessions area in which the police station named in the recognizance is situated."; and

    (b) the following subsection shall be substituted for section 117(3)—

        "(3) Where a warrant has been endorsed for bail under subsection (1) above—

        (a) where the person arrested is to be released on bail on his entering into a recognizance without sureties, it shall not be necessary to take him to a police station, but if he is so taken, he shall be released from custody on his entering into the recognizance; and

        (b) where he is to be released on his entering into a recognizance with sureties, he shall be taken to a police station on his arrest, and the custody officer there shall (subject to his approving any surety tendered in compliance with the endorsement) release him from custody as directed in the endorsement.".

---

[1] Repealed by Criminal Justice and Public Order Act 1994 (c.33), Sched. 11, para. 1.

² Words substituted by Criminal Justice and Public Order Act 1994 (c.33), Pt II, s.29(4)(d).
³ Words inserted by Criminal Justice and Public Order Act 1994 (c.33), Pt II, s.29(4)(e).

[Early administrative hearings conducted by justices' clerks

51–049 **47A.** Where a person has been charged with an offence at a police station, any requirement imposed under this Part for the person to appear or be brought before a magistrates' court shall be taken to be satisfied if the person appears or is brought before the clerk to the justices for a petty sessions area in order for the clerk to conduct a hearing under section 50 of the Crime and Disorder Act 1998 (early administrative hearings).]¹

¹ Added by Crime and Disorder Act 1998 (c.37), Sched. 8, para. 62.

Remands to police detention

51–050 **48.** In section 128 of the Magistrates' Courts Act 1980—

> (a) in subsection (7) for the words "the custody of a constable" there shall be substituted the words "detention at a police station";
> (b) after subsection (7) there shall be inserted the following subsection—

> "(8) Where a person is committed to detention at a police station under subsection (7) above—

> (a) he shall not be kept in such detention unless there is a need for him to be so detained for the purposes of inquiries into other offences;
> (b) if kept in such detention, he shall be brought back before the magistrates' court which committed him as soon as that need ceases;
> (c) he shall be treated as a person in police detention to whom the duties under section 39 of the Police and Criminal Evidence Act 1984 (responsibilities in relation to persons detained) relate;
> (d) his detention shall be subject to periodic review at the times set out in section 40 of that Act (review of police detention).".

Police detention to count towards custodial sentence

51–051 **49.**—(1) In subsection (1) of section 67 of the Criminal Justice Act 1967 (computation of custodial sentences) for the words from "period", in the first place where it occurs, to "the offender" there shall be substituted the words "relevant period, but where he".

(2) The following subsection shall be inserted after that subsection—

> "(1A) In subsection (1) above "relevant period" means —

> (a) any period during which the offender was in police detention in connection with the offence for which the sentence was passed; or

> (b) any period during which he was in custody—

> (i) by reason only of having been committed to custody by an order of a court made in connection with any proceedings relating to that sentence or the offence for which it was passed or any proceedings from which those proceedings arose; or
> (ii) by reason of his having been so committed and having been concurrently detained otherwise than by order of a court.".

(3) The following subsections shall be added after subsection (6) of that section—

"(7) A person is in police detention for the purposes of this section—

(a) at any time when he is in police detention for the purposes of the Police and Criminal Evidence Act 1984; and

(b) at any time when he is detained under section 12 of the Prevention of Terrorism (Temporary Provisions) Act 1984.

(8) No period of police detention shall be taken into account under this section unless it falls after the coming into force of section 49 of the Police and Criminal Evidence Act 1984.".

Records of detention

50.—(1) Each police force shall keep written records showing on an annual basis—   **51–052**

(a) the number of persons kept in police detention for more than 24 hours and subsequently released without charge;
(b) the number of applications for warrants of further detention and the results of the applications; and
(c) in relation to each warrant of further detention—

  (i) the period of further detention authorised by it;
  (ii) the period which the person named in it spent in police detention on its authority; and
  (iii) whether he was charged or released without charge.

(2) Every annual report—

[(a) under section 22 of the Police Act 1996; or]¹
(b) made by the Commissioner of Police of the Metropolis,

shall contain information about the matters mentioned in subsection (1) above in respect of the period to which the report relates.

¹ Substituted by Police Act 1996 (c.16), Sched. 7 Pt II, para. 35.

Savings

51. Nothing in this Part of this Act shall affect—   **51–053**

(a) the powers conferred on immigration officers by section 4 of and Schedule 2 to the Immigration Act 1971 (administrative provisions as to control on entry etc.);
[(b) the powers conferred by virtue of section 41 of, or Schedule 7 to, the Terrorism Act 2000 (powers of arrest and detention);]
(c) any duty of a police officer under—

  (i) section 129, 190 or 202 of the Army Act 1955 (duties of governors of prisons and others to receive prisoners, deserters, absentees and persons under escort);
  (ii) section 129, 190 or 202 of the Air Force Act 1955 (duties of governors of prisons and others to receive prisoners, deserters, absentees and persons under escort);

(iii) section 107 of the Naval Discipline Act 1957 (duties of governors of civil prisons etc.); or

(iv) paragraph 5 of Schedule 5 to the Reserve Forces Act 1980 (duties of governors of civil prisons); or

(d) any right of a person in police detention to apply for a writ of habeas corpus or other prerogative remedy.

¹ Substituted by Terrorism Act 2000 (c.11), Sched. 15, para. 5(4).

PART V

QUESTIONING AND TREATMENT OF PERSONS BY POLICE

Abolition of certain powers of constables to search persons

51–054   **53.**—(1) Subject to subsection (2) below, there shall cease to have effect any Act (including a local Act) passed before this Act in so far as it authorises—

(a) any search by a constable of a person in police detention at a police station; or

(b) an intimate search of a person by a constable;

and any rule of common law which authorises a search such as is mentioned in paragraph (a) or (b) above is abolished.
(2) [. . .]¹

¹ Repealed by Prevention of Terrorism (Temporary Provisions) Act 1989 (c.4), s.25(2), Sched. 9, Pt. I.

Searches of detained persons

51–055   **54.**—(1) The custody officer at a police station shall ascertain and record or cause to be recorded everything which a person has with him when he is—

(a) brought to the station after being arrested elsewhere or after being committed to custody by an order or sentence of a court; or

[(b) arrested at the station or detained there, [as a person falling within section 34(7), under section 37 above].]

(2) In the case of an arrested person the record shall be made as part of his custody record.
(3) Subject to subsection (4) below, a custody officer may seize and retain any such thing or cause any such thing to be seized and retained.
(4) Clothes and personal effects may only be seized if the custody officer—

(a) believes that the person from whom they are seized may use them—

(i) to cause physical injury to himself or any other person;
(ii) to damage property;
(iii) to interfere with evidence; or
(iv) to assist him to escape; or

(b) has reasonable grounds for believing that they may be evidence relating to an offence.

(5) Where anything is seized, the person from whom it is seized shall be told the reason for the seizure unless he is—

(a) violent or likely to become violent; or

(b) incapable of understanding what is said to him.

(6) Subject to subsection (7) below, a person may be searched if the custody officer considers it necessary to enable him to carry out his duty under subsection (1) above and to the extent that the custody officer considers necessary for that purpose.

[(6A) A person who is in custody at a police station or is in police detention otherwise than at a police station may at any time be searched in order to ascertain whether he has with him anything which he could use for any of the purposes specified in subsection (4)(a) above.

(6B) Subject to subsection (6C) below, a constable may seize and retain, or cause to be seized and retained, anything found on such a search.

(6C) A constable may only seize clothes and personal effects in the circumstances specified in subsection (4) above.][1]

(7) An intimate search may not be conducted under this section.

(8) A search under this section shall be carried out by a constable.

(9) The constable carrying out a search shall be of the same sex as the person searched.

[1] s. 54(6A)–(6C) inserted by Criminal Justice Act 1988 (c.33), s.147(b).

Searches and examination to ascertain identity

[**54A.** (1) If an officer of at least the rank of inspector authorises it, a person who is detained in a police station may be searched or examined, or both— **51–056**

(a) for the purpose of ascertaining whether he has any mark that would tend to identify him as a person involved in the commission of an offence; or

(b) for the purpose of facilitating the ascertainment of his identity.

(2) An officer may only give an authorisation under subsection (1) for the purpose mentioned in paragraph (a) of that subsection if—

(a) the appropriate consent to a search or examination that would reveal whether the mark in question exists has been withheld; or

(b) it is not practicable to obtain such consent.

(3) An officer may only give an authorisation under subsection (1) in a case in which subsection (2) does not apply if—

(a) the person in question has refused to identify himself; or

(b) the officer has reasonable grounds for suspecting that that person is not who he claims to be.

(4) An officer may give an authorisation under subsection (1) orally or in writing but, if he gives it orally, he shall confirm it in writing as soon as is practicable.

(5) Any identifying mark found on a search or examination under this section may be photographed—

(a) with the appropriate consent; or

(b) if the appropriate consent is withheld or it is not practicable to obtain it, without it.

(6) Where a search or examination may be carried out under this section, or

a photograph may be taken under this section, the only persons entitled to carry out the search or examination, or to take the photograph, are—

(a) constables; and
(b) persons who (without being constables) are designated for the purposes of this section by the chief officer of police for the police area in which the police station in question is situated;

and section 117 (use of force) applies to the exercise by a person falling within paragraph (b) of the powers conferred by the preceding provisions of this section as it applies to the exercise of those powers by a constable.

(7) A person may not under this section carry out a search or examination of a person of the opposite sex or take a photograph of any part of the body of a person of the opposite sex.

(8) An intimate search may not be carried out under this section.

(9) A photograph taken under this section—

(a) may be used by, or disclosed to, any person for any purpose related to the prevention or detection of crime, the investigation of an offence or the conduct of a prosecution; and
(b) after being so used or disclosed, may be retained but may not be used or disclosed except for a purpose so related.

(10) In subsection (9)—

(a) the reference to crime includes a reference to any conduct which—

(i) constitutes one or more criminal offences (whether under the law of a part of the United Kingdom or of a country or territory outside the United Kingdom); or
(ii) is, or corresponds to, any conduct which, if it all took place in any one part of the United Kingdom, would constitute one or more criminal offences; and

(b) the references to an investigation and to a prosecution include references, respectively, to any investigation outside the United Kingdom of any crime or suspected crime and to a prosecution brought in respect of any crime in a country or territory outside the United Kingdom.

(11) In this section—

(a) references to ascertaining a person's identity include references to showing that he is not a particular person; and
(b) references to taking a photograph include references to using any process by means of which a visual image may be produced, and references to photographing a person shall be construed accordingly.

(12) In this section "mark" includes features and injuries; and a mark is an identifying mark for the purposes of this section if its existence in any person's case facilitates the ascertainment of his identity or his identification as a person involved in the commission of an offence.][1]

[1] Added by Anti-terrorism, Crime and Security Act 2001 (c.24) Pt 10, s.90(1).

Intimate searches

51–057 55.—(1) Subject to the following provisions of this section, if an officer of at least the rank of superintendent has reasonable grounds for believing—

(a) that a person who has been arrested and is in police detention may have concealed on him anything which—

    (i) he could use to cause physical injury to himself or others; and

    (ii) he might so use while he is in police detention or in the custody of a court; or

(b) that such a person—

    (i) may have a Class A drug concealed on him; and

    (ii) was in possession of it with the appropriate criminal intent before his arrest,

he may authorise [an intimate search] of that person.

(2) An officer may not authorise an intimate search of a person for anything unless he has reasonable grounds for believing that it cannot be found without his being intimately searched.

(3) An officer may give an authorisation under subsection (1) above orally or in writing but, if he gives it orally, he shall confirm it in writing as soon as is practicable.

(4) An intimate search which is only a drug offence search shall be by way of examination by a suitably qualified person.

(5) Except as provided by subsection (4) above, an intimate search shall be by way of examination by a suitably qualified person unless an officer of at least the rank of superintendent considers that this is not practicable.

(6) An intimate search which is not carried out as mentioned in subsection (5) above shall be carried out by a constable.

(7) A constable may not carry out an intimate search of a person of the opposite sex.

(8) No intimate search may be carried out except—

(a) at a police station;

(b) at a hospital;

(c) at a registered medical practitioner's surgery; or

(d) at some other place used for medical purposes.

(9) An intimate search which is only a drug offence search may not be carried out at a police station.

(10) If an intimate search of a person is carried out, the custody record relating to him shall state—

(a) which parts of his body were searched; and

(b) why they were searched.

(11) The information required to be recorded by subsection (10) above shall be recorded as soon as practicable after the completion of the search.

(12) The custody officer at a police station may seize and retain anything which is found on an intimate search of a person, or cause any such thing to be seized and retained—

(a) if he believes that the person from whom it is seized may use it—

    (i) to cause physical injury to himself or any other person;

    (ii) to damage property;

    (iii) to interfere with evidence; or

    (iv) to assist him to escape; or

(b) if he has reasonable grounds for believing that it may be evidence relating to an offence.

(13) Where anything is seized under this section, the person from whom it is seized shall be told the reason for the seizure unless he is—

(a) violent or likely to become violent; or
(b) incapable of understanding what is said to him.

(14) Every annual report—

[(a) under section 22 of the Police Act 1996; or]
(b) made by the Commissioner of Police of the Metropolis,

shall contain information about searches under this section which have been carried out in the area to which the report relates during the period to which it relates.

[(14A) Every annual report under section 57 of the Police Act 1997 (reports by Director General of the National Crime Squad) shall contain information about searches authorised under this section by members of the National Crime Squad during the period to which the report relates.]

(15) The information about such searches shall include—

(a) the total number of searches;
(b) the number of searches conducted by way of examination by a suitably qualified person;
(c) the number of searches not so conducted but conducted in the presence of such a person; and
(d) the result of the searches carried out.

(16) The information shall also include, as separate items—

(a) the total number of drug offence searches; and
(b) the result of those searches.

(17) In this section—

"the appropriate criminal intent" means an intent to commit an offence under—

(a) section 5(3) of the Misuse of Drugs Act 1971 (possession of controlled drug with intent to supply to another); or
(b) section 68(2) of the Customs and Excise Management Act 1979 (exportation etc. with intent to evade a prohibition or restriction);

"Class A drug" has the meaning assigned to it by section 2(1)(b) of the Misuse of Drugs Act 1971;
"drug offence search" means an intimate search for a Class A drug which an officer has authorised by virtue of subsection (1)(b) above; and
"suitably qualified person" means —

(a) a registered medical practitioner; or
(b) a registered nurse.

Right to have someone informed when arrested

51–058   56.—(1) Where a person has been arrested and is being held in custody in a police station or other premises, he shall be entitled, if he so requests, to have one friend or relative or other person who is known to him or who is likely to take an interest in his welfare told, as soon as is practicable except to the extent that delay is permitted by this section, that he has been arrested and is being detained there.

(2) Delay is only permitted—

(a) in the case of a person who is in police detention for a serious arrestable offence; and

(b) if an officer of at least the rank of superintendent authorises it.

(3) In any case the person in custody must be permitted to exercise the right conferred by subsection (1) above within 36 hours from the relevant time, as defined in section 41(2) above.

(4) An officer may give an authorisation under subsection (2) above orally or in writing but, if he gives it orally, he shall confirm it in writing as soon as is practicable.

(5) [Subject to sub-section (5A) below] an officer may only authorise delay where he has reasonable grounds for believing that telling the named person of the arrest—

(a) will lead to interference with or harm to evidence connected with a serious arrestable offence or interference with or physical injury to other persons; or

(b) will lead to the alerting of other persons suspected of having committed such an offence but not yet arrested for it; or

(c) will hinder the recovery of any property obtained as a result of such an offence.

[(5A) An officer may also authorise delay where the serious arrestable offence is a drug trafficking offence [or an offence to which Part VI of the Criminal Justice Act 1988 applies (offences in respect of which confiscation orders under that Part may be made)] and the officer has reasonable grounds for believing—

[(a) where the offence is a drug trafficking offence, that the detained person has benefited from drug trafficking and that the recovery of the value of that person's proceeds of drug trafficking will be hindered by telling the named person of the arrest; and

(b) where the offence is one to which Part VI of the Criminal Justice Act 1988 applies, that the detained person has benefited from the offence and that the recovery of the value of the property obtained by that person from or in connection with the offence or of the pecuniary advantage derived by him from or in connection with it will be hindered by telling the named person of the arrest.]¹]²

(6) If a delay is authorised—

(a) the detained person shall be told the reason for it; and

(b) the reason shall be noted on his custody record.

(7) The duties imposed by subsection (6) above shall be performed as soon as is practicable.

(8) The rights conferred by this section on a person detained at a police station or other premises are exercisable whenever he is transferred from one place to another; and this section applies to each subsequent occasion on which they are exercisable as it applies to the first such occasion.

(9) There may be no further delay in permitting the exercise of the right conferred by subsection (1) above once the reason for authorising delay ceases to subsist.

[(10) Nothing in this section applies to a person arrested or detained under the terrorism provisions.][3]

[1] s.56(5A)(a)(b) substituted by Criminal Justice Act 1988 (c.33), s.99(2)(b).
[2] s.56(5A) inserted by Drug Trafficking Offences Act 1986 (c.32), s.32(1) and as amended as indicated below subs. (5A).
[3] Substituted by Terrorism Act 2000 (c.11), Sched. 15, para. 5(5).

Additional rights of children and young persons

51–059   **57.** The following subsections shall be substituted for section 34(2) of the Children and Young Persons Act 1933

"(2) Where a child or young person is in police detention, such steps as are practicable shall be taken to ascertain the identity of a person responsible for his welfare.

(3) If it is practicable to ascertain the identity of a person responsible for the welfare of the child or young person, that person shall be informed, unless it is not practicable to do so—

(a) that the child or young person has been arrested;
(b) why he has been arrested; and
(c) where he is being detained.

(4) Where information falls to be given under subsection (3) above, it shall be given as soon as it is practicable to do so.

(5) For the purposes of this section the persons who may be responsible for the welfare of a child or young person are—

(a) his parent or guardian; or
(b) any other person who has for the time being assumed responsibility for his welfare.

(6) If it is practicable to give a person responsible for the welfare of the child or young person the information required by subsection (3) above, that person shall be given it as soon as it is practicable to do so.

(7) If it appears that at the time of his arrest a supervision order, as defined in section 11 of the Children and Young Persons Act 1969, is in force in respect of him, the person responsible for his supervision shall also be informed as described in subsection (3) above as soon as it is reasonably practicable to do so.

(8) The reference to a parent or guardian in subsection (5) above is—

(a) in the case of a child or young person in the care of a local authority, a reference to that authority; and
(b) in the case of a child or young person in the care of a voluntary organisation in which parental rights and duties with respect to him are vested by virtue of a resolution under section 64(1) of the Child Care Act 1980, a reference to that organisation.

(9) The rights conferred on a child or young person by subsections (2) to (8) above are in addition to his rights under section 56 of the Police and Criminal Evidence Act 1984.

(10) The reference in subsection (2) above to a child or young person who is in police detention includes a reference to a child or young person who has been detained under the terrorism provisions; and in subsection (3) above "arrest" includes such detention.

(11) In subsection (10) above "the terrorism provisions" has the meaning assigned to it by section 65 of the Police and Criminal Evidence Act 1984".

Access to legal advice

58.—(1) A person arrested and held in custody in a police station or other premises shall be entitled, if he so requests, to consult a solicitor privately at any time.   **51–060**

(2) Subject to subsection (3) below, a request under subsection (1) above and the time at which it was made shall be recorded in the custody record.

(3) Such a request need not be recorded in the custody record of a person who makes it at a time while he is at a court after being charged with an offence.

(4) If a person makes such a request, he must be permitted to consult a solicitor as soon as is practicable except to the extent that delay is permitted by this section.

(5) In any case he must be permitted to consult a solicitor within 36 hours from the relevant time, as defined in section 41(2) above.

(6) Delay in compliance with a request is only permitted—

    (a) in the case of a person who is in police detention for a serious arrestable offence; and

    (b) if an officer of at least the rank of superintendent authorises it.

(7) An officer may give an authorisation under subsection (6) above orally or in writing but, if he gives it orally, he shall confirm it in writing as soon as is practicable.

(8) [Subject to sub-section (8A) below] an officer may only authorise delay where he has reasonable grounds for believing that the exercise of the right conferred by subsection (1) above at the time when the person detained desires to exercise it—

    (a) will lead to interference with or harm to evidence connected with a serious arrestable offence or interference with or physical injury to other persons; or

    (b) will lead to the alerting of other persons suspected of having committed such an offence but not yet arrested for it; or

    (c) will hinder the recovery of any property obtained as a result of such an offence.

[(8A) An officer may also authorise delay where the serious arrestable offence is a drug trafficking offence [or an offence to which Part VI of the Criminal Justice Act 1988 applies] and the officer has reasonable grounds for believing—

    [(a) where the offence is a drug trafficking offence, that the detained person has benefited from drug trafficking and that the recovery of the value of that person's proceeds of drug trafficking will be hindered by the exercise of the right conferred by subsection (1) above; and

    (b) where the offence is one to which Part VI of the Criminal Justice Act 1988 applies, that the detained person has benefited from the offence and that the recovery of the value of the property obtained by that person from or in connection with the offence or of the pecuniary advantage derived by him from or in connection with it will be hindered by the exercise of the right conferred by subsection (1) above.]¹]²

(9) If delay is authorised—

    (a) the detained person shall be told the reason for it; and

    (b) the reason shall be noted on his custody record.

(10) The duties imposed by subsection (9) above shall be performed as soon as is practicable.

(11) There may be no further delay in permitting the exercise of the right conferred by subsection (1) above once the reason for authorising delay ceases to subsist.

[(12) Nothing in this section applies to a person arrested or detained under the terrorism provisions.][3]

---

[1] s.58(8A)(a)(b) substituted by Criminal Justice Act 1988 (c.33), s.99(3)(b).
[2] s.58(8A) inserted by Drug Trafficking Offences Act 1986 (c.32), s.32(2).
[3] Substituted by Terrorism Act 2000 (c.11), Sched. 15, para. 5(6).

. . . . . .

Tape-recording of interviews

51–061   60.—(1) It shall be the duty of the Secretary of State—

(a) to issue a code of practice in connection with the tape-recording of interviews of persons suspected of the commission of criminal offences which are held by police officers at police stations; and

(b) to make an order requiring the tape-recording of interviews of persons suspected of the commission of criminal offences, or of such descriptions of criminal offences as may be specified in the order, which are so held, in accordance with the code as it has effect for the time being.

(2) An order under subsection (1) above shall be made by statutory instrument and shall be subject to annulment in pursuance of a resolution of either House of Parliament.

Visual recording of interviews

51–062   [60A.—(1) The Secretary of State shall have power—

(a) to issue a code of practice for the visual recording of interviews held by police officers at police stations; and

(b) to make an order requiring the visual recording of interviews so held, and requiring the visual recording to be in accordance with the code for the time being in force under this section.

(2) A requirement imposed by an order under this section may be imposed in relation to such cases or police stations in such areas, or both, as may be specified or described in the order.

(3) An order under subsection (1) above shall be made by statutory instrument and shall be subject to annulment in pursuance of a resolution of either House of Parliament.

(4) In this section—

(a) references to any interview are references to an interview of a person suspected of a criminal offence; and

(b) references to a visual recording include references to a visual recording in which an audio recording is comprised.][1]

---

[1] Added by Criminal Justice and Police Act 2001 (c.16), Pt 3, s.76(1).

Finger-printing

61.—(1) Except as provided by this section no person's fingerprints may be taken without the appropriate consent.

51–063

(2) Consent to the taking of a person's fingerprints must be in writing if it is given at a time when he is at a police station.

(3) The fingerprints of a person detained at a police station may be taken without the appropriate consent—

    (a) if an officer of at least the rank of superintendent authorises them to be taken; or

    (b) if—

        (i) he has been charged with a recordable offence or informed that he will be reported for such an offence; and

        (ii) he has not had his fingerprints taken in the course of the investigation of the offence by the police.

(4) An officer may only give an authorisation under subsection (3)(a) above if he has reasonable grounds—

    (a) for suspecting the involvement of the person whose fingerprints are to be taken in a criminal offence; and

    (b) for believing that his fingerprints will tend to confirm or disprove his involvement [or will facilitate the ascertainment of his identity (within the meaning of section 54A), or both][1].

[but an authorisation shall not be given for the purpose only of facilitating the ascertainment of that person's identity except where he has refused to identify himself or the officer has reasonable grounds for suspecting that he is not who he claims to be.][2]

(5) An officer may give an authorisation under subsection (3)(a) above orally or in writing but, if he gives it orally, he shall confirm it in writing as soon as is practicable.

(6) Any person's fingerprints may be taken without the appropriate consent if he has been convicted of a recordable offence.

(7) In a case where by virtue of subsection (3) or (6) above a person's fingerprints are taken without the appropriate consent—

    (a) he shall be told the reason before his fingerprints are taken; and

    (b) the reason shall be recorded as soon as is practicable after the fingerprints are taken.

[(7A) If a person's fingerprints are taken at a police station, whether with or without the appropriate consent—

    (a) before the fingerprints are taken, an officer shall inform him that they may be the subject of a speculative search; and

    (b) the fact that the person has been informed of this possibility shall be recorded as soon as is practicable after the fingerprints have been taken.][3]

(8) If he is detained at a police station when the fingerprints are taken, the reason for taking them [and, in the case falling within subsection (7A) above, the fact referred to in paragraph (b) of that subsection][4] shall be recorded on his custody record.

(9) Nothing in this section—

(a) affects any power conferred by paragraph 18(2) of Schedule 2 to the Immigration Act 1971; or

[(b) applies to a person arrested or detained under the terrorism provisions.]⁵

¹ Words inserted by Anti-terrorism, Crime and Security Act 2001 (c.24), Pt 10, s.90(2)(a).
² Words inserted by Anti-terrorism, Crime and Security Act 2001 (c.24), Pt 10, s.90(2)(b).
³ Added by Criminal Justice and Public Order Act 1994 (c.33), Sched. 10, para. 56(a).
⁴ Words inserted by Criminal Justice and Public Order Act 1994 (c.33), Sched. 10, para. 56(b).
⁵ Substituted by Terrorism Act 2000 (c.11), Sched. 15, para. 5(7).

Intimate samples

51–064   62.—(1) [Subject to section 63B below a]n intimate sample may be taken from a person in police detention only—

(a) if a police officer of at least the rank of superintendent authorises it to be taken; and
(b) if the appropriate consent is given.

[(1A) An intimate sample may be taken from a person who is not in police detention but from whom, in the course of the investigation of an offence, two or more non-intimate samples suitable for the same means of analysis have been taken which have proved insufficient—

(a) if a police officer of at least the rank of superintendent authorises it to be taken; and
(b) if the appropriate consent is given.]

(2) An officer may only give an authorisation [under subsection (1) or (1A) above] if he has reasonable grounds—

(a) for suspecting the involvement of the person from whom the sample is to be taken in a [recordable offence]; and
(b) for believing that the sample will tend to confirm or disprove his involvement.

(3) An officer may give an authorisation under subsection (1) [or (1A)] above orally or in writing but, if he gives it orally, he shall confirm it in writing as soon as is practicable.

(4) The appropriate consent must be given in writing.

(5) Where—

(a) an authorisation has been given; and
(b) it is proposed that an intimate sample shall be taken in pursuance of the authorisation,

an officer shall inform the person from whom the sample is to be taken—

(i) of the giving of the authorisation; and
(ii) of the grounds for giving it.

(6) The duty imposed by subsection (5)(ii) above includes a duty to state the nature of the offence in which it is suspected that the person from whom the sample is to be taken has been involved.

(7) If an intimate sample is taken from a person—

(a) the authorisation by virtue of which it was taken;

    (b) the grounds for giving the authorisation; and
    (c) the fact that the appropriate consent was given,

shall be recorded as soon as is practicable after the sample is taken.
    [(7A) If an intimate sample is taken from a person at a police station—

    (a) before the sample is taken, an officer shall inform him that it may be the subject of a speculative search; and
    (b) the fact that the person has been informed of this possibility shall be recorded as soon as practicable after the sample has been taken.]

    (8) If an intimate sample is taken from a person detained at a police station, the matters required to be recorded by subsection (7) [or (7A)] above shall be recorded in his custody record.
    (9) An intimate sample, other than a sample of urine [or a dental impression], may only be taken from a person by a registered medical practitioner [and a dental impression may only be taken by a registered dentist].
    (10) Where the appropriate consent to the taking of an intimate sample from a person was refused without good cause, in any proceedings against that person for an offence—

    (a) the court, in determining—

        (i) whether to commit that person for trial; or
       (ii) whether there is a case to answer; and

    [(aa) a judge, in deciding whether to grant an application made by the accused under—

        (i) section 6 of the Criminal Justice Act 1987 (application for dismissal of charge of serious fraud in respect of which notice of transfer has been given under section 4 of that Act); or
       (ii) paragraph 5 of Schedule 6 to the Criminal Justice Act 1991 (application for dismissal of charge of violent or sexual offence involving child in respect of which notice of transfer has been given under section 53 of that Act; and]

    (b) the court or jury, in determining whether that person is guilty of the offence charged,

may draw such inferences from the refusal as appear proper.
    (11) Nothing in this section affects [sections 4 to 11 of the Road Traffic Act 1988][12].
    [(12) Nothing in this section applies to a person arrested or detained under the terrorism provisions; and subsection (1A) shall not apply where the non-intimate samples mentioned in that subsection were taken under paragraph 10 of Schedule 8 to the Terrorism Act 2000.][1]

[1] Substituted by Terrorism Act 2000 (c.11), Sched. 15, para. 5(8).

Other samples

    63.—(1) Except as provided by this section, a non-intimate sample may not   **51–065** be taken from a person without the appropriate consent.
    (2) Consent to the taking of a non-intimate sample must be given in writing.
    (3) A non-intimate sample may be taken from a person without the appropriate consent if—

    (a) he is in police detention or is being held in custody by the police on the authority of a court; and

(b) an officer of at least the rank of superintendent authorises it to be taken without the appropriate consent.

[(3A) A non-intimate sample may be taken from a person (whether or not he falls within subsection (3)(a) above) without the appropriate consent if—

(a) he has been charged with a recordable offence or informed that he will be reported for such an offence; and
(b) either he has not had a non-intimate sample taken from him in the course of the investigation of the offence by the police or he had a non-intimate sample taken from him but either it was not suitable for the same means of analysis or, though so suitable, the sample proved insufficient.

(3B) A non-intimate sample may be taken from a person without the appropriate consent if he has been convicted of a recordable offence.]

[(3C) A non-intimate sample may also be taken from a person without the appropriate consent if he is a person to whom section 2 of the Criminal Evidence (Amendment) Act 1997 applies (persons detained following acquittal on grounds of insanity or finding of unfitness to plead).]

(4) An officer may only give an authorisation under subsection (3) above if he has reasonable grounds—

(a) for suspecting the involvement of the person from whom the sample is to be taken in a [recordable offence]; and
(b) for believing that the sample will tend to confirm or disprove his involvement.

(5) An officer may give an authorisation under subsection (3) above orally or in writing but, if he gives it orally, he shall confirm it in writing as soon as is practicable.

(6) Where—

(a) an authorisation has been given; and
(b) it is proposed that a non-intimate sample shall be taken in pursuance of the authorisation,

an officer shall inform the person from whom the sample is to be taken—

(i) of the giving of the authorisation; and
(ii) of the grounds for giving it.

(7) The duty imposed by subsection (6)(ii) above includes a duty to state the nature of the offence in which it is suspected that the person from whom the sample is to be taken has been involved.

(8) If a non-intimate sample is taken from a person by virtue of subsection (3) above—

(a) the authorisation by virtue of which it was taken; and
(b) the grounds for giving the authorisation,

shall be recorded as soon as is practicable after the sample is taken.

[(8A) In a case where by virtue of subsection (3A) [, (3B) or (3C) above] a sample is taken from a person without the appropriate consent—

(a) he shall be told the reason before the sample is taken; and
(b) the reason shall be recorded as soon as practicable after the sample is taken.]

[(8B) If a non-intimate sample is taken from a person at a police station, whether with or without the appropriate consent—

(a) before the sample is taken, an officer shall inform him that it may be the subject of a speculative search; and
(b) the fact that the person has been informed of this possibility shall be recorded as soon as practicable after the sample has been taken.]

(9) If a non-intimate sample is taken from a person detained at a police station, the matters required to be recorded by subsection (8) [or (8A)]⁷ [or (8B)]⁸ above shall be recorded in his custody record.

[[(9A) Subsection (3B) above shall not apply to any person convicted before 10th April 1995 unless he is a person to whom section 1 of the Criminal Evidence (Amendment) Act 1997 applies (persons imprisoned or detained by virtue of pre-existing conviction for sexual offence, etc).]]

[(10) Nothing in this section applies to a person arrested or detained under the terrorism provisions.]¹

¹ Substituted by Terrorism Act 2000 (c.11), Sched. 15, para. 5(9).

Fingerprints and samples: supplementary provisions

[**63A.**—[(1) Where a person has been arrested on suspicion of being involved   **51–066** in a recordable offence or has been charged with such an offence or has been informed that he will be reported for such an offence, fingerprints or samples or the information derived from samples taken under any power conferred by this Part of this Act from the person may be checked against—

(a) other fingerprints or samples to which the person seeking to check has access and which are held by or on behalf of [any one or more relevant law-enforcement authorities or which] are held in connection with or as a result of an investigation of an offence;
(b) information derived from other samples if the information is contained in records to which the person seeking to check has access and which are held as mentioned in paragraph (a) above.]

[(1A) In subsection (1) above "relevant law-enforcement authority" means—

(a) a police force;
(b) the National Criminal Intelligence Service;
(c) the National Crime Squad;
(d) a public authority (not falling within paragraphs (a) to (c)) with functions in any part of the British Islands which consist of or include the investigation of crimes or the charging of offenders;
(e) any person with functions in any country or territory outside the United Kingdom which—

    (i) correspond to those of a police force; or
    (ii) otherwise consist of or include the investigation of conduct contrary to the law of that country or territory, or the apprehension of persons guilty of such conduct;

(f) any person with functions under any international agreement which consist of or include the investigation of conduct which is—

    (i) unlawful under the law of one or more places,
    (ii) prohibited by such an agreement, or
    (iii) contrary to international law,

or the apprehension of persons guilty of such conduct.

(1B) The reference in subsection (1A) above to a police force is a reference to any of the following—

    (a) any police force maintained under section 2 of the Police Act 1996 (c.16) (police forces in England and Wales outside London);

    (b) the metropolitan police force;

    (c) the City of London police force;

    (d) any police force maintained under or by virtue of section 1 of the Police (Scotland) Act 1967 (c.77);

    (e) the Police Service of Northern Ireland;

    (f) the Police Service of Northern Ireland Reserve;

    (g) the Ministry of Defence Police;

    (h) the Royal Navy Regulating Branch;

    (i) the Royal Military Police;

    (j) the Royal Air Force Police;

    (k) the Royal Marines Police;

    (l) the British Transport Police;

    (m) the States of Jersey Police Force;

    (n) the salaried police force of the Island of Guernsey;

    (o) the Isle of Man Constabulary.

(1C) Where—

    (a) fingerprints or samples have been taken from any person in connection with the investigation of an offence but otherwise than in circumstances to which subsection (1) above applies, and

    (b) that person has given his consent in writing to the use in a speculative search of the fingerprints or of the samples and of information derived from them,

the fingerprints or, as the case may be, those samples and that information may be checked against any of the fingerprints, samples or information mentioned in paragraph (a) or (b) of that subsection.

(1D) A consent given for the purposes of subsection (1C) above shall not be capable of being withdrawn.][1]

(2) Where a sample of hair other than public hair is to be taken the sample may be taken either by cutting hairs or by plucking hairs with their roots so long as no more are plucked than the person taking the sample reasonably considers to be necessary for a sufficient sample.

(3) Where any power to take a sample is exercisable in relation to a person the sample may be taken in a prison or other institution to which the Prison Act 1952 applies.

[(3A) Where—

    (a) the power to take a non-intimate sample under section 63(3B) above is exercisable in relation to any person who is detained under Part III of the Mental Health Act 1983 in pursuance of—

        (i) a hospital order or interim hospital order made following his conviction for the recordable offence in question, or

        (ii) a transfer direction given at a time when he was detained in pursuance of any sentence or order imposed following that conviction, or

    (b) the power to take a non-intimate sample under section 63(3C) above is exercisable in relation to any person, the sample may be taken in the hospital in which he is detained under that Part of that Act. Expressions used in this subsection and in the Mental Health Act 1983 have the same meaning as in that Act.

(3B) Where the power to take a non-intimate sample under section 63(3B) above is exercisable in relation to a person detained in pursuance of directions of the Secretary of State under [section 92 of the Powers of Criminal Courts (Sentencing) Act 2000] the sample may be taken at the place where he is so detained.]

(4) Any constable may, within the allowed period, require a person who is neither in police detention nor held in custody by the police on the authority of a court to attend a police station in order to have a sample taken where—

    (a) the person has been charged with a recordable offence or informed that he will be reported for such an offence and either he has not had a sample taken from him in the course of the investigation of the offence by the police or he has had a sample so taken from him but either it was not suitable for the same means of analysis or, though so suitable, the sample proved insufficient; or

    (b) the person has been convicted of a recordable offence and either he has not had a sample taken from him since the conviction or he has had a sample taken from him (before or after his conviction) but either it was not suitable for the same means of analysis or, though so suitable, the sample proved insufficient.

(5) The period allowed for requiring a person to attend a police station for the purpose specified in subsection (4) above is—

    (a) in the case of a person falling within paragraph (a), one month beginning with the date of the charge [or of his being informed as mentioned in that paragraph] or one month beginning with the date on which the appropriate officer is informed of the fact that the sample is not suitable for the same means of analysis or has proved insufficient, as the case may be;

    (b) in the case of a person falling within paragraph (b), one month beginning with the date of the conviction or one month beginning with the date on which the appropriate officer is informed of the fact that the sample is not suitable for the same means of analysis or has proved insufficient, as the case may be.

(6) A requirement under subsection (4) above—

    (a) shall give the person at least 7 days within which he must so attend; and

    (b) may direct him to attend at a specified time of day or between specified times of day.

(7) Any constable may arrest without a warrant a person who has failed to comply with a requirement under subsection (4) above.

(8) In this section "the appropriate officer" is—

    (a) in the case of a person falling within subsection (4)(a), the officer investigating the offence with which that person has been charged or as to which he was informed that he would be reported;

    (b) in the case of a person falling within subsection (4)(b), the officer in charge of the police station from which the investigation of the offence of which he was convicted was conducted.]

[1] subss. (1A), (1B), (1C) and (1D) substituted for subs. (1A) by Criminal Justice and Police Act 2001 (c.16), Pt 3, s.81(2).

Testing for presence of Class A drugs

51–067   [**63B.**—(1) A sample of urine or a non-intimate sample may be taken from a person in police detention for the purpose of ascertaining whether he has any specified Class A drug in his body if the following conditions are met.

(2) The first condition is—

    (a) that the person concerned has been charged with a trigger offence; or

    (b) that the person concerned has been charged with an offence and a police officer of at least the rank of inspector, who has reasonable grounds for suspecting that the misuse by that person of any specified Class A drug caused or contributed to the offence, has authorised the sample to be taken.

(3) The second condition is that the person concerned has attained the age of 18.

(4) The third condition is that a police officer has requested the person concerned to give the sample.

(5) Before requesting the person concerned to give a sample, an officer must—

    (a) warn him that if, when so requested, he fails without good cause to do so he may be liable to prosecution, and

    (b) in a case within subsection (2)(b) above, inform him of the giving of the authorisation and of the grounds in question.

(6) A sample may be taken under this section only by a person prescribed by regulations made by the Secretary of State by statutory instrument.

No regulations shall be made under this subsection unless a draft has been laid before, and approved by resolution of, each House of Parliament.

(7) Information obtained from a sample taken under this section may be disclosed—

    (a) for the purpose of informing any decision about granting bail in criminal proceedings (within the meaning of the Bail Act 1976) to the person concerned;

    (b) where the person concerned is in police detention or is remanded in or committed to custody by an order of a court or has been granted such bail, for the purpose of informing any decision about his supervision;

    (c) where the person concerned is convicted of an offence, for the purpose of informing any decision about the appropriate sentence to be passed by a court and any decision about his supervision or release;

    (d) for the purpose of ensuring that appropriate advice and treatment is made available to the person concerned.

(8) A person who fails without good cause to give any sample which may be taken from him under this section shall be guilty of an offence.][1]

[1] Added by Criminal Justice and Court Services Act 2000 (c.43), Pt III, c.II s.57(2).

Testing for presence of Class A drugs: supplementary

51–068   [**63C.**—(1) A person guilty of an offence under section 63B above shall be liable on summary conviction to imprisonment for a term not exceeding three months, or to a fine not exceeding level 4 on the standard scale, or to both.

(2) A police officer may give an authorisation under section 63B above orally or in writing but, if he gives it orally, he shall confirm it in writing as soon as is practicable.

(3) If a sample is taken under section 63B above by virtue of an authorisation, the authorisation and the grounds for the suspicion shall be recorded as soon as is practicable after the sample is taken.

(4) If the sample is taken from a person detained at a police station, the matters required to be recorded by subsection (3) above shall be recorded in his custody record.

(5) Subsections (11) and (12) of section 62 above apply for the purposes of section 63B above as they do for the purposes of that section; and section 63B above does not prejudice the generality of sections 62 and 63 above.

(6) In section 63B above—

"Class A drug" and "misuse" have the same meanings as in the Misuse of Drugs Act 1971;
"specified" (in relation to a Class A drug) and "trigger offence" have the same meanings as in Part III of the Criminal Justice and Court Services Act 2000.]¹

¹ Added by Criminal Justice and Court Services Act 2000 (c.43) Pt III, c.II, s.57(2).

Destruction of fingerprints and samples

64.—[(1A) Where—   **51–069**

(a) fingerprints or samples are taken from a person in connection with the investigation of an offence, and
(b) subsection (3) below does not require them to be destroyed,

the fingerprints or samples may be retained after they have fulfilled the purposes for which they were taken but shall not be used by any person except for purposes related to the prevention or detection of crime, the investigation of an offence or the conduct of a prosecution.

(1B) In subsection (1A) above—

(a) the reference to using a fingerprint includes a reference to allowing any check to be made against it under section 63A(1) or (1C) above and to disclosing it to any person;
(b) the reference to using a sample includes a reference to allowing any check to be made under section 63A(1) or (1C) above against it or against information derived from it and to disclosing it or any such information to any person;
(c) the reference to crime includes a reference to any conduct which—

(i) constitutes one or more criminal offences (whether under the law of a part of the United Kingdom or of a country or territory outside the United Kingdom); or
(ii) is, or corresponds to, any conduct which, if it all took place in any one part of the United Kingdom, would constitute one or more criminal offences; and

    (d) the references to an investigation and to a prosecution include references, respectively, to any investigation outside the United Kingdom of any crime or suspected crime and to a prosecution brought in respect of any crime in a country or territory outside the United Kingdom.][1]

(3) If—

    (a) fingerprints or samples are taken from a person in connection with the investigation of an offence; and
    (b) that person is not suspected of having committed the offence,

they must, [except as provided in [the following provisions of this section],] be destroyed as soon as they have fulfilled the purpose for which they were taken.

    [(3AA) Samples and fingerprints are not required to be destroyed under subsection (3) above if—

    (a) they were taken for the purposes of the investigation of an offence of which a person has been convicted; and
    (b) a sample or, as the case may be, fingerprint was also taken from the convicted person for the purposes of that investigation.

    (3AB) Subject to subsection (3AC) below, where a person is entitled under subsection (3) above to the destruction of any fingerprint or sample taken from him (or would be but for subsection (3AA) above), neither the fingerprint nor the sample, nor any information derived from the sample, shall be used—

    (a) in evidence against the person who is or would be entitled to the destruction of that fingerprint or sample; or
    (b) for the purposes of the investigation of any offence;

and subsection (1B) above applies for the purposes of this subsection as it applies for the purposes of subsection (1A) above.

    (3AC) Where a person from whom a fingerprint or sample has been taken consents in writing to its retention—

    (a) that sample need not be destroyed under subsection (3) above;
    (b) subsection (3AB) above shall not restrict the use that may be made of the fingerprint or sample or, in the case of a sample, of any information derived from it; and
    (c) that consent shall be treated as comprising a consent for the purposes of section 63A(1C) above;

and a consent given for the purpose of this subsection shall not be capable of being withdrawn.

    (3AD) For the purposes of subsection (3AC) above it shall be immaterial whether the consent is given at, before or after the time when the entitlement to the destruction of the fingerprint or sample arises.][2]

    (4) [. . .][3]

    [(5) If fingerprints are destroyed—

    (a) any copies of the fingerprints shall also be destroyed; and
    (b) any chief officer of police controlling access to computer data relating to the fingerprints shall make access to the data impossible, as soon as it is practicable to do so.]

    (6) A person who asks to be allowed to witness the destruction of his fingerprints or copies of them shall have a right to witness it.

[(6A) If—

(a) subsection (5)(b) above falls to be complied with; and
(b) the person to whose fingerprints the data relate asks for a certificate that it has been complied with;

such a certificate shall be issued to him, not later than the end of the period of three months beginning with the day on which he asks for it, by the responsible chief officer of police or a person authorised by him or on his behalf for the purposes of this section.

(6B) In this section—

"the responsible chief officer of police" means the chief officer of police in whose [police] area the computer data were put on to the computer.][4]

(7) Nothing in this section—

(a) affects any power conferred by paragraph 18(2) of Schedule 2 to the Immigration Act 1971 [or section 20 of the Immigration and Asylum Act 1999 (c.33) (disclosure of police information to the Secretary of State for use for immigration purposes)]; or
(b) applies to a person arrested or detained under the terrorism provisions.

[1] subss. (1A) and (1B) substituted for subss. (1) and (2) by Criminal Justice and Police Act 2001 (c.16), Pt 3, s.82(2).
[2] subss. (3AA), (3AB), (3AC) and (3AD) substituted for subss. (3A) and (3B) by Criminal Justice and Police Act 2001 (c.16), Pt 3, s.82(4).
[3] Repealed by Criminal Justice and Police Act 2001 (c.16) Sched. 7(2)(1), para. 1.
[4] ss. 64(6A)(6B) inserted by Criminal Justice Act 1988 (c.33), s.148(2).

Photographing of suspects, etc.

[64A.—(1) A person who is detained at a police station may be photograph-ed—   **51–070**

(a) with the appropriate consent; or
(b) if the appropriate consent is withheld or it is not practicable to obtain it, without it.

(2) A person proposing to take a photograph of any person under this sec-tion—

(a) may, for the purpose of doing so, require the removal of any item or substance worn on or over the whole or any part of the head or face of the person to be photographed; and
(b) if the requirement is not complied with, may remove the item or sub-stance himself.

(3) Where a photograph may be taken under this section, the only persons entitled to take the photograph are—

(a) constables; and
(b) persons who (without being constables) are designated for the purposes of this section by the chief officer of police for the police area in which the police station in question is situated;

and section 117 (use of force) applies to the exercise by a person falling within paragraph (b) of the powers conferred by the preceding provisions of this section as it applies to the exercise of those powers by a constable.

(4) A photograph taken under this section—

(a) may be used by, or disclosed to, any person for any purpose related to the prevention or detection of crime, the investigation of an offence or the conduct of a prosecution; and

(b) after being so used or disclosed, may be retained but may not be used or disclosed except for a purpose so related.

(5) In subsection (4)—

(a) the reference to crime includes a reference to any conduct which—

(i) constitutes one or more criminal offences (whether under the law of a part of the United Kingdom or of a country or territory outside the United Kingdom); or

(ii) is, or corresponds to, any conduct which, if it all took place in any one part of the United Kingdom, would constitute one or more criminal offences; and

(b) the references to an investigation and to a prosecution include references, respectively, to any investigation outside the United Kingdom of any crime or suspected crime and to a prosecution brought in respect of any crime in a country or territory outside the United Kingdom.

(6) References in this section to taking a photograph include references to using any process by means of which a visual image may be produced; and references to photographing a person shall be construed accordingly.][1]

[1] Added by Anti-terrorism, Crime and Security Act 2001 (c.24), Pt 10, s.92.

. . . . . .

PART VI

CODES OF PRACTICE—GENERAL

Codes of practice

51–071   **66.**—[(1) The Secretary of State shall issue codes of practice in connection with—

(a) the exercise by police officers of statutory powers—

(i) to search a person without first arresting him; or

(ii) to search a vehicle without making an arrest;

(b) the detention, treatment, questioning and identification of persons by police officers;

(c) searches of premises by police officers; and

(d) the seizure of property found by police officers on persons or premises.

(2) Codes shall (in particular) include provision in connection with the exercise by police officers of powers under section 63B above.][1]

[1] Added by Criminal Justice and Court Services Act 2000 (c.43), Pt III, c.II, s.57(4).

Codes of practice—supplementary

67.—(1) When the Secretary of State proposes to issue a code of practice to **51–072** which this section applies, he shall prepare and publish a draft of that code, shall consider any representations made to him about the draft and may modify the draft accordingly.

(2) This section applies to a code of practice under [section 60, 60A or 66][1] above.

(3) The Secretary of State shall lay before both Houses of Parliament a draft of any code of practice prepared by him under this section.

(4) When the Secretary of State has laid the draft of a code before Parliament, he may bring the code into operation by order made by statutory instrument.

(5) No order under subsection (4) above shall have effect until approved by a resolution of each House of Parliament.

(6) An order bringing a code of practice into operation may contain such transitional provisions or savings as appear to the Secretary of State to be necessary or expedient in connection with the code of practice thereby brought into operation.

(7) The Secretary of State may from time to time revise the whole or any part of a code of practice to which this section applies and issue that revised code; and the foregoing provisions of this section shall apply (with appropriate modifications) to such a revised code as they apply to the first issue of a code.

[(7A) Subject to subsection (7B) below, the Secretary of State may by order provide that a code of practice for the time being in force is to be treated as having effect with such modifications as may be set out in the order.

(7B) The effect of the modifications made by an order under subsection (7A) above must be confined to one or more of the following—

(a) the effect of the code in relation to such area of England and Wales as may be specified in the order;
(b) the effect of the code during such period, not exceeding two years, as may be so specified;
(c) the effect of the order in relation to such offences or descriptions of offender as may be so specified.

(7C) An order under subsection (7A) above shall be made by statutory instrument and shall be subject to annulment in pursuance of a resolution of either House of Parliament.][2]

(8) [. . .][3]

(9) Persons other than police officers who are charged with the duty of investigating offences or charging offenders shall in the discharge of that duty have regard to any relevant provision of such a code.

(10) A failure on the part—

(a) of a police officer to comply with any provision of such a code; or
(b) of any person other than a police officer who is charged with the duty of investigating offences or charging offenders to have regard to any relevant provision of such a code in the discharge of that duty,

shall not of itself render him liable to any criminal or civil proceedings.

(11) In all criminal and civil proceedings any such code shall be admissible in evidence; and if any provision of such a code appears to the court or tribunal conducting the proceedings to be relevant to any question arising in the proceedings it shall be taken into account in determining that question.

(12) In this section "criminal proceedings" includes—

(a) proceedings in the United Kingdom or elsewhere before a court-martial constituted under the Army Act 1955, the Air Force Act 1955 or the Naval Discipline Act 1957 [. . .][4];

(b) proceedings before the Courts-Martial Appeal Court; and
(c) proceedings before a Standing Civilian Court.

[1] Word inserted by Criminal Justice and Police Act 2001 (c.16), Pt 3, s.76(2).
[2] Added by Criminal Justice and Police Act 2001 (c.16), Pt 3, s.77.
[3] Repealed by Police Act 1996 (c.16), Sched. 9, Pt II, para. 1.
[4] Words repealed by Armed Forces Act 2001 (c.19), Sched. 7, Pt 1, para. 1.

. . . . . .

Part VII

Documentary Evidence in Criminal Proceedings

Microfilm copies

51–073   **71.** In any proceedings the contents of a document may (whether or not the document is still in existence) be proved by the production of an enlargement of a microfilm copy of that document or of the material part of it, authenticated in such manner as the court may approve. [Where the proceedings concerned are proceedings before a magistrates' court inquiring into an offence as examining justices this section shall have effect with the omission of the words "authenticated in such manner as the court may approve."][1]

[1] Words inserted by Criminal Procedure and Investigations Act 1996 (c.25) Sched. 1, Pt II, para. 24.

Part VII—supplementary

51–074   **72.**—(1) In this Part of this Act—

["copy", in relation to a document, means anything onto which information recorded in the document has been copied, by whatever means and whether directly or indirectly and "statement" means any representation of fact, however made; and] "proceedings" means criminal proceedings, including—

(a) proceedings in the United Kingdom or elsewhere before a court martial constituted under the Army Act 1955 [, the Air Force Act 1955 or the Naval Discipline Act 1957];
(b) proceedings in the United Kingdom or elsewhere before the Courts-Martial Appeal Court—

(i) on an appeal from a court-martial so constituted; or
(ii) on a reference under section 34 of the Courts-Martial (Appeals) Act 1968; and

(c) proceedings before a Standing Civilian Court.

(2) Nothing in this Part of this Act shall prejudice any power of a court to exclude evidence (whether by preventing questions from being put or otherwise) at its discretion.

PART VIII

Convictions and acquittals

Proof of convictions and acquittals

73.—(1) Where in any proceedings the fact that a person has in the United **51–075**
Kingdom been convicted or acquitted of an offence otherwise than by a Service
court is admissible in evidence, it may be proved by producing a certificate of
conviction or, as the case may be, of acquittal relating to that offence, and
proving that the person named in the certificate as having been convicted or
acquitted of the offence is the person whose conviction or acquittal of the
offence is to be proved.

(2) For the purposes of this section a certificate of conviction or of acquittal—

  (a) shall, as regards a conviction or acquittal on indictment, consist of a
      certificate, signed by the [proper officer] of the court where the convic-
      tion or acquittal took place, giving the substance and effect (omitting
      the formal parts) of the indictment and of the conviction or acquittal;
      and
  (b) shall, as regards a conviction or acquittal on a summary trial, consist
      of a copy of the conviction or of the dismissal of the information,
      signed by the of the court where the conviction or acquittal took place
      or by the [proper officer] of the court, if any, to which a memorandum
      of the conviction or acquittal was sent;

and a document purporting to be a duly signed certificate of conviction or acquittal under this section shall be taken to be such a certificate unless the contrary
is proved.

[(3) In subsection (2) above "proper officer" means—

  (a) in relation to a magistrates' court in England and Wales, the justices'
      chief executive for the court; and
  (b) in relation to any other court, the clerk of the court, his deputy or any
      other person having custody of the court record.]

(4) The method of proving a conviction or acquittal authorised by this section
shall be in addition to and not to the exclusion of any other authorised manner
of proving a conviction or acquittal.

Conviction as evidence of commission of offence

74.—(1) In any proceedings the fact that a person other than the accused has **51–076**
been convicted of an offence by or before any court in the United Kingdom or
by a Service court outside the United Kingdom shall be admissible in evidence
for the purpose of proving, where to do so is relevant to any issue in those
proceedings, that that person committed that offence, whether or not any other
evidence of his having committed that offence is given.

(2) In any proceedings in which by virtue of this section a person other than
the accused is proved to have been convicted of an offence by or before any
court in the United Kingdom or by a Service court outside the United Kingdom,
he shall be taken to have committed that offence unless the contrary is proved.

(3) In any proceedings where evidence is admissible of the fact that the
accused has committed an offence, in so far as that evidence is relevant to any

matter in issue in the proceedings for a reason other than a tendency to show in the accused a disposition to commit the kind of offence with which he is charged, if the accused is proved to have been convicted of the offence—

    (a) by or before any court in the United Kingdom; or
    (b) by a Service court outside the United Kingdom,

he shall be taken to have committed that offence unless the contrary is proved.

    (4) Nothing in this section shall prejudice—

    (a) the admissibility in evidence of any conviction which would be admissible apart from this section; or
    (b) the operation of any enactment whereby a conviction or a finding of fact in any proceedings is for the purposes of any other proceedings made conclusive evidence of any fact.

Provisions supplementary to section 74

51–077   **75.**—(1) Where evidence that a person has been convicted of an offence is admissible by virtue of section 74 above, then without prejudice to the reception of any other admissible evidence for the purpose of identifying the facts on which the conviction was based—

    (a) the contents of any document which is admissible as evidence of the conviction; and
    (b) the contents of the information, complaint, indictment or charge-sheet on which the person in question was convicted,

shall be admissible in evidence for that purpose.

    (2) Where in any proceedings the contents of any document are admissible in evidence by virtue of subsection (1) above, a copy of that document, or of the material part of it, purporting to be certified or otherwise authenticated by or on behalf of the court or authority having custody of that document shall be admissible in evidence and shall be taken to be a true copy of that document or part unless the contrary is shown.

    (3) Nothing in any of the following—

    (a) [section 14 of the Powers of Criminal Courts (Sentencing) Act 2000] (under which a conviction leading to probation or discharge is to be disregarded except as mentioned in that section);
    (b) [section 247 of the Criminal Procedure (Scotland) Act 1995] (which makes similar provision in respect of convictions on indictment in Scotland); and
    (c) section 8 of the Probation Act (Northern Ireland) 1950 (which corresponds to section 13 of the Powers of Criminal Courts Act 1973) or any legislation which is in force in Northern Ireland for the time being and corresponds to that section,

shall affect the operation of section 74 above; and for the purposes of that section any order made by a court of summary jurisdiction in Scotland under [section 228 or section 246(3) of the said Act of 1995] shall be treated as a conviction.

(4) Nothing in section 74 above shall be construed as rendering admissible in any proceedings evidence of any conviction other than a subsisting one.

Confessions

Confessions

76.—(1) In any proceedings a confession made by an accused person may be given in evidence against him in so far as it is relevant to any matter in issue in the proceedings and is not excluded by the court in pursuance of this section.

51–078

(2) If, in any proceedings where the prosecution proposes to give in evidence a confession made by an accused person, it is represented to the court that the confession was or may have been obtained—

(a) by oppression of the person who made it; or
(b) in consequence of anything said or done which was likely, in the circumstances existing at the time, to render unreliable any confession which might be made by him in consequence thereof;

the court shall not allow the confession to be given in evidence against him except in so far as the prosecution proves to the court beyond reasonable doubt that the confession (notwithstanding that it may be true) was not obtained as aforesaid.

(3) In any proceedings where the prosecution proposes to give in evidence a confession made by an accused person, the court may of its own motion require the prosecution, as a condition of allowing it to do so, to prove that the confession was not obtained as mentioned in subsection (2) above.

(4) The fact that a confession is wholly or partly excluded in pursuance of this section shall not affect the admissibility in evidence—

(a) of any facts discovered as a result of the confession; or
(b) where the confession is relevant as showing that the accused speaks, writes or expresses himself in a particular way, of so much of the confession as is necessary to show that he does so.

(5) Evidence that a fact to which this subsection applies was discovered as a result of a statement made by an accused person shall not be admissible unless evidence of how it was discovered is given by him or on his behalf.

(6) Subsection (5) above applies—

(a) to any fact discovered as a result of a confession which is wholly excluded in pursuance of this section; and
(b) to any fact discovered as a result of a confession which is partly so excluded, if the fact is discovered as a result of the excluded part of the confession.

(7) Nothing in Part VII of this Act shall prejudice the admissibility of a confession made by an accused person.

(8) In this section "oppression" includes torture, inhuman or degrading treatment, and the use or threat of violence (whether or not amounting to torture).

[(9) Where the proceedings mentioned in subsection (1) above are proceedings before a magistrates' court inquiring into an offence as examining justices this section shall have effect with the omission of—

(a) in subsection (1) the words "and is not excluded by the court in pursuance of this section", and

(b) subsections (2) to (6) and (8).][1]

[1] Inserted by Criminal Procedure and Investigations Act 1996 (c.25), Sched. 1, Pt II, para.25.

Confessions by mentally handicapped persons

51–079   **77.**—(1) Without prejudice to the general duty of the court at a trial on indictment to direct the jury on any matter on which it appears to the court appropriate to do so, where at such a trial—

(a) the case against the accused depends wholly or substantially on a confession by him; and
(b) the court is satisfied—

   (i) that he is mentally handicapped; and
   (ii) that the confession was not made in the presence of an independent person,

the court shall warn the jury that there is special need for caution before convicting the accused in reliance on the confession, and shall explain that the need arises because of the circumstances mentioned in paragraphs (a) and (b) above.

(2) In any case where at the summary trial of a person for an offence it appears to the court that a warning under subsection (1) above would be required if the trial were on indictment, the court shall treat the case as one in which there is a special need for caution before convicting the accused on his confession.

(3) In this section—

"independent person" does not include a police officer or a person employed for, or engaged on, police purposes;
"mentally handicapped", in relation to a person, means that he is in a state of arrested or incomplete development of mind which includes significant impairment of intelligence and social functioning; and
"police purposes" has the meaning assigned to it by [section 101(2) of the Police Act 1996].

Miscellaneous

Exclusion of unfair evidence

51–080   **78.**—(1) In any proceedings the court may refuse to allow evidence on which the prosecution proposes to rely to be given if it appears to the court that, having regard to all the circumstances, including the circumstances in which the evidence was obtained, the admission of the evidence would have such an adverse effect on the fairness of the proceedings that the court ought not to admit it.

(2) Nothing in this section shall prejudice any rule of law requiring a court to exclude evidence.

[(3) This section shall not apply in the case of proceedings before a magistrates' court inquiring into an offences as examining justices.][1]

[1] Inserted by Criminal Procedure and Investigations Act 1996 (c.25), Sched. 1, Pt II, para. 26.

Time for taking accused's evidence

51–081   **79.** If at the trial of any person for an offence—

(a) the defence intends to call two or more witnesses to the facts of the case; and

(b) those witnesses include the accused,

the accused shall be called before the other witness or witnesses unless the court in its discretion otherwise directs.

Competence and compellability of accused's spouse

80.—(1) In any proceedings the wife or husband of the accused shall be competent to give evidence—   **51–082**

(a) subject to subsection (4) below, for the prosecution; and

(b) on behalf of the accused or any person jointly charged with the accused.

(2) In any proceedings the wife or husband of the accused shall, subject to subsection (4) below, be compellable to give evidence on behalf of the accused.

(3) In any proceedings the wife or husband of the accused shall, subject to subsection (4) below, be compellable to give evidence for the prosecution or on behalf of any person jointly charged with the accused if and only if—

(a) the offence charged involves an assault on, or injury or a threat of injury to, the wife or husband of the accused or a person who was at the material time under the age of sixteen; or

(b) the offence charged is a sexual offence alleged to have been committed in respect of a person who was at the material time under that age; or

(c) the offence charged consists of attempting or conspiring to commit, or of aiding, abetting, counselling, procuring or inciting the commission of, an offence falling within paragraph (a) or (b) above.

(4) Where a husband and wife are jointly charged with an offence neither spouse shall at the trial be competent or compellable by virtue of subsection (1)(a), (2) or (3) above to give evidence in respect of that offence unless that spouse is not, or is no longer, liable to be convicted of that offence at the trial as a result of pleading guilty or for any other reason.

(5) In any proceedings a person who has been but is no longer married to the accused shall be competent and compellable to give evidence as if that person and the accused had never been married.

(6) Where in any proceedings the age of any person at any time is material for the purposes of subsection (3) above, his age at the material time shall for the purposes of that provision be deemed to be or to have been that which appears to the court to be or to have been his age at that time.

(7) In subsection (3)(b) above "sexual-offence" means an offence under the Sexual Offences Act 1956, the Indecency with Children Act 1960, the Sexual Offences Act 1967, section 54 of the Criminal Law Act 1977 or the Protection of Children Act 1978.

(8) The failure of the wife or husband of the accused to give evidence shall not be made the subject of any comment by the prosecution.

(9) Section 1(d) of the Criminal Evidence Act 1898 (communications between husband and wife) and section 43(1) of the Matrimonial Causes Act 1965 (evidence as to marital intercourse) shall cease to have effect.

Advance notice of expert evidence in Crown Court

51–083   81.—(1) Crown Court Rules may make provision for—

(a) requiring any party to proceedings before the court to disclose to the other party or parties any expert evidence which he proposes to adduce in the proceedings; and
(b) prohibiting a party who fails to comply in respect of any evidence with any requirement imposed by virtue of paragraph (a) above from adducing that evidence without the leave of the court.

(2) Crown Court Rules made by virtue of this section may specify the kinds of expert evidence to which they apply and may exempt facts or matters of any description specified in the rules.

Part VIII—supplementary

Part VIII—interpretation

51–084   82.—(1) In this Part of this Act—

"confession", includes any statement wholly or partly adverse to the person who made it, whether made to a person in authority or not and whether made in words or otherwise;
"court-martial" means a court-martial constituted under the Army Act 1955, the Air Force Act 1955 or the Naval Discipline Act 1957;
"proceedings" means criminal proceedings, including—

(a) proceedings in the United Kingdom or elsewhere before a court-martial constituted under the Army Act 1955 [, the Air Force Act 1955 or the Naval Discipline Act 1957];
(b) proceedings in the United Kingdom or elsewhere before the Courts-Martial Appeal Court—

(i) on an appeal from a court-martial so constituted; or
(ii) on a reference under section 34 of the Courts-Martial (Appeals) Act 1968; and

(c) proceedings before a Standing Civilian Court; and

"Service court" means a court-martial or a Standing Civilian Court.

[(2) In this Part of this Act references to conviction before a Service court are references to a finding of guilty which is, or falls to be treated as, the finding of the court; and "convicted" shall be construed accordingly.]

(3) Nothing in this Part of this Act shall prejudice any power of a court to exclude evidence (whether by preventing questions from being put or otherwise) at its discretion.

. . . . . .

Part XI

Miscellaneous and Supplementary

Meaning of "serious arrestable offence"

116.—(1) This section has effect for determining whether an offence is a   **51–085**
serious arrestable offence for the purposes of this Act.

(2) The following arrestable offences are always serious—

  (a) an offence (whether at common law or under any enactment) specified
     in Part I of Schedule 5 to this Act; and
  (b) an offence under an enactment specified in Part II of that Schedule;
     [and]
  [(c) any of the offences mentioned in paragraphs (a) to (f) of section 1(3)
     of the Drug Trafficking Act 1994.]

(3) Subject to [subsection (4)][1] below, any other arrestable offence is serious
only if its commission—

  (a) has led to any of the consequences specified in subsection (6) below; or
  (b) is intended or is likely to lead to any of those consequences.

(4) An arrestable offence which consists of making a threat is serious if carrying out the threat would be likely to lead to any of the consequences specified
in subsection (6) below.

(5) [. . .][2]

(6) The consequences mentioned in subsections (3) and (4) above are—

  (a) serious harm to the security of the State or to public order;
  (b) serious interference with the administration of justice or with the
     investigation of offences or of a particular offence;
  (c) the death of any person;
  (d) serious injury to any person;
  (e) substantial financial gain to any person; and
  (f) serious financial loss to any person.

(7) Loss is serious for the purposes of this section if, having regard to all the
circumstances, it is serious for the person who suffers it.

(8) In this section "injury" includes any disease and any impairment of a
person's physical or mental condition.

[1] Words substituted by Terrorism Act 2000 (c.11), Sched. 15, para. 5(11)(a).
[2] repealed by Terrorism Act 2000 (c.11), Sched. 16, Pt I, para. 1.

Power of constable to use reasonable force

117. Where any provision of this Act—   **51–086**

  (a) confers a power on a constable; and
  (b) does not provide that the power may only be exercised with the consent
     of some person, other than a police officer,
the officer may use reasonable force, if necessary, in the exercise of the power.[[1]]

[1] In relation to the investigation of offences conducted by a service policeman under the Army Act
1955, the Air Force Act 1955 or the Naval Discipline Act 1957:

Power of constable to use reasonable force

117. Where any provision of this Act—

(a) confers a power on a service policeman; and
(b) does not provide that the power may only be exercised with the consent of some person, other than a service policeman,

the service policeman may use reasonable force, if necessary, in the exercise of the power.

General interpretation

51–087   **118.**—(1) In this Act—

"arrestable offence" has the meaning assigned to it by section 24 above;
["British Transport Police Force" means the constables appointed under section 53 of the British Transport Commission Act 1949 (c. xxix);][1]
"designated police station" has the meaning assigned to it by section 35 above;
"document" has the same meaning as in Part I of the Civil Evidence Act 1968;
"item subject to legal privilege" has the meaning assigned to it by section 10 above;
"parent or guardian" means —

(a) in the case of a child or young person in the care of a local authority, that authority;

"premises" has the meaning assigned to it by section 23 above;
"recordable offence" means any offence to which regulations under section 27 above apply;
"vessel" includes any ship, boat, raft or other apparatus constructed or adapted for floating on water.

(2) A person is in police detention for the purposes of this Act if—

[(a) he has been taken to a police station after being arrested for an offence or after being arrested under asection 41 of the Terrorism Act 2000, or][2]
(b) he is arrested at a police station after attending voluntarily at the station or accompanying a constable to it,

and is detained there or is detained elsewhere in the charge of a constable, except that a person who is at a court after being charged is not in police detention for those purposes.

---

[1] Definition inserted by Anti-terrorism, Crime and Security Act 2001 (c.24), Sched. 7, para. 14.
[4] Substituted by Terrorism Act 2000 (c.11), Sched. 15, para. 5(12).

. . . . . .

SCHEDULE 1

SPECIAL PROCEDURE

Making of orders by circuit judge

1. If on an application made by a constable a circuit judge is satisfied that one or other of the sets of access conditions is fulfilled, he may make an order under paragraph 4 below.   **51–088**

2. The first set of access conditions is fulfilled if—   **51–089**

    (a) there are reasonable grounds for believing—

        (i) that a serious arrestable offence has been committed;
        (ii) that there is material which consists of special procedure material or includes special procedure material and does not also include excluded material on premises specified in the application;
        (iii) that the material is likely to be of substantial value (whether by itself or together with other material) to the investigation in connection with which the application is made; and
        (iv) that the material is likely to be relevant evidence;

    (b) other methods of obtaining the material—

        (i) have been tried without success; or
        (ii) have not been tried because it appeared that they

were bound to fail; and

    (c) it is in the public interest, having regard—

        (i) to the benefit likely to accrue to the investigation if the material is obtained; and
        (ii) to the circumstances under which the person in possession of the material holds it,

that the material should be produced or that access to it should be given.

3. The second set of access conditions is fulfilled if—   **51–090**

    (a) there are reasonable grounds for believing that there is material which consists of or includes excluded material or special procedure material on premises specified in the application;
    (b) but for section 9(2) above a search of the premises for that material could have been authorised by the issue of a warrant to a constable under an enactment other than this Schedule; and
    (c) the issue of such a warrant would have been appropriate.

4. An order under this paragraph is an order that the person who appears to the circuit judge to be in possession of the material to which the application relates shall—   **51–091**

    (a) produce it to a constable for him to take away; or
    (b) give a constable access to it,

not later than the end of the period of seven days from the date of the order or the end of such longer period as the order may specify.

5. Where the material consists of information contained in a computer—   **51–092**

    (a) an order under paragraph 4(a) above shall have effect as an order to produce the material in a form in which it can be taken away and in which it is visible and legible; and
    (b) an order under paragraph 4(b) above shall have effect as an order to give a constable access to the material in a form in which it is visible and legible.

6. For the purposes of sections 21 and 22 above material produced in pursuance of an order under paragraph 4(a) above shall be treated as if it were material seized by a constable.   **51–093**

Notices of applications for orders

7. An application for an order under paragraph 4 above shall be made inter partes.   **51–094**

8. Notice of an application for such an order may be served on a person either by delivering it to him or by leaving it at his proper address or by sending it by post to him in a registered letter or by the recorded delivery service.   **51–095**

51–096   9. Such a notice may be served—

(a) on a body corporate, by serving it on the body's secretary or clerk or other similar officer; and
(b) on a partnership, by serving it on one of the partners.

51–097   10. For the purposes of this Schedule, and of section 7 of the Interpretation Act 1978 in its application to this Schedule, the proper address of a person, in the case of secretary or clerk or other similar officer of a body corporate, shall be that of the registered or principal office of that body, in the case of a partner of a firm shall be that of the principal office of the firm, and in any other case shall be the last known address of the person to be served.

51–098   11. Where notice of an application for an order under paragraph 4 above has been served on a person, he shall not conceal, destroy, alter or dispose of the material to which the application relates except—

(a) with the leave of a judge; or
(b) with the written permission of a constable,

until—

(i) the application is dismissed or abandoned; or
(ii) he has complied with an order under paragraph 4 above made on the application.

Issue of warrants by circuit judge

51–099   12. If on an application made by a constable a circuit judge—

(a) is satisfied—

(i) that either set of access conditions is fulfilled; and
(ii) that any of the further conditions set out in paragraph 14 below is also fulfilled; or

(b) is satisfied—

(i) that the second set of access conditions is fulfilled; and
(ii) that an order under paragraph 4 above relating to the material has not been complied with,

he may issue a warrant authorising a constable to enter and search the premises.

51–100   13. A constable may seize and retain anything for which a search has been authorised under paragraph 12 above.

51–101   14. The further conditions mentioned in paragraph 12(a)(ii) above are—

(a) that it is not practicable to communicate with any person entitled to grant entry to the premises to which the application relates;
(b) that it is practicable to communicate with a person entitled to grant entry to the premises but it is not practicable to communicate with any person entitled to grant access to the material;
(c) that the material contains information which—

(i) is subject to a restriction or obligation such as is mentioned in section 11(2)(b) above; and
(ii) is likely to be disclosed in breach of it if a warrant is not issued;

(d) that service of notice of an application for an order under paragraph 4 above may seriously prejudice the investigation.

51–102   15.—(1) If a person fails to comply with an order under paragraph 4 above, a circuit judge may deal with him as if he had committed a contempt of the Crown Court.
(2) Any enactment relating to contempt of the Crown Court shall have effect in relation to such a failure as if it were such a contempt.

Costs

16. The costs of any application under this Schedule and of anything done or to be done in pursuance of an order made under it shall be in the discretion of the judge.

51–103

. . . . . .

Section 116

SCHEDULE 5

SERIOUS ARRESTABLE OFFENCES

PART I

OFFENCES MENTIONED IN SECTION 116(2)(a)

1. Treason.

51–104

2. Murder.

3. Manslaughter.

4. Rape.

5. Kidnapping.

6. Incest with a girl under the age of 13.

[**7.** Buggery with a person under the age of 16.]¹

8. Indecent assault which constitutes an act of gross indecency.

[**9.** An offence under section 170 of the Customs and Excise Management Act 1979 (c.2) of being knowingly concerned, in relation to any goods, in any fraudulent evasion or attempt at evasion of a prohibition in force with respect to the goods under section 42 of the Customs Consolidation Act 1876 (c.36) (prohibition on importing indecent or obscene articles).]²

¹ Item substituted by Criminal Justice and Public Order Act 1994 (c.33), Sched. 10, para. 59.
² Added by Criminal Justice and Police Act 2001 (c.16), Pt 3, s.72.

PART II

OFFENCES MENTIONED IN SECTION 116(2)(b)

Explosive Substances Act 1883 (c.3)

1. Section 2 (causing explosion likely to endanger life or property).

51–105

Sexual Offences Act 1956 (c.69)

2. Section 5 (intercourse with a girl under the age of 13).

51–106

Firearms Act 1968 (c.27)

3. Section 16 (possession of firearms with intent to injure).
4. Section 17(1) (use of firearms and imitation firearms to resist arrest).
5. Section 18 (carrying firearms with criminal intent).
6. [. . .]¹

51–107

¹ Repealed by Road Traffic (Consequential Provisions) Act 1988 (c.54), s.3, Sched. 1, Pt I.

Taking of Hostages Act 1982 (c.28)

7. Section 1 (hostage-taking).

51–108

Aviation Security Act 1982 (c.36)

8. Section 1 (hi-jacking).

51–109

Criminal Justice Act 1988 (c.33)

[**9.** Section 134 (Torture).]¹

51–110

¹ Sched. 5, Pt II, para. 9 inserted by Criminal Justice Act 1988 (c.33), s.170(1), Sched. 15, para. 102.

The Road Traffic Act 1988 (c.52)

51–111   [Section 1 (causing death by [dangerous]¹ driving).
[Section 3A (causing death by careless driving when under the influence of drink or drugs).]²]³

¹ Word substituted by Road Traffic Act 1991 (c.40) Sched. 4, para. 39(a).
² Words inserted by Road Traffic Act 1991 (c.40), Sched. 4, para. 39(b).
³ Entry inserted by Road Traffic Act 1988 (c.52), s.4, Sched. 3, para. 27(5).

Aviation and Maritime Security Act 1990 (c.31)

51–112   [**11.** Section 1 (endangering safety at aerodromes).]¹
[**12.** Section 9 (hijacking of ships).]
[**13.** Section 10 (seizing or exercising control of fixed platforms).]

¹ Sched. 5, paras. 11, 12 and 13 inserted by Aviation and Maritime Security Act 1990 (c.31), ss.53(1), Sched. 3, para. 8.

Channel Tunnel (Security) Order 1994 No.

51–113   [**14.** Article 4 (hijacking of Channel Tunnel trains).]
[**15.** Article 5 (seizing or exercising control of the tunnel system).]

Protection of Children Act 1978 (c.37)

51–114   [**14.** Section 1 (indecent photographs and pseudo-photographs of children).]

Obscene Publications Act 1959 (c.66.)

51–115   [**15.** Section 2 (publication of obscene matter).]

Video Recordings Act 1984

(1984, c. 39)

52–001   *An Act to make provision for regulating the distribution of video recordings and for connected purposes.*   [12th July 1984]

Preliminary

Interpretation of terms

52–002   **1.**—(1) The provisions of this section shall have effect for the interpretation of terms used in this Act.

(2) "Video work" means any series of visual images (with or without sound)—

(a) produced electronically by the use of information contained on any disc magnetic tape [or any other device capable of storing data electronically], and
(b) shown as a moving picture.

(3) "Video recording" means any disc magnetic tape [any other device capable of storing data electronically] containing information by the use of which the whole or a part of a video work may be produced.

(4) "Supply" means supply in any manner, whether or not for reward, and, therefore, includes supply by way of sale, letting on hire, exchange or loan; and references to a supply are to be interpreted accordingly.

Exempted works

2.—(1) Subject to subsection (2) [or (3)] below, a video work is for the   **52–003**
purposes of this Act an exempted work if, taken as a whole—

    (a) it is designed to inform, educate or instruct;
    (b) it is concerned with sport, religion or music; or
    (c) it is a video game.
    [(d) techniques likely to be useful in the commission of offences;]

(2) A video work is not an exempted work for those purposes if, to any
significant extent, it depicts—

    (a) human sexual activity or acts of force or restraint associated with such
        activity;
    (b) mutilation or torture of, or other acts of gross violence towards, humans
        or animals;
    (c) human genital organs or human urinary or excretory functions;

or is [likely] to any significant extent to stimulate or encourage anything falling
within paragraph (a) or, in the case of anything falling within paragraph (b), is
[likely] to any extent to do so.
    [(3) A video work is not an exempted work for those purposes if, to any
significant extent, it depicts criminal activity which is likely to any significant
extent to stimulate or encourage the commission of offences.]

Exempted supplies

3.—(1) The provisions of this section apply to determine whether or not a   **52–004**
supply of a video recording is an exempted supply for the purposes of this Act.
    (2) The supply of a video recording by any person is an exempted supply if
it is neither—

    (a) a supply for reward, nor
    (b) a supply in the course or furtherance of a business.

(3) Where on any premises facilities are provided in the course or furtherance
of a business for supplying video recordings, the supply by any person of a
video recording on those premises is to be treated for the purposes of subsection
(2) above as a supply in the course or furtherance of a business.
    (4) Where a person (in this subsection referred to as the "original supplier")
supplies a video recording to a person who, in the course of a business, makes
video works or supplies video recordings, the supply is an exempted supply—

    (a) if it is not made with a view to any further supply of that recording, or
    (b) if it is so made, but is not made with a view to the eventual supply of
        that recording to the public or is made with a view to the eventual
        supply of that recording to the original supplier.

For the purposes of this subsection, any supply is a supply to the public unless
it is—

    (i) a supply to a person who, in the course of a business, makes video
       works or supplies video recordings,
    (ii) an exempted supply by virtue of subsection (2) above or subsections
        (5) to (10) below, or
    (iii) a supply outside the United Kingdom.

(5) Where a video work—

  (a) is designed to provide a record of an event or occasion for those who took part in the event or occasion or are connected with those who did so,
  (b) does not, to any significant extent, depict anything falling within paragraph (a), (b) or (c) of section 2(2) of this Act, and
  (c) is not designed to any significant extent to stimulate or encourage anything falling within paragraph (a) of that subsection or, in the case of anything falling within paragraph (b) of that subsection, is not designed to any extent to do so,

the supply of a video recording containing only that work to a person who took part in the event or occasion or is connected with someone who did so is an exempted supply.

(6) The supply of a video recording for the purpose only of the exhibition of any video work contained in the recording in premises other than a dwelling-house—

  (a) being premises mentioned in subsection (7) below, or
  (b) being an exhibition which in England and Wales or Scotland would be [a film exhibition to which section 6 of the Cinemas Act 1985 applies (film] exhibition to which public not admitted or are admitted without payment), or in Northern Ireland would be an exempted exhibition within the meaning of section 5 of the Cinematograph Act (Northern Ireland) 1959 (similar provisions for Northern Ireland),

is an exempted supply.

[(7) The premises referred to in subsection (6) above are—

  (a) premises in respect of which a licence under section 1 of the Cinemas Act 1985 is in force,
  (b) premises falling within section 7 of that Act (premises used only occasionally and exceptionally for film exhibitions), or
  (c) premises falling within section 8 of that Act (building or structure of a movable character) in respect of which such a licence as is mentioned in subsection (1)(a) of that section has been granted.]

(8) The supply of a video recording with a view only to its use for or in connection with [a programme service (within the meaning of the Broadcasting Act 1990)] is an exempted supply.

(9) The supply of a video recording for the purpose only of submitting a video work contained in the recording for the issue of a classification certificate or otherwise only for purposes of arrangements made by the designated authority is an exempted supply.

(10) The supply of a video recording with a view only to its use—

  (a) in training for or carrying on any medical or related occupation,
  (b) for the purpose of—

    (i) services provided in pursuance of the National Health Service Act 1977 or the National Health Service (Scotland) Act 1978, or
    (ii) such of the services provided in pursuance of the Health and Personal Social Services (Northern Ireland) Order 1972 as are health services (within the meaning of that Order), or

  (c) in training persons employed in the course of services falling within paragraph (b) above,

is an exempted supply.

(11) For the purposes of subsection (10) above, an occupation is a medical or related occupation if, to carry on the occupation, a person is required to be registered under the Professions Supplementary to Medicine Act 1960, [the Nurses, Midwives and Health Visitors Act 1997] [the Medical Act 1983, the Osteopaths Act 1993 or the Chiropractors Act 1994].

(12) The supply of a video recording otherwise than for reward, being a supply made for the purpose only of supplying it to a person who previously made an exempted supply of the recording, is also an exempted supply.

Designated authority

Authority to determine suitability of video works for classification

4.—(1) The Secretary of State may by notice under this section designate any person as the authority responsible for making arrangements—   **52–005**

(a) for determining for the purposes of this Act whether or not video works are suitable for classification certificates to be issued in respect of them, having special regard to the likelihood of video works in respect of which such certificates have been issued being viewed in the home,

(b) in the case of works which are determined in accordance with the arrangements to be so suitable—

[(i) for assigning a unique title to each video work in respect of which a classification certificate is to be issued]

(ii) for making such other determinations as are required for the issue of classification certificates, and

(iii) for issuing such certificates, and

(c) for maintaining a record of such determinations (whether determinations made in pursuance of arrangements made by that person or by any person previously designated under this section).

[(1A) A title assigned to a video work under subsection (1)(b)(ia) above shall consist of—

(a) the title under which the video work was determined to be suitable for the issue of a classification certificate; and

(b) a registration number (which may contain letters and other symbols as well as figures).

(1B) The record maintained under subsection (1)(c) above shall include, in relation to each video work in respect of which a classification certificate has been issued, a video recording which—

(a) contains the video work; and

(b) shows, or shows on its spool, case or other thing on or in which the recording is kept—

(i) the title assigned to the video work under subsection (1)(b)(ia) above; and

(ii) the determination or determinations made in respect of the video work.]

(2) The power to designate any person by notice under this section includes power—

(a) to designate two or more persons jointly as the authority responsible for making those arrangements, and

(b) to provide that any person holding an office or employment specified in the notice is to be treated as designated while holding that office or employment.

(3) The Secretary of State shall not make any designation under this section unless he is satisfied that adequate arrangements will be made for an appeal by any person against a determination that a video work submitted by him for the issue of a classification certificate—

(a) is not suitable for a classification certificate to be issued in respect of it, or

(b) is not suitable for viewing by persons who have not attained a particular age,

or against a determination that no video recording containing the work is to be supplied other than in a licensed sex shop.

(4) The Secretary of State may at any time designate another person in place of any person designated under this section and, if he does so, may give directions as to the transfer of any record kept in pursuance of the arrangements referred to in subsection (1) above; and it shall be the duty of any person having control of any such record or any part of it to comply with the directions.

(5) No fee shall be recoverable by the designated authority in connection with any determination falling within subsection (1)(a) or (b) above or the issue of any classification certificate unless the fee is payable in accordance with a tariff approved by the Secretary of State.

(6) The Secretary of State may for the purposes of subsection (5) above approve a tariff providing for different fees for different classes of video works and for different circumstances.

(7) Any notice under this section shall be published in the London, Edinburgh and Belfast Gazettes.

(8) In this Act, references to the designated authority, in relation to any transaction, are references to the person or persons designated under this section at the time of that transaction.

Criteria for suitability to which special regard to be had

52–006   [**4A.**—(1) The designated authority shall, in making any determination as to the suitability of a video work, have special regard (among the other relevant factors) to any harm that may be caused to potential viewers or, through their behaviour, to society by the manner in which the work deals with—

(a) criminal behaviour;

(b) illegal drugs;

(c) violent behaviour or incidents;

(d) horrific behaviour or incidents; or

(e) human sexual activity.

(2) For the purposes of this section—

"potential viewer" means any person (including a child or young person) who is likely to view the video work in question if a classification certificate or a classification certificate of a particular description were issued;

"suitability" means suitability for the issue of a classification certificate or suitability for the issue of a certificate of a particular description;

"violent behaviour" includes any act inflicting or likely to result in the infliction of injury;

and any behaviour or activity referred to in subsection (1)(a) to (e) above shall be taken to include behaviour or activity likely to stimulate or encourage it.]¹

¹ Added by Criminal Justice and Public Order Act 1994 (c.33), Pt VII, s.90(1).

Review of determinations as to suitability

[**4B.**—(1) The Secretary of State may by order make provision enabling the designated authority to review any determination made by them, before the coming into force of section 4A of this Act, as to the suitability of a video work.   **52–007**
(2) The order may in particular provide—

(a) for the authority's power of review to be exercisable in relation to such determinations as the authority think fit;
(b) for the authority to determine, on any review, whether, if they were then determining the suitability of the video work to which the determination under review relates, they—

(i) would issue a classification certificate, or
(ii) would issue a different classification certificate;

(c) for the cancellation of a classification certificate, where they determine that they would not issue a classification certificate;
(d) for the cancellation of a classification certificate and issue of a new classification certificate, where they determine that they would issue a different classification certificate;
(e) for any such cancellation or issue not to take effect until the end of such period as may be determined in accordance with the order;
(f) for such persons as may appear to the authority to fall within a specified category of person to be notified of any such cancellation or issue in such manner as may be specified;
(g) for treating a classification certificate, in relation to any act or omission occurring after its cancellation, as if it had not been issued;
(h) for specified provisions of this Act to apply to determinations made on a review subject to such modifications (if any) as may be specified;
(i) for specified regulations made under section 8 of this Act to apply to a video work in respect of which a new classification certificate has been issued subject to such modifications (if any) as may be specified.

(3) In subsection (2) above "specified" means specified by an order made under this section.
(4) The Secretary of State shall not make any order under this section unless he is satisfied that adequate arrangements will be made for an appeal against determinations made by the designated authority on a review.
(5) The power to make an order under this section shall be exercisable by statutory instrument which shall be subject to annulment in pursuance of a resolution of either House of Parliament.
(6) In this section "suitability" has the same meaning as in section 4A of this Act.]¹

¹ Added by Criminal Justice and Public Order Act 1994 (c.33), Pt VII, s.90(1).

Parliamentary procedure for designation

5.—(1) Where the Secretary of State proposes to make a designation under section 4 of this Act, he shall lay particulars of his proposal before both Houses   **52–008**

of Parliament and shall not make the proposed designation until after the end of the period of forty days beginning with the day on which the particulars of his proposal were so laid.

(2) If, within the period mentioned in subsection (1) above, either House resolves that the Secretary of State should not make the proposed designation, the Secretary of State shall not do so (but without prejudice to his power to lay before Parliament particulars of further proposals in accordance with that subsection).

(3) For the purposes of subsection (1) above—

    (a) where particulars of a proposal are laid before each House of Parliament on different days, the later day shall be taken to be the day on which the particulars were laid before both Houses;

    (b) in reckoning any period of forty days, no account shall be taken of any time during which Parliament is dissolved or prorogued or during which both Houses are adjourned for more than four days.

Annual report

52–009   **6.**—(1) The designated authority shall, as soon as it is reasonably practicable to do so after 31st December, make a report to the Secretary of State on the carrying out in the year ending with that date of the arrangements referred to in section 4(1) and (3) of this Act (together with a statement of accounts) and on such other matters (if any) as the designated authority consider appropriate or the Secretary of State may require.

(2) The Secretary of State shall lay a copy of any report made to him under this section before each House of Parliament.

Classification and labelling

Classification certificates

52–010   **7.**—(1) In this Act "classification certificate" means a certificate—

    (a) issued in respect of a video work in pursuance of arrangements made by the designated authority; and

    (b) satisfying the requirements of subsection (2) below.

(2) Those requirements are that the certificate must contain [the title assigned to the video work in accordance with section 4(1)(b)(ia) of this Act and][1]—

    (a) a statement that the video work concerned is suitable for general viewing and unrestricted supply (with or without any advice as to the desirability of parental guidance with regard to the viewing of the work by young children or as to the particular suitability of the work for viewing by children[or young children][2]); or

    (b) a statement that the video work concerned is suitable for viewing only by persons who have attained the age (not being more than eighteen years) specified in the certificate and that no video recording containing that work is to be supplied to any person who has not attained the age so specified; or

    (c) the statement mentioned in paragraph (b) above together with a statement that no video recording containing that work is to be supplied other than in a licensed sex shop.

---

[1] Words inserted by Video Recordings Act 1993 (c.24), s.1(3).
[2] Words inserted by Criminal Justice and Public Order Act 1994 (c.33), Pt VII, s.90(2).

Requirements as to labelling, etc.

8.—(1) The Secretary of State may, in relation to video works in respect of   **52–011**
which classification certificates have been issued, by regulations require such
indication as may be specified by the regulations of any of the contents of any
classification certificate to be shown in such a manner as may be so specified
on any video recording containing the video work in respect of which the certificate was issued or any spool, case or other thing on or in which such a video
recording is kept.

(2) Regulations under this section may make different provision for different
video works and for different circumstances.

(3) The power to make regulations under this section shall be exercisable by
statutory instrument which shall be subject to annulment in pursuance of a resolution of either House of Parliament.

Offences and penalties

Supplying video recording of unclassified work

9.—(1) A person who supplies or offers to supply a video recording con-   **52–012**
taining a video work in respect of which no classification certificate has been
issued is guilty of an offence unless—

    (a) the supply is, or would if it took place be, an exempted supply, or
    (b) the video work is an exempted work.

(2) It is a defence to a charge of committing an offence under this section to
prove that the accused believed on reasonable grounds—

    (a) that the video work concerned or, if the video recording contained more
        than one work to which the charge relates, each of those works was
        either an exempted work or a work in respect of which a classification
        certificate had been issued, or
    (b) that the supply was, or would if it took place be, an exempted supply
        by virtue of section 3(4) or (5) of this Act.

[(3) A person guilty of an offence under this section shall be liable—

    (a) on conviction on indictment, to imprisonment for a term not exceeding
        two years or a fine or both,
    (b) on summary conviction, to imprisonment for a term not exceeding six
        months or a fine not exceeding £20,000 or both.][1]

[1] Added by Criminal Justice and Public Order Act 1994 (c.33), Pt VII, s.88(2).

**Possession of video recording of unclassified work for the purposes of
supply**

10.—(1) Where a video recording contains a video work in respect of which   **52–013**
no classification certificate has been issued, a person who has the recording in
his possession for the purpose of supplying it is guilty of an offence unless—

    (a) he has it in his possession for the purpose only of a supply which, if it
        took place, would be an exempted supply, or
    (b) the video work is an exempted work.

(2) It is a defence to a charge of committing an offence under this section to
prove—

(a) that the accused believed on reasonable grounds that the video work concerned or, if the video recording contained more than one work to which the charge relates, each of those works was either an exempted work or a work in respect of which a classification certificate had been issued,

(b) that the accused had the video recording in his possession for the purpose only of a supply which he believed on reasonable grounds would, if it took place, be an exempted supply by virtue of section 3(4) or (5) of this Act, or

(c) that the accused did not intend to supply the video recording until a classification certificate had been issued in respect of the video work concerned.

[(3) A person guilty of an offence under this section shall be liable—

(a) on conviction on indictment, to imprisonment for a term not exceeding two years or a fine or both,

(b) on summary conviction, to imprisonment for a term not exceeding six months or a fine not exceeding £20,000 or both.]¹

¹ Added by Criminal Justice and Public Order Act 1994 (c.33), Pt VII, s.88(3).

Supplying video recording of classified work in breach of classification

52–014
11.—(1) Where a classification certificate issued in respect of a video work states that no video recording containing that work is to be supplied to any person who has not attained the age specified in the certificate, a person who supplies or offers to supply a video recording containing that work to a person who has not attained the age so specified is guilty of an offence unless the supply is, or would if it took place be, an exempted supply.

(2) It is a defence to a charge of committing an offence under this section to prove—

(a) that the accused neither knew nor had reasonable grounds to believe that the classification certificate contained the statement concerned,

(b) that the accused neither knew nor had reasonable grounds to believe that the person concerned had not attained that age, or

(c) that the accused believed on reasonable grounds that the supply was, or would if it took place be, an exempted supply by virtue of section 3(4) or (5) of this Act.

[(3) A person guilty of an offence under this section shall be liable, on summary conviction, to imprisonment for a term not exceeding six months or a fine not exceeding level 5 on the standard scale or both.]¹

¹ Added by Criminal Justice and Public Order Act 1994 (c.33), Pt VII, s.88(4).

Cinemas Act 1985

(1985, c. 13)

53–001 *An Act to consolidate the Cinematograph Acts 1909 to 1982 and certain related enactments, with an amendment to give effect to a recommendation of the Law Commission.* [27th March 1985]

Control of exhibitions

Licence required for exhibitions

1.—(1) Subject to sections 5 to 8 below, no premises shall be used for a film **53–002**
exhibition unless they are licensed for the purpose under this section.

(2) A licensing authority may [grant to an applicant and from time to time
renew or transfer a licence] to use any premises specified in the licence for the
purpose of film exhibitions on such terms and conditions and subject to such
restrictions as, subject to regulations under section 4 below, [they may so spe-
cify].

(3) Without prejudice to the generality of subsection (2) above, it shall be the
duty of a licensing authority, in granting a licence under this section as respects
any premises,—

   (a) to impose conditions or restrictions prohibiting the admission of chil-
       dren to film exhibitions involving the showing of works designated, by
       the authority or by such other body as may be specified in the licence,
       as works unsuitable for children; and
   (b) to consider what (if any) conditions or restrictions should be imposed
       as to the admission of children to other film exhibitions involving the
       showing of works designated, by the authority or by such other body
       as may be specified in the licence, as works of such other description
       as may be so specified.

Consent required for exhibitions for children

2.—(1) Subject to sections 5 and 6 below, no premises shall be used, except **53–003**
with the consent of the licensing authority, for a film exhibition organised
wholly or mainly as an exhibition for children.

(2) Subject to regulations under section 4 below, a licensing authority may,
without prejudice to any conditions or restrictions imposed by them on the granting of a licence, impose special conditions or restrictions on the granting of a
consent under this section.

Exempted exhibitions

. . . . . .

Exhibitions in private dwelling-houses

5.—(1) This section applies to any film exhibition which— **53–004**

   (a) is given in a private dwelling-house,
   (b) is one to which the public are not admitted, and
   (c) satisfies the condition mentioned in subsection (2) below.

(2) The condition referred to in subsection (1)(c) above is that either—

   (a) the exhibition is not promoted for private gain, or
   (b) the sole or main purpose of the exhibition is to demonstrate any prod-
       uct, to advertise any goods or services or to provide information, educa-
       tion or instruction.

(3) The following exemptions have effect in relation to any film exhibition to
which this section applies, that is to say—

(a) a licence shall not be required by reason only of the giving of the exhibition;

(b) where the exhibition is given in premises in respect of which a licence is in force, no condition or restriction on or subject to which the licence was granted shall apply to the exhibition;

(c) regulations under section 4 above shall not apply to the exhibition.

Other non-commercial exhibitions

53–005   **6.**—(1) Subject to subsections (4) and (5) below, this section applies to any film exhibition (other than one to which section 5 above applies) which—

(a) is one to which the public are not admitted or are admitted without payment, or

(b) does not fall within paragraph (a) above but is given by an exempted organisation,

and (in either case) satisfies the condition mentioned in subsection (2) below.
    (2) The condition referred to in subsection (1) above is that either—

(a) the exhibition is not promoted for private gain, or

(b) the sole or main purpose of the exhibition is to demonstrate any product, to advertise any goods or services or to provide information, education or instruction.

(3) The following exemptions have effect in relation to any film exhibition to which this section applies, that is to say—

(a) a licence under section 1 above shall not be required by reason only of the giving of the exhibition unless the pictures are produced by means specified in regulations under section 4 above as means involving such risk that it is inexpedient that this paragraph should have effect;

(b) where the exhibition is given in premises in respect of which a licence under section 1 above is in force, no condition or restriction on or subject to which the licence was granted shall apply to the exhibition except so far as it relates to the matters specified in section 4(2)(a) above;

(c) a consent under section 2 above shall not be required by reason only of the giving of the exhibition;

(d) where the exhibition is given in premises in respect of which a consent under section 2 above is in force, no condition or restriction on or subject to which the consent was granted shall apply to the exhibition;

(e) regulations under section 4 above making such provision as is mentioned in subsection (2)(b) of that section shall not apply to the exhibition and regulations under that section making such provision as is mentioned in subsection (2)(a) of that section shall not apply to the exhibition unless it is given in premises in respect of which a licence under section 1 above is in force.

(4) A film exhibition is excluded from being one to which this section applies if it is organised solely or mainly as an exhibition for children who are members of a club, society or association the principal object of which is attendance at film exhibitions, unless the exhibition is given in a private dwelling-house or as part of the activities of an educational or religious institution.
    (5) A film exhibition is excluded from being one to which this section applies by virtue of paragraph (b) of subsection (1) above if on more than three out of

the last preceding seven days the premises in question were used for the giving of a film exhibition to which this section applied by virtue of that paragraph.

(6) In this section "exempted organisation" means a society, institution, committee or other organisation with respect to which there is in force at the time of the exhibition in question a certificate given by the Secretary of State certifying that he is satisfied that the organisation is not conducted or established for profit; and there shall be paid to the Secretary of State in respect of the giving of such a certificate such reasonable fee as he may determine.

(7) The Secretary of State shall not give such a certificate with respect to any organisation—

(a) the activities of which appear to him to consist of or include the giving of film exhibitions promoted for private gain, or
(b) the objects of which do not appear to him to consist of or include the giving of film exhibitions to which the public are admitted;

and the Secretary of State may revoke such a certificate at any time if it appears to him that, since the certificate was given, the activities of the organisation have consisted of or included the giving of film exhibitions promoted for private gain.

(8) Any certificate given by the Commissioners of Customs and Excise under section 5(4) of the Cinematograph Act 1952 before the commencement of the Cinematograph (Amendment) Act 1982 shall have effect as if given by the Secretary of State.

Exhibitions in premises used occasionally

7.—(1) Where the premises in which it is proposed to give a film exhibition **53–006** are premises used occasionally and exceptionally only, and not on more than six days in any one calendar year, for the purposes of such an exhibition, it shall not be necessary to obtain a licence under section 1 above if—

(a) the occupier of the premises has given to the licensing authority, to the fire authority and to the chief officer of police, not less than seven days' notice in writing of his intention so to use the premises; and
(b) he complies with any regulations under section 4 above and, subject to any such regulations, with any conditions imposed by the licensing authority and notified to him in writing.

(2) For the purposes of subsection (1) above, the giving in any premises of an exhibition to which section 5 or 6 above applies shall be disregarded.

. . . . . .

Appeals

Appeals against decisions of licensing authority

16.—(1) Any person aggrieved— **53–007**

(a) by the refusal or revocation of a licence,
(b) by any terms, conditions or restrictions on or subject to which a licence is granted, or
(c) by the refusal of a renewal or transfer of a licence,

may appeal to the Crown Court or, in Scotland, to the sheriff.

(2) Any person aggrieved—

 (a) by the refusal to allow any premises in England and Wales to be opened and used on Sundays for the purpose of film exhibitions under subsection (2) of section 9 above, or

 (b) by any conditions imposed under that subsection,

may appeal to the Crown Court.

(3) Where the decision against which an appeal under this section is brought was given on an application of which (in accordance with section 3(1) above) notice was required to be given to a fire authority and a chief officer of police, any notice of appeal under this section against that decision shall be given to that authority and that officer as well as to any other person to whom it is required to be given apart from this subsection.

(4) [Subject to section 16A below] here a licence is revoked it shall be deemed to remain in force during the period within which an appeal under this section may be brought and, if such an appeal is brought, until the determination or abandonment of the appeal.

(5) [Subject to section 16A below], where an application for the renewal or transfer of a licence is refused, the licence shall be deemed to remain in force or, as the case may require, to have effect with any necessary modifications—

 (a) during any period within which an appeal under this section may be brought and, if such an appeal is brought, until the determination or abandonment of the appeal; and

 (b) where such an appeal is successful, until the licence is renewed or transferred by the licensing authority.

. . . . . .

Interpretation

53–008 **21.**—(1) In this Act, except where the contrary intention appears,—

"chief officer of police" has the meaning given by section 3(10) above;

"child" means a person under the age of sixteen;

"film exhibition" means any exhibition of moving pictures which is produced otherwise than by the simultaneous reception and exhibition of [programmes included in a programme service (within the meaning of the Broadcasting Act 1990);]

"fire authority" has the meaning given by section 3(10) above;

"licence" and references to a licence of either kind shall be construed in accordance with section 3(10) above;

"licensing authority" has the meaning given by section 3(10) above;

"local authority" means—

 (a) in England, [a London borough council, the Common Council of the City of London] [or a] district council;

 [(aa) in Wales, a county council or a county borough council;]

 (b) in Scotland, [a council constituted under section 2 of the Local Government etc. (Scotland) Act 1994];

(2) Any reference in this Act to an exhibition which requires a licence under section 1 above is a reference to an exhibition to which that section applies; and any reference in this Act to an exhibition which requires a consent under section 2 above is a reference to an exhibition to which that section applies.

Prosecution of Offences Act 1985

(1985, c. 23)

An Act to provide for the establishment of a Crown Prosecution Service for England and Wales; to make provision as to costs in criminal cases; to provide for the imposition of time limits in relation to preliminary stages of criminal proceedings; to amend section 42 of the Supreme Court Act 1981 and section 3 of the Children and Young Persons Act 1969; to make provision with respect to consents to prosecutions; to repeal section 9 of the Perjury Act 1911; and for connected purposes. [23rd May 1985] **54–001**

PART I

THE CROWN PROSECUTION SERVICE

Constitution and functions of Service

The Crown Prosecution Service

1.—(1) There shall be a prosecuting service for England and Wales (to be **54–002** known as the "Crown Prosecution Service") consisting of—

    (a) the Director of Public Prosecutions, who shall be head of the Service;
    (b) the Chief Crown Prosecutors, designated under subsection (4) below, each of whom shall be the member of the Service responsible to the Director for supervising the operation of the Service in his area; and
    (c) the other staff appointed by the Director under this section.

(2) The Director shall appoint such staff for the Service as, with the approval of the Treasury as to numbers, remuneration and other terms and conditions of service, he considers necessary for the discharge of his functions.

(3) The Director may designate any member of the Service [who has a general qualification (within the meaning of section 71 of the Courts and Legal Services Act 1990] for the purposes of this subsection, and any person so designated shall be known as a Crown Prosecutor.

(4) The Director shall divide England and Wales into areas and, for each of those areas, designate a Crown Prosecutor for the purposes of this subsection and any person so designated shall be known as a Chief Crown Prosecutor.

(5) The Director may, from time to time, vary the division of England and Wales made for the purposes of subsection (4) above.

(6) Without prejudice to any functions which may have been assigned to him in his capacity as a member of the Service, every Crown Prosecutor shall have all the powers of the Director as to the institution and conduct of proceedings but shall exercise those powers under the direction of the Director.

(7) Where any enactment (whenever passed)—

(a) prevents any step from being taken without the consent of the Director or without his consent or the consent of another; or

(b) requires any step to be taken by or in relation to the Director;

any consent given by or, as the case may be, step taken by or in relation to, a Crown Prosecutor shall be treated, for the purposes of that enactment, as given by or, as the case may be, taken by or in relation to the Director.

The Director of Public Prosecutions

54–003   **2.**—(1) The Director of Public Prosecutions shall be appointed by the Attorney General.

(2) The Director must be a [person who has a ten year general qualification, within the meaning of section 71 of the Courts and Legal Services Act 1990]

(3) There shall be paid to the Director such remuneration as the Attorney General may, with the approval of the Treasury, determine.

Functions of the Director

54–004   **3.**—(1) The Director shall discharge his functions under this or any other enactment under the superintendence of the Attorney General.

(2) It shall be the duty of the Director, [subject to any provisions contained in the Criminal Justice Act 1987]—

(a) to take over the conduct of all criminal proceedings, other than specified proceedings, instituted on behalf of a police force (whether by a member of that force or by any other person);

(b) to institute and have the conduct of criminal proceedings in any case where it appears to him that—

(i) the importance or difficulty of the case makes it appropriate that proceedings should be instituted by him; or

(ii) it is otherwise appropriate for proceedings to be instituted by him;

(c) to take over the conduct of all binding over proceedings instituted on behalf of a police force (whether by a member of that force or by any other person);

(d) to take over the conduct of all proceedings begun by summons issued under section 3 of the Obscene Publications Act 1959 (forfeiture of obscene articles);

(e) to give, to such extent as he considers appropriate, advice to police forces on all matters relating to criminal offences;

(f) to appear for the prosecution, when directed by the court to do so, on any appeal under—

(i) section 1 of the Administration of Justice Act 1960 (appeal from the High Court in criminal cases);

(ii) Part I or Part II of the Criminal Appeal Act 1968 (appeals from the Crown Court to the criminal division of the Court of Appeal and thence to the House of Lords); or

(iii) section 108 of the Magistrates' Courts Act 1980 (right of appeal to Crown Court) as it applies, by virtue of subsection (5) of section 12 of the Contempt of Court Act 1981, to orders made under section 12 (contempt of magistrates' courts); and

(g) to discharge such other functions as may from time to time be assigned to him by the Attorney General in pursuance of this paragraph.

(3) In this section—

"the court" means—

    (a) in the case of an appeal to or from the criminal division of the Court of Appeal, that division;

    (b) in the case of an appeal from a Divisional Court of the Queen's Bench Division, the Divisional Court; and

    (c) in the case of an appeal against an order of a magistrates' court, the Crown Court;

"police force" means any police force maintained by a police authority under [the Police Act 1996] [, the National Crime Squad] and any other body of constables for the time being specified by order made by the Secretary of State for the purposes of this section; and

"specified proceedings" means proceedings which fall within any category for the time being specified by order made by the Attorney General for the purposes of this section.

(4) The power to make orders under subsection (3) above shall be exercisable by statutory instrument subject to annulment in pursuance of a resolution of either House of Parliament.

. . . . . .

Prosecutions instituted and conducted otherwise than by the Service

6.—(1) Subject to subsection (2) below, nothing in this Part shall preclude any person from instituting any criminal proceedings or conducting any criminal proceedings to which the Director's duty to take over the conduct of proceedings does not apply.   **54–005**

(2) Where criminal proceedings are instituted in circumstances in which the Director is not under a duty to take over their conduct, he may nevertheless do so at any stage.

Local Government Act 1986

(1986, c. 10)

An Act to require rating authorities to set a rate on or before 1st April; to prohibit political publicity and otherwise restrain local authority publicity; to require the mortgagor's consent and make other provision in connection with the disposal of local authority mortgages; to amend the law as to the effect of retirement and re-election of, and the allowances payable to, members of certain authorities; and for connected purposes.   **55–001**

[26th March 1986]

. . . . . .

PART II

LOCAL AUTHORITY PUBLICITY

Prohibition of political publicity

55–002   2.—(1) A local authority shall not publish any material which, in whole or in part, appears to be designed to affect public support for a political party.

[(2) In determining whether material falls within the prohibition regard shall be had to the content and style of the material, the time and other circumstances of publication and the likely effect on those to whom it is directed and, in particular, to the following matters—

   (a) whether the material refers to a political party or to persons identified with a political party or promotes or opposes a point of view on a question of political controversy which is identifiable as the view of one political party and not of another;
   (b) where the material is part of a campaign, the effect which the campaign appears to be designed to achieve.]¹

(3) A local authority shall not give financial or other assistance to a person for the publication of material which the authority are prohibited by this section from publishing themselves.

¹ s. 2(2) substituted by Local Government Act 1988 (c.9), s.27(1).

Prohibition on promoting homosexuality by teaching or by publishing material

55–003   [2A.—(1) A local authority shall not—

   (a) intentionally promote homosexuality or publish material with the intention of promoting homosexuality;
   (b) promote the teaching in any maintained school of the acceptability of homosexuality as a pretended family relationship.

(2) Nothing in subsection (1) above shall be taken to prohibit the doing of anything for the purpose of treating or preventing the spread of disease[; or]

   [(b) prevent the headteacher or governing body of a maintained school, or a teacher employed by a maintained school, from taking steps to prevent any form of bullying.]

(3) In any proceedings in connection with the application of this section a court shall draw such inferences as to the intention of the local authority as may reasonably be drawn from the evidence before it.

(4) In subsection (1)(b) above "maintained school" means,—

   (a) in England and Wales, [a maintained school or maintained nursery school, within the meaning of the School Standards and Framework Act 1998;] and
   (b) in Scotland, a public school, nursery school or special school,within the meaning of the Education (Scotland) Act 1980.[¹]]²

¹ In relation to Scotland: s.2A is repealed.
² s. 2A inserted by Local Government Act 1988 (c.9), s.28(1).

Parliamentary Constituencies Act 1986

(1986, c. 56)

An Act to consolidate the House of Commons (Redistribution of Seats) Acts **56–001**
1949 to 1979 and certain related enactments.   [7th November 1986]

Parliamentary constituencies

1.—(1) There shall for the purpose of parliamentary elections be the county **56–002**
and borough constituencies (or in Scotland the county and burgh constituencies),
each returning a single member, which are described in Orders in Council made
under this Act.

(2) In this Act and, except where the context otherwise requires, in any Act
passed after the Representation of the People Act 1948, "constituency" means
an area having separate representation in the House of Commons.

The Boundary Commissions

2.—(1) For the purpose of the continuous review of the distribution of seats **56–003**
at parliamentary elections, there shall continue to be four permanent Boundary
Commissions, namely a Boundary Commission for England, a Boundary Commission for Scotland, a Boundary Commission for Wales and a Boundary Commission for Northern Ireland.

(2) Schedule 1 to this Act shall have effect with respect to the constitution
of, and other matters relating to, the Boundary Commissions.

Reports of the Commissions

3.—(1) Each Boundary Commission shall keep under review the representa- **56–004**
tion in the House of Commons of the part of the United Kingdom with which
they are concerned and shall, in accordance with subsection (2) below, submit
to the Secretary of State reports with respect to the whole of that part of the
United Kingdom, either—

  (a) showing the constituencies into which they recommend that it should
      be divided in order to give effect to the rules set out in paragraphs 1 to
      6 of Schedule 2 to this Act (read with paragraph 7 of that Schedule), or
  (b) stating that, in the opinion of the Commission, no alteration is required
      to be made in respect of that part of the United Kingdom in order to
      give effect to the said rules (read with paragraph 7).

(2) Reports under subsection (1) above shall be submitted by a Boundary
Commission [not less than eight or more than twelve years] from the date of
the submission of their last report under that subsection.

[(2A) A failure by a Boundary Commission to submit a report within the time
limit which is appropriate to that report shall not be regarded as invalidating the
report for the purposes of any enactment.]

(3) Any Boundary Commission may also from time to time submit to the
Secretary of State reports with respect to the area comprised in any particular
constituency or constituencies in the part of the United Kingdom with which
they are concerned, showing the constituencies into which they recommend that
that area should be divided in order to give effect to the rules set out in paragraph
1 to 6 of Schedule 2 to this Act (read with paragraph 7 of that Schedule).

(4) A report of a Boundary Commission under this Act showing the constituencies into which they recommend that any area should be divided shall state,
as respects each constituency, the name by which they recommend that it should

be known, and whether they recommend that it should be a county constituency or a borough constituency (or in Scotland a county constituency or a burgh constituency).

(5) As soon as may be after a Boundary Commission have submitted a report to the Secretary of State under this Act, he shall lay the report before Parliament together, except in a case where the report states that no alteration is required to be made in respect of the part of the United Kingdom with which the Commission are concerned, with the draft of an Order in Council for giving effect, whether with or without modifications, to the recommendations contained in the report.

(6) Schedule 2 to this Act which contains the rules referred to above and related provisions shall have effect.

[(7) For the purposes of the application of the rules in paragraph 4 of Schedule 2 to this Act (relationship between constituencies and certain local government boundaries) a report of a Boundary Commission under subsection (1) above shall take account only of those boundaries (whether of counties, London boroughs, local authority areas in Scotland or wards in Northern Ireland) which are in operation at whichever is the earlier of—

(a) the date of the report; and
(b) the tenth anniversary of the date of the submission of the most recent report of the Commission under subsection (1) above;

but nothing in this subsection shall prevent a Boundary Commission publishing proposed recommendations which take account of boundaries which at the time of publication are prospective only.[¹]

(8) For the purposes of subsection (7) above, a boundary shall be regarded as prospective at any time if, at that time, it is specified in a provision of an Act, Measure of the Northern Ireland Assembly, statutory instrument or statutory rule but the boundary has not yet come into operation.]

¹ In relation to the first mandatory report of each Boundary Commission

(7) For the purposes of the application of the rules in paragraph 4 of Schedule 2 to this Act (relationship between constituencies and certain local government boundaries) a report of a Boundary Commission under subsection (1) above shall take account only of those boundaries (whether of counties, London boroughs, local authority areas in Scotland or wards in Northern Ireland) which are in operation at whichever is the earlier of—

(a) the date of the report; and
(b) 1st June 1994;

but nothing in this subsection shall prevent a Boundary Commission publishing proposed recommendations which take account of boundaries which at the time of publication are prospective only.

. . . . . .

Section 3   SCHEDULE 2

RULES FOR REDISTRIBUTION OF SEATS

The rules

56–005   **1.**—(1) The number of constituencies in Great Britain shall not be substantially greater or less than 613.
(2) [. . .]¹
(3) The number of constituencies in Wales shall not be less than 35.

(4) The number of constituencies in Northern Ireland shall not be greater than 18 or less than 16, and shall be 17 unless it appears to the Boundary Commission for Northern Ireland that Northern Ireland should for the time being be divided into 16 or (as the case may be) into 18 constituencies.

[1] Repealed by Scotland Act 1998 (c.46), Sched. 9, para. 1.

2. Every constituency shall return a single member.   **56–006**

3. There shall continue to be a constituency which shall include the whole of the City of London   **56–007**
and the name of which shall refer to the City of London.

[**3A.** A constituency which includes the Orkney Islands or the Shetland Islands shall not include   **56–008**
the whole or any part of a local government area other than the Orkney Islands and the Shetland Islands.][1]

[1] Added by Scotland Act 1998 (c.46), Pt V, s.86(3).

4.—(1) So far as is practicable having regard to [rules 1 to 3A]—   **56–009**

    (a) in England and Wales,—

        (i) no county or any part of a county shall be included in a constituency which includes
        the whole or part of any other county or the whole or part of a London borough,
        (ii) no London borough or any part of a London borough shall be included in a constitu-
        ency which includes the whole or part of any other London borough,

    (b) in Scotland, regard shall be had to the boundaries of local authority areas,
    (c) in Northern Ireland, no ward shall be included partly in one constituency and partly in
    another.

[(1A) In sub-paragraph (1)(a) above "county" means, in relation to Wales, a preserved county
(as defined by section 64 of the Local Government (Wales) Act 1994).][1]
(2) In sub-paragraph (1)(b) above "area" and "local authority" have the same meanings as in the
Local Government (Scotland) Act 1973.

[1] Added by Local Government (Wales) Act 1994 (c.19), Sched. 2, para. 13.

5. The electorate of any constituency shall be as near the electoral quota as is practicable having   **56–010**
regard to rules 1 to 4; and a Boundary Commission may depart from the strict application of rule 4
if it appears to them that a departure is desirable to avoid an excessive disparity between the electorate of any constituency and the electoral quota, or between the electorate of any constituency and that
of neighbouring constituencies in the part of the United Kingdom with which they are concerned.

6. A Boundary Commission may depart from the strict application of rules 4 and 5 if special   **56–011**
geographical considerations, including in particular the size, shape and accessibility of a constituency, appear to them to render a departure desirable.

General and supplementary

7. It shall not be the duty of a Boundary Commission to aim at giving full effect in all circum-   **56–012**
stances to the above rules [(except rule 3A)][1], but they shall take account, so far as they reasonably
can—

    (a) of the inconveniences attendant on alterations of constituencies other than alterations made
    for the purposes of rule 4, and
    (b) of any local ties which would be broken by such alterations.

[1] Words inserted by Scotland Act 1998 (c.46), Pt V, s.86(5).

8. In the application of rule 5 to each part of the United Kingdom for which there is a Boundary   **56–013**
Commission—

    (a) the expression "electoral quota" means a number obtained by dividing the electorate for
    that part of the United Kingdom by the number of constituencies in it existing on the
    enumeration date,
    (b) the expression "electorate" means —

        (i) in relation to a constituency, the number of persons whose names appear on the regis-
        ter of parliamentary electors in force on the enumeration date under the Representation
        of the People Acts for the constituency,
        (ii) in relation to the part of the United Kingdom, the aggregate electorate as defined in
        sub-paragraph (i) above of all the constituencies in that part,

(c) the expression "enumeration date" means, in relation to any report of a Boundary Commission under this Act, the date on which the notice with respect to that report is published in accordance with section 5(1) of this Act.

56–014 **9.** In this Schedule, a reference to a rule followed by a number is a reference to the rule set out in the correspondingly numbered paragraph of this Schedule.

Section 7   SCHEDULE 3

CONSEQUENTIAL AMENDMENTS

The Northern Ireland Constitution Act 1973

56–015 **1.** [. . .]¹

¹ Repealed by Northern Ireland Act 1998 (c.47), Sched. 15, para. 1.
  2. [. . .]¹

¹ Repealed by Northern Ireland Act 1998 (c.47), Sched. 15, para. 1.

The House of Commons Disqualification Act 1975

56–016 **3.** In Part III of Schedule 1 to the House of Commons Disqualification Act 1975 for the words "Part I or Part II of Schedule 1 to the House of Commons (Redistribution of Seats) Act 1949" there shall be substituted the words "Schedule 1 to the Parliamentary Constituencies Act 1986".

The Northern Ireland Assembly Disqualification Act 1975

56–017 **4.** In Part III of Schedule 1 to the Northern Ireland Assembly Disqualification Act 1975 for the words "Part I or Part II of Schedule 1 to the House of Commons (Redistribution of Seats) Act 1949" there shall be substituted the words "Schedule 1 to the Parliamentary Constituencies Act 1986".

The European Parliamentary Elections Act 1978

56–018 **5.** [. . .]¹

¹ Repealed by European Parliamentary Elections Act 1999 (c.1), Sched. 4, para. 1.

The Finance (No. 2) Act 1983

56–019 **6.** [. . .]¹

¹ Repealed by Taxation of Chargeable Gains Act 1992 (c.12), Sched. 12, para. 1.

Public Order Act 1986

(1986, c. 64)

57–001 *An Act to abolish the common law offences of riot, rout, unlawful assembly and affray and certain statutory offences relating to public order; to create new offences relating to public order; to control public processions and assemblies; to control the stirring up of racial hatred; to provide for the exclusion of certain offenders from sporting events; to create a new offence relating to the contamination of or interference with goods; to confer power to direct certain trespassers to leave land; to amend section 7 of the Conspiracy and Protection of Property Act 1875, section 1 of the Prevention of Crime Act 1953, Part V of the Criminal Justice (Scotland) Act 1980 and the Sporting Events (Control of Alcohol etc.) Act 1985; to repeal certain obsolete or unnecessary enactments; and for connected purposes.*

[7th November 1986]

PART I

NEW OFFENCES

Riot

1.—(1) Where 12 or more persons who are present together use or threaten unlawful violence for a common purpose and the conduct of them (taken together) is such as would cause a person of reasonable firmness present at the scene to fear for his personal safety, each of the persons using unlawful violence for the common purpose is guilty of riot.

(2) It is immaterial whether or not the 12 or more use or threaten unlawful violence simultaneously.

(3) The common purpose may be inferred from conduct.

(4) No person of reasonable firmness need actually be, or be likely to be, present at the scene.

(5) Riot may be committed in private as well as in public places.

(6) A person guilty of riot is liable on conviction on indictment to imprisonment for a term not exceeding ten years or a fine or both.

57–002

Violent disorder

2.—(1) Where 3 or more persons who are present together use or threaten unlawful violence and the conduct of them (taken together) is such as would cause a person of reasonable firmness present at the scene to fear for his personal safety, each of the persons using or threatening unlawful violence is guilty of violent disorder.

(2) It is immaterial whether or not the 3 or more use or threaten unlawful violence simultaneously.

(3) No person of reasonable firmness need actually be, or be likely to be, present at the scene.

(4) Violent disorder may be committed in private as well as in public places.

(5) A person guilty of violent disorder is liable on conviction on indictment to imprisonment for a term not exceeding 5 years or a fine or both, or on summary conviction to imprisonment for a term not exceeding 6 months or a fine not exceeding the statutory maximum or both.

57–003

Affray

3.—(1) A person is guilty of affray if he uses or threatens unlawful violence towards another and his conduct is such as would cause a person of reasonable firmness present at the scene to fear for his personal safety.

(2) Where 2 or more persons use or threaten the unlawful violence, it is the conduct of them taken together that must be considered for the purposes of subsection (1).

(3) For the purposes of this section a threat cannot be made by the use of words alone.

(4) No person of reasonable firmness need actually be, or be likely to be, present at the scene.

(5) Affray may be committed in private as well as in public places.

(6) A constable may arrest without warrant anyone he reasonably suspects is committing affray.

(7) A person guilty of affray is liable on conviction on indictment to imprisonment for a term not exceeding 3 years or a fine or both, or on summary conviction to imprisonment for a term not exceeding 6 months or a fine not exceeding the statutory maximum or both.

57–004

Fear or provocation of violence

57–005   **4.**—(1) A person is guilty of an offence if he—

(a) uses towards another person threatening, abusive or insulting words or behaviour, or
(b) distributes or displays to another person any writing, sign or other visible representation which is threatening, abusive or insulting,

with intent to cause that person to believe that immediate unlawful violence will be used against him or another by any person, or to provoke the immediate use of unlawful violence by that person or another, or whereby that person is likely to believe that such violence will be used or it is likely that such violence will be provoked.

(2) An offence under this section may be committed in a public or a private place, except that no offence is committed where the words or behaviour are used, or the writing, sign or other visible representation is distributed or displayed, by a person inside a dwelling and the other person is also inside that or another dwelling.

(3) A constable may arrest without warrant anyone he reasonably suspects is committing an offence under this section.

(4) A person guilty of an offence under this section is liable on summary conviction to imprisonment for a term not exceeding 6 months or a fine not exceeding level 5 on the standard scale or both.

Intentional harassment, alarm or distress

57–006   [**4A.**—(1) A person is guilty of an offence if, with intent to cause a person harassment, alarm or distress, he—

(a) uses threatening, abusive or insulting words or behaviour, or disorderly behaviour, or
(b) displays any writing, sign or other visible representation which is threatening, abusive or insulting,

thereby causing that or another person harassment, alarm or distress.

(2) An offence under this section may be committed in a public or a private place, except that no offence is committed where the words or behaviour are used, or the writing, sign or other visible representation is displayed, by a person inside a dwelling and the person who is harassed, alarmed or distressed is also inside that or another dwelling.

(3) It is a defence for the accused to prove—

(a) that he was inside a dwelling and had no reason to believe that the words or behaviour used, or the writing, sign or other visible representation displayed, would be heard or seen by a person outside that or any other dwelling, or
(b) that his conduct was reasonable.

(4) A constable may arrest without warrant anyone he reasonably suspects is committing an offence under this section.

(5) A person guilty of an offence under this section is liable on summary conviction to imprisonment for a term not exceeding 6 months or a fine not exceeding level 5 on the standard scale or both.][1]

---

[1] Added by Criminal Justice and Public Order Act 1994 (c.33), Pt XII, s.154.

Harassment, alarm or distress

5.—(1) A person is guilty of an offence if he—   **57–007**

(a) uses threatening, abusive or insulting words or behaviour, or disorderly behaviour, or

(b) displays any writing, sign or other visible representation which is threatening, abusive or insulting,

within the hearing or sight of a person likely to be caused harassment, alarm or distress thereby.

(2) An offence under this section may be committed in a public or a private place, except that no offence is committed where the words or behaviour are used, or the writing, sign or other visible representation is displayed, by a person inside a dwelling and the other person is also inside that or another dwelling.

(3) It is a defence for the accused to prove—

(a) that he had no reason to believe that there was any person within hearing or sight who was likely to be caused harassment, alarm or distress, or

(b) that he was inside a dwelling and had no reason to believe that the words or behaviour used, or the writing, sign or other visible representation displayed, would be heard or seen by a person outside that or any other dwelling, or

(c) that his conduct was reasonable.

(4) A constable may arrest a person without warrant if—

(a) he engages in offensive conduct which [a]¹ constable warns him to stop, and

(b) he engages in further offensive conduct immediately or shortly after the warning.

(5) In subsection (4) "offensive conduct" means conduct the constable reasonably suspects to constitute an offence under this section, and the conduct mentioned in paragraph (a) and the further conduct need not be of the same nature.

(6) A person guilty of an offence under this section is liable on summary conviction to a fine not exceeding level 3 on the standard scale.

¹ Word substitued by Public Order (Amendment) Act 1996 (c.59), s.1.

Mental element: miscellaneous

6.—(1) A person is guilty of riot only if he intends to use violence or is aware   **57–008**
that his conduct may be violent.

(2) A person is guilty of violent disorder or affray only if he intends to use or threaten violence or is aware that his conduct may be violent or threaten violence.

(3) A person is guilty of an offence under section 4 only if he intends his words or behaviour, or the writing, sign or other visible representation, to be threatening, abusive or insulting, or is aware that it may be threatening, abusive or insulting.

(4) A person is guilty of an offence under section 5 only if he intends his words or behaviour, or the writing, sign or other visible representation, to be threatening, abusive or insulting, or is aware that it may be threatening, abusive or insulting or (as the case may be) he intends his behaviour to be or is aware that it may be disorderly.

(5) For the purposes of this section a person whose awareness is impaired by intoxication shall be taken to be aware of that of which he would be aware if not intoxicated, unless he shows either that his intoxication was not self-induced or that it was caused solely by the taking or administration of a substance in the course of medical treatment.

(6) In subsection (5) "intoxication" means any intoxication, whether caused by drink, drugs or other means, or by a combination of means.

(7) Subsections (1) and (2) do not affect the determination for the purposes of riot or violent disorder of the number of persons who use or threaten violence.

Procedure: miscellaneous

57–009 **7.**—(1) No prosecution for an offence of riot or incitement to riot may be instituted except by or with the consent of the Director of Public Prosecutions.

(2) For the purposes of the rules against charging more than one offence in the same count or information, each of sections 1 to 5 creates one offence.

(3) If on the trial on indictment of a person charged with violent disorder or affray the jury find him not guilty of the offence charged, they may (without prejudice to section 6(3) of the Criminal Law Act 1967) find him guilty of an offence under section 4.

(4) The Crown Court has the same powers and duties in relation to a person who is by virtue of subsection (3) convicted before it of an offence under section 4 as a magistrates' court would have on convicting him of the offence.

Interpretation

57–010 **8.** In this Part—

"dwelling" means any structure or part of a structure occupied as a person's home or as other living accommodation (whether the occupation is separate or shared with others) but does not include any part not so occupied, and for this purpose "structure" includes a tent, caravan, vehicle, vessel or other temporary or movable structure;
"violence" means any violent conduct, so that—

(a) except in the context of affray, it includes violent conduct towards property as well as violent conduct towards persons, and
(b) it is not restricted to conduct causing or intended to cause injury or damage but includes any other violent conduct (for example, throwing at or towards a person a missile of a kind capable of causing injury which does not hit or falls short).

Offences abolished

57–011 **9.**—(1) The common law offences of riot, rout, unlawful assembly and affray are abolished.

(2) The offences under the following enactments are abolished—

(a) section 1 of the Tumultuous Petitioning Act 1661 (presentation of petition to monarch or Parliament accompanied by excessive number of persons),
(b) section 1 of the Shipping Offences Act 1793 (interference with operation of vessel by persons riotously assembled),
(c) section 23 of the Seditious Meetings Act 1817 (prohibition of certain meetings within one mile of West-minster Hall when Parliament sitting), and
(d) section 5 of the Public Order Act 1936 (conduct conducive to breach of the peace).

PART II

PROCESSIONS AND ASSEMBLIES

Advance notice of public processions

11.—(1) Written notice shall be given in accordance with this section of any   **57–012**
proposal to hold a public procession intended—

    (a) to demonstrate support for or opposition to the views or actions of any
        person or body of persons,
    (b) to publicise a cause or campaign, or
    (c) to mark or commemorate an event,

unless it is not reasonably practicable to give any advance notice of the procession.

(2) Subsection (1) does not apply where the procession is one commonly or customarily held in the police area (or areas) in which it is proposed to be held or is a funeral procession organised by a funeral director acting in the normal course of his business.

(3) The notice must specify the date when it is intended to hold the procession, the time when it is intended to start it, its proposed route, and the name and address of the person (or of one of the persons) proposing to organise it.

(4) Notice must be delivered to a police station—

    (a) in the police area in which it is proposed the procession will start, or
    (b) where it is proposed the procession will start in Scotland and cross into
        England, in the first police area in England on the proposed route.

(5) If delivered not less than 6 clear days before the date when the procession is intended to be held, the notice may be delivered by post by the recorded delivery service; but section 7 of the Interpretation Act 1978 (under which a document sent by post is deemed to have been served when posted and to have been delivered in the ordinary course of post) does not apply.

(6) If not delivered in accordance with subsection (5), the notice must be delivered by hand not less than 6 clear days before the date when the procession is intended to be held or, if that is not reasonably practicable, as soon as delivery is reasonably practicable.

(7) Where a public procession is held, each of the persons organising it is guilty of an offence if—

    (a) the requirements of this section as to notice have not been satisfied, or
    (b) the date when it is held, the time when it starts, or its route, differs
        from the date, time or route specified in the notice.

(8) It is a defence for the accused to prove that he did not know of, and neither suspected nor had reason to suspect, the failure to satisfy the requirements or (as the case may be) the difference of date, time or route.

(9) To the extent that an alleged offence turns on a difference of date, time or route, it is a defence for the accused to prove that the difference arose from circumstances beyond his control or from something done with the agreement of a police officer or by his direction.

(10) A person guilty of an offence under subsection (7) is liable on summary conviction to a fine not exceeding level 3 on the standard scale.

Imposing conditions on public processions

57–013 **12.**—(1) If the senior police officer, having regard to the time or place at which and the circumstances in which any public procession is being held or is intended to be held and to its route or proposed route, reasonably believes that—

(a) it may result in serious public disorder, serious damage to property or serious disruption to the life of the community, or
(b) the purpose of the persons organising it is the intimidation of others with a view to compelling them not to do an act they have a right to do, or to do an act they have a right not to do,

he may give directions imposing on the persons organising or taking part in the procession such conditions as appear to him necessary to prevent such disorder, damage, disruption or intimidation, including conditions as to the route of the procession or prohibiting it from entering any public place specified in the directions.

(2) In subsection (1) "the senior police officer" means —

(a) in relation to a procession being held, or to a procession intended to be held in a case where persons are assembling with a view to taking part in it, the most senior in rank of the police officers present at the scene, and
(b) in relation to a procession intended to be held in a case where paragraph (a) does not apply, the chief officer of police.

(3) A direction given by a chief officer of police by virtue of subsection (2)(b) shall be given in writing.

(4) A person who organises a public procession and knowingly fails to comply with a condition imposed under this section is guilty of an offence, but it is a defence for him to prove that the failure arose from circumstances beyond his control.

(5) A person who takes part in a public procession and knowingly fails to comply with a condition imposed under this section is guilty of an offence, but it is a defence for him to prove that the failure arose from circumstances beyond his control.

(6) A person who incites another to commit an offence under subsection (5) is guilty of an offence.

(7) A constable in uniform may arrest without warrant anyone he reasonably suspects is committing an offence under subsection (4), (5) or (6).

(8) A person guilty of an offence under subsection (4) is liable on summary conviction to imprisonment for a term not exceeding 3 months or a fine not exceeding level 4 on the standard scale or both.

(9) A person guilty of an offence under subsection (5) is liable on summary conviction to a fine not exceeding level 3 on the standard scale.

(10) A person guilty of an offence under subsection (6) is liable on summary conviction to imprisonment for a term not exceeding 3 months or a fine not exceeding level 4 on the standard scale or both, notwithstanding section 45(3) of the Magistrates' Courts Act 1980 (inciter liable to same penalty as incited).

(11) In Scotland this section applies only in relation to a procession being held, and to a procession intended to be held in a case where persons are assembling with a view to taking part in it.

Prohibiting public processions

57–014 **13.**—(1) If at any time the chief officer of police reasonably believes that, because of particular circumstances existing in any district or part of a district, the powers under section 12 will not be sufficient to prevent the holding of public processions in that district or part from resulting in serious public disorder, he shall apply to the council of the district for an order prohibiting for such period not exceeding 3 months as may be specified in the application the holding of all public processions (or of any class of public procession so specified) in the district or part concerned.

(2) On receiving such an application, a council may with the consent of the Secretary of State make an order either in the terms of the application or with such modifications as may be approved by the Secretary of State.

(3) Subsection (1) does not apply in the City of London or the metropolitan police district.

(4) If at any time the Commissioner of Police for the City of London or the Commissioner of Police of the Metropolis reasonably believes that, because of particular circumstances existing in his police area or part of it, the powers under section 12 will not be sufficient to prevent the holding of public processions in that area or part from resulting in serious public disorder, he may with the consent of the Secretary of State make an order prohibiting for such period not exceeding 3 months as may be specified in the order the holding of all public processions (or of any class of public procession so specified) in the area or part concerned.

(5) An order made under this section may be revoked or varied by a subsequent order made in the same way, that is, in accordance with subsections (1) and (2) or subsection (4), as the case may be.

(6) Any order under this section shall, if not made in writing, be recorded in writing as soon as practicable after being made.

(7) A person who organises a public procession the holding of which he knows is prohibited by virtue of an order under this section is guilty of an offence.

(8) A person who takes part in a public procession the holding of which he knows is prohibited by virtue of an order under this section is guilty of an offence.

(9) A person who incites another to commit an offence under subsection (8) is guilty of an offence.

(10) A constable in uniform may arrest without warrant anyone he reasonably suspects is committing an offence under subsection (7), (8) or (9).

(11) A person guilty of an offence under subsection (7) is liable on summary conviction to imprisonment for a term not exceeding 3 months or a fine not exceeding level 4 on the standard scale or both.

(12) A person guilty of an offence under subsection (8) is liable on summary conviction to a fine not exceeding level 3 on the standard scale.

(13) A person guilty of an offence under subsection (9) is liable on summary conviction to imprisonment for a term not exceeding 3 months or a fine not exceeding level 4 on the standard scale or both, notwithstanding section 45(3) of the Magistrates' Courts Act 1980.

Imposing conditions on public assemblies

14.—(1) If the senior police officer, having regard to the time or place at   **57–015**
which and the circumstances in which any public assembly is being held or is intended to be held, reasonably believes that—

    (a) it may result in serious public disorder, serious damage to property or serious disruption to the life of the community, or

    (b) the purpose of the persons organising it is the intimidation of others with a view to compelling them not to do an act they have a right to do, or to do an act they have a right not to do, he may give directions imposing on the persons organising or taking part in the assembly such conditions as to the place at which the assembly may be (or continue to be) held, its maximum duration, or the maximum number of persons who may constitute it, as appear to him necessary to prevent such disorder, damage, disruption or intimidation.

(2) In subsection (1) "the senior police officer" means—

(a) in relation to an assembly being held, the most senior in rank of the police officers present at the scene, and
(b) in relation to an assembly intended to be held, the chief officer of police.

(3) A direction given by a chief officer of police by virtue of subsection (2)(b) shall be given in writing.

(4) A person who organises a public assembly and knowingly fails to comply with a condition imposed under this section is guilty of an offence, but it is a defence for him to prove that the failure arose from circumstances beyond his control.

(5) A person who takes part in a public assembly and knowingly fails to comply with a condition imposed under this section is guilty of an offence, but it is a defence for him to prove that the failure arose from circumstances beyond his control.

(6) A person who incites another to commit an offence under subsection (5) is guilty of an offence.

(7) A constable in uniform may arrest without warrant anyone he reasonably suspects is committing an offence under subsection (4), (5) or (6).

(8) A person guilty of an offence under subsection (4) is liable on summary conviction to imprisonment for a term not exceeding 3 months or a fine not exceeding level 4 on the standard scale or both.

(9) A person guilty of an offence under subsection (5) is liable on summary conviction to a fine not exceeding level 3 on the standard scale.

(10) A person guilty of an offence under subsection (6) is liable on summary conviction to imprisonment for a term not exceeding 3 months or a fine not exceeding level 4 on the standard scale or both, notwithstanding section 45(3) of the Magistrates' Courts Act 1980.

Prohibiting trespassory assemblies

57–016   [**14A.**—(1) If at any time the chief officer of police reasonably believes that an assembly is intended to be held in any district at a place on land to which the public has no right of access or only a limited right of access and that the assembly—

(a) is likely to be held without the permission of the occupier of the land or to conduct itself in such a way as to exceed the limits of any permission of his or the limits of the public's right of access, and
(b) may result—

(i) in serious disruption to the life of the community, or
(ii) where the land, or a building or monument on it, is of historical, architectural, archaeological or scientific importance, in significant damage to the land, building or monument,

he may apply to the council of the district for an order prohibiting for a specified, period the holding of all trespassory assemblies in the district or a part of it, as specified.

(2) On receiving such an application, a council may—

(a) in England and Wales, with the consent of the Secretary of State make an order either in the terms of the application or with such modifications as may be approved by the Secretary of State; or

(b) in Scotland, make an order in the terms of the application.

(3) Subsection (1) does not apply in the City of London or the metropolitan police district.

(4) If at any time the Commissioner of Police for the City of London or the Commissioner of Police of the Metropolis reasonably believes that an assembly is intended to be held at a place on land to which the public has no right of access or only a limited right of access in his police area and that the assembly—

(a) is likely to be held without the permission of the occupier of the land or to conduct itself in such a way as to exceed the limits of any permission of his or the limits of the public's right of access, and

(b) may result—

(i) in serious disruption to the life of the community, or

(ii) where the land, or a building or monument on it, is of historical, architectural, archaeological or scientific importance, in significant damage to the land, building or monument,

he may with the consent of the Secretary of State make an order prohibiting for a specified period the holding of all trespassory assemblies in the area or a part of it, as specified.

(5) An order prohibiting the holding of trespassory assemblies operates to prohibit any assembly which—

(a) is held on land to which the public has no right of access or only a limited right of access, and

(b) takes place in the prohibited circumstances, that is to say, without the permission of the occupier of the land or so as to exceed the limits of any permission of his or the limits of the public's right of access.

(6) No order under this section shall prohibit the holding of assemblies for a period exceeding 4 days or in an area exceeding an area represented by a circle with a radius of 5 miles from a specified centre.

(7) An order made under this section may be revoked or varied by a subsequent order made in the same way, that is, in accordance with subsection (1) and (2) or subsection (4), as the case may be.

(8) Any order under this section shall, if not made in writing, be recorded in writing as soon as practicable after being made.

(9) In this section and sections 14B and 14C—

"assembly" means an assembly of 20 or more persons;

"land" means land in the open air;

"limited", in relation to a right of access by the public to land, means that their use of it is restricted to use for a particular purpose (as in the case of a highway or road) or is subject to other restrictions;

"occupier" means—

(a) in England and Wales, the person entitled to possession of the land by virtue of an estate or interest held by him; or

(b) in Scotland, the person lawfully entitled to natural possession of the land,

and in subsections (1) and (4) includes the person reasonably believed by the authority applying for or making the order to be the occupier;

"public" includes a section of the public; and
"specified"means specified in an order under this section.

(10) In relation to Scotland, the references in subsection (1) above to a district and to the council of the district shall be construed—

(a) as respects applications before 1st April 1996, as references to the area of a regional or islands authority and to the authority in question; and

(b) as respects applications on and after that date, as references to a local government area and to the council for that area.

(11) In relation to Wales, the references in subsection (1) above to a district and to the council of the district shall be construed, as respects applications on and after 1st April 1996, as references to a county or county borough and to the council for that county or county borough.]¹

¹ Added by Criminal Justice and Public Order Act 1994 (c.33), Pt V, s.70.

Offences in connection with trespassory assemblies and arrest therefor

57–017   [**14B.**—(1) A person who organises an assembly the holding of which he knows is prohibited by an order under section 14A is guilty of an offence.

(2) A person who takes part in an assembly which he knows is prohibited by an order under section 14A is guilty of an offence.

(3) In England and Wales, a person who incites another to commit an offence under subsection (2) is guilty of an offence.

(4) A constable in uniform may arrest without a warrant anyone he reasonably suspects to be committing an offence under this section.

(5) A person guilty of an offence under subsection (1) is liable on summary conviction to imprisonment for a term not exceeding 3 months or a fine not exceeding level 4 on the standard scale or both.

(6) A person guilty of an offence under subsection (2) is liable on summary conviction to a fine not exceeding level 3 on the standard scale.

(7) A person guilty of an offence under subsection (3) is liable on summary conviction to imprisonment for a term not exceeding 3 months or a fine not exceeding level 4 on the standard scale or both, notwithstanding section 45(3) of the Magistrates' Courts Act 1980.

(8) Subsection (3) above is without prejudice to the application of any principle of Scots Law as respects art and part guilt to such incitement as is mentioned in that subsection.]¹

¹ Added by Criminal Justice and Public Order Act 1994 (c.33), Pt V, s.70.

Stopping persons from proceeding to trespassory assemblies

57–018   [**14C.**—(1) If a constable in uniform reasonably believes that a person is on his way to an assembly within the area to which an order under section 14A applies which the constable reasonably believes is likely to be an assembly which is prohibited by that order, he may, subject to subsection (2) below—

(a) stop that person, and

(b) direct him not to proceed in the direction of the assembly.

(2) The power conferred by subsection (1) may only be exercised within the area to which the order applies.

(3) A person who fails to comply with a direction under subsection (1) which he knows has been given to him is guilty of an offence.

(4) A constable in uniform may arrest without a warrant anyone he reasonably suspects to be committing an offence under this section.

(5) A person guilty of an offence under subsection (3) is liable on summary conviction to a fine not exceeding level 3 on the standard scale.][1]

[1] Added by Criminal Justice and Public Order Act 1994 (c.33), Pt V, s.71.

Delegation

15.—(1) The chief officer of police may delegate, to such extent and subject to such conditions as he may specify, any of his functions under [sections 12 to 14A][1] to [an][2] assistant chief constable; and references in those sections to the person delegating shall be construed accordingly.   **57–019**

(2) Subsection (1) shall have effect in the City of London and the metropolitan police district as if "[an][3] assistant chief constable" read "an assistant commissioner of police".

[1] Word substituted by Criminal Justice and Public Order Act 1994 (c.33) Sched. 10, para. 60.
[2] Words substituted by Police and Magistrates' Courts Act 1994 (c.29), Sched. 5 Pt II, para. 37.
[3] *ibid.*

Interpretation

16. In this Part—   **57–020**

"the City of London" means the City as defined for the purposes of the Acts relating to the City of London police;
"the metropolitan police district" means that district as defined in section 76 of the London Government Act 1963;
"public assembly" means an assembly of 20 or more persons in a public place which is wholly or partly open to the air;
"public place" means—

(a) any highway, or in Scotland any road within the meaning of the Roads (Scotland) Act 1984, and
(b) any place to which at the material time the public or any section of the public has access, on payment or otherwise, as of right or by virtue of express or implied permission;

"public procession" means a procession in a public place.

PART III

RACIAL HATRED

Meaning of "racial hatred"

Meaning of "racial hatred"

17. In this Part "racial hatred" means hatred against a group of persons [. . .][1]   **57–021**
defined by reference to colour, race, nationality (including citizenship) or ethnic or national origins.

[1] Words repealed by Anti-terrorism, Crime and Security Act 2001 (c.24), Sched. 8(4), para. 1.

Acts intended or likely to stir up racial hatred

Use of words or behaviour or display of written material.

57–022   **18.**—(1) A person who uses threatening, abusive or insulting words or behaviour, or displays any written material which is threatening, abusive or insulting, is guilty of an offence if—

    (a) he intends thereby to stir up racial hatred, or
    (b) having regard to all the circumstances racial hatred is likely to be stirred up thereby.

(2) An offence under this section may be committed in a public or a private place, except that no offence is committed where the words or behaviour are used, or the written material is displayed, by a person inside a dwelling and are not heard or seen except by other persons in that or another dwelling.

(3) A constable may arrest without warrant anyone he reasonably suspects is committing an offence under this section.

(4) In proceedings for an offence under this section it is a defence for the accused to prove that he was inside a dwelling and had no reason to believe that the words or behaviour used, or the written material displayed, would be heard or seen by a person outside that or any other dwelling.

(5) A person who is not shown to have intended to stir up racial hatred is not guilty of an offence under this section if he did not intend his words or behaviour, or the written material, to be, and was not aware that it might be, threatening, abusive or insulting.

(6) This section does not apply to words or behaviour used, or written material displayed, solely for the purpose of being included in a programme [included in a programme service][1].

[1] Words substituted by Broadcasting Act 1990 (c.42), s.164(2).

Publishing or distributing written material

57–023   **19.**—(1) A person who publishes or distributes written material which is threatening, abusive or insulting is guilty of an offence if—

    (a) he intends thereby to stir up racial hatred, or
    (b) having regard to all the circumstances racial hatred is likely to be stirred up thereby.

(2) In proceedings for an offence under this section it is a defence for an accused who is not shown to have intended to stir up racial hatred to prove that he was not aware of the content of the material and did not suspect, and had no reason to suspect, that it was threatening, abusive or insulting.

(3) References in this Part to the publication or distribution of written material are to its publication or distribution to the public or a section of the public.

Public performance of play

57–024   **20.**—(1) If a public performance of a play is given which involves the use of threatening, abusive or insulting words or behaviour, any person who presents or directs the performance is guilty of an offence if—

    (a) he intends thereby to stir up racial hatred, or
    (b) having regard to all the circumstances (and, in particular, taking the performance as a whole) racial hatred is likely to be stirred up thereby.

(2) If a person presenting or directing the performance is not shown to have intended to stir up racial hatred, it is a defence for him to prove—

(a) that he did not know and had no reason to suspect that the performance would involve the use of the offending words or behaviour, or

(b) that he did not know and had no reason to suspect that the offending words or behaviour were threatening, abusive or insulting, or

(c) that he did not know and had no reason to suspect that the circumstances in which the performance would be given would be such that racial hatred would be likely to be stirred up.

(3) This section does not apply to a performance given solely or primarily for one or more of the following purposes—

(a) rehearsal,

(b) making a recording of the performance, or

(c) enabling the performance to be [included in a programme service][1],

but if it is proved that the performance was attended by persons other than those directly connected with the giving of the performance or the doing in relation to it of the things mentioned in paragraph (b) or (c), the performance shall, unless the contrary is shown, be taken not to have been given solely or primarily for the purposes mentioned above.

(4) For the purposes of this section—

(a) a person shall not be treated as presenting a performance of a play by reason only of his taking part in it as a performer,

(b) a person taking part as a performer in a performance directed by another shall be treated as a person who directed the performance if without reasonable excuse he performs otherwise than in accordance with that person's direction, and

(c) a person shall be taken to have directed a performance of a play given under his direction notwithstanding that he was not present during the performance;

and a person shall not be treated as aiding or abetting the commission of an offence under this section by reason only of his taking part in a performance as a performer.

(5) In this section "play" and "public performance" have the same meaning as in the Theatres Act 1968.

(6) The following provisions of the Theatres Act 1968 apply in relation to an offence under this section as they apply to an offence under section 2 of that Act—

section 9 (script as evidence of what was performed),
section 10 (power to make copies of script),
section 15 (powers of entry and inspection).

[1] Words substituted by Broadcasting Act 1990 (c.42), s.164(2).

Distributing, showing or playing a recording

21.—(1) A person who distributes, or shows or plays, a recording of visual images or sounds which are threatening, abusive or insulting is guilty of an offence if—   **57–025**

(a) he intends thereby to stir up racial hatred, or

(b) having regard to all the circumstances racial hatred is likely to be stirred up thereby.

(2) In this Part "recording" means any record from which visual images or sounds may, by any means, be reproduced; and references to the distribution, showing or playing of a recording are to its distribution, showing or playing to the public or a section of the public.

(3) In proceedings for an offence under this section it is a defence for an accused who is not shown to have intended to stir up racial hatred to prove that he was not aware of the content of the recording and did not suspect, and had no reason to suspect, that it was threatening, abusive or insulting.

(4) This section does not apply to the showing or playing of a recording solely for the purpose of enabling the recording to be [included in a programme service]¹.

¹ Words substituted by Broadcasting Act 1990 (c.42), s.164(2).

Broadcasting or including programme in cable programme service

57–026   **22.**—(1) If a programme involving threatening, abusive or insulting visual images or sounds is [included in a programme service], each of the persons mentioned in subsection (2) is guilty of an offence if—

(a) he intends thereby to stir up racial hatred, or
(b) having regard to all the circumstances racial hatred is likely to be stirred up thereby.

(2) The persons are—

(a) the person providing the programme service,
(b) any person by whom the programme is produced or directed, and
(c) any person by whom offending words or behaviour are used.

(3) If the person providing the service, or a person by whom the programme was produced or directed, is not shown to have intended to stir up racial hatred, it is a defence for him to prove that—

(a) he did not know and had not reason to suspect that the programme would involve the offending material, and
(b) having regard to the circumstances in which the programme was [included in a programme service], it was not reasonably practicable for him to secure the removal of the material.

(4) It is a defence for a person by whom the programme was produced or directed who is not shown to have intended to stir up racial hatred to prove that he did not know and had not reason to suspect—

(a) that the programme would be [included in a programme service], or
(b) that the circumstances in which the programme would be so included would be such that racial hatred would be likely to be stirred up.

(5) It is a defence for a person by whom offending words or behaviour were used and who is not shown to have intended to stir up racial hatred to prove that he did not know and had no reason to suspect—

(a) that a programme involving the use of the offending material would be [included in a programme service], or

(b) that the circumstances in which a programme involving the use of the offending material would be so included, or in which a programme so included would involve the use of the offending material, would be such that racial hatred would be likely to be stirred up.

(6) A person who is not shown to have intended to stir up racial hatred is not guilty of an offence under this section if he did not know, and had no reason to suspect, that the offending material was threatening, abusive or insulting.

Racially inflammatory material

Possession of racially inflammatory material

23.—(1) A person who has in his possession written material which is threatening, abusive or insulting, or a recording of visual images or sounds which are threatening, abusive or insulting, with a view to—   **57–027**

(a) in the case of written material, its being displayed, published, distributed, [or included in a cable programme service], whether by himself or another, or

(b) in the case of a recording, its being distributed, shown, played, [or included in a cable programme service], whether by himself or another,

is guilty of an offence if he intends racial hatred to be stirred up thereby or, having regard to all the circumstances, racial hatred is likely to be stirred up thereby.

(2) For this purpose regard shall be had to such display, publication, distribution, showing, playing, [or inclusion in a programme service] as he has, or it may reasonably be inferred that he has, in view.

(3) In proceedings for an offence under this section it is a defence for an accused who is not shown to have intended to stir up racial hatred to prove that he was not aware of the content of the written material or recording and did not suspect, and had no reason to suspect, that it was threatening, abusive or insulting.

Powers of entry and search

24.—(1) If in England and Wales a justice of the peace is satisfied by information on oath laid by a constable that there are reasonable grounds for suspecting that a person has possession of written material or a recording in contravention of section 23, the justice may issue a warrant under his hand authorising any constable to enter and search the premises where it is suspected the material or recording is situated.   **57–028**

(2) If in Scotland a sheriff or justice of the peace is satisfied by evidence on oath that there are reasonable grounds for suspecting that a person has possession of written material or a recording in contravention of section 23, the sheriff or justice may issue a warrant authorising any constable to enter and search the premises where it is suspected the material or recording is situated.

(3) A constable entering or searching premises in pursuance of a warrant issued under this section may use reasonable force if necessary.

(4) In this section "premises" means any place and, in particular, includes—

(a) any vehicle, vessel, aircraft or hovercraft,

(b) any offshore installation as defined in section 1(3)(b) of the Mineral Workings (Offshore Installations) Act 1971, and

(c) any tent or movable structure.

Supplementary provisions

Savings for reports of parliamentary or judicial proceedings

57–029   **26.**—(1) Nothing in this Part applies to a fair and accurate report of proceedings in Parliament [or in the Scottish Parliament]¹.

(2) Nothing in this Part applies to a fair and accurate report of proceedings publicly heard before a court or tribunal exercising judicial authority where the report is published contemporaneously with the proceedings or, if it is not reasonably practicable or would be unlawful to publish a report of them contemporaneously, as soon as publication is reasonably practicable and lawful.

¹ Words inserted by Scotland Act 1998 (c.46), Sched. 8, para. 24.

Procedure and punishment

57–030   **27.**—(1) No proceedings for an offence under this Part may be instituted in England and Wales except by or with the consent of the Attorney General.

(2) For the purposes of the rules in England and Wales against charging more than one offence in the same count or information, each of sections 18 to 23 creates one offence.

(3) A person guilty of an offence under this Part is liable—

    (a) on conviction on indictment to imprisonment for a term not exceeding [seven years]¹ or a fine or both;

    (b) on summary conviction to imprisonment for a term not exceeding six months or a fine not exceeding the statutory maximum or both.

¹ Words substituted by Anti-terrorism, Crime and Security Act 2001 (c.24), Pt 5, s.40.

PART V

MISCELLANEOUS AND GENERAL

Amendments, repeals and savings

57–031   **40.**—(1) Schedule 1, which amends the Sporting Events (Control of Alcohol etc.) Act 1985 and Part V of the Criminal Justice (Scotland) Act 1980, shall have effect.

(2) Schedule 2, which contains miscellaneous and consequential amendments, shall have effect.

(3) The enactments mentioned in Schedule 3 (which include enactments related to the subject matter of this Act but already obsolete or unnecessary) are repealed to the extent specified in column 3.

(4) Nothing in this Act affects the common law powers in England and Wales to deal with or prevent a breach of the peace.

(5) As respects Scotland, nothing in this Act affects any power of a constable under any rule of law.

Copyright, Designs and Patents Act 1988

(1988, c. 48)

An Act to restate the law of copyright, with amendments; to make fresh provision   **58–001**
as to the rights of performers and others in performances; to confer a design right in original designs; to amend the Registered Designs Act 1949; to make provision with respect to patent agents and trade mark agents; to confer patents and designs jurisdiction on certain county courts; to amend the law of patents; to make provision with respect to devices designed to circumvent copy-protection of works in electronic form; to make fresh provision penalising the fraudulent reception of transmissions; to make the fraudulent application or use of a trade mark an offence; to make provision for the benefit of the Hospital for Sick Children, Great Ormond Street, London; to enable financial assistance to be given to certain international bodies; and for connected purposes.   [15th November 1988]

PART I

COPYRIGHT

. . . . . .

First ownership of copyright

11.—(1) The author of a work is the first owner of any copyright in it, subject   **58–002**
to the following provisions.

(2) Where a literary, dramatic, musical or artistic work, [or a film,] is made by an employee in the course of his employment, his employer is the first owner of any copyright in the work subject to any agreement to the contrary.

(3) This section does not apply to Crown copyright or Parliamentary copyright (see sections 163 and 165) or to copyright which subsists by virtue of section 168 (copyright of certain international organisations).

. . . . . .

CHAPTER III

ACTS PERMITTED IN RELATION TO COPYRIGHT WORKS

Public administration

Parliamentary and judicial proceedings

45.—(1) Copyright is not infringed by anything done for the purposes of   **58–003**
parliamentary or judicial proceedings.

(2) Copyright is not infringed by anything done for the purposes of reporting such proceedings; but this shall not be construed as authorising the copying of a work which is itself a published report of the proceedings.

. . . . . .

Public records

58–004   **49.** Material which is comprised in public records within the meaning of the Public Records Act 1958, the Public Records (Scotland) Act 1937 or the Public Records Act (Northern Ireland) 1923 [, or in Welsh public records (as defined in the Government of Wales Act 1998),][1] which are open to public inspection in pursuance of that Act, may be copied, and a copy may be supplied to any person, by or with the authority of any officer appointed under that Act, without infringement of copyright.

[1] Words inserted by Government of Wales Act 1998 (c.38), Sched. 12, para. 27.

. . . . . .

Right to privacy of certain photographs and films

Right to privacy of certain photographs and films

58–005   **85.**—(1) A person who for private and domestic purposes commissions the taking of a photograph or the making a film has, where copyright subsists in the resulting work, the right not to have—

    (a) copies of the work issued to the public,
    (b) the work exhibited or shown in in public, or
    (c) the work broadcast or included in a cable programme service;

and, except as mentioned in subsection (2), a person who does or authorises the doing of any of those acts infringes that right.

    (2) The right is not infringed by an act which by virtue of any of the following provisions would not infringe copyright in the work—

    (a) section 31 (incidental inclusion of work in an artistic work, film, broadcast or cable programme);
    (b) section 45 (parliamentary and judicial proceedings);
    (c) section 46 (Royal Commissions and statutory inquiries);
    (d) section 50 (acts done under statutory authority);
    (e) [section 57 or 66A (acts permitted on assumptions as to expiry of copyright, etc.)].

. . . . . .

Consent and waiver of rights

58–006   **87.**—(1) It is not an infringement of any of the rights conferred by this Chapter to do any act to which the person entitled to the right has consented.

    (2) Any of those rights may be waived by instrument in writing signed by the person giving up the right.

    (3) A waiver—

    (a) may relate to a specific work, to works of a specified description or to works generally, and may relate to existing or future works, and
    (b) may be conditional or unconditional and may be expressed to be subject to revocation;

and if made in favour of the owner or prospective owner of the copyright in the work or works to which it relates, it shall be presumed to extend to his licensees and successors in title unless a contrary intention is expressed.

(4) Nothing in this Chapter shall be construed as excluding the operation of the general law of contract or estoppel in relation to an informal waiver or other transaction in relation to any of the rights mentioned in subsection (1).

. . . . . .

CHAPTER X

MISCELLANEOUS AND GENERAL

Crown and Parliamentary copyright

Crown copyright

163.—(1) Where a work is made by Her Majesty or by an officer or servant **58–007** of the Crown in the course of his duties—

   (a) the work qualifies for copyright protection notwithstanding section 153(1) (ordinary requirement as to qualification for copyright protection), and
   (b) Her Majesty is the first owner of any copyright in the work.

[(1A) For the purposes of this section, works made by Her Majesty include any sound recording, film, live broadcast or live cable programme of the proceedings of the National Assembly for Wales (including proceedings of a committee of the Assembly or of a sub-committee of such a committee) which is made by or under the direction or control of the Assembly; but a work shall not be regarded as made by or under the direction or control of the Assembly by reason only of its being commissioned by or on behalf of the Assembly.][1]

(2) Copyright in such a work is referred to in this Part as "Crown copyright", notwithstanding that it may be, or have been, assigned to another person.

(3) Crown copyright in a literary, dramatic, musical or artistic work continues to subsist—

   (a) until the end of the period of 125 years from the end of the calendar year in which the work was made, or
   (b) if the work is published commercially before the end of the period of 75 years from the end of the calendar year in which it was made, until the end of the period of 50 years from the end of the calendar year in which it was first so published.

(4) In the case of a work of joint authorship where one or more but not all of the authors are persons falling within subsection (1), this section applies only in relation to those authors and the copyright subsisting by virtue of their contribution to the work.

(5) Except as mentioned above, and subject to any express exclusion elsewhere in this Part, the provisions of this Part apply in relation to Crown copyright as to other copyright.

(6) This section does not apply to a work if, or to the extent that, Parliamentary copyright subsists in the work (see [sections 165 to 166A]).

[1] Added by Government of Wales Act 1998 (c.38), Sched. 12, para. 28.

Copyright in Acts and Measures

58–008
164.—(1) Her Majesty is entitled to copyright in every Act of Parliament [, Act of the Scottish Parliament][1] or Measure of the General Synod of the Church of England.

(2) The copyright subsists from Royal Assent until the end of the period of 50 years from the end of the calendar year in which Royal Assent was given.

(3) References in this Part to Crown copyright (except in section 163) include copyright under this section; and, except as mentioned above, the provisions of this Part apply in relation to copyright under this section as to other Crown copyright.

(4) No other copyright, or right in the nature of copyright, subsists in an Act or Measure.

[1] Words inserted by Scotland Act 1998 (c.46), Sched. 8, para. 25(5).

Parliamentary copyright

58–009
165.—(1) Where a work is made by or under the direction or control of the House of Commons or the House of Lords—

    (a) the work qualifies for copyright protection notwithstanding section 153(1) (ordinary requirement as to qualification for copyright protection), and

    (b) the House by whom, or under whose direction or control, the work is made is the first owner of any copyright in the work, and if the work is made by or under the direction or control of both Houses, the two Houses are joint first owners of copyright.

(2) Copyright in such a work is referred to in this Part as "Parliamentary copyright", notwithstanding that it may be, or have been, assigned to another person.

(3) Parliamentary copyright in a literary, dramatic, musical or artistic work continues to subsist until the end of the period of 50 years from the end of the calendar year in which the work was made.

(4) For the purposes of this section, works made by or under the direction or control of the House of Commons or the House of Lords include—

    (a) any work made by an officer or employee of that House in the course of his duties, and

    (b) any sound recording, film, live broadcast or live cable programme of the proceedings of that House;

but a work shall not be regarded as made by or under the direction or control of either House by reason only of its being commissioned by or on behalf of that House.

(5) In the case of a work of joint authorship where one or more but not all of the authors are acting on behalf of, or under the direction or control of, the House of Commons or the House of Lords, this section applies only in relation to those authors and the copyright subsisting by virtue of their contribution to the work.

(6) Except as mentioned above, and subject to any express exclusion elsewhere in this Part, the provisions of this Part apply in relation to Parliamentary copyright as to other copyright.

(7) The provisions of this section also apply, subject to any exceptions or modifications specified by Order in Council, to works made by or under the direction or control of any other legislative body of a country to which this Part

extends; and references in this Part to "Parliamentary copyright" shall be construed accordingly.

(8) A statutory instrument containing an Order in Council under subsection (7) shall be subject to annulment in pursuance of a resolution of either House of Parliament.

Copyright in Parliamentary Bills

166.—(1) Copyright in every Bill introduced into Parliament belongs, in accordance with the following provisions, to one or both of the Houses of Parliament.   **58–010**

(2) Copyright in a public Bill belongs in the first instance to the House into which the Bill is introduced, and after the Bill has been carried to the second House to both Houses jointly, and subsists from the time when the text of the Bill is handed in to the House in which it is introduced.

(3) Copyright in a private Bill belongs to both Houses jointly and subsists from the time when a copy of the Bill is first deposited in either House.

(4) Copyright in a personal Bill belongs in the first instance to the House of Lords, and after the Bill has been carried to the House of Commons to both Houses jointly, and subsists from the time when it is given a First Reading in the House of Lords.

(5) Copyright under this section ceases—

(a) on Royal Assent, or
(b) if the Bill does not receive Royal Assent, on the withdrawal or rejection of the Bill or the end of the Session:

Provided that, copyright in a Bill continues to subsist notwithstanding its rejection in any Session by the House of Lords if, by virtue of the Parliament Acts 1911 and 1949, it remains possible for it to be presented for Royal Assent in that Session.

(6) References in this Part to Parliamentary copyright (except in section 165) include copyright under this section; and, except as mentioned above, the provisions of this Part apply in relation to copyright under this section as to other Parliamentary copyright.

(7) No other copyright, or right in the nature of copyright, subsists in a Bill after copyright has once subsisted under this section; but without prejudice to the subsequent operation of this section in relation to a Bill which, not having passed in one Session, is reintroduced in a subsequent Session.

Criminal Justice Act 1988

(1988, c. 33)

An Act to make fresh provision for extradition; to amend the rules of evidence in criminal proceedings; to provide for the reference by the Attorney General of certain questions relating to sentencing to the Court of Appeal; to amend the law with regard to the jurisdiction and powers of criminal courts, the collection, enforcement and remission of fines imposed by coroners, juries, supervision orders, the detention of children and young persons, probation and the probation service, criminal appeals, anonymity in cases of rape and similar cases, orders under sections 4 and 11 of the   **59–001**

Contempt of Court Act 1981 relating to trials on indictment, orders restricting the access of the public to the whole or any part of a trial on indictment or to any proceedings ancillary to such a trial and orders restricting the publication of any report of the whole or any part of a trial on indictment or any such ancillary proceedings, the alteration of names of petty sessions areas, officers of inner London magistrates' courts and the costs and expenses of prosecution witnesses and certain other persons; to make fresh provision for the payment of compensation by the Criminal Injuries Compensation Board; . . .   [29th July 1988]

. . . . . .

Part XI

Miscellaneous

Miscarriages of justice

Compensation for miscarriages of justice

59–002   **133.**—(1) Subject to subsection (2) below, when a person has been convicted of a criminal offence and when subsequently his conviction has been reversed or he has been pardoned on the ground that a new or newly discovered fact shows beyond reasonable doubt that there has been a miscarriage of justice, the Secretary of State shall pay compensation for the miscarriage of justice to the person who has suffered punishment as a result of such conviction or, if he is dead, to his personal representatives, unless the non-disclosure of the unknown fact was wholly or partly attributable to the person convicted.

(2) No payment of compensation under this section shall be made unless an application for such compensation has been made to the Secretary of State.

(3) The question whether there is a right to compensation under this section shall be determined by the Secretary of State.

(4) If the Secretary of State determines that there is a right to such compensation, the amount of the compensation shall be assessed by an assessor appointed by the Secretary of State.

[(4A) In assessing so much of any compensation payable under this section to or in respect of a person as is attributable to suffering, harm to reputation or similar damage, the assessor shall have regard in particular to—

    (a) the seriousness of the offence of which the person was convicted and the severity of the punishment resulting from the conviction;

    (b) the conduct of the investigation and prosecution of the offence; and

    (c) any other convictions of the person and any punishment resulting from them.]¹

(5) In this section "reversed" shall be construed as referring to a conviction having been quashed—

    (a) on an appeal out of time; or

    (b) on a reference—

        [(i) under the Criminal Appeal Act 1995; or]

        (ii) under section 263 of the Criminal Procedure (Scotland) Act 1975[; or]

        (iii) [. . .]

    [(c) on an appeal under section 7 of the Terrorism Act 2000.]

(6) For the purposes of this section a person suffers punishment as a result of a conviction when sentence is passed on him for the offence of which he was convicted.

(7) Schedule 12 shall have effect.

[1] Added by Criminal Appeal Act 1995 (c.35), Pt III, s.28.

Torture

Torture

134.—(1) A public official or person acting in an official capacity, whatever his nationality, commits the offence of torture if in the United Kingdom or elsewhere he intentionally inflicts severe pain or suffering on another in the performance or purported performance of his official duties.

(2) A person not falling within subsection (1) above commits the offence of torture, whatever his nationality, if—

    (a) in the United Kingdom or elsewhere he intentionally inflicts severe pain or suffering on another at the instigation or with the consent or acquiescence—

        (i) of a public official; or
        (ii) of a person acting in an official capacity; and

    (b) the official or other person is performing or purporting to perform his official duties when he instigates the commission of the offence or consents to or acquiesces in it.

(3) It is immaterial whether the pain or suffering is physical or mental and whether it is caused by an act or an omission.

(4) It shall be a defence for a person charged with an offence under this section in respect of any conduct of his to prove that he had lawful authority, justification or excuse for that conduct.

(5) For the purposes of this section "lawful authority, justification or excuse" means—

    (a) in relation to pain or suffering inflicted in the United Kingdom, lawful authority, justification or excuse under the law of the part of the United Kingdom where it was inflicted;
    (b) in relation to pain or suffering inflicted outside the United Kingdom—

        (i) if it was inflicted by a United Kingdom official acting under the law of the United Kingdom or by a person acting in an official capacity under that law, lawful authority, justification or excuse under that law;
        (ii) if it was inflicted by a United Kingdom official acting under the law of any part of the United Kingdom or by a person acting in an official capacity under such law, lawful authority, justification or excuse under the law of the part of the United Kingdom under whose law he was acting; and
        (iii) in any other case, lawful authority, justification or excuse under the law of the place where it was inflicted.

(6) A person who commits the offence of torture shall be liable on conviction on indictment to imprisonment for life.

59–003

Requirement of Attorney General's consent for prosecutions

59–004   **135.** Proceedings for an offence under section 134 above shall not be begun—

(a) in England and Wales, except by, or with the consent of, the Attorney General; or
(b) in Northern Ireland, except by, or with the consent of, the Attorney General for Northern Ireland.

. . . . . .

Articles with blades or points and offensive weapons

Offence of having article with blade or point in public place

59–005   **139.**—(1) Subject to subsections (4) and (5) below, any person who has an article to which this section applies with him in a public place shall be guilty of an offence.

(2) Subject to subsection (3) below, this section applies to any article which has a blade or is sharply pointed except a folding pocketknife.

(3) This section applies to a folding pocketknife if the cutting edge of its blade exceeds 3 inches.

(4) It shall be a defence for a person charged with an offence under this section to prove that he had good reason or lawful authority for having the article with him in a public place.

(5) Without prejudice to the generality of subsection (4) above, it shall be a defence for a person charged with an offence under this section to prove that he had the article with him—

(a) for use at work;
(b) for religious reasons; or
(c) as part of any national costume.

(6) A person guilty of an offence under subsection (1) above shall be liable[—][1]

[(a) on summary conviction, to imprisonment for a term not exceeding six months, or a fine not exceeding the statutory maximum, or both;
(b) on conviction on indictment, to imprisonment for a term not exceeding two years, or a fine, or both.][2]

(7) In this section "public place" includes any place to which at the material time the public have or are permitted access, whether on payment or otherwise.

(8) This section shall not have effect in relation to anything done before it comes into force.

[1] Words substituted by Offensive Weapons Act 1996 (c.26), s.3(1).
[2] *ibid.*

Offence of having article with blade or point (or offensive weapon) on school premises

59–006   [**139A.**—(1) Any person who has an article to which section 139 of this Act applies with him on school premises shall be guilty of an offence.

(2) Any person who has an offensive weapon within the meaning of section

1 of the Prevention of Crime Act 1953 with him on school premises shall be guilty of an offence.

(3) It shall be a defence for a person charged with an offence under subsection (1) or (2) above to prove that he had good reason or lawful authority for having the article or weapon with him on the premises in question.

(4) Without prejudice to the generality of subsection (3) above, it shall be a defence for a person charged with an offence under subsection (1) or (2) above to prove that he had the article or weapon in question with him—

(a) for use at work,
(b) for educational purposes,
(c) for religious reasons, or
(d) as part of any national costume.

(5) A person guilty of an offence—

(a) under subsection (1) above shall be liable—

    (i) on summary conviction to imprisonment for a term not exceeding six months, or a fine not exceeding the statutory maximum, or both;
    (ii) on conviction on indictment, to imprisonment for a term not exceeding two years, or a fine, or both;

(b) under subsection (2) above shall be liable—

    (i) on summary conviction, to imprisonment for a term not exceeding six months, or a fine not exceeding the statutory maximum, or both;
    (ii) on conviction on indictment, to imprisonment for a term not exceeding four years, or a fine, or both.

(6) In this section and section 139B, "school premises" means land used for the purposes of a school excluding any land occupied solely as a dwelling by a person employed at the school; and "school" has the meaning given by [section 4 of the Education Act 1996][1].

(7) In the application of this section to Northern Ireland—

(a) the reference in subsection (2) above to section 1 of the Prevention of Crime Act 1953 is to be construed as a reference to Article 22 of the Public Order (Northern Ireland) Order 1987; and
(b) the reference in subsection (6) above to [section 4 of the Education Act 1996][2] is to be construed as a reference to Article 2(2) of the Education and Libraries (Northern Ireland) Order 1986.][3]

[1] Words substituted by Education Act 1996 (c.56), Sched. 37, Pt I, para. 69.
[2] *ibid.*
[3] Added by Offensive Weapons Act 1996 (c.26), s.4(1).

Power of entry to search for articles with a blade or point and offensive weapons

[**139B.**—(1) A constable may enter school premises and search those premises **59–007** and any person on those premises for—

(a) any article to which section 139 of this Act applies, or
(b) any offensive weapon within the meaning of section 1 of the Prevention of Crime Act 1953,

if he has reasonable grounds for believing that an offence under section 139A of this Act is being, or has been, committed.

(2) If in the course of a search under this section a constable discovers an article or weapon which he has reasonable grounds for suspecting to be an article or weapon of a kind described in subsection (1) above, he may seize and retain it.

(3) The constable may use reasonable force, if necessary, in the exercise of the power of entry conferred by this section.

(4) In the application of this section to Northern Ireland the reference in subsection (1)(b) above to section 1 of the Prevention of Crime Act 1953 is to be construed as a reference to Article 22 of the Public Order (Northern Ireland) Order 1987.]¹

¹ Added by Offensive Weapons Act 1996 (c.26), s.4(1).

. . . . . .

Power of justice of the peace to authorise entry and search of premises for offensive weapons

59–008   142.—(1) If on an application made by a constable a justice of the peace (including, in Scotland, the sheriff) is satisfied that there are reasonable grounds for believing—

(a) that there are on premises specified in the application—

  (i) knives such as are mentioned in section 1(1) of the Restriction of Offensive Weapons Act 1959; or
  (ii) weapons to which section 141 above applies; and

(b) that an offence under section 1 of the Restriction of Offensive Weapons Act 1959 or section 141 above has been or is being committed in relation to them; and
(c) that any of the conditions specified in subsection (3) below applies,

he may issue a warrant authorising a constable to enter and search the premises.

(2) A constable may seize and retain anything for which a search has been authorised under subsection (1) above.

(3) The conditions mentioned in subsection (1)(b) above are—

(a) that it is not practicable to communicate with any person entitled to grant entry to the premises;
(b) that it is practicable to communicate with a person entitled to grant entry to the premises but it is not practicable to communicate with any person entitled to grant access to the knives or weapons to which the application relates;
(c) that entry to the premises will not be granted unless a warrant is produced;
(d) that the purpose of a search may be frustrated or seriously prejudiced unless a constable arriving at the premises can secure immediate entry to them.

(4) Subsection (1)(a)(i) shall be omitted in the application of this section to Northern Ireland.

. . . . . .

Reports of criminal proceedings

Crown Court proceedings—orders restricting or preventing reports or restricting public access

159.—(1) A person aggrieved may appeal to the Court of Appeal, if that court grants leave, against— **59–009**

(a) an order under section 4 or 11 of the Contempt of Court Act 1981 made in relation to a trial on indictment;

[(aa) an order made by the Crown Court under section 58(7) or (8) of the Criminal Procedure and Investigations Act 1996 in a case where the Court has convicted a person on a trial on indictment;.]¹

(b) any order restricting the access of the public to the whole or any part of a trial on indictment or to any proceedings ancillary to such a trial; and

(c) any order restricting the publication of any report of the whole or any part of a trial on indictment or any such ancillary proceedings;

and the decision of the Court of Appeal shall be final.

(2) Subject to Rules of Court, the jurisdiction of the Court of Appeal under this section shall be exercised by the criminal division of the Court, and references to the Court of Appeal in this section shall be construed as references to that division.

(3) On an application for leave to appeal under this section a judge shall have power to give such directions as appear to him to be appropriate and, without prejudice to the generality of this subsection, power—

(a) to order the production in court of any transcript or note of proceedings or other document;

(b) to give directions as to persons who are to be parties to the appeal or who may be parties to it if they wish and as to service of documents on any person;

and the Court of Appeal shall have the same powers as the single judge.

(4) Subject to Rules of Court made by virtue of subsection (6) below, any party to an appeal under this section may give evidence before the Court of Appeal orally or in writing.

(5) On the hearing of an appeal under this section the Court of Appeal shall have power—

(a) to stay any proceedings in any other court until after the appeal is disposed of;

(b) to confirm, reverse or vary the order complained of; and

(c) to make such order as to costs as it thinks fit.

(6) Without prejudice to the generality of section 84 of the Supreme Court Act 1981, Rules of Court may make in relation to trials satisfying specified conditions special provision as to the practice and procedure to be followed in relation to hearings in camera and appeals from orders for such hearings and may in particular, but without prejudice to the generality of this subsection, provide that subsection (4) above shall not have effect.

(7) In the application of this section to Northern Ireland—

(a) subsection (2) shall be omitted; and

(b) the reference in subsection (6) to section 84 of the Supreme Court Act

1981 shall be construed as a reference to sections 52 and 55 of the Judicature (Northern Ireland) Act 1978.

¹ Added by Criminal Procedure and Investigations Act 1996 (c.25) Pt VII, s.61(6).

Possession of indecent photograph of child

Summary offence of possession of indecent photograph of child

59–010   **160.**—(1) It is an offence for a person to have any indecent photograph [or pseudo-photograph]¹ of a child in his possession.

(2) Where a person is charged with an offence under subsection (1) above, it shall be a defence for him to prove—

(a) that he had a legitimate reason for having the photograph [or pseudo-photograph]² in his possession; or

(b) that he had not himself seen the photograph [or pseudo-photograph]³ and did not know, nor had any cause to suspect, it to be indecent; or

(c) that the photograph [or pseudo-photograph]⁴ was sent to him without any prior request made by him or on his behalf and that he did not keep it for an unreasonable time.

[(2A) A person shall be liable on conviction on indictment of an offence under this section to imprisonment for a term not exceeding five years or a fine, or both.]⁵

(3) A person shall be liable on summary conviction of an offence under this section to [imprisonment for a term not exceeding six months or]⁶ a fine not exceeding level 5 on the standard scale, [or both]⁷.

(4) Sections 1(3), 2(3), 3 and 7 of the Protection of Children Act 1978 shall have effect as if any reference in them to that Act included a reference to this section.

¹ Words inserted by Criminal Justice and Public Order Act 1994 (c.33), Pt VII, s.84(4)(a).
² Words inserted by Criminal Justice and Public Order Act 1994 (c.33), Pt VII, s.84(4)(b).
³ *ibid.*
⁴ *ibid.*
⁵ Added by Criminal Justice and Court Services Act 2000 (c.43) Pt II, s.41(3)(a).
⁶ Words inserted by Criminal Justice and Public Order Act 1994 (c.33) Pt VII, s.86(1).
⁷ *ibid.*

Malicious Communications Act 1988¹

(1988, c. 27)

¹ As amended by Criminal Justice and Police Act 2001, s.43.

60–001   *An Act to make provision for the punishment of persons who send or deliver letters or other articles for the purpose of causing distress or anxiety.*

[29th July 1988]

Offence of sending letters etc. with intent to cause distress or anxiety

1.—(1) Any person who sends to another person—   **60–002**

(a) a [letter, electronic communication or article of any description] which conveys—

   (i) a message which is indecent or grossly offensive;

   (ii) a threat; or

   (iii) information which is false and known or believed to be false by the sender; or

(b) any [article or electronic communication] which is, in whole or part, of an indecent or grossly offensive nature,

is guilty of an offence if his purpose, or one of his purposes, in sending it is that it should, so far as falling within paragraph (a) or (b) above, cause distress or anxiety to the recipient or to any other person to whom he intends that it or its contents or nature should be communicated.

(2) A person is not guilty of an offence by virtue of subsection (1)(a)(ii) above if he shows—

(a) that the threat was used to reinforce a demand [made by him on reasonable grounds]; and

(b) that he believed, [and had reasonable grounds for believing,] that the use of the threat was a proper means of reinforcing the demand.

[(2A) In this section "electronic communication" includes—

(a) any oral or other communication by means of a telecommunication system (within the meaning of the Telecommunications Act 1984 (c. 12)); and

(b) any communication (however sent) that is in electronic form.]

(3) In this section references to sending include references to delivering [or transmitting] and to causing to be sent, [delivered or transmitted] and "sender" shall be construed accordingly.

(4) A person guilty of an offence under this section shall be liable on summary conviction to [imprisonment for a term not exceeding six months or to a fine not exceeding level 5 on the standard scale, or to both].

Elected Authorities (Northern Ireland) Act 1989

(1989, c. 3)

An Act to amend the law relating to the franchise at elections to district councils   **61–001**
in Northern Ireland, to make provision in relation to a declaration against terrorism to be made by candidates at such elections and at elections to the Northern Ireland Assembly and by persons co-opted as members of district councils, to amend sections 3 and 4 of the Local Government Act (Northern Ireland) 1972, and for connected purposes. [15th March 1989]

. . . . . .

Disqualification for breach of declaration against terrorism or in consequence
of imprisonment or detention

Declaration against terrorism: local elections

61–002   **3.**—(1) A person is not validly nominated as a candidate at a local election unless his consent to nomination includes a declaration in the form set out in Part I of Schedule 2 to this Act.

(2) In Schedule 5 to the Electoral Law Act (Northern Ireland) 1962, in the Appendix of Forms, in the form headed "Candidate's consent to nomination", after the paragraph beginning "I further declare" there is inserted the paragraph set out in Part I of Schedule 2 to this Act.

Declaration against terrorism: councillors co-opted to fill casual vacancies

61–003   **4.**—(1) A person is not eligible to be chosen by a district council to fill a casual vacancy in the council unless he has made, and served on the clerk of the council, a declaration in the form set out in Part II of Schedule 2 to this Act.

(2) In section 11(4B) of the Electoral Law Act (Northern Ireland) 1962 (procedure for filling casual vacancy) in paragraph (c) for the words from "any person" to "meeting" there is substituted—

> "any person who—
>
> (i) is qualified to be a member of the council;
> (ii) has made, and served on the clerk of the council, a declaration in the form set out in Part II of Schedule 2 to the Elected Authorities (Northern Ireland) Act 1989; and
> (iii) is not objected to by any member of the council present at the meeting;"

Declaration against terrorism: Assembly elections

61–004   **5.** A person is not validly nominated as a candidate at an election to the Northern Ireland Assembly unless his consent to nomination includes a declaration in the form set out in Part I of Schedule 2 to this Act.

Breach of terms of declaration

61–005   **6.**—(1) A person who has made a declaration required for the purposes of section 3, 4 or 5 of this Act in connection with a local election, an election to the Northern Ireland Assembly or the filling of a casual vacancy in a district council acts in breach of the terms of the declaration if at any time after he is declared to be elected at that election or is chosen to fill that vacancy and while he remains a member of the district council or of the Assembly—

(a) he expresses support for or approval of—

(i) a proscribed organisation, or
(ii) acts of terrorism (that is to say, violence for political ends) connected with the affairs of Northern Ireland, and

(b) he does so—

(i) at a public meeting, or
(ii) knowing, or in such circumstances that he can reasonably be expected to know, that the fact that he has made that expression of support or approval is likely to become known to the public.

(2) For the purposes of subsection (1) above a person shall be taken to express support for, or approval of, any matter if his words or actions could reasonably be understood as expressing support for, or approval of, it.

(3) It is immaterial for the purposes of subsection (1) above—

(a) whether the expression of support or approval is made by spoken or written words, by the display of written matter or by other behaviour, and

(b) whether it is made in the United Kingdom or elsewhere.

(4) This section has effect notwithstanding section 26(1) of the Northern Ireland Constitution Act 1973 (privileges of the Northern Ireland Assembly).

(5) In this section—

"proscribed organisation" has the same meaning as in [section 3 of the Terrorism Act 2000][1],
"public meeting" includes—

(a) any meeting in a public place,

(b) any meeting which the public or any section of the public is permitted to attend, whether on payment or otherwise, and

(c) any meeting of the Northern Ireland Assembly, a district council or any committee or sub-committee of the Assembly or such a council (whether or not a meeting which the public is permitted to attend), and

"public place" means —

(a) any highway, and

(b) any place to which at the material time the public or any section of the public has access, on payment or otherwise, as of right or by virtue of express or implied permission.

[1] Words substituted by Terrorism Act 2000 (c.11), Sched. 15, para. 7(2).

Extradition Act 1989

(1989, c. 33)

An Act to consolidate enactments relating to extradition under the Criminal Justice Act 1988, the Fugitive Offenders Act 1967 and the Extradition Acts 1870 to 1935, with amendments to give effect to recommendations of the Law Commission and the Scottish Law Commission.   [27th July 1989]   **62–001**

PART I

INTRODUCTORY

General

Liability to extradition

1.—(1) Where extradition procedures under Part III of this Act are available   **62–002**

as between the United Kingdom and a foreign state, a person in the United Kingdom who—

(a) is accused in that state of the commission of an extradition crime; or
(b) is alleged to be unlawfully at large after conviction of an extradition crime by a court in that state,

may be arrested and returned to that state in accordance with those procedures.

(2) Subject to the provisions of this Act, a person in the United Kingdom who is accused of an extradition crime—

(a) in a Commonwealth country designated for the purposes of this subsection under section 5(1) below; or
(b) in a colony,

or who is alleged to be unlawfully at large after conviction of such an offence in any such country or in a colony, may be arrested and returned to that country or colony in accordance with extradition procedures under Part III of this Act.

[(2A) Subject to the provisions of this Act, a person in the United Kingdom who—

(a) is accused in the Hong Kong Special Administrative Region of an extradition crime, or
(b) is alleged to be unlawfully at large after conviction for such an offence in that Region,

may be arrested and returned to that Region in accordance with extradition procedures under Part III of this Act.]

(3) Where an Order in Council under section 2 of the Extradition Act 1870 is in force in relation to a foreign state, Schedule 1 to this Act (the provisions of which derive from that Act and certain associated enactments) shall have effect in relation to that state, but subject to the limitations, restrictions, conditions, exceptions and qualifications, if any, contained in the Order.

Extradition crimes

Meaning of "extradition crime"

62–003   2.—(1) In this Act, except in Schedule 1, "extradition crime" means—

(a) conduct in the territory of a foreign state, a designated Commonwealth country [, a colony or the Hong Kong Special Administrative Region] which, if it occurred in the United Kingdom, would constitute an offence punishable with imprisonment for a term of 12 months, or any greater punishment, and which, however described in the law of the foreign state, Commonwealth country or colony [or of the Hong Kong Special Administrative Region], is so punishable under that law;
(b) an extra-territorial offence against the law of a foreign state, designated Commonwealth country or colony, [or of the Hong Kong Special Administrative Region,] which is punishable under that law with imprisonment for a term of 12 months, or any greater punishment, and which satisfies—

(i) the condition specified in subsection (2) below; or
(ii) all the conditions specified in subsection (3) below; [or]¹
[(iii) the condition specified in subsection (3A) below.]²

(2) The condition mentioned in subsection (1)(b)(i) above is that in corres-

ponding circumstances equivalent conduct would constitute an extra-territorial offence against the law of the United Kingdom punishable with imprisonment for a term of 12 months, or any greater punishment.

(3) The conditions mentioned in subsection (1)(b)(ii) above are—

(a) that the foreign state, Commonwealth country or colony [or the Hong Kong Special Administrative Region] bases its jurisdiction on the nationality of the offender;

(b) that the conduct constituting the offence occurred outside the United Kingdom; and

(c) that, if it occurred in the United Kingdom, it would constitute an offence under the law of the United Kingdom punishable with imprisonment for a term of 12 months, or any greater punishment.

[(3A) The condition mentioned in subsection (1)(b)(iii) above is that the conduct constituting the offence constitutes or, if committed in the United Kingdom would constitute—

(a) an offence under section 51 or 58 of the International Criminal Court Act 2001 (genocide, crimes against humanity and war crimes),

(b) an offence under section 52 or 59 of that Act (conduct ancillary to genocide, etc. committed outside the jurisdiction), or

(c) an ancillary offence, as defined in section 55 or 62 of that Act, in relation to any such offence.][3]

(4) For the purposes of [this Act, except Schedule 1][4]—

(a) the law of a foreign state, designated Commonwealth country or colony includes the law of any part of it and the law of the United Kingdom includes the law of any part of the United Kingdom;

(b) conduct in a colony or dependency of a foreign state or of a designated Commonwealth country, or a vessel, aircraft or hovercraft of a foreign state or of such a country, shall be treated as if it were conduct in the territory of that state or country;

(c) conduct in a vessel, aircraft or hovercraft of a colony of the United Kingdom shall be treated as if it were conduct in that colony; [but]

[(d) reference shall be made to the law of the colony or dependency of a foreign state or of a designated Commonwealth country, and not (where different) to the law of the foreign state or Commonwealth country, to determine the level of punishment applicable to conduct in that colony or dependency.]

[(d) conduct in a vessel, aircraft or hovercraft of the Hong Kong Special Administrative Region shall be treated as if it were conduct in that Region]

[(5) References in this section to an offence under any provision of the International Criminal Court Act 2001, or to an offence ancillary to such an offence, include any corresponding offence under the law of Scotland.][5]

[1] Added by International Criminal Court Act 2001 (c.17), Pt 5, s. 72(2).
[2] *ibid.*
[3] Added by International Criminal Court Act 2001 (c.17), Pt 5, s. 72(3).
[4] Words substituted by Criminal Justice and Public Order Act 1994 (c.33), Sched. 9, para. 37(2)(a).
[5] Added by International Criminal Court Act 2001 (c.17) Pt 5, s. 72(4).

Return to foreign states

Arrangements for availability of Part III procedure

62–004   **3.**—(1) In this Act "extradition arrangements" means arrangements made with a foreign state under which extradition procedures under Part III of this Act will be available as between the United Kingdom and that state.

(2) For this purpose "foreign state" means any state other than—

(i)   the United Kingdom;
(ii) a country mentioned in Schedule 3 to the British Nationality Act 1981 (countries whose citizens are Commonwealth citizens);
(iii) a colony;
(iv) the Republic of Ireland; [or]
[(v) the Hong Kong Special Administrative Region.]

but a state which is a party to the European Convention on Extradition done at Paris on 13th December 1957 may be treated as a foreign state.

(3) Extradition arrangements may be—

(a) arrangements of a general nature made with one or more states and relating to the operation of extradition procedures under Part III of this Act (in this Act referred to as "general extradition arrangements"); or
(b) arrangements relating to the operation of those procedures in particular cases (in this Act referred to as "special extradition arrangements") made with a state with which there are no general extradition arrangements.

Orders in Council as to extradition

62–005   **4.**—(1) Where general extradition arrangements have been made, Her Majesty may, by Order in Council reciting or embodying their terms, direct that this Act, so far as it relates to extradition procedures under Part III of this Act, shall apply as between the United Kingdom and the foreign state, or any foreign state, with which they have been made, subject to the limitations, restrictions, exceptions and qualifications, if any, contained in the Order.

(2) An Order in Council under this section shall not be made unless the general extradition arrangements to which it relates—

(a) provide for their determination after the expiration of a notice given by a party to them and not exceeding one year or for their denunciation by means of such a notice; and
(b) are in conformity with the provisions of this Act, and in particular with the restrictions on return contained in Part II of this Act.

(3) An Order in Council under this section shall be conclusive evidence that the arrangements therein referred to comply with this Act and that this Act, so far as it relates to extradition procedures under Part III of this Act, applies in the case of the foreign state, or any foreign state, mentioned in the Order.

(4) An Order in Council under this section shall be laid before Parliament after being made.

(5) An Order in Council under this section which does not provide that a person may only be returned to the foreign state requesting his return if the court of committal is satisfied that the evidence would be sufficient to [make a case requiring an answer by that person if the proceedings were a summary trial of an information against him and][1] the extradition crime had taken place within

the jurisdiction of the court shall be subject to annulment in pursuance of a resolution of either House of Parliament.

¹ Words substituted by Criminal Justice and Public Order Act 1994 (c.33), Pt XII, s. 158(2).

Return to Commonwealth countries and colonies

Procedure for designation etc.

5.—(1) Her Majesty may by Order in Council designate for the purposes of **62–006** section 1(2) above any country for the time being mentioned in Schedule 3 to the British Nationality Act 1981 (countries whose citizens are Commonwealth citizens); and any country so designated is in this Act referred to as a "designated Commonwealth country".

(2) This Act has effect in relation to all colonies.

(3) Her Majesty may by Order in Council direct that this Act shall have effect in relation to the return of persons to, or in relation to persons returned from, any designated Commonwealth country or any colony subject to such exceptions, adaptations or modifications as may be specified in the Order.

(4) Any Order under this section may contain such transitional or other incidental and supplementary provisions as may appear to Her Majesty to be necessary or expedient.

(5) For the purposes of any Order in Council under subsection (1) above, any territory for the external relations of which a Commonwealth country is responsible may be treated as part of that country or, if the Government of that country so requests, as a separate country.

(6) Any Order in Council under this section, other than an Order to which subsection (7) below applies, shall be subject to annulment in pursuance of a resolution of either House of Parliament.

(7) No recommendation shall be made to Her Majesty in Council to make an Order containing any such direction as is authorised by subsection (3) above unless a draft of the Order has been laid before Parliament and approved by resolution of each House of Parliament.

PART II

RESTRICTIONS ON RETURN

General restrictions on return

6.—(1) A person shall not be returned under Part III of this Act, or committed **62–007** or kept in custody for the purposes of return, if it appears to an appropriate authority—

(a) that the offence of which that person is accused or was convicted is an offence of a political character;

(b) that it is an offence under military law which is not also an offence under the general criminal law;

(c) that the request for his return (though purporting to be made on account of an extradition crime) is in fact made for the purpose of prosecuting or punishing him on account of his race, religion, nationality or political opinions; or

(d) that he might, if returned, be prejudiced at his trial or punished, detained or restricted in his personal liberty by reason of his race, religion, nationality or political opinions.

(2) A person who is alleged to be unlawfully at large after conviction of an

extradition crime shall not be returned to a foreign state [or to the Hong Kong Special Administrative Region], or committed or kept in custody for the purposes of return to a foreign state [or to that region], if it appears to an appropriate authority—

    (a) that the conviction was obtained in his absence; and

    (b) that it would not be in the interests of justice to return him on the ground of that conviction.

(3) A person accused of an offence shall not be returned, or committed or kept in custody for the purposes of return, if it appears to an appropriate authority that if charged with that offence in the United Kingdom he would be entitled to be discharged under any rule of law relating to previous acquittal or conviction.

(4) A person shall not be returned, or committed or kept in custody for the purposes of such return, unless provision is made by the relevant law, or by an arrangement made with the relevant foreign state, Commonwealth country or colony [or with the Hong Kong Special Administrative Region][3], for securing that he will not, unless he has first had an opportunity to leave it, be dealt with there for or in respect of any offence committed before his return to it other than—

    (a) the offence in respect of which his return is ordered;

    (b) an offence, other than an offence excluded by subsection (5) below, which is disclosed by the facts in respect of which his return was ordered; or

    (c) subject to subsection (6) below, any other offence being an extradition crime in respect of which the Secretary of State [or the Scottish Ministers] may consent to his being dealt with.

(5) The offences excluded from paragraph (b) of subsection (4) above are offences in relation to which an order for the return of the person concerned could not lawfully be made.

(6) The Secretary of State [or the Scottish Ministers] may not give consent under paragraph (c) of that subsection in respect of an offence in relation to which it appears to him [or them] that an order for the return of the person concerned could not lawfully be made, or would not in fact be made.

(7) Any such arrangement as is mentioned in subsection (4) above which is made with a designated Commonwealth country or a colony may be an arrangement made for the particular case or an arrangement of a more general nature; and for the purposes of that subsection a certificate issued by or under the authority of the Secretary of State [or the Scottish Ministers] confirming the existence of an arrangement with a Commonwealth country or a colony and stating its terms shall be conclusive evidence of the matters contained in the certificate.

(8) In relation to a Commonwealth country or a colony the reference in subsection (1) above to an offence of a political character does not include an offence against the life or person of the Head of the Commonwealth or attempting or conspiring to commit, or assisting, counselling or procuring the commission of or being accessory before or after the fact to such an offence, or of impeding the apprehension or prosecution of persons guilty of such an offence.

(9) In this Act "appropriate authority" means—

    [(a) the Secretary of State, or, except in section 25(1), in the case of a function that is exercisable in or as regards Scotland, the Scottish Ministers;]

    (b) the court of committal;

(c) the High Court or High Court of Justiciary on an application for habeas corpus or for review of the order of committal.

(10) In this section, in relation to Commonwealth countries and colonies, "race" includes tribe.

PART III

PROCEDURE

General

Extradition request and authority to proceed

7.—(1) Subject to the provisions of this Act relating to provisional warrants, **62–008** a person shall not be dealt with under this Part of this Act except in pursuance of an order of the Secretary of State [or the Scottish Ministers] (in this Act referred to as an "authority to proceed") issued in pursuance of a request (in this Act referred to as an "extradition request") for the surrender of a person under this Act made [to the Secretary of State]—

[(a) by—

> (i) an authority in a foreign state which appears to the Secretary of State to have the function of making extradition requests in that foreign state, or
> (ii) some person recognised by the Secretary of State as a diplomatic or consular representative of a foreign state; or]

(b) by or on behalf of the Government of a designated Commonwealth country, or the Governor of a colony; [or]

[(c) by or on behalf of the Government of the Hong Kong Special Administrative Region.]
[and an extradition request may be made by facsimile transmission and an authority to proceed issued without waiting to receive the original.]

(2) There shall be furnished with any such request—

(a) particulars of the person whose return is requested;

(b) particulars of the offence of which he is accused or was convicted (including evidence [or, in a case falling within subsection (2A) below, information] sufficient to justify the issue of a warrant for his arrest under this Act);

(c) in the case of a person accused of an offence, a warrant [or a duly authenticated copy of a warrant] for his arrest issued in the foreign state, Commonwealth country or colony [or in the Hong Kong Special Administrative Region]; and

(d) in the case of a person unlawfully at large after conviction of an offence, a certificate [or a duly authenticated copy of a certificate] of the conviction and sentence,

and copies of them shall be served on the person whose return is requested before he is brought before the court of committal.

[(2A) Where—

(a) the extradition request is made by a foreign state; and

(b) an Order in Council falling within section 4(5) above is in force in relation to that state, it shall be a sufficient compliance with subsection (2)(b) above to furnish information sufficient to justify the issue of a warrant for his arrest under this Act.]

(3) Rules under section 144 of the Magistrates' Courts Act 1980 may make provision as to the procedure for service under subsection (2) above in England and Wales and the High Court of Justiciary may, by Act of Adjournal, make rules as to such procedure in Scotland.

(4) On receipt of any such request the Secretary of State [or the Scottish Ministers] may issue an authority to proceed unless it appears to him [or them] that an order for the return of the person concerned could not lawfully be made, or would not in fact be made, in accordance with the provisions of this Act.

(5) An authority to proceed shall specify the offence or offences under the law of the United Kingdom which it appears to the Secretary of State [or the Scottish Ministers] would be constituted by equivalent conduct in the United Kingdom.

(6) In this section "warrant", in the case of any foreign state, includes any judicial document authorising the arrest of a person accused of a crime.

[(7) Where an extradition request is made by facsimile transmission this Act (including subsection (2) above) shall have effect as if the foreign documents so sent were the originals used to make the transmission and receivable in evidence accordingly.]

Arrest for purposes of committal

62–009   **8.**—(1) For the purposes of this Part of this Act a warrant for the arrest of a person may be issued—

   (a) on receipt of an authority to proceed—

      (i) by the [Senior District Judge (Chief Magistrate) or another District Judge (Magistrates' Courts) designated by him];
      (ii) by the sheriff of Lothian and Borders;

   (b) without such an authority—

      (ii) by a justice of the peace in any part of the United Kingdom; and
      (iii) in Scotland, by a sheriff,

upon information that the said person is or is believed to be in or on his way to the United Kingdom;

and any warrant issued by virtue of paragraph (b) above is in this Act referred to as a "provisional warrant".

(3) A person empowered to issue warrants of arrest under this section may issue such a warrant if he is supplied with such evidence [or, in a case falling within subsection (3A) below, information] as would in his opinion justify the issue of a warrant for the arrest of a person accused or, as the case may be, convicted within his jurisdiction and it appears to him that the conduct alleged would constitute an extradition crime.

[(3A) Where—

   (a) the extradition request or, where a provisional warrant is applied for, the request for the person's arrest is made by a foreign state; and
   (b) an Order in Council falling within section 4(5) above is in force in relation to that state,

it shall be sufficient for the purposes of subsection (3) above to supply such information as would, in the opinion of the person so empowered, justify the issue of a warrant of arrest.]

(4) Where a provisional warrant is issued under this section, the authority by whom it is issued shall forthwith give notice to the Secretary of State [or the Scottish Ministers], and transmit to him [or them] the information and evidence, or certified copies of the information and evidence, upon which it was issued; and the Secretary of State [or the Scottish Ministers] may in any case, and shall if he decides [or, they decide] not to issue an authority to proceed in respect of the person to whom the warrant relates, by order cancel the warrant and, if that person has been arrested under it, discharge him from custody.

(5) A warrant of arrest issued under this section may, without being backed, be executed in any part of the United Kingdom and may be so executed by any person to whom it is directed or by any constable.

(6) Where a warrant is issued under this section for the arrest of a person accused of an offence of stealing or receiving stolen property in a designated Commonwealth country or a colony or any other offence committed in such a country or in a colony in respect of property, a justice of the peace in any part of the United Kingdom and in Scotland a sheriff shall have the like power to issue a warrant to search for the property as if the offence had been committed within his jurisdiction.

Proceedings for committal

9.—(1) A person arrested in pursuance of a warrant under section 8 above shall (unless previously discharged under subsection (4) of that section) be brought as soon as practicable before a court (in this Act referred to as "the court of committal").   **62–010**

(2) For the purposes of proceedings under this section a court of committal in England and Wales [shall consist of the Senior District Judge (Chief Magistrate) or another District Judge (Magistrates' Courts) designated by him and] shall have the like [powers, as nearly as may be, including powers to adjourn the case and meanwhile to remand the person arrested under the warrant either in custody or on bail, as if the proceedings were the summary trial of an information against him; and section 16(1)(c) of the Prosecution of Offences Act 1985 (costs on dismissal) shall apply accordingly reading the reference to the dismissal of the information as a reference to the discharge of the person arrested.]

[(2A) If a court of committal in England and Wales exercises its power to adjourn the case it shall on so doing remand the person arrested in custody or on bail.]

(3) For the purposes of proceedings under this section a court of committal in Scotland [shall consist of the sheriff of Lothian and Borders and] shall have the like powers, including power to adjourn the case and meanwhile to remand the person arrested under the warrant either in custody or on bail, and the proceedings shall be conducted as nearly as may be in the like manner, as if the proceedings were summary proceedings in respect of an offence alleged to have been committed by that person; and the provisions of the Legal Aid (Scotland) Act 1986 relating to such proceedings or any appellate proceedings following thereon shall apply accordingly to that person.

(4) Where—

    (a) the extradition request is made by a foreign state; and
    (b) an Order in Council such as is mentioned in subsection (8) below is in force in relation to that state,

there is no need to furnish the court of committal with evidence sufficient to [make a case requiring an answer by the arrested person if the proceedings were the summary trial of an information against him.]

(5) Where the person arrested is in custody by virtue of a provisional warrant

and no authority to proceed has been received in respect of him, the court of committal may fix a period (of which the court shall give notice to the Secretary of State [or the Scottish Ministers]) after which he will be discharged from custody unless such an authority has been received.

(6) In exercising the power conferred by subsection (5) above in a case where the extradition request is made under general extradition arrangements the court shall have regard to any period specified for the purpose in the Order in Council relating to the arrangements.

(7) Where—

    (a) the extradition request is made under general extradition arrangements but no period is so specified; or

    (b) the application is made under special extradition arrangements,

the court of committal may fix a reasonable period.

[(7A) In exercising the power conferred by subsection (5) above in a case where the extradition request is made by or on behalf of the Government of the Hong Kong Special Administrative Region the court shall not fix a period ending more than 60 days after the day of the person's arrest, unless the exceptional circumstances of the case justify a longer period.]

(8) Where an authority to proceed has been issued in respect of the person arrested and the court of committal is satisfied, after hearing any representations made in support of the extradition request or on behalf of that person, that the offence to which the authority relates is an extradition crime, and is further satisfied—

    (a) where that person is accused of the offence, unless an Order in Council giving effect to general extradition arrangements under which the extradition request was made otherwise provides, that the evidence would be sufficient to [make a case requiring an answer by that person if the proceedings were the summary trial of an information against him.]

    (b) where that person is alleged to be unlawfully at large after conviction of the offence, that he has been so convicted and appears to be so at large,

the court, unless his committal is prohibited by any other provision of this Act, shall commit him to custody or on bail—

    (i) to await the Secretary of State's [or the Scottish Ministers] decision as to his return; and

    (ii) if the Secretary of State decides [or the Scottish Ministers decide] that he shall be returned, to await his return.

(9) If the court commits a person under subsection (8) above, it shall issue a certificate of the offence against the law of the United Kingdom which would be constituted by his conduct.

(10) If the court commits a person to custody in the exercise of that power, it may subsequently grant bail if it considers it appropriate to do so.

(11) If—

    (a) the court is not satisfied as mentioned in subsection (8) above in relation to the person arrested; or

    (b) his committal is prohibited by a provision of this Act,

it shall discharge him.

Statement of case by court

10.—(1) If the court of committal refuses to make an order in relation to a **62–011** person under section 9 above in respect of the offence or, as the case may be, any of the offences to which the authority to proceed relates, the foreign state, Commonwealth country or colony seeking the surrender of that person to it may question the proceeding on the ground that it is wrong in law by applying to the court to state a case for the opinion of the High Court or, in Scotland, the High Court of Justiciary on the question of law involved.

(2) If the state, country or colony seeking return immediately informs the court of committal that it intends to make such an application, the court shall make an order providing for the detention of the person to whom the authority to proceed relates, or directing that he shall not be released except on bail.

(3) Rules of Court may specify—

(a) a period within which such an application must be made unless the court grants a longer period; and

(b) a period within which the court of committal must comply with such an application.

(4) Where the court of committal fails to comply with an application under subsection (1) above within the period specified by Rules of Court, the High Court or, in Scotland, the High Court of Justiciary may, on the application of the state, country or colony that applied for the case to be stated, make an order requiring the court to state a case.

(5) The High Court or High Court of Justiciary shall have power—

(a) to remit the case to the court of committal to decide it according to the opinion of the High Court or High Court of Justiciary on the question of law; or

(b) to dismiss the appeal.

(6) Where the court dismisses an appeal relating to an offence, it shall by order declare that that offence is not an offence in respect of which the Secretary of State has [or the Scottish Ministers have] power to make an order for return in respect of the person whose return was requested.

(7) An order made by a [District Judge (Magistrates' Courts)] under subsection (2) above shall cease to have effect if—

(a) the court dismisses the appeal in respect of the offence or all the offences to which it relates; and

(b) the foreign state, Commonwealth country or colony does not immediately—

(i) apply for leave to appeal to the House of Lords; or

(ii) inform the court that it intends to apply for leave.

(8) An order made by the sheriff of Lothian and Borders under subsection (2) above shall cease to have effect if the court dismisses the appeal in respect of the offence or all the offences to which it relates.

(9) In relation to a decision of a court on an appeal under this section, section 1 of the Administration of Justice Act 1960 (right of appeal to House of Lords) shall have effect as if so much of subsection (2) as restricts the grant of leave to appeal were omitted.

(10) The House of Lords may exercise any powers of the High Court under subsection (5) above and subsection (6) above shall apply to them as it applies to that Court.

(11) Subject to subsections (7) and (8) above, an order under subsection (2) above shall have effect so long as the case is pending.

(12) For the purposes of this section a case is pending (unless proceedings are discontinued) until (disregarding any power of a court to grant leave to take any step out of time) there is no step that the state, country or colony can take.

(13) In the application of this section to Scotland subsections (9) and (10) above shall be omitted and in relation to an appeal under this section in Scotland the court may make an order providing for the detention of the person to whom it relates or it may grant bail; and [section 177(2) and (3) of the Criminal Procedure (Scotland) Act 1995] shall apply for the purpose of such an appeal as it applies for the purpose of an appeal such as is mentioned in [section 176] of that Act.

[(14) This section shall apply to the Hong Kong Special Administrative Region in the same way as it applies to any foreign state, Commonwealth country or colony.]

Application for habeas corpus, etc.

62–012   **11.**—(1) Where a person is committed under section 9 above, the court shall inform him in ordinary language of his right to make an application for habeas corpus, and shall forthwith give notice of the committal to the Secretary of State [or the Scottish Ministers].

(2) A person committed shall not be returned—

    (a) in any case, until the expiration of the period of 15 days beginning with the day on which the order for his committal is made;

    (b) if an application for habeas corpus is made in his case, so long as proceedings on that application are pending.

(3) Without prejudice to any jurisdiction of the High Court apart from this section, the court shall order the applicant's discharge if it appears to the court in relation to the offence, or each of the offences, in respect of which the applicant's return is sought, that—

    (a) by reason of the trivial nature of the offence; or

    (b) by reason of the passage of time since he is alleged to have committed it or to have become unlawfully at large, as the case may be; or

    (c) because the accusation against him is not made in good faith in the interests of justice;

it would, having regard to all the circumstances, be unjust or oppressive to return him.

(4) On any such application the court may receive additional evidence relevant to the exercise of its jurisdiction under section 6 above or subsection (3) above.

(5) Proceedings on an application for habeas corpus shall be treated for the purposes of this section as pending (unless they are discontinued) until (disregarding any power of a court to grant leave to appeal out of time) there is no further possibility of an appeal.

(6) In the application of this section to Scotland references to an application for habeas corpus shall be construed as references to an application for review of the order of committal and references to the High Court shall be construed as references to the High Court of Justiciary.

Order for return

12.—(1) Where a person is committed under section 9 above and is not dis-   **62–013**
charged by order of the High Court or the High Court of Justiciary, the Secretary
of State [or the Scottish Ministers] may by warrant order him to be returned
unless his return is prohibited, or prohibited for the time being, by this Act, or
the Secretary of State decides [or the Scottish Ministers decide] under this section to make no such order in his case.

(2) Without prejudice to his general discretion as to the making of an order
for the return of a person to a foreign state, Commonwealth country or colony
[or to the Hong Kong Special Administrative Region]—

- (a) the Secretary of State [or the Scottish Minsters] shall not make an order
  in the case of any person if it appears to the Secretary of State in
  relation to the offence, or each of the offences, in respect of which his
  return is sought, that—

  - (i) by reason of its trivial nature; or
  - (ii) by reason of the passage of time since he is alleged to have com-
    mitted it or to have become unlawfully at large, as the case may
    be; or
  - (iii) because the accusation against him is not made in good faith in
    the interests of justice,

  it would, having regard to all the circumstances, be unjust or oppressive
  to return him; and

- (b) the Secretary of State [or the Scottish Minsters] may decide to make
  no order for the return of a person accused or convicted of an offence
  not punishable with death in Great Britain if that person could be or
  has been sentenced to death for that offence in the country by which
  the request for his return is made.

(3) An order for return shall not be made in the case of a person who is
serving a sentence of imprisonment or detention, or is charged with an offence,
in the United Kingdom—

- (a) in the case of a person serving such a sentence, until the sentence has
  been served;
- (b) in the case of a person charged with an offence, until the charge is
  disposed of or withdrawn or unless an order is made for it to lie on the
  file and, if it results in his serving a term of imprisonment or detention,
  until the sentence has been served.

(4) In the application of this section to Scotland, the reference in subsection
(3) above to an order being made for the charge to lie on the file shall be
construed as a reference to the diet being deserted pro loco et tempore.

(5) The Secretary of State [or the Scottish Minsters] may decide to make no
order under this section for the return of a person committed in consequence of
an extradition request if another extradition request or a requisition under Schedule 1 to this Act has been made in respect of him and it appears to the Secretary
of State [or the Scottish Minsters], having regard to all the circumstances of the
case and in particular—

- (a) the relative seriousness of the offences in question;
- (b) the date on which each such request was made; and
- (c) the nationality or citizenship of the person concerned and his ordinary
  residence,

that preference should be given to that other request or requisition.

(6) Notice of the issue of a warrant under this section for the return of a person to a Commonwealth country or colony shall forthwith be given to the person to be returned.

Return to foreign states-supplementary

62–014   **13.**—(1) The Secretary of State [or the Scottish Ministers] shall give the person to whom an order under section 12(1) above for return to a foreign state [or to the Hong Kong Special Administrative Region] would relate notice in writing that he is contemplating making such an order.

(2) The person to whom such an order would relate shall have a right to make representations, at any time before the expiration of the period of 15 days commencing with the date on which the notice is given, as to why he should not be returned to the foreign state, and unless he waives that right, no such order shall be made in relation to him before the end of that period.

(3) A notice under subsection (1) above shall explain in ordinary language the right conferred by subsection (2) above.

(4) It shall be the duty of the Secretary of State [or the Scottish Ministers] to consider any representations made in the exercise of that right.

(5) Unless the person to whom it relates waives the right conferred on him by subsection (6) below, he shall not be returned to the foreign state [or to the Hong Kong Special Administrative Region] until the expiration of the period of 7 days commencing with the date on which the warrant is issued or such longer period as—

(a) in England and Wales, rules under section 84 of the Supreme Court Act 1981 may provide; or

(b) in Scotland, the High Court of Justiciary may provide by Act of Adjournal.

(6) At any time within that period he may apply for leave to seek judicial review of the Secretary of State's [or the Scottish Ministers] decision to make the order.

(7) If he applies for judicial review, he may not be returned so long as the proceedings for judicial review are pending.

(8) Proceedings for judicial review shall be treated for the purposes of this section as pending (unless they are discontinued) until (disregarding any power of a court to grant leave to appeal out of time) there is no further possibility of an appeal.

(9) A warrant under section 12 above—

(a) shall state in ordinary language that the Secretary of State has [or the Scottish Ministers have] considered any representations made in the exercise of the right conferred by subsection (2) above; and

(b) shall explain in ordinary language the rights conferred by this section on a person whose return to a foreign state [or to the Hong Kong Special Administrative Region] has been ordered under section 12 above,

and a copy shall be given to the person to whom it relates as soon as the order for his return is made.

Simplified procedure

62–015   **14.**—(1) A person may give notice that he waives the rights conferred on him by section 11 above.

(2) A notice under this section shall be given in England and Wales in the manner prescribed by rules under section 144 of the Magistrates' Courts Act 1980, and without prejudice to the generality of subsection (1) of that section, the power to make such rules shall include power to make provision for a magistrate to order the committal for return of a person with his consent at any time after his arrest.

(3) A notice under this section shall be given in Scotland in the manner prescribed by the High Court of Justiciary by Act of Adjournal and the sheriff may order the committal for return of a person with his consent at any time after his arrest.

(4) Where an order is made by virtue of this section, this Act shall cease to apply to the person in respect of whom it is made, except that, if he is not surrendered within one month after the order is made, the High Court or, in Scotland, the High Court of Justiciary, upon application by or on behalf of that person, may, unless reasonable cause is shown for the delay, order him to be discharged.

Special extradition arrangements

Special extradition arrangements

15.—(1) Where special extradition arrangements have been made in respect of a person, extradition procedures shall be available in the case of that person, as between the United Kingdom and the foreign state with which the arrangements have been made, subject to the limitations, restrictions, exceptions and qualifications, if any, contained in the arrangements.   **62–016**

(2) If the Secretary of State issues a certificate of special extradition arrangements, it shall be conclusive evidence of all matters stated in it.

(3) In subsection (2) above "certificate of special extradition arrangements" means a certificate—

(a) that special extradition arrangements have been made in respect of a person as between the United Kingdom and a foreign state specified in the certificate; and

(b) that extradition procedures are available in the case of that person as between the United Kingdom and the foreign state to the extent specified in the certificate.

Effect of delay

Custody

17.—(1) Any person remanded or committed to custody under this Part of this Act shall be committed to the like institution as a person charged with an offence before the court of committal.   **62–017**

(2) If any person who is in custody by virtue of a warrant under this Act escapes out of custody, he may be retaken in any part of the United Kingdom in like manner as a person escaping from custody under a warrant for his arrest issued in that part in respect of an offence committed in that part.

(3) Where a person, being in custody in any part of the United Kingdom whether under this Part of this Act or otherwise, is required to be removed in custody under this Act to another part of the United Kingdom and is so removed by sea or by air, he shall be deemed to continue in legal custody until he reaches the place to which he is required to be removed.

(4) A warrant for the return of any person shall be sufficient authority for all persons to whom it is directed and all constables to receive that person, keep him in custody and convey him into the jurisdiction to which he is to be returned.

. . . . . .

PART V

SPECIAL CASES

International Convention cases

Extension of purposes of extradition for offences under Acts giving effect to international Conventions

62–018 22.—(1) Except as provided by subsection (6) below, this section has effect where—

(a) general extradition arrangements have not been made with a state which is a party to a Convention to which this section applies; and
(b) no Order in Council under section 2 of the Extradition Act 1870 is in force in relation to that state.

(2) The Conventions to which this section applies are—

(a) the Convention on Offences and certain other Acts committed on board Aircraft, which was signed at Tokyo on 14th September 1963 ("the Tokyo Convention");
(b) the Convention for the Suppression of Unlawful Seizure of Aircraft, which was signed at the Hague on 16th December 1970 ("the Hague Convention");
(c) the Convention for the Suppression of Unlawful Acts against the Safety of Civil Aviation, which was signed at Montreal on 23rd September 1971 ("the Montreal Convention");
(d) the Convention on the Prevention and Punishment of Crimes against Internationally Protected Persons adopted by the United Nations General Assembly in 1973 ("the Internationally Protected Persons Convention");
(e) the International Convention against the Taking of Hostages opened for signature at New York on 18th December 1979 ("the Hostages Convention");
(f) the Convention on the Physical Protection of Nuclear Material opened for signature at Vienna and New York on 3rd March 1980 ("the Nuclear Material Convention");
(g) the United Nations Convention Against Torture and other Cruel, Inhuman or Degrading Treatment or Punishment adopted by the United Nations General Assembly on 10th December 1984 ("the Torture Convention").
[[(h) the United Nations Convention against Illicit Traffic in Narcotic Drugs and Psychotropic Substances which was signed in Vienna on 20th December 1988 ("the Vienna Convention").]
(i) the Protocol for the Suppression of Unlawful Acts of Violence at Airports Serving International Civil Aviation, supplementary to the Montreal Convention, which was signed at Montreal on 24th February 1988 ("the Montreal Protocol");
(j) the Convention for the Suppression of Unlawful Acts against the Safety

of Maritime Navigation, which was signed at Rome on 10th March 1988 ("the Rome Convention");

(k) the Protocol for the Suppression of Unlawful Acts against the Safety of Fixed Platforms Located on the Continental Shelf, which was also signed at Rome on 10th March 1988 ("the Rome Protocol").]

[(l) the Convention on the Safety of United Nations and Associated Personnel adopted by the General Assembly of the United Nations on 9th December 1994 ("the UN Personnel Convention").]

[(m) the Convention for the Suppression of Terrorist Bombings, which was opened for signature at New York on 12th January 1998 ("the Terrorist Bombings Convention");

(n) the Convention for the Suppression of the Financing of Terrorism which was opened for signature at New York on 10th January 2000 ("the Terrorist Finance Convention").]

(3) Where this section has effect, an Order in Council applying this Act may be made under section 4 above as if a Convention to which this section applies that is specified in the Order constituted general extradition arrangements between the United Kingdom and the foreign state, or any foreign state, party to the Convention; but where this Act is so applied, it shall have effect only in respect—

(a) of the relevant offences;
(b) of an attempt to commit a relevant offence;
(c) of counselling, procuring, commanding, aiding or abetting a relevant offence; and
(d) of being accessory before or after the fact to a relevant offence.

(4) The relevant offences are—

(a) in relation to the Tokyo Convention, any offence committed on board an aircraft in flight;
(b) in relation to the Hague Convention, any offence under or by virtue of section 1 or 6(1) or (2)(a) of the Aviation Security Act 1982;
(c) in relation to the Montreal Convention, any offence under or by virtue of section 2, 3 or 6(2)(b) or (c) of that Act;
(d) in relation to the Internationally Protected Persons Convention—

(i) an offence mentioned in paragraph (a) of subsection (1) of section 1 of the Internationally Protected Persons Act 1978 which is committed against a protected person within the meaning of that section;
(ii) an offence mentioned in paragraph (b) of that subsection which is committed in connection with such an attack as is so mentioned; and
(iii) an offence under section 1(3) of that Act;

(e) in relation to the Hostages Convention, an offence under the Taking of Hostages Act 1982;
(f) in relation to the Nuclear Material Convention—

(i) an offence mentioned in paragraph (a), (b), (c) or (d) of subsection (1) of section 1 of the Nuclear Material (Offences) Act 1983 which is committed by doing an act in relation to or by means of nuclear material; and
(ii) an offence under section 2 of that Act;

(g) in relation to the Torture Convention, torture;
[[(h) in relation to the Vienna Convention—

> (i) any drug trafficking offence within the meaning of the [Drug Trafficking Act 1994;]
>
> (ii) an offence to which section 1 of the Criminal Justice (Scotland) Act 1987 relates; [and]
>
> [(iii) any drug trafficking offence within the meaning of the Proceeds of Crime (Northern Ireland) Order 1996;]]

(i) in relation to the Montreal Protocol, an offence under section 1 of the Aviation and Maritime Security Act 1990;

(j) in relation to the Rome Convention, an offence under section 9 or 12 of that Act or an offence under section 11 or 13 of that Act committed in relation to a ship (within the meaning of Part II of that Act); and

(k) in relation to the Rome Protocol, an offence under section 10 of that Act or an offence under section 11 or 13 of that Act committed in relation to a fixed platform (within the meaning of Part II of that Act).]

[(l) in relation to the UN Personnel Convention—

> (i) an offence mentioned in section 1(2) of the United Nations Personnel Act 1997 which is committed against a UN worker within the meaning of that Act;
>
> (ii) an offence mentioned in subsection (2) of section 2 of that Act which is committed in connection with such an attack as is mentioned in subsection (1) of that section; and
>
> (iii) an offence under section 3 of that Act.]

[(m) in relation to the Terrorist Bombings Convention, an offence, committed as an act of terrorism or for the purposes of terrorism, under—

> (i) section 2, 3 or 5 of the Explosive Substances Act 1883 (causing explosions, &c.),
>
> (ii) section 1 of the Biological Weapons Act 1974 (biological weapons), or
>
> (iii) section 2 of the Chemical Weapons Act 1996 (chemical weapons);

(n) in relation to the Terrorist Finance Convention, an offence under any of sections 15 to 18 of the Terrorism Act 2000 (terrorist property: offences).]

(5) An Order in Council such as is mentioned in subsection (3) above may not provide that a court dealing with a person arrested for an offence shall not be under a duty to determine whether the evidence would be sufficient to [make a case requiring an answer by that person if the proceedings were the summary trial of an information against him].

(6) For the purposes of general extradition procedures under Part III of this Act, in their application (whether or not by virtue of such an Order in Council) as between the United Kingdom and any other state, any act or omission, wherever it takes place, which constitutes—

(a) an offence mentioned in this section; and

(b) an offence against the law of that state;

shall be deemed to be an offence committed within the territory of that state.

(7) Subsections (4) and (5) of section 92 of the Civil Aviation Act 1982 shall apply for the purposes of this section as they apply for the purposes of that section.

(8) Section 98 of that Act shall have effect as if the reference to sections 92 to 95 included a reference to this section.

Genocide, crimes against humanity and war crimes

[**23.**—(1) This section applies to—   **62–019**

(a) any offence that if committed in the United Kingdom would be punishable as—

    (i) an offence under section 51 or 58 of the International Criminal Court Act 2001 (genocide, crimes against humanity and war crimes),

    (ii) an offence under section 52 or 59 of that Act (conduct ancillary to genocide, etc. committed outside the jurisdiction), or

    (iii) an ancillary offence, as defined in section 55 or 62 of that Act, in relation to any such offence as is mentioned in sub-paragraph (i) or (ii); and

(b) any offence punishable in the United Kingdom under section 1 of the Geneva Conventions Act 1957 (grave breach of scheduled conventions).

(2) For the purposes of this Act—

(a) an offence to which this section applies shall not be regarded as an offence of a political character, and

(b) no proceedings in respect of such an offence shall be regarded as a criminal matter of a political character.

(3) It is not an objection to proceedings against a person in respect of an offence to which this section applies that under the law in force at the time when and in the place where he is alleged to have committed the act of which he is accused, or of which he was convicted, he could not have been punished for it.

(4) References in this section to an offence under any provision of the International Criminal Court Act 2001, or to an offence ancillary to such an offence, include any corresponding offence under the law of Scotland.]

¹ Substituted by International Criminal Court Act 2001 (c.17), Pt 5, s. 73(1).

Suppression of terrorism

24.—(1) For the purposes mentioned in subsection (2) below—   **62–020**

(a) no offence to which section 1 of the Suppression of Terrorism Act 1978 applies shall be regarded as an offence of a political character; and

(b) no proceedings in respect of an offence to which that section applies shall be regarded as a criminal matter of a political character or as criminal proceedings of a political character.

(2) Those purposes are the purposes—

(a) of a request for the return of a person in accordance with extradition procedures under Part III of this Act made by a country to which this subsection applies; and

(b) of a requisition under Schedule 1 to this Act which is made by such a country.

(3) Subsection (2) above applies—

(a) to a country for the time being designated in an order made by the Secretary of State as a party to the European Convention on the Suppression of Terrorism signed at Strasbourg on 27th January 1977; and

(b) to a country in relation to which the Secretary of State has made an order under section 5 of the Suppression of Terrorism Act 1978 applying that subsection.

(4) In relation to a requisition under Schedule 1 to this Act which is made by a country to which subsection (2) above applies that Schedule shall have effect as if at the end of paragraph 1(2)(b) there were added—

"or

(c) he proves to the satisfaction of the [District Judge (Magistrates' Courts)] or the court before whom he is brought on habeas corpus, or to the Secretary of State—

    (i) that the requisition for his surrender has in fact been made with a view to try or punish him on account of his race, religion, nationality or political opinions; or

    (ii) that he might, if surrendered, be prejudiced at his trial or punished, detained or restricted in his personal liberty by reason of his race, religion, nationality or political opinions.".

[(5) Subsections (1) and (2) above shall have effect in relation to an offence to which section 22(4)(m) or (n) above applies as they have effect in relation to an offence to which section 1 of the Suppression of Terrorism Act 1978 applies.

(6) For that purpose subsection (2) applies to a country which is a party to—

(a) the Convention for the Suppression of Terrorist Bombings mentioned in section 22(2)(m) above, or

(b) the Convention for the Suppression of the Financing of Terrorism mentioned in section 22(2)(n) above.][1]

[1] Added by Terrorism Act 2000, c.11, Pt VI, s. 64(4).

Hostage-taking

62–021   **25.**—(1) A person shall not be returned under this Act to a designated Commonwealth country which is party to the Convention referred to in subsection (3) below, or committed or kept in custody for the purposes of such return, if it appears to the appropriate authority—

(a) that he might, if returned, be prejudiced at his trial by reason of the impossibility of effecting communications between him and the appropriate authorities of the state entitled to exercise rights of protection in relation to him; and

(b) that the act or omission constituting the offence of which he has been accused or convicted also constituted an offence under section 1 of the Taking of Hostages Act 1982 or an attempt to commit such an offence.

(2) Where the Secretary of State certifies that a country is a party to the Convention, the certificate shall, in any proceedings under this Act, be conclusive evidence of that fact.

(3) The Convention mentioned in subsections (1) and (2) above is the International Convention against the Taking of Hostages opened for signature at New York on 18th December 1979.

Official Secrets Act 1989

(1989, c. 6)

An Act to replace section 2 of the Official Secrets Act 1911 by provisions pro-   **63–001**
tecting more limited classes of official information.   [11th May 1989]

Security and intelligence

1.—(1) A person who is or has been—   **63–002**

    (a) a member of the security and intelligence services; or
    (b) a person notified that he is subject to the provisions of this subsection,

is guilty of an offence if without lawful authority he discloses any information, document or other article relating to security or intelligence which is or has been in his possession by virtue of his position as a member of any of those services or in the course of his work while the notification is or was in force.

(2) The reference in subsection (1) above to disclosing information relating to security or intelligence includes a reference to making any statement which purports to be a disclosure of such information or is intended to be taken by those to whom it is addressed as being such a disclosure.

(3) A person who is or has been a Crown servant or government contractor is guilty of an offence if without lawful authority he makes a damaging disclosure of any information, document or other article relating to security or intelligence which is or has been in his possession by virtue of his position as such but otherwise than as mentioned in subsection (1) above.

(4) For the purposes of subsection (3) above a disclosure is damaging if—

    (a) it causes damage to the work of, or of any part of, the security and intelligence services; or
    (b) it is of information or a document or other article which is such that its unauthorised disclosure would be likely to cause such damage or which falls within a class or description of information, documents or articles the unauthorised disclosure of which would be likely to have that effect.

(5) It is a defence for a person charged with an offence under this section to prove that at the time of the alleged offence he did not know, and had no reasonable cause to believe, that the information, document or article in question related to security or intelligence or, in the case of an offence under subsection (3), that the disclosure would be damaging within the meaning of that subsection.

(6) Notification that a person is subject to subsection (1) above shall be effected by a notice in writing served on him by a Minister of the Crown; and such a notice may be served if, in the Minister's opinion, the work undertaken by the person in question is or includes work connected with the security and intelligence services and its nature is such that the interests of national security require that he should be subject to the provisions of that subsection.

(7) Subject to subsection (8) below, a notification for the purposes of subsection (1) above shall be in force for the period of five years beginning with the day on which it is served but may be renewed by further notices under subsection (6) above for periods of five years at a time.

(8) A notification for the purposes of subsection (1) above may at any time be revoked by a further notice in writing served by the Minister on the person concerned; and the Minister shall serve such a further notice as soon as, in his

opinion, the work undertaken by that person ceases to be such as is mentioned in subsection (6) above.

(9) In this section "security or intelligence" means the work of, or in support of, the security and intelligence services or any part of them, and references to information relating to security or intelligence include references to information held or transmitted by those services or by persons in support of, or of any part of, them.

Defence

63–003   **2.**—(1) A person who is or has been a Crown servant or government contractor is guilty of an offence if without lawful authority he makes a damaging disclosure of any information, document or other article relating to defence which is or has been in his possession by virtue of his position as such.

(2) For the purposes of subsection (1) above a disclosure is damaging if—

    (a) it damages the capability of, or of any part of, the armed forces of the Crown to carry out their tasks or leads to loss of life or injury to members of those forces or serious damage to the equipment or installations of those forces; or

    (b) otherwise than as mentioned in paragraph (a) above, it endangers the interests of the United Kingdom abroad, seriously obstructs the promotion or protection by the United Kingdom of those interests or endangers the safety of British citizens abroad; or

    (c) it is of information or of a document or article which is such that its unauthorised disclosure would be likely to have any of those effects.

(3) It is a defence for a person charged with an offence under this section to prove that at the time of the alleged offence he did not know, and had no reasonable cause to believe, that the information, document or article in question related to defence or that its disclosure would be damaging within the meaning of subsection (1) above.

(4) In this section "defence" means —

    (a) the size, shape, organisation, logistics, order of battle, deployment, operations, state of readiness and training of the armed forces of the Crown;

    (b) the weapons, stores or other equipment of those forces and the invention, development, production and operation of such equipment and research relating to it;

    (c) defence policy and strategy and military planning and intelligence;

    (d) plans and measures for the maintenance of essential supplies and services that are or would be needed in time of war.

International relations

63–004   **3.**—(1) A person who is or has been a Crown servant or government contractor is guilty of an offence if without lawful authority he makes a damaging disclosure of—

    (a) any information, document or other article relating to international relations; or

    (b) any confidential information, document or other article which was obtained from a State other than the United Kingdom or an international organisation, being information or a document or article which is or has been in his possession by virtue of his position as a Crown servant or government contractor.

(2) For the purposes of subsection (1) above a disclosure is damaging if—

    (a) it endangers the interests of the United Kingdom abroad, seriously obstructs the promotion or protection by the United Kingdom of those interests or endangers the safety of British citizens abroad; or

    (b) it is of information or of a document or article which is such that its unauthorised disclosure would be likely to have any of those effects.

(3) In the case of information or a document or article within subsection (1)(b) above—

    (a) the fact that it is confidential, or

    (b) its nature or contents,

may be sufficient to establish for the purposes of subsection (2)(b) above that the information, document or article is such that its unauthorised disclosure would be likely to have any of the effects there mentioned.

(4) It is a defence for a person charged with an offence under this section to prove that at the time of the alleged offence he did not know, and had no reasonable cause to believe, that the information, document or article in question was such as is mentioned in subsection (1) above or that its disclosure would be damaging within the meaning of that subsection.

(5) In this section "international relations" means the relations between States, between international organisations or between one or more States and one or more such organisations and includes any matter relating to a State other than the United Kingdom or to an international organisation which is capable of affecting the relations of the United Kingdom with another State or with an international organisation.

(6) For the purposes of this section any information, document or article obtained from a State or organisation is confidential at any time while the terms on which it was obtained require it to be held in confidence or while the circumstances in which it was obtained make it reasonable for the State or organisation to expect that it would be so held.

Crime and special investigation powers

4.—(1) A person who is or has been a Crown servant or government con-   **63–005**
tractor is guilty of an offence if without lawful authority he discloses any information, document or other article to which this section applies and which is or has been in his possession by virtue of his position as such.

(2) This section applies to any information, document or other article—

    (a) the disclosure of which—

        (i) results in the commission of an offence; or

        (ii) facilitates an escape from legal custody or the doing of any other act prejudicial to the safekeeping of persons in legal custody; or

        (iii) impedes the prevention or detection of offences or the apprehension or prosecution of suspected offenders; or

    (b) which is such that its unauthorised disclosure would be likely to have any of those effects.

(3) This section also applies to—

    (a) any information obtained by reason of the interception of any communication in obedience to a warrant issued under section 2 of the Interception of Communications Act 1985[or under the authority of an interception warrant under section 5 of the Regulation of Investigatory Powers Act 2000][1], any information relating to the obtaining of information by reason of any such interception and any document or other article which is or has been used or held for use in, or has been obtained by reason of, any such interception; and

   (b) any information obtained by reason of action authorised by a warrant issued under section 3 of the Security Service Act 1989 [or under section 5 of the Intelligence Services Act 1994 or by an authorisation given under section 7 of that Act][2], any information relating to the obtaining of information by reason of any such action and any document or other article which is or has been used or held for use in, or has been obtained by reason of, any such action.

(4) It is a defence for a person charged with an offence under this section in respect of a disclosure falling within subsection (2)(a) above to prove that at the time of the alleged offence he did not know, and had no reasonable cause to believe, that the disclosure would have any of the effects there mentioned.

(5) It is a defence for a person charged with an offence under this section in respect of any other disclosure to prove that at the time of the alleged offence he did not know, and had no reasonable cause to believe, that the information, document or article in question was information or a document or article to which this section applies.

(6) In this section "legal custody" includes detention in pursuance of any enactment or any instrument made under an enactment.

[1] Words added by Regulation of Investigatory Powers Act 2000 (c.23), Sched. 4, para. 5.
[2] Words added by Intelligence Services Act 1994 (c.13), Sched. 4, para. 4.

Information resulting from unauthorised disclosures or entrusted in confidence

63–006   **5.**—(1) Subsection (2) below applies where—

   (a) any information, document or other article protected against disclosure by the foregoing provisions of this Act has come into a person's possession as a result of having been—

     (i) disclosed (whether to him or another) by a Crown servant or government contractor without lawful authority; or

     (ii) entrusted to him by a Crown servant or government contractor on terms requiring it to be held in confidence or in circumstances in which the Crown servant or government contractor could reasonably expect that it would be so held; or

     (iii) disclosed (whether to him or another) without lawful authority by a person to whom it was entrusted as mentioned in sub-paragraph (ii) above; and

   (b) the disclosure without lawful authority of the information, document or article by the person into whose possession it has come is not an offence under any of those provisions.

(2) Subject to subsections (3) and (4) below, the person into whose possession the information, document or article has come is guilty of an offence if he discloses it without lawful authority knowing, or having reasonable cause to believe, that it is protected against disclosure by the foregoing provisions of this Act and that it has come into his possession as mentioned in subsection (1) above.

(3) In the case of information or a document or article protected against disclosure by sections 1 to 3 above, a person does not commit an offence under
subsection (2) above unless—

(a) the disclosure by him is damaging; and
(b) he makes it knowing, or having reasonable cause to believe, that it
would be damaging;

and the question whether a disclosure is damaging shall be determined for the
purposes of this subsection as it would be in relation to a disclosure of that
information, document or article by a Crown servant in contravention of section
1(3), 2(1) or 3(1) above.

(4) A person does not commit an offence under subsection (2) above in
respect of information or a document or other article which has come into his
possession as a result of having been disclosed—

(a) as mentioned in subsection (1)(a)(i) above by a government contractor; or
(b) as mentioned in subsection (1)(a)(iii) above,

unless that disclosure was by a British citizen or took place in the United Kingdom, in any of the Channel Islands or in the Isle of Man or a colony.

(5) For the purposes of this section information or a document or article is
protected against disclosure by the foregoing provisions of this Act if—

(a) it relates to security or intelligence, defence or international relations
within the meaning of section 1, 2 or 3 above or is such as is mentioned
in section 3(1)(b) above; or
(b) it is information or a document or article to which section 4 above
applies;

and information or a document or article is protected against disclosure by sections 1 to 3 above if it falls within paragraph (a) above.

(6) A person is guilty of an offence if without lawful authority he discloses
any information, document or other article which he knows, or has reasonable
cause to believe, to have come into his possession as a result of a contravention
of section 1 of the Official Secrets Act 1911.

Information entrusted in confidence to other States or international organisations

6.—(1) This section applies where—   **63–007**

(a) any information, document or other article which—

(i) relates to security or intelligence, defence or international relations; and
(ii) has been communicated in confidence by or on behalf of the
United Kingdom to another State or to an international organisation,

has come into a person's possession as a result of having been disclosed
(whether to him or another) without the authority of that State or organisation or, in the case of an organisation, of a member of it; and
(b) the disclosure without lawful authority of the information, document
or article by the person into whose possession it has come is not an
offence under any of the foregoing provisions of this Act.

(2) Subject to subsection (3) below, the person into whose possession the information, document or article has come is guilty of an offence if he makes a damaging disclosure of it knowing, or having reasonable cause to believe, that it is such as is mentioned in subsection (1) above, that it has come into his possession as there mentioned and that its disclosure would be damaging.

(3) A person does not commit an offence under subsection (2) above if the information, document or article is disclosed by him with lawful authority or has previously been made available to the public with the authority of the State or organisation concerned or, in the case of an organisation, of a member of it.

(4) For the purposes of this section "security or intelligence", "defence" and "international relations" have the same meaning as in section 1, 2 and 3 above and the question whether a disclosure is damaging shall be determined as it would be in relation to a disclosure of the information, document or article in question by a Crown servant in contravention of section 1(3), 2(1) and 3(1) above.

(5) For the purposes of this section information or a document or article is communicated in confidence if it is communicated on terms requiring it to be held in confidence or in circumstances in which the person communicating it could reasonably expect that it would be so held.

Authorised disclosures

63–008   7.—(1) For the purposes of this Act a disclosure by—

  (a) a Crown servant; or
  (b) a person, not being a Crown servant or government contractor, in whose case a notification for the purposes of section 1(1) above is in force,

is made with lawful authority if, and only if, it is made in accordance with his official duty.

(2) For the purposes of this Act a disclosure by a government contractor is made with lawful authority if, and only if, it is made—

  (a) in accordance with an official authorisation; or
  (b) for the purposes of the functions by virtue of which he is a government contractor and without contravening an official restriction.

(3) For the purposes of this Act a disclosure made by any other person is made with lawful authority if, and only if, it is made—

  (a) to a Crown servant for the purposes of his functions as such; or
  (b) in accordance with an official authorisation.

(4) It is a defence for a person charged with an offence under any of the foregoing provisions of this Act to prove that at the time of the alleged offence he believed that he had lawful authority to make the disclosure in question and had no reasonable cause to believe otherwise.

(5) In this section "official authorisation" and "official restriction" mean, subject to subsection (6) below, an authorisation or restriction duly given or imposed by a Crown servant or government contractor or by or on behalf of a prescribed body or a body of a prescribed class.

(6) In relation to section 6 above "official authorisation" includes an authorisation duly given by or on behalf of the State or organisation concerned or, in the case of an organisation, a member of it.

Safeguarding of information

8.—(1) Where a Crown servant or government contractor, by virtue of his **63–009** position as such, has in his possession or under his control any document or other article which it would be an offence under any of the foregoing provisions of this Act for him to disclose without lawful authority he is guilty of an offence if—

(a) being a Crown servant, he retains the document or article contrary to his official duty; or

(b) being a government contractor, he fails to comply with an official direction for the return or disposal of the document or article;

or if he fails to take such care to prevent the unauthorised disclosure of the document or article as a person in his position may reasonably be expected to take.

(2) It is a defence for a Crown servant charged with an offence under subsection (1)(a) above to prove that at the time of the alleged offence he believed that he was acting in accordance with his official duty and had no reasonable cause to believe otherwise.

(3) In subsections (1) and (2) above references to a Crown servant include any person, not being a Crown servant or government contractor, in whose case a notification for the purposes of section 1(1) above is in force.

(4) Where a person has in his possession or under his control any document or other article which it would be an offence under section 5 above for him to disclose without lawful authority, he is guilty of an offence if—

(a) he fails to comply with an official direction for its return or disposal; or

(b) where he obtained it from a Crown servant or government contractor on terms requiring it to be held in confidence or in circumstances in which that servant or contractor could reasonably expect that it would be so held, he fails to take such care to prevent its unauthorised disclosure as a person in his position may reasonably be expected to take.

(5) Where a person has in his possession or under his control any document or other article which it would be an offence under section 6 above for him to disclose without lawful authority, he is guilty of an offence if he fails to comply with an official direction for its return or disposal.

(6) A person is guilty of an offence if he discloses any official information, document or other article which can be used for the purpose of obtaining access to any information, document or other article protected against disclosure by the foregoing provisions of this Act and the circumstances in which it is disclosed are such that it would be reasonable to expect that it might be used for that purposes without authority.

(7) For the purposes of subsection (6) above a person discloses information or a document or article which is official if—

(a) he has or has had it in his possession by virtue of his position as a Crown servant or government contractor; or

(b) he knows or has reasonable cause to believe that a Crown servant or government contractor has or has had it in his possession by virtue of his position as such.

(8) Subsection (5) of section 5 above applies for the purposes of subsection (6) above as it applies for the purposes of that section.

(9) In this section "official direction" means a direction duly given by a

Crown servant or government contractor or by or on behalf of a prescribed body or a body of a prescribed class.

Prosecutions

63–010   9.—(1) Subject to subsection (2) below, no prosecution for an offence under this Act shall be instituted in England and Wales or in Northern Ireland except by or with the consent of the Attorney General or, as the case may be, the Attorney General for Northern Ireland.

(2) Subsection (1) above does not apply to an offence in respect of any such information, document or article as is mentioned in section 4(2) above but no prosecution for such an offence shall be instituted in England and Wales or in Northern Ireland except by or with the consent of the Director of Public Prosecutions or, as the case may be, the Director of Public Prosecutions for Northern Ireland.

Penalties

63–011   10.—(1) A person guilty of an offence under any provision of this Act other than section 8(1), (4) or (5) shall be liable—

    (a) on conviction on indictment, to imprisonment for a term not exceeding two years or a fine or both;

    (b) on summary conviction, to imprisonment for a term not exceeding six months or a fine not exceeding the statutory maximum or both.

(2) A person guilty of an offence under section 8(1), (4) or (5) above shall be liable on summary conviction to imprisonment for a term not exceeding three months or a fine not exceeding level 5 on the standard scale or both.

Arrest, search and trial

63–012   11.—(1) In section 24(2) of the Police and Criminal Evidence Act 1984 (arrestable offences) in paragraph (b) for the words "the Official Secrets Acts 1911 and 1920" there shall be substituted the words "the Official Secrets Act 1920" and after that paragraph there shall be inserted—

"(bb) offences under any provision of the Official Secrets Act 1989 except section 8(1), (4) or (5);".

(2) Offences under any provision of this Act other than section 8(1), (4) or (5) and attempts to commit them shall be arrestable offences within the meaning of section 2 of the Criminal Law Act (Northern Ireland) 1967.

(3) Section 9(1) of the Official Secrets Act 1911 (search warrants) shall have effect as if references to offences under that Act included references to offences under any provision of this Act other than section 8(1), (4) or (5); and the following provisions of the Police and Criminal Evidence Act 1984, that is to say—

    (a) section 9(2) (which excludes items subject to legal privilege and certain other material from powers of search conferred by previous enactments); and

    (b) paragraph 3(b) of Schedule 1 (which prescribes access conditions for the special procedure laid down in that Schedule);

shall apply to section 9(1) of the said Act of 1911 as extended by this subsection as they apply to that section as originally enacted.

(4) Section 8(4) of the Official Secrets Act 1920 (exclusion of public from hearing on grounds of national safety) shall have effect as if references to offences under that Act included references to offences under any provision of this Act other than section 8(1), (4) or (5).

(5) Proceedings for an offence under this Act may be taken in any place in the United Kingdom.

"Crown servant" and "government contractor"

12.—(1) In this Act "Crown servant" means —

63–013

  (a) a Minister of the Crown;
 [(aa) a member of the Scottish Executive or a junior Scottish Minister;]
  (c) any person employed in the civil service of the Crown, including Her Majesty's Diplomatic Service, Her Majesty's Overseas Civil Service, the civil service of Northern Ireland and the Northern Ireland Court Service;
  (d) any member of the naval, military or air forces of the Crown, including any person employed by an association established for the purposes of [Part XI of the Reserve Forces Act 1996];
  (e) any constable and any other person employed or appointed in or for the purposes of any police force (including a police force within the meaning of the [Police (Northern Ireland) Act 1998]) [or of the National Criminal Intelligence Service or the National Crime Squad];
  (f) any person who is a member or employee of a prescribed body or a body of a prescribed class and either is prescribed for the purposes of this paragraph or belongs to a prescribed class of members or employees of any such body;
  (g) any person who is the holder of a prescribed office or who is an employee of such a holder and either is prescribed for the purposes of this paragraph or belongs to a prescribed class of such employees.

(2) In this Act "government contractor" means, subject to subsection (3) below, any person who is not a Crown servant but who provides, or is employed in the provision of, goods or services—

  (a) for the purposes of any Minister or person mentioned in paragraph (a) or (b) of subsection (1) above, [of any office-holder in the Scottish Administration,] of any of the services, forces or bodies mentioned in that subsection or of the holder of any office prescribed under that subsection; or
 [(aa) for the purposes of the National Assembly for Wales;]
  (b) under an agreement or arrangement certified by the Secretary of State as being one to which the government of a State other than the United Kingdom or an international organisation is a party or which is subordinate to, or made for the purposes of implementing, any such agreement or arrangement.

(3) Where an employee or class of employees of any body, or of any holder of an office, is prescribed by an order made for the purposes of subsection (1) above—

  (a) any employee of that body, or of the holder of that office, who is not prescribed or is not within the prescribed class; and
  (b) any person who does not provide, or is not employed in the provision of, goods or services for the purposes of the performance of those

functions of the body or the holder of the office in connection with which the employee or prescribed class of employees is engaged,

shall not be a government contractor for the purposes of this Act.

[(4) In this section "office-holder in the Scottish Administration" has the same meaning as in section 126(7)(a) of the Scotland Act 1998.]

[(5) This Act shall apply to the following as it applies to persons falling within the definition of Crown servant—

(a) the First Minister and deputy First Minister in Northern Ireland; and
(b) Northern Ireland Ministers and junior Ministers.]

Other interpretation provisions

63–014   13.—(1) In this Act—

"disclose" and "disclosure", in relation to a document or other article, include parting with possession of it;
"international organisation" means, subject to subsections (2) and (3) below, an organisation of which only States are members and includes a reference to any organ of such an organisation;
"prescribed" means prescribed by an order made by the Secretary of State;
"State" includes the government of a State and any organ of its government and references to a State other than the United Kingdom include references to any territory outside the United Kingdom.

(2) In section 12(2)(b) above the reference to an international organisation includes a reference to any such organisation whether or not one of which only States are members and includes a commercial organisation.

(3) In determining for the purposes of subsection (1) above whether only States are members of an organisation, any member which is itself an organisation of which only States are members, or which is an organ of such an organisation, shall be treated as a State.

Security Service Act 1989

(1989, c. 5)

64–001   *An Act to place the Security Service on a statutory basis; to enable certain actions to be taken on the authority of warrants issued by the Secretary of State, with provision for the issue of such warrants to be kept under review by a Commissioner; to establish a procedure for the investigation by a Tribunal or, in some cases, by the Commissioner of complaints about the Service; and for connected purposes.*   [27th April 1989]

The Security Service

64–002   1.—(1) There shall continue to be a Security Service (in this Act referred to as "the Service") under the authority of the Secretary of State.

(2) The function of the Service shall be the protection of national security and, in particular, its protection against threats from espionage, terrorism and sabotage, from the activities of agents of foreign powers and from actions

intended to overthrow or undermine parliamentary democracy by political, industrial or violent means.

(3) It shall also be the function of the Service to safeguard the economic well-being of the United Kingdom against threats posed by the actions or intentions of persons outside the British Islands.

[(4) It shall also be the function of the Service to act in support of the activities of police forces [, the National Criminal Intelligence Service, the National Crime Squad] and other law enforcement agencies in the prevention and detection of serious crime.]

[(5) Section 81(5) of the Regulation of Investigatory Powers Act 2000 (meaning of "prevention" and "detection"), so far as it relates to serious crime, shall apply for the purposes of this Act as it applies for the purposes of the provisions of that Act not contained in Chapter I of Part I.][1]

[1] Added by Regulation of Investigatory Powers Act 2000 (c.23), Sched. 4, para. 4(1).

The Director-General

2.—(1) The operations of the Service shall continue to be under the control of a Director-General appointed by the Secretary of State.   **64–003**

(2) The Director-General shall be responsible for the efficiency of the Service and it shall be his duty to ensure—

(a) that there are arrangements for securing that no information is obtained by the Service except so far as necessary for the proper discharge of its functions or disclosed by it except so far as necessary for that purpose or for the purpose of [the prevention or detection of] serious crime [or for the purpose of any criminal proceedings]; and

[(b) that the Service does not take any action to further the interests of any political party; and

(c) that there are arrangements, agreed with [the Director General of the National Criminal Intelligence Service], for co-ordinating the activities of the Service in pursuance of section 1(4) of this Act with the activities of police forces, [the National Criminal Intelligence Service, the National Crime Squad] and other law enforcement agencies.]

(3) The arrangements mentioned in subsection (2)(a) above shall be such as to ensure that information in the possession of the Service is not disclosed for use in determining whether a person should be employed, or continue to be employed, by any person, or in any office or capacity, except in accordance with provision in that behalf approved by the Secretary of State.

[(3A) Without prejudice to the generality of subsection (2)(a) above, the disclosure of information shall be regarded as necessary for the proper discharge of the functions of the Security Service if it consists of—

(a) the disclosure of records subject to and in accordance with the Public Records Act 1958; or

(b) the disclosure, subject to and in accordance with arrangements approved by the Secretary of State, of information to the Comptroller and Auditor General for the purposes of his functions.]

(4) The Director-General shall make an annual report on the work of the Service to the Prime Minister and the Secretary of State and may at any time report to either of them on any matter relating to its work.

Broadcasting Act 1990

(1990, c. 42)

65–001   An Act to make new provision with respect to the provision and regulation of
independent television and sound programme services and of other services
provided on television or radio frequencies; to make provision with respect
to the provision and regulation of local delivery services; to amend in other
respects the law relating to broadcasting and the provision of television
and sound programme services and to make provision with respect to the
supply and use of information about programmes; to make provision with
respect to the transfer of the property, rights and liabilities of the Independent Broadcasting Authority and the Cable Authority and the dissolution of
those bodies; to make new provision relating to the Broadcasting Complaints Commission; to provide for the establishment and functions of a
Broadcasting Standards Council; to amend the Wireless Telegraphy Acts
1949 to 1967 and the Marine, &c., Broadcasting (Offences) Act 1967; to
revoke a class licence granted under the Telecommunications Act 1984 to
run broadcast relay systems; and for connected purposes.

[1st November 1990]

Part I

Independent Television Services

Chapter 1

Regulation by Commission of Television Services Generally

Establishment of Independent Television Commission

The Independent Television Commission

65–002   **1.**—(1) There shall be a commission to be called the Independent Television
Commission (in this Part referred to as "the Commission").
       (2) The Commission shall consist of—

  (a) a chairman and a deputy chairman appointed by the Secretary of State;
      and
  (b) such number of other members appointed by the Secretary of State, not
      being less than eight nor more than ten, as he may from time to time
      determine.

       (3) Schedule 1 to this Act shall have effect with respect to the Commission.

Function of Commission

Regulation by Commission of provision of television services

65–003   **2.**—(1) It shall be the function of the Commission to regulate, in accordance
with this Part [and Part I of the Broadcasting Act 1996], the provision of the
following services, namely—

  (a) television programme services [(other than satellite television services
      and digital programme services)] which are provided from places in
      the United Kingdom by persons other than the BBC and the Welsh
      Authority,

[(b) satellite television services (as defined by section 43(1)) provided by persons other than the BBC and the Welsh Authority,]

(c) additional services which are provided from places in the United Kingdom,

[(d) multiplex services (as defined by section 1(1) of the Broadcasting Act 1996) which are provided from places in the United Kingdom by persons other than the BBC, and

[(e) digital programme services (as defined by section 1(4) of the Broadcasting Act 1996) provided by persons who for the purposes of Council Directive 89/552/EEC are under the jurisdiction of the United Kingdom, other than the BBC and the Welsh Authority,]]

[(f) digital additional services (as defined by section 24(1) of the Broadcasting Act 1996) provided by persons who for the purposes of Council Directive 89/552/EEC are under the jurisdiction of the United Kingdom, other than the BBC.]

and to regulate, in accordance with Part II, the provision of local delivery services (within the meaning of that Part) which are so provided.

(2) It shall be the duty of the Commission—

(a) to discharge their functions under this Part and Part II [and under Part I of the Broadcasting Act 1996] as respects the licensing of the services referred to in subsection (1) in the manner which they consider is best calculated—

(i) to ensure that a wide range of such services is available throughout the United Kingdom, and

(ii) to ensure fair and effective competition in the provision of such services and services connected with them; and

(b) to discharge their functions under this Part [and Part I of the Broadcasting Act 1996] as respects the licensing of television programme services [and multiplex services (as defined by section 1(1) of that Act)] in the manner which they consider is best calculated to ensure the provision of [television programme services] [and multiplex services (as defined by section 1(1) of that Act)] which (taken as a whole) are of high quality and offer a wide range of programmes calculated to appeal to a variety of tastes and interests.

(3) Subsection (2)(a)(ii) shall not be construed as affecting the discharge by the Director General of Fair Trading, the Secretary of State or the [Competition Commission] of any of his or their functions in connection with competition.

(4) In this Part—

"additional service" has the meaning given by section 48(1); and
"television programme service" means—

(a) a television broadcasting service (as defined by subsection (5));

[(b) a restricted service (as defined by section 42A);]

[(c) a satellite television service (as defined by section 43(1));]

(d) a licensable programme service (as defined by section 46(1))[; or]

[(e) a digital programme service (as defined by section 1(4) of the Broadcasting Act 1996).]

(5) In this Part "television broadcasting service" means (subject to subsection (6)) a service consisting in the broadcasting of television programmes for general reception in, or in any area in, the United Kingdom, [but not including a restricted service (as defined by section 42A) [, a satellite television service (as

defined by section 43(1))] or a multiplex service (as defined by section 1(1) of the Broadcasting Act 1996)].

(6) Subsection (5) does not apply to any teletext service or any other service in the case of which the visual images broadcast in the service consist wholly or mainly of non-representational images, that is to say visual images which are neither still pictures nor comprised within sequences of visual images capable of being seen as moving pictures.

. . . . . .

General provisions about licensed services

General requirements as to licensed services

65–004   **6.**—(1) The Commission shall do all that they can to secure that every licensed service complies with the following requirements, namely—

    (a) that nothing is included in its programmes which offends against good taste or decency or is likely to encourage or incite to crime or to lead to disorder or to be offensive to public feeling;

    (b) that any news given (in whatever form) in its programmes is presented with due accuracy and impartiality;

    (c) that due impartiality is preserved on the part of the person providing the service as respects matters of political or industrial controversy or relating to current public policy;

    (d) that due responsibility is exercised with respect to the content of any of its programmes which are religious programmes, and that in particular any such programmes do not involve—

        (i) any improper exploitation of any susceptibilities of those watching the programmes, or

        (ii) any abusive treatment of the religious views and beliefs of those belonging to a particular religious or religious denomination; and

    (e) that its programmes do not include any technical device which, by using images of very brief duration or by any other means, exploits the possibility of conveying a message to, or otherwise influencing the minds of, persons watching the programmes without their being aware, or fully aware, of what has occurred.

(2) In applying subsection (1)(c) a series of programmes may be considered as a whole.

(3) The Commission shall—

    (a) draw up, and from time to time review, a code giving guidance as to the rules to be observed in connection with the application of subsection (1)(c) in relation to licensed services; and

    (b) do all that they can to secure that the provisions of the code are observed in the provision of licensed services;

and the Commission may make different provision in the code for different cases or circumstances.

(4) Without prejudice to the generality of subsection (1), the Commission shall do all that they can to secure that there are excluded from the programmes included in a licensed service all expressions of the views and opinions of the person providing the service on matters (other than the provision of programme

services) which are of political or industrial controversy or relate to current public policy.

(5) The rules specified in the code referred to in subsection (3) shall, in particular, take account of the following matters—

(a) that due impartiality should be preserved on the part of the person providing a licensed service as respects major matters falling within subsection (1)(c) as well as matters falling within that provision taken as a whole; and

(b) the need to determine what constitutes a series of programmes for the purposes of subsection (2).

(6) The rules so specified shall, in addition, indicate to such extent as the Commission consider appropriate—

(a) what due impartiality does and does not require, either generally or in relation to particular circumstances;

(b) the ways in which due impartiality may be achieved in connection with programmes of particular descriptions;

(c) the period within which a programme should be included in a licensed service if its inclusion is intended to secure that due impartiality is achieved for the purposes of subsection (1)(c) in connection with that programme and any programme previously included in that service taken together; and

(d) in relation to any inclusion in a licensed service of a series of programmes which is of a description specified in the rules—

(i) that the dates and times of the other programmes comprised in the series should be announced at the time when the first programme so comprised is included in that service, or

(ii) if that is not practicable, that advance notice should be given by other means of subsequent programmes so comprised which include material intended to secure, or assist in securing, that due impartiality is achieved in connection with the series as a whole;

and those rules shall, in particular, indicate that due impartiality does not require absolute neutrality on every issue or detachment from fundamental democratic principles.

(7) The Commission shall publish the code drawn up under subsection (3), and every revision of it, in such manner as they consider appropriate.

(8) Nothing in this section or in sections 7 to 12 has effect in relation to any licensed service which is an additional service other than [a teletext service].

General code for programmes

7.—(1) The Commission shall draw up, and from time to time review, a code   **65–005**
giving guidance—

(a) as to the rules to be observed with respect to the showing of violence, or the inclusion of sounds suggestive of violence, in programmes included in licensed services, particularly when large numbers of children and young persons may be expected to be watching the programmes;

(b) as to the rules to be observed with respect to the inclusion in such programmes of appeals for donations; and

(c) as to such other matters concerning standards and practice for such programmes as the Commission may consider suitable for inclusion in the code;

and the Commission shall do all that they can to secure that the provisions of the code are observed in the provision of licensed services.

(2) In considering what other matters ought to be included in the code in pursuance of subsection (1)(c), the Commission shall have special regard to programmes included in licensed services in circumstances such that large numbers of children and young persons may be expected to be watching the programmes.

(3) The Commission shall, in drawing up or revising the code under this section, take account of such of the international obligations of the United Kingdom as the Secretary of State may notify to them for the purposes of this subsection.

(4) The Commission shall publish the code drawn up under this section, and every revision of it, in such manner as they consider appropriate.

General provisions as to advertisements

65–006 8.—(1) The Commission shall do all that they can to secure that the rules specified in subsection (2) are complied with in relation to licensed services.

(2) Those rules are as follows—

    (a) a licensed service must not include—

        (i) any advertisement which is inserted by or on behalf of any body whose objects are wholly or mainly of a political nature,

        (ii) any advertisement which is directed towards any political end, or

        (iii) any advertisement which has any relation to any industrial dispute (other than an advertisement of a public service nature inserted by, or on behalf of, a government department);

    (b) in the acceptance of advertisements for inclusion in a licensed service there must be no unreasonable discrimination either against or in favour of any particular advertiser; and

    (c) a licensed service must not, without the previous approval of the Commission, include a programme which is sponsored by any person whose business consists, wholly or mainly, in the manufacture or supply of a product, or in the provision of a service, which the licence holder is prohibited from advertising by virtue of any provision of section 9.

(3) Nothing in subsection (2) shall be construed as prohibiting the inclusion in a licensed service of any party political broadcast which complies with the rules (so far as applicable) made by the Commission for the purposes of section 36.

(4) After consultation with the Commission the Secretary of State may make regulations amending, repealing, or adding to the rules specified in subsection (2); but no such regulations shall be made unless a draft of the regulations has been laid before and approved by a resolution of each House of Parliament.

(5) The Commission shall not act as an advertising agent.

Control of advertisements

65–007 9.—(1) It shall be the duty of the Commission—

    (a) after the appropriate consultation, to draw up, and from time to time review, a code—

(i) governing standards and practice in advertising and in the sponsoring of programmes, and

(ii) prescribing the advertisements and methods of advertising or sponsorship to be prohibited, or to be prohibited in particular circumstances; and

(b) to do all that they can to secure that the provisions of the code are observed in the provision of licensed services;

and the Commission may make different provision in the code for different kinds of licensed services.

(2) In subsection (1) "the appropriate consultation" means consultation with—

(a) the Radio Authority;

(b) every person who is the holder of a licence under this Part;

(c) such bodies or persons appearing to the Commission to represent each of the following, namely—

(i) viewers,

(ii) advertisers, and

(iii) professional organisations qualified to give advice in relation to the advertising of particular products,

as the Commission think fit; and

(d) such other bodies or persons who are concerned with standards of conduct in advertising as the Commission think fit.

(3) The Commission shall publish the code drawn up under this section, and every revision of it, in such manner as they consider appropriate.

(4) The Commission shall—

(a) from time to time consult the Secretary of State as to the classes and descriptions of advertisements which must not be included in licensed services and the methods of advertising or sponsorship which must not be employed in, or in connection with, the provision of such services; and

(b) carry out any directions which he may give to them in respect of such matters.

(5) The Commission may, in the discharge of a general responsibility with respect to advertisements and methods of advertising and sponsorship, impose requirements as to advertisements or methods of advertising or sponsorship which go beyond the requirements imposed by the code.

(6) The methods of control exercisable by the Commission for the purpose of securing that the provisions of the code are complied with, and for the purpose of securing compliance with requirements imposed under subsection (5) which go beyond the requirements of the code, shall include a power to give directions to the holder of a licence—

(a) with respect to the classes and descriptions of advertisements and methods of advertising or sponsorship to be excluded, or to be excluded in particular circumstances, or

(b) with respect to the exclusion of a particular advertisement, or its exclusion in particular circumstances.

(7) The Commission may give directions to persons holding any class of licences with respect to the times when advertisements are to be allowed.

(8) Directions under this section may be, to any degree, either general or specific and qualified or unqualified; and directions under subsection (7) may, in particular, relate to—

(a) the maximum amount of time to be given to advertisements in any hour or other period,

(b) the minimum interval which must elapse between any two periods given over to advertisements and the number of such periods to be allowed in any programme or in any hour or day,

(c) the exclusion of advertisements from a specified part of a licensed service,

and may make different provision for different parts of the day, different days of the week, different types of programmes or for other differing circumstances.

(9) The Commission shall—

(a) in drawing up or revising the code, or

(b) in giving any directions under subsection (7),

take account of such of the international obligations of the United Kingdom as the Secretary of State may notify to them for the purposes of this subsection.

Government control over licensed services

65–008   **10.**—(1) If it appears to him to be necessary or expedient to do so in connection with his functions as such, the Secretary of State or any other Minister of the Crown may at any time by notice require the Commission to direct the holders of any licences specified in the notice to publish in their licensed services, at such times as may be specified in the notice, such announcement as is so specified, with or without visual images of any picture, scene or object mentioned in the announcement; and it shall be the duty of the Commission to comply with the notice.

(2) Where the holder of a licence publishes any announcement in pursuance of a direction under subsection (1), he may announce that he is doing so in pursuance of such a direction.

(3) The Secretary of State may at any time by notice require the Commission to direct the holders of any licences specified in the notice to refrain from including in the programmes included in their licensed services any matter or classes of matter specified in the notice; and it shall be the duty of the Commission to comply with the notice.

(4) Where the Commission—

(a) have given the holder of any licence a direction in accordance with a notice under subsection (3), or

(b) in consequence of the revocation by the Secretary of State of such a notice, have revoked such a direction,

or where such a notice has expired, the holder of the licence in question may publish in the licensed service an announcement of the giving or revocation of the direction or of the expiration of the notice, as the case may be.

(5) The powers conferred by this section are in addition to any power specifically conferred on the Secretary of State by any other provision of this Act.

(6) In relation to any licensed service provided from a place in Northern Ireland, the reference in subsection (1) to a Minister of the Crown includes a reference to the head of any Northern Ireland department.

. . . . . .

Prohibition on providing unlicensed television services

Prohibition on providing television services without a licence

13.—(1) Subject to subsection (2), any person who provides any service fal- **65–009**
ling within [section 2(1)(a), (aa), (b), (c), (cc), or (d)] without being authorised
to do so by or under a licence under this Part [or Part I of the Broadcasting
Act 1996] shall be guilty of an offence.

(2) The Secretary of State may, after consultation with the Commission, by
order provide that subsection (1) shall not apply to such services or descriptions
of services as are specified in the order.

(3) A person guilty of an offence under this section shall be liable—

    (a) on summary conviction, to a fine not exceeding the statutory maximum;
    (b) on conviction on indictment, to a fine.

(4) No proceedings in respect of an offence under this section shall be instituted—

    (a) in England and Wales, except by or with the consent of the Director
       of Public Prosecutions;
    (b) in Northern Ireland, except by or with the consent of the Director of
       Public Prosecutions for Northern Ireland.

(5) Without prejudice to subsection (3), compliance with this section shall be
enforceable by civil proceedings by the Crown for an injunction or interdict or
for any other appropriate relief.

(6) Any order under this section shall be subject to annulment in pursuance
of a resolution of either House of Parliament.

. . . . . .

CHAPTER II

TELEVISION BROADCASTING ON CHANNEL 3, 4 AND 5

Channel 3

Party political broadcasts

36.—(1) Subject to subsection (2), any regional Channel 3 licence or licence **65–010**
to provide Channel 4 or 5 shall include—

    (a) conditions requiring the licence holder to include party political broad-
       casts in the licensed service; and
    (b) conditions requiring the licence holder to observe such rules with
       respect to party political broadcasts as the Commission may determine.

(2) Where any determination under section 28(3) is in force, a licence to
provide Channel 5 may (but need not) include any such conditions as are mentioned in subsection (1)(a) and (b).

(3) Without prejudice to the generality of paragraph (b) of subsection (1) [but
subject to section 37 of the Political Parties, Elections and Referendums Act
2000 (prohibition of broadcasts by unregistered parties)][1], the Commission may
determine for the purposes of that subsection—

    (a) the political parties on whose behalf party political broadcasts may be
       made; and

    (b) in relation to any political party on whose behalf such broadcasts may be made, the length and frequency of such broadcasts.

(4) Any rules made by the Commission for the purposes of this section may make different provision for different cases or circumstances.

[(5) Before making any rules for the purposes of this section the Commission shall have regard to any views expressed by the Electoral Commission.][2]

[1] Words substituted by Political Parties, Elections and Referendums Act 2000 (c.41), Sched. 21, para. 8.
[2] Added by Political Parties, Elections and Referendums Act 2000 (c.41), Pt I, s. 11(1).

Civil Service (Management Functions) Act 1992

(1992, c. 61)

66–001   *An Act to make provision with respect to functions relating to the management of Her Majesty's Home Civil Service; and to make provision about parliamentary procedure in relation to legislation for Northern Ireland making corresponding provision with respect to the Northern Ireland Civil Service.*
                                                        [17th December 1992]

Home Civil Service

Delegation of functions

66–002   **1.**—(1) This section applies to any function delegated by Her Majesty with respect to the management of Her Majesty's Home Civil Service which has been the subject of a transfer of functions Order.

(2) A Minister of the Crown in whom a function to which this section applies is vested may, to such extent and subject to such conditions as he thinks fit, delegate the function to any other servant of the Crown.

(3) Without prejudice to the generality of subsection (2) above, the conditions subject to which a function may be delegated under that subsection include a condition prohibiting, to such extent as may be specified in the condition, the carrying out of the function under the authority of the person to whom it is delegated.

(4) Without prejudice to any rule of law with respect to the carrying out of functions under the authority of a person in charge of a government department, where a function is delegated under subsection (2) above otherwise than to such a person, the person to whom the function is delegated may, subject to the terms of the delegation, authorise a servant of the Crown for whom he is responsible to carry out the function on his behalf.

(5) In this section, "transfer of functions Order" means an Order in Council under section 1 of the Ministers of the Crown (Transfer of Functions) Act 1946 or section 1 of the Ministers of the Crown Act 1975 (transfer of functions from one Minister of the Crown to another).

Power to authorise exercise of functions without approval etc.

66–003   **2.**—(1) This section applies to any statutory power which—

    (a) relates to the appointment or management of members of Her Majesty's Home Civil Service, and

(b) requires for its exercise the sanction of a Minister of the Crown (whether by way of approval, consent, agreement or otherwise).

(2) The Minister whose sanction is required for the exercise of a power to which this section applies may, to such extent and subject to such conditions as he thinks fit, authorise its exercise without his sanction.

(3) Without prejudice to the generality of subsection (2) above, the conditions which may be imposed on an authorisation under that subsection include a condition prohibiting, to such extent as may be specified in the condition, the exercise of the power concerned under the authority of the person by whom it is exercisable.

(4) Where by virtue of any statutory provision the sanction required for the exercise of a power to which this section applies itself requires the sanction (whether by way of approval, consent, agreement or otherwise) of a Minister of the Crown, the power conferred by subsection (2) above shall be exercisable subject to the approval of that Minister.

Local Government Act 1992

(1992, c. 19)

An Act to make new provision, by giving effect to proposals in Cm. 1599 (The **67–001**
Citizen's Charter) relating to publicity and competition, for securing economy, efficiency and effectiveness in the manner in which local authorities carry on certain activities; and to make new provision in relation to local government in England for effecting structural, boundary and electoral changes. [6th March 1992]

PART II

LOCAL GOVERNMENT CHANGES FOR ENGLAND

The Local Government Commission

The Local Government Commission for England

12.—(1) There shall be a body corporate to be known as the Local Govern-   **67–002**
ment Commission for England (in this Part referred to as "the Local Government Commission") for the purpose of carrying out the functions assigned to it by section 13 below.

(2) Schedule 2 to this Act shall have effect with respect to the Local Government Commission.

Functions of the Local Government Commission

Duty to conduct reviews and make recommendations

13.—[(1) The Secretary of State may direct the Local Government Commis-   **67–003**
sion to conduct a review of such areas in England as are specified in the direction or are of a description so specified.

(1AA) A direction under subsection (1) above shall, in respect of each area to which it relates, specify which of the following kinds of changes, namely—

    (a) structural changes,
    (b) boundary changes, and
    (c) electoral changes,

is or are to be considered in the review of that area.

(1A) Where the Secretary of State gives a direction under subsection (1) above requiring the Local Government Commission to conduct any review, the Local Government Commission shall conduct the review in accordance with this Part and any directions given under it and, in respect of each of the areas to which the direction relates, recommend in the case of each kind of changes required to be considered in the review of the area either—

    (a) that the Secretary of State should make such changes of that kind as are specified in the recommendations; or
    (b) that he should make no changes of that kind.]¹

(1B) Recommendations under subsection (1A) above for parish boundary changes may include recommendations for the related alteration of the boundaries of any electoral division of a county or ward of a district and any consequential alteration in the number of councillors to be elected for the ward.

(1C) For the purposes of [subsection (1B)]² above—

    (a) a parish boundary change means a boundary change which is the alteration of the area of a parish, the constitution of a new parish or the abolition of a parish;

(2) It shall also be the duty of the Local Government Commission—

    (a) independently of any reviews under subsection (1) above, to conduct periodic reviews of every principal area in England for the purpose of determining whether recommendations should be made for electoral changes in that area; and
    (b) as respects any area reviewed, to recommend to the Secretary of State either—

        (i) that he should make such electoral changes as are specified in the recommendations; or
        (ii) that he should make no such changes.

(5) Any structural, boundary or electoral changes recommended to the Secretary of State under this section shall be such as appear to the Local Government Commission desirable having regard to the need—

    (a) to reflect the identities and interests of local communities; and
    (b) to secure effective and convenient local government.

(6) The Secretary of State may give directions as to the exercise by the Local Government Commission of any functions under this section; and such directions may require that Commission to have regard to any guidance given by the Secretary of State as respects matters to be taken into account.

---

¹ Substituted by Political Parties, Elections and Referendums Act 2000 (c.41), Sched. 21, para. 9(2).
² Words substituted by Political Parties, Elections and Referendums Act 2000 (c.41), Sched. 21, para. 9(3)(a).

Changes that may be recommended

14.—(1) For the purposes of this Part—

67–004

(a) a structural change is the replacement, in any non-metropolitan area, of the two principal tiers of local government with a single tier;

(b) a boundary change is any of the changes specified in subsection (3) below, whether made for the purpose of facilitating a structural change or independently of any such change; and

(c) an electoral change is a change of electoral arrangements for any local government area, whether made in consequence of any structural or boundary change or independently of any such change;

and recommendations by the Local Government Commission for any structural or boundary changes shall include such recommendations as to the matters mentioned in subsection (5) below as the Commission thinks appropriate in connection with the recommended changes.

(2) In subsection (1)(a) above—

(a) the reference to a non-metropolitan area is a reference to any area which is or, as a result of any recommended boundary change would be, a non-metropolitan county or a non-metropolitan district; and

(b) the reference to the replacement, in any such area, of the two principal tiers of local government with a single tier is a reference to either—

(i) the transfer to a council for a county consisting of that area of the functions in relation to that area of district councils; or

(ii) the transfer to a district council for that area of the functions in relation to that area of a county council.

[(c) the establishment of a parish council for any new parish which would result from any recommended boundary change and the electoral arrangements (as defined in subsection (4)(b) above) for the council.]

(3) The changes mentioned in subsection (1)(b) above are—

(a) the alteration of a local government area, including the alteration of so much of the boundary of any such area as lies below the high-water mark of medium tides, but excluding the extension of any local government area into Wales;

(b) the constitution of a new local government area of any description outside Greater London by the amalgamation of two or more such areas of the like description or by the aggregation of parts of such areas of the like description or by the separation of part of any local government area;

(c) the abolition of a principal area of any description outside Greater London, or of a metropolitan county, and its distribution among other areas of the like description;

(d) the constitution of a new London borough by the amalgamation of two or more London boroughs or by the aggregation of parts of London boroughs or by the separation of part of a London borough;

(e) the abolition of a London borough and the distribution of its area among other London boroughs;

(f) the constitution of a new parish by—

(i) the establishment as a parish of any area which is not a parish or part of one; or

(ii) the aggregation of the whole or any part of any such area with one or more parishes or parts of parishes; and

(g) the abolition of a parish, with or without the distribution of its area among other parishes.

(4) In subsection (1)(c) above "electoral arrangements" means—

(a) in relation to a principal area—

(i) the number of councillors of the council for that area;
(ii) the number and boundaries of the electoral areas into which that area is for the time being divided for the purposes of the election of councillors;
(iii) the number of councillors to be elected for any electoral area in that principal area and the years in which they are to be so elected; and
(iv) the name of any electoral area;

(b) in relation to a parish council—

(i) the number of councillors;
(ii) the question whether or not the parish or (in the case of a common parish council) any of the parishes should be divided into wards for the purposes of the election of councillors;
(iii) the number and boundaries of any such wards;
(iv) the number of councillors to be elected for any such ward or, in the case of a common parish, for each parish; and
(v) the name of any such ward.

(5) The matters mentioned in subsection (1) above are—

(a) the abolition of any local authority whose functions would all vest in another as a result of any recommended structural change or whose area would be abolished or otherwise substantially affected by any recommended boundary change;
(b) the establishment, as a county or district council, of a new authority for any area which would result from any recommended boundary change involving the amalgamation or aggregation of areas or parts of areas or involving other substantial alterations of areas;
(c) the extent to which a structural or boundary change requires (whether because functions become vested in an authority for a smaller area or for any other reason connected with the change) that joint arrangements should be made in relation to functions affected by the change;
(d) whether, in connection with any recommended structural change, any authority should, for the purpose of the vesting of functions under Part II of the Town and Country Planning Act 1990 (development plans) in that authority—

(i) be treated as an authority to whose area Chapter I of that Part (unitary plans) applies, instead of Chapter II (structure and local plans); or
(ii) be authorised to include any of the policies mentioned in section 37 or 38 of that Act (mineral and waste plans) in their local plan.

[(e) Whether, in connection with any recommended structural or boundary change, there should be any change in police areas (including any change resulting in a reduction or increase in the number of police areas)]

(6) For the purposes of this Part the establishment of a new authority as the county or district council for any area shall be taken to include provision, subject to any necessary electoral changes—

(a) for an existing county council to become the district council for any area comprising a part of a county or for any two or more such areas; or

(b) for an existing district council to become the county council for an area comprising any one or more districts.

(7) For the purposes of this section—

(a) a metropolitan district and a non-metropolitan district shall be regarded as local government areas of a like description and so shall a metropolitan county and a non-metropolitan county; and

(b) any county or district resulting from the amalgamation or aggregation of the whole or any part of a metropolitan area with the whole or any part of a non-metropolitan area shall be regarded as a non-metropolitan county or, as the case may be, district.

[(8) Notwithstanding section 6(2)(a) of the Local Government Act 1972, the Local Government Commission may recommend under [section 13(1A) above][1] that an electoral division of a non-metropolitan county should return more than one councillor.][2]

[1] Words substituted by Political Parties, Elections and Referendums Act 2000 (c.41), Sched. 21, para. 10.
[2] Added by Local Government Act 2000 (c.22), Pt IV, s. 89(2).

Procedure on a review

15.—(1) As soon as reasonably practicable after being directed to conduct a **67–005** review, the Local Government Commission shall take such steps as it considers sufficient to secure that persons who may be interested in the review are informed of—

(a) the direction requiring that review to be conducted;

(b) any other directions under this Part which are relevant to the review; and

(c) the period within which representations with respect to the subject-matter of the review may be made.

(2) As soon as reasonably practicable after deciding to conduct a periodic review of any area under section 13(2) above, the Local Government Commission shall take such steps as it considers sufficient to secure that persons who may be interested in the review are informed of—

(a) the fact that the Commission is to conduct a periodic review of that area;

(b) any directions under this Part which are relevant to the review; and

(c) the period within which representations with respect to the subject-matter of the review may be made.

(3) In conducting a review, the Local Government Commission shall—

(a) take into consideration any representations made to it within the period mentioned in subsection (1)(c) or (2)(c) above;

(b) prepare draft recommendations and take such steps as it considers sufficient to secure that persons who may be interested in the recommendations are informed of them and of the period within which representations with respect to them may be made;

    (c) deposit copies of the draft recommendations at the principal office of any principal council [or police authority] appearing to that Commission to be likely to be affected by them; and

    (d) take into consideration any representations made to that Commission within that period.

(4) As soon as the Local Government Commission is in a position to submit to the Secretary of State a report on a review, it shall—

    (a) submit such a report to him together with its recommendations;

    (b) take such steps as it considers sufficient to secure that persons who may be interested in the recommendations are informed of them and of the period within which they may be inspected; and

    (c) deposit copies of the recommendations at the principal office of any principal council [or police authority] appearing to that Commission to be likely to be affected by them.

(5) Copies of any draft recommendations deposited at the principal office of a principal council under subsection (3)(c) above, and of any recommendations deposited at any such office under subsection (4)(c) above, shall be kept available for inspection at that office throughout the period within which representations with respect to them may be made or, as the case may be, within which they may be inspected.

(6) Where the report on a review is submitted to the Secretary of State under subsection (4) above, he may, if he thinks fit, direct the Local Government Commission to conduct a further review of any area to which the report relates and to make revised recommendations as respects that area; and this section shall apply in relation to the further review with such modifications as may be specified in the direction.

(7) The Secretary of State may give directions as to the exercise by the Local Government Commission of any functions under this section; and such directions may require that Commission to have regard to any guidance given by the Secretary of State as respects matters to be taken into account.

(8) This section shall have effect as if the Common Council of the City of London were a principal council and the City of London included the Inner Temple and the Middle Temple.

Implementation of recommendations

Implementation of recommendations by order

67–006   **17.**—(1) Where the Local Government Commission submit to the Secretary of State a report on a review together with its recommendations, he may, if he thinks fit, by order give effect to all or any of the recommendations, with or without modifications.

(2) No order under this section shall be made before the end of the period of six weeks beginning with the submission of the report; and before making such an order, the Secretary of State may by a direction require the Local Government Commission to supply him with such additional information as may be described in the direction.

(3) An order under this section may, in particular, include provision which, for the purpose of giving effect (with or without modifications) to recommendations of the Local Government Commission, makes provision with respect to—

(a) the area of any authority and the name of any such area;
(b) the name of any authority;
(c) the establishment of any new authority for any county or district or the winding up and dissolution of any existing authority;
(d) the total number of councillors of any authority, the apportionment of councillors among electoral areas, the assignment of existing council-lors to new or altered electoral areas, and the first election of council-lors for any new or altered electoral area;
(e) without prejudice to paragraph (d) above, the holding of a fresh elec-tion of councillors for all electoral areas in a local government area where substantial changes have been made to some of those areas, or the order of retirement of councillors for any electoral areas in the local government area in question;
[(f) in the case of an order containing provision for a structural change by which the functions of district councils in relation to any area are trans-ferred to a council for a county consisting of that area, the ordinary year of election and the order of retirement of parish councillors for any parish situated in the area;]
(g) in the case of an order relating to the system of election of district councillors, the ordinary year of election and the order of retirement of parish councillors for any parish situated in the district;
(h) the constitution [, election and membership] of public bodies in any area affected by the order;
(i) the abolition or establishment, or the restriction or extension, of the jurisdiction of any public body in or over any part of any area affected by the order.

(4) The power to make an order under this section shall include power to make any such provision in relation to the other provisions of that order, or to the provisions of any previous order under this section, as is equivalent to that which may be contained in regulations under section 19 below or in an agree-ment under section 20 below.

(5) Without prejudice to the preceding provisions of this section, where char-ter trustees have been constituted under section 246 of the 1972 Act for an area which is altered by an order under this section and subsection (8) of that section (incorporation of whole or part of trustees' area in parish) does not apply, the order may make such provision with respect to the charter trustees as appears to the Secretary of State to be appropriate.

[(6) The Secretary of State shall exercise his power to make orders under this section in relation to police areas in such a way as to ensure that none of the following areas—

(a) a county in which there are no district councils,
(b) a district in any other county, and
(c) a London borough,

is divided between two or more police areas; but this subsection shall not have effect so as to prevent the maintenance of any part of the boundary of the metropolitan police district as it exists [on 1st April 1995].]

[(7) An order under this section may provide for an electoral division of a non-metropolitan county to return more than one councillor; and in such a case section 6(2)(a) of the Local Government Act 1972 shall not apply.]

Trade Union and Labour Relations (Consolidation) Act 1992

(1992, c. 52)

68–001   *An Act to consolidate the enactments relating to collective labour relations, that is to say, to trade unions, employers' associations, industrial relations and industrial action.*   [16th July 1992]

. . . . . .

PART IV

INDUSTRIAL RELATIONS

CHAPTER III

CODES OF PRACTICE

Codes of Practice issued by the Secretary of State

Issue of Codes of Practice by the Secretary of State

68–002   **203.**—(1) The Secretary of State may issue Codes of Practice containing such practical guidance as he thinks fit for the purpose—

    (a) of promoting the improvement of industrial relations, or

    (b) of promoting what appear to him to be to be desirable practices in relation to the conduct by trade unions of ballots and elections.

(2) The Secretary of State may from time to time revise the whole or any part of a Code of Practice issued by him and issue that revised Code.

Procedure for issue of Code by Secretary of State

68–003   **204.**—(1) When the Secretary of State proposes to issue a Code of Practice, or a revised Code, he shall after consultation with ACAS prepare and publish a draft of the Code, shall consider any representations made to him about the draft and may modify the draft accordingly.

(2) If he determines to proceed with the draft, he shall lay it before both Houses of Parliament and, if it is approved by resolution of each House, shall issue the Code in the form of the draft.

(3) A Code issued under this section shall come into effect on such day as the Secretary of State may by order appoint.

The order may contain such transitional provisions or savings as appear to him to be necessary or expedient.

(4) An order under subsection (3) shall be made by statutory instrument, which shall be subject to annulment in pursuance of a resolution of either House of Parliament.

. . . . . .

Revocation of Code issued by Secretary of State

68–004   **206.**—(1) A Code of Practice issued by the Secretary of State may be revoked by him by order made by statutory instrument.

The order may contain such transitional provisions and savings as appear to him to be appropriate.

(2) An order shall not be made under this section unless a draft of it has been laid before and approved by resolution of each House of Parliament.

Supplementary provisions

Effect of failure to comply with Code

207.—(1) A failure on the part of any person to observe any provision of a Code of Practice issued under this Chapter shall not of itself render him liable to any proceedings.

(2) In any proceedings before an [employment tribunal] or the Central Arbitration Committee any Code of Practice issued under this Chapter by ACAS shall be admissible in evidence, and any provision of the Code which appears to the tribunal or Committee to be relevant to any question arising in the proceedings shall be taken into account in determining that question.

(3) In any proceedings before a court or [employment tribunal] or the Central Arbitration Committee any Code of Practice issued under this Chapter by the Secretary of State shall be admissible in evidence, and any provision of the Code which appears to the court, tribunal or Committee to be relevant to any question arising in the proceedings shall be taken into account in determining that question.

68–005

. . . . . .

PART V

INDUSTRIAL ACTION

Protection of acts in contemplation or furtherance of trade dispute

Peaceful picketing

220.—(1) It is lawful for a person in contemplation or furtherance of a trade dispute to attend—

(a) at or near his own place of work, or

(b) if he is an official of a trade union, at or near the place of work of a member of the union whom he is accompanying and whom he represents,

for the purpose only of peacefully obtaining or communicating information, or peacefully persuading any person to work or abstain from working.

(2) If a person works or normally works—

(a) otherwise than at any one place, or

(b) at a place the location of which is such that attendance there for a purpose mentioned in subsection (1) is impracticable,

his place of work for the purposes of that subsection shall be any premises of his employer from which he works or from which his work is administered.

(3) In the case of a worker not in employment where—

(a) his last employment was terminated in connection with a trade dispute, or

68–006

(b) the termination of his employment was one of the circumstances giving rise to a trade dispute,

in relation to that dispute his former place of work shall be treated for the purposes of subsection (1) as being his place of work.

(4) A person who is an official of a trade union by virtue only of having been elected or appointed to be a representative of some of the members of the union shall be regarded for the purposes of subsection (1) as representing only those members; but otherwise an official of a union shall be regarded for those purposes as representing all its members.

. . . . . .

Criminal offences

Intimidation or annoyance by violence or otherwise

68–007   **241.**—(1) A person commits an offence who, with a view to compelling another person to abstain from doing or to do any act which that person has a legal right to do or abstain from doing, wrongfully and without legal authority—

(a) uses violence to or intimidates that person or his wife or children, or injures his property,
(b) persistently follows that person about from place to place,
(c) hides any tools, clothes or other property owned or used by that person, or deprives him of or hinders him in the use thereof,
(d) watches or besets the house or other place where that person resides, works, carries on business or happens to be, or the approach to any such house or place, or
(e) follows that person with two or more other persons in a disorderly manner in or through any street or road.

(2) A person guilty of an offence under this section is liable on summary conviction to imprisonment for a term not exceeding six months or a fine not exceeding level 5 on the standard scale, or both.

(3) A constable may arrest without warrant anyone he reasonably suspects is committing an offence under this section.

Tribunals and Inquiries Act 1992

(1992, c. 53)

69–001   *An Act to consolidate the Tribunals and Inquiries Act 1971 and certain other enactments relating to tribunals and inquiries.*   [16th July 1992]

The Council on Tribunals and their functions

The Council on Tribunals

69–002   **1.**—(1) There shall continue to be a council entitled the Council on Tribunals (in this Act referred to as "the Council")—

(a) to keep under review the constitution and working of the tribunals specified in Schedule 1 (being the tribunals constituted under or for the purposes of the statutory provisions specified in that Schedule) and, from time to time, to report on their constitution and working;

(b) to consider and report on such particular matters as may be referred to the Council under this Act with respect to tribunals other than the ordinary courts of law, whether or not specified in Schedule 1, or any such tribunal; and

(c) to consider and report on such matters as may be referred to the Council under this Act, or as the Council may determine to be of special importance, with respect to administrative procedures involving, or which may involve, the holding by or on behalf of a Minister of a statutory inquiry, or any such procedure.

(2) Nothing in this section authorises or requires the Council to deal with any matter with respect to which the Parliament of Northern Ireland had power to make laws.

Composition of the Council and the Scottish Committee

2.—(1) Subject to subsection (3), the Council shall consist of not more than fifteen nor less than ten members appointed by the Lord Chancellor and the [Scottish Ministers], and one of the members shall be so appointed to be chairman of the Council.   **69–003**

(2) There shall be a Scottish Committee of the Council (in this Act referred to as "the Scottish Committee") which, subject to subsection (3), shall consist of—

(a) either two or three members of the Council designated by the [Scottish Ministers], and

(b) either three or four persons, not being members of the Council, appointed by the [Scottish Ministers];

and the [Scottish Ministers] shall appoint one of the members of the Scottish Committee (being a member of the Council) to be chairman of the Scottish Committee.

(3) In addition to the persons appointed or designated under subsection (1) or (2), the Parliamentary Commissioner for Administration shall, by virtue of his office, be a member of the Council and of the Scottish Committee.

(4) In appointing members of the Council regard shall be had to the need for representation of the interests of persons in Wales.

. . . . . .

Composition and procedure of tribunals and inquiries

Recommendations of Council as to appointment of members of tribunals

5.—(1) Subject to section 6 but without prejudice to the generality of section 1(1)(a), the Council may make to the appropriate Minister general recommendations as to the making of appointments to membership of any tribunals mentioned in Schedule 1 or of panels constituted for the purposes of any such tribunals; and (without prejudice to any statutory provisions having effect with respect to such appointments) the appropriate Minister shall have regard to recommendations under this section.   **69–004**

(2) In this section "the appropriate Minister", in relation to appointments of

any description, means the Minister making the appointments or, if they are not made by a Minister, the Minister in charge of the government department concerned with the tribunals in question.

(3) The following provisions shall have effect as respects any tribunal specified in Part II of Schedule 1—

(a) the Council shall not make any recommendations under this section until—

(i) they have referred the matter of the recommendations for consideration, and report to the Council, by the Scottish Committee, and

(ii) they have considered the report of that Committee,

(b) without prejudice to the generality of section 4(5), the Scottish Committee may of its own motion propose any such general recommendations as expedient to be made by the Council to the appropriate Minister, and

(c) if the Council—

(i) in making recommendations under this section on any matter which they have referred to the Scottish Committee or on which that Committee has made proposals, do not adopt the report or proposals of that Committee without modification, or

(ii) do not make recommendations on matters on which the Scottish Committee has made proposals to the Council,

the Scottish Committee may submit its report or proposals to the [Scottish Ministers].

Appointment of chairmen of certain tribunals

69–005 **6.**—(1) The chairman, or any person appointed to act as chairman, of any of the tribunals to which this subsection applies shall (without prejudice to any statutory provisions as to qualifications) be selected by the appropriate authority from a panel of persons appointed by the Lord Chancellor.

(2) Members of panels constituted under this section shall hold and vacate office under the terms of the instruments under which they are appointed, but may resign office by notice in writing to the Lord Chancellor; and any such member who ceases to hold office shall be eligible for re-appointment.

(3) Subsection (1) applies to any tribunal specified in [paragraph 7(b) or 38(a)][1] of Schedule 1.

(4) [. . .][2]

(5) The person or persons constituting any tribunal specified in paragraph 31 of Schedule 1 shall be appointed by the Lord Chancellor, and where such a tribunal consists of more than one person the Lord Chancellor shall designate which of them is to be the chairman.

(6) In this section, "the appropriate authority" means the Minister who apart from this Act would be empowered to appoint or select the chairman, person to act as chairman, members or member of the tribunal in question.

(7) A panel may be constituted under this section for the purposes either of a single tribunal or of two or more tribunals, whether or not of the same description.

(8) In relation to any of the tribunals referred to in this section which sits in Scotland, this section shall have effect with the substitution for any reference to the Lord Chancellor of a reference to the Lord President of the Court of Session.

(9) In relation to any of the tribunals referred to in this section which sits in Northern Ireland, this section shall have effect with the substitution for any

reference to the Lord Chancellor of a reference to the Lord Chief Justice of Northern Ireland.

¹ Words repealed by Social Security Act 1998 (c.14), Sched. 7, para. 118(1).
² Repealed by Social Security Act 1998 (c.14), Sched. 8, para. 1.

Concurrence required for removal of members of certain tribunals

7.—(1) Subject to subsection (2), the power of a Minister, other than the Lord Chancellor, to terminate a person's membership of any tribunal specified in Schedule 1, or of a panel constituted for the purposes of any such tribunal, shall be exercisable only with the consent of—

    (a) the Lord Chancellor, the Lord President of the Court of Session and the Lord Chief Justice of Northern Ireland, if the tribunal sits in all parts of the United Kingdom;
    (b) the Lord Chancellor and the Lord President of the Court of Session, if the tribunal sits in all parts of Great Britain;
    (c) the Lord Chancellor and the Lord Chief Justice of Northern Ireland, if the tribunal sits both in England and Wales and in Northern Ireland;
    (d) the Lord Chancellor, if the tribunal does not sit outside England and Wales;
    (e) the Lord President of the Court of Session, if the tribunal sits only in Scotland;
    (f) the Lord Chief Justice of Northern Ireland, if the tribunal sits only in Northern Ireland.

69–006

(2) This section does not apply to any tribunal specified in paragraph 3, 12, 14, 17, 18, 26, 33(a), 34, 35(d) or (e), 36(a), 39(b), 40, 43, 48 [, 56(a) or 57A] of Schedule 1.

(3) For the purposes of this section in its application to any tribunal specified in paragraph 22(a) of Schedule 1, an adjudicator who has sat only in England and Wales, who has sat only in Scotland or who has sat only in Northern Ireland shall be deemed to constitute a tribunal which does not sit outside England and Wales, which sits only in Scotland or which sits only in Northern Ireland, as the case may be.

Procedural rules for tribunals

8.—(1) The power of a Minister, the Lord President of the Court of Session, the Commissioners of Inland Revenue or the Foreign Compensation Commission to make, approve, confirm or concur in procedural rules for any tribunal specified in Schedule 1 shall be exercisable only after consultation with the Council.

69–007

(3) The Council shall consult the Scottish Committee in relation to the exercise of their functions under this section[with respect to any tribunal specified in Part 2 of Schedule 1.]

(4) In this section "procedural rules" includes any statutory provision relating to the procedure of the tribunal in question.

Procedure in connection with statutory inquiries

9.—(1) The Lord Chancellor, after consultation with the Council, may make rules regulating the procedure to be followed in connection with statutory inquiries held by or on behalf of Ministers; and different provision may be made by any such rules in relation to different classes of such inquiries.

69–008

(2) Any rules made by the Lord Chancellor under this section shall have

effect, in relation to any statutory inquiry, subject to the provisions of the enactment under which the inquiry is held, and of any rules or regulations made under that enactment.

(3) Subject to subsection (2), rules made under this section may regulate procedure in connection with matters preparatory to such statutory inquiries as are mentioned in subsection (1), and in connection with matters subsequent to such inquiries, as well as in connection with the conduct of proceedings at such inquiries.

(4) In the application of this section to inquiries held in Scotland—

> (a) for any reference to the Lord Chancellor there shall be substituted a reference to the Lord Advocate, and
> (b) the Council, in exercising their functions under this section in relation to rules to be made by the Lord Advocate, shall consult with the Scottish Committee.

Judicial control of tribunals etc.

Reasons to be given for decisions of tribunals and Ministers

69–009   **10.**—(1) Subject to the provisions of this section and of section 14, where—

> (a) any tribunal specified in Schedule 1 gives any decision, or
> (b) any Minister notifies any decision taken by him—
>
>> (i) after a statutory inquiry has been held by him or on his behalf, or
>> (ii) in a case in which a person concerned could (whether by objecting or otherwise) have required a statutory inquiry to be so held,

it shall be the duty of the tribunal or Minister to furnish a statement, either written or oral, of the reasons for the decision if requested, on or before the giving or notification of the decision, to state the reasons.

(2) The statement referred to in subsection (1) may be refused, or the specification of the reasons restricted, on grounds of national security.

(3) A tribunal or Minister may refuse to furnish a statement under subsection (1) to a person not primarily concerned with the decision if of the opinion that to furnish it would be contrary to the interests of any person primarily concerned.

(4) Subsection (1) does not apply to any decision taken by a Minister after the holding by him or on his behalf of an inquiry or hearing which is a statutory inquiry by virtue only of an order made under section 16(2) unless the order contains a direction that this section is to apply in relation to any inquiry or hearing to which the order applies.

(5) Subsection (1) does not apply—

> (a) to decisions in respect of which any statutory provision has effect, apart from this section, as to the giving of reasons;
> (b) to decisions of a Minister in connection with the preparation, making, approval, confirmation, or concurrence in regulations, rules or byelaws, or orders or schemes of a legislative and not executive character; or
> [(ba) to decisions of the Pensions Compensation Board referred to in paragraph 35(h) of Schedule 1.]

(6) Any statement of the reasons for a decision referred to in paragraph (a) or (b) of subsection (1), whether given in pursuance of that subsection or of any other statutory provision, shall be taken to form part of the decision and accordingly to be incorporated in the record.

(7) If, after consultation with the Council, it appears to the Lord Chancellor that it is expedient that—

(a) decisions of any particular tribunal or any description of such decisions, or
(b) any description of decisions of a Minister,

should be excluded from the operation of subsection (1) on the ground that the subject-matter of such decisions, or the circumstances in which they are made, make the giving of reasons unnecessary or impracticable, the Lord Chancellor may by order direct that subsection (1) shall not apply to such decisions.

(8) Where an order relating to any decisions has been made under subsection (7), the Lord Chancellor may, by a subsequent order made after consultation with the Council, revoke or vary the earlier order so that subsection (1) applies to any of those decisions.

. . . . . .

Supervisory functions of superior courts not excluded by Acts passed before 1st August 1958

12.—(1) As respects England and Wales—   **69–010**

(a) any provision in an Act passed before 1st August 1958 that any order or determination shall not be called into question in any court, or
(b) any provision in such an Act which by similar words excludes any of the powers of the High Court,

shall not have effect so as to prevent the removal of the proceedings into the High Court by order of certiorari or to prejudice the powers of the High Court to make orders of mandamus.

(2) As respects Scotland—

(a) any provision in an Act passed before 1st August 1958 that any order or determination shall not be called into question in any court, or
(b) any provision in such an Act which by similar words excludes any jurisdiction which the Court of Session would otherwise have to entertain an application for reduction or suspension of any order or determination, or otherwise to consider the validity of any order or determination,

shall not have effect so as to prevent the exercise of any such jurisdiction.

(3) Nothing in this section shall apply—

(a) to any order or determination of a court of law, or
(b) where an Act makes special provision for application to the High Court or the Court of Session within a time limited by the Act.

European Communities (Amendment) Act 1993

(1993, c. 32)

70–001 *An Act to make provision consequential on the Treaty on European Union signed at Maastricht on 7th February 1992.* [20th July 1993]

Treaty on European Union

70–002 **1.**—(1) In section 1(2) of the European Communities Act 1972, in the definition of "the Treaties" and "the Community Treaties", after paragraph (j) (inserted by the European Communities (Amendment) Act 1986) there shall be inserted the words—

> "and
>
> (k) Titles II, III and IV of the Treaty on European Union signed at Maastricht on 7th February 1992, together with the other provisions of the Treaty so far as they relate to those Titles, and the Protocols adopted at Maastricht on that date and annexed to the Treaty establishing the European Community with the exception of the Protocol on Social Policy on page 117 of Cm 1934".

(2) For the purpose of section 6 of the European Parliamentary Elections Act 1978 (approval of treaties increasing the Parliament's powers) the Treaty on European Union signed at Maastricht on 7th February 1992 is approved.

Economic and monetary union

70–003 **2.** No notification shall be given to the Council of the European Communities that the United Kingdom intends to move to the third stage of economic and monetary union (in accordance with the Protocol on certain provisions relating to the United Kingdom adopted at Maastricht on 7th February 1992) unless a draft of the notification has first been approved by Act of Parliament and unless Her Majesty's Government has reported to Parliament on its proposals for the co-ordination of economic policies, its role in the European Council of Finance Ministers (ECOFIN) in pursuit of the objectives of Article 2 of the Treaty establishing the European Community as provided for in Articles 103 and 102a, and the work of the European Monetary Institute in preparation for economic and monetary union.

Criminal Justice and Public Order Act 1994

(1994, c. 33)

71–001 *An Act to make further provision in relation to criminal justice (including employment in the prison service); to amend or extend the criminal law and powers for preventing crime and enforcing that law; to amend the Video Recordings Act 1984; and for purposes connected with those purposes.* [3rd November 1994]

. . . . . .

PART II

BAIL

No bail for defendants charged with or convicted of homicide or rape after previous conviction of such offences

25.—(1) A person who in any proceedings has been charged with or convicted **71–002** of an offence to which this section applies in circumstances to which it applies [shall be granted bail in those proceedings only if the court or, as the case may be, the constable considering the grant of bail is satisfied that there are exceptional circumstances which justify it][1].

(2) This section applies, subject to subsection (3) below, to the following offences, that is to say—

    (a) murder;
    (b) attempted murder;
    (c) manslaughter;
    (d) rape; or
    (e) attempted rape.

(3) This section applies to a person charged with or convicted of any such offence only if he has been previously convicted by or before a court in any part of the United Kingdom of any such offence or of culpable homicide and, in the case of a previous conviction of manslaughter or of culpable homicide, if he was then sentenced to imprisonment or, if he was then a child or young person, to long-term detention under any of the relevant enactments.

(4) This section applies whether or not an appeal is pending against conviction or sentence.

(5) In this section—

"conviction" includes—

    (a) a finding that a person is not guilty by reason of insanity;
    (b) a finding under section 4A(3) of the Criminal Procedure (Insanity) Act 1964 (cases of unfitness to plead) that a person did the act or made the omission charged against him; and
    (c) a conviction of an offence for which an order is made placing the offender on probation or discharging him absolutely or conditionally;

and "convicted" shall be construed accordingly; and
"the relevant enactments" means—

    (a) as respects England and Wales, [section 91 of the Powers of Criminal Courts (Sentencing) Act 2000][2];
    [(b) as respects Scotland, sections 205(1) to (3) and 208 of the Criminal Procedure (Scotland) Act 1995;][3]
    (c) as respects Northern Ireland, section 73(2) of the Children and Young Persons Act (Northern Ireland) 1968.

(6) This section does not apply in relation to proceedings instituted before its commencement.

---

[1] Words substituted by Crime and Disorder Act 1998 (c.37), Pt III, s. 56.
[2] Words substituted by Powers of Criminal Courts (Sentencing) Act 2000 (c.6), Sched. 9, para. 160.
[3] Substituted by Criminal Procedure (Consequential Provisions) (Scotland) Act 1995 (c.40), Sched. 4, para. 93(2).

PART III

COURSE OF JUSTICE: EVIDENCE, PROCEDURE, ETC.

Corroboration

Abolition of corroboration rules

71–003   **32.**—(1) Any requirement whereby at a trial on indictment it is obligatory for the court to give the jury a warning about convicting the accused on the uncorroborated evidence of a person merely because that person is—

> (a) an alleged accomplice of the accused, or
> (b) where the offence charged is a sexual offence, the person in respect of whom it is alleged to have been committed,

is hereby abrogated.

(2) In section 34(2) of the Criminal Justice Act 1988 (abolition of requirement of corroboration warning in respect of evidence of a child) the words from "in relation to" to the end shall be omitted.

(3) Any requirement that—

> (a) is applicable at the summary trial of a person for an offence, and
> (b) corresponds to the requirement mentioned in subsection (1) above or that mentioned in section 34(2) of the Criminal Justice Act 1988,

is hereby abrogated.

(4) Nothing in this section applies in relation to—

> (a) any trial, or
> (b) any proceedings before a magistrates' court as examining justices,

which began before the commencement of this section.

Inferences from accused's silence

Effect of accused's failure to mention facts when questioned or charged

71–004   **34.**—(1) Where, in any proceedings against a person for an offence, evidence is given that the accused—

> (a) on being questioned under caution by a [service policeman] trying to discover whether or by whom the offence had been committed, [or during the taking of evidence as a preliminary to the trial of the offence by court-martial,] failed to mention any fact relied on in his defence in those proceedings; or
> (b) on being charged [by a service policeman] with the offence or officially informed [by a service policeman] that he might be prosecuted for it, failed to mention any such fact,

being a fact which in the circumstances existing at the time the accused could reasonably have been expected to mention when so questioned, charged or informed, as the case may be, subsection (2) below applies.

(2) Where this subsection applies—

> [(a) a magistrates' court inquiring into the offence as examining justices;][1]

(b) a judge, in deciding whether to grant an application made by the accused under—

> (i) section 6 of the Criminal Justice Act 1987 (application for dismissal of charge of serious fraud in respect of which notice of transfer has been given under section 4 of that Act; or
> (ii) paragraph 5 of Schedule 6 to the Criminal Justice Act 1991 (application for dismissal of charge of violent or sexual offence involving child in respect of which notice of transfer has been given under section 53 of that Act);

(c) the court, in determining whether there is a case to answer; and
(d) the court, in determining whether the accused is guilty of the offence charged,

may draw such inferences from the failure as appear proper.

(3) Subject to any directions by the court, evidence tending to establish the failure may be given before or after evidence tending to establish the fact which the accused is alleged to have failed to mention.

(4) This section applies in relation to questioning by persons (other than constables) charged with the duty of investigating offences or charging offenders as it applies in relation to questioning by constables; and in subsection (1) above "officially informed" means informed by a constable or any such person.

(5) This section does not—

(a) prejudice the admissibility in evidence of the silence or other reaction of the accused in the face of anything said in his presence relating to the conduct in respect of which he is charged, in so far as evidence thereof would be admissible apart from this section; or
(b) preclude the drawing of any inference from any such silence or other reaction of the accused which could properly be drawn apart from this section.

(6) This section does not apply in relation to a failure to mention a fact if the failure occurred before [the coming into force of the 1997 Order].

(7) [. . .]²

¹ Substituted by Criminal Procedure and Investigations Act 1996 (c.25), Pt V, s. 44(3).
² Repealed by Criminal Procedure and Investigations Act 1996 (c.25), Sched. 5, para. 1.

Effect of accused's silence at trial

35.—(1) At the trial of any person [. . .]¹ for an offence, subsections (2) and **71–005**
(3) below apply unless—

(a) the accused's guilt is not in issue; or
(b) it appears to the court that the physical or mental condition of the accused makes it undesirable for him to give evidence;

but subsection (2) below does not apply if, at the conclusion of the evidence for the prosecution, his [representative] informs the court that the accused will give evidence or, where he is unrepresented, the court ascertains from him that he will give evidence.

(2) Where this subsection applies, the court shall, at the conclusion of the evidence for the prosecution, satisfy itself that the accused is aware that the stage has been reached at which evidence can be given for the defence and that he can, if he wishes, give evidence and that, if he chooses not to give evidence, or having been sworn, without good cause refuses to answer any question, it

will be permissible for the court to draw such inferences as appear proper from his failure to give evidence or his refusal, without good cause, to answer any question.

(3) Where this subsection applies, the court, in determining whether the accused is guilty of the offence charged, may draw such inferences as appear proper from the failure of the accused to give evidence or his refusal, without good cause, to answer any question.

(4) This section does not render the accused compellable to give evidence on his own behalf, and he shall accordingly not be guilty of contempt of court by reason of a failure to do so.

(5) For the purposes of this section a person who, having been sworn, refuses to answer any question shall be taken to do so without good cause unless—

(a) he is entitled to refuse to answer the question by virtue of any enactment, whenever passed or made, or on the ground of privilege; or
(b) the court in the exercise of its general discretion excuses him from answering it.

(6) [. . .]²
(7) This section applies—

(a) [only if the time when the court begins to receive evidence in the proceedings falls after the coming into force of the 1997 Order];
(b) in relation to proceedings in a magistrates' court, only if the time when the court begins to receive evidence in the proceedings falls after the commencement of this section.

¹ Words repealed by Crime and Disorder Act 1998 (c.37), Sched. 10, para. 1.
² Repealed by Crime and Disorder Act 1998 (c.37), Sched. 10, para. 1.

Effect of accused's failure or refusal to account for objects, substances or marks

71–006 36.—(1) Where—

(a) a person is arrested by a [service policeman], and there is—

(i) on his person; or
(ii) in or on his clothing or footwear; or
(iii) otherwise in his possession; or
(iv) in any place in which he is at the time of his arrest,

any object, substance or mark, or there is any mark on any such object; and
(b) that or another [service policeman] investigating the case reasonably believes that the presence of the object, substance or mark may be attributable to the participation of the person arrested in the commission of an offence specified by the [service policeman]; and
(c) the [service policeman] informs the person arrested that he so believes, and requests him to account for the presence of the object, substance or mark; and
(d) the person fails or refuses to do so,

then if, in any proceedings against the person for the offence so specified, evidence of those matters is given, subsection (2) below applies.

(2) Where this subsection applies—

[(a) a magistrates' court inquiring into the offence as examining justices;]¹

(b) a judge, in deciding whether to grant an application made by the accused under—

  (i) section 6 of the Criminal Justice Act 1987 (application for dismissal of charge of serious fraud in respect of which notice of transfer has been given under section 4 of that Act); or

  (ii) paragraph 5 of Schedule 6 to the Criminal Justice Act 1991 (application for dismissal of charge of violent or sexual offence involving child in respect of which notice of transfer has been given under section 53 of that Act);

(c) the court, in determining whether there is a case to answer; and

(d) the court, in determining whether the accused is guilty of the offence charged,

may draw such inferences from the failure or refusal as appear proper.

(3) Subsections (1) and (2) above apply to the condition of clothing or footwear as they apply to a substance or mark thereon.

(4) Subsections (1) and (2) above do not apply unless the accused was told in ordinary language by the when making the request mentioned in subsection (1)(c) above what the effect of this section would be if he failed or refused to comply with the request.

(5) This section applies in relation to officers of customs and excise as it applies in relation to constables.

(6) This section does not preclude the drawing of any inference from a failure or refusal of the accused to account for the presence of an object, substance or mark or from the condition of clothing or footwear which could properly be drawn apart from this section.

(7) This section does not apply in relation to a failure or refusal which occurred before [the coming into force of the 1997 Order].

(8) [. . .]²

---

¹ Substituted by Criminal Procedure and Investigations Act 1996 (c.25), Pt V, s. 44(3).
² Repealed by Criminal Procedure and Investigations Act 1996 (c.25), Sched. 5, para. 1.

Effect of accused's failure or refusal to account for presence at a particular place

37.—(1) Where—   **71–007**

(a) a person arrested by a [service policeman] was found by him at a place at or about the time the offence for which he was arrested is alleged to have been committed; and

(b) that or another [service policeman] investigating the offence reasonably believes that the presence of the person at that place and at that time may be attributable to his participation in the commission of the offence; and

(c) the [service policeman] informs the person that he so believes, and requests him to account for that presence; and

(d) the person fails or refuses to do so,

then if, in any proceedings against the person for the offence, evidence of those matters is given, subsection (2) below applies.

(2) Where this subsection applies—

  [(a) a magistrates' court inquiring into the offence as examining justices;.]¹
  (b) a judge, in deciding whether to grant an application made by the accused under—

(i) section 6 of the Criminal Justice Act 1987 (application for dismissal of charge of serious fraud in respect of which notice of transfer has been given under section 4 of that Act); or

(ii) paragraph 5 of Schedule 6 to the Criminal Justice Act 1991 (application for dismissal of charge of violent or sexual offence involving child in respect of which notice of transfer has been given under section 53 of that Act);

(c) the court, in determining whether there is a case to answer; and

(d) the court, in determining whether the accused is guilty of the offence charged,

may draw such inferences from the failure or refusal as appear proper.

(3) Subsections (1) and (2) do not apply unless the accused was told in ordinary language by the [service policeman] when making the request mentioned in subsection (1)(c) above what the effect of this section would be if he failed or refused to comply with the request.

(4) This section applies in relation to officers of customs and excise as it applies in relation to constables.

(5) This section does not preclude the drawing of any inference from a failure or refusal of the accused to account for his presence at a place which could properly be drawn apart from this section.

(6) This section does not apply in relation to a failure or refusal which occurred before [the coming into force of the 1997 Order].

(7) [. . .][2]

---

[1] Substituted by Criminal Procedure and Investigations Act 1996 (c.25), Pt V, s. 44(3).
[2] Repealed by Criminal Procedure and Investigations Act 1996 (c.25), Sched. 5, para. 1.

Juries

. . . . . .

PART IV

POLICE POWERS

Powers of police to stop and search

Powers to stop and search in anticipation of violence

71–008   **60.**—[(1) If a police officer of or above the rank of inspector reasonably believes—

(a) that incidents involving serious violence may take place in any locality in his police area, and that it is expedient to give an authorisation under this section to prevent their occurrence, or

(b) that persons are carrying dangerous instruments or offensive weapons in any locality in his police area without good reason,

he may give an authorisation that the powers conferred by this section are to be exercisable at any place within that locality for a specified period not exceeding 24 hours.]

(3) If it appears to [an officer of or above the rank of] superintendent that it is expedient to do so, having regard to offences which have, or are reasonably suspected to have, been committed in connection with any [activity] falling

within the authorisation, he may direct that the authorisation shall continue in being for a further [24] hours.

[(3A) If an inspector gives an authorisation under subsection (1) he must, as soon as it is practicable to do so, cause an officer of or above the rank of superintendent to be informed.]

(4) This section confers on any constable in uniform power—

(a) to stop any pedestrian and search him or anything carried by him for offensive weapons or dangerous instruments;

(b) to stop any vehicle and search the vehicle, its driver and any passenger for offensive weapons or dangerous instruments.

(c) [. . .]¹

(5) A constable may, in the exercise of [the powers conferred by subsection (4) above]², stop any person or vehicle and make any search he thinks fit whether or not he has any grounds for suspecting that the person or vehicle is carrying weapons or articles of that kind.

(6) If in the course of a search under this section a constable discovers a dangerous instrument or an article which he has reasonable grounds for suspecting to be an offensive weapon, he may seize it.

(7) This section applies (with the necessary modifications) to ships, aircraft and hovercraft as it applies to vehicles.

(8) [A person who fails—

(a) to stop, or to stop a vehicle[. . .]³ [,]⁴

(b) [. . .]⁵

when required to do so by a constable in the exercise of his powers under this section shall be liable on summary conviction to imprisonment for a term not exceeding one month or to a fine not exceeding level 3 on the standard scale or both.]⁶

(9) Any authorisation under this section shall be in writing signed by the officer giving it and shall specify [the grounds on which it is given and] the locality in which and the period during which the powers conferred by this section are exercisable and a direction under subsection (3) above shall also be given in writing or, where that is not practicable, recorded in writing as soon as it is practicable to do so.

[(9A) The preceding provisions of this section, so far as they relate to an authorisation by a member of the British Transport Police Force (including one who for the time being has the same powers and privileges as a member of a police force for a police area), shall have effect as if the references to a locality in his police area were references to any locality in or in the vicinity of any policed premises, or to the whole or any part of any such premises.]⁷

(10) Where a vehicle is stopped by a constable under this section, the driver shall be entitled to obtain a written statement that the vehicle was stopped under the powers conferred by this section if he applies for such a statement not later than the end of the period of twelve months from the day on which the vehicle was stopped as respects a pedestrian who is stopped and searched under this section.

[(10A) A person who is searched by a constable under this section shall be entitled to obtain a written statement that he was searched under the powers conferred by this section if he applies for such a statement not later than the end of the period of twelve months from the day on which he was searched.]

(11) In this section—

["British Transport Police Force" means the constables appointed under section 53 of the British Transport Commission Act 1949;]⁸

"dangerous instruments" means instruments which have a blade or are sharply pointed;

"offensive weapon" has the meaning given by section 1(9) of the Police and Criminal Evidence Act 1984 [or, in relation to Scotland, section 47(4) of the Criminal Law (Consolidation) (Scotland) Act 1995]; and

["policed premises", in relation to England and Wales, has the meaning given by section 53(3) of the British Transport Commission Act 1949 and, in relation to Scotland, means those places where members of the British Transport Police Force have the powers, protection and privileges of a constable under section 53(4)(a) of that Act (as it relates to Scotland);][9]

"vehicle" includes a caravan as defined in section 29(1) of the Caravan Sites and Control of Development Act 1960.

[(11A) For the purposes of this section, a person carries a dangerous instrument or an offensive weapon if he has it in his possession.]

(12) The powers conferred by this section are in addition to and not in derogation of, any power otherwise conferred.

---

[1] Repealed by Anti-terrorism, Crime and Security Act 2001 (c.24), Sched. 8(6), para. 1.
[2] Words substituted by Crime and Disorder Act 1998 (c.37), Pt I, c.III, s.25(2).
[3] Repealed by Anti-terrorism, Crime and Security Act 2001 (c.24), Sched. 8(6), para. 1.
[4] *ibid.*
[5] *ibid.*
[6] Words substituted and new paragraphs created by Crime and Disorder Act 1998 (c.37), Pt I, c.III, s.25(3).
[7] Added by Anti-terrorism, Crime and Security Act 2001 (c.24), Sched. 7, para. 16(2).
[8] Definition inserted by Anti-terrorism, Crime and Security Act 2001 (c.24), Sched. 7, para. 16(3)(a).
[9] Definition inserted by Anti-terrorism, Crime and Security Act 2001 (c.24), Sched. 7, para. 16(3)(b).

PART V

PUBLIC ORDER: COLLECTIVE TRESPASS OR NUISANCE ON LAND

Powers to remove trespassers on land

Power to remove trespassers on land

71–009   **61.**—(1) If the senior police officer present at the scene reasonably believes that two or more persons are trespassing on land and are present there with the common purpose of residing there for any period, that reasonable steps have been taken by or on behalf of the occupier to ask them to leave and—

(a) that any of those persons has caused damage to the land or to property on the land or used threatening, abusive or insulting words or behaviour towards the occupier, a member of his family or an employee or agent of his, or

(b) that those persons have between them six or more vehicles on the land,

he may direct those persons, or any of them, to leave the land and to remove any vehicles or other property they have with them on the land.

(2) Where the persons in question are reasonably believed by the senior police officer to be persons who were not originally trespassers but have become trespassers on the land, the officer must reasonably believe that the other conditions specified in subsection (1) are satisfied after those persons became trespassers before he can exercise the power conferred by that subsection.

(3) A direction under subsection (1) above, if not communicated to the persons referred to in subsection (1) by the police officer giving the direction, may be communicated to them by any constable at the scene.

(4) If a person knowing that a direction under subsection (1) above has been given which applies to him—

(a) fails to leave the land as soon as reasonably practicable, or
(b) having left again enters the land as a trespasser within the period of three months beginning with the day on which the direction was given,

he commits an offence and is liable on summary conviction to imprisonment for a term not exceeding three months or a fine not exceeding level 4 on the standard scale, or both.

(5) A constable in uniform who reasonably suspects that a person is committing an offence under this section may arrest him without a warrant.

(6) In proceedings for an offence under this section it is a defence for the accused to show—

(a) that he was not trespassing on the land, or
(b) that he had a reasonable excuse for failing to leave the land as soon as reasonably practicable or, as the case may be, for again entering the land as a trespasser.

(7) In its application in England and Wales to common land this section has effect as if in the preceding subsections of it—

(a) references to trespassing or trespassers were references to acts and persons doing acts which constitute either a trespass as against the occupier or an infringement of the commoners' rights; and
(b) references to "the occupier" included the commoners or any of them or, in the case of common land to which the public has access, the local authority as well as any commoner.

(8) Subsection (7) above does not—

(a) require action by more than one occupier; or
(b) constitute persons trespassers as against any commoner or the local authority if they are permitted to be there by the other occupier.

(9) In this section—

"common land" means common land as defined in section 22 of the Commons Registration Act 1965;
"commoner" means a person with rights of common as defined in section 22 of the Commons Registration Act 1965;
"land" does not include—

(a) buildings other than—

(i) agricultural buildings within the meaning of, in England and Wales, paragraphs 3 to 8 of Schedule 5 to the Local Government Finance Act 1988 or, in Scotland, section 7(2) of the Valuation and Rating (Scotland) Act 1956, or
(ii) scheduled monuments within the meaning of the Ancient Monuments and Archaeological Areas Act 1979;

(b) land forming part of—

(i) a highway unless it falls within the classifications in section 54 of the Wildlife and Countryside Act 1981 (footpath, bridleway or byway open to all traffic or road used as a public path) or is a cycle track under the Highways Act 1980 or the Cycle Tracks Act 1984; or

(ii) a road within the meaning of the Roads (Scotland) Act 1984 unless it falls within the definitions in section 151(2)(a)(ii) or (b) (footpaths and cycle tracks) of that Act or is a bridleway within the meaning of section 47 of the Countryside (Scotland) Act 1967;

"the local authority", in relation to common land, means any local authority which has powers in relation to the land under section 9 of the Commons Registration Act 1965;

"occupier" (and in subsection (8) "the other occupier") means—

(a) in England and Wales, the person entitled to possession of the land by virtue of an estate or interest held by him; and

(b) in Scotland, the person lawfully entitled to natural possession of the land;

"property", in relation to damage to property on land, means—

(a) in England and Wales, property within the meaning of section 10(1) of the Criminal Damage Act 1971; and

(b) in Scotland, either—

(i) heritable property other than land; or

(ii) corporeal movable property; and

"damage" includes the deposit of any substance capable of polluting the land;

"trespass" means, in the application of this section—

(a) in England and Wales, subject to the extensions effected by subsection (7) above, trespass as against the occupier of the land;

(b) in Scotland, entering, or as the case may be remaining on, land without lawful authority and without the occupier's consent; and

"trespassing" and "trespasser" shall be construed accordingly;

"vehicle" includes—

(a) any vehicle, whether or not it is in a fit state for use on roads, and includes any chassis or body, with or without wheels, appearing to have formed part of such a vehicle, and any load carried by, and anything attached to, such a vehicle; and

(b) a caravan as defined in section 29(1) of the Caravan Sites and Control of Development Act 1960;

and a person may be regarded for the purposes of this section as having a purpose of residing in a place notwithstanding that he has a home elsewhere.

Supplementary powers of seizure

71–010   **62.**—(1) If a direction has been given under section 61 and a constable reasonably suspects that any person to whom the direction applies has, without reasonable excuse—

(a) failed to remove any vehicle on the land which appears to the constable to belong to him or to be in his possession or under his control; or

(b) entered the land as a trespasser with a vehicle within the period of three months beginning with the day on which the direction was given,

the constable may seize and remove that vehicle.

(2) In this section "trespasser" and "vehicle" have the same meaning as in section 61.

Powers in relation to raves

Powers to remove persons attending or preparing for a rave

63.—(1) This section applies to a gathering on land in the open air of 100 or more persons (whether or not trespassers) at which amplified music is played during the night (with or without intermissions) and is such as, by reason of its loudness and duration and the time at which it is played, is likely to cause serious distress to the inhabitants of the locality; and for this purpose—

71–011

  (a) such a gathering continues during intermissions in the music and, where the gathering extends over several days, throughout the period during which amplified music is played at night (with or without intermissions); and
  (b) "music" includes sounds wholly or predominantly characterised by the emission of a succession of repetitive beats.

(2) If, as respects any land in the open air, a police officer of at least the rank of superintendent reasonably believes that—

  (a) two or more persons are making preparations for the holding there of a gathering to which this section applies,
  (b) ten or more persons are waiting for such a gathering to begin there, or
  (c) ten or more persons are attending such a gathering which is in progress,

he may give a direction that those persons and any other persons who come to prepare or wait for or to attend the gathering are to leave the land and remove any vehicles or other property which they have with them on the land.

(3) A direction under subsection (2) above, if not communicated to the persons referred to in subsection (2) by the police officer giving the direction, may be communicated to them by any constable at the scene.

(4) Persons shall be treated as having had a direction under subsection (2) above communicated to them if reasonable steps have been taken to bring it to their attention.

(5) A direction under subsection (2) above does not apply to an exempt person.

(6) If a person knowing that a direction has been given which applies to him—

  (a) fails to leave the land as soon as reasonably practicable, or
  (b) having left again enters the land within the period of 7 days beginning with the day on which the direction was given,

he commits an offence and is liable on summary conviction to imprisonment for a term not exceeding three months or a fine not exceeding level 4 on the standard scale, or both.

(7) In proceedings for an offence under this section it is a defence for the accused to show that he had a reasonable excuse for failing to leave the land as soon as reasonably practicable or, as the case may be, for again entering the land.

(8) A constable in uniform who reasonably suspects that a person is committing an offence under this section may arrest him without a warrant.

(9) This section does not apply—

(a) in England and Wales, to a gathering licensed by an entertainment licence; or

(b) in Scotland, to a gathering in premises which, by virtue of section 41 of the Civic Government (Scotland) Act 1982, are licensed to be used as a place of public entertainment.

(10) In this section—

"entertainment licence" means a licence granted by a local authority under—

(a) Schedule 12 to the London Government Act 1963;

(b) section 3 of the Private Places of Entertainment (Licensing) Act 1967; or

(c) Schedule 1 to the Local Government (Miscellaneous Provisions) Act 1982;

"exempt person", in relation to land (or any gathering on land), means the occupier, any member of his family and any employee or agent of his and any person whose home is situated on the land;

"land in the open air" includes a place partly open to the air;

"local authority" means—

(a) in Greater London, a London borough council or the Common Council of the City of London;

(b) in England outside Greater London, a district council or the council of the Isles of Scilly;

(c) in Wales, a county council or county borough council; and

"occupier", "trespasser" and "vehicle" have the same meaning as in section 61.

(11) Until 1st April 1996, in this section "local authority" means, in Wales, a district council.

Supplementary powers of entry and seizure

71–012   **64.**—(1) If a police officer of at least the rank of superintendent reasonably believes that circumstances exist in relation to any land which would justify the giving of a direction under section 63 in relation to a gathering to which that section applies he may authorise any constable to enter the land for any of the purposes specified in subsection (2) below.

(2) Those purposes are—

(a) to ascertain whether such circumstances exist; and

(b) to exercise any power conferred on a constable by section 63 or subsection (4) below.

(3) A constable who is so authorised to enter land for any purpose may enter the land without a warrant.

(4) If a direction has been given under section 63 and a constable reasonably suspects that any person to whom the direction applies has, without reasonable excuse—

(a) failed to remove any vehicle or sound equipment on the land which appears to the constable to belong to him or to be in his possession or under his control; or

(b) entered the land as a trespasser with a vehicle or sound equipment within the period of 7 days beginning with the day on which the direction was given,

the constable may seize and remove that vehicle or sound equipment.

(5) Subsection (4) above does not authorise the seizure of any vehicle or sound equipment of an exempt person.

(6) In this section—

"exempt person" has the same meaning as in section 63;
"sound equipment" means equipment designed or adapted for amplifying music and any equipment suitable for use in connection with such equipment, and "music" has the same meaning as in section 63; and
"vehicle" has the same meaning as in section 61.

Raves: power to stop persons from proceeding

65.—(1) If a constable in uniform reasonably believes that a person is on his way to a gathering to which section 63 applies in relation to which a direction under section 63(2) is in force, he may, subject to subsections (2) and (3) below—

71–013

   (a) stop that person, and
   (b) direct him not to proceed in the direction of the gathering.

(2) The power conferred by subsection (1) above may only be exercised at a place within 5 miles of the boundary of the site of the gathering.

(3) No direction may be given under subsection (1) above to an exempt person.

(4) If a person knowing that a direction under subsection (1) above has been given to him fails to comply with that direction, he commits an offence and is liable on summary conviction to a fine not exceeding level 3 on the standard scale.

(5) A constable in uniform who reasonably suspects that a person is committing an offence under this section may arrest him without a warrant.

(6) In this section, "exempt person" has the same meaning as in section 63.

Power of court to forfeit sound equipment

66.—(1) Where a person is convicted of an offence under section 63 in relation to a gathering to which that section applies and the court is satisfied that any sound equipment which has been seized from him under section 64(4), or which was in his possession or under his control at the relevant time, has been used at the gathering the court may make an order for forfeiture under this subsection in respect of that property.

71–014

(2) The court may make an order under subsection (1) above whether or not it also deals with the offender in respect of the offence in any other way and without regard to any restrictions on forfeiture in any enactment.

(3) In considering whether to make an order under subsection (1) above in respect of any property a court shall have regard—

   (a) to the value of the property; and
   (b) to the likely financial and other effects on the offender of the making of the order (taken together with any other order that the court contemplates making).

(4) An order under subsection (1) above shall operate to deprive the offender

of his rights, if any, in the property to which it relates, and the property shall (if not already in their possession) be taken into the possession of the police.

(5) Except in a case to which subsection (6) below applies, where any property has been forfeited under subsection (1) above, a magistrates' court may, on application by a claimant of the property, other than the offender from whom it was forfeited under subsection (1) above, make an order for delivery of the property to the applicant if it appears to the court that he is the owner of the property.

(6) In a case where forfeiture under subsection (1) above has been by order of a Scottish court, a claimant such as is mentioned in subsection (5) above may, in such manner as may be prescribed by act of adjournal, apply to that court for an order for the return of the property in question.

(7) No application shall be made under subsection (5), or by virtue of subsection (6), above by any claimant of the property after the expiration of 6 months from the date on which an order under subsection (1) above was made in respect of the property.

(8) No such application shall succeed unless the claimant satisfies the court either that he had not consented to the offender having possession of the property or that he did not know, and had no reason to suspect, that the property was likely to be used at a gathering to which section 63 applies.

(9) An order under subsection (5), or by virtue of subsection (6), above shall not affect the right of any person to take, within the period of 6 months from the date of an order under subsection (5), or as the case may be by virtue of subsection (6), above, proceedings for the recovery of the property from the person in possession of it in pursuance of the order, but on the expiration of that period the right shall cease.

(10) The Secretary of State may make regulations for the disposal of property, and for the application of the proceeds of sale of property, forfeited under subsection (1) above where no application by a claimant of the property under subsection (5), or by virtue of subsection (6), above has been made within the period specified in subsection (7) above or no such application has succeeded.

(11) The regulations may also provide for the investment of money and for the audit of accounts.

(12) The power to make regulations under subsection (10) above shall be exercisable by statutory instrument which shall be subject to annulment in pursuance of a resolution of either House of Parliament.

(13) In this section—

"relevant time", in relation to a person—

    (a) convicted in England and Wales of an offence under section 63, means the time of his arrest for the offence or of the issue of a summons in respect of it;

    (b) so convicted in Scotland, means the time of his arrest for, or of his being cited as an accused in respect of, the offence;

"sound equipment" has the same meaning as in section 64.

Retention and charges for seized property

Retention and charges for seized property

71–015   **67.**—(1) Any vehicles which have been seized and removed by a constable under section 62(1) or 64(4) may be retained in accordance with regulations made by the Secretary of State under subsection (3) below.

(2) Any sound equipment which has been seized and removed by a constable under section 64(4) may be retained until the conclusion of proceedings against the person from whom it was seized for an offence under section 63.

(3) The Secretary of State may make regulations—

(a) regulating the retention and safe keeping and the disposal and the destruction in prescribed circumstances of vehicles; and
(b) prescribing charges in respect of the removal, retention, disposal and destruction of vehicles.

(4) Any authority shall be entitled to recover from a person from whom a vehicle has been seized such charges as may be prescribed in respect of the removal, retention, disposal and destruction of the vehicle by the authority.

(5) Regulations under subsection (3) above may make different provisions for different classes of vehicles or for different circumstances.

(6) Any charges under subsection (4) above shall be recoverable as a simple contract debt.

(7) Any authority having custody of vehicles under regulations under subsection (3) above shall be entitled to retain custody until any charges under subsection (4) are paid.

(8) The power to make regulations under subsection (3) above shall be exercisable by statutory instrument which shall be subject to annulment in pursuance of a resolution of either House of Parliament.

(9) In this section—

"conclusion of proceedings" against a person means—

(a) his being sentenced or otherwise dealt with for the offence or his acquittal;
(b) the discontinuance of the proceedings; or
(c) the decision not to prosecute him,
whichever is the earlier;

"sound equipment" has the same meaning as in section 64, and
"vehicle" has the same meaning as in section 61.

Disruptive trespassers

Offence of aggravated trespass

68.—(1) A person commits the offence of aggravated trespass if he trespasses **71–016** on land in the open air and, in relation to any lawful activity which persons are engaging in or are about to engage in on that or adjoining land in the open air, does there anything which is intended by him to have the effect—

(a) of intimidating those persons or any of them so as to deter them or any of them from engaging in that activity,
(b) of obstructing that activity, or
(c) of disrupting that activity.

(2) Activity on any occasion on the part of a person or persons on land is "lawful" for the purposes of this section if he or they may engage in the activity on the land on that occasion without committing an offence or trespassing on the land.

(3) A person guilty of an offence under this section is liable on summary conviction to imprisonment for a term not exceeding three months or a fine not exceeding level 4 on the standard scale, or both.

(4) A constable in uniform who reasonably suspects that a person is committing an offence under this section may arrest him without a warrant.

(5) In this section "land" does not include—

    (a) the highways and roads excluded from the application of section 61 by paragraph (b) of the definition of land in subsection (9) of that section; or

    (b) a road within the meaning of the Roads (Northern Ireland) Order 1993.

Powers to remove persons committing or participating in aggravated trespass

71–017   **69.**—(1) If the senior police officer present at the scene reasonably believes—

    (a) that a person is committing, has committed or intends to commit the offence of aggravated trespass on land in the open air; or

    (b) that two or more persons are trespassing on land in the open air and are present there with the common purpose of intimidating persons so as to deter them from engaging in a lawful activity or of obstructing or disrupting a lawful activity,

he may direct that person or (as the case may be) those persons (or any of them) to leave the land.

(2) A direction under subsection (1) above, if not communicated to the persons referred to in subsection (1) by the police officer giving the direction, may be communicated to them by any constable at the scene.

(3) If a person knowing that a direction under subsection (1) above has been given which applies to him—

    (a) fails to leave the land as soon as practicable, or

    (b) having left again enters the land as a trespasser within the period of three months beginning with the day on which the direction was given,

he commits an offence and is liable on summary conviction to imprisonment for a term not exceeding three months or a fine not exceeding level 4 on the standard scale, or both.

(4) In proceedings for an offence under subsection (3) it is a defence for the accused to show—

    (a) that he was not trespassing on the land, or

    (b) that he had a reasonable excuse for failing to leave the land as soon as practicable or, as the case may be, for again entering the land as a trespasser.

(5) A constable in uniform who reasonably suspects that a person is committing an offence under this section may arrest him without a warrant.

(6) In this section "lawful activity" and "land" have the same meaning as in section 68.

. . . . . .

Squatters

Interim possession orders: false or misleading statements

71–018   **75.**—(1) A person commits an offence if, for the purpose of obtaining an interim possession order, he—

    (a) makes a statement which he knows to be false or misleading in a material particular; or

    (b) recklessly makes a statement which is false or misleading in a material particular.

(2) A person commits an offence if, for the purpose of resisting the making of an interim possession order, he—

    (a) makes a statement which he knows to be false or misleading in a material particular; or

    (b) recklessly makes a statement which is false or misleading in a material particular.

(3) A person guilty of an offence under this section shall be liable—

    (a) on conviction on indictment, to imprisonment for a term not exceeding two years or a fine or both;

    (b) on summary conviction, to imprisonment for a term not exceeding six months or a fine not exceeding the statutory maximum or both.

(4) In this section—

    "interim possession order" means an interim possession order (so entitled) made under rules of court for the bringing of summary proceedings for possession of premises which are occupied by trespassers;

    "premises" has the same meaning as in Part II of the Criminal Law Act 1977 (offences relating to entering and remaining on property); and

    "statement", in relation to an interim possession order, means any statement, in writing or oral and whether as to fact or belief, made in or for the purposes of the proceedings.

Interim possession orders: trespassing during currency of order

76.—(1) This section applies where an interim possession order has been **71–019** made in respect of any premises and served in accordance with rules of court; and references to "the order" and "the premises" shall be construed accordingly.

(2) Subject to subsection (3), a person who is present on the premises as a trespasser at any time during the currency of the order commits an offence.

(3) No offence under subsection (2) is committed by a person if—

    (a) he leaves the premises within 24 hours of the time of service of the order and does not return; or

    (b) a copy of the order was not fixed to the premises in accordance with rules of court.

(4) A person who was in occupation of the premises at the time of service of the order but leaves them commits an offence if he re-enters the premises as a trespasser or attempts to do so after the expiry of the order but within the period of one year beginning with the day on which it was served.

(5) A person guilty of an offence under this section shall be liable on summary conviction to imprisonment for a term not exceeding six months or a fine not exceeding level 5 on the standard scale or both.

(6) A person who is in occupation of the premises at the time of service of the order shall be treated for the purposes of this section as being present as a trespasser.

(7) A constable in uniform may arrest without a warrant anyone who is, or whom he reasonably suspects to be, guilty of an offence under this section.

(8) In this section—

    "interim possession order" has the same meaning as in section 75 above and "rules of court" is to be construed accordingly; and "premises" has the same meaning as in that section that is to say the same meaning as in Part II of the Criminal Law Act 1977 (offences relating to entering and remaining on property).

Powers to remove unauthorised campers

Power of local authority to direct unauthorised campers to leave land

71–020   **77.**—(1) If it appears to a local authority that persons are for the time being residing in a vehicle or vehicles within that authority's area—

(a) on any land forming part of a highway;
(b) on any other unoccupied land; or
(c) on any occupied land without the consent of the occupier,

the authority may give a direction that those persons and any others with them are to leave the land and remove the vehicle or vehicles and any other property they have with them on the land.

(2) Notice of a direction under subsection (1) must be served on the persons to whom the direction applies, but it shall be sufficient for this purpose for the direction to specify the land and (except where the direction applies to only one person) to be addressed to all occupants of the vehicles on the land, without naming them.

(3) If a person knowing that a direction under subsection (1) above has been given which applies to him—

(a) fails, as soon as practicable, to leave the land or remove from the land any vehicle or other property which is the subject of the direction, or
(b) having removed any such vehicle or property again enters the land with a vehicle within the period of three months beginning with the day on which the direction was given,

he commits an offence and is liable on summary conviction to a fine not exceeding level 3 on the standard scale.

(4) A direction under subsection (1) operates to require persons who re-enter the land within the said period with vehicles or other property to leave and remove the vehicles or other property as it operates in relation to the persons and vehicles or other property on the land when the direction was given.

(5) In proceedings for an offence under this section it is a defence for the accused to show that his failure to leave or to remove the vehicle or other property as soon as practicable or his re-entry with a vehicle was due to illness, mechanical breakdown or other immediate emergency.

(6) In this section—

"land" means land in the open air;
"local authority" means—

(a) in Greater London, a London borough or the Common Council of the City of London;
(b) in England outside Greater London, a county council, a district council or the Council of the Isles of Scilly;
(c) in Wales, a county council or a county borough council;

"occupier" means the person entitled to possession of the land by virtue of an estate or interest held by him;
"vehicle" includes—

(a) any vehicle, whether or not it is in a fit state for use on roads, and includes any body, with or without wheels, appearing to have formed part of such a vehicle, and any load carried by, and anything attached to, such a vehicle; and

(b) a caravan as defined in section 29(1) of the Caravan Sites and Control of Development Act 1960;

and a person may be regarded for the purposes of this section as residing on any land notwithstanding that he has a home elsewhere.

(7) Until 1st April 1996, in this section "local authority" means, in Wales, a county council or a district council.

Orders for removal of persons and their vehicles unlawfully on land

78.—(1) A magistrates' court may, on a complaint made by a local authority, if satisfied that persons and vehicles in which they are residing are present on land within that authority's area in contravention of a direction given under section 77, make an order requiring the removal of any vehicle or other property which is so present on the land and any person residing in it.   **71–021**

(2) An order under this section may authorise the local authority to take such steps as are reasonably necessary to ensure that the order is complied with and, in particular, may authorise the authority, by its officers and servants—

(a) to enter upon the land specified in the order; and

(b) to take, in relation to any vehicle or property to be removed in pursuance of the order, such steps for securing entry and rendering it suitable for removal as may be so specified.

(3) The local authority shall not enter upon any occupied land unless they have given to the owner and occupier at least 24 hours notice of their intention to do so, or unless after reasonable inquiries they are unable to ascertain their names and addresses.

(4) A person who wilfully obstructs any person in the exercise of any power conferred on him by an order under this section commits an offence and is liable on summary conviction to a fine not exceeding level 3 on the standard scale.

(5) Where a complaint is made under this section, a summons issued by the court requiring the person or persons to whom it is directed to appear before the court to answer to the complaint may be directed—

(a) to the occupant of a particular vehicle on the land in question; or

(b) to all occupants of vehicles on the land in question, without naming him or them.

(6) Section 55(2) of the Magistrates' Courts Act 1980 (warrant for arrest of defendant failing to appear) does not apply to proceedings on a complaint made under this section.

(7) Section 77(6) of this Act applies also for the interpretation of this section.

Provisions as to directions under s. 77 and orders under s. 78

79.—(1) The following provisions apply in relation to the service of notice of a direction under section 77 and of a summons under section 78, referred to in those provisions as a "relevant document".   **71–022**

(2) Where it is impracticable to serve a relevant document on a person named in it, the document shall be treated as duly served on him if a copy of it is fixed in a prominent place to the vehicle concerned; and where a relevant document is directed to the unnamed occupants of vehicles, it shall be treated as duly

served on those occupants if a copy of it is fixed in a prominent place to every vehicle on the land in question at the time when service is thus effected.

(3) A local authority shall take such steps as may be reasonably practicable to secure that a copy of any relevant document is displayed on the land in question (otherwise than by being fixed to a vehicle) in a manner designed to ensure that it is likely to be seen by any person camping on the land.

(4) Notice of any relevant document shall be given by the local authority to the owner of the land in question and to any occupier of that land unless, after reasonable inquiries, the authority is unable to ascertain the name and address of the owner or occupier; and the owner of any such land and any occupier of such land shall be entitled to appear and to be heard in the proceedings.

(5) Section 77(6) applies also for the interpretation of this section.

PART VI

PREVENTION OF TERRORISM

71–023   **81.** [. . .][1]

[1] Repealed by Terrorism Act 2000 (c.11), Sched. 16, Pt I, para. 1.

82. [. . .][1]

[1] Repealed by Terrorism Act 2000 (c.11), Sched. 16, Pt I, para. 1.

83. [. . .][1]

[1] Repealed by Terrorism Act 2000 (c.11), Sched. 16, Pt I, para. 1.

PART VII

OBSCENITY AND PORNOGRAPHY AND VIDEOS

Obscene publications and indecent photographs of children

. . . . . .

PART XII

MISCELLANEOUS AND GENERAL

Closed-circuit television by local authorities

Local authority powers to provide closed-circuit television

71–024   **163.**—(1) Without prejudice to any power which they may exercise for those purposes under any other enactment, a local authority may take such of the following steps as they consider will, in relation to their area, promote the prevention of crime or the welfare of the victims of crime—

- (a) providing apparatus for recording visual images of events occurring on any land in their area;
- (b) providing within their area a telecommunications system which, under Part II of the Telecommunications Act 1984, may be run without a licence;
- (c) arranging   for   the   provision   of   any   other   description   of

telecommunications system within their area or between any land in their area and any building occupied by a public authority.

(2) Any power to provide, or to arrange for the provision of, any apparatus includes power to maintain, or operate, or, as the case may be, to arrange for the maintenance or operation of, that apparatus.

(3) Before taking such a step under this section; a local authority shall consult the chief officer of police for the police area in which the step is to be taken.

(4) In this section—

"chief officer of police", in relation to a police area in Scotland, means the chief constable of a police force maintained for that area;

"local authority"—

(a) in England, means a county council or district council;
(b) in Wales, means a county council or county borough council; and
(c) in Scotland, has the meaning given by section 235(1) of the Local Government (Scotland) Act 1973; and

"telecommunications system" has the meaning given in section 4 of the Telecommunications Act 1984 and "licence" means a licence under section 7 of that Act.

(5) Until 1st April 1996, in this section "local authority" means, in Wales, a county council or district council.

Drug Trafficking Act 1994

(1994, c. 37)

An Act to consolidate the Drug Trafficking Offences Act 1986 and certain provi-   **72–001**
sions of the Criminal Justice (International Cooperation) Act 1990 relating
to drug trafficking.   [3rd November 1994]

PART I

CONFISCATION ORDERS

Introductory

Meaning of "drug trafficking" and "drug trafficking offence"

1.—(1) In this Act "drug trafficking" means, subject to subsection (2) below,   **72–002**
doing or being concerned in any of the following, whether in England and Wales
or elsewhere—

(a) producing or supplying a controlled drug where the production or supply contravenes section 4(1) of the Misuse of Drugs Act 1971 or a corresponding law;
(b) transporting or storing a controlled drug where possession of the drug contravenes section 5(1) of that Act or a corresponding law;
(c) importing or exporting a controlled drug where the importation or exportation is prohibited by section 3(1) of that Act or a corresponding law;

(d) manufacturing or supplying a scheduled substance within the meaning of section 12 of the Criminal Justice (International Cooperation) Act 1990 where the manufacture or supply is an offence under that section or would be such an offence if it took place in England and Wales;

(e) using any ship for illicit traffic in controlled drugs in circumstances which amount to the commission of an offence under section 19 of that Act;

(f) conduct which is an offence under section 49 of this Act or which would be such an offence if it took place in England and Wales;

(g) acquiring, having possession of or using property in circumstances which amount to the commission of an offence under section 51 of this Act or which would amount to such an offence if it took place in England and Wales.

(2) "Drug trafficking" also includes a person doing the following, whether in England and Wales or elsewhere, that is to say, entering into or being otherwise concerned in an arrangement whereby—

(a) the retention or control by or on behalf of another person of the other person's proceeds of drug trafficking is facilitated; or

(b) the proceeds of drug trafficking by another person are used to secure that funds are placed at the other person's disposal or are used for the other person's benefit to acquire property by way of investment.

(3) In this Act "drug trafficking offence" means any of the following—

(a) an offence under section 4(2) or (3) or 5(3) of the Misuse of Drugs Act 1971 (production, supply and possession for supply of controlled drugs);

(b) an offence under section 20 of that Act (assisting in or inducing commission outside United Kingdom of offence punishable under a corresponding law);

(c) an offence under—

(i) section 50(2) or (3) of the Customs and Excise Management Act 1979 (improper importation).

(ii) section 68(2) of that Act (exportation), or

(iii) section 170 of that Act (fraudulent evasion),

in connection with a prohibition or restriction on importation or exportation having effect by virtue of section 3 of the Misuse of Drugs Act 1971;

(d) an offence under section 12 of the Criminal Justice (International Co-operation) Act 1990 (manufacture or supply of substance specified in Schedule 2 to that Act;

(e) an offence under section 19 of that Act (using ship for illicit traffic in controlled drugs),

(f) an offence under section 49, 50 or 51 of this Act or section 14 of the Criminal Justice (International Co-operation) Act 1990 (which makes, in relation to Scotland and Northern Ireland, provision corresponding to section 49 of this Act);

(g) an offence under section 1 of the Criminal Law Act 1977 of conspiracy to commit any of the offences in paragraphs (a) to (f) above;

(h) an offence under section 1 of the Criminal Attempts Act 1981 of attempting to commit any of those offences; and

(i) an offence of inciting another person to commit any of those offences, whether under section 19 of the Misuse of Drugs Act 1971 or at common law;

and includes aiding, abetting, counselling or procuring the commission of any of the offences in paragraphs (a) to (f) above.

(4) In this section "corresponding law" has the same meaning as in the Misuse of Drugs Act 1971.

(5) For the purposes of the application of Part II of this Act in Scotland and Northern Ireland, "drug trafficking" shall be construed in accordance with section 48(2) of this Act.

Confiscation orders

Confiscation orders

2.—(1) Subject to subsection (7) below, where a defendant appears before **72–003** the Crown Court to be sentenced in respect of one or more drug trafficking offences (and has not previously been sentenced or otherwise dealt with in respect of his conviction for the offence or, as the case may be, any of the offences concerned), then—

(a) if the prosecutor asks the court to proceed under this section, or
(b) if the court considers that, even though the prosecutor has not asked it to do so, it is appropriate for it to proceed under this section,

it shall act as follows.

(2) The court shall first determine whether the defendant has benefited from drug trafficking.

(3) For the purposes of this Act, a person has benefited from drug trafficking if he has at any time (whether before or after the commencement of this Act) received any payment or other reward in connection with drug trafficking carried on by him or another person.

(4) If the court determines that the defendant has so benefited, the court shall, before sentencing or otherwise dealing with him in respect of the offence or, as the case may be, any of the offences concerned, determine in accordance with section 5 of this Act the amount to be recovered in his case by virtue of this section.

(5) The court shall then, in respect of the offence or offences concerned—

(a) order the defendant to pay that amount;
(b) take account of the order before—

    (i) imposing any fine on him;
    (ii) making any order involving any payment by him; or
    (iii) making any order under section 27 of the Misuse of Drugs Act 1971 (forfeiture orders) or [section 143 of the Powers of Criminal Courts (Sentencing) Act 2000] (deprivation orders); and

(c) subject to paragraph (b) above, leave the order out of account in determining the appropriate sentence or other manner of dealing with him.

(6) No enactment restricting the power of a court dealing with an offender in a particular way from dealing with him also in any other way shall by reason only of the making of an order under this section restrict the Crown Court from dealing with an offender in any way the court considers appropriate in respect of a drug trafficking offence.

(7) Subsection (1) above does not apply in relation to any offence for which a defendant appears before the Crown Court to be sentenced if—

(b) the powers of the court (apart from this section to deal with him in respect of that offence are limited to dealing with him in any way in which a magistrates' court might have dealt with him in respect of the offence.

(8) The standard of proof required to determine any question arising under this Act as to—

(a) whether a person has benefited from drug trafficking, or
(b) the amount to be recovered in his case by virtue of this section,

shall be that applicable in civil proceedings.

(9) In this Act "confiscation order" means an order under this section and includes, in particular, such an order made by virtue of section 13, 14 or 19 of this Act.

. . . . . .

Assessing the proceeds of drug trafficking

72–004   **4.**—(1) For the purposes of this Act—

(a) any payments or other rewards received by a person at any time (whether before or after the commencement of this Act) in connection with drug trafficking carried on by him or another person are his proceeds of drug trafficking; and
(b) the value of his proceeds of drug trafficking is the aggregate of the values of the payments or other rewards.

(2) Subject to subsection (4) and (5) below, the Crown Court shall, for the purpose—

(a) of determining whether the defendant has benefited from drug trafficking, and
(b) if he has, of assessing the value of his proceeds of drug trafficking,

make the required assumptions.

(3) The required assumptions are—

(a) that any property appearing to the court—

(i) to have been held by the defendant at any time since his conviction, or
(ii) to have been transferred to him at any time since the beginning of the period of six years ending when the proceedings were instituted against him,

was received by him, at the earliest time at which he appears to the court to have held it, as a payment or reward in connection with drug trafficking carried on by him;
(b) that any expenditure of his since the beginning of that period was met out of payments received by him in connection with drug trafficking carried on by him; and
(c) that, for the purpose of valuing any property received or assumed to have been received by him at any time as such a reward, he received the property free of any other interests in it.

(4) The court shall not make any required assumption in relation to any particular property or expenditure if—

(a) that assumption is shown to be incorrect in the defendant's case; or

(b) the court is satisfied that there would be a serious risk of injustice in the defendant's case if the assumption were to be made;

and where, by virtue of this subsection, the court does not make one or more of the required assumptions, it shall state its reasons.

(5) Subsection (2) above does not apply if the only drug trafficking offence in respect of which the defendant appears before the court to be sentenced is an offence under section 49, 50 or 51 of this Act.

(6) For the purpose of assessing the value of the defendant's proceeds of drug trafficking in a case where a confiscation order has previously been made against him, the court shall leave out of account any of his proceeds of drug trafficking that are shown to the court to have been taken into account in determining the amount to be recovered under that order.

(7) References in subsection (6) above to a confiscation order include a reference to a confiscation order within the meaning of—

(a) the Drug Trafficking Offences Act 1986; or

[(b) the Proceeds of Crime (Scotland) Act 1995;]

(8) For the purposes of the application of Part II of this Act in Scotland and Northern Ireland, the expression "proceeds of drug trafficking" shall be construed in accordance with section 48(2) of this Act.

Intelligence Services Act 1994

(1994, c. 13)

An Act to make provision about the Secret Intelligence Service and the Government Communications Headquarters, including provision for the issue of warrants and authorisations enabling certain actions to be taken and for the issue of such warrants and authorisations to be kept under review; to make further provision about warrants issued on applications by the Security Service; to establish a procedure for the investigation of complaints about the Secret Intelligence Service and the Government Communications Headquarters; to make provision for the establishment of an Intelligence and Security Committee to scrutinise all three of those bodies; and for connected purposes. [26th May 1994]   **73–001**

The Secret Intelligence Service

The Secret Intelligence Service

1.—(1) There shall continue to be a Secret Intelligence Service (in this Act referred to as "the Intelligence Service") under the authority of the Secretary of State; and, subject to subsection   **73–002**

(2) below, its functions shall be—

(a) to obtain and provide information relating to the actions or intentions of persons outside the British Islands; and

(b) to perform other tasks relating to the actions or intentions of such persons.

(2) The functions of the Intelligence Service shall be exercisable only—

(a) in the interests of national security, with particular reference to the defence and foreign policies of Her Majesty's Government in the United Kingdom; or

(b) in the interests of the economic well-being of the United Kingdom; or

(c) in support of the prevention or detection of serious crime.

The Chief of the Intelligence Service

73–003   **2.**—(1) The operations of the Intelligence Service shall continue to be under the control of a Chief of that Service appointed by the Secretary of State.

(2) The Chief of the Intelligence Service shall be responsible for the efficiency of that Service and it shall be his duty to ensure—

(a) that there are arrangements for securing that no information is obtained by the Intelligence Service except so far as necessary for the proper discharge of its functions and that no information is disclosed by it except so far as necessary—

(i) for that purpose;

(ii) in the interests of national security;

(iii) for the purpose of the prevention or detection of serious crime; or

(iv) for the purpose of any criminal proceedings; and

(b) that the Intelligence Service does not take any action to further the interests of any United Kingdom political party.

(3) Without prejudice to the generality of subsection (2)(a) above, the disclosure of information shall be regarded as necessary for the proper discharge of the functions of the Intelligence Service if it consists of—

(a) the disclosure of records subject to and in accordance with the Public Records Act 1958; or

(b) the disclosure, subject to and in accordance with arrangements approved by the Secretary of State, of information to the Comptroller and Auditor General for the purposes of his functions.

(4) The Chief of the Intelligence Service shall make an annual report on the work of the Intelligence Service to the Prime Minister and the Secretary of State and may at any time report to either of them on any matter relating to its work.

GCHQ

The Government Communications Headquarters

73–004   **3.**—(1) There shall continue to be a Government Communications Headquarters under the authority of the Secretary of State; and, subject to subsection (2) below, its functions shall be—

(a) to monitor or interfere with electromagnetic, acoustic and other emissions and any equipment producing such emissions and to obtain and provide information derived from or related to such emissions or equipment and from encrypted material; and

(b) to provide advice and assistance about—

(i) languages, including terminology used for technical matters, and

(ii) cryptography and other matters relating to the protection of information and other material, to the armed forces of the Crown, to Her Majesty's Government in the United Kingdom or to a Northern Ireland Department or to any other organisation which is determined for the purposes of this section in such manner as may be specified by the Prime Minister.

(2) The functions referred to in subsection (1)(a) above shall be exercisable only—

(a) in the interests of national security, with particular reference to the defence and foreign policies of Her Majesty's Government in the United Kingdom; or

(b) in the interests of the economic well-being of the United Kingdom in relation to the actions or intentions of persons outside the British Islands; or

(c) in support of the prevention or detection of serious crime.

(3) In this Act the expression "GCHQ"refers to the Government Communications Headquarters and to any unit or part of a unit of the armed forces of the Crown which is for the time being required by the Secretary of State to assist the Government Communications Headquarters in carrying out its functions.

The Director of GCHQ

4.—(1) The operations of GCHQ shall continue to be under the control of a Director appointed by the Secretary of State.   **73–005**

(2) The Director shall be responsible for the efficiency of GCHQ and it shall be his duty to ensure—

(a) that there are arrangements for securing that no information is obtained by GCHQ except so far as necessary for the proper discharge of its functions and that no information is disclosed by it except so far as necessary for that purpose or for the purpose of any criminal proceedings; and

(b) that GCHQ does not take any action to further the interests of any United Kingdom political party:

(3) Without prejudice to the generality of subsection (2)(a) above, the disclosure of information shall be regarded as necessary for the proper discharge of the functions of GCHQ if it consists of—

(a) the disclosure of records subject to and in accordance with the Public Records Act 1958; or

(b) the disclosure, subject to and in accordance with arrangements approved by the Secretary of State, of information to the Comptroller and Auditor General for the purposes of his functions.

(4) The Director shall make an annual report on the work of GCHQ to the Prime Minister and the Secretary of State and may at any time report to either of them on any matter relating to its work.

Authorisation of certain actions

Warrants: general

5.—(1) No entry on or interference with property or with wireless telegraphy shall be unlawful if it is authorised by a warrant issued by the Secretary of State under this section.   **73–006**

(2) The Secretary of State may, on an application made by the Security Service, the Intelligence Service or GCHQ, issue a warrant under this section authorising the taking, subject to subsection (3) below, of such action as is specified in the warrant in respect of any property so specified or in respect of wireless telegraphy so specified if the Secretary of State—

    (a) thinks it necessary for the action to be taken on the ground that it is likely to be of substantial value in assisting, as the case may be,—

        (i) the Security Service in carrying out any of its functions under the 1989 Act; or

        (ii) the Intelligence Service in carrying out any of its functions under section 1 above; or

        (iii) GCHQ in carrying out any function which falls within section 3(1)(a) above; and

    (b) is satisfied that what the action seeks to achieve cannot reasonably be achieved by other means; and

    (c) is satisfied that satisfactory arrangements are in force under section 2(2)(a) of the 1989 Act (duties of the Director-General of the Security Service), section 2(2)(a) above or section 4(2)(a) above with respect to the disclosure of information obtained by virtue of this section and that any information obtained under the warrant will be subject to those arrangements.

[(3) A warrant issued on the application of the Intelligence Service or GCHQ for the purposes of the exercise of their functions by virtue of section 1(2)(c) or 3(2)(c) above may not relate to property in the British Islands.

(3A) A warrant issued on the application of the Security Service for the purposes of the exercise of their function under section 1(4) of the Security Service Act 1989 may not relate to property in the British Islands unless it authorises the taking of action in relation to conduct within subsection (3B) below.

(3B) Conduct is within this subsection if it constitutes (or, if it took place in the United Kingdom, would constitute) one or more offences, and either—

    (a) it involves the use of violence, results in substantial financial gain or is conduct by a large number of persons in pursuit of a common purpose; or

    (b) the offence or one of the offences is an offence for which a person who has attained the age of twenty-one and has no previous convictions could reasonably be expected to be sentenced to imprisonment for a term of three years or more.]

(4) Subject to subsection (5) below, the Security Service may make an application under subsection (2) above for a warrant to be issued authorising that Service (or a person acting on its behalf) to take such action as is specified in the warrant on behalf of the Intelligence Service or GCHQ and, where such a warrant is issued, the functions of the Security Service shall include the carrying out of the action so specified, whether or not it would otherwise be within its functions.

(5) The Security Service may not make an application for a warrant by virtue of subsection (4) above except where the action proposed to be authorised by the warrant—

    (a) is action in respect of which the Intelligence Service or, as the case may be, GCHQ could make such an application; and

    (b) is to be taken otherwise than in support of the prevention or detection of serious crime.

Warrants: procedure and duration, etc.

6.—(1) A warrant shall not be issued except—   **73–007**

(a) under the hand of the Secretary of State [or, in the case of a warrant by the Scottish Ministers (by virtue of provision made under section 63 of the Scotland Act 1998), a member of the Scottish Executive]; or

(b) in an urgent case where the Secretary of State has expressly authorised its issue and a statement of that fact is endorsed on it, under the hand of a senior official;

[(c) in an urgent case where, the Scottish Ministers have (by virtue of provision made under section 63 of the Scotland Act 1998) expressly authorised its issue and a statement of that fact is endorsed thereon, under the hand of a member of the staff of the Scottish Administration who is in the Senior Civil Service and is designated by the Scottish Ministers as a person under whose hand a warrant may be issued in such a case.]

(2) A warrant shall, unless renewed under subsection (3) below, cease to have effect—

(a) if the warrant was under the hand of the Secretary of State [or, in the case of a warrant issued by the Scottish Ministers (by virtue of provision made under section 63 of the Scotland Act 1998), a member of the Scottish Executive], at the end of the period of six months beginning with the day on which it was issued; and

(b) in any other case, at the end of the period ending with the second working day following that day.

(3) If at any time before the day on which a warrant would cease to have effect the Secretary of State considers it necessary for the warrant to continue to have effect for the purpose for which it was issued, he may by an instrument under his hand renew it for a period of six months beginning with that day.

(4) The Secretary of State shall cancel a warrant if he is satisfied that the action authorised by it is no longer necessary.

(5) In the preceding provisions of this section "warrant" means a warrant under section 5 above.

(6) As regards the Security Service, this section and section 5 above have effect in place of section 3 (property warrants) of the 1989 Act, and accordingly—

(a) a warrant issued under that section of the 1989 Act and current when this section and section 5 above come into force shall be treated as a warrant under section 5 above, but without any change in the date on which the warrant was in fact issued or last renewed; and

(b) section 3 of the 1989 Act shall cease to have effect.

Authorisation of acts outside the British Islands

7.—(1) If, apart from this section; a person would be liable in the United   **73–008** Kingdom for any act done outside the British Islands, he shall not be so liable if the act is one which is authorised to be done by virtue of an authorisation given by the Secretary of State under this section.

(2) In subsection (1) above "liable in the United Kingdom" means liable under the criminal or civil law of any part of the United Kingdom.

(3) The Secretary of State shall not give an authorisation under this section unless he is satisfied—

(a) that any acts which may be done in reliance on the authorisation or, as the case may be, the operation in the course of which the acts may be done will be necessary for the proper discharge of a function of the Intelligence Service [or GCHQ]; and

(b) that there are satisfactory arrangements in force to secure—

    (i) that nothing will be done in reliance on the authorisation beyond what is necessary for the proper discharge of a function of the Intelligence Service [or GCHQ]; and

    (ii) that, in so far as any acts may be done in reliance on the authorisation, their nature and likely consequences will be reasonable, having regard to the purposes for which they are carried out; and

(c) that there are satisfactory arrangements in force under [section 2(2)(a) or 4(2)(a)] above with respect to the disclosure of information obtained by virtue of this section and that any information obtained by virtue of anything done in reliance on the authorisation will be subject to those arrangements.

(4) Without prejudice to the generality of the power of the Secretary of State to give an authorisation under this section, such an authorisation—

(a) may relate to a particular act or acts, to acts of a description specified in the authorisation or to acts undertaken in the course of an operation so specified;

(b) may be limited to a particular person or persons of a description so specified; and

(c) may be subject to conditions so specified.

(5) An authorisation shall not be given under this section except—

(a) under the hand of the Secretary of State; or

(b) in an urgent case where the Secretary of State has expressly authorised it to be given and a statement of that fact is endorsed on it, under the hand of a senior official.

(6) An authorisation shall, unless renewed under subsection (7) below, cease to have effect—

(a) if the authorisation was given under the hand of the Secretary of State, at the end of the period of six months beginning with the day on which it was given;

(b) in any other case, at the end of the period ending with the second working day following the day on which it was given.

(7) If at any time before the day on which an authorisation would cease to have effect the Secretary of State considers it necessary for the authorisation to continue to have effect for the purpose for which it was given, he may by an instrument under his hand renew it for a period of six months beginning with that day.

(8) The Secretary of State shall cancel an authorisation if he is satisfied that any act authorised by it is no longer necessary.

[(9) For the purposes of this section the reference in subsection (1) to an act done outside the British Islands includes a reference to any act which—

(a) is done in the British Islands; but

(b) is or is intended to be done in relation to apparatus that is believed to be outside the British Islands, or in relation to anything appearing to originate from such apparatus;

and in this subsection "apparatus" has the same meaning as in the Regulation of Investigatory Powers Act 2000 (c. 23).]

8. [. . .]¹   **73–009**

¹ Repealed by Regulation of Investigatory Powers Act 2000 (c.23), Sched. 5, para. 1.

The Intelligence and Security Committee

The Intelligence and Security Committee

10.—(1) There shall be a Committee, to be known as the Intelligence and   **73–010** Security Committee and in this section referred to as "the Committee", to examine the expenditure, administration and policy of—

(a) the Security Service;
(b) the Intelligence Service; and
(c) GCHQ.

(2) The Committee shall consist of nine members—

(a) who shall be drawn both from the members of the House of Commons and from the members of the House of Lords; and
(b) none of whom shall be a Minister of the Crown.

(3) The members of the Committee shall be appointed by the Prime Minister after consultation with the Leader of the Opposition, within the meaning of the Ministerial and other Salaries Act 1975; and one of those members shall be so appointed as Chairman of the Committee.

(4) Schedule 3 to this Act shall have effect with respect to the tenure of office of members of, the procedure of and other matters relating to, the Committee; and in that Schedule "the Committee" has the same meaning as in this section.

(5) The Committee shall make an annual report on the discharge of their functions to the Prime Minister and may at any time report to him on any matter relating to the discharge of those functions.

(6) The Prime Minister shall lay before each House of Parliament a copy of each annual report made by the Committee under subsection (5) above together with a statement as to whether any matter has been excluded from that copy in pursuance of subsection (7) below.

(7) If it appears to the Prime Minister, after consultation with the Committee, that the publication of any matter in a report would be prejudicial to the continued discharge of the functions of either of the Services or, as the case may be, GCHQ, the Prime Minister may exclude that matter from the copy of the report as laid before each House of Parliament.

Interpretation and consequential amendments

11.—(1) In this Act—   **73–011**

(a) "the 1989 Act" means the Security Service Act 1989;
(b) [. . .]¹
(c) "Minister of the Crown" has the same meaning as in the Ministers of the Crown Act 1975;
(d) "senior official" in relation to a department is a reference to an officer

of or above Grade 3 or, as the case may require, Diplomatic Service Senior Grade;

(e) "wireless telegraphy" has the same meaning as in the Wireless Telegraphy Act 1949 and, in relation to wireless telegraphy, "interfere" has the same meaning as in that Act;

(f) "working day" means any day other than a Saturday, a Sunday, Christmas Day, Good Friday or a day which is a bank holiday under the Banking and Financial Dealings Act 1971 in any part of the United Kingdom.

[(1A) Section 81(5) of the Regulation of Investigatory Powers Act 2000 (meaning of "prevention" and "detection"), so far as it relates to serious crime, shall apply

(a) for the purposes of section 3 above, as it applies for the purposes of Chapter 1 of Part 1 of that Act; and

(b) for the other purposes of this Act, as it applies for the purposes of the provisions of that Act not contained in that Chapter.]

(2) In consequence of the preceding provisions of this Act, the 1989 Act, the Official Secrets Act 1989 and the Official Secrets Act 1989 (Prescription) Order 1990 shall have effect subject to the amendments in Schedule 4 to this Act.

[1] Repealed by Regulation of Investigatory Powers Act 2000 (c.23), Sched. 5, para. 1.
[2] Added by Regulation of Investigatory Powers Act 2000 (c.23), Sched. 4, para. 6.

Trade Marks Act 1994

(1994, c. 26)

74–001   *An Act to make new provision for registered trade marks, implementing Council Directive No. 89/104/EEC of 21st December 1988 to approximate the laws of the Member States relating to trade marks; to make provision in connection with Council Regulation (EC) No. 40/94 of 20th December 1993 on the Community trade mark; to give effect to the Madrid Protocol Relating to the International Registration of Marks of 27th June 1989, and to certain provisions of the Paris Convention for the Protection of Industrial Property of 20th March 1883, as revised and amended; and for connected purposes.*
[21st July 1994]

PART I

REGISTERED TRADE MARKS

Introductory

Trade marks

74–002   **1.**—(1) In this Act a "trade mark" means any sign capable of being represented graphically which is capable of distinguishing goods or services of one undertaking from those of other undertakings.

A trade mark may, in particular, consist of words (including personal names), designs, letters, numerals or the shape of goods or their packaging.

(2) References in this Act to a trade mark include, unless the context otherwise requires, references to a collective mark (see section 49) or certification mark (see section 50).

Registered trade marks

2.—(1) A registered trade mark is a property right obtained by the registration of the trade mark under this Act and the proprietor of a registered trade mark has the rights and remedies provided by this Act.

74–003

(2) No proceedings he to prevent or recover damages for the infringement of an unregistered trade mark as such; but nothing in this Act affects the law relating to passing off.

Grounds for refusal of registration

Absolute grounds for refusal of registration

3.—(1) The following shall not be registered—

74–004

   (a) signs which do not satisfy the requirements of section 1(1).
   (b) trade marks which are devoid of any distinctive character.
   (c) trade marks which consist exclusively of signs or indications which may serve, in trade, to designate the kind, quality, quantity, intended purpose, value, geographical origin, the time of production of goods or of rendering of services, or other characteristics of goods or services,
   (d) trade marks which consist exclusively of signs or indications which have become customary in the current language or in the bona fide and established practices of the trade:
   Provided that, a trade mark shall not be refused registration by virtue of paragraph (b), (c) or (d) above if, before the date of application for registration, it has in fact acquired a distinctive character as a result of the use made of it.

(2) A sign shall not be registered as a trade mark if it consists exclusively of—

   (a) the shape which results from the nature of the goods themselves,
   (b) the shape of goods which is necessary to obtain a technical result, or
   (c) the shape which gives substantial value to the goods.

(3) A trade mark shall not be registered if it is—

   (a) contrary to public policy or to accepted principles of morality, or
   (b) of such a nature as to deceive the public (for instance as to the nature, quality or geographical origin of the goods or service).

(4) A trade mark shall not be registered if or to the extent that its use is prohibited in the United Kingdom by any enactment or rule of law or by any provision of Community law.

(5) A trade mark shall not be registered in the cases specified, or referred to, in section 4 (specially protected emblems).

(6) A trade mark shall not be registered if or to the extent that the application is made in bad faith.

Specially protected emblems

74–005   4.—(1) A trade mark which consists of or contains—

(a) the Royal arms, or any of the principal armorial bearings of the Royal arms, or any insignia or device so nearly resembling the Royal arms or any such armorial bearing as to be likely to be mistaken for them or it;

(b) a representation of the Royal crown or any of the Royal flags;

(c) a representation of Her Majesty or any member of the Royal family, or any colourable imitation thereof; or

(d) words, letters or devices likely to lead persons to think that the applicant either has or recently has had Royal patronage or authorisation,

shall not be registered unless it appears to the registrar that consent has been given by or on behalf of Her Majesty or, as the case may be, the relevant member of the Royal family.

(2) A trade mark which consists of or contains a representation of—

(a) the national flag of the United Kingdom (commonly known as the Union Jack), or

(b) the flag of England, Wales, Scotland, Northern Ireland or the Isle of Man,

shall not be registered if it appears to the registrar that the use of the trade mark would be misleading or grossly offensive.

Provision may be made by rules identifying the flags to which paragraph (b) applies.

(3) A trade mark shall not be registered in the cases specified in—

section 57 (national emblems, etc. of Convention countries), or section 58 (emblems, etc. of certain international organisations).

(4) Provision may be made by rules prohibiting in such cases as may be prescribed the registration of a trade mark which consists of or contains—

(a) arms to which a person is entitled by virtue of a grant of arms by the Crown, or

(b) insignia so nearly resembling such arms as to be likely to be mistaken for them,

unless it appears to the registrar that consent has been given by or on behalf of that person.

Where such a mark is registered, nothing in this Act shall be construed as authorising its use in any way contrary to the laws of arms.

[(5) A trade mark which consists of or contains a controlled representation within the meaning of the Olympic Symbol etc. (Protection) Act 1995 shall not be registered unless it appears to the registrar—

(a) that the application is made by the person for the time being appointed under section 1(2) of the Olympic Symbol etc. (Protection) Act 1995 (power of Secretary of State to appoint a person as the proprietor of the Olympics association right), or

(b) that consent has been given by or on behalf of the person mentioned in paragraph (a) above.]

. . . . . .

PART IV

MISCELLANEOUS AND GENERAL PROVISIONS

Miscellaneous

Unauthorised use of Royal arms, etc.

99.—(1) A person shall not without the authority of Her Majesty use in con-   **74–006**
nection with any business the Royal arms (or arms so closely resembling the
Royal arms as to be calculated to deceive) in such manner as to be calculated
to lead to the belief that he is duly authorised to use the Royal arms.

(2) A person shall not without the authority of Her Majesty or of a member
of the Royal family use in connection with any business any device, emblem or
title in such a manner as to be calculated to lead to the belief that he is employed
by, or supplies goods or services to Her Majesty or that member of the Royal
family.

(3) A person who contravenes subsection (1) commits an offence and is liable
on summary conviction to a fine not exceeding level 2 on the standard scale.

(4) Contravention of subsection (1) or (2) may be restrained by injunction in
proceedings brought by—

(a) any person who is authorised to use the arms, device, emblem or title
in question, or
(b) any person authorised by the Lord Chamberlain to take such proceedings

(5) Nothing in this section affects any right of the proprietor of a trade mark
containing any such arms, device, emblem or title to use that trade mark.

Criminal Appeal Act 1995

(1995, c. 35)

An Act to amend provisions relating to appeals and references to the Court of   **75–001**
Appeal in criminal cases; to establish a Criminal Cases Review Commis-
sion and confer functions on, and make other provision in relation to, the
Commission; to amend section 142 of the Magistrates' Courts Act 1980 and
introduce in Northern Ireland provisions similar to those of that section; to
amend section 133 of the Criminal Justice Act 1988; and for connected
purposes.   [19th July 1995]

. . . . . .

Part II

The Criminal Cases Review Commission

The Commission

The Commission

75–002　　**8.**—(1) There shall be a body corporate to be known as the Criminal Cases Review Commission.

(2) The Commission shall not be regarded as the servant or agent of the Crown or as enjoying any status, immunity or privilege of the Crown; and the Commission's property shall not be regarded as property of, or held on behalf of, the Crown.

(3) The Commission shall consist of not fewer than eleven members.

(4) The members of the Commission shall be appointed by Her Majesty on the recommendation of the Prime Minister.

(5) At least one third of the members of the Commission shall be persons who are legally qualified; and for this purpose a person is legally qualified if—

> (a) he has a ten year general qualification, within the meaning of section 71 of the Courts and Legal Services Act 1990, or
> (b) he is a member of the Bar of Northern Ireland, or solicitor of the Supreme Court of Northern Ireland, of at least ten years' standing.

(6) At least two thirds of the members of the Commission shall be persons who appear to the Prime Minister to have knowledge or experience of any aspect of the criminal justice system and of them at least one shall be a person who appears to him to have knowledge or experience of any aspect of the criminal justice system in Northern Ireland; and for the purposes of this subsection the criminal justice system includes, in particular, the investigation of offences and the treatment of offenders.

(7) Schedule 1 (further provisions with respect to the Commission) shall have effect.

References to court

Cases dealt with on indictment in England and Wales

75–003　　**9.**—(1) Where a person has been convicted of an offence on indictment in England and Wales, the Commission—

> (a) may at any time refer the conviction to the Court of Appeal, and
> (b) (whether or not they refer the conviction) may at any time refer to the Court of Appeal any sentence (not being a sentence fixed by law) imposed on, or in subsequent proceedings relating to, the conviction.

(2) A reference under subsection (1) of a person's conviction shall be treated for all purposes as an appeal by the person under section 1 of the 1968 Act against the conviction.

(3) A reference under subsection (1) of a sentence imposed on, or in subsequent proceedings relating to, a person's conviction on an indictment shall be treated for all purposes as an appeal by the person under section 9 of the 1968 Act against—

> (a) the sentence, and
> (b) any other sentence (not being a sentence fixed by law) imposed on,

or in subsequent proceedings relating to, the conviction or any other conviction on the indictment.

(4) On a reference under subsection (1) of a person's conviction on an indictment the Commission may give notice to the Court of Appeal that any other conviction on the indictment which is specified in the notice is to be treated as referred to the Court of Appeal under subsection (1).

(5) Where a verdict of not guilty by reason of insanity has been returned in England and Wales in the case of a person, the Commission may at any time refer the verdict to the Court of Appeal; and a reference under this subsection shall be treated for all purposes as an appeal by the person under section 12 of the 1968 Act against the verdict.

(6) Where a jury in England and Wales has returned findings that a person is under a disability and that he did the act or made the omission charged against him, the Commission may at any time refer either or both of those findings to the Court of Appeal; and a reference under this subsection shall be treated for all purposes as an appeal by the person under section 15 of the 1968 Act against the finding or findings referred.

. . . . . .

Cases dealt with summarily in England and Wales

11.—(1) Where a person has been convicted of an offence by a magistrates'   **75–004**
court in England and Wales, the Commission—

(a) may at any time refer the conviction to the Crown Court, and
(b) (Whether or not they refer the conviction) may at any time refer to the Crown Court any sentence imposed on, or in subsequent proceedings relating to, the conviction.

(2) A reference under subsection (1) of a person's conviction shall be treated for all purposes as an appeal by the person under section 108(1) of the Magistrates' Courts Act 1980 against the conviction (whether or not he pleaded guilty).

(3) A reference under subsection (1) of a sentence imposed on, or in subsequent proceedings relating to, a person's conviction shall be treated for all purposes as an appeal by the person under section 108(1) of the Magistrates' Courts Act 1980 against—

(a) the sentence, and
(b) any other sentence imposed on, or in subsequent proceedings relating to, the conviction or any related conviction.

(4) On a reference under subsection (1) of a person's conviction the Commission may give notice to the Crown Court that any related conviction which is specified in the notice is to be treated as referred to the Crown Court under subsection (1).

(5) For the purposes of this section convictions are related if they are convictions of the same person by the same court on the same day.

(6) On a reference under this section the Crown Court may not award any punishment more severe than that awarded by the court whose decision is referred.

(7) The Crown Court may grant bail to a person whose conviction or sentence has been referred under this section; and any time during which he is released

on bail shall not count as part of any term of imprisonment or detention under his sentence.

. . . . . .

Conditions for making of references

75–005   13.—(1) A reference of a conviction, verdict, finding or sentence shall not be made under any of section 9 to 12 unless—

  (a) the Commission consider that there is a real possibility that the conviction, verdict, finding or sentence would not be upheld were the reference to be made,

  (b) the Commission so consider—

    (i) in the case of a conviction, verdict or finding, because of an argument, or evidence, not raised in the proceedings which led to it or on any appeal or application for leave to appeal against it, or

    (ii) in the case of a sentence, because of an argument on a point of law, or information, not so raised, and

  (c) an appeal against the conviction, verdict, finding or sentence has been determined or leave to appeal against it has been refused.

(2) Nothing in subsection (1)(b)(i) or (c) shall prevent the making of a reference if it appears to the Commission that there are exceptional circumstances which justify making it.

Further provisions about references

75–006   14.—(1) A reference of a conviction, verdict, finding or sentence may be made under any of sections 9 to 12 either after an application has been made by or on behalf of the person to whom it relates or without an application having been so made.

(2) In considering whether to make a reference of a conviction, verdict, finding or sentence under any of sections 9 to 12 the Commission shall have regard to—

  (a) any application or representations made to the Commission by or on behalf of the person to whom it relates,

  (b) any other representations made to the Commission in relation to it, and

  (c) any other matters which appear to the Commission to be relevant.

(3) In considering whether to make a reference under section 9 or 10 the Commission may at any time refer any point on which they desire the assistance of the Court of Appeal to that Court for the Court's opinion on it; and on a reference under this subsection the Court of Appeal shall consider the point referred and furnish the Commission with the Court's opinion on the point.

(4) Where the Commission make a reference under any of sections 9 to 12 the Commission shall—

  (a) give to the court to which the reference is made a statement of the Commission's reasons for making the reference, and

  (b) send a copy of the statement to every person who appears to the Commission to be likely to be a party to any proceedings on the appeal arising from the reference.

(5) Where a reference under any of sections 9 to 12 is treated as an appeal against any conviction, verdict, finding or sentence, the appeal may be on any ground relating to the conviction, verdict, finding or sentence (whether or not the ground is related to any reason given by the Commission for making the reference).

(6) In every case in which—

(a) an application has been made to the Commission by or on behalf of any person for the reference under any of sections 9 to 12 of any conviction, verdict, finding or sentence, but

(b) the Commission decide not to make a reference of the conviction, verdict, finding or sentence,

the Commission shall give a statement of the reasons for their decision to the person who made the application.

Investigations and assistance

Investigations for Court of Appeal

15.—(1) Where a direction is given by the Court of Appeal under section 23A(1) of the 1968 Act or section 25A(1) of the 1980 Act the Commission shall investigate the matter specified in the direction in such manner as the Commission think fit.   **75–007**

(2) Where, in investigating a matter specified in such a direction, it appears to the Commission that—

(a) another matter (a "related matter") which is relevant to the determination of the case by the Court of Appeal ought, if possible, to be resolved before the case is determined by that Court, and

(b) an investigation of the related matter is likely to result in the Court's being able to resolve it,

the Commission may also investigate the related matter.

(3) The Commission shall—

(a) keep the Court of Appeal informed as to the progress of the investigation of any matter specified in a direction under section 23A(1) of the 1968 Act or section 25A(1) of the 1980 Act, and

(b) if they decide to investigate any related matter, notify the Court of Appeal of their decision and keep the Court informed as to the progress of the investigation.

(4) The Commission shall report to the Court of Appeal on the investigation of any matter specified in a direction under section 23A(1) of the 1968 Act or section 25A(1) of the 1980 Act when—

(a) they complete the investigation of that matter and of any related matter investigated by them, or

(b) they are directed to do so by the Court of Appeal,

whichever happens first.

(5) A report under subsection (4) shall include details of any inquiries made by or for the Commission in the investigation of the matter specified in the direction or any related matter investigated by them.

(6) Such a report shall be accompanied—

(a) by any statements and opinions received by the Commission in the investigation of the matter specified in the direction or any related matter investigated by them, and

(b) subject to subsection (7), by any reports so received.

(7) Such a report need not be accompanied by any reports submitted to the Commission under section 20(6) by an investigating officer.

Assistance in connection with prerogative of mercy

75–008 **16.**—(1) Where the Secretary of State refers to the Commission any matter which arises in the consideration of whether to recommend the exercise of Her Majesty's prerogative of mercy in relation to a conviction and on which he desires their assistance, the Commission shall—

(a) consider the matter referred, and

(b) give to the Secretary of State a statement of their conclusions on it;

and the Secretary of State shall, in considering whether so to recommend, treat the Commission's statement as conclusive of the matter referred.

(2) Where in any case the Commission are of the opinion that the Secretary of State should consider whether to recommend the exercise of Her Majesty's prerogative of mercy in relation to the case they shall give him the reasons for their opinion.

Supplementary powers

Power to obtain documents, etc.

75–009 **17.**—(1) This section applies where the Commission believe that a person serving in a public body has possession or control of a document or other material which may assist the Commission in the exercise of any of their functions.

(2) Where it is reasonable to do so, the Commission may require the person who is the appropriate person in relation to the public body—

(a) to produce the document or other material to the Commission or to give the Commission access to it, and

(b) to allow the Commission to take away the document or other material or to make and take away a copy of it in such form as they think appropriate,

and may direct that person that the document or other material must not be destroyed, damaged or altered before the direction is withdrawn by the Commission.

(3) The documents and other material covered by this section include, in particular, any document or other material obtained or created during any investigation or proceedings relating to—

(a) the case in relation to which the Commission's function is being or may be exercised, or

(b) any other case which may be in any way connected with that case (whether or not any function of the Commission could be exercised in relation to that other case).

(4) The duty to comply with a requirement under this section is not affected by any obligation of secrecy or other limitation on disclosure (including any such obligation or limitation imposed by or by virtue of an enactment) which

would otherwise prevent the production of the document or other material to the Commission or the giving of access to it to the Commission.

Criminal Procedure (Scotland) Act 1995

(1995, c. 46)

An Act to consolidate certain enactments relating to criminal procedure in Scotland.　　　　　　　　[8th November 1995]　　　**76–001**

. . . . . .

Part II

Police Functions

Lord Advocate's instructions

Instructions by Lord Advocate as to reporting of offences

12. The Lord Advocate may, from time to time, issue instructions to a chief **76–002** constable with regard to the reporting, for consideration of the question of prosecution, of offences alleged to have been committed within the area of such chief constable, and it shall be the duty of a chief constable to whom any such instruction is issued to secure compliance therewith.

Detention and questioning

Powers relating to suspects and potential witnesses

13.—(1) Where a constable has reasonable grounds for suspecting that a **76–003** person has committed or is committing an offence at any place, he may require—

(a) that person, if the constable finds him at that place or at any place where the constable is entitled to be, to give his name and address and may ask him for an explanation of the circumstances which have given rise to the constable's suspicion;

(b) any other person whom the constable finds at that place or at any place where the constable is entitled to be and who the constable believes has information relating to the offence, to give his name and address.

(2) The constable may require the person mentioned in paragraph (a) of subsection (1) above to remain with him while he (either or both)—

(a) subject to subsection (3) below, verifies any name and address given by the person;

(b) notes any explanation proffered by the person.

(3) The constable shall exercise his power under paragraph (a) of subsection

(2) above only where it appears to him that such verification can be obtained quickly.

(4) A constable may use reasonable force to ensure that the person mentioned in paragraph (a) of subsection (1) above remains with him.

(5) A constable shall inform a person, when making a requirement of that person under—

(a) paragraph (a) of subsection (1) above, of his suspicion and of the general nature of the offence which he suspects that the person has committed or is committing;

(b) paragraph (b) of subsection (1) above, of his suspicion, of the general nature of the offence which he suspects has been or is being committed and that the reason for the requirement is that he believes the person has information relating to the offence;

(c) subsection (2) above, why the person is being required to remain with him;

(d) either of the said subsections, that failure to comply with the requirement may constitute an offence.

(6) A person mentioned in—

(a) paragraph (a) of subsection (1) above who having been required—

(i) under that subsection to give his name and address; or

(ii) under subsection (2) above to remain with a constable,

fails, without reasonable excuse, to do so, shall be guilty of an offence and liable on summary conviction to a fine not exceeding level 3 on the standard scale;

(b) paragraph (b) of the said subsection (1) who having been required under that subsection to give his name and address fails, without reasonable excuse, to do so shall be guilty of an offence and liable on summary conviction to a fine not exceeding level 2 on the standard scale.

(7) A constable may arrest without warrant any person who he has reasonable grounds for suspecting has committed an offence under subsection (6) above.

Detention and questioning at police station

76–004   14.—(1) Where a constable has reasonable grounds for suspecting that a person has committed or is committing an offence punishable by imprisonment, the constable may, for the purpose of facilitating the carrying out of investigations—

(a) into the offence; and

(b) as to whether criminal proceedings should be instigated against the person,

detain that person and take him as quickly as is reasonably practicable to a police station or other premises and may thereafter for that purpose take him to any other place and, subject to the following provisions of this section, the detention may continue at the police station or, as the case may be, the other premises or place.

(2) Detention under subsection (1) above shall be terminated not more than six hours after it begins or (if earlier)—

(a) when the person is arrested;

(b) when he is detained in pursuance of any other enactment; or

(c) where there are no longer such grounds as are mentioned in the said subsection (1),

and when a person has been detained under subsection (1) above, he shall be informed immediately upon the termination of his detention in accordance with this subsection that his detention has been terminated.

(3) Where a person has been released at the termination of a period of detention under subsection (1) above he shall not thereafter be detained, under that subsection, on the same grounds or on any grounds arising out of the same circumstances.

(4) Subject to subsection (5) below, where a person has previously been detained in pursuance of any other enactment, and is detained under subsection (1) above on the same grounds or on grounds arising from the same circumstances as those which led to his earlier detention, the period of six hours mentioned in subsection (2) above shall be reduced by the length of that earlier detention.

(5) Subsection (4) above shall not apply in relation to detention under section 41(3) of the Prisons (Scotland) Act 1989 (detention in relation to introduction etc. into prison of prohibited article), but where a person was detained under section 41(3) immediately prior to his detention under subsection (1) above the period of six hours mentioned in subsection (2) above shall be reduced by the length of that earlier detention.

(6) At the time when a constable detains a person under subsection (1) above, he shall inform the person of his suspicion, of the general nature of the offence which he suspects has been or is being committed and of the reason for the detention; and there shall be recorded—

(a) the place where detention begins and the police station or other premises to which the person is taken;

(b) any other place to which the person is, during the detention, thereafter taken;

(c) the general nature of the suspected offence;

(d) the time when detention under subsection (1) above begins and the time of the person's arrival at the police station or other premises;

(e) the time when the person is informed of his rights in terms of subsection (9) below and of subsection (1)(b) of section 15 of this Act and the identity of the constable so informing him;

(f) where the person requests such intimation to be sent as is specified in section 15(1)(b) of this Act, the time when such request is—

(i) made;

(ii) complied with; and

(g) the time of the person's release from detention or, where instead of being released he is arrested in respect of the alleged offence, the time of such arrest.

(7) Where a person is detained under subsection (1) above, a constable may—

(a) without prejudice to any relevant rule of law as regards the admissibility in evidence of any answer given, put questions to him in relation to the suspected offence;

(b) exercise the same powers of search as are available following an arrest.

(8) A constable may use reasonable force in exercising any power conferred by subsection (1), or by paragraph (b) of subsection (7), above.

(9) A person detained under subsection (1) above shall be under no obligation to answer any question other than to give his name and address, and a constable shall so inform him both on so detaining him and on arrival at the police station or other premises.

Rights of person arrested or detained

76–005   **15.**—(1) Without prejudice to section 17 of this Act, a person who, not being a person in respect of whose custody or detention subsection (4) below applies—

(a) has been arrested and is in custody in a police station or other premises, shall be entitled to have intimation of his custody and of the place where he is being held sent to a person reasonably named by him;

(b) is being detained under section 14 of this Act and has been taken to a police station or other premises or place, shall be entitled to have intimation of his detention and of the police station or other premises or place sent to a solicitor and to one other person reasonably named by him,

without delay or, where some delay is necessary in the interest of the investigation or the prevention of crime or the apprehension of offenders, with no more delay than is so necessary.

(2) A person shall be informed of his entitlement under subsection (1) above—

(a) on arrival at the police station or other premises; or

(b) where he is not arrested, or as the case may be detained, until after such arrival, on such arrest or detention.

(3) Where the person mentioned in paragraph (a) of subsection (1) above requests such intimation to be sent as is specified in that paragraph there shall be recorded the time when such request is—

(a) made;

(b) complied with.

(4) Without prejudice to the said section 17, a constable shall, where a person who has been arrested and is in such custody as is mentioned in paragraph (a) of subsection (1) above or who is being detained as is mentioned in paragraph (b) of that subsection appears to him to be a child, send without delay such intimation as is mentioned in the said paragraph (a), or as the case may be paragraph (b), to that person's parent if known; and the parent—

(a) in a case where there is reasonable cause to suspect that he has been involved in the alleged offence in resect of which the person has been arrested or detained, may; and

(b) in any other case shall,

be permitted access to the person.

(5) The nature and extent of any access permitted under subsection (4) above shall be subject to any restriction essential for the furtherance of the investigation or the well-being of the person.

(6) In subsection (4) above—

(a) "child" means a person under 16 years of age; and

(b) "parent" includes guardian and any person who has the [care][1] of a
    child.

[1] Words substituted by Crime and Punishment (Scotland) Act 1997 (c.48), Sched. 1, para. 21(2).

Drunken persons: power to take to designated place

16.—(1) Where a constable has power to arrest a person without a warrant   **76–006**
for any offence and the constable has reasonable grounds for suspecting that
that person is drunk, the constable may, if he thinks fit, take him to any place
designated by the Secretary of State for the purposes of this section as a place
suitable for the care of drunken persons.

(2) A person shall not by virtue of this section be liable to be detained in any
such place as is mentioned in subsection (1) above, but the exercise in his case
of the power conferred by this section shall not preclude his being charged with
any offence.

Arrest: access to solicitor

Right of accused to have access to solicitor

17.—(1) Where an accused has been arrested on any criminal charge, he shall   **76–007**
be entitled immediately upon such arrest—

(a) to have intimation sent to a solicitor that his professional assistance is
    required by the accused, and informing the solicitor—

    (i) of the place where the person is being detained;
    (ii) whether the person is to be liberated; and
    (iii) if the person is not to be liberated, the court to which he is to be
          taken and the date when he is to be so taken; and

(b) to be told what rights there are under—

    (i) paragraph (a) above;
    (ii) subsection (2) below; and
    (iii) section 35(1) and (2) of this Act.

(2) The accused and the solicitor shall be entitled to have a private interview
before the examination or, as the case may be, first appearance.

Prints and samples

Prints, samples, etc. in criminal investigations

18.—(1) This section applies where a person has been arrested and is in   **76–008**
custody or is detained under section 14(1) of this Act.

(2) A constable may take from the person [, or require the person to provide
him with, such relevant physical data] as the constable may, having regard to
the circumstances of the suspected offence in respect of which the person has
been arrested or detained, reasonably consider it appropriate to take [from him
or require him to provide, and the person so required shall comply with that
requirement].

[(3) Subject to subsection (4) below, all record of any relevant physical data
taken from or provided by a person under subsection (2) above, all samples
taken under subsection (6) below and all information derived from such samples
shall be destroyed as soon as possible following a decision not to institute criminal proceedings against the person or on the conclusion of such proceedings

otherwise than with a conviction or an order under section 246(3) of this Act.]

(4) The duty under subsection (3) above to destroy samples taken under subsection (6) below and information derived from such samples shall not apply—

(a) where the destruction of the sample or the information could have the effect of destroying any sample, or any information derived therefrom, lawfully held in relation to a person other than the person from whom the sample was taken; or

(b) where the record, sample or information in question is of the same kind as a record, a sample or, as the case may be, information lawfully held by or on behalf of any police force in relation to the person.

(5) No sample, or information derived from a sample, retained by virtue of subsection (4) above shall be used—

(a) in evidence against the person from whom the sample was taken; or
(b) for the purposes of the investigation of any offence.

(6) A constable may, with the authority of an officer of a rank no lower than inspector, take from the person—

(a) from the hair of an external part of the body other than pubic hair, by means of cutting, combing or plucking, a sample of hair or other material;

(b) from a fingernail or toenail or from under any such nail, a sample of nail or other material;

(c) from an external part of the body, by means of swabbing or rubbing, a sample of blood or other body fluid, of body tissue or of other material;

(d) from the inside of the mouth, by means of swabbing, a sample of saliva or other material.

[(7A) For the purposes of this section and sections 19 to 20 of this Act "relevant physical data" means any—

(a) fingerprint;
(b) palm print;
(c) print or impression other than those mentioned in paragraph (a) and (b) above, of an external part of the body;
(d) record of a person's skin on an external part of the body created by a device approved by the Secretary of State.

(7B) The Secretary of State by order made by statutory instrument may approve a device for the purpose of creating such records as are mentioned in paragraph (d) of subsection (7A) above.]

(8) Nothing in this section shall prejudice—

(a) any power of search;
(b) any power to take possession of evidence where there is imminent danger of its being lost or destroyed; or
(c) any power to take prints, impressions or samples under the authority of a warrant.

Prints, samples, etc. in criminal investigations: supplementary provisions

76–009   **19.**—(1) [Without prejudice to any power exercisable under section 19A of this Act, this] section applies where a person convicted of an offence—

(a) has not, since the conviction, had a sample, print or impression taken from him; or
(b) [has at any time had—

   (i) taken from him or been required (whether under paragraph (a) above or under section 18 or 19A of this Act or otherwise) to provide any relevant physical data; or
   (ii) any impression or sample taken from him,

which was not suitable for the means of analysis for which the data were taken or required or the impression or sample was taken or, though suitable, was insufficient (either in quantity or in quality) to enable information to be obtained by that means of analysis.]

(2) Where this section applies, a constable may, within the permitted period—

[(a) take from or require the convicted person to provide him with such relevant physical data as he reasonably considers it appropriate to take or, as the case may be, require the provision of;]
(b) with the authority of an officer of a rank no lower than inspector, take from the person any sample mentioned in any of paragraphs (a) to (d) of subsection (6) of section 18 of this Act by the means specified in that paragraph in relation to that sample.

(3) A constable—

(a) may require the convicted person to attend a police station for the purposes of subsection (2) above;
(b) may, where the convicted person is in legal custody by virtue of section 295 of this Act, exercise the powers conferred by subsection (2) above in relation to the person in the place where he is for the time being.

(4) In subsection (2) above, "the permitted period" means —

(a) in a case to which paragraph (a) of subsection (1) above applies, the period of one month beginning with the date of the conviction;
(b) in a case to which paragraph (b) of that subsection applies, the period of one month beginning with the date on which a constable of the police force which instructed the analysis receives written intimation that [the relevant physical data were or] the sample was unsuitable or, as the case may be, insufficient as mentioned in that paragraph.

(5) A requirement under subsection (3)(a) above—

(a) shall give the person at least seven days' notice of the date on which he is required to attend;
(b) may direct him to attend at a specified time of day or between specified times of day.

(6) Any constable may arrest without warrant a person who fails to comply with a requirement under subsection (3)(a) above.

Samples, etc. from persons convicted of sexual and violent offences

[**19A.**—(1) This section applies where a person—   **76–010**

(a) is convicted on or after the relevant date of a relevant offence and is sentenced to imprisonment;

(b) was convicted before the relevant date of a relevant offence, was sentenced to imprisonment and is serving that sentence on or after the relevant date;

(c) was convicted before the relevant date of a specified relevant offence, was sentenced to imprisonment, is not serving that sentence on that date or at any time after that date but was serving it at any time during the period of five years ending with the day before that date.

(2) Subject to subsections (3) and (4) below, where this section applies a constable may—

(a) take from the person or require the person to provide him with such relevant physical data as the constable reasonably considers appropriate; and

(b) with the authority of an officer of a rank no lower than inspector, take from the person any sample mentioned in any of paragraphs (a) to (d) of subsection (6) of section 18 of this Act by the means specified in that paragraph in relation to that sample.

(3) The power conferred by subsection (2) above shall not be exercised where the person has previously had taken from him or been required to provide relevant physical data or any sample under section 19(1)(a) of this Act or under this section unless the data so taken or required have been or, as the case may be, the sample so taken or required has been lost or destroyed.

(4) Where this section applies by virtue of—

(a) paragraph (a) or (b) of subsection (1) above, the powers conferred by subsection (2) above may be exercised at any time when the person is serving his sentence; and

(b) paragraph (c) of the said subsection (1), those powers may only be exercised within a period of three months beginning on the relevant date.

(5) Where a person in respect of whom the power conferred by subsection (2) above may be exercised—

(a) is no longer serving his sentence of imprisonment, subsections (3)(a), (5) and (6);

(b) is serving his sentence of imprisonment, subsection (3)(b),

of section 19 of this Act shall apply for the purposes of subsection (2) above as they apply for the purposes of subsection (2) of that section.

(6) In this section—

"conviction" includes—

(a) an acquittal, by virtue of section 54(6) or 55(3) of this Act, on the ground of the person's insanity at the time at which he committed the act constituting the relevant offence;

(b) a finding under section 55(2) of this Act,

and "convicted" shall be construed accordingly;

"relevant date" means the date on which section 48 of the Crime and Punishment (Scotland) Act 1997 is commenced;

"relevant offence" means any relevant sexual offence or any relevant violent offence;

"relevant sexual offence" means any of the following offences—

(a) rape;
(b) clandestine injury to women;
(c) abduction of a woman with intent to rape;
(d) assault with intent to rape or ravish;
(e) indecent assault;
(f) lewd, indecent or libidinous behaviour or practices;
(g) shameless indecency;
(h) sodomy; and
(i) any offence which consists of a contravention of any of the following statutory provisions—

　　(i) section 52 of the Civic Government (Scotland) Act 1982
　　　(taking and distribution of indecent images of children);
　　(ii) section 52A of that Act (possession of indecent images of
　　　children);
　　(iii) section 106 of the Mental Health (Scotland) Act 1984
　　　(protection of mentally handicapped females);
　　(iv) section 107 of that Act (protection of patients);
　　(v) section 1 of the Criminal Law (Consolidation)(Scotland) Act
　　　1995 (incest);
　　(vi) section 2 of that Act (intercourse with step-child);
　　(vii) section 3 of that Act (intercourse with child under 16 years
　　　by person in position of trust);
　　(viii) section 5(1) or (2) of that Act (unlawful intercourse with girl
　　　under 13 years);
　　(ix) section 5(3) of that Act (unlawful intercourse with girl aged
　　　between 13 and 16 years);
　　(x) section 6 of that Act (indecent behaviour towards girl
　　　between 12 and 16 years);
　　(xi) section 7 of that Act (procuring);
　　(xii) section 8 of that Act (abduction and unlawful detention of
　　　women and girls);
　　(xiii) section 9 of that Act (permitting use of premises for unlawful
　　　sexual intercourse);
　　(xiv) section 10 of that Act (liability of parents etc in respect of
　　　offences against girls under 16 years);
　　(xv) section 11(1)(b) of that Act (soliciting for immoral purpose);
　　(xvi) section 13(5)(b) and (c) of that Act (homosexual offences).

"relevant violent offence" means any of the following offences—

(a) murder or culpable homicide;
(b) uttering a threat to the life of another person;
(c) perverting the course of justice in connection with an offence of
　　murder;
(d) fire raising;
(e) assault;
(f) reckless conduct causing actual injury;
(g) abduction; and
(h) any offence which consists of a contravention of any of the following statutory provisions—

　　(i) sections 2 (causing explosion likely to endanger life) or 3
　　　(attempting to cause such an explosion) of the Explosive
　　　Substances Act 1883;
　　(ii) section 12 of the Children and Young Persons (Scotland) Act
　　　1937 (cruelty to children);
　　(iii) sections 16 (possession of firearm with intent to endanger life

or cause serious injury), 17 (use of firearm to resist arrest) or 18 (having a firearm for purpose of committing an offence listed in Schedule 2) of the Firearms Act 1968;

(iv) section 6 of the Child Abduction Act 1984 (taking or sending child out of the United Kingdom); and

"sentence of imprisonment" means the sentence imposed in respect of the relevant offence and includes—

(a) a hospital order, a restriction order, a hospital direction and any order under section 57(2)(a) or (b) of this Act; and

(b) a sentence of detention imposed under section 207 or 208 of this Act,

and "sentenced to imprisonment" shall be construed accordingly; and any reference to a person serving his sentence shall be construed as a reference to the person being detained in a prison, hospital or other place in pursuance of a sentence of imprisonment; and
"specified relevant offence" means —

(a) any relevant sexual offence mentioned in paragraphs (a), (b), (f) and (i)(viii) of the definition of that expression and any such offence as is mentioned in paragraph (h) of that definition where the person against whom the offence was committed did not consent; and

(b) any relevant violent offence mentioned in paragraph (a) or (g) of the definition of that expression and any such offence as is mentioned in paragraph (e) of that definition where the assault is to the victim's severe injury,

but, notwithstanding subsection (7) below, does not include— (i) conspiracy or incitement to commit; and (ii) aiding and abetting, counselling or procuring the commission of, any of those offences.

(7) In this section—

(a) any reference to a relevant offence includes a reference to any attempt, conspiracy or incitement to commit such an offence; and

(b) any reference to—

(i) a relevant sexual offence mentioned in paragraph (i); or
(ii) a relevant violent offence mentioned in paragraph (h);

of the definition of those expressions in subsection (6) above includes a reference to aiding and abetting, counselling or procuring the commission of such an offence.][1]

[1] Added by Crime and Punishment (Scotland) Act 1997 (c.48), Pt IV, s. 48(2).

Power of constable in obtaining relevant physical data, etc.

76–011 [**19B.** A constable may use reasonable force in—

(a) taking any relevant physical data from a person or securing a person's compliance with a requirement made under section 18(2), 19(2)(a) or 19A(2)(a) of this Act;

(b) exercising any power conferred by section 18(6), 19(2)(b) or 19A(2)(b) of this Act.][1]

[1] Added by Crime and Punishment (Scotland) Act 1997 (c.48), Pt IV, s. 48(2).

Use of prints, samples etc.

20. Without prejudice to any power to do so apart from this section, [relevant **76–012** physical data]¹, impressions and samples lawfully held by or on behalf of any police force or in connection with or as a result of an investigation of an offence and information derived therefrom may be checked against other such [data]², impressions, samples and information.

¹ Words substituted by Crime and Punishment (Scotland) Act 1997 (c.48), Pt IV, s. 47(3)(a).
² Word substituted by Crime and Punishment (Scotland) Act 1997 (c.48), Pt IV, s. 47(3)(b).

Schedule 1 offences

Schedule 1 offences: power of constable to take offender into custody

21.—(1) Without prejudice to any other powers of arrest, a constable may **76–013** take into custody without warrant—

    (a) any person who within his view commits any of the offences mentioned in Schedule 1 to this Act, if the constable does not know and cannot ascertain his name and address;

    (b) any person who has committed, or whom he had reason to believe to have committed, any of the offences mentioned in that Schedule, if the constable does not know and cannot ascertain his name and address or has reasonable ground for believing that he will abscond.

(2) Where a person has been arrested under this section, the officer in charge of a police station may—

    (a) liberate him upon a written undertaking, signed by him and certified by the said officer, in terms of which that person undertakes to appear at a specified court at a specified time; or

    (b) liberate him without any such undertaking; or

    (c) refuse to liberate him, and such refusal and the detention of that person until his case is tried in the usual form shall not subject the officer to any claim whatsoever.

(3) A person in breach of an undertaking given by him under subsection (2)(a) above without reasonable excuse shall be guilty of an offence and liable to the following penalties—

    (a) a fine not exceeding level 3 on the standard scale; and

    (b) imprisonment for a period—

        (i) where conviction is in the district court, not exceeding 60 days; or

        (ii) in any other case, not exceeding 3 months.

(4) The penalties provided for in subsection (3) above may be imposed in addition to any other penalty which it is competent for the court to impose, notwithstanding that the total of penalties imposed may exceed the maximum penalty which it is competent to impose in respect of the original offence.

(5) In any proceedings relating to an offence under this section, a writing, purporting to be such an undertaking as is mentioned in subsection (2)(a) above and bearing to be signed and certified, shall be sufficient evidence of the terms of the undertaking given by the arrested person.

Police liberation

Liberation by police

76–014   **22.**—(1) Where a person has been arrested and charged with an offence which may be tried summarily, the officer in charge of a police station may—

(a) liberate him upon a written undertaking, signed by him and certified by the officer, in terms of which the person undertakes to appear at a specified court at a specified time; or

(b) liberate him without any such undertaking; or

(c) refuse to liberate him.

(2) A person in breach of an undertaking given by him under subsection (1) above without reasonable excuse shall be guilty of an offence and liable on summary conviction to the following penalties—

(a) a fine not exceeding level 3 on the standard scale; and

(b) imprisonment for a period—

(i) where conviction is in the district court, not exceeding 60 days; or

(ii) where conviction is in the sheriff court, not exceeding 3 months.

(3) The refusal of the officer in charge to liberate a person under subsection (1)(c) above and the detention of that person until his case is tried in the usual form shall not subject the officer to any claim whatsoever.

(4) The penalties provided for in subsection (2) above may be imposed in addition to any other penalty which it is competent for the court to impose, notwithstanding that the total of penalties imposed may exceed the maximum penalty which it is competent to impose in respect of the original offence.

(5) In any proceedings relating to an offence under this section, a writing, purporting to be such an undertaking as is mentioned in subsection (1)(a) above and bearing to be signed and certified, shall be sufficient evidence of the terms of the undertaking given by the arrested person.

. . . . . .

PART IV

PETITION PROCEDURE

Judicial examination

Judicial examination

76–015   **35.**—(1) The accused's solicitor shall be entitled to be present at the examination.

(2) The sheriff may delay the examination for a period not exceeding 48 hours from and after the time of the accused's arrest, in order to allow time for the attendance of the solicitor.

(3) Where the accused is brought before the sheriff for examination on any charge and he or his solicitor intimates that he does not desire to emit a declaration in regard to such a charge, it shall be unnecessary to take a declaration, and, subject to section 36 of this Act, the accused may be committed for further examination or until liberated in due course of law without a declaration being taken.

(4) Nothing in subsection (3) above shall prejudice the right of the accused subsequently to emit a declaration on intimating to the prosecutor his desire to do so; and that declaration shall be taken in further examination.

(5) Where, subsequent to examination or further examination on any charge, the prosecutor desires to question the accused as regards an extrajudicial confession, whether or not a full admission, allegedly made by him to or in the hearing of a constable, which is relevant to the charge and as regards which he has not previously been examined, the accused may be brought before the sheriff for further examination.

(6) Where the accused is brought before the sheriff for further examination the sheriff may delay that examination for a period not exceeding 24 hours in order to allow time for the attendance of the accused's solicitor.

(7) Any proceedings before the sheriff in examination or further examination shall be conducted in chambers and outwith the presence of any co-accused.

(8) This section applies to procedure on petition; without prejudice to the accused being tried summarily by the sheriff for any offence in respect of which he has been committed until liberated in due course of law.

Judicial examination: questioning by prosecutor

36.—(1) Subject to the following provisions of this section an accused on being brought before the sheriff for examination on any charge (whether the first or a further examination) may be questioned by the prosecutor in so far as such questioning is directed towards eliciting any admission, denial, explanation, justification or comment which the accused may have as regards anything to which subsections (2) to (4) below apply.

76–016

(2) This subsection applies to matters averred in the charge, and the particular aims of a line of questions under this subsection shall be to determine—

(a) whether any account which the accused can give ostensibly discloses a defence; and
(b) the nature and particulars of that defence.

(3) This subsection applies to the alleged making by the accused, to or in the hearing of a constable, of an extrajudicial confession (whether or not a full admission) relevant to the charge, and questions under this subsection may only be put if the accused has, before the examination, received from the prosecutor or from a constable a written record of the confession allegedly made.

(4) This subsection applies to what is said in any declaration emitted in regard to the charge by the accused at examination.

(5) The prosecutor shall, in framing questions in exercise of his power under subsection (1) above, have regard to the following principles—

(a) the question should not be designed to challenge the truth of anything said by the accused;
(b) there should be no reiteration of a question which the accused has refused to answer at the examination; and
(c) there should be no leading questions,

and the sheriff shall ensure that all questions are fairly put to, and understood by, the accused.

(6) The accused shall be told by the sheriff—

(a) where he is represented by a solicitor at the judicial examination, that he may consult that solicitor before answering any question; and
(b) that if he answers any question put to him at the examination under

this section in such a way as to disclose an ostensible defence, the prosecutor shall be under the duty imposed by subsection (10) below.

(7) With the permission of the sheriff, the solicitor for the accused may ask the accused any question the purpose of which is to clarify any ambiguity in an answer given by the accused to the prosecutor at the examination or to give the accused an opportunity to answer any question which he has previously refused to answer.

(8) An accused may decline to answer a question under subsection (1) above; and, where he is subsequently tried on the charge mentioned in that subsection or on any other charge arising out of the circumstances which gave rise to the charge so mentioned, his having so declined may be commented upon by the prosecutor, the judge presiding at the trial, or any co-accused, only where and in so far as the accused (or any witness called on his behalf) in evidence avers something which could have been stated appropriately in answer to that question.

(9) The procedure in relation to examination under this section shall be prescribed by Act of Adjournal.

(10) Without prejudice to any rule of law, on the conclusion of an examination under this section the prosecutor shall secure the investigation, to such extent as is reasonably practicable, of any ostensible defence disclosed in the course of the examination.

(11) The duty imposed by subsection (10) above shall not apply as respects any ostensible defence which is not reasonably capable of being investigated.

Judicial examination: record of proceedings

76–017   **37.**—(1) The prosecutor shall provide for a verbatim record to be made by means of shorthand notes or by mechanical means of all questions to and answers and declarations by the accused in examination, or further examination, under sections 35 and 36 of this Act.

(2) A shorthand writer shall—

>   (a) sign the shorthand notes taken by him of the questions, answers and declarations mentioned in subsection (1) above and certify the notes as being complete and correct; and
>   (b) retain the notes.

(3) A person recording the questions, answers and declarations mentioned in subsection (1) above by mechanical means shall—

>   (a) certify that the record is true and complete;
>   (b) specify in the certificate the proceedings to which the record relates; and
>   (c) retain the record.

(4) The prosecutor shall require the person who made the record mentioned in subsection (1) above, or such other competent person as he may specify, to make a transcript of the record in legible form; and that person shall—

>   (a) comply with the requirement;
>   (b) certify the transcript as being a complete and correct transcript of the record purporting to have been made and certified, and in the case of shorthand notes signed, by the person who made the record; and
>   (c) send the transcript to the prosecutor.

(5) A transcript certified under subsection (4)(b) above shall, subject to section

38(1) of this Act, be deemed for all purposes to be a complete and correct record of the questions, answers and declarations mentioned in subsection (1) above.

(6) Subject to subsections (7) to (9) below, within 14 days of the date of examination or further examination, the prosecutor shall—

(a) serve a copy of the transcript on the accused examined; and
(b) serve a further such copy on the solicitor (if any) for that accused.

(7) Where at the time of further examination a trial diet is already fixed and the interval between the further examination and that diet is not sufficient to allow of the time limits specified in subsection (6) above and subsection (1) of section 38 of this Act the sheriff shall (either or both)—

(a) direct that those subsections shall apply in the case with such modifications as to time limits as he shall specify;
(b) subject to subsection (8) below, postpone the trial diet.

(8) Postponement under paragraph (b) of subsection (7) above alone shall only be competent where the sheriff considers that to proceed under paragraph (a) of that subsection alone, or paragraphs (a) and (b) together, would not be practicable.

(9) Any time limit mentioned in subsection (6) above and subsection (1) of section 38 of this Act (including any such time limit as modified by a direction under subsection (7) above) may be extended, in respect of the case, by the High Court; [and an application to the High Court for any such extension shall be disposed of by the High Court or any Lord Commissioner of Justiciary in court or in chambers].

(10) A copy of—

(a) a transcript required by paragraph (a) of subsection (6) above to be served on an accused or by paragraph (b) of that subsection to be served on his solicitor; or
(b) a notice required by paragraph (a) of section 38(1) of this Act to be served on an accused or on the prosecutor,

shall be served in such manner as may be prescribed by Act of Adjournal; and a written execution purporting to be signed by the person who served such transcript or notice, together with, where appropriate, the relevant post office receipt shall be sufficient evidence of service of such a copy.

. . . . . .

Committal

Committal until liberated in due course of law

40.—(1) Every petition shall be signed and no accused shall be committed **76–018** until liberated in due course of law for any crime or offence without a warrant in writing expressing the particular charge in respect of which he is committed.

(2) Any such warrant for imprisonment which either proceeds on an unsigned petition or does not express the particular charge shall be null and void.

(3) The accused shall immediately be given a true copy of the warrant for imprisonment signed by the constable or person executing the warrant before imprisonment or by the prison officer receiving the warrant.

. . . . . .

PART XIII

MISCELLANEOUS

Lord Advocate

Demission of office by Lord Advocate

76–019   **287.**—(1) All indictments which have been raised by a Lord Advocate shall remain effective notwithstanding his subsequently having died or demitted office and may be taken up and proceeded with by his successor.

(2) During any period when the office of Lord Advocate is vacant it shall be lawful to indict accused persons in name of the Solicitor General then in office.

(3) The advocates depute shall not demit office when a Lord Advocate dies or demits office but shall continue in office until their successors receive commissions.

(4) The advocates depute and procurators fiscal shall have power, notwithstanding any vacancy in the office of Lord Advocate, to take up and proceed with any indictment which—

(a) by virtue of subsection (1) above, remains effective; or
(b) by virtue of subsection (2) above, is in the name of the Solicitor General.

(5) For the purposes of this Act, where, but for this subsection, demission of office by one Law Officer would result in the offices of both being vacant, he or, where both demit office on the same day, the person demitting the office of Lord Advocate shall be deemed to continue in office until the warrant of appointment of the person succeeding to the office of Lord Advocate is granted.

(6) The Lord Advocate shall enter upon the duties of his office immediately upon the grant of his warrant of appointment.

Rights of appeal for Advocate General: devolution issues

76–020   [**288A.**—(1) This section applies where—

(a) a person is acquitted or convicted of a charge (whether on indictment or in summary proceedings), and
(b) the Advocate General for Scotland was a party to the proceedings in pursuance of paragraph 6 of Schedule 6 to the Scotland Act 1998 (devolution issues).

(2) The Advocate General for Scotland may refer any devolution issue which has arisen in the proceedings to the High Court for their opinion; and the Clerk of Justiciary shall send to the person acquitted or convicted and to any solicitor who acted for that person at the trial, a copy of the reference and intimation of the date fixed by the Court for a hearing.

(3) The person may, not later than seven days before the date so fixed, intimate in writing to the Clerk of Justiciary and to the Advocate General for Scotland either—

(a) that he elects to appear personally at the hearing, or
(b) that he elects to be represented by counsel at the hearing, but, except by leave of the Court on cause shown, and without prejudice to his right to attend, he shall not appear or be represented at the hearing other than by and in conformity with an election under this subsection.

(4) Where there is no intimation under subsection (3)(b), the High Court shall appoint counsel to act at the hearing as amicus curiae.

(5) The costs of representation elected under subsection (3)(b) or of an appointment under subsection (4) shall, after being taxed by the Auditor of the Court of Session, be paid by the Advocate General for Scotland out of money provided by Parliament.

(6) The opinion on the point referred under subsection (2) shall not affect the acquittal or (as the case may be) conviction in the trial.]¹

¹ Added by Scotland Act 1998 (c.46), Sched. 8, para. 32(2).

Appeals to Judicial Committee of the Privy Council

[**288B.**—(1) This section applies where the Judicial Committee of the Privy Council determines an appeal under paragraph 13(a) of Schedule 6 to the Scotland Act 1998 against a determination of a devolution issue by the High Court in the ordinary course of proceedings.

76–021

(2) The determination of the appeal shall not affect any earlier acquittal or earlier quashing of any conviction in the proceedings.

(3) Subject to subsection (2) above, the High Court shall have the same powers in relation to the proceedings when remitted to it by the Judicial Committee as it would have if it were considering the proceedings otherwise than as a trial court.]¹

¹ Added by Scotland Act 1998 (c.46), Sched. 8, para. 32(2).

. . . . . .

Certain rights of accused

Accused's right to request identification parade

290.—(1) Subject to subsection (2) below, the sheriff may, on an application by an accused at any time after the accused has been charged with an offence, order that, in relation to the alleged offence, the prosecutor shall hold an identification parade in which the accused shall be one of those constituting the parade.

76–022

(2) The sheriff shall make an order in accordance with subsection (1) above only after giving the prosecutor an opportunity to be heard and only if—

(a) an identification parade, such as is mentioned in subsection (1) above, has not been held at the instance of the prosecutor;
(b) after a request by the accused, the prosecutor has refused to hold, or has unreasonably delayed holding, such an identification parade; and
(c) the sheriff considers the application under subsection (1) above to be reasonable.

Disability Discrimination Act 1995

(1995, c. 50)

An Act to make it unlawful to discriminate against disabled persons in connection with employment, the provision of goods, facilities and services or the

77–001

disposal or management of premises; to make provision about the employ-
ment of disabled persons; and to establish a National Disability Council.

[8th November 1995]

PART I

DISABILITY

Meaning of "disability" and "disabled person"

77–002   **1.**—(1) Subject to the provisions of Schedule 1, a person has a disability for
the purposes of this Act if he has a physical or mental impairment which has a
substantial and long-term adverse effect on his ability to carry out normal day-
to-day activities.

(2) In this Act "disabled person" means a person who has a disability.

Past disabilities

77–003   **2.**—(1) The provisions of this Part and Parts II and III apply in relation to a
person who has had a disability as they apply in relation to a person who has
that disability.

(2) Those provisions are subject to the modifications made by Schedule 2.

(3) Any regulations or order made under this Act may include provision with
respect to persons who have had a disability.

(4) In any proceedings under Part II or Part III of this Act, the question
whether a person had a disability at a particular time ("the relevant time") shall
be determined, for the purposes of this section, as if the provisions of, or under,
this Act in force when the act complained of was done had been in force at the
relevant time.

(5) The relevant time may be a time before the passing of this Act.

Guidance

77–004   **3.**—(1) The Secretary of State may issue guidance about the matters to be
taken into account in determining—

 (a) whether an impairment has a substantial adverse effect on a person's
     ability to carry out normal day-to-day activities; or
 (b) whether such an impairment has a long-term effect.

(2) The guidance may, among other things, give examples of—

 (a) effects which it would be reasonable, in relation to particular activities,
     to regard for purposes of this Act as substantial adverse effects;
 (b) effects which it would not be reasonable, in relation to particular activ-
     ities, to regard for such purposes as substantial adverse effects;
 (c) substantial adverse effects which it would be reasonable to regard, for
     such purposes, as long-term;
 (d) substantial adverse effects which it would not be reasonable to regard,
     for such purposes, as long-term.

(3) A tribunal or court determining, for any purpose of this Act, whether an
impairment has a substantial and long-term adverse effect on a person's ability
to carry out normal day-to-day activities, shall take into account any guidance
which appears to it to be relevant.

(4) In preparing a draft of any guidance, the Secretary of State shall consult
such persons as he considers appropriate.

(5) Where the Secretary of State proposes to issue any guidance, he shall publish a draft of it, consider any representations that are made to him about the draft and, if he thinks it appropriate, modify his proposals in the light of any of those representations.

(6) If the Secretary of State decides to proceed with any proposed guidance, he shall lay a draft of it before each House of Parliament.

(7) If, within the 40-day period, either House resolves not to approve the draft, the Secretary of State shall take no further steps in relation to the proposed guidance.

(8) If no such resolution is made within the 40-day period, the Secretary of State shall issue the guidance in the form of his draft.

(9) The guidance shall come into force on such date as the Secretary of State may appoint by order.

(10) Subsection (7) does not prevent a new draft of the proposed guidance from being laid before Parliament.

(11) The Secretary of State may—

(a) from time to time revise the whole or part of any guidance and re-issue it;

(b) by order revoke any guidance.

(12) In this section—

"40-day period", in relation to the draft of any proposed guidance, means—

(a) if the draft is laid before one House on a day later than the day on which it is laid before the other House, the period of 40 days beginning with the later of the two days, and

(b) in any other case, the period of 40 days beginning with the day on which the draft is laid before each House,

no account being taken of any period during which Parliament is dissolved or prorogued or during which both Houses are adjourned for more than 4 days; and

"guidance" means guidance issued by the Secretary of State under this section and includes guidance which has been revised and re-issued.

Part II

Employment

Discrimination by employers

Discrimination against applicants and employees

4.—(1) It is unlawful for an employer to discriminate against a disabled **77–005** person—

(a) in the arrangements which he makes for the purpose of determining to whom he should offer employment;

(b) in the terms on which he offers that person employment; or

(c) by refusing to offer, or deliberately not offering, him employment.

(2) It is unlawful for an employer to discriminate against a disabled person whom he employs—

(a) in the terms of employment which he affords him;

(b) in the opportunities which he affords him for promotion, a transfer, training or receiving any other benefit;

(c) by refusing to afford him, or deliberately not affording him, any such opportunity; or

(d) by dismissing him, or subjecting him to any other detriment.

(3) Subsection (2) does not apply to benefits of any description if the employer is concerned with the provision (whether or not for payment) of benefits of that description to the public, or to a section of the public which includes the employee in question, unless—

(a) that provision differs in a material respect from the provision of the benefits by the employer to his employees; or

(b) the provision of the benefits to the employee in question is regulated by his contract of employment; or

(c) the benefits relate to training.

(4) In this Part "benefits" includes facilities and services.

(5) In the case of an act which constitutes discrimination by virtue of section 55, this section also applies to discrimination against a person who is not disabled.

(6) This section applies only in relation to employment at an establishment in Great Britain.

Meaning of "discrimination"

77–006   **5.**—(1) For the purposes of this Part, an employer discriminates against a disabled person if—

(a) for a reason which relates to the disabled person's disability, he treats him less favourably than he treats or would treat others to whom that reason does not or would not apply; and

(b) he cannot show that the treatment in question is justified.

(2) For the purposes of this Part, an employer also discriminates against a disabled person if—

(a) he fails to comply with a section 6 duty imposed on him in relation to the disabled person; and

(b) he cannot show that his failure to comply with that duty is justified.

(3) Subject to subsection (5), for the purposes of subsection (1) treatment is justified if, but only if, the reason for it is both material to the circumstances of the particular case and substantial.

(4) For the purposes of subsection (2), failure to comply with a section 6 duty is justified if, but only if, the reason for the failure is both material to the circumstances of the particular case and substantial.

(5) If, in a case falling within subsection (1), the employer is under a section 6 duty in relation to the disabled person but fails without justification to comply with that duty, his treatment of that person cannot be justified under subsection (3) unless it would have been justified even if he had complied with the section 6 duty.

(6) Regulations may make provision, for purposes of this section, as to circumstances in which—

(a) treatment is to be taken to be justified;

(b) failure to comply with a section 6 duty is to be taken to be justified;

(c) treatment is to be taken not to be justified;

(d) failure to comply with a section 6 duty is to be taken not to be justified.

(7) Regulations under subsection (6) may, in particular—

(a) make provision by reference to the cost of affording any benefit; and

(b) in relation to benefits under occupational pension schemes, make provision with a view to enabling uniform rates of contributions to be maintained.

Duty of employer to make adjustments

6.—(1) Where—   **77–007**

(a) any arrangements made by or on behalf of an employer, or

(b) any physical feature of premises occupied by the employer,

place the disabled person concerned at a substantial disadvantage in comparison with persons who are not disabled [and who have not had a disability], it is the duty of the employer to take such steps as it is reasonable, in all the circumstances of the case, for him to have to take in order to prevent the arrangements or feature having that effect.

(2) Subsection (1)(a) applies only in relation to—

(a) arrangements for determining to whom employment should be offered;

(b) any term, condition or arrangements on which employment, promotion, a transfer, training or any other benefit is offered or afforded.

(3) The following are examples of steps which an employer may have to take in relation to a disabled person in order to comply with subsection (1)—

(a) making adjustments to premises;

(b) allocating some of the disabled person's duties to another person;

(c) transferring him to fill an existing vacancy;

(d) altering his working hours;

(e) assigning him to a different place of work;

(f) allowing him to be absent during working hours for rehabilitation, assessment or treatment;

(g) giving him, or arranging for him to be given, training;

(h) acquiring or modifying equipment;

(i) modifying instructions or reference manuals;

(j) modifying procedures for testing or assessment;

(k) providing a reader or interpreter;

(l) providing supervision.

(4) In determining whether it is reasonable for an employer to have to take a particular step in order to comply with subsection (1), regard shall be had, in particular, to—

(a) the extent to which taking the step would prevent the effect in question;

(b) the extent to which it is practicable for the employer to take the step;

(c) the financial and other costs which would be incurred by the employer in taking the step and the extent to which taking it would disrupt any of his activities;

(d) the extent of the employer's financial and other resources;

(e) the availability to the employer of financial or other assistance with respect to taking the step.

This subsection is subject to any provision of regulations made under subsection (8).

(5) In this section, "the disabled person concerned" means —

(a) in the case of arrangements for determining to whom employment should be offered, any disabled person who is, or has notified the employer that he may be, an applicant for that employment;

(b) in any other case, a disabled person who is—

(i) an applicant for the employment concerned; or

(ii) an employee of the employer concerned.

(6) Nothing in this section imposes any duty on an employer in relation to a disabled person if the employer does not know, and could not reasonably be expected to know—

(a) in the case of an applicant or potential applicant, that the disabled person concerned is, or may be, an applicant for the employment; or

(b) in any case, that that person has [had] a disability and is likely to be affected in the way mentioned in subsection (1).

(7) Subject to the provisions of this section, nothing in this Part is to be taken to require an employer to treat a disabled person more favourably than he treats or would treat others.

(8) Regulations may make provision, for the purposes of subsection (1)—

(a) as to circumstances in which arrangements are, or a physical feature is, to be taken to have the effect mentioned in that subsection;

(b) as to circumstances in which arrangements are not, or a physical feature is not, to be taken to have that effect;

(c) as to circumstances in which it is reasonable for an employer to have to take steps of a prescribed description;

(d) as to steps which it is always reasonable for an employer to have to take;

(e) as to circumstances in which it is not reasonable for an employer to have to take steps of a prescribed description;

(f) as to steps which it is never reasonable for an employer to have to take;

(g) as to things which are to be treated as physical features;

(h) as to things which are not to be treated as such features.

(9) Regulations made under subsection (8)(c), (d), (e) or (f) may, in particular, make provision by reference to the cost of taking the steps concerned.

(10) Regulations may make provision adding to the duty imposed on employers by this section, including provision of a kind which may be made under subsection (8).

(11) This section does not apply in relation to any benefit under an occupational pension scheme or any other benefit payable in money or money's worth under a scheme or arrangement for the benefit of employees in respect of—

(a) termination of service;

(b) retirement, old age or death;

(c) accident, injury, sickness or invalidity; or

(d) any other prescribed matter.

(12) This section imposes duties only for the purpose of determining whether an employer has discriminated against a disabled person; and accordingly a breach of any such duty is not actionable as such.

Exemption for small businesses

7.—(1) Nothing in this Part applies in relation to an employer who has fewer than [15] employees.

77–008

(2) The Secretary of State may by order amend subsection (1) by substituting a different number (not greater than 20) for the number for the time being specified there.

[(3) Before making an order under subsection (2) the Secretary of State shall consult—

    (a) the Disability Rights Commission;

    (b) such organisations representing the interests of employers as he considers appropriate; and

    (c) such organisations representing the interests of disabled persons in employment or seeking employment as he considers appropriate.

(4) The Secretary of State shall, before laying an order under this section before Parliament, publish a summary of the views expressed to him in his consultations.]

Enforcement, etc.

Enforcement, remedies and procedure

8.—(1) A complaint by any person that another person—

77–009

    (a) has discriminated against him in a way which is unlawful under this Part, or

    (b) is, by virtue of section 57 or 58, to be treated as having discriminated against him in such a way,

may be presented to an [employment tribunal].

(2) Where an [employment tribunal] finds that a complaint presented to it under this section is well-founded, it shall take such of the following steps as it considers just and equitable—

    (a) making a declaration as to the rights of the complainant and the respondent in relation to the matters to which the complaint relates;

    (b) ordering the respondent to pay compensation to the complainant;

    (c) recommending that the respondent take, within a specified period, action appearing to the tribunal to be reasonable, in all the circumstances of the case, for the purpose of obviating or reducing the adverse effect on the complainant of any matter to which the complaint relates.

(3) Where a tribunal orders compensation under subsection (2)(b), the amount of the compensation shall be calculated by applying the principles applicable to the calculation of damages in claims in tort or (in Scotland) in reparation for breach of statutory duty.

(4) For the avoidance of doubt it is hereby declared that compensation in respect of discrimination in a way which is unlawful under this Part may include compensation for injury to feelings whether or not it includes compensation under any other head.

(5) If the respondent to a complaint fails, without reasonable justification, to

comply with a recommendation made by an [employment tribunal] under subsection (2)(c) the tribunal may, if it thinks it just and equitable to do so—

(a) increase the amount of compensation required to be paid to the complainant in respect of the complaint, where an order was made under subsection (2)(b); or
(b) make an order under subsection (2)(b).

(6) Regulations may make provision—

(a) for enabling a tribunal, where an amount of compensation falls to be awarded under subsection (2)(b), to include in the award interest on that amount; and
(b) specifying, for cases where a tribunal decides that an award is to include an amount in respect of interest, the manner in which and the periods and rate by reference to which the interest is to be determined.

(7) Regulations may modify the operation of any order made under [section 14 of the Employment Tribunals Act 1996] (power to make provision as to interest on sums payable in pursuance of [employment tribunal] decisions) to the extent that it relates to an award of compensation under subsection (2)(b).

(8) Part I of Schedule 3 makes further provision about the enforcement of this Part and about procedure.

Validity of certain agreements

77–010 **9.**—(1) Any term in a contract of employment or other agreement is void so far as it purports to—

(a) require a person to do anything which would contravene any provision of, or made under, this Part;
(b) exclude or limit the operation of any provision of this Part; or
(c) prevent any person from presenting a complaint to an [employment tribunal] under this Part.

(2) Paragraphs (b) and (c) of subsection (1) do not apply to an agreement not to institute proceedings under section 8(1), or to an agreement not to continue such proceedings, if—

(a) a conciliation officer has acted under [section 18 of the Employment Tribunals Act 1996] in relation to the matter; or
(b) the conditions set out in subsection (3) are satisfied.

(3) The conditions are that—

(a) the complainant must have received [advice from a relevant independent adviser] as to the terms and effect of the proposed agreement (and in particular its effect on his ability to pursue his complaint before an [employment tribunal]);
(b) when the adviser gave the advice there must have been in force a [contract of insurance, or an indemnity provided for members of a profession or professional body] covering the risk of a claim by the complainant in respect of loss arising in consequence of the advice; and
(c) the agreement must be in writing, relate to the particular complaint, identify the adviser and state that the conditions are satisfied.

[(4) A person is a relevant independent adviser for the purposes of subsection (3)(a)—

    (a) if he is a qualified lawyer,

    (b) if he is an officer, official, employee or member of an independent trade union who has been certified in writing by the trade union as competent to give advice and as authorised to do so on behalf of the trade union,

    (c) if he works at an advice centre (whether as an employee or a volunteer) and has been certified in writing by the centre as competent to give advice and as authorised to do so on behalf of the centre, or

    (d) if he is a person of a description specified in an order made by the Secretary of State.

(4A) But a person is not a relevant independent adviser for the purposes of subsection (3)(a) in relation to the complainant—

    (a) if he is, is employed by or is acting in the matter for the other party or a person who is connected with the other party;

    (b) in the case of a person within subsection (4)(b) or (c), if the trade union or advice centre is the other party or a person who is connected with the other party,

    (c) in the case of a person within subsection (4)(c), if the complainant makes a payment for the advice received from him; or

    (d) in the case of a person of a description specified in an order under subsection (4)(d), if any condition specified in the order in relation to the giving of advice by persons of that description is not satisfied.

(4B) In subsection (4)(a) "qualified lawyer" means—

    (a) as respects England and Wales, a barrister (whether in practice as such or employed to give legal advice), a solicitor who holds a practising certificate, or a person other than a barrister or solicitor who is an authorised advocate or authorised litigator (within the meaning of the Courts and Legal Services Act 1990), and

    (b) as respects Scotland, an advocate (whether in practice as such or employed to give legal advice), or a solicitor who holds a practising certificate.

(4C) In subsection (4)(b) "independent trade union" has the same meaning as in the Trade Union and Labour Relations (Consolidation) Act 1992.

(5) For the purposes of subsection (4A) any two persons are to be treated as connected—

    (a) if one is a company of which the other (directly or indirectly) has control, or

    (b) if both are companies of which a third person (directly or indirectly) has control.]

[(6) An agreement under which the parties agree to submit a dispute to arbitration—

    (a) shall be regarded for the purposes of subsection (2) as being an agreement not to institute, or an agreement not to continue, proceedings if—

        (i) the dispute is covered by a scheme having effect by virtue of an order under section 212A of the Trade Union and Labour Relations (Consolidation) Act 1992, and

(ii) the agreement is to submit it to arbitration in accordance with the scheme, but

(b) shall be regarded as neither being nor including such an agreement in any other case.]

Charities and support for particular groups of persons

77–011

10.—(1) Nothing in this Part—

(a) affects any charitable instrument which provides for conferring benefits on one or more categories of person determined by reference to any physical or mental capacity; or

(b) makes unlawful any act done by a charity or recognised body in pursuance of any of its charitable purposes, so far as those purposes are connected with persons so determined.

(2) Nothing in this Part prevents—

(a) a person who provides supported employment from treating members of a particular group of disabled persons more favourably than other persons in providing such employment; or

(b) the Secretary of State from agreeing to arrangements for the provision of supported employment which will, or may, have that effect.

(3) In this section—

"charitable instrument" means an enactment or other instrument (whenever taking effect) so far as it relates to charitable purposes;

"charity" has the same meaning as in the Charities Act 1993;

"recognised body" means a body which is a recognised body for the purposes of Part I of the Law Reform (Miscellaneous Provisions) (Scotland) Act 1990; and

"supported employment" means facilities provided, or in respect of which payments are made, under section 15 of the Disabled Persons (Employment) Act 1944.

(4) In the application of this section to England and Wales, "charitable purposes" means purposes which are exclusively charitable according to the law of England and Wales.

(5) In the application of this section to Scotland, "charitable purposes" shall be construed in the same way as if it were contained in the Income Tax Acts.

Advertisements suggesting that employers will discriminate against disabled persons

77–012

11.—(1) This section applies where—

(a) a disabled person has applied for employment with an employer;

(b) the employer has refused to offer, or has deliberately not offered, him the employment;

(c) the disabled person has presented a complaint under section 8 against the employer;

(d) the employer has advertised the employment (whether before or after the disabled person applied for it); and

(e) the advertisement indicated, or might reasonably be understood to have indicated, that any application for the advertised employment would, or might, be determined to any extent by reference to—

(i) the successful applicant not having any disability or any category of disability which includes the disabled person's disability; or

(ii) the employer's reluctance to take any action of a kind mentioned in section 6.

(2) The tribunal hearing the complaint shall assume, unless the contrary is shown, that the employer's reason for refusing to offer, or deliberately not offering, the employment to the complainant was related to the complainant's disability.

(3) In this section "advertisement" includes every form of advertisement or notice, whether to the public or not.

Discrimination by other persons

Discrimination against contract workers

12.—(1) It is unlawful for a principal, in relation to contract work, to discriminate against a disabled person—   **77–013**

(a) in the terms on which he allows him to do that work;

(b) by not allowing him to do it or continue to do it;

(c) in the way he affords him access to any benefits or by refusing or deliberately omitting to afford him access to them; or

(d) by subjecting him to any other detriment.

(2) Subsection (1) does not apply to benefits of any description if the principal is concerned with the provision (whether or not for payment) of benefits of that description to the public, or to a section of the public which includes the contract worker in question, unless that provision differs in a material respect from the provision of the benefits by the principal to contract workers.

(3) The provisions of this Part (other than subsections (1) to (3) of section 4) apply to any principal, in relation to contract work, as if he were, or would be, the employer of the contract worker and as if any contract worker supplied to do work for him were an employee of his.

(4) In the case of an act which constitutes discrimination by virtue of section 55, this section also applies to discrimination against a person who is not disabled.

(5) This section applies only in relation to contract work done at an establishment in Great Britain (the provisions of section 68 about the meaning of "employment at an establishment in Great Britain" applying for the purposes of this subsection with the appropriate modifications).

(6) In this section—

"principal" means a person ("A") who makes work available for doing by individuals who are employed by another person who supplies them under a contract made with A;

"contract work" means work so made available; and

"contract worker" means any individual who is supplied to the principal under such a contract.

Discrimination by trade organisations

13.—(1) It is unlawful for a trade organisation to discriminate against a disabled person—   **77–014**

(a) in the terms on which it is prepared to admit him to membership of the organisation; or

(b) by refusing to accept, or deliberately not accepting, his application for membership.

(2) It is unlawful for a trade organisation, in the case of a disabled person who is a member of the organisation, to discriminate against him—

    (a) in the way it affords him access to any benefits or by refusing or deliberately omitting to afford him access to them;

    (b) by depriving him of membership, or varying the terms on which he is a member; or

    (c) by subjecting him to any other detriment.

(3) In the case of an act which constitutes discrimination by virtue of section 55, this section also applies to discrimination against a person who is not disabled.

(4) In this section "trade organisation" means an organisation of workers, an organisation of employers or any other organisation whose members carry on a particular profession or trade for the purposes of which the organisation exists.

Meaning of "discrimination" in relation to trade organisations

77–015   **14.**—(1) For the purposes of this Part, a trade organisation discriminates against a disabled person if—

    (a) for a reason which relates to the disabled person's disability, it treats him less favourably than it treats or would treat others to whom that reason does not or would not apply; and

    (b) it cannot show that the treatment in question is justified.

(2) For the purposes of this Part, a trade organisation also discriminates against a disabled person if—

    (a) it fails to comply with a section 15 duty imposed on it in relation to the disabled person; and

    (b) it cannot show that its failure to comply with that duty is justified.

(3) Subject to subsection (5), for the purposes of subsection (1) treatment is justified if, but only if, the reason for it is both material to the circumstances of the particular case and substantial.

(4) For the purposes of subsection (2), failure to comply with a section 15 duty is justified if, but only if, the reason for the failure is both material to the circumstances of the particular case and substantial.

(5) If, in a case falling within subsection (1), the trade organisation is under a section 15 duty in relation to the disabled person concerned but fails without justification to comply with that duty, its treatment of that person cannot be justified under subsection (3) unless the treatment would have been justified even if the organisation had complied with the section 15 duty.

(6) Regulations may make provision, for purposes of this section, as to circumstances in which—

    (a) treatment is to be taken to be justified;

    (b) failure to comply with a section 15 duty is to be taken to be justified;

    (c) treatment is to be taken not to be justified;

    (d) failure to comply with a section 15 duty is to be taken not to be justified.

. . . . . .

PART III

DISCRIMINATION IN OTHER AREAS

Goods, facilities and services

Discrimination in relation to goods, facilities and services

19.—(1) It is unlawful for a provider of services to discriminate against a **77–016** disabled person—

(a) in refusing to provide, or deliberately not providing, to the disabled person any service which he provides, or is prepared to provide, to members of the public;

(b) in failing to comply with any duty imposed on him by section 21 in circumstances in which the effect of that failure is to make it impossible or unreasonably difficult for the disabled person to make use of any such service;

(c) in the standard of service which he provides to the disabled person or the manner in which he provides it to him; or

(d) in the terms on which he provides a service to the disabled person.

(2) For the purposes of this section and sections 20 and 21—

(a) the provision of services includes the provision of any goods or facilities;

(b) a person is "a provider of services" if he is concerned with the provision, in the United Kingdom, of services to the public or to a section of the public; and

(c) it is irrelevant whether a service is provided on payment or without payment.

(3) The following are examples of services to which this section and sections 20 and 21 apply—

(a) access to and use of any place which members of the public are permitted to enter;

(b) access to and use of means of communication;

(c) access to and use of information services;

(d) accommodation in a hotel, boarding house or other similar establishment;

(e) facilities by way of banking or insurance or for grants, loans, credit or finance;

(f) facilities for entertainment, recreation or refreshment;

(g) facilities provided by employment agencies or under section 2 of the Employment and Training Act 1973;

(h) the services of any profession or trade, or any local or other public authority.

(4) In the case of an act which constitutes discrimination by virtue of section 55, this section also applies to discrimination against a person who is not disabled.

(5) Except in such circumstances as may be prescribed, this section and sections 20 and 21 do not apply to—

(a) education which is funded, or secured, by a relevant body or provided at—

    (i) an establishment which is funded by such a body or by a Minister of the Crown; or

    (ii) any other establishment which is a school as defined in [section 4(1) and (2) of the Education Act 1996] or section 135(1) of the Education (Scotland) Act 1980;

[(aa) education which is provided by an institution within the further education sector (within the meaning given by section 91(3) of the Further and Higher Education Act 1992);

(ab) education which is provided by such establishments as may be specified by the Secretary of State by order;]

(b) any service so far as it consists of the use of any means of transport; or

(c) such other services as may be prescribed.

(6) In subsection (5)"relevant body" means—

(a) a local education authority in England and Wales;

(b) an education authority in Scotland;

(f) the Further Education Funding Council for Wales;

[(ff) the Scottish Further Education Funding Council established by an order under section 7(1) of the Further and Higher Education (Scotland) Act 1992;]

(g) the Higher Education Funding Council for England;

(h) the Scottish Higher Education Funding Council;

(i) the Higher Education Funding Council for Wales;

(j) the Teacher Training Agency;

(k) a voluntary organisation; or

(l) a body of a prescribed kind.

Meaning of "discrimination"

77–017   **20.**—(1) For the purposes of section 19, a provider of services discriminates against a disabled person if—

(a) for a reason which relates to the disabled person's disability, he treats him less favourably than he treats or would treat others to whom that reason does not or would not apply; and

(b) he cannot show that the treatment in question is justified.

(2) For the purposes of section 19, a provider of services also discriminates against a disabled person if—

(a) he fails to comply with a section 21 duty imposed on him in relation to the disabled person; and

(b) he cannot show that his failure to comply with that duty is justified.

(3) For the purposes of this section, treatment is justified only if—

(a) in the opinion of the provider of services, one or more of the conditions mentioned in subsection (4) are satisfied; and

(b) it is reasonable, in all the circumstances of the case, for him to hold that opinion.

(4) The conditions are that—

(a) in any case, the treatment is necessary in order not to endanger the health or safety of any person (which may include that of the disabled person);

(b) in any case, the disabled person is incapable of entering into an enforceable agreement, or of giving an informed consent, and for that reason the treatment is reasonable in that case;

(c) in a case falling within section 19(1)(a), the treatment is necessary because the provider of services would otherwise be unable to provide the service to members of the public;

(d) in a case falling within section 19(1)(c) or (d), the treatment is necessary in order for the provider of services to be able to provide the service to the disabled person or to other members of the public;

(e) in a case falling within section 19(1)(d), the difference in the terms on which the service is provided to the disabled person and those on which it is provided to other members of the public reflects the greater cost to the provider of services in providing the service to the disabled person.

(5) Any increase in the cost of providing a service to a disabled person which results from compliance by a provider of services with a section 21 duty shall be disregarded for the purposes of subsection (4)(e).

(6) Regulations may make provision, for purposes of this section, as to circumstances in which—

(a) it is reasonable for a provider of services to hold the opinion mentioned in subsection (3)(a);

(b) it is not reasonable for a provider of services to hold that opinion.

(7) Regulations may make provision for subsection (4)(b) not to apply in prescribed circumstances where—

(a) a person is acting for a disabled person under a power of attorney;

(b) functions conferred by or under Part VII of the Mental Health Act 1983 are exercisable in relation to a disabled person's property or affairs; or

(c) powers are exercisable in Scotland in relation to a disabled person's property or affairs in consequence of the appointment of a curator bonis, tutor or judicial factor.

(8) Regulations may make provision, for purposes of this section, as to circumstances (other than those mentioned in subsection (4)) in which treatment is to be taken to be justified.

(9) In subsections (3), (4) and (8)"treatment"includes failure to comply with a section 21 duty.

Duty of providers of services to make adjustments

21.—(1) Where a provider of services has a practice, policy or procedure **77–018** which makes it impossible or unreasonably difficult for disabled persons to make use of a service which he provides, or is prepared to provide, to other members of the public, it is his duty to take such steps as it is reasonable, in all the circumstances of the case, for him to have to take in order to change that practice, policy or procedure so that it no longer has that effect.

(2) Where a physical feature (for example, one arising from the design or construction of a building or the approach or access to premises) makes it impossible or unreasonably difficult for disabled persons to make use of such a service, it is the duty of the provider of that service to take such steps as it is reasonable, in all the circumstances of the case, for him to have to take in order to—

(a) remove the feature;
(b) alter it so that it no longer has that effect;
(c) provide a reasonable means of avoiding the feature; or
(d) provide a reasonable alternative method of making the service in question available to disabled persons.

(3) Regulations may prescribe—

(a) matters which are to be taken into account in determining whether any provision of a kind mentioned in subsection (2)(c) or (d) is reasonable; and
(b) categories of providers of services to whom subsection (2) does not apply.

(4) Where an auxiliary aid or service (for example, the provision of information on audio tape or of a sign language interpreter) would—

(a) enable disabled persons to make use of a service which a provider of services provides, or is prepared to provide, to members of the public, or
(b) facilitate the use by disabled persons of such a service,

it is the duty of the provider of that service to take such steps as it is reasonable, in all the circumstances of the case, for him to have to take in order to provide that auxiliary aid or service.

(5) Regulations may make provision, for the purposes of this section—

(a) as to circumstances in which it is reasonable for a provider of services to have to take steps of a prescribed description;
(b) as to circumstances in which it is not reasonable for a provider of services to have to take steps of a prescribed description;
(c) as to what is to be included within the meaning of "practice, policy or procedure";
(d) as to what is not to be included within the meaning of that expression;
(e) as to things which are to be treated as physical features;
(f) as to things which are not to be treated as such features;
(g) as to things which are to be treated as auxiliary aids or services;
(h) as to things which are not to be treated as auxiliary aids or services.

(6) Nothing in this section requires a provider of services to take any steps which would fundamentally alter the nature of the service in question or the nature of his trade, profession or business.

(7) Nothing in this section requires a provider of services to take any steps which would cause him to incur expenditure exceeding the prescribed maximum.

(8) Regulations under subsection (7) may provide for the prescribed maximum to be calculated by reference to—

(a) aggregate amounts of expenditure incurred in relation to different cases;
(b) prescribed periods;
(c) services of a prescribed description;
(d) premises of a prescribed description; or
(e) such other criteria as may be prescribed.

(9) Regulations may provide, for the purposes of subsection (7), for expenditure incurred by one provider of services to be treated as incurred by another.

(10) This section imposes duties only for the purposes of determining whether a provider of services has discriminated against a disabled person; and accordingly a breach of any such duty is not actionable as such.

Premises

Discrimination in relation to premises

22.—(1) It is unlawful for a person with power to dispose of any premises to discriminate against a disabled person—   **77–019**

    (a) in the terms on which he offers to dispose of those premises to the disabled person;

    (b) by refusing to dispose of those premises to the disabled person; or

    (c) in his treatment of the disabled person in relation to any list of persons in need of premises of that description.

(2) Subsection (1) does not apply to a person who owns an estate or interest in the premises and wholly occupies them unless, for the purpose of disposing of the premises, he—

    (a) uses the services of an estate agent, or

    (b) publishes an advertisement or causes an advertisement to be published.

(3) It is unlawful for a person managing any premises to discriminate against a disabled person occupying those premises—

    (a) in the way he permits the disabled person to make use of any benefits or facilities;

    (b) by refusing or deliberately omitting to permit the disabled person to make use of any benefits or facilities; or

    (c) by evicting the disabled person, or subjecting him to any other detriment.

(4) It is unlawful for any person whose licence or consent is required for the disposal of any premises comprised in, or (in Scotland) the subject of, a tenancy to discriminate against a disabled person by withholding his licence or consent for the disposal of the premises to the disabled person.

(5) Subsection (4) applies to tenancies created before as well as after the passing of this Act.

(6) In this section—

    "advertisement" includes every form of advertisement or notice, whether to the public or not;

    "dispose", in relation to premises, includes granting a right to occupy the premises, and, in relation to premises comprised in, or (in Scotland) the subject of, a tenancy, includes—

        (a) assigning the tenancy, and

        (b) sub-letting or parting with possession of the premises or any part of the premises;

    and "disposal" shall be construed accordingly;

    "estate agent" means a person who, by way of profession or trade, provides services for the purpose of finding premises for persons seeking to acquire them or assisting in the disposal of premises; and

    "tenancy" means a tenancy created—

(a) by a lease or sub-lease,
(b) by an agreement for a lease or sub-lease,
(c) by a tenancy agreement, or
(d) in pursuance of any enactment.

(7) In the case of an act which constitutes discrimination by virtue of section 55, this section also applies to discrimination against a person who is not disabled.

(8) This section applies only in relation to premises in the United Kingdom.

Exemption for small dwellings

77–020   **23.**—(1) Where the conditions mentioned in subsection (2) are satisfied, subsection (1), (3) or (as the case may be (4) of section 22 does not apply.

(2) The conditions are that—

(a) the relevant occupier resides, and intends to continue to reside, on the premises;
(b) the relevant occupier shares accommodation on the premises with persons who reside on the premises and are not members of his household;
(c) the shared accommodation is not storage accommodation or a means of access; and
(d) the premises are small premises.

(3) For the purposes of this section, premises are "small premises" if they fall within subsection (4) or (5).

(4) Premises fall within this subsection if—

(a) only the relevant occupier and members of his household reside in the accommodation occupied by him;
(b) the premises comprise, in addition to the accommodation occupied by the relevant occupier, residential accommodation for at least one other household;
(c) the residential accommodation for each other household is let, or available for letting, on a separate tenancy or similar agreement; and
(d) there are not normally more than two such other households.

(5) Premises fall within this subsection if there is not normally residential accommodation on the premises for more than six persons in addition to the relevant occupier and any members of his household.

(6) For the purposes of this section "the relevant occupier" means —

(a) in a case falling within section 22(1), the person with power to dispose of the premises, or a near relative of his;
(b) in a case falling within section 22(4), the person whose licence or consent is required for the disposal of the premises, or a near relative of his.

(7) For the purposes of this section—

"near relative" means a person's spouse, partner, parent, child, grandparent, grandchild, or brother or sister (whether of full or half blood or by affinity); and
"partner" means the other member of a couple consisting of a man and a woman who are not married to each other but are living together as husband and wife.

Meaning of "discrimination"

24.—(1) For the purposes of section 22, a person ("A") discriminates against   **77–021**
a disabled person if—

- (a) for a reason which relates to the disabled person's disability, he treats
  him less favourably than he treats or would treat others to whom that
  reason does not or would not apply; and
- (b) he cannot show that the treatment in question is justified.

(2) For the purposes of this section, treatment is justified only if—

- (a) in A's opinion, one or more of the conditions mentioned in subsection
  (3) are satisfied; and
- (b) it is reasonable, in all the circumstances of the case, for him to hold
  that opinion.

(3) The conditions are that—

- (a) in any case, the treatment is necessary in order not to endanger the
  health or safety of any person (which may include that of the disabled
  person);
- (b) in any case, the disabled person is incapable of entering into an
  enforceable agreement, or of giving an informed consent, and for that
  reason the treatment is reasonable in that case;
- (c) in a case falling within section 22(3)(a), the treatment is necessary in
  order for the disabled person or the occupiers of other premises forming
  part of the building to make use of the benefit or facility;
- (d) in a case falling within section 22(3)(b), the treatment is necessary in
  order for the occupiers of other premises forming part of the building
  to make use of the benefit or facility.

(4) Regulations may make provision, for purposes of this section, as to circumstances in which—

- (a) it is reasonable for a person to hold the opinion mentioned in subsection 2(a);
- (b) it is not reasonable for a person to hold that opinion.

(5) Regulations may make provision, for purposes of this section, as to circumstances (other than those mentioned in subsection (3)) in which treatment is
to be taken to be justified.

Enforcement, etc.

Enforcement, remedies and procedure

25.—(1) A claim by any person that another person—   **77–022**

- (a) has discriminated against him in a way which is unlawful under this
  Part; or
- (b) is by virtue of section 57 or 58 to be treated as having discriminated
  against him in such a way,

may be made the subject of civil proceedings in the same way as any other
claim in tort or (in Scotland) in reparation for breach of statutory duty.

(2) For the avoidance of doubt it is hereby declared that damages in respect

of discrimination in a way which is unlawful under this Part may include compensation for injury to feelings whether or not they include compensation under any other head.

(3) Proceedings in England and Wales shall be brought only in a county court.

(4) Proceedings in Scotland shall be brought only in a sheriff court.

(5) The remedies available in such proceedings are those which are available in the High Court or (as the case may be) the Court of Session.

(6) Part II of Schedule 3 makes further provision about the enforcement of this Part and about procedure.

. . . . . .

PART V

PUBLIC TRANSPORT

Taxis

Taxi accessibility regulations

77–023 32.—(1) The Secretary of State may make regulations ("taxi accessibility regulations") for the purpose of securing that it is possible—

(a) for disabled persons—

(i) to get into and out of taxis in safety;
(ii) to be carried in taxis in safety and in reasonable comfort; and

(b) for disabled persons in wheelchairs—

(i) to be conveyed in safety into and out of taxis while remaining in their wheelchairs; and
(ii) to be carried in taxis in safety and in reasonable comfort while remaining in their wheelchairs.

(2) Taxi accessibility regulations may, in particular—

(a) require any regulated taxi to conform with provisions of the regulations as to—

(i) the size of any door opening which is for the use of passengers;
(ii) the floor area of the passenger compartment;
(iii) the amount of headroom in the passenger compartment;
(iv) the fitting of restraining devices designed to ensure the stability of a wheelchair while the taxi is moving;

(b) require the driver of any regulated taxi which is plying for hire, or which has been hired, to comply with provisions of the regulations as to the carrying of ramps or other devices designed to facilitate the loading and unloading of wheelchairs;

(c) require the driver of any regulated taxi in which a disabled person who is in a wheelchair is being carried (while remaining in his wheelchair) to comply with provisions of the regulations as to the position in which the wheelchair is to be secured.

(3) The driver of a regulated taxi which is plying for hire, or which has been hired, is guilty of an offence if—

(a) he fails to comply with any requirement imposed on him by the regulations; or

(b) the taxi fails to conform with any provision of the regulations with which it is required to conform.

(4) A person who is guilty of such an offence is liable, on summary conviction, to a fine not exceeding level 3 on the standard scale.

(5) In this section—

"passenger compartment" has such meaning as may be prescribed;

"regulated taxi" means any taxi to which the regulations are expressed to apply;

"taxi" means a vehicle licensed under—

(a) section 37 of the Town Police Clauses Act 1847, or

(b) section 6 of the Metropolitan Public Carriage Act 1869,

but does not include a taxi which is drawn by a horse or other animal.

. . . . . .

PSV accessibility regulations

40.—(1) The Secretary of State may make regulations ("PSV accessibility regulations") for the purpose of securing that it is possible for disabled persons—   **77–024**

(a) to get on to and off regulated public service vehicles in safety and without unreasonable difficulty (and, in the case of disabled persons in wheelchairs, to do so while remaining in their wheelchairs); and

(b) to be carried in such vehicles in safety and in reasonable comfort.

(2) PSV accessibility regulations may, in particular, make provision as to the construction, use and maintenance of regulated public service vehicles including provision as to—

(a) the fitting of equipment to vehicles;

(b) equipment to be carried by vehicles;

(c) the design of equipment to be fitted to, or carried by, vehicles;

(d) the fitting and use of restraining devices designed to ensure the stability of wheelchairs while vehicles are moving;

(e) the position in which wheelchairs are to be secured while vehicles are moving.

(3) Any person who—

(a) contravenes or fails to comply with any provision of the PSV accessibility regulations,

(b) uses on a road a regulated public service vehicle which does not conform with any provision of the regulations with which it is required to conform, or

(c) causes or permits to be used on a road such a regulated public service vehicle,

is guilty of an offence.

(4) A person who is guilty of such an offence is liable, on summary conviction, to a fine not exceeding level 4 on the standard scale.

(5) In this section—

"public service vehicle" means a vehicle which is—

(a) adapted to carry more than eight passengers; and
(b) a public service vehicle for the purposes of the Public Passenger Vehicles Act 1981;

"regulated public service vehicle" means any public service vehicle to which the PSV accessibility regulations are expressed to apply.

(6) Different provision may be made in regulations under this section—

(a) as respects different classes or descriptions of vehicle;
(b) as respects the same class or description of vehicle in different circumstances.

(7) Before making any regulations under this section or section 41 or 42 the Secretary of State shall consult the Disabled Persons Transport Advisory Committee and such other representative organisations as he thinks fit.

(8) In this section "operator" has the same meaning as in the Public Passenger Vehicles Act 1981.

. . . . . .

Rail vehicles

Rail vehicle accessibility regulations

77–025   **46.**—(1) The Secretary of State may make regulations ("rail vehicle accessibility regulations") for the purpose of securing that it is possible—

(a) for disabled persons—

(i) to get on to and off regulated rail vehicles in safety and without unreasonable difficulty;
(ii) to be carried in such vehicles in safety and in reasonable comfort; and

(b) for disabled persons in wheelchairs—

(i) to get on to and off such vehicles in safety and without unreasonable difficulty while remaining in their wheelchairs, and
(ii) to be carried in such vehicles in safety and in reasonable comfort while remaining in their wheelchairs.

(2) Rail vehicle accessibility regulations may, in particular, make provision as to the construction, use and maintenance of regulated rail vehicles including provision as to—

(a) the fitting of equipment to vehicles;
(b) equipment to be carried by vehicles;
(c) the design of equipment to be fitted to, or carried by, vehicles;
(d) the use of equipment fitted to, or carried by, vehicles;
(e) the toilet facilities to be provided in vehicles;

(f) the location and floor area of the wheelchair accommodation to be provided in vehicles;

(g) assistance to be given to disabled persons.

(3) If a regulated rail vehicle which does not conform with any provision of the rail vehicle accessibility regulations with which it is required to conform is used for carriage, the operator of the vehicle is guilty of an offence.

(4) A person who is guilty of such an offence is liable, on summary conviction, to a fine not exceeding level 4 on the standard scale.

(5) Different provision may be made in rail vehicle accessibility regulations—

(a) as respects different classes or descriptions of rail vehicle;

(b) as respects the same class or description of rail vehicle in different circumstances;

(c) as respects different networks.

(6) In this section—

"network" means any permanent way or other means of guiding or supporting rail vehicles or any section of it;

"operator", in relation to any rail vehicle, means the person having the management of that vehicle;

"rail vehicle" means a vehicle—

(a) constructed or adapted to carry passengers on any railway, tramway or prescribed system; and

(b) first brought into use, or belonging to a class of vehicle first brought into use, after 31st December 1998;

"regulated rail vehicle" means any rail vehicle to which the rail vehicle accessibility regulations are expressed to apply; and

"wheelchair accommodation" has such meaning as may be prescribed.

(7) In subsection (6)—

"prescribed system" means a system using a prescribed mode of guided transport ("guided transport" having the same meaning as in the Transport and Works Act 1992); and

"railway" and "tramway" have the same meaning as in that Act.

(8) The Secretary of State may by regulations make provision as to the time when a rail vehicle, or a class of rail vehicle, is to be treated, for the purposes of this section, as first brought into use.

(9) Regulations under subsection (8) may include provision for disregarding periods of testing and other prescribed periods of use.

(10) For the purposes of this section and section 47, a person uses a vehicle for carriage if he uses it for the carriage of members of the public for hire or reward at separate fares.

(11) Before making any regulations under subsection (1) or section 47 the Secretary of State shall consult the Disabled Persons Transport Advisory Committee and such other representative organisations as he thinks fit.

. . . . . .

PART VII

SUPPLEMENTAL

Victimisation

77–026 55.—(1) For the purposes of Part II or Part III, a person ("A") discriminates against another person ("B") if—

> (a) he treats B less favourably than he treats or would treat other persons whose circumstances are the same as B's; and
> (b) he does so for a reason mentioned in subsection (2).

(2) The reasons are that—

> (a) B has—
>> (i) brought proceedings against A or any other person under this Act; or
>> (ii) given evidence or information in connection with such proceedings brought by any person; or
>> (iii) otherwise done anything under this Act in relation to A or any other person; or
>> (iv) alleged that A or any other person has (whether or not the allegation so states) contravened this Act; or
>
> (b) A believes or suspects that B has done or intends to do any of those things.

(3) Where B is a disabled person, or a person who has had a disability, the disability in question shall be disregarded in comparing his circumstances with those of any other person for the purposes of subsection (1)(a).

(4) Subsection (1) does not apply to treatment of a person because of an allegation made by him if the allegation was false and not made in good faith.

. . . . . .

Aiding unlawful acts

77–027 57.—(1) A person who knowingly aids another person to do an act made unlawful by this Act is to be treated for the purposes of this Act as himself doing the same kind of unlawful act.

(2) For the purposes of subsection (1), an employee or agent for whose act the employer or principal is liable under section 58 (or would be so liable but for section 58(5)) shall be taken to have aided the employer or principal to do the act.

(3) For the purposes of this section, a person does not knowingly aid another to do an unlawful act if—

> (a) he acts in reliance on a statement made to him by that other person that, because of any provision of this Act, the act would not be unlawful; and
> (b) it is reasonable for him to rely on the statement.

(4) A person who knowingly or recklessly makes such a statement which is false or misleading in a material respect is guilty of an offence.

(5) Any person guilty of an offence under subsection (4) shall be liable on summary conviction to a fine not exceeding level 5 on the standard scale.

Liability of employers and principals

58.—(1) Anything done by a person in the course of his employment shall   **77–028**
be treated for the purposes of this Act as also done by his employer, whether or
not it was done with the employer's knowledge or approval.

(2) Anything done by a person as agent for another person with the authority
of that other person shall be treated for the purposes of this Act as also done by
that other person.

(3) Subsection (2) applies whether the authority was—

(a) express or implied; or
(b) given before or after the act in question was done.

(4) Subsections (1) and (2) do not apply in relation to an offence under section
57(4).

(5) In proceedings under this Act against any person in respect of an act
alleged to have been done by an employee of his, it shall be a defence for that
person to prove that he took such steps as were reasonably practicable to prevent
the employee from—

(a) doing that act; or
(b) doing, in the course of his employment, acts of that description.

Statutory authority and national security etc.

59.—(1) Nothing in this Act makes unlawful any act done—   **77–029**

(a) in pursuance of any enactment; or
(b) in pursuance of any instrument made by a Minister of the Crown under
any enactment; or
(c) to comply with any condition or requirement imposed by a Minister of
the Crown (whether before or after the passing of this Act) by virtue
of any enactment.

(2) In subsection (1) "enactment" includes one passed or made after the date
on which this Act is passed and "instrument" includes one made after that date.

(3) Nothing in this Act makes unlawful any act done for the purpose of
safeguarding national security.

Asylum and Immigration Act 1996

(1996, c. 49)

An Act to amend and supplement the Immigration Act 1971 and the Asylum and   **78–001**
Immigration Appeals Act 1993; to make further provision with respect to
persons subject to immigration control and the employment of such per-
sons; and for connected purposes.   [24th July 1996]

. . . . . .

Persons subject to immigration control

Restrictions on employment

78–002   **8.**—(1) Subject to subsection (2) below, if any person ("the employer") employs a person subject to immigration control ("the employee") who has attained the age of 16, the employer shall be guilty of an offence if—

    (a) the employee has not been granted leave to enter or remain in the United Kingdom; or

    (b) the employee's leave is not valid and subsisting, or is subject to a condition precluding him from taking up the employment,

and (in either case) the employee does not satisfy such conditions as may be specified in an order made by the Secretary of State.

(2) Subject to subsection (3) below, in proceedings under this section, it shall be a defence to prove that—

    (a) before the employment began, there was produced to the employer a document which appeared to him to relate to the employee and to be of a description specified in an order made by the Secretary of State; and

    (b) either the document was retained by the employer, or a copy or other record of it was made by the employer in a manner specified in the order in relation to documents of that description.

(3) The defence afforded by subsection (2) above shall not be available in any case where the employer knew that his employment of the employee would constitute an offence under this section.

(4) A person guilty of an offence under this section shall be liable on summary conviction to a fine not exceeding level 5 on the standard scale.

(5) Where an offence under this section committed by a body corporate is proved to have been committed with the consent or connivance of, or to be attributable to any neglect on the part of—

    (a) any director, manager, secretary or other similar officer of the body corporate, or

    (b) any person who was purporting to act in any such capacity,

he as well as the body corporate shall be guilty of the offence and shall be liable to be proceeded against and punished accordingly.

(6) Where the affairs of a body corporate are managed by its members, subsection (5) above shall apply in relation to the acts and defaults of a member in connection with his functions of management as if he were a director of the body corporate.

(7) An order under this section shall be made by statutory instrument which shall be subject to annulment in pursuance of a resolution of either House of Parliament.

(8) In this section—

    "contract of employment" means a contract of service or apprenticeship, whether express or implied, and (if it is express) whether it is oral or in writing;

    "employ" means employ under a contract of employment and "employment" shall be construed accordingly.

Code of practice

[**8A.**—(1) The Secretary of State must issue a code of practice as to the **78–003** measures which an employer is to be expected to take, or not to take, with a view to securing that, while avoiding the commission of an offence under section 8, he also avoids unlawful discrimination.

(2) "Unlawful discrimination" means—

(a) discrimination in contravention of section 4(1) of the Race Relations Act 1976 ("the 1976 Act"); or
(b) in relation to Northern Ireland, discrimination in contravention of Article 6(1) of the Race Relations (Northern Ireland) Order 1997 ("the 1997 Order").

(3) Before issuing the code, the Secretary of State must—

(a) prepare and publish a draft of the proposed code; and
(b) consider any representations about it which are made to him.

(4) In preparing the draft, the Secretary of State must consult—

(a) the Commission for Racial Equality;
(b) the Equality Commission for Northern Ireland; and
(c) such organisations and bodies (including organisations or associations of organisations representative of employers or of workers) as he considers appropriate.

(5) If the Secretary of State decides to proceed with the code, he must lay a draft of the code before both Houses of Parliament.

(6) The draft code may contain modifications to the original proposals made in the light of representations to the Secretary of State.

(7) After laying the draft code before Parliament, the Secretary of State may bring the code into operation by an order made by statutory instrument.

(8) An order under subsection (7)—

(a) shall be subject to annulment in pursuance of a resolution of either House of Parliament;
(b) may contain such transitional provisions or savings as appear to the Secretary of State to be necessary or expedient in connection with the code.

(9) A failure on the part of any person to observe a provision of the code does not of itself make him liable to any proceedings.

(10) But the code is admissible in evidence—

(a) in proceedings under the 1976 Act before an employment tribunal;
(b) in proceedings under the 1997 Order before an industrial tribunal.

(11) If any provision of the code appears to the tribunal to be relevant to any question arising in such proceedings, that provision is to be taken into account in determining the question.

(12) The Secretary of State may from time to time revise the whole or any part of the code and issue the code as revised.

(13) The provisions of this section also apply (with appropriate modifications) to any revision, or proposed revision, of the code.]¹

¹ Added by Immigration and Asylum Act 1999 (c.33), Pt I, s. 22.

Broadcasting Act 1996

(1996, c. 55)

79–001   *An Act to make new provision about the broadcasting in digital form of television and sound programme services and the broadcasting in that form on television or radio frequencies of other services; to amend the Broadcasting Act 1990; to make provision about rights to televise sporting or other events of national interest; to amend in other respects the law relating to the provision of television and sound programme services; to provide for the establishment and functions of a Broadcasting Standards Commission and for the dissolution of the Broadcasting Complaints Commission and the Broadcasting Standards Council; to make provision for the transfer to other persons of property, rights and liabilities of the British Broadcasting Corporation relating to their transmission network; and for connected purposes.*   [24th July 1996]

PART I

DIGITAL TERRESTRIAL TELEVISION BROADCASTING

Introductory

Multiplex services and digital programme services

79–002   **1.**—(1) In this Part "multiplex service" means a service provided by any person which consists in the broadcasting for general reception of two or more services specified in subsection (3) by combining the relevant information in digital form, together with any broadcasting in digital form of digital additional services (as defined by section 24(1)).

[(1A) In subsection (1) "for general reception" means for general reception in, or in any area in, the United Kingdom.]

(2) A service in respect of which a licence under section 7 is in force is not prevented from being a multiplex service at a particular time merely because only one service specified in subsection (3) is being broadcast in digital form at that time.

(3) The services referred to in subsections (1) and (2) are—

(a) a digital programme service (as defined by subsection (4))), or
(b) a qualifying service (as defined by section 2(2)).

(4) In this Part "digital programme service" means a service consisting in the provision by any person of television programmes (together with any ancillary services, as defined by section 24(2)) with a view to their being broadcast in digital form for general reception, whether by him or by some other person, but does not include—

(a) a qualifying service,

(b) a teletext service, or

(c) any service in the case of which the visual images to be broadcast do not consist wholly or mainly of images capable of being seen as moving pictures,

except, in the case of a service falling within paragraph (b) or (c), to the extent that it is an ancillary service.

[(4A) In subsection (4) "for general reception" means for general reception in, or in any area in, the United Kingdom or any other EEA State.]

(5) The Secretary of State may, if having regard to developments in broadcasting technology he considers it appropriate to do so, by order amend the definition of "digital programme service" in subsection (4).

(6) No order under subsection (5) shall be made unless a draft of the order has been laid before and approved by a resolution of each House of Parliament.

(7) In this section—

"broadcast" means broadcast otherwise than—

(a) by satellite, or

(b) in the provision of a local delivery service (as defined by section 72(1) of the 1990 Act.

......

General provisions about licences

Licences under Part I

3.—(1) Any licence granted by the Independent Television Commission (in this Part referred to as "the Commission") under this Part shall be in writing and (subject to the provisions of this Part) shall continue in force for such period as is provided, in relation to a licence of the kind in question, by the relevant provision of this Part.   **79–003**

(2) A licence may be so granted for the provision of such a service as is specified in the licence or for the provision of a service of such a description as is so specified.

(3) The Commission—

(a) shall not grant a licence to any person unless they are satisfied that he is a fit and proper person to hold it, and

(b) shall do all that they can to secure that, if they cease to be so satisfied in the case of any person holding a licence, that person does not remain the holder of the licence;

and nothing in this Part shall be construed as affecting the operation of this subsection or of section 5(1) or (2)(b) or (c).

(4) The Commission may vary a licence by a notice served on the licence holder if—

(a) in the case of a variation of the period for which a licence having effect for a specified period is to continue in force, the licence holder consents, or

(b) in the case of any other variation, the licence holder has been given a reasonable opportunity of making representations to the Commission about the variation.

(5) Paragraph (a) of subsection (4) does not affect the operation of section 17(1)(b); and that subsection shall not authorise the variation of any conditions included in a licence in pursuance of section 13(1).

(6) A licence granted to any person under this Part shall not be transferable to any other person without the previous consent in writing of the Commission.

(7) Without prejudice to the generality of subsection (6), the Commission shall not give their consent for the purposes of that subsection unless they are satisfied that any such other person would be in a position to comply with all of the conditions included in the licence which would have effect during the period for which it is to be in force.

(8) The holding by any person of a licence to provide any service shall not relieve him of any requirement to hold a licence under section 1 of the Wireless Telegraphy Act 1949 or section 7 of the Telecommunications Act 1984 in connection with the provision of that service.

. . . . . .

Digital programme services

Licensing of digital programme services

79–004 **18.**—(1) An application for a licence to provide digital programme services (in this Part referred to as a "digital programme licence") shall—

(a) be made in such manner as the Commission may determine, and

(b) be accompanied by such fee (if any) as they may determine.

(2) At any time after receiving such an application and before determining it, the Commission may require the applicant to furnish such additional information as they may consider necessary for the purpose of considering the application.

(3) Any information to be furnished to the Commission under this section shall, if they so require, be in such form or verified in such manner as they may specify.

(4) Where an application for a digital programme licence is made to the Commission in accordance with the provisions of this section, they shall grant the licence unless precluded from doing so by section 3(3)(a) or 5(1).

(5) Subject to subsection (6), sections 6 to 12 of the 1990 Act (general provisions relation to services licensed under Part I of that Act) shall apply in relation to a digital programme service licensed under this Part as they apply in relation to a service licensed under that Part of that Act.

(6) In its application in relation to a digital programme service—

(a) section 6 of the 1990 Act shall have effect with the omission of subsection (8), and

(b) section 12(1)(b) of that Act shall have effect as if the reference to the Commission's functions under Chapter II of Part I of that Act included a reference to their functions under this Part.

. . . . . .

Miscellaneous and supplemental

Promotion of equal opportunities and fair treatment

79–005 **34.**—(1) Any multiplex licence or digital programme licence shall include conditions requiring the licence holder—

(a) to make arrangements for promoting, in relation to employment by him, equality of opportunity between men and women and between persons of different racial groups,

(b) to make arrangements for promoting, in relation to employment by him, the fair treatment of disabled persons, and

(c) to review those arrangements from time to time.

(2) In subsection (1) "racial group" has the same meaning as in the Race Relations Act 1976 and "disabled person" has the same meaning as in the Disability Discrimination Act 1995.

. . . . . .

PART IV

SPORTING AND OTHER EVENTS OF NATIONAL INTEREST

Listed events

97.—(1) For the purposes of this Part, a listed event is a sporting or other event of national interest which is for the time being included in a list drawn up by the Secretary of State for the purposes of this Part.   **79–006**

(2) The Secretary of State shall not at any time draw up, revise or cease to maintain such a list as is mentioned in subsection (1) unless he has first consulted—

(a) the BBC,

(b) the Welsh Authority,

(c) the Commission, and

(d) in relation to a relevant event, the person from whom the rights to televise that event may be acquired;

and for the purposes of this subsection a relevant event is a sporting or other event of national interest which the Secretary of State proposes to include in, or omit from, the list.

(3) As soon as he has drawn up or revised such a list as is mentioned in subsection (1) the Secretary of State shall publish the list in such manner as he considers appropriate for bringing it to the attention of—

(a) the persons mentioned in subsection (2), and

(b) every person who is the holder of a licence granted by the Commission under Part I of the 1990 Act or a digital programme licence granted by them under Part I of this Act.

(4) In this section "national interest" includes interest within England, Scotland, Wales or Northern Ireland.

(5) The addition of any relevant event to such a list as is mentioned in subsection (1) shall not affect—

(a) the validity of any contract entered into before the date on which the Secretary of State consulted, the persons mentioned in subsection (2) in relation to the proposed addition, or

(b) the exercise of any rights acquired under such a contract.

(6) The list drawn up by the Secretary of State for the purposes of section 182 of the 1990 Act, as that list is in force immediately before the commencement

of this section, shall be taken to have been drawn up for the purposes of this Part.

· · · · · ·

PART V

THE BROADCASTING STANDARDS COMMISSION

Complaints

Complaints of unfair treatment etc.

79–007   **111.**—(1) A fairness complaint may be made by an individual or by a body of persons, whether incorporated or not, but, subject to subsection (2), shall not be entertained by the BSC unless made by the person affected or by a person authorised by him to make the complaint for him.

(2) Where the person affected is an individual who has died, a fairness complaint may be made by his personal representative or by a member of the family of the person affected, or by some other person or body closely connected with him (whether as his employer, or as a body of which he was at his death a member, or in any other way).

(3) Where the person affected is an individual who is for any reason both unable to make a complaint himself and unable to authorise another person to do so for him, a fairness complaint may be made by a member of the family of the person affected, or by some other person or body closely connected with him (whether as his employer, or as a body of which he is a member, or in any other way).

(4) The BSC shall not entertain, or proceed with the consideration of, a fairness complaint if it appears to them that the complaint relates to the broadcasting of the relevant programme, or to its inclusion in a licensed service, on an occasion more than five years after the death of the person affected, unless it appears to them that in the particular circumstances it is appropriate to do so.

(5) The BSC may refuse to entertain a fairness complaint if it appears to them not to have been made within a reasonable time after the last occasion on which the relevant programme was broadcast or, as the case may be, included in a licensed service.

(6) Where, in the case of a fairness complaint, the relevant programme was broadcast or included in a licensed service after the death of the person affected, subsection (5) shall apply as if at the end there were added "within five years (or such longer period as may be allowed by the BSC in the particular case under subsection (4) after the death of the person affected".

(7) The BSC may refuse to entertain—

(a) a fairness complaint which is a complaint of unjust or unfair treatment if the person named as the person affected was not himself the subject of the treatment complained of and it appears to the BSC that he did not have a sufficiently direct interest in the subject-matter of that treatment to justify the making of a complaint with him as the person affected, or

(b) a complaint made under subsection (2) or (3) by a person other than the person affected or a person authorised by him, if it appears to the BSC that the complainant's connection with the person affected is not sufficiently close to justify the making of the complaint by him.

Criminal Procedure and Investigations Act 1996

(1996, c. 25)

An Act to make provision about criminal procedure and criminal investigations. **80–001**
[4th July 1996]

. . . . . .

Part I

Disclosure

Confidentiality

Confidentiality of disclosed information

17.—(1) If the accused is given or allowed to inspect a document or other **80–002**
object under—

(a) section 3, 4, 7, 9, 14 or 15, or
(b) an order under section 8,

then, subject to subsections (2) to (4), he must not use or disclose it or any
information recorded in it.

(2) The accused may use or disclose the object or information—

(a) in connection with the proceedings for whose purposes he was given
the object or allowed to inspect it,
(b) with a view to the taking of further criminal proceedings (for instance,
by way of appeal) with regard to the matter giving rise to the proceedings mentioned in paragraph (a), or
(c) in connection with the proceedings first mentioned in paragraph (b).

(3) The accused may use or disclose—

(a) the object to the extent that it has been displayed to the public in open
court, or
(b) the information to the extent that it has been communicated to the
public in open court;

but the preceding provisions of this subsection do not apply if the object is
displayed or the information is communicated in proceedings to deal with a
contempt of court under section 18.

(4) If—

(a) the accused applies to the court for an order granting permission to use
or disclose the object or information, and
(b) the court makes such an order,

the accused may use or disclose the object or information for the purpose and
to the extent specified by the court.

(5) An application under subsection (4) may be made and dealt with at any
time, and in particular after the accused has been acquitted or convicted or the
prosecutor has decided not to proceed with the case concerned: but this is subject
to rules made by virtue of section 19(2).

(6) Where—

(a) an application is made under subsection (4), and
(b) the prosecutor or a person claiming to have an interest in the object or information applies to be heard by the court,

the court must not make an order granting permission unless the person applying under paragraph (b) has been given an opportunity to be heard.

(7) References in this section to the court are to—

(a) a magistrates' court, where this Part applies by virtue of section 1(1);
(b) the Crown Court, where this Part applies by virtue of section 1(2).

(8) Nothing in this section affects any other restriction or prohibition on the use or disclosure of an object or information, whether the restriction or prohibition arises under an enactment (whenever passed) or otherwise.

Confidentiality: contravention

80–003   **18.**—(1) It is a contempt of court for a person knowingly to use or disclose an object or information recorded in it if the use or disclosure is in contravention of section 17.

(2) The following courts have jurisdiction to deal with a person who is guilty of a contempt under this section—

(a) a magistrates' court, where this Part applies by virtue of section 1(1),
(b) the Crown Court, where this Part applies by virtue of section 1(2).

(3) A person who is guilty of a contempt under this section may be dealt with as follows—

(a) a magistrates' court may commit him to custody for a specified period not exceeding six months or impose on him a fine not exceeding £5,000 or both;
(b) the Crown Court may commit him to custody for a specified period not exceeding two years or impose a fine on him or both.

(4) If—

(a) a person is guilty of a contempt under this section, and
(b) the object concerned is in his possession,

the court finding him guilty may order that the object shall be forfeited and dealt with in such manner as the court may order.

(5) The power of the court under subsection (4) includes power to order the object to be destroyed or to be given to the prosecutor or to be placed in his custody for such period as the court may specify.

(6) If—

(a) the court proposes to make an order under subsection (4), and
(b) the person found guilty, or any other person claiming to have an interest in the object, applies to be heard by the court,

the court must not make the order unless the applicant has been given an opportunity to be heard.

(7) If—

(a) a person is guilty of a contempt under this section and

(b) a copy of the object concerned is in his possession,

the court finding him guilty may order that the copy shall be forfeited and dealt with in such manner as the court may order.

(8) Subsections (5) and (6) apply for the purposes of subsection (7) as they apply for the purposes of subsection (4), but as if references to the object were references to the copy.

(9) An object or information shall be inadmissible as evidence in civil proceedings if to adduce it would in the opinion of the court be likely to constitute a contempt under this section and "the court" here means the court before which the civil proceedings are being taken.

(10) The powers of a magistrates' court under this section may be exercised either of the court's own motion or by order on complaint.

. . . . . .

PART II

CRIMINAL INVESTIGATIONS

Introduction

22.—(1) For the purposes of this Part a criminal investigation is an investigation conducted by police officers with a view to it being ascertained— **80–004**

(a) whether a person should be charged with an offence, or

(b) whether a person charged with an offence is guilty of it.

(2) In this Part references to material are to material of all kinds, and in particular include references to—

(a) information, and

(b) objects of all descriptions.

(3) In this Part references to recording information are to putting it in a durable or retrievable form (such as writing or tape).

Code of practice

23.—(1) The Secretary of State shall prepare a code of practice containing provisions designed to secure— **80–005**

(a) that where a criminal investigation is conducted all reasonable steps are taken for the purposes of the investigation and, in particular, all reasonable lines of inquiry are pursued;

(b) that information which is obtained in the course of a criminal investigation and may be relevant to the investigation is recorded;

(c) that any record of such information is retained;

(d) that any other material which is obtained in the course of a criminal investigation and may be relevant to the investigation is retained;

(e) that information falling within paragraph (b) and material falling within paragraph (d) is revealed to a person who is involved in the prosecution of criminal proceedings arising out of or relating to the investigation and who is identified in accordance with prescribed provisions;

(f) that where such a person inspects information or other material in pursuance of a requirement that it be revealed to him, and he requests that it be disclosed to the accused, the accused is allowed to inspect it or is given a copy of it;

(g) that where such a person is given a document indicating the nature of information or other material in pursuance of a requirement that it be revealed to him, and he requests that it be disclosed to the accused, the accused is allowed to inspect it or is given a copy of it;

(h) that the person who is to allow the accused to inspect information or other material or to give him a copy of it shall decide which of those (inspecting or giving a copy) is appropriate;

(i) that where the accused is allowed to inspect material as mentioned in paragraph (f) or (g) and he requests a copy, he is given one unless the person allowing the inspection is of opinion that it is not practicable or not desirable to give him one;

(j) that a person mentioned in paragraph (e) is given a written statement that prescribed activities which the code requires have been carried out.

(2) The code may include provision—

(a) that a police officer identified in accordance with prescribed provisions must carry out a prescribed activity which the code requires;

(b) that a police officer so identified must take steps to secure the carrying out by a person (whether or not a police officer) of a prescribed activity which the code requires;

(c) that a duty must be discharged by different people in succession in prescribed circumstances (as where a person dies or retires).

(3) The code may include provision about the form in which information is to be recorded.

(4) The code may include provision about the manner in which and the period for which—

(a) a record of information is to be retained, and

(b) any other material is to be retained;

and if a person is charged with an offence the period may extend beyond a conviction or an acquittal.

(5) The code may include provision about the time when, the form in which, the way in which, and the extent to which, information or any other material is to be revealed to the person mentioned in subsection (1)(c).

(6) The code must be so framed that it does not apply to material intercepted in obedience to a warrant issued under section 2 of the Interception of Communications Act 1985[or under the authority of an interception warrant under section 5 of the Regulation of Investigatory Powers Act 2000.][1]

(7) The code may—

(a) make different provision in relation to different cases or descriptions of case;

(b) contain exceptions as regards prescribed cases or descriptions of case.

(8) In this section "prescribed" means prescribed by the code.

[1] Words added by Regulation of Investigatory Powers Act 2000 (c.23), Sched. 4, para. 7(2).

Effect of code

80–006   26.—(1) A person other than a police officer who is charged with the duty of conducting an investigation with a view to it being ascertained—

(a) whether a person should be charged with an offence, or

(b) whether a person charged with an offence is guilty of it,

shall in discharging that duty have regard to any relevant provision of a code which would apply if the investigation were conducted by police officers.

(2) A failure—

(a) by a police officer to comply with any provision of a code for the time being in operation by virtue of an order under section 25, or

(b) by a person to comply with subsection (1),

shall not in itself render him liable to any criminal or civil proceedings.

(3) In all criminal and civil proceedings a code in operation at any time by virtue of an order under section 25 shall be admissible in evidence.

(4) If it appears to a court or tribunal conducting criminal or civil proceedings that—

(a) any provision of a code in operation at any time by virtue of an order under section 25, or

(b) any failure mentioned in subsection (2)(a) or (b),

is relevant to any question arising in the proceedings, the provision or failure shall be taken into account in deciding the question.

. . . . . .

PART III

PREPARATORY HEARINGS

Reporting restrictions

Restrictions on reporting

37.—(1) Except as provided by this section—

80–007

(a) no written report of proceedings falling within subsection (2) shall be published in Great Britain;

(b) no report of proceedings falling within subsection (2) shall be included in a relevant programme for reception in Great Britain.

(2) The following proceedings fall within this subsection—

(a) a preparatory hearing;

(b) an application for leave to appeal in relation to such a hearing,

(c) an appeal in relation to such a hearing.

(3) The judge dealing with a preparatory hearing may order that subsection (1) shall not apply, or shall not apply to a specified extent, to a report of—

(a) the preparatory hearing, or

(b) an application to the judge for leave to appeal to the Court of Appeal under section 35(1) in relation to the preparatory hearing.

(4) The Court of Appeal may order that subsection (1) shall not apply, or shall not apply to a specified extent, to a report of—

    (a) an appeal to the Court of Appeal under section 35(1) in relation to a preparatory hearing,

    (b) an application to that Court for leave to appeal to it under section 35(1) in relation to a preparatory hearing, or

    (c) an application to that Court for leave to appeal to the House of Lords under Part II of the Criminal Appeal Act 1968 in relation to a preparatory hearing.

(5) The House of Lords may order that subsection (1) shall not apply, or shall not apply to a specified extent, to a report of—

    (a) an appeal to that House under Part II of the Criminal Appeal Act 1968 in relation to a preparatory hearing, or

    (b) an application to that House for leave to appeal to it under Part II of the Criminal Appeal Act 1968 in relation to a preparatory hearing.

(6) Where there is only one accused and he objects to the making of an order under subsection (3), (4) or (5) the judge or the Court of Appeal or the House of Lords shall make the order if (and only if) satisfied after hearing the representations of the accused that it is in the interests of justice to do so; and if the order is made it shall not apply to the extent that a report deals with any such objection or representations.

(7) Where there are two or more accused and one or more of them objects to the making of an order under subsection (3), (4) or (5) the judge or the Court of Appeal or the House of Lords shall make the order if (and only if) satisfied after hearing the representations of each of the accused that it is in the interests of justice to do so; and if the order is made it shall not apply to the extent that a report deals with any such objection or representations.

(8) Subsection (1) does not apply to—

    (a) the publication of a report of a preparatory hearing.

    (b) the publication of a report of an appeal in relation to a preparatory hearing or of an application for leave to appeal in relation to such a hearing,

    (c) the inclusion in a relevant programme of a report of a preparatory hearing, or

    (d) the inclusion in a relevant programme of a report of an appeal in relation to a preparatory hearing or of an application for leave to appeal in relation to such a hearing,

at the conclusion of the trial of the accused or of the last of the accused to be tried.

(9) Subsection (1) does not apply to a report which contains only one or more of the following matters—

    (a) the identity of the court and the name of the judge;

    (b) the names, ages, home addresses and occupations of the accused and witnesses;

    (c) the offence or offences, or a summary of them, with which the accused is or are charged;

    (d) the names of counsel and solicitors in the proceedings;

    (e) where the proceedings are adjourned, the date and place to which they are adjourned;

    (f) any arrangements as to bail;

    [(g) whether a right to representation funded by the Legal Services Commission as part of the Criminal Defence Service was granted to the accused or any of the accused.]

(10) The addresses that may be published or included in a relevant programme under subsection (9) are addresses—

(a) at any relevant time, and
(b) at the time of their publication or inclusion in a relevant programme;

and "relevant time" here means a time when events giving rise to the charges to which the proceedings relate occurred.

(11) Nothing in this section affects any prohibition or restriction imposed by virtue of any other enactment on a publication or on matter included in a programme.

(12) In this section—

(a) "publish", in relation to a report, means publish the report either by itself or as part of a newspaper or periodical, for distribution to the public;
(b) expressions cognate with "publish"shall be construed accordingly,
(c) "relevant programme" means a programme included in a programme service, within the meaning of the Broadcasting Act 1990.

Offences in connection with reporting

38.—(1) If a report is published or included in a relevant programme in con-   **80–008**
travention of section 37 each of the following persons is guilty of an offence—

(a) in the case of a publication of a written report as part of a newspaper or periodical, any proprietor, editor or publisher of the newspaper or periodical;
(b) in the case of a publication of a written report otherwise than as part of a newspaper or periodical, the person who publishes it;
(c) in the case of the inclusion of a report in a relevant programme, any body corporate which is engaged in providing the service in which the programme is included and any person having functions in relation to the programme corresponding to those of an editor of a newspaper.

(2) A person guilty of an offence under this section is liable on summary conviction to a fine of an amount not exceeding level 5 on the standard scale.

(3) Proceedings for an offence under this section shall not be instituted in England and Wales otherwise than by or with the consent of the Attorney General.

(4) Subsection (12) of section 37 applies for the purposes of this section as it applies for the purposes of that.

PART IV

RULINGS

Meaning of pre-trial hearing

39.—(1) For the purposes of this Part a hearing is a pre-trial hearing if it   **80–009**
relates to a trial on indictment and it takes place—

(a) after the accused has been committed for trial for the offence concerned, [after the accused has been sent for trial for the offence under section 51 of the Crime and Disorder Act 1998,][1] or after the proceedings for the trial have been transferred to the Crown Court, and

(b) before the start of the trial.

(2) For the purposes of this Part a hearing is also a pre-trial hearing if—

    (a) it relates to a trial on indictment to be held in pursuance of a bill of indictment preferred under the authority of section 2(2)(b) of the Administration of Justice (Miscellaneous Provisions) Act 1933 (bill preferred by direction of Court of Appeal, or by direction or with consent of a judge), and

    (b) it takes place after the bill of indictment has been preferred and before the start of the trial.

(3) For the purposes of this section the start of a trial on indictment occurs when a jury is sworn to consider the issue of guilt or fitness to plead or, if the court accepts a plea of guilty before a jury is sworn, when that plea is accepted; but this is subject to section 8 of the Criminal Justice Act 1987 and section 30 of this Act (preparatory hearings).

¹ Words inserted by Crime and Disorder Act 1998 (c.37), Sched. 8, para. 129.

Power to make rulings

80–010   **40.**—(1) A judge may make at a pre-trial hearing a ruling as to—

    (a) any question as to the admissibility of evidence;

    (b) any other question of law relating to the case concerned.

(2) A ruling may be made under this section—

    (a) on an application by a party to the case, or

    (b) of the judge's own motion.

(3) Subject to subsection (4), a ruling made under this section has binding effect from the time it is made until the case against the accused or, if there is more than one, against each of them is disposed of; and the case against an accused is disposed of if—

    (a) he is acquitted or convicted, or

    (b) the prosecutor decides not to proceed with the case against him.

(4) A judge may discharge or vary (or further vary) a ruling made under this section if it appears to him that it is in the interests of justice to do so; and a judge may act under this subsection—

    (a) on an application by a party to the case, or

    (b) of the judge's own motion.

(5) No application may be made under subsection (4)(a) unless there has been a material change of circumstances since the ruling was made or, if a previous application has been made, since the application (or last application) was made.

(6) The judge referred to in subsection (4) need not be the judge who made the ruling or, if it has been varied, the judge (or any of the judges) who varied it.

(7) For the purposes of this section the prosecutor is any person acting as prosecutor, whether an individual or a body.

Restrictions on reporting

41.—(1) Except as provided by this section—   **80–011**

    (a) no written report of matters falling within subsection (2) shall be published in Great Britain;

    (b) no report of matters falling within subsection (2) shall be included in a relevant programme for reception in Great Britain.

(2) The following matters fall within this subsection—

    (a) a ruling made under section 40;

    (b) proceedings on an application for a ruling to be made under section 40;

    (c) an order that a ruling made under section 40 be discharged or varied or further varied;

    (d) proceedings on an application for a ruling made under section 40 to be discharged or varied or further varied.

(3) The judge dealing with any matter falling within subsection (2) may order that subsection (1) shall not apply, or shall not apply to a specified extent, to a report of the matter.

(4) Where there is only one accused and he objects to the making of an order under subsection (3) the judge shall make the order if (and only if) satisfied after hearing the representations of the accused that it is in the interests of justice to do so; and if the order is made it shall not apply to the extent that a report deals with any such objection or representations.

(5) Where there are two or more accused and one or more of them objects to the making of an order under subsection (3) the judge shall make the order if (and only if) satisfied after hearing the representations of each of the accused that it is in the interests of justice to do so; and if the order is made it shall not apply to the extent that a report deals with any such objection or representations.

(6) Subsection (1) does not apply to—

    (a) the publication of a report of matters, or

    (b) the inclusion in a relevant programme of a report of matters,

at the conclusion of the trial of the accused or of the last of the accused to be tried.

(7) Nothing in this section affects any prohibition or restriction imposed by virtue of any other enactment on a publication or on matter included in a programme.

(8) In this section—

    (a) "publish", in relation to a report, means publish the report, either by itself or as part of a newspaper or periodical, for distribution to the public;

    (b) expressions cognate with "publish" shall be construed accordingly;

    (c) "relevant programme" means a programme included in a programme service, within the meaning of the Broadcasting Act 1990.

. . . . . .

PART VII

MISCELLANEOUS AND GENERAL

Derogatory assertions

Orders in respect of certain assertions

80–012 **58.**—(1) This section applies where a person has been convicted of an offence and a speech in mitigation is made by him or on his behalf before—

 (a) a court determining what sentence should be passed on him in respect of the offence, or
 (b) a magistrates' court determining whether he should be committed to the Crown Court for sentence.

(2) This section also applies where a sentence has been passed on a person in respect of an offence and a submission relating to the sentence is made by him or on his behalf before—

 (a) a court hearing an appeal against or reviewing the sentence, or
 (b) a court determining whether to grant leave to appeal against the sentence.

(3) Where it appears to the court that there is a real possibility that an order under subsection (8) will be made in relation to the assertion, the court may make an order under subsection (7) in relation to the assertion.

(4) Where there are substantial grounds for believing—

 (a) that an assertion forming part of the speech or submission is derogatory to a person's character (for instance, because it suggests that his conduct is or has been criminal, immoral or improper), and
 (b) that the assertion is false or that the facts asserted are irrelevant to the sentence,

the court may make an order under subsection (8) in relation to the assertion.

(5) An order under subsection (7) or (8) must not be made in relation to an assertion if it appears to the court that the assertion was previously made—

 (a) at the trial at which the person was convicted of the offence, or
 (b) during any other proceedings relating to the offence.

(6) Section 59 has effect where a court makes an order under subsection (7) or (8).

(7) An order under this subsection—

 (a) may be made at any time before the court has made a determination with regard to sentencing;
 (b) may be revoked at any time by the court;
 (c) subject to paragraph (b), shall cease to have effect when the court makes a determination with regard to sentencing.

(8) An order under this subsection—

 (a) may be made at any time before the court has made a determination with regard to sentencing, but only if it is made as soon as is reasonably practicable after the making of the determination;

(b) may be revoked at any time by the court;

(c) subject to paragraph (b), shall cease to have effect at the end of the period of 12 months beginning with the day on which it is made;

(d) may be made whether or not an order has been made under subsection (7) with regard to the case concerned.

(9) For the purposes of subsection (7) and (8) the court makes a determination with regard to sentencing—

(a) when it determines what sentence should be passed (where this section applies by virtue of subsection (1)(a);

(b) when it determines whether the person should be committed to the Crown Court for sentence (where this section applies by virtue of sub-section (1)(b));

(c) when it determines what the sentence should be (where this section applies by virtue of subsection (2)(a));

(d) when it determines whether to grant leave to appeal (where this section applies by virtue of subsection (2)(b).

Restriction on reporting of assertions

59.—(1) Where a court makes an order under section 58(7) or (8) in relation   **80–013** to any assertion, at any time when the order has effect the assertion must not—

(a) be published in Great Britain in a written publication available to the public, or

(b) be included in a relevant programme for reception in Great Britain.

(2) In this section—

"relevant programme" means a programme included in a programme ser-vice, within the meaning of the Broadcasting Act 1990;

"written publication" includes a film, a soundtrack and any other record in permanent form but does not include an indictment or other document prepared for use in particular legal proceedings.

(3) For the purposes of this section an assertion is published or included in a programme if the material published or included—

(a) names the person about whom the assertion is made or, without naming him, contains enough to make it likely that members of the public will identify him as the person about whom it is made, and

(b) reproduces the actual wording of the matter asserted or contains its substance.

Reporting of assertions: offences

60.—(1) If an assertion is published or included in a relevant programme   **80–014** in contravention of section 59, each of the following persons is guilty of an offence—

(a) in the case of publication in a newspaper or periodical, any proprietor, any editor and any publisher of the newspaper or periodical;

(b) in the case of publication in any other form, the person publishing the assertion;

(c) in the case of an assertion included in a relevant programme, any body corporate engaged in providing the service in which the programme is included and any person having functions in relation to the programme corresponding to those of an editor of a newspaper.

(2) A person guilty of an offence under this section is liable on summary conviction to a fine of an amount not exceeding level 5 on the standard scale.

(3) Where a person is charged with an offence under this section it is a defence to prove that at the time of the alleged offence—

(a) he was not aware, and neither suspected nor had reason to suspect, that an order under section 58(7) or (8) had effect at that time, or
(b) he was not aware, and neither suspected nor had reason to suspect, that the publication or programme in question was of, or (as the case may be) included, the assertion in question.

(4) Where an offence under this section committed by a body corporate is proved to have been committed with the consent or connivance of, or to be attributable to any neglect on the part of—

(a) a director, manager, secretary or other similar officer of the body corporate, or
(b) a person purporting to act in any such capacity,

he as well as the body, corporate is guilty of the offence and liable to be proceeded against and punished accordingly.

(5) In relation to a body corporate whose affairs are managed by its members "director" in subsection (4) means a member of the body corporate.

(6) Subsections (2) and (3) of section 59 apply for the purposes of this section as they apply for the purposes of that.

Defamation Act 1996

(1996, c. 31)

81–001   *An Act to amend the law of defamation and to amend the law of limitation with respect to actions for defamation or malicious falsehood.*   [4th July 1996]

Responsibility for publication

Responsibility for publication

81–002   **1.**—(1) In defamation proceedings a person has a defence if he shows that—

(a) he was not the author, editor or publisher of the statement complained of,
(b) he took reasonable care in relation to its publication, and
(c) he did not know, and had no reason to believe, that what he did caused or contributed to the publication of a defamatory statement.

(2) For this purpose "author", "editor" and "publisher" have the following meanings, which are further explained in subsection (3)—

"author" means the originator of the statement, but does not include a person who did not intend that his statement be published at all;

"editor" means a person having editorial or equivalent responsibility for the content of the statement or the decision to publish it; and

"publisher" means a commercial publisher, that is, a person whose business is issuing material to the public, or a section of the public, who issues material containing the statement in the course of that business.

(3) A person shall not be considered the author, editor or publisher of a statement if he is only involved—

(a) in printing, producing, distributing or selling printed material containing the statement;

(b) in processing, making copies of, distributing, exhibiting or selling a film or sound recording (as defined in Part I of the Copyright, Designs and Patents Act 1988) containing the statement;

(c) in processing, making copies of, distributing or selling any electronic medium in or on which the statement is recorded, or in operating or providing any equipment, system or service by means of which the statement is retrieved, copied, distributed or made available in electronic form;

(d) as the broadcaster of a live programme containing the statement in circumstances in which he has no effective control over the maker of the statement;

(e) as the operator of or provider of access to a communications system by means of which the statement is transmitted, or made available, by a person over whom he has no effective control.

In a case not within paragraphs (a) to (e) the court may have regard to those provisions by way of analogy in deciding whether a person is to be considered the author, editor or publisher of a statement.

(4) Employees or agents of an author, editor or publisher are in the same position as their employer or principal to the extent that they are responsible for the content of the statement or the decision to publish it.

(5) In determining for the purposes of this section whether a person took reasonable care, or had reason to believe that what he did caused or contributed to the publication of a defamatory statement, regard shall be had to—

(a) the extent of his responsibility for the content of the statement or the decision to publish it,

(b) the nature or circumstances of the publication, and

(c) the previous conduct or character of the author, editor or publisher.

(6) This section does not apply to any cause of action which arose before the section came into force.

Offer to make amends

Offer to make amends

2.—(1) A person who has published a statement alleged to be defamatory of another may offer to make amends under this section.   **81–003**

(2) The offer may be in relation to the statement generally or in relation to a specific defamatory meaning which the person making the offer accepts that the statement conveys ("a qualified offer").

(3) An offer to make amends—

(a) must be in writing,

(b) must be expressed to be an offer to make amends under section 2 of the Defamation Act 1996, and

(c) must state whether it is a qualified offer and, if so, set out the defamatory meaning in relation to which it is made.

(4) An offer to make amends under this section is an offer—

(a) to make a suitable correction of the statement complained of and a sufficient apology to the aggrieved party,

(b) to publish the correction and apology in a manner that is reasonable and practicable in the circumstances, and

(c) to pay to the aggrieved party such compensation (if any), and such costs, as may be agreed or determined to be payable.

The fact that the offer is accompanied by an offer to take specific steps does not affect the fact that an offer to make amends under this section is an offer to do all the things mentioned in paragraphs (a) to (c).

(5) An offer to make amends under this section may not be made by a person after serving a defence in defamation proceedings brought against him by the aggrieved party in respect of the publication in question.

(6) An offer to make amends under this section may be withdrawn before it is accepted; and a renewal of an offer which has been withdrawn shall be treated as a new offer.

Accepting an offer to make amends

81–004   **3.**—(1) If an offer to make amends under section 2 is accepted by the aggrieved party, the following provisions apply.

(2) The party accepting the offer may not bring or continue defamation proceedings in respect of the publication concerned against the person making the offer, but he is entitled to enforce the offer to make amends, as follows.

(3) If the parties agree on the steps to be taken in fulfilment of the offer, the aggrieved party may apply to the court for an order that the other party fulfil his offer by taking the steps agreed.

(4) If the parties do not agree on the steps to be taken by way of correction, apology and publication, the party who made the offer may take such steps as he thinks appropriate, and may in particular—

(a) make the correction and apology by a statement in open court in terms approved by the court, and

(b) give an undertaking to the court as to the manner of their publication.

(5) If the parties do not agree on the amount to be paid by way of compensation, it shall be determined by the court on the same principles as damages in defamation proceedings. The court shall take account of any steps taken in fulfilment of the offer and (so far as not agreed between the parties) of the suitability of the correction, the sufficiency of the apology and whether the manner of their publication was reasonable in the circumstances, and may reduce or increase the amount of compensation accordingly.

(6) If the parties do not agree on the amount to be paid by way of costs, it shall be determined by the court on the same principles as costs awarded in court proceedings.

(7) The acceptance of an offer by one person to make amends does not affect any cause of action against another person in respect of the same publication, subject as follows.

(8) In England and Wales or Northern Ireland, for the purposes of the Civil Liability (Contribution) Act 1978—

(a) the amount of compensation paid under the offer shall be treated as paid in bona fide settlement or compromise of the claim; and

(b) where another person is liable in respect of the same damage (whether jointly or otherwise), the person whose offer to make amends was accepted is not required to pay by virtue of any contribution under section 1 of that Act a greater amount than the amount of the compensation payable in pursuance of the offer.

(9) In Scotland—

(a) subsection (2) of section 3 of the Law Reform (Miscellaneous Provisions) (Scotland) Act 1940 (right of one joint wrongdoer as respects another to recover contribution towards damages) applies in relation to compensation paid under an offer to make amends as it applies in relation to damages in an action to which that section applies; and

(b) where another person is liable in respect of the same damage (whether jointly or otherwise), the person whose offer to make amends was accepted is not required to pay by virtue of any contribution under section 3(2) of that Act a greater amount than the amount of compensation payable in pursuance of the offer.

(10) Proceedings under this section shall be heard and determined without a jury.

Failure to accept offer to make amends

4.—(1) If an offer to make amends under section 2, duly made and not with-   **81–005** drawn, is not accepted by the aggrieved party, the following provisions apply.

(2) The fact that the offer was made is a defence (subject to subsection (3)) to defamation proceedings in respect of the publication in question by that party against the person making the offer.

A qualified offer is only a defence in respect of the meaning to which the offer related.

(3) There is no such defence if the person by whom the offer was made knew or had reason to believe that the statement complained of—

(a) referred to the aggrieved party or was likely to be understood as referring to him, and

(b) was both false and defamatory of that party.

but it shall be presumed until the contrary is shown that he did not know and had no reason to believe that was the case.

(4) The person who made the offer need not rely on it by way of defence, but if he does he may not rely on any other defence.

If the offer was a qualified offer, this applies only in respect of the meaning to which the offer related.

(5) The offer may be relied on in mitigation of damages whether or not it was relied on as a defence.

. . . . . .

Evidence concerning proceedings in Parliament

Evidence concerning proceedings in Parliament

81–006   **13.**—(1) Where the conduct of a person in or in relation to proceedings in Parliament is in issue in defamation proceedings, he may waive for the purposes of those proceedings, so far as concerns him, the protection of any enactment or rule of law which prevents proceedings in Parliament being impeached or questioned in any court or place out of Parliament.

(2) Where a person waives that protection—

  (a) any such enactment or rule of law shall not apply to prevent evidence being given, questions being asked or statements, submissions, comments or findings being made about his conduct, and

  (b) none of those things shall be regarded as infringing the privilege of either House of Parliament.

(3) The waiver by one person of that protection does not affect its operation in relation to another person who has not waived it.

(4) Nothing in this section affects any enactment or rule of law so far as it protects a person (including a person who has waived the protection referred to above) from legal liability for words spoken or things done in the course of, or for the purposes of or incidental to, any proceedings in Parliament.

(5) Without prejudice to the generality of subsection (4), that subsection applies to—

  (a) the giving of evidence before either House or a committee;

  (b) the presentation or submission of a document to either House or a committee;

  (c) the preparation of a document for the purposes of or incidental to the transacting of any such business;

  (d) the formulation, making or publication of a document, including a report, by or pursuant to an order to either House or a committee; and

  (e) any communication with the Parliamentary Commissioner for Standards or any person having functions in connection with the registration of members' interests.

In this subsection "a committee" means a committee of either House or a joint committee of both House of Parliament.

Statutory privilege

Reports of court proceedings absolutely privileged

81–007   **14.**—(1) A fair and accurate report of proceedings in public before a court to which this section applies, if published contemporaneously with the proceedings, is absolutely privileged.

(2) A report of proceedings which by an order of the court, or as a consequence of any statutory provision, is required to be postponed shall be treated as published contemporaneously if it is published as soon as practicable after publication is permitted.

(3) This section applies to—

  (a) any court in the United Kingdom,

  (b) the European Court of Justice or any court attached to that court,

  (c) the European Court of Human Rights, and

  (d) any international criminal tribunal established by the Security Council of the United Nations or by an international agreement to which the United Kingdom is a party.

In paragraph (a) "court" includes any tribunal or body exercising the judicial power of the State.

(4) In section 8(6) of the Rehabilitation of Offenders Act 1974 and in Article 9(6) of the Rehabilitation of Offenders (Northern Ireland) Order 1978 (defamation actions: reports of court proceedings), for "section 3 of the Law of Libel Amendment Act 1888" substitute "section 14 of the Defamation Act 1996".

Reports, etc. protected by qualified privilege

15.—(1) The publication of any report or other statement mentioned in Schedule 1 to this Act is privileged unless the publication is shown to be made with malice, subject as follows. **81–008**

(2) In defamation proceedings in respect of the publication of a report or other statement mentioned in Part IIof that Schedule, there is no defence under this section if the plaintiff shows that the defendant—

(a) was requested by him to publish in a suitable manner a reasonable letter or statement by way of explanation or contradiction, and
(b) refused or neglected to do so.

For this purpose "in a suitable manner" means in the same manner as the publication complained of or in a manner that is adequate and reasonable in the circumstances.

(3) This section does not apply to the publication to the public, or a section of the public, of matter which is not of public concern and the publication of which is not for the public benefit.

(4) Nothing in this section shall be construed—

(a) as protecting the publication of matter the publication of which is prohibited by law, or
(b) as limiting or abridging any privilege subsisting apart from this section.

. . . . . .

General provisions

Short title and saving

20.—(1) This Act may be cited as the Defamation Act 1996. **81–009**

(2) Nothing in this Act affects the law relating to criminal libel.

. . . . . .

SCHEDULE 1

QUALIFIED PRIVILEGE

PART II

STATEMENTS PRIVILEGED SUBJECT TO EXPLANATION OR
CONTRADICTION

81–010   **15.**—(1) A fair and accurate report of, or copy of or extract from, any adjudication, report, statement or notice issued by a body, officer or other person designated for the purposes of this paragraph—

(a) for England and Wales or Northern Ireland, by order of the Lord Chancellor, and
(b) for Scotland, by order of the Secretary of State.

(2) An order under this paragraph shall be made by statutory instrument which shall be subject to annulment in pursuance of a resolution of either House of Parliament.

Education Act 1996

(1996, c. 56)

82–001 *An Act to consolidate the Education Act 1944 and certain other enactments relating to education, with amendments to give effect to recommendations of the Law Commission.*   [24th July 1996]

. . . . . .

PART V

THE CURRICULUM

CHAPTER IV

MISCELLANEOUS AND SUPPLEMENTARY PROVISIONS

Sex education

Sex education: manner of provision

82–002   **403.**—(1) The governing body and head teacher shall take such steps as are reasonably practicable to secure that where sex education is given to any registered pupils at a maintained school, it is given in such a manner as to encourage those pupils to have due regard to moral considerations and the value of family life.

[(1A) The Secretary of State must issue guidance designed to secure that when sex education is given to registered pupils at maintained schools—

(a) they learn the nature of marriage and its importance for family life and the bringing up of children, and
(b) they are protected from teaching and materials which are inappropriate having regard to the age and the religious and cultural background of the pupils concerned.

(1B) In discharging their functions under subsection (1) governing bodies and head teachers must have regard to the Secretary of State's guidance.

(1C) Guidance under subsection (1A) must include guidance about any material which may be produced by NHS bodies for use for the purposes of sex education in schools.

(1D) The Secretary of State may at any time revise his guidance under subsection (1A).]

[(2) In this section "maintained school" includes a community or foundation special school established in a hospital and"NHS body" has the same meaning as in section 22 of the National Health Service Act 1977.]

Sex education: statements of policy

404.—(1) The governing body of a maintained school shall—   **82–003**

(a) make, and keep up to date, a separate written statement of their policy with regard to the provision of sex education, and
(b) make copies of the statement available for inspection (at all reasonable times) by parents of registered pupils at the school and provide a copy of the statement free of charge to any such parent who asks for one.

[(1A) A statement under subsection (1) must include a statement of the effect of section 405.]

(2) In subsection (1) "maintained school" includes, in relation to pupils who are provided with secondary education, [a community or foundation special school] established in a hospital.

Exemption from sex education

405. If the parent of any pupil in attendance at a maintained school requests   **82–004** that he may be wholly or partly excused from receiving sex education at the school, the pupil shall, except so far as such education is comprised in the National Curriculum, be so excused accordingly until the request is withdrawn.

Politics

Political indoctrination

406.—(1) The local education authority, governing body and head teacher   **82–005** shall forbid—

(a) the pursuit of partisan political activities by any of those registered pupils at a maintained school who are junior pupils, and
(b) the promotion of partisan political views in the teaching of any subject in the school.

(2) In the case of activities which take place otherwise than on the school premises, subsection (1)(a) applies only where arrangements for junior pupils to take part in the activities are made by—

(a) any member of the school's staff (in his capacity as such), or
(b) anyone acting on behalf of the school or of a member of the school's staff (in his capacity as such).

(3) In this section "maintained school" includes [a community or foundation special school] established in a hospital.

Duty to secure balanced treatment of political issues

82–006   **407.**—(1) The local education authority, governing body and head teacher shall take such steps as are reasonably practicable to secure that where political issues are brought to the attention of pupils while they are—

    (a) in attendance at a maintained school, or
    (b) taking part in extra-curricular activities which are provided or organised for registered pupils at the school by or on behalf of the school,

they are offered a balanced presentation of opposing views.

    (2) In this section "maintained school" includes [a community or foundation special school] established in a hospital.

Employment Rights Act 1996

(1996, c. 18)

83–001   *An Act to consolidate enactments relating to employment rights.*

                                            [22nd May 1996]

. . . . . .

PART IVA

PROTECTED DISCLOSURES

Meaning of "protected disclosure"

83–002   [**43A.** In this Act a "protected disclosure" means a qualifying disclosure (as defined by section 43B) which is made by a worker in accordance with any of sections 43C to 43H.][1]

[1] Added by Public Interest Disclosure Act 1998 (c.23), s. 1.

Disclosures qualifying for protection

83–003   [**43B.**—(1) In this Part a "qualifying disclosure" means any disclosure of information which, in the reasonable belief of the worker making the disclosure, tends to show one or more of the following—

    (a) that a criminal offence has been committed, is being committed or is likely to be committed,
    (b) that a person has failed, is failing or is likely to fail to comply with any legal obligation to which he is subject,
    (c) that a miscarriage of justice has occurred, is occurring or is likely to occur,
    (d) that the health or safety of any individual has been, is being or is likely to be endangered,

(e) that the environment has been, is being or is likely to be damaged, or

(f) that information tending to show any matter falling within any one of the preceding paragraphs has been, is being or is likely to be deliberately concealed.

(2) For the purposes of subsection (1), it is immaterial whether the relevant failure occurred, occurs or would occur in the United Kingdom or elsewhere, and whether the law applying to it is that of the United Kingdom or of any other country or territory.

(3) A disclosure of information is not a qualifying disclosure if the person making the disclosure commits an offence by making it.

(4) A disclosure of information in respect of which a claim to legal professional privilege (or, in Scotland, to confidentiality as between client and professional legal adviser) could be maintained in legal proceedings is not a qualifying disclosure if it is made by a person to whom the information had been disclosed in the course of obtaining legal advice.

(5) In this Part "the relevant failure", in relation to a qualifying disclosure, means the matter falling within paragraphs (a) to (f) of subsection (1).][1]

[1] Added by Public Interest Disclosure Act 1998 (c.23) s. 1.

Disclosure to employer or other responsible person

[**43C.**—(1) A qualifying disclosure is made in accordance with this section if the worker makes the disclosure in good faith— **83–004**

(a) to his employer, or

(b) where the worker reasonably, believes that the relevant failure relates solely or mainly to—

(i) the conduct of a person other than his employer, or

(ii) any other matter for which a person other than his employer has legal responsibility,

to that other person.

(2) A worker who, in accordance with a procedure whose use by him is authorised by his employer, makes a qualifying disclosure to a person other than his employer, is to be treated for the purposes of this Part as making the qualifying disclosure to his employer.][1]

[1] Added by Public Interest Disclosure Act 1998 (c.23) s. 1.

Disclosure to legal adviser

[**43D.** A qualifying disclosure is made in accordance with this section if it is made in the course of obtaining legal advice.][1] **83–005**

[1] Added by Public Interest Disclosure Act 1998 (c.23), s. 1.

Disclosure to Minister of the Crown

[**43E.** A qualifying disclosure is made in accordance with this section if— **83–006**

(a) the worker's employer is—

(i) an individual appointed under any enactment [(including any enactment comprised in, or in an instrument made under, an Act of the Scottish Parliament)] by a Minister of the Crown [or a member of the Scottish Executive]², or

(ii) a body any of whose members are so appointed, and

(b) the disclosure is made in good faith to a Minister of the Crown [or a member of the Scottish Executive].]¹

¹ Added by Public Interest Disclosure Act 1998 (c.23), s. 1.

Disclosure to prescribed person

83–007   [**43F.**—(1) A qualifying disclosure is made in accordance with this section if the worker—

(a) makes the disclosure in good faith to a person prescribed by an order made by the Secretary of State for the purposes of this section, and

(b) reasonably believes—

(i) that the relevant failure falls within any description of matters in respect of which that person is so prescribed, and

(ii) that the information disclosed, and any allegation contained in it, are substantially true.

(2) An order prescribing persons for the purposes of this section may specify persons or descriptions of persons, and shall specify the descriptions of matters in respect of which each person, or persons of each description, is or are prescribed.]¹

¹ Added by Public Interest Disclosure Act 1998 (c.23), s. 1.

Disclosure in other cases

83–008   [**43G.**—(1) A qualifying disclosure is made in accordance with this section if—

(a) the worker makes the disclosure in good faith,

(b) he reasonably believes that the information disclosed, and any allegation contained in it, are substantially true,

(c) he does not make the disclosure for purposes of personal gain,

(d) any of the conditions in subsection (2) is met, and

(e) in all the circumstances of the case, it is reasonable for him to make the disclosure.

(2) The conditions referred to in subsection (1)(d) are—

(a) that, at the time he makes the disclosure, the worker reasonably believes that he will be subjected to a detriment by his employer if he makes a disclosure to his employer or in accordance with section 43F,

(b) that, in a case where no person is prescribed for the purposes of section 43F in relation to the relevant failure, the worker reasonably believes that it is likely that evidence relating to the relevant failure will be concealed or destroyed if he makes a disclosure to his employer, or

(c) that the worker has previously made a disclosure of substantially the same information—

(i) to his employer, or

(ii) in accordance with section 43F.

(3) In determining for the purposes of subsection (1)(e) whether it is reason-

able for the worker to make the disclosure, regard shall be had, in particular, to—

  (a) the identity of the person to whom the disclosure is made,

  (b) the seriousness of the relevant failure,

  (c) whether the relevant failure is continuing or is likely to occur in the future,

  (d) whether the disclosure is made in breach of a duty of confidentiality owed by the employer to any other person,

  (e) in a case falling within subsection (2)(c)(i) or (ii), any action which the employer or the person to whom the previous disclosure in accordance with section 43F was made has taken or might reasonably be expected to have taken as a result of the previous disclosure, and

  (f) in a case falling within subsection (2)(c)(i), whether in making the disclosure to the employer the worker complied with any procedure whose use by him was authorised by the employer.

(4) For the purposes of this section a subsequent disclosure may be regarded as a disclosure of substantially the same information as that disclosed by a previous disclosure as mentioned in subsection (2)(c) even though the subsequent disclosure extends to information about action taken or not taken by any person as a result of the previous disclosure.]¹

¹ Added by Public Interest Disclosure Act 1998 (c.23), s. 1.

Disclosure of exceptionally serious failure

[**43H.**—(1) A qualifying disclosure is made in accordance with this section if—   **83–009**

  (a) the worker makes the disclosure in good faith,

  (b) he reasonably believes that the information disclosed, and any allegation contained in it, are substantially true,

  (c) he does not make the disclosure for purposes of personal gain,

  (d) the relevant failure is of an exceptionally serious nature, and

  (e) in all the circumstances of the case, it is reasonable for him to make the disclosure.

(2) In determining for the purposes of subsection (1)(e) whether it is reasonable for the worker to make the disclosure, regard shall be had, in particular, to the identity of the person to whom the disclosure is made.]¹

¹ Added by Public Interest Disclosure Act 1998 (c.23), s. 1.

Contractual duties of confidentiality

[**43J.**—(1) Any provision in an agreement to which this section applies is void in so far as it purports to preclude the worker from making a protected disclosure.   **83–010**

(2) This section applies to any agreement between a worker and his employer (whether a worker's contract or not), including an agreement to refrain from instituting or continuing any proceedings under this Act or any proceedings for breach of contract.]¹

¹ Added by Public Interest Disclosure Act 1998 (c.23), s. 1.

Extension of meaning of "worker" etc. for Part IVA

83–011   [**43K.**—(1) For the purposes of this Part "worker" includes an individual who is not a worker as defined by section 230(3) but who—

(a) works or worked for a person in circumstances in which—

(i) he is or was introduced or supplied to do that work by a third person, and

(ii) the terms on which he is or was engaged to do the work are or were in practice substantially determined not by him but by the person for whom he works or worked, by the third person or by both of them,

(b) contracts or contracted with a person, for the purposes of that person's business, for the execution of work to be done in a place not under the control or management of that person and would fall within section 230(3)(b) if for "personally" in that provision there were substituted "(whether personally or otherwise)",

(c) works or worked as a person providing general medical services, general dental services, general ophthalmic services or pharmaceutical services in accordance with arrangements made—

(i) by a Health Authority under section 29, 35, 38 or 41 of the National Health Service Act 1977, or

(ii) by a Health Board under section 19, 25, 26 or 27 of the National Health Service (Scotland) Act 1978, or

(d) is or was provided with work experience provided pursuant to a training course or programme or with training for employment (or with both) otherwise than—

(i) under a contract of employment, or

(ii) by an educational establishment on a course run by that establishment;

and any reference to a worker's contract, to employment or to a worker being "employed" shall be construed accordingly.

(2) For the purposes of this Part "employer" includes—

(a) in relation to a worker falling within paragraph (a) of subsection (1), the person who substantially determines or determined the terms on which he is or was engaged,

(b) in relation to a worker falling within paragraph (c) of that subsection, the authority or board referred to in that paragraph, and

(c) in relation to a worker falling within paragraph (d) of that subsection, the person providing the work experience or training.

(3) In this section "educational establishment" includes any university, college, school or other educational establishment,][1]

[1] Added by Public Interest Disclosure Act 1998 (c.23), s. 1.

. . . . . .

PART V

PROTECTION FROM SUFFERING DETRIMENT IN EMPLOYMENT

Rights not to suffer detriment

Protected disclosures

[**47B.**—(1) A worker has the right not to be subjected to any detriment by   **83–012**
any act, or any deliberate failure to act, by his employer done on the ground
that the worker has made a protected disclosure.

(2) [T]his section does not apply where—

(a) the worker is an employee, and
(b) the detriment in question amounts to dismissal (within the meaning of [Part X]).

(3) For the purposes of this section, and of sections 48 and 49 so far as relating to this section, "worker" "worker's contract", "employment" and "employer" have the extended meaning given by section 43K.]¹

¹ Added by Public Interest Disclosure Act 1998 (c.23), s. 2.

. . . . . .

PART X

UNFAIR DISMISSAL

CHAPTER I

RIGHT NOT TO BE UNFAIRLY DISMISSED

Fairness

Protected disclosure

[**103A.** An employee who is dismissed shall be regarded for the purposes of   **83–013**
this Part as unfairly dismissed if the reason (or, if more than one, the principal
reason) for the dismissal is that the employee made a protected disclosure.]¹

¹ Added by Public Interest Disclosure Act 1998 (c.23), s. 5.

. . . . . .

PART XIII

MISCELLANEOUS

CHAPTER I

PARTICULAR TYPES OF EMPLOYMENT

Crown employment etc.

Crown employment

83–014   **191.**—(1) Subject to sections 192 and 193, the provisions of this Act to which this section applies have effect in relation to Crown employment and persons in Crown employment as they have effect in relation to other employment and other employees or workers.

(2) This section applies to—

    (a) Part I to III,

[(aa) Part IVA,]¹

    (b) Part V, apart from section 45,

    (c) Parts VI to VIII,

    (d) in Part IX, sections 92 and 93,

    (e) Part X, apart from section 101, and

    (f) this Part and Parts XIV and XV.

(3) In this Act "Crown employment" means employment under or for the purposes of a government department or any officer or body exercising on behalf of the Crown functions conferred by a statutory provision.

(4) For the purposes of the application of provisions of this Act in relation to Crown employment in accordance with subsection (1)—

    (a) references to an employee or a worker shall be construed as references to a person in Crown employment,

    (b) references to a contract of employment, or a worker's contract, shall be construed as references to the terms of employment of a person in Crown employment,

    (c) references to dismissal, or to the termination of a worker's contract, shall be construed as references to the termination of Crown employment,

    (d) references to redundancy shall be construed as references to the existence of such circumstances as are treated, in accordance with any arrangements falling within section 177(3) for the time being in force, as equivalent to redundancy in relation to Crown employment, and

    (e) references to an undertaking shall be construed—

        (i) in relation to a Minister of the Crown, as references to his functions or (as the context may require) to the department of which he is in charge, and

        (ii) in relation to a government department, officer or body, as references to the functions of the department, officer or body or (as the context may require) to the department, officer or body.

(5) Where the terms of employment of a person in Crown employment restrict his right to take part in—

    (a) certain political activities, or

(b) activities which may conflict with his official functions,

nothing in section 50 requires him to be allowed time off work for public duties connected with any such activities.

(6) Sections 159 and 160 are without prejudice to any exemption or immunity of the Crown.

¹ Added by Public Interest Disclosure Act 1998 (c.23), s. 10.

Armed forces

192.—(1) Section 191—   **83–015**

    (a) applies to service as a member of the naval, military or air forces of the Crown but subject to the following provisions of this section, and

    (b) applies to employment by an association established for the purposes of Part XI of the Reserve Forces Act 1996.

(2) The provisions of this Act which have effect by virtue of section 191 in relation to service as a member of the naval, military or air forces of the Crown are—

    (a) Part I,

    [(b) in Part V, section 45A, and sections 48 and 49 so far as relating to that section,]

    [(c) section 47C,]

    (d) in [Part VI, sections 55 to 57B],

    (e) Parts VII and VIII,

    (f) in Part IX, sections 92 and 93,

    (g) Part X, apart from sections 100 to 103 and 134, and

    (h) this Part and Parts XIV and XV.

(3) Her Majesty may by Order in Council—

    (a) amend subsection (2) by making additions to, or omissions from, the provisions for the time being specified in that subsection, and

    (b) make any provision for the time being so specified apply to service as a member of the naval, military or air forces of the Crown subject to such exceptions and modifications as may be specified in the Order in Council,

but no provision contained in Part II may be added to the provisions for the time being specified in subsection (2).

(4) Modifications made by an Order in Council under subsection (3) may include provision precluding the making of a complaint or reference to any [employment tribunal] unless [—]

    [(a) the person aggrieved has made a complaint to an officer under the service procedures for the redress of complaints applicable to him and has submitted that complaint to the Defence Council under those procedures; and

    (b) the Defence Council have made a determination with respect to the complaint.]

    [(5) Where modifications made by an Order in Council under subsection (3) include provision such as is mentioned in subsection (4), the Order in Council shall also include provision—

(a) enabling a complaint or reference to be made to an [employment tribunal] in such circumstances as may be specified in the Order, notwithstanding that provision such as is mentioned in subsection (4) would otherwise preclude the making of the complaint or reference; and

(b) where a complaint or reference is made to an [employment tribunal] by virtue of provision such as is mentioned in paragraph (a), enabling the service procedures for the redress of complaints to continue after the complaint or reference is made.]

(6) In subsection (4) and (5) "the service redress procedures" means the procedures, excluding those which relate to the making of a report on a complaint to Her Majesty, referred to in—

(a) [section 180 of the Army Act 1955],
(b) [section 180 of the Air Force Act 1955], and
(c) section 130 of the Naval Discipline Act 1957.

(7) No provision shall be made by virtue of subsection (4) which has the effect of substituting a period longer than six months for any period specified as the normal period for a complaint or reference.

(8) In subsection (7) "the normal period for a complaint or reference", in relation to any matter within the jurisdiction of an [employment tribunal], means the period specified in the relevant enactment as the period within which the complaint or reference must be made (disregarding any provision permitting an extension of that period at the discretion of the tribunal).

National security

83–016   [**193.** Part IVA and section 47B of this Act do not apply in relation to employment for the purposes of—

(a) the Security Service,
(b) the Secret Intelligence Service, or
(c) the Government Communications Headquarters.]

Police Act 1996

(1996, c. 16)

84–001   *An Act to consolidate the Police Act 1964, Part IX of the Police and Criminal Evidence Act 1984, Chapter I of Part I of the Police and Magistrates' Courts Act 1994 and certain other enactments relating to the police.*
[22nd May 1996]

PART I

ORGANISATION OF POLICE FORCES

Police areas

Police areas

84–002   **1.**—(1) England and Wales shall be divided into police areas.

(2) The police areas referred to in subsection (1) shall be—

(a) those listed in Schedule 1 (subject to any amendment made to that Schedule by an order under section 32 below, section 58 of the Local Government Act 1972, or section 17 of the Local Government Act 1992).
(b) the metropolitan police district, and
(c) the City of London police area.

(3) References in Schedule 1 to any local government area are to that area as it is for the time being [. . .]¹.

¹ Repealed by Greater London Authority Act 1999 (c.29), Sched. 34, Pt VII, para. 1.

Forces outside London

Maintenance of police forces

2. A police force shall be maintained for every police area for the time being listed in Schedule 1.   **84–003**

Establishment of police authorities

3.—(1) There shall be a police authority for every police area for the time being listed in Schedule 1.   **84–004**

(2) A police authority established under this section for any area shall be a body corporate to be known by the name of the area with the addition of the words "Police Authority".

Membership of police authorities etc.

4.—(1) Subject to subsection (2), each police authority established under section 3 shall consist of seventeen members.   **84–005**

(2) The Secretary of State may by order provide in relation to a police authority specified in the order that the number of its members shall be a specified odd number greater than seventeen.

(3) A statutory instrument containing an order under subsection (2) shall be laid before Parliament after being made.

(4) Schedules 2 and 3 shall have effect in relation to police authorities established under section 3 and the appointment of their members.

Reductions in size of police authorities

5.—(1) This section applies to any order under section 4(2) which varies of revokes an earlier order so as to reduce the number of a police authority's members.   **84–006**

(2) Before making an order to which this section applies, the Secretary of State shall consult—

(a) the authority,
(b) the councils which are relevant councils in relation to the authority for the purposes of Schedule 2, and
(c) any selection panel, constituted under regulations made in accordance with [section 29(2) of the Justices of the Peace Act 1997]¹, which is responsible, for is represented on a joint committee which is responsible, for the appointment of members of the authority.

(3) An order to which this section applies may include provision as to the termination of the appointment of the existing members of the authority and the making of new appointments or re-appointments.

¹ Words substituted. by Justices of the Peace Act 1997 (c.25), Sched. 5, para. 37(2).

The metropolitan police force

Maintenance of the metropolitan police force

84–007   [**5A.** A police force shall be maintained for the metropolitan police district.]¹

¹ ss. 5A, 5B, 5C and the section group titles immediately preceeding and following them inserted by Greater London Authority Act 1999 (c.29), Pt VI, s. 310(1).

Establishment of the Metropolitan Police Authority

84–008   [**5B.**—(1) There shall be a police authority for the metropolitan police district.
(2) The police authority established under this section shall be a body corporate to be known as the Metropolitan Police Authority.]

Membership etc of the Metropolitan Police Authority

84–009   [**5C.**—(1) The Metropolitan Police Authority shall consist of twenty three members (subject to subsection (2)).
(2) The Secretary of State may by order provide that the number of members of the Metropolitan Police Authority shall be a specified odd number not less than seventeen.
(3) Before making an order under subsection (2) which reduces the number of members of the Metropolitan Police Authority, the Secretary of State shall consult—

(a) the Greater London Authority;
(b) the Metropolitan Police Authority; and
(c) the person or body responsible for the appointment of members of the Greater London Magistrates' Courts Authority under regulations made under section 30B of the Justices of the Peace Act 1997 (which, by virtue of paragraph 5(b) of Schedule 2A to this Act, appoints magistrates to be members of the Metropolitan Police Authority).

(4) An order under subsection (2) which reduces the number of members of the Metropolitan Police Authority may include provision as to the termination of the appointment of the existing members of the Metropolitan Police Authority and the making of new appointments or re-appointments.
(5) A statutory instrument containing an order under subsection (2) shall be laid before Parliament after being made.
(6) Schedules 2A and 3 shall have effect in relation to the Metropolitan Police Authority and the appointment of its members.]

The metropolitan police and forces outside London

General functions of police authorities

84–010   [**6.**—(1) Every police authority established under section 3 shall secure the maintenance of an efficient and effective police force for its area.
(2) In discharging its functions, every police authority established under section 3 shall have regard to—

(a) any objectives determined by the Secretary of State under section 37,
(b) any objectives determined by the authority under section 7,
(c) any performance targets established by the authority, whether in compliance with a direction under section 38 or otherwise, and
(d) any local policing plan issued by the authority under section 8.

(3) In discharging any function to which a code of practice issued under section 39 relates, a police authority established under section 3 shall have regard to the code.

(4) A police authority shall comply with any direction given to it by the Secretary of State under section 38 or 40.

[(5) This section shall apply in relation to the Metropolitan Police Authority as it applies in relation to a police authority established under section 3.]¹]

¹ Added by Greater London Authority Act 1999 (c.29), Pt VI, s. 311.

Local policing objectives

[**7.**—(1) Every police authority established under section 3 shall, before the beginning of each financial year, determine objectives for the policing of the authority's area during that year.   **84–011**

(2) Objectives determined under this section may relate to matters to which objectives determined under section 37 also relate, or to other matters, but in any event shall be so framed as to be consistent with the objectives determined under that section.

(3) Before determining objectives under this section, a police authority shall—

(a) consult the chief constable for the area, and
(b) consider any views obtained by the authority in accordance with arrangements made under section 96.

[(4) This section shall apply in relation to the Metropolitan Police Authority as it applies to a police authority established under section 3, but taking the reference to the chief constable for the area as a reference to the Commissioner of Police of the Metropolis.]¹]

¹ Added by Greater London Authority Act 1999 (c.29), Sched. 27, para. 70.

Local policing plans

[**8.**—(1) Every police authority established under section 3 shall, before the beginning of each financial year, issue a plan setting out the proposed arrangements for the policing of the authority's area during the year ("the local policing plan").   **84–012**

(2) The local policing plan shall include a statement of the authority's priorities for the year, of the financial resources expected to be available and of the proposed allocation of those resources, and shall give particulars of—

(a) any objectives determined by the Secretary of State under section 37,
(b) any objectives determined by the authority under section 7,
(c) any performance targets established by the authority, whether in compliance with a direction under section 38 or otherwise, and
(d) The inspectors of constabulary may inspect, and report to the Secretary of State on, a police authority's compliance with the requirements of Part I of the Local Government Act 1999 (best value).

(3) A draft of the local policing plan shall be prepared by the chief constable for the area and submitted by him to the police authority for it to consider.

(4) Before issuing a local policing plan which differs from the draft submitted by the chief constable under subsection (3), a police authority shall consult the chief constable.

(5) A police authority shall arrange for every local policing plan issued by it under this section to be published in such manner as appears to it to be appropriate, and shall send a copy of the plan to the Secretary of State.

[(6) This section shall apply in relation to the Metropolitan Police Authority as it applies to a police authority established under section 3, but taking the references to the chief constable for the area as references to the Commissioner of Police of the Metropolis.]¹]

¹ Added by Greater London Authority Act 1999 (c.29), Sched. 27, para. 71.

Annual reports by police authorities

84–013   [9.—(1) As soon as possible after the end of each financial year every police authority established under section 3 shall issue a report relating to the policing of the authority's area for the year.

(2) A report issued by a police authority under this section for any year shall include an assessment of the extent to which the local policing plan for that year issued under section 8 has been carried out.

(3) A police authority shall arrange for every report issued by it under this section to be published in such manner as appears to it to be appropriate, and shall send a copy of the report to the Secretary of State.

[(4) This section shall apply in relation to the Metropolitan Police Authority as it applies to a police authority established under section 3.]¹]

¹ Added by Greater London Authority Act 1999 (c.29), Sched. 27, para. 72.

General functions of the Commissioner of Police of the Metropolis

84–014   [9A.—(1) The metropolitan police force shall be under the direction and control of the Commissioner of Police of the Metropolis appointed under section 9B.

(2) In discharging his functions, the Commissioner of Police of the Metropolis shall have regard to the local policing plan issued by the Metropolitan Police Authority under section 8.]¹

¹ Added by Greater London Authority Act 1999 (c.29), Pt VI, s. 314.

Appointment of Commissioner of Police of the Metropolis

84–015   [9B.—(1) There shall be a Commissioner of Police of the Metropolis.

(2) Any appointment of a Commissioner of Police of the Metropolis shall be made by Her Majesty by warrant under Her sign manual.

(3) A person appointed as Commissioner of Police of the Metropolis shall hold office at Her Majesty's pleasure.

(4) Any appointment of a Commissioner of Police of the Metropolis shall be subject to regulations under section 50.

(5) Before recommending to Her Majesty that She appoint a person as the Commissioner of Police of the Metropolis, the Secretary of State shall have regard to—

    (a) any recommendations made to him by the Metropolitan Police Authority; and

    (b) any representations made to him by the Mayor of London.

(6) Any functions exercisable by the Mayor of London under subsection (5) may only be exercised by him personally.]¹

¹ Added by Greater London Authority Act 1999 (c.29), Pt VI, s. 315.

Functions of Deputy Commissioner of Police of the Metropolis

[**9C.**—(1) The Deputy Commissioner of Police of the Metropolis may exercise any or all of the powers and duties of the Commissioner of Police of the Metropolis— **84–016**

    (a) during any absence, incapacity or suspension from duty of the Commissioner,

    (b) during any vacancy in the office of the Commissioner, or

    (c) at any other time, with the consent of the Commissioner.

(2) The Deputy Commissioner of Police of the Metropolis shall not have power to act by virtue of subsection (1)(a) or (b) for a continuous period exceeding three months, except with the consent of the Secretary of State.

(3) The Deputy Commissioner of Police of the Metropolis shall also have all the powers and duties of an Assistant Commissioner of Police of the Metropolis.]¹

¹ Added by Greater London Authority Act 1999 (c.29), Pt VI, s. 316.

Appointment of Deputy Commissioner of Police of the Metropolis

[**9D.**—(1) There shall be a Deputy Commissioner of Police of the Metropolis. **84–017**

(2) Any appointment of a Deputy Commissioner shall be made by Her Majesty by warrant under Her sign manual.

(3) A person appointed as the Deputy Commissioner shall hold office at Her Majesty's pleasure.

(4) Any appointment of a Deputy Commissioner shall be subject to regulations under section 50.

(5) Before recommending to Her Majesty that She appoint a person as the Deputy Commissioner, the Secretary of State shall have regard to—

    (a) any recommendations made to him by the Metropolitan Police Authority; and

    (b) any representations made to him by the Commissioner.

(6) In this section—

    "the Commissioner" means the Commissioner of Police of the Metropolis;
    "Deputy Commissioner" means Deputy Commissioner of Police of the Metropolis.]¹

¹ Added by Greater London Authority Act 1999 (c.29), Pt VI, s. 317.

Removal of Commissioner or Deputy Commissioner

[**9E.**—(1) The Metropolitan Police Authority, acting with the approval of the Secretary of State, may call upon the Commissioner of Police of the Metropolis to retire in the interests of efficiency or effectiveness. **84–018**

(2) Before seeking the approval of the Secretary of State under subsection (1), the Metropolitan Police Authority shall give the Commissioner of Police of the Metropolis an opportunity to make representations and shall consider any representations that he makes.

(3) Where the Commissioner of Police of the Metropolis is called upon to retire under subsection (1), he shall retire on such date as the Metropolitan Police Authority may specify or on such earlier date as may be agreed upon between him and the Authority.

(4) This section shall apply in relation to the Deputy Commissioner of Police of the Metropolis as it applies to the Commissioner of Police of the Metropolis.

(5) This section is without prejudice to—

    (a) section 9B(3),
    (b) section 9D(3),
    (c) any regulations under section 50, or
    (d) any regulations under the Police Pensions Act 1976.][1]

[1] Added by Greater London Authority Act 1999 (c.29), Pt VI, s. 318.

Assistant Commissioners of Police of the Metropolis

84–019   [9F.—(1) The ranks that may be held in the metropolitan police force shall include that of Assistant Commissioner of Police of the Metropolis ("Assistant Commissioner").

(2) Any appointment of an Assistant Commissioner shall be made by the Metropolitan Police Authority, but subject to the approval of the Secretary of State and to regulations under section 50.

(3) Subsections (1) to (3) of section 9E shall apply in relation to an Assistant Commissioner as they apply to the Commissioner of Police of the Metropolis.

(4) Subsection (3) is without prejudice to—

    (a) any regulations under section 50, or
    (b) any regulations under the Police Pensions Act 1976.

(5) An Assistant Commissioner may exercise any of the powers and duties of the Commissioner of Police of the Metropolis with the consent of the Commissioner.

(6) Subsection (5) is without prejudice to any regulations under section 50.][1]

[1] Added by Greater London Authority Act 1999 (c.29), Pt VI, s. 319.

Commanders

84–020   [9G.—(1) The ranks that may be held in the metropolitan police force shall include that of Commander.

(2) Any appointment of a Commander in the metropolitan police force shall be made by the Metropolitan Police Authority, but subject to the approval of the Secretary of State and to regulations under section 50.

(3) Subsections (1) to (3) of section 9E shall apply in relation to a Commander in the metropolitan police force as they apply to the Commissioner of Police of the Metropolis.

(4) Subsection (3) is without prejudice to—

    (a) any regulations under section 50, or
    (b) any regulations under the Police Pensions Act 1976.][1]

[1] Added by Greater London Authority Act 1999 (c.29), Pt VI, s. 320.

Other members of the metropolitan police force

84–021   [9H.—(1) The ranks that may be held in the metropolitan police force shall be such as may be prescribed by regulations under section 50.

(2) The ranks so prescribed in the case of the metropolitan police force shall include, in addition to the ranks of—

    (a) Commissioner of Police of the Metropolis,
    (b) Deputy Commissioner of Police of the Metropolis,
    (c) Assistant Commissioner of Police of the Metropolis,
    [(d) Deputy Assistant Commissioner of Police of the Metropolis, and][1]
    (e) Commander,

those of [chief superintendent,][2] superintendent, chief inspector, inspector, sergeant and constable.

(3) In the metropolitan police force, appointments and promotions to any rank below that of Commander shall be made in accordance with regulations under section 50 by the Commissioner of Police of the Metropolis.][3]

[1] Substituted by Criminal Justice and Police Act 2001 (c.16), Pt 5, s. 122(2).
[2] Words inserted by Criminal Justice and Police Act 2001 (c.16), Pt 5, s. 125(1).
[3] Added by Greater London Authority Act 1999 (c.29), Pt VI, s. 322.

General functions of chief constables

[**10.**—(1) A police force maintained under section 2 shall be under the direction and control of the chief constable appointed under section 11.

(2) In discharging his functions, every chief constable shall have regard to the local policing plan issued by the police authority for his area under section 8.][1]

84–022

[1] ss. 5A, 5B, 5C and the section group titles immediately preceeding and following them inserted by Greater London Authority Act 1999 (c.29), Pt VI, s. 310(1).

Appointment and removal of chief constables

[**11.**—(1) The chief constable of a police force maintained under section 2 shall be appointed by the police authority responsible for maintaining the force, but subject to the approval of the Secretary of State and to regulations under section 50.

84–023

(2) Without prejudice to any regulations under section 50 or under the Police Pensions Act 1976, the police authority, acting with the approval of the Secretary of State, may call upon the chief constable to retire in the interests of efficiency or effectiveness.

(3) Before seeking the approval of the Secretary of State under subsection (2), the police authority shall give the chief constable an opportunity to make representations and shall consider any representations that he makes.

(4) A chief constable who is called upon to retire under subsection (2) shall retire on such date as the police authority may specify or on such earlier date as may be agreed upon between him and the authority.]

Appointment and removal of deputy chief constables

[**11A.**—(1) Every police force maintained under section 2 shall have a deputy chief constable.

84–024

(2) The appointment of a person to be the deputy chief constable of a police force shall be made, in accordance with regulations under section 50, by the police authority responsible for maintaining that force, but only after consultation with the chief constable and subject to the approval of the Secretary of State.

(3) Subsections (2) to (4) of section 11 shall apply in relation to a deputy chief constable as they apply in relation to a chief constable.]¹

¹ Added by Criminal Justice and Police Act 2001 (c.16), Pt 5, s. 123(1).

Assistant chief constables

84–025   [**12.**—(1) The ranks that may be held in a police force maintained under section 2 shall include that of assistant chief constable; and in every such police force there shall be at least one person holding that rank.

(2) Appointments and promotions to the rank of assistant chief constable shall be made, in accordance with regulations under section 50, by the police authority after consultation with the chief constable and subject to the approval of the Secretary of State.

(3) Subsections (2), (3) and (4) of section 11 shall apply to an assistant chief constable as they apply to a chief constable.

(4) [. . .]¹]

¹ Repealed by Criminal Justice and Police Act 2001 (c.16), Sched. 7(4), para. 1.

Power of deputy to exercise functions of chief constable

84–026   [**12A.**—(1) A deputy chief constable of a police force may exercise or perform any or all of the powers or duties of the chief constable of that force—

    (a) during any absence, incapacity or suspension from duty of the chief constable,

    (b) during any vacancy in the office of the chief constable, or

    (c) at any other time, with the consent of the chief constable.

(2) A police authority responsible for maintaining a police force may designate a person holding the rank of assistant chief constable in that force to exercise or perform any or all of the powers or duties of the chief constable of that force—

    (a) during any absence, incapacity or suspension from duty of both the chief constable and the deputy chief constable, or

    (b) during any vacancy in the offices of both the chief constable and the deputy chief constable.

(3) Only one person shall be authorised to act at any one time by virtue of a designation under subsection (2).

(4) The power to act by virtue of subsection (1)(a) or (b) or subsection (2) shall not be exercisable for a continuous period exceeding three months except with the consent of the Secretary of State.

(5) The provisions of subsections (1) and (2) shall be without prejudice to any other enactment that makes provision for the exercise by any other person of powers conferred on a chief constable.]¹

¹ Added by Criminal Justice and Police Act 2001 (c.16), Pt 5, s. 124(2).

Other members of police forces

84–027   [**13.**—(1) The ranks that may be held in a police force maintained under section 2 shall be such as may be prescribed by regulations under section 50 and the ranks so prescribed shall include, in addition to chief constable, [deputy chief constable]¹ and assistant chief constable, the ranks of [chief superintendent,]² superintendent, chief inspector, inspector, sergeant and constable.

(2) [. . .]³

(3) Appointments and promotions to any rank below that of assistant chief constable in any police force maintained under section 2 shall be made, in accordance with regulations under section 50, by the chief constable.]

¹ Words inserted by Criminal Justice and Police Act 2001 (c.16), Pt 5, s. 123(2)(a).
² Words inserted by Criminal Justice and Police Act 2001 (c.16), Pt 5, s. 125(2).
³ Repealed by Criminal Justice and Police Act 2001 (c.16), Sched. 7(4), para. 1.

Police fund

[**14.**—(1) Each police authority established under section 3 shall keep a fund   **84–028** to be known as the police fund.

(2) Subject to any regulations under the Police Pensions Act 1976, all receipts of the police authority shall be paid into the police fund and all expenditure of the authority shall be paid out of that fund.

(3) Accounts shall be kept by each police authority of payments made into or out of the police fund.

[(4) This section shall apply in relation to the Metropolitan Police Authority as it applies in relation to a police authority established under section 3.]¹]

¹ Added by Greater London Authority Act 1999 (c.29), Sched 27, para. 73.

Questions on police matters at council meetings

[**20.**—(1) Every relevant council shall make arrangements (whether by   **84–029** standing orders or otherwise) for enabling questions on the discharge of the functions of a police authority [established under section 3]¹ to be put by members of the council at a meeting of the council for answer by a person nominated by the authority for that purpose.

(2) On being given reasonable notice by a relevant council of a meeting of that council at which questions on the discharge of the police authority's functions are to be put, the police authority shall nominate one or more of its members to attend the meeting to answer those questions.

(3) In this section "relevant council" has the same meaning as in Schedule 2.]

¹ Words added by Greater London Authority Act 1999 (c.29) Sched. 27, para. 78.

General provisions

Reports by chief constables to police authorities

22.—(1) Every [chief officer of police of a police force] shall, as soon as   **84–030** possible after the end of each financial year, submit to the police authority a general report on the policing during that year of the area for which his force is maintained.

(2) A [chief officer] shall arrange for a report submitted by him under subsection (1) to be published in such manner as appears to him to be appropriate.

(3) The [chief officer of police] of a police force shall, whenever so required by the police authority, submit to that authority a report on such matters as may be specified in the requirement, being matters connected with the policing of the area for which the force is maintained.

(4) A report submitted under subsection (3) shall be in such form as the police authority may specify.

(5) If it appears to the [chief officer] that a report in compliance with subsection (3) would contain information which in the public interest ought not to be disclosed, or is not needed for the discharge of the functions of the police authority, he may request that authority to refer the requirement to submit the report

to the Secretary of State; and in any such case the requirement shall be of no effect unless it is confirmed by the Secretary of State.

(6) The police authority may arrange, or require the [chief officer] to arrange, for a report submitted under subsection (3) to be published in such manner as appears to the authority to be appropriate.

. . . . . .

Provision of special services

84–031   **25.**—(1) The chief officer of police of a police force may provide, at the request of any person, special police services at any premises or in any locality in the police area for which the force is maintained, subject to the payment to the police authority of charges on such scales as may be determined by that authority.

[(1A) The Chief Constable of the British Transport Police Force may provide special police services at the request of any person, subject to the payment to the Strategic Rail Authority of charges on such scales as may be determined by that Authority.][1]

(2) [. . .][2]

[1] Added by Anti-terrorism, Crime and Security Act 2001 (c.24), Sched. 7, para. 23.
[2] Repealed by Greater London Authority Act 1999 (c.29) Sched. 34, Pt VII, para. 1.

. . . . . .

Attestation of constables

84–032   **29.** Every member of a police force maintained for a police area and every special constable appointed for a police area shall, on appointment, be attested as a constable by making a declaration in the form set out in Schedule 4—

    (a) [. . .][1]
    (b) [. . .][2] before a justice of the peace having jurisdiction within the police area.

[1] Repealed by Greater London Authority Act 1999 (c.29), Sched. 34, Pt VII, para. 1.
[2] Words repealed by Greater London Authority Act 1999 (c.29), Sched. 34, Pt VII, para. 1.

Jurisdiction of constables

84–033   **30.**—(1) A member of a police force shall have all the powers and privileges of a constable throughout England and Wales and the adjacent United Kingdom waters.

(2) A special constable shall have all the powers and privileges of a constable in the police area for which he is appointed and, where the boundary of that area includes the coast, in the adjacent United Kingdom waters.

(3) Without prejudice to subsection (2), a special constable appointed for a police area shall have all the powers and privileges of a constable—

    (a) in the case of a special constable appointed for a police area other than the City of London police area, in any other police area which is contiguous to his own police area; and
    (b) in the case of a special constable appointed for the City of London police area, in the metropolitan police district and in any police area which is contiguous to that district.

[(3A) A member of the British Transport Police Force who is for the time being required by virtue of section 23 or 24 to serve with a police force maintained by a police authority shall have all the powers and privileges of a member of that police force.][1]

(4) A special constable who is for the time being required by virtue of section 23 or 24 to serve with another police force shall have all the powers and privileges of a constable in any area in which special constables appointed for the area for which that force is maintained have those powers and privileges under this section.

(5) In this section—

"powers"includes powers under any enactment, whenever passed or made;
"United Kingdom waters" means the sea and other waters within the seaward limits of the territorial sea;

and this section, so far as it relates to powers under any enactment, makes them exercisable throughout the United Kingdom waters whether or not the enactment applies to those waters apart from this provision.

(6) This section is without prejudice to—

(a) section 98 and 99 below, and
(b) any other enactment conferring powers on constables for particular purposes.

[1] Added by Anti-terrorism, Crime and Security Act 2001 (c.24), Sched. 7, para. 24.

. . . . . .

Alteration of police areas

Power to alter police areas by order

32.—(1) The Secretary of State may by order make alterations in police areas in England and Wales other than the City of London police area. **84–034**

(2) The alterations that may be made by an order under this section include alterations that result in a reduction or an increase in the number of police areas, but not alterations that result in the abolition of the metropolitan police district.

(3) The Secretary of State shall not exercise his power under this section to make alterations unless either—

(a) he has received a request to make the alterations from the police authority for each of the areas affected by them, or
(b) it appears to him to be expedient to make the alterations in the interests of efficiency or effectiveness.

(4) The Secretary of State shall exercise his power to make orders under this section in such a way as to ensure that none of the following areas—

(a) a county in which there are no district councils,
(b) a district in any other county,
(c) a county borough in Wales, and
(d) a London borough,

is divided between two or more police areas.

(5) [. . .][1]

[1] Repealed by Greater London Authority Act 1999 (c.29), Sched. 34, Pt. VII, para. 1.

. . . . . .

Part II

Central Supervision, Direction and Facilities

Functions of Secretary of State

General duty of Secretary of State

84–035   **36.**—(1) The Secretary of State shall exercise his powers under the provisions of this Act referred to in subsection (2) in such manner and to such extent as appears to him to be best calculated to promote the efficiency and effectiveness of the police.

(2) The provisions of this Act mentioned in subsection (1) are—

(a) Part I;
(b) this Part;
(c) Part III (other than sections 61 and 62; and
(d) in Chapter II of Part IV, section 85 and Schedule 6; and
(e) in Part V, section 95.

Setting of objectives for police authorities

84–036   **37.**—(1) The Secretary of State may by order determine objectives for the policing of the areas of all police authorities [to which this section applies].

[(1A) The police authorities to which this section applies are those established under section 3 and the Metropolitan Police Authority.]¹

(2) Before making an order under this section the Secretary of State shall consult—

(a) persons whom he considers to represent the interests of police authorit- ies [to which this section applies], and
(b) persons whom he considers to represent the interests of [chief officers of police] of forces maintained by those authorities.

(3) A statutory instrument containing an order under this section shall be laid before Parliament after being made.

² Words added by Greater London Authority Act 1999 (c.29), Sched. 27, para. 86(3).

Setting of performance targets

84–037   **38.**—(1) Where an objective has been determined under section 37, the Sec- retary of State may direct police authorities to establish levels of performance ("performance targets") to be aimed at in seeking to achieve the objective.

(2) A direction under this section may be given to all police authorities [to which section 37 applies] or to one or more particular authorities.

(3) A direction given under this section may impose conditions with which the performance targets must conform, and different conditions may be imposed for different authorities.

(4) The Secretary of State shall arrange for any direction given under this section to be published in such manner as appears to him to be appropriate.

Codes of practice

84–038   **39.**—(1) The Secretary of State may issue codes of practice relating to the discharge by police authorities established under section 3 [and the Metropolitan Police Authority] of any of their functions.

(2) The Secretary of State may from time to time revise the whole or part of any code of practice issued under this section.

(3) The Secretary of State shall lay before Parliament a copy of any code of practice, and of any revision of a code of practice, issued by him under this section.

Power to give directions to police authorities after adverse reports

40.—(1) The Secretary of State may at any time require the inspectors of constabulary to carry out, for the purposes of this section, an inspection under section 54 of any police force maintained under section 2 [or of the metropolitan police force].

84–039

(2) Where a report made to the Secretary of State under section 54 on an inspection carried out for the purposes of this section states—

- (a) that, in the opinion of the person making the report, the force inspected is not efficient or not effective, or
- (b) that in his opinion, unless remedial measures are taken, the force will cease to be efficient or will cease to be effective,

the Secretary of State may direct the police authority responsible for maintaining the force to take such measures as may be specified in the direction.

Directions as to minimum budget

41.—(1) The power of the Secretary of State to give directions under section 40 to a police authority established under section 3 shall include power to direct the authority that the amount of its budget requirement for any financial year (under section 43 of the Local Government Finance Act 1992) shall not be less than an amount specified in the direction.

84–040

(2) The power exercisable by virtue of subsection (1) and any direction given under that power, are subject to any limitation imposed under [Chapter IVA of Part I of the Local Government Finance Act 1992].

(3) A direction shall not be given by virtue of subsection (1) in relation to a financial year at any time after the end of the preceding December.

(4) Where the Secretary of State gives a direction to a police authority by virtue of subsection (1), any precept issued or calculation made by the authority under Part I of the Local Government Finance Act 1992 which is inconsistent with the direction shall be void.

Removal of chief constables, etc.

42.—(1) The Secretary of State may require a police authority to exercise its power under section 11 to call upon the chief constable to retire in the interests of efficiency or effectiveness.

84–041

(2) Before requiring the exercise of that power or approving the exercise of that or the similar power exercisable with respect to [a deputy chief constable or] an assistant chief constable, the Secretary of State shall give the chief constable[, the deputy chief constable or, as the case may be, the assistant chief constable] an opportunity to make representations to him and shall consider any representations so made.

(3) Where representations are made under this section the Secretary of State may, and in a case where he proposes to require the exercise of the power mentioned in subsection (1) shall, appoint one or more persons (one at least of whom shall be a person who is not an officer of police or of a Government department) to hold an inquiry and report to him and shall consider any report made under this subsection.

(4) The costs incurred by a chief constable[, deputy chief constable] or assist-

ant chief constable in respect of an inquiry under this section, taxed in such manner as the Secretary of State may direct, shall be defrayed out of the police fund.

[(5) This section shall apply to the power of the Metropolitan Police Authority under section 9E to call upon—

(a) the Commissioner of Police of the Metropolis,
(b) the Deputy Commissioner of Police of the Metropolis,
(c) an Assistant Commissioner of Police of the Metropolis,
[(d) a Deputy Assistant Commissioner of Police of the Metropolis, or]
(e) a Commander in the metropolitan police force,

to retire in the interests of efficiency or effectiveness as it applies to the power of a police authority under section 11.]

Reports from police authorities

84–042   **43.**—(1) A police authority shall, whenever so required by the Secretary of State, submit to the Secretary of State a report on such matters connected with the discharge of the authority's functions, or otherwise with the policing of its area, as may be specified in the requirement.

(2) A requirement under subsection (1) may specify the form in which a report is to be given.

(3) The Secretary of State may arrange, or require the police authority to arrange, for a report under this section to be published in such manner as appears to him to be appropriate.

Reports from chief constables

84–043   **44.**—(1) The Secretary of State may require a [chief officer of police of any police force] to submit to him a report on such matters as may be specified in the requirement, being matters connected with the policing of the [chief officer's] police area.

(2) A requirement under subsection (1) may specify the form in which a report is to be given.

(3) The Secretary of State may arrange, or require the [chief officer] to arrange, for a report under this section to be published in such manner as appears to the Secretary of State to be appropriate.

(4) [The chief officer of police of every police force] shall, as soon as possible after the end of each financial year, submit to the Secretary of State the like report as is required by section 22(1) to be submitted to the police authority.

. . . . . .

Police grant

84–044   **46.**—(1) Subject to the following provisions of this section, the Secretary of State shall for each financial year make grants for police purposes to—

(a) police authorities for areas other than the metropolitan police district, and
(b) the [Greater London Authority];

and in those provisions references to police authorities shall be taken as including references to the [Greater London Authority].

(2) For each financial year the Secretary of State shall with the approval of the Treasury determine—

(a) the aggregate amount of grants to be made under this section, and
(b) the amount of the grant to be made to each authority;

and any determination may be varied by further determinations under this subsection.

(3) The Secretary of State shall prepare a report setting out any determination under subsection (2), and stating the considerations which he took into account in making the determination.

(4) In determining the allocation among police authorities of the whole or any part of the aggregate amount of grants, the Secretary of State may exercise his discretion by applying such formulae or other rules as he considers appropriate.

(5) The considerations which the Secretary of State takes into account in making a determination under subsection (2), and the formulae and other rules referred to in subsection (4), may be different for different authorities or different classes of authority.

(6) A copy of every report prepared under subsection (3) shall be laid before the House of Commons, and no payment of grant shall be made unless the report setting out the determination of its amount has been approved by resolution of that House.

(7) A grant to a police authority under this section shall be paid at such time, or in instalments of such amounts and at such times, as the Secretary of State may with the approval of the Treasury determine; and any such time may fall within or after the financial year concerned.

[(7A) Where the Greater London Authority receives a grant under this section, it shall forthwith account for the grant to the Metropolitan Police Authority and pay it over to that Authority.]

(8) Where in consequence of a further determination under subsection (2) the amount of an authority's grant is less than the amount already paid to it for the year concerned, a sum equal to the difference shall be paid by the authority to the Secretary of State on such day as he may specify; but no sum shall be payable by an authority under this subsection unless the report setting out the further determination has been approved by resolution of the House of Commons.

[(9) Where the Greater London Authority is required to pay a sum under subsection (8) above, the Mayor of London may direct the Metropolitan Police Authority to pay an amount not exceeding that sum to the Greater London Authority on such day as he may specify in the direction.]

. . . . . .

Regulations for police forces

50.—(1) Subject to the provisions of this section, the Secretary of State may make regulations as to the government, administration and conditions of service of police forces.   **84–045**

(2) Without prejudice to the generality of subsection (1), regulations under this section may make provision with respect to—

(a) the ranks to be held by members of police forces;
(b) the qualifications for appointment and promotion of members of police forces;
(c) periods of service on probation;
(d) voluntary retirement of members of police forces;

(e) the conduct, efficiency and effectiveness of members of police forces and the maintenance of discipline;

(f) the suspension of members of a police force from membership of that force and from their office as constable;

(g) the maintenance of personal records of members of police forces;

(h) the duties which are or are not to be performed by members of police forces;

(i) the treatment as occasions of police duty of attendance at meetings of the Police Federations and of any body recognised by the Secretary of State for the purposes of section 64;

(j) the hours of duty, leave, pay and allowances of members of police forces; and

(k) the issue, use and return of police clothing, personal equipment and accoutrements.

(3) Without prejudice to the powers conferred by this section, regulations under this section shall—

(a) establish, or make provision for the establishment of, procedures for cases in which a member of a police force may be dealt with by dismissal, requirement to resign, reduction in rank, reduction in rate of pay, fine, reprimand or caution, and

[(b) make provision for securing that any case in which a senior officer may be dismissed or dealt with in any of the other ways mentioned in paragraph (a) is decided by the police authority which maintains the force or by a committee of that authority.]

For the purposes of this subsection"senior officer" means a member of a police force holding a rank above that of [chief] superintendent.

(4) In relation to any matter as to which provision may be made by regulations under this section, the regulations may, subject to subsection (3)(b),—

(a) authorise or require provision to be made by, or confer discretionary powers on, the Secretary of State, police authorities, chief officers of police or other persons, or

(b) authorise or require the delegation by any person of functions conferred on that person by or under the regulations.

(5) Regulations under this section for regulating pay and allowances may be made with retrospective effect to any date specified in the regulations, but nothing in this subsection shall be construed as authorising pay or allowances payable to any person to be reduced retrospectively.

(6) Regulations under this section as to conditions of service shall secure that appointments for fixed terms are not made except where the person appointed holds the rank of superintendent or a higher rank.

(7) Regulations under this section may make different provision for different cases and circumstances.

(8) Any statutory instrument containing regulations under this section shall be subject to annulment in pursuance of a resolution of either House of Parliament.

. . . . . .

Inspectors of constabulary

Appointment and functions of inspectors of constabulary

54.—(1) Her Majesty may appoint such number of inspectors (to be known **84–046** as "Her Majesty's Inspectors of Constabulary") as the Secretary of State may with the consent of the Treasury determine, and of the persons so appointed one may be appointed as chief inspector of constabulary.

(2) The inspectors of constabulary shall inspect, and report to the Secretary of State on the efficiency and effectiveness of, every police force maintained for a police area [and the National Criminal Intelligence Service and the National Crime Squad]¹.

[(2A) The inspectors of constabulary may inspect, and report to the Secretary of State on, a police authority's compliance with the requirements of Part I of the Local Government Act 1999 (best value).]²

(3) The inspectors of constabulary shall carry out such other duties for the purpose of furthering police efficiency and effectiveness as the Secretary of State may from time to time direct.

(4) The chief inspector of constabulary shall in each year submit to the Secretary of State a report in such form as the Secretary of State may direct, and the Secretary of State shall lay a copy of that report before Parliament.

(5) The inspectors of constabulary shall be paid such salary and allowances as the Secretary of State may with the consent of the Treasury determine.

¹ Words added by Police Act 1997 (c.50), Sched. 9, para. 76.
² Added by Local Government Act 1999 (c.27), Pt I, s. 24(2).

Publication of reports

55.—(1) Subject to subsection (2), the Secretary of State shall arrange for any **84–047** report received by him under section 54(2) [or (2A)] to be published in such manner as appears to him to be appropriate.

(2) The Secretary of State may exclude from publication under subsection (1) any part of a report if, in his opinion, the publication of that part—

(a) would be against the interests of national security, or
(b) might jeopardise the safety of any person.

(3) The Secretary of State shall send a copy of the published report—

(a) to the police authority maintaining the police force to which the report relates, and
(b) to the chief officer of police of that police force.

(4) The police authority shall invite the chief officer of police to submit comments on the published report to the authority before such date as it may specify.

(5) The police authority shall prepare comments on the published report and shall arrange for—

(a) its comments,
(b) any comments submitted by the chief officer of police in accordance with subsection (4), and
(c) any response which the authority has to the comments submitted by the chief officer of police,

to be published in such manner as appears to the authority to be appropriate.

(6) The police authority (except where it is the Secretary of State) shall send a copy of any document published under subsection (5) to the Secretary of State.

[(7) Subsections (3) to (6) above shall apply in relation to a report relating to the National Criminal Intelligence Service or the National Crime Squad as if—

(a) the body to which the report relates were a police force,
(b) the Service Authority which maintains that body were the police authority which maintains that force, and
(c) the Director General of that body were the chief officer of police of that force.]

. . . . . .

PART III

POLICE REPRESENTATIVE INSTITUTIONS

Police Federations

84–048   **59.**—(1) There shall continue to be a Police Federation for England and Wales and a Police Federation for Scotland for the purpose of representing members of the police forces in those countries respectively in all matters affecting their welfare and efficiency, except for—

(a) questions of promotion affecting individuals, and
(b) (subject to subsection (2)) questions of discipline affecting individuals.

(2) A Police Federation may represent a member of a police force at any [proceedings brought under regulations made in accordance with section 50(3) above or section 26(2A) of the Police (Scotland) Act 1967] or on an appeal from any such proceedings.

(3) Except on an appeal to [a police appeals tribunal] or as provided by section 84, a member of a police force may only be represented under subsection (2) by another member of a police force.

(4) The Police Federations shall act through local and central representative bodies.

(5) The Police Federations and every branch of a Federation shall be entirely independent of, and subject to subsection (6) unassociated with, any body or person outside the Police service, but may employ persons outside the police service in an administrative or advisory capacity.

(6) The Secretary of State—

(a) may authorise a Police Federation or a branch of a Federation to be associated with a person or body outside the police service in such cases and manner, and subject to such conditions and restrictions, as he may specify, and
(b) may vary or withdraw an authorisation previously given;

and anything for the time being so authorised shall not be precluded by subsection (5).

(7) This section applies to police cadets as it applies to members of police forces, and references to the police service shall be construed accordingly.

[(8) For the purposes of subsection (1)—

(a) the Director General of the National Criminal Intelligence Service and persons within section 9(2)(a) of the Police Act 1997 (former members of police forces) appointed as police members of the National Criminal Intelligence Service, and

(b) the Director General of the National Crime Squad and persons within section 55(2)(a) of that Act (former members of police forces) appointed as police members of the National Crime Squad,

shall be treated as members of a police force in England and Wales, and references in this section to police service shall be construed accordingly.]

Regulations for Police Federations

60.—(1) The Secretary of State may by regulations—

(a) prescribe the constitution and proceedings of the Police Federations, or
(b) authorise the Federations to make rules concerning such matters relating to their constitution and proceedings as may be specified in the regulations.

(2) Without prejudice to the generality of subsection (1), regulations under this section may make provision—

(a) with respect to the membership of the Federations;
(b) with respect to the raising of funds by the Federations by voluntary subscription and the use and management of funds derived from such subscriptions;
(c) with respect to the manner in which representations may be made by committees or bodies of the Federations to police authorities, chief officers of police and the Secretary of State;
(d) for the payment by the Secretary of State of expenses incurred in connection with the Federations and for the use by the Federations of premises provided by police authorities for police purposes; and
(e) for modifying any regulations under the Police Pensions Act 1976, section 50 above or section 26 of the Police (Scotland) Act 1967 in relation to any member of a police force who is the secretary or an officer of a Police Federation and for requiring the appropriate Federation to make contributions in respect of the pay, pension or allowances payable to or in respect of any such person.

[(2A) For the purposes of paragraphs (c) and (d) of subsection (2)—

(a) the Service Authority for the National Criminal Intelligence Service and the Service Authority for the National Crime Squad shall be treated as police authorities, and
(b) the Director General of the National Criminal Intelligence Service and the Director General of the National Crime Squad shall be treated as chief officers of police,

and the reference in paragraph (d) of that subsection to "police purposes" shall be construed accordingly.]¹
(3) Regulations under this section may contain such supplementary and transitional provisions as appear to the Secretary of State to be appropriate, including provisions adapting references in any enactment (including this Act) to committees or other bodies of the Federations.
(4) Before making any regulations under this section the Secretary of State shall consult the three Central Committees of the Police Federation to which the regulations will relate, sitting together as a Joint Committee.
(5) A statutory instrument containing regulations under this section shall be subject to annulment in pursuance of a resolution of either House of Parliament.

(6) This section applies to police cadets as it applies to members of police forces.

---

[1] Added by Police Act 1997 (c.50), Sched. 9, para. 80.

The Police Negotiating Board for the United Kingdom

84–050   **61.**—(1) There shall continue to be a Police Negotiating Board for the United Kingdom for the consideration by persons representing the interests of—

(a) the authorities who between them maintain the police forces in Great Britain and the Royal Ulster Constabulary,

[(aa) the Service Authority for the National Criminal Intelligence Service and the Service Authority for the National Crime Squad;][1]

(b) the persons who are members of those police forces or of that Constabulary or are police cadets,

[(c) the persons who are members of the National Criminal Intelligence Service within section 9(1)(a) or the Police Act 1997 or members of the National Crime Squad within section 55(1)(a) or (b) of that Act;][2]

(d) the Commissioner of Police of the Metropolis,

(e) the Secretary of State, [and]

[(f) the Scottish Ministers,]

of questions relating to hours of duty, leave, pay and allowances, pensions or the issue, use and return of police clothing, personal equipment and accoutrements.

(2) The Chairman and any deputy chairman or chairmen of the Board shall be appointed by the Prime Minister [after consultation with the Scottish Ministers].

(3) Subject to subsection (2), the Board shall continue to be constituted in accordance with such arrangements, made after consultations between the Secretary of State and organisations representing the interests of the persons referred to in [paragraphs (a), (b), (c) and (e)] of subsection (1), as appear to the Secretary of State to be satisfactory.

(4) The Secretary of State may—

(a) pay to the Chairman and to any deputy chairman or chairmen of the Board such fees as the Secretary of State may, with the approval of the Treasury, determine, and

(b) defray any expenses incurred by the Board.

[(5) The Scottish Ministers may make payments towards the expenses incurred by the Board in relation to the exercise by it of its function in or as regards Scotland.

(6) For the purposes of section 36(3) of the Police (Scotland) Act 1967, any expenditure under subsection (5) above shall be treated as expenditure incurred under section 36(1) of the said Act of 1967.]

---

[1] Added by Police Act 1997 (c.50), Sched. 9, para. 81(a).
[2] Added by Police Act 1997 (c.50), Sched. 9, para. 81(b).

. . . . . .

PART IV

COMPLAINTS, DISCIPLINARY PROCEEDINGS ETC.

CHAPTER I

COMPLAINTS

Interpretation

Interpretation of Chapter I

65. In this Chapter— **84–051**

"the appropriate authority" means —

(b) in relation to a member of any police force—

(i) if he is a senior officer, the police authority for the force's area, and
(ii) if he is not a senior officer, the chief officer of police of the force;

"the Authority" means the Police Complaints Authority;
"complaint" means a complaint about the conduct of a member of a police force which is submitted—

(a) by a member of the public, or
(b) on behalf of a member of the public and with his written consent;

"disciplinary proceedings" means proceedings identified as such by regulations under section 50;
"investigating officer" means [a person (whether a member of the police force or not) appointed under section 68(2B) or] a member of a police force appointed under section 68(3) or, as the case may be, section 69(5) or (6) to investigate a complaint;
"senior officer" means a member of a police force holding a rank above that of [chief] superintendent;
"serious injury" means a fracture, damage to an internal organ, impairment of bodily function, a deep cut or a deep laceration.

The Police Complaints Authority

The Police Complaints Authority

66.—(1) The authority known as "the Police Complaints Authority" shall **84–052**
continue in existence as a body corporate.
(2) Schedule 5 shall have effect in relation to the Authority.

Handling of Complaints etc.

Preliminary

67.—(1) Where a complaint is submitted to the chief officer of police for a **84–053**
police area, he shall taken any steps that appear to him to be desirable for the

purpose of obtaining or preserving evidence relating to the conduct complained of.

(2) After complying with subsection (1), the chief officer shall determine whether he is the appropriate authority in relation to the member of a police force whose conduct is the subject of the complaint.

(3) If the chief officer determines that he is not the appropriate authority, he shall—

(a) send the complaint or, if it was submitted orally, particulars of it, to the appropriate authority, and
(b) give notice that he has done so to the person by whom or on whose behalf the complaint was submitted.

(4) Nothing in this Chapter shall have effect in relation to a complaint in so far as it relates to the direction or control of a police force by the chief officer of police or the person performing the functions of the chief officer of police.

(5) If any conduct to which a complaint wholly or partly relates is or has been the subject of criminal or disciplinary proceedings, none of the provisions of this Chapter which relate to the recording and investigation of complaints shall have effect in relation to the complaint in so far as it relates to that conduct.

Investigation of complaints senior officers

84–054   **68.**—(1) Where a complaint about the conduct of a senior officer—

(a) is submitted to the appropriate authority, or
(b) is sent to the appropriate authority under section 67(3),

the appropriate authority shall record and, subject to subsection (2), investigate it.

(2) If satisfied that the conduct complained of, even if proved, would not justify criminal or disciplinary proceedings, the appropriate authority may deal with the complaint according to the appropriate authority's discretion.

[(2A) In any other case, subsection (2B) or (3) shall apply.

(2B) If the complaint is about the conduct of the Commissioner of Police of the Metropolis or the Deputy Commissioner of Police of the Metropolis—

(a) the appropriate authority shall notify the Secretary of State; and
(b) the Secretary of State shall appoint a person to investigate the complaint.]

(3) In any other case, the appropriate authority shall appoint a member of the appropriate authority's force or of some other force to investigate the complaint.

[(4) If—

(a) in a case where subsection (2B) applies, the Secretary of State, or
(b) in a case where subsection (3) applies, the appropriate authority,

requests the chief officer of police of a police force to provide a member of his force for appointment under subsection [(2B) or] (3), the chief officer shall comply with the request.]

(5) No member of a police force of a rank lower than that of the member whose conduct is the subject of the complaint may be appointed under subsection (3).

(6) Unless an investigation under this section is supervised by the Authority under section 72, the investigating officer shall submit his report on it to the appropriate authority.

Investigation of complaints: standard procedure

69.—(1) If a chief officer of police determines that he is the appropriate **84–055**
authority in relation to a member of a police force—

(a) whose conduct is the subject of a complaint, and
(b) who is not a senior officer,

he shall record the complaint.

(2) After recording a complaint under subsection (1), the chief officer of
police shall consider whether the complaint is suitable for informal resolution
and may appoint a member of his force to assist him.

(3) A complaint is not suitable for informal resolution unless—

(a) the member of the public concerned gives his consent, and
(b) the chief officer of police is satisfied that the conduct complained of,
even if proved, would not justify criminal or disciplinary proceedings.

(4) If it appears to the chief officer of police that the complaint is suitable for
informal resolution, he shall seek to resolve it informally and may appoint a
member of his force to do so on his behalf.

(5) If it appears to the chief officer of police that the complaint is not suitable
for informal resolution, he shall appoint a member of his own or some other
force to investigate it formally.

(6) If, after attempts have been made to resolve a complaint informally, it
appears to the chief officer of police—

(a) that informal resolution of the complaint is impossible, or
(b) that the complaint is for any other reason not suitable for informal
resolution,

he shall appoint a member of his own or some other force to investigate it
formally.

(7) A member of a police force may not be appointed to investigate a complaint formally if he has previously been appointed to act in relation to it under
subsection (4).

(8) If a chief officer of police requests the chief officer of police of some
other force to provide a member of that other force for appointment under subsection (5) or (6), that chief officer shall comply with the request.

(9) Unless the investigation is supervised by the Authority under section 72,
the investigating officer shall submit his report on it to the chief officer of police
who appointed him.

References of complaints to Authority

70.—(1) The appropriate authority— **84–056**

(a) shall refer to the Authority—

(i) any complaint alleging that the conduct complained of resulted in
the death of, or serious injury to, some other person, and
(ii) any complaint of a description specific for the purposes of this
section in regulations made by the Secretary of State, and

(b) may refer to the Authority any complaint which is not required to be
referred to them.

(2) The Authority may require the submission to them for consideration of any

complaint not referred to them by the appropriate authority; and the appropriate authority shall comply with any such requirement not later than the end of the period specified for the purposes of this subsection in regulations made by the Secretary of State.

(3) Where a complaint falls to be referred to the Authority under subsection (1)(a), the appropriate authority shall refer it to them not later than the end of the period specified for the purposes of sub-paragraph (i) or, as the case may be, (ii) of that subsection in regulations made by the Secretary of State.

References of other matters to Authority

84–057   **71.**—(1) The appropriate authority may refer to the Authority any matter to which this section applies, if it appears to the appropriate authority that the matter ought to be referred by reason—

  (a) of its gravity, or
  (b) of exceptional circumstances.

(2) This section applies to any matter which—

  (a) appears to the appropriate authority to indicate that a member of a police force may have committed a criminal offence or behaved in a manner which would justify disciplinary proceedings, and
  (b) is not the subject of a complaint.

Supervision of investigations by Authority

84–058   **72.**—(1) The Authority shall supervise the investigation of—

  (a) any complaint alleging that the conduct of a member of a police force resulted in the death of, or serious injury to, some other person,
  (b) any other description of complaint specified for the purposes of this section in regulations made by the Secretary of State, and
  (c) any complaint which is not within paragraph (a) or (b), and any matter referred to the Authority under section 71, if the Authority determine that it is desirable in the public interest that they should do so.

(2) Where the Authority have made a determination under subsection (1)(c), they shall notify it to the appropriate authority.

(3) Where an investigation is to be supervised by the Authority, they may require—

  (a) that no appointment is made under [section 68(2B) or (3) or 69(5)] unless they have given notice to the appropriate authority that they approve the person whom that authority propose to appoint, or
  (b) if such an appointment has already been made and the Authority are not satisfied with the person appointed, that—

    (i) the appropriate authority, as soon as is reasonably practicable, select another member of a police force and notify the Authority that it proposes to appoint him, and
    (ii) the appointment is not made unless the Authority give notice to the appropriate authority that they approve that person.

[(3A) In the application of subsection (3) in relation to appointment under section 68(2B)—

    (a) any reference to the appropriate authority shall be taken as a reference to the Secretary of State; and

    (b) the reference in paragraph (b)(i) to another member of a police force shall be taken as a reference to another person.]

(4) The Secretary of State shall by regulations authorise the Authority, subject to any restrictions or conditions specified in the regulations, to impose requirements as to a particular investigation additional to any requirements imposed by virtue of subsection (3).

(5) A member of a police force shall comply with any requirement imposed on him by virtue of regulations under subsection (4).

Reports on investigations, etc.

73.—(1) At the end of an investigation which the Authority have supervised, **84–059** the investigating officer shall—

    (a) submit a report on the investigation to the Authority, and

    (b) send a copy of the report to the appropriate authority.

(2) After considering a report submitted to them under subsection (1), the Authority shall submit an appropriate statement to the appropriate authority.

(3) If it is practicable to do so, the Authority, when submitting the appropriate statement under subsection (2), shall send a copy of it to the member of a police force whose conduct has been investigated.

    (4) If—

    (a) the investigation related to a complaint, and

    (b) it is practicable to do so,

the Authority shall also send a copy of the appropriate statement to the person by or on behalf of whom the complaint was submitted.

(5) The power to issue an appropriate statement includes power to issue separate statements in respect of the disciplinary and criminal aspects of an investigation.

(6) No disciplinary proceedings shall be brought before the appropriate statement is submitted to the appropriate authority.

(7) Subject to subsection (8) neither the appropriate authority nor the Director of Public Prosecutions shall bring criminal proceedings before the appropriate statement is submitted to the appropriate authority.

(8) The restriction imposed by subsection (7) does not apply if it appears to the Director that there are exceptional circumstances which make it undesirable to wait for the submission of the appropriate statement.

(9) In this section "appropriate statement" means a statement—

    (a) as to whether the investigation was or was not conducted to the Authority's satisfaction,

    (b) specifying any respect in which it was not so conducted, and

    (c) dealing with any such other matters as the Secretary of State may by regulations provide.

Steps to be taken after investigation: senior officers

74. On receiving—   **84–060**

    (a) a report concerning the conduct of a senior officer which is submitted to it under section 68(6), or

(b) a copy of a report concerning the conduct of a senior officer which is sent to it under section 73(1),

the appropriate authority shall send a copy of the report to the Director of Public Prosecutions unless the report satisfies the appropriate authority that no criminal offence has been committed.

Steps to be taken after investigation: standard procedure

84–061   **75.**—(1) Nothing in this section or section 76 has effect in relation to senior officers.

(2) On receiving—

(a) a report concerning the conduct of a member of a police force who is not a senior officer which is submitted to him under section 69(9), or

(b) a copy of a report concerning the conduct of such a member which is sent to him under section 73(1).

a chief officer of police shall determine whether the report indicates that a criminal offence may have been committed by a member of the police force for his area.

(3) If the chief officer determines that the report indicates that a criminal offence may have been committed by a member of the police force for his area, he shall send a copy of the report to the Director of Public Prosecutions.

(4) After the Director has dealt with the question of criminal proceedings, the chief officer shall, in such cases as may be prescribed by regulations made by the Secretary of State, send the Authority a memorandum which—

(a) is signed by the chief officer,

(b) states whether he has brought (or proposes to bring) disciplinary proceedings in respect of the conduct which was the subject of the investigation, and

(c) if he has not brought (or does not propose to bring) such proceedings, gives his reasons.

(5) If the chief officer considers that the report does not indicate that a criminal offence may have been committed by a member of the police force for his area, he shall, in such cases as may be prescribed by regulations made by the Secretary of State, send the Authority a memorandum to that effect which—

(a) is signed by the chief officer,

(b) states whether he has brought (or proposes to bring) disciplinary proceedings in respect of the conduct which was the subject of the investigation, and

(c) if he has not brought (or does not propose to bring) such proceedings, gives his reasons.

(6) Where the investigation—

(a) related to conduct which was the subject of a complaint, and

(b) was not supervised by the Authority,

the chief officer shall, if he is required by virtue of regulations under subsection (4) or (5) to send the Authority a memorandum, at the same time send them a copy of the complaint, or of the record of the complaint, and a copy of the report of the investigation.

(7) Where a chief officer has sent the Authority a memorandum under subsection (4) or (5), he shall—

(a) if the memorandum states that he proposes to bring disciplinary proceedings, bring and proceed with them, and
(b) if the memorandum states that he has brought such proceedings, proceed with them.

Powers of Authority as to disciplinary proceedings

76.—(1) Where a memorandum under section 75 states that a chief officer of police has not brought disciplinary proceedings or does not propose to bring such proceedings, the Authority may recommend him to bring such proceedings.   **84–062**

(2) Where a chief officer has brought disciplinary proceedings in accordance with a recommendation under subsection (1), he shall proceed with them.

(3) If after the Authority have made a recommendation under this section and consulted the chief officer he is still unwilling to bring disciplinary proceedings, they may direct him to do so.

(4) Where the Authority give a chief officer a direction under this section, they shall supply him with a written statement of their reasons for doing so.

(5) Subject to subsection (6), it shall be the duty of a chief officer to comply with such a direction.

(6) The Authority may withdraw a direction given under this section.

(7) A chief officer shall—

(a) advise the Authority of what action he has taken in response to a recommendation or direction under this section, and
(b) supply the Authority with such other information as they may reasonably require for the purposes of discharging their functions under this section.

Information as to the manner of dealing with complaints, etc.

77. Every police authority in carrying out its duty with respect to the maintenance of an efficient and effective police force, and inspectors of constabulary in carrying out their duties with respect to the efficiency and effectiveness of any police force, shall keep themselves informed as to the working of sections 67 to 76 in relation to the force.   **84–063**

Constabularies maintained by authorities other than police authorities

78.—(1) An agreement for the establishment in relation to any body of constables maintained by an authority, other than a police authority, of procedures corresponding or similar to any of those established by or by virtue of this Chapter may, with the approval of the Secretary of State, be made between the Authority and the authority maintaining the body of constables.   **84–064**

(2) Where no such procedures are in force in relation to a body of constables, the Secretary of State may by order establish such procedures.

(3) An agreement under this section may at any time be varied or terminated with the approval of the Secretary of State.

(4) Before making an order under this section the Secretary of State shall consult—

(a) the Authority, and
(b) the authority maintaining the body of constables to whom the order would relate.

(5) A statutory instrument containing an order under this section shall be

subject to annulment in pursuance of a resolution of either House of Parliament.

(6) Nothing in any other enactment passed or made before 31st October 1984 shall prevent an authority who maintain a body of constables from carrying into effect procedures established by virtue of this section.

(7) No such procedures shall have effect in relation to anything done by a constable outside England and Wales.

Reports

84–065

79.—(1) The Authority shall, at the request of the Secretary of State, report to him on such matters relating generally to their functions as the Secretary of State may specify, and the Authority may for that purpose carry out research into any such matters.

(2) The Authority may make a report to the Secretary of State on any matters coming to their notice under this Chapter to which they consider that his attention should be drawn by reason of their gravity or of other exceptional circumstances.

(3) The Authority shall send a copy of any report under subsection (2)—

- (a) to the police authority and the chief officer of police of any police force which appears to the Authority to be concerned, or
- (b) if the report concerns a body of constables such as is mentioned in section 78, to the authority maintaining it and the officer having the direction and the control of it.

(4) As soon as practicable after the end of each calendar year the Authority shall make to the Secretary of State a report on the discharge of their functions during that year.

(5) The Secretary of State shall lay before Parliament a copy of every report received by him under this section and shall cause every such report to be published.

(6) The Authority shall send to each police authority—

- (a) a copy of every report made under subsection (4), and
- (b) any statistical or other general information—
  - (i) which relates to the year dealt with by the report and to the area of that police authority, and
  - (ii) which the Authority consider should be brought to the police authority's attention in connection with its functions under section 77.

Restriction on disclosure of information

84–066

80.—(1) No information received by the Authority in connection with any of their functions under sections 67 to 79 or regulations made by virtue of section 81 shall be disclosed by any person who is or has been a member, officer or servant of the Authority except—

- (a) to the Secretary of State or to a member, officer or servant of the Authority or, so far as may be necessary for the proper discharge of the functions of the Authority, to other persons.
- (b) for the purposes of any criminal, civil or disciplinary proceedings, or
- (c) in the form of a summary or other general statement made by the Authority which does not identify the person from whom the information was received or any person to whom it relates.

(2) Any person who discloses information in contravention of this section

shall be guilty of an offence and liable on summary conviction to a fine of an amount not exceeding level 5 on the standard scale.

. . . . . .

CHAPTER II

DISCIPLINARY AND OTHER PROCEEDINGS

Representation at disciplinary and other proceedings

84.—(1) A member of a police force of the rank of [chief] superintendent or below may not be dismissed, required to resign or reduced in rank by a decision taken in proceedings under regulations made in accordance with section 50(3)(a) unless he has been given an opportunity to elect to be legally represented at any hearing held in the course of those proceedings.   **84–067**

(2) Where a member of a police force makes an election to which subsection (1) refers, he may be represented at the hearing, at his option, either by counsel or by a solicitor.

(3) Except in a case where a member of a police force of the rank of [chief] superintendent or below has been given an opportunity to elect to be legally represented and has so elected, he may be represented at the hearing only by another member of a police force.

(4) Regulations under section 50 shall specify—

(a) a procedure for notifying a member of a police force of the effect of subsections (1) to (3) above.
(b) when he is to be notified of the effect of those subsections, and
(c) when he is to give notice whether he wishes to be legally represented at the hearing.

(5) If a member of a police force—

(a) fails without reasonable cause to give notice in accordance with the regulations that he wishes to be legally represented, or
(b) gives notice in accordance with the regulations that he does not wish to be legally represented.

he may be dismissed, required to resign or reduced in rank without his being legally represented.

(6) If a member of a police force has given notice in accordance with the regulations that he wishes to be legally represented, the case against him may be presented by counsel or a solicitor whether or not he is actually so represented.

¹ Words inserted by Criminal Justice and Police Act 2001 (c.16), Pt 5, s. 125(3).

Appeals against dismissal etc.

85.—(1) A member of a police force who is dismissed, required to resign or reduced in rank by a decision taken in proceedings under regulations made in accordance with section 50(3) may appeal to a police appeals tribunal against the decision except where he has a right of appeal to some other person; and in that case he may appeal to a police appeals tribunal from any decision of that other person as a result of which he is dismissed, required to resign or reduced in rank.   **84–068**

(2) Where a police appeals tribunal allows an appeal it may, if it considers

that it is appropriate to do so, make an order dealing with the appellant in a way—

> (a) which appears to the tribunal to be less severe than the way in which he was dealt with by the decision appealed against, and
> (b) in which he could have been dealt with by the person who made that decision.

(3) The Secretary of State may make rules as to the procedure on appeals to police appeals tribunals under this section.

(4) Rules made under this section may make provision for enabling a police appeals tribunal to require any person to attend a hearing to give evidence or to produce documents, and may, in particular, apply subsections (2) and (3) of section 250 of the Local Government Act 1972 with such modifications as may be set out in the rules.

(5) A statutory instrument containing rules made under this section shall be laid before Parliament after being made.

(6) Schedule 6 shall have effect in relation to appeals under this section.

Admissibility of statements in subsequent proceedings

84–069   **86.**—(1) Subject to subsection (2), no statement made by a person for the purpose of the informal resolution of a complaint shall be admissible in any subsequent criminal, civil or disciplinary proceedings.

(2) A statement is not rendered inadmissible by subsection (1) if it consists of or includes an admission relating to a matter which does not fall to be resolved informally.

(3) In this section "complaint" and "disciplinary proceedings" have the meanings given in section 65.

. . . . . .

Liability for wrongful acts of constables

84–070   **88.**—(1) The chief officer of police for a police area shall be liable in respect of torts committed by constables under his direction and control in the performance or purported performance of their functions in like manner as a master is liable in respect of torts committed by his servants in the course of their employment, and accordingly shall in respect of any such tort be treated for all purposes as a joint tortfeasor.

(2) There shall be paid out of the police fund—

> (a) any damages or costs awarded against the chief officer of police in any proceedings brought against him by virtue of this section and any costs incurred by him in any such proceedings so far as not recovered by him in the proceedings, and
> (b) any sum required in connection with the settlement of any claim made against the chief officer of police by virtue of this section, if the settlement is approved by the police authority.

(3) Any proceedings in respect of a claim made by virtue of this section shall be brought against the chief officer of police for the time being or, in the case of a vacancy in that office, against the person for the time being performing the functions of the chief officer of police; and references in subsections (1) and (2) to the chief officer of police shall be construed accordingly.

(4) A police authority may, in such cases and to such extent as appear to it to be appropriate, pay out of the police fund—

    (a) any damages or costs awarded against a person to whom this subsection applies in proceedings for a tort committed by that person,

    (b) any costs incurred and not recovered by such a person in such proceedings, and

    (c) any sum required in connection with the settlement of a claim that has or might have given rise to such proceedings.

(5) Subsection (4) applies to a person who is—

    (a) a member of the police force maintained by the police authority.

    (b) a constable for the time being required to serve with that force by virtue of section 24 or 98[of this Act or section 23 of the Police Act 1997], or

    (c) a special constable appointed for the authority's police area.

Part V

Miscellaneous and General

Offences

Assaults on constables

89.—(1) Any person who assaults a constable in the execution of his duty, or a person assisting a constable in the execution of his duty, shall be guilty of an offence and liable on summary conviction to imprisonment for a term not exceeding six months or to a fine not exceeding level 5 on the standard scale, or to both.   **84–071**

(2) Any person who resists or wilfully obstructs a constable in the execution of his duty, or a person assisting a constable in the execution of his duty, shall be guilty of an offence and liable on summary conviction to imprisonment for a term not exceeding one month or to a fine not exceeding level 3 on the standard scale, or to both.

(3) This section also applies to a constable who is a member of a police force maintained in Scotland or Northern Ireland when he is executing a warrant, or otherwise acting in England or Wales, by virtue of any enactment conferring powers on him in England and Wales.

Impersonation, etc.

90.—(1) Any person who with intent to deceive impersonates a member of a police force or special constable, or makes any statement or does any act calculated falsely to suggest that he is such a member or constable, shall be guilty of an offence and liable on summary conviction to imprisonment for a term not exceeding six months or to a fine not exceeding level 5 on the standard scale, or to both.   **84–072**

(2) Any person who, not being a constable, wears any article of police uniform in circumstances where it gives him an appearance so nearly resembling that of a member of a police force as to be calculated to deceive shall be guilty of an offence and liable on summary conviction to a fine not exceeding level 3 on the standard scale.

(3) Any person who, not being a member of a police force or special constable, has in his possession any article of police uniform shall, unless he proves

that he obtained possession of that article lawfully and has possession of it for a lawful purpose, be guilty of an offence and liable on summary conviction to a fine not exceeding level 1 on the standard scale.

(4) In this section—

(a) "article of police uniform" means any article of uniform or any distinctive badge or mark or document of identification usually issued to members of police forces or special constables, or anything having the appearance of such an article, badge, mark or document,

[(aa) "member of a police force" includes a member of the British Transport Police Force, and]¹

(b) "special constable" means a special constable appointed for a police area.

¹ Added by Anti-terrorism, Crime and Security Act 2001 (c.24), Sched. 7, para. 25.

Causing disaffection

84–073   **91.**—(1) Any person who causes, or attempts to cause, or does any act calculated to cause, disaffection amongst the members of any police force, or induces or attempts to induce, or does any act calculated to induce, any member of a police force to withhold his services, shall be guilty of an offence and liable—

(a) on summary conviction, to imprisonment for a term not exceeding six months or to a fine not exceeding the statutory maximum, or to both;

(b) on conviction on indictment, to imprisonment for a term not exceeding two years or to a fine, or to both.

(2) This section applies to [members of the British Transport Police Force and] special constables appointed for a police area as it applies to members of a police force.

¹ Words inserted by Anti-terrorism, Crime and Security Act 2001 (c.24), Sched. 7, para. 26.

. . . . . .

Acceptance of gifts and loans

84–074   **93.**—(1) A police authority may, in connection with the discharge of any of its functions, accept gifts of money, and gifts or loans of other property, on such terms as appear to the authority to be appropriate.

(2) The terms on which gifts or loans are accepted under subsection (1) may include terms providing for the commercial sponsorship of any activity of the police authority or of the police force maintained by it.

. . . . . .

Miscellaneous

Arrangements for obtaining the views of the community on policing

84–075   **96.**—(1) Arrangements shall be made for each police area for obtaining—

(a) the views of people in that area about matters concerning the policing of the area, and

(b) their co-operation with the police in preventing crime in that area.

(2) Except as provided by [subsection (6)], arrangements for each police area shall be made by the police authority after consulting the chief constable [or in the case of the metropolitan police district, the Commissioner of Police of the Metropolis] as to the arrangements that would be appropriate.

(6) The Common Council of the City of London shall issue guidance to the Commissioner of Police for the City of London concerning arrangements for the City of London police area; and the Commissioner shall make arrangements under this section after taking account of that guidance.

(7) A body or person whose duty it is to make arrangements under this section shall review the arrangements so made from time to time.

(8) If it appears to the Secretary of State that arrangements for a police area are not adequate for the purposes set out in subsection (1), he may require the body or person whose duty it is to make arrangements for that area to submit a report to him concerning the arrangements.

(9) After considering a report submitted under subsection (8), the Secretary of State may require the body or person who submitted it to review the arrangements and submit a further report to him concerning them.

(10) A body or person whose duty it is to make arrangements shall be under the same duties to consult when reviewing arrangements as when making them.

. . . . . .

Section 4.   SCHEDULE 2

POLICE AUTHORITIES ESTABLISHED UNDER SECTION 3

Membership of police authorities

1.—(1) Where, by virtue of section 4, a police authority is to consist of seventeen members—   **84–076**

(a) nine of those members shall be members of a relevant council appointed under paragraph 2,
(b) five shall be persons appointed under paragraph 5, and
(c) three shall be magistrates appointed under paragraph 8.

(2) Where, by virtue of an order under subsection (2) of that section, a police authority is to consist of more than seventeen members—

(a) a number which is greater by one than the number of members provided for in paragraph (b) and (c) below shall be members of a relevant council appointed under paragraph 2.
(b) such number as may be prescribed by the order, not exceeding one third of the total membership, shall be persons appointed under paragraph 5, and
(c) the remainder shall be magistrates appointed under paragraph 8.

Appointment of members by relevant councils

2.—(1) In the case of a police authority in relation to which there is only one relevant council,   **84–077**
the members of the police authority referred to in paragraph 1(1)(a) or (2)(a) shall be appointed by that council.

(2) In any other case, those members shall be appointed by a joint committee consisting of persons appointed by the relevant councils from among their own members.

3. The number of members of the joint committee, and the number of those members to be   **84–078**
appointed by each relevant council, shall be such as the councils may agree or, in the absence of agreement, as may be determined by the Secretary of State.

4.—(1) A council or joint committee shall exercise its power to appoint members of a police   **84–079**
authority under paragraph 2 so as to ensure that, so far as practicable, [in the case of the members for whose appointment it is responsible, the proportion who are members of any given party—]

[(a) where it is a council that is responsible for their appointment, is the same as the proportion of the members of the council who are members of that party; and

(b) where it is a joint committee that is so responsible, is the same as the proportion of the members of the relevant councils taken as a whole who are members of that party.]

Appointment of independent members

84–080   **5.** The members of a police authority referred to in paragraph 1(1)(b) or (2)(b) shall be appointed—

(a) by the members of the police authority appointed under paragraph 2 or 8,
(b) from among persons on a short-list prepared by the Secretary of State in accordance with Schedule 3.

84–081   **6.**—(1) Every police authority shall arrange for a notice stating—

(a) the name of each of its members appointed under paragraph 5, and
(b) such other information relating to him as the authority considers appropriate,

to be published in such manner as appears to it to be appropriate.

(2) A police authority shall send to the Secretary of State a copy of any notice which it has arranged to be published under sub-paragraph (1).

Appointment of magistrates

84–082   **7.** The members of a police authority referred to in paragraph 1(1)(c) or (2)(c)—

(a) must be magistrates for an area all or part of which constitutes or forms part of the authority's area, and
(b) shall be appointed in accordance with paragraph 8;

and in that paragraph references to a panel are references to a selection panel constituted under regulations made in accordance with [section 29(2) of the Justices of the Peace Act 1997][1].

[1] Words substituted. by Justices of the Peace Act 1997 (c.25), Sched. 5, para. 37(3)(a).

84–083   **8.**—(1) Where there is a panel for an area which constitutes or includes the police authority's area, that panel shall make the appointment.

(2) Where the area of more than one panel falls wholly or partly within the police authority's area, the appointment shall be made by a joint committee consisting of representatives from the panels concerned.

(3) The number of members of a joint committee, and the number of those members to be appointed by each panel, shall be such as the panels may agree or, in the absence of agreement, as may be determined by the Lord Chancellor.

Chairman

84–084   **9.**—(1) A police authority shall at each annual meeting appoint a chairman from among its members.

(2) The appointment under sub-paragraph (1) shall be the first business transacted at the meeting.

(3) On a casual vacancy occurring in the office of chairman, an appointment to fill the vacancy shall be made—

(a) at the next meeting of the authority (other than an extraordinary meeting), or
(b) if that meeting is held within fourteen days after the date on which the vacancy occurs and is not an annual meeting, not later than the next following meeting.

Vice-chairmen

84–085   [**9A.**—(1) At an annual meeting a police authority may appoint one or more vice-chairmen from among its members.

(2) The making of appointments under sub-paragraph (1) shall be the first business transacted at the meeting after the appointment of the chairman.

(3) Where a vice-chairman ceases to hold office at any time between annual meetings, a police authority may make an appointment to fill the vacancy at any meeting of the authority held more than fourteen days after the occurrence of the vacancy.

(4) Subject to any standing orders made by a police authority, anything authorised or required to be done by, to or before their chairman may be done by, to or before any vice-chairman of the authority.][1]

[1] Added by Criminal Justice and Police Act 2001 (c.16), Pt 5, s. 104(1).

Disqualification

10. [. . .]¹   **84–086**

¹ Repealed by Criminal Justice and Police Act 2001 (c.16), Sched. 7(4), para. 1.

11.—(1) Subject to sub-paragraph (3) and (4), a person shall be disqualified for being appointed   **84–087**
as or being a member of a police authority if—

    (a) he holds any paid office or employment appointments to which are or may be made or
        confirmed by the police authority or any committee or sub-committee of the authority, or
        by a joint committee on which the authority is represented, or by any person holding any
        such office or employment;
    (b) a bankruptcy order has been made against him or his estate has been sequestrated or he
        has made a composition or arrangement with, or granted a trust deed for, his creditors;
    (c) he is subject to a disqualification order under the Company Directors Disqualification Act
        1986[to a disqualification order under Part II of the Companies (Northern Ireland) Order
        1989], or to an order made under section 429(2)(b) of the Insolvency Act 1986 (failure to
        pay under county court administration order); or
    (d) he has within five years before the date of his appointment or since his appointment been
        convicted in the United Kingdom, the Channel Islands or the Isle of Man of an offence,
        and has had passed on him a sentence of imprisonment (whether suspended or not) for a
        period of not less than three months.

    (2) A paid employee of a police authority who is employed under the direction of a joint board,
joint authority or joint committee on which the authority is represented and any member of which
is appointed on the nomination of some other police authority shall be disqualified for being
appointed as or being a member of that other police authority.
    (3) Where a person is disqualified under sub-paragraph (1)(b) by reason that a bankruptcy order
has been made against him or his estate has been sequestrated, the disqualification shall cease—

    (a) unless the bankruptcy order is previously annulled or the sequestration of his estate is
        recalled or reduced, on his obtaining a discharge; and
    (b) if the bankruptcy order is annulled or the sequestration of his estate is recalled or reduced,
        on the date of that event.

    (4) Where a person is disqualified under sub-paragraph (1)(b) by reason of his having made a
composition or arrangement with, or granted a trust deed for, his creditors and he pays his debts in
full, the disqualification shall cease on the date on which the payment is completed, and in any other
case it shall cease at the end of the period of five years beginning with the date on which the terms
of the deed of composition or arrangement or trust deed are fulfilled.
    (5) For the purposes of sub-paragraph (1)(d), the date of a conviction shall be taken to be the
ordinary date on which the period allowed for making an appeal or application expires or, if an
appeal or application is made, the date on which the appeal or application is finally disposed of or
abandoned or fails by reason of its non-prosecution.

13.—(1) Without prejudice to [paragraph 11], a person shall be disqualified for being appointed   **84–088**
as a member of a police authority under paragraph 5 if—

    (a) he has not yet attained the age of twenty-one years, or
    (b) neither his principal or only place of work, nor his principal or only place of residence,
        has been in the area of the authority during the whole of the period of twelve months
        ending with the day of appointment.

    (2) Without prejudice to [paragraph 11], a person shall be disqualified for being a member so
appointed if, at any time, neither his principal or only place of work, nor his principal or only place
of residence, is within that area.

14.—(1) Without prejudice to [paragraph 11], a person shall be disqualified for being appointed   **84–089**
as a member of a police authority under paragraph 5, and for being a member so appointed, if he
is—

    (a) a member of the council for a county, district, county borough or London borough which
        is wholly or partly within the area of the police authority;
    (b) a magistrate eligible for appointment to the police authority under paragraph 8;
    (c) a member of the selection panel for the police authority's area established under Schedule 3;
    (d) a member of a police force;
    (e) an officer or employee of a police authority; or
    (f) an officer or employee of a relevant council.

    (2) A person shall not be regarded for the purposes of sub-paragraph (1)(f) as an employee of a
relevant council by reason of his holding—

(a) the post of head teacher or principal of a school, college or other educational institution or establishment which is maintained or assisted by a local education authority; or

(b) any other post as a teacher or lecturer in any such school, college, institution or establishment.

Tenure of office

84–090   **15.** Subject to the following paragraphs (and to the provisions of any order under section 4(2)) a person shall hold and vacate office as a member of a police authority in accordance with the terms of his appointment.

84–091   **16.**—(1) A person shall be appointed to hold office as a member for—

(a) a term of four years, or
(b) such shorter term as the body appointing him may determine in any particular case.

(2) A person shall not, by virtue of sub-paragraph (1)(b), be appointed under paragraph 5 for a term shorter than four years without the approval of the Secretary of State.

84–092   **17.**—(1) A person may at any time resign his office as a member, or as chairman [or vice-chairman], by notice in writing to the police authority.

(2) Where a member appointed under paragraph 5 resigns his office as a member under sub-paragraph (1) of this paragraph, he shall send a copy of the notice to the Secretary of State.

84–093   **18.**—(1) A member of a relevant council appointed to be a member of a police authority under paragraph 2 shall cease to be a member of the authority if he ceases to be a member of the council (and does not on the same day again become a member of the council).

(2) A magistrate appointed to be a member of a police authority under paragraph 8 shall cease to be a member of the authority if he ceases to be a magistrate for an area all or part of which constitutes or forms part of the authority's area.

84–094   **19.**—(1) A police authority may remove a member from office by notice in writing if—

(a) he has been absent from meetings of the police authority for a period longer than three consecutive months without the consent of the authority,
(b) he has been convicted of a criminal offence (but is not disqualified for being a member under paragraph 11),
(c) the police authority is satisfied that the member is incapacitated by physical or mental illness, or
(d) the police authority is satisfied that the member is otherwise unable or unfit to discharge his functions as a member.

(2) Where a police authority removes a member under sub-paragraph (1), it shall give notice of that fact—

(a) in the case of a member appointed under paragraph 2 or 8, to the body which appointed him, and
(b) in the case of a member appointed under paragraph 5, to the Secretary of State.

84–095   **20.** A council or joint committee may remove from office a member of a police authority appointed by it under paragraph 2 with a view to appointing another in his place if it considers that to do so would further the object provided for by paragraph 4.

84–096   **21.** If a chairman of a police authority ceases to be a member, he shall also cease to be chairman [or vice-chairman].

Eligibility for re-appointment

84–097   **22.** A person who ceases to be a member, otherwise than by virtue of paragraph 19, or ceases to be chairman[or vice-chairman], may (if otherwise eligible) be re-appointed.

Validity of acts

84–098   **23.** The acts and proceedings of any person appointed to be a member or chairman [or vice-chairman] of a police authority and acting in that office shall, notwithstanding his disqualification or want of qualification, be as valid and effectual as if he had been qualified.

84–099   **24.** The proceedings of a police authority shall not be invalidated by a vacancy in the membership of the authority or in the office of chairman [by a vacancy for a vice-chairman] or by any defect in the appointment of a person as a member or as chairman [or vice-chairman].

Allowances

25.—(1) A police authority may make to its chairman [, vice-chairmen] and other members such payments by way of reimbursement of expenses as the Secretary of State may, with the approval of the Treasury, determine.   **84–100**

(2) Payments made under sub-paragraph (1) may differ according to whether the recipient is a chairman[, a vice-chairman,] or other member or was appointed under paragraph 2, 5 or 8.

[Allowances for members, etc.

25A.—(1) Subject to the following provisions of this paragraph, a police authority may make to its chairman, vice-chairmen and other members such payments by way of allowances as the authority may determine.   **84–101**

(2) Subject to sub-paragraph (6), no payment shall be made under this paragraph except in accordance with arrangements published by the authority not more than twelve months before the making of the payment.

(3) A police authority may from time to time revise any arrangements made for the purposes of this paragraph; but, no revisions shall take effect until published by the authority.

(4) It shall be the duty of a police authority, when making or revising any arrangements made for the purposes of this paragraph, to have regard to any guidance given by the Secretary of State about the payment of allowances.

(5) Payments made under this paragraph may differ according to whether the recipient is the chairman, a vice chairman or other member or is appointed under paragraph 2, 5 or 8.

(6) The Secretary of State may by regulations impose such limits as may be provided for by or under the regulations on the payments that may be made under this paragraph.

(7) A statutory instrument containing regulations under sub-paragraph (6) shall be subject to annulment in pursuance of a resolution of either House of Parliament.][1]

[1] Added by Criminal Justice and Police Act 2001 (c.16), Pt 5, s. 107(2).

[Members of standards committees

25B Paragraphs 25 and 25A shall have effect in relation to a police authority as if references to members of the authority included references to persons who are not members of the authority but are members of the authority's standards committee; and the power to make different payments according to the recipient shall include power to make different payments to persons who are not members of the authority but are members of the authority's standards committee.][1]   **84–102**

[1] Added by Criminal Justice and Police Act 2001 (c.16), Pt 5, s. 107(2).

Interpretation

26.—(1) For the purposes of this Schedule, a council is a "relevant council" in relation to a police authority if—   **84–103**

    (a) it is the council for a county, district [or county borough][1] which constitutes, or is wholly within, the authority's police area, and

    (b) in the case of a district council, the district is not in a county having a county council within paragraph (a).

(2) [. . .][2]

[1] Words substituted by Greater London Authority Act 1999 (c.29), Sched. 27, para. 105(4)(a).
[2] Repealed by Greater London Authority Act 1999 (c.29), Sched. 34, Pt VII, para. 1.

27. In this Schedule "magistrate" has the same meaning as in [the Justices of the Peace Act 1997][1].   **84–104**

[1] Words substituted. by Justices of the Peace Act 1997 (c.25), Sched. 5, para. 37(3)(b).

Schedule 2A

THE METROPOLITAN POLICE AUTHORITY

Membership

[1.—(1) Where the Metropolitan Police Authority is to consist of twenty three members—   **84–105**

    (a) twelve of those members shall be members of the London Assembly appointed under paragraph 2,

    (b) seven shall be persons appointed under paragraph 3, and

    (c) four shall be magistrates appointed under paragraph 5.

(2) Where, by virtue of an order under section 5C(2), the Metropolitan Police Authority is to consist of a number of members other than twenty three—

    (a) a number which is greater by one than the number of members provided for in paragraphs (b) and (c) shall be members of the London Assembly appointed under paragraph 2,

    (b) such number as may be prescribed by the order, not exceeding one third of the total membership, shall be persons appointed under paragraph 3, and

    (c) the remainder shall be magistrates appointed under paragraph 5.]¹

Appointment of members by the Mayor

84–106
    [**2.**—(1) The members of the Metropolitan Police Authority referred to in paragraph 1(1)(a) or (2)(a) shall be appointed by the Mayor of London in accordance with this paragraph.

    (2) One of those members must be the Deputy Mayor, except as provided by paragraphs 9(2)(b) and 17(b) of Schedule 4 to the Greater London Authority Act 1999 or unless the Deputy Mayor is disqualified for being appointed as or being a member of the Metropolitan Police Authority under paragraph 7 below.

    (3) The Mayor (or, where paragraph 9(2)(b) or 17(b) of Schedule 4 to that Act applies, the Chair of the London Assembly) shall ensure that, so far as practicable, [in the case of the members of the Authority who are members of the London Assembly appointed under this paragraph, the proportion who are members of any given party is the same as the proportion of the members of the London Assembly who are members of that party].]

Appointment of independent members

84–107
    [**3.**—(1) The members of the Metropolitan Police Authority referred to in paragraph 1(1)(b) or 2(b) shall be appointed in accordance with this paragraph.

    (2) One shall be appointed by the Secretary of State.

    (3) The remainder shall be appointed—

    (a) by the members of the Metropolitan Police Authority appointed under paragraph 2 or 5,

    (b) from among persons on a short-list prepared by the Secretary of State in accordance with Schedule 3.

    (4) In the application of Schedule 3 in relation to the appointment of the first members of the Metropolitan Police Authority, the selection panel referred to in paragraph 1(1)(b) of that Schedule shall, instead of being constituted in accordance with sub-paragraphs (2) and (3) of that paragraph, be constituted in accordance with sub-paragraph (5) below.

    (5) The selection panel shall consist of three members, of whom—

    (a) one shall be appointed by the Secretary of State;

    (b) one shall be appointed by the Secretary of State after consultation with persons whom, or organisations which, he considers represent the interests of local government in Greater London; and

    (c) one shall be appointed by the two members of the panel appointed by virtue of paragraphs (a) and (b).

    (6) Notwithstanding paragraph 3(1A) of Schedule 3, the persons appointed under paragraphs (b) and (c) of sub-paragraph (5) shall cease to hold office when all the first members of the Metropolitan Police Authority have been appointed (but shall be eligible for further appointment under Schedule 3); but an appointment under paragraph (a) of that sub-paragraph shall have effect thereafter as if it had been an appointment under paragraph 1(2)(b) of that Schedule.]

84–108
    [**4.**—(1) The Metropolitan Police Authority shall arrange for a notice stating—

    (a) the name of each of its members appointed under paragraph 3(2) or (3), and

    (b) such other information relating to any such member as the Metropolitan Police Authority considers appropriate,

to be published in such manner as appears to it to be appropriate.

    (2) The Metropolitan Police Authority shall send to the Secretary of State a copy of any notice which it has arranged to be published under sub-paragraph (1).]

Appointment of magistrates

84–109
    [**5.** The members of the Metropolitan Police Authority referred to in paragraph 1(1)(c) or (2)(c)—

    (a) must be magistrates for commission areas which are wholly or partly within the metropolitan police district, and

    (b) shall be appointed by the person or body responsible for the appointment of members of the Greater London Magistrates' Courts Authority under regulations made under section 30B of the Justices of the Peace Act 1997.]

Chairman

[**6.**—(1) The Metropolitan Police Authority shall at each annual meeting appoint a chairman from among its members.   **84–110**

(2) The appointment under sub-paragraph (1) shall be the first business transacted at the meeting.

(3) On a casual vacancy occurring in the office of chairman, an appointment to fill the vacancy shall be made—

- (a) at the next meeting of the Metropolitan Police Authority (other than an extraordinary meeting), or
- (b) if that meeting is held within fourteen days after the date on which the vacancy occurs and is not an annual meeting, not later than the next following meeting.]

[Vice-chairmen

6A.—(1) At an annual meeting the Metropolitan Police Authority may appoint one or more vice-chairmen from among its members.   **84–111**

(2) The making of appointments under sub-paragraph (1) shall be the first business transacted at the meeting after the appointment of the chairman.

(3) Where a vice-chairman ceases to hold office at any time between annual meetings, the Metropolitan Police Authority may make an appointment to fill the vacancy at any meeting of the Authority held more than fourteen days after the occurrence of the vacancy.

(4) Subject to any standing orders made by the Metropolitan Police Authority, anything authorised or required to be done by, to or before their chairman may be done by, to or before any vice-chairman of the authority.]

Disqualification

[**7.**—(1) Subject to sub-paragraphs (3) and (4), a person shall be disqualified for being appointed as or being a member of the Metropolitan Police Authority if—   **84–112**

- (a) he holds any paid office or employment appointments to which are or may be made or confirmed by the Metropolitan Police Authority or any committee or sub-committee of the Metropolitan Police Authority, or by a joint committee on which the Metropolitan Police Authority is represented, or by a person holding any such office or employment;
- (b) a bankruptcy order has been made against him, or his estate has been sequestrated or he has made a composition or arrangement with, or granted a trust deed for, his creditors;
- (c) he is subject to a disqualification order under the Company Directors Disqualification Act 1986[to a disqualification order under Part II of the Companies (Northern Ireland) Order 1989], or to an order made under section 429(2)(b) of the Insolvency Act 1986 (failure to pay under county court administration order); or
- (d) he has within five years before the date of his appointment or since his appointment been convicted in the United Kingdom, the Channel Islands or the Isle of Man of an offence, and has had passed on him a sentence of imprisonment (whether suspended or not) for a period of not less than three months.

(2) A paid employee of a police authority who is employed under the direction of a joint board, joint authority or joint committee—

- (a) on which that police authority is represented, and
- (b) any member of which is appointed on the nomination of some other police authority,

shall be disqualified for being appointed as, or being, a member of that other police authority if either of those police authorities is the Metropolitan Police Authority.

(3) Where a person is disqualified under sub-paragraph (1)(b) by reason that a bankruptcy order has been made against him or his estate has been sequestrated, the disqualification shall cease—

- (a) unless the bankruptcy order is previously annulled or the sequestration of his estate is recalled or reduced, on his obtaining a discharge; and
- (b) if the bankruptcy order is annulled or the sequestration of his estate is recalled or reduced, on the date of that event.

(4) Where a person is disqualified under sub-paragraph (1)(b) by reason of his having made a composition or arrangement with, or granted a trust deed for, his creditors and he pays his debts in full, the disqualification shall cease on the date on which the payment is completed, and in any other case it shall cease at the end of the period of five years beginning with the date on which the terms of the deed of composition or arrangement or trust deed are fulfilled.

(5) For the purposes of sub-paragraph (1)(d), the date of a conviction shall be taken to be the ordinary date on which the period allowed for making an appeal or application expires or, if an

appeal or application is made, the date on which the appeal or application is finally disposed of or abandoned or fails by reason of its non-prosecution.]

84–113   [**8.**—(1) Without prejudice to paragraph 7, a person shall be disqualified for being appointed as a member of the Metropolitan Police Authority under paragraph 3 if—

(a) he has not yet attained the age of twenty-one years, or
(b) neither his principal or only place of work, nor his principal or only place of residence, has been in the metropolitan police district during the whole of the period of twelve months ending with the day of appointment.

(2) Without prejudice to paragraph 7, a person shall be disqualified for being a member so appointed if, at any time, neither his principal or only place of work, nor his principal or only place of residence, is within the metropolitan police district.]

84–114   [**9.**—(1) Without prejudice to paragraph 7, a person shall be disqualified for being appointed as a member of the Metropolitan Police Authority under paragraph 3, and for being a member so appointed, if he is—

(a) a member of a London borough council;
(b) the Mayor of London;
(c) a member of the London Assembly;
(d) a magistrate for a commission area which is wholly or partly within the metropolitan police district;
(e) a member of the selection panel for the metropolitan police district established under Schedule 3;
(f) a member of a police force;
(g) an officer or employee of a police authority; or
(h) an officer or employee of the Greater London Authority or of a London borough council.

(2) A person shall not be regarded for the purposes of sub-paragraph (1)(h) as an employee of a London borough council by reason of his holding—

(a) the post of head teacher or principal of a school, college or other educational institution or establishment which is maintained or assisted by a local education authority; or
(b) any other post as a teacher or lecturer in any such school, college, institution or establishment.]

Tenure of office

84–115   [**10.** Subject to the following paragraphs (and to the provision of any order under section 5C(2)) a person shall hold and vacate office as a member of the Metropolitan Police Authority in accordance with the terms of his appointment.][1]

[1] Added by Greater London Authority Act 1999 (c.29), Sched. 26, para. 1.

84–116   [**11.**—(1) A person shall be appointed to hold office as a member for—

(a) a term of four years, or
(b) such shorter term as the person or body appointing him may determine in any particular case.

(2) A person shall not, by virtue of sub-paragraph (1)(b), be appointed under paragraph 3(3) for a term shorter than four years without the approval of the Secretary of State.]

84–117   [**12.**—(1) A person may at any time resign his office as a member, or as chairman[or vice-chairman], by notice in writing to the Metropolitan Police Authority.
(2) Where a member appointed under paragraph 3 resigns his office as a member under sub-paragraph (1) of this paragraph, he shall send a copy of the notice to the Secretary of State.]

84–118   [**13.**—(1) A member of the London Assembly appointed to be a member of the Metropolitan Police Authority under paragraph 2 shall cease to be a member of the Metropolitan Police Authority if he ceases to be a member of the London Assembly (and does not immediately again become a member of the London Assembly).
(2) The Deputy Mayor appointed to be a member of the Metropolitan Police Authority under paragraph 2 shall cease to be a member of that Authority if he ceases to be Deputy Mayor.
(3) A magistrate appointed to be a member of the Metropolitan Police Authority under paragraph 5 shall cease to be a member of that Authority if he ceases to be one of the magistrates for commission areas which are wholly or partly within the metropolitan police district.]

84–119   [**14.**—(1) The Metropolitan Police Authority may remove a member from office by notice in writing if—

(a) he has been absent from meetings of the Metropolitan Police Authority for a period longer than three consecutive months without the consent of the Metropolitan Police Authority,

(b) he has been convicted of a criminal offence (but is not disqualified for being a member under paragraph 7),

(c) the Metropolitan Police Authority is satisfied that the member is incapacitated by physical or mental illness, or

(d) the Metropolitan Police Authority is satisfied that the member is otherwise unable or unfit to discharge his functions as a member.

(2) Where the Metropolitan Police Authority removes a member under sub-paragraph (1), it shall give notice of that fact—

(a) in the case of a member appointed under paragraph 2 or 5, to the body or person which appointed him, and

(b) in the case of a member appointed under paragraph 3, to the Secretary of State.]

[15. The Mayor of London may remove from office a member of the Metropolitan Police Authority appointed by him under paragraph 2 with a view to appointing another in his place if he considers that to do so would further the object provided for by paragraph 2(3).]   **84–120**

[16. If the chairman of the Metropolitan Police Authority ceases to be a member, he shall also cease to be chairman[or vice-chairman].]   **84–121**

Eligibility for re-appointment

[17. A person who ceases to be a member, otherwise than by virtue of paragraph 14, or ceases to be chairman [or vice-chairman] may (if otherwise eligible) be re-appointed.]   **84–122**

Validity of acts

[18. The acts and proceedings of any person appointed to be a member or chairman [or vice-chairman] of the Metropolitan Police Authority and acting in that office shall, notwithstanding his disqualification or want of qualification, be as valid and effectual as if he had been qualified.]   **84–123**

[19. The proceedings of the Metropolitan Police Authority shall not be invalidated by a vacancy in the membership of the Metropolitan Police Authority or in the office of chairman [by a vacancy for a vice-chairman] or by any defect in the appointment of a person as a member or as chairman [or vice-chairman].]   **84–124**

Allowances

[20.—(1) The Metropolitan Police Authority may make to its chairman [, vice-chairmen] and other members such payments by way of reimbursement of expenses as the Secretary of State may determine.   **84–125**

(3) Payments made under sub-paragraph (1) may differ according to whether the recipient is the chairman [a vice-chairman,] or one of the other members of the Metropolitan Police Authority or was appointed under paragraph 2, 3 or 5.]

[Allowances for members etc.

20A.—(1) Subject to the following provisions of this paragraph, the Metropolitan Police Authority may make to its chairman, vice-chairmen and other members such payments by way of allowances as that Authority may determine.   **84–126**

(2) Subject to sub-paragraphs (6) and (7), no payment shall be made under this paragraph except in accordance with arrangements published by the Metropolitan Police Authority not more than twelve months before the making of the payment.

(3) The Metropolitan Police Authority may from time to time revise any arrangements made for the purposes of this paragraph; but, no revisions shall take effect until published by that Authority.

(4) It shall be the duty of the Metropolitan Police Authority, when making or revising any arrangements made for the purposes of this paragraph, to have regard to any guidance given by the Secretary of State about the payment of allowances.

(5) Payments made under this paragraph may differ according to whether the recipient is the chairman, a vice chairman or one of the other members of the Metropolitan Police Authority, or is appointed under paragraph 3 or 5.

(6) No payment shall be made under this paragraph to any member of the Metropolitan Police Authority who is also a member of the London Assembly.

(7) The Secretary of State may by regulations impose such limits as may be provided for by or under the regulations on the payments that may be made under this paragraph.

(8) A statutory instrument containing regulations under sub-paragraph (7) shall be subject to annulment in pursuance of a resolution of either House of Parliament.][1]

[1] Added by Criminal Justice and Police Act 2001 (c.16), Pt 5, s. 107(3).

[Members of standards committees

84–127   **20B.** Paragraphs 20 and 20A shall have effect in relation to the Metropolitan Police Authority as if references to the members of that Authority included references to persons who are not members of that Authority but are members of the Authority's standards committee; and the power to make different payments according to the recipient shall include power to make different payments to persons who are not members of that Authority but are members of the Authority's standards committee.]¹

¹ Added by Criminal Justice and Police Act 2001 (c.16), Pt 5, s. 107(3).

Mayor's functions to be exercised by him personally

84–128   **[21.** Any functions exercisable by the Mayor of London under this Schedule may only be exercised by him personally.]¹

¹ Added by Greater London Authority Act 1999 (c.29), Sched. 26, para. 1.

Interpretation

84–129   **[22.** In this Schedule—

"commission area" has the same meaning as in the Justices of the Peace Act 1997;
"magistrate" has the same meaning as in the Justices of the Peace Act 1997.]¹

¹ Added by Greater London Authority Act 1999 (c.29), Sched. 26, para. 1.

. . . . . .

Section 66.   SCHEDULE 5

THE POLICE COMPLAINTS AUTHORITY

Constitution of Authority

84–130   **1.**—(1) The Police Complaints Authority shall consist of a chairman and not less than eight other members.
(2) The chairman shall be appointed by Her Majesty.
(3) The other members shall be appointed by the Secretary of State.
(4) The members of the Authority shall not include any person who is or has been a constable in any part of the United Kingdom.
(5) Persons may be appointed as whole-time or part-time members of the Authority.
(6) The Secretary of State may appoint not more than two of the members of the Authority to be deputy chairmen.

Status of Authority

84–131   **2.** The Authority shall not be regarded as the servant or agent of the Crown or as enjoying any status, privilege or immunity of the Crown; and the Authority's property shall not be regarded as property of or property held on behalf of the Crown.

Members

84–132   **3.**—(1) Subject to the following provisions of this Schedule, a person shall hold an office to which he is appointed under paragraph 1(2), (3) or (6) in accordance with the terms of his appointment.
(2) A person shall not be appointed to such an office for more than three years at a time.
(3) A person may at any time resign such an office.
(4) The Secretary of State may at any time remove a person from such an office if satisfied that—

(a) he has without reasonable excuse failed to carry out his duties for a continuous period of three months beginning not earlier than six months before that time;
(b) he has been convicted of a criminal offence;
(c) he has become bankrupt or made an arrangement with his creditors;
(d) he is incapacitated by physical or mental illness;
(e) he has acted improperly in relation to his duties; or
(f) he is otherwise unable or unfit to perform his duties.

4. The Secretary of State may pay, or make such payments towards the provision of, such remuneration, persons, allowances or gratuities to or in respect of persons appointed to office under paragraph 1(2), (3) or (6) or any of them as he may, with the consent of the Treasury, determine.

84–133

5. Where a person ceases to hold such an office otherwise than on the expiry of his term of office, and it appears to the Secretary of State that there are special circumstances which make it right for that person to receive compensation, the Secretary of State may, with the consent of the Treasury, direct the Authority to make to the person a payment of such amount as the Secretary of State may, with the consent of the Treasury, determine.

84–134

Staff

6. The Authority may, after consultation with the Secretary of State, appoint such officers and servants as appear to the Authority to be appropriate, subject to the approval of the Treasury as to numbers and as to remuneration and other terms and conditions of service.

84–135

7. Where a person who is employed by the Authority and is by reference to that employment a participant in a scheme under section 1 of the Superannuation Act 1972 is appointed to an office under paragraph 1(2), (3) or (6), the Treasury may determine that his service in that office shall be treated for the purposes of the scheme as service as an employee of the Authority; and his rights under the scheme shall not be affected by paragraph 4.

84–136

8. The Employers' Liability (Compulsory Insurance) Act 1969 shall not require insurance to be effected by the Authority.

84–137

Power of Authority to set up regional offices

9.—(1) If it appears to the Authority that it is necessary to do so in order to discharge their duties efficiently, the Authority may, with the consent of the Secretary of State and the Treasury, set up a regional office in any place in England and Wales.

(2) The Authority may delegate any of their functions to a regional office.

84–138

Proceedings

10.—(1) Subject to the provisions of Chapter I of Part IV and section 87, the arrangements for the proceedings of the Authority (including the quorum for meetings) shall be such as the Authority may determine.

(2) The arrangements may, with the approval of the Secretary of State, provide for the discharge, under the general direction of the Authority, of any of the Authority's functions by a committee or by one or more of the members, officers or servants of the Authority.

84–139

11. The validity of any proceedings of the Authority shall not be affected by—

(a) any defect in the appointment of the chairman or any other member, or
(b) any vacancy in the office of chairman or among the other members.

84–140

Finance

12. The Secretary of State—

(a) shall pay to the Authority expenses incurred or to be incurred by the Authority under paragraph 5 and 6, and
(b) shall, with the consent of the Treasury, pay to the Authority such sums as appear to the Secretary of State to be appropriate for enabling the Authority to meet other expenses.

84–141

13.—(1) The Authority shall—

(a) keep proper accounts and proper records in relation to the accounts,
(b) prepare in respect of each financial year of the Authority a statement of accounts in such form as the Secretary of State may, with the approval of the Treasury, direct, and
(c) send copies of the statement to the Secretary of State and the Comptroller and Auditor General before the end of the month of August next following the financial year to which the statement relates.

84–142

(2) The Comptroller and Auditor General shall examine, certify and report on each statement received by him in pursuance of this paragraph and shall lay copies of each statement and of his report before Parliament.

(3) The financial year of the Authority shall be the twelve months ending on 31st March.

Justices of the Peace Act 1997

(1997, c. 25)

85–001 *An Act to consolidate the Justices of the Peace Act 1979 and provisions of Part IV of the Police and Magistrates' Courts Act 1994.* [19th March 1997]

. . . . . .

PART V

PROTECTION AND INDEMNIFICATION OF JUSTICES AND JUSTICES' CLERKS

Immunity for acts within jurisdiction

85–002 **51.**—[(1) No action shall lie against any justice of the peace or justices' clerk in respect of any act or omission of his—

    (a) in the execution of his duty—

        (i) as such a justice; or
        (ii) as such a clerk exercising, by virtue of any statutory provision, any of the functions of a single justice; and

    (b) with respect to any matter within his jurisdiction.

(2) In this section references to a justices' clerk include any person appointed by a magistrates' courts committee to assist a justices' clerk.]

Immunity for certain acts beyond jurisdiction

85–003 **52.**—[(1) An action shall lie against any justice of the peace or justices' clerk in respect of any act or omission of his—

    (a) in the purported execution of his duty—

        (i) as such a justice; or
        (ii) as such a clerk exercising, by virtue of any statutory provision, any of the functions of a single justice; but

    (b) with respect to a matter which is not within his jurisdiction,

if, but only if, it is proved that he acted in bad faith.
(2) In this section references to a justices' clerk include any person appointed by a magistrates' courts committee to assist a justices' clerk.]

Where action prohibited, proceedings may be set aside

85–004 **53.**—If any action is brought in circumstances in which this Part of this Act provides that no action is to lie, a judge of the court in which the action is brought may, on the application of the defendant and upon an affidavit as to the facts, set aside the proceedings in the action, with or without costs, as the judge thinks fit.

[Costs in legal proceedings

85–005 **53A.**—(1) A court may not order any justice of the peace or justices' clerk to pay costs in any proceedings in respect of any act or omission of his in the execution (or purported execution) of his duty—

(a) as such a justice; or

(b) as such a clerk exercising, by virtue of any statutory provision, any of the functions of a single justice.

(2) Subsection (1) above does not apply in relation to—

(a) any proceedings in which a justice or justices' clerk is being tried for an offence or is appealing against a conviction; or

(b) any proceedings in which it is proved that a justice or justices' clerk acted in bad faith in respect of the matters giving rise to the proceedings.

(3) Where a court is prevented by subsection (1) above from ordering a justice or justices' clerk to pay costs in any proceedings, the court may instead order the making by the Lord Chancellor of a payment in respect of the costs of a person in the proceedings.

(4) The Lord Chancellor may by statutory instrument make regulations specifying—

(a) circumstances when a court shall or shall not exercise the power conferred on it by subsection (3) above; and

(b) how the amount of any payment ordered under that subsection is to be determined.

(5) No regulations may be made under subsection (4) above unless a draft of the statutory instrument containing them has been laid before, and approved by a resolution of, each House of Parliament.

(6) In this section references to a justices' clerk include any person appointed by a magistrates' courts committee to assist a justices' clerk.]

Indemnification of justices and justices' clerks

54.—(1) For the purposes of subsection (2) below, the following amounts are "relevant amounts" in relation to a justice of the peace or justices' clerk—   **85–006**

(a) any costs which he reasonably incurs—

  (i) in or in connection with proceedings in respect of anything done or omitted in the exercise (or purported exercise) of his duty as a justice of the peace or justices' clerk; or

  (ii) in taking steps to dispute any claim which might be made in such proceedings;

(b) any damages awarded against him or costs ordered to be paid by him in any such proceedings; and

(c) any sums payable by him in connection with a reasonable settlement of any such proceedings or claim,

and relevant amounts relate to criminal matters if the duty mentioned in paragraph (a)(i) above relates to criminal matters.

(2) Subject to the provisions of this section, a justice of the peace or justices' clerk—

(a) shall be indemnified [by the appropriate authority] in respect of relevant amounts which relate to criminal matters unless it is proved, in respect of the matters giving rise to the proceedings or claim, that he acted in bad faith; and

    (b) in respect of other relevant amounts—

        (i) may be indemnified [by the appropriate authority] [unless it is proved, in respect of the matters giving rise to the proceedings or claim, that he acted in bad faith]; and

        (ii) shall be so indemnified if, in respect of the matters giving rise to the proceedings or claim, he acted reasonably and in good faith.

[(2A) In subsection (2) above the "appropriate authority" means—

    (a) the Greater London Magistrates' Courts Authority, where at the material time the justice or justices' clerk was acting for an area consisting of or falling within Greater London; or

    (b) the paying authority or authorities, where at the material time the justice or justices' clerk was acting for an area outside Greater London.]

(3) Any question whether, or to what extent, a person is to be indemnified under this section shall be determined by the magistrates' courts committee for the area for which he acted at the material time.

(4) A determination under subsection (3) above with respect to any such costs or sums as are mentioned in subsection (1)(a) or (c) above may, if the person claiming to be indemnified so requests, be made in advance before those costs are incurred or the settlement made, as the case may be.

(5) Any such determination in advance for indemnity in respect of costs to be incurred shall be subject to such limitations, if any, as the committee think proper and to the subsequent determination of the amount of the costs reasonably incurred and shall not affect any other determination which may fall to be made in connection with the proceedings or claim in question.

(6) An appeal shall lie to a person appointed for the purpose by the Lord Chancellor—

    (a) on the part of the person claiming to be indemnified, from any decision of the magistrates' courts committee under subsection (3) or (4) above, other than a decision to postpone until after the conclusion of the proceedings any determination with respect to his own costs or to impose limitations on making a determination in advance for indemnity in respect of such costs;

    (b) on the part of any paying authority, from any determination of the magistrates' courts committee under subsection (3) above other than a determination in advance for indemnity in respect of costs to be incurred by the person claiming to be indemnified.

(7) Where[, in relation to any justice or justices' clerk acting for an area outside Greater London, there are two or more paying authorities,] any question as to the extent to which the funds required to indemnify him are to be provided by each authority shall be determined by agreement between those authorities and the magistrates' courts committee concerned or, in default of such agreement, shall be determined by the Lord Chancellor.

(8) The Lord Chancellor may by statutory instrument make rules prescribing the procedure to be followed in any appeal under subsection (6) above; and any statutory instrument made by virtue of this subsection shall be subject to annulment in pursuance of a resolution of either House of Parliament.

(9) In this section—

"justices' clerk" includes any person appointed by a magistrates' courts committee to assist a justices' clerk;

["paying authority"

(a) in relation to any justice or justices' clerk who at the material time acted for an area outside Greater London, means any authority which is a paying authority for the purposes of section 55 below in relation to the magistrates' courts committee for that area; and

(b) in relation to a justices' clerk who at the material time acted for an area consisting of or falling within Greater London, means the council of any London borough or the Common Council of the City of London.]

Law Officers Act 1997

(1997, c. 60)

An Act to enable functions of the Attorney General and of the Attorney General for Northern Ireland to be exercised by the Solicitor General; and for connected purposes.   [31st July 1997]

86–001

The Attorney General and the Solicitor General

1.—(1) Any function of the Attorney General may be exercised by the Solicitor General.

(2) Anything done by or in relation to the Solicitor General in the exercise of or in connection with a function of the Attorney General has effect as if done by or in relation to the Attorney General.

(3) The validity of anything done in relation to the Attorney General, or done by or in relation to the Solicitor General, is not affected by a vacancy in the office of Attorney General.

(4) Nothing in this section—

(a) prevents anything being done by or in relation to the Attorney General in the exercise of or in connection with any function of his; or

(b) requires anything done by the Solicitor General to be done in the name of the Solicitor General instead of the name of the Attorney General.

(5) It is immaterial for the purposes of this section whether a function of the Attorney General arises under an enactment or otherwise.

86–002

Local Government (Contracts) Act 1997

(1997, c. 65)

An Act to make provision about the powers of local authorities (including probation committees and the Receiver for the Metropolitan Police District) to enter into contracts; to enable expenditure of local authorities making administrative arrangements for magistrates' courts to be treated for some purposes as not being capital expenditure; and for connected purposes.
[27th November 1997]

87–001

Contracts for provision of assets or services

Functions to include power to enter into contracts

87–002 **1.** (1) Every statutory provision conferring or imposing a function on a local authority confers power on the local authority to enter into a contract with another person for the provision or making available of assets or services, or both, (whether or not together with goods) for the purposes of, or in connection with, the discharge of the function by the local authority.

(2) Where—

 (a) a local authority enters into a contract such as is mentioned in subsection (1) ("the provision contract") under any statutory provision, and

 (b) in connection with the provision contract, a person ("the financier") makes a loan to, or provides any other form of finance for, a party to the provision contract other than the local authority,

the statutory provision also confers power on the local authority to enter into a contract with the financier, or any insurer of or trustee for the financier, in connection with the provision contract.

(3) The following are local authorities for the purposes of this Act—

 (a) any authority with respect to the finances of which Part IV of the Local Government and Housing Act 1989 has effect at the time in question.

 (b) any probation committee,

 (c) the Receiver for the Metropolitan Police District, and

 (d) any local authority or joint board as defined in section 235(1) of the Local Government (Scotland) Act 1973.

(4) In this Act "assets" means assets of any description (whether tangible or intangible), including (in particular) land, buildings, roads, works, plant, machinery, vehicles, vessels, apparatus, equipment and computer software.

(5) Regulations may be made amending subsection (4)[1]

---

[1] In relation to contracts entered into by the National Assembly for Wales on or after, July 1, 1999, s. 1 reads:

Functions to include power to enter into contracts

1. (1) Every statutory provision conferring or imposing a function on the Assembly confers power on the Assembly to enter into a contract with another person for the provision or making available of assets or services, or both, (whether or not together with goods) for the purposes of, or in connection with, the discharge of the function by the Assembly.

(2) Where—

 (a) the Assembly enters into a contract such as is mentioned in subsection (1) ("the provision contract") under any statutory provision, and

 (b) in connection with the provision contract, a person ("the financier") makes a loan to, or provides any other form of finance for, a party to the provision contract other than the Assembly,

the statutory provision also confers power on the Assembly to enter into a contract with the financier, or any insurer of or trustee for the financier, in connection with the provision contract.

[(3) In this Act references to "the Assembly" means the National Assembly for Wales.]

(4) In this Act "assets" means assets of any description (whether tangible or intangible), including (in particular) land, buildings, roads, works, plant, machinery, vehicles, vessels, apparatus, equipment and computer software.

Certified contracts

Certified contracts to be *intra vires*

2.—(1) Where a local authority has entered into a contract, the contract shall, **87–003** if it is a certified contract, have effect (and be deemed always to have had effect) as if the local authority had had power to enter into it (and had exercised that power properly in entering into it).

(2) For the purposes of this Act a contract entered into by a local authority is a certified contract if (and, subject to subsections (3) and (4), only if) the certification requirements have been satisfied by the local authority with respect to the contract and they were so satisfied before the end of the certification period.

(3) A contract entered into by a local authority shall be treated as a certified contract during the certification period if the contract provides that the certification requirements are intended to be satisfied by the local authority with respect to the contract before the end of that period.

(4) Where a local authority has entered into a contract which is a certified contract ("the existing contract") and the existing contract is replaced by a contract entered into by it with a person or persons not identical with the person or persons with whom it entered into the existing contract, the replacement contract is also a certified contract if—

(a) the period for which it operates or is intended to operate ends at the same time as the period for which the existing contract was to operate, and

(b) apart from that, its provisions are the same as those of the existing contract.

(5) In this Act "the certification period", in relation to a contract entered into by a local authority, means the period of six weeks beginning with the day on which the local authority entered into the contract.

(6) Subsection (1) is subject to section 5 (special provisions about judicial reviews and audit reviews).

(7) The application of subsection (1) in relation to a contract entered into by a local authority does not affect any claim for damages made by a person who is not (and has never been) a party to the contract in respect of a breach by the local authority of any duty to do, or not to do, something before entering into the contract (including, in particular, any such duty imposed by a statutory provision for giving effect to any Community obligation relating to public procurement or by section 17(1) of the Local Government Act 1988).[1]

[1] In relation to contracts entered into by the National Assembly for Wales on or after, July 1, 1999, s. 2 reads:

Certified contracts to be *intra vires*

2.—(1) Where the Assembly has entered into a contract, the contract shall, if it is a certified contract, have effect (and be deemed always to have had effect) as if the Assembly had had power to enter into it (and had exercised that power properly in entering into it).

(2) For the purposes of this Act a contract entered into by the Assembly is a certified contract if (and, subject to subsections (3) and (4), only if) the certification requirements have been satisfied by the Assembly with respect to the contract and they were so satisfied before the end of the certification period.

(3) A contract entered into by the Assembly shall be treated as a certified contract during the certification period if the contract provides that the certification requirements are intended to be satisfied by the Assembly with respect to the contract before the end of that period.

(4) Where the Assembly has entered into a contract which is a certified contract ("the existing

contract") and the existing contract is replaced by a contract entered into by it with a person or persons not identical with the person or persons with whom it entered into the existing contract, the replacement contract is also a certified contract if—

(a) the period for which it operates or is intended to operate ends at the same time as the period for which the existing contract was to operate, and

(b) apart from that, its provisions are the same as those of the existing contract.

(5) In this Act "the certification period", in relation to a contract entered into by the Assembly, means the period of six weeks beginning with the day on which the Assembly entered into the contract.

[(6) Subsection (1) is subject to section 5 (special provisions about judicial reviews).]

(7) The application of subsection (1) in relation to a contract entered into by the Assembly does not affect any claim for damages made by a person who is not (and has never been) a party to the contract in respect of a breach by the Assembly of any duty to do, or not to do, something before entering into the contract (including, in particular, any such duty imposed by a statutory provision for giving effect to any Community obligation relating to public procurement).

The certification requirements

87–004   **3.**—(1) In this Act "the certification requirements", in relation to a contract entered into by a local authority, means the requirements specified in subsections (2) to (4).

(2) The requirement specified in this subsection is that the local authority must have issued a certificate (whether before or after the contract is entered into)—

(a) including details of the period for which the contract operates or is to operate,

(b) describing the purpose of the contract,

(c) containing a statement that the contract is or is to be a contract falling within section 4(3) or (4),

(d) stating that the local authority had or has power to enter into the contract and specifying the statutory provision, or each of the statutory provisions, conferring the power,

(e) stating that a copy of the certificate has been or is to be given to each person to whom a copy is required to be given by regulations,

(f) dealing in a manner prescribed by regulations with any matters required by regulations to be dealt with in certificates under this section, and

(g) confirming that the local authority has complied with or is to comply with any requirement imposed by regulations with respect to the issue of certificates under this section.

(3) The requirement specified in this subsection is that the local authority must have secured that the certificate is signed by any person who is required by regulations to sign it.

(4) The requirement specified in this subsection is that the local authority must have obtained consent to the issue of a certificate under this section from each of the persons with whom the local authority has entered, or is to enter, into the contract.[1]

[1] In relation to contracts entered into by the National Assembly for Wales on or after, July 1, 1999, s. 3 reads:

The certification requirements

3.—(1) In this Act "the certification requirements", in relation to a contract entered into by the Assembly, means the requirements specified in subsections (2) to (4).

(2) The requirement specified in this subsection is that [the Assembly] must have issued a certificate (whether before or after the contract is entered into)—

(a) including details of the period for which the contract operates or is to operate,

(b) describing the purpose of the contract,

(c) containing a statement that the contract is or is to be a contract falling within section 4(3) or (4),

[(d) stating that the Assembly had or has power to enter into the contract, specifying the statutory provision, or each of the statutory provision, conferring the power and, where that provision or one such provision is section 40 of the Government of Wales Act 1998, specifying each function of the Assembly which the contract is calculated to facilitate, or is conducive or incidental to, the exercise of that function,

(e) stating that a copy of the certificate has been or is to be given to—

    (i) each of the persons with whom the Assembly has entered or is to enter into the contract in relation to which the certificate is issued,

    (ii) the presiding officer or deputy presiding officer of the Assembly, and

    (iii) the Auditor General for Wales, and

(f) confirming that the Assembly has complied with or is to comply with the requirements imposed by subsection (4) with respect to the issue of certificates under this section.]

[(3) The requirement specified in this subsection is that the Assembly must have secured that the certificate issued by it is signed by the Assembly First Secretary or on his behalf pursuant to section 63 of the Government of Wales Act 1998 (exercise of functions by the Assembly staff).]

(4) The requirement specified in this subsection is that [the Assembly] must have obtained consent to the issue of a certificate under this section from each of the persons with whom [the Assembly] has entered, or is to enter, into the contract.

Certified contracts: supplementary

4.—(1) Where the certification requirements have been satisfied in relation to a contract by a local authority, the certificate which has been issued shall have effect (and be deemed always to have had effect) as if the local authority had had power to issue it (and had exercised that power properly in issuing it); and a certificate which has been so issued is not invalidated by reason that anything in the certificate is inaccurate or untrue.

87–005

(2) Where the certification requirements have been satisfied in relation to a contract by a local authority within section 1(3)(a) or (d), the local authority shall secure that throughout the period for which the contract operates—

    (a) a copy of the certificate which has been issued is open to inspection by members of the public at all reasonable times without payment, and

    (b) members of the public are afforded facilities for obtaining copies of that certificate on payment of a reasonable fee.

(3) A contract entered into by a local authority falls within this subsection if—

    (a) it is entered into with another person for the provision or making available of services (whether or not together with assets or goods) for the purposes of, or in connection with, the discharge by the local authority of any of its functions, and

    (b) it operates, or is intended to operate, for a period of at least five years.

(4) A contract entered into by a local authority falls within this subsection if it is entered into, in connection with a contract falling within subsection (3), with—

    (a) a person who, in connection with that contract, makes a loan to, or provides any other form of finance for, a party to that contract other than the local authority, or

    (b) any insurer of or trustee for such a person.

(5) Regulations may be made amending subsection (3) or (4).[¹]

[¹] In relation to contracts entered into by the National Assembly for Wales on or after, July 1, 1999, s. 4 reads:

Certified contracts: supplementary

4.—(1) Where the certification requirements have been satisfied in relation to a contract by the Assembly, the certificate which has been issued shall have effect (and be deemed always to have had effect) as if the Assembly had had power to issue it (and had exercised that power properly in issuing it); and a certificate which has been so issued is not invalidated by reason that anything in the certificate is inaccurate or untrue.

(2) Where the certification requirements have been satisfied [by it in relation to a contract, the Assembly] shall secure that throughout the period for which the contract operates—

(a) a copy of the certificate which has been issued is open to inspection by members of the public at all reasonable times without payment, and

(b) members of the public are afforded facilities for obtaining copies of that certificate on payment of a reasonable fee.

(3) A contract entered into by [the Assembly] falls within this subsection if—

(a) it is entered into with another person for the provision or making available of services (whether or not together with assets or goods) for the purposes of, or in connection with, the discharge by [the Assembly] of any of its functions, and

(b) it operates, or is intended to operate, for a period of at least five years.

(4) A contract entered into by [the Assembly][¹] falls within this subsection if it is entered into, in connection with a contract falling within subsection (3), with—

(a) a person who, in connection with that contract, makes a loan to, or provides any other form of finance for, a party to that contract other than [the Assembly], or

(b) any insurer of or trustee for such a person.

Special provision for judicial reviews and audit reviews

87–006   **5.**—(1) Section 2(1) does not apply for the purposes of determining any question arising on

(a) an application for judicial review, or

(b) an audit review.

as to whether a local authority had power to enter into a contract (or exercised any power properly in entering into a contract).

(2) Section 2(1) has effect subject to any determination or order made in relation to a certified contract on—

(a) an application for judicial review, or

(b) an audit review.

(3) Where, on an application for judicial review or an audit review relating to a certified contract entered into by a local authority, a court—

(a) is of the opinion that the local authority did not have power to enter into the contract (or exercised any power improperly in entering into it), but

(b) (having regard in particular to the likely consequences for the financial position of the local authority, and for the provision of services to the public, of a decision that the contract should not have effect) considers that the contract should have effect,

the court may determine that the contract has (and always has had) effect as if the local authority had had power to enter into it (and had exercised that power properly in entering into it).

(4) In this section and sections 6 and 7 references to an application for judicial review include any appeal (or further appeal) against a determination or order made on such an application.[¹]

---

¹ In relation to contracts entered into by the National Assembly for Wales on or after July 1, 1999, s. 5 reads:

Special provision for judicial reviews and audit reviews

5.—(1) Section 2(1) does not apply for the purposes of determining any question arising on [an application for judicial review as to whether the Assembly had power to enter into a contract (or exercised any power properly in entering into a contract).]

(2) Section 2(1) has effect subject to any determination or order made in relation to a certified contract on [an application for judicial review.]

(3) Where, on an application for judicial review relating to a certified contract entered into by [the Assembly], a court—

(a) is of the opinion that [the Assembly] did not have power to enter into the contract (or exercised any power improperly in entering into it), but
(b) (having regard in particular to the likely consequences for the financial position of [the Assembly], and for the provision of services to the public, of a decision that the contract should not have effect) considers that the contract should have effect,

the court may determine that the contract has (and always has had) effect as if [the Assembly] had had power to enter into it (and had exercised that power properly in entering into it).

(4) In this section and sections 6 and 7 references to an application for judicial review include any appeal (or further appeal) against a determination or order made on such an application[and include a reference of a devolution issue under Schedule 8 to the Government of Wales Act 1998].

Relevant discharge terms

6.—(1) No determination or order made in relation to a certified contract on— **87–007**

(a) an application for judicial review, or
(b) an audit review,

shall affect the enforceability of any relevant discharge terms relating to the contract.

(2) In this section and section 7 "relevant discharge terms", in relation to a contract entered into by a local authority, means terms—

(a) which have been agreed by the local authority and any person with whom the local authority entered into the contract,
(b) which either form part of the contract or constitute or form part of another agreement entered into by them not later than the day on which the contract was entered into, and
(c) which provide for a consequence mentioned in subsection (3) to ensue in the event of the making of a determination or order in relation to the contract on an application for judicial review or an audit review.

(3) Those consequences are—

(a) the payment of compensatory damages (measured by reference to loss incurred or loss of profits or to any other circumstances) by one of the parties to the other,
(b) the adjustment between the parties of rights and liabilities relating to any assets or goods provided or made available under the contract, or
(c) both of those things.

(4) Where a local authority has agreed relevant discharge terms with any person with whom it has entered into a contract and the contract is a certified contract, the relevant discharge terms shall have effect (and be deemed always to have had effect) as if the local authority had had power to agree them (and had exercised that power properly in agreeing them).[1]

[1] In relation to contracts entered into by the National Assembly for Wales on or after, July 1, 1999, s. 6 reads:

Relevant discharge terms

6.—(1) No determination or order made in relation to a certified contract on an application for judicial review shall affect the enforceability of any relevant discharge terms relating to the contract.

(2) In this section and section 7 "relevant discharge terms", in relation to a contract entered into by [the Assembly], means terms—

  (a) which have been agreed by [the Assembly] and any person with whom [the Assembly] entered into the contract,
  (b) which either form part of the contract or constitute or form part of another agreement entered into by them not later than the day on which the contract was entered into, and
  (c) which provide for a consequence mentioned in subsection (3) to ensue in the event of the making of a determination or order in relation to the contract on an application for judicial review.

(3) Those consequences are—

  (a) the payment of compensatory damages (measured by reference to loss incurred or loss of profits or to any other circumstances) by one of the parties to the other,
  (b) the adjustment between the parties of rights and liabilities relating to any assets or goods provided or made available under the contract, or
  (c) both of those things.

(4) Where [the Assembly] has agreed relevant discharge terms with any person with whom it has entered into a contract and the contract is a certified contract, the relevant discharge terms shall have effect (and be deemed always to have had effect) as if [the Assembly] had had power to agree them (and had exercised that power properly in agreeing them).

Absence of relevant discharge terms

87–008 **7.**—(1) Subsection (2) applies where—

  (a) the result of a determination or order made by a court on an application for judicial review or an audit review is that a certified contract does not have effect, and
  (b) there are no relevant discharge terms having effect between the local authority and a person who is a party to the contract.

(2) That person shall be entitled to be paid by the local authority such sums (if any) as he would have been entitled to be paid by the local authority if the contract—

  (a) had had effect until the time when the determination or order was made, but
  (b) had been terminated at that time by acceptance by him of a repudiatory breach by the local authority.

(3) For the purposes of this section the circumstances in which there are no relevant discharge terms having effect between the local authority and a person who is a party to the contract include (as well as circumstances in which no such terms have been agreed) circumstances in which the result of a determination or order of a court, made (despite section 6(4)) on an application for judicial review or an audit review, is that such terms do not have effect.[1]

¹ In relation to contracts entered into by the National Assembly for Wales on or after, July 1, 1999, s. 7 reads:

Absence of relevant discharge terms

7.—(1) Subsection (2) applies where—

(a) the result of a determination or order made by a court on an application for judicial review is that a certified contract does not have effect, and

(b) there are no relevant discharge terms having effect between [the Assembly] and a person who is a party to the contract.

(2) That person shall be entitled to be paid by [the Assembly] such sums (if any) as he would have been entitled to be paid by [the Assembly] if the contract—

(a) had had effect until the time when the determination or order was made, but

(b) had been terminated at that time by acceptance by him of a repudiatory breach by [the Assembly].

(3) For the purposes of this section the circumstances in which there are no relevant discharge terms having effect between [the Assembly] and a person who is a party to the contract include (as well as circumstances in which no such terms have been agreed) circumstances in which the result of a determination or order of a court, made (despite section 6(4)) on an application for judicial review, is that such terms do not have effect.

National Health Service (Private Finance) Act 1997

(1997, c. 56)

An Act to make provision about the powers of National Health Service trusts to   **88–001**
enter into agreements.   [15th July 1997]

Powers of NHS trusts to enter into agreements

1.—(1) The powers of a National Health Service trust include power to enter   **88–002**
into externally financed development agreements.

(2) For the purposes of this section, an agreement is an externally financed development agreement if it is certified as such in writing by the Secretary of State.

(3) The Secretary of State may give a certificate under this section if—

(a) in his opinion the purpose or main purpose of the agreement is the provision of facilities in connection with the discharge by the trust of any of its functions; and

(b) a person proposes to make a loan to, or provide any other form of finance for, another Party in connection with the agreement.

(4) If a National Health Service trust enters into an externally financed development agreement it may also, in connection with that agreement, enter into an agreement with a person who falls within subsection (3)(b) in relation to the externally financed development agreement.

(5) In subsection (3)—

"another Party" means any Party to the agreement other than the trust; and
"facilities" includes—

(a) works, buildings, plant, equipment or other property; and

(b) services.

(6) The fact that an agreement made by a National Health Service trust has not been certified under this section does not affect its validity.

Northern Ireland Arms Decommissioning Act 1997

(1997, c. 7)

89–001   *An Act to make provision connected with Northern Ireland about the decommissioning of firearms, ammunition and explosives; and for connected purposes.*   [27th February 1997]

Decommissioning scheme

89–002   1.—(1) In this Act a "decommissioning scheme"is any scheme which—

    (a) is made by the Secretary of State to facilitate the decommissioning of firearms, ammunition and explosives in Northern Ireland, and

    (b) includes provisions satisfying the requirements of sections 2 and 3 (whether or not it also includes other provisions).

(2) Section 2 of the Documentary Evidence Act 1868 (mode of proving certain documents) shall apply to a decommissioning scheme.

Duration of decommissioning scheme

89–003   2.—(1) A decommissioning scheme must identify a period during which firearms, ammunition and explosives may be dealt with in accordance with the scheme ("the amnesty period").

(2) The amnesty period must end before—

    (a) the first anniversary of the day on which this Act is passed, or

    (b) such later day as the Secretary of State may by order from time to time appoint.

(3) A day appointed by an order under subsection (2)(b) must not be—

    (a) more than twelve months after the day on which the order is made, or

    (b) more than five years after the day on which this Act is passed.

(4) An order under subsection (2)(b) shall be made by statutory instrument; and no order shall be made unless a draft has been laid before, and approved by resolution of, each House of Parliament.

Methods of decommissioning

89–004   3.—(1) A decommissioning scheme must make provision for one or more of the following ways of dealing with firearms, ammunition and explosives (and may make provision for others)—

(a) transfer to the Commission mentioned in section 7, or to a designated person, for destruction;

(b) depositing for collection and destruction by the Commission or a designated person;

(c) provision of information for the purpose of collection and destruction by the Commission or a designated person;

(d) destruction by persons in unlawful possession.

(2) In subsection (1)"designated person" means a person designated by the Secretary of State or, in the case of firearms, ammunition or explosives transferred or collected in the Republic of Ireland, a person designated by the Minister for Justice of the Republic.

Amnesty

4.—(1) No proceedings shall be brought for an offence listed in the Schedule to this Act in respect of anything done in accordance with a decommissioning scheme.   **89–005**

(2) The Secretary of State may by order add any offence or description of offence to, or remove any offence or description of offence from, the list in the Schedule to this Act.

(3) An order under subsection (2)—

(a) shall be made by statutory instrument, and

(b) may include such transitional provisions as appear to the Secretary of State to be expedient.

(4) No order shall be made under subsection (2) unless a draft has been laid before, and approved by resolution of, each House of Parliament.

Evidence

5.—(1) A decommissioned article, or information derived from it, shall not be admissible in evidence in criminal proceedings.   **89–006**

(2) Evidence of anything done, and of any information obtained, in accordance with a decommissioning scheme shall not be admissible in criminal proceedings.

(3) Subsections (1) and (2) shall not apply to the admission of evidence adduced in criminal proceedings on behalf of the accused.

(4) Subsection (1) shall not apply to proceedings for an offence alleged to have been committed by the use of, or in relation to, something which was a decommissioned article at the time when the offence is alleged to have been committed.

Testing decommissioned articles

6.—(1) A person who has received a decommissioned article shall not carry out, or cause or permit anyone else to carry out, a test or procedure in relation to the article the purpose of which is—   **89–007**

(a) to discover information about anything done with or in relation to any decommissioned article,

(b) to discover who has been in contact with, or near to, any decommissioned article,

(c) to discover where any decommissioned article was at any time (including the conditions under which it was kept),

(d) to discover when any decommissioned article was in contact with, or near to, a particular person or when it was in a particular place or kept under particular conditions,

(e) to discover when or where any decommissioned article was made, or

(f) to discover the composition of any decommissioned article.

(2) Subsection (1)(f) does not prohibit a test or procedure the purpose of which is—

(a) to determine whether an article is, or contains, an explosive or ammunition,

(b) to determine the quantity of explosive or ammunition present, or

(c) to determine whether an article can safely be moved or otherwise dealt with.

(3) Subsection (1) does not prohibit a test or procedure the purpose of which is to discover information in relation to a decommissioned article where the information—

(a) is sought for the purposes of the investigation of an offence alleged to have been committed at a time after the article became a decommissioned article, and

(b) does not concern the treatment of the article in accordance with a decommissioning scheme.

The Commission

89–008   **7.**—(1) In this section"the Commission" means an independent organisation established by an agreement, made in connection with the affairs of Northern Ireland between Her Majesty's Government in the United Kingdom and the Government of the Republic of Ireland, to facilitate the decommissioning of firearms, ammunition and explosives.

(2) The Secretary of State may be order—

(a) confer on the Commission the legal capacities of a body corporate;

(b) confer on the Commission, in such cases, to such extent and with such modifications as the order may specify, any of the privileges and immunities set out in Part I of Schedule 1 to the International Organisations Act 1968;

(c) confer on members and servants of the Commission and members of their families who form part of their households, in such cases, to such extent and with such modifications as the order may specify any of the privileges and immunities set out in Parts II, III and V of that Schedule;

(d) make provision about the waiver of privileges and immunities.

In this subsection "servants of the Commission"includes agents of, and persons carrying out work for or giving advice to, the Commission.

(3) An order under subsection (2)—

(a) may make different provision for different cases (including different provision for different persons);

(b) shall be made by statutory instrument which shall be subject to annulment in pursuance of a resolution of either House of Parliament.

(4) The Secretary of State may—

(a) make payments to the Commission or to members of the Commission;

(b) provide for the Commission such premises and facilities, and the services of such staff, as he thinks appropriate.

(5) This section shall come into force on such day as the Secretary of State, after consulting the Minister for Justice of the Republic of Ireland, may by order made by statutory instrument appoint.

(6) This section shall cease to have effect at the end of such day as the Secretary of State, after consulting the Minister for Justice of the Republic of Ireland, may by order made by statutory instrument appoint; and an order under this subsection may include such transitional provisions as appear to the Secretary of State to be expedient.

Arms in England and Wales and Scotland

8.—(1) This section applies to any scheme which— **89–009**

    (a) is made by the Secretary of State, for purposes relating to the affairs of Northern Ireland, to facilitate the decommissioning of firearms, ammunition and explosives in England and Wales or in Scotland, and

    (b) includes provisions satisfying the requirements of section 2 and 3 (whether or not it also includes other provisions).

(2) The Secretary of State may by order provide that a scheme to which this section applies shall be a decommissioning scheme for the purposes of this Act.

(3) In relation to a scheme which is a decommissioning scheme by virtue of subsection (2), the Schedule to this Act shall have effect with the substitution for any offence under the law of Northern Ireland of such similar offence under the law of England and Wales, or as the case may be of Scotland, as the Secretary of State may specify by order.

(4) An order under this section shall be made by statutory instrument; and no order shall be made unless a draft has been laid before, and approved by resolution of, each House of Parliament.

Expenses

9. Any expenses incurred by the Secretary of State in connection with a **89–010** decommissioning scheme or under section 7(4) shall be paid out of money provided by Parliament.

Interpretation

10.—(1) In this Act— **89–011**

"ammunition" means anything which is—

    (a) ammunition within the meaning of the Firearms (Northern Ireland) Order 1981, or

    (b) a component of such ammunition;

"decommissioned article" means—

    (a) anything which has been transferred, deposited or collected in accordance with a decommissioning scheme,

    (b) anything found on or in, or received with, something falling within paragraph (a), and

    (c) a part of, or thing derived from, something falling within paragraph (a) or (b);

"destruction"includes making permanently inaccessible or permanently unusable;

"firearm" means anything which—

(a) is a firearm within the meaning of the Firearms (Northern Ireland) Order 1981,

(b) is an accessory to such a firearm,

(c) is a weapon designed or adapted for the discharge of any thing, or

(d) has the appearance of being one of the things described in paragraphs (a) to (c);

"explosive" means anything which is—

(a) an explosive within the meaning of the Explosives Act 1875, or

(b) an explosive substance within the meaning of the Explosive Substances Act 1883.

(2) In this Act, references to things done in accordance with a decommissioning scheme include references to things done in accordance with arrangements provided for by a scheme.

Police Act 1997

(1997, c. 50)

90–001 *An Act to make provision for the National Criminal Intelligence Service and the National Crime Squad; to make provision about entry on and interference with property and with wireless telegraphy in the course of the prevention or detection of serious crime; to make provision for the Police Information Technology Organisation; to provide for the issue of certificates about criminal records; to make provision about the administration and organisation of the police; to repeal certain enactments about rehabilitation of offenders; and for connected purposes.* [21st March 1997]

. . . . . .

Part III

Authorisation of Action in Respect of Property

The Commissioners

The Commissioners

90–002 **91.**—(1) The Prime Minister, [after consultation with the Scottish Ministers,] shall appoint for the purposes of this Part—

(a) a Chief Commissioner, and

(b) such number of other Commissioners as the Prime Minister thinks fit.

(2) The persons appointed under subsection (1) shall be persons who hold or have held high judicial office within the meaning of the Appellate Jurisdiction Act 1876.

(3) Subject to subsections (4) to (7), each Commissioner shall hold and vacate office in accordance with the terms of his appointment.

(4) Each Commissioner shall be appointed for a term of three years.

(5) A person who ceases to be a Commissioner (otherwise than under subsection (7)) may be reappointed under this section.

[(6) Subject to subsection (7), a Commissioner shall not be removed from office before the end of the term for which he is appointed unless—

    (a) a resolution approving his removal has been passed by each House of Parliament; and

    (b) a resolution approving his removal has been passed by the Scottish Parliament.]

(7) A Commissioner may be removed from office by the Prime Minister if after his appointment—

    (a) a bankruptcy order is made against him or his estate is sequestrated or he makes a composition or arrangement with, or grants a trust deed for, his creditors;

    (b) a disqualification order under the Company Directors Disqualification Act 1986 or Part II of the Companies (Northern Ireland) Order 1989, or an order under section 429(2)(b) of the Insolvency Act 1986 (failure to pay under county court administration order), is made against him[or his disqualification undertaking is accepted under section 7 or 8 of the Company Directors Disqualification Act 1986][1]; or

    (c) he is convicted in the United Kingdom, the Channel Islands or the Isle of Man of an offence and has passed on him a sentence of imprisonment (whether suspended or not).

(8) The Secretary of State shall pay to each Commissioner [, other than a Commissioner carrying out functions as mentioned in subsection (8A),] such allowances as the Secretary of State considers appropriate.

[(8A) The Scottish Ministers shall pay to any Commissioner who carries out his functions under this Part wholly or mainly in Scotland such allowances as the Scottish Ministers consider appropriate.]

(9) The Secretary of State shall, after consultation with the Chief Commissioner [and subject to the approval of the Treasury as to numbers][2], provide the Commissioners [[and any Assistant Surveillance Commissioners holding office under section 63 of the Regulation of Investigatory Powers Act 2000][3], other than any Commissioner carrying out functions as mentioned in subsection (9A),] with such staff as the Secretary of State considers necessary for the discharge of their functions.

[(9A) The Scottish Ministers shall, after consultation with the Chief Commissioner, provide any Commissioner who carries out his functions under this Part wholly or mainly in Scotland with such staff as the Scottish Ministers consider necessary for the discharge of his functions.]

(10) The decisions of the Chief Commissioner or, subject to sections 104 and 106, any other Commissioner (including decisions as to his jurisdiction) shall not be subject to appeal or liable to be questioned in any court.

[1] Words inserted by Insolvency Act 2000 (c.39), Sched. 4, Pt II, para. 22(2).
[2] Words added by Regulation of Investigatory Powers Act 2000 (c.23), Sched. 4, para. 8(1)(a).
[3] Words added by Regulation of Investigatory Powers Act 2000 (c.23), Sched. 4, para. 8(1)(b).

Effect of authorisation under Part III

90–003 **92.** No entry on or interference with property or with wireless telegraphy shall be unlawful if it is authorised by an authorisation having effect under this Part.

Authorisations to interfere with property, etc.

90–004 **93.**—(1) Where subsection (2) applies, an authorising officer may authorise—

  (a) the taking of such action, in respect of such property in the relevant area, as he may specify, or
  (b) the taking of such action in the relevant area as he may specify, in respect of wireless telegraphy.

(2) This subsection applies where the authorising officer believes—

  (a) that it is necessary for the action specified to be taken on the ground that it is likely to be of substantial value in the prevention or detection of serious crime, and
  (b) that what the action seeks to achieve cannot reasonably be achieved by other means.

(3) An authorising officer shall not give an authorisation under this section except on an application made—

  (a) if the authorising officer is within subsection (5)(a) to [(ea) or (ee)]¹, by a member of his police force,
  [(aa) if the authorising officer is within subsection (5) (eb) to (ed), by a member, as the case may be, of the Royal Navy Regulating Branch, the Royal Military Police or the Royal Air Force Police;]²
  (b) if the authorising officer is within subsection (5)(f), by a member of the National Criminal Intelligence Service,
  (c) if the authorising officer is within subsection (5)(g), by a member of the National Crime Squad, or
  (d) if the authorising officer is within subsection (5)(h), by a customs officer.

(4) For the purposes of subsection (2), conduct which constitutes one or more offences shall be regarded as serious crime if, and only if,—

  (a) it involves the use of violence, results in substantial financial gain or is conduct by a large number of persons in pursuit of a common purpose, or
  (b) the offence or one of the offences is an offence for which a person who has attained the age of twenty-one and has no previous convictions could reasonably be expected to be sentenced to imprisonment for a term of three years or more,

and, where the authorising officer is within subsection (5)(h), it relates to an assigned matter within the meaning of section 1(1) of the Customs and Excise Management Act 1979.

(5) In this section "authorising officer" means —

  (a) the chief constable of a police force maintained under section 2 of the

Police Act 1996 (maintenance of police forces for areas in England and Wales except London);

(b) the Commissioner, or an Assistant Commissioner, of Police of the Metropolis;

(c) the Commissioner of Police for the City of London;

(d) the chief constable of a police force maintained under or by virtue of section 1 of the Police (Scotland) Act 1967 (maintenance of police forces for areas in Scotland);

(e) the Chief Constable or a Deputy Chief Constable of the Royal Ulster Constabulary;

(f) the Director General of the National Criminal Intelligence Service;

(g) the Director General of the National Crime Squad; or

(h) the customs officer designated by the Commissioners of Customs and Excise for the purposes of this paragraph.

(6) In this section "relevant area"—

(a) in relation to a person within paragraph (a), (b) or (c) of subsection (5), means the area in England and Wales for which his police force is maintained;

(b) in relation to a person within paragraph (d) of that subsection means the area in Scotland for which his police force is maintained;

(c) in relation to a person within paragraph (e) of that subsection, means Northern Ireland;

(d) in relation to the Director General of the National Criminal Intelligence Service, means the United Kingdom;

(e) in relation to the Director General of the National Crime Squad, means England and Wales;

and in each case includes the adjacent United Kingdom waters.

(7) The powers conferred by, or by virtue of, this section are additional to any other powers which a person has as a constable either at common law or under or by virtue of any other enactment and are not to be taken to affect any of those other powers.

---

[1] Words substituted by Regulation of Investigatory Powers Act 2000 (c.23), Sched. 4, para. 8(2)(a).
[2] Added by Regulation of Investigatory Powers Act 2000 (c.23), Sched. 4, para. 8(2)(b).

Authorisations given in absence of authorising officer

94.—(1) Subsection (2) applies where it is not reasonably practicable for an authorising officer to consider an application for an authorisation under section 93 and—   **90–005**

(a) if the authorising officer is within paragraph (b) or (e) of section 93(5), it is also not reasonably practicable for the application to be considered by any of the other persons within the paragraph concerned;

(b) if the authorising officer is within paragraph (a), (c), (d), or (f) of section 93(5), it is also not reasonably practicable for the application to be considered by his designated deputy; or

(c) if the authorising officer is within paragraph (g) of section 93(5), it is also not reasonably practicable for the application to be considered either—

(i) by any other person designated for the purposes of that paragraph; or

(ii) by the designated deputy of the Director General of the National Crime Squad.

(2) Where this subsection applies, the powers conferred on the authorising officer by section 93 may, in an urgent case, be exercised—

(a) where the authorising officer is within paragraph (a) or (d) of subsection (5) of that section, by a person holding the rank of assistant chief constable in his force;

(b) where the authorising officer is within paragraph (b) of that subsection, by a person holding the rank of commander in the metropolitan police force;

(c) where the authorising officer is within paragraph (c) of that subsection, by a person holding the rank of commander in the City of London police force;

(d) where the authorising officer is within paragraph (e) of that subsection, by a person holding the rank of assistant chief constable in the Royal Ulster Constabulary;

(da) where the authorising officer is within paragraph (ea) of that subsection, by a person holding the rank of deputy or assistant chief constable in the Ministry of Defence Police;

(db) where the authorising officer is within paragraph (eb) of that subsection, by a person holding the position of assistant Provost Marshal in the Royal Navy Regulating Branch;

(dc) where the authorising officer is within paragraph (ec) or (ed) of that subsection, by a person holding the position of deputy Provost Marshal in the Royal Military Police or, as the case may be, in the Royal Air Force Police;

(dd) where the authorising officer is within paragraph (ee) of that subsection, by a person holding the rank of deputy or assistant chief constable in the British Transport Police;

(e) where the authorising officer is within paragraph (f) of that subsection by a person designated for the purposes of this section by the Director General of the National Criminal Intelligence Service;

(ea) where the authorising officer is within paragraph (g) of that subsection, by a person designated for the purposes of this paragraph by the Director General of the National Crime Squad as a person entitled to act in an urgent case;

(f) where the authorising officer is within paragraph (h) of that subsection, by a customs officer designated by the Commissioners of Customs and Excise for the purposes of this section.

(3) A police member of the National Criminal Intelligence Service or the National Crime Squad appointed under section 9(1)(b) or 55(1)(b) may not be designated under subsection (2)(e) [or (2)(ea)] unless he holds the rank of assistant chief constable in that Service or Squad.

(4) In subsection (1), "designated deputy"—

(a) in the case of an authorising officer within paragraph (a) or (d) of section 93(5), means the person holding the rank of assistant chief constable designated to act under section 12(4) of the Police Act 1996 or, as the case may be, section 5(4) of the Police (Scotland) Act 1967;

(b) in the case of an authorising officer within paragraph (c) of section 93(5), means the person authorised to act under section 25 of the City of London Police Act 1839;

(c) in the case of an authorising officer within paragraph (f) or (g) of section 93(5), means the person designated to act under section 8 or 54.

Authorisations: form and duration, etc.

95.—(1) An authorisation shall be in writing, except that in an urgent case an **90–006** authorisation (other than one given by virtue of section 94) may be given orally.

(2) An authorisation shall, unless renewed under subsection (3), cease to have effect—

  (a) if given orally or by virtue of section 94, at the end of the period of 72 hours beginning with the time when it took effect;
  (b) in any other case, at the end of the period of three months beginning with the day on which it took effect.

(3) If at any time before an authorisation would cease to have effect the authorising officer who gave the authorisation, or in whose absence it was given, considers it necessary for the authorisation to continue to have effect for the purpose for which it was issued, he may, in writing, renew it for a period of three months beginning with the day on which it would cease to have effect.

(4) A person shall cancel an authorisation given by him if satisfied that [the authorisation is one in relation to which the requirements of paragraphs (a) and (b) of section 93(2) are no longer satisfied.]

(5) An authorising officer shall cancel an authorisation given in his absence if satisfied that [the authorisation is one in relation to which the requirements of paragraphs (a) and (b) of section 93(2) are no longer satisfied.]

(6) If the authorising officer who gave the authorisation is within [paragraph (b) or (e), or (g) of section 93(5)], the power conferred on that person by subsections (3) and (4) above shall also be exercisable by each of the other persons within the paragraph concerned.

(7) Nothing in this section shall prevent a designated deputy from exercising the powers conferred on an authorising officer within paragraph (a), (c), (d), (f) or (g) of section 93(5) by subsections (3), (4) and (5) above.

Notification of authorisations, etc.

96.—(1) Where a person gives, renews or cancels an authorisation, he shall, **90–007** as soon as is reasonably practicable and in accordance with arrangements made by the Chief Commissioner, give notice in writing that he has done so to a Commissioner appointed under section 91(1)(b).

(2) Subject to subsection (3), a notice under this section shall specify such matters as the Secretary of State may by order prescribe.

(3) A notice under this section of the giving or renewal of an authorisation shall specify—

  (a) whether section 97 applies to the authorisation or renewal, and
  (b) where that section does not apply by virtue of subsection (3) of that section, the grounds on which the case is believed to be one of urgency.

(4) Where a notice is given to a Commissioner under this section, he shall, as soon as is reasonably practicable, scrutinise the notice.

(5) An order under subsection (2) shall be made by statutory instrument.

(6) A statutory instrument which contains an order under subsection (2) shall not be made unless a draft has been laid before, and approved by a resolution of, each House of Parliament.

Authorisations requiring approval

90–008   **97.**—(1) An authorisation to which this section applies shall not take effect until—

> (a) it has been approved in accordance with this section by a Commissioner appointed under section 91(1)(b), and
> (b) the person who gave the authorisation has been notified under subsection (4).

(2) Subject to subsection (3), this section applies to an authorisation if, at the time it is given, the person who gives it believes—

> (a) that any of the property specified in the authorisation—
>
>> (i) is used wholly or mainly as a dwelling or as a bedroom in a hotel, or
>> (ii) constitutes office premises, or
>
> (b) that the action authorised by it is likely to result in any person acquiring knowledge of—
>
>> (i) matters subject to legal privilege,
>> (ii) confidential personal information, or
>> (iii) confidential journalistic material.

(3) This section does not apply to an authorisation where the person who gives it believes that the case is one of urgency.

(4) Where a Commissioner receives a notice under section 96 which specifies that this section applies to the authorisation, he shall as soon as is reasonably practicable—

> (a) decide whether to approve the authorisation or refuse approval, and
> (b) give written notice of his decision to the person who gave the authorisation.

(5) A Commissioner shall approve an authorisation if, and only if, he is satisfied that there are reasonable grounds for believing the matters specified in section 93(2).

(6) Where a Commissioner refuses to approve an authorisation, he shall, as soon as is reasonably practicable, make a report of his findings to the authorising officer who gave it or in whose absence it was given.

[(6A) The reference in subsection (6) to the authorising officer who gave the authorisation or in whose absence it was given shall be construed, in the case of an authorisation given by or in the absence of a person within paragraph (b), (e) or (g) of section 93(5), as a reference to the Commissioner of Police, Chief Constable or, as the case may be, Director General mentioned in the paragraph concerned.]¹

(7) This section shall apply in relation to a renewal of an authorisation as it applies in relation to an authorisation (the references in subsection (2)(a) and (b) to the authorisation being construed as references to the authorisation renewed).

(8) In this section—

> "office premises" has the meaning given in section 1(2) of the Offices, Shops and Railway Premises Act 1963;

"hotel" means premises used for the reception of guests who desire to sleep in the premises.

¹ Added by Regulation of Investigatory Powers Act 2000 (c.23), Sched. 4, para. 8(7).

Matters subject to legal privilege

98.—(1) Subject to subsection (5) below, in section 97 "matters subject to legal privilege" means matters to which subsection (2), (3) or (4) below applies.

    (2) This subsection applies to communications between a professional legal adviser and—

    (a) his client, or
    (b) any person representing his client,

which are made in connection with the giving of legal advice to the client.

    (3) This subsection applies to communications—

    (a) between a professional legal adviser and his client or any person representing his client, or
    (b) between a professional legal adviser or his client or any such representative and any other person,

which are made in connection with or in contemplation of legal proceedings and for the purposes of such proceedings.

    (4) This subsection applies to items enclosed with or referred to in communications of the kind mentioned in subsection (2) or (3) and made—

    (a) in connection with the giving of legal advice, or
    (b) in connection with or in contemplation of legal proceedings and for the purposes of such proceedings.

    (5) For the purposes of section 97—

    (a) communications and items are not matters subject to legal privilege when they are in the possession of a person who is not entitled to possession of them, and
    (b) communications and items held, or oral communications made, with the intention of furthering a criminal purpose are not matters subject to legal privilege.

90–009

Confidential personal information

99.—(1) In section 97 "confidential personal information" means—

    (a) personal information which a person has acquired or created in the course of any trade, business, profession or other occupation or for the purposes of any paid or unpaid office, and which he holds in confidence, and
    (b) communications as a result of which personal information—

      (i) is acquired or created as mentioned in paragraph (a), and
      (ii) is held in confidence.

    (2) For the purposes of this section "personal information" means information concerning an individual (whether living or dead) who can be identified from it and relating—

90–010

(a) to his physical or mental health, or

(b) to spiritual counselling or assistance given or to be given to him.

(3) A person holds information in confidence for the purposes of this section if he holds it subject—

(a) to an express or implied undertaking to hold it in confidence, or

(b) to a restriction on disclosure or an obligation of secrecy contained in any enactment (including an enactment contained in an Act passed after this Act).

Confidential journalistic material

90–011   **100.**—(1) In section 97 "confidential journalistic material" means —

(a) material acquired or created for the purposes of journalism which—

   (i) is in the possession of persons who acquired or created it for those purposes,

   (ii) is held subject to an undertaking, restriction or obligation of the kind mentioned in section 99(3), and

   (iii) has been continuously held (by one or more persons) subject to such an undertaking, restriction or obligation since it was first acquired or created for the purposes of journalism, and

(b) communications as a result of which information is acquired for the purposes of journalism and held as mentioned in paragraph (a)(ii).

(2) For the purposes of subsection (1), a person who receives material, or acquires information, from someone who intends that the recipient shall use it for the purposes of journalism is to be taken to have acquired it for those purposes.

. . . . . .

Complaints, etc.

Quashing of authorisations, etc.

90–012   **103.**—(1) Where, at any time, a Commissioner appointed under section 91(1)(b) is satisfied that, at the time an authorisation was given or renewed, there were no reasonable grounds for believing the matters specified in section 93(2), he may quash the authorisation or, as the case may be, renewal.

(2) Where, in the case of an authorisation or renewal to which section 97 does not apply, a Commissioner appointed under section 91(1)(b) is at any time satisfied that, at the time the authorisation was given or, as the case may be, renewed,—

(a) there were reasonable grounds for believing any of the matters specified in subsection (2) of section 97, and

(b) there were no reasonable grounds for believing the case to be one of urgency for the purposes of subsection (3) of that section,

he may quash the authorisation or, as the case may be, renewal.

(3) Where a Commissioner quashes an authorisation or renewal under subsection (1) or (2), he may order the destruction of any records relating to information obtained by virtue of the authorisation (or, in the case of a renewal, relating

wholly or partly to information so obtained after the renewal) other than records required for pending criminal or civil proceedings.

(4) If a Commissioner appointed under section 91(1)(b) is satisfied that, at any time after an authorisation was given or, in the case of an authorisation renewed under section 95, after it was renewed, there were no reasonable grounds for believing the matters specified in section 93(2), he may cancel the authorisation.

(5) Where—

(a) an authorisation has ceased to have effect (otherwise than by virtue of subsection (1) or (2)), and

(b) a Commissioner appointed under section 91(1)(b) is satisfied that, at any time during the period of the authorisation, there were no reasonable grounds for believing the matters specified in section 93(2),

he may order the destruction of any records relating, wholly or partly, to information which was obtained by virtue of the authorisation after that time (other than records required for pending criminal or civil proceedings).

(6) Where a Commissioner exercises his powers under subsection (1), (2) or (4), he shall, if he is satisfied that there are reasonable grounds for doing so, order that the authorisation shall be effective, for such period as he shall specify, so far as it authorises the taking of action to retrieve anything left on property in accordance with the authorisation.

(7) Where a Commissioner exercises a power conferred by this section, he shall, as soon as is reasonably practicable, make a report of his findings—

(a) to the authorising officer who gave the authorisation or in whose absence it was given, and

(b) to the Chief Commissioner;

[and subsection (6A) of section 97 shall apply for the purposes of this subsection as it applies for the purposes of subsection (6) of that section.][1]

(8) Where—

(a) a decision is made under subsection (1) or (2) and an order for the destruction of records is made under subsection (3), or

(b) a decision to order the destruction of records is made under subsection (5),

the order shall not become operative until the period for appealing against the decision has expired and, where an appeal is made, a decision dismissing it has been made by the Chief Commissioner.

(9) A Commissioner may exercise any of the powers conferred by this section notwithstanding any approval given under section 97.

[1] Words substituted by Regulation of Investigatory Powers Act 2000 (c.23), Sched. 4, para. 8(8).

Appeals

Appeals by authorising officers

104.—(1) An authorising officer who gives an authorisation, or in whose **90–013** absence it is given, may, within the prescribed period, appeal to the Chief Commissioner against—

(a) any refusal to approve the authorisation or any renewal of it under section 97;

(b) any decision to quash the authorisation, or any renewal of it, under sub-section (1) of section 103;

(c) any decision to quash the authorisation, or any renewal of it, under subsection (2) of that section;

(d) any decision to cancel the authorisation under subsection (4) of that section;

(e) any decision to order the destruction of records under subsection (5)of that section;

(f) any refusal to make an order under subsection (6) of that section;

(2) In subsection (1), "the prescribed period" means the period of seven days beginning with the day on which the refusal, decision or, as the case may be, determination appealed against is reported to the authorising officer.

(3) In determining an appeal within subsection (1)(a), the Chief Commissioner shall, if he is satisfied that there are reasonable grounds for believing the matters specified in section 93(2), allow the appeal and direct the Commissioner to approve the authorisation or renewal under that section.

(4) In determining—

(a) an appeal within subsection (1)(b),

the Chief Commissioner shall allow the appeal unless he is satisfied that, at the time the authorisation was given or, as the case may be, renewed there were no reasonable grounds for believing the matters specified in section 93(2).

(5) In determining—

(a) an appeal within subsection (1)(c),

the Chief Commissioner shall allow the appeal unless he is satisfied as mentioned in section 103(2).

(6) In determining—

(a) an appeal within subsection (1)(d) or (e),

the Chief Commissioner shall allow the appeal unless he is satisfied that at the time to which the decision relates there were no reasonable grounds for believing the matters specified in section 93(2).

(7) In determining an appeal within subsection (1)(f), the Chief Commissioner shall allow the appeal and order that the authorisation shall be effective to the extent mentioned in section 103(6), for such period as he shall specify, if he is satisfied that there are reasonable grounds for making such an order.

(8) Where an appeal is allowed under this section, the Chief Commissioner shall—

(a) in the case of an appeal within subsection (1)(b) or (c), also quash any order made by the Commissioner to destroy records relating to information obtained by virtue of the authorisation concerned.

. . . . . .

General

Supplementary provisions relating to Commissioners

90–014   **107.**—(1) The Chief Commissioner shall keep under review the performance of functions under this Part.

(2) The Chief Commissioner shall make an annual report on [the matters with which he is concerned][1] to the Prime Minister [and to the Scottish Ministers] and may at any time report to him [or them (as the case may require)] on [anything relating to any of those matters][2].

(3) The Prime Minister shall lay before each House of Parliament a copy of each annual report made by the Chief Commissioner under subsection (2) together with a statement as to whether any matter has been excluded from that copy in pursuance of subsection (4) below.

[(3A) The Scottish Ministers shall lay before the Scottish Parliament a copy of each annual report made by the Chief Commissioner under subsection (2), together with a statement as to whether any matter has been excluded from that copy in pursuance of subsection (4) below.]

(4) The Prime Minister may exclude a matter from the copy of a report as laid before each House of Parliament, if it appears to him, after consultation with the Chief Commissioner [and the Scottish Ministers], that the publication of that matter in the report would be prejudicial to [any of the purposes for which authorisations may be given or granted under this Part of this Act or Part II of the Regulation of Investigatory Powers Act 2000 or under any enactment contained in or made under an Act of the Scottish Parliament which makes provision equivalent to that made by Part II of that Act of 2000 or][3] to the discharge of—

(a) the functions of any police authority,
(b) the functions of the Service Authority for the National Criminal Intelligence Service or the Service Authority for the National Crime Squad, or
(c) the duties of the Commissioners of Customs and Excise.

(5) Any person having functions under this Part, and any person taking action in relation to which an authorisation was given, shall comply with any request of a Commissioner for documents or information required by him for the purpose of enabling him to discharge his functions.

[(5A) It shall be the duty of—

(a) every person by whom, or on whose application, there has been given or granted any authorisation the function of giving or granting which is subject to review by the Chief Commissioner,
(b) every person who has engaged in conduct with the authority of such an authorisation,
(c) every person who holds or has held any office, rank or position with the same public authority as a person falling within paragraph (a),
(d) every person who holds or has held any office, rank or position with any public authority for whose benefit (within the meaning of Part II of the Regulation of Investigatory Powers Act 2000) activities which are or may be subject to any such review have been or may be carried out, and
(e) every person to whom a notice under section 49 of the Regulation of Investigatory Powers Act 2000 (notices imposing a disclosure requirement in respect of information protected by a key) has been given in relation to any information obtained by conduct to which such an authorisation relates,

to disclose or provide to the Chief Commissioner all such documents and information as he may require for the purpose of enabling him to carry out his functions.

(5B) It shall be the duty of every Commissioner to give the tribunal established under section 65 of the Regulation of Investigatory Powers Act 2000 all such assistance (including his opinion as to any issue falling to be determined by that tribunal) as that tribunal may require—

    (a) in connection with the investigation of any matter by that tribunal; or

    (b) otherwise for the purposes of that tribunal's consideration or determination of any matter.

(5C) In this section "public authority" means any public authority within the meaning of section 6 of the Human Rights Act 1998 (acts of public authorities) other than a court or tribunal.][4]

---

[1] Words substituted by Regulation of Investigatory Powers Act 2000 (c.23), Sched. 4, para. 8(10)(a)(i).

[2] Words substituted by Regulation of Investigatory Powers Act 2000 (c.23), Sched. 4, para. 8(10)(a)(ii).

[3] Words substituted by Regulation of Investigatory Powers Act 2000 (c.23), Sched. 4, para. 8(10)(b).

[4] Added by Regulation of Investigatory Powers Act 2000 (c.23), Sched. 4, para. 8(11).

Protection from Harassment Act 1997

(1997, c. 40)

91–001   *An Act to make provision for protecting persons from harassment and similar conduct.*   [21st March 1997]

England and Wales

Prohibition of harassment

91–002   **1.**—(1) A person must not pursue a course of conduct—

    (a) which amounts to harassment of another, and

    (b) which he knows or ought to know amounts to harassment of the other.

(2) For the purposes of this section, the person whose course of conduct is in question ought to know that it amounts to harassment of another if a reasonable person in possession of the same information would think the course of conduct amounted to harassment of the other.

(3) Subsection (1) does not apply to a course of conduct if the person who pursued it shows—

    (a) that it was pursued for the purpose of preventing or detecting crime,

    (b) that it was pursued under any enactment or rule of law or to comply with any condition or requirement imposed by any person under any enactment, or

    (c) that in the particular circumstances the pursuit of the course of conduct was reasonable.

Offence of harassment

91–003   **2.**—(1) A person who pursues a course of conduct in breach of section 1 is guilty of an offence.

(2) A person guilty of an offence under this section is liable on summary conviction to imprisonment for a term not exceeding six months, or a fine not exceeding level 5 on the standard scale, or both.

(3) In section 24(2) of the Police and Criminal Evidence Act 1984 (arrestable offences), after paragraph (m) there is inserted—

> "(n) an offence under section 2 of the Protection from Harassment Act 1997 (harassment)."

Civil remedy

3.—(1) An actual or apprehended breach of section 1 may be the subject of a claim in civil proceedings by the person who is or may be the victim of the course of conduct in question.   **91–004**

(2) On such a claim, damages may be awarded for (among other things) any anxiety caused by the harassment and any financial loss resulting from the harassment.

(3) Where—

(a) in such proceedings the High Court or a county court grants an injunction for the purpose of restraining the defendant from pursuing any conduct which amounts to harassment, and
(b) the plaintiff considers that the defendant has done anything which he is prohibited from doing by the injunction,

the plaintiff may apply for the issue of a warrant for the arrest of the defendant.

(4) An application under subsection (3) may be made—

(a) where the injunction was granted by the High Court, to a judge of that court, and
(b) where the injunction was granted by a county court, to a judge or district judge of that or any other county court.

(5) The judge or district judge to whom an application under subsection (3) is made may only issue a warrant if—

(a) the application is substantiated on oath, and
(b) the judge or district judge has reasonable grounds for believing that the defendant has done anything which he is prohibited from doing by the injunction.

(6) Where—

(a) the High Court or a county court grants an injunction for the purpose mentioned in subsection (3)(a), and
(b) without reasonable excuse the defendant does anything which he is prohibited from doing by the injunction,

he is guilty of an offence.

(7) Where a person is convicted of an offence under subsection (6) in respect of any conduct, that conduct is not punishable as a contempt of court.

(8) A person cannot be convicted of an offence under subsection (6) in respect of any conduct which has been punished as a contempt of court.

(9) A person guilty of an offence under subsection (6) is liable—

(a) on conviction on indictment, to imprisonment for a term not exceeding five years, or a fine, or both, or

(b) on summary conviction, to imprisonment for a term not exceeding six months, or a fine not exceeding the statutory maximum, or both.

Putting people in fear of violence

91–005 **4.**—(1) A person whose course of conduct causes another to fear, on at least two occasions, that violence will be used against him is guilty of an offence if he knows or ought to know that his course of conduct will cause the other so to fear on each of those occasions.

(2) For the purposes of this section, the person whose course of conduct is in question ought to know that it will cause another to fear that violence will be used against him on any occasion if a reasonable person in possession of the same information would think the course of conduct would cause the other so to fear on that occasion.

(3) It is a defence for a person charged with an offence under this section to show that—

(a) his course of conduct was pursued for the purpose of preventing or detecting crime,

(b) his course of conduct was pursued under any enactment or rule of law or to comply with any condition or requirement imposed by any person under any enactment, or

(c) the pursuit of his course of conduct was reasonable for the protection of himself or another or for the protection of his or another's property.

(4) A person guilty of an offence under this section is liable—

(a) on conviction on indictment, to imprisonment for a term not exceeding five years, or a fine, or both, or

(b) on summary conviction, to imprisonment for a term not exceeding six months, or a fine not exceeding the statutory maximum, or both.

(5) If on the trial on indictment of a person charged with an offence under this section the jury find him not guilty of the offence charged, they may find him guilty of an offence under section 2.

(6) The Crown Court has the same powers and duties in relation to a person who is by virtue of subsection (5) convicted before it of an offence under section 2 as a magistrates' court would have on convicting him of the offence.

Restraining orders

91–006 **5.**—(1) A court sentencing or otherwise dealing with a person ("the defendant") convicted of an offence under section 2 or 4 may (as well as sentencing him or dealing with him in any other way) make an order under this section.

(2) The order may, for the purpose of protecting the victim of the offence, or any other person mentioned in the order, from further conduct which—

(a) amounts to harassment, or

(b) will cause a fear of violence,

prohibit the defendant from doing anything described in the order.

(3) The order may have effect for a specified period or until further order.

(4) The prosecutor, the defendant or any other person mentioned in the order may apply to the court which made the order for it to be varied or discharged by a further order.

(5) If without reasonable excuse the defendant does anything which he is

prohibited from doing by an order under this section, he is guilty of an offence.
(6) A person guilty of an offence under this section is liable—

(a) on conviction on indictment, to imprisonment for a term not exceeding five years, or a fine, or both, or
(b) on summary conviction, to imprisonment for a term not exceeding six months, or a fine not exceeding the statutory maximum, or both.

Limitation

6. In section 11 of the Limitation Act 1980 (special time limit for actions in respect of personal injuries), after subsection (1) there is inserted—   **91–007**

"(1A) This section does not apply to any action brought for damages under section 3 of the Protection from Harassment Act 1997."

Interpretation of this group of sections

7.—(1) This section applies for the interpretation of sections 1 to 5.   **91–008**
(2) References to harassing a person include alarming the person or causing the person distress.
(3) A "course of conduct"must involve conduct on at least two occasions.
[(3A) A person's conduct on any occasion shall be taken, if aided, abetted, counselled or procured by another—

(a) to be conduct on that occasion of the other (as well as conduct of the person whose conduct it is); and
(b) to be conduct in relation to which the other's knowledge and purpose, and what he ought to have known, are the same as they were in relation to what was contemplated or reasonably foreseeable at the time of the aiding, abetting, counselling or procuring.][1]

(4) "Conduct"includes speech.

[1] Added by Criminal Justice and Police Act 2001 (c.16), Pt 1, c. 3, s. 44(1).

Special Immigration Appeals Commission Act 1997

(1997, c. 68)

An Act to establish the Special Immigration Appeals Commission; to make provision with respect to its jurisdiction; and for connected purposes.   **92–001**
[17th December 1997]

Establishment of the Commission

1.—(1) There shall be a commission, known as the Special Immigration Appeals Commission, for the purpose of exercising the jurisdiction conferred by this Act.   **92–002**
(2) Schedule 1 to this Act shall have effect in relation to the Commission.
[(3) The Commission shall be a superior court of record.

(4) A decision of the Commission shall be questioned in legal proceedings only in accordance with—

>   (a) section 7, or
>   (b) section 30(5)(a) of the Anti-terrorism, Crime and Security Act 2001 (derogation).][1]

[1] Added by Anti-terrorism, Crime and Security Act 2001 (c.24), Pt 4, s. 35.

Jurisdiction: appeals

92–003 **2.**—[(1) A person may appeal to the Special Immigration Appeals Commission against a decision which he would be entitled to appeal against under Part IV of the Immigration and Asylum Act 1999 ("the 1999 Act") but for a public interest provision.

(1A) Subsection (1) does not apply to an appeal under section 59(2) of the 1999 Act.

(1B) "Public interest provision" means any of sections 60(9), 62(4), 64(1) or (2) or 70(1) to (6) of the 1999 Act.

(1C) A reference in this Act to an appeal under this section includes a reference to an appeal under regulation 29(1) of the Immigration (European Economic Area) Regulations 2000 (other than on the ground mentioned in paragraph (2) of that regulation) which lies to the Commission as a result of regulation 31 of those Regulations.]

(2) A person may appeal to the Special Immigration Appeals Commission against the refusal of an entry clearance if he would be entitled to appeal against the refusal under subsection (2) of section 13 of the Immigration Act 1971 but for subsection (5) of that section (exclusion conducive to public good), and—

>   (a) he seeks to rely on an enforceable Community right or any provision made under section 2(2) of the European Communities Act 1972, or
>   (b) he seeks to enter the United Kingdom under immigration rules making provision about entry—
>
>> (i) to exercise rights of access to a child resident there,
>> (ii) as the spouse or fiance of a person present and settled there, or
>> (iii) as the parent, grandparent or other dependent relative of a person present and settled there.

(3) Schedule 2 to this Act (which makes supplementary provision relating to appeals under this section) shall have effect.

(4) In this section, "immigration rules" has the same meaning as in the Immigration Act 1971.

[Jurisdiction: racial discrimination and human rights

92–004 **2A.**—(1) A person who alleges that an authority has, in taking an appealable decision, racially discriminated against him or acted in breach of his human rights may appeal to the Commission against that decision.

(2) For the purposes of this section—

>   (a) an authority racially discriminates against a person if he acts, or fails to act, in relation to that other person in a way which is unlawful by virtue of section 19B of the Race Relations Act 1976; and
>   (b) an authority acts in breach of a person's human rights if he acts, or fails to act, in relation to that other person in a way which is made unlawful by section 6(1) of the Human Rights Act 1998.

(3) Subsections (4) and (5) apply if, in any appellate proceedings being heard by the Commission, a question arises as to whether an authority has, in taking a decision which is the subject of the proceedings, racially discriminated against the appellant or acted in breach of the appellant's human rights.

(4) The Commission has jurisdiction to consider the question.

(5) If the Commission decides that the authority concerned—

(a) racially discriminated against the appellant; or
(b) acted in breach of the appellant's human rights, the appeal may be allowed on [the ground in question] [¹]

(6) "Authority" means —

(a) the Secretary of State;
(b) an immigration officer;
(c) a person responsible for the grant or refusal of entry clearance.

(7) "Appealable decision" means a decision against which a person would be entitled to appeal under Part IV of the 1999 Act but for a public interest provision.

(8) "The 1999 Act" and "public interest provision" have the same meaning as in section 2.

(9) A reference in this Act to an appeal under this section includes a reference to an appeal under regulation 29(1) of the Immigration (European Economic Area) Regulations 2000, on the ground mentioned in paragraph (2) of that regulation, which lies to the Commission as a result of regulation 31 of those Regulations.

¹ Words substituted by Race Relations (Amendment) Act 2000 (c.34), Sched. 2, para. 26(b).

. . . . . .

Determination of appeals

4.—(1) The Special Immigration Appeals Commission on an appeal to it **92–005** under this Act—

(a) shall allow the appeal if it considers—
   (i) that the decision or action against which the appeal is brought was not in accordance with the law or with any immigration rules applicable to the case, or
   (ii) where the decision or action involved the exercise of a discretion by the Secretary of State or an officer, that the discretion should have been exercised differently, and

(b) in any other case, shall dismiss the appeal.

(2) Where an appeal is allowed, the Commission shall give such directions for giving effect to the determination as it thinks requisite, and may also make recommendations with respect to any other action which it considers should be taken in the case under the Immigration Act 1971; and it shall be the duty of the Secretary of State and of any officer to whom directions are given under this subsection to comply with them.

(3) In this section "immigration rules" has the same meaning as in the Immigration Act 1971.

Procedure in relation to jurisdiction under sections 2 and 3

92–006   5.—(1) The Lord Chancellor may make rules—

    (a) for regulating the exercise of the rights of appeal conferred by [section 2 or 2A][1] above,

    (b) for prescribing the practice and procedure to be followed on or in connection with appeals under [section 2 or 2A above][2] including the mode and burden of proof and admissibility of evidence on such appeals, and

    (c) for other matters preliminary or incidental to or arising out of such appeals, including proof of the decisions of the Special Immigration Appeals Commission.

(2) Rules under this section shall provide that an appellant has the right to be legally represented in any proceedings before the Commission on an appeal under [section 2 or 2A][3] above, subject to any power conferred on the Commission by such rules.

(3) Rules under this section may, in particular—

    (a) make provision enabling proceedings before the Commission to take place without the appellant being given full particulars of the reasons for the decision which is the subject of the appeal,

    (b) make provision enabling the Commission to hold proceedings in the absence of any person, including the appellant and any legal representative appointed by him,

    (c) make provision about the functions in proceedings before the Commission of persons appointed under section 6 below, and

    (d) make provision enabling the Commission to give the appellant a summary of any evidence taken in his absence.

(4) Rules under this section may also include provision—

    (a) enabling any functions of the Commission which relate to matters preliminary or incidental to an appeal, or which are conferred by Part II of Schedule 2 to the Immigration Act 1971, to be performed by a single member of the Commission, or

    (b) conferring on the Commission such ancillary powers as the Lord Chancellor thinks necessary for the purposes of the exercise of its functions.

(5) The power to make rules under this section shall include power to make rules with respect to applications to the Commission under paragraphs 22 to 24 of Schedule 2 to the Immigration Act 1971 and matters arising out of such applications.

(6) In making rules under this section the Lord Chancellor shall have regard, in particular, to—

    (a) the need to secure that decisions which are the subject of appeals are properly reviewed, and

    (b) the need to secure that information is not disclosed contrary to the public interest.

(7) . . .

(8) The power to make rules under this section shall be exercisable by statutory instrument.

(9) No rules shall be made under this section unless a draft of them has been laid before and approved by resolution of each House of Parliament.

[1] Words inserted by Race Relations (Amendment) Act 2000 (c.34), Sched. 2, para. 28(a).

² Words substituted by Race Relations (Amendment) Act 2000 (c.34), Sched. 2, para. 28(b).
³ Words inserted by Race Relations (Amendment) Act 2000 (c.34), Sched. 2, para. 28(c).

Appointment of person to represent the appellant's interests

6.—(1) The relevant law officer may appoint a person to represent the interests of an appellant in any proceedings before the Special Immigration Appeals Commission from which the appellant and any legal representative of his are excluded.

92–007

(2) For the purposes of subsection (1) above, the relevant law officer is—

  (a) in relation to proceedings before the Commission in England and Wales, the Attorney General,
  (b) in relation to proceedings before the Commission in Scotland, the Lord Advocate, and
  (c) in relation to proceedings before the Commission in Northern Ireland, the Attorney General for Northern Ireland.

(3) A person appointed under subsection (1) above—

  (a) if appointed for the purposes of proceedings in England and Wales, shall have a general qualification for the purposes of section 71 of the Courts and Legal Services Act 1990,
  (b) if appointed for the purposes of proceedings in Scotland, shall be

    (i) an advocate, or
    (ii) a solicitor who has by virtue of section 25A of the Solicitors (Scotland) Act 1980 rights of audience in the Court of Session and the High Court of Justiciary, and

  (c) if appointed for the purposes of proceedings in Northern Ireland, shall be a member of the Bar of Northern Ireland.

(4) A person appointed under subsection (1) above shall not be responsible to the person whose interests he is appointed to represent.

Appeals from the Commission

7.—(1) Where the Special Immigration Appeals Commission has made a final determination of an appeal, any party to the appeal may bring a further appeal to the appropriate appeal court on any question of law material to that determination.

92–008

(2) An appeal under this section may be brought only with the leave of the Commission or, if such leave is refused, with the leave of the appropriate appeal court.

(3) In this section "the appropriate appeal court" means —

  (a) in relation to a determination made by the Commission in England and Wales, the Court of Appeal,
  (b) in relation to a determination made by the Commission in Scotland, the Court of Session, and
  (c) in relation to a determination made by the Commission in Northern Ireland, the Court of Appeal in Northern Ireland.

Audit Commission Act 1998

(1998, c. 18)

93–001   *An Act to consolidate Part III of the Local Government Finance Act 1982 and other enactments relating to the Audit Commission for Local Authorities and the National Health Service in England and Wales.* [11th June 1998]

PART I

THE AUDIT COMMISSION

The Audit Commission

93–002   **1.**—(1) There shall continue to be a body known as the Audit Commission for Local Authorities and the National Health Service in England and Wales.

(2) The Commission shall consist of not less than 15 nor more than 20 members appointed by the Secretary of State.

(3) The Secretary of State shall appoint one of the members to be chairman and another to be deputy chairman.

(4) An appointment under subsection (2) or (3) shall be made after consultation with such organisations and other bodies as appear to the Secretary of State to be appropriate.

(5) Schedule 1 has effect with respect to the Commission.

. . . . . .

PART II

ACCOUNTS AND AUDIT OF PUBLIC BODIES

Audit of accounts

Appointment of auditors

93–003   **3.**—(1) An auditor appointed by the Commission to audit the accounts of a body whose accounts are required to be audited in accordance with this Act ("a body subject to audit") may be—

    (a) an officer of the Commission,
    (b) an individual who is not an officer of the Commission, or
    (c) a firm of individuals who are not officers of the Commission.

(2) Where two or more auditors are appointed in relation to the accounts of a body, some but not others may be officers of the Commission and they may be appointed—

    (a) to act jointly;
    (b) to act separately in relation to different parts of the accounts; or
    (c) to discharge different functions in relation to the audit.

(3) Before appointing an auditor or auditors to audit the accounts of a body other than a health service body the Commission shall consult that body.

(4) For the purpose of assisting the Commission in deciding on the appointment of an auditor or auditors in relation to the accounts of a body other than a health service body, the Commission may require the body to make available

for inspection by or on behalf of the Commission such documents relating to any accounts of the body as the Commission may reasonably require for that purpose.

(5) A person shall not be appointed by the Commission as an auditor unless—

    (a) he is a member of one or more of the bodies mentioned in subsection (7);

    (b) he has such other qualifications as may be approved for the purposes of this section by the Secretary of State; or

    (c) he was approved before 1st April 1996 by the Secretary of State under section 13(5) of the Local Government Finance Act 1982, and the approval has not been withdrawn.

(6) A firm shall not be appointed by the Commission as an auditor unless each of its members is a member of one or more of the bodies mentioned in subsection (7).

(7) The bodies referred to in subsections (5) and (6) are—

    (a) the Institute of Chartered Accountants in England and Wales;

    (b) the Institute of Chartered Accountants of Scotland;

    (c) the Association of Certified Accountants;

    (d) the Chartered Institute of Public Finance and Accountancy;

    (e) the Institute of Chartered Accountants in Ireland; and

    (f) any other body of accountants established in the United Kingdom and for the time being approved by the Secretary of State for the purposes of this section.

(8) The appointment by the Commission of an auditor who is not an officer of the Commission shall be on such terms and for such period as the Commission may determine.

(9) Arrangements may be approved by the Commission, either generally or in a particular case, for a person or persons to assist an auditor appointed by the Commission (whether the auditor is an officer of the Commission or not) by carrying out such of the auditor's functions under this Act as may be specified in the arrangements.

(10) Subsection (9) does not apply to functions under section 19.

(11) References in the following provisions of this Act to an auditor include, in relation to any function of an auditor, a reference to any person carrying out that function under arrangements approved under subsection (9).

Code of audit practice

4.—(1) The Commission shall prepare, and keep under review, a code of **93–004** audit practice prescribing the way in which auditors are to carry out their functions under this Act.

(2) A different code may be prepared with respect to the audit of the accounts of health service bodies as compared with the code applicable to the accounts of other bodies.

(3) A code prepared under this section shall embody what appears to the Commission to be the best professional practice with respect to the standards, procedures and techniques to be adopted by auditors.

(4) A code does not come into force until approved by a resolution of each House of Parliament, and its continuation in force is subject to its being so approved at intervals of not more than five years.

(5) Subsection (4) does not preclude alterations to a code being made by the Commission in the intervals between its being approved in accordance with that subsection.

(6) The Commission shall send copies of any code prepared under this section, and of any alterations made to such a code, to the Secretary of State who shall lay them before Parliament; and the Commission shall from time to time publish any such code as for the time being in force.

(7) Before preparing or altering a code applicable to any accounts, the Commission shall consult—

(a) if the accounts are or include those of health service bodies, such organisations connected with the health service as appear to the Commission to be concerned;

(b) if the accounts are or include those of other bodies, such associations of local authorities as appear to the Commission to be concerned; and

(c) in any case, such bodies of accountants as appear to the Commission to be appropriate.

General duties of auditors

93–005   **5.**—(1) In auditing accounts required to be audited in accordance with this Act, an auditor shall by examination of the accounts and otherwise satisfy himself—

(a) if they are accounts of a health service body, that they are prepared in accordance with directions under [subsection (2) or (2B) of section 98 of the National Health Service Act 1977];

(b) in any other case, that they are prepared in accordance with regulations under section 27;

(c) that they comply with the requirements of all other statutory provisions applicable to the accounts;

(d) that proper practices have been observed in the compilation of the accounts;

(e) that the body whose accounts are being audited has made proper arrangements for securing economy, efficiency and effectiveness in its use of resources; and

(f) that that body, if required to publish information in pursuance of a direction under section 44 (performance information), has made such arrangements for collecting and recording the information and for publishing it as are required for the performance of its duties under that section.

(2) The auditor shall comply with the code of audit practice applicable to the accounts being audited as that code is for the time being in force.

Auditors' right to documents and information

93–006   **6.**—(1) An auditor has a right of access at all reasonable times to every document relating to a body subject to audit which appears to him necessary for the purposes of his functions under this Act.

(2) An auditor may—

(a) require a person holding or accountable for any such document to give him such information and explanation as he thinks necessary for the purposes of his functions under this Act; and

(b) if he thinks it necessary, require the person to attend before him in person to give the information or explanation or to produce the document.

(3) . . .

(4) Without prejudice to subsection (2), the auditor may—

    (a) require any officer or member of a body subject to audit to give him such information or explanation as he thinks necessary for the purposes of his functions under this Act; and

    (b) if he thinks it necessary, require the officer or member to attend before him in person to give the information or explanation.

(5) Without prejudice to subsections (1) to (4), every body subject to audit shall provide the auditor with every facility and all information which he may reasonably require for the purposes of his functions under this Act.

(6) A person who without reasonable excuse fails to comply with any requirement of an auditor under subsection (1), (2) or (4) is guilty of an offence and liable on summary conviction—

    (a) to a fine not exceeding level 3 on the standard scale, and

    (b) to an additional fine not exceeding £20 for each day on which the offence continues after conviction for that offence.

(7) Any expenses incurred by an auditor in connection with proceedings for an offence under subsection (6) alleged to have been committed in relation to the audit of the accounts of any body, so far as not recovered from any other source, are recoverable from that body.

. . . . . .

Auditors' reports and recommendations

Immediate and other reports in public interest

8. In auditing accounts required to be audited in accordance with this Act, the auditor shall consider—　**93–007**

    (a) whether, in the public interest, he should make a report on any matter coming to his notice in the course of the audit, in order for it to be considered by the body concerned or brought to the attention of the public, and

    (b) whether the public interest requires any such matter to be made the subject of an immediate report rather than of a report to be made at the conclusion of the audit.

General report

9.—(1) When an auditor has concluded his audit of the accounts of any body　**93–008**
under this Act he shall, subject to subsection (2), enter on the relevant statement of accounts prepared pursuant to regulations under section 27 (or, where no such statement is required to be prepared, on the accounts)—

    (a) a certificate that he has completed the audit in accordance with this Act, and

    (b) his opinion on the statement (or, as the case may be, on the accounts).

(2) Where an auditor makes a report to the body concerned under section 8 at the conclusion of the audit, he may include the certificate and opinion referred

to in subsection (1) in that report instead of making an entry on the statement or accounts.

. . . . . .

Public inspection etc. and action by the auditor

Inspection of statements of accounts and auditors' reports

93–009   **14.**—(1) A local government elector for the area of a body subject to audit, other than a health service body, may—

(a) inspect and make copies of any statement of accounts prepared by the body pursuant to regulations under section 27;
(b) inspect and make copies of any report, other than an immediate report, made to the body by an auditor; and
(c) require copies of any such statement or report to be delivered to him on payment of a reasonable sum for each copy.

(2) A document which a person is entitled to inspect under this section may be inspected by him at all reasonable times and without payment.

(3) A person who has the custody of any such document and—

(a) obstructs a person in the exercise of a right under this section to inspect or make copies of the document, or
(b) refuses to give copies of the document to a person entitled under this section to obtain them,

is guilty of an offence and liable on summary conviction to a fine not exceeding level 3 on the standard scale.

(4) References in this section to copies of a document include references to copies of any part of it.

Inspection of documents and questions at audit

93–010   **15.**—(1) At each audit under this Act, other than an audit of accounts of a health service body, any persons interested may—

(a) inspect the accounts to be audited and all books, deeds, contracts, bills, vouchers and receipts relating to them, and
(b) make copies of all or any part of the accounts and those other documents.

(2) At the request of a local government elector for any area to which the accounts relate, the auditor shall give the elector, or any representative of his, an opportunity to question the auditor about the accounts.

(3) Nothing in this section entitles a person—

(a) to inspect so much of any accounts or other document as contains personal information about a member of the staff of the body whose accounts are being audited; or
(b) to require any such information to be disclosed in answer to any question.

(4) For the purposes of subsection (3), information is to be regarded as personal information about a member of a body's staff if it relates specifically to a

particular individual and is available to the body for reasons connected with the fact—

(a) that that individual holds or has held an office or employment under that body; or

(b) that payments or other benefits in respect of an office or employment under any other person are or have been made or provided to that individual by that body.

(5) For the purposes of subsection (4)(b), payments made or benefits provided to an individual in respect of an office or employment include any payment made or benefit provided to him in respect of his ceasing to hold the office or employment.

Right to make objections at audit

16.—(1) At each audit of accounts under this Act, other than an audit of accounts of a health service body, a local government elector for an area to which the accounts relate, or any representative of his, may attend before the auditor and (in accordance with subsection (2)) make objections—   **93–011**

(a) as to any matter in respect of which the auditor could take action under section 17 or 18; or

(b) as to any other matter in respect of which the auditor could make a report under section 8.

(2) No objection may be made under subsection (1) unless the auditor has received written notice of the proposed objection and of the grounds on which it is to be made.

(3) An elector sending a notice to an auditor for the purposes of subsection (2) shall at the same time send a copy of the notice to the body whose accounts are being audited.

. . . . . .

Prevention of unlawful expenditure etc.

Power of auditor to apply for judicial review

24.—(1) Subject to section 31(3) of the Supreme Court Act 1981 (no application for judicial review without leave) the auditor appointed in relation to the accounts of a body other than a health service body may make an application for judicial review with respect to—   **93–012**

(a) any decision of that body, or

(b) any failure by that body to act,

which it is reasonable to believe would have an effect on the accounts of that body.

(2) The existence of the powers conferred on an auditor under this Act is not a ground for refusing an application falling within subsection (1) (or an application for leave to make such an application).

(3) On an application for judicial review made as mentioned in subsection (1), the court may make such order as it thinks fit for the payment, by the body to whose decision the application relates, of expenses incurred by the auditor in connection with the application.

Bank of England Act 1998

(1998, c. 11)

94–001 *An Act to make provision about the constitution, regulation, financial arrangements and functions of the Bank of England, including provision for the transfer of supervisory functions; to amend the Banking Act 1987 in relation to the provision and disclosure of information; to make provision relating to appointments to the governing body of a designated agency under the Financial Services Act 1986; to amend Schedule 5 to that Act; to make provision relating to the registration of Government stocks and bonds; to make provision about the application of section 207 of the Companies Act 1989 to bearer securities; and for connected purposes.*

[23rd April 1998]

PART I

CONSTITUTION, REGULATION AND FINANCIAL ARRANGEMENTS

Constitution and regulation

Court of directors

94–002 **1.**—(1) There shall continue to be a court of directors of the Bank.

(2) The court shall consist of a Governor, 2 Deputy Governors and 16 directors of the Bank, all of whom shall be appointed by Her Majesty.

(3) On the day on which this Act comes into force, all persons who are, immediately before that day, holding office as director of the Bank shall vacate their office.

(4) Schedule 1 shall have effect with respect to the court.

Functions of court of directors

94–003 **2.**—(1) The court of directors of the Bank shall manage the Bank's affairs, other than the formulation of monetary policy.

(2) In particular, the court's functions under subsection (1) shall include determining the Bank's objectives (including objectives for its financial management) and strategy.

(3) In determining the Bank's objectives and strategy, the court's aim shall be to ensure the effective discharge of the Bank's functions.

(4) Subject to that, in determining objectives for the financial management of the Bank, the court's aim shall be to ensure the most efficient use of the Bank's resources.

. . . . . .

PART II

MONETARY POLICY

Role of the Bank

Objectives

11. In relation to monetary policy, the objectives of the Bank of England shall   **94–004**
be—

    (a) to maintain price stability, and
    (b) subject to that, to support the economic policy of Her Majesty's Gov-
        ernment, including its objectives for growth and employment.

Specification of matters relevant to objectives

12.—(1) The Treasury may by notice in writing to the Bank specify for the   **94–005**
purposes of section 11—

    (a) what price stability is to be taken to consist of, or
    (b) what the economic policy of Her Majesty's Government is to be taken
        to be.

(2) The Treasury shall specify under subsection (1) both of the matters mentioned there—

    (a) before the end of the period of 7 days beginning with the day on which
        this Act comes into force, and
    (b) at least once in every period of 12 months beginning on the anniversary
        of the day on which this Act comes into force.

(3) Where the Treasury give notice under this section they shall—

    (a) publish the notice in such manner as they think fit, and
    (b) lay a copy of it before Parliament.

. . . . . .

Treasury's reserve powers

Reserve powers

19.—(1) The Treasury, after consultation with the Governor of the Bank, may   **94–006**
by order give the Bank directions with respect to monetary policy if they are
satisfied that the directions are required in the public interest and by extreme
economic circumstances.

(2) An order under this section may include such consequential modifications
of the provisions of this Part relating to the Monetary Policy Committee as the
Treasury think fit.

(3) A statutory instrument containing an order under this section shall be laid
before Parliament after being made.

(4) Unless an order under this section is approved by resolution of each House
of Parliament before the end of the period of 28 days beginning with the day
on which it is made, it shall cease to have effect at the end of that period.

(5) In reckoning the period of 28 days for the purposes of subsection (4), no account shall be taken of any time during which Parliament is dissolved or prorogued or during which either House is adjourned for more than 4 days.

(6) An order under this section which does not cease to have effect before the end of the period of 3 months beginning with the day on which it is made shall cease to have effect at the end of that period.

(7) While an order under this section has effect, section 11 shall not have effect.

Crime and Disorder Act 1998

(1998, c. 37)

95–001 *An Act to make provision for preventing crime and disorder; to create certain racially-aggravated offences; to abolish the rebuttable presumption that a child is doli incapax and to make provision as to the effect of a child's failure to give evidence at his trial; to abolish the death penalty for treason and piracy; to make changes to the criminal justice system; to make further provision for dealing with offenders; to make further provision with respect to remands and committals for trial and the release and recall of prisoners; to amend Chapter I of Part II of the Crime (Sentences) Act 1997 and to repeal Chapter I of Part III of the Crime and Punishment (Scotland) Act 1997; to make amendments designed to facilitate, or otherwise desirable in connection with, the consolidation of certain enactments; and for connected purposes.* [31st July 1998]

PART I

PREVENTION OF CRIME AND DISORDER

CHAPTER I

ENGLAND AND WALES

Crime and disorder: general

Anti-social behaviour orders

95–002   1.—(1) An application for an order under this section may be made by a relevant authority if it appears to the authority that the following conditions are fulfilled with respect to any person aged 10 or over, namely—

(a) that the person has acted, since the commencement date, in an anti-social manner, that is to say, in a manner that caused or was likely to cause harassment, alarm or distress to one or more persons not of the same household as himself; and

(b) that such an order is necessary to protect persons in the local government area in which the harassment, alarm or distress was caused or was likely to be caused from further anti-social acts by him;

and in this section "relevant authority" means the council for the local government area or any chief officer of police any part of whose police area lies within that area.

(2) A relevant authority shall not make such an application without consulting each other relevant authority.

(3) Such an application shall be made by complaint to the magistrates' court whose commission area includes the place where it is alleged that the harassment, alarm or distress was caused or was likely to be caused.

(4) If, on such an application, it is proved that the conditions mentioned in subsection (1) above are fulfilled, the magistrates' court may make an order under this section (an "anti-social behaviour order") which prohibits the defendant from doing anything described in the order.

(5) For the purpose of determining whether the condition mentioned in subsection (1)(a) above is fulfilled, the court shall disregard any act of the defendant which he shows was reasonable in the circumstances.

(6) The prohibitions that may be imposed by an anti-social behaviour order are those necessary for the purpose of protecting from further anti-social acts by the defendant—

(a) persons in the local government area; and
(b) persons in any adjoining local government area specified in the application for the order;

and a relevant authority shall not specify an adjoining local government area in the application without consulting the council for that area and each chief officer of police any part of whose police area lies within that area.

(7) An anti-social behaviour order shall have effect for a period (not less than two years) specified in the order or until further order.

(8) Subject to subsection (9) below, the applicant or the defendant may apply by complaint to the court which made an anti-social behaviour order for it to be varied or discharged by a further order.

(9) Except with the consent of both parties, no anti-social behaviour order shall be discharged before the end of the period of two years beginning with the date of service of the order.

(10) If without reasonable excuse a person does anything which he is prohibited from doing by an anti-social behaviour order, he shall be liable—

(a) on summary conviction, to imprisonment for a term not exceeding six months or to a fine not exceeding the statutory maximum, or to both; or
(b) on conviction on indictment, to imprisonment for a term not exceeding five years or to a fine, or to both.

(11) Where a person is convicted of an offence under subsection (10) above, it shall not be open to the court by or before which he is so convicted to make an order under subsection (1)(b) (conditional discharge) of [section 12 of the Powers of Criminal Courts (Sentencing) Act 2000][1] in respect of the offence.

(12) In this section—

"the commencement date" means the date of the commencement of this section;
"local government area" means—

(a) in relation to England, a district or London borough, the City of London, the Isle of Wight and the Isles of Scilly;
(b) in relation to Wales, a county or county borough.

[1] Words substituted by Powers of Criminal Courts (Sentencing) Act 2000 (c.6), Sched. 9, para. 192.

Sex offender orders

95–003 **2.**—(1) If it appears to a chief officer of police that the following conditions are fulfilled with respect to any person in his police area, namely—

(a) that the person is a sex offender; and

(b) that the person has acted, since the relevant date, in such a way as to give reasonable cause to believe that an order under this section is necessary to protect the public from serious harm from him,

the chief officer may apply for an order under this section to be made in respect of the person.

(2) Such an application shall be made by complaint to the magistrates' court whose commission area includes any place where it is alleged that the defendant acted in such a way as is mentioned in subsection (1)(b) above.

(3) If, on such an application, it is proved that the conditions mentioned in subsection (1) above are fulfilled, the magistrates' court may make an order under this section (a "sex offender order") which prohibits the defendant from doing anything described in the order.

(4) The prohibitions that may be imposed by a sex offender order are those necessary for the purpose of protecting the public from serious harm from the defendant.

(5) A sex offender order shall have effect for a period (not less than five years) specified in the order or until further order; and while such an order has effect, Part I of the Sex Offenders Act 1997 shall have effect as if—

(a) the defendant were subject to the notification requirements of that Part; and

(b) in relation to the defendant, the relevant date (within the meaning of that Part) were the date of service of the order.

(6) Subject to subsection (7) below, the applicant or the defendant may apply by complaint to the court which made a sex offender order for it to be varied or discharged by a further order.

(7) Except with the consent of both parties, no sex offender order shall be discharged before the end of the period of five years beginning with the date of service of the order.

(8) If without reasonable excuse a person does anything which he is prohibited from doing by a sex offender order, he shall be liable—

(a) on summary conviction, to imprisonment for a term not exceeding six months or to a fine not exceeding the statutory maximum, or to both; or

(b) on conviction on indictment, to imprisonment for a term not exceeding five years or to a fine, or to both.

(9) Where a person is convicted of an offence under subsection (8) above, it shall not be open to the court by or before which he is so convicted to make an order under subsection (1)(b) (conditional discharge) of [section 12 of the Powers of Criminal Courts (Sentencing) Act 2000][1] in respect of the offence.

[1] Words substituted by Powers of Criminal Courts (Sentencing) Act 2000 (c.6), Sched. 9, para. 193.

Sex offender orders: supplemental

95–004 **3.**—(1) In section 2 above and this section "sex offender" means a person who—

(a) has been convicted of a sexual offence to which Part I of the Sex Offenders Act 1997 applies;

(b) has been found not guilty of such an offence by reason of insanity, or found to be under a disability and to have done the act charged against him in respect of such an offence;

(c) has been cautioned by a constable, in England and Wales or Northern Ireland, in respect of such an offence which, at the time when the caution was given, he had admitted; or

(d) has been punished under the law in force in a country or territory outside the United Kingdom for an act which—

    (i) constituted an offence under that law; and

    (ii) would have constituted a sexual offence to which that Part applies if it had been done in any part of the United Kingdom.

(2) In subsection (1) of section 2 above "the relevant date", in relation to a sex offender, means—

(a) the date or, as the case may be, the latest date on which he has been convicted, found, cautioned or punished as mentioned in subsection (1) above; or

(b) if later, the date of the commencement of that section.

(3) Subsections (2) and (3) of section 6 of the Sex Offenders Act 1997 apply for the construction of references in subsections (1) and (2) above as they apply for the construction of references in Part I of that Act.

(4) In subsections (1) and (2) above, any reference to a person having been cautioned shall be construed as including a reference to his having been reprimanded or warned (under section 65 below) as a child or young person.

(5) An act punishable under the law in force in any country or territory outside the United Kingdom constitutes an offence under that law for the purposes of subsection (1) above, however it is described in that law.

(6) Subject to subsection (7) below, the condition in subsection (1)(d)(i) above shall be taken to be satisfied unless, not later than rules of court may provide, the defendant serves on the applicant a notice—

(a) stating that, on the facts as alleged with respect to the act in question, the condition is not in his opinion satisfied;

(b) showing his grounds for that opinion; and

(c) requiring the applicant to show that it is satisfied.

(7) The court, if it thinks fit, may permit the defendant to require the applicant to show that the condition is satisfied without the prior service of a notice under subsection (6) above.

Appeals against orders

4.—(1) An appeal shall lie to the Crown Court against the making by a magistrates' court of an anti-social behaviour order or sex offender order.   **95–005**

(2) On such an appeal the Crown Court—

(a) may make such orders as may be necessary to give effect to its determination of the appeal; and

(b) may also make such incidental or consequential orders as appear to it to be just.

(3) Any order of the Crown Court made on an appeal under this section (other

than one directing that an application be re-heard by a magistrates' court) shall, for the purposes of section 1(8) or 2(6) above, be treated as if it were an order of the magistrates' court from which the appeal was brought and not an order of the Crown Court.

......

Youth crime and disorder

Child safety orders

95–006 **11.**—(1) Subject to subsection (2) below, if a magistrates' court, on the application of a local authority, is satisfied that one or more of the conditions specified in subsection (3) below are fulfilled with respect to a child under the age of 10, it may make an order (a "child safety' order") which—

  (a) places the child, for a period (not exceeding the permitted maximum) specified in the order, under the supervision of the responsible officer; and
  (b) requires the child to comply with such requirements as are so specified.

(2) A court shall not make a child safety order unless it has been notified by the Secretary of State that arrangements for implementing such orders are available in the area in which it appears that the child resides or will reside and the notice has not been withdrawn.

(3) The conditions are—

  (a) that the child has committed an act which, if he had been aged 10 or over, would have constituted an offence;
  (b) that a child safety order is necessary for the purpose of preventing the commission by the child of such act as is mentioned in paragraph (a) above;
  (c) that the child has contravened a ban imposed by a curfew notice; and
  (d) that the child has acted in a manner that caused or was likely to cause harassment, alarm or distress to one or more persons not of the same household as himself.

(4) The maximum period permitted for the purposes of subsection (1)(a) above is three months or, where the court is satisfied that the circumstances of the case are exceptional, 12 months.

(5) The requirements that may be specified under subsection (1)(b) above are those which the court considers desirable in the interests of—

  (a) securing that the child receives appropriate care, protection and support and is subject to proper control; or
  (b) preventing any repetition of the kind of behaviour which led to the child safety order being made.

(6) Proceedings under this section or section 12 below shall be family proceedings for the purposes of the 1989 Act or section 65 of the Magistrates' Courts Act 1980 ("the 1980 Act"); and the standard of proof applicable to such proceedings shall be that applicable to civil proceedings.

(7) In this section "local authority"has the same meaning as in the 1989 Act.

(8) In this section and section 12 below, "responsible officer", in relation to a child safety order, means one of the following who is specified in the order, namely—

(a) a social worker of a local authority social services department; and

(b) a member of a youth offending team.

Appeals against child safety orders

13.—(1) An appeal shall lie to the High Court against the making by a magis-   **95–007**
trates' court of a child safety order; and on such an appeal the High Court—

(a) may make such orders as may be necessary to give effect to its determination of the appeal; and

(b) may also make such incidental or consequential orders as appear to it
to be just.

(2) Any order of the High Court made on an appeal under this section (other
than one directing that an application be re-heard by a magistrates' court) shall,
for the purposes of subsections (4) to (6) of section 12 above, be treated as if it
were an order of the magistrates' court from which the appeal was brought and
not an order of the High Court.

(3) Subsections (6) and (7) of section 10 above shall apply for the purposes
of subsection (1) above as they apply for the purposes of subsection (1)(a) of
that section.

Local child curfew schemes

14.—(1) A local authority or a chief officer of police may make a scheme (a   **95–008**
"local child curfew scheme") for enabling the authority or (as the case may be)
the officer—

(a) subject to and in accordance with the provisions of the scheme; and

(b) if, after such consultation as is required by the scheme, the authority
or (as the case may be) the officer considers it necessary to do so for
the purpose of maintaining order,

to give a notice imposing, for a specified period (not exceeding 90 days), a ban
to which subsection (2) below applies.

(2) This subsection applies to a ban on children of specified ages ([under 16])
being in a public place within a specified area—

(a) during specified hours (between 9 pm and 6 am); and

(b) otherwise than under the effective control of a parent or a responsible
person aged 18 or over.

(3) Before making a local child curfew scheme, a local authority shall consult—

(a) every chief officer of police any part of whose police area lies within
its area; and

(b) such other persons or bodies as it considers appropriate.

[(3A) Before making a local child curfew scheme, a chief officer of police
shall consult—

(a) every local authority any part of whose area lies within the area to be
specified; and

(b) such other persons or bodies as he considers appropriate.]¹

[(4) A local child curfew scheme shall, if made by a local authority, be made
under the common seal of the authority.

(4A) A local child curfew scheme shall not have effect until it is confirmed by the Secretary of State.][2]

(5) The Secretary of State—

(a) may confirm, or refuse to confirm, a local child curfew scheme submitted under this section for confirmation; and

(b) may fix the date on which such a scheme is to come into operation;

and if no date is so fixed, the scheme shall come into operation at the end of the period of one month beginning with the date of its confirmation.

(6) A notice given under a local child curfew scheme (a "curfew notice") may specify different hours in relation to children of different ages.

(7) A curfew notice shall be given—

(a) by posting the notice in some conspicuous place or places within the specified area; and

(b) in such other manner, if any, as appears to the local authority or (as the case may be) the chief officer of police to be desirable for giving publicity to the notice.

(8) In this section—

"local authority" means—

(a) in relation to England, the council of a district or London brought, the Common Council of the City of London, the Council of the Isle of Wight and the Council of the Isles of Scilly;

(b) in relation to Wales, the council of a county or county borough;

"public place" has the same meaning as in Part II of the Public Order Act 1986.

[1] Added by Criminal Justice and Police Act 2001 (c.16), Pt 1, c. 3, s. 49(3).
[2] subss. (4) and (4A) substituted for subs. (4) by Criminal Justice and Police Act 2001 (c.16), Pt 1, c. 3, s. 49(4).

Contravention of curfew notices

95–009

15.—(1) Subsections (2) and (3) below apply where a constable has reasonable cause to believe that a child is in contravention of a ban imposed by a curfew notice.

(2) The constable shall, as soon as practicable, inform the local authority for the area that the child has contravened the ban.

(3) The constable may remove the child to the child's place of residence unless he has reasonable cause to believe that the child would, if removed to that place, be likely to suffer significant harm.

(4) In subsection (1) of section 47 of the 1989 Act (local authority's duty to investigate)—

(a) in paragraph (a), after sub-paragraph (ii) there shall be inserted the following sub-paragraph—

"(iii) has contravened a ban imposed by a curfew notice within the meaning of Chapter I of Part I of the Crime and Disorder Act 1998; or"; and

(b) at the end there shall be inserted the following paragraph—

"In the case of a child falling within paragraph (a)(iii) above, the enquiries shall be commenced as soon as practicable and, in any event, within 48 hours of the authority receiving the information."

. . . . . .

CHAPTER II

SCOTLAND

Anti-social behaviour orders

19.—(1) A local authority may make an application for an order under this **95–010** section if it appears to the authority that the following conditions are fulfilled with respect to any person of or over the age of 16, namely—

(a) that the person has—

    (i) acted in an anti-social manner, that is to say, in a manner that caused or was likely to cause alarm or distress; or

    (ii) pursued a course of anti-social conduct, that is to say, pursued a course of conduct that caused or was likely to cause alarm or distress,

to one or more persons not of the same household as himself in the authority's are (and in this section "anti-social acts" and "anti-social conduct" shall be construed accordingly); and

(b) that such an order is necessary to protect persons in the authority's area from further anti-social acts or conduct by him.

(2) An application under subsection (1) above shall be made by summary application to the sheriff within whose sheriffdom the alarm or distress was alleged to have been caused or to have been likely to be caused.

(3) On an application under subsection (1) above, the sheriff may, if he is satisfied that the conditions mentioned in that subsection are fulfilled, make an order under this section (an "anti-social behaviour order") which, for the purpose of protecting persons in the area of the local authority from further anti-social acts or conduct by the person against whom the order is sought, prohibits him from doing anything described in the order.

(4) For the purpose of determining whether the condition mentioned in sub-section (1)(a) is fulfilled, the sheriff shall disregard any act of the person in respect of whom the application is made which that person shows was reasonable in the circumstances.

(5) This section does not apply in relation to anything done before the commencement of this section.

(6) Nothing in this section shall prevent a local authority from instituting any legal proceedings otherwise than under this section against any person in relation to any anti-social act or conduct.

(7) In this section "conduct" includes speech and a course of conduct must involve conduct on at least two occasions.

(8) In this section and section 21 below "local authority" means a council constituted under section 2 of the Local Government etc. (Scotland) Act 1994 and any reference to the area of such an authority is a reference to the local government area within the meaning of that Act for which it is so constituted.

Sex offender orders

95–011   **20.**—(1) An application for an order under this section may be made by a chief constable if it appears to him that the conditions mentioned in subsection (2) below are fulfilled with respect to any person in the area of his police force.

(2) The conditions are—

> (a) that the person in respect of whom the application for the order is made is—
>
>> (i) of or over the age of 16 years; and
>> (ii) a sex offender; and
>
> (b) that the person has acted, since the relevant date, in such a way as to give reasonable cause to believe that an order under this section is necessary to protect the public from serious harm from him.

(3) An application under subsection (1) above shall be made by summary application to the sheriff within whose sheriffdom the person is alleged to have acted as mentioned in subsection (2)(b) above.

(4) On an application under subsection (1) above the sheriff may—

> (a) pending the determination of the application, make any such interim order as he considers appropriate; and
> (b) if he is satisfied that the conditions mentioned in subsection (2) above are fulfilled, make an order under this section ("a sex offender order") which prohibits the person in respect of whom it is made from doing anything described in the order.

(5) The prohibitions that may be imposed by an order made under subsection (4) above are those necessary for the purpose of protecting the public from serious harm from the person in respect of whom the order is made.

(6) While a sex offender order has effect, Part I of the Sex Offenders Act 1997 shall have effect as if—

> (a) the person in respect of whom the order has been obtained were subject to the notification requirements of that Part; and
> (b) in relation to that person, the relevant date (within the meaning of that Part) were the date on which the copy of the order was given or delivered to that person in accordance with subsections (8) and (9) of section 21 below.

(7) Section 3 above applies for the purposes of this section as it applies for the purposes of section 2 above with the following modifications—

> (a) any reference in that section to the defendant shall be construed as a reference to the person in respect of whom the order is sought; and
> (b) in subsection (2) of that section, the reference to subsection (1) of the said section 2 shall be construed as a reference to subsection (2)(b) of this section.

(8) A constable may arrest without warrant a person whom he reasonably suspects of doing, or having done, anything prohibited by an order under subsection (4)(a) above or a sex offender order.

Procedural provisions with respect to orders

95–012   **21.**—(1) Before making an application under—

(a) section 19(1) above;

(b) subsection (7)(b)(i) below,

the local authority shall consult the relevant chief constable.

(2) Before making an application under section 20(1) above or subsection (7)(b)(i) below, the chief constable shall consult the local authority within whose area the person in respect of whom the order is sought is for the time being.

(3) In subsection (1) above "relevant chief constable" means the chief constable of the police force maintained under the Police (Scotland) Act 1967 the area of which includes the area of the local authority making the application.

(4) A failure to comply with subsection (1) or (2) above shall not affect the validity of an order made on any application to which either of those subsections applies.

(5) A record of evidence shall be kept on any summary application under section 19 or 20 above or subsection (7)(b) below.

(6) Subsections (7) to (9) below apply to anti-social behaviour orders and sex offender orders and subsections (8) and (9) below apply to an order made under section 20(4)(a) above.

(7) An order to which this subsection applies—

(a) shall have effect for a period specified in the order or indefinitely; and

(b) may at any time be varied or revoked on a summary application by—

(i) the local authority or, as the case may be, chief constable who obtained the order; or

(ii) the person subject to the order.

(8) The clerk of the court by which an order to which this subsection applies is made or varied shall cause a copy of the order as so made or varied to be—

(a) given to the person named in the order; or

(b) sent to the person so named by registered post or by the recorded delivery service.

(9) An acknowledgement or certificate of delivery of a letter sent under subsection (8)(b) above issued by the Post Office shall be sufficient evidence of the delivery of the letter on the day specified in such acknowledgement or certificate.

(10) Where an appeal is lodged against the determination of an application under section 19 or 20 above or subsection (7)(b) above, any order made on the application shall, without prejudice to the determination of an application under subsection (7)(b) above made after the lodging of the appeal, continue to have effect pending the disposal of the appeal.

Offences in connection with breach of orders

22.—(1) Subject to subsection (3) below, if without reasonable excuse a **95–013** person breaches an anti-social behaviour order by doing anything which he is prohibited from doing by the order, he shall be guilty of an offence and shall be liable—

(a) on summary conviction, to a term of imprisonment not exceeding six months or to a fine not exceeding the statutory maximum or to both; or

(b) on conviction on indictment, to imprisonment for a term not exceeding five years or to a fine or to both.

(2) Subsection (3) applies where—

(a) the breach of the anti-social behaviour order referred to in subsection

(1) above consists in the accused having acted in a manner prohibited by the order which constitutes a separate offence (in this section referred to as the "separate offence"); and

(b) the accused has been charged with that separate offence.

(3) Where this subsection applies, the accused shall not be liable to be proceeded against for an offence under subsection (1) above but, subject to subsection (4) below, the court which sentences him for that separate offence shall, in determining the appropriate sentence or disposal for that offence, have regard to—

(a) the fact that the offence was committed by him while subject to an anti-social behaviour order;

(b) the number of such orders to which he was subject at the time of the commission of the offence;

(c) any previous conviction of the accused of an offence under subsection (1) above; and

(d) the extent to which the sentence or disposal in respect of any such previous conviction of the accused differed, by virtue of this subsection, from that which the court would have imposed but for this subsection.

(4) The court shall not, under subsection (3) above, have regard to the fact that the separate offence was committed while the accused was subject to an anti-social behaviour order unless that fact is libelled in the indictment or, as the case may be, specified in the complaint.

(5) The fact that the separate offence was committed while the accused was subject to an anti-social behaviour order shall, unless challenged—

(a) in the case of proceedings on indictment, by giving notice of a preliminary objection under paragraph (b) of section 72 of the Criminal Procedure (Scotland) Act 1995 ("the 1995 Act") or under that paragraph as applied by section 71(2) of that Act; or

(b) in summary proceedings, by preliminary objection before his plea is recorded,

be held as admitted.

(6) Subject to subsection (7) below, subsections (1) to (5) above apply in relation to an order under section 20(4)(a) above and to a sex offender order as they apply in relation to an anti-social behaviour order.

(7) Subsection (2) above as applied for the purposes of subsection (6) above shall have effect with the substitution of the words "at the time at which he committed" for the words "which constitutes".

. . . . . .

Part II

Criminal Law

Racially or religiously aggravated offences: England and Wales

Meaning of "[racially or religiously aggravated]"

95–014   **28.**—(1) An offence is [racially or religiously aggravated] for the purposes of sections 29 to 32 below if—

(a) at the time of committing the offence, or immediately before or after doing so, the offender demonstrates towards the victim of the offence hostility based on the victim's membership (or presumed membership) of a [racial or religious group]; or

(b) the offence is motivated (wholly or partly) by hostility towards members of a [racial or religious group] based on their membership of that group.

(2) In subsection (1)(a) above—

"membership", in relation to a [racial or religious group], includes association with members of that group;
"presumed" means presumed by the offender.

(3) It is immaterial for the purposes of paragraph (a) or (b) of subsection (1) above whether or not the offender's hostility is also based, to any extent, [on any other factor not mentioned in that paragraph.]

(4) In this section "racial group" means a group of persons defined by reference to race, colour, nationality (including citizenship) or ethnic or national origins.

[(5) In this section "religious group" means a group of persons defined by reference to religious belief or lack of religious belief.]

[Racially or religiously aggravated][1] assaults

29.—(1) A person is guilty of an offence under this section if he commits—   **95–015**

(a) an offence under section 20 of the Offences Against the Person Act 1861 (malicious wounding or grievous bodily harm);

(b) an offence under section 47 of that Act (actual bodily harm); or

(c) common assault,

which is [racially or religiously aggravated][2] for the purposes of this section.

(2) A person guilty of an offence falling within subsection (1)(a) or (b) above shall be liable—

(a) on summary conviction, to imprisonment for a term not exceeding six months or to a fine not exceeding the statutory maximum, or to both;

(b) on conviction on indictment, to imprisonment for a term not exceeding seven years or to a fine, or to both.

(3) A person guilty of an offence falling within subsection (1)(c) above shall be liable—

(a) on summary conviction, to imprisonment for a term not exceeding six months or to a fine not exceeding the statutory maximum, or to both;

(b) on conviction on indictment, to imprisonment for a term not exceeding two years or to a fine, or to both.

[1] Words substituted by Anti-terrorism, Crime and Security Act 2001 (c.24), Pt 5, s. 39(6)(a).
[2] *ibid.*

[Racially or religiously aggravated][1] criminal damage

30.—(1) A person is guilty of an offence under this section if he commits an   **95–016**
offence under section 1(1) of the Criminal Damage Act 1971 (destroying or damaging property belonging to another) which is [racially or religiously aggravated][2] for the purposes of this section.

(2) A person guilty of an offence under this section shall be liable—

(a) on summary conviction, to imprisonment for a term not exceeding six months or to a fine not exceeding the statutory maximum, or to both;
(b) on conviction on indictment, to imprisonment for a term not exceeding fourteen years or to a fine, or to both.

(3) For the purposes of this section, section 28(1)(a) above shall have effect as if the person to whom the property belongs or is treated as belonging for the purposes of that Act were the victim of the offence.

[1] Words substituted by Anti-Terrorism, Crime and Security Act 2001 (c.24), Pt 5, s. 39(6)(b).
[2] *ibid.*

[Racially or religiously aggravated][1] public order offences

95–017   31.—(1) A person is guilty of an offence under this section if he commits—

(a) an offence under section 4 of the Public Order Act 1986 (fear or provocation of violence);
(b) an offence under section 4A of that Act (intentional harassment, alarm or distress); or
(c) an offence under section 5 of that Act (harassment, alarm or distress),

which is [racially or religiously aggravated][2] for the purposes of this section.

(2) A constable may arrest without warrant anyone whom he reasonably suspects to be committing an offence falling within subsection (1)(a) or (b) above.

(3) A constable may arrest a person without warrant if—

(a) he engages in conduct which a constable reasonably suspects to constitute an offence falling within subsection (1)(c) above;
(b) he is warned by that constable to stop; and
(c) he engages in further such conduct immediately or shortly after the warning.

The conduct mentioned in paragraph (a) above and the further conduct need not be of the same nature.

(4) A person guilty of an offence falling within subsection (1)(a) or (b) above shall be liable—

(a) on summary conviction, to imprisonment for a term not exceeding six months or to a fine not exceeding the statutory maximum, or to both;
(b) on conviction on indictment, to imprisonment for a term not exceeding two years or to a fine, or to both.

(5) A person guilty of an offence falling within subsection (1)(c) above shall be liable on summary conviction to a fine not exceeding level 4 on the standard scale.

(6) If, on the trial on indictment of a person charged with an offence falling within subsection (1)(a) or (b) above, the jury find him not guilty of the offence charged, they may find him guilty of the basic offence mentioned in that provision.

(7) For the purposes of subsection (1)(c) above, section 28(1)(a) above shall have effect as if the person likely to be caused harassment, alarm or distress were the victim of the offence.

[1] Words substituted by Anti-Terrorism, Crime and Security Act 2001 (c.24) Pt 5, s. 39(6)(c).
[2] *ibid.*

[Racially or religiously aggravated]¹ harassment etc.

32.—(1) A person is guilty of an offence under this section if he commits—   **95–018**

    (a) an offence under section 2 of the Protection from Harassment Act 1997 (offence of harassment); or

    (b) an offence under section 4 of that Act (putting people in fear of violence),

which is [racially or religiously aggravated]² for the purposes of this section.

(2) In section 24(2) of the 1984 Act (arrestable offences), after paragraph (o) there shall be inserted—

    "(p) an offence falling within section 32(1)(a) of the Crime and Disorder Act 1998 (racially-aggravated harassment);".

(3) A person guilty of an offence falling within subsection (1)(a) above shall be liable—

    (a) on summary conviction, to imprisonment for a term not exceeding six months or to a fine not exceeding the statutory maximum, or to both;

    (b) on conviction on indictment, to imprisonment for a term not exceeding two years or to a fine, or to both.

(4) A person guilty of an offence falling within subsection (1)(b) above shall be liable—

    (a) on summary conviction, to imprisonment for a term not exceeding six months or to a fine not exceeding the statutory maximum, or to both;

    (b) on conviction on indictment, to imprisonment for a term not exceeding seven years or to a fine, or to both.

(5) If, on the trial on indictment of a person charged with an offence falling within subsection (1)(a) above, the jury find him not guilty of the offence charged, they may find him guilty of the basic offence mentioned in that provision.

(6) If, on the trial on indictment of a person charged with an offence falling within subsection (1)(b) above, the jury find him not guilty of the offence charged, they may find him guilty of an offence falling within subsection (1)(a) above.

(7) Section 5 of the Protection from Harassment Act 1997 (restraining orders) shall have effect in relation to a person convicted of an offence under this section as if the reference in subsection (1) of that section to an offence under section 2 or 4 included a reference to an offence under this section.

¹ Words substituted by Anti-terrorism, Crime and Security Act 2001 (c.24), Pt 5, s. 39(6)(d).
² *ibid.*

. . . . . .

Miscellaneous

Abolition of rebuttable presumption that a child is doli incapax

34. The rebuttable presumption of criminal law that a child aged 10 or over   **95–019**
is incapable of committing an offence is hereby abolished.

. . . . . .

Abolition of death penalty for treason and piracy

95–020   **36.**—(1) In section I of the Treason Act (Ireland) 1537 (practising any harm etc. to, or slandering, the King, Queen or heirs apparent punishable as high treason), for the words "have and suffer such pains of death and" there shall be substituted the words "be liable to imprisonment for life and to such".

(2) In the following enactments, namely—

(a) section II of the Crown of Ireland Act 1542 (occasioning disturbance etc. to the crown of Ireland punishable as high treason);

(b) section XII of the Act of Supremacy (Ireland) 1560 (penalties for maintaining or defending foreign authority);

(c) section 3 of the Treason Act 1702 (endeavouring to hinder the succession to the Crown etc. punishable as high treason);

(d) section I of the Treason Act (Ireland) 1703 (which makes corresponding provision), for the words "suffer pains of death" there shall be substituted the words "be liable to imprisonment for life".

(3) The following enactments shall cease to have effect, namely—

(a) the Treason Act 1790;

(b) the Treason Act 1795.

(4) In section 1 of the Treason Act 1814 (form of sentence in case of high treason), for the words "such person shall be hanged by the neck until such person be dead", there shall be substituted the words "such person shall be liable to imprisonment for life".

(5) In section 2 of the Piracy Act 1837 (punishment of piracy when murder is attempted), for the words "and being convicted thereof shall suffer death" there shall be substituted the words "and being convicted thereof shall be liable to imprisonment for life".

(6) The following enactments shall cease to have effect, namely—

(a) the Sentence of Death (Expectant Mothers) Act 1931; and

(b) sections 32 and 33 of the Criminal Justice Act (Northern Ireland) 1945 (which make corresponding provision).

. . . . . .

PART IV

DEALING WITH OFFENDERS

CHAPTER I

ENGLAND AND WALES

Young offenders: reprimands and warnings

Reprimands and warnings

95–021   **65.**—(1) Subsections (2) to (5) below apply where—

(a) a constable has evidence that a child or young person ("the offender") has committed an offence;

(b) the constable considers that the evidence is such that, if the offender were prosecuted for the offence, there would be a realistic prospect of his being convicted;

(c) the offender admits to the constable that he committed the offence;

(d) the offender has not previously been convicted of an offence; and

(e) the constable is satisfied that it would not be in the public interest for the offender to be prosecuted.

(2) Subject to subsection (4) below, the constable may reprimand the offender if the offender has not previously been reprimanded or warned.

(3) The constable may warn the offender if—

(a) the offender has not previously been warned; or

(b) where the offender has previously been warned, the offence was committed more than two years after the date of the previous warning and the constable considers the offence to be not so serious as to require a charge to be brought;

but no person may be warned under paragraph (b) above more than once.

(4) Where the offender has not been previously reprimanded, the constable shall warn rather than reprimand the offender if he considers the offence to be so serious as to require a warning.

(5) The constable shall—

(a) where the offender is under the age of 17, give any reprimand or warning in the presence of an appropriate adult; and

(b) explain to the offender and, where he is under that age, the appropriate adult in ordinary language—

  (i) in the case of a reprimand, the effect of subsection (5)(a) of section 66 below;

  (ii) in the case of a warning, the effect of subsections (1), (2), (4) and (5)(b) and (c) of that section, and any guidance issued under subsection (3) of that section.

(6) The Secretary of State shall publish, in such manner as he considers appropriate, guidance as to—

(a) the circumstances in which it is appropriate to give reprimands or warnings, including criteria for determining—

  (i) for the purposes of subsection (3)(b) above, whether an offence is not so serious as to require a charge to be brought; and

  (ii) for the purposes of subsection (4) above, whether an offence is so serious as to require a warning;

[(aa) the places where reprimands and warnings may be given.] [¹]

(b) the category of constable by whom reprimands and warnings may be given; and

(c) the form which reprimands and warnings are to take and the manner in which they are to be given and recorded.

(7) In this section "appropriate adult", in relation to a child or young person, means—

(a) his parent or guardian or, if he is in the care of a local authority or voluntary organisation, a person representing that authority or organisation;

(b) a social worker of a local authority social services department;

(c) if no person falling within paragraph (a) or (b) above is available, any responsible person aged 18 or over who is not a police officer or a person employed by the police.

(8) No caution shall be given to a child or young person after the commencement of this section.

(9) Any reference (however expressed) in any enactment passed before or in the same Session as this Act to a person being cautioned shall be construed, in relation to any time after that commencement, as including a reference to a child or young person being reprimanded or warned.

[1] Added by Criminal Justice and Court Services Act 2000 (c.43), Pt III, c. II, s. 56(1)(b).

Data Protection Act 1998

(1998, c. 29)

96–001   *An Act to make new provision for the regulation of the processing of information relating to individuals, including the obtaining, holding, use or disclosure of such information.*   [16th July 1998]

PART I

PRELIMINARY

Basic interpretative provisions

96–002   **1.**—(1) In this Act, unless the context otherwise requires—

"data" means information which—

(a) is being processed by means of equipment operating automatically in response to instructions given for that purpose,

(b) is recorded with the intention that it should be processed by means of such equipment,

(c) is recorded as part of a relevant filing system or with the intention that it should form part of a relevant filing system, or

(d) does not fall within paragraph (a), (b) or (c) but forms part of an accessible record as defined by section 68;

"data controller" means, subject to subsection (4), a person who (either alone or jointly or in common with other persons) determines the purposes for which and the manner in which any personal data are, or are to be, processed;

"data processor", in relation to personal data, means any person (other than an employee of the data controller) who processes the data on behalf of the data controller;

"data subject" means an individual who is the subject of personal data;

"personal data" means data which relate to a living individual who can be identified—

(a) from those data, or

(b) from those data and other information which is in the possession of, or is likely to come into the possession of, the data controller, and includes any expression of opinion about the individual and any indication of the intentions of the data controller or any other person in respect of the individual;

"processing", in relation to information or data, means obtaining, recording or holding the information or data or carrying out any operation or set of operations on the information or data, including—

  (a) organisation, adaptation or alteration of the information or data,
  (b) retrieval, consultation or use of the information or data,
  (c) disclosure of the information or data by transmission, dissemination or otherwise making available, or
  (d) alignment, combination, blocking, erasure or destruction of the information or data;

"relevant filing system" means any set of information relating to individuals to the extent that, although the information is not processed by means of equipment operating automatically in response to instructions given for that purpose, the set is structured, either by reference to individuals or by reference to criteria relating to individuals, in such a way that specific information relating to a particular individual is readily accessible.

(2) In this Act, unless the context otherwise requires—

  (a)"obtaining" or "recording", in relation to personal data, includes obtaining or recording the information to be contained in the data, and
  (b) "using" or "disclosing", in relation to personal data, includes using or disclosing the information contained in the data.

(3) In determining for the purposes of this Act whether any information is recorded with the intention—

  (a) that it should be processed by means of equipment operating automatically in response to instructions given for that purpose, or
  (b) that it should form part of a relevant filing system,

it is immaterial that it is intended to be so processed or to form part of such a system only after being transferred to a country or territory outside the European Economic Area.

(4) Where personal data are processed only for purposes for which they are required by or under any enactment to be processed, the person on whom the obligation to process the data is imposed by or under that enactment is for the purposes of this Act the data controller.

Sensitive personal data

2. In this Act "sensitive personal data" means personal data consisting of information as to—   **96–003**

  (a) the racial or ethnic origin of the data subject,
  (b) his political opinions,
  (c) his religious beliefs or other beliefs of a similar nature,
  (d) whether he is a member of a trade union (within the meaning of the Trade Union and Labour Relations (Consolidation) Act 1992),
  (e) his physical or mental health or condition,
  (f) his sexual life,
  (g) the commission or alleged commission by him of any offence, or

(h) any proceedings for any offence committed or alleged to have been committed by him, the disposal of such proceedings or the sentence of any court in such proceedings.

The special purposes

96–004   **3.** In this Act "the special purposes" means any one or more of the following—

(a) the purposes of journalism,
(b) artistic purposes, and
(c) literary purposes.

The data protection principles

96–005   **4.**—(1) References in this Act to the data protection principles are to the principles set out in Part I of Schedule 1.

(2) Those principles are to be interpreted in accordance with Part II of Schedule 1.

(3) Schedule 2 (which applies to all personal data) and Schedule 3 (which applies only to sensitive personal data) set out conditions applying for the purposes of the first principle; and Schedule 4 sets out cases in which the eighth principle does not apply.

(4) Subject to section 27(1), it shall be the duty of a data controller to comply with the data protection principles in relation to all personal data with respect to which he is the data controller.

Application of Act

96–006   **5.**—(1) Except as otherwise provided by or under section 54, this Act applies to a data controller in respect of any data only if—

(a) the data controller is established in the United Kingdom and the data are processed in the context of that establishment, or
(b) the data controller is established neither in the United Kingdom nor in any other EEA State but uses equipment in the United Kingdom for processing the data otherwise than for the purposes of transit through the United Kingdom.

(2) A data controller falling within subsection (1)(b) must nominate for the purposes of this Act a representative established in the United Kingdom.

(3) For the purposes of subsections (1) and (2), each of the following is to be treated as established in the United Kingdom—

(a) an individual who is ordinarily resident in the United Kingdom,
(b) a body incorporated under the law of, or of any part of, the United Kingdom,
(c) a partnership or other unincorporated association formed under the law of any part of the United Kingdom, and
(d) any person who does not fall within paragraph (a), (b) or (c) but maintains in the United Kingdom—

(i) an office, branch or agency through which he carries on any activity, or
(ii) a regular practice;

and the reference to establishment in any other EEA State has a corresponding meaning.

The Commissioner and the Tribunal

6.—[(1) For the purposes of this Act and of the Freedom of Information Act 2000 there shall be an officer known as the Information Commissioner (in this Act referred to as "the Commissioner").][1]

96–007

(2) The Commissioner shall be appointed by Her Majesty by Letters Patent.

[(3) For the purposes of this Act and of the Freedom of Information Act 2000 there shall be a tribunal known as the Information Tribunal (in this Act referred to as "the Tribunal").][2]

(4) The Tribunal shall consist of—

(a) a chairman appointed by the Lord Chancellor after consultation with the Lord Advocate,

(b) such number of deputy chairmen so appointed as the Lord Chancellor may determine, and

(c) such number of other members appointed by the [Lord Chancellor] as he may determine.

(5) The members of the Tribunal appointed under subsection (4)(a) and (b) shall be—

(a) persons who have a 7 year general qualification, within the meaning of section 71 of the Courts and Legal Services Act 1990,

(b) advocates or solicitors in Scotland of at least 7 years' standing, or

(c) members of the bar of Northern Ireland or solicitors of the Supreme Court of Northern Ireland of at least 7 years' standing.

(6) The members of the Tribunal appointed under subsection (4)(c) shall be—

(a) persons to represent the interests of data subjects,

[(aa) persons to represent the interests of those who make requests for information under the Freedom of Information Act 2000,][3]

(b) persons to represent the interests of data controllers, [and][4]

[(bb) persons to represent the interests of public authorities.][5]

(7) Schedule 5 has effect in relation to the Commissioner and the Tribunal.

[1] Substituted by Freedom of Information Act 2000 (c.36), Sched. 2, Pt I, para. 13(2).
[2] Substituted by Freedom of Information Act 2000 (c.36), Sched. 2, Pt I, para. 13(3).
[3] Word substituted and s.6(6)(aa) added by Freedom of Information Act 2000 (c.36) Sched. 2, Pt II, para. 16(a).
[4] Added by Freedom of Information Act 2000 (c.36) Sched. 2, Pt II, para. 16(b).
[5] *ibid.*

PART II

RIGHTS OF DATA SUBJECTS AND OTHERS

Right of access to personal data

7.—(1) Subject to the following provisions of this section and to sections 8 and 9, an individual is entitled—

96–008

(a) to be informed by any data controller whether personal data of which that individual is the data subject are being processed by or on behalf of that data controller,

(b) if that is the case, to be given by the data controller a description of—

(i) the personal data of which that individual is the data subject,
(ii) the purposes for which they are being or are to be processed, and
(iii) the recipients or classes of recipients to whom they are or may be disclosed,

(c) to have communicated to him in an intelligible form—

(i) the information constituting any personal data of which that individual is the data subject, and
(ii) any information available to the data controller as to the source of those data, and

(d) where the processing by automatic means of personal data of which that individual is the data subject for the purpose of evaluating matters relating to him such as, for example, his performance at work, his credit worthiness, his reliability or his conduct, has constituted or is likely to constitute the sole basis for any decision significantly affecting him, to be informed by the data controller of the logic involved in that decision-taking.

(2) A data controller is not obliged to supply any information under subsection (1) unless he has received—

(a) a request in writing, and
(b) except in prescribed cases, such fee (not exceeding the prescribed maximum) as he may require.

[(3) Where a data controller—

(a) reasonably requires further information in order to satisfy himself as to the identity of the person making a request under this section and to locate the information which that person seeks, and
(b) has informed him of that requirement,

the data controller is not obliged to comply with the request unless he is supplied with that further information.]¹

(4) Where a data controller cannot comply with the request without disclosing information relating to another individual who can be identified from that information, he is not obliged to comply with the request unless—

(a) the other individual has consented to the disclosure of the information to the person making the request, or
(b) it is reasonable in all the circumstances to comply with the request without the consent of the other individual.

(5) In subsection (4) the reference to information relating to another individual includes a reference to information identifying that individual as the source of the information sought by the request; and that subsection is not to be construed as excusing a data controller from communicating so much of the information sought by the request as can be communicated without disclosing the identity of the other individual concerned, whether by the omission of names or other identifying particulars or otherwise.

(6) In determining for the purposes of subsection (4)(b) whether it is reasonable in all the circumstances to comply with the request without the consent of the other individual concerned, regard shall be had, in particular, to—

(a) any duty of confidentiality owed to the other individual,
(b) any steps taken by the data controller with a view to seeking the consent of the other individual,

(c) whether the other individual is capable of giving consent, and

(d) any express refusal of consent by the other individual.

(7) An individual making a request under this section may, in such cases as may be prescribed, specify that his request is limited to personal data of any prescribed description.

(8) Subject to subsection (4), a data controller shall comply with a request under this section promptly and in any event before the end of the prescribed period beginning with the relevant day.

(9) If a court is satisfied on the application of any person who has made a request under the foregoing provisions of this section that the data controller in question has failed to comply with the request in contravention of those provisions, the court may order him to comply with the request.

(10) In this section—

"prescribed" means prescribed by the [Lord Chancellor] by regulations:

"the prescribed maximum" means such amount as may be prescribed:

"the prescribed period" means forty days or such other period as may be prescribed:

"the relevant day", in relation to a request under this section, means the day on which the data controller receives the request or, if later, the first day on which the data controller has both the required fee and the information referred to in subsection (3).

(11) Different amounts or periods may be prescribed under this section in relation to different cases.

¹ Substituted by Freedom of Information Act 2000 (c.36), Sched. 6, para. 1.

Provisions supplementary to section 7

8.—(1) The [Lord Chancellor] may by regulations provide that, in such cases **96–009** as may be prescribed, a request for information under any provision of subsection (1) of section 7 is to be treated as extending also to information under other provisions of that subsection.

(2) The obligation imposed by section 7(1)(c)(i) must be complied with by supplying the data subject with a copy of the information in permanent form unless—

(a) the supply of such a copy is not possible or would involve disproportionate effort, or

(b) the data subject agrees otherwise;

and where any of the information referred to in section 7(1)(c)(i) is expressed in terms which are not intelligible without explanation the copy must be accompanied by an explanation of those terms.

(3) Where a data controller has previously complied with a request made under section 7 by an individual, the data controller is not obliged to comply with a subsequent identical or similar request under that section by that individual unless a reasonable interval has elapsed between compliance with the previous request and the making of the current request.

(4) In determining for the purposes of subsection (3) whether requests under section 7 are made at reasonable intervals, regard shall be had to the nature of the data, the purposes for which the data are processed and the frequency with which the data are altered.

(5) Section 7(1)(d) is not to be regarded as requiring the provision of information as to the logic involved in any decision-taking if, and to the extent that, the information constitutes a trade secret.

(6) The information to be supplied pursuant to a request under section 7 must be supplied by reference to the data in question at the time when the request is received, except that it may take account of any amendment or deletion made between that time and the time when the information is supplied, being an amendment or deletion that would have been made regardless of the receipt of the request.

(7) For the purposes of section 7(4) and (5) another individual can be identified from the information being disclosed if he can be identified from that information, or from that and any other information which, in the reasonable belief of the data controller, is likely to be in, or to come into, the possession of the data subject making the request.

Application of section 7 where data controller is credit reference agency

96–010

9.—(1) Where the data controller is a credit reference agency, section 7 has effect subject to the provisions of this section.

(2) An individual making a request under section 7 may limit his request to personal data relevant to his financial standing, and shall be taken to have so limited his request unless the request shows a contrary intention.

(3) Where the data controller receives a request under section 7 in a case where personal data of which the individual making the request is the data subject are being processed by or on behalf of the data controller, the obligation to supply information under that section includes an obligation to give the individual making the request a statement, in such form as may be prescribed by the [Lord Chancellor] by regulations, of the individual's rights—

(a) under section 159 of the Consumer Credit Act 1974, and
(b) to the extent required by the prescribed form, under this Act.

Right to prevent processing likely to cause damage or distress

96–011

10.—(1) Subject to subsection (2), an individual is entitled at any time by notice in writing to a data controller to require the data controller at the end of such period as is reasonable in the circumstances to cease, or not to begin, processing, or processing for a specified purpose or in a specified manner, any personal data in respect of which he is the data subject, on the ground that, for specified reasons—

(a) the processing of those data or their processing for that purpose or in that manner is causing or is likely to cause substantial damage or substantial distress to him or to another, and
(b) that damage or distress is or would be unwarranted.

(2) Subsection (1) does not apply—

(a) in a case where any of the conditions in paragraphs 1 to 4 of Schedule 2 is met, or
(b) in such other cases as may be prescribed by the [Lord Chancellor] by order.

(3) The data controller must within twenty-one days of receiving a notice under subsection (1) ("the data subject notice") give the individual who gave it a written notice—

(a) stating that he has complied or intends to comply with the data subject notice, or
(b) stating his reasons for regarding the data subject notice as to any extent

unjustified and the extent (if any) to which he has complied or intends to comply with it.

(4) If a court is satisfied, on the application of any person who has given a notice under subsection (1) which appears to the court to be justified (or to be justified to any extent), that the data controller in question has failed to comply with the notice, the court may order him to take such steps for complying with the notice (or for complying with it to that extent) as the court thinks fit.

(5) The failure by a data subject to exercise the right conferred by subsection (1) or section 11(1) does not affect any other right conferred on him by this Part.

Right to prevent processing for purposes of direct marketing

11.—(1) An individual is entitled at any time by notice in writing to a data controller to require the data controller at the end of such period as is reasonable in the circumstances to cease, or not to begin, processing for the purposes of direct marketing personal data in respect of which he is the data subject. **96–012**

(2) If the court is satisfied, on the application of any person who has given a notice under subsection (1), that the data controller has failed to comply with the notice, the court may order him to take such steps for complying with the notice as the court thinks fit.

[(2A) This section shall not apply in relation to the processing of such data as are mentioned in paragraph (1) of regulation 8 of the Telecommunications (Data Protection and Privacy) Regulations 1999 (processing of telecommunications billing data for certain marketing purposes) for the purposes mentioned in paragraph (2) of that regulation.]

(3) In this section "direct marketing" means the communication (by whatever means) of any advertising or marketing material which is directed to particular individuals.

Rights in relation to automated decision-taking

12.—(1) An individual is entitled at any time, by notice in writing to any data controller, to require the data controller to ensure that no decision taken by or on behalf of the data controller which significantly affects that individual is based solely on the processing by automatic means of personal data in respect of which that individual is the data subject for the purpose of evaluating matters relating to him such as, for example, his performance at work, his credit worthiness, his reliability or his conduct. **96–013**

(2) Where, in a case where no notice under subsection (1) has effect, a decision which significantly affects an individual is based solely on such processing as is mentioned in subsection (1)—

   (a) the data controller must as soon as reasonably practicable notify the individual that the decision was taken on that basis, and

   (b) the individual is entitled, within twenty-one days of receiving that notification from the data controller, by notice in writing to require the data controller to reconsider the decision or to take a new decision otherwise than on that basis.

(3) The data controller must, within twenty-one days of receiving a notice under subsection (2)(b) ("the data subject notice") give the individual a written notice specifying the steps that he intends to take to comply with the data subject notice.

(4) A notice under subsection (1) does not have effect in relation to an exempt decision; and nothing in subsection (2) applies to an exempt decision.

(5) In subsection (4) "exempt decision" means any decision—

(a) in respect of which the condition in subsection (6) and the condition in subsection (7) are met, or
(b) which is made in such other circumstances as may be prescribed by the [Lord Chancellor] by order.

(6) The condition in this subsection is that the decision—

(a) is taken in the course of steps taken—

    (i) for the purpose of considering whether to enter into a contract with the data subject,
    (ii) with a view to entering into such a contract, or
    (iii) in the course of performing such a contract, or

(b) is authorised or required by or under any enactment.

(7) The condition in this subsection is that either—

(a) the effect of the decision is to grant a request of the data subject, or
(b) steps have been taken to safeguard the legitimate interests of the data subject (for example, by allowing him to make representations).

(8) If a court is satisfied on the application of a data subject that a person taking a decision in respect of him ("the responsible person") has failed to comply with subsection (1) or (2)(b), the court may order the responsible person to reconsider the decision, or to take a new decision which is not based solely on such processing as is mentioned in subsection (1).

(9) An order under subsection (8) shall not affect the rights of any person other than the data subject and the responsible person.

[Rights of data subjects in relation to exempt manual data

96–014   **12A.**—(1) A data subject is entitled at any time by notice in writing—

(a) to require the data controller to rectify, block, erase or destroy exempt manual data which are inaccurate or incomplete, or
(b) to require the data controller to cease holding exempt manual data in a way incompatible with the legitimate purposes pursued by the data controller.

(2) A notice under subsection (1)(a) or (b) must state the data subject's reasons for believing that the data are inaccurate or incomplete or, as the case may be, his reasons for believing that they are held in a way incompatible with the legitimate purposes pursued by the data controller.

(3) If the court is satisfied, on the application of any person who has given a notice under subsection (1) which appears to the court to be justified (or to be justified to any extent) that the data controller in question has failed to comply with the notice, the court may order him to take such steps for complying with the notice (or for complying with it to that extent) as the court thinks fit.

(4) In this section "exempt manual data" means —

(a) in relation to the first transitional period, as defined by paragraph 1(2) of Schedule 8, data to which paragraph 3 or 4 of that Schedule applies, and
(b) in relation to the second transitional period, as so defined, data to which paragraph 14 of that Schedule applies.

(5) For the purposes of this section personal data are incomplete if, and only if, the data, although not inaccurate, are such that their incompleteness would constitute a contravention of the third or fourth data protection principles, if those principles applied to the data.]

Compensation for failure to comply with certain requirements

13.—(1) An individual who suffers damage by reason of any contravention by a data controller of any of the requirements of this Act is entitled to compensation from the data controller for that damage.

(2) An individual who suffers distress by reason of any contravention by a data controller of any of the requirements of this Act is entitled to compensation from the data controller for that distress if—

(a) the individual also suffers damage by reason of the contravention, or
(b) the contravention relates to the processing of personal data for the special purposes.

(3) In proceedings brought against a person by virtue of this section it is a defence to prove that he had taken such care as in all the circumstances was reasonably required to comply with the requirement concerned.

96–015

Rectification, blocking, erasure and destruction

14.—(1) If a court is satisfied on the application of a data subject that personal data of which the applicant is the subject are inaccurate, the court may order the data controller to rectify, block, erase or destroy those data and any other personal data in respect of which he is the data controller and which contain an expression of opinion which appears to the court to be based on the inaccurate data.

(2) Subsection (1) applies whether or not the data accurately record information received or obtained by the data controller from the data subject or a third party but where the data accurately record such information, then—

(a) if the requirements mentioned in paragraph 7 of Part II of Schedule 1 have been complied with, the court may, instead of making an order under subsection (1), make an order requiring the data to be supplemented by such statement of the true facts relating to the matters dealt with by the data as the court may approve, and
(b) if all or any of those requirements have not been complied with, the court may, instead of making an order under that subsection, make such order as it thinks fit for securing compliance with those requirements with or without a further order requiring the data to be supplemented by such a statement as is mentioned in paragraph (a).

(3) Where the court—

(a) makes an order under subsection (1), or
(b) is satisfied on the application of a data subject that personal data of which he was the data subject and which have been rectified, blocked, erased or destroyed were inaccurate,

it may, where it considers it reasonably practicable, order the data controller to notify third parties to whom the data have been disclosed of the rectification, blocking, erasure or destruction.

(4) If a court is satisfied on the application of a data subject—

96–016

(a) that he has suffered damage by reason of any contravention by a data controller of any of the requirements of this Act in respect of any personal data, in circumstances entitling him to compensation under section 13, and

(b) that there is a substantial risk of further contravention in respect of those data in such circumstances,

the court may order the rectification, blocking, erasure or destruction of any of those data.

(5) Where the court makes an order under subsection (4) it may, where it considers it reasonably practicable, order the data controller to notify third parties to whom the data have been disclosed of the rectification, blocking, erasure or destruction.

(6) In determining whether it is reasonably practicable to require such notification as is mentioned in subsection (3) or (5) the court shall have regard, in particular, to the number of persons who would have to be notified.

Jurisdiction and procedure

96–017 **15.**—(1) The jurisdiction conferred by sections 7 to 14 is exercisable by the High Court or a county court or, in Scotland, by the Court of Session or the sheriff.

(2) For the purpose of determining any question whether an applicant under subsection (9) of section 7 is entitled to the information which he seeks (including any question whether any relevant data are exempt from that section by virtue of Part IV) a court may require the information constituting any data processed by or on behalf of the data controller and any information as to the logic involved in any decision-taking as mentioned in section 7(1)(d) to be made available for its own inspection but shall not, pending the determination of that question in the applicant's favour, require the information sought by the applicant to be disclosed to him or his representatives whether by discovery (or, in Scotland, recovery) or otherwise.

. . . . . .

PART IV

EXEMPTIONS

Preliminary

96–018 **27.**—(1) References in any of the data protection principles or any provision of Parts II and III to personal data or to the processing of personal data do not include references to data or processing which by virtue of this Part are exempt from that principle or other provision.

(2) In this Part "the subject information provisions" means —

(a) the first data protection principle to the extent to which it requires compliance with paragraph 2 of Part II of Schedule 1, and

(b) section 7.

(3) In this Part "the non-disclosure provisions" means the provisions specified in subsection (4) to the extent to which they are inconsistent with the disclosure in question.

(4) The provisions referred to in subsection (3) are—

(a) the first data protection principle, except to the extent to which it requires compliance with the conditions in Schedules 2 and 3,

(b) the second, third, fourth and fifth data protection principles, and

(c) sections 10 and 14(1) to (3).

(5) Except as provided by this Part, the subject information provisions shall have effect notwithstanding any enactment or rule of law prohibiting or restricting the disclosure, or authorising the withholding, of information.

National security

28.—(1) Personal data are exempt from any of the provisions of—   **96–019**

(a) the data protection principles,

(b) Parts II, III and V, and

(c) section 55,

if the exemption from that provision is required for the purpose of safeguarding national security.

(2) Subject to subsection (4), a certificate signed by a Minister of the Crown certifying that exemption from all or any of the provisions mentioned in subsection (1) is or at any time was required for the purpose there mentioned in respect of any personal data shall be conclusive evidence of that fact.

(3) A certificate under subsection (2) may identify the personal data to which it applies by means of a general description and may be expressed to have prospective effect.

(4) Any person directly affected by the issuing of a certificate under subsection (2) may appeal to the Tribunal against the certificate.

(5) If on an appeal under subsection (4), the Tribunal finds that, applying the principles applied by the court on an application for judicial review, the Minister did not have reasonable grounds for issuing the certificate, the Tribunal may allow the appeal and quash the certificate.

(6) Where in any proceedings under or by virtue of this Act it is claimed by a data controller that a certificate under subsection (2) which identifies the personal data to which it applies by means of a general description applies to any personal data, any other party to the proceedings may appeal to the Tribunal on the ground that the certificate does not apply to the personal data in question and, subject to any determination under subsection (7), the certificate shall be conclusively presumed so to apply.

(7) On any appeal under subsection (6), the Tribunal may determine that the certificate does not so apply.

(8) A document purporting to be a certificate under subsection (2) shall be received in evidence and deemed to be such a certificate unless the contrary is proved.

(9) A document which purports to be certified by or on behalf of a Minister of the Crown as a true copy of a certificate issued by that Minister under subsection (2) shall in any legal proceedings be evidence (or, in Scotland, sufficient evidence) of that certificate.

(10) The power conferred by subsection (2) on a Minister of the Crown shall not be exercisable except by a Minister who is a member of the Cabinet or by the Attorney General or the Lord Advocate.

(11) No power conferred by any provision of Part V may be exercised in relation to personal data which by virtue of this section are exempt from that provision.

(12) Schedule 6 shall have effect in relation to appeals under subsection (4) or (6) and the proceedings of the Tribunal in respect of any such appeal.

Crime and taxation

96–020   29.—(1) Personal data processed for any of the following purposes—

   (a) the prevention or detection of crime,
   (b) the apprehension or prosecution of offenders, or
   (c) the assessment or collection of any tax or duty or of any imposition of
        a similar nature,

are exempt from the first data protection principle (except to the extent to which
it requires compliance with the conditions in Schedules 2 and 3) and section 7
in any case to the extent to which the application of those provisions to the data
would be likely to prejudice any of the matters mentioned in this subsection.
   (2) Personal data which—

   (a) are processed for the purpose of discharging statutory functions, and
   (b) consist of information obtained for such a purpose from a person who
        had it in his possession for any of the purposes mentioned in subsection
        (1),

are exempt from the subject information provisions to the same extent as personal data processed for any of the purposes mentioned in that subsection.
   (3) Personal data are exempt from the non-disclosure provisions in any case
in which—

   (a) the disclosure is for any of the purposes mentioned in subsection (1),
        and
   (b) the application of those provisions in relation to the disclosure would
        be likely to prejudice any of the matters mentioned in that subsection.

   (4) Personal data in respect of which the data controller is a relevant authority
and which—

   (a) consist of a classification applied to the data subject as part of a system
        of risk assessment which is operated by that authority for either of the
        following purposes—

      (i) the assessment or collection of any tax or duty or any imposition
           of a similar nature, or
      (ii) the prevention or detection of crime, or apprehension or prosecu-
           tion of offenders, where the offence concerned involves any
           unlawful claim for any payment out of, or any unlawful applica-
           tion of, public funds, and

   (b) are processed for either of those purposes,

are exempt from section 7 to the extent to which the exemption is required in
the interests of the operation of the system.
   (5) In subsection (4)—

   "public funds" includes funds provided by any Community institution;
   "relevant authority" means—

      (a) a government department,
      (b) a local authority, or
      (c) any other authority administering housing benefit or council tax
           benefit.

Health, education and social work

30.—(1) The [Lord Chancellor] may by order exempt from the subject **96–021** information provisions, or modify those provisions in relation to, personal data consisting of information as to the physical or mental health or condition of the data subject.

(2) The [Lord Chancellor] may by order exempt from the subject information provisions, or modify those provisions in relation to—

(a) personal data in respect of which the data controller is the proprietor of, or a teacher at, a school, and which consist of information relating to persons who are or have been pupils at the school, or

(b) personal data in respect of which the data controller is an education authority in Scotland, and which consist of information relating to persons who are receiving, or have received, further education provided by the authority.

(3) The [Lord Chancellor] may by order exempt from the subject information provisions, or modify those provisions in relation to, personal data of such other descriptions as may be specified in the order, being information—

(a) processed by government departments or local authorities or by voluntary organisations or other bodies designated by or under the order, and

(b) appearing to him to be processed in the course of, or for the purposes of, carrying out social work in relation to the data subject or other individuals;

but the [Lord Chancellor] shall not under this subsection confer any exemption or make any modification except so far as he considers that the application to the data of those provisions (or of those provisions without modification) would be likely to prejudice the carrying out of social work.

(4) An order under this section may make different provision in relation to data consisting of information of different descriptions.

(5) In this section—

"education authority" and "further education" have the same meaning as in the Education (Scotland) Act 1980 ("the 1980 Act"), and
"proprietor"—

(a) in relation to a school in England or Wales, has the same meaning as in the Education Act 1996,

(b) in relation to a school in Scotland, means—

(i) in the case of a self-governing school, the board of management within the meaning of the Self-Governing Schools etc. (Scotland) Act 1989,

(ii) in the case of an independent school, the proprietor within the meaning of the 1980 Act,

(iii) in the case of a grant-aided school, the managers within the meaning of the 1980 Act, and

(iv) in the case of a public school, the education authority within the meaning of the 1980 Act, and

(c) in relation to a school in Northern Ireland, has the same meaning as in the Education and Libraries (Northern Ireland) Order 1986 and includes, in the case of a controlled school, the Board of Governors of the school.

Regulatory activity

96–022 31.—(1) Personal data processed for the purposes of discharging functions to which this subsection applies are exempt from the subject information provisions in any case to the extent to which the application of those provisions to the data would be likely to prejudice the proper discharge of those functions.

(2) Subsection (1) applies to any relevant function which is designed—

  (a) for protecting members of the public against—

    (i) financial loss due to dishonesty, malpractice or other seriously improper conduct by, or the unfitness or incompetence of, persons concerned in the provision of banking, insurance, investment or other financial services or in the management of bodies corporate,

    (ii) financial loss due to the conduct of discharged or undischarged bankrupts, or

    (iii) dishonesty, malpractice or other seriously improper conduct by, or the unfitness or incompetence of, persons authorised to carry on any profession or other activity,

  (b) for protecting charities against misconduct or mismanagement (whether by trustees or other persons) in their administration,

  (c) for protecting the property of charities from loss or misapplication,

  (d) for the recovery of the property of charities,

  (e) for securing the health, safety and welfare of persons at work, or

  (f) for protecting persons other than persons at work against risk to health or safety arising out of or in connection with the actions of persons at work.

(3) In subsection (2) "relevant function" means—

  (a) any function conferred on any person by or under any enactment,

  (b) any function of the Crown, a Minister of the Crown or a government department, or

  (c) any other function which is of a public nature and is exercised in the public interest.

(4) Personal data processed for the purpose of discharging any function which—

  (a) is conferred by or under any enactment on—

    (i) the Parliamentary Commissioner for Administration,

    (ii) the Commission for Local Administration in England, the Commission for Local Administration in Wales or the Commissioner for Local Administration in Scotland,

    (iii) the Health Service Commissioner for England, the Health Service Commissioner for Wales or the Health Service Commissioner for Scotland,

    (iv) the Welsh Administration Ombudsman,

    (v) the Assembly Ombudsman for Northern Ireland, or

    (vi) the Northern Ireland Commissioner for Complaints, and

  (b) is designed for protecting members of the public against—

    (i) maladministration by public bodies,

    (ii) failures in services provided by public bodies, or

    (iii) a failure of a public body to provide a service which it was a function of the body to provide, are exempt from the subject information provisions in any case to the extent to which the application of those provisions to the data would be likely to prejudice the proper discharge of that function.

[(4A) Personal data processed for the purpose of discharging any function which is conferred by or under Part XVI of the Financial Services and Markets Act 2000 on the body established by the Financial Services Authority for the purposes of that Part are exempt from the subject information provisions in any case to the extent to which the application of those provisions to the data would be likely to prejudice the proper discharge of the function.]¹

(5) Personal data processed for the purpose of discharging any function which—

    (a) is conferred by or under any enactment on the Director General of Fair Trading, and

    (b) is designed—

        (i) for protecting members of the public against conduct which may adversely affect their interests by persons carrying on a business,

        (ii) for regulating agreements or conduct which have as their object or effect the prevention, restriction or distortion of competition in connection with any commercial activity, or

        (iii) for regulating conduct on the part of one or more undertakings which amounts to the abuse of a dominant position in a market,

are exempt from the subject information provisions in any case to the extent to which the application of those provisions to the data would be likely to prejudice the proper discharge of that function.

¹ Added by Financial Services and Markets Act 2000 (c.8), Pt XVI, s. 233.

Journalism, literature and art

32.—(1) Personal data which are processed only for the special purposes are exempt from any provision to which this subsection relates if— **96–023**

    (a) the processing is undertaken with a view to the publication by any person of any journalistic, literary or artistic material,

    (b) the data controller reasonably believes that, having regard in particular to the special importance of the public interest in freedom of expression, publication would be in the public interest, and

    (c) the data controller reasonably believes that, in all the circumstances, compliance with that provision is incompatible with the special purposes.

(2) Subsection (1) relates to the provisions of—

    (a) the data protection principles except the seventh data protection principle,

    (b) section 7,

    (c) section 10,

    (d) section 12, and

    [(e) section 12A,]

    (f) section 14(1) to (3).

(3) In considering for the purposes of subsection (1)(b) whether the belief of a data controller that publication would be in the public interest was or is a reasonable one, regard may be had to his compliance with any code of practice which—

    (a) is relevant to the publication in question, and

    (b) is designated by the [Lord Chancellor] by order for the purposes of this subsection.

(4) Where at any time ("the relevant time") in any proceedings against a data controller under section 7(9), 10(4), 12(8) [, 12A(3)] or 14 or by virtue of section 13 the data controller claims, or it appears to the court, that any personal data to which the proceedings relate are being processed—

    (a) only for the special purposes, and

    (b) with a view to the publication by any person of any journalistic, literary or artistic material which, at the time twenty-four hours immediately before the relevant time, had not previously been published by the data controller,

the court shall stay the proceedings until either of the conditions in subsection (5) is met.

    (5) Those conditions are—

    (a) that a determination of the Commissioner under section 45 with respect to the data in question takes effect, or

    (b) in a case where the proceedings were stayed on the making of a claim, that the claim is withdrawn.

(6) For the purposes of this Act "publish", in relation to journalistic, literary or artistic material, means make available to the public or any section of the public.

Research, history and statistics

96–024   **33.**—(1) In this section—

"research purposes" includes statistical or historical purposes;
"the relevant conditions", in relation to any processing of personal data, means the conditions—

    (a) that the data are not processed to support measures or decisions with respect to particular individuals, and

    (b) that the data are not processed in such a way that substantial damage or substantial distress is, or is likely to be, caused to any data subject.

(2) For the purposes of the second data protection principle, the further processing of personal data only for research purposes in compliance with the relevant conditions is not to be regarded as incompatible with the purposes for which they were obtained.

(3) Personal data which are processed only for research purposes in compliance with the relevant conditions may, notwithstanding the fifth data protection principle, be kept indefinitely.

(4) Personal data which are processed only for research purposes are exempt from section 7 if—

    (a) they are processed in compliance with the relevant conditions, and

    (b) the results of the research or any resulting statistics are not made available in a form which identifies data subjects or any of them.

(5) For the purposes of subsections (2) to (4) personal data are not to be

treated as processed otherwise than for research purposes merely because the data are disclosed—

(a) to any person, for research purposes only;
(b) to the data subject or a person acting on his behalf,
(c) at the request, or with the consent, of the data subject or a person acting on his behalf, or
(d) in circumstances in which the person making the disclosure has reasonable grounds for believing that the disclosure falls within paragraph (a), (b) or (c).

Information available to the public by or under enactment

34. Personal data are exempt from—   **96–025**

(a) the subject information provisions,
(b) the fourth data protection principle and [sections 12A and 14(1) to (3)], and
(c) the non-disclosure provisions,

if the data consist of information which the data controller is obliged by or under any enactment to make available to the public, whether by publishing it, by making it available for inspection, or otherwise and whether gratuitously or on payment of a fee.

Disclosures required by law or made in connection with legal proceedings etc.

35.—(1) Personal data are exempt from the non-disclosure provisions where   **96–026**
the disclosure is required by or under any enactment, by any rule of law or by the order of a court.

(2) Personal data are exempt from the non-disclosure provisions where the disclosure is necessary—

(a) for the purpose of, or in connection with, any legal proceedings (including prospective legal proceedings), or
(b) for the purpose of obtaining legal advice,

or is otherwise necessary for the purposes of establishing, exercising or defending legal rights.

Domestic purposes

36. Personal data processed by an individual only for the purposes of that   **96–027**
individual's personal, family or household affairs (including recreational purposes) are exempt from the data protection principles and the provisions of Parts II and III.

Miscellaneous exemptions

37. Schedule 7 (which confers further miscellaneous exemptions) has effect.   **96–028**

Powers to make further exemptions by order

38.—(1) The [Lord Chancellor] may by order exempt from the subject   **96–029**
information provisions personal data consisting of information the disclosure of which is prohibited or restricted by or under any enactment if and to the extent

that he considers it necessary for the safeguarding of the interests of the data subject or the rights and freedoms of any other individual that the prohibition or restriction ought to prevail over those provisions.

(2) The [Lord Chancellor] may by order exempt from the non-disclosure provisions any disclosures of personal data made in circumstances specified in the order, if he considers the exemption is necessary for the safeguarding of the interests of the data subject or the rights and freedoms of any other individual.

. . . . . .

PART V

ENFORCEMENT

Enforcement notices

96–030   **40.**—(1) If the Commissioner is satisfied that a data controller has contravened or is contravening any of the data protection principles, the Commissioners may serve him with a notice (in this Act referred to as "an enforcement notice") requiring him, for complying with the principle or principles in question, to do either or both of the following—

(a) to take within such time as may be specified in the notice, or to refrain from taking after such time as may be so specified, such steps as are so specified, or

(b) to refrain from processing any personal data, or any personal data of a description specified in the notice, or to refrain from processing them for a purpose so specified or in a manner so specified, after such time as may be so specified.

(2) In deciding whether to serve an enforcement notice, the Commissioner shall consider whether the contravention has caused or is likely to cause any person damage or distress.

(3) An enforcement notice in respect of a contravention of the fourth data protection principle which requires the data controller to rectify, block, erase or destroy any inaccurate data may also require the data controller to rectify, block, erase or destroy any other data held by him and containing an expression of opinion which appears to the Commissioner to be based on the inaccurate data.

(4) An enforcement notice in respect of a contravention of the fourth data protection principle, in the case of data which accurately record information received or obtained by the data controller from the data subject or a third party, may require the data controller either—

(a) to rectify, block, erase or destroy any inaccurate data and any other data held by him and containing an expression of opinion as mentioned in subsection (3), or

(b) to take such steps as are specified in the notice for securing compliance with the requirements specified in paragraph 7 of Part II of Schedule 1 and, if the Commissioner thinks fit, for supplementing the data with such statement of the true facts relating to the matters dealt with by the data as the Commissioner may approve.

(5) Where—

(a) an enforcement notice requires the data controller to rectify, block, erase or destroy any personal data, or

(b) the Commissioner is satisfied that personal data which have been rectified, blocked, erased or destroyed had been processed in contravention of any of the data protection principles,

an enforcement notice may, if reasonably practicable, require the data controller to notify third parties to whom the data have been disclosed of the rectification, blocking, erasure or destruction; and in determining whether it is reasonably practicable to require such notification regard shall be had, in particular, to the number of persons who would have to be notified.

(6) An enforcement notice must contain—

(a) a statement of the data protection principle or principles which the Commissioner is satisfied have been or are being contravened and his reasons for reaching that conclusion, and

(b) particulars of the rights of appeal conferred by section 48.

(7) Subject to subsection (8), an enforcement notice must not require any of the provisions of the notice to be complied with before the end of the period within which an appeal can be brought against the notice and, if such an appeal is brought, the notice need not be complied with pending the determination or withdrawal of the appeal.

(8) If by reason of special circumstances the Commissioner considers that an enforcement notice should be complied with as a matter of urgency he may include in the notice a statement to that effect and a statement of his reasons for reaching that conclusion; and in that event subsection (7) shall not apply but the notice must not require the provisions of the notice to be complied with before the end of the period of seven days beginning with the day on which the notice is served.

(9) Notification regulations (as defined by section 16(2)) may make provision as to the effect of the service of an enforcement notice on any entry in the register maintained under section 19 which relates to the person on whom the notice is served.

(10) This section has effect subject to section 46(1).

. . . . . .

Failure to comply with notice

47.—(1) A person who fails to comply with an enforcement notice, an **96–031** information notice or a special information notice is guilty of an offence.

(2) A person who, in purported compliance with an information notice or a special information notice—

(a) makes a statement which he knows to be false in a material respect, or

(b) recklessly makes a statement which is false in a material respect,

is guilty of an offence.

(3) It is a defence for a person charged with an offence under subsection (1) to prove that he exercised all due diligence to comply with the notice in question.

. . . . . .

Powers of entry and inspection

96–032   **50.** Schedule 9 (powers of entry and inspection) has effect.

Schedules

Section 4(1) and (2)   SCHEDULE 1

THE DATA PROTECTION PRINCIPLES

PART I

THE PRINCIPLES

96–033   **1.** Personal data shall be processed fairly and lawfully and, in particular, shall not be processed unless—

> (a) at least one of the conditions in Schedule 2 is met, and
> (b) in the case of sensitive personal data, at least one of the conditions in Schedule 3 is also met.

2. Personal data shall be obtained only for one or more specified and lawful purposes, and shall not be further processed in any manner incompatible with that purpose or those purposes.

3. Personal data shall be adequate, relevant and not excessive in relation to the purpose or purposes for which they are processed.

4. Personal data shall be accurate and, where necessary, kept up to date.

5. Personal data processed for any purpose or purposes shall not be kept for longer than is necessary for that purpose or those purposes.

6. Personal data shall be processed in accordance with the rights of data subjects under this Act.

7. Appropriate technical and organisational measures shall be taken against unauthorised or unlawful processing of personal data and against accidental loss or destruction of, or damage to, personal data.

8. Personal data shall not be transferred to a country or territory outside the European Economic Area unless that country or territory ensures an adequate level of protection for the rights and freedoms of data subjects in relation to the processing of personal data.

PART II

INTERPRETATION OF THE PRINCIPLES IN PART I

The first principle

96–034   **1.**—(1) In determining for the purposes of the first principle whether personal data are processed fairly, regard is to be had to the method by which they are obtained, including in particular whether any person from whom they are obtained is deceived or misled as to the purpose or purposes for which they are to be processed.

(2) Subject to paragraph 2, for the purposes of the first principle data are to be treated as obtained fairly if they consist of information obtained from a person who—

> (a) is authorised by or under any enactment to supply it, or
> (b) is required to supply it by or under any enactment or by any convention or other instrument imposing an international obligation on the United Kingdom.

96–035   **2.**—(1) Subject to paragraph 3, for the purposes of the first principle personal data are not to be treated as processed fairly unless—

> (a) in the case of data obtained from the data subject, the data controller ensures so far as practicable that the data subject has, is provided with, or has made readily available to him, the information specified in sub-paragraph (3), and
> (b) in any other case, the data controller ensures so far as practicable that, before the relevant time or as soon as practicable after that time, the data subject has, is provided with, or has made readily available to him, the information specified in sub-paragraph (3).

(2) In sub-paragraph (1)(b) "the relevant time" means—

> (a) the time when the data controller first processes the data, or
> (b) in a case where at that time disclosure to a third party within a reasonable period is envisaged—
>
> > (i) if the data are in fact disclosed to such a person within that period, the time when the data are first disclosed,

(ii) if within that period the data controller becomes, or ought to become, aware that the data are unlikely to be disclosed to such a person within that period, the time when the data controller does become, or ought to become, so aware, or

(iii) in any other case, the end of that period.

(3) The information referred to in sub-paragraph (1) is as follows, namely—

(a) the identity of the data controller,

(b) if he has nominated a representative for the purposes of this Act, the identity of that representative,

(c) the purpose or purposes for which the data are intended to be processed, and

(d) any further information which is necessary, having regard to the specific circumstances in which the data are or are to be processed, to enable processing in respect of the data subject to be fair.

3.—(1) Paragraph 2(1)(b) does not apply where either of the primary conditions in sub-paragraph (2), together with such further conditions as may be prescribed by the [Lord Chancellor] by order, are met.   **96–036**

(2) The primary conditions referred to in sub-paragraph (1) are—

(a) that the provision of that information would involve a disproportionate effort, or

(b) that the recording of the information to be contained in the data by, or the disclosure of the data by, the data controller is necessary for compliance with any legal obligation to which the data controller is subject, other than an obligation imposed by contract.

4.—(1) Personal data which contain a general identifier falling within a description prescribed by the [Lord Chancellor] by order are not to be treated as processed fairly and lawfully unless they are processed in compliance with any conditions so prescribed in relation to general identifiers of that description.   **96–037**

(2) In sub-paragraph (1) "a general identifier" means any identifier (such as, for example, a number or code used for identification purposes) which—

(a) relates to an individual, and

(b) forms part of a set of similar identifiers which is of general application.

The second principle

5. The purpose or purposes for which personal data are obtained may in particular be specified—   **96–038**

(a) in a notice given for the purposes of paragraph 2 by the data controller to the data subject, or

(b) in a notification given to the Commissioner under Part III of this Act.

6. In determining whether any disclosure of personal data is compatible with the purpose or purposes for which the data were obtained, regard is to be had to the purpose or purposes for which the personal data are intended to be processed by any person to whom they are disclosed.   **96–039**

The fourth principle

7. The fourth principle is not to be regarded as being contravened by reason of any inaccuracy in personal data which accurately record information obtained by the data controller from the data subject or a third party in a case where—   **96–040**

(a) having regard to the purpose or purposes for which the data were obtained and further processed, the data controller has taken reasonable steps to ensure the accuracy of the data, and

(b) if the data subject has notified the data controller of the data subject's view that the data are inaccurate, the data indicate that fact.

The sixth principle

8. A person is to be regarded as contravening the sixth principle if, but only if—   **96–041**

(a) he contravenes section 7 by failing to supply information in accordance with that section,

(b) he contravenes section 10 by failing to comply with a notice given under subsection (1) of that section to the extent that the notice is justified or by failing to give a notice under subsection (3) of that section,

(c) he contravenes section 11 by failing to comply with a notice given under subsection (1) of that section, [. . .]¹

(d) he contravenes section 12 by failing to comply with a notice given under subsection (1) or (2)(b) of that section or by failing to give a notification under subsection (2)(a) of that section or a notice under subsection (3) of that section, [or

(e) he contravenes section 12A by failing to comply with a notice given under subsection (1) of that section to the extent that the notice is justified.]²

¹ Word repealed by Data Protection Act 1998 (c.29), Sched. 13, para. 5.
² para. (e) and the word "or" immediatley preceeding it inserted by Data Protection Act 1998 (c.29), Sched. 13, para. 5.

The seventh principle

96–042   9. Having regard to the state of technological development and the cost of implementing any measures, the measures must ensure a level of security appropriate to—

(a) the harm that might result from such unauthorised or unlawful processing or accidental loss, destruction or damage as are mentioned in the seventh principle, and
(b) the nature of the data to be protected.

96–043   10. The data controller must take reasonable steps to ensure the reliability of any employees of his who have access to the personal data.

96–044   11. Where processing of personal data is carried out by a data processor on behalf of a data controller, the data controller must in order to comply with the seventh principle—

(a) choose a data processor providing sufficient guarantees in respect of the technical and organisational security measures governing the processing to be carried out, and
(b) take reasonable steps to ensure compliance with those measures.

96–045   12. Where processing of personal data is carried out by a data processor on behalf of a data controller; the data controller is not to be regarded as complying with the seventh principle unless—

(a) the processing is carried out under a contract—

(i) which is made or evidenced in writing, and
(ii) under which the data processor is to act only on instructions from the data controller, and
(b) the contract requires the data processor to comply with obligations equivalent to those imposed on a data controller by the seventh principle.

The eighth principle

96–046   13. An adequate level of protection is one which is adequate in all the circumstances of the case, having regard in particular to—

(a) the nature of the personal data,
(b) the country or territory of origin of the information contained in the data,
(c) the country or territory of final destination of that information,
(d) the purposes for which and period during which the data are intended to be processed,
(e) the law in force in the country or territory in question,
(f) the international obligations of that country or territory,
(g) any relevant codes of conduct or other rules which are enforceable in that country or territory (whether generally or by arrangement in particular cases), and
(h) any security measures taken in respect of the data in that country or territory.

96–047   14. The eighth principle does not apply to a transfer falling within any paragraph of Schedule 4, except in such circumstances and to such extent as the [Lord Chancellor]¹ may by order provide.

96–048   15.—(1) Where—

(a) in any proceedings under this Act any question arises as to whether the requirement of the eighth principle as to an adequate level of protection is met in relation to the transfer of any personal data to a country or territory outside the European Economic Area, and
(b) a Community finding has been made in relation to transfers of the kind in question,

that question is to be determined in accordance with that finding.
(2) In sub-paragraph (1) "Community finding" means a finding of the European Commission, under the procedure provided for in Article 31(2) of the Data Protection Directive, that a country or territory outside the European Economic Area does, or does not, ensure an adequate level of protection within the meaning of Article 25(2) of the Directive.

CONDITIONS RELEVANT FOR PURPOSES OF THE FIRST PRINCIPLE: PROCESSING OF ANY PERSONAL DATA

1. The data subject has given his consent to the processing.   **96–049**

2. The processing is necessary—

(a) for the performance of a contract to which the data subject is a party, or
(b) for the taking of steps at the request of the data subject with a view to entering into a contract.

3. The processing is necessary for compliance with any legal obligation to which the data controller is subject, other than an obligation imposed by contract.

4. The processing is necessary in order to protect the vital interests of the data subject.

5. The processing is necessary—

(a) for the administration of justice,
(b) for the exercise of any functions conferred on any person by or under any enactment,
(c) for the exercise of any functions of the Crown, a Minister of the Crown or a government department, or
(d) for the exercise of any other functions of a public nature exercised in the public interest by any person.

6.—(1) The processing is necessary for the purposes of legitimate interests pursued by the data controller or by the third party or parties to whom the data are disclosed, except where the processing is unwarranted in any particular case by reason of prejudice to the rights and freedoms or legitimate interests of the data subject.

(2) The [Lord Chancellor] may by order specify particular circumstances in which this condition is, or is not, to be taken to be satisfied.

CONDITIONS RELEVANT FOR PURPOSES OF THE FIRST PRINCIPLE: PROCESSING OF SENSITIVE PERSONAL DATA

1. The data subject has given his explicit consent to the processing of the personal data.   **96–050**

2.—(1) The processing is necessary for the purposes of exercising or performing any right or   **96–051**
obligation which is conferred or imposed by law on the data controller in connection with employment.

(2) The [Lord Chancellor] may by order—

(a) exclude the application of sub-paragraph (1) in such cases as may be specified, or
(b) provide that, in such cases as may be specified, the condition in sub-paragraph (1) is not to be regarded as satisfied unless such further conditions as may be specified in the order are also satisfied.

3. The processing is necessary—   **96–052**

(a) in order to protect the vital interests of the data subject or another person, in a case where—

(i) consent cannot be given by or on behalf of the data subject, or
(ii) the data controller cannot reasonably be expected to obtain the consent of the data subject, or

(b) in order to protect the vital interests of another person, in a case where consent by or on behalf of the data subject has been unreasonably withheld.

4. The processing—   **96–053**

(a) is carried out in the course of its legitimate activities by any body or association which—

(i) is not established or conducted for profit, and
(ii) exists for political, philosophical, religious or trade-union purposes,

(b) is carried out with appropriate safeguards for the rights and freedoms of data subjects,
(c) relates only to individuals who either are members of the body or association or have regular contact with it in connection with its purposes, and

(d) does not involve disclosure of the personal data to a third party without the consent of the data subject.

96–054 5. The information contained in the personal data has been made public as a result of steps deliberately taken by the data subject.

96–055 6. The processing—

(a) is necessary for the purpose of, or in connection with, any legal proceedings (including prospective legal proceedings),

(b) is necessary for the purpose of obtaining legal advice, or

(c) is otherwise necessary for the purposes of establishing, exercising or defending legal rights.

96–056 7.— (1) The processing is necessary—

(a) for the administration of justice,

(b) for the exercise of any functions conferred on any person by or under an enactment, or

(c) for the exercise of any functions of the Crown, a Minister of the Crown or a government department.

(2) The [Lord Chancellor] may by order—

(a) exclude the application of sub-paragraph (1) in such cases as may be specified, or

(b) provide that, in such cases as may be specified, the condition in sub-paragraph (1) is not to be regarded as satisfied unless such further conditions as may be specified in the order are also satisfied.

96–057 8.— (1) The processing is necessary for medical purposes and is undertaken by—

(a) a health professional, or

(b) a person who in the circumstances owes a duty of confidentiality which is equivalent to that which would arise if that person were a health professional.

(2) In this paragraph "medical purposes" includes the purposes of preventative medicine, medical diagnosis, medical research, the provision of care and treatment and the management of health care services.

96–058 9.—(1) The processing—

(a) is of sensitive personal data consisting of information as to racial or ethnic origin,

(b) is necessary for the purpose of identifying or keeping under review the existence or absence of equality of opportunity or treatment between persons of different racial or ethnic origins, with a view to enabling such equality to be promoted or maintained, and

(c) is carried out with appropriate safeguards for the rights and freedoms of data subjects.

(2) The [Lord Chancellor] may by order specify circumstances in which processing falling within sub-paragraph (1)(a) and (b) is, or is not, to be taken for the purposes of sub-paragraph (1)(c) to be carried out with appropriate safeguards for the rights and freedoms of data subjects.

96–059 10. The personal data are processed in circumstances specified in an order made by the [Lord Chancellor] for the purposes of this paragraph.

. . . . . .

Section 37   SCHEDULE 7

MISCELLANEOUS EXEMPTIONS

Confidential references given by the data controller

96–060 1. Personal data are exempt from section 7 if they consist of a reference given or to be given in confidence by the data controller for the purposes of—

(a) the education, training or employment, or prospective education, training or employment, of the data subject,

(b) the appointment, or prospective appointment, of the data subject to any office, or

(c) the provision, or prospective provision, by the data subject of any service.

Armed forces

2. Personal data are exempt from the subject information provisions in any case to the extent to which the application of those provisions would be likely to prejudice the combat effectiveness of any of the armed forces of the Crown.

96–061

Judicial appointments and honours

3. Personal data processed for the purposes of—

96–062

    (a) assessing any person's suitability for judicial office or the office of Queen's Counsel, or
    (b) the conferring by the Crown of any honour[or dignity][1],

are exempt from the subject information provisions.

[1] Words added by Freedom of Information Act 2000 (c.36), Sched. 6, para. 6.

Crown employment and Crown or Ministerial appointments

[**4.** (1) The [Lord Chancellor] may by order exempt from the subject information provisions personal data processed for the purposes of assessing any person's suitability for—

96–063

    (a) employment by or under the Crown, or
    (b) any office to which appointments are made by Her Majesty, by a Minister of the Crown or by a Northern Ireland authority.

(2) In this paragraph "Northern Ireland authority" means the First Minister, the deputy First Minister, a Northern Ireland Minister or a Northern Ireland department.]

Management forecasts etc.

5. Personal data processed for the purposes of management forecasting or management planning to assist the data controller in the conduct of any business or other activity are exempt from the subject information provisions in any case to the extent to which the application of those provisions would be likely to prejudice the conduct of that business or other activity.

96–064

Corporate finance

6.—(1) Where personal data are processed for the purposes of, or in connection with, a corporate finance service provided by a relevant person—

96–065

    (a) the data are exempt from the subject information provisions in any case to the extent to which either—

        (i) the application of those provisions to the data could affect the price of any instrument which is already in existence or is to be or may be created, or
        (ii) the data controller reasonably believes that the application of those provisions to the data could affect the price of any such instrument, and

    (b) to the extent that the data are not exempt from the subject information provisions by virtue of paragraph (a), they are exempt from those provisions if the exemption is required for the purpose of safeguarding an important economic or financial interest of the United Kingdom.

(2) For the purposes of sub-paragraph (1)(b) the [Lord Chancellor] may by order specify—

    (a) matters to be taken into account in determining whether exemption from the subject information provisions is required for the purpose of safeguarding an important economic or financial interest of the United Kingdom, or
    (b) circumstances in which exemption from those provisions is, or is not, to be taken to be required for that purpose.

(3) In this paragraph—

    "corporate finance service" means a service consisting in—

        (a) underwriting in respect of issues of, or the placing of issues of, any instrument,
        (b) advice to undertakings on capital structure, industrial strategy and related matters and advice and service relating to mergers and the purchase of undertakings, or
        (c) services relating to such underwriting as is mentioned in paragraph (a);

    "instrument" means any instrument listed in section B of the Annex to the Council Directive on investment services in the securities field (93/22/EEC), as set out in Schedule 1 to the Investment Services Regulations 1995;

"price" includes value;
"relevant person" means—

    (a) any person who is authorised under Chapter III of Part I of the Financial Services Act 1986 or is an exempted person under Chapter IV of Part I of that Act,

    (b) any person who, but for Part III or IV of Schedule 1 to that Act, would require authorisation under that Act,

    (c) any European investment firm within the meaning given by Regulation 3 of the Investment Services Regulations 1995,

    (d) any person who, in the course of his employment, provides to his employer a service falling within paragraph (b) or (c) of the definition of "corporate finance service", or

    (e) any partner who provides to other partners in the partnership a service falling within either of those paragraphs.

Negotiations

96–066   7. Personal data which consist of records of the intentions of the data controller in relation to any negotiations with the data subject are exempt from the subject information provisions in any case to the extent to which the application of those provisions would be likely to prejudice those negotiations.

Examination marks

96–067   8.—(1) Section 7 shall have effect subject to the provisions of sub-paragraphs (2) to (4) in the case of personal data consisting of marks or other information processed by a data controller—

    (a) for the purpose of determining the results of an academic, professional or other examination or of enabling the results of any such examination to be determined, or

    (b) in consequence of the determination of any such results.

(2) Where the relevant day falls before the day on which the results of the examination are announced, the period mentioned in section 7(8) shall be extended until—

    (a) the end of five months beginning with the relevant day, or

    (b) the end of forty days beginning with the date of the announcement,

whichever is the earlier.

(3) Where by virtue of sub-paragraph (2) a period longer than the prescribed period elapses after the relevant day before the request is complied with, the information to be supplied pursuant to the request shall be supplied both by reference to the data in question at the time when the request is received and (if different) by reference to the data as from time to time held in the period beginning when the request is received and ending when it is complied with.

(4) For the purposes of this paragraph the results of an examination shall be treated as announced when they are first published or (if not published) when they are first made available or communicated to the candidate in question.

(5) In this paragraph—

"examination" includes any process for determining the knowledge, intelligence, skill or ability of a candidate by reference to his performance in any test, work or other activity;
"the prescribed period" means forty days or such other period as is for the time being prescribed under section 7 in relation to the personal data in question;
"relevant day" has the same meaning as in section 7.

Examination scripts etc.

96–068   9.—(1) Personal data consisting of information recorded by candidates during an academic, professional or other examination are exempt from section 7.

(2) In this paragraph "examination" has the same meaning as in paragraph 8.

Legal professional privilege

96–069   10. Personal data are exempt from the subject information provisions if the data consist of information in respect of which a claim to legal professional privilege [or, in Scotland, to confidentiality of communications][1] could be maintained in legal proceedings.

---

[1] Words substituted by Freedom of Information Act 2000 (c.36), Sched. 6, para. 7.

Self-incrimination

11.—(1) A person need not comply with any request or order under section 7 to the extent that compliance would, by revealing evidence of the commission of any offence other than an offence under this Act, expose him to proceedings for that offence.

(2) Information disclosed by any person in compliance with any request or order under section 7 shall not be admissible against him in proceedings for an offence under this Act.

96–070

Finance Act 1998

(1998, c. 36)

An Act to grant certain duties, to alter other duties, and to amend the law relating to the National Debt and the Public Revenue, and to make further provision in connection with Finance.   [31st July 1998]

97–001

. . . . . .

The European single currency

Adoption of single currency by other member States

163.—(1) The Treasury may, to such extent as appears to them appropriate in connection with any of the matters falling within subsection (2) below, by regulations modify the application and effect as respects—

97–002

   (a) transactions in a currency other than sterling,
   (b) instruments denominated in such a currency, and
   (c) the bringing into account of amounts expressed in, or by reference to, such a currency,

of any enactment or subordinate legislation relating to any matter under the care and management of the Commissioners of Inland Revenue.

(2) The matters falling within this subsection are—

   (a) the adoption or proposed adoption by other member States of the single currency; and
   (b) any transitional measures or other arrangements applying or likely to apply in relation to the adoption of the single currency by other member States.

(3) Without prejudice to the generality of subsection (1) above, the power conferred by that subsection includes power by regulations to provide—

   (a) for liabilities to pay amounts to the Commissioners of Inland Revenue under any enactment or subordinate legislation relating to taxation to be capable of being discharged, in accordance with the regulations, by payments in the single currency;
   (b) for elections made for the purposes of section 93(1)(b) or 94(2)(b) of the Finance Act 1993 (computation of a company's profits in a foreign currency) to have effect as modified in accordance with the regulations; and

(c) for such persons as may be described in the regulations to be treated as having made elections for any of those purposes in such terms as may be provided for in the regulations.

(4) The power to make regulations under this section includes—

(a) power to impose charges to taxation;
(b) power to amend or repeal any enactment; and
(c) power to make such incidental, supplemental, consequential and transitional provision as appears to the Treasury to be appropriate.

(5) The power to make regulations under this section shall be exercisable by statutory instrument subject to annulment in pursuance of a resolution of the House of Commons.

(6) In this section—

"enactment" includes any enactment contained in this Act (other than this section) and any enactment passed after this Act;
"other member State" means a member State other than the United Kingdom;
"subordinate legislation" has the same meaning as in the Interpretation Act 1978.

(7) References in this section to the adoption of the single currency are references to the adoption of the single currency in accordance with the Treaty establishing the European Community, and the reference in subsection (3)(a) above to that currency shall be construed accordingly.

Government of Wales Act 1998

(1998, c. 38)

98–001 *An Act to establish and make provision about the National Assembly for Wales and the offices of Auditor General for Wales and Welsh Administration Ombudsman; to reform certain Welsh public bodies and abolish certain other Welsh Public bodies; and for connected purposes.* [31st July 1998]

PART I

THE NATIONAL ASSEMBLY FOR WALES

The Assembly

The Assembly

98–002 1.—(1) There shall be an Assembly for Wales to be known as the National Assembly for Wales or Cynulliad Cenedlaethol Cymru (but referred to in this Act as the Assembly).

(2) The Assembly shall be a body corporate.

(3) The exercise by the Assembly of its functions is to be regarded as done on behalf of the Crown.

Membership

2.—(1) The Assembly shall consist of—   **98–003**

(a) one member for each Assembly constituency, and
(b) members for each Assembly electoral region.

(2) The Assembly constituencies and Assembly electoral regions, and the number of Assembly seats for each Assembly electoral region, shall be as provided for by or in accordance with Schedule 1.

(3) Members of the Assembly (referred to in this Act as Assembly members) shall be returned in accordance with the provision made by and under this Act for—

(a) the holding of ordinary elections of Assembly members, and
(b) the filling of vacancies in Assembly seats.

(4) An ordinary election involves the holding of elections for the return of the entire Assembly.

(5) The term of office of an Assembly member—

(a) begins when he is declared to be returned as an Assembly member, and
(b) continues until the end of the day before the day of the poll at the next ordinary election.

(6) But an Assembly member may at any time resign his seat by giving notice to—

(a) the presiding officer, or
(b) any person authorised by the standing orders of the Assembly to receive the notice.

(7) The validity of anything done by the Assembly is not affected by any vacancy in its membership.

Ordinary elections

Time of ordinary elections

3.—(1) The poll at the first ordinary election shall be held on a day appointed   **98–004**
by order made by the Secretary of State.

(2) The poll at each subsequent ordinary election shall be held on the first Thursday in May in the fourth calendar year following that in which the previous ordinary election was held.

(3) But the Secretary of State may by order require the poll at such an ordinary election to be held on a day which is neither—

(a) more than one month earlier, nor
(b) more than one month later,

than the first Thursday in May.

(4) Where the poll at an ordinary election would be held on the same day as polls at ordinary elections of community councillors, the Secretary of State may by order provide for the polls at ordinary elections of community councillors to be postponed, for not more than three months, to a day specified in the order.

(5) An order under subsection (4) may make provision for—

(a) any provision of, or made under, the Representation of the People
   Acts, or
(b) any other enactment relating to elections of community councillors,

to have effect with such modifications or exceptions as the Secretary of State
considers appropriate in connection with the postponement of polls for which it
provides.

(6) No order shall be made under subsection (3), and no order in connection
with an ordinary election subsequent to the first shall be made under subsection
(4), unless the Secretary of State has consulted the Assembly.

Voting at ordinary elections

98–005   **4.**—(1) Each person entitled to vote at an ordinary election in an Assembly
constituency shall have two votes.

(2) One (referred to in this Act as a constituency vote) is to be given for a
candidate to be the Assembly member for the Assembly constituency.

(3) The other (referred to in this Act as an electoral region vote) is to be given
for—

(a) a registered political party which has submitted a list of candidates to
   be Assembly members for the Assembly electoral region in which the
   Assembly constituency is included, or
(b) an individual who is a candidate to be an Assembly member for that
   Assembly electoral region.

(4) The Assembly member for the Assembly constituency shall be returned
under the simple majority system.

(5) The Assembly members for the Assembly electoral region shall be
returned under the additional member system of proportional representation in
accordance with sections 5 to 7.

(6) The person who is to be returned as the Assembly member for each
Assembly constituency in the Assembly electoral region must be determined
before it is determined who are to be returned as the Assembly members for
that Assembly electoral region.

(7) At an ordinary election a person may not be a candidate to be the Assembly member for more than one Assembly constituency.

(8) In this Act "registered political party" means [a party registered under
Part II of the Political Parties, Elections and Referendums Act 2000][1].

[1] Words substituted by Political Parties, Elections and Referendums Act 2000 (c.41), Sched. 21,
para. 12(2).

Party lists and individual candidates

98–006   **5.**—(1) Any registered political party may submit a list of candidates to be
Assembly members for the Assembly electoral region.

(2) The list is to be submitted to the regional returning officer.

(3) The list has effect in relation to—

(a) the ordinary election, and
(b) any vacancies in seats of Assembly members returned for Assembly
   electoral regions which occur after that election and before the next
   ordinary election.

(4) The list must not include more than twelve persons (but may include only
one).

(5) The list must not include a person—

  (a) who is included on any other list submitted for the Assembly electoral region or any list submitted for another Assembly electoral region,
  (b) who is an individual candidate to be an Assembly member for the Assembly electoral region or another Assembly electoral region,
  (c) who is a candidate to be the Assembly member for an Assembly constituency which is not included in the Assembly electoral region, or
  (d) who is a candidate to be the Assembly member for an Assembly constituency included in the Assembly electoral region but is not a candidate of the party.

(6) A person may not be an individual candidate to be an Assembly member for the Assembly electoral region if he is—

  (a) included on a list submitted by a registered political party for the Assembly electoral region or another Assembly electoral region,
  (b) an individual candidate to be an Assembly member for another Assembly electoral region,
  (c) a candidate to be the Assembly member for an Assembly constituency which is not included in the Assembly electoral region, or
  (d) a candidate of any registered political party to be the Assembly member for an Assembly constituency included in the Assembly electoral region.

Calculation of electoral region figures

6.—(1) For each registered political party by which a list of candidates has **98–007** been submitted for the Assembly electoral region—

  (a) there shall be added together the number of electoral region votes given for the party in the Assembly constituencies included in the Assembly electoral region, and
  (b) the number arrived at under paragraph (a) shall then be divided by the aggregate of one and the number of candidates of the party returned as Assembly members for any of those Assembly constituencies.

(2) For each individual candidate to be an Assembly member for the Assembly electoral region there shall be added together the number of electoral region votes given for him in the Assembly constituencies included in the Assembly electoral region.
(3) The number arrived at—

  (a) in the case of a registered political party, under subsection (1)(b), or
  (b) in the case of an individual candidate, under subsection (2),

is referred to in this Act as the electoral region figure for that party or individual candidate.

Return of electoral region members

7.—(1) The first seat for the Assembly electoral region shall be allocated to **98–008** the party or individual candidate with the highest electoral region figure.
(2) The second and subsequent seats for the Assembly electoral region shall be allocated to the party or individual candidate with the highest electoral region figure after any recalculation required by subsection (3) has been carried out.

(3) This subsection requires a recalculation under section 6(1)(b) in relation to a party—

    (a) for the first application of subsection (2), if the application of subsection (1) resulted in the allocation of a seat to the party, or

    (b) for any subsequent application of subsection (2), if the previous application of that subsection did so;

and a recalculation shall be carried out after adding one to the aggregate mentioned in section 6(1)(b).

(4) An individual candidate already returned as an Assembly member shall be disregarded.

(5) Seats for the Assembly electoral region which are allocated to a party shall be filled by the persons on the party's list in the order in which they appear on the list.

(6) Once a party's list has been exhausted (by the return of persons included on it as Assembly members for Assembly constituencies or by the previous application of subsection (1) or (2)) the party shall be disregarded.

(7) If (on the application of subsection (1) or any application of subsection (2)) the highest electoral region figure is the electoral region figure of two or more parties or individual candidates, the subsection shall apply to each of them.

(8) However, where subsection (7) would mean that more than the full number of seats for the Assembly electoral region were allocated, subsection (1) or (2) shall not apply until—

    (a) a recalculation has been carried out under section 6(1)(b) after adding one to the number of votes given for each party with that electoral region figure, and

    (b) one has been added to the number of votes given for each individual candidate with that electoral region figure.

(9) If, after that, the highest electoral region figure is still the electoral region figure of two or more parties or individual candidates, the regional returning officer shall decide between them by lots.

(10) For the purposes of subsection (5) and section 9 a person included on a list submitted by a registered political party who is returned as an Assembly member shall be treated as ceasing to be on the list (even if his return is void).

Vacancies

Constituency seats

98–009   **8.**—(1) This section applies where the seat of an Assembly member returned for an Assembly constituency is vacant.

(2) Subject to subsection (6), an election shall be held in the Assembly constituency to fill the vacancy.

(3) At the election to fill the vacancy, each person entitled to vote at the election shall have only a constituency vote; and the Assembly member for the Assembly constituency shall be returned under the simple majority system.

(4) The date of the poll at the election shall be fixed by the presiding officer in accordance with subsection (5).

(5) The date fixed shall be not later than three months after the occurrence of the vacancy, except that if the vacancy does not come to the presiding officer's notice within one month of its occurrence the date fixed shall be not later than three months after the vacancy comes to his notice.

(6) An election shall not be held if it appears to the presiding officer that the

latest date which may be fixed for the poll would fall within the period of three months preceding an ordinary election.

(7) A person may not be a candidate in an election to fill a vacancy if he is an Assembly member or a candidate in another such election.

(8) For the purposes of this section a vacancy shall be taken to have occurred on such date as may be determined under the standing orders of the Assembly.

(9) References in this section and section 9 to the presiding officer include references to any person for the time being performing the functions of presiding officer.

Electoral region seats

9.—(1) This section applies where the seat of an Assembly member returned for an Assembly electoral region is vacant.   **98–010**

(2) If the Assembly member was returned (under section 7 or this section) from the list of a registered political party, the regional returning officer shall notify to the presiding officer the name of the person who is to fill the vacancy.

(3) A person's name may only be so notified if he—

  (a) is included on that list,
  (b) is willing to serve as an Assembly member for the Assembly electoral region, and
  (c) is not a person to whom subsection (4) applies.

(4) This subsection applies to a person if—

  (a) he is not a member of the party, and
  (b) the party gives notice to the regional returning officer that his name is not to be notified to the presiding officer as the name of the person who is to fill the vacancy.

(5) But where there is more than one person who satisfies the conditions in subsection (3), the regional returning officer may only notify the name of whichever of them was the higher, or highest, on that list.

(6) A person whose name is notified under subsection (2) shall be treated as declared to be returned as an Assembly member for the Assembly electoral region on the day on which notification of his name is received by the presiding officer.

(7) If—

  (a) the Assembly member whose seat is vacant was returned as an individual candidate, or
  (b) he was returned from the list of a registered political party but there is no-one who satisfies the conditions in subsection (3),

the seat shall remain vacant until the next ordinary election.

The franchise and conduct of elections

Entitlement to vote

10.—(1) The persons entitled to vote at an election of Assembly members (or of an Assembly member) in an Assembly constituency are those who on the day of the poll—   **98–011**

  (a) would be entitled to vote as electors at a local government election in an electoral area wholly or partly included in the Assembly constituency, and

(b) are registered in the register of local government electors at an address within the Assembly constituency.

(2) But a person is not entitled as an elector—

(a) to cast more than one constituency vote, or more than one electoral region vote, in the same Assembly constituency at any ordinary election,

(b) to vote in more than one Assembly constituency at any ordinary election, or

(c) to cast more than one vote in an election held under section 8.

Power to make provision about elections etc.

98–012   11.—(1) The Secretary of State may by order make provision as to—

(a) the conduct of elections for the return of Assembly members,

(b) the questioning of an elections for the return of Assembly members and the consequences of irregularities, and

(c) the return of an Assembly member otherwise than at an election.

(2) The provision which may be made under subsection (1)(a) includes, in particular, provision—

(a) about the registration of electors,

(b) for disregarding alterations in a register of electors,

(c) about the limitation of the election expenses of candidates (and the creation of criminal offences in connection with the limitation of such expenses),

(d) for the combination of polls at elections for the return of Assembly members and other elections, and

(e) for modifying the operation of section 4 in a case where the poll at an election for the return of the Assembly member for an Assembly constituency is abandoned (or notice of it is countermanded).

(3) An order under this section may—

(a) apply or incorporate, with or without modifications or exceptions, any provision of, or made under, the Representation of the People Acts or the European Parliamentary Elections Act 1978 or any other enactment relating to parliamentary elections, European Parliamentary elections or local government elections,

(b) modify any form contained in, or in regulations or rules made under, the Representation of the People Acts so far as may be necessary to enable it to be used both for the original purpose and in relation to elections for the return of Assembly members, and

(c) so far as may be necessary in consequences of any provision made by this Act or an order under this section, amend any provision made by or under any enactment relating to the registration of parliamentary electors or local government electors.

(4) An order under this section may require sums to be paid by the Assembly.

(5) No return of an Assembly member at an election shall be questioned except by an election petition under the provisions of Part III of the

Representation of the People Act 1983 as applied by or incorporated in an order under this section.

(6) In this Act "regional returning officer", in relation to any Assembly electoral region, means the person designated as the regional returning officer for the Assembly electoral region in accordance with an order under this section.

Disqualification

Disqualification from being Assembly member

12.—(1) A person is disqualified from being an Assembly member if—   **98–013**

(a) he is disqualified from being a member of the House of Commons under paragraphs (a) to (e) of section 1(1) of the House of Commons Disqualification Act 1975 (judges, civil servants, members of the armed forces, members of police forces and members of foreign legislatures),

(b) he holds any of the offices for the time being designated by Order in Council as offices disqualifying persons from being Assembly members,

(c) he holds the office of Auditor General for Wales or the office of Welsh Administration Ombudsman, or

(d) he is disqualified from being a member of a local authority under section 17(2)(b) or 18(7) of the Audit Commission Act 1998 (members of local authorities who are responsible for incurring or authorising unlawful expenditure or whose wilful misconduct has caused a loss or deficiency).

(2) Subject to section 13(1) and (2), a person is also disqualified from being an Assembly member if he is disqualified otherwise than under the House of Commons Disqualification Act 1975 (either generally or in relation to a particular constituency) from being a member of the House of Commons or from sitting and voting in it.

(3) For the purposes of subsection (2) the references to the Republic of Ireland in section 1 of the Representation of the People Act 1981 (disqualification of offenders detained in, or unlawfully at large from detention in, the British Islands or the Republic of Ireland) shall be treated as references to any member State (other than the United Kingdom).

(4) A person who holds office as lord-lieutenant, lieutenant or high sheriff of any area in Wales is disqualified from being an Assembly member for any Assembly constituency or Assembly electoral region wholly or partly included in that area.

(5) An Order in Council under paragraph (b) of subsection (1) may designate particular offices or offices of any description and may designate an office by reference to any characteristic of a person holding it; and in that paragraph and this subsection "office" includes any post or employment.

(6) No recommendation shall be made to Her Majesty in Council to make an Order in Council under subsection (1)(b) unless a draft of the statutory instrument containing the Order in Council has been laid before, and approved by a resolution of, each House of Parliament.

(7) But subsection (6) does not apply in the case of an Order in Council varying or revoking a previous Order in Council if the Assembly has resolved that the Secretary of State be requested to recommend the making of the Order in Council.

Exceptions and relief from disqualification

98–014   **13.**—(1) A person is not disqualified from being an Assembly member merely because—

    (a) he is a peer (whether of the United Kingdom, Great Britain, England or Scotland), or

    [(b) he is a Lord Spiritual.]¹

(2) A citizen of the European Union who is resident in the United Kingdom is not disqualified from being an Assembly member merely because of section 3 of the Act of Settlement (disqualification of persons born outside the United Kingdom other than Commonwealth citizens and citizens of the Republic of Ireland).

(3) Where a person was, or is alleged to have been, disqualified from being an Assembly member on a ground within section 12(1)(a), (b) or (c) or (4), the Assembly may resolve that any disqualification incurred by that person on that ground is to be disregarded if it appears to the Assembly—

    (a) that that ground has been removed, and

    (b) that it is proper so to resolve.

(4) A resolution under subsection (3) shall not—

    (a) affect any proceedings under Part III of the Representation of the People Act 1983 as applied by or incorporated in an order under section 11, or

    (b) enable the Assembly to disregard any disqualification which has been established in such proceedings or in proceedings under section 15.

¹ Substituted by House of Commons (Removal of Clergy Disqualification) Act 2001 (c.13), Sched. 1, para. 3.

Effect of disqualification

98–015   **14.**—(1) If a person who is disqualified from being an Assembly member, or from being an Assembly member for a particular Assembly constituency or Assembly electoral region, is returned as an Assembly member or as an Assembly member for that Assembly constituency or Assembly electoral region, his return shall be void and his seat vacant.

(2) If an Assembly member becomes disqualified from being an Assembly member or from being an Assembly member for the Assembly constituency or Assembly electoral region for which he is sitting, he shall cease to be an Assembly member (so that his seat is vacant).

(3) Subsections (1) and (2) have effect subject to any resolution of the Assembly under section 13(3).

(4) Subsection (2) also has effect subject to section 141 of the Mental Health Act 1983 (mental illness) and section 427 of the Insolvency Act 1986 (bankruptcy etc.); and where, in consequence of either of those sections, the seat of a disqualified Assembly member is not vacant he shall not cease to be an Assembly member until his seat becomes vacant but—

    (a) he shall not participate in any proceedings of the Assembly (including proceedings of a committee of the Assembly or of a sub-committee of such a committee), and

    (b) any of his other rights and privileges as an Assembly member may be withdrawn by the Assembly.

(5) The validity of anything done by the Assembly is not affected by the disqualification of any person from being an Assembly member or from being an Assembly member for the Assembly constituency or Assembly electoral region for which he purports to sit.

. . . . . .

PART II

ASSEMBLY FUNCTIONS

Introduction

Introductory

21. The Assembly shall have the functions which are—   **98–016**

(a) transferred to, or made exercisable by, the Assembly by virtue of this Act, or

(b) conferred or imposed on the Assembly by or under this Act or any other Act.

Transfer of Ministerial functions to Assembly

Transfer of Ministerial functions

22.—(1) Her Majesty may by Order in Council—   **98–017**

(a) provide for the transfer to the Assembly of any function so far as exercisable by a Minister of the Crown in relation to Wales,

(b) direct that any function so far as so exercisable shall be exercisable by the Assembly concurrently with the Minister of the Crown, or

(c) direct that any function so far as exercisable by a Minister of the Crown in relation to Wales shall be exercisable by the Minister only with the agreement of, or after consultation with, the Assembly.

(2) The Secretary of State shall, before the first ordinary election, lay before each House of Parliament the draft of an Order in Council under this section making provision for the transfer of such functions in each of the fields specified in Schedule 2 as the Secretary of State considers appropriate.

(3) An Order in Council under this section may contain any appropriate consequential, incidental, supplementary or transitional provisions or savings (including provisions in the form of amendments or repeals of enactments).

(4) No recommendation shall be made to Her Majesty in Council to make an Order in Council under this section—

(a) unless a draft of the statutory instrument containing the Order in Council has been laid before, and approved by a resolution of, each House of Parliament, and

(b) in the case of an Order in Council varying or revoking a previous Order in Council, unless such a draft has also been laid before, and approved by a resolution of, the Assembly.

(5) Schedule 3 (which makes further provision about the transfer etc. of functions by Order in Council under this section) has effect.

General transfer of property, rights and liabilities, etc.

98–018   **23.**—(1) There shall be transferred to and vest in the Assembly by virtue of this subsection all property, rights and liabilities to which a Minister of the Crown is entitled or subject, at the coming into force of an Order in Council under section 22, in connection with any function exercisable by the Minister which is transferred by the Order in Council.

(2) There may be continued by or in relation to the Assembly anything (including legal proceedings) which relates to—

(a) any function exercisable by a Minister of the Crown which is transferred by an Order in Council under section 22, or

(b) any property, rights or liabilities transferred by subsection (1) as the result of the transfer of any such function by such an Order in Council,

and which is in the process of being done by or in relation to the Minister immediately before the coming into force of the Order in Council.

(3) Anything which was done by a Minister of the Crown for the purpose of or in connection with—

(a) any function exercisable by the Minister which is transferred by an Order in Council under section 22, or

(b) any property, rights or liabilities transferred by subsection (1) as the result of the transfer of any such function by such an Order in Council,

and which is in effect immediately before the coming into force of the Order in Council shall have effect as if done by the Assembly.

(4) The Assembly shall be substituted for any Minister of the Crown in any instruments, contracts or legal proceedings which relate to—

(a) any function exercisable by the Minister which is transferred by an Order in Council under section 22, or

(b) any property, rights or liabilities transferred by subsection (1) as the result of the transfer of any such function by such an Order in Council,

and which are made or commenced before the coming into force of the Order in Council.

. . . . . .

Other functions

Implementation of Community law

98–019   **29.**—(1) The power to designate a Minister of the Crown or government department under section 2(2) of the European Communities Act 1972 may be exercised to designate the Assembly.

(2) Accordingly, the Assembly may exercise the power to make regulations conferred by section 2(2) of the European Communities Act 1972 in relation to any matter, or for any purpose, if the Assembly has been designated in relation to that matter or for that purpose, but subject to such restrictions or conditions (if any) as may be specified by the Order in Council designating the Assembly.

(3) Paragraph 2(2) of Schedule 2 to the European Communities Act 1972 (Parliamentary procedure) shall not apply to a statutory instrument containing regulations made by the Assembly unless the statutory instrument contains regulations—

(a) made by a Minister of the Crown or government department (whether or not jointly with the Assembly),

(b) relating to an English border area, or

(c) relating to a cross-border body (and not relating only to the exercise of functions, or the carrying on of activities, by the body in or with respect to Wales or a part of Wales).

(4) The power conferred by section 56 of the Finance Act 1973 (services provided in pursuance of a Community obligation etc.) on the Minister in charge of a government department to make (with the consent of the Treasury) regulations prescribing, or providing for the determination of, fees and charges in respect of things done by the department may be exercised by the Assembly (with the consent of the Treasury) for prescribing, or providing for the determination of, fees and charges in respect of corresponding things done by the Assembly.

(5) Section 56(4) of the Finance Act 1973 shall not cause a statutory instrument containing regulations made by the Assembly to be subject to annulment in pursuance of a resolution of either House of Parliament unless the statutory instrument contains regulations—

(a) made by a Minister of the Crown (whether or not jointly with the Assembly),

(b) relating to an English border area, or

(c) relating to a cross-border body (and not relating only to the exercise of functions, or the carrying on of activities, by the body in or with respect to Wales or a part of Wales).

Consultation about public appointments

30.—(1) Her Majesty may by Order in Council make provision requiring any Minister of the Crown or other person to consult the Assembly before—   **98–020**

(a) appointing a person to a specified public post,

(b) recommending, consenting to or approving the appointment of a person to a specified public post,

(c) nominating a person for appointment to a specified public post, or

(d) selecting persons with a view to the appointment of one or more of them to a specified public post (whether or not by the person subject to the requirement).

(2) In subsection (1) "a specified public post" means —

(a) a public office specified, or of a description specified, in the Order in Council, or

(b) membership, or membership of a description so specified, of a public body so specified or of a description so specified.

(3) An Order in Council under this section may not specify any public office or body, or public offices or bodies of any description, unless the office or body exercises, or all offices or bodies of the description exercise, functions in or in relation to Wales or a part of Wales (whether or not they also exercise functions in or in relation to any other area).

(4) An Order in Council under this section may impose a requirement on a person even where—

(a) he is required to consult, or obtain the consent or approval of, another person before acting, or

(b) he is required to act at the request of another person or after a recommendation, nomination or selection has been made by another person.

(5) A requirement imposed by an Order in Council under this section need not be complied with in relation to an appointment if—

(a) it is not reasonably practicable to comply with it because of the urgency of making the appointment, or
(b) the appointment is a temporary one.

(6) Where a person is appointed to an office or membership of a body, any failure to comply with a requirement imposed by an Order in Council under this section in relation to the appointment does not affect the validity of anything done by or in relation to him as the holder of the office, or by or in relation to the body while he is a member of it.

(7) An Order in Council under this section may contain any appropriate consequential, incidental, transitional or supplementary provisions or savings (including provisions in the form of amendments or repeals of enactments).

(8) No recommendation shall be made to Her Majesty in Council to make an Order in Council under this section which contains provisions in the form of amendments or repeals of enactments contained in an Act unless a draft of the statutory instrument containing the Order in Council has been laid before, and approved by a resolution of, each House of Parliament.

(9) A statutory instrument containing an Order in Council under this section shall (unless a draft of it has been approved by a resolution of each House of Parliament) be subject to annulment in pursuance of a resolution of either House of Parliament.

Consultation about government's legislative programme

98–021 **31.**—(1) As soon as is reasonably practicable after the beginning of each session of Parliament, the Secretary of State for Wales shall undertake with the Assembly such consultation about the government's legislative programme for the session as appears to him to be appropriate but including attending and participating in proceedings of the Assembly relating to the programme on at least one occasion.

(2) For this purpose the government's legislative programme for a session of Parliament consists of the bills which (at the beginning of the session) are intended to be introduced into either House of Parliament during the session by a Minister of the Crown.

(3) If at any time after the beginning of a session of Parliament—

(a) it is decided that a bill should be introduced into either House of Parliament during the session by a Minister of the Crown, and
(b) no consultation about the bill has been undertaken under subsection (1),

the Secretary of State for Wales shall undertake with the Assembly such consultation about the bill as appears to him to be appropriate.

(4) This section does not require the Secretary of State for Wales to undertake consultation with the Assembly about a bill if he considers that there are considerations relating to the bill which make it inappropriate for him to do so.

Support of culture etc.

98–022 32. The Assembly may do anything it considers appropriate to support—

(a) museums,galleries or libraries in Wales,

    (b) buildings of historical or architectural interest, or other places of historical interest, in Wales,

    (c) the Welsh language, or

    (d) the arts, crafts, sport or other cultural or recreational activities in Wales.

Consideration of matters affecting Wales

33. The Assembly may consider, and make appropriate representations about, any matter affecting Wales.   **98–023**

Ancillary powers etc.

Inquiries

35.—(1) The Assembly may cause an inquiry to be held into any matter relevant to the exercise of any of its functions.   **98–024**

(2) Subsections (2) to (5) of section 250 of the Local Government Act 1972 (witnesses and costs at local inquiries) shall apply in relation to an inquiry held under subsection (1) as if it were a local inquiry held under that section and the Assembly were the Minister causing it to be held.

Polls for ascertaining views of the public

36.—(1) The Assembly may hold a poll in an area consisting of Wales or any part (or parts) of Wales for the purpose of ascertaining the views of those polled about whether or how any of the Assembly's functions (other than those under section 33) should be exercised.   **98–025**

(2) The persons entitled to vote in a poll under this section are those who—

    (a) would be entitled to vote as electors at a local government election in an electoral area wholly or partly included in the area in which the poll is held, and

    (b) are registered in the register of local government electors at an address within the area in which the poll is held.

(3) The Assembly may not delegate the function of deciding—

    (a) whether to hold a poll under this section,

    (b) when, and in which area, a poll is to be held, and

    (c) the wording of any questions or propositions to be put to those polled.

(4) The Assembly may by order make provision as to the conduct of polls (or any poll) under this section.

(5) The Secretary of State may by order make provision for the combination of polls (or any poll) under this section with polls at any elections.

(6) An order under subsection (4) or (5) may apply or ncorporate, with or without modifications or exceptions, any provision of or made under any enactment relating to any elections; and the provision which may be made under subsection (4) includes, in particular, provision for disregarding alterations in a register of electors.

(7) The costs of polls under this section shall be met by the Assembly.

Private bills

37.—(1) The Assembly may promote private bills in Parliament and may oppose any private bill in Parliament.   **98–026**

(2) But the Assembly shall not promote or oppose any private bill in

Parliament unless a motion to authorise the Assembly to promote or oppose the bill is passed by the Assembly on a vote in which at least two-thirds of the Assembly members voting support the motion.

(3) Subsection (1) shall not cause the Assembly to have power to apply for orders under section 1 or 3 of the Transport and Works Act 1992 by virtue of section 20 of that Act (which gives a body with power to promote and oppose private bills power to apply for and object to such orders).

Legal proceedings

98–027   **38.** Where the Assembly considers it appropriate for the promotion or protection of the public interest it may institute in its own name, defend or appear in any legal proceedings relating to matters with respect to which any functions of the Assembly are exercisable.

Contracts

98–028   **39.** The Secretary of State may by order provide that the Local Government (Contracts) Act 1997 shall apply in relation to contracts entered into by the Assembly but subject to any appropriate modifications.

Supplementary powers

98–029   **40.** The Assembly may do anything (including the acquisition or disposal of any property or rights) which is calculated to facilitate, or is conducive or incidental to, the exercise of any of its functions.

. . . . . .

Supplementary

Parliamentary procedures for subordinate legislation

98–030   **44.**—(1) This section applies where a function to make subordinate legislation (including a function conferred or imposed by, or after the passing of, this Act) has been transferred to, or made exercisable by, the Assembly by an Order in Council under section 22.

(2) Subject to subsections (4) and (5), any relevant Parliamentary procedural provision relating to the function shall not have effect in relation to the exercise of the function by the Assembly.

(3) For the purposes of this Act "relevant Parliamentary procedural provision" means provision—

(a) requiring any instrument made in the exercise of the function, or a draft of any such instrument, to be laid before Parliament or either House of Parliament,

(b) for the annulment or approval of any such instrument or draft by or in pursuance of a resolution of either House of Parliament or of both Houses,

(c) prohibiting the making of any such instrument without that approval,

(d) for any such instrument to be a provisional order (that is, an order which requires to be confirmed by Act of Parliament), or

(e) requiring any order (within the meaning of the Statutory Orders (Special Procedure) Act 1945) to be subject to special parliamentary procedure.

(4) Subsection (2) does not apply in the case of any instrument made in the exercise of the function, or a draft of any such instrument, if it—

    (a) contains subordinate legislation made or to be made by a Minister of the Crown or government department (whether or not jointly with the Assembly),

    (b) contains (or confirms or approves) subordinate legislation relating to an English border area, or

    (c) contains (or confirms or approves) subordinate legislation relating to a cross-border body (and not relating only to the exercise of functions, or the carrying on of activities, by the body in or with respect to Wales or a part of Wales).

(5) Where a function transferred to, or made exercisable by, the Assembly by an Order in Council under section 22 is subject to a provision of the description specified in subsection (3)(e), the Order in Council may provide that—

    (a) any order made by the Assembly in the exercise of the function, or

    (b) any order so made in circumstances specified in the Order in Council,

is to be subject to special parliamentary procedure.

(6) In this section "make" includes confirm or approve and related expressions (except "made exercisable") shall be construed accordingly; but an instrument (or draft) does not fall within subsection (4)(a) just because it contains subordinate legislation made (or to be made) by the Assembly with the agreement of a Minister of the Crown or government department.

Human Rights Act 1998

(1998, c. 42)

An Act to give further effect to rights and freedoms guaranteed under the European Convention on Human Rights; to make provision with respect to holders of certain judicial offices who become judges of the European Court of Human Rights; and for connected purposes.　　[9th November 1998]　　**99–001**

Introduction

The Convention Rights

1.—(1) In this Act "the Convention rights" means the rights and fundamental freedoms set out in—　　**99–002**

    (a) Articles 2 to 12 and 14 of the Convention,

    (b) Articles 1 to 3 of the First Protocol, and

    (c) Articles 1 and 2 of the Sixth Protocol,

as read with Articles 16 to 18 of the Convention.

(2) Those Articles are to have effect for the purposes of this Act subject to any designated derogation or reservation (as to which see sections 14 and 15).

(3) The Articles are set out in Schedule 1.

(4) The [Lord Chancellor] may by order make such amendments to this Act

as he considers appropriate to reflect the effect, in relation to the United Kingdom, of a protocol.

(5) In subsection (4) "protocol" means a protocol to the Convention—

(a) which the United Kingdom has ratified; or
(b) which the United Kingdom has signed with a view to ratification.

(6) No amendment may be made by an order under subsection (4) so as to come into force before the protocol concerned is in force in relation to the United Kingdom.

Interpretation of Convention rights

99–003 **2.**—(1) A court or tribunal determining a question which has arisen in connection with a Convention right must take into account any—

(a) judgment, decision, declaration or advisory opinion of the European Court of Human Rights,
(b) opinion of the Commission given in a report adopted under Article 31 of the Convention,
(c) decision of the Commission in connection with Article 26 or 27(2) of the Convention, or
(d) decision of the Committee of Ministers taken under Article 46 of the Convention,

whenever made or given, so far as, in the opinion of the court or tribunal, it is relevant to the proceedings in which that question has arisen.

(2) Evidence of any judgment, decision, declaration or opinion of which account may have to be taken under this section is to be given in proceedings before any court or tribunal in such manner as may be provided by rules.

(3) In this section "rules" means rules of court or, in the case of proceedings before a tribunal, rules made for the purposes of this section—

(a) by the Lord Chancellor or the Secretary of State, in relation to any proceedings outside Scotland;
(b) by the Secretary of State, in relation to proceedings in Scotland; or
(c) by a Northern Ireland department, in relation to proceedings before a tribunal in Northern Ireland—

(i) which deals with transferred matters; and
(ii) for which no rules made under paragraph (a) are in force.

Legislation

Interpretation of legislation

99–004 **3.**—(1) So far as it is possible to do so, primary legislation and subordinate legislation must be read and given effect in a way which is compatible with the Convention rights.

(2) This section—

(a) applies to primary legislation and subordinate legislation whenever enacted;
(b) does not affect the validity, continuing operation or enforcement of any incompatible primary legislation; and
(c) does not affect the validity, continuing operation or enforcement of any

incompatible subordinate legislation if (disregarding any possibility of revocation) primary legislation prevents removal of the incompatibility.

Declaration of incompatibility

4.—(1) Subsection (2) applies in any proceedings in which a court determines whether a provision of primary legislation is compatible with a Convention right.

(2) If the court is satisfied that the provision is incompatible with a Convention right, it may make a declaration of that incompatibility.

(3) Subsection (4) applies in any proceedings in which a court determines whether a provision of subordinate legislation, made in the exercise of a power conferred by primary legislation, is compatible with a Convention right.

(4) If the court is satisfied—

    (a) that the provision is incompatible with a Convention right, and

    (b) that (disregarding any possibility of revocation) the primary legislation concerned prevents removal of the incompatibility,

it may make a declaration of that incompatibility.

(5) In this section "court" means —

    (a) the House of Lords;

    (b) the Judicial Committee of the Privy Council;

    (c) the Courts-Martial Appeal Court;

    (d) in Scotland, the High Court of Justiciary sitting otherwise than as a trial court or the Court of Session;

    (e) in England and Wales or Northern Ireland, the High Court or the Court of Appeal.

(6) A declaration under this section ("a declaration of incompatibility")—

    (a) does not affect the validity, continuing operation or enforcement of the provision in respect of which it is given; and

    (b) is not binding on the parties to the proceedings in which it is made.

Right of Crown to intervene

5.—(1) Where a court is considering whether to make a declaration of incompatibility, the Crown is entitled to notice in accordance with rules of court.

(2) In any case to which subsection (1) applies—

    (a) a Minister of the Crown (or a person nominated by him),

    (b) a member of the Scottish Executive,

    (c) a Northern Ireland Minister,

    (d) a Northern Ireland department,

is entitled, on giving notice in accordance with rules of court, to be joined as a party to the proceedings.

(3) Notice under subsection (2) may be given at any time during the proceedings.

(4) A person who has been made a party to criminal proceedings (other than in Scotland) as the result of a notice under subsection (2) may, with leave, appeal to the House of Lords against any declaration of incompatibility made in the proceedings.

(5) In subsection (4)—

    "criminal proceedings" includes all proceedings before the Courts-Martial Appeal Court; and

99–005

99–006

"leave" means leave granted by the court making the declaration of incompatibility or by the House of Lords.

Public authorities

Acts of public authorities

99–007   **6.**—(1) It is unlawful for a public authority to act in a way which is incompatible with a Convention right.

(2) Subsection (1) does not apply to an act if—

(a) as the result of one or more provisions of primary legislation, the authority could not have acted differently; or

(b) in the case of one or more provisions of, or made under, primary legislation which cannot be read or given effect in a way which is compatible with the Convention rights, the authority was acting so as to give effect to or enforce those provisions.

(3) In this section "public authority" includes—

(a) a court or tribunal, and

(b) any person certain of whose functions are functions of a public nature,

but does not include either House of Parliament or a person exercising functions in connection with proceedings in Parliament.

(4) In subsection (3) "Parliament" does not include the House of Lords in its judicial capacity.

(5) In relation to a particular act, a person is not a public authority by virtue only of subsection (3)(b) if the nature of the act is private.

(6) "An act" includes a failure to act but does not include a failure to—

(a) introduce in, or lay before, Parliament a proposal for legislation; or

(b) make any primary legislation or remedial order.

Proceedings

99–008   **7.**—(1) A person who claims that a public authority has acted (or proposes to act) in a way which is made unlawful by section 6(1) may—

(a) bring proceedings against the authority under this Act in the appropriate court or tribunal, or

(b) rely on the Convention right or rights concerned in any legal proceedings,

but only if he is (or would be) a victim of the unlawful act.

(2) In subsection (1)(a) "appropriate court or tribunal" means such court or tribunal as may be determined in accordance with rules; and proceedings against an authority include a counterclaim or similar proceedings.

(3) If the proceedings are brought on an application for judicial review, the applicant is to be taken to have a sufficient interest in relation to the unlawful act only if he is, or would be, a victim of that act.

(4) If the proceedings are made by way of a petition for judicial review in Scotland, the applicant shall be taken to have title and interest to sue in relation to the unlawful act only if he is, or would be, a victim of that act.

(5) Proceedings under subsection (1)(a) must be brought before the end of—

(a) the period of one year beginning with the date on which the act complained of took place; or

(b) such longer period as the court or tribunal considers equitable having regard to all the circumstances,

but that is subject to any rule imposing a stricter time limit in relation to the procedure in question.

(6) In subsection (1)(b) "legal proceedings" includes—

(a) proceedings brought by or at the instigation of a public authority; and

(b) an appeal against the decision of a court or tribunal.

(7) For the purposes of this section, a person is a victim of an unlawful act only if he would be a victim for the purposes of Article 34 of the Convention if proceedings were brought in the European Court of Human Rights in respect of that act.

(8) Nothing in this Act creates a criminal offence.

(9) In this section "rules" means —

(a) in relation to proceedings before a court or tribunal outside Scotland, rules made by the Lord Chancellor or the Secretary of State for the purposes of this section or rules of court,

(b) in relation to proceedings before a court or tribunal in Scotland, rules made by the Secretary of State for those purposes,

(c) in relation to proceedings before a tribunal in Northern Ireland—

(i) which deals with transferred matters; and

(ii) for which no rules made under paragraph (a) are in force,

rules made by a Northern Ireland department for those purposes,

and includes provision made by order under section 1 of the Courts and Legal Services Act 1990.

(10) In making rules, regard must be had to section 9.

(11) The Minister who has power to make rules in relation to a particular tribunal may, to the extent he considers it necessary to ensure that the tribunal can provide an appropriate remedy in relation to an act (or proposed act) of a public authority which is (or would be) unlawful as a result of section 6(1), by order add to—

(a) the relief or remedies which the tribunal may grant; or

(b) the grounds on which it may grant any of them.

(12) An order made under subsection (11) may contain such incidental, supplemental, consequential or transitional provision as the Minister making it considers appropriate.

(13) "The Minister" includes the Northern Ireland department concerned.

Judicial remedies

8.—(1) In relation to any act (or proposed act) of a public authority which **99–009** the court finds is (or would be) unlawful, it may grant such relief or remedy, or make such order, within its powers as it considers just and appropriate.

(2) But damages may be awarded only by a court which has power to award damages, or to order the payment of compensation, in civil proceedings.

(3) No award of damages is to be made unless, taking account of all the circumstances of the case, including—

(a) any other relief or remedy granted, or order made, in relation to the act in question (by that or any other court), and

(b) the consequences of any decision (of that or any other court) in respect of that act,

the court is satisfied that the award is necessary to afford just satisfaction to the person in whose favour it is made.

(4) In determining—

(a) whether to award damages, or

(b) the amount of an award,

the court must take into account the principles applied by the European Court of Human Rights in relation to the award of compensation under Article 41 of the Convention.

(5) A public authority against which damages are awarded is to be treated—

(a) in Scotland, for the purposes of section 3 of the Law Reform (Miscellaneous Provisions) (Scotland) Act 1940 as if the award were made in an action of damages in which the authority has been found liable in respect of loss or damage to the person to whom the award is made;

(b) for the purposes of the Civil Liability (Contribution) Act 1978 as liable in respect of damage suffered by the person to whom the award is made.

(6) In this section—

"court" includes a tribunal;
"damages" means damages for an unlawful act of a public authority; and
"unlawful" means unlawful under section 6(1).

Judicial acts

99–010   **9.**—(1) Proceedings under section 7(1)(a) in respect of a judicial act may be brought only—

(a) by exercising a right of appeal;

(b) on an application (in Scotland a petition) for judicial review; or

(c) in such other forum as may be prescribed by rules.

(2) That does not affect any rule of law which prevents a court from being the subject of judicial review.

(3) In proceedings under this Act in respect of a judicial act done in good faith, damages may not be awarded otherwise than to compensate a person to the extent required by Article 5(5) of the Convention.

(4) An award of damages permitted by subsection (3) is to be made against the Crown; but no award may be made unless the appropriate person, if not a party to the proceedings, is joined.

(5) In this section—

"appropriate person" means the Minister responsible for the court concerned, or a person or government department nominated by him;
"court" includes a tribunal;
"judge" includes a member of a tribunal, a justice of the peace and a clerk or other officer entitled to exercise the jurisdiction of a court;

"judicial act" means a judicial act of a court and includes an act done on the instructions, or on behalf, of a judge; and

"rules" has the same meaning as in section 7(9).

Remedial action

Power to take remedial action

10.—(1) This section applies if—   **99–011**

(a) a provision of legislation has been declared under section 4 to be incompatible with a Convention right and, if an appeal lies—

(i) all persons who may appeal have stated in writing that they do not intend to do so;

(ii) the time for bringing an appeal has expired and no appeal has been brought within that time; or

(iii) an appeal brought within that time has been determined or abandoned; or

(b) it appears to a Minister of the Crown or Her Majesty in Council that, having regard to a finding of the European Court of Human Rights made after the coming into force of this section in proceedings against the United Kingdom, a provision of legislation is incompatible with an obligation of the United Kingdom arising from the Convention.

(2) If a Minister of the Crown considers that there are compelling reasons for proceeding under this section, he may by order make such amendments to the legislation as he considers necessary to remove the incompatibility.

(3) If, in the case of subordinate legislation, a Minister of the Crown considers—

(a) that it is necessary to amend the primary legislation under which the subordinate legislation in question was made, in order to enable the incompatibility to be removed, and

(b) that there are compelling reasons for proceeding under this section,

he may by order make such amendments to the primary legislation as he considers necessary.

(4) This section also applies where the provision in question is in subordinate legislation and has been quashed, or declared invalid, by reason of incompatibility with a Convention right and the Minister proposes to proceed under paragraph 2(b) of Schedule 2.

(5) If the legislation is an Order in Council, the power conferred by subsection (2) or (3) is exercisable by Her Majesty in Council.

(6) In this section "legislation" does not include a Measure of the Church Assembly or of the General Synod of the Church of England.

(7) Schedule 2 makes further provision about remedial orders.

Other rights and proceedings

Safeguard for existing human rights

11. A person's reliance on a Convention right does not restrict—   **99–012**

(a) any other right or freedom conferred on him by or under any law having effect in any part of the United Kingdom; or

(b) his right to make any claim or bring any proceedings which he could make or bring apart from sections 7 to 9.

Freedom of expression

99–013   **12.**—(1) This section applies if a court is considering whether to grant any relief which, if granted, might affect the exercise of the Convention right to freedom of expression.

(2) If the person against whom the application for relief is made ("the respondent") is neither present nor represented, no such relief is to be granted unless the court is satisfied—

(a) that the applicant has taken all practicable steps to notify the respondent; or
(b) that there are compelling reasons why the respondent should not be notified.

(3) No such relief is to be granted so as to restrain publication before trial unless the court is satisfied that the applicant is likely to establish that publication should not be allowed.

(4) The court must have particular regard to the importance of the Convention right to freedom of expression and, where the proceedings relate to material which the respondent claims, or which appears to the court, to be journalistic, literary or artistic material (or to conduct connected with such material), to—

(a) the extent to which—

(i) the material has, or is about to, become available to the public; or
(ii) it is, or would be, in the public interest for the material to be published;

(b) any relevant privacy code.

(5) In this section—

"court" includes a tribunal; and
"relief" includes any remedy or order (other than in criminal proceedings).

Freedom of thought, conscience and religion

99–014   **13.**—(1) If a court's determination of any question arising under this Act might affect the exercise by a religious organisation (itself or its members collectively) of the Convention right to freedom of thought, conscience and religion, it must have particular regard to the importance of that right.

(2) In this section "court" includes a tribunal.

Derogations and reservations

Derogations

99–015   **14.**—[(1) In this Act "designated derogation" means any derogation by the United Kingdom from an Article of the Convention, or of any protocol to the Convention, which is designated for the purposes of this Act in an order made by the [Lord Chancellor].]

(3) If a designated derogation is amended or replaced it ceases to be a designated derogation.

(4) But subsection (3) does not prevent the [Lord Chancellor] from exercising

his power under subsection (1) to make a fresh designation order in respect of the Article concerned.

(5) The [Lord Chancellor] must by order make such amendments to Schedule 3 as he considers appropriate to reflect—

(a) any designation order; or

(b) the effect of subsection (3).

(6) A designation order may be made in anticipation of the making by the United Kingdom of a proposed derogation.

Reservations

15.—(1) In this Act "designated reservation" means—   **99–016**

(a) the United Kingdom's reservation to Article 2 of the First Protocol to the Convention; and

(b) any other reservation by the United Kingdom to an Article of the Convention, or of any protocol to the Convention, which is designated for the purposes of this Act in an order made by the [Lord Chancellor].

(2) The text of the reservation referred to in subsection (1)(a) is set out in Part II of Schedule 3.

(3) If a designated reservation is withdrawn wholly or in part it ceases to be a designated reservation.

(4) But subsection (3) does not prevent the [Lord Chancellor] from exercising his power under subsection (1)(b) to make a fresh designation order in respect of the Article concerned.

(5) The [Lord Chancellor] must by order make such amendments to this Act as he considers appropriate to reflect—

(a) any designation order; or

(b) the effect of subsection (3).

Period for which designated derogations have effect

16.—[(1) If it has not already been withdrawn by the United Kingdom, a   **99–017** designated derogation ceases to have effect for the purposes of this Act, at the end of the period of five years beginning with the date on which the order designating it was made.]

(2) At any time before the period—

(a) fixed by subsection (1), or

(b) extended by an order under this subsection,

comes to an end, the [Lord Chancellor] may by order extend it by a further period of five years.

(3) An order under [section 14(1)] ceases to have effect at the end of the period for consideration, unless a resolution has been passed by each House approving the order.

(4) Subsection (3) does not affect—

(a) anything done in reliance on the order; or

(b) the power to make a fresh order under section 14(1).

(5) In subsection (3) "period for consideration" means the period of forty days beginning with the day on which the order was made.

(6) In calculating the period for consideration, no account is to be taken of any time during which—

(a) Parliament is dissolved or prorogued; or
(b) both Houses are adjourned for more than four days.

(7) If a designated derogation is withdrawn by the United Kingdom, the [Lord Chancellor] must by order make such amendments to this Act as he considers are required to reflect that withdrawal.

Periodic review of designated reservations

99–018   **17.**—(1) The appropriate Minister must review the designated reservation referred to in section 15(1)(a)—

(a) before the end of the period of five years beginning with the date on which section 1(2) came into force; and
(b) if that designation is still in force, before the end of the period of five years beginning with the date on which the last report relating to it was laid under subsection (3).

(2) The appropriate Minister must review each of the other designated reservations (if any)—

(a) before the end of the period of five years beginning with the date on which the order designating the reservation first came into force; and
(b) if the designation is still in force, before the end of the period of five years beginning with the date on which the last report relating to it was laid under subsection (3).

(3) The Minister conducting a review under this section must prepare a report on the result of the review and lay a copy of it before each House of Parliament.

. . . . . .

Parliamentary procedure

Statements of compatibility

99–019   **19.**—(1) A Minister of the Crown in charge of a Bill in either House of Parliament must, before Second Reading of the Bill—

(a) make a statement to the effect that in his view the provisions of the Bill are compatible with the Convention rights ("a statement of compatibility"); or
(b) make a statement to the effect that although he is unable to make a statement of compatibility the government nevertheless wishes the House to proceed with the Bill.

(2) The statement must be in writing and be published in such manner as the Minister making it considers appropriate.

. . . . . .

Short title, commencement, application and extent

22.—(1) This Act may be cited as the Human Rights Act 1998.   **99–020**

(2) Sections 18, 20 and 21(5) and this section come into force on the passing of this Act.

(3) The other provisions of this Act come into force on such days as the Secretary of State may by order appoint; and different days may be appointed for different purposes.

(4) Paragraph (b) of subsection (1) of section 7 applies to proceedings brought by or at the instigation of a public authority whenever the act in question took place; but otherwise that subsection does not apply to an act taking place before the coming into force of that section.

(5) This Act binds the Crown.

(6) This Act extends to Northern Ireland.

(7) Section 21(5), so far as it relates to any provision contained in the Army Act 1955, the Air Force Act 1955 or the Naval Discipline Act 1957, extends to any place to which that provision extends.

. . . . . .

Section 1(3)   SCHEDULE 1

THE ARTICLES

PART I

THE CONVENTION RIGHTS AND FREEDOMS

Right to life

Article 2

1. Everyone's right to life shall be protected by law. No one shall be deprived of his life intention- **99–021**
ally save in the execution of a sentence of a court following his conviction of a crime for which this penalty is provided by law.

2. Deprivation of life shall not be regarded as inflicted in contravention of this Article when it results from the use of force which is no more than absolutely necessary:

    (a) in defence of any person from unlawful violence;

    (b) in order to effect a lawful arrest or to prevent the escape of a person lawfully detained;

    (c) in action lawfully taken for the purpose of quelling a riot or insurrection.

Prohibition of torture

Article 3

No one shall be subjected to torture or to inhuman or degrading treatment or punishment.   **99–022**

Prohibition of slavery and forced labour

Article 4

1. No one shall be held in slavery or servitude.   **99–023**

2. No one shall be required to perform forced or compulsory labour.

3. For the purpose of this Article the term "forced or compulsory labour" shall not include:

    (a) any work required to be done in the ordinary course of detention imposed according to the provisions of Article 5 of this Convention or during conditional release from such detention;

    (b) any service of a military character or, in case of conscientious objectors in countries where they are recognised, service exacted instead of compulsory military service;

    (c) any service exacted in case of an emergency or calamity threatening the life or well-being of the community;

    (d) any work or service which forms part of normal civic obligations.

Right to liberty and security

Article 5

99–024
1. Everyone has the right to liberty and security of a person. No one shall be deprived of his liberty save in the following cases and in accordance with a procedure prescribed by law:

(a) the lawful detention of a person after conviction by a competent court;
(b) the lawful arrest or detention of a person for non-compliance with the lawful order of a court or in order to secure the fulfilment of any obligation prescribed by law;
(c) the lawful arrest or detention of a person effected for the purpose of bringing him before the competent legal authority on reasonable suspicion of having committed an offence or when it is reasonably considered necessary to prevent his committing an offence or fleeing after having done so;
(d) the detention of a minor by lawful order for the purpose of educational supervision or his lawful detention for the purpose of bringing him before the competent legal authority;
(e) the lawful detention of persons for the prevention of the spreading of infectious diseases, of persons of unsound mind, alcoholics or drug addicts or vagrants;
(f) the lawful arrest or detention of a person to prevent his effecting an unauthorised entry into the country or of a person against whom action is being taken with a view to deportation or extradition.

2. Everyone who is arrested shall be informed promptly, in a language which he understands, of the reasons for his arrest and of any charge against him.

3. Everyone arrested or detained in accordance with the provisions of paragraph 1(c) of this Article shall be brought promptly before a judge or other officer authorised by law to exercise judicial power and shall be entitled to trial within a reasonable time or to release pending trial. Release may be conditioned by guarantees to appear for trial.

4. Everyone who is deprived of his liberty by arrest or detention shall be entitled to take proceedings by which the lawfulness of his detention shall be decided speedily by a court and his release ordered if the detention is not lawful.

5. Everyone who has been the victim of arrest or detention in contravention of the provisions of this Article shall have an enforceable right to compensation.

Right to a fair trial

Article 6

99–025
1. In the determination of his civil rights and obligations or of any criminal charge against him, everyone is entitled to a fair and public hearing within a reasonable time by an independent and impartial tribunal established by law. Judgment shall be pronounced publicly but the press and public may be excluded from all or part of the trial in the interest of morals, public order or national security in a democratic society, where the interests of juveniles or the protection of the private life of the parties so require, or to the extent strictly necessary in the opinion of the court in special circumstances where publicity would prejudice the interests of justice.

2. Everyone charged with a criminal offence shall be presumed innocent until proved guilty according to law.

3. Everyone charged with a criminal offence has the following minimum rights:

(a) to be informed promptly, in a language which he understands and in detail, of the nature and cause of the accusation against him;
(b) to have adequate time and facilities for the preparation of his defence;
(c) to defend himself in person or through legal assistance of his own choosing or, if he has not sufficient means to pay for legal assistance, to be given it free when the interests of justice so require;
(d) to examine or have examined witnesses against him and to obtain the attendance and examination of witnesses on his behalf under the same conditions as witnesses against him;
(e) to have the free assistance of an interpreter if he cannot understand or speak the language used in court.

No punishment without law

Article 7

99–026
1. No one shall be held guilty of any criminal offence on account of any act or omission which did not constitute a criminal offence under national or international law at the time when it was committed. Nor shall a heavier penalty be imposed than the one that was applicable at the time the criminal offence was committed.

2. This Article shall not prejudice the trial and punishment of any person for any act or omission which, at the time when it was committed, was criminal according to the general principles of law recognised by civilised nations.

Right to respect for private and family life

Article 8
1. Everyone has the right to respect for his private and family life, his home and his correspond-ence.
2. There shall be no interference by a public authority with the exercise of this right except such as is in accordance with the law and is necessary in a democratic society in the interests of national security, public safety or the economic well-being of the country, for the prevention of disorder or crime, for the protection of health or morals, or for the protection of the rights and freedoms of others.

99–027

Freedom of thought, conscience and religion

Article 9
1. Everyone has the right to freedom of thought, conscience and religion, this right includes freedom to change his religion or belief and freedom, either alone or in community with others and in public or private, to manifest his religion or belief, in worship, teaching, practice and observance.
2. Freedom to manifest one's religion or beliefs shall be subject only to such limitation as are prescribed by law and are necessary in a democratic society in the interests of public safety, for the protection of public order, health or morals, or for the protection of the rights and freedoms of others.

99–028

Freedom of expression

Article 10
1. Everyone has the right to freedom of expression. This right shall include freedom to hold opinions and to receive and impart information and ideas without interference by public authority and regardless of frontiers. This Article shall not prevent States from requiring the licensing of broadcasting, television or cinema enterprises.
2. The exercise of these freedoms, since it carries with it duties and responsibilities, may be subject to such formalities, conditions, restrictions or penalties as are prescribed by law and are necessary in a democratic society, in the interests of national security, territorial integrity or public safety, for the prevention of disorder or crime, for the protection of health or morals, for the protec-tion of the reputation or rights of others, for preventing the disclosure of information received in confidence, or for maintaining the authority and impartiality of the judiciary.

99–029

Freedom of assembly and association

Article 11
1. Everyone has the right to freedom of peaceful assembly and to freedom of association with others, including the right to form and to join trade unions for the protection of his interests.
2. No restrictions shall be placed on the exercise of these rights other than such as are prescribed by law and are necessary in a democratic society in the interests of national security or public safety, for the prevention of disorder or crime, for the protection of health or morals or for the protection of the rights and freedoms of others. This Article shall not prevent the imposition of lawful restric-tions on the exercise of these rights by members of the armed forces, of the police or of the adminis-tration of the State.

99–030

Right to marry

Article 12
Men and women of marriageable age have the right to marry and to found a family, according to the national laws governing the exercise of this right.

99–031

Prohibition of discrimination

Article 14
The enjoyment of the rights and freedoms set forth in this Convention shall be secured without discrimination on any ground such as sex, race, colour, language, religion, political or other opinion, national or social origin, association with a national minority, property, birth or other status.

99–032

Restrictions on political activity of aliens

Article 16
Nothing in Articles 10, 11 and 14 shall be regarded as preventing the High Contracting Parties from imposing restrictions on the political activity of aliens.

99–033

Prohibition of abuse of rights

Article 17
Nothing in this Convention may be interpreted as implying for any State, group or person any right to engage in any activity or perform any act aimed at the destruction of any of the rights

99–034

and freedoms set forth herein or at their limitation to a greater extent than is provided for in the Convention.

Limitation on use of restrictions on rights

99–035

Article 18
The restrictions permitted under this Convention to the said rights and freedoms shall not be applied for any purpose other than those for which they have been prescribed.

PART II

THE FIRST PROTOCOL

Protection of property

99–036

Article 1
Every natural or legal person is entitled to the peaceful enjoyment of his possessions. No one shall be deprived of his possessions except in the public interest and subject to the conditions provided for by law and by the general principles of international law.
The preceding provisions shall not, however, in any way impair the right of a State to enforce such laws as it deems necessary to control the use of property in accordance with the general interest or to secure the payment of taxes or other contributions or penalties.

Right to education

99–037

Article 2
No person shall be denied the right to education. In the exercise of any functions which it assumes in relation to education and to teaching, the State shall respect the right of parents to ensure such education and teaching in conformity with their own religious and philosophical convictions.

Right to free elections

99–038

Article 3
The High Contracting Parties undertake to hold free elections at reasonable intervals by secret ballot, under conditions which will ensure the free expression of the opinion of the people in the choice of the legislature.

PART III

THE SIXTH PROTOCOL

Abolition of the death penalty

99–039

Article 1
The death penalty shall be abolished. No one shall be condemned to such penalty or executed.

Death penalty in time of war

99–040

Article 2
A State may make provision in its law for the death penalty in respect of acts committed in time of war or of imminent threat of war; such penalty shall be applied only in the instances laid down in the law and in accordance with its provisions. The State shall communicate to the Secretary General of the Council of Europe the relevant provisions of that law.

Section 10   SCHEDULE 2

REMEDIAL ORDERS

Orders

99–041

1.—(1) A remedial order may—

    (a) contain such incidental, supplemental, consequential or transitional provision as the person making it considers appropriate;
    (b) be made so as to have effect from a date earlier than that on which it is made;
    (c) make provision for the delegation of specific functions;
    (d) make different provision for different cases.

(2) The power conferred by sub-paragraph (1)(a) includes—

(a) power to amend primary legislation (including primary legislation other than that which contains the incompatible provision); and

(b) power to amend or revoke subordinate legislation (including subordinate legislation other than that which contains the incompatible provision).

(3) A remedial order may be made so as to have the same extent as the legislation which it affects.

(4) No person is to be guilty of an offence solely as a result of the retrospective effect of a remedial order.

Procedure

2. No remedial order may be made unless—   **99–042**

(a) a draft of the order has been approved by a resolution of each House of Parliament made after the end of the period of 60 days beginning with the day on which the draft was laid; or

(b) it is declared in the order that it appears to the person making it that, because of the urgency of the matter, it is necessary to make the order without a draft being so approved.

Orders laid in draft

3.—(1) No draft may be laid under paragraph 2(a) unless—   **99–043**

(a) the person proposing to make the order has laid before Parliament a document which contains a draft of the proposed order and the required information; and

(b) the period of 60 days, beginning with the day on which the document required by this sub-paragraph was laid, has ended.

(2) If representations have been made during that period, the draft laid under paragraph 2(a) must be accompanied by a statement containing—

(a) a summary of the representations; and

(b) if, as a result of the representations, the proposed order has been changed, details of the changes.

Urgent cases

4.—(1) If a remedial order ("the original order") is made without being approved in draft, the   **99–044**
person making it must lay it before Parliament, accompanied by the required information, after it is made.

(2) If representations have been made during the period of 60 days beginning with the day on which the original order was made, the person making it must (after the end of that period) lay before Parliament a statement containing—

(a) a summary of the representations; and

(b) if, as a result of the representations, he considers it appropriate to make changes to the original order, details of the changes.

(3) If sub-paragraph (2)(b) applies, the person making the statement must—

(a) make a further remedial order replacing the original order; and

(b) lay the replacement order before Parliament.

(4) If, at the end of the period of 120 days beginning with the day on which the original order, was made, a resolution has not been passed by each House approving the original or replacement order, the order ceases to have effect (but without that affecting anything previously done under either order or the power to make a fresh remedial order).

Definitions

5. In this Schedule—   **99–045**

"representations" means representations about a remedial order (or proposed remedial order) made to the person making (or proposing to make) it and includes any relevant Parliamentary report or resolution; and
"required information" means—

(a) an explanation of the incompatibility which the order (or proposed order) seeks to remove, including particulars of the relevant declaration, finding or order; and

(b) a statement of the reasons for proceeding under section 10 and for making an order in those terms.

Calculating periods

99–046   **6.** In calculating any period for the purposes of this Schedule, no account is to be taken of any time during which—

(a) Parliament is dissolved or prorogued; or
(b) both Houses are adjourned for more than four days.

99–047   [**7.**—(1) This paragraph applies in relation to—

(a) any remedial order made, and any draft of such an order proposed to be made,—

(i) by the Scottish Ministers; or
(ii) within devolved competence (within the meaning of the Scotland Act 1998) by Her Majesty in Council; and

(b) any document or statement to be laid in connection with such an order (or proposed order).

(2) This Schedule has effect in relation to any such order (or proposed order), document or statement subject to the following modifications.

(3) Any reference to Parliament, each House of Parliament or both Houses of Parliament shall be construed as a reference to the Scottish Parliament.

(4) Paragraph 6 does not apply and instead, in calculating any period for the purposes of this Schedule, no account is to be taken of any time during which the Scottish Parliament is dissolved or is in recess for more than four days.]¹

¹ Added by S.I. 2000 No. 2040, Sched. 1, Pt I, para. 21.

Northern Ireland Act 1998

(1998, c. 47)

100–001 *An Act to make new provision for the government of Northern Ireland for the purpose of implementing the agreement reached at multi-party talks on Northern Ireland set out in Command Paper 3883.* [19th November 1998]

Part I

Preliminary

Status of Northern Ireland

100–002   **1.**—(1) It is hereby declared that Northern Ireland in its entirety remains part of the United Kingdom and shall not cease to be so without the consent of a majority of the people of Northern Ireland voting in a poll held for the purposes of this section in accordance with Schedule 1.

(2) But if the wish expressed by a majority in such a poll is that Northern Ireland should cease to be part of the United Kingdom and form part of a united Ireland, the Secretary of State shall lay before Parliament such proposals to give effect to that wish as may be agreed between Her Majesty's Government in the United Kingdom and the Government of Ireland.

. . . . . .

PART II

LEGISLATIVE POWERS

General

Acts of the Northern Ireland Assembly

5.—(1) Subject to sections 6 to 8, the Assembly may make laws, to be known **100–003** as Acts.

(2) A Bill shall become an Act when it has been passed by the Assembly and has received Royal Assent.

(3) A Bill receives Royal Assent at the beginning of the day on which Letters Patent under the Great Seal of Northern Ireland signed with Her Majesty's own hand signifying Her Assent are notified to the Presiding Officer.

(4) The date of Royal Assent shall be written on the Act by the Presiding Officer, and shall form part of the Act.

(5) The validity of any proceedings leading to the enactment of an Act of the Assembly shall not be called into question in any legal proceedings.

(6) This section does not affect the power of the Parliament of the United Kingdom to make laws for Northern Ireland, but an Act of the Assembly may modify any provision made by or under an Act of Parliament in so far as it is part of the law of Northern Ireland.

Legislative competence

6.—(1) A provision of an Act is not law if it is outside the legislative compet- **100–004** ence of the Assembly.

(2) A provision is outside that competence if any of the following paragraphs apply—

(a) it would form part of the law of a country or territory other than Northern Ireland, or confer or remove functions exercisable otherwise than in or as regards Northern Ireland;

(b) it deals with an excepted matter and is not ancillary to other provisions (whether in the Act or previously enacted) dealing with reserved or transferred matters;

(c) it is incompatible with any of the Convention rights;

(d) it is incompatible with Community law;

(e) it discriminates against any person or class of person on the ground of religious belief or political opinion;

(f) it modifies an enactment in breach of section 7.

(3) For the purposes of this Act, a provision is ancillary to other provisions if it is a provision—

(a) which provides for the enforcement of those other provisions or is otherwise necessary or expedient for making those other provisions effective; or

(b) which is otherwise incidental to, or consequential on, those provisions;

and references in this Act to provisions previously enacted are references to provisions contained in, or in any instrument made under, other Northern Ireland legislation or an Act of Parliament.

(4) Her Majesty may by Order in Council specify functions which are to be treated, for such purposes of this Act as may be specified, as being, or as not being, functions which are exercisable in or as regards Northern Ireland.

(5) No recommendation shall be made to Her Majesty to make an Order in Council under subsection (4) unless a draft of the Order has been laid before and approved by resolution of each House of Parliament.

Entrenched enactments

100–005   **7.**—(1) Subject to subsection (2), the following enactments shall not be modified by an Act of the Assembly or subordinate legislation made, confirmed or approved by a Minister or Northern Ireland department—

    (a) the European Communities Act 1972;
    (b) the Human Rights Act 1998; and
    (c) section 43(1) to (6) and (8), section 67, sections 84 to 86, section 95(3) and (4) and section 98.

(2) Subsection (1) does not prevent an Act of the Assembly or subordinate legislation modifying section 3(3) or (4) or 11(1) of the European Communities Act 1972.

(3) In this Act "Minister", unless the context otherwise requires, means the First Minister, the deputy First Minister or a Northern Ireland Minister.

. . . . . .

Scrutiny and stages of Bills

Scrutiny by Ministers

100–006   **9.**—(1) A Minister in charge of a Bill shall, on or before introduction of it in the Assembly, make a statement to the effect that in his view the Bill would be within the legislative competence of the Assembly.

(2) The statement shall be in writing and shall be published in such manner as the Minister making the statement considers appropriate.

Scrutiny by Presiding Officer

100–007   **10.**—(1) Standing orders shall ensure that a Bill is not introduced in the Assembly if the Presiding Officer decides that any provision of it would not be within the legislative competence of the Assembly.

(2) Subject to subsection (3)—

    (a) the Presiding Officer shall consider a Bill both on its introduction and before the Assembly enters on its final stage; and
    (b) if he considers that the Bill contains—

        (i) any provision which deals with an excepted matter and is ancillary to other provisions (whether in the Bill or previously enacted) dealing with reserved or transferred matters; or
        (ii) any provision which deals with a reserved matter, he shall refer it to the Secretary of State; and

    (c) the Assembly shall not proceed with the Bill or, as the case may be, enter on its final stage unless—

        (i) the Secretary of State's consent to the consideration of the Bill by the Assembly is signified; or
        (ii) The Assembly is informed that in his opinion the Bill does not contain any such provision as is mentioned in paragraph (b)(i) or (ii).

(3) Subsection (2)(b) and (c) shall not apply—

(a) where, in the opinion of the Presiding Officer, each provision of the Bill which deals with an excepted or reserved matter is ancillary to other provisions (whether in the Bill or previously enacted) dealing with transferred matters only; or

(b) on the introduction of a Bill, where the Bill has been endorsed with a statement that the Secretary of State has consented to the Assembly considering the Bill.

(4) In this section and section 14 "final stage", in relation to a Bill, means the stage in the Assembly's proceedings at which the Bill falls finally to be passed or rejected.

. . . . . .

Stages of Bills

13.—(1) Standing orders shall include provision—   **100–008**

(a) for general debate on a Bill with an opportunity for members to vote on its general principles;

(b) for the consideration of, and an opportunity for members to vote on, the details of a Bill; and

(c) for a final stage at which a Bill can be passed or rejected but not amended.

(2) Standing orders may, in relation to different types of Bill, modify provisions made in pursuance of subsection (1)(a) or (b).

(3) Standing orders—

(a) shall include provision for establishing such a committee as is mentioned in paragraph 11 of Strand One of the Belfast Agreement;

(b) may include provision for the details of a Bill to be considered by the committee in such circumstances as may be specified in the orders.

(4) Standing orders shall include provision—

(a) requiring the Presiding Officer to send a copy of each Bill, as soon as reasonably practicable after introduction, to the Northern Ireland Human Rights Commission; and

(b) enabling the Assembly to ask the Commission, where the Assembly thinks fit, to advise whether a Bill is compatible with human rights (including the Convention rights).

(5) Standing orders shall provide for an opportunity for the reconsideration of a Bill after its passing if (and only if)—

(a) the Judicial Committee decide that any provision of the Bill would not be within the legislative competence of the Assembly;

(b) a reference made in relation to a provision of the Bill under section 11 has been withdrawn following a request for withdrawal under section 12;

(c) a decision is made in relation to the Bill under section 14(4) or (5); or

(d) a motion under section 15(1) is passed by either House of Parliament.

(6) Standing orders shall, in particular, ensure that any Bill amended on reconsideration is subject to a final stage at which it can be approved or rejected but not amended.

(7) References in subsection (5) and other provisions of this Act to the passing of a Bill shall, in the case of a Bill which has been amended on reconsideration, be read as references to the approval of the Bill.

Royal Assent

Submission by Secretary of State

100–009   **14.**—(1) It shall be the Secretary of State who submits Bills for Royal Assent.

(2) The Secretary of State shall not submit a Bill for Royal Assent at any time when—

>   (a) the Attorney General for Northern Ireland is entitled to make a reference in relation to a provision of the Bill under section 11; or
>   (b) any such reference has been made but has not been decided or otherwise disposed of by the Judicial Committee.

(3) If—

>   (a) the Judicial Committee have decided that any provision of a Bill would not be within the legislative competence of the Assembly; or
>   (b) a reference made in relation to a provision of the Bill under section 11 has been withdrawn following a request for withdrawal under section 12,

the Secretary of State shall not submit the Bill in its unamended form for Royal Assent.

(4) The Secretary of State may, unless he consents to it, decide not to submit for Royal Assent a Bill containing a provision—

>   (a) which the Secretary of State considers deals with an excepted matter and is ancillary to other provisions (whether in the Bill or previously enacted) dealing with reserved or transferred matters; or
>   (b) which the Secretary of State considers deals with a reserved matter,

if the Bill has not been referred to him under subsection (2) of section 10 (whether by virtue of subsection (3)(a) of that section or otherwise) before the Assembly enters on its final stage.

(5) The Secretary of State may decide not to submit for Royal Assent a Bill which contains a provision which he considers—

>   (a) would be incompatible with any international obligations, with the interests of defence or national security or with the protection of public safety or public order; or
>   (b) would have an adverse effect on the operation of the single market in goods and services within the United Kingdom.

Parliamentary control where consent given

100–010   **15.**—(1) Subject to subsections (2) and (3), a Bill to which the Secretary of State has consented under this Part shall not be submitted by him for Royal Assent unless he has first laid it before Parliament and either—

(a) the period of 20 days beginning with the date on which it is laid has expired without notice having been given in either House of a motion that the Bill shall not be submitted for Royal Assent; or

(b) if notice of such a motion is given within that period, the motion has been rejected or withdrawn.

(2) Subsection (1) shall not apply to a Bill if the Secretary of State considers that it contains no provision which deals with an excepted or reserved matter except a provision which is ancillary to other provisions (whether in the Bill or previously enacted) dealing with transferred matters only.

(3) Subsection (1) shall not apply to a Bill if the Secretary of State considers that by reason of urgency it should be submitted for Royal Assent without first being laid before Parliament.

(4) Any Bill submitted by virtue of subsection (3) shall, if given Royal Assent, be laid before Parliament by the Secretary of State after Royal Assent, and if—

(a) within the period of 20 days beginning with the date on which it is laid notice is given in either House of a motion praying that the Act of the Assembly shall cease to have effect; and

(b) that motion is carried,

Her Majesty may by Order in Council repeal that Act with effect from such date as may be specified in the Order.

(5) An Order in Council under subsection (4) may make such consequential and transitional provisions and such savings in connection with the repeal as appear to Her Majesty to be necessary or expedient.

(6) Any notice of motion for the purposes of subsection (1) or (4) must be signed by not less than 20 members of the House in which it is given; and the period mentioned in that subsection shall be computed, in relation to each House, by reference only to days on which that House sits.

PART III

EXECUTIVE AUTHORITIES

Authorities

First Minister and deputy First Minister

16.—(1) Each Assembly shall, within a period of six weeks beginning with **100–011** its first meeting, elect from among its members the First Minister and the deputy First Minister.

(2) Each candidate for either office must stand for election jointly with a candidate for the other office.

(3) Two candidates standing jointly shall not be elected to the two offices without the support of a majority of the members voting in the election, a majority of the designated Nationalists voting and a majority of the designated Unionists voting.

(4) The first Minister and the deputy First Minister—

(a) shall not take up office until each of them has affirmed the terms of the pledge of office; and

(b) subject to the provisions of this Part, shall hold office until the conclusion of the next election for First Minister and deputy First Minister.

(5) The holder of the office of First Minister or deputy First Minister may by notice in writing to the Presiding Officer designate a Northern Ireland Minister to exercise the functions of that office—

(a) during any absence or incapacity of the holder; or
(b) during any vacancy in that office arising otherwise than under subsection (7)(a);

but a person shall not have power to act by virtue of paragraph (a) for a continuous period exceeding 6 weeks.

(6) The First Minister or the deputy First Minister—

(a) may at any time resign by notice in writing to the Presiding Officer; and
(b) shall cease to hold office if he ceases to be a member of the Assembly otherwise than by virtue of a dissolution.

(7) If either the First Minister or the deputy First Minister ceases to hold office at any time, whether by resignation or otherwise, the other—

(a) shall also cease to hold office at that time; but
(b) may continue to exercise the functions of his office until the election required by subsection (8).

(8) Where the offices of the First Minister and the deputy First Minister become vacant at any time an election shall be held under this section to fill the vacancies within a period of six weeks beginning with that time.

(9) Standing orders may make provision with respect to the holding of elections under this section.

(10) In this Act "the pledge of office" means the pledge of office which, together with the code of conduct to which it refers, is set out in Annex A to Strand One of the Belfast Agreement (the text of which Annex is reproduced in Schedule 4).

Ministerial offices

100–012   **17.**—(1) The First Minister and the deputy First Minister acting jointly may at any time, and shall where subsection (2) applies, determine—

(a) the number of Ministerial offices to be held by Northern Ireland Ministers; and
(b) the functions to be exercisable by the holder of each such office.

(2) This subsection applies where provision is made by an Act of the Assembly for establishing a new Northern Ireland department or dissolving an existing one.

(3) In making a determination under subsection (1), the First Minister and the deputy First Minister shall ensure that the functions exercisable by those in charge of the different Northern Ireland departments existing at the date of the determination are exercisable by the holders of different Ministerial offices.

(4) The number of Ministerial offices shall not exceed 10 or such greater number as the Secretary of State may by order provide.

(5) A determination under subsection (1) shall not have effect unless it is approved by a resolution of the Assembly passed with cross-community support.

Northern Ireland Ministers

18.—(1) Where—   **100–013**

(a) an Assembly is elected under section 31 or 32;

(b) a determination under section 17(1) takes effect;

(c) a resolution which causes one or more Ministerial offices to become vacant is passed under section 30(2);

(d) the period of exclusion imposed by a resolution under section 30(2) comes to an end; or

(e) such other circumstances obtain as may be specified in standing orders,

all Northern Ireland Ministers shall cease to hold office and the Ministerial offices shall be filled by applying subsections (2) to (6) within a period so specified.

(2) The nominating officer of the political party for which the formula in subsection (5) gives the highest figure may select a Ministerial office and nominate a person to hold it who is a member of the party and of the Assembly.

(3) If—

(a) the nominating officer does not exercise the power conferred by subsection (2) within a period specified in standing orders; or

(b) the nominated person does not take up the selected Ministerial office within that period,

that power shall become exercisable by the nominating officer of the political party for which the formula in subsection (5) gives the next highest figure.

(4) Subsections (2) and (3) shall be applied as many times as may be necessary to secure that each of the Ministerial offices is filled.

(5) The formula is—

$$S/1 + M$$

where—

S = the number of seats in the Assembly which were held by members of the party on the day on which the Assembly first met following its election;

M = the number of Ministerial offices (if any) which are held by members of the party.

(6) Where the figures given by the formula for two or more political parties are equal, each of those figures shall be recalculated with S being equal to the number of first preference votes cast for the party at the last general election of members of the Assembly.

(7) The holding of office as First Minister or deputy First Minister shall not prevent a person being nominated to hold a Ministerial office.

(8) A Northern Ireland Minister shall not take up office until he has affirmed the terms of the pledge of office.

(9) A Northern Ireland Minister shall cease to hold office if—

(a) he resigns by notice in writing to the First Minister and the deputy First Minister;

(b) he ceases to be a member of the Assembly otherwise than by virtue of a dissolution; or

(c) he is dismissed by the nominating officer who nominated him (or that officer's successor) and the Presiding Officer is notified of his dismissal.

(10) Where a Ministerial office is vacant otherwise than by virtue of subsection (1), the nominating officer of the party on whose behalf the previous incumbent was nominated may nominate a person to hold the office who is a member of the party and of the Assembly.

(11) If—

(a) the nominating officer does not exercise the power conferred by subsection (10) within a period specified in standing orders; or

(b) the nominated person does not take up the office within that period,

the vacancy shall be filled by applying subsections (2) to (6) within a period specified in standing orders.

(12) Where—

(a) the Assembly has resolved under section 30(2) that a political party does not enjoy its confidence; and

(b) the party's period of exclusion has not come to an end,

the party shall be disregarded for the purposes of any application of subsections (2) to (6).

(13) In this section "nominating officer"—

(a) in relation to [a party registered under Part II of the Political Parties, Elections and Referendums Act 2000][1], means the registered nominating officer or a member of the Assembly nominated by him for the purposes of this section;

(b) in relation to any other political party, means the person who appears to the Presiding Officer to be the leader of the party, or a member of the Assembly nominated by that person for the purposes of this section.

[1] Words substituted by Political Parties, Elections and Referendums Act 2000 (c.41), Sched. 21, para. 14(2).

Junior Ministers

100–014 **19.**—(1) The First Minister and the deputy First Minister acting jointly may at any time determine—

(a) that a number of members of the Assembly specified in the determination shall be appointed as junior Ministers in accordance with such procedures for their appointment as are so specified; and

(b) that the functions exercisable by virtue of each junior Ministerial office shall be those specified in relation to that office in the determination.

(2) Procedures specified in a determination under this section may apply such formulae or other rules as the First Minister and the deputy First Minister consider appropriate.

(3) A determination under this section shall—

(a) make provision as to the circumstances in which a junior Minister shall cease to hold office, and for the filling of vacancies; and

(b) provide that a junior Minister shall not take up office until he has affirmed the terms of the pledge of office.

(4) A determination under this section shall not take effect until it has been approved by a resolution of the Assembly.

(5) Where a determination under this section takes effect—

(a) any junior Ministers previously appointed shall cease to hold office; and

(b) the procedures specified in the determination shall be applied within a period specified in standing orders.

[Disqualification for certain offices which may be held by members of the Assembly

19A.—(1) No person may—   **100–015**

(a) stand for election as First Minister or as deputy First Minister, or be elected as such,

(b) be nominated to hold a Ministerial office,

(c) be appointed as a junior Minister, or

(d) be nominated under paragraph 7 of Schedule 1 to the Police (Northern Ireland) Act 2000 (members of the Northern Ireland Policing Board drawn from the Northern Ireland Assembly),

if he is the holder of a disqualifying office.

(2) A Minister or junior Minister ceases to hold that office on becoming the holder of a disqualifying office.

(3) A person holding office as a member of the Northern Ireland Policing Board in accordance with paragraph 7 of Schedule 1 to the Police (Northern Ireland) Act 2000 ceases to hold that office on becoming the holder of a disqualifying office.

(4) In this section "disqualifying office" means—

(a) Minister of the Government of Ireland; or

(b) chairman or deputy chairman of—

    (i) a committee of the Dáil Éireann (House of Representatives of Ireland);

    (ii) a committee of the Seanad Éireann (Senate of Ireland); or

    (iii) a joint committee of the Oireachtas (National Parliament of Ireland).][1]

[1] Added by Disqualifications Act 2000 (c.42), s. 2.

The Executive Committee

20.—(1) There shall be an Executive Committee of each Assembly consisting **100–016** of the First Minister, the deputy First Minister and the Northern Ireland Ministers.

(2) The First Minister and the deputy First Minister shall be chairmen of the Committee.

(3) The Committee shall have the functions set out in paragraphs 19 and 20 of Strand One of the Belfast Agreement.

. . . . . .

Functions

Statutory functions

22.—(1) An Act of the Assembly or other enactment may confer functions **100–017** on a Minister (but not a junior Minister) or a Northern Ireland department by name.

(2) Functions conferred on a Northern Ireland department by an enactment passed or made before the appointed day shall, except as provided by an Act of the Assembly or other subsequent enactment, continue to be exercisable by that department.

Prerogative and executive powers

100–018   **23.**—(1) The executive power in Northern Ireland shall continue to be vested in Her Majesty.

(2) As respects transferred matters, the prerogative and other executive powers of Her Majesty in relation to Northern Ireland shall, subject to subsection (3), be exercisable on Her Majesty's behalf by any Minister or Northern Ireland department.

(3) As respects the Northern Ireland Civil Service and the Commissioner for Public Appointments for Northern Ireland, the prerogative and other executive powers of Her Majesty in relation to Northern Ireland shall be exercisable on Her Majesty's behalf by the First Minister and the deputy First Minister acting jointly.

(4) The First Minister and deputy First Minister acting jointly may by prerogative order under subsection (3) direct that such of the powers mentioned in that subsection as are specified in the order shall be exercisable on Her Majesty's behalf by a Northern Ireland Minister or Northern Ireland department so specified.

Community law, Convention rights, etc.

100–019   **24.**—(1) A Minister or Northern Ireland department has no power to make, confirm or approve any subordinate legislation, or to do any act, so far as the legislation or act—

(a) is incompatible with any of the Convention rights;
(b) is incompatible with Community law;
(c) discriminates against a person or class of person on the ground of religious belief or political opinion;
(d) in the case of an act, aids or incites another person to discriminate against a person or class of person on that ground; or
(e) in the case of legislation, modifies an enactment in breach of section 7.

(2) Subsection (1)(c) and (d) does not apply in relation to any act which is unlawful by virtue of the Fair Employment (Northern Ireland) Act 1976, or would be unlawful but for some exception made by virtue of Part V of that Act.

Excepted and reserved matters

100–020   **25.**—(1) If any subordinate legislation made, confirmed or approved by a Minister or Northern Ireland department contains a provision dealing with an excepted or reserved matter, the Secretary of State may by order revoke the legislation.

(2) An order made under subsection (1) shall recite the reasons for revoking the legislation and may make provision having retrospective effect.

International obligations

100–021   **26.**—(1) If the Secretary of State considers that any action proposed to be taken by a Minister or Northern Ireland department would be incompatible with any international obligations, with the interest of defence or national security or with the protection of public safety or public order, he may by order direct that the proposed action shall not be taken.

(2) If the Secretary of State considers that any action capable of being taken by a Minister or Northern Ireland department is required for the purpose of giving effect to any international obligations, of safeguarding the interests of defence or national security or of protecting public safety or public order, he may by order direct that the action shall be taken.

(3) In subsections (1) and (2), "action" includes making, confirming or approving subordinate legislation and, in subsection (2), includes introducing a Bill in the Assembly.

(4) If any subordinate legislation made, confirmed or approved by a Minister or Northern Ireland department contains a provision which the Secretary of State considers—

(a) would be incompatible with any international obligations, with the interests of defence or national security or with the protection of public safety or public order; or

(b) would have an adverse effect on the operation of the single market in goods and services within the United Kingdom,

the Secretary of State may by order revoke the legislation.

(5) An order under this section shall recite the reasons for making the order and may make provision having retrospective effect.

. . . . . .

Part IV

The Northern Ireland Assembly

Presiding Officer and Commission

Presiding Officer

39.—(1) Each Assembly shall as its first business elect from among its members a Presiding Officer and deputies. **100–022**

(2) A person elected Presiding Officer or deputy shall hold office until the conclusion of the next election for Presiding Officer under subsection (1) unless—

(a) he previously resigns;

(b) he ceases to be a member of the Assembly otherwise than by virtue of a dissolution; or

(c) the Assembly elects from among its members a person to hold office as Presiding Officer or deputy in his place.

(3) If the Presiding Officer or a deputy ceases to hold office (otherwise than under subsection (2)(c) before the Assembly is dissolved, the Assembly shall elect another from among its members to fill his place.

(4) The Presiding Officer's functions may be exercised by a deputy if the office of Presiding Officer is vacant or the Presiding Officer is for any reason unable to act.

(5) The Presiding Officer may (subject to standing orders) authorise a deputy to exercise functions on his behalf.

(6) Standing orders may include provision as to the participation (including voting) of the Presiding Officer and deputies in the proceedings of the Assembly.

(7) A person shall not be elected under subsections (1) to (3) without cross-community support.

Commission

100–023   **40.**—(1) There shall be a body corporate, to be known as the Northern Ireland Assembly Commission ("the Commission"), to perform—

    (a) the functions conferred on the Commission by virtue of any enactment; and

    (b) any functions conferred on the Commission by resolution of the Assembly.

(2) the members of the Commission shall be—

    (a) the Presiding Officer; and

    (b) the prescribed number of members of the Assembly appointed in accordance with standing orders.

(3) In subsection (2) "the prescribed number" means 5 or such other number as may be prescribed by standing orders.

[(3A) A member of the Assembly who is—

    (a) a Minister of the Government of Ireland, or

    (b) chairman or deputy chairman of—

        (i) a committee of the Dáil Éireann (House of Representatives of Ireland),

        (ii) a committee of the Seanad Éireann (Senate of Ireland), or

        (iii) a joint committee of the Oireachtas (National Parliament of Ireland),

may not be appointed as a member of the Commission.][1]

(4) The Commission shall provide the Assembly, or ensure that the Assembly is provided, with the property, staff and services required for the Assembly's purposes.

(5) The Assembly may give special or general directions to the Commission for the purpose of or in connection with the exercise of the Commission's functions.

(6) Proceedings by or against the Assembly (other than proceedings on the Crown side of the Queen's Bench Division) shall be instituted by or against the Commission on behalf of the Assembly.

(7) Any property or liabilities acquired or incurred in relation to matters within the general responsibility of the Commission to which (apart from this subsection) the Assembly would be entitled or subject shall be treated for all purposes as property or liabilities of the Commission.

(8) Any expenses of the Commission shall be defrayed out of money appropriated by Act of the Assembly.

(9) Any sums received by the Commission shall be paid into the Consolidated Fund of Northern Ireland, subject to any provision made by Act of the Assembly for the disposal of or accounting for such sums.

(10) Schedule 5 (which makes further provision about the Commission) shall have effect.

---

[1] Added by Disqualifications Act 2000 (c.42), s. 3(2).

Proceedings etc.

Standing orders

41.—(1) The proceedings of the Assembly shall be regulated by standing **100–024** orders.

(2) Standing orders shall not be made, amended or repealed without cross-community support.

(3) Schedule 6 (which makes provision as to how certain matters are to be dealt with by standing orders) shall have effect.

Petitions of concern

42.—(1) If 30 members petition the Assembly expressing their concern about **100–025** a matter which is to be voted on by the Assembly, the vote on that matter shall require cross-community support.

(2) Standing orders shall make provision with respect to the procedure to be followed in petitioning the Assembly under this section, including provision with respect to the period of notice required.

(3) Standing orders shall provide that the matter to which a petition under this section relates may be referred, in accordance with paragraphs 11 and 13 of Strand One of the Belfast Agreement, to the committee established under section 13(3)(a).

Members' interests

43.—(1) Standing orders shall include provision for a register of interests of **100–026** members of the Assembly, and for—

(a) registrable interests (as defined in standing orders) to be registered in it; and

(b) the register to be published and made available for public inspection.

(2) Standing orders shall include provision requiring that any member of the Assembly who has—

(a) a financial interest (as defined in standing orders) in any matter; or

(b) any other interest, or an interest of any other kind, specified in standing orders in any matter,

declares that interest before taking part in any proceedings of the Assembly relating to that matter.

(3) Standing orders made in pursuance of subsection (1) or (2) may include provision for preventing or restricting the participation in proceedings of the Assembly of a member with a registrable interest, or an interest mentioned in subsection (2), in a matter to which the proceedings relate.

(4) Standing orders shall include provision prohibiting a member of the Assembly from—

(a) advocating or initiating any cause or matter on behalf of any person, by any means specified in standing orders, in consideration of any payment or benefit in kind of a description so specified; or

(b) urging, in consideration of any such payment or benefit in kind, any other member of the Assembly to advocate or initiate any cause or matter on behalf of any person by any such means.

(5) Standing orders may include provision—

(a) for excluding from proceedings of the Assembly any member who fails to comply with, or contravenes, any provision made in pursuance of subsections (1) to (4); and

(b) for withdrawing his rights and privileges as a member for the period of his exclusion.

(6) Any member of the Assembly who—

(a) takes part in any proceedings of the Assembly without having complied with, or in contravention of, any provision made in pursuance of subsections (1) to (3); or

(b) contravenes any provision made in pursuance of subsection (4), is guilty of an offence.

(7) A person guilty of an offence under subsection (6) is liable on summary conviction to a fine not exceeding level 5 on the standard scale.

(8) Proceedings for an offence under subsection (6) shall not be taken without the consent of the Director of Public Prosecutions for Northern Ireland.

. . . . . .

Miscellaneous

Privilege

100–027 **50.**—(1) For the purposes of the law of defamation, absolute privilege shall attach to—

(a) the making of a statement in proceedings of the Assembly; and

(b) the publication of a statement under the Assembly's authority.

(2) A person is not guilty of contempt of court under the strict liability rule as the publisher of any matter—

(a) in the course of proceedings of the Assembly which relate to a Bill or subordinate legislation; or

(b) to the extent that it consists of a fair and accurate report of such proceedings which is made in good faith.

(3) In this section—

"statement" has the same meaning as in the Defamation Act 1996;
"the strict liability rule" has the same meaning as in the Contempt of Court Act 1981.

. . . . . .

Part VII

Human Rights and Equal Opportunities

Human rights

The Northern Ireland Human Rights Commission

68.—(1) There shall be a body corporate to be known as the Northern Ireland **100–028** Human Rights Commission.

(2) The Commission shall consist of a Chief Commissioner and other Commissioners appointed by the Secretary of State.

(3) In making appointments under this section, the Secretary of State shall as far as practicable secure that the Commissioners, as a group, are representative of the community in Northern Ireland.

(4) Schedule 7 (which makes supplementary provision about the Commission) shall have effect.

The Commission's functions

69.—(1) The Commission shall keep under review the adequacy and effect- **100–029** iveness in Northern Ireland of law and practice relating to the protection of human rights.

(2) The Commission shall, before the end of the period of two years beginning with the commencement of this section, make to the Secretary of State such recommendations as it thinks fit for improving—

(a) its effectiveness;

(b) the adequacy and effectiveness of the functions conferred on it by this Part; and

(c) the adequacy and effectiveness of the provisions of this Part relating to it.

(3) The Commission shall advise the Secretary of State and the Executive Committee of the Assembly of legislative and other measures which ought to be taken to protect human rights—

(a) as soon as reasonably practicable after receipt of a general or specific request for advice; and

(b) on such other occasions as the Commission thinks appropriate.

(4) The Commission shall advise the Assembly whether a Bill is compatible with human rights—

(a) as soon as reasonably practicable after receipt of a request for advice; and

(b) on such other occasions as the Commission thinks appropriate.

(5) The Commission may—

(a) give assistance to individuals in accordance with section 70; and

(b) bring proceedings involving law or practice relating to the protection of human rights.

(6) The Commission shall promote understanding and awareness of the importance of human rights in Northern Ireland; and for this purpose it may undertake, commission or provide financial or other assistance for—

(a) research; and

(b) educational activities.

(7) The Secretary of State shall request the Commission to provide advice of the kind referred to in paragraph 4 of the Human Rights section of the Belfast Agreement.

(8) For the purpose of exercising its functions under this section the Commission may conduct such investigations as it considers necessary or expedient.

(9) The Commission may decide to publish its advice and the outcome of its research and investigations.

(10) The Commission shall do all that it can to ensure the establishment of the committee referred to in paragraph 10 of that section of that Agreement.

(11) In this section—

(a) a reference to the Assembly includes a reference to a committee of the Assembly;

(b) "human rights" includes the Convention rights.

Assistance by Commission

100–030   **70.**—(1) This section applies to—

(a) proceedings involving law or practice relating to the protection of human rights which a person in Northern Ireland has commenced, or wishes to commence; or

(b) proceedings in the course of which such a person relies, or wishes to rely, on such law or practice.

(2) Where the person applies to the Northern Ireland Human Rights Commission for assistance in relation to proceedings to which this section applies, the Commission may grant the application on any of the following grounds—

(a) that the case raises a question of principle;

(b) that it would be unreasonable to expect the person to deal with the case without assistance because of its complexity, or because of the person's position in relation to another person involved, or for some other reason;

(c) that there are other special circumstances which make it appropriate for the Commission to provide assistance.

(3) Where the Commission grants an application under subsection (2) it may—

(a) provide, or arrange for the provision of, legal advice;

(b) arrange for the provision of legal representation;

(c) provide any other assistance which it thinks appropriate.

(4) Arrangements made by the Commission for the provision of assistance to a person may include provision for recovery of expenses from the person in certain circumstances.

Restriction on application of rights

100–031   **71.**—(1) Nothing in section 6(2)(c), 24(1)(a) or 69(5)(b) shall enable a person—

(a) to bring any proceedings in a court or tribunal on the ground that any legislation or act is incompatible with the Convention rights; or

(b) to rely on any of the Convention rights in any such proceedings, unless he would be a victim for the purposes of article 34 of the Convention if proceedings in respect of the legislation or act were brought in the European Court of Human Rights.

(2) Subsection (1) does not apply to the Attorney General, the Attorney General for Northern Ireland, the Advocate General for Scotland or the Lord Advocate.

(3) Section 6(2)(c)—

(a) does not apply to a provision of an Act of the Assembly if the passing of the Act is, by virtue of subsection (2) of section 6 of the Human Rights Act 1998, not unlawful under subsection (1) of that section; and

(b) does not enable a court or tribunal to award in respect of the passing of an Act of the Assembly any damages which it could not award on finding the passing of the Act unlawful under that subsection.

(4) Section 24(1)(a)—

(a) does not apply to an act which, by virtue of subsection (2) of section 6 of the Human Rights Act 1998, is not unlawful under subsection (1) of that section; and

(b) does not enable a court or tribunal to award in respect of an act any damages which it could not award on finding the act unlawful under that subsection.

(5) In this section "the Convention" has the same meaning as in the Human Rights Act 1998.

. . . . . .

PART VIII

MISCELLANEOUS

Judicial scrutiny

Legislative power to remedy ultra vires acts

80.—(1) The Secretary of State may by order make such provisions as he **100–032** considers necessary or expedient in consequence of—

(a) any provision of an Act of the Assembly which is not, or may not be, within the legislative competence of the Assembly; or

(b) any purported exercise by a Minister or Northern Ireland department of his or its functions which is not, or may not be, a valid exercise of those functions.

(2) An order under this section may—

(a) make provision having retrospective effect;

(b) make consequential or supplementary provision, including provision amending or repealing any Northern Ireland legislation, or any instrument made under such legislation;

(c) make transitional or saving provision.

Powers of courts or tribunals to vary retrospective decisions

100–033   81.—(1) This section applies where any court or tribunal decides that—

   (a) any provision of an Act of the Assembly is not within the legislative competence of the Assembly; or
   (b) a Minister or Northern Ireland department does not have the power to make, confirm or approve a provision of subordinate legislation that he or it has purported to make, confirm or approve.

   (2) The court or tribunal may make an order—

   (a) removing or limiting any retrospective effect of the decision; or
   (b) suspending the effect of the decision for any period and on any conditions to allow the defect to be corrected.

   (3) In deciding whether to make an order under this section, the court or tribunal shall (among other things) have regard to the extent to which persons who are not parties to the proceedings would otherwise be adversely affected.
   (4) Where a court or tribunal is considering whether to make an order under this section, it shall order notice of that fact to be given to—

   (a) the Attorney General for Northern Ireland; and
   (b) where the decision mentioned in subsection (1) relates to a devolution issue (within the meaning of Schedule 10), the appropriate authority, unless the person to whom the notice would be given is a party to the proceedings.

   (5) A person to whom notice is given under subsection (4) or, where such notice is given to the First Minister and the deputy First Minister, those Ministers acting jointly may take part as a party in the proceedings so far as they relate to the making of the order.
   (6) Paragraphs 37 and 38 of Schedule 10 apply with necessary modifications for the purposes of subsections (4) and (5) as they apply for the purposes of that Schedule.
   (7) In this section "the appropriate authority" means—

   (a) in relation to proceedings in Northern Ireland, the First Minister and the deputy First Minister;
   (b) in relation to proceedings in England and Wales, the Attorney General;
   (c) in relation to proceedings in Scotland, the Lord Advocate and the Advocate General for Scotland.

The Judicial Committee

100–034   82.—(1) Any decision of the Judicial Committee in proceedings under this Act shall be stated in open court and shall be binding in all legal proceedings (other than proceedings before the Committee).
   (2) No member of the Judicial Committee shall sit and act as a member of the Committee in proceedings under this Act unless he holds or has held—

   (a) the office of a Lord of Appeal in Ordinary; or
   (b) high judicial office as defined in section 25 of the Appellate Jurisdiction Act 1876 (ignoring for this purpose section 5 of the Appellate Jurisdiction Act 1887).

   (3) Her Majesty may by Order in Council—

(a) confer on the Judicial Committee in relation to proceedings under this Act such powers as Her Majesty considers necessary or expedient;

(b) apply the Judicial Committee Act 1833 in relation to proceedings under this Act with exceptions or modifications;

(c) make rules for regulating the procedure in relation to proceedings under this Act before the Judicial Committee.

(4) A statutory instrument containing an Order in Council under subsection (3)(a) or (b) shall be subject to annulment in pursuance of a resolution of either House of Parliament.

(5) In this section "proceedings under this Act" means proceedings on a question referred to the Judicial Committee under section 11 or proceedings under Schedule 10.

Interpretation of Acts of the Assembly, etc.

83.—(1) This section applies where—   **100–035**

(a) any provision of an Act of the Assembly, or of a Bill for such an Act, could be read either—

   (i) in such a way as to be within the legislative competence of the Assembly; or

   (ii) in such a way as to be outside that competence; or

(b) any provision of subordinate legislation made, confirmed or approved, or purporting to be made, confirmed or approved, by a Northern Ireland authority could be read either—

   (i) in such a way as not to be invalid by reason of section 24 or, as the case may be, section 76; or

   (ii) in such a way as to be invalid by reason of that section.

(2) The provision shall be read in the way which makes it within that competence or, as the case may be, does not make it invalid by reason of that section, and shall have effect accordingly.

(3) In this section "Northern Ireland authority" means a Minister, a Northern Ireland department or a public authority (within the meaning of section 76) carrying out functions relating to Northern Ireland.

Northern Ireland (Sentences) Act 1998

(1998, c. 35)

An Act to make provision about the release on licence of certain persons serving **101–001**
sentences of imprisonment in Northern Ireland.   [28th July 1998]

Sentence Review Commissioners

Sentence Review Commissioners

1.—(1) The Secretary of State shall appoint Sentence Review Commissioners. **101–002**
(2) The Secretary of State shall so far as reasonably practicable ensure that at any time—

(a) at least one of the Commissioners is a lawyer, and
(b) at least one is a psychiatrist or a psychologist.

(3) In making appointments the Secretary of State shall have regard to the desirability of the Commissioners, as a group, commanding widespread acceptance throughout the community in Northern Ireland.

(4) Schedule 1 (which makes further provision about the Commissioners) shall have effect.

(5) In subsection (2)(a) "lawyer" means a person who holds a legal qualification in the United Kingdom.

. . . . . .

Eligibility for release

Applications

101–003   **3.**—(1) A prisoner may apply to Commissioners for a declaration that he is eligible for release in accordance with the provisions of this Act.

(2) The Commissioners shall grant the application if (and only if)—

(a) the prisoner is serving a sentence of imprisonment for a fixed term in Northern Ireland and the first three of the following four conditions are satisfied, or
(b) the prisoner is serving a sentence of imprisonment for life in Northern Ireland and the following four conditions are satisfied.

(3) The first condition is that the sentence—

(a) was passed in Northern Ireland for a qualifying offence, and
(b) is one of imprisonment for life or for a term of at least five years.

(4) The second condition is that the prisoner is not a supporter of a specified organisation.

(5) The third condition is that, if the prisoner were released immediately, he would not be likely—

(a) to become a supporter of a specified organisation, or
(b) to become concerned in the commission, preparation or instigation of acts of terrorism connected with the affairs of Northern Ireland.

(6) The fourth condition is that, if the prisoner were released immediately, he would not be a danger to the public.

(7) A qualifying offence is an offence which—

(a) was committed before 10th April 1998,
(b) was when committed a scheduled offence within the meaning of the Northern Ireland (Emergency Provisions) Act 1973, 1978, 1991 or 1996, and
(c) was not the subject of a certificate of the Attorney General for Northern Ireland that it was not to be treated as a scheduled offence in the case concerned.

(8) A specified organisation is an organisation specified by order of the Secretary of State; and he shall specify any organisation which he believes—

(a) is concerned in terrorism connected with the affairs of Northern Ireland, or in promoting or encouraging it, and

(b) has not established or is not maintaining a complete and unequivocal ceasefire.

(9) In applying subsection (8)(b) the Secretary of State shall in particular take into account whether an organisation—

(a) is committed to the use now and in the future of only democratic and peaceful means to achieve its objectives;

(b) has ceased to be involved in any acts of violence or of preparation for violence;

(c) is directing or promoting acts of violence by other organisations;

(d) is co-operating fully with any Commission of the kind referred to in section 7 of the Northern Ireland Arms Decommissioning Act 1997 in implementing the Decommissioning section of the agreement reached at multi-party talks on Northern Ireland set out in Command Paper 3883.

(10) The Secretary of State shall from time to time review the list of organisations specified under subsection (8); and if he believes—

(a) that paragraph (a) or (b) of that subsection does not apply to a specified organisation, or

(b) that paragraphs (a) and (b) apply to an organisation which is not specified,

he shall make a new order under subsection (8).

Fixed term prisoners

4.—(1) If a fixed term prisoner is granted a declaration in relation to a sentence he has a right to be released on licence (so far as that sentence is concerned) on the day on which he has served— **101–004**

(a) one third of his sentence, plus

[(b) one day for every day of remission which he has lost and not had restored (or additional day which he has been awarded and which has not been remitted) in accordance with prison rules.][1]

(2) If the day arrived at under subsection (1) falls on or before the day of the declaration, the prisoner's right to be released under that subsection is a right to be released by the end of the day after the day of the declaration.

(3) If a prisoner would have a right to be released on or by the end of a listed day he has a right to be released on or by the end of the next non-listed day; and the listed days are—

(a) Saturday,

(b) Sunday,

(c) Christmas Day,

(d) Good Friday, and

(e) a public holiday in Northern Ireland.

(4) If a prisoner is released on licence under this section his sentence shall expire (and the licence shall lapse) at the time when he could have been discharged on the ground of good conduct under prison rules.

---

[1] Substituted by Northern Ireland (Sentences) Act 1998 (c.35), Sched. 3, para. 4(1).

Fixed term prisoners: special cases

101–005　　**5.**—(1) If the length of a sentence is treated as reduced by a period of custody in accordance with section 26 of the Treatment of Offenders Act (Northern Ireland) 1968 (duration of sentence) for the purposes of section 4(1) above the period of custody must be treated as having been served as part of the sentence.

(2) If a sentence of at least five years is supplemented by a period of imprisonment in accordance with [section 80(2) of the Terrorism Act 2000][1] (conviction of scheduled offence during period of remission) for the purposes of section 4(1) above the supplementary period must be treated as part of the sentence.

(3) If—

    (a) a sentence of less than five years is supplemented by a period of imprisonment in accordance with [section 80(2) of the 2000 Act][2], and

    (b) the supplementary period relates to an earlier sentence of at least five years for a qualifying offence (within the meaning of section 3 above),

the prisoner may make an application under section 3 in respect of the supplementary period and the application shall be granted if (and only if) the second and third conditions are satisfied.

(4) References in this section to section [section 80(2) of the 2000 Act][3] Act include references to—

    (a) section 23(2) of the Prevention of Terrorism (Temporary Provisions) Act 1989, and

    (b) section 15(2) of the Northern Ireland (Emergency Provisions) Act 1991[, and][4]

    [(c) section 16(2) of the Northern Ireland (Emergency Provisions) Act 1996.][5]

[1] Words substituted by Terrorism Act 2000 (c.11), Sched. 15, para. 16(2)(a).
[2] Words substituted by Terrorism Act 2000 (c.11), Sched. 15, para. 16(2)(b).
[3] Words substituted by Terrorism Act 2000 (c.11), Sched. 15, para. 16(2)(c).
[4] Word added by Terrorism Act 2000 (c.11), Sched. 15, para. 16(2)(d).
[5] Added by Terrorism Act 2000 (c.11), Sched. 15, para. 16(2)(d).

Life prisoners

101–006　　**6.**—(1) When Commissioners grant a declaration to a life prisoner in relation to a sentence they must specify a day which they believe marks the completion of about two thirds of the period which the prisoner would have been likely to spend in prison under the sentence.

(2) The prisoner has a right to be released on licence (so far as that sentence is concerned)—

    (a) on the day specified under subsection (1), or

    (b) if that day falls on or before the day of the declaration, by the end of the day after the day of the declaration.

(3) But if he would have a right to be released on or by the end of a listed day (within the meaning of section 4(3)) he has a right to be released on or by the end of the next non-listed day.

Life prisoners: specified dates

101–007　　**7.**—(1) The Secretary of State must inform the Commissioners of the length of time served by persons—

(a) sentenced in Northern Ireland to imprisonment for life, and

(b) released on licence after 1982 and before 1999.

(2) In specifying a day under section 6(1) Commissioners must have regard to—

(a) information given under subsection (1) above, and

(b) previous decisions of Commissioners.

(3) Before Commissioners specify a day under section 6(1) the Secretary of State may notify them of cases which he believes are particularly relevant in the prisoner's case; and the Commissioners may take the notification into account.[¹]²

¹ In relation to a declaration granted under 1998 (c.35), s.3:

7.—Life prisoners: specified dates

7. In specifying a day for a prisoner under section 6 the Commissioners must have regard to—

(a) any order or direction made in relation to the prisoner under section 28 of the Crime (Sentences) Act 1997 (duty to release certain life prisoners);

(b) any order made in relation to the prisoner under section 34 of the Criminal Justice Act 1991 (duty to release discretionary life prisoners) or certificate under paragraph 9 of Schedule 12 to that Act (transitional provisions);

(c) any certificate issued by the Lord Justice General in relation to the prisoner under section 16(2) of the Crime and Punishment (Scotland) Act 1997 or paragraph 6 of Schedule 6 to the Prisoners and Criminal Proceedings (Scotland) Act 1993 (transitional provisions);

(d) any order made in relation to the prisoner under section 2 of the Prisoners and Criminal Proceedings (Scotland) Act 1993 (duty to release designated life prisoners);

(e) any other information, whether relating to the prisoner's case or to other cases, which the Secretary of State submits; and

(f) previous decisions of Commissioners.

² Substituted by Northern Ireland (Sentences) Act 1998 (c.35), Sched. 3, para. 6.

Revocation of declaration

8.—(1) The Secretary of State shall apply to Commissioners to revoke a **101–008** declaration under section 3(1) if, at any time before the prisoner is released under section 4 or 6, the Secretary of State believes—

(a) that as a result of an order under section 3(8), or a change in the prisoner's circumstances, an applicable condition in section 3 is not satisfied, or

(b) that evidence or information which was not available to the Commissioners when they granted the declaration suggests that an applicable condition in section 3 is not satisfied.

(2) The Commissioners shall grant an application under this section if (and only if) the prisoner has not been released under section 4 or 6 and they believe—

(a) that as a result of an order under section 3(8), or a change in the prisoner's circumstances, an applicable condition in section 3 is not satisfied, or

(b) that evidence or information which was not available to them when they granted the declaration suggests that an applicable condition in section 3 is not satisfied.

Licences: conditions

101–009   **9.**—(1) A person's licence under section 4 or 6 is subject only to the conditions—

    (a) that he does not support a specified organisation (within the meaning of section 3),

    (b) that he does not become concerned in the commission, preparation or instigation of acts of terrorism connected with the affairs of Northern Ireland, and

    (c) in the case of a life prisoner, that he does not become a danger to the public.

(2) The Secretary of State may suspend a licence under section 4 or 6 if he believes the person concerned has broken or is likely to break a condition imposed by this section.

(3) Where a person's licence is suspended—

    (a) he shall be detained in pursuance of his sentence and, if at large, shall be taken to be unlawfully at large, and

    (b) Commissioners shall consider his case.

(4) On consideration of a person's case—

    (a) if the Commissioners think he has not broken and is not likely to break a condition imposed by this section, they shall confirm his licence, and

    (b) otherwise, they shall revoke his licence.

(5) Where a person's licence is confirmed—

    (a) he has a right to be released (so far as the relevant sentence is concerned) by the end of the day after the day of confirmation, or

    (b) if he is at large, he has a right (so far as the relevant sentence is concerned) to remain at large.

(6) But if he would have a right to be released by the end of a listed day (within the meaning of section 4(3)) he has a right to be released by the end of the next non-listed day.

(7) Detention during suspension of a licence shall not be made unlawful by the subsequent confirmation of the licence.

Nuclear Explosions (Prohibition and Inspections) Act 1998

(1998, c. 7)

102–001   *An Act to enable effect to be given to certain provisions of the Comprehensive Nuclear-Test-Ban Treaty adopted in New York on 10th September 1996 and the Protocol to that Treaty; and for connected purposes.*

[18th March 1998]

Causing a nuclear explosion

1.—(1) Any person who knowingly causes a nuclear weapon test explosion **102–002** or any other nuclear explosion is guilty of an offence and liable on conviction on indictment to imprisonment for life.

(2) Nothing in subsection (1) shall apply to a nuclear weapon explosion carried out in the course of an armed conflict.

(3) If in proceedings for an offence under this section any question arises as to whether a nuclear weapon explosion was or was not carried out in the course of an armed conflict, that question shall be determined by the Secretary of State; and a certificate purporting to set out any such determination and to be signed by the Secretary of State shall be received in evidence and be deemed to be so signed without further proof, unless the contrary is shown.

Application of section 1

2.—(1) Section 1 shall apply to acts done in the United Kingdom or else- **102–003** where.

(2) So far as it applies to acts done outside the United Kingdom, section 1 applies to—

    (a) United Kingdom nationals,
    (b) Scottish partnerships, and
    (c) bodies incorporated under the law of any part of the United Kingdom.

(3) For the purposes of subsection (2), a United Kingdom national is an individual who is—

    (a) a British citizen, a [British overseas territories citizen][1], a British National (Overseas) or a British Overseas citizen,
    (b) a person who under the British Nationality Act 1981 is a British subject, or
    (c) a British protected person within the meaning of that Act.

(4) Her Majesty may by Order in Council extend the application of section 1, so far as it applies to acts done outside the United Kingdom, to bodies incorporated under the law of any of the Channel Islands, the Isle of Man or any colony.

(5) Proceedings for an offence committed under section 1 outside the United Kingdom may be taken, and the offence may for incidental purposes be treated as having been committed, in any place in the United Kingdom.

[1] Words substituted by British Overseas Territories Act 2002 (c.8), s. 2(3).

Provision supplementary to section 1

3.—(1) Proceedings for an offence under section 1 shall not be instituted— **102–004**

    (a) in England and Wales, except by or with the consent of the Attorney General;
    (b) in Northern Ireland, except by or with the consent of the Attorney General for Northern Ireland.

(2) The court by or before which a person is convicted of an offence under section 1 may order that anything shown to the court's satisfaction to relate to

the offence shall be forfeited, and either destroyed or otherwise dealt with in such manner as the court may order.

(3) In particular, the court may order the thing to be dealt with as the Secretary of State may see fit; and in such a case the Secretary of State may direct that it be destroyed or otherwise dealt with.

(4) Where—

(a) the court proposes to order anything to be forfeited under this section, and
(b) a person claiming to have an interest in it applies to be heard by the court,

the court must not order it to be forfeited unless he has been given an opportunity to show cause why the order should not be made.

. . . . . .

Offences: Miscellaneous

Offences by bodies corporate and Scottish partnerships

102–005   **11.**—(1) Where an offence under this Act is committed by a body corporate and is proved to have been committed with the consent or connivance of, or to be attributable to any neglect on the part of—

(a) a director, manager, secretary or other similar officer of the body corporate, or
(b) any person who was purporting to act in any such capacity,

he as well as the body corporate shall be guilty of that offence and shall be liable to be proceeded against and punished accordingly.

(2) In subsection (1) "director", in relation to a body corporate whose affairs are managed by its members, means a member of the body corporate.

(3) Where an offence under this Act is committed by a Scottish partnership and is proved to have been committed with the consent or connivance of a partner, he as well as the partnership shall be guilty of that offence and shall be liable to be proceeded against and punished accordingly.

Other miscellaneous provisions

Amendment of Army, Air Force and Naval Discipline Acts

102–006   **12.** In each of the following provisions, namely—

(a) section 70(4) of the Army Act 1955 (civil offences),
(b) section 70(4) of the Air Force Act 1955 (civil offences), and
(c) section 48(2) of the Naval Discipline Act 1957 (exclusion of jurisdiction of courts-martial),

after the words "Chemical Weapons Act 1996" there shall be inserted "or an offence under section 1 of the Nuclear Explosions (Prohibition and Inspections) Act 1998".

Public Processions (Northern Ireland) Act 1998

(1998, c. 2)

An Act to amend the law relating to public processions in Northern Ireland; to **103–001**
provide for the establishment and functions of the Parades Commission for
Northern Ireland; and for connected purposes. [16th February 1998]

The Commission

The Commission

1.—(1) There shall be established a body to be known as the Parades Com- **103–002**
mission for Northern Ireland (in this Act referred to as "the Commission").
(2) Schedule 1 has effect in relation to the Commission.

Functions of the Commission

2.—(1) It shall be the duty of the Commission— **103–003**

    (a) to promote greater understanding by the general public of issues concerning public processions;
    (b) to promote and facilitate mediation as a means of resolving disputes concerning public processions;
    (c) to keep itself generally informed as to the conduct of public processions and protest meetings;
    (d) to keep under review, and make such recommendations as it thinks fit to the Secretary of State concerning, the operation of this Act.

(2) The Commission may in accordance with the following provisions of this Act—

    (a) facilitate mediation between parties to particular disputes concerning proposed public processions and take such other steps as appear to the Commission to be appropriate for resolving such disputes;
    (b) issue determinations in respect of particular proposed public processions.

(3) For the purposes of its functions under this section, the Commission may, with the approval of the Secretary of State—

    (a) provide financial or other assistance to any person or body on such terms and conditions as the Commission may determine;
    (b) commission research.

Code of Conduct

3.—(1) The Commission shall issue a code (in this Act referred to as "the **103–004**
Code of Conduct")—

    (a) providing guidance to persons organising a public procession or protest meeting; and
    (b) regulating the conduct of persons organising or taking part in a public procession or protest meeting.

(2) The Commission—

(a) shall keep the Code of Conduct under review; and
(b) may from time to time revise the whole or any part of the Code of Conduct and issue the revised Code of Conduct.

(3) Schedule 2 has effect in relation to the Code of Conduct.

Procedural rules

103–005   **4.**—(1) The Commission shall issue a set of rules (in this Act referred to as "the procedural rules") for the purpose of regulating and prescribing the practice and procedure to be followed—

(a) by the Commission in exercising the functions mentioned in section 2(2); and
(b) by other persons or bodies in their dealings with the Commission in connection with the exercise of those functions.

(2) In particular (but without prejudice to the generality of subsection (1)) the procedural rules may—

(a) provide for the determination by the Commission of the particular cases in relation to which the functions mentioned in section 2(2) are to be exercised;
(b) prescribe the manner in which, and the time within which, specified actions may or must be taken (whether by the Commission or by other persons or bodies) for the purposes of the exercise by the Commission of those functions;
(c) require notice of specified determinations of the Commission made in the exercise of those functions to be published in such form and manner as may be specified.

(3) In subsection (2) "specified" means specified in the procedural rules.
(4) The Commission—

(a) shall keep the procedural rules under review; and
(b) may from time to time revise the whole or any part of the procedural rules and issue the revised procedural rules.

(5) Schedule 2 has effect in relation to the procedural rules.

Guidelines

103–006   **5.**—(1) The Commission shall issue a set of guidelines (in this Act referred to as "the guidelines") as to the exercise by the Commission of its functions under section 8.
(2) The Commission—

(a) shall keep the guidelines under review; and
(b) may from time to time revise the whole or any part of the guidelines and issue the revised guidelines.

(3) Schedule 2 has effect in relation to the guidelines.

Advance notice of public processions and related protest meetings

Advance notice of public processions

6.—(1) A person proposing to organise a public procession shall give notice **103–007** of that proposal in accordance with subsections (2) to (4) to a member of the Royal Ulster Constabulary not below the rank of sergeant by leaving the notice with him at the police station nearest to the proposed starting place of that procession.

(2) Notice under this section shall be given—

    (a) not less than 28 days before the date on which the procession is to be held; or

    (b) if that is not reasonably practicable, as soon as it is reasonably practicable to give such notice.

(3) Notice under this section shall—

    (a) be given in writing in such form as may be prescribed by regulations made by the Secretary of State; and

    (b) be signed by the person giving the notice.

(4) The form prescribed under subsection (3)(a) shall require a person giving notice under this section to specify—

    (a) the date and time when the procession is to be held;

    (b) its route;

    (c) the number of persons likely to take part in it;

    (d) the names of any bands which are to take part in it;

    (e) the arrangements for its control being made by the person proposing to organise it;

    (f) the name and address of that person;

    (g) where the notice is given as mentioned in paragraph (b) of subsection (2), the reason why it was not reasonably practicable to give notice in accordance with paragraph (a) of that subsection; and

    (h) such other matters as appear to the Secretary of State to be necessary for, or appropriate for facilitating, the exercise by the Commission, the Secretary of State or members of the Royal Ulster Constabulary of any function in relation to the procession.

(5) This section does not apply where the procession is—

    (a) a funeral procession; or

    (b) a procession of a class or description specified in an order made by the Secretary of State.

(6) The Chief Constable shall ensure that a copy of a notice given under this section is immediately sent to the Commission.

(7) A person who organises or takes part in a public procession—

    (a) in respect of which the requirements of this section as to notice have not been satisfied; or

    (b) which is held on a date, at a time or along a route which differs from the date, time or route specified in relation to it in the notice given under this section,

shall be guilty of an offence.

(8) In proceedings for an offence under subsection (7) it is a defence for the accused to prove that he did not know of, and neither suspected nor had reason to suspect, the failure to satisfy the requirements of this section or (as the case may be) the difference of date, time or route.

(9) To the extent that an alleged offence under subsection (7) turns on a difference of date, time or route it is a defence for the accused to prove that the difference arose from—

(a) circumstances beyond his control;
(b) something done in compliance with conditions imposed under section 8; or
(c) something done with the agreement of a member of the Royal Ulster Constabulary not below the rank of inspector or by his direction.

(10) A person guilty of an offence under subsection (7) shall be liable on summary conviction to imprisonment for a term not exceeding 6 months or to a fine not exceeding level 5 on the standard scale, or to both.

Advance notice of protest meetings related to public processions

103–008   7.—(1) Where notice has been given under section 6 in relation to a public procession, a person proposing to organise a related protest meeting shall give notice of that proposal in accordance with subsections (2) to (4) to a member of the Royal Ulster Constabulary not below the rank of sergeant by leaving the notice with him at the police station nearest to the place at which the meeting is to be held.

(2) Notice under this section shall be given—

(a) not later than 14 days before the date on which the meeting is to be held; or
(b) if that is not reasonably practicable, as soon as it is reasonably practicable to give such notice.

(3) Notice under this section shall—

(a) be given in writing in such form as may be prescribed by regulations made by the Secretary of State; and
(b) be signed by the person giving the notice.

(4) The form prescribed under subsection (3)(a) shall require a person giving notice under this section to specify—

(a) the date and time when the meeting is to be held;
(b) the place at which it is to be held;
(c) the number of persons likely to take part in it;
(d) the arrangements for its control being made by the person proposing to organise it;
(e) the name and address of that person;
(f) where the notice is given as mentioned in paragraph (b) of subsection (2), the reason why it was not reasonably practicable to give notice in accordance with paragraph (a) of that subsection; and
(g) such other matters as appear to the Secretary of State to be necessary for, or appropriate for facilitating, the exercise by the Secretary of State or members of the Royal Ulster Constabulary of any function in relation to the meeting.

(5) The Chief Constable shall ensure that a copy of a notice given under this section is immediately sent to the Commission.

(6) A person who organises or takes part in a protest meeting—

(a) in respect of which the requirements of this section as to notice have not been satisfied; or

(b) which is held on a date or at a time or place which differs from the date, time or place specified in relation to it in the notice given under this section,

shall be guilty of an offence.

(7) In proceedings for an offence under subsection (6) it is a defence for the accused to prove that he did not know of, and neither suspected nor had reason to suspect, the failure to satisfy the requirements of this section or (as the case may be) the difference of date, time or place.

(8) To the extent that an alleged offence under subsection (6) turns on a difference of date, time or place it is a defence for the accused to prove that the difference arose from—

(a) circumstances beyond his control;

(b) something done in compliance with conditions imposed under Article 4(2) of the Public Order (Northern Ireland) Order 1987; or

(c) something done with the agreement of a member of the Royal Ulster Constabulary not below the rank of inspector or by his direction.

(9) A person guilty of an offence under subsection (6) shall be liable on summary conviction to imprisonment for a term not exceeding 6 months or to a fine not exceeding level 5 on the standard scale, or to both.

The Commission's powers to impose conditions on public processions

The Commission's powers to impose conditions on public processions

8.—(1) The Commission may issue a determination in respect of a proposed **103–009** public procession imposing on the persons organising or taking part in it such conditions as the Commission considers necessary.

(2) Without prejudice to the generality of subsection (1), the conditions imposed under that subsection may include conditions as to the route of the procession or prohibiting it from entering any place.

(3) Conditions imposed under subsection (1) may incorporate or be framed by reference to—

(a) the Code of Conduct; or

(b) any other document—

(i) prepared by the person or body organising the procession in question; and

(ii) approved by the Commission for the purposes of this section.

(4) The Commission may, in accordance with the procedural rules, amend or revoke any determination issued under this section.

(5) In considering in any particular case—

(a) whether to issue a determination under this section;

(b) whether to amend or revoke a determination issued under this section; or

(c) what conditions should be imposed by a determination (or amended determination) issued under this section,

the Commission shall have regard to the guidelines.

(6) The guidelines shall in particular (but without prejudice to the generality of section 5(1)) provide for the Commission to have regard to—

    (a) any public disorder or damage to property which may result from the procession;

    (b) any disruption to the life of the community which the procession may cause;

    (c) any impact which the procession may have on relationships within the community;

    (d) any failure of a person of a description specified in the guidelines to comply with the Code of Conduct (whether in relation to the procession in question or any related protest meeting or in relation to any previous procession or protest meeting); and

    (e) the desirability of allowing a procession customarily held along a particular route to be held along that route.

(7) A person who knowingly fails to comply with a condition imposed under this section shall be guilty of an offence, but it is a defence for him to prove that the failure arose—

    (a) from circumstances beyond his control; or

    (b) from something done by direction of a member of the Royal Ulster Constabulary not below the rank of inspector.

(8) A person who incites another to commit an offence under subsection (7) shall be guilty of an offence.

(9) A person guilty of an offence under subsection (7) or (8) shall be liable on summary conviction to imprisonment for a term not exceeding 6 months or to a fine not exceeding level 5 on the standard scale, or to both.

Review by Secretary of State of determination of Commission under section 8

103–010   9.—(1) The Secretary of State shall, on an application made by the Chief Constable, review a determination issued by the Commission under section 8.

(2) On a review of a determination under this section the Secretary of State may—

    (a) revoke the determination;

    (b) amend the determination by amending or revoking any condition imposed by the determination or by adding any new condition; or

    (c) confirm the determination.

(3) In considering in any particular case—

    (a) whether to revoke, amend or confirm a determination; or

    (b) what amendments should be made to a determination,

the Secretary of State shall have regard to the guidelines.

(4) Wherever practicable the Secretary of State shall before revoking, amending or confirming a determination under this section consult the Commission; but nothing in this subsection shall affect the validity of any revocation, amendment or confirmation under this section.

(5) A determination of the Commission which is amended by the Secretary of State under this section shall be treated for the purposes of this Act (except section 8(4)) as if it had been issued by the Commission as so amended.

(6) Where a determination of the Commission in relation to a public pro-

cession has been revoked by the Secretary of State under this section, the Commission shall not issue any further determination under section 8 in relation to that procession.

(7) The Secretary of State shall immediately notify the Commission where any determination of the Commission is revoked, amended or confirmed under this section.

Saving for powers of a constable

10. Nothing in section 8 or 9 or in any determination of the Commission **103–011** affects the common law powers of a constable to take action to deal with or prevent a breach of the peace.

Secretary of State's powers to prohibit public processions

Secretary of State's powers to prohibit public processions

11.—(1) If, in the case of any proposed public procession, the Secretary of **103–012** State is of the opinion that, having regard to—

(a) any serious public disorder or serious damage to property which may result from the procession;

(b) any serious disruption to the life of the community which the procession may cause;

(c) any serious impact which the procession may have on relationships within the community; and

(d) any undue demands which the procession may cause to be made on the police or military forces,

it is necessary in the public interest to do so, he may by order prohibit the holding of that procession.

(2) If, in relation to any area and any period of time not exceeding 28 days, the Secretary of State is of the opinion that, having regard to—

(a) any serious public disorder or serious damage to property which may result from public processions of a particular class or description in that area in that period;

(b) any serious disruption to the life of the community which such processions may cause;

(c) any serious impact which such processions may have on relationships within the community;

(d) any undue demands which such processions may cause to be made on the police or military forces; and

(e) the extent of the powers exercisable under subsection (1),

it is necessary in the public interest to do so, he may by order prohibit the holding of all public processions of that class or description in that area in that period.

(3) If, in relation to any area and any period of time not exceeding 28 days, the Secretary of State is of the opinion that, having regard to—

(a) any serious public disorder or serious damage to property which may result from public processions in that area in that period;

(b) any serious disruption to the life of the community which such processions may cause;

(c) any serious impact which such processions may have on relationships within the community;

(d) any undue demands which such processions may cause to be made on the police or military forces; and

(e) the extent of the powers exercisable under subsections (1) and (2),

it is necessary in the public interest to do so, he may by order prohibit the holding of all public processions in that area in that period.

(4) An order under subsection (2) or (3) may exempt any procession, or any procession of any class or description, specified in the order.

(5) Wherever practicable the Secretary of State shall before making an order under this section consult—

(a) the Commission; and

(b) the Chief Constable,

but nothing in this subsection shall affect the validity of any such order.

(6) The power to make an order under this section includes power to revoke or amend any such order.

(7) An order made under subsection (1) in relation to a public procession has effect to revoke any previous determination made by the Commission under section 8 in relation to that procession, and an order made under subsection (2) or (3) has effect to revoke any previous determination made by the Commission under that section in relation to any public procession the holding of which is prohibited by the order.

(8) A person who organises or takes part in a public procession the holding of which he knows is prohibited by an order under this section shall be guilty of an offence.

(9) A person guilty of an offence under subsection (8) shall be liable on summary conviction to imprisonment for a term not exceeding 6 months or to a fine not exceeding level 5 on the standard scale, or to both.

General regulation of public processions

Registration of bands taking part in public processions

103–013   **12.**—(1) The Secretary of State may by order provide for the registration of bands.

(2) Without prejudice to the generality of subsection (1), an order under that subsection may provide for—

(a) applications for registration or the renewal of registration to be made to such court or other body or person as may be specified in the order;

(b) the procedure for the making and hearing of such applications (including the making and hearing of objections);

(c) the grounds on which such applications may be refused;

(d) the issue and duration of certificates of registration;

(e) appeals against decisions made in relation to such applications;

(f) the cancellation of registration and the procedure in relation thereto;

(g) registration to be subject to such conditions as may be specified in or determined under the order;

(h) the order not to apply to such bands or bands of such descriptions as may be specified in or determined under the order;

(i) such other matters as appear to the Secretary of State to be necessary or expedient for the proper functioning of the system of registration provided for by the order.

(3) Any power to make rules of court regulating the practice or procedure of a court specified as mentioned in subsection (2)(a) includes power to make such

provision as may be necessary or expedient for carrying into effect the provisions of an order under subsection (1).

(4) A person who knowingly takes part in a public procession as a member of a band which—

(a) is one to which an order under subsection (1) applies, but is not registered under that order; or

(b) does not comply with any condition subject to which it is registered under such an order,

shall be guilty of an offence.

(5) A person guilty of an offence under subsection (4) shall be liable on summary conviction to imprisonment for a term not exceeding 6 months or to a fine not exceeding level 5 on the standard scale, or to both.

Control of alcohol at public processions

13.—(1) Where a constable in uniform reasonably suspects that a person to **103–014** whom this subsection applies is consuming intoxicating liquor, the constable may require that person—

(a) to surrender anything in his possession which is, or which the constable reasonably believes to be, intoxicating liquor; and

(b) to state his name and address.

(2) Subsection (1) applies to a person—

(a) who is taking part in a public procession; or

(b) who is among those who have assembled with a view to taking part in a public procession; or

(c) who—

(i) is otherwise present at, or is in the vicinity of, a place on the route or proposed route of a public procession; and

(ii) is in a public place, other than licensed premises.

(3) Where a constable in uniform reasonably suspects that a person to whom this subsection applies is in possession of intoxicating liquor, the constable may require that person—

(a) to surrender anything in his possession which is, or which the constable reasonably believes to be, intoxicating liquor; and

(b) to state his name and address.

(4) Subsection (3) applies to a person who is in a passenger vehicle which is being used for the principal purpose of carrying passengers for the whole or any part of a journey to a place in the vicinity of the route or proposed route of a public procession.

(5) A constable may dispose of anything surrendered to him under this section in such manner as he considers appropriate.

(6) A person who fails without reasonable cause to comply with a requirement imposed on him under subsection (1) or (3) shall be guilty of an offence and liable on summary conviction to a fine not exceeding level 2 on the standard scale.

(7) A constable who imposes a requirement on a person under subsection (1) or (3) shall inform that person of his suspicion and that failing without reasonable cause to comply with a requirement imposed under that subsection is an offence.

(8) A constable in uniform may—

    (a) stop a passenger vehicle; and
    (b) search the vehicle and any person in the vehicle,

if he has reasonable grounds to suspect that intoxicating liquor is being carried on the vehicle and that the vehicle is being used for the principal purpose mentioned in subsection (4).

(9) The powers of a constable under this section may only be exercised in relation to a particular public procession in the period—

    (a) beginning 6 hours before the proposed starting time of that procession; and
    (b) ending at midnight on the day on which the persons taking part in the procession disperse.

(10) Where a proposed public procession does not take place but persons have assembled with a view to taking part in the procession, subsection (9) shall have effect as if for the reference in paragraph (b) to the persons taking part in the procession there were substituted reference to the persons assembled with a view to taking part in the procession.

Breaking up public procession

103–015   **14.**—(1) A person who for the purpose of preventing or hindering any lawful public procession or of annoying persons taking part in or endeavouring to take part in any such procession—

    (a) hinders, molests or obstructs those persons or any of them;
    (b) acts in a disorderly way towards those persons or any of them; or
    (c) behaves offensively and abusively towards those persons or any of them,

shall be guilty of an offence.

(2) A person guilty of an offence under subsection (1) shall be liable on summary conviction to imprisonment for a term not exceeding 6 months or to a fine not exceeding level 5 on the standard scale, or to both.

Supplementary

Powers of arrest

103–016   **15.** A constable in uniform may arrest without warrant anyone he reasonably suspects is committing an offence under this Act.

Regulations and orders

103–017   **16.**—(1) Any power of the Secretary of State to make orders or regulations under this Act, except an order under section 11, shall be exercised by statutory instrument.

(2) A statutory instrument containing any regulations under this Act shall be subject to annulment in pursuance of a resolution of either House of Parliament.

(3) A statutory instrument containing an order under paragraph 4 of Schedule 2 shall not be made unless a draft has been laid before, and approved by resolution of, each House of Parliament.

(4) A statutory instrument containing—

(a) an order under paragraph 8 of Schedule 2 made without a draft having been laid before, and approved by resolution of, each House of Parliament; or

(b) an order under section 6(5)(b) or 12(1) or paragraph 2(2) or 12(6) of Schedule 1,

shall be subject to annulment in pursuance of a resolution of either House of Parliament.

(5) An order or regulations under this Act—

(a) may make different provision for different cases, circumstances or areas; and

(b) may contain such incidental, supplemental or transitional provisions and savings as the Secretary of State considers appropriate.

Interpretation

17.—(1) In this Act—   **103–018**

"area" means the whole or any part of Northern Ireland;

"band" means a group of two or more persons who carry for the purpose of playing or sounding, or engage in the playing or sounding of, musical instruments;

"the Code of Conduct" has the meaning assigned by section 3(1);

"the Commission" means the Parades Commission for Northern Ireland;

"constable" means a member of the Royal Ulster Constabulary or the Royal Ulster Constabulary Reserve;

"the guidelines" has the meaning assigned by section 5(1);

"intoxicating liquor" and "licensed premises" have the same meanings as in the Licensing (Northern Ireland) Order 1996;

"passenger vehicle" means a motor vehicle (within the meaning of the Road Traffic (Northern Ireland) Order 1995) which is adapted to carry more than 8 passengers;

"the procedural rules" has the meaning assigned by section 4(1);

"protest meeting" means an open-air public meeting (within the meaning of the Public Order (Northern Ireland) Order 1987)—

(a) which is, or is to be, held—

(i) at a place which is on or in the vicinity of the route or proposed route of a public procession; and

(ii) at or about the same time as the procession is being or is to be held; and

(b) the purpose (or one of the purposes) of which is to demonstrate opposition to the holding of that procession on that route or proposed route;

"public place" means —

(a) any road within the meaning of the Roads (Northern Ireland) Order 1993; and

(b) any place to which at the material time the public or any section of the public has access, on payment or otherwise, as of right or by virtue of express or implied permission;

"public procession" means a procession in a public place, whether or not involving the use of vehicles or other conveyances.

(2) For the purposes of this Act a protest meeting is "related" to a public

procession if the purpose (or one of the purposes) of the meeting is to demonstrate opposition to the holding of that procession on its route or proposed route.

(3) References in this Act to the Chief Constable are to the Chief Constable of the Royal Ulster Constabulary; but the Chief Constable may delegate, to such extent and subject to such conditions as he may specify, any of his functions under this Act to a member of the Royal Ulster Constabulary not below the rank of Assistant Chief Constable.

<hr />

Scotland Act 1998

(1998, c. 46)

104–001 *An Act to provide for the establishment of a Scottish Parliament and Administration and other changes in the government of Scotland; to provide for changes in the constitution and functions of certain public authorities; to provide for the variation of the basic rate of income tax in relation to income of Scottish taxpayers in accordance with a resolution of the Scottish Parliament; to amend the law about parliamentary constituencies in Scotland; and for connected purposes.* [19th November 1998]

PART I

THE SCOTTISH PARLIAMENT

The Scottish Parliament

The Scottish Parliament

104–002   **1.**—(1) There shall be a Scottish Parliament.

(2) One member of the Parliament shall be returned for each constituency (under the simple majority system) at an election held in the constituency.

(3) Members of the Parliament for each region shall be returned at a general election under the additional member system of proportional representation provided for in this Part and vacancies among such members shall be filled in accordance with this Part.

(4) The validity of any proceedings of the Parliament is not affected by any vacancy in its membership.

(5) Schedule 1 (which makes provision for the constituencies and regions for the purposes of this Act and the number of regional members) shall have effect.

General elections

Ordinary general elections

104–003   **2.**—(1) The day on which the poll at the first ordinary general election for membership of the Parliament shall be held, and the day, time and place for the meeting of the Parliament following that poll, shall be appointed by order made by the Secretary of State.

(2) The poll at subsequent ordinary general elections shall be held on the first Thursday in May in the fourth calendar year following that in which the previous ordinary general election was held, unless the day of the poll is determined by a proclamation under subsection (5).

(3) If the poll is to be held on the first Thursday in May, the Parliament—

    (a) is dissolved by virtue of this section at the beginning of the minimum period which ends with that day, and

    (b) shall meet within the period of seven days beginning immediately after the day of the poll.

(4) In subsection (3), "the minimum period" means the period determined in accordance with an order under section 12(1).

(5) If the Presiding Officer proposes a day for the holding of the poll which is not more than one month earlier, not more than one month later, than the first Thursday in May, Her Majesty may by proclamation under the Scottish Seal—

    (a) dissolve the Parliament,

    (b) require the poll at the election to be held on the day proposed, and

    (c) require the Parliament to meet within the period of seven days beginning immediately after the day of the poll.

(6) In this Act "the Scottish Seal" means Her Majesty's Seal appointed by the Treaty of Union to be kept and used in Scotland in place of the Great Seal of Scotland.

Extraordinary general elections

    3.—(1) The Presiding Officer shall propose a day for the holding of a poll **104–004** if—

    (a) the Parliament resolves that it should be dissolved and, if the resolution is passed on a division, the number of members voting in favour of it is not less than two-thirds of the total number of seats for members of the Parliament, or

    (b) any period during which the Parliament is required under section 46 to nominate one of its members for appointment as First Minister ends without such a nomination being made.

(2) If the Presiding Officer makes such a proposal, Her Majesty may by proclamation under the Scottish Seal—

    (a) dissolve the Parliament and require an extraordinary general election to be held,

    (b) require the poll at the election to be held on the day proposed, and

    (c) require the Parliament to meet within the period of seven days beginning immediately after the day of the poll.

(3) If a poll is held under this section within the period of six months ending with the day on which the poll at the next ordinary general election would be held (disregarding section 2(5)), that ordinary general election shall not be held.

(4) Subsection (3) does not affect the year in which the subsequent ordinary general election is to be held.

Candidates

    5.—(1) At a general election, the candidates may stand for return as constitu- **104–005** ency members or regional members.

(2) A person may not be a candidate to be a constituency member for more than one constituency.

(3) The candidates to be regional members shall be those included in a list submitted under subsection (4) or individual candidates.

(4) Any registered political party may submit to the regional returning officer a list of candidates to be regional members for a particular region (referred to in this Act, in relation to the region, as the party's "regional list").

(5) A registered political party's regional list has effect in relation to the general election and any vacancy occurring among the regional members after that election and before the next general election.

(6) Not more than twelve persons may be included in the list (but the list may include only one person).

(7) A registered political party's regional list must not include a person—

    (a) who is included in any other list submitted under subsection (4) for the region of any list submitted under that subsection for another region,

    (b) who is an individual candidate to be a regional member for the region or another region,

    (c) who is a candidate to be a constituency member for a constituency not included in the region, or

    (d) who is a candidate to be a constituency member for a constituency included in the region but is not a candidate of that party.

(8) A person may not be an individual candidate to be a regional member for a particular region if he is—

    (a) included in a list submitted under subsection (4) for the region or another region,

    (b) an individual candidate to be a regional member for another region,

    (c) a candidate to be a constituency member for a constituency not included in the region, or

    (d) a candidate of any registered political party to be a constituency member for a constituency included in the region.

(9) In this Act, "registered political party" means a party registered under [Part II of the Political Parties, Elections and Referendums Act 2000][1].

[1] Words substituted by Political Parties, Elections and Referendums Act 2000 (c.41), Sched. 21, para. 13(2).

Poll for regional members

104–006   **6.**—(1) This section and sections 7 and 8 are about the return of regional members at a general election.

(2) In each of the constituencies for the Parliament, a poll shall be held at which each person entitled to vote as elector may give a vote (referred to in this Act as a "regional vote") for—

    (a) a registered political party which has submitted a regional list, or

    (b) an individual candidate to be a regional member for the region.

(3) The right conferred on a person by subsection (2) is in addition to any right the person may have to vote in any poll for the return of a constituency member.

Calculation of regional figures

104–007   **7.**—(1) The persons who are to be returned as constituency members for constituencies included in the region must be determined before the persons who are to be returned as the regional members for the region.

(2) For each registered political party which has submitted a regional list, the regional figure for the purposes of section 8 is—

    (a) the total number of regional votes given for the party in all the constituencies included in the region, divided by

    (b) the aggregate of one plus the number of candidates of the party returned as constituency members for any of those constituencies.

(3) Each time a seat is allocated to the party under section 8, that figure shall be recalculated by increasing (or further increasing) the aggregate in subsection (2)(b) by one.

(4) For each individual candidate to be a regional member for the region, the regional figure for the purposes of section 8 is the total number of regional votes given for him in all the constituencies included in the region.

Allocation of seats to regional members

8.—(1) The first regional member seat shall be allocated to the registered **104–008** political party or individual candidate with the highest regional figure.

(2) The second and subsequent regional member seats shall be allocated to the registered political party or individual candidate with the highest regional figure, after any recalculation required by section 7(3) has been carried out.

(3) An individual candidate already returned as a constituency or regional member shall be disregarded.

(4) Seats for the region which are allocated to a registered political party shall be filled by the persons in the party's regional list in the order in which they appear in the list.

(5) For the purposes of this section and section 10, a person in a registered political party's regional list who is returned as a member of the Parliament shall be treated as ceasing to be in the list (even if his return is void).

(6) Once a party's regional list has been exhausted (by the return of persons included in it as constituency members or by the previous application of subsection (1) or (2)) the party shall be disregarded.

(7) If (on the application of subsection (1) or any application of subsection (2)) the highest regional figure is the regional figure of two or more parties or individual candidates

    [(a) the subsection in question shall apply to each of them; or

    (b) if paragraph (a) would result in more than the correct number of seats for the region being allocated, the subsection in question shall apply as if the regional figure for each of those parties or candidates had been adjusted in accordance with subsection (8).]

[(8) The regional figure for a party or candidate is adjusted in accordance with this subsection by—

    (a) adding one vote to the total number of regional votes given for the party or candidate in all the constituencies included in the region; and

    (b) (in the case of a party) recalculating the regional figure accordingly.

(9) If, on the application of the subsection in question in accordance with subsection (7)(b), seats would be allocated to two or more parties or individual candidates and that would result in more than the correct number of seats for the region being allocated, the regional returning officer shall decide between them by lot.]

Vacancies

Constituency vacancies

104–009   **9.**—(1) Where the seat of a constituency member is vacant, an election shall be held to fill the vacancy (subject to subsection (4)).

(2) The date of the poll shall be fixed by the Presiding Officer.

(3) The date shall fall within the period of three months—

(a) beginning with the occurrence of the vacancy, or

(b) if the vacancy does not come to the notice of the Presiding Officer within the period of one month beginning with its occurrence, beginning when it does come to his notice.

(4) The election shall not be held if the latest date for holding the poll would fall within the period of three months ending with the day on which the poll at the next ordinary general election would be held (disregarding section 2(5)).

(5) For the purposes of this section, the date on which a vacancy is to be treated as occurring shall be determined under standing orders.

(6) A person may not be a candidate at such an election if he is a member of the Parliament or a candidate in another election to fill a vacancy.

Regional vacancies

104–010   **10.**—(1) This section applies where the seat of a regional member is vacant.

(2) If the regional member was returned as an individual candidate, or the vacancy is not filled in accordance with the following provisions, the seat shall remain vacant until the next general election.

(3) If the regional member was returned (under section 8 or this section) from a registered political party's regional list, the regional returning officer shall notify the Presiding Officer of the name of the person who is to fill the vacancy.

[(4) The regional returning officer shall ascertain from that party's regional list the name and address of the person whose name appears highest on that list ("the first choice") and shall take such steps as appear to him to be reasonable to contact the first choice to ask whether he will—

(a) state in writing that he is willing and able to serve as a regional member for that region; and

(b) deliver a certificate signed by or on behalf of the nominating officer of the registered party which submitted that regional list stating that he may be returned as a regional member from that list.

(4A) Where—

(a) within such period as the regional returning officer considers reasonable—

(i) he decides that the steps he has taken to contact the first choice have been unsuccessful; or

(ii) he has not received from that person the statement and certificate referred to in subsection (4) above; or

(b) that person has—

(i) stated in writing that he is not willing to serve as a regional member for that region; or

(ii) failed to deliver the certificate referred to in subsection (4)(b) above, the regional returning officer shall repeat the procedure required by subsection (4) above in respect of the person (if any) whose name and address appears next in that list ("the second choice") or, where sub-paragraph (a) or (b) of this subsection applies in respect of that person, in respect of the person (if any) whose name and address appear next highest after the second choice in that list and the regional returning officer shall continue to repeat the procedure until the regional returning officer has notified the Presiding Officer of the name of the person who is to fill the vacancy or the names in the list are exhausted.

(5) Where a person whose name appears on that list provides the statement and certificate referred to in subsection (4) above, the regional returning officer shall notify to the Presiding Officer the name of that person.

(5A) Where—

    (a) under subsection (4A) above, the regional returning officer has asked a second or other subsequent choice the questions referred to in subsection (4) above; and

    (b) the person who was asked those questions on an earlier occasion then provides the statement and certificate referred to in that subsection,

that statement and certificate shall have no effect unless and until the circumstances described in sub-paragraph (a) or (b) of subsection (4A) apply in respect of the second or other subsequent choice.]

(6) Where a person's name has been notified under subsection (3), this Act shall apply as if he had been declared to be returned as a regional member for the region on the day on which notification of his name was received by the Presiding Officer.

(7) For the purposes of this section, the date on which a vacancy is to be treated as occurring shall be determined under standing orders.

Franchise and conduct of elections

Electors

11.—(1) The persons entitled to vote as electors at an election for membership **104–011** of the Parliament held in any constituency are those who on the day of the poll—

    (a) would be entitled to vote as electors at a local government election in an electoral area falling wholly or partly within the constituency, and

    (b) are registered in the register of local government electors at an address within the constituency.

(2) A person is not entitled to vote as elector in any constituency—

    (a) more than once at a poll for the return of a constituency member, or

    (b) more than once at a poll for the return of regional members, or to vote as elector in more than one constituency at a general election.

. . . . . .

Duration of membership

Term of office of members

13. The term of office of a member of the Parliament begins on the day on **104–012** which the member is declared to be returned and ends with the dissolution of the Parliament.

Resignation of members

104–013   **14.** A member of the Parliament may at any time resign his seat by giving notice in writing to the Presiding Officer.

Disqualification

Disqualification from membership of the Parliament

104–014   **15.**—(1) A person is disqualified from being a member of the Parliament (subject to section 16) if—

    (a) he is disqualified from being a member of the House of Commons under paragraphs (a) to (e) of section 1(1) of the House of Commons Disqualification Act 1975 (judges, civil servants, members of the armed forces, members of police forces and members of foreign legislatures),

    (b) he is disqualified otherwise than under that Act (either generally or in relation to a particular parliamentary constituency) from being a member of the House of Commons or from sitting and voting in it,

    (c) he is a Lord of Appeal in Ordinary, or

    (d) he is an office-holder of a description specified in an Order in Council made by Her Majesty under this subsection.

(2) An office-holder of a description specified in an Order in Council made by Her Majesty under this subsection is disqualified from being a member of the Parliament for any constituency or region of a description specified in the Order in relation to the office-holder.

(3) In this section "office-holder" includes employee or other post-holder.

Exceptions and relief from disqualification

104–015   **16.**—(1) A person is not disqualified from being a member of the Parliament merely because—

    (a) he is a peer (whether of the United Kingdom, Great Britain, England or Scotland), or

    [(b) he is a Lord Spiritual.]¹

(2) A citizen of the European Union who is resident in the United Kingdom is not disqualified from being a member of the Parliament merely because of section 3 of the Act of Settlement (disqualification of persons born outside the United Kingdom other than Commonwealth citizens and citizens of the Republic of Ireland).

(3) Subsection (4) applies where a person was, or is alleged to have been, disqualified from being a member of the Parliament (either generally or in relation to a particular constituency or region) on any ground other than one falling within section 15(1)(b).

(4) The Parliament may resolve to disregard any disqualification incurred by that person on the ground in question if it considers that—

    (a) the ground has been removed, and

    (b) it is proper to disregard any disqualification so incurred.

(5) A resolution under this section shall not—

    (a) affect any proceedings under Part III of the Representation of the People Act 1983 as applied by an order under section 12, or

(b) enable the Parliament to disregard any disqualification which has been established in such proceedings or in proceedings under section 18.

¹ Substituted by House of Commons (Removal of Clergy Disqualification) Act 2001 (c.13), Sched. 1, para. 4.

Effect of disqualification

17.—(1) If a person who is disqualified from being a member of the Parlia- **104–016** ment or from being a member for a particular constituency or region is returned as a member of the Parliament or (as the case may be) as a member for the constituency or region, his return shall be void and his seat vacant.

(2) If a member of the Parliament becomes disqualified from being a member of the Parliament or from being a member for the particular constituency or region for which he is sitting, he shall cease to be a member of the Parliament (so that his seat is vacant).

(3) Subsections (1) and (2) have effect subject to any resolution of the Parliament under section 16.

(4) Subsection (2) also has effect subject to section 141 of the Mental Health Act 1983 (mental illness) and section 427 of the Insolvency Act 1986 (sequestration etc); and where, in consequence of either of those sections, the seat of a disqualified member of the Parliament is not vacant he shall not cease to be a member of the Parliament until his seat becomes vacant but—

(a) he shall not participate in any proceedings of the Parliament, and
(b) any of his rights and privileges as a member of the Parliament may be withdrawn by a resolution of the Parliament.

(5) The validity of any proceedings of the Parliament is not affected by the disqualification of any person from being a member of the Parliament or from being a member for the constituency or region for which he purports to sit.

. . . . . .

Presiding Officer and administration

Presiding Officer

19.—(1) The Parliament shall, at its first meeting following a general election, **104–017** elect from among its members a Presiding Officer and two deputies.

(2) A person elected Presiding Officer or deputy shall hold office until the conclusion of the next election for Presiding Officer under subsection (1) unless he previously resigns, ceases to be a member of the Parliament otherwise than by virtue of a dissolution or is removed from office by resolution of the Parliament.

(3) If the Presiding Officer or a deputy ceases to hold office before the Parliament is dissolved, the Parliament shall elect another from among its members to fill his place.

(4) The Presiding Officer's functions may be exercised by a deputy if the office of Presiding Officer is vacant or the Presiding Officer is for any reason unable to act.

(5) The Presiding Officer may (subject to standing orders) authorise any deputy to exercise functions on his behalf.

(6) Standing orders may include provision as to the participation (including voting) of the Presiding Officer and deputies in the proceedings of the Parliament.

(7) The validity of any act of the Presiding Officer or a deputy is not affected by any defect in his election.

Clerk of the Parliament

104–018   **20.**—(1) There shall be a Clerk of the Parliament.

(2) The clerk shall be appointed by the Scottish Parliamentary Corporate Body (established under section 21).

(3) The Clerk's functions may be exercised by any Assistant Clerk if the office of Clerk is vacant or the Clerk is for any reason unable to act.

(4) The clerk may authorise any Assistant Clerk or other member of the staff of the Parliament to exercise functions on his behalf.

Scottish Parliamentary Corporate Body

104–019   **21.**—(1) There shall be a body corporate to be known as "The Scottish Parliamentary Corporate Body" (referred to in this Act as the Parliamentary corporation) to perform the functions conferred on the corporation by virtue of this Act or any other enactment.

(2) The members of the corporation shall be—

    (a) the Presiding Officer, and

    (b) four members of the Parliament appointed in accordance with standing orders.

(3) The corporation shall provide the Parliament, or ensure that the Parliament is provided, with the property, staff and services required for the Parliament's purposes.

(4) The Parliament may give special or general directions to the corporation for the purpose of or in connection with the exercise of the corporation's functions.

(5) Any property or liabilities acquired or incurred in relation to matters within the general responsibility of the corporation to which (apart from this subsection) the Parliament would be entitled or subject shall be treated for all purposes as property or (as the case may be) liabilities of the corporation.

(6) Any expenses of the corporation shall be payable out of the Scottish Consolidated Fund.

(7) Any sums received by the corporation shall be paid into that Fund, subject to any provision made by or under an Act of the Scottish Parliament for the disposal of or accounting for such sums.

(8) Schedule 2 (which makes further provision about the corporation) shall have effect.

Proceedings, etc.

Standing orders

104–020   **22.**—(1) The proceedings of the Parliament shall be regulated by standing orders.

(2) Schedule 3 (which makes provision as to how certain matters are to be dealt with by standing orders) shall have effect.

Power to call for witnesses and documents

104–021   **23.**—(1) The Parliament may require any person—

    (a) to attend its proceedings for the purpose of giving evidence, or

    (b) to produce documents in his custody or under his control, concerning any subject for which any member of the Scottish Executive has general responsibility.

(2) Subject to subsection (3), the Parliament may impose such a requirement on a person outside Scotland only in connection with the discharge by him of—

(a) functions of the Scottish Administration, or
(b) functions of a Scottish public authority or cross-border public authority, or Border rivers functions (within the meaning of section 111(4)), which concern a subject for which any member of the Scottish Executive has general responsibility.

(3) In relation to the exercise of functions of a Minister of the Crown, the Parliament may not impose such a requirement on—

(a) him (whether or not he continues to be a Minister of the Crown), or
(b) a person who is or has been in Crown employment, within the meaning of section 191(3) of the Employment Rights Act 1996, unless the exercise concerns a subject for which any member of the Scottish Executive has general responsibility.

(4) But the Parliament may not impose such a requirement in pursuance of subsection (3) in connection with the exercise of functions which are exercisable—

(a) by the Scottish Ministers as well as by a Minister of the Crown, or
(b) by a Minister of the Crown only with the agreement of, or after consultation with, the Scottish Ministers.

(5) Subsection (4)(b) does not prevent the Parliament imposing such a requirement in connection with the exercise of functions which do not relate to reserved matters.

(6) Where all the functions of a body relate to reserved matters, the Parliament may not impose such a requirement on any person in connection with the discharge by him of those functions.

(7) The Parliament may not impose such a requirement on—

(a) a judge of any court, or
(b) a member of any tribunal in connection with the discharge by him of his functions as such.

(8) Such a requirement may be imposed by a committee or sub-committee of the Parliament only if the committee or sub-committee is expressly authorised to do so (whether by standing orders or otherwise).

(9) A person is not obliged under this section to answer any question or produce any document which he would be entitled to refuse to answer or produce in proceedings in a court in Scotland.

(10) A procurator fiscal is not obliged under this section to answer any question or produce any document concerning the operation of the system of criminal prosecution in any particular case if the Lord Advocate—

(a) considers that answering the question or producing the document might prejudice criminal proceedings in that case or would otherwise be contrary to the public interest, and
(b) has authorised the procurator fiscal to decline to answer the question or produce the document on that ground.

. . . . . .

Participation of the Scottish Law Officers

104–022   **27.**—(1) If the Lord Advocate or the Solicitor General for Scotland is not a member of the Parliament—

(a) he may participate in the proceedings of the Parliament to the extent permitted by standing orders, but may not vote, and
(b) standing orders may in other respects provide that they are to apply to him as if he were such a member.

(2) Subsection (1) is without prejudice to section 39.

(3) The Lord Advocate or the Solicitor General for Scotland may, in any proceedings of the Parliament, decline to answer any question or produce any document relating to the operation of the system of criminal prosecution in any particular case if he considers that answering the question or producing the document—

(a) might prejudice criminal proceedings in that case, or
(b) would otherwise be contrary to the public interest.

Legislation

Acts of the Scottish Parliament

104–023   **28.**—(1) Subject to section 29, the Parliament may make laws, to be known as Acts of the Scottish Parliament.

(2) Proposed Acts of the Scottish Parliament shall be known as Bills; and a Bill shall become an Act of the Scottish Parliament when it has been passed by the Parliament and has received Royal Assent.

(3) A Bill receives Royal Assent at the beginning of the day on which Letters Patent under the Scottish Seal signed with Her Majesty's own hand signifying Her Assent are recorded in the Register of the Great Seal.

(4) The date of Royal Assent shall be written on the Act of the Scottish Parliament by the Clerk, and shall form part of the Act.

(5) The validity of an Act of the Scottish Parliament is not affected by any invalidity in the proceedings of the Parliament leading to its enactment.

(6) Every Act of the Scottish Parliament shall be judicially noticed.

(7) This section does not affect the power of the Parliament of the United Kingdom to make laws for Scotland.

Legislative competence

104–024   **29.**—(1) An Act of the Scottish Parliament is not law so far as any provision of the Act is outside the legislative competence of the Parliament.

(2) A provision is outside that competence so far as any of the following paragraphs apply—

(a) it would form part of the law of a country or territory other than Scotland, or confer or remove functions exercisable otherwise than in or as regards Scotland,
(b) it relates to reserved matters,
(c) it is in breach of the restrictions in Schedule 4,
(d) it is incompatible with any of the Convention rights or with Community law,
(e) it would remove the Lord Advocate from his position as head of the systems of criminal prosecution and investigation of deaths in Scotland.

(3) For the purposes of this section, the question whether a provision of an Act of the Scottish Parliament relates to a reserved matter is to be determined, subject to subsection (4), by reference to the purpose of the provision, having regard (among other things) to its effect in all the circumstances.

(4) A provision which—

(a) would otherwise not relate to reserved matters, but

(b) makes modifications of Scots private law, or Scots criminal law, as it applies to reserved matters,

is to be treated as relating to reserved matters unless the purpose of the provision is to make the law in question apply consistently to reserved matters and otherwise.

Legislative competence; supplementary

30.—(1) Schedule 5 (which defines reserved matters) shall have effect.   **104–025**

(2) Her Majesty may by Order in Council make any modifications of Schedule 4 or 5 which She considers necessary or expedient.

(3) Her Majesty may be Order in Council specify functions which are to be treated, for such purposes of this Act as may be specified, as being, or as not being, functions which are exercisable in or as regards Scotland.

(4) An Order in Council under this section may also make such modifications of—

(a) any enactment or prerogative instrument (including any enactment comprised in or made under this Act), or

(b) any other instrument or document,

as Her Majesty considers necessary or expedient in connection with other provision made by the Order.

Scrutiny of Bills before introduction

31.—(1) A member of the Scottish Executive in charge of a Bill shall, on or **104–026** before introduction of the Bills in the Parliament state that in his view the provisions of the Bill would be within the legislative competence of the Parliament.

(2) The Presiding Officer shall, on or before the introduction of a Bill in the Parliament, decide whether or not in his view the provisions of the Bill would be within the legislative competence of the Parliament and state his decision.

(3) The form of any statement, and the manner in which it is to be made, shall be determined under standing orders, and standing orders may provide for any statement to be published.

Submission of Bills for Royal Assent

32.—(1) It is for the Presiding Officer to submit Bills for Royal Assent.   **104–027**

(2) The Presiding Officer shall not submit a Bill for Royal Assent at any time when—

(a) the Advocate General, the Lord Advocate or the Attorney General is entitled to make a reference in relation to the Bill under section 33,

(b) any such reference has been made but has not been decided or otherwise disposed of by the Judicial Committee, or

(c) an order may be made in relation to the Bill under section 35.

(3) The Presiding Officer shall not submit a Bill in its unamended form for Royal Assent if—

    (a) the Judicial Committee have decided that the Bill or any provision of it would not be within the legislative competence of the Parliament, or

    (b) a reference made in relation to the Bill under section 33 has been withdrawn following a request for withdrawal of the reference under section 34(2)(b).

(4) In this Act—

    "Advocate General" means the Advocate General for Scotland,
    "Judicial Committee" means the Judicial Committee of the Privy Council.

Scrutiny of Bills by the Judicial Committee

104–028   **33.**—(1) The Advocate General, the Lord Advocate or the Attorney General may refer the question of whether a Bill or any provision of a Bill would be within the legislative competence of the Parliament to the Judicial Committee for decision.

(2) Subject to subsection (3), he may make a reference in relation to a Bill at any time during—

    (a) the period of four weeks beginning with the passing of the Bill, and

    (b) any period of four weeks beginning with any subsequent approval of the Bill in accordance with standing orders made by virtue of section 36(5).

(3) He shall not make a reference in relation to a Bill if he has notified the Presiding Officer that he does not intend to make a reference in relation to the Bill, unless the Bill has been approved as mentioned in subsection (2)(b) since the notification.

ECJ references

104–029   **34.**—(1) This section applies where—

    (a) a reference has been made in relation to a Bill under section 33,

    (b) a reference for a preliminary ruling has been made by the Judicial Committee in connection with that reference, and

    (c) neither of those references has been decided or otherwise disposed of.

(2) If the Parliament resolves that it wishes to reconsider the Bill—

    (a) the Presiding Officer shall notify the Advocate General, the Lord Advocate and the Attorney General of that fact, and

    (b) the person who made the reference in relation to the Bill under section 33 shall request the withdrawal of the reference.

(3) In this section "a reference for a preliminary ruling" means a reference of a question to the European Court under Article 177 of the Treaty establishing the European Community, Article 41 of the Treaty establishing the European Coal and Steel Community or Article 150 of the Treaty establishing the European Atomic Energy Community.

Power to intervene in certain cases

35.—(1) If a Bill contains provisions—

(a) which the Secretary of State has reasonable grounds to believe would be incompatible with any international obligations or the interests of defence or national security, or

(b) which make modifications of the law as it applies to reserved matters and which the Secretary of State has reasonable grounds to believe would have an adverse effect on the operation of the law as it applies to reserved matters,

he may make an order prohibiting the Presiding Officer from submitting the Bill for Royal Assent.

(2) The order must identify the Bill and the provisions in question and state the reasons for making the order.

(3) The order may be made at any time during—

(a) the period of four weeks beginning with the passing of the Bill,

(b) any period of four weeks beginning with any subsequent approval of the Bill in accordance with standing order made by virtue of section 36(5),

(c) if a reference is made in relation to the Bill under section 33, the period of four weeks beginning with the reference being decided or otherwise disposed of by the Judicial Committee.

(4) The Secretary of State shall not make an order in relation to a Bill if he has notified the Presiding Officer that he does not intend to do so, unless the Bill has been approved as mentioned in subsection (3)(b) since the notification.

(5) An order in force under this section at a time when such approval is given shall cease to have effect.

Stages of Bills

36.—(1) Standing orders shall include provision—

(a) for general debate on a Bill with an opportunity for members to vote on its general principles,

(b) for the consideration of, and an opportunity for members to vote on, the details of a Bill, and

(c) for a final stage at which a Bill can be passed or rejected.

(2) Subsection (1) does not prevent standing orders making provision to enable the Parliament to expedite proceedings in relation to a particular Bill.

(3) Standing orders may make provision different from that required by subsection (1) for the procedure applicable to Bills of any of the following kinds—

(a) Bills which restate the law,

(b) Bills which repeal spent enactments,

(c) private Bills.

(4) Standing orders shall provide for an opportunity for the reconsideration of a Bill after its passing if (and only if)—

(a) the Judicial Committee decide that a Bill or any provision of it would not be within the legislative competence of the Parliament,

(b) a reference made in relation to the Bill under section 33 is withdrawn following a request for withdrawal of the reference under section 34(2)(b), or

(c) an order is made in relation to the Bill under section 35.

(5) Standing orders shall, in particular, ensure that any Bill amended on reconsideration is subject to a final stage at which it can be approved or rejected.

(6) References in subsection (4), sections 28(2) and 38(1)(a) and paragraph 7 of Schedule 3 to the passing of a Bill shall, in the case of a Bill which has been amended on reconsideration, be read as references to the approval of the Bill.

Other provisions

Acts of Unions

104–032   **37.** The Union with Scotland Act 1706 and the Union with England Act 1707 have effect subject to this Act.

. . . . . .

Members' interests

104–033   **39.**—(1) Provision shall be made for a register of interests of members of the Parliament and for the register to be published and made available for public inspection.

(2) Provision shall be made—

(a) requiring members of the Parliament to register in that register financial interests (including benefits in kind), as defined for the purposes of this paragraph,

(b) requiring that any member of the Parliament who has a financial interest (including benefits in kind), as defined for the purposes of this paragraph, in any matter declares that interest before taking part in any proceedings of the Parliament relating to that matter.

(3) Provision made in pursuance of subsection (2) shall include any provision which the Parliament considers appropriate for preventing or restricting the participation in proceedings of the Parliament of a member within interest defined for the purposes of subsection (2)(a) or (b) in a matter to which the proceedings relate.

(4) Provision shall be made prohibiting a member of the Parliament from—

(a) advocating or initiating any cause or matter on behalf of any person, by any means specified in the provision, in consideration of any payment or benefit in kind of a description so specified, or

(b) urging, in consideration of any such payment or benefit in kind, any other member of the Parliament to advocate or initiate any cause or matter on behalf of any person by any such means.

(5) Provision made in pursuance of subsections (2) to (4) shall include any provision which the Parliament considers appropriate for excluding from proceedings of the Parliament any member who fails to comply with, or contravenes, any provision made in pursuance of those subsections.

(6) Any member of the Parliament who—

(a) takes part in any proceedings of the Parliament without having complied with, or in contravention of, any provision made in pursuance of subsection (2) or (3), or

   (b) contravenes any provision made in pursuance of subsection (4). is guilty of an offence.

(7) A person guilty of an offence under subsection (6) is liable on summary conviction to a fine not exceeding level 5 on the standard scale.

   (8) In this section—

   (a) "provision" means provision made by or under an Act of the Scottish Parliament,

   (b) references to members of the parliament include references to the Lord Advocate and the Solicitor General for Scotland, whether or not they are such members.

. . . . . .

Legal issues

Defamatory statements

41.—(1) For the purposes of the law of defamation—   **104–034**

   (a) any statement made in proceedings of the Parliament, and

   (b) the publication under the authority of the Parliament of any statement,

shall be absolutely privileged.

   (2) In subsection (1), "statement" has the same meaning as in the Defamation Act 1996.

Contempt of court

42.—(1) The strict liability rule shall not apply in relation to any publica- **104–035**
tion—

   (a) made in proceedings of the Parliament in relation to a Bill or subordinate legislation, or

   (b) to the extent that it consists of a fair and accurate report of such proceedings made in good faith.

   (2) In subsection (1), "the strict liability rule" and "publication" have the same meanings as in the Contempt of Court Act 1981.

Corrupt practices

43. The Parliament shall be a public body for the purposes of the Prevention **104–036**
of Corruption Acts 1889 to 1916.

PART II

THE SCOTTISH ADMINISTRATION

Ministers and their staff

The Scottish Executive

44.—(1) There shall be a Scottish Executive, whose members shall be—   **104–037**

   (a) the First Minister,

(b) such Minister as the First Minister may appoint under section 47, and
(c) the Lord Advocate and the Solicitor General for Scotland.

(2) The members of the Scottish Executive are referred to collectively as the Scottish Ministers.

(3) A person who holds a Ministerial office may not be appointed a member of the Scottish Executive; and if a member of the Scottish Executive is appointed to a Ministerial office he shall cease to hold office as a member of the Scottish Executive.

(4) In subsection (3), references to a member of the Scottish Executive include a junior Scottish Minister and "Ministerial office" has the same meaning as in section 2 of the House of Commons Disqualification Act 1975.

The First Minister

104–038 **45.**—(1) The First Minister shall be appointed by Her Majesty from among the members of the Parliament and shall hold office at Her Majesty's pleasure.

(2) The First Minister may at any time tender his resignation to Her Majesty and shall do so if the Parliament resolves that the Scottish Executive no longer enjoys the confidence of the Parliament.

(3) The First Minister shall cease to hold office if a person is appointed in his place.

(4) If the office of First Minister is vacant or he is for any reason unable to act, the functions exercisable by him shall be exercisable by a person designated by the Presiding Officer.

(5) A person shall be so designated only if—

(a) he is a member of the Parliament, or
(b) if the Parliament has been dissolved, he is a person who ceased to be a member by virtue of the dissolution.

(6) Functions exercisable by a person by virtue of subsection (5)(a) shall continue to be exercisable by him even if the Parliament is dissolved.

(7) The First Minister shall be the Keeper of the Scottish Seal.

Choice of the First Minister

104–039 **46.**—(1) If one of the following events occurs, the Parliament shall within the period allowed nominate one of its members for appointment as First Minister.

(2) The events are—

(a) the holding of a poll at a general election,
(b) the First Minister tendering his resignation to Her Majesty,
(c) the office of First Minister becoming vacant (otherwise than in consequence of his so tendering his resignation),
(d) the First Minister ceasing to be a member of Parliament otherwise than by virtue of a dissolution.

(3) The period allowed is the period of 28 days which begins with the day on which the event in question occurs; but—

(a) if another of those events occurs within the period allowed, that period shall be extended (subject to paragraph (b)) so that it ends with the period of 28 days beginning with the day on which that other event occurred, and
(b) the period shall end if the parliament passes a resolution under section 3(1)(a) or when Her Majesty appoints a person as First Minister.

(4) The Presiding Officer shall recommend to Her Majesty the appointment of any member of the Parliament who is nominated by the Parliament under this section.

Ministers

47.—(1) The First Minister may, with the approval of Her Majesty, appoint **104–040** Ministers from among the members of the Parliament.

(2) The First Minister shall not seek Her Majesty's approval for any appointment under this section without the agreement of the Parliament.

(3) A Minister appointed under this section—

(a) shall hold office at Her Majesty's pleasure,
(b) may be removed from office by the First Minister,
(c) may at any time resign and shall do so if the Parliament resolves that the Scottish Executive no longer enjoys the confidence of the Parliament,
(d) if he resigns, shall cease to hold office immediately, and
(e) shall cease to hold office if the ceases to be a member of the Parliament otherwise than by virtue of a dissolution.

The Scottish Law Officers

48.—(1) It is for the First Minister to recommend to Her Majesty the appoint- **104–041** ment or removal of a person as Lord Advocate or Solicitor General for Scotland; but he shall not do so without the agreement of the Parliament.

(2) The Lord Advocate and the Solicitor General for Scotland may at any time resign and shall do so if the parliament resolves that the Scottish Executive no longer enjoys the confidence of the Parliament.

(3) Where the Lord Advocate resigns in consequence of such a resolution, he shall be deemed to continue in office until the warrant of appointment of the person succeeding to the office of Lord Advocate is granted, but only for the purpose of exercising his retained functions.

(4) Subsection (3) is without prejudice to section 287 of the Criminal Procedure (Scotland) Act 1995 (demission of office by Lord Advocate).

(5) Any decision of the Lord Advocate in his capacity as head of the systems of criminal prosecution and investigation of deaths in Scotland shall continue to be taken by him independently of any other person.

(6) In Schedule 2 to the House of Commons Disqualification Act 1975 (Ministerial offices) and Part III of Schedule 1 to the Ministerial and other Salaries Act 1975 (salaries of the Law Officers), the entries for the Lord Advocate and the Solicitor General for Scotland are omitted.

Junior Scottish Ministers

49.—(1) The First Minister may, with the approval of Her Majesty, appoint **104–042** persons from among the members of the Parliament to assist the Scottish Ministers in the exercise of their functions.

(2) They shall be known as junior Scottish Ministers.

(3) The First Minister shall not seek Her Majesty's approval for any appointment under this section without the agreement of the Parliament.

(4) A junior Scottish Minister—

(a) shall hold office at Her Majesty's pleasure,
(b) may be removed from office by the First Minister,
(c) may at any time resign and shall do so if the Parliament resolves that

the Scottish Executive no longer enjoys the confidence of the Parliament,

(d) if he resigns, shall cease to hold office immediately, and

(e) shall cease to hold office if he ceases to be a member of the Parliament otherwise than by virtue of a dissolution.

Validity of acts of Scottish Ministers, etc.

104–043   **50.** The validity of any act of a member of the Scottish Executive or junior Scottish Minister is not affected by any defect in his nomination by the Parliament or (as the case may be) in the Parliament's agreement to his appointment.

The Civil Service

104–044   **51.**—(1) The Scottish Ministers may appoint persons to be members of the staff of the Scottish Administration.

(2) Service as—

(a) the holder of any office in the Scottish Administration which is not a ministerial office, or

(b) a member of the staff of the Scottish Administration,

shall be service in the Home Civil Service.

(3) Subsection (1) and the other enactments conferring power to appoint such person shall have effect subject to any provision made in relation to the Home Civil Service by or under any Order in Council.

(4) Any Civil Service managements function shall be exercisable by the Minister for the Civil Service in relation to the persons mentioned in subsection (2) as it is exercisable in relation to other members of the Home Civil Service; and, accordingly, section 1 of the Civil Service (Management Functions) Act 1992 (delegation of functions by Ministers) shall apply to any such function as extended by this section.

(5) Any salary or allowance payable to or in respect of the persons mentioned in subsection (2) (including contributions to any pension scheme shall be payable out of the Scottish Consolidated Fund.

(6) Section 1(2) and (3) of the Superannuation Act 1972 (delegation of functions relating to civil service superannuation schemes etc.) shall have effect as if references to a Minister of the Crown (other than the Minister for the Civil Service) included the Scottish Ministers.

(7) The Scottish Ministers shall make payments to the Minister for the Civil Service, at such times as he may determine, of such amounts as he may determine in respect of—

(a) the provision of pensions, allowances or gratuities by virtue of section 1 of the Superannuation Act 1972 to or in respect of persons who are or have been in such service as is mentioned in subsection (2), and

(b) any expenses to be incurred in administering those pension, allowances or gratuities.

(8) Amounts required for payments under subsection (7) shall be charged on the Scottish Consolidated Fund.

(9) In this section—

"Civil Service management function" means any function to which section 1 of the Civil Service (Management Functions) Act 1992 applies and which is vested in the Minister for the Civil Service,

"the Home Civil Service" means Her Majesty's Home Civil Service.

. . . . . .

Ministerial functions

General transfer of functions

53.—(1) The functions mentioned in subsection (2) shall, so far as they are **104–045** exercisable within devolved competence, be exercisable by the Scottish Ministers instead of by a Minister of the Crown.

(2) Those functions are—

- (a) those of Her Majesty's prerogative and other executive functions which are exercisable on behalf of Her Majesty by a Minister of the Crown,
- (b) other functions conferred on a Minister of the Crown by a prerogative instrument, and
- (c) functions conferred on a Minister of the Crown by any pre-commencement enactment,

but do not include any retained functions of the Lord Advocate.

(3) In this Act, "pre-commencement enactment" means—

- (a) an Act passed before or in the same session as this Act and any other enactment made before the passing of this Act,
- (b) an enactment made, before the commencement of this section, under such an Act or such other enactment,
- (c) subordinate legislation under section 106, to the extent that the legislation states that it is to be treated as a pre-commencement enactment.

(4) This section and section 54 are modified by Part III of Schedule 4.

Developed competence

54.—(1) References in this Act to the exercise of a function being within or **104–046** outside devolved competence are to be read in accordance with this section.

(2) It is outside devolved competence—

- (a) to make any provision by subordinate legislation which would be outside the legislative competence of the Parliament if it were included in an Act of the Scottish Parliament, or
- (b) to confirm or approve any subordinate legislation containing such provision.

(3) In the case of any function other than a function of making, confirming or approving subordinate legislation, it is outside devolved competence to exercise the functions (or exercise it in any way) so far as a provision of an Act of the Scottish Parliament conferring the function (or, as the case may be, conferring it so as to be exercisable in that way) would be outside the legislative competence of the Parliament.

. . . . . .

Community law and Convention rights

104–047   **57.**—(1) Despite the transfer to the Scottish Ministers by virtue of section 53 of functions in relation to observing and implementing obligations under Community law, any function of a Minister of the Crown in relation to any matter shall continue to be exercisable by him as regards Scotland for the purposes specified in section 2(2) of the European Communities Act 1972.

(2) A member of the Scottish Executive has no power to make any subordinate legislation, or to do any other act, so far as the legislation or act is incompatible with any of the Convention rights or with Community law.

(3) Subsection (2) does not apply to an act of the Lord Advocate—

(a) in prosecuting any offence, or
(b) in his capacity as head of the systems of criminal prosecution and investigation of deaths in Scotland,

which, because of subsection (2) of section 6 of the Human Rights Act 1998, is not unlawful under subsection (1) of that section.

Power to prevent or require action

104–048   **58.**—(1) If the Secretary of State has reasonable grounds to believe that any action proposed to be taken by a member of the Scottish Executive would be incompatible with any international obligations, he may by order direct that the proposed action shall not be taken.

(2) If the Secretary of State has reasonable grounds to believe that any action capable of being taken by a member of the Scottish Executive is required for the purpose of giving effect to any such obligations, he may by order direct that the action shall be taken.

(3) If any subsections (1) and (2), "action" includes making, confirming or approving subordinate legislation and, in subsection (2), includes introducing a Bill in the Parliament.

(4) If any subordinate legislation made or which could be revoked by a member of the Scottish Executive contains provisions—

(a) which the Secretary of State has reasonable grounds to believe to be incompatible with any international obligations or the interests of defence or national security, or
(b) which make modifications of the law as it applies to reserved matters and which the Secretary of State has reasonable grounds to believe to have an adverse effect on the operation of the law as it applies to reserved matters,

the Secretary of State may by order revoke the legislation.

(5) An order under this section must state the reasons for making the order.

. . . . . .

PART IV

THE TAX-VARYING POWER

Power to fix basic rate for Scottish taxpayers

104–049   **73.**—(1) Subject to section 74, this section applies for any year of assessment for which become tax is charged if—

(a) the Parliament has passed a resolution providing for the percentage determined to be the basic rate for that year to be increased or reduced for Scottish taxpayers in accordance with resolution.

(b) the increase or reduction provided for is confined to an increase or reduction by a number not exceeding three which is specified in the resolution and is either a whole number or half of a whole number, and

(c) the resolution has not been cancelled by a subsequent resolution of the Parliament.

(2) Where this section applies for any year of assessment the Income Tax Acts (excluding this Part) shall have effect in relation to the income of Scottish taxpayers as if any rate determined by the parliament of the United Kingdom to be the basic rate for that year were increased or reduced in accordance with the resolution of the Scottish Parliament.

(3) In subsection (2) the reference to the income of Scottish taxpayers does not include a reference to any income of Scottish taxpayers which had it been income for the year 1998–99, would have been income to which section 1A of the Income and Corporation Taxes Act 1998 (income from savings and distributions) applied for that year.

(4) In this section—

(a) a reference, in relation to any year of assessment, to income tax being charged for that year includes a reference to the passing of a PCTA resolution that provides for the charging of that tax for that year, and

(b) a reference, in relation to a year of assessment, to the determination by the Parliament of the United Kingdom of a rate to be the basic rate for that year includes a reference to the passing of a PCTA resolution specifying a percentage to be the basic rate for that year.

(5) In this section "a PCTA resolution" means a resolution of the House of Commons containing such a declaration as is mentioned in section 1(2)(b) of the Provincial Collection of Taxes Act 1968.

Supplemental provision with respect to resolutions

74.—(1) This section applies to any resolution of the Parliament ("a tax- **104–050** varying resolution") which—

(a) provides, in accordance with section 73, for an increase or reduction for Scottish taxpayers of the basic rate for any year of assessment, or

(b) cancels a previous resolution of the Parliament providing for such an increase or reduction.

(2) Subject to subsection (3), a tax-varying resolution—

(a) must be expressed so as to relate to no more than a single year of assessment beginning after, but no more than twelve months after, the passing of the resolution, but

(b) shall have effect in relation to a determination by the Parliament of the United kingdom of the rate to be the basic rate for that year irrespective of whether that determination had been made at the time of the passing of the resolution.

(3) Subsection (2) shall not prevent a tax-varying resolution relating to any year of assessment from being passed and having effect where—

(a) a determination by the Parliament of the United Kingdom of the rate to be the basic rate for that year is made after, or less than a month before, the beginning of that year,

   (b) that determination is not confined to the passing of the enactment by which a determination of the same rate by a PCTA resolution is ratified, and

   (c) the tax-varying resolution is passed within the period of one month beginning with the day of the making by the Parliament of the United Kingdom of its determination.

(4) Where, in a case to which subsection (3) applies, a tax-varying resolution is passed after the beginning of the year of assessment to which it relates—

   (a) the resolution shall have effect as from the beginning of that year, and

   (b) all such payments, repayments, deductions and other adjustments shall be made as are required to restore the position to what it would have been if the resolution had been passed before the beginning of that year.

(5) Standing orders shall ensure that only a member of the Scottish Executive may move a motion for a tax-varying resolution.

(6) A tax-varying resolution shall not be passed so as to have effect in relation to any year of assessment before the year 2000–01.

(7) Subsections (4) and (5) of section 73 apply for the purposes of this section as they apply for the purposes of that section.

. . . . . .

PART V

MISCELLANEOUS AND GENERAL

Miscellaneous

Maladministration

104–051   **91.**—(1) The Parliament shall make provision for the investigation of relevant complaints made to its members in respect of any action taken by or on behalf of—

   (a) a member of the Scottish Executive in the exercise of functions conferred on the Scottish Ministers, or

   (b) any other office-holder in the Scottish Administration.

(2) For the purposes of subsection (1), a complaint is a relevant complaint if it is a complaint of a kind which could be investigated under the Parliamentary Commissioner Act 1967 if it were made to a member of the House of Commons in respect of a government department or other authority to which that Act applies.

(3) The Parliament may make provision for the investigation of complaints in respect of—

   (a) any action taken by or on behalf of an office-holder in the Scottish Administration,

   (b) any action taken by or on behalf of the Parliamentary corporation,

   (c) any action taken by or on behalf of a Scottish public authority with mixed functions or no reserved functions, or

(d) any action concerning Scotland and not relating to reserved matters which is taken by or on behalf of a cross-border public authority.

(4) In making provision of the kind required by subsection (1), the Parliament shall have regard (among other things) to the Act of 1967.

(5) Sections 53 and 117 to 121 shall not apply in relation to functions conferred by or under the Act of 1967.

(6) In this section—

"action" includes failure to act (and related expressions shall be read accordingly),

"provision" means provision by an Act of the Scottish Parliament;

and the references to the Act of 1967 are to that Act as it has effect on the commencement of this section.

Queen's Printer for Scotland

92.—(1) There shall be a Queen's Printer for Scotland who shall—   **104–052**

(a) exercise the Queen's Printer functions in relation to Acts of the Scottish Parliament and subordinate legislation to which this section applies, and

(b) exercise any other functions conferred on her by this Act or any other enactment.

(2) In subsection (1), "the Queen's Printer functions" means the printing functions in relation to Acts of Parliament and subordinate legislation of the Queen's Printer of Acts of Parliament.

(3) The Queen's Printer for Scotland shall also on behalf of Her Majesty exercise Her rights and privileges in connection with—

(a) Crown copyright in Acts of the Scottish Parliament,

(b) Crown copyright in any in subordinate legislation to which this section applies,

(c) Crown copyright in any existing or future works (other than subordinate legislation) made in the exercise of a function which is exercisable by any office-holder in, or member of the staff of, the Scottish Administration (or would be so exercisable if the function had not ceased to exist),

(d) other copyright assigned to Her Majesty in works made in connection with the exercise of functions by any such office-holder or member.

(4) This section applies to subordinate legislation made, confirmed or approved—

(a) by a member of the Scottish Executive,

(b) by a Scottish public authority with mixed functions or no reserved functions, or

(c) within devolved competence by a person other than a Minister of the Crown or such a member or authority.

(5) The Queen's Printer of Acts of Parliament shall hold the office of Queen's Printer for Scotland.

(6) References in this Act to a Scottish public authority include the Queen's Printer for Scotland.

. . . . . .

Appointment and removal of judges

104–053   95.—(1) It shall continue to be for the Prime Minister to recommend to Her Majesty the appointment of a person as Lord President of the Court of Session or Lord Justice Clerk.

(2) The Prime Minister shall not recommend to Her Majesty the appointment of any person who has not been nominated by the First Minister for such appointment.

(3) Before nominating persons for such appointment the First Minister shall consult the Lord President and the Lord Justice Clerk (unless, in either case, the office is vacant).

(4) It is for the First Minister, after consulting the Lord President, to recommend to Her Majesty the appointment of a person as—

(a) a judge of the Court of Session (other than the Lord President or the Lord Justice Clerk), or

(b) a sheriff principal or a sheriff.

(5) The First Minister shall comply with any requirements in relation to—

(a) a nomination under subsection (2), or

(b) a recommendation under subsection (4),

imposed by virtue of any enactment.

(6) A judge of the Court of Session and the Chairman of the Scottish Land Court may be removed from office only by Her Majesty; and any recommendation to Her Majesty for such removal shall be made by the First Minister.

(7) The First Minister shall make such a recommendation if (and only if) the Parliament, on a motion made by the First Minister, resolves that such a recommendation should be made.

(8) Provision shall be made for a tribunal constituted by the First Minister to investigate and report on whether a judge of the Court of Session or the Chairman of the Scottish Land Court is unfit for office by reason of inability, neglect of duty or misbehaviour and for the report to be laid before the Parliament.

(9) Such provision shall include provision—

(a) for the constitution of the tribunal by the First Minister when requested by the Lord President to do so and in such other circumstances as the First Minister thinks fit, and

(b) for the appointment to chair the tribunal of a member of the Judicial Committee who holds or has held any of the offices referred to in section 103(2).

and may include provision for suspension from office.

(10) The First Minister may make a motion under subsection (7) only if—

(a) he has received from a tribunal constituted in pursuance of subsection (8) a written report concluding that the person in question is unfit for office by reason of inability, neglect of duty or misbehaviour and giving reasons for that conclusion,

(b) where the person in question is the Lord President or the Lord Justice Clerk, he has consulted the Prime Minister, and

(c) he has complied with any other requirement imposed by virtue of any enactment.

(11) In subsections (8) to (10)—

"provision" means provision by or under an Act of the Scottish Parliament,
"tribunal" means a tribunal of at least three persons.

Provision of information to the Treasury

96.—(1) The Treasury may require the Scottish Ministers to provide within **104–054**
such period as the Treasury may reasonably specify, such information, in such
form and prepared in such manner, as the Treasury may reasonably specify.

(2) If the information is not in their possession or under their control, their
duty under subsection (1) is to take all reasonable steps to comply with the
requirement.

Assistance for opposition parties

97.—(1) Her Majesty may by Order in Council provide for the Parliamentary **104–055**
corporation to make payments to registered political parties for the purpose of
assisting members of the Parliament who are connected with such parties to
perform their Parliamentary duties.

(2) The corporation shall not make any payment to a party in pursuance of
such an Order if any of the members of the Parliament who are connected
with the party are also members of the Scottish Executive or Junior Scottish
Ministers.

(3) But such an Order may, in any circumstances specified in the Order,
require the fact that any members who are connected with a party are also
members of the Scottish Executive or junior Scottish Ministers to be disregarded.

(4) Such an Order may determine the circumstances in which a member of
the Parliament and a registered political party are to be regarded for the purposes
of this section as connected.

Juridical

Devolution issues

98. Schedule 6 (which makes provision in relation to devolution issues) shall **104–056**
have effect.

Rights and liabilities of the Crown in different capacities

99.—(1) Rights and liabilities may arise between the Crown in right of Her **104–057**
Majesty's Government in the United Kingdom and the Crown in right of the
Scottish Administration by virtue of a contract, by operation of law or by virtue
of an enactment as they may arise between subjects.

(2) Property and liabilities may be transferred between the Crown in one of
those capacities and the Crown in the other capacity as they may be transferred
between subjects; and they may together create, vary or extinguish any property
or liability as subjects may.

(3) Proceedings in respect of—

(a) any property or liabilities to which the Crown in one of those capacities
is entitled or subject under subsection (1) or (2), or
(b) the exercise of, or failure to exercise, any function exercisable by an
office-holder of the Crown in one of those capacities,

may be instituted by the Crown in either capacity; and the Crown in the other
capacity may be a separate party in the proceedings.

(4) This section applies to a unilateral obligation as it applies to a contract.

(5) In this section—

"office-holder", in relation to the Crown in right of Her Majesty's Government in the United Kingdom, means any Minister of the Crown or other office-holder under the Crown in that capacity and, in relation to the Crown in right of the Scottish Administration, means any office-holder in the Scottish Administration,

"subject" means a person not acting on behalf of the Crown.

Human rights

104–058   **100.**—(1) This Act does not enable a person—

    (a) to bring any proceedings in a court or tribunal on the ground that an act is incompatible with the Convention rights, or

    (b) to rely on any of the Convention rights in any such proceedings, unless he would be a victim for the purposes of Article 34 of the Convention (within the meaning of the Human Rights Act 1998) if proceedings in respect of the act were brought in the European Court of Human Rights.

(2) Subsection (1) does not apply to the Lord Advocate the Advocate General, the Attorney General or the Attorney General for Northern Ireland.

(3) This Act does not enable a court or tribunal to award any damages in respect of an act which is incompatible with any of the Convention rights which it could not award if section 8(3) and (4) of the Human Rights Act 1998 applied.

(4) In this section "act" means—

    (a) making any legislation,

    (b) any other act or failure to act, if it is the act or failure of a member of the Scottish Executive.

Interpretation of Acts of the Scottish Parliament, etc.

104–059   **101.**—(1) This section applies to—

    (a) any provision of an Act of the Scottish Parliament, or of a Bill for such an Act, and

    (b) any provision of subordinate legislation made, confirmed or approved, or purporting to be made, confirmed or approved, by a member of the Scottish Executive,

which could be read in such a way as to be outside competence.

(2) Such a provision is to be read as narrowly as is required for it to be within competence, if such a reading is possible, and is to have effect accordingly.

(3) In this section "competence" —

    (a) in relation to an Act of the Scottish Parliament, or a Bill for such an Act, means the legislative competence of the Parliament, and

    (b) in relation to subordinate legislation, means the powers conferred by virtue of this Act.

Powers of courts or tribunals to vary retrospective decisions

102.—(1) This section applies where any court or tribunal decides that— **104–060**

(a) an Act of the Scottish Parliament or any provision of such an Act is not within the legislative competence of the Parliament, or

(b) a member of the Scottish Executive does not have the power to make, confirm or approve a provision of subordinate legislation that he has purported to make, confirm or approve.

(2) The court or tribunal may make an order—

(a) removing or limiting any retrospective effect of the decision, or

(b) suspending the effect of the decision for any period and on any conditions to allow the defect to be corrected.

(3) In deciding whether to make an order under this section, the court or tribunal shall (among other things) have regard to the extent to which persons who are not parties to the proceedings would otherwise be adversely affected.

(4) Where a court or tribunal is considering whether to make an order under this section, it shall order intimation of that fact to be given to—

(a) the Lord Advocate, and

(b) the appropriate law officer, where the decision mentioned in subsection (1) relates to a devolution issue (within the meaning of Schedule 6),

unless the person to whom the intimation would be given is a party to the proceedings.

(5) A person to whom intimation is given under subsection (4) may take part as a party in the proceedings so far as they relate to the making of the order.

(6) Paragraphs 36 and 37 of Schedule 6 apply with necessary modifications for the purposes of subsections (4) and (5) as they apply for the purposes of that Schedule.

(7) In this section—

"intimation" includes notice,

"the appropriate law officer" means—

(a) in relation to proceedings in Scotland, the Advocate General,

(b) in relation to proceedings in England and Wales, the Attorney General,

(c) in relation to proceedings in Northern Ireland, the Attorney General for Northern Ireland.

The Judicial Committee

103.—(1) Any decision of the Judicial Committee in proceedings under this **104–061**
Act shall be stated in open court and shall be binding in all legal proceedings (other than proceedings before the Committee).

(2) No member of the Judicial Committee shall sit and act as a member of the Committee in proceedings under this Act unless he holds or has held—

(a) the office of a Lord of Appeal in Ordinary, or

(b) high judicial office as defined in section 25 of the Appellate Jurisdiction Act 1876 (ignoring for this purpose section 5 of the Appellate Jurisdiction Act 1887).

(3) Her Majesty may by Order in Council—

  (a) confer on the Judicial Committee in relation to proceedings under this Act such powers as Her Majesty considers necessary or expedient,
  (b) apply the Judicial Committee Act 1833 in relation to proceedings under this Act with exceptions or modifications,
  (c) make rules for regulating the procedure in relation to proceedings under this Act before the Judicial Committee.

(4) In this section "proceedings under this Act" means proceedings on a question referred to the Judicial Committee under section 33 or proceedings under Schedule 6.

Access to Justice Act 1999

(1999, c. 22)

105–001 *An Act to establish the Legal Services Commission, the Community Legal Service and the Criminal Defence Service; to amend the law of legal aid in Scotland; to make further provision about legal services; to make provision about appeals, courts, judges and court proceedings; to amend the law about magistrates and magistrates' courts; and to make provision about immunity from action and costs and indemnities for certain officials exercising judicial functions.* [27th July 1999]

. . . . . .

PART III

PROVISION OF LEGAL SERVICES

Legal Services Complaints Commissioner

Commissioner

105–002 51.—(1) The Lord Chancellor may appoint a person as Legal Services Complaints Commissioner.

(2) Any appointment of a person as Commissioner shall be for a period of not more than three years; and a person appointed as Commissioner shall hold and vacate office in accordance with the terms of his appointment.

(3) At the end of his term of appointment the Commissioner shall be eligible for re-appointment.

(4) The Commissioner shall not be an authorised advocate, authorised litigator, licensed conveyancer or authorised practitioner (within the meaning of the Courts and Legal Services Act 1990) or a notary.

(5) Schedule 8 (which makes further provision about the Commissioner) has effect.

Commissioner's functions

105–003 52.—(1) If it appears to the Lord Chancellor that complaints about members of any professional body are not being handled effectively and efficiently, he may by direction require the Legal Services Complaints Commissioner to consider exercising in relation to the body such of the powers in subsection (2) as are specified in the direction.

(2) Those powers are—

(a) to require a professional body to provide information, or make reports, to the Commissioner about the handling of complaints about its members,

(b) to investigate the handling of complaints about the members of a professional body,

(c) to make recommendations in relation to the handling of complaints about the members of a professional body,

(d) to set targets in relation to the handling of complaints about the members of a professional body, and

(e) to require a professional body to submit to the Commissioner a plan for the handling of complaints about its members.

(3) Where the Commissioner requires a professional body to submit to him a plan for the handling of complaints about its members but the body—

(a) fails to submit to him a plan which he considers adequate for securing that such complaints are handled effectively and efficiently, or

(b) submits to him such a plan but fails to handle complaints in accordance with it,

he may require the body to pay a penalty.

(4) Before requiring a professional body to pay a penalty under subsection (3) the Commissioner shall afford it a reasonable opportunity of appearing before him to make representations.

(5) The Lord Chancellor shall by order made by statutory instrument specify the maximum amount of any penalty under subsection (3).

(6) In determining the amount of any penalty which a professional body is to be required to pay under subsection (3) the Commissioner shall have regard to all the circumstances of the case, including in particular—

(a) the total number of complaints about members of the body and, where the penalty is imposed in respect of a failure to handle complaints in accordance with a plan, the number of complaints not so handled, and

(b) the assets of the body and the number of its members.

(7) A penalty under subsection (3) shall be paid to the Commissioner who shall pay it to the Lord Chancellor.

(8) Where a direction under subsection (1) in relation to a professional body has been given (and not revoked), section 24(1) of the Courts and Legal Services Act 1990 (power of Legal Services Ombudsman to make recommendations about arrangements for investigation of complaints) shall not have effect in relation to the body.

(9) No order shall be made under subsection (5) unless a draft of the order has been laid before, and approved by a resolution of, each House of Parliament.

(10) In this section "professional body" has the same meaning as in section 22 of the Courts and Legal Services Act 1990.

Greater London Authority Act 1999

(1999, c. 29)

106–001 *An Act to establish and make provision about the Greater London Authority, the Mayor of London and the London Assembly; to make provision in relation to London borough councils and the Common Council of the City of London with respect to matters consequential on the establishment of the Greater London Authority; to make provision with respect to the functions of other local authorities and statutory bodies exercising functions in Greater London; to make provision about transport and road traffic in and around Greater London; to make provision about policing in Greater London and to make an adjustment of the metropolitan police district; and for connected purposes.* [11th November 1999]

PART I

THE GREATER LONDON AUTHORITY

The Authority

106–002   **1.**—(1) There shall be an authority for Greater London, to be known. The Authority as the Greater London Authority.

(2) The Authority shall be a body corporate.

(3) The Authority shall have the functions which are transferred to, or conferred or imposed on, the Authority by or under this Act or any other Act.

Membership

Membership of the Authority and the Assembly

106–003   **2.**—(1) The Authority shall consist of—

    (a) the Mayor of London; and
    (b) an Assembly for London, to be known as the London Assembly.

(2) The Assembly shall consist of twenty five members, of whom—

    (a) fourteen shall be members for Assembly constituencies ("constituency members"); and
    (b) eleven shall be members for the whole of Greater London ("London members").

(3) There shall be one constituency member for each Assembly constituency.

(4) The Assembly constituencies shall be the areas, and shall be known by the names, specified in an order made by the Secretary of State.

(5) Schedule 1 to this Act (which makes further provision about Assembly constituencies and orders under subsection (4) above) shall have effect.

(6) The Mayor and the Assembly members shall be returned in accordance with the provision made in or by virtue of this Act for—

    (a) the holding of ordinary elections of the Mayor, the constituency members and the London members; and
    (b) the filling of vacancies in the office of Mayor or among the constituency members or the London members.

(7) An ordinary election involves the holding of—

(a) an election for the return of the Mayor;

(b) an election for the return of the London members; and

(c) elections for the return of the constituency members.

(8) The term of office of the Mayor and Assembly members returned at an ordinary election shall—

(a) begin on the second day after the day on which the last of the successful candidates at the ordinary election is declared to be returned; and

(b) end on the second day after the day on which the last of the successful candidates at the next ordinary election is declared to be returned;

but this subsection is subject to the other provisions of this Act and, in particular, to any provision made by order by virtue of subsection (4) of section 3 below.

(9) If at any ordinary election the poll at the election of an Assembly member for an Assembly constituency is countermanded or abandoned for any reason, the day on which the last of the successful candidates at the ordinary election is declared to be returned shall be determined for the purposes of subsection (8) above without regard to the return of the Assembly member for that Assembly constituency.

(10) The validity of proceedings of the Assembly is not affected by any vacancy in its membership.

(11) The validity of anything done by the Authority is not affected by any vacancy in the office of Mayor or any vacancy in the membership of the Assembly.

. . . . . .

Qualifications and disqualifications

Qualification to be the Mayor or an Assembly member

20.—(1) Subject to any disqualification by virtue of this Act or any other **106–004** enactment, a person is qualified to be elected and to be the Mayor or an Assembly member if he satisfies the requirements of subsections (2) to (4) below.

(2) The person must be—

(a) a Commonwealth citizen;

(b) a citizen of the Republic of Ireland; or

(c) a relevant citizen of the Union.

(3) On the relevant day, the person must have attained the age of 21 years.

(4) The person must satisfy at least one of the following conditions—

(a) on the relevant day he is, and from that day continues to be, a local government elector for Greater London;

(b) he has, during the whole of the twelve months preceding that day, occupied as owner or tenant any land or other premises in Greater London;

(c) his principal or only place of work during that twelve months has been in Greater London;

(d) he has during the whole of that twelve months resided in Greater London.

(5) This section applies in relation to being returned as a London member

under section 11 above otherwise than at an election as it applies in relation to being elected.

(6) References in this section to election shall accordingly be construed as if a London member so returned were elected at an election on the day on which he is to be treated as returned.

(7) In the application of this section by virtue of subsection (5) above, any reference to the day on which a person is nominated as a candidate shall be taken as a reference to the day on which notification of the person's name is given under section 11(3) above by the Greater London returning officer.

(8) In this section—

"citizen of the Union" shall be construed in accordance with Article 8.1 of the Treaty establishing the European Community (as amended by Title II of the Treaty on European Union);

"relevant citizen of the Union" means a citizen of the Union who is not—

(a) a Commonwealth citizen; or
(b) a citizen of the Republic of Ireland;

"the relevant day", in relation to any candidate, means—

(a) the day on which he is nominated as a candidate and also, if there is a poll, the day of the election; or
(b) if the election is not preceded by the nomination of candidates, the day of the election.

Disqualification from being the Mayor or an Assembly member

106–005   **21.**—(1) A person is disqualified from being elected or being the Mayor or an Assembly member if—

(a) he is a member of staff of the Authority;
(b) he holds any of the offices or appointments for the time being designated by the Secretary of State in an order as offices or appointments disqualifying persons from being the Mayor or an Assembly member;
(c) he has been adjudged bankrupt, or made a composition or arrangement with his creditors;
(d) he has within five years before the day of the election, or since his election, been convicted in the United Kingdom, the Channel Islands or the Isle of Man of any offence and has had passed on him a sentence of imprisonment (whether suspended or not) for a period of not less than three months without the option of a fine; or
(e) he is disqualified under—

(i) section 85A or Part III of the Representation of the People Act 1983, or
(ii) section 17 or 18 of the Audit Commission Act 1998,

from being elected or being the Mayor or an Assembly member.

(2) A paid officer of a London borough council who is employed under the direction of—

(a) any of that council's committees or sub-committees the membership of which includes the Mayor or one or more persons appointed on the nomination of the Authority acting by the Mayor, or
(b) a joint committee the membership of which includes one or more members appointed on the nomination of that council and one or more

members appointed on the nomination of the Authority acting by the Mayor,

(c) the executive or any committee of the executive of that council, where that council are operating executive arrangements and the membership of that executive includes the Mayor or one or more persons appointed on the nomination of the Authority acting by the Mayor, or

(d) a member of the executive of that council, where that council are operating executive arrangements and that member is also the Mayor or a person appointed on the nomination of the Authority acting by the Mayor,

shall be disqualified from being elected or being the Mayor or an Assembly member.

(2A) In this section "executive" and "executive arrangements" have the same meaning as in Part II of the Local Government Act 2000.

(3) Where a person is disqualified under subsection (1)(c) above by reason of having been adjudged bankrupt, the disqualification shall cease—

(a) unless the bankruptcy order made against the person is previously annulled, on his discharge from bankruptcy; and

(b) if the bankruptcy order is so annulled, on the date of the annulment.

(4) Where a person is disqualified under subsection (1)(c) above by reason of having made a composition or arrangement with his creditors, the disqualification shall cease—

(a) if he pays his debts in full, on the date on which the payment is completed; and

(b) in any other case, on the expiration of five years from the date on which the terms of the deed of composition or arrangement are fulfilled.

(5) For the purposes of subsection (1)(d) above—

(a) the ordinary date on which the period allowed for making an appeal or application with respect to the conviction expires, or

(b) if such an appeal or application is made, the date on which the appeal or application is finally disposed of or abandoned or fails by reason of its non-prosecution,

shall be deemed to be the date of the conviction.

(6) This section shall apply in relation to being returned as a London member under section 11 above otherwise than at an election as it applies in relation to being elected.

(7) References in this section to election shall accordingly be construed as if a London member so returned were elected at an election on the day on which he is to be treated as returned.

. . . . . .

PART II

GENERAL FUNCTIONS AND PROCEDURE

The general and subsidiary powers of the Authority

The general power of the Authority

106–006 **30.**—(1) The Authority shall have power to do anything which it considers will further any one or more of its principal purposes.

(2) Any reference in this Act to the principal purposes of the Authority is a reference to the purposes of—

(a) promoting economic development and wealth creation in Greater London;

(b) promoting social development in Greater London; and

(c) promoting the improvement of the environment in Greater London.

(3) In determining whether or how to exercise the power conferred by subsection (1) above to further any one or more of its principal purposes, the Authority shall have regard to the desirability of so exercising that power as to—

(a) further the remaining principal purpose or purposes, so far as reasonably practicable to do so; and

(b) secure, over a period of time, a reasonable balance between furthering each of its principal purposes.

(4) In determining whether or how to exercise the power conferred by subsection (1) above, the Authority shall have regard to the effect which the proposed exercise of the power would have on—

(a) the health of persons in Greater London; and

(b) the achievement of sustainable development in the United Kingdom.

(5) Where the Authority exercises the power conferred by subsection (1) above, it shall do so in the way which it considers best calculated—

(a) to promote improvements in the health of persons in Greater London, and

(b) to contribute towards the achievement of sustainable development in the United Kingdom,

except to the extent that the Authority considers that any action that would need to be taken by virtue of paragraph (a) or (b) above is not reasonably practicable in all the circumstances of the case.

(6) In subsection (5)(a) above, the reference to promoting improvements in health includes a reference to mitigating any detriment to health which would otherwise be occasioned by the exercise of the power.

(7) The Secretary of State may issue guidance to the Authority concerning the exercise by the Authority of the power conferred by subsection (1) above.

(8) In deciding whether or how to exercise that power, the Authority shall have regard to any guidance issued under subsection (7) above.

(9) Any guidance issued under subsection (7) above shall be published by the Secretary of State in such manner as he considers appropriate.

(10) The functions conferred or imposed on the Authority under or by virtue of this section shall be functions of the Authority which are exercisable by the Mayor acting on behalf of the Authority.

Limits of the general power

31.—(1) The Authority shall not by virtue of section 30(1) above incur **106–007** expenditure in doing anything which may be done by a functional body other than the London Development Agency.

(2) In determining whether to exercise the power conferred by section 30(1) above, the Authority shall seek to secure that it does not incur expenditure in doing anything which is being done by the London Development Agency.

(3) The Authority shall not by virtue of section 30(1) above incur expenditure in providing—

    (a) any housing,
    (b) any education services,
    (c) any social services, or
    (d) any health services,

in any case where the provision in question may be made by a London borough council, the Common Council or any other public body.

(4) Any reference in subsection (3) above to the provision of housing—

    (a) includes a reference to the management of housing; but
    (b) does not include a reference to the acquisition by the Authority of existing housing accommodation and the making of that accommodation available on a temporary basis for one or more of the principal purposes of the Authority or for purposes incidental to such a purpose.

(5) Any reference in subsection (3) above to the provision of social services is a reference to the exercise of[any social services function within the meaning of the Local Authority Social Services Act 1970][1]

(6) Nothing in subsections (1) to (5) above shall be taken to prevent the Authority incurring expenditure in co-operating with, or facilitating or co-ordinating the activities of, the bodies mentioned in those subsections.

(7) The Secretary of State may by order amending this section make further provision for preventing the Authority from doing by virtue of section 30(1) above anything—

    (a) which may be done by a London borough council, the Common Council or a public body, and
    (b) which is specified, or is of a description specified, in the order.

(8) The Secretary of State may by order impose limits on the expenditure which may be incurred by the Authority by virtue of section 30(1) above.

(9) The Secretary of State may by order amending this section make provision removing or restricting any prohibitions or limitations imposed by this section on what may be done by the Authority by virtue of section 30(1) above.

[1] Words substituted by Local Government Act 2000 (c.22), Sched. 5, para. 33.

Consultation

32.—(1) The power conferred by section 30(1) above is exercisable only **106–008** after consultation with such bodies or persons as the Authority may consider appropriate in the particular case.

(2) In determining what consultation (if any) is appropriate under subsection (1) above, the bodies which, and persons whom, the Authority considers consulting must include—

    (a) any London borough council;

(b) the Common Council; and
(c) bodies of each of the descriptions specified in subsection (3) below.

(3) Those descriptions are—

(a) voluntary bodies some or all of whose activities benefit the whole or part of Greater London;
(b) bodies which represent the interests of different racial, ethnic or national groups in Greater London;
(c) bodies which represent the interests of different religious groups in Greater London;
(d) bodies which represent the interests of persons carrying on business in Greater London.

(4) The Authority may make arrangements with—

(a) any London borough council,
(b) the Common Council,
(c) bodies of the descriptions specified in subsection (3) above, and
(d) such other bodies or persons as it may consider appropriate,

for the purpose of facilitating the carrying out by the Authority of consultation pursuant to this section or any other provision of this Act.

(5) The functions conferred on the Authority under or by virtue of this section shall be functions of the Authority which are exercisable by the Mayor acting on behalf of the Authority.

Equality of opportunity

106–009 33.—(1) The Authority shall make appropriate arrangements with a view to securing that—

(a) in the exercise of the power conferred on the Authority by section 30 above,
(b) in the formulation of the policies and proposals to be included in any of the strategies mentioned in section 41(1) below, and
(c) in the implementation of any of those strategies,

there is due regard to the principle that there should be equality of opportunity for all people.

(2) After each financial year the Authority shall publish a report containing—

(a) a statement of the arrangements made in pursuance of subsection (1) above which had effect during that financial year; and
(b) an assessment of how effective those arrangements were in promoting equality of opportunity.

(3) The functions conferred or imposed on the Authority under or by virtue of this section shall be functions of the Authority which are exercisable by the Mayor acting on behalf of the Authority.

Subsidiary powers of the Authority

106–010 34.—(1) The Authority, acting by the Mayor, by the Assembly, or by both jointly, may do anything (including the acquisition or disposal of any property or rights) which is calculated to facilitate, or is conducive or incidental to, the exercise of any functions of the Authority exercisable by the Mayor or, as the case may be, by the Assembly or by both acting jointly.

(2) The Authority shall not by virtue of this section raise money (whether by precepts, borrowing or otherwise) or lend money, except in accordance with the enactments relating to those matters.

Exercise of functions: general principles

Authority functions to be exercisable by Mayor, Assembly or both

35.—(1) Any function transferred to, or conferred or imposed on, the Author- **106–011** ity by or under this Act or any other Act (whenever passed) shall, in accordance with the provisions of this Act, be exercisable—

    (a) only by the Mayor acting on behalf of the Authority;
    (b) only by the Assembly so acting; or
    (c) only by the Mayor and Assembly jointly so acting.

(2) Any function—

    (a) which is transferred to, or conferred or imposed on, the Authority by or under this Act or any other Act (whenever passed), and
    (b) which (apart from this subsection) is not made exercisable on behalf of the Authority by the Mayor, by the Assembly, or by the Mayor and the Assembly acting jointly,

shall be exercisable only by the Mayor acting on behalf of the Authority.

(3) Any function transferred to, or conferred or imposed on, the Mayor by or under this Act or any other Act (whenever passed) shall be taken to be a function of the Authority exercisable only by the Mayor acting on behalf of the Authority.

(4) Any function transferred to, or conferred or imposed on, the Assembly by or under this Act or any other Act (whenever passed) shall be taken to be a function of the Authority exercisable only by the Assembly acting on behalf of the Authority.

(5) Any function transferred to, or conferred or imposed on, the Mayor and the Assembly by or under this Act or any other Act (whenever passed) shall be taken to be a function of the Authority exercisable only by the Mayor and Assembly acting jointly on behalf of the Authority.

(6) Subsections (3) and (4) above are subject to subsection (5) above.

(7) Any reference in this Act to—

    (a) functions of the Authority,
    (b) functions of the Mayor,
    (c) functions of the Assembly, or
    (d) functions of the Mayor and Assembly,

shall be construed in accordance with the foregoing provisions of this section.

(8) Subsections (1) to (7) above are subject to any express provision to the contrary in this Act.

(9) Subsections (2) and (3) above are without prejudice to sections 38 and 380[1] below and Schedule 4 to this Act.

(10) This section is subject, in particular, to Part II of the Deregulation and Contracting Out Act 1994 (contracting out).

Standing orders of the Authority

36.—(1) The Assembly, in consultation with the Mayor, may make standing **106–012** orders of the Authority.

(2) The procedure of the Assembly, and of any committees or sub-committees of the Assembly, shall be regulated by the standing orders of the Authority.

(3) Standing orders of the Authority may make provision regulating the procedure to be followed—

(a) by any member of the Assembly, or
(b) by any member of staff of the Authority,

by whom functions of the Authority are exercisable pursuant to arrangements under section 54 below.

(4) Standing orders of the Authority may make provision regulating the procedure to be followed by the Mayor or by the Assembly in discharging any functions of the Mayor or the Assembly, to the extent that the functions—

(a) consist of consultation, or any other interaction or relationship, between the Mayor and the Assembly; or
(b) are exercisable by the Mayor in relation to the Assembly or by the Assembly in relation to the Mayor.

(5) Standing orders of the Authority may make provision for any other matter for which provision by standing orders of the Authority is authorised or required by or under any other provision of this Act or any other enactment.

(6) Subsections (2) to (5) above are subject to any other provision of this Act or any other enactment which regulates, or provides for the regulation of, the procedure of the Assembly or any procedure to be followed by the Mayor.

(7) Standing orders of the Authority may make different provision for different circumstances.

(8) The Assembly, after consultation with the Mayor, may at any time vary or revoke any standing orders of the Authority.

(9) Neither section 38 below nor section 54 below shall apply in relation to the functions of the Mayor or the Assembly under this section.

. . . . . .

Meetings and procedure of the Assembly

Meetings of the whole Assembly

106–013   **52.**—(1) The Assembly may hold, in addition to any meetings required to be held by or under this section or any other enactment, such other meetings as it may determine.

(2) Before the expiration of the period of ten days following the day of the poll at an ordinary election, there shall be a meeting of the Assembly to elect—

(a) the Chair of the Assembly; and
(b) the Deputy Chair of the Assembly.

(3) On such ten occasions in each calendar year as the Assembly may determine, there shall be a meeting of the Assembly—

(a) to consider the written report submitted for the meeting by the Mayor under section 45 above,
(b) to enable Assembly members to put—

(i) oral or written questions to the Mayor; and
(ii) oral questions to any employees of the Authority who are required

to attend such meetings and answer questions put to them by Assembly members; and

(c) to transact any other business on the agenda for the meeting.

(4) The first meeting under subsection (3) above after an ordinary election shall be held not later than 25 days after the day of the poll at the election.

(5) Notice of the time and place of any meeting of the Assembly—

(a) shall be given to the Mayor and the Assembly members, and
(b) shall be published,

in accordance with the standing orders of the Authority.

(6) In the case of a meeting of the Assembly under subsection (3) above, the notice required by subsection (5) above must be given and published—

(a) if the meeting is the first such meeting after an ordinary election, as soon as reasonably practicable after the day of the poll at that election; or
(b) in any other case, at least 28 clear days before the meeting.

(7) If notice of a meeting to be held under subsection (3) above has been given pursuant to subsection (6) above, then, until that meeting has been held or the notice has been withdrawn, notice must not be given of another such meeting.

(8) An extraordinary meeting of the Assembly may be called at any time by the Chair of the Assembly.

(9) If—

(a) the Chair of the Assembly refuses to call an extraordinary meeting of the Assembly after a requisition for that purpose, signed by five Assembly members, has been presented to him, or
(b) if, without so refusing, the Chair of the Assembly does not call an extraordinary meeting within seven days after such a requisition has been presented to him,

any five Assembly members may forthwith call an extraordinary meeting of the Assembly.

(10) Section 54 below shall not apply in relation to any function of the Assembly under this section.

Assembly procedure

53.—(1) All questions coming before, or to be decided by, the Assembly shall **106–014** be decided by a majority of the members of the Assembly present and voting at a meeting of the Assembly.

(2) In the case of an equality of votes, the person chairing the meeting of the Assembly shall have a second or casting vote.

(3) Subsections (1) and (2) above are subject to any provision to the contrary contained in this or any other enactment.

(4) The Assembly may determine its own procedure and that of its committees and sub-committees (including quorum).

(5) Subsection (4) above is subject to—

(a) subsections (1) and (2) above;
(b) sections 50 to 52 above;
(c) section 56 below;

(d) Schedules 6 and 7 to this Act; and
(e) any other provision made by or under this Act or any other Act (whenever passed) which regulates, or provides for the regulation of, the procedure of the Assembly or committees of the Assembly.

Discharge of functions by committees or single members

106–015 **54.**—(1) The Assembly may arrange for any of the functions exercisable by it to be discharged on its behalf—

(a) by a committee or sub-committee of the Assembly; or
(b) by a single member of the Assembly.

(2) The Assembly may arrange for a member of staff of the Authority appointed under section 67(2) below to exercise on the Assembly's behalf any function exercisable by the Assembly under section 67(2) or 70(2) below.

(3) Where by virtue of this section any functions exercisable by the Assembly may be discharged by a committee of the Assembly, then, unless the Assembly otherwise directs, the committee may arrange for the discharge of any, of those functions by a sub-committee or by a single member of the Assembly.

(4) Where by virtue of this section any functions exercisable by the Assembly may be discharged by a sub-committee of the Assembly, then, unless the Assembly or the committee concerned otherwise directs, the sub-committee may arrange for the discharge of any of those functions by a single member of the Assembly.

(5) Any arrangements made under this section by the Assembly, or by a committee or sub-committee of the Assembly, for the discharge of any functions by—

(a) a committee or sub-committee of the Assembly,
(b) a member of the Assembly, or
(c) a member of staff of the Authority,

shall not prevent the Assembly, or the committee or sub-committee by whom the arrangements are made, from exercising those functions.

(6) Subsection (1)(b) above does not apply in relation to functions under or by virtue of section 20A of the Police Act 1996 (questions by Assembly members to representatives of the Metropolitan Police Authority).

(7) Subsections (1) to (3) of section 53 above shall apply in relation to a meeting of a committee or sub-committee of the Assembly as they apply in relation to a meeting of the Assembly.

(8) Subsections (1) to (5) above are subject to any express provision contained in this Act or any Act passed after this Act.

Assembly committees and sub-committees

106–016 **55.**—(1) For the purpose of discharging, in pursuance of arrangements under section 54(1)(a) above, any functions exercisable by the Assembly—

(a) the Assembly may appoint a committee of the Assembly (an "ordinary committee"); and
(b) an ordinary committee may appoint one or more sub-committees ("ordinary sub-committees").

(2) Subject to the provisions of this section—

(a) the number of members, and

(b) their term of office,

shall be fixed in the case of an ordinary committee by the Assembly or, in the case of an ordinary sub-committee, by the appointing committee.

(3) An ordinary committee or sub-committee must not include any person who is not an Assembly member.

(4) The Assembly may appoint one or more committees. ("advisory committees") to advise it on any matter relating to the discharge of its functions.

(5) An advisory committee—

(a) may consist of such persons (whether Assembly members or not) appointed for such term as may be determined by the Assembly; and

(b) may appoint one or more sub-committees ("advisory sub-committees") to advise the committee with respect to any matter on which the committee has been appointed to advise.

Minutes

56.—(1) Minutes of the proceedings of a meeting of the Assembly, or of any **106–017** committee or sub-committee of the Assembly, shall be kept in such form as the Assembly may determine.

(2) Any such minutes shall be signed at the same or next suitable meeting of the Assembly, committee or sub-committee by the person presiding at that meeting.

(3) Any minute purporting to be signed as mentioned in subsection (2) above shall be received in evidence without further proof.

(4) For the purposes of subsection (2) above, the next suitable meeting of the Assembly, or of a committee or sub-committee of the Assembly, is their next following meeting or, where standing orders of the Authority provide for another meeting to be regarded as suitable, either the next following meeting or that other meeting.

(5) In the application of this section in the case of a meeting of the Assembly under section 52(3) above, "minutes" includes—

(a) the text of any question put pursuant to section 52(3) above at the meeting, and

(b) the text of the answer given to any such question,

whether the question was put, or the answer given, orally or in writing.

Political composition of Assembly committees

57.—(1) Sections 15 to 17 of, and Schedule 1 to, the Local Government and **106–018** Housing Act 1989 (political balance on committees etc) shall have effect in relation to the Assembly, so far as relating to the appointment of members of its committees, as if the Assembly were a relevant authority and its ordinary committees and advisory committees were ordinary or, as the case may be, advisory committees within the meaning of those provisions (and accordingly bodies to which section 15 of that Act applies).

(2) In the case of any committee of the Assembly, the first appointment of members of the committee shall be an occasion on which the duty imposed by subsection (1) of section 15 of that Act arises in relation to the committee.

Openness

106–019   **58.**—(1) Part VA of the Local Government Act 1972 (access to meetings and documents of certain authorities, committees and sub-committees) shall have effect as if—

(a) the Assembly were a principal council, and
(b) any committee or sub-committee of the Assembly were a committee or sub-committee of a principal council, within the meaning of that Part,

but with the following modifications.

(2) In the application of Part VA of that Act by subsection (1) above—

(a) any information furnished to the Authority and available to the Assembly shall be treated as information furnished to the Assembly;
(b) any offices of, or belonging to, the Authority shall be treated as also being offices of or belonging to the Assembly; and
(c) the proper officer of the Authority shall be taken to be the proper officer in relation to the Assembly.

(3) In the following provisions of that Act, namely—

(a) section 100A(2) (which requires the exclusion of the public from meetings and makes other provision to prevent disclosure of confidential information in breach of the obligation of confidence), and
(b) section 100D(4) (which prevents the inclusion in a list of documents of any document which would so disclose such information),

any reference to the disclosure (or likelihood of disclosure) of confidential information in breach of the obligation of confidence includes a reference to the disclosure of information of any of the descriptions specified in subsection (4) below without the consent of the relevant body concerned.

(4) The descriptions are—

(a) any information relating to the financial or business affairs of any particular person which was acquired in consequence of a relationship between that person and a relevant body;
(b) the amount of any expenditure proposed to be incurred by a relevant body under any particular contract; if and so long as disclosure would be likely to give an advantage to a person entering into, or seeking to enter into, a contract with the relevant body, whether the advantage would arise against the relevant body or another such person;
(c) any terms proposed or to be proposed by or to a relevant body in the course of negotiations for any particular contract, if and so long as disclosure would prejudice the relevant body in those or any other negotiations concerning the subject matter of the contract;
(d) the identity of any person as the person offering any particular tender for a contract for the supply of goods or services to a relevant body;

and in this subsection "relevant body" means Transport for London or the London Development Agency.

(5) In section 100C of that Act (inspection of minutes and other documents after meetings) any reference to the minutes of a meeting shall, in the case of a meeting of the Assembly under section 52(3) above, be taken to include a reference to—

(a) the text of any question put pursuant to section 52(3) above at the meeting, and

(b) the text of the answer given to any such question,

whether the question was put, or the answer given, orally or in writing.

(6) Nothing in section 100D of that Act (inspection of background papers) requires or authorises the inclusion in any such list as is referred to in subsection (1) of that section of any document which discloses anything which, by virtue of subsection (6) of section 45 above, is not required to be disclosed under subsection (3) or (4) of that section.

(7) In section 100E of that Act (application to committees and sub-committees) subsection (3)(a) shall have effect as if section 55 above were included among the enactments specified in section 101(9) of that Act.

(8) For the purposes of section 100F of that Act (additional rights of access to documents for members of principal councils) any document which is in the possession or under the control of the Authority and which is available to the Assembly shall be treated as a document which is in the possession or under the control of the Assembly.

(9) In the case of the Assembly, the register of members required to be maintained under section 100G(1) of that Act shall, instead of stating the ward or division which a member represents, state—

(a) whether the member is a London member or a constituency member; and

(b) if he is a constituency member, the Assembly constituency for which he is the member.

(10) For the purposes of section 100H(3) of that Act (acts which infringe copyright) the Authority shall be treated as a principal council.

(11) In the application in relation to the Assembly of Schedule 12A to that Act (access to information: exempt information) any reference to "the authority" includes a reference to the Authority.

General functions of the Assembly

Review and investigation

59.—(1) The Assembly shall keep under review the exercise by the Mayor of **106–020** the statutory functions exercisable by him.

(2) For the purposes of subsection (1) above, the powers, of the Assembly include in particular power to investigate, and prepare reports about,—

(a) any actions and decisions of the Mayor,

(b) any actions and decisions of any member of staff of the Authority,

(c) matters relating to the principal purposes of the Authority,

(d) matters in relation to which statutory functions are exercisable by the Mayor, or

(e) any other matters which the Assembly considers to be of importance to Greater London.

Proposals to the Mayor

60.—(1) Where the Assembly decides to do so, the Assembly may submit a **106–021** proposal to the Mayor.

(2) Section 54 above shall not apply in relation to the function of the Assembly under subsection (1) above.

. . . . . .

Bills in Parliament

Power of Authority to promote or oppose Bills in Parliament

106–022   77.—(1) The Authority may—

    (a) promote a local Bill in Parliament for any purpose which is for the public benefit of the inhabitants of, or of any part of, Greater London; or

    (b) oppose any local Bill in Parliament which affects any such inhabitants.

(2) Section 70 of the Local Government Act 1972 (prohibition on promoting Bills for changing local government areas etc) shall have effect in relation to the Authority as it has effect in relation to a local authority.

(3) The functions conferred on the Authority by subsection (1) above shall be functions of the Authority which are exercisable by the Mayor acting on behalf of the Authority.

(4) The functions conferred on the Authority by subsection (1)(a) above are exercisable subject to, and in accordance with, the provisions of Schedule 5 to this Act.

(5) Before exercising the functions conferred on the Authority by subsection (1)(b) above, the Mayor shall consult the Assembly.

(6) No payment shall be made by the Authority (whether acting by the Mayor, the Assembly or the Mayor and Assembly acting jointly) to the Mayor or an Assembly member for acting as counsel or agent in promoting or opposing a Bill under this section.

(7) A London borough council or the Common Council may contribute towards the expenses of the Authority in promoting a local Bill in Parliament.

Power to request provisions in Bills promoted by London local authorities

106–023   78.—(1) A local Bill promoted in Parliament by a London local authority may include provisions requested by the Authority.

(2) Subsection (1) above applies only if the Authority confirms the request in writing as soon as practicable after the expiration of 14 days after the Bill has been deposited in Parliament.

(3) If the Authority does not confirm the request as required by subsection (2) above, it shall give notice of that fact to the London local authority promoting the Bill.

(4) Where notice under subsection (3) above is given to a London local authority, that authority shall take all necessary steps for the omission from the Bill of the provisions in question or, if those provisions were requested also by other London local authorities under section 87 of the Local Government Act 1985, of those provisions so far as relating to the Authority.

(5) The functions conferred or imposed on the Authority by subsections (1) to (3) above shall be functions of the Authority which are exercisable by the Mayor acting on behalf of the Authority.

(6) Before exercising the functions conferred on the Authority by subsection (1) or (2) above, the Mayor shall consult the Assembly.

(7) If, in accordance with this section, the Authority requests the inclusion of provisions in a Bill promoted by a London local authority, the Authority may contribute towards the expenses of the London local authority in connection with the Bill.

(8) In consequence of the other provisions of this section, in section 87(3) of the Local Government Act 1985 (consequences of non-confirmation of requests by London local authorities for inclusion of provisions in Bills promoted by

others) after "other councils" there shall be inserted ", or by the Greater London Authority under section 78 of the Greater London Authority Act 1999,".

(9) In this section "London local authority" means—

(a) a London borough council; or
(b) the Common Council:

Authority's consent to inclusion of certain provisions in local Bills

79.—(1) A local Bill promoted in Parliament by a London local authority **106–024** may include provisions which affect the exercise of statutory functions by the Authority or any of the functional bodies

(2) Subsection (1) above applies only if the Authority—

(a) gives its written consent; and
(b) confirms that consent in writing as soon as practicable after the expiration of 14 days after the Bill has been deposited in Parliament.

(3) If the Authority does not confirm the consent as required by subsection (2)(b) above, the Authority shall give notice of that fact to the London local authority promoting the Bill.

(4) Where notice under subsection (3) above is given to a London local authority, that authority shall take all necessary steps for the omission from the Bill of the provisions in question or, if those provisions were requested by other London local authorities under section 87 of the Local Government Act 1985, of those provisions so far as relating to the Authority or the functional body concerned.

(5) The functions conferred or imposed on the Authority by subsections (2) and (3) above shall be functions of the Authority which are exercisable by the Mayor acting on behalf of the Authority.

(6) Before exercising the functions conferred on the Authority by subsection (2)(a) or (b) above, the Mayor shall consult the Assembly.

(7) Nothing in this section applies in relation to provisions requested under section 78 above.

(8) In this section "London local authority" means—

(a) a London borough council; or
(b) the Common Council.

House of Lords Act 1999

(1999 c. 34)

An Act to restrict membership of the House of Lords by virtue of a hereditary **107–001**
peerage; to make related provision about disqualifications for voting
at elections to, and for membership of, the House of Commons; and for
connected purposes. [11th November 1999]

Exclusion of hereditary peers

1. No-one shall be a member of the House of Lords by virtue of a hereditary **107–002** peerage.

Exception from section 1

107–003   **2.**—(1) Section 1 shall not apply in relation to anyone excepted from it by or in accordance with Standing Orders of the House.

(2) At any one time 90 people shall be excepted from section 1; but anyone excepted as holder of the office of Earl Marshal, or as performing the office of Lord Great Chamberlain, shall not count towards that limit.

(3) Once excepted from section 1, a person shall continue to be so throughout his life (until an Act of Parliament provides to the contrary).

(4) Standing Orders shall make provision for filling vacancies among the people excepted from section 1; and in any case where—

(a) the vacancy arises on a death occurring after the end of the first Session of the next Parliament after that in which this Act is passed, and

(b) the deceased person was excepted in consequence of an election,

that provision shall require the holding of a by-election.

(5) A person may be excepted from section 1 by or in accordance with Standing Orders made in anticipation of the enactment or commencement of this section.

(6) Any question whether a person is excepted from section 1 shall be decided by the Clerk of the Parliaments, whose certificate shall be conclusive.

Removal of disqualifications in relation to the House of Commons

107–004   **3.**—(1) The holder of a hereditary peerage shall not be disqualified by virtue of that peerage for—

(a) voting at elections to the House of Commons, or

(b) being, or being elected as, a member of that House.

(2) Subsection (1) shall not apply in relation to anyone excepted from section 1 by virtue of section 2.

Commencement and transitional provision

107–005   **5.**—(1) Sections 1 to 4 (including Schedules 1 and 2) shall come into force at the end of the Session of Parliament in which this Act is passed.

(2) Accordingly, any writ of summons issued for the present Parliament in right of a hereditary peerage shall not have effect after that Session unless it has been issued to a person who, at the end of the Session is excepted from section 1 by virtue of section 2.

(3) The Secretary of State may by order make such transitional provision about the entitlement of holders of hereditary peerages to vote at elections to the House of Commons or the European Parliament as he considers appropriate.

(4) An order under this section—

(a) may modify the effect of any enactment or any provision made under an enactment, and

(b) shall be made by statutory instrument which shall be subject to annulment in pursuance of a resolution of either House of Parliament.

ment in pursuance of a resolution of either House of Parliament.

Interpretation and short title
6.—(1) In this Act "hereditary peerage" includes the principality of Wales and the earldom of Chester.

(2) This Act may be cited as the House of Lords Act 1999.

Immigration and Asylum Act 1999

(1999, c. 33)

An Act to make provision about immigration and asylum; to make provision **108–001**
about procedures in connection with marriage on superintendent regis-
trar's certificate; and for connected purposes.   [11th November 1999]

. . . . . .

PART I

IMMIGRATION: GENERAL

Removal from the United Kingdom

Removal of certain persons unlawfully in the United Kingdom

10.—(1) A person who is not a British citizen may be removed from the **108–002**
United Kingdom, in accordance with directions given by an immigration officer, if—

    (a) having only a limited leave to enter or remain, he does not observe a condition attached to the leave or remains beyond the time limited by the leave;
    (b) he has obtained leave to remain by deception; or
    (c) directions ("the first directions") have been given for the removal, under this section, of a person ("the other person") to whose family he belongs.

(2) Directions may not be given under subsection (1)(a) if the person concerned has made an application for leave to remain in accordance with regulations made under section 9.

(3) Directions may not be given under subsection (1)(c) unless the Secretary of State has given the person concerned written notice, not more than eight weeks after the other person left the United Kingdom in accordance with the first directions, that he intends to remove the person concerned from the United Kingdom.

(4) If such a notice is sent by the Secretary of State by first class post, addressed to the person concerned's last known address, it is to be taken to have been received by that person on the second day after the day on which it was posted.

(5) Directions for the removal of a person under subsection (1)(c) cease to have effect if he ceases to belong to the family of the other person.

(6) Directions under this section—

(a) may be given only to persons falling within a prescribed class;

(b) may impose any requirements of a prescribed kind.

(7) In relation to any such directions, paragraphs 10, 11, 16 to 18, 21 and 22 to 24 of Schedule 2 to the 1971 Act (administrative provisions as to control of entry), apply as they apply in relation to directions given under paragraph 8 of that Schedule.

(8) Directions for the removal of a person given under this section invalidate any leave to enter or remain in the United Kingdom given to him before the directions are given or while they are in force.

(9) The costs of complying with a direction given under this section (so far as reasonably incurred) must be met by the Secretary of State.

Removal of asylum claimants under standing arrangements with member States

108–003 **11.**—(1) In determining whether a person in relation to whom a certificate has been issued under subsection (2) may be removed from the United Kingdom, a member State is to be regarded as—

(a) a place where a person's life and liberty is not threatened by reason of his race, religion, nationality, membership of a particular social group, or political opinion; and

(b) a place from which a person will not be sent to another country otherwise than in accordance with the Refugee Convention.

(2) Nothing in section 15 prevents a person who has made a claim for asylum ("the claimant") from being removed from the United Kingdom to a member State if—

(a) the Secretary of State has certified that—

(i) the member State has accepted that, under standing arrangements, it is the responsible State in relation to the claimant's claim for asylum; and

(ii) in his opinion, the claimant is not a national or citizen of the member State to which he is to be sent;

(b) the certificate has not been set aside on an appeal under section 65.

(3) Unless a certificate has been issued under section 72(2)(a) in relation to a person, he is not to be removed from the United Kingdom—

(a) if he has an appeal under section 65 against the decision to remove him in accordance with this section pending; or

(b) before the time for giving notice of such an appeal has expired.

(4) "Standing arrangements" means arrangements in force as between member States for determining which state is responsible for considering applications for asylum.

. . . . . .

Protection of claimants from removal or deportation

108–004 **15.**—(1) During the period beginning when a person makes a claim for asylum and ending when the Secretary of State gives him notice of the decision on the claim, he may not be removed from, or required to leave, the United Kingdom.

(2) Subsection (1) does not prevent—

(a) directions for his removal being given during that period;
(b) a deportation order being made against him during that period.

(3) But no such direction or order is to have effect during that period.
(4) This section is to be treated as having come into force on 26 July 1993.

. . . . . .

Part II

Carriers' Liability

Clandestine entrants

Penalty for carrying clandestine entrants

32.—(1) A person is a clandestine entrant if—

108–005

(a) he arrives in the United Kingdom concealed in a vehicle, ship or aircraft,
(b) he passes, or attempts to pass, through immigration control concealed in a vehicle, or
(c) he arrives in the United Kingdom on a ship or aircraft, having embarked—

(i) concealed in a vehicle; and

(ii) at a time when the ship or aircraft was outside the United Kingdom,

and claims, or indicates that he intends to seek, asylum in the United Kingdom or evades, or attempts to evade, immigration control.

(2) The person (or persons) responsible for a clandestine entrant is (or are together) liable to—

(a) a penalty of the prescribed amount in respect of the clandestine entrant; and
(b) an additional penalty of that amount in respect of each person who was concealed with the clandestine entrant in the same transporter.

(3) A penalty imposed under this section must be paid to the Secretary of State before the end of the prescribed period.
(4) Payment of the full amount of a penalty by one or more of the persons responsible for the clandestine entrant discharges the liability of each of the persons responsible for that entrant.
(5) In the case of a clandestine entrant to whom subsection (1)(a) applies, each of the following is a responsible person—

(a) if the transporter is a ship or aircraft, the owner or captain;
(b) if it is a vehicle (but not a detached trailer), the owner, hirer or driver of the vehicle;
(c) if it is a detached trailer, the owner, hirer or operator of the trailer.

(6) In the case of a clandestine entrant to whom subsection (1)(b) or (c) applies, each of the following is a responsible person—

  (a) if the transporter is a detached trailer, the owner, hirer or operator of the trailer;
  (b) if it is not, the owner, hirer or driver of the vehicle.

(7) Subject to any defence provided by section 34, it is immaterial whether a responsible person knew or suspected—

  (a) that the clandestine entrant was concealed in the transporter; or
  (b) that there were one or more other persons concealed with the clandestine entrant in the same transporter.

(8) Subsection (9) applies if a transporter ("the carried transporter") is itself being carried in or on another transporter.

(9) If a person is concealed in the carried transporter, the question whether any other person is concealed with that person in the same transporter is to be determined by reference to the carried transporter and not by reference to the transporter in or on which it is carried.

(10) "Immigration control" means United Kingdom immigration control and includes any United Kingdom immigration control operated in a prescribed control zone outside the United Kingdom.[1]

---

[1] In relation to enabling penalties to be imposed on a clandestine entrant who arrives on a rail freight wagon and claims or indicates that he intends to seek asylum in the United Kingdom:

Penalty for carrying clandestine entrants

32.—(1) A person is a clandestine entrant if—

(a) he arrives in the United Kingdom concealed in a vehicle, ship or aircraft,
(b) he passes, or attempts to pass, through immigration control concealed in a vehicle, or
(c) he arrives in the United Kingdom on a ship or aircraft, having embarked—

  (i) concealed in a vehicle; and
  (ii) at a time when the ship or aircraft was outside the United Kingdom,

  and claims, or indicates that he intends to seek, asylum in the United Kingdom or evades, or attempts to evade, immigration control.

(2) The person (or persons) responsible for a clandestine entrant is (or are together) liable to—

(a) a penalty of the prescribed amount in respect of the clandestine entrant; and
(b) an additional penalty of that amount in respect of each person who was concealed with the clandestine entrant in the same rail freight wagon.

(3) A penalty imposed under this section must be paid to the Secretary of State before the end of the prescribed period.

(4) Payment of the full amount of a penalty by one or more of the persons responsible for the clandestine entrant discharges the liability of each of the persons responsible for that entrant.

(5) Each of the following persons is responsible for a clandestine entrant who arrives in the United Kingdom concealed in a train—

(a) the railway operator who, at its last scheduled stop before arrival in the United Kingdom, had the duty of certifying the train as fit to travel to the United Kingdom;
(b) any other railway operator who has entered into an arrangement with that operator under which they share profits or liabilities arising from that train's journey from the last scheduled stop into the United Kingdom.

[(5A) In the case of a clandestine entrant who arrives in the United Kingdom concealed in a freight shuttle wagon, the responsible person is the operator of the shuttle train which includes that freight shuttle wagon.]

(6) In the case of a clandestine entrant to whom subsection (1)(b) or (c) applies, each of the following is a responsible person—

(a) if the transporter is a detached trailer, the owner, hirer or operator of the trailer;
(b) if it is not, the owner, hirer or driver of the vehicle.

(7) Subject to any defence provided by section 34, it is immaterial whether a responsible person knew or suspected—

    (a) that the clandestine entrant was concealed in the rail freight wagon; or

    (b) that there were one or more other persons concealed with the clandestine entrant in the same rail freight wagon.

(8) Subsection (9) applies if a transporter ("the carried transporter") is itself being carried in or on another transporter.

(9) If a person is concealed in the carried transporter, the question whether any other person is concealed with that person in the same transporter is to be determined by reference to the carried transporter and not by reference to the transporter in or on which it is carried.

(10) "Immigration control" means United Kingdom immigration control and includes any United Kingdom immigration control operated in a prescribed control zone outside the United Kingdom.

. . . . . .

Defences to claim that penalty is due under section 32

34.—(1) This section applies if it is alleged that a person ("the carrier") is **108–006** liable to a penalty under section 32.

(2) It is a defence for the carrier to show that he, or an employee of his who was directly responsible for allowing the clandestine entrant to be concealed, was acting under duress.

(3) It is also a defence for the carrier to show that—

    (a) he did not know, and had no reasonable grounds for suspecting, that a clandestine entrant was, or might be, concealed in the transporter;

    (b) an effective system for preventing the carriage of clandestine entrants was in operation in relation to the transporter; and

    (c) that on the occasion in question the person or persons responsible for operating that system did so properly.[1]

(4) In determining, for the purposes of this section, whether a particular system is effective, regard is to be had to the code of practice issued by the Secretary of State under section 33.

(5) If there are two or more persons responsible for a clandestine entrant, the fact that one or more of them has a defence under subsection (3) does not affect the liability of the others.

(6) But if a person responsible for a clandestine entrant has a defence under subsection (2), the liability of any other person responsible for that entrant is discharged.

[1] In relation to enabling penalties to be imposed on a clandestine entrant who arrives in a rail freight wagon and claims or indicates that he intends to seek asylum in the United Kingdom:

    (3) It is also a defence for the carrier to show that—

    (a) he did not know, and had no reasonable grounds for suspecting, that a clandestine entrant was, or might be, concealed in the [rail freight wagon, or, knowing, or having reasonable grounds for suspecting, that a clandestine entrant was, or might be, concealed in the rail freight wagon in circumstances where the clandestine entrant had boarded the train or shuttle train after it had commenced its journey to the United Kingdom, he was not able to stop the train or shuttle train without endangering safety];

    (b) an effective system for preventing the carriage of clandestine entrants was in operation in relation to the [train, or shuttle train, including the rail freight wagon]; and

    (c) that on the occasion in question the person or persons responsible for operating that system did so properly.

Procedure

35.—(1) If the Secretary of State decides that a person ("P") is liable to one **108–007** or more penalties under section 32, he must notify P of his decision.

(2) A notice under subsection (1) (a "penalty notice") must—

(a) state the Secretary of State's reasons for deciding that P is liable to the penalty (or penalties);
(b) state the amount of the penalty (or penalties) to which P is liable;
(c) specify the date before which, and the manner in which, the penalty (or penalties) must be paid; and
(d) include an explanation of the steps—

    (i) that P must take if he objects to the penalty;

    (ii) that the Secretary of State may take under this Part to recover any unpaid penalty.

(3) Subsection (4) applies if more than one person is responsible for a clandestine entrant.

(4) If a penalty notice is served on one of the responsible persons, the Secretary of State is to be taken to have served the required penalty notice on each of them.

(5) The Secretary of State must nevertheless take reasonable steps, while the penalty remains unpaid, to secure that the penalty notice is actually served on each of those responsible persons.

(6) If a person on whom a penalty notice is served, or who is treated as having had a penalty notice served on him, alleges that he is not liable for one or more, or all, of the penalties specified in the penalty notice, he may give written notice of his allegation to the Secretary of State.[1]

(7) Notice under subsection (6) ("a notice of objection") must—

(a) give reasons for the allegation; and
(b) be given before the end of such period as may be prescribed;

(8) If a notice of objection is given before the end of the prescribed period, the Secretary of State must consider it and determine whether or not any penalty to which it relates is payable.

(9) The Secretary of State may by regulations provide, in relation to detached trailers, for a penalty notice which is served in such manner as may be prescribed to have effect as a penalty notice properly served on the responsible person or persons concerned under this section.

(10) Any sum payable to the Secretary of State as a penalty under section 32 may be recovered by the Secretary of State as a debt due to him.

[1] In relation to enabling penalties to be imposed on a clandestine entrant who arrives in a rail freight wagon and claims or indicates that he intends to seek asylum in the United Kingdom:

(6) If a person on whom a penalty notice is served, alleges that he is not liable for one or more, or all, of the penalties specified in the penalty notice, he may give written notice of his allegation to the Secretary of State.

Power to detain vehicles etc. in connection with penalties under section 32

108–008   **36.**—(1) If a penalty notice has been given under section 35, a senior officer may detain any relevant—

(a) vehicle,
(b) small ship, or
(c) small aircraft,

until all penalties to which the notice relates, and any expenses reasonably incurred by the Secretary of State in connection with the detention, have been paid.

(2) That power—

    (a) may be exercised only if, in the opinion of the senior officer concerned, there is a significant risk that the penalty (or one or more of the penalties) will not be paid before the end of the prescribed period if the transporter is not detained; and

    (b) may not be exercised if alternative security which the Secretary of State considers is satisfactory, has been given.

(3) If a transporter is detained under this section, the owner, consignor or any other person who has an interest in any freight or other thing carried in or on the transporter may remove it, or arrange for it to be removed, at such time and in such way as is reasonable.

(4) The detention of a transporter under this section is lawful even though it is subsequently established that the penalty notice on which the detention was based was ill-founded in respect of all or any of the penalties to which it related.

(5) But subsection (4) does not apply if the Secretary of State was acting unreasonably in issuing the penalty notice.[1]

---

[1] In relation to enabling penalties to be imposed on a clandestine entrant who arrives in a rail freight wagon and claims or indicates that he intends to seek asylum in the United Kingdom:

Power to detain vehicles etc. in connection with penalties under section 32

    36.—(1) If a penalty notice has been given under section 35, a senior officer may detain any relevant transporter until all penalties to which the notice relates, and any expenses reasonably incurred by the Secretary of State in connection with the detention, have been paid.

    (1A) For those purposes, "transporter" means the rail freight wagon in which the clandestine entrant arrived in the United Kingdom.

    (2) That power—

    (a) may be exercised only if, in the opinion of the senior officer concerned, there is a significant risk that the penalty (or one or more of the penalties) will not be paid before the end of the prescribed period if the transporter is not detained; and

    (b) may not be exercised if alternative security which the Secretary of State considers is satisfactory, has been given.

    (3) If a transporter is detained under this section, the owner, consignor or any other person who has an interest in any freight or other thing carried in or on the transporter may remove it, or arrange for it to be removed, at such time and in such way as is reasonable.

    (4) The detention of a transporter under this section is lawful even though it is subsequently established that the penalty notice on which the detention was based was ill-founded in respect of all or any of the penalties to which it related.

    (5) But subsection (4) does not apply if the Secretary of State was acting unreasonably in issuing the penalty notice.

. . . . . .

Passengers without proper documents

Charges in respect of passengers without proper documents

    40.—(1) This section applies if a person requiring leave to enter the United **108–009** Kingdom arrives in the United Kingdom by ship, aircraft, road passenger vehicle or train and, on being required to do so by an immigration officer, fails to produce—

    (a) a valid passport with photograph or some other document satisfactorily establishing his identity and nationality or citizenship; and

(b) if he requires a visa, a valid visa of the required kind.

(2) The Secretary of State may charge the owner of the ship, aircraft or vehicle or the train operator, in respect of that person, the sum of £2,000 or such other sum as may be prescribed.

(3) The charge is payable to the Secretary of State on demand.

(4) No charge is payable in respect of any person who is shown by the owner or train operator to have produced the required document or documents to him or his representative when embarking—

(a) on the ship or aircraft for the voyage or flight to the United Kingdom; or

(b) on the vehicle or train for the journey to the United Kingdom.

(5) No charge is payable by a train operator, or by the owner of a road passenger vehicle, in respect of a person ("A"), if he shows that—

(a) neither he nor his representative was permitted, under the law applicable to the place where A embarked on the journey to the United Kingdom, to require A to produce to him when embarking the required document or documents;

(b) he had in place satisfactory arrangements (including, where appropriate, arrangements with other persons) designed to ensure that he did not carry passengers who did not, or might not, have documents of the required kind;

(c) all such steps as were practicable were taken in accordance with the arrangements to establish whether A had the required document or documents; and

(d) all such steps as were practicable were taken in accordance with the arrangements to prevent A's arrival in the United Kingdom where—

(i) A refused to produce the required document or documents to a person acting in accordance with the arrangements; or

(ii) for other reasons it appeared to that person that A did not, or might not, have the required document or documents

(6) For the purposes of subsections (4) and (5), a document—

(a) is to be regarded as being what it purports to be unless its falsity is reasonably apparent; and

(b) is to be regarded as relating to the person producing it unless it is reasonably apparent that it relates to another person.

(7) Subsection (8) applies if—

(a) a person arrives in the United Kingdom in circumstances in which the Secretary of State is entitled to impose on the owner of a road passenger vehicle a charge under this section in respect of that person; and

(b) the vehicle arrived in the United Kingdom in a ship or aircraft.

(8) The Secretary of State may impose a charge in respect of the arrival of the vehicle, or a charge in respect of the arrival of the ship or aircraft, but not in respect of both.

(9) The Secretary of State may by order provide that this section is not to apply in relation to passengers arriving in the United Kingdom on a train who embarked on the journey to the United Kingdom—

(a) in a country specified in the order; or

(b) at places so specified within a country so specified.

(10) The Secretary of State may make an order under subsection (9) only if he is satisfied that there is in force between the United Kingdom and the country concerned an agreement providing for the operation of United Kingdom immigration control in that country or for the checking of passports and visas there.

(11) "Road passenger vehicle" means a vehicle—

(a) which is adapted to carry more than eight passengers and is being used for carrying passengers for hire or reward; or

(b) which is not so adapted but is being used for carrying passengers for hire or reward at separate fares in the course of a business of carrying passengers.

(12) For the purposes of this section a person requires a visa if—

(a) under the immigration rules he requires a visa for entry into the United Kingdom; or

(b) as a result of section 41 he requires a visa for passing through the United Kingdom.

(13) "Representative", in relation to a person, means an employee or agent of his.

. . . . . .

PART IV

APPEALS

Leave to enter

Leave to enter the United Kingdom

59.—(1) A person who is refused leave to enter the United Kingdom under **108–010** any provision of the 1971 Act may appeal to an adjudicator against—

(a) the decision that he requires leave, or

(b) the refusal.

(2) A person who, on an application duly made, is refused a certificate of entitlement or an entry clearance may appeal to an adjudicator against the refusal.

(3) Subsection (4) applies if a person appeals under this section on being refused leave to enter the United Kingdom and—

(a) before he appeals, directions have been given for his removal from the United Kingdom; or

(b) before or after he appeals, the Secretary of State or an immigration officer serves on him notice that any directions which may be given for his removal as a result of the refusal will be for his removal to a country or one of several countries specified in the notice.

(4) The appellant may—

(a) object to the country to which he would be removed in accordance with the directions, or

(b) object to the country specified in the notice (or to one or more of those specified),

and claim that he ought to be removed (if at all) to a different country specified by him.

Limitations on rights of appeal under section 59

108–011 **60.**—(1) Section 59 does not entitle a person to appeal, on the ground that he has a right of abode in the United Kingdom, against a decision that he requires leave to enter the United Kingdom if he does not hold—

   (a) a United Kingdom passport describing him as a British citizen or as a citizen of the United Kingdom and Colonies having the right of abode in the United Kingdom; or
   (b) a certificate of entitlement.

(2) Section 59 does not entitle a person to appeal, on the ground that he does not require leave to enter the United Kingdom, against a decision that he does require such leave if he is required by immigration rules or an order under section 8(2) of the 1971 Act to hold a specified document but does not do so.

(3) Section 59 does not entitle a person to appeal against a refusal of leave to enter while he is in the United Kingdom unless, at the time of the refusal, he held a current entry clearance or was a person named in a current work permit.

(4) Subsection (5) applies to a person who seeks to enter the United Kingdom—

   (a) as a visitor;
   (b) in order to follow a course of study of not more than six months' duration for which he has been accepted;
   (c) with the intention of studying but without having been accepted for any course of study; or
   (d) as a dependant of a person within paragraph (a), (b) or (c).

(5) That person—

   (a) is not entitled to appeal under section 59 against a refusal of an entry clearance unless he is a family visitor; and
   (b) is not entitled to appeal against a refusal of leave to enter if he does not hold a current entry clearance at the time of the refusal.

(6) The Secretary of State may by regulations make provision—

   (a) requiring a family visitor appealing under section 59 to pay such fee as may be fixed by the regulations;
   (b) for such an appeal not to be entertained unless the required fee has been paid by the appellant;
   (c) for the repayment of any such fee if the appeal is successful.

(7) Section 59 does not entitle a person to appeal against a refusal of leave to enter, or against a refusal of an entry clearance, if the refusal is on the ground that he or any person whose dependant he is—

   (a) does not hold a relevant document required by the immigration rules;
   (b) does not satisfy a requirement of the immigration rules as to age or nationality or citizenship; or

(c) seeks entry for a period exceeding that permitted by the immigration rules.

(8) The following are relevant documents—

(a) entry clearances;
(b) passports or other identity documents; and
(c) work permits.

(9) Section 59 does not entitle a person to appeal against a refusal of leave to enter, or against a refusal of an entry clearance, if—

(a) the Secretary of State certifies that directions have been given by the Secretary of State (and not by a person acting under his authority) for the appellant not to be given entry to the United Kingdom on the ground that his exclusion is conducive to the public good; or
(b) the leave to enter, or entry clearance, was refused in compliance with any such directions.

(10) "Family visitor" has such meaning as may be prescribed.

. . . . . .

Deportation

Deportation orders

63.—(1) A person may appeal to an adjudicator against— **108–012**

(a) a decision of the Secretary of State to make a deportation order against him under section 5(1) of the 1971 Act as a result of his liability to deportation under section 3(5) of that Act; or
(b) a refusal by the Secretary of State to revoke a deportation order made against him.

(2) A deportation order is not to be made against a person under section 5(1) of the 1971 Act while an appeal may be brought against the decision to make it.
(3) Subsection (4) applies if—

(a) a person appeals under this section; and
(b) before or after he appeals, the Secretary of State serves on him notice that any directions which may be given for his removal as a result of the deportation order will be for his removal to a country or one of several countries specified in the notice.

(4) The appellant may object to the country specified in the notice (or to one or more of those specified), and claim that he ought to be removed (if at all) to a different country specified by him.

Limitations on rights of appeal under section 63

64.—(1) Section 63 does not entitle a person to appeal against a decision to **108–013** make a deportation order against him if the ground of the decision was that his deportation is conducive to the public good as being in the interests of national security or of the relations between the United Kingdom and any other country or for other reasons of a political nature.

(2) Section 63 does not entitle a person to appeal against a refusal to revoke a deportation order, if—

(a) the Secretary of State has certified that the appellant's exclusion from the United Kingdom would be conducive to the public good; or
(b) revocation was refused on that ground by the Secretary of State (and not by a person acting under his authority).

(3) Section 63 does not entitle a person to appeal against a refusal to revoke a deportation order while he is in the United Kingdom, whether because he has not complied with the requirement to leave or because he has contravened the prohibition on entering.

(4) Subsection (5) applies to—

(a) an appeal against a decision to make a deportation order against a person as belonging to the family of another person; or
(b) an appeal against a refusal to revoke a deportation order so made.

(5) The appellant is not to be allowed, for the purpose of showing that he does not or did not belong to another person's family, to dispute any statement made with a view to obtaining leave for the appellant to enter or remain in the United Kingdom (including any statement made to obtain an entry clearance).

(6) But subsection (5) does not apply if the appellant shows—

(a) that the statement was not so made by him or by any person acting with his authority; and
(b) that, when he took the benefit of the leave, he did not know any such statement had been made to obtain it or, if he did know, he was under the age of eighteen.

Human rights

[Racial discrimination and breach of human rights][1]

108–014   65.—(1) A person who alleges that an authority has, in taking any decision under the Immigration Acts relating to that person's entitlement to enter or remain in the United Kingdom [racially discriminated against him or][2], acted in breach of his human rights may appeal to an adjudicator against that decision unless he has grounds for bringing an appeal against the decision under the Special Immigration Appeals Commission Act 1997.

[(2) For the purposes of this Part—

(a) an authority racially discriminates against a person if he acts, or fails to act, in relation to that other person in a way which is unlawful by virtue of section 19B of the Race Relations Act 1976; and
(b) an authority acts in breach of a person's human rights if he acts, or fails to act, in relation to that other person in a way which is made unlawful by section 6(1) of the Human Rights Act 1998.]

(3) Subsections (4) and (5) apply if, in proceedings before an adjudicator or the Immigration Appeal Tribunal on an appeal, a question arises as to whether an authority has, in taking any decision under the Immigration Acts relating to the appellant's entitlement to enter or remain in the United Kingdom, [racially discriminated against the appellant or][3] acted in breach of the appellant's human rights.

(4) The adjudicator, or the Tribunal, has jurisdiction to consider the question.

(5) [If the adjudicator, or the Tribunal, decides that the authority concerned

(a) racially discriminated against the appellant; or
(b) acted in breach of the appellant's human rights, the appeal may be allowed on the ground in question.]

(6) No appeal may be brought under this section by any person in respect of a decision if—

(a) that decision is already the subject of an appeal brought by him under the Special Immigration Appeals Commission Act 1997; and
(b) the appeal under that Act has not been determined.

(7) "Authority" means —

(a) the Secretary of State;
(b) an immigration officer;
(c) a person responsible for the grant or refusal of entry clearance.

[1] Words substituted by Race Relations (Amendment) Act 2000 (c.34), Sched. 2, para. 34.
[2] Words inserted by Race Relations (Amendment) Act 2000 (c.34), s. 6(3).
[3] Words inserted by Race Relations (Amendment) Act 2000 (c.34), Sched. 2, para. 32.

. . . . . .

"One-stop" procedure

Duty to disclose grounds for appeal etc.

74.—(1) This section applies if—   **108–015**

(a) the decision on an application for leave to enter or remain in the United Kingdom is that the application be refused; and
(b) the applicant, while he is in the United Kingdom, is entitled to appeal against the refusal under the Special Immigration Appeals Commission Act 1997 or this Act.

(2) This section also applies if—

(a) as a result of a decision to vary, or to refuse to vary, any limited leave to enter or remain in the United Kingdom which a person has, he may be required to leave the United Kingdom within 28 days of being notified of the decision; and
(b) that person is entitled to appeal against the decision under the Special Immigration Appeals Commission Act 1997 or this Act.

(3) This section also applies if—

(a) the Secretary of State has decided to make a deportation order against a person under section 5(1) of the 1971 Act as a result of his liability to deportation under section 3(5) of that Act; and
(b) that person, while he is in the United Kingdom, is entitled to appeal against that decision under the Special Immigration Appeals Commission Act 1997 or this Act.

(4) The decision-maker must serve on the applicant and on any relevant

member of his family a notice requiring the recipient of the notice to state any additional grounds which he has or may have for wishing to enter or remain in the United Kingdom.

(5) "Decision-maker" means the Secretary of State or (as the case may be) an immigration officer.

(6) The statement must be—

(a) in writing; and
(b) served on the Secretary of State before the end of such period as may be prescribed.

(7) A statement required under this section must—

(a) if the person making it wishes to claim asylum, include a claim for asylum; and
[(aa) if he claims that he was racially discriminated against, include notice of that claim;][1]
(b) if he claims that an act breached his human rights, include notice of that claim.

(8) Regulations may prescribe the persons who, in relation to an applicant, are relevant members of his family.

(9) Regulations may prescribe the procedure to be followed in connection with notices given and statements made in accordance with this section and, in particular, may prescribe the form in which such notices and statements are to be given or made.

[1] Added by Race Relations (Amendment) Act 2000 (c.34), Sched. 2, para. 37.

Duty to disclose grounds for entering, etc. the United Kingdom

108–016   75.—(1) This section applies if a person who—

(a) is an illegal entrant,
(b) is liable to be removed under section 10, or
(c) has arrived in the United Kingdom without—

(i) leave to enter;
(ii) an entry clearance; or
(iii) a current work permit in which he is named,

makes a claim for asylum or a claim that it would be contrary to the United Kingdom's obligations under the Human Rights Convention for him to be removed from, or required to leave, the United Kingdom.

(2) The person responsible for the determination of the claim must serve on the claimant and on any relevant member of his family a notice requiring the recipient of the notice to state any additional grounds which he has or may have for wishing to enter or remain in the United Kingdom.

(3) The statement must be—

(a) in writing; and
(b) served on the person who is responsible for the determination of the claim before the end of such period as may be prescribed.

(4) Regulations may prescribe the procedure to be followed in connection with notices given and statements made in accordance with this section and, in particular, may prescribe the form in which such notices and statements are to be given or made.

(5) Regulations may prescribe the persons who, in relation to a claimant, are relevant members of his family.

(6) Regulations may provide that, if a claim is determined against the claimant, prescribed provisions of section 73, 76, or 77 are to apply to an appeal against that determination by a person on whom a notice has been served under subsection (2), with such modifications (if any) as may be prescribed.

Result of failure to comply with section 74

76.—(1) In this section—

    108–017

  (a) "the applicant" means the person on whom a notice has been served under section 74(4);

  (b) "notice" means a notice served under that section; and

  (c) "statement" means the statement which the notice requires the applicant to make to the Secretary of State.

(2) If the applicant's statement does not mention a particular ground—

  (a) on which he wishes to enter or remain in the United Kingdom, and

  (b) of which he is aware at the material time,

he may not rely on that ground in any appeal under the Special Immigration Appeals Commission Act 1997 or this Part.

(3) Subsection (2) does not apply if—

  (a) the ground is a claim for asylum or a claim that an act [racially discriminated against the applicant or breached his][1] human rights; or

  (b) the Secretary of State considers that the applicant had a reasonable excuse for the omission.

(4) Subsection (5) applies if the applicant's statement does not include a claim for asylum.

(5) If the applicant claims asylum after the end of the period prescribed under section 74(6)(b), no appeal may be made under section 69 if the Secretary of State has certified that in his opinion —

  (a) one purpose of making the claim for asylum was to delay the removal from the United Kingdom of the applicant or of any member of his family; and

  (b) the applicant had no other legitimate purpose for making the application.

(6) "Member of the family" has such meaning as may be prescribed.

[1] Words substituted by Race Relations (Amendment) Act 2000 (c.34), Sched. 2, para. 38.

"One-stop" appeals

77.—(1) This section applies in relation to—

    108–018

  (a) an appeal brought on any of the grounds mentioned in section 69;

  (b) any other appeal against a decision—

    (i) to refuse an application for leave to enter or remain in the United Kingdom;

    (ii) to vary, or to refuse to vary, any limited leave to enter or remain in the United Kingdom, which has the result mentioned in section 74(2)(a); or

   (iii) to make a deportation order against a person under section 5(1) of the 1971 Act as a result of his liability to deportation under section 3(5) of that Act.

(2) Subject to section 72(2), the appellant is to be treated as also appealing on any additional grounds—

   (a) which he may have for appealing against the refusal, variation, decision or directions in question under any other provision of this Act; and

   (b) which he is not prevented (by any provision of section 76) from relying on.

(3) In considering—

   (a) any ground mentioned in section 69, or

   (b) any question relating to the appellant's rights under Article 3 of the Human Rights Convention,

the appellate authority may take into account any evidence which it considers to be relevant to the appeal (including evidence about matters arising after the date on which the decision appealed against was taken).

(4) In considering any other ground, the appellate authority may take into account only evidence—

   (a) which was available to the Secretary of State at the time when the decision appealed against was taken; or

   (b) which relates to relevant facts as at that date.

(5) "Additional grounds", in relation to an appeal, means any grounds specified in a statement made to the Secretary of State under section 74(4) other than those on which the appeal has been brought.

(6) "Appellate authority" means an adjudicator, the Tribunal or the Special Immigration Appeals Commission.

Transfer of appellate proceedings

108–019   **78.**—(1) Subsection (3) applies if—

   (a) a person who has brought an appeal under this Part has been notified of the Secretary of State's decision to make a deportation order against him; and

   (b) as a result of section 64(1), he is not entitled to appeal against that decision under section 63.

(2) Subsection (3) also applies if—

   (a) a person who has brought an appeal under this Part has been notified of the Secretary of State's decision to refuse to revoke a deportation order made against him; and

   (b) as a result of section 64(2), he is not entitled to appeal against that refusal under section 63.

(3) If he appeals against that decision under section 2(1) or 2A of the Special Immigration Appeals Commission Act 1997, any appeal under this Part is transferred to, and must be heard by, the Commission.

(4) Subsection (5) applies if a person, in a statement required by a notice under section 74 or 75, states an additional ground which relates to a matter which may be the subject of an appeal under section 2(1) or 2A of the Special Immigration Appeals Commission Act 1997.

(5) The appeal under this Part is transferred to, and must be heard by, the Commission.

. . . . . .

Provision of support

Persons for whom support may be provided

95.—(1) The Secretary of State may provide, or arrange for the provision of, **108–020** support for—

    (a) asylum-seekers, or
    (b) dependants of asylum-seekers,

who appear to the Secretary of State to be destitute or to be likely to become destitute within such period as may be prescribed.

(2) In prescribed circumstances, a person who would otherwise fall within subsection (1) is excluded.

(3) For the purposes of this section, a person is destitute if—

    (a) he does not have adequate accommodation or any means of obtaining it (whether or not his other essential living needs are met); or
    (b) he has adequate accommodation or the means of obtaining it, but cannot meet his other essential living needs.

(4) If a person has dependants, subsection (3) is to be read as if the references to him were references to him and his dependants taken together.

(5) In determining, for the purposes of this section, whether a person's accommodation is adequate, the Secretary of State—

    (a) must have regard to such matters as may be prescribed for the purposes of this paragraph; but
    (b) may not have regard to such matters as may be prescribed for the purposes of this paragraph or to any of the matters mentioned in subsection (6).

(6) Those matters are—

    (a) the fact that the person concerned has no enforceable right to occupy the accommodation;
    (b) the fact that he shares the accommodation, or any part of the accommodation, with one or more other persons;
    (c) the fact that the accommodation is temporary;
    (d) the location of the accommodation.

(7) In determining, for the purposes of this section, whether a person's other essential living needs are met, the Secretary of State—

    (a) must have regard to such matters as may be prescribed for the purposes of this paragraph; but

(b) may not have regard to such matters as may be prescribed for the purposes of this paragraph.

(8) The Secretary of State may by regulations provide that items or expenses of such a description as may be prescribed are, or are not, to be treated as being an essential living need of a person for the purposes of this Part.

(9) Support may be provided subject to conditions.

(10) The conditions must be set out in writing.

(11) A copy of the conditions must be given to the supported person.

(12) Schedule 8 gives the Secretary of State power to make regulations supplementing this section.

(13) Schedule 9 makes temporary provision for support in the period before the coming into force of this section.

Ways in which support may be provided

108–021   **96.**—(1) Support may be provided under section 95—

> (a) by providing accommodation appearing to the Secretary of State to be adequate for the needs of the supported person and his dependants (if any);
> (b) by providing what appear to the Secretary of State to be essential living needs of the supported person and his dependants (if any);
> (c) to enable the supported person (if he is the asylum-seeker) to meet what appear to the Secretary of State to be expenses (other than legal expenses or other expenses of a prescribed description) incurred in connection with his claim for asylum;
> (d) to enable the asylum-seeker and his dependants to attend bail proceedings in connection with his detention under any provision of the Immigration Acts; or
> (e) to enable the asylum-seeker and his dependants to attend bail proceedings in connection with the detention of a dependant of his under any such provision.

(2) If the Secretary of State considers that the circumstances of a particular case are exceptional, he may provide support under section 95 in such other ways as he considers necessary to enable the supported person and his dependants (if any) to be supported.

(3) Unless the circumstances of a particular case are exceptional, support provided by the Secretary of State under subsection (1)(a) or (b) or (2) must not be wholly or mainly by way of payments made (by whatever means) to the supported person or to his dependants (if any).

(4) But the Secretary of State may by order provide for subsection (3) not to apply—

> (a) in all cases, for such period as may be specified;
> (b) in such circumstances as may be specified;
> (c) in relation to specified categories of person; or
> (d) in relation to persons whose accommodation is in a specified locality.

(5) The Secretary of State may by order repeal subsection (3).

(6) "Specified" means specified in an order made under subsection (4).

Supplemental

108–022   **97.**—(1) When exercising his power under section 95 to provide accommodation, the Secretary of State must have regard to—

(a) the fact that the accommodation is to be temporary pending determination of the asylum-seeker's claim;

(b) the desirability, in general, of providing accommodation in areas in which there is a ready supply of accommodation; and

(c) such other matters (if any) as may be prescribed.

(2) But he may not have regard to—

(a) any preference that the supported person or his dependants (if any) may have as to the locality in which the accommodation is to be provided; or

(b) such other matters (if any) as may be prescribed.

(3) The Secretary of State may by order repeal all or any of the following—

(a) subsection (1)(a);

(b) subsection (1)(b);

(c) subsection (2)(a).

(4) When exercising his power under section 95 to provide essential living needs, the Secretary of State—

(a) must have regard to such matters as may be prescribed for the purposes of this paragraph; but

(b) may not have regard to such other matters as may be prescribed for the purposes of this paragraph.

(5) In addition, when exercising his power under section 95 to provide essential living needs, the Secretary of State may limit the overall amount of the expenditure which he incurs in connection with a particular supported person—

(a) to such portion of the income support applicable amount provided under section 124 of the Social Security Contributions and Benefits Act 1992, or

(b) to such portion of any components of that amount,

as he considers appropriate having regard to the temporary nature of the support that he is providing.

(6) For the purposes of subsection (5), any support of a kind falling within section 96(1)(c) is to be treated as if it were the provision of essential living needs.

(7) In determining how to provide, or arrange for the provision of, support under section 95, the Secretary of State may disregard any preference which the supported person or his dependants (if any) may have as to the way in which the support is to be given.

Temporary support

98.—(1) The Secretary of State may provide, or arrange for the provision of, **108–023** support for—

(a) asylum-seekers, or

(b) dependants of asylum-seekers,

who it appears to the Secretary of State may be destitute.

(2) Support may be provided under this section only until the Secretary of State is able to determine whether support may be provided under section 95.

(3) Subsections (2) to (11) of section 95 apply for the purposes of this section as they apply for the purposes of that section.

. . . . . .

Reception zones

108–024   **101.**—(1) The Secretary of State may by order designate as reception zones—

(a) areas in England and Wales consisting of the areas of one or more local authorities;
(b) areas in Scotland consisting of the areas of one or more local authorities;
(c) Northern Ireland.

(2) Subsection (3) applies if the Secretary of State considers that—

(a) a local authority whose area is within a reception zone has suitable housing accommodation within that zone; or
(b) the Executive has suitable housing accommodation.

(3) The Secretary of State may direct the local authority or the Executive to make available such of the accommodation as may be specified in the direction for a period so specified—

(a) to him for the purpose of providing support under section 95; or
(b) to a person with whom the Secretary of State has made arrangements under section 95.

(4) A period specified in a direction under subsection (3)—

(a) begins on a date so specified; and
(b) must not exceed five years.

(5) A direction under subsection (3) is enforceable, on an application made on behalf of the Secretary of State, by injunction or in Scotland an order under section 45(b) of the Court of Session Act 1988.

(6) The Secretary of State's power to give a direction under subsection (3) in respect of a particular reception zone must be exercised by reference to criteria specified for the purposes of this subsection in the order designating that zone.

(7) The Secretary of State may not give a direction under subsection (3) in respect of a local authority in Scotland unless the Scottish Ministers have confirmed to him that the criteria specified in the designation order concerned are in their opinion met in relation to that authority.

(8) Housing accommodation is suitable for the purposes of subsection (2) if it—

(a) is unoccupied;
(b) would be likely to remain unoccupied for the foreseeable future if not made available; and
(c) is appropriate for the accommodation of persons supported under this Part or capable of being made so with minor work.

(9) If housing accommodation for which a direction under this section is, for the time being, in force—

(a) is not appropriate for the accommodation of persons supported under this Part, but

(b) is capable of being made so with minor work,

the direction may require the body to whom it is given to secure that that work is done without delay.

(10) The Secretary of State must make regulations with respect to the general management of any housing accommodation for which a direction under subsection (3) is, for the time being, in force.

(11) Regulations under subsection (10) must include provision—

(a) as to the method to be used in determining the amount of rent or other charges to be payable in relation to the accommodation;

(b) as to the times at which payments of rent or other charges are to be made;

(c) as to the responsibility for maintenance of, and repairs to, the accommodation;

(d) enabling the accommodation to be inspected, in such circumstances as may be prescribed, by the body to which the direction was given;

(e) with respect to the condition in which the accommodation is to be returned when the direction ceases to have effect.

(12) Regulations under subsection (10) may, in particular, include provision—

(a) for the cost, or part of the cost, of minor work required by a direction under this section to be met by the Secretary of State in prescribed circumstances;

(b) as to the maximum amount of expenditure which a body may be required to incur as a result of a direction under this section.

(13) The Secretary of State must by regulations make provision ("the dispute resolution procedure") for resolving disputes arising in connection with the operation of any regulations made under subsection (10).

(14) Regulations under subsection (13) must include provision—

(a) requiring a dispute to be resolved in accordance with the dispute resolution procedure;

(b) requiring the parties to a dispute to comply with obligations imposed on them by the procedure; and

(c) for the decision of the person resolving a dispute in accordance with the procedure to be final and binding on the parties

(15) Before—

(a) designating a reception zone in Great Britain,

(b) determining the criteria to be included in the order designating the zone, or

(c) making regulations under subsection (13),

the Secretary of State must consult such local authorities, local authority associations and other persons as he thinks appropriate.

(16) Before—

(a) designating Northern Ireland as a reception zone, or

(b) determining the criteria to be included in the order designating Northern Ireland, the Secretary of State must consult the Executive and such other persons as he thinks appropriate.

(17) Before making regulations under subsection (10) which extend only to Northern Ireland, the Secretary of State must consult the Executive and such other persons as he thinks appropriate.

(18) Before making any other regulations under subsection (10), the Secretary of State must consult—

    (a) such local authorities, local authority associations and other persons as he thinks appropriate; and

    (b) if the regulations extend to Northern Ireland, the Executive.

Local Government Act 1999

(1999, c. 7)

109–001 *An Act to make provision imposing on local and certain other authorities requirements relating to economy, efficiency and effectiveness; and to make provision for the regulation of council tax and precepts.* [27th July 1999]

PART I

BEST VALUE

Best value authorities

Best value authorities

109–002   **1.**—(1) For the purposes of this Part each of these is a best value authority—

    (a) a local authority;

    (b) a National Park authority;

    (c) the Broads Authority;

    (d) a police authority;

    (e) a fire authority constituted by a combination scheme and a metropolitan county fire and civil defence authority;

    (f) the London Fire and Emergency Planning Authority;

    (g) a waste disposal authority;

    (h) a metropolitan county passenger transport authority;

    (i) Transport for London;

    (j) the London Development Agency.

(2) In relation to England "local authority" in subsection (1)(a) means —

    (a) a county council, a district council, a London borough council, a parish council or a parish meeting of a parish which does not have a separate parish council;

    (b) the Council of the Isles of Scilly;

    (c) the Common Council of the City of London in its capacity as a local authority;

    (d) the Greater London Authority so far as it exercises its functions through the Mayor.

(3) In relation to Wales "local authority" in subsection (1)(a) means a county council, a county borough council or a community council.

(4) In subsection (1)(d) "police authority" means —

(a) a police authority established under section 3 of the Police Act 1996;

(b) the Common Council of the City of London in its capacity as a police authority;

(c) the Metropolitan Police Authority.

(5) In subsection (1)(g) "waste disposal authority" means an authority which—

(a) is a waste disposal authority for the purposes of Part II of the Environmental Protection Act 1990, or

(b) is established under section 10 of the Local Government Act 1985 (joint arrangements).

. . . . . .

Duties

The general duty

3.—(1) A best value authority must make arrangements to secure continuous **109–003** improvement in the way in which its functions are exercised, having regard to a combination of economy, efficiency and effectiveness.

(2) For the purpose of deciding how to fulfil the duty arising under subsection (1) an authority must consult—

(a) representatives of persons liable to pay any tax, precept or levy to or in respect of the authority,

(b) representatives of persons liable to pay non-domestic rates in respect of any area within which the authority carries out functions,

(c) representatives of persons who use or are likely to use services provided by the authority, and

(d) representatives of persons appearing to the authority to have an interest in any area within which the authority carries out functions.

(3) For the purposes of subsection (2) "representatives" in relation to a group of persons means persons who appear to the authority to be representative of that group.

(4) In deciding on—

(a) the persons to be consulted, and

(b) the form, content and timing of consultations,

an authority must have regard to any guidance issued by the Secretary of State.

Performance indicators and standards

4.—(1) The Secretary of State may by order specify—   **109–004**

(a) factors ("performance indicators") by reference to which a best value authority's performance in exercising functions can be measured;

(b) standards ("performance standards") to be met by best value authorities in relation to performance indicators specified under paragraph (a).

(2) An order may specify different performance indicators or standards—

    (a) for different functions;
    (b) for different authorities;
    (c) to apply at different times.

(3) Before specifying performance indicators or standards the Secretary of State shall consult—

    (a) persons appearing to him to represent the best value authorities concerned, and
    (b) such other persons (if any) as he thinks fit.

(4) In specifying performance indicators and standards, and in deciding whether to do so, the Secretary of State—

    (a) shall aim to promote improvement of the way in which the functions of best value authorities are exercised, having regard to a combination of economy, efficiency and effectiveness, and
    (b) shall have regard to any recommendations made to him by the Audit Commission.

(5) In exercising a function a best value authority must meet any applicable performance standard specified under subsection (1)(b).

Youth Justice and Criminal Evidence Act 1999

(1999, c. 23)

110–001 *An Act to provide for the referral of offenders under 18 to youth offender panels; to make provision in connection with the giving of evidence or information for the purposes of criminal proceedings; to amend section 51 of the Criminal Justice and Public Order Act 1994; to make pre-consolidation amendments relating to youth justice; and for connected purposes.*

[27th July 1999]

. . . . . .

PART II

GIVING OF EVIDENCE OR INFORMATION FOR PURPOSES OF CRIMINAL PROCEEDINGS

CHAPTER I

SPECIAL MEASURES DIRECTIONS IN CASE OF VULNERABLE AND INTIMIDATED WITNESSES

Preliminary

Witnesses eligible for assistance on grounds of age or incapacity

110–002   **16.**—(1) For the purposes of this Chapter a witness in criminal proceedings (other than the accused) is eligible for assistance by virtue of this section—

(a) if under the age of 17 at the time of the hearing; or

(b) if the court considers that the quality of evidence given by the witness is likely to be diminished by reason of any circumstances falling within subsection (2).

(2) The circumstances falling within this subsection are—

(a) that the witness—

(i) suffers from mental disorder within the meaning of the Mental Health Act 1983, or

(ii) otherwise has a significant impairment of intelligence and social functioning;

(b) that the witness has a physical disability or is suffering from a physical disorder.

(3) In subsection (1)(a) "the time of the hearing", in relation to a witness, means the time when it falls to the court to make a determination for the purposes of section 19(2) in relation to the witness.

(4) In determining whether a witness falls within subsection (1)(b) the court must consider any views expressed by the witness.

(5) In this Chapter references to the quality of a witness's evidence are to its quality in terms of completeness, coherence and accuracy; and for this purpose "coherence" refers to a witness's ability in giving evidence to give answers which address the questions put to the witness and can be understood both individually and collectively.

Witnesses eligible for assistance on grounds of fear or distress about testifying

17.—(1) For the purposes of this Chapter a witness in criminal proceedings **110–003** (other than the accused) is eligible for assistance by virtue of this subsection if the court is satisfied that the quality of evidence given by the witness is likely to be diminished by reason of fear or distress on the part of the witness in connection with testifying in the proceedings.

(2) In determining whether a witness falls within subsection (1) the court must take into account, in particular—

(a) the nature and alleged circumstances of the offence to which the proceedings relate;

(b) the age of the witness;

(c) such of the following matters as appear to the court to be relevant, namely—

(i) the social and cultural background and ethnic origins of the witness,

(ii) the domestic and employment circumstances of the witness, and

(iii) any religious beliefs or political opinions of the witness;

(d) any behaviour towards the witness on the part of—

(i) the accused,

(ii) members of the family or associates of the accused, or

(iii) any other person who is likely to be an accused or a witness in the proceedings.

(3) In determining that question the court must in addition consider any views expressed by the witness.

(4) Where the complainant in respect of a sexual offence is a witness in proceedings relating to that offence (or to that offence and any other offences), the witness is eligible for assistance in relation to those proceedings by virtue of this subsection unless the witness has informed the court of the witness' wish not to be so eligible by virtue of this subsection.

. . . . . .

Special measures directions

Special measures direction relating to eligible witness

110–004   **19.**—(1) This section applies where in any criminal proceedings—

    (a) a party to the proceedings makes an application for the court to give a direction under this section in relation to a witness in the proceedings other than the accused, or

    (b) the court of its own motion raises the issue whether such a direction should be given.

(2) Where the court determines that the witness is eligible for assistance by virtue of section 16 or 17, the court must then—

    (a) determine whether any of the special measures available in relation to the witness (or any combination of them) would, in its opinion, be likely to improve the quality of evidence given by the witness; and

    (b) if so—

        (i) determine which of those measures (or combination of them) would, in its opinion, be likely to maximise so far as practicable the quality of such evidence; and

        (ii) give a direction under this section providing for the measure or measures so determined to apply to evidence given by the witness.

(3) In determining for the purposes of this Chapter whether any special measure or measures would or would not be likely to improve, or to maximise so far as practicable, the quality of evidence given by the witness, the court must consider all the circumstances of the case, including in particular—

    (a) any views expressed by the witness; and

    (b) whether the measures or measures must tend to inhibit such evidence being effectively tested by a party to the proceedings.

(4) A special measures direction must specify particulars of the provision made by the direction in respect of each special measure which is to apply to the witness's evidence.

(5) In this Chapter "special measures direction" means a direction under this section.

(6) Nothing in this Chapter is to be regarded as affecting any power of a court to make an order or give leave of any description (in the exercise of its inherent jurisdiction or otherwise)—

    (a) in relation to a witness who is not an eligible witness, or

    (b) in relation to an eligible witness where (as, for example, in a case where a foreign language interpreter is to be provided) the order is made or the leave is given otherwise than by reason of the fact that the witness is an eligible witness.

Further provisions about directions: general

20.—(1) Subject to subsection (2) and section 21(8), a special measures direc- **110–005**
tion has binding effect from the time it is made until the proceedings for the
purposes of which it is made are either—

(a) determined (by acquittal, conviction or otherwise), or
(b) abandoned,

in relation to the accused or (if there is more than one) in relation to each of the
accused.

(2) The court may discharge or vary (or further vary) a special measures
direction if it appears to the court to be in the interests of justice to do so, and
may do so either—

(a) on an application made by a party to the proceedings, if there has been
a material change of circumstances since the relevant time, or
(b) of its own motion.

(3) In subsection (2) "the relevant time" means —

(a) the time when the direction was given, or
(b) if a previous application has been made under that subsection, the time
when the application (or last application) was made.

(4) Nothing in section 24(2) and (3), 27(4) to (7) or 28(4) to (6) is to be
regarded as affecting the power of the court to vary or discharge a special measures direction under subsection (2).

(5) The court must state in open court its reasons for—

(a) giving or varying,
(b) refusing an application for, or for the variation or discharge of, or
(c) discharging,

a special measures direction and, if it is a magistrates' court, must cause them
to be entered in the register of its proceedings.

(6) Rules of court may make provision—

(a) for uncontested applications to be determined by the court without a
hearing;
(b) for preventing the renewal of an unsuccessful application for a special
measures direction except where there has been a material change of
circumstances;
(c) for expert evidence to be given in connection with an application for,
or for varying or discharging, such a direction;
(d) for the manner in which confidential or sensitive information is to be
treated in connection with such an application and in particular as to
its being disclosed to, or withheld from, a party to the proceedings.

Special provisions relating to child witnesses

21.—(1) For the purposes of this section— **110–006**

(a) a witness in criminal proceedings is a "child witness" if he is an eligible witness by reason of section 16(1)(a) (whether or not he is an
eligible witness by reason of any other provision of section 16 or 17);

    (b) a child witness is "in need of special protection" if the offence (or any of the offences) to which the proceedings relate is—

        (i) an offence falling within section 35(3)(a) (sexual offences etc.), or
      (ii) an offence falling within section 35(3)(b), (c) or (d) (kidnapping, assaults etc.); and

    (c) a "relevant recording", in relation to a child witness, is a video recording of an interview of the witness made with a view to its admission as evidence in chief of the witness.

(2) Where the court, in making a determination for the purposes of section 19(2), determines that a witness in criminal proceedings is a child witness, the court must—

    (a) first have regard to subsections (3) to (7) below; and
    (b) then have regard to section 19(2);

and for the purposes of section 19(2), as it then applies to the witness, any special measures required to be applied in relation to him by virtue of this section shall be treated as if they were measures determined by the court, pursuant to section 19(2)(a) and (b)(i), to be ones that (whether on their own or with any other special measures) would be likely to maximise, so far as practicable, the quality of his evidence.

(3) The primary rule in the case of a child witness is that the court must give a special measures direction in relation to the witness which complies with the following requirements—

    (a) it must provide for any relevant recording to be admitted under section 27 (video recorded evidence in chief); and
    (b) it must provide for any evidence given by the witness in the proceedings which is not given by means of a video recording (whether in chief or otherwise) to be given by means of a live link in accordance with section 24.

(4) The primary rule is subject to the following limitations—

    (a) the requirement contained in subsection (3)(a) or (b) has effect subject to the availability (within the meaning of section 18(2)) of the special measure in question in relation to the witness;
    (b) the requirement contained in subsection (3)(a) also has effect subject to section 27(2); and
    (c) the rule does not apply to the extent that the court is satisfied that compliance with it would not be likely to maximise the quality of the witness's evidence so far as practicable (whether because the application to that evidence of one or more other special measures available in relation to the witness would have that result or for any other reason).

(5) However, subsection (4)(c) does not apply in relation to a child witness in need of special protection.

(6) Where a child witness is in need of special protection by virtue of subsection (1)(b)(i), any special measures direction given by the court which complies with the requirement contained in subsection (3)(a) must in addition provide for the special measure available under section 28 (video recorded cross-examination or re-examination) to apply in relation to—

    (a) any cross-examination of the witness otherwise than by the accused in person, and

(b) any subsequent re-examination.

(7) The requirement contained in subsection (6) has effect subject to the following limitations—

(a) it has effect subject to the availability (within the meaning of section 18(2)) of that special measure in relation to the witness; and
(b) it does not apply if the witness has informed the court that he does not want that special measure to apply in relation to him.

(8) Where a special measures direction is given in relation to a child witness who is an eligible witness by reason only of section 16(1)(a), then—

(a) subject to subsection (9) below, and
(b) except where the witness has already begun to give evidence in the proceedings,

the direction shall cease to have effect at the time when the witness attains the age of 17.

(9) Where a special measures direction is given in relation to a child witness who is an eligible witness by reason only of section 16(1)(a) and—

(a) the direction provides—

(i) for any relevant recording to be admitted under section 27 as evidence in chief of the witness, or
(ii) for the special measure available under section 28 to apply in relation to the witness, and

(b) if it provides for that special measure to so apply, the witness is still under the age of 17 when the video recording is made for the purposes of section 28,

then, so far as it provides as mentioned in paragraph (a)(i) or (ii) above, the direction shall continue to have effect in accordance with section 20(1) even though the witness subsequently attains that age.

Extension of provisions of section 21 to certain witnesses over 17

22.—(1) For the purposes of this section—   **110–007**

(a) a witness in criminal proceedings (other than the accused) is a "qualifying witness" if he—

(i) is not an eligible witness at the time of the hearing (as defined by section 16(3)), but
(ii) was under the age of 17 when a relevant recording was made;

(b) a qualifying witness is "in need of special protection" if the offence (or any of the offences) to which the proceedings relate is—

(i) an offence falling within section 35(3)(a) (sexual offences etc.), or
(ii) an offence falling within section 35(3)(b), (c) or (d) (kidnapping, assaults etc.); and

(c) a "relevant recording", in relation to a witness, is a video recording of an interview of the witness made with a view to its admission as evidence in chief of the witness.

(2) Subsections (2) to (7) of section 21 shall apply as follows in relation to a qualifying witness—

    (a) subsections (2) to (4), so far as relating to the giving of a direction complying with the requirement contained in subsection (3)(a), shall apply to a qualifying witness in respect of the relevant recording as they apply to a child witness (within the meaning of that section);

    (b) subsection (5), so far as relating to the giving of such a direction, shall apply to a qualifying witness in need of special protection as it applies to a child witness in need of special protection (within the meaning of that section); and

    (c) subsections (6) and (7) shall apply to a qualifying witness in need of special protection by virtue of subsection (1)(b)(i) above as they apply to such a child witness as is mentioned in subsection (6).

Screening witness from accused

110–008   **23.**—(1) A special measures direction may provide for the witness, while giving testimony or being sworn in court, to be prevented by means of a screen or other arrangement from seeing the accused.

(2) But the screen or other arrangement must not prevent the witness from being able to see, and to be seen by—

    (a) the judge or justices (or both) and the jury (if there is one);

    (b) legal representatives acting in the proceedings; and

    (c) any interpreter or other person appointed (in pursuance of the direction or otherwise) to assist the witness.

(3) Where two or more legal representatives are acting for a party to the proceedings, subsection (2)(b) is to be regarded as satisfied in relation to those representatives if the witness is able at all material times to see and be seen by at least one of them.

Evidence by live link

110–009   **24.**—(1) A special measures direction may provide for the witness to give evidence by means of a live link.

(2) Where a direction provides for the witness to give evidence by means of a live link, the witness may not give evidence in any other way without the permission of the court.

(3) The court may give permission for the purposes of subsection (2) if it appears to the court to be in the interests of justice to do so, and may do so either—

    (a) on an application by a party to the proceedings, if there has been a material change of circumstances since the relevant time, or

    (b) of its own motion.

(4) In subsection (3) "the relevant time" means —

    (a) the time when the direction was given, or

    (b) if a previous application has been made under that subsection, the time when the application (or last application) was made.

(5) Where in proceedings before a magistrates' court—

    (a) evidence is to be given by means of a live link in accordance with a special measures direction, but

    (b) suitable facilities for receiving such evidence are not available at any petty-sessional court-house in which that court can (apart from this subsection) lawfully sit,

the court may sit for the purposes of the whole or any part of those proceedings at a place where such facilities are available and which has been appointed for the purposes of this subsection by the justices acting for the petty sessions area for which the court acts.

(6) A place appointed under subsection (5) may be outside the petty sessions area for which it is appointed; but (if so) it is to be regarded as being in that area for the purpose of the jurisdiction of the justices acting for that area.

(7) In this section "petty-sessional court-house" has the same meaning as in the Magistrates' Courts Act 1980 and "petty sessions area" has the same meaning as in the Justices of the Peace Act 1997.

(8) In this Chapter "live link" means a live television link or other arrangement whereby a witness, while absent from the courtroom or other place where the proceedings are being held, is able to see and hear a person there and to be seen and heard by the persons specified in section 23(2)(a) to (c).

Evidence given in private

25.—(1) A special measures direction may provide for the exclusion from the **110–010** court, during the giving of the witness's evidence, of persons of any description specified in the direction.

(2) The persons who may be so excluded do not include—

(a) the accused,
(b) legal representatives acting in the proceedings, or
(c) any interpreter or other person appointed (in pursuance of the direction or otherwise) to assist the witness.

(3) A special measures direction providing for representatives of news gathering or reporting organisations to be so excluded shall be expressed not to apply to one named person who—

(a) is a representative of such an organisation, and
(b) has been nominated for the purpose by one or more such organisations,

unless it appears to the court that no such nomination has been made.

(4) A special measures direction may only provide for the exclusion of persons under this section where—

(a) the proceedings relate to a sexual offence; or
(b) it appears to the court that there are reasonable grounds for believing that any person other than the accused has sought, or will seek, to intimidate the witness in connection with testifying in the proceedings.

(5) Any proceedings from which persons are excluded under this section (whether or not those persons include representatives of news gathering or reporting organisations) shall nevertheless be taken to be held in public for the purposes of any privilege or exemption from liability available in respect of fair, accurate and contemporaneous reports of legal proceedings held in public.

Removal of wigs and gowns

26. A special measures direction may provide for the wearing of wigs or **110–011** gowns to be dispensed with during the giving of the witness's evidence.

Video recorded evidence in chief

110–012   **27.**—(1) A special measures direction may provide for a video recording of an interview of the witness to be admitted as evidence in chief of the witness.

(2) A special measures direction may, however, not provide for a video recording, or a part of such a recording, to be admitted under this section if the court is of the opinion, having regard to all the circumstances of the case, that in the interests of justice the recording, or that part of it, should not be so admitted.

(3) In considering for the purposes of subsection (2) whether any part of a recording should not be admitted under this section, the court must consider whether any prejudice to the accused which might result from that part being so admitted is outweighed by the desirability of showing the whole, or substantially the whole, of the recorded interview.

(4) Where a special measures direction provides for a recording to be admitted under this section, the court may nevertheless subsequently direct that it is not to be so admitted if—

(a) it appears to the court that—

    (i) the witness will not be available for cross-examination (whether conducted in the ordinary way or in accordance with any such direction), and

    (ii) the parties to the proceedings have not agreed that there is no need for the witness to be so available; or

(b) any rules of court requiring disclosure of the circumstances in which the recording was made have not been complied with to the satisfaction of the court.

(5) Where a recording is admitted under this section—

(a) the witness must be called by the party tendering it in evidence, unless—

    (i) a special measures direction provides for the witness's evidence on cross-examination to be given otherwise than by testimony in court, or

    (ii) the parties to the proceedings have agreed as mentioned in subsection (4)(a)(ii); and

(b) the witness may not give evidence in chief otherwise than by means of the recording—

    (i) as to any matter which, in the opinion of the court, has been dealt with adequately in the witness's recorded testimony, or

    (ii) without the permission of the court, as to any other matter which, in the opinion of the court, is dealt with in that testimony.

(6) Where in accordance with subsection (2) a special measures direction provides for part only of a recording to be admitted under this section, references in subsections (4) and (5) to the recording or to the witness's recorded testimony are references to the part of the recording or testimony which is to be so admitted.

(7) The court may give permission for the purposes of subsection (5)(b)(ii) if it appears to the court to be in the interests of justice to do so, and may do so either—

(a) on an application by a party to the proceedings, if there has been a material change of circumstances since the relevant time, or

(b) of its own motion.

(8) In subsection (7) "the relevant time" means—

(a) the time when the direction was given, or

(b) if a previous application has been made under that subsection, the time when the application (or last application) was made.

(9) The court may, in giving permission for the purposes of subsection (5)(b)(ii), direct that the evidence in question is to be given by the witness by means of a live link; and, if the court so directs, subsections (5) to (7) of section 24 shall apply in relation to that evidence as they apply in relation to evidence which is to be given in accordance with a special measures direction.

(10) A magistrates' court inquiring into an offence as examining justices under section 6 of the Magistrates' Courts Act 1980 may consider any video recording in relation to which it is proposed to apply for a special measures direction providing for it to be admitted at the trial in accordance with this section.

(11) Nothing in this section affects the admissibility of any video recording which would be admissible apart from this section.

Video recorded cross-examination or re-examination

28.—(1) Where a special measures direction provides for a video recording **110–013** to be admitted under section 27 as evidence in chief of the witness, the direction may also provide—

(a) for any cross-examination of the witness, and any re-examination, to be recorded by means of a video recording; and

(b) for such a recording to be admitted, so far as it relates to any such cross-examination or re-examination, as evidence of the witness under cross-examination or on re-examination, as the case may be.

(2) Such a recording must be made in the presence of such persons as rules of court or the direction may provide and in the absence of the accused, but in circumstances in which—

(a) the judge or justices (or both) and legal representatives acting in the proceedings are able to see and hear the examination of the witness and to communicate with the persons in whose presence the recording is being made, and

(b) the accused is able to see and hear any such examination and to communicate with any legal representative acting for him.

(3) Where two or more legal representatives are acting for a party to the proceedings, subsection (2)(a) and (b) are to be regarded as satisfied in relation to those representatives if at all material times they are satisfied in relation to at least one of them.

(4) Where a special measures direction provides for a recording to be admitted under this section, the court may nevertheless subsequently direct that it is not to be so admitted if any requirement of subsection (2) or rules of court or the direction has not been complied with to the satisfaction of the court.

(5) Where in pursuance of subsection (1) a recording has been made of any examination of the witness, the witness may not be subsequently cross-examined or re-examined in respect of any evidence given by the witness in the proceedings (whether in any recording admissible under section 27 or this section or otherwise than in such a recording) unless the court gives a further special

measures direction making such provision as is mentioned in subsection (1)(a) and (b) in relation to any subsequent cross-examination, and re-examination, of the witness.

(6) The court may only give such a further direction if it appears to the court—

(a) that the proposed cross-examination is sought by a party to the proceedings as a result of that party having become aware, since the time when the original recording was made in pursuance of subsection (1), of a matter which that party could not with reasonable diligence have ascertained by then, or

(b) that for any other reason it is in the interests of justice to give the further direction.

(7) Nothing in this section shall be read as applying in relation to any cross-examination of the witness by the accused in person (in a case where the accused is to be able to conduct any such cross-examination).

. . . . . .

Aids to communication

110–014   **30.** A special measures direction may provide for the witness, while giving evidence (whether by testimony in court or otherwise), to be provided with such device as the court considers appropriate with a view to enabling questions or answers to be communicated to or by the witness despite any disability or disorder or other impairment which the witness has or suffers from.

. . . . . .

Supplementary

Warning to jury

110–015   **32.** Where on a trial on indictment evidence has been given in accordance with a special measures direction, the judge must give the jury such warning (if any) as the judge considers necessary to ensure that the fact that the direction was given in relation to the witness does not prejudice the accused.

. . . . . .

CHAPTER II

PROTECTION OF WITNESSES FROM CROSS-EXAMINATION BY ACCUSED IN PERSON

General prohibitions

Complainants in proceedings for sexual offences

110–016   **34.** No person charged with a sexual offence may in any criminal proceedings cross-examine in person a witness who is the complainant, either—

(a) in connection with that offence, or

(b) in connection with any other offence (of whatever nature) with which that person is charged in the proceedings.

Child complainants and other child witnesses

35.—(1) No person charged with an offence to which this section applies **110–017** may in any criminal proceedings cross-examine in person a protected witness, either—

    (a) in connection with that offence, or

    (b) in connection with any other offence (of whatever nature) with which that person is charged in the proceedings.

(2) For the purposes of subsection (1) a "protected witness" is a witness who—

    (a) either is the complainant or is alleged to have been a witness to the commission of the offence to which this section applies, and

    (b) either is a child or falls to be cross-examined after giving evidence in chief (whether wholly or in part)—

        (i) by means of a video recording made (for the purposes of section 27) at a time when the witness was a child, or

        (ii) in any other way at any such time.

(3) The offences to which this section applies are—

    (a) any offence under—

        (i) the Sexual Offences Act 1956,

        (ii) the Indecency with Children Act 1960,

        (iii) the Sexual Offences Act 1967,

        (iv) section 54 of the Criminal Law Act 1977, or

        (v) the Protection of Children Act 1978;

    (b) kidnapping, false imprisonment or an offence under section 1 or 2 of the Child Abduction Act 1984;

    (c) any offence under section 1 of the Children and Young Persons Act 1933;

    (d) any offence (not within any of the preceding paragraphs) which involves an assault on, or injury or a threat of injury to, any person.

(4) In this section "child" means—

    (a) where the offence falls within subsection (3)(a), a person under the age of 17; or

    (b) where the offence falls within subsection (3)(b), (c) or (d), a person under the age of 14.

(5) For the purposes of this section "witness" includes a witness who is charged with an offence in the proceedings.

Prohibition imposed by court

Direction prohibiting accused from cross-examining particular witness

36.—(1) This section applies where, in a case where neither of sections 34 **110–018** and 35 operates to prevent an accused in any criminal proceedings from cross-examining a witness in person—

(a) the prosecutor makes an application for the court to give a direction under this section in relation to the witness, or

(b) the court of its own motion raises the issue whether such a direction should be given.

(2) If it appears to the court—

(a) that the quality of evidence given by the witness on cross-examination—

(i) is likely to be diminished if the cross-examination (or further cross-examination) is conducted by the accused in person, and

(ii) would be likely to be improved if a direction were given under this section, and

(b) that it would not be contrary to the interests of justice to give such a direction,

the court may give a direction prohibiting the accused from cross-examining (or further cross-examining) the witness in person.

(3) In determining whether subsection (2)(a) applies in the case of a witness the court must have regard, in particular, to—

(a) any views expressed by the witness as to whether or not the witness is content to be cross-examined by the accused in person;

(b) the nature of the questions likely to be asked, having regard to the issues in the proceedings and the defence case advanced so far (if any);

(c) any behaviour on the part of the accused at any stage of the proceedings, both generally and in relation to the witness;

(d) any relationship (of whatever nature) between the witness and the accused;

(e) whether any person (other than the accused) is or has at any time been charged in the proceedings with a sexual offence or an offence to which section 35 applies, and (if so) whether section 34 or 35 operates or would have operated to prevent that person from cross-examining the witness in person;

(f) any direction under section 19 which the court has given, or proposes to give, in relation to the witness.

(4) For the purposes of this section—

(a) "witness", in relation to an accused, does not include any other person who is charged with an offence in the proceedings; and

(b) any reference to the quality of a witness's evidence shall be construed in accordance with section 16(5).

. . . . . .

Cross-examination on behalf of accused

Defence representation for purposes of cross-examination

110–019   **38.**—(1) This section applies where an accused is prevented from cross-examining a witness in person by virtue of section 34, 35 or 36.

(2) Where it appears to the court that this section applies, it must—

(a) invite the accused to arrange for a legal representative to act for him for the purpose of cross-examining the witness; and

(b) require the accused to notify the court, by the end of such period as it may specify, whether a legal representative is to act for him for that purpose.

(3) If by the end of the period mentioned in subsection (2)(b) either—

(a) the accused has notified the court that no legal representative is to act for him for the purpose of cross-examining the witness, or
(b) no notification has been received by the court and it appears to the court that no legal representative is to so act,

the court must consider whether it is necessary in the interests of justice for the witness to be cross-examined by a legal representative appointed to represent the interests of the accused.

(4) If the court decides that it is necessary in the interests of justice for the witness to be so cross-examined, the court must appoint a qualified legal representative (chosen by the court) to cross-examine the witness in the interests of the accused.

(5) A person so appointed shall not be responsible to the accused.

(6) Rules of court may make provision—

(a) as to the time when, and the manner in which, subsection (2) is to be complied with;
(b) in connection with the appointment of a legal representative under subsection (4), and in particular for securing that a person so appointed is provided with evidence or other material relating to the proceedings.

(7) Rules of court made in pursuance of subsection (6)(b) may make provision for the application, with such modifications as are specified in the rules, of any of the provisions of—

(a) Part I of the Criminal Procedure and Investigations Act 1996 (disclosure of material in connection with criminal proceedings), or
(b) the Sexual Offences (Protected Material) Act 1997.

(8) For the purposes of this section—

(a) any reference to cross-examination includes (in a case where a direction is given under section 36 after the accused has begun cross-examining the witness) a reference to further cross-examination; and
(b) "qualified legal representative" means a legal representative who has a right of audience (within the meaning of the Courts and Legal Services Act 1990) in relation to the proceedings before the court.

Warning to jury

39.—(1) Where on a trial on indictment an accused is prevented from cross-examining a witness in person by virtue of section 34, 35 or 36, the judge must give the jury such warning (if any) as the judge considers necessary to ensure that the accused is not prejudiced—   **110–020**

(a) by any inferences that might be drawn from the fact that the accused has been prevented from cross-examining the witness in person;
(b) where the witness has been cross-examined by a legal representative appointed under section 38(4), by the fact that the cross-examination

was carried out by such a legal representative and not by a person acting as the accused's own legal representative.

(2) Subsection (8)(a) of section 38 applies for the purposes of this section as it applies for the purposes of section 38.

. . . . . .

Chapter III

Protection of Complainants in Proceedings for Sexual Offences

Restriction on evidence or questions about complainant's sexual history

110–021 **41.**—(1) If at a trial a person is charged with a sexual offence, then, except with the leave of the court—

(a) no evidence may be adduced, and
(b) no question may be asked in cross-examination,

by or on behalf of any accused at the trial, about any sexual behaviour of the complainant.

(2) The court may give leave in relation to any evidence or question only on an application made by or on behalf of an accused, and may not give such leave unless it is satisfied—

(a) that subsection (3) or (5) applies, and
(b) that a refusal of leave might have the result of rendering unsafe a conclusion of the jury or (as the case may be) the court on any relevant issue in the case.

(3) This subsection applies if the evidence or question relates to a relevant issue in the case and either—

(a) that issue is not an issue of consent; or
(b) it is an issue of consent and the sexual behaviour of the complainant to which the evidence or question relates is alleged to have taken place at or about the same time as the event which is the subject matter of the charge against the accused; or
(c) it is an issue of consent and the sexual behaviour of the complainant to which the evidence or question relates is alleged to have been, in any respect, so similar—

(i) to any sexual behaviour of the complainant which (according to evidence adduced or to be adduced by or on behalf of the accused) took place as part of the event which is the subject matter of the charge against the accused, or
(ii) to any other sexual behaviour of the complainant which (according to such evidence) took place at or about the same time as that event,

that the similarity cannot reasonably be explained as a coincidence.

(4) For the purposes of subsection (3) no evidence or question shall be regarded as relating to a relevant issue in the case if it appears to the court to be reasonable to assume that the purpose (or main purpose) for which it would

be adduced or asked is to establish or elicit material for impugning the credibility of the complainant as a witness.

(5) This subsection applies if the evidence or question—

(a) relates to any evidence adduced by the prosecution about any sexual behaviour of the complainant; and

(b) in the opinion of the court, would go no further than is necessary to enable the evidence adduced by the prosecution to be rebutted or explained by or on behalf of the accused.

(6) For the purposes of subsections (3) and (5) the evidence or question must relate to a specific instance (or specific instances) of alleged sexual behaviour on the part of the complainant (and accordingly nothing in those subsections is capable of applying in relation to the evidence or question to the extent that it does not so relate).

(7) Where this section applies in relation to a trial by virtue of the fact that one or more of a number of persons charged in the proceedings is or are charged with a sexual offence—

(a) it shall cease to apply in relation to the trial if the prosecutor decides not to proceed with the case against that person or those persons in respect of that charge; but

(b) it shall not cease to do so in the event of that person or those persons pleading guilty to, or being convicted of, that charge.

(8) Nothing in this section authorises any evidence to be adduced or any question to be asked which cannot be adduced or asked apart from this section.

. . . . . .

Chapter IV

Reporting Restrictions

Reports relating to persons under 18

Restrictions on reporting alleged offences involving persons under 18

44.—(1) This section applies (subject to subsection (3)) where a criminal **110–022** investigation has begun in respect of—

(a) an alleged offence against the law of—

(i) England and Wales, or
(ii) Northern Ireland; or

(b) an alleged civil offence (other than an offence falling within paragraph (a)) committed (whether or not in the United Kingdom) by a person subject to service law.

(2) No matter relating to any person involved in the offence shall while he is under the age of 18 be included in any publication if it is likely to lead members of the public to identify him as a person involved in the offence.

(3) The restrictions imposed by subsection (2) cease to apply once there are proceedings in a court (whether a court in England and Wales, a service court or a court in Northern Ireland) in respect of the offence.

(4) For the purposes of subsection (2) any reference to a person involved in the offence is to—

(a) a person by whom the offence is alleged to have been committed; or
(b) if this paragraph applies to the publication in question by virtue of subsection (5)—

    (i) a person against or in respect of whom the offence is alleged to have been committed, or
    (ii) a person who is alleged to have been a witness to the commission of the offence;

except that paragraph (b)(i) does not include a person in relation to whom section 1 of the Sexual Offences (Amendment) Act 1992 (anonymity of victims of certain sexual offences) applies in connection with the offence.

(5) Subsection (4)(b) applies to a publication if—

(a) where it is a relevant programme, it is transmitted, or
(b) in the case of any other publication, it is published,

on or after such date as may be specified in an order made by the Secretary of State.

(6) The matters relating to a person in relation to which the restrictions imposed by subsection (2) apply (if their inclusion in any publication is likely to have the result mentioned in that subsection) include in particular—

(a) his name,
(b) his address,
(c) the identity of any school or other educational establishment attended by him,
(d) the identity of any place of work, and
(e) any still or moving picture of him.

(7) Any appropriate criminal court may by order dispense, to any extent specified in the order, with the restrictions imposed by subsection (2) in relation to a person if it is satisfied that it is necessary in the interests of justice to do so.

(8) However, when deciding whether to make such an order dispensing (to any extent) with the restrictions imposed by subsection (2) in relation to a person, the court shall have regard to the welfare of that person.

(9) In subsection (7) "appropriate criminal court" means—

(a) in a case where this section applies by virtue of subsection (1)(a)(i) or (ii), any court in England and Wales or (as the case may be) in Northern Ireland which has any jurisdiction in, or in relation to, any criminal proceedings (but not a service court unless the offence is alleged to have been committed by a person subject to service law);
(b) in a case where this section applies by virtue of subsection (1)(b), any court falling within paragraph (a) or a service court.

(10) The power under subsection (7) of a magistrates' court in England and Wales may be exercised by a single justice.

(11) In the case of a decision of a magistrates' court in England and Wales, or a court of summary jurisdiction in Northern Ireland, to make or refuse to make an order under subsection (7), the following persons, namely—

(a) any person who was a party to the proceedings on the application for the order, and

(b) with the leave of the Crown Court, any other person,

may, in accordance with rules of court, appeal to the Crown Court against that decision or appear or be represented at the hearing of such an appeal.

(12) On such an appeal the Crown Court—

(a) may make such order as is necessary to give effect to its determination of the appeal; and

(b) may also make such incidental or consequential orders as appear to it to be just.

(13) In this section—

(a) "civil offence" means an act or omission which, if committed in England and Wales, would be an offence against the law of England and Wales;

(b) any reference to a criminal investigation, in relation to an alleged offence, is to an investigation conducted by police officers, or other persons charged with the duty of investigating offences, with a view to it being ascertained whether a person should be charged with the offence;

(c) any reference to a person subject to service law is to—

(i) a person subject to military law, air-force law or the Naval Discipline Act 1957, or

(ii) any other person to whom provisions of Part II of the Army Act 1955, Part II of the Air Force Act 1955 or Parts I and II of the Naval Discipline Act 1957 apply (whether with or without any modifications).

Power to restrict reporting of criminal proceedings involving persons under 18

45.—(1) This section applies (subject to subsection (2)) in relation to—   **110–023**

(a) any criminal proceedings in any court (other than a service court) in England and Wales or Northern Ireland; and

(b) any proceedings (whether in the United Kingdom or elsewhere) in any service court.

(2) This section does not apply in relation to any proceedings to which section 49 of the Children and Young Persons Act 1933 applies.

(3) The court may direct that no matter relating to any person concerned in the proceedings shall while he is under the age of 18 be included in any publication if it is likely to lead members of the public to identify him as a person concerned in the proceedings.

(4) The court or an appellate court may by direction ("an excepting direction") dispense, to any extent specified in the excepting direction, with the restrictions imposed by a direction under subsection (3) if it is satisfied that it is necessary in the interests of justice to do so.

(5) The court or an appellate court may also by direction ("an excepting direction") dispense, to any extent specified in the excepting direction, with the restrictions imposed by a direction under subsection (3) if it is satisfied—

(a) that their effect is to impose a substantial and unreasonable restriction on the reporting of the proceedings, and

(b) that it is in the public interest to remove or relax that restriction;

but no excepting direction shall be given under this subsection by reason only of the fact that the proceedings have been determined in any way or have been abandoned.

(6) When deciding whether to make—

(a) a direction under subsection (3) in relation to a person, or
(b) an excepting direction under subsection (4) or (5) by virtue of which the restrictions imposed by a direction under subsection (3) would be dispensed with (to any extent) in relation to a person,

the court or (as the case may be) the appellate court shall have regard to the welfare of that person.

(7) For the purposes of subsection (3) any reference to a person concerned in the proceedings is to a person—

(a) against or in respect of whom the proceedings are taken, or
(b) who is a witness in the proceedings.

(8) The matters relating to a person in relation to which the restrictions imposed by a direction under subsection (3) apply (if their inclusion in any publication is likely to have the result mentioned in that subsection) include in particular—

(a) his name,
(b) his address,
(c) the identity of any school or other educational establishment attended by him,
(d) the identity of any place of work, and
(e) any still or moving picture of him.

(9) A direction under subsection (3) may be revoked by the court or an appellate court.

(10) An excepting direction—

(a) may be given at the time the direction under subsection (3) is given or subsequently; and
(b) may be varied or revoked by the court or an appellate court.

(11) In this section "appellate court", in relation to any proceedings in a court, means a court dealing with an appeal (including an appeal by way of case stated) arising out of the proceedings or with any further appeal.

Reports relating to adult witnesses

Power to restrict reports about certain adult witness in criminal proceedings

110–024   46.—(1) This section applies where—

(a) in any criminal proceedings in any court (other than a service court) in England and Wales or Northern Ireland, or
(b) in any proceedings (whether in the United Kingdom or elsewhere) in any service court,

a party to the proceedings makes an application for the court to give a reporting direction in relation to a witness in the proceedings (other than the accused) who has attained the age of 18.

In this section "reporting direction" has the meaning given by subsection (6).
(2) If the court determines—

(a) that the witness is eligible for protection, and
(b) that giving a reporting direction in relation to the witness is likely to improve—

(i) the quality of evidence given by the witness, or
(ii) the level of co-operation given by the witness to any party to the proceedings in connection with that party's preparation of its case,

the court may give a reporting direction in relation to the witness.

(3) For the purposes of this section a witness is eligible for protection if the court is satisfied—

(a) that the quality of evidence given by the witness, or
(b) the level of co-operation given by the witness to any party to the proceedings in connection with that party's preparation of its case,

is likely to be diminished by reason of fear or distress on the part of the witness in connection with being identified by members of the public as a witness in the proceedings.
(4) In determining whether a witness is eligible for protection the court must take into account, in particular—

(a) the nature and alleged circumstances of the offence to which the proceedings relate;
(b) the age of the witness;
(c) such of the following matters as appear to the court to be relevant, namely—

(i) the social and cultural background and ethnic origins of the witness,
(ii) the domestic and employment circumstances of the witness, and
(iii) any religious beliefs or political opinions of the witness;

(d) any behaviour towards the witness on the part of—

(i) the accused,
(ii) members of the family or associates of the accused, or
(iii) any other person who is likely to be an accused or a witness in the proceedings.

(5) In determining that question the court must in addition consider any views expressed by the witness.
(6) For the purposes of this section a reporting direction in relation to a witness is a direction that no matter relating to the witness shall during the witness's lifetime be included in any publication if it is likely to lead members of the public to identify him as being a witness in the proceedings.
(7) The matters relating to a witness in relation to which the restrictions imposed by a reporting direction apply (if their inclusion in any publication is likely to have the result mentioned in subsection (6)) include in particular—

(a) the witness's name,
(b) the witness's address,
(c) the identity of any educational establishment attended by the witness,
(d) the identity of any place of work, and
(e) any still or moving picture of the witness.

(8) In determining whether to give a reporting direction the court shall consider—

    (a) whether it would be in the interests of justice to do so, and

    (b) the public interest in avoiding the imposition of a substantial and unreasonable restriction on the reporting of the proceedings.

(9) The court or an appellate court may by direction ("an excepting direction") dispense, to any extent specified in the excepting direction, with the restrictions imposed by a reporting direction if—

    (a) it is satisfied that it is necessary in the interests of justice to do so, or

    (b) it is satisfied—

        (i) that the effect of those restrictions is to impose a substantial and unreasonable restriction on the reporting of the proceedings, and

        (ii) that it is in the public interest to remove or relax that restriction;

    but no excepting direction shall be given under paragraph (b) by reason only of the fact that the proceedings have been determined in any way or have been abandoned.

(10) A reporting direction may be revoked by the court or an appellate court.

(11) An excepting direction—

    (a) may be given at the time the reporting direction is given or subsequently; and

    (b) may be varied or revoked by the court or an appellate court.

(12) In this section—

    (a) "appellate court", in relation to any proceedings in a court, means a court dealing with an appeal (including an appeal by way of case stated) arising out of the proceedings or with any further appeal;

    (b) references to the quality of a witness's evidence are to its quality in terms of completeness, coherence and accuracy (and for this purpose "coherence" refers to a witness's ability in giving evidence to give answers which address the questions put to the witness and can be understood both individually and collectively);

    (c) references to the preparation of the case of a party to any proceedings include, where the party is the prosecution, the carrying out of investigations into any offence at any time charged in the proceedings.

Freedom of Information Act 2000

(2000, c. 36)

111–001 *An Act to make provision for the disclosure of information held by public authorities or by persons providing services for them and to amend the Data Protection Act 1998 and the Public Records Act 1958; and for connected purposes.* [30th November 2000]

Part I

Access to Information held by Public Authorities

Right to information

General right of access to information held by public authorities

1.—(1) Any person making a request for information to a public authority is **111–002**
entitled—

(a) to be informed in writing by the public authority whether it holds
information of the description specified in the request, and
(b) if that is the case, to have that information communicated to him.

(2) Subsection (1) has effect subject to the following provisions of this section
and to the provisions of sections 2, 9, 12 and 14.
(3) Where a public authority—

(a) reasonably requires further information in order to identify and locate
the information requested, and
(b) has informed the applicant of that requirement,

the authority is not obliged to comply with subsection (1) unless it is supplied
with that further information.
(4) The information—

(a) in respect of which the applicant is to be informed under subsection
(1)(a), or
(b) which is to be communicated under subsection (1)(b),

is the information in question held at the time when the request is received,
except that account may be taken of any amendment or deletion made between
that time and the time when the information is to be communicated under subsection (1)(b), being an amendment or deletion that would have been made
regardless of the receipt of the request.
(5) A public authority is to be taken to have complied with subsection (1)(a)
in relation to any information if it has communicated the information to the
applicant in accordance with subsection (1)(b).
(6) In this Act, the duty of a public authority to comply with subsection (1)(a)
is referred to as "the duty to confirm or deny".

Effect of the exemptions in Part II

2.—(1) Where any provision of Part II states that the duty to confirm or deny **111–003**
does not arise in relation to any information, the effect of the provision is that
where either—

(a) the provision confers absolute exemption, or
(b) in all the circumstances of the case, the public interest in maintaining
the exclusion of the duty to confirm or deny outweighs the public interest in disclosing whether the public authority holds the information,

section 1(1)(a) does not apply.
(2) In respect of any information which is exempt information by virtue of
any provision of Part II, section 1(1)(b) does not apply if or to the extent that—

   (a) the information is exempt information by virtue of a provision conferring absolute exemption, or

   (b) in all the circumstances of the case, the public interest in maintaining
the exemption outweighs the public interest in disclosing the information.

(3) For the purposes of this section, the following provisions of Part II (and
no others) are to be regarded as conferring absolute exemption—

   (a) section 21,

   (b) section 23,

   (c) section 32,

   (d) section 34,

   (e) section 36 so far as relating to information held by the House of Commons or the House of Lords,

   (f) in section 40—

      (i) subsection (1), and

      (ii) subsection (2) so far as relating to cases where the first condition
referred to in that subsection is satisfied by virtue of subsection
(3)(a)(i) or (b) of that section,

   (g) section 41, and

   (h) section 44.

Public authorities

111–004   **3.**—(1) In this Act "public authority" means—

   (a) subject to section 4(4), any body which, any other person who, or the
holder of any office which—

      (i) is listed in Schedule 1, or

      (ii) is designated by order under section 5, or

   (b) a publicly-owned company as defined by section 6.

(2) For the purposes of this Act, information is held by a public authority if—

   (a) it is held by the authority, otherwise than on behalf of another
person, or

   (b) it is held by another person on behalf of the authority.

Amendment of Schedule 1

111–005   **4.**—(1) The Lord Chancellor may by order amend Schedule 1 by adding to
that Schedule a reference to any body or the holder of any office which (in
either case) is not for the time being listed in that Schedule but as respects which
both the first and the second conditions below are satisfied.

(2) The first condition is that the body or office—

   (a) is established by virtue of Her Majesty's prerogative or by an enactment or by subordinate legislation, or

   (b) is established in any other way by a Minister of the Crown in his
capacity as Minister, by a government department or by the National
Assembly for Wales.

(3) The second condition is—

    (a) in the case of a body, that the body is wholly or partly constituted by appointment made by the Crown, by a Minister of the Crown, by a government department or by the National Assembly for Wales, or

    (b) in the case of an office, that appointments to the office are made by the Crown, by a Minister of the Crown, by a government department or by the National Assembly for Wales.

(4) If either the first or the second condition above ceases to be satisfied as respects any body or office which is listed in Part VI or VII of Schedule 1, that body or the holder of that office shall cease to be a public authority by virtue of the entry in question.

(5) The Lord Chancellor may by order amend Schedule 1 by removing from Part VI or VII of that Schedule an entry relating to any body or office—

    (a) which has ceased to exist, or

    (b) as respects which either the first or the second condition above has ceased to be satisfied.

(6) An order under subsection (1) may relate to a specified person or office or to persons or offices falling within a specified description.

(7) Before making an order under subsection (1), the [Lord Chancellor] shall—

    (a) if the order adds to Part II, III, IV or VI of Schedule 1 a reference to—

        (i) a body whose functions are exercisable only or mainly in or as regards Wales, or

        (ii) the holder of an office whose functions are exercisable only or mainly in or as regards Wales,

    consult the National Assembly for Wales, and

    (b) if the order relates to a body which, or the holder of any office who, if the order were made, would be a Northern Ireland public authority, consult the First Minister and deputy First Minister in Northern Ireland.

(8) This section has effect subject to section 80.

(9) In this section "Minister of the Crown" includes a Northern Ireland Minister.

Further power to designate public authorities

5.—(1) The Lord Chancellor may by order designate as a public authority for **111–006** the purposes of this Act any person who is neither listed in Schedule 1 nor capable of being added to that Schedule by an order under section 4(1), but who—

    (a) appears to the Lord Chancellor to exercise functions of a public nature, or

    (b) is providing under a contract made with a public authority any service whose provision is a function of that authority.

(2) An order under this section may designate a specified person or office or persons or offices falling within a specified description.

(3) Before making an order under this section, the [Lord Chancellor] shall consult every person to whom the order relates, or persons appearing to him to represent such persons.

(4) This section has effect subject to section 80.

Publicly-owned companies

111–007   6.—(1) A company is a "publicly-owned company" for the purposes of section 3(1)(b) if—

(a) it is wholly owned by the Crown, or
(b) it is wholly owned by any public authority listed in Schedule 1 other than—

    (i) a government department, or
    (ii) any authority which is listed only in relation to particular information.

(2) For the purposes of this section—

(a) a company is wholly owned by the Crown if it has no members except—

    (i) Ministers of the Crown, government departments or companies wholly owned by the Crown, or
    (ii) persons acting on behalf of Ministers of the Crown, government departments or companies wholly owned by the Crown, and

(b) a company is wholly owned by a public authority other than a government department if it has no members except—

    (i) that public authority or companies wholly owned by that public authority, or
    (ii) persons acting on behalf of that public authority or of companies wholly owned by that public authority.

(3) In this section—

"company" includes any body corporate;
"Minister of the Crown" includes a Northern Ireland Minister.

Public authorities to which Act has limited application

111–008   7.—(1) Where a public authority is listed in Schedule 1 only in relation to information of a specified description, nothing in Parts I to V of this Act applies to any other information held by the authority.
(2) An order under section 4(1) may, in adding an entry to Schedule 1, list the public authority only in relation to information of a specified description.
(3) The Lord Chancellor may by order amend Schedule 1—

(a) by limiting to information of a specified description the entry relating to any public authority, or
(b) by removing or amending any limitation to information of a specified description which is for the time being contained in any entry.

(4) Before making an order under subsection (3), the Lord Chancellor shall—

(a) if the order relates to the National Assembly for Wales or a Welsh public authority, consult the National Assembly for Wales,
(b) if the order relates to the Northern Ireland Assembly, consult the Presiding Officer of that Assembly, and
(c) if the order relates to a Northern Ireland department or a Northern

Ireland public authority, consult the First Minister and deputy First Minister in Northern Ireland.

(5) An order under section 5(1)(a) must specify the functions of the public authority designated by the order with respect to which the designation is to have effect; and nothing in Parts I to V of this Act applies to information which is held by the authority but does not relate to the exercise of those functions.

(6) An order under section 5(1)(b) must specify the services provided under contract with respect to which the designation is to have effect; and nothing in Parts I to V of this Act applies to information which is held by the public authority designated by the order but does not relate to the provision of those services.

(7) Nothing in Parts I to V of this Act applies in relation to any information held by a publicly-owned company which is excluded information in relation to that company.

(8) In subsection (7) "excluded information", in relation to a publicly-owned company, means information which is of a description specified in relation to that company in an order made by the [Lord Chancellor] for the purposes of this subsection.

(9) In this section "publicly-owned company" has the meaning given by section 6.

Request for information

8.—(1) In this Act any reference to a "request for information" is a reference to such a request which— **111–009**

(a) is in writing,
(b) states the name of the applicant and an address for correspondence, and
(c) describes the information requested.

(2) For the purposes of subsection (1)(a), a request is to be treated as made in writing where the text of the request—

(a) is transmitted by electronic means,
(b) is received in legible form, and
(c) is capable of being used for subsequent reference.

Fees

9.—(1) A public authority to whom a request for information is made may, within the period for complying with section 1(1), give the applicant a notice in writing (in this Act referred to as a "fees notice") stating that a fee of an amount specified in the notice is to be charged by the authority for complying with section 1(1). **111–010**

(2) Where a fees notice has been given to the applicant, the public authority is not obliged to comply with section 1(1) unless the fee is paid within the period of three months beginning with the day on which the fees notice is given to the applicant.

(3) Subject to subsection (5), any fee under this section must be determined by the public authority in accordance with regulations made by the Secretary of State.

(4) Regulations under subsection (3) may, in particular, provide—

(a) that no fee is to be payable in prescribed cases,

    (b) that any fee is not to exceed such maximum as may be specified in, or determined in accordance with, the regulations, and

    (c) that any fee is to be calculated in such manner as may be prescribed by the regulations.

(5) Subsection (3) does not apply where provision is made by or under any enactment as to the fee that may be charged by the public authority for the disclosure of the information.

Time for compliance with request

111–011   **10.**—(1) Subject to subsections (2) and (3), a public authority must comply with section 1(1) promptly and in any event not later than the twentieth working day following the date of receipt.

(2) Where the authority has given a fees notice to the applicant and the fee is paid in accordance with section 9(2), the working days in the period beginning with the day on which the fees notice is given to the applicant and ending with the day on which the fee is received by the authority are to be disregarded in calculating for the purposes of subsection (1) the twentieth working day following the date of receipt.

(3) If, and to the extent that—

    (a) section 1(1)(a) would not apply if the condition in section 2(1)(b) were satisfied, or

    (b) section 1(1)(b) would not apply if the condition in section 2(2)(b) were satisfied,

the public authority need not comply with section 1(1)(a) or (b) until such time as is reasonable in the circumstances; but this subsection does not affect the time by which any notice under section 17(1) must be given.

(4) The Secretary of State may by regulations provide that subsections (1) and (2) are to have effect as if any reference to the twentieth working day following the date of receipt were a reference to such other day, not later than the sixtieth working day following the date of receipt, as may be specified in, or determined in accordance with, the regulations.

(5) Regulations under subsection (4) may—

    (a) prescribe different days in relation to different cases, and

    (b) confer a discretion on the Commissioner.

(6) In this section—

    "the date of receipt" means—

        (a) the day on which the public authority receives the request for information, or

        (b) if later, the day on which it receives the information referred to in section 1(3);

    "working day" means any day other than a Saturday, a Sunday, Christmas Day, Good Friday or a day which is a bank holiday under the Banking and Financial Dealings Act 1971 in any part of the United Kingdom.

Means by which communication to be made

111–012   **11.**—(1) Where, on making his request for information, the applicant expresses a preference for communication by any one or more of the following means, namely—

(a) the provision to the applicant of a copy of the information in permanent form or in another form acceptable to the applicant,

(b) the provision to the applicant of a reasonable opportunity to inspect a record containing the information, and

(c) the provision to the applicant of a digest or summary of the information in permanent form or in another form acceptable to the applicant,

the public authority shall so far as reasonably practicable give effect to that preference.

(2) In determining for the purposes of this section whether it is reasonably practicable to communicate information by particular means, the public authority may have regard to all the circumstances, including the cost of doing so.

(3) Where the public authority determines that it is not reasonably practicable to comply with any preference expressed by the applicant in making his request, the authority shall notify the applicant of the reasons for its determination.

(4) Subject to subsection (1), a public authority may comply with a request by communicating information by any means which are reasonable in the circumstances.

Exemption where cost of compliance exceeds appropriate limit

12.—(1) Section 1(1) does not oblige a public authority to comply with a **111–013** request for information if the authority estimates that the cost of complying with the request would exceed the appropriate limit.

(2) Subsection (1) does not exempt the public authority from its obligation to comply with paragraph (a) of section 1(1) unless the estimated cost of complying with that paragraph alone would exceed the appropriate limit.

(3) In subsections (1) and (2) "the appropriate limit" means such amount as may be prescribed, and different amounts may be prescribed in relation to different cases.

(4) The Secretary of State may by regulations provide that, in such circumstances as may be prescribed, where two or more requests for information are made to a public authority—

(a) by one person, or

(b) by different persons who appear to the public authority to be acting in concert or in pursuance of a campaign,

the estimated cost of complying with any of the requests is to be taken to be the estimated total cost of complying with all of them.

(5) The Secretary of State may by regulations make provision for the purposes of this section as to the costs to be estimated and as to the manner in which they are to be estimated.

Fees for disclosure where cost of compliance exceeds appropriate limit

13.—(1) A public authority may charge for the communication of any **111–014** information whose communication—

(a) is not required by section 1(1) because the cost of complying with the request for information exceeds the amount which is the appropriate limit for the purposes of section 12(1) and (2), and

(b) is not otherwise required by law,

such fee as may be determined by the public authority in accordance with regulations made by the Secretary of State.

(2) Regulations under this section may, in particular, provide—

(a) that any fee is not to exceed such maximum as may be specified in, or determined in accordance with, the regulations, and

(b) that any fee is to be calculated in such manner as may be prescribed by the regulations.

(3) Subsection (1) does not apply where provision is made by or under any enactment as to the fee that may be charged by the public authority for the disclosure of the information.

Vexatious or repeated requests

111–015 **14.**—(1) Section 1(1) does not oblige a public authority to comply with a request for information if the request is vexatious.

(2) Where a public authority has previously complied with a request for information which was made by any person, it is not obliged to comply with a subsequent identical or substantially similar request from that person unless a reasonable interval has elapsed between compliance with the previous request and the making of the current request.

Special provisions relating to public records transferred to Public Record Office, etc.

111–016 **15.**—(1) Where—

(a) the appropriate records authority receives a request for information which relates to information which is, or if it existed would be, contained in a transferred public record, and

(b) either of the conditions in subsection (2) is satisfied in relation to any of that information,

that authority shall, within the period for complying with section 1(1), send a copy of the request to the responsible authority.

(2) The conditions referred to in subsection (1)(b) are—

(a) that the duty to confirm or deny is expressed to be excluded only by a provision of Part II not specified in subsection (3) of section 2, and

(b) that the information is exempt information only by virtue of a provision of Part II not specified in that subsection.

(3) On receiving the copy, the responsible authority shall, within such time as is reasonable in all the circumstances, inform the appropriate records authority of the determination required by virtue of subsection (3) or (4) of section 66.

(4) In this Act "transferred public record" means a public record which has been transferred—

(a) to the Public Record Office,

(b) to another place of deposit appointed by the Lord Chancellor under the Public Records Act 1958, or

(c) to the Public Record Office of Northern Ireland.

(5) In this Act—

"appropriate records authority", in relation to a transferred public record, means—

(a) in a case falling within subsection (4)(a), the Public Record Office,

(b) in a case falling within subsection (4)(b), the Lord Chancellor, and

    (c) in a case falling within subsection (4)(c), the Public Record Office of Northern Ireland;

"responsible authority", in relation to a transferred public record, means—

    (a) in the case of a record transferred as mentioned in subsection (4)(a) or (b) from a government department in the charge of a Minister of the Crown, the Minister of the Crown who appears to the Lord Chancellor to be primarily concerned,

    (b) in the case of a record transferred as mentioned in subsection (4)(a) or (b) from any other person, the person who appears to the Lord Chancellor to be primarily concerned,

    (c) in the case of a record transferred to the Public Record Office of Northern Ireland from a government department in the charge of a Minister of the Crown, the Minister of the Crown who appears to the appropriate Northern Ireland Minister to be primarily concerned,

    (d) in the case of a record transferred to the Public Record Office of Northern Ireland from a Northern Ireland department, the Northern Ireland Minister who appears to the appropriate Northern Ireland Minister to be primarily concerned, or

    (e) in the case of a record transferred to the Public Record Office of Northern Ireland from any other person, the person who appears to the appropriate Northern Ireland Minister to be primarily concerned.

Duty to provide advice and assistance

16.—(1) It shall be the duty of a public authority to provide advice and assistance, so far as it would be reasonable to expect the authority to do so, to persons who propose to make, or have made, requests for information to it.   **111–017**

    (2) Any public authority which, in relation to the provision of advice or assistance in any case, conforms with the code of practice under section 45 is to be taken to comply with the duty imposed by subsection (1) in relation to that case.

Refusal of request

Refusal of request

17.—(1) A public authority which, in relation to any request for information, is to any extent relying on a claim that any provision of Part II relating to the duty to confirm or deny is relevant to the request or on a claim that information is exempt information must, within the time for complying with section 1(1), give the applicant a notice which—   **111–018**

    (a) states that fact,

    (b) specifies the exemption in question, and

    (c) states (if that would not otherwise be apparent) why the exemption applies.

  (2) Where—

    (a) in relation to any request for information, a public authority is, as respects any information, relying on a claim—

        (i) that any provision of Part II which relates to the duty to confirm or deny and is not specified in section 2(3) is relevant to the request, or

   (ii) that the information is exempt information only by virtue of a provision not specified in section 2(3), and

(b) at the time when the notice under subsection (1) is given to the applicant, the public authority (or, in a case falling within section 66(3) or (4), the responsible authority) has not yet reached a decision as to the application of subsection (1)(b) or (2)(b) of section 2,

the notice under subsection (1) must indicate that no decision as to the application of that provision has yet been reached and must contain an estimate of the date by which the authority expects that such a decision will have been reached.

(3) A public authority which, in relation to any request for information, is to any extent relying on a claim that subsection (1)(b) or (2)(b) of section 2 applies must, either in the notice under subsection (1) or in a separate notice given within such time as is reasonable in the circumstances, state the reasons for claiming—

(a) that, in all the circumstances of the case, the public interest in maintaining the exclusion of the duty to confirm or deny outweighs the public interest in disclosing whether the authority holds the information, or

(b) that, in all the circumstances of the case, the public interest in maintaining the exemption outweighs the public interest in disclosing the information.

(4) A public authority is not obliged to make a statement under subsection (1)(c) or (3) if, or to the extent that, the statement would involve the disclosure of information which would itself be exempt information.

(5) A public authority which, in relation to any request for information, is relying on a claim that section 12 or 14 applies must, within the time for complying with section 1(1), give the applicant a notice stating that fact.

(6) Subsection (5) does not apply where—

(a) the public authority is relying on a claim that section 14 applies,

(b) the authority has given the applicant a notice, in relation to a previous request for information, stating that it is relying on such a claim, and

(c) it would in all the circumstances be unreasonable to expect the authority to serve a further notice under subsection (5) in relation to the current request.

(7) A notice under subsection (1), (3) or (5) must—

(a) contain particulars of any procedure provided by the public authority for dealing with complaints about the handling of requests for information or state that the authority does not provide such a procedure, and

(b) contain particulars of the right conferred by section 50.

The Information Commissioner and the Information Tribunal

The Information Commissioner and the Information Tribunal

111–019   **18.**—(1) The Data Protection Commissioner shall be known instead as the Information Commissioner.

(2) The Data Protection Tribunal shall be known instead as the Information Tribunal.

(3) In this Act—

(a) the Information Commissioner is referred to as "the Commissioner", and

(b) the Information Tribunal is referred to as "the Tribunal".

(4) Schedule 2 (which makes provision consequential on subsections (1) and (2) and amendments of the Data Protection Act 1998 relating to the extension by this Act of the functions of the Commissioner and the Tribunal) has effect.

(5) If the person who held office as Data Protection Commissioner immediately before the day on which this Act is passed remains in office as Information Commissioner at the end of the period of two years beginning with that day, he shall vacate his office at the end of that period.

(6) Subsection (5) does not prevent the re-appointment of a person whose appointment is terminated by that subsection.

(7) In the application of paragraph 2(4)(b) and (5) of Schedule 5 to the Data Protection Act 1998 (Commissioner not to serve for more than fifteen years and not to be appointed, except in special circumstances, for a third or subsequent term) to anything done after the passing of this Act, there shall be left out of account any term of office served by virtue of an appointment made before the passing of this Act.

Publication schemes

Publication schemes

19.—(1) It shall be the duty of every public authority—   **111–020**

(a) to adopt and maintain a scheme which relates to the publication of information by the authority and is approved by the Commissioner (in this Act referred to as a "publication scheme"),

(b) to publish information in accordance with its publication scheme, and

(c) from time to time to review its publication scheme.

(2) A publication scheme must—

(a) specify classes of information which the public authority publishes or intends to publish,

(b) specify the manner in which information of each class is, or is intended to be, published, and

(c) specify whether the material is, or is intended to be, available to the public free of charge or on payment.

(3) In adopting or reviewing a publication scheme, a public authority shall have regard to the public interest—

(a) in allowing public access to information held by the authority, and

(b) in the publication of reasons for decisions made by the authority.

(4) A public authority shall publish its publication scheme in such manner as it thinks fit.

(5) The Commissioner may, when approving a scheme, provide that his approval is to expire at the end of a specified period.

(6) Where the Commissioner has approved the publication scheme of any public authority, he may at any time give notice to the public authority revoking his approval of the scheme as from the end of the period of six months beginning with the day on which the notice is given.

(7) Where the Commissioner—

(a) refuses to approve a proposed publication scheme, or
(b) revokes his approval of a publication scheme,

he must give the public authority a statement of his reasons for doing so.

Model publication schemes

111–021   **20.**—(1) The Commissioner may from time to time approve, in relation to public authorities falling within particular classes, model publication schemes prepared by him or by other persons.

(2) Where a public authority falling within the class to which an approved model scheme relates adopts such a scheme without modification, no further approval of the Commissioner is required so long as the model scheme remains approved; and where such an authority adopts such a scheme with modifications, the approval of the Commissioner is required only in relation to the modifications.

(3) The Commissioner may, when approving a model publication scheme, provide that his approval is to expire at the end of a specified period.

(4) Where the Commissioner has approved a model publication scheme, he may at any time publish, in such manner as he thinks fit, a notice revoking his approval of the scheme as from the end of the period of six months beginning with the day on which the notice is published.

(5) Where the Commissioner refuses to approve a proposed model publication scheme on the application of any person, he must give the person who applied for approval of the scheme a statement of the reasons for his refusal.

(6) Where the Commissioner refuses to approve any modifications under subsection (2), he must give the public authority a statement of the reasons for his refusal.

(7) Where the Commissioner revokes his approval of a model publication scheme, he must include in the notice under subsection (4) a statement of his reasons for doing so.

PART II

EXEMPT INFORMATION

Information accessible to applicant by other means

111–022   **21.**—(1) Information which is reasonably accessible to the applicant otherwise than under section 1 is exempt information.

(2) For the purposes of subsection (1)—

(a) information may be reasonably accessible to the applicant even though it is accessible only on payment, and
(b) information is to be taken to be reasonably accessible to the applicant if it is information which the public authority or any other person is obliged by or under any enactment to communicate (otherwise than by making the information available for inspection) to members of the public on request, whether free of charge or on payment.

(3) For the purposes of subsection (1), information which is held by a public authority and does not fall within subsection (2)(b) is not to be regarded as reasonably accessible to the applicant merely because the information is available from the public authority itself on request, unless the information is made

available in accordance with the authority's publication scheme and any payment required is specified in, or determined in accordance with, the scheme.

Information intended for future publication

22.—(1) Information is exempt information if—

111–023

(a) the information is held by the public authority with a view to its publication, by the authority or any other person, at some future date (whether determined or not),

(b) the information was already held with a view to such publication at the time when the request for information was made, and

(c) it is reasonable in all the circumstances that the information should be withheld from disclosure until the date referred to in paragraph (a).

(2) The duty to confirm or deny does not arise if, or to the extent that, compliance with section 1(1)(a) would involve the disclosure of any information (whether or not already recorded) which falls within subsection (1).

Information supplied by, or relating to, bodies dealing with security matters

23.—(1) Information held by a public authority is exempt information if it 111–024
was directly or indirectly supplied to the public authority by, or relates to, any of the bodies specified in subsection (3).

(2) A certificate signed by a Minister of the Crown certifying that the information to which it applies was directly or indirectly supplied by, or relates to, any of the bodies specified in subsection (3) shall, subject to section 60, be conclusive evidence of that fact.

(3) The bodies referred to in subsections (1) and (2) are—

(a) the Security Service,

(b) the Secret Intelligence Service,

(c) the Government Communications Headquarters,

(d) the special forces,

(e) the Tribunal established under section 65 of the Regulation of Investigatory Powers Act 2000,

(f) the Tribunal established under section 7 of the Interception of Communications Act 1985,

(g) the Tribunal established under section 5 of the Security Service Act 1989,

(h) the Tribunal established under section 9 of the Intelligence Services Act 1994,

(i) the Security Vetting Appeals Panel,

(j) the Security Commission,

(k) the National Criminal Intelligence Service, and

(l) the Service Authority for the National Criminal Intelligence Service.

(4) In subsection (3)(c) "the Government Communications Headquarters" includes any unit or part of a unit of the armed forces of the Crown which is for the time being required by the Secretary of State to assist the Government Communications Headquarters in carrying out its functions.

(5) The duty to confirm or deny does not arise if, or to the extent that, compliance with section 1(1)(a) would involve the disclosure of any information (whether or not already recorded) which was directly or indirectly supplied to the public authority by, or relates to, any of the bodies specified in subsection (3).

National security

111–025   24.—(1) Information which does not fall within section 23(1) is exempt information if exemption from section 1(1)(b) is required for the purpose of safeguarding national security.

(2) The duty to confirm or deny does not arise if, or to the extent that, exemption from section 1(1)(a) is required for the purpose of safeguarding national security.

(3) A certificate signed by a Minister of the Crown certifying that exemption from section 1(1)(b), or from section 1(1)(a) and (b), is, or at any time was, required for the purpose of safeguarding national security shall, subject to section 60, be conclusive evidence of that fact.

(4) A certificate under subsection (3) may identify the information to which it applies by means of a general description and may be expressed to have prospective effect.

. . . . . .

Defence

111–026   26.—(1) Information is exempt information if its disclosure under this Act would, or would be likely to, prejudice—

    (a) the defence of the British Islands or of any colony, or
    (b) the capability, effectiveness or security of any relevant forces.

(2) In subsection (1)(b) "relevant forces" means —

    (a) the armed forces of the Crown, and
    (b) any forces co-operating with those forces,

or any part of any of those forces.

(3) The duty to confirm or deny does not arise if, or to the extent that, compliance with section 1(1)(a) would, or would be likely to, prejudice any of the matters mentioned in subsection (1).

International relations

111–027   27.—(1) Information is exempt information if its disclosure under this Act would, or would be likely to, prejudice—

    (a) relations between the United Kingdom and any other State,
    (b) relations between the United Kingdom and any international organisation or international court,
    (c) the interests of the United Kingdom abroad, or
    (d) the promotion or protection by the United Kingdom of its interests abroad.

(2) Information is also exempt information if it is confidential information obtained from a State other than the United Kingdom or from an international organisation or international court.

(3) For the purposes of this section, any information obtained from a State, organisation or court is confidential at any time while the terms on which it was obtained require it to be held in confidence or while the circumstances in which it was obtained make it reasonable for the State, organisation or court to expect that it will be so held.

(4) The duty to confirm or deny does not arise if, or to the extent that, compliance with section 1(1)(a)—

(a) would, or would be likely to, prejudice any of the matters mentioned in subsection (1), or

(b) would involve the disclosure of any information (whether or not already recorded) which is confidential information obtained from a State other than the United Kingdom or from an international organisation or international court.

(5) In this section—

"international court" means any international court which is not an international organisation and which is established—

(a) by a resolution of an international organisation of which the United Kingdom is a member, or

(b) by an international agreement to which the United Kingdom is a party;

"international organisation" means any international organisation whose members include any two or more States, or any organ of such an organisation;

"State" includes the government of any State and any organ of its government, and references to a State other than the United Kingdom include references to any territory outside the United Kingdom.

Relations within the United Kingdom

28.—(1) Information is exempt information if its disclosure under this Act **111–028** would, or would be likely to, prejudice relations between any administration in the United Kingdom and any other such administration.

(2) In subsection (1) "administration in the United Kingdom" means—

(a) the government of the United Kingdom,

(b) the Scottish Administration,

(c) the Executive Committee of the Northern Ireland Assembly, or

(d) the National Assembly for Wales.

(3) The duty to confirm or deny does not arise if, or to the extent that, compliance with section 1(1)(a) would, or would be likely to, prejudice any of the matters mentioned in subsection (1).

The economy

29.—(1) Information is exempt information if its disclosure under this Act **111–029** would, or would be likely to, prejudice—

(a) the economic interests of the United Kingdom or of any part of the United Kingdom, or

(b) the financial interests of any administration in the United Kingdom, as defined by section 28(2).

(2) The duty to confirm or deny does not arise if, or to the extent that, compliance with section 1(1)(a) would, or would be likely to, prejudice any of the matters mentioned in subsection (1).

Investigations and proceedings conducted by public authorities

111–030 **30.**—(1) Information held by a public authority is exempt information if it has at any time been held by the authority for the purposes of—

    (a) any investigation which the public authority has a duty to conduct with a view to it being ascertained—

        (i) whether a person should be charged with an offence, or
        (ii) whether a person charged with an offence is guilty of it,

    (b) any investigation which is conducted by the authority and in the circumstances may lead to a decision by the authority to institute criminal proceedings which the authority has power to conduct, or
    (c) any criminal proceedings which the authority has power to conduct.

(2) Information held by a public authority is exempt information if—

    (a) it was obtained or recorded by the authority for the purposes of its functions relating to—

        (i) investigations falling within subsection (1)(a) or (b),
        (ii) criminal proceedings which the authority has power to conduct,
        (iii) investigations (other than investigations falling within subsection (1)(a) or (b)) which are conducted by the authority for any of the purposes specified in section 31(2) and either by virtue of Her Majesty's prerogative or by virtue of powers conferred by or under any enactment, or
        (iv) civil proceedings which are brought by or on behalf of the authority and arise out of such investigations, and

    (b) it relates to the obtaining of information from confidential sources.

(3) The duty to confirm or deny does not arise in relation to information which is (or if it were held by the public authority would be) exempt information by virtue of subsection (1) or (2).

(4) In relation to the institution or conduct of criminal proceedings or the power to conduct them, references in subsection (1)(b) or (c) and subsection (2)(a) to the public authority include references—

    (a) to any officer of the authority,
    (b) in the case of a government department other than a Northern Ireland department, to the Minister of the Crown in charge of the department, and
    (c) in the case of a Northern Ireland department, to the Northern Ireland Minister in charge of the department.

(5) In this section—

"criminal proceedings" includes—

    (a) proceedings before a court-martial constituted under the Army Act 1955, the Air Force Act 1955 or the Naval Discipline Act 1957,
    (b) proceedings on dealing summarily with a charge under the Army Act 1955 or the Air Force Act 1955 or on summary trial under the Naval Discipline Act 1957,
    (c) proceedings before a court established by section 83ZA of the Army Act 1955, section 83ZA of the Air Force Act 1955 or section 52FF of the Naval Discipline Act 1957 (summary appeal courts),

(d) proceedings before the Courts-Martial Appeal Court, and

(e) proceedings before a Standing Civilian Court;

"offence" includes any offence under the Army Act 1955, the Air Force Act 1955 or the Naval Discipline Act 1957.

(6) In the application of this section to Scotland—

(a) in subsection (1)(b), for the words from "a decision" to the end there is substituted "a decision by the authority to make a report to the procurator fiscal for the purpose of enabling him to determine whether criminal proceedings should be instituted",

(b) in subsections (1)(c) and (2)(a)(ii) for "which the authority has power to conduct" there is substituted "which have been instituted in consequence of a report made by the authority to the procurator fiscal", and

(c) for any reference to a person being charged with an offence there is substituted a reference to the person being prosecuted for the offence.

Law enforcement

31.—(1) Information which is not exempt information by virtue of section 30 **111–031** is exempt information if its disclosure under this Act would, or would be likely to, prejudice—

(a) the prevention or detection of crime,

(b) the apprehension or prosecution of offenders,

(c) the administration of justice,

(d) the assessment or collection of any tax or duty or of any imposition of a similar nature,

(e) the operation of the immigration controls,

(f) the maintenance of security and good order in prisons or in other institutions where persons are lawfully detained,

(g) the exercise by any public authority of its functions for any of the purposes specified in subsection (2),

(h) any civil proceedings which are brought by or on behalf of a public authority and arise out of an investigation conducted, for any of the purposes specified in subsection (2), by or on behalf of the authority by virtue of Her Majesty's prerogative or by virtue of powers conferred by or under an enactment, or

(i) any inquiry held under the Fatal Accidents and Sudden Deaths Inquiries (Scotland) Act 1976 to the extent that the inquiry arises out of an investigation conducted, for any of the purposes specified in subsection (2), by or on behalf of the authority by virtue of Her Majesty's prerogative or by virtue of powers conferred by or under an enactment.

(2) The purposes referred to in subsection (1)(g) to (i) are—

(a) the purpose of ascertaining whether any person has failed to comply with the law,

(b) the purpose of ascertaining whether any person is responsible for any conduct which is improper,

(c) the purpose of ascertaining whether circumstances which would justify regulatory action in pursuance of any enactment exist or may arise,

(d) the purpose of ascertaining a person's fitness or competence in relation to the management of bodies corporate or in relation to any profession or other activity which he is, or seeks to become, authorised to carry on,

(e) the purpose of ascertaining the cause of an accident,

(f) the purpose of protecting charities against misconduct or mismanagement (whether by trustees or other persons) in their administration,

(g) the purpose of protecting the property of charities from loss or misapplication,

(h) the purpose of recovering the property of charities,

(i) the purpose of securing the health, safety and welfare of persons at work, and

(j) the purpose of protecting persons other than persons at work against risk to health or safety arising out of or in connection with the actions of persons at work.

(3) The duty to confirm or deny does not arise if, or to the extent that, compliance with section 1(1)(a) would, or would be likely to, prejudice any of the matters mentioned in subsection (1).

Court records, etc.

111–032　32.—(1) Information held by a public authority is exempt information if it is held only by virtue of being contained in—

(a) any document filed with, or otherwise placed in the custody of, a court for the purposes of proceedings in a particular cause or matter,

(b) any document served upon, or by, a public authority for the purposes of proceedings in a particular cause or matter, or

(c) any document created by—

　(i) a court, or

　(ii) a member of the administrative staff of a court,

for the purposes of proceedings in a particular cause or matter.

(2) Information held by a public authority is exempt information if it is held only by virtue of being contained in—

(a) any document placed in the custody of a person conducting an inquiry or arbitration, for the purposes of the inquiry or arbitration, or

(b) any document created by a person conducting an inquiry or arbitration, for the purposes of the inquiry or arbitration.

(3) The duty to confirm or deny does not arise in relation to information which is (or if it were held by the public authority would be) exempt information by virtue of this section.

(4) In this section—

(a) "court" includes any tribunal or body exercising the judicial power of the State,

(b) "proceedings in a particular cause or matter" includes any inquest or post-mortem examination,

(c) "inquiry" means any inquiry or hearing held under any provision contained in, or made under, an enactment, and

(d) except in relation to Scotland, "arbitration" means any arbitration to which Part I of the Arbitration Act 1996 applies.

Audit functions

33.—(1) This section applies to any public authority which has functions in **111–033**
relation to—

    (a) the audit of the accounts of other public authorities, or

    (b) the examination of the economy, efficiency and effectiveness with
which other public authorities use their resources in discharging their
functions.

(2) Information held by a public authority to which this section applies is
exempt information if its disclosure would, or would be likely to, prejudice the
exercise of any of the authority's functions in relation to any of the matters
referred to in subsection (1).

(3) The duty to confirm or deny does not arise in relation to a public authority
to which this section applies if, or to the extent that, compliance with section
1(1)(a) would, or would be likely to, prejudice the exercise of any of the authority's functions in relation to any of the matters referred to in subsection (1).

Parliamentary privilege

34.—(1) Information is exempt information if exemption from section 1(1)(b) **111–034**
is required for the purpose of avoiding an infringement of the privileges of either
House of Parliament.

(2) The duty to confirm or deny does not apply if, or to the extent that,
exemption from section 1(1)(a) is required for the purpose of avoiding an
infringement of the privileges of either House of Parliament.

(3) A certificate signed by the appropriate authority certifying that exemption
from section 1(1)(b), or from section 1(1)(a) and (b), is, or at any time was,
required for the purpose of avoiding an infringement of the privileges of either
House of Parliament shall be conclusive evidence of that fact.

(4) In subsection (3) "the appropriate authority" means—

    (a) in relation to the House of Commons, the Speaker of that House, and

    (b) in relation to the House of Lords, the Clerk of the Parliaments.

Formulation of government policy, etc.

35.—(1) Information held by a government department or by the National **111–035**
Assembly for Wales is exempt information if it relates to—

    (a) the formulation or development of government policy,

    (b) Ministerial communications,

    (c) the provision of advice by any of the Law Officers or any request for
the provision of such advice, or

    (d) the operation of any Ministerial private office.

(2) Once a decision as to government policy has been taken, any statistical
information used to provide an informed background to the taking of the
decision is not to be regarded—

    (a) for the purposes of subsection (1)(a), as relating to the formulation or
development of government policy, or

    (b) for the purposes of subsection (1)(b), as relating to Ministerial com-
munications.

(3) The duty to confirm or deny does not arise in relation to information which is (or if it were held by the public authority would be) exempt information by virtue of subsection (1).

(4) In making any determination required by section 2(1)(b) or (2)(b) in relation to information which is exempt information by virtue of subsection (1)(a), regard shall be had to the particular public interest in the disclosure of factual information which has been used, or is intended to be used, to provide an informed background to decision-taking.

(5) In this section—

"government policy" includes the policy of the Executive Committee of the Northern Ireland Assembly and the policy of the National Assembly for Wales;

"the Law Officers" means the Attorney General, the Solicitor General, the Advocate General for Scotland, the Lord Advocate, the Solicitor General for Scotland and the Attorney General for Northern Ireland;

"Ministerial communications" means any communications—

(a) between Ministers of the Crown,

(b) between Northern Ireland Ministers, including Northern Ireland junior Ministers, or

(c) between Assembly Secretaries, including the Assembly First Secretary,

and includes, in particular, proceedings of the Cabinet or of any committee of the Cabinet, proceedings of the Executive Committee of the Northern Ireland Assembly, and proceedings of the executive committee of the National Assembly for Wales;

"Ministerial private office" means any part of a government department which provides personal administrative support to a Minister of the Crown, to a Northern Ireland Minister or a Northern Ireland junior Minister or any part of the administration of the National Assembly for Wales providing personal administrative support to the Assembly First Secretary or an Assembly Secretary;

"Northern Ireland junior Minister" means a member of the Northern Ireland Assembly appointed as a junior Minister under section 19 of the Northern Ireland Act 1998.

Prejudice to effective conduct of public affairs

111–036   **36.**—(1) This section applies to—

(a) information which is held by a government department or by the National Assembly for Wales and is not exempt information by virtue of section 35, and

(b) information which is held by any other public authority.

(2) Information to which this section applies is exempt information if, in the reasonable opinion of a qualified person, disclosure of the information under this Act—

(a) would, or would be likely to, prejudice—

(i) the maintenance of the convention of the collective responsibility of Ministers of the Crown, or

(ii) the work of the Executive Committee of the Northern Ireland Assembly, or

(iii) the work of the executive committee of the National Assembly for Wales,

(b) would, or would be likely to, inhibit—

(i) the free and frank provision of advice, or
(ii) the free and frank exchange of views for the purposes of deliberation, or

(c) would otherwise prejudice, or would be likely otherwise to prejudice, the effective conduct of public affairs.

(3) The duty to confirm or deny does not arise in relation to information to which this section applies (or would apply if held by the public authority) if, or to the extent that, in the reasonable opinion of a qualified person, compliance with section 1(1)(a) would, or would be likely to, have any of the effects mentioned in subsection (2).

(4) In relation to statistical information, subsections (2) and (3) shall have effect with the omission of the words "in the reasonable opinion of a qualified person".

(5) In subsections (2) and (3) "qualified person"—

(a) in relation to information held by a government department in the charge of a Minister of the Crown, means any Minister of the Crown,
(b) in relation to information held by a Northern Ireland department, means the Northern Ireland Minister in charge of the department,
(c) in relation to information held by any other government department, means the commissioners or other person in charge of that department,
(d) in relation to information held by the House of Commons, means the Speaker of that House,
(e) in relation to information held by the House of Lords, means the Clerk of the Parliaments,
(f) in relation to information held by the Northern Ireland Assembly, means the Presiding Officer,
(g) in relation to information held by the National Assembly for Wales, means the Assembly First Secretary,
(h) in relation to information held by any Welsh public authority other than the Auditor General for Wales, means—

(i) the public authority, or
(ii) any officer or employee of the authority authorised by the Assembly First Secretary,

(i) in relation to information held by the National Audit Office, means the Comptroller and Auditor General,
(j) in relation to information held by the Northern Ireland Audit Office, means the Comptroller and Auditor General for Northern Ireland,
(k) in relation to information held by the Auditor General for Wales, means the Auditor General for Wales,
(l) in relation to information held by any Northern Ireland public authority other than the Northern Ireland Audit Office, means—

(i) the public authority, or
(ii) any officer or employee of the authority authorised by the First Minister and deputy First Minister in Northern Ireland acting jointly,

(m) in relation to information held by the Greater London Authority, means the Mayor of London,
(n) in relation to information held by a functional body within the meaning

of the Greater London Authority Act 1999, means the chairman of that functional body, and

(o) in relation to information held by any public authority not falling within any of paragraphs (a) to (n), means—

(i) a Minister of the Crown,
(ii) the public authority, if authorised for the purposes of this section by a Minister of the Crown, or
(iii) any officer or employee of the public authority who is authorised for the purposes of this section by a Minister of the Crown.

(6) Any authorisation for the purposes of this section—

(a) may relate to a specified person or to persons falling within a specified class,
(b) may be general or limited to particular classes of case, and
(c) may be granted subject to conditions.

(7) A certificate signed by the qualified person referred to in subsection (5)(d)or (e) above certifying that in his reasonable opinion—

(a) disclosure of information held by either House of Parliament, or
(b) compliance with section 1(1)(a) by either House,

would, or would be likely to, have any of the effects mentioned in subsection (2) shall be conclusive evidence of that fact.

Communications with Her Majesty, etc. and honours

111–037 37.—(1) Information is exempt information if it relates to—

(a) communications with Her Majesty, with other members of the Royal Family or with the Royal Household, or
(b) the conferring by the Crown of any honour or dignity.

(2) The duty to confirm or deny does not arise in relation to information which is (or if it were held by the public authority would be) exempt information by virtue of subsection (1).

Health and safety

111–038 38.—(1) Information is exempt information if its disclosure under this Act would, or would be likely to—

(a) endanger the physical or mental health of any individual, or
(b) endanger the safety of any individual.

(2) The duty to confirm or deny does not arise if, or to the extent that, compliance with section 1(1)(a) would, or would be likely to, have either of the effects mentioned in subsection (1).

Environmental information

111–039 39.—(1) Information is exempt information if the public authority holding it—

(a) is obliged by regulations under section 74 to make the information available to the public in accordance with the regulations, or

(b) would be so obliged but for any exemption contained in the regulations.

(2) The duty to confirm or deny does not arise in relation to information which is (or if it were held by the public authority would be) exempt information by virtue of subsection (1).

(3) Subsection (1)(a) does not limit the generality of section 21(1).

Personal information

40.—(1) Any information to which a request for information relates is exempt **111–040** information if it constitutes personal data of which the applicant is the data subject.

(2) Any information to which a request for information relates is also exempt information if—

(a) it constitutes personal data which do not fall within subsection (1), and

(b) either the first or the second condition below is satisfied.

(3) The first condition is—

(a) in a case where the information falls within any of paragraphs (a) to (d) of the definition of "data" in section 1(1) of the Data Protection Act 1998, that the disclosure of the information to a member of the public otherwise than under this Act would contravene—

(i) any of the data protection principles, or

(ii) section 10 of that Act (right to prevent processing likely to cause damage or distress), and

(b) in any other case, that the disclosure of the information to a member of the public otherwise than under this Act would contravene any of the data protection principles if the exemptions in section 33A(1) of the Data Protection Act 1998 (which relate to manual data held by public authorities) were disregarded.

(4) The second condition is that by virtue of any provision of Part IV of the Data Protection Act 1998 the information is exempt from section 7(1)(c) of that Act (data subject's right of access to personal data).

(5) The duty to confirm or deny—

(a) does not arise in relation to information which is (or if it were held by the public authority would be) exempt information by virtue of subsection (1), and

(b) does not arise in relation to other information if or to the extent that either—

(i) the giving to a member of the public of the confirmation or denial that would have to be given to comply with section 1(1)(a) would (apart from this Act) contravene any of the data protection principles or section 10 of the Data Protection Act 1998 or would do so if the exemptions in section 33A(1) of that Act were disregarded, or

(ii) by virtue of any provision of Part IV of the Data Protection Act 1998 the information is exempt from section 7(1)(a) of that Act (data subject's right to be informed whether personal data being processed).

(6) In determining for the purposes of this section whether anything done before 24th October 2007 would contravene any of the data protection

principles, the exemptions in Part III of Schedule 8 to the Data Protection Act 1998 shall be disregarded.

(7) In this section—

"the data protection principles" means the principles set out in Part I of Schedule 1 to the Data Protection Act 1998, as read subject to Part II of that Schedule and section 27(1) of that Act;
"data subject" has the same meaning as in section 1(1) of that Act;
"personal data" has the same meaning as in section 1(1) of that Act.

Information provided in confidence

111–041   **41.**—(1) Information is exempt information if—

(a) it was obtained by the public authority from any other person (including another public authority), and
(b) the disclosure of the information to the public (otherwise than under this Act) by the public authority holding it would constitute a breach of confidence actionable by that or any other person.

(2) The duty to confirm or deny does not arise if, or to the extent that, the confirmation or denial that would have to be given to comply with section 1(1)(a) would (apart from this Act) constitute an actionable breach of confidence.

Legal professional privilege

111–042   **42.**—(1) Information in respect of which a claim to legal professional privilege or, in Scotland, to confidentiality of communications could be maintained in legal proceedings is exempt information.

(2) The duty to confirm or deny does not arise if, or to the extent that, compliance with section 1(1)(a) would involve the disclosure of any information (whether or not already recorded) in respect of which such a claim could be maintained in legal proceedings.

Commercial interests

111–043   **43.**—(1) Information is exempt information if it constitutes a trade secret.

(2) Information is exempt information if its disclosure under this Act would, or would be likely to, prejudice the commercial interests of any person (including the public authority holding it).

(3) The duty to confirm or deny does not arise if, or to the extent that, compliance with section 1(1)(a) would, or would be likely to, prejudice the interests mentioned in subsection (2).

Prohibitions on disclosure

111–044   **44.**—(1) Information is exempt information if its disclosure (otherwise than under this Act) by the public authority holding it—

(a) is prohibited by or under any enactment,
(b) is incompatible with any Community obligation, or
(c) would constitute or be punishable as a contempt of court.

(2) The duty to confirm or deny does not arise if the confirmation or denial that would have to be given to comply with section 1(1)(a) would (apart from this Act) fall within any of paragraphs (a) to (c) of subsection (1).

PART III

GENERAL FUNCTIONS OF SECRETARY OF STATE, LORD CHANCELLOR AND
INFORMATION COMMISSIONER

Issue of code of practice by Secretary of State

45.—(1) The Secretary of State shall issue, and may from time to time revise, **111–045**
a code of practice providing guidance to public authorities as to the practice
which it would, in his opinion, be desirable for them to follow in connection
with the discharge of the authorities' functions under Part I.

(2) The code of practice must, in particular, include provision relating to—

(a) the provision of advice and assistance by public authorities to persons
who propose to make, or have made, requests for information to them,

(b) the transfer of requests by one public authority to another public
authority by which the information requested is or may be held,

(c) consultation with persons to whom the information requested relates or
persons whose interests are likely to be affected by the disclosure of
information,

(d) the inclusion in contracts entered into by public authorities of terms
relating to the disclosure of information, and

(e) the provision by public authorities of procedures for dealing with complaints about the handling by them of requests for information.

(3) The code may make different provision for different public authorities.

(4) Before issuing or revising any code under this section, the Secretary of
State shall consult the Commissioner.

(5) The Secretary of State shall lay before each House of Parliament any code
or revised code made under this section.

Issue of code of practice by Lord Chancellor

46.—(1) The Lord Chancellor shall issue, and may from time to time revise, **111–046**
a code of practice providing guidance to relevant authorities as to the practice
which it would, in his opinion, be desirable for them to follow in connection
with the keeping, management and destruction of their records.

(2) For the purpose of facilitating the performance by the Public Record
Office, the Public Record Office of Northern Ireland and other public authorities
of their functions under this Act in relation to records which are public records
for the purposes of the Public Records Act 1958 or the Public Records Act
(Northern Ireland) 1923, the code may also include guidance as to—

(a) the practice to be adopted in relation to the transfer of records under
section 3(4) of the Public Records Act 1958 or section 3 of the Public
Records Act (Northern Ireland) 1923, and

(b) the practice of reviewing records before they are transferred under
those provisions.

(3) In exercising his functions under this section, the Lord Chancellor shall
have regard to the public interest in allowing public access to information held
by relevant authorities.

(4) The code may make different provision for different relevant authorities.

(5) Before issuing or revising any code under this section the Lord Chancellor
shall consult—

(a) the Secretary of State,

(b) the Commissioner, and

(c) in relation to Northern Ireland, the appropriate Northern Ireland Minister.

(6) The Lord Chancellor shall lay before each House of Parliament any code or revised code made under this section.

(7) In this section "relevant authority" means—

(a) any public authority, and

(b) any office or body which is not a public authority but whose administrative and departmental records are public records for the purposes of the Public Records Act 1958 or the Public Records Act (Northern Ireland) 1923.

General functions of Commissioner

111–047   **47.**—(1) It shall be the duty of the Commissioner to promote the following of good practice by public authorities and, in particular, so to perform his functions under this Act as to promote the observance by public authorities of—

(a) the requirements of this Act, and

(b) the provisions of the codes of practice under sections 45 and 46.

(2) The Commissioner shall arrange for the dissemination in such form and manner as he considers appropriate of such information as it may appear to him expedient to give to the public—

(a) about the operation of this Act,

(b) about good practice, and

(c) about other matters within the scope of his functions under this Act,

and may give advice to any person as to any of those matters.

(3) The Commissioner may, with the consent of any public authority, assess whether that authority is following good practice.

(4) The Commissioner may charge such sums as he may with the consent of the [Lord Chancellor] determine for any services provided by the Commissioner under this section.

(5) The Commissioner shall from time to time as he considers appropriate—

(a) consult the Keeper of Public Records about the promotion by the Commissioner of the observance by public authorities of the provisions of the code of practice under section 46 in relation to records which are public records for the purposes of the Public Records Act 1958, and

(b) consult the Deputy Keeper of the Records of Northern Ireland about the promotion by the Commissioner of the observance by public authorities of those provisions in relation to records which are public records for the purposes of the Public Records Act (Northern Ireland) 1923.

(6) In this section "good practice", in relation to a public authority, means such practice in the discharge of its functions under this Act as appears to the Commissioner to be desirable, and includes (but is not limited to) compliance with the requirements of this Act and the provisions of the codes of practice under sections 45 and 46.

. . . . . .

PART IV

ENFORCEMENT

Application for decision by Commissioner

50.—(1) Any person (in this section referred to as "the complainant") may **111–048** apply to the Commissioner for a decision whether, in any specified respect, a request for information made by the complainant to a public authority has been dealt with in accordance with the requirements of Part I.

(2) On receiving an application under this section, the Commissioner shall make a decision unless it appears to him—

(a) that the complainant has not exhausted any complaints procedure which is provided by the public authority in conformity with the code of practice under section 45,

(b) that there has been undue delay in making the application,

(c) that the application is frivolous or vexatious, or

(d) that the application has been withdrawn or abandoned.

(3) Where the Commissioner has received an application under this section, he shall either—

(a) notify the complainant that he has not made any decision under this section as a result of the application and of his grounds for not doing so, or

(b) serve notice of his decision (in this Act referred to as a "decision notice") on the complainant and the public authority.

(4) Where the Commissioner decides that a public authority—

(a) has failed to communicate information, or to provide confirmation or denial, in a case where it is required to do so by section 1(1), or

(b) has failed to comply with any of the requirements of sections 11 and 17,

the decision notice must specify the steps which must be taken by the authority for complying with that requirement and the period within which they must be taken.

(5) A decision notice must contain particulars of the right of appeal conferred by section 57.

(6) Where a decision notice requires steps to be taken by the public authority within a specified period, the time specified in the notice must not expire before the end of the period within which an appeal can be brought against the notice and, if such an appeal is brought, no step which is affected by the appeal need be taken pending the determination or withdrawal of the appeal.

(7) This section has effect subject to section 53.

. . . . . .

Enforcement notices

52.—(1) If the Commissioner is satisfied that a public authority has failed to **111–049** comply with any of the requirements of Part I, the Commissioner may serve the authority with a notice (in this Act referred to as "an enforcement notice") requiring the authority to take, within such time as may be specified in the notice, such steps as may be so specified for complying with those requirements.

(2) An enforcement notice must contain—

(a) a statement of the requirement or requirements of Part I with which the Commissioner is satisfied that the public authority has failed to comply and his reasons for reaching that conclusion, and

(b) particulars of the right of appeal conferred by section 57.

(3) An enforcement notice must not require any of the provisions of the notice to be complied with before the end of the period within which an appeal can be brought against the notice and, if such an appeal is brought, the notice need not be complied with pending the determination or withdrawal of the appeal.

(4) The Commissioner may cancel an enforcement notice by written notice to the authority on which it was served.

(5) This section has effect subject to section 53.

Exception from duty to comply with decision notice or enforcement notice

111–050 53.—(1) This section applies to a decision notice or enforcement notice which—

(a) is served on—

(i) a government department,

(ii) the National Assembly for Wales, or

(iii) any public authority designated for the purposes of this section by an order made by the Secretary of State, and

(b) relates to a failure, in respect of one or more requests for information—

(i) to comply with section 1(1)(a) in respect of information which falls within any provision of Part II stating that the duty to confirm or deny does not arise, or

(ii) to comply with section 1(1)(b) in respect of exempt information.

(2) A decision notice or enforcement notice to which this section applies shall cease to have effect if, not later than the twentieth working day following the effective date, the accountable person in relation to that authority gives the Commissioner a certificate signed by him stating that he has on reasonable grounds formed the opinion that, in respect of the request or requests concerned, there was no failure falling within subsection (1)(b).

(3) Where the accountable person gives a certificate to the Commissioner under subsection (2) he shall as soon as practicable thereafter lay a copy of the certificate before—

(a) each House of Parliament,

(b) the Northern Ireland Assembly, in any case where the certificate relates to a decision notice or enforcement notice which has been served on a Northern Ireland department or any Northern Ireland public authority, or

(c) the National Assembly for Wales, in any case where the certificate relates to a decision notice or enforcement notice which has been served on the National Assembly for Wales or any Welsh public authority.

(4) In subsection (2) "the effective date", in relation to a decision notice or enforcement notice, means—

(a) the day on which the notice was given to the public authority, or

(b) where an appeal under section 57 is brought, the day on which that appeal (or any further appeal arising out of it) is determined or withdrawn.

(5) Before making an order under subsection (1)(a)(iii), the Secretary of State shall—

(a) if the order relates to a Welsh public authority, consult the National Assembly for Wales,
(b) if the order relates to the Northern Ireland Assembly, consult the Presiding Officer of that Assembly, and
(c) if the order relates to a Northern Ireland public authority, consult the First Minister and deputy First Minister in Northern Ireland.

(6) Where the accountable person gives a certificate to the Commissioner under subsection (2) in relation to a decision notice, the accountable person shall, on doing so or as soon as reasonably practicable after doing so, inform the person who is the complainant for the purposes of section 50 of the reasons for his opinion.

(7) The accountable person is not obliged to provide information under subsection (6) if, or to the extent that, compliance with that subsection would involve the disclosure of exempt information.

(8) In this section "the accountable person"—

(a) in relation to a Northern Ireland department or any Northern Ireland public authority, means the First Minister and deputy First Minister in Northern Ireland acting jointly,
(b) in relation to the National Assembly for Wales or any Welsh public authority, means the Assembly First Secretary, and
(c) in relation to any other public authority, means—

(i) a Minister of the Crown who is a member of the Cabinet, or
(ii) the Attorney General, the Advocate General for Scotland or the Attorney General for Northern Ireland.

(9) In this section "working day" has the same meaning as in section 10.

. . . . . .

Appeal against notice served under Part IV

57.—(1) Where a decision notice has been served, the complainant or the **111–051** public authority may appeal to the Tribunal against the notice.

(2) A public authority on which an information notice or an enforcement notice has been served by the Commissioner may appeal to the Tribunal against the notice.

(3) In relation to a decision notice or enforcement notice which relates—

(a) to information to which section 66 applies, and
(b) to a matter which by virtue of subsection (3) or (4) of that section falls to be determined by the responsible authority instead of the appropriate records authority,

subsections (1) and (2) shall have effect as if the reference to the public authority were a reference to the public authority or the responsible authority.

. . . . . .

SCHEDULE 1

PUBLIC AUTHORITIES

PART I

GENERAL

111–052

1. Any government department.
2. The House of Commons.
3. The House of Lords.
4. The Northern Ireland Assembly.
5. The National Assembly for Wales.
6. The armed forces of the Crown, except—

    (a) the special forces, and
    (b) any unit or part of a unit which is for the time being required by the Secretary of State to assist the Government Communications Headquarters in the exercise of its functions.

PART II

LOCAL GOVERNMENT

ENGLAND AND WALES

111–053

7. A local authority within the meaning of the Local Government Act 1972, namely—

    (a) in England, a county council, a London borough council, a district council or a parish council,
    (b) in Wales, a county council, a county borough council or a community council.

8. The Greater London Authority.
9. The Common Council of the City of London, in respect of information held in its capacity as a local authority, police authority or port health authority.
10. The Sub-Treasurer of the Inner Temple or the Under-Treasurer of the Middle Temple, in respect of information held in his capacity as a local authority.
11. The Council of the Isles of Scilly.
12. A parish meeting constituted under section 13 of the Local Government Act 1972.
13. Any charter trustees constituted under section 246 of the Local Government Act 1972.
14. A fire authority constituted by a combination scheme under section 5 or 6 of the Fire Services Act 1947.
15. A waste disposal authority established by virtue of an order under section 10(1) of the Local Government Act 1985.
16. A port health authority constituted by an order under section 2 of the Public Health (Control of Disease) Act 1984.
17. A licensing planning committee constituted under section 119 of the Licensing Act 1964.
18. An internal drainage board which is continued in being by virtue of section 1 of the Land Drainage Act 1991.
19. A joint authority established under Part IV of the Local Government Act 1985 (fire services, civil defence and transport).
20. The London Fire and Emergency Planning Authority.

Local Government Act 2000

(2000, c. 22)

112–001 *An Act to make provision with respect to the functions and procedures of local authorities and provision with respect to local authority elections; to make provision with respect to grants and housing benefit in respect of certain welfare services; to amend section 29 of the Children Act 1989; and for connected purposes.* [28th July 2000]

Part I

Promotion of Economic, Social or Environmental Well-Being, etc.

Interpretation

Meaning of "local authority" in Part I

1. In this Part "local authority" means— **112–002**

(a) in relation to England—

(i) a county council,
(ii) a district council,
(iii) a London borough council,
(iv) the Common Council of the City of London in its capacity as a local authority,
(v) the Council of the Isles of Scilly,

(b) in relation to Wales, a county council or a county borough council.

Promotion of well-being

Promotion of well-being

2.—(1) Every local authority are to have power to do anything which they **112–003** consider is likely to achieve any one or more of the following objects—

(a) the promotion or improvement of the economic well-being of their area,
(b) the promotion or improvement of the social well-being of their area, and
(c) the promotion or improvement of the environmental well-being of their area.

(2) The power under subsection (1) may be exercised in relation to or for the benefit of—

(a) the whole or any part of a local authority's area, or
(b) all or any persons resident or present in a local authority's area.

(3) In determining whether or how to exercise the power under subsection (1), a local authority must have regard to their strategy under section 4.

(4) The power under subsection (1) includes power for a local authority to—

(a) incur expenditure,
(b) give financial assistance to any person,
(c) enter into arrangements or agreements with any person,
(d) co-operate with, or facilitate or co-ordinate the activities of, any person,
(e) exercise on behalf of any person any functions of that person, and
(f) provide staff, goods, services or accommodation to any person.

(5) The power under subsection (1) includes power for a local authority to do anything in relation to, or for the benefit of, any person or area situated outside their area if they consider that it is likely to achieve any one or more of the objects in that subsection.

(6) Nothing in subsection (4) or (5) affects the generality of the power under subsection (1).

Limits on power to promote well-being

112–004   **3.**—(1) The power under section 2(1) does not enable a local authority to do anything which they are unable to do by virtue of any prohibition, restriction or limitation on their powers which is contained in any enactment (whenever passed or made).

(2) The power under section 2(1) does not enable a local authority to raise money (whether by precepts, borrowing or otherwise).

(3) The Secretary of State may by order make provision preventing local authorities from doing, by virtue of section 2(1), anything which is specified, or is of a description specified, in the order.

(4) Before making an order under subsection (3), the Secretary of State must consult such representatives of local government and such other persons (if any) as he considers appropriate.

(5) Before exercising the power under section 2(1), a local authority must have regard to any guidance for the time being issued by the Secretary of State about the exercise of that power.

(6) Before issuing any guidance under subsection (5), the Secretary of State must consult such representatives of local government and such other persons (if any) as he considers appropriate.

(7) In its application to Wales, this section has effect as if for any reference to the Secretary of State there were substituted a reference to the National Assembly for Wales.

(8) In this section "enactment" includes an enactment comprised in subordinate legislation (within the meaning of the Interpretation Act 1978).

Strategies for promoting well-being

112–005   **4.**—(1) Every local authority must prepare a strategy (referred to in this section as a community strategy) for promoting or improving the economic, social and environmental well-being of their area and contributing to the achievement of sustainable development in the United Kingdom.

(2) A local authority may from time to time modify their community strategy.

(3) In preparing or modifying their community strategy, a local authority—

(a) must consult and seek the participation of such persons as they consider appropriate, and

(b) must have regard to any guidance for the time being issued by the Secretary of State.

(4) Before issuing any guidance under this section, the Secretary of State must consult such representatives of local government and such other persons (if any) as he considers appropriate.

(5) In its application to Wales, this section has effect as if for any reference to the Secretary of State there were substituted a reference to the National Assembly for Wales.

Power to amend or repeal enactments

112–006   **5.**—(1) If the Secretary of State thinks that an enactment (whenever passed or made) prevents or obstructs local authorities from exercising their power under section 2(1) he may by order amend, repeal, revoke or disapply that enactment.

(2) The power under subsection (1) may be exercised in relation to—

(a) all local authorities,
(b) particular local authorities, or
(c) particular descriptions of local authority.

(3) The power under subsection (1) to amend or disapply an enactment includes a power to amend or disapply an enactment for a particular period.
(4) In exercising the power under subsection (1), the Secretary of State—

(a) must not make any provision which has effect in relation to Wales unless he has consulted the National Assembly for Wales, and
(b) must not make any provision in relation to legislation made by the National Assembly for Wales without the consent of the Assembly.

(5) The National Assembly for Wales may submit proposals to the Secretary of State that the power under subsection (1) should be exercised in relation to Wales in accordance with those proposals.
(6) In this section "enactment" includes an enactment comprised in subordinate legislation (within the meaning of the Interpretation Act 1978).

. . . . . .

PART II

ARRANGEMENTS WITH RESPECT TO EXECUTIVES ETC.

Executive arrangements

Executive arrangements

10.—(1) In this Part "executive arrangements" means arrangements by a local **112–007** authority—

(a) for and in connection with the creation and operation of an executive of the authority, and
(b) under which certain functions of the authority are the responsibility of the executive.

(2) Executive arrangements by a local authority must conform with any provisions made by or under this Part which relate to such arrangements.

Local authority executives

Local authority executives

11.—(1) The executive of a local authority must take one of the forms speci- **112–008** fied in subsections (2) to (5).
(2) It may consist of—

(a) an elected mayor of the authority, and
(b) two or more councillors of the authority appointed to the executive by the elected mayor.

(3) It may consist of—

(a) a councillor of the authority (referred to in this Part as the executive leader) elected as leader of the executive by the authority, and

(b) two or more councillors of the authority appointed to the executive by one of the following—

    (i) the executive leader, or
    (ii) the authority.

(4) It may consist of—

(a) an elected mayor of the authority, and
(b) an officer of the authority (referred to in this Part as the council manager) appointed to the executive by the authority.

(5) It may take any such form as may be prescribed in regulations made by the Secretary of State.

(6) Regulations under subsection (5) may, in particular, provide for—

(a) a form of executive some or all of the members of which are elected by the local government electors for the authority's area to a specified post in the executive associated with the discharge of particular functions,
(b) a form of executive some or all of the members of which are elected by those elected but not to any such post,
(c) the system of voting that will be used for elections under paragraph (a) or (b).

(7) A local authority executive may not include the chairman or vice-chairman of the authority.

(8) The number of members of a mayor and cabinet executive or a leader and cabinet executive may not exceed 10.

(9) The Secretary of State may by regulations amend subsection (8) so as to provide for a different maximum number of members of an executive to which that subsection applies, but the power under this subsection may not be exercised so as to provide for a maximum number which exceeds 10.

(10) Section 101 of the Local Government Act 1972 (arrangements for discharge of functions by local authorities) does not apply to the function of electing a leader under subsection (3)(a) or appointing councillors or an officer to the executive under subsection (3)(b)(ii) or (4)(b).

. . . . . .

Executive functions

Functions which are the responsibility of an executive

112–009   **13.**—(1) This section has effect for the purposes of determining the functions of a local authority which are the responsibility of an executive of the authority under executive arrangements.

(2) Subject to any provision made by this Act or by any enactment which is passed or made after the day on which this Act is passed, any function of a local authority which is not specified in regulations under subsection (3) is to be the responsibility of an executive of the authority under executive arrangements.

(3) The Secretary of State may by regulations make provision for any function of a local authority specified in the regulations—

(a) to be a function which is not to be the responsibility of an executive of the authority under executive arrangements,

(b) to be a function which may be the responsibility of such an executive under such arrangements, or

(c) to be a function which—

    (i) to the extent provided by the regulations is to be the responsibility of such an executive under such arrangements, and

    (ii) to the extent provided by the regulations is not to be the responsibility of such an executive under such arrangements.

(4) Executive arrangements must make provision for any function of a local authority falling within subsection (3)(b)—

(a) to be a function which is to be the responsibility of an executive of the authority,

(b) to be a function which is not to be the responsibility of such an executive, or

(c) to be a function which—

    (i) to the extent provided by the arrangements is to be the responsibility of such an executive, and

    (ii) to the extent provided by the arrangements is not to be the responsibility of such an executive.

(5) The power under subsection (3)(c) or (4)(c) includes power in relation to any function of a local authority—

(a) to designate any action in connection with the discharge of that function which is to be the responsibility of an executive of a local authority, and

(b) to designate any action in connection with the discharge of that function which is not to be the responsibility of such an executive.

(6) The Secretary of State may by regulations specify cases or circumstances in which any function of a local authority which, by virtue of the preceding provisions of this section, would otherwise be the responsibility of an executive of the authority to any extent is not to be the responsibility of such an executive to that or any particular extent.

(7) A function of a local authority may, by virtue of this section, be the responsibility of an executive of the authority to any extent notwithstanding that section 101 of the Local Government Act 1972, or any provision of that section, does not apply to that function.

(8) Any reference in the following provisions of this Part to any functions which are, or are not, the responsibility of an executive of a local authority under executive arrangements is a reference to the functions of the authority to the extent to which they are or (as the case may be) are not, by virtue of this section, the responsibility of the executive under such arrangements.

(9) Any function which is the responsibility of an executive of a local authority under executive arrangements—

(a) is to be regarded as exercisable by the executive on behalf of the authority, and

(b) may be discharged only in accordance with any provisions made by or under this Part which apply to the discharge of any such function by that form of executive.

(10) Accordingly any function which is the responsibility of an executive of a local authority under executive arrangements—

(a) may not be discharged by the authority,

(b) is not to be a function to which section 101(1) of the Local Government Act 1972 applies, and

(c) may be the subject of arrangements made under section 101(5) of that Act only if permitted by any provision made under section 20.

(11) Subject to any provision made under subsection (12), any function which, under executive arrangements, is not the responsibility of an executive of a local authority is to be discharged in any way which would be permitted or required apart from the provisions made by or under this Part.

(12) The Secretary of State may by regulations make provision with respect to the discharge of any function which, under executive arrangements, is not the responsibility of an executive of a local authority (including provision disapplying section 101 of the Local Government Act 1972 or any provision of that section).

(13) Any reference in this section to a function specified in regulations includes a reference to a function of a description specified in regulations.

(14) In this section—

"action" in relation to any function includes any action (of whatever nature and whether or not separately identified by any enactment) involving—

(a) the taking of any step in the course of, or otherwise for the purposes of or in connection with, the discharge of the function,

(b) the doing of anything incidental or conducive to the discharge of the function, or

(c) the doing of anything expedient in connection with the discharge of the function or any action falling within paragraph (a) or (b),

"function" means a function of any nature, whether conferred or otherwise arising before, on or after the passing of this Act.

Provisions with respect to executive arrangements

Discharge of functions: mayor and cabinet executive

112–010 **14.**—(1) Subject to any provision made under section 18, 19 or 20, any functions which, under executive arrangements, are the responsibility of a mayor and cabinet executive are to be discharged in accordance with this section.

(2) The elected mayor—

(a) may discharge any of those functions, or

(b) may arrange for the discharge of any of those functions—

(i) by the executive,

(ii) by another member of the executive,

(iii) by a committee of the executive, or

(iv) by an officer of the authority.

(3) Where by virtue of this section any functions may be discharged by a local authority executive, then, unless the elected mayor otherwise directs, the executive may arrange for the discharge of any of those functions—

(a) by a committee of the executive, or

(b) by an officer of the authority.

(4) Where by virtue of this section any functions may be discharged by a member of a local authority executive, then, unless the elected mayor otherwise directs, that member may arrange for the discharge of any of those functions by an officer of the authority.

(5) Where by virtue of this section any functions may be discharged by a committee of a local authority executive, then, unless the elected mayor otherwise directs, the committee may arrange for the discharge of any of those functions by an officer of the authority.

(6) Any arrangements made by virtue of this section by an elected mayor, executive, member or committee for the discharge of any functions by an executive, member, committee or officer are not to prevent the elected mayor, executive, member or committee by whom the arrangements are made from exercising those functions.

. . . . . .

Access to information, etc.

22.—(1) Meetings of a local authority executive, or a committee of such an **112–011** executive, are to be open to the public or held in private.

(2) Subject to regulations under subsection (9), it is for a local authority executive to decide which of its meetings, and which of the meetings of any committee of the executive, are to be open to the public and which of those meetings are to be held in private.

(3) A written record must be kept of prescribed decisions made at meetings of local authorities executives, or committees of such executives, which are held in private.

(4) A written record must be kept of prescribed decisions made by individual members of local authority executives.

(5) Written records under subsection (3) or (4) must include reasons for the decisions to which they relate.

(6) Written records under subsections (3) and (4), together with such reports, background papers or other documents as may be prescribed, must be made available to members of the public in accordance with regulations made by the Secretary of State.

(7) Regulations under subsection (6) may make provision for or in connection with preventing the whole or part of any record or document containing prescribed information from being made available to members of the public.

(8) The Secretary of State may by regulations make provision—

    (a) with respect to the access of the public to meetings of joint committees, or sub-committees of such committees, at which decisions are made in connection with the discharge of functions which are the responsibility of executives (including provision enabling such meetings to be held in private),

    (b) for or in connection with requiring written records to be kept of decisions made at meetings which by virtue of paragraph (a) are held in private,

    (c) for or in connection with requiring written records falling within paragraph (b) to include reasons,

    (d) for or in connection with requiring any such written records to be made available to members of the public,

    (e) for or in connection with requiring documents connected with decisions to which any such written records relate to be made available to members of the public.

(9) The Secretary of State may by regulations make provision—

(a) as to the circumstances in which meetings mentioned in subsection (2), or particular proceedings at such meetings, must be open to the public,

(b) as to the circumstances in which meetings mentioned in subsection (2), or particular proceedings at such meetings, must be held in private,

(c) with respect to the information which is to be included in written records kept by virtue of this section,

(d) with respect to the reasons which are to be included in any such written records,

(e) with respect to the persons who are to produce, keep or make available any such written records,

(f) for or in connection with requiring any such written records to be made available to members of local authorities or to overview and scrutiny committees or sub-committees,

(g) for or in connection with requiring documents connected with decisions to which any such written records relate to be made available to members of local authorities or to overview and scrutiny committees or sub-committees,

(h) for or in connection with requiring information to be made available by electronic means,

(i) for or in connection with conferring rights on members of the public, members of local authorities or overview and scrutiny committees or sub-committees in relation to records or documents,

(j) for or in connection with the creation of offences in respect of any rights or requirements conferred or imposed by virtue of this section.

(10) The Secretary of State may by regulations make provision for or in connection with requiring prescribed information about prescribed decisions made in connection with the discharge of functions which are the responsibility of a local authority executive to be made available to members of the public or members of the authority.

(11) The provision which may be made under subsection (10) includes provision—

(a) requiring prescribed information to be made available in advance of the prescribed decisions mentioned in that subsection,

(b) as to the way or form in which prescribed information is to be made available.

(12) The Secretary of State may by regulations make provision which, in relation to meetings of—

(a) local authority executives or committees of such executives, or

(b) joint committees, or sub-committees of such committees, falling within subsection (8)(a),

applies or reproduces (with or without modifications) any provisions of Part VA of the Local Government Act 1972.

(13) In this section—

"joint committee" means a joint committee falling within section 101(5)(a) of the Local Government Act 1972,

"prescribed" means prescribed by regulations made by the Secretary of State.

. . . . . .

PART III

CHAPTER I

CONDUCT OF MEMBERS

Standards of conduct

Model code of conduct

50.—(1) The Secretary of State may by order issue a model code as regards **112–012** the conduct which is expected of members and co-opted members of relevant authorities in England and police authorities in Wales (referred to in this Part as a model code of conduct).

(2) The National Assembly for Wales may by order issue a model code as regards the conduct which is expected of members and co-opted members of relevant authorities in Wales other than police authorities (also referred to in this Part as a model code of conduct).

(3) The power under subsection (1) or (2) to issue a model code of conduct includes power to revise any such model code which has been issued.

(4) A model code of conduct—

(a) must be consistent with the principles for the time being specified in an order under section 49(1) or 49(2) (as the case may be),

(b) may include provisions which are mandatory, and

(c) may include provisions which are optional.

(5) Before making an order under this section, the Secretary of State or the National Assembly for Wales must carry out such consultation as is required, by virtue of section 49, before an order is made under that section.

(6) For the purpose of facilitating the making of an order under this section, the Secretary of State may invite such body as he considers appropriate to draw up, and send to him, a proposed model code of conduct or proposed revisions to such a model code.

(7) An invitation under subsection (6)—

(a) must be made in writing,

(b) may be made to more than one body,

(c) may be limited to particular descriptions of authority,

(d) must specify the period within which the proposals are to be drawn up and sent to the Secretary of State,

(e) may require different proposals to be drawn up for different authorities or descriptions of authority, and

(f) may require any body to which the invitation is made to consult such persons as may be specified in the invitation.

Duty of relevant authorities to adopt codes of conduct

51.—(1) It is the duty of a relevant authority, before the end of the period of **112–013** six months beginning with the day on which the first order under section 50 which applies to them is made, to pass a resolution adopting a code as regards the conduct which is expected of members and co-opted members of the authority (referred to in this Part as a code of conduct).

(2) It is the duty of a relevant authority, before the end of the period of six months beginning with the day on which any subsequent order under section 50 which applies to them is made, to pass a resolution—

(a) adopting a code of conduct in place of their existing code of conduct under this section, or

(b) revising their existing code of conduct under this section.

(3) A relevant authority may by resolution—

(a) adopt a code of conduct in place of their existing code of conduct under this section, or

(b) revise their existing code of conduct under this section.

(4) A code of conduct or revised code of conduct—

(a) must incorporate any mandatory provisions of the model code of conduct which for the time being applies to that authority,

(b) may incorporate any optional provisions of that model code, and

(c) may include other provisions which are consistent with that model code.

(5) Where a relevant authority fail to comply with the duty under subsection (1) or (2) before the end of the period mentioned in that subsection—

(a) they must comply with that duty as soon as reasonably practicable after the end of that period, and

(b) any mandatory provisions of the model code of conduct which for the time being applies to the authority are to apply in relation to the members and co-opted members of the authority for so long as the authority fail to comply with that duty.

(6) As soon as reasonably practicable after adopting or revising a code of conduct under this section, a relevant authority must—

(a) ensure that copies of the code or revised code are available at an office of the authority for inspection by members of the public at all reasonable hours,

(b) publish in one or more newspapers circulating in their area a notice which—

(i) states that they have adopted or revised a code of conduct,

(ii) states that copies of the code or revised code are available at an office of the authority for inspection by members of the public at such times as may be specified in the notice, and

(iii) specifies the address of that office, and

(c) send a copy of the code or revised code—

(i) in the case of a relevant authority in England or a police authority in Wales, to the Standards Board for England,

(ii) in the case of a relevant authority in Wales, to the Commission for Local Administration in Wales.

(7) Where a relevant authority themselves publish a newspaper, the duty to publish a notice under subsection (6)(b) is to be construed as a duty to publish that notice in their newspaper and at least one other newspaper circulating in their area.

(8) A relevant authority may publicise their adoption or revision of a code of conduct under this section in any other manner that they consider appropriate.

(9) A relevant authority's function with respect to the passing of a resolution under this section may be discharged only by the authority (and accordingly, in

the case of a relevant authority to which section 101 of the Local Government Act 1972 applies, is not to be a function to which that section applies).

Duty to comply with code of conduct

52.—(1) A person who is a member or co-opted member of a relevant author- **112–014** ity at a time when the authority adopt a code of conduct under section 51 for the first time—

(a) must, before the end of the period of two months beginning with the date on which the code of conduct is adopted, give to the authority a written undertaking that in performing his functions he will observe the authority's code of conduct for the time being under section 51, and

(b) if he fails to do so, is to cease to be a member or co-opted member at the end of that period.

(2) The form of declaration of acceptance of office which may be prescribed by an order under section 83 of the Local Government Act 1972 may include an undertaking by the declarant that in performing his functions he will observe the authority's code of conduct for the time being under section 51.

(3) A person who becomes a member of a relevant authority to which section 83 of that Act does not apply at any time after the authority have adopted a code of conduct under section 51 for the first time may not act in that office unless he has given the authority a written undertaking that in performing his functions he will observe the authority's code of conduct for the time being under section 51.

(4) A person who becomes a co-opted member of a relevant authority at any time after the authority have adopted a code of conduct under section 51 for the first time may not act as such unless he has given the authority a written undertaking that in performing his functions he will observe the authority's code of conduct for the time being under section 51.

Standards committees

Standards committees

53.—(1) Subject to subsection (2), every relevant authority must establish a **112–015** committee (referred to in this Part as a standards committee) which is to have the functions conferred on it by or under this Part.

(2) Subsection (1) does not apply to a parish council or community council.

(3) The number of members of a standards committee of a relevant authority in England or a police authority in Wales and their term of office are to be fixed by the authority (subject to any provision made by virtue of subsection (6)(a)).

(4) A standards committee of a relevant authority in England or a police authority in Wales must include—

(a) at least two members of the authority, and

(b) at least one person who is not a member, or an officer, of that or any other relevant authority.

(5) A standards committee of a relevant authority in England which are operating executive arrangements—

(a) may not include the elected mayor or executive leader, and

(b) may not be chaired by a member of the executive.

(6) The Secretary of State may by regulations make provision—

    (a) as to the size and composition of standards committees of relevant authorities in England and police authorities in Wales,

    (b) as to the appointment to such committees of persons falling within subsection (4)(b),

    (c) with respect to the access of the public to meetings of such committees,

    (d) with respect to the publicity to be given to meetings of such committees,

    (e) with respect to the production of agendas for, or records of, meetings of such committees,

    (f) with respect to the availability to the public or members of relevant authorities of agendas for, records of or information connected with meetings of such committees,

    (g) as to the proceedings and validity of proceedings of such committees.

(7) The Standards Board for England—

    (a) may issue guidance with respect to the size and composition of standards committees of relevant authorities in England and police authorities in Wales, and

    (b) must send a copy of any such guidance to the Secretary of State.

(8) A member of a standards committee of a relevant authority in England or a police authority in Wales who is not a member of the authority is entitled to vote at meetings of the committee.

(9) A relevant authority in England and a police authority in Wales must send a statement which sets out the terms of reference, or any revised terms of reference, of their standards committee to the Standards Board for England.

(10) A standards committee of a relevant authority in England or a police authority in Wales is not to be regarded as a body to which section 15 of the Local Government and Housing Act 1989 (duty to allocate seats to political groups) applies.

(11) The National Assembly for Wales may by regulations make provision—

    (a) as to the size and composition of standards committees of relevant authorities in Wales other than police authorities (including provision with respect to the appointment to any such committee of persons who are not members of the relevant authority concerned),

    (b) as to the term of office of members of any such committees,

    (c) as to the persons who may, may not or must chair any such committees,

    (d) as to the entitlement to vote of members of any such committee who are not members of the relevant authority concerned,

    (e) for or in connection with treating any such committees as bodies to which section 15 of the Local Government and Housing Act 1989 does not apply,

    (f) with respect to the access of the public to meetings of such committees,

    (g) with respect to the publicity to be given to meetings of such committees,

    (h) with respect to the production of agendas for, or records of, meetings of such committees,

    (i) with respect to the availability to the public or members of relevant authorities of agendas for, records of or information connected with meetings of any such committees,

    (j) as to the proceedings and validity of proceedings of any such committees,

    (k) for or in connection with requiring relevant authorities in Wales (other than police authorities) to send to the Commission for Local Administration in Wales statements which set out the terms of reference of their standards committees.

(12) The provision which may be made by virtue of subsection (6)(c) to (f) or (11)(f) to (i) includes provision which applies or reproduces (with or without modifications) any provisions of Part VA of the Local Government Act 1972.

Functions of standards committees

54.—(1) The general functions of a standards committee of a relevant authority are— **112–016**

(a) promoting and maintaining high standards of conduct by the members and co-opted members of the authority, and
(b) assisting members and co-opted members of the authority to observe the authority's code of conduct.

(2) Without prejudice to its general functions, a standards committee of a relevant authority has the following specific functions—

(a) advising the authority on the adoption or revision of a code of conduct,
(b) monitoring the operation of the authority's code of conduct, and
(c) advising, training or arranging to train members and co-opted members of the authority on matters relating to the authority's code of conduct.

(3) A relevant authority may arrange for their standards committee to exercise such other functions as the authority consider appropriate.

(4) The Secretary of State may by regulations make provision with respect to the exercise of functions by standards committees of relevant authorities in England and police authorities in Wales.

(5) The National Assembly for Wales may by regulations make provision with respect to the exercise of functions by standards committees of relevant authorities in Wales (other than police authorities).

(6) The Standards Board for England may issue guidance with respect to the exercise of functions by standards committees of relevant authorities in England and police authorities in Wales.

(7) The National Assembly for Wales may issue guidance with respect to the exercise of functions by standards committees of relevant authorities in Wales (other than police authorities).

. . . . . .

CHAPTER II

INVESTIGATIONS ETC: ENGLAND

Standards Board for England

Standards Board for England

57.—(1) There is to be a body corporate known as the Standards Board for **112–017** England.

(2) The Standards Board for England is to consist of not less than three members appointed by the Secretary of State.

(3) The Standards Board for England is to have the functions conferred on it

by this Part and such other functions as may be conferred on it by order made by the Secretary of State under this subsection.

(4) In exercising its functions the Standards Board for England must have regard to the need to promote and maintain high standards of conduct by members and co-opted members of relevant authorities in England.

(5) The Standards Board for England—

(a) must appoint employees known as ethical standards officers who are to have the functions conferred on them by this Part,

(b) may issue guidance to relevant authorities in England and police authorities in Wales on matters relating to the conduct of members and co-opted members of such authorities,

(c) may issue guidance to relevant authorities in England and police authorities in Wales in relation to the qualifications or experience which monitoring officers should possess, and

(d) may arrange for any such guidance to be made public.

(6) Schedule 4 makes further provision in relation to the Standards Board for England.

Written allegations

112–018 58.—(1) A person may make a written allegation to the Standards Board for England that a member or co-opted member (or former member or co-opted member) of a relevant authority in England has failed, or may have failed, to comply with the authority's code of conduct.

(2) If the Standards Board for England considers that a written allegation under subsection (1) should be investigated, it must refer the case to one of its ethical standards officers.

(3) If the Standards Board for England considers that a written allegation under subsection (1) should not be investigated, it must take reasonable steps to give written notification to the person who made the allegation of the decision and the reasons for the decision.

Functions of ethical standards officers.

Functions of ethical standards officers

112–019 59.—(1) The functions of ethical standards officers are to investigate—

(a) cases referred to them by the Standards Board for England under section 58(2), and

(b) other cases in which any such officer considers that a member or co-opted member (or former member or co-opted member) of a relevant authority in England has failed, or may have failed, to comply with the authority's code of conduct and which have come to the attention of any such officer as a result of an investigation under paragraph (a).

(2) The Standards Board for England may make arrangements in relation to the assignment of investigations under this section to particular ethical standards officers.

(3) The purpose of an investigation under this section is to determine which of the findings mentioned in subsection (4) is appropriate.

(4) Those findings are—

(a) that there is no evidence of any failure to comply with the code of conduct of the relevant authority concerned,

(b) that no action needs to be taken in respect of the matters which are the subject of the investigation,

(c) that the matters which are the subject of the investigation should be referred to the monitoring officer of the relevant authority concerned, or

(d) that the matters which are the subject of the investigation should be referred to the president of the Adjudication Panel for England for adjudication by a tribunal falling within section 76(1).

(5) Where a person is no longer a member or co-opted member of the relevant authority concerned but is a member or co-opted member of another relevant authority in England, the reference in subsection (4)(c) to the monitoring officer of the relevant authority concerned is to be treated as a reference either to the monitoring officer of the relevant authority concerned or to the monitoring officer of that other relevant authority (and accordingly an ethical standards officer who reaches a finding under subsection (4)(c) must decide to which of those monitoring officers to refer the matters concerned).

. . . . . .

Reports etc.

Reports etc.

64.—(1) Where an ethical standards officer determines in relation to any case **112–020** that a finding under section 59(4)(a) or (b) is appropriate—

(a) he may produce a report on the outcome of his investigation,

(b) he may provide a summary of any such report to any newspapers circulating in the area of the relevant authority concerned,

(c) he must send to the monitoring officer of the relevant authority concerned a copy of any such report, and

(d) where he does not produce any such report, he must inform the monitoring officer of the relevant authority concerned of the outcome of the investigation.

(2) Where an ethical standards officer determines in relation to any case that a finding under section 59(4)(c) is appropriate he must—

(a) produce a report on the outcome of his investigation,

(b) subject to subsection (4)(b), refer the matters which are the subject of the investigation to the monitoring officer of the relevant authority concerned, and

(c) send a copy of the report to the monitoring officer, and the standards committee, of the relevant authority concerned.

(3) Where an ethical standards officer determines in relation to any case that a finding under section 59(4)(d) is appropriate he must—

(a) produce a report on the outcome of his investigation,

(b) refer the matters which are the subject of the investigation to the president of the Adjudication Panel for England for adjudication by a tribunal falling within section 76(1), and

(c) send a copy of the report to the monitoring officer of the relevant authority concerned and to the president of the Adjudication Panel for England.

(4) Where a person is no longer a member or co-opted member of the relevant authority concerned but is a member or co-opted member of another relevant authority in England—

(a) the references in subsections (1)(b), (c) and (d), (2)(c) and (3)(c) to the relevant authority concerned are to be treated as including references to that other relevant authority, and

(b) an ethical standards officer who reaches a finding under section 59(4)(c) must refer the matters concerned either to the monitoring officer of the relevant authority concerned or to the monitoring officer of that other relevant authority.

(5) A report under this section may cover more than one investigation under section 59 in relation to any members or co-opted members (or former members or co-opted members) of the same relevant authority.

(6) An ethical standards officer must—

(a) inform any person who is the subject of an investigation under section 59, and

(b) take reasonable steps to inform any person who made any allegation which gave rise to the investigation,

of the outcome of the investigation.

. . . . . .

CHAPTER IV

ADJUDICATIONS

Adjudication Panels

Adjudication Panels

112–021   **75.**—(1) There is to be a panel of persons, known as the Adjudication Panel for England, eligible for membership of tribunals drawn from the Panel.

(2) There is to be a panel of persons, known as the Adjudication Panel for Wales or Panel Dyfarnu Cymru, eligible for membership of tribunals drawn from the Panel.

(3) The members of the Adjudication Panel for England are to be appointed by the Lord Chancellor.

(4) The Lord Chancellor—

(a) must appoint one of the members of the Adjudication Panel for England as president of the Panel, and

(b) may appoint one of those members as deputy president of the Panel.

(5) The members of the Adjudication Panel for Wales are to be appointed by the National Assembly for Wales on such terms and conditions as it may determine.

(6) The National Assembly for Wales—

(a) must appoint one of the members of the Adjudication Panel for Wales as president of the Panel, and

(b) may appoint one of those members as deputy president of the Panel.

(7) Such members of the Adjudication Panel for England as the Lord Chancellor thinks fit must possess such qualifications as may be determined by the Lord Chancellor.

(8) Such members of the Adjudication Panel for Wales as the National Assembly for Wales thinks fit must possess such qualifications as may be determined by the National Assembly for Wales.

(9) The president and deputy president (if any) of the Adjudication Panel for England are to be responsible—

(a) for training the members of the Panel,
(b) for issuing guidance on how tribunals drawn from the Panel are to reach decisions.

(10) The president and deputy president (if any) of the Adjudication Panel for Wales are to be responsible—

(a) for training the members of the Panel,
(b) for issuing guidance on how tribunals drawn from the Panel are to reach decisions.

(11) The Lord Chancellor must obtain the consent of the Secretary of State before making any appointment under subsection (3) or (4) or any determination under subsection (7).

Case tribunals and interim case tribunals

Case tribunals and interim case tribunals

76.—(1) Adjudications in respect of matters referred to the president of the **112–022** relevant Adjudication Panel under section 64(3) or 71(3) are to be conducted by tribunals (referred to in this Part as case tribunals) consisting of not less than three members of the Panel.

(2) Adjudications in respect of matters referred to the president of the relevant Adjudication Panel under section 65(4) or 72(4) are to be conducted by tribunals (referred to in this Part as interim case tribunals) consisting of not less than three members of the Panel.

(3) The president of the relevant Adjudication Panel (or in his absence the deputy president) is to appoint the members of any case tribunal or interim case tribunal.

(4) A case tribunal drawn from the relevant Adjudication Panel may conduct a single adjudication in relation to two or more matters which are referred to the president of the Panel under section 64(3) or 71(3).

(5) An interim case tribunal drawn from the relevant Adjudication Panel may conduct a single adjudication in relation to two or more matters which are referred to the president of the Panel under section 65(4) or 72(4).

(6) The president or the deputy president of the relevant Adjudication Panel may be a member of a case tribunal or interim case tribunal drawn from the Panel.

(7) A member of the relevant Adjudication Panel may not at any time be a member of a case tribunal or interim case tribunal drawn from the Panel which is to adjudicate on a matter relating to a member or co-opted member (or former member or co-opted member) of a relevant authority if, within the period of five years ending with that time, the member of the Panel has been a member or an officer of the authority or a member of any committee, sub-committee, joint committee or joint sub-committee of the authority.

(8) A member of the relevant Adjudication Panel who is directly or indirectly

interested in any matter which is, or is likely to be, the subject of an adjudication conducted by a case tribunal or interim case tribunal—

(a) must disclose the nature of his interest to the president or deputy president of that Panel, and

(b) may not be a member of a case tribunal or interim case tribunal which conducts an adjudication in relation to that matter.

(9) Where there is no deputy president of the relevant Adjudication Panel, the reference in subsection (3) and (8) to the deputy president is to be treated as a reference to such member of the Panel as the Lord Chancellor or (as the case may require) the National Assembly for Wales may specify.

(10) A person who is a member of an interim case tribunal which, as a result of an investigation under section 59 or 69, conducts an adjudication in relation to any person may not be a member of a case tribunal which, on the conclusion of that investigation, subsequently conducts an adjudication in relation to that person.

(11) The Lord Chancellor may issue guidance with respect to the composition of case tribunals or interim case tribunals drawn from the Adjudication Panel for England.

(12) The Lord Chancellor must obtain the consent of the Secretary of State before issuing any guidance under subsection (11).

(13) The National Assembly for Wales may issue guidance with respect to the composition of case tribunals or interim case tribunals drawn from the Adjudication Panel for Wales.

(14) The National Assembly for Wales may incur expenditure for the purpose of providing administrative support to the Adjudication Panel for Wales.

Adjudications

Adjudications

112–023   77.—(1) A person who is the subject of an adjudication conducted by a case tribunal or interim case tribunal may appear before the tribunal in person or be represented by—

(a) counsel or a solicitor, or

(b) any other person whom he desires to represent him.

(2) The Secretary of State may be regulations make such provision as appears to him to be necessary or expedient with respect to adjudications by case tribunals or interim case tribunals drawn from the Adjudication Panel for England.

(3) The president of the Adjudication Panel for England may, after consultation with the Secretary of State, give directions as to the practice and procedure to be followed by tribunals drawn from the Panel.

(4) The National Assembly for Wales may by regulations make such provision as appears to it to be necessary or expedient with respect to adjudications by case tribunals or interim case tribunals drawn from the Adjudication Panel for Wales.

(5) The president of the Adjudication Panel for Wales may, after consultation with the National Assembly for Wales, give directions as to the practice and procedure to be followed by tribunals drawn from the Panel.

(6) Regulations under this section may, in particular, include provision—

(a) for requiring persons to attend adjudications to give evidence and produce documents and for authorising the administration of oaths to witnesses,

(b) for requiring persons to furnish further particulars,

(c) for prescribing the procedure to be followed in adjudications, including provision as to the persons entitled to appear and to be heard on behalf of persons giving evidence,

(d) for the award of costs or expenses (including provision with respect to interest and provision with respect to the enforcement of any such award),

(e) for taxing or otherwise settling any such costs or expenses (and for enabling such costs to be taxed in a county court),

(f) for the registration and proof of decisions and awards of tribunals.

(7) A person who without reasonable excuse fails to comply with any requirement imposed by virtue of subsection (6)(a) or (b) is guilty of an offence and liable on summary conviction to a fine not exceeding level 3 on the standard scale.

(8) In this section any reference to documents includes a reference to information held by means of a computer or in any other electronic form.

Decisions of interim case tribunals

78.—(1) An interim case tribunal which adjudicates on any matters which are the subject of an interim report must reach one of the following decisions— **112–024**

(a) that the person to whom the recommendation mentioned in section 65(3) or 72(3) relates should not be suspended or partially suspended from being a member or co-opted member of the relevant authority concerned,

(b) that that person should be suspended or partially suspended from being a member or co-opted member of the authority concerned for a period which does not exceed six months or (if shorter) the remainder of the person's term of office.

(2) An interim case tribunal must give notice of its decision to the standards committee of the relevant authority concerned.

(3) If the decision of an interim case tribunal is that a person should be suspended or partially suspended from being a member or co-opted member of the relevant authority concerned—

(a) the notice must give details of the suspension or partial suspension and specify the date on which the suspension or partial suspension is to begin, and

(b) the relevant authority must suspend or partially suspend the person in accordance with the notice.

(4) A decision of an interim case tribunal under this section shall not prevent an ethical standards officer from continuing with the investigation under section 59 which gave rise to the interim report concerned and producing a report under section 64, or a further interim report under section 65, in respect of any matters which are the subject of the investigation.

(5) A decision of an interim case tribunal under this section shall not prevent a Local Commissioner in Wales from continuing with the investigation under section 69 which gave rise to the interim report concerned and producing a report under section 71, or a further interim report under section 72, in respect of any matters which are the subject of the investigation.

(6) The suspension or partial suspension of any person under this section shall not extend beyond the day on which a notice under section 79 is given to the

standards committee of the relevant authority concerned with respect to that person.

(7) A copy of any notice under this section must be given—

(a) to any person who is the subject of the notice, and
(b) to the monitoring officer of the relevant authority concerned.

(8) In a case where section 65(6) or 72(6) applies, the references in subsections (2) and (7)(b) to the relevant authority concerned are to be treated as including a reference to the relevant authority of which the person concerned was formerly a member or co-opted member.

(9) An interim case tribunal must take reasonable steps to inform any person who made any allegation which gave rise to the investigation under section 59 or 69 of its decision under this section.

(10) A person who is suspended or partially suspended under this section may appeal to the High Court—

(a) against the suspension or partial suspension, or
(b) against the length of the suspension or partial suspension.

Decisions of case tribunals

112–025   **79.**—(1) A case tribunal which adjudicates on any matter must decide whether or not any person to which that matter relates has failed to comply with the code of conduct of the relevant authority concerned.

(2) Where a case tribunal decides that a person has not failed to comply with the code of conduct of the relevant authority concerned, it must give notice to that effect to the standards committee of the relevant authority concerned.

(3) Where a case tribunal decides that a person has failed to comply with the code of conduct of the relevant authority concerned, it must decide whether the nature of the failure is such that the person should be suspended or disqualified in accordance with subsection (4).

(4) A person may be—

(a) suspended or partially suspended from being a member or co-opted member of the relevant authority concerned, or
(b) disqualified for being, or becoming (whether by election or otherwise), a member of that or any other relevant authority.

(5) Where a case tribunal makes such a decision as is mentioned in subsection (4)(a), it must decide the period for which the person should be suspended or partially suspended (which must not exceed one year or, if shorter, the remainder of the person's term of office).

(6) Where a case tribunal makes such a decision as is mentioned in subsection (4)(b), it must decide the period for which the person should be disqualified (which must not exceed five years).

(7) Where a case tribunal decides that a person has failed to comply with the code of conduct of the relevant authority concerned but should not be suspended or disqualified as mentioned in subsection (4), it must give notice to the standards committee of the relevant authority concerned—

(a) stating that the person has failed to comply with that code of conduct, and
(b) specifying the details of that failure.

(8) Where a case tribunal decides that a person has failed to comply with the code of conduct of the relevant authority concerned and should be suspended or

partially suspended as mentioned in subsection (4)(a), it must give notice to the standards committee of the relevant authority concerned—

  (a) stating that the person has failed to comply with that code of conduct,
  (b) specifying the details of that failure, and
  (c) stating that the person must be suspended or partially suspended by the relevant authority concerned for the period, and in the way, which the tribunal has decided.

(9) A relevant authority must comply with any notice given to its standards committee under subsection (8).

(10) Where a case tribunal decides that a person has failed to comply with the code of conduct of the relevant authority concerned and should be disqualified as mentioned in subsection (4)(b), it must give notice to the standards committee of the relevant authority concerned—

  (a) stating that the person has failed to comply with that code of conduct,
  (b) specifying the details of that failure, and
  (c) stating that the person is disqualified for being, or becoming (whether by election or otherwise), a member of that or any other relevant authority for the period which the tribunal has decided.

(11) The effect of a notice given to the standards committee of a relevant authority under subsection (10) is to disqualify the person concerned as mentioned in subsection (10)(c).

(12) A copy of any notice under this section—

  (a) must be given—

      (i) to the Standards Board for England, where the relevant authority concerned is in England,
      (ii) to the Commission for Local Administration in Wales, where the relevant authority concerned is in Wales,

  (b) must be given to any person who is the subject of the decision to which the notice relates, and
  (c) must be published in one or more newspapers circulating in the area of the relevant authority concerned.

(13) Where the person concerned is no longer a member or co-opted member of the relevant authority concerned but is a member or co-opted member of another relevant authority in the same country (that is to say, England or Wales)—

  (a) a copy of any notice under subsection (2), (7) or (10) must also be given to the standards committee of that other relevant authority,
  (b) the references in subsections (4)(a) and (8)(c) to the relevant authority concerned are to be treated as references to that other relevant authority,
  (c) the duty to give notice to the standards committee of the relevant authority concerned under subsection (8) is to be treated as a duty—

      (i) to give that notice to the standards committee of that other relevant authority, and
      (ii) to give a copy of that notice to the standards committee of the relevant authority concerned,

  (d) the reference in subsection (12)(c) to the relevant authority concerned is to be treated as including a reference to that other relevant authority.

(14) A case tribunal must take reasonable steps to inform any person who made any allegation which gave rise to the adjudication of the decision of the case tribunal under this section.

(15) Where a case tribunal decides under this section that a person has failed to comply with the code of conduct of the relevant authority concerned, that person may appeal to the High Court against that decision, or any other decision under this section which relates to him.

. . . . . .

CHAPTER V

SUPPLEMENTARY

Disclosure and registration of members' interests etc.

Disclosure and registration of members' interests etc.

112–026 **81.**—(1) The monitoring officer of each relevant authority must establish and maintain a register of interests of the members and co-opted members of the authority.

(2) The mandatory provisions of the model code applicable to each relevant authority ("the mandatory provisions") must require the members and co-opted members of each authority to register in that authority's register maintained under subsection (1) such financial and other interests as are specified in the mandatory provisions.

(3) The mandatory provisions must also—

    (a) require any member or co-opted member of a relevant authority who has an interest specified in the mandatory provisions under subsection (2) to disclose that interest before taking part in any business of the authority relating to that interest,

    (b) make provision for preventing or restricting the participation of a member or co-opted member of a relevant authority in any business of the authority to which an interest disclosed under paragraph (a) relates.

(4) Any participation by a member or co-opted member of a relevant authority in any business which is prohibited by the mandatory provisions is not a failure to comply with the authority's code of conduct if the member or co-opted member has acted in accordance with a dispensation from the prohibition granted by the authority's standards committee in accordance with regulations made under subsection (5).

(5) The Secretary of State may prescribe in regulations the circumstances in which standards committees may grant dispensations under subsection (4).

(6) A relevant authority must ensure that copies of the register for the time being maintained by their monitoring officer under this section are available at an office of the authority for inspection by members of the public at all reasonable hours.

(7) As soon as practicable after the establishment by their monitoring officer of a register under this section, a relevant authority must—

    (a) publish in one or more newspapers circulating in their area a notice which—

        (i) states that copies of the register are available at an office of the authority for inspection by members of the public at all reasonable hours, and

(ii) specifies the address of that office, and

(b) inform the Standards Board for England that copies of the register are so available.

(8) In its application to standards committees of relevant authorities in Wales (other than police authorities), subsection (5) has effect as if for the reference to the Secretary of State there were substituted a reference to the National Assembly for Wales.

Code of conduct for local government employees

Code of conduct for local government employees

82.—(1) The Secretary of State may by order issue a code as regards the **112–027** conduct which is expected of qualifying employees of relevant authorities in England and police authorities in Wales.

(2) The National Assembly for Wales may by order issue a code as regards the conduct which is expected of qualifying employees of relevant authorities in Wales (other than police authorities).

(3) The power under subsection (1) or (2) to issue a code includes power—

(a) to issue a separate code for council managers (within the meaning of Part II of this Act), and

(b) to revise any code which has been issued.

(4) Before making an order under this section, the Secretary of State must consult—

(a) such representatives of relevant authorities in England, and of employees of such authorities, as he considers appropriate,

(b) the Audit Commission, and

(c) the Commission for Local Administration in England.

(5) Before making an order under this section so far as it relates to police authorities in Wales, the Secretary of State must consult—

(a) such representatives of police authorities in Wales, and of employees of such authorities, as he considers appropriate,

(b) the Commission for Local Administration in Wales, and

(c) the National Assembly for Wales.

(6) Before making an order under this section, the National Assembly for Wales must consult—

(a) such representatives of relevant authorities in Wales, and of employees of such authorities, as it considers appropriate,

(b) the Audit Commission, and

(c) the Commission for Local Administration in Wales.

(7) The terms of appointment or conditions of employment of every qualifying employee of a relevant authority (whether appointed or employed before or after the commencement of this section) are to be deemed to incorporate any code for the time being under this section which is applicable.

(8) In this section "qualifying employee", in relation to a relevant authority, means an employee of the authority other than an employee falling within any description of employee specified in regulations under this subsection.

(9) The power to make regulations under subsection (8) is to be exercised—

(a) in relation to England, by the Secretary of State, and
(b) in relation to Wales, by the National Assembly for Wales.

. . . . . .

PART V

MISCELLANEOUS

Maladministration etc

Payments in cases of maladministration etc.

112–028 92.—(1) Where a relevant authority consider—

(a) that action taken by or on behalf of the authority in the exercise of their functions amounts to, or may amount to, maladministration, and
(b) that a person has been, or may have been, adversely affected by that action,

the authority may, if they think appropriate, make a payment to, or provide some other benefit for, that person.

(2) Any function which is conferred on the Greater London Authority under this section is to be exercisable by the Mayor of London and the London Assembly acting jointly on behalf of the Authority.

(3) In this section—

"action" includes failure to act,
"relevant authority" has the same meaning as in Part III of this Act.

Police (Northern Ireland) Act 2000

(2000, c. 32)

113–001 *An Act to make provision about policing in Northern Ireland; and for connected purposes.*   [23rd November 2000]

PART I

NAME OF THE POLICE IN NORTHERN IRELAND

Name of the police in Northern Ireland

113–002 **1.**—(1) The body of constables known as the Royal Ulster Constabulary shall continue in being as the Police Service of Northern Ireland (incorporating the Royal Ulster Constabulary).

(2) The body of constables referred to in subsection (1) shall be styled for operational purposes the "Police Service of Northern Ireland".

(3) The body of constables known as the Royal Ulster Constabulary Reserve shall continue in being as the Police Service of Northern Ireland Reserve (incorporating the Royal Ulster Constabulary Reserve).

(4) The body of constables referred to in subsection (3) shall be styled for operational purposes "The Police Service of Northern Ireland Reserve".

PART II

THE NORTHERN IRELAND POLICING BOARD

The Northern Ireland Policing Board

2.—(1) There shall be a body corporate to be known as the Northern Ireland **113–003** Policing Board (in this Act referred to as "the Board").

(2) Schedule 1 shall have effect in relation to the Board.

(3) The Police Authority for Northern Ireland is hereby dissolved.

(4) Schedule 2 (which contains provisions for the transfer of the functions, assets, liabilities and staff of the Police Authority for Northern Ireland to the Board and other supplementary provisions) shall have effect.

General functions of the Board

3.—(1) The Board shall secure the maintenance of the police in Northern **113–004** Ireland.

(2) The Board shall secure that—

(a) the police,
(b) the police support staff, and
(c) traffic wardens appointed by the Board under section 71,

are efficient and effective.

(3) In carrying out its functions under subsections (1) and (2) the Board shall—

(a) in accordance with the following provisions of this Act, hold the Chief Constable to account for the exercise of his functions and those of the police, the police support staff and traffic wardens;

(b) monitor the performance of the police in—

(i) carrying out the general duty under section 32(1);
(ii) complying with the Human Rights Act 1998;
(iii) carrying out the policing plan;

(c) keep itself informed as to—

(i) the workings of Part VII of the 1998 Act (police complaints and disciplinary proceedings) and trends and patterns in complaints under that Part;
(ii) the manner in which complaints from members of the public against traffic wardens are dealt with by the Chief Constable under section 71;
(iii) trends and patterns in crimes committed in Northern Ireland;
(iv) trends and patterns in recruitment to the police and the police support staff;
(v) the extent to which the membership of the police and the police support staff is representative of the community in Northern Ireland;

(d) assess—

    (i) the effectiveness of measures taken to secure that the membership of the police and the police support staff is representative of that community;

    (ii) the level of public satisfaction with the performance of the police and of district policing partnerships;

    (iii) the effectiveness of district policing partnerships in performing their functions and, in particular, of arrangements made under Part III in obtaining the views of the public about matters concerning policing and the co-operation of the public with the police in preventing crime;

    (iv) the effectiveness of the code of ethics issued under section 52;

  (e) make arrangements for obtaining the co-operation of the public with the police in the prevention of crime.

(4) In carrying out its functions, the Board shall have regard to—

  (a) the principle that the policing of Northern Ireland is to be conducted in an impartial manner;

  (b) the policing plan;

  (c) any code of practice issued by the Secretary of State under section 27; and

  (d) the need—

    (i) to co-ordinate its activities with those of other statutory authorities; and

    (ii) to co-operate with such authorities.

. . . . . .

PART VI

THE POLICE

General

Regulations as to emblems and flags

113–005   **54.**—(1) The Secretary of State may make regulations—

  (a) prescribing the design of an emblem for the police; and

  (b) regulating the use of that or any other emblem—

    (i) on equipment or property used for the purposes of the police; or

    (ii) otherwise in connection with the police.

(2) The Secretary of State may make regulations—

  (a) prescribing the design of a flag for the police; and

  (b) regulating the flying or carrying of that or any other flag—

    (i) on land or buildings used for the purposes of the police; or

    (ii) otherwise in connection with the police.

(3) Before making any regulations under this section the Secretary of State shall consult—

  (a) the Board;

(b) the Chief Constable;

(c) the Police Association; and

(d) any other person or body appearing to him to have an interest in the matter.

Political Parties, Elections and Referendums Act 2000

(2000, c. 41)

An Act to establish an Electoral Commission; to make provision about the regis- **114–001**
tration and finances of political parties; to make provision about donations and expenditure for political purposes; to make provision about election and referendum campaigns and the conduct of referendums; to make provision about election petitions and other legal proceedings in connection with elections; to reduce the qualifying periods set out in sections 1 and 3 of the Representation of the People Act 1985; to make pre-consolidation amendments relating to European Parliamentary Elections; and for con-
nected purposes.   [30th November 2000]

PART I

THE ELECTORAL COMMISSION

Establishment of Electoral Commission and bodies with related functions

Establishment of the Electoral Commission

1.—(1) There shall be a body corporate to be known as the Electoral Commis- **114–002**
sion or, in Welsh, Comisiwn Etholiadol (in this Act referred to as "the Commission").

(2) The Commission shall consist of members to be known as Electoral Commissioners.

(3) There shall be not less than five, but not more than nine, Electoral Commissioners.

(4) The Electoral Commissioners shall be appointed by Her Majesty (in accordance with section 3).

(5) Her Majesty shall (in accordance with section 3) appoint one of the Electoral Commissioners to be the chairman of the Commission.

(6) Schedule 1, which makes further provision in relation to the Commission, shall have effect.

Speaker's Committee

2.—(1) There shall be a Committee (to be known as "the Speaker's **114–003**
Committee") to perform the functions conferred on the Committee by this Act.

(2) The Speaker's Committee shall consist of the Speaker of the House of Commons, who shall be the chairman of the Committee, and the following other members, namely—

(a) the Member of the House of Commons who is for the time being the Chairman of the Home Affairs Select Committee of the House of Commons;

(b) the [Secretary of State for Transport, Local Government and the Regions][1] (whether or not a Member of the House of Commons);

(c) a Member of the House of Commons who is a Minister of the Crown with responsibilities in relation to local government; and

(d) five Members of the House of Commons who are not Ministers of the Crown.

(3) The member of the Committee mentioned in subsection (2)(c) shall be appointed to membership of the Committee by the Prime Minister.

(4) The members of the Committee mentioned in Subsection (2)(d) shall be appointed to membership of the Committee by the Speaker of the House of Commons.

(5) Schedule 2, which makes further provision in relation to the Speaker's Committee, shall have effect.

(6) In this section and that Schedule, references to the Home Affairs Select Committee shall—

(a) if the name of that Committee is changed, be taken (subject to paragraph (b)) to be references to the Committee by its new name;

(b) if the functions of that Committee at the passing of this Act with respect to electoral matters (or functions substantially corresponding thereto) become functions of a different committee of the House of Commons, be taken to be references to the committee by whom the functions are for the time being exercisable.

[1] Words substituted by S.I. 2001 No. 3500 Sched. 2 Pt II, para. 9(1).

. . . . . .

Part II

Registration of Political Parties

Requirement for registration

Parties to be registered in order to field candidates at elections

114–004   **22.**—(1) Subject to subsection (4), no nomination may be made in relation to a relevant election unless the nomination is in respect of—

(a) a person who stands for election in the name of a qualifying registered party; or

(b) a person who does not purport to represent any party; or

(c) a qualifying registered party, where the election is one for which registered parties may be nominated.

(2) For the purposes of subsection (1) a party (other than a minor party) is a "qualifying registered party" in relation to a relevant election if—

(a) the constituency, local government area or electoral region in which the election is held—

(i) is in England, Scotland or Wales, or

(ii) is the electoral region of Scotland or Wales,

and the party was, on the last day for publication of notice of the election, registered in respect of that part of Great Britain in the Great Britain register maintained by the Commission under section 23, or

(b) the constituency, district electoral area or electoral region in which the election is held—

(i) is in Northern Ireland, or
(ii) is the electoral region of Northern Ireland,

and the party was, on that day, registered in the Northern Ireland register maintained by the Commission under that section.

(3) For the purposes of subsection (1) a person does not purport to represent any party if either—

(a) the description of the candidate given in his nomination paper, is—

(i) "Independent", or
(ii) where the candidate is the Speaker of the House of Commons seeking re-election, "The Speaker seeking re-election"; or

(b) no description of the candidate is given in his nomination paper.

(4) Subsection (1) does not apply in relation to any parish or community election.

(5) The following elections are relevant elections for the purposes of this Part—

(a) parliamentary elections,
(b) elections to the European Parliament,
(c) elections to the Scottish Parliament,
(d) elections to the National Assembly for Wales,
(e) elections to the Northern Ireland Assembly,
(f) local government elections, and
(g) local elections in Northern Ireland.

(6) For the purposes of this Act a person stands for election in the name of a registered party if his nomination paper includes a description authorised by a certificate issued by or on behalf of the registered nominating officer of the party.

The registers of political parties

The new registers

23.—(1) In place of the register of political parties maintained by the registrar **114–005** of companies under the Registration of Political Parties Act 1998, there shall be the new registers of political parties mentioned in subsection (2) which—

(a) shall be maintained by the Commission, and
(b) (subject to the provisions of this section) shall be so maintained in such form as the Commission may determine.

(2) The new registers of political parties are—

(a) a register of parties that intend to contest relevant elections in one or more of England, Scotland and Wales (referred to in this Act as "the Great Britain register"); and
(b) a register of parties that intend to contest relevant elections in Northern Ireland (referred to in this Act as "the Northern Ireland register").

(3) Each party registered in the Great Britain register shall be so registered in respect of one or more of England, Scotland and Wales; and the entry for each party so registered shall be marked so as to indicate—

    (a) the part or parts of Great Britain in respect of which it is registered; and

    (b) if the party is a minor party, that it is such a party.

(4) A party may be registered under this Part in both of the new registers, but where a party is so registered—

    (a) the party as registered in the Great Britain register, and

    (b) the party as registered in the Northern Ireland register,

shall constitute two separate registered parties.

(5) In such a case—

    (a) the party shall for the purposes of this Act be so organised and administered as to secure that the financial affairs of the party in Great Britain are conducted separately from those of the party in Northern Ireland;

    (b) the financial affairs of the party in Great Britain or (as the case may be) Northern Ireland, shall accordingly constitute for those purposes the financial affairs of the party as registered in the Great Britain register or (as the case may be) the Northern Ireland register; and

    (c) any application for the registration of a party in accordance with subsection (4) shall similarly be made and determined by reference to the party's organisation and activities in Great Britain and Northern Ireland respectively.

(6) The Secretary of State may by order make provision for the transfer to the Commission of any property, rights and liabilities to which the registrar of companies is entitled or subject in connection with his functions under the Registration of Political Parties Act 1998an order under this subsection may in particular provide for the order to have effect despite any provision (of whatever nature) which would prevent or restrict the transfer of the property, rights or liabilities otherwise than by the order.

. . . . . .

Supplemental

Party political broadcasts

114–006   **37.**—(1) A broadcaster shall not include in its broadcasting services any party political broadcast made on behalf of a party which is not a registered party.

(2) In this Act "broadcaster" means—

    (a) the holder of a licence under the Broadcasting Act 1990 or 1996,

    (b) the British Broadcasting Corporation, or

    (c) Sianel Pedwar Cymru.

. . . . . .

PART IV

CONTROL OF DONATIONS TO REGISTERED PARTIES AND THEIR MEMBERS ETC.

CHAPTER I

DONATIONS TO REGISTERED PARTIES

Sponsorship

51.—(1) For the purposes of this Part sponsorship is provided in relation to **114–007** a registered party if—

(a) any money or other property is transferred to the party or to any person for the benefit of the party, and
(b) the purpose (or one of the purposes) of the transfer is (or must, having regard to all the circumstances, reasonably be assumed to be)—

(i) to help the party with meeting, or to meet, to any extent any defined expenses incurred or to be incurred by or on behalf of the party, or
(ii) to secure that to any extent any such expenses are not so incurred.

(2) In subsection (1) "defined expenses" means expenses in connection with—

(a) any conference, meeting or other event organised by or on behalf of the party;
(b) the preparation, production or dissemination of any publication by or on behalf of the party; or
(c) any study or research organised by or on behalf of the party.

(3) The following do not, however, constitute sponsorship by virtue of subsection (1)—

(a) the making of any payment in respect of—

(i) any charge for admission to any conference, meeting or other event, or
(ii) the purchase price of, or any other charge for access to, any publication;

(b) the making of any payment in respect of the inclusion of an advertisement in any publication where the payment is made at the commercial rate payable for the inclusion of such an advertisement in any such publication;

and subsection (1) also has effect subject to section 52(3).

(4) The Secretary of State may by order made on the recommendation of the Commission amend subsection (2) or (3).

(5) In this section "publication" means a publication made available in whatever form and by whatever means (whether or not to the public at large or any section of the public).

. . . . . .

CHAPTER II

RESTRICTIONS ON DONATIONS TO REGISTERED PARTIES

Permissible donations

Permissible donors

114–008 **54.**—(1) A donation received by a registered party must not be accepted by the party if—

(a) the person by whom the donation would be made is not, at the time of its receipt by the party, a permissible donor; or

(b) the party is (whether because the donation is given anonymously or by reason of any deception or concealment or otherwise) unable to ascertain the identity of that person.

(2) For the purposes of this Part the following are permissible donors—

(a) an individual registered in an electoral register;

(b) a company—

(i) registered under the Companies Act 1985 or the Companies (Northern Ireland) Order 1986, and

(ii) incorporated within the United Kingdom or another member State,

which carries on business in the United Kingdom;

(c) a registered party;

(d) a trade union entered in the list kept under the Trade Union and Labour Relations (Consolidation) Act 1992 or the Industrial Relations (Northern Ireland) Order 1992;

(e) a building society (within the meaning of the Building Societies Act 1986);

(f) a limited liability partnership registered under the Limited Liability Partnerships Act 2000, or any corresponding enactment in force in Northern Ireland, which carries on business in the United Kingdom;

(g) a friendly society registered under the Friendly Societies Act 1974 or a society registered (or deemed to be registered) under the Industrial and Provident Societies Act 1965 or the Industrial and Provident Societies Act (Northern Ireland) 1969; and

(h) any unincorporated association of two or more persons which does not fall within any of the preceding paragraphs but which carries on business or other activities wholly or mainly in the United Kingdom and whose main office is there.

(3) In relation to a donation in the form of a bequest subsection (2)(a) shall be read as referring to an individual who was, at any time within the period of five years ending with the date of his death, registered in an electoral register.

(4) Where any person ("the principal donor") causes an amount ("the principal donation") to be received by a registered party by way of a donation—

(a) on behalf of himself and one or more other persons, or

(b) on behalf of two or more other persons,

then for the purposes of this Part each individual contribution by a person falling within paragraph (a) or (b) of more than £200 shall be treated as if it were a separate donation received from that person.

(5) In relation to each such separate donation, the principal donor must ensure

that, at the time when the principal donation is received by the party, the party is given—

(a) (except in the case of a donation which the principal donor is treated as making) all such details in respect of the person treated as making the donation as are required by virtue of paragraph 2 of Schedule 6 to be given in respect of the donor of a recordable donation; and

(b) (in any case) all such details in respect of the donation as are required by virtue of paragraph 4 of Schedule 6 to be given in respect of a recordable donation.

(6) Where—

(a) any person ("the agent") causes an amount to be received by a registered party by way of a donation on behalf of another person ("the donor"), and

(b) the amount of that donation is more than £200,

the agent must ensure that, at the time when the donation is received by the party, the party is given all such details in respect of the donor as are required by virtue of paragraph 2 of Schedule 6 to be given in respect of the donor of a recordable donation.

(7) A person commits an offence if, without reasonable excuse, he fails to comply with subsection (5) or (6).

(8) In this section "electoral register" means any of the following—

(a) a register of parliamentary or local government electors maintained under section 9 of the Representation of the People Act 1983;

(b) a register of relevant citizens of the European Union prepared under [the European Parliamentary Elections (Franchise of Relevant Citizens of the Union) Regulations 2001]; or

(c) a register of peers prepared under regulations under section 3 of the Representation of the People Act 1985.

. . . . . .

Acceptance or return of donations: general

56.—(1) Where—   **114–009**

(a) a donation is received by a registered party, and

(b) it is not immediately decided that the party should (for whatever reason) refuse the donation,

all reasonable steps must be taken forthwith by or on behalf of the party to verify (or, so far as any of the following is not apparent, ascertain) the identity of the donor, whether he is a permissible donor, and (if that appears to be the case) all such details in respect of him as are required by virtue of paragraph 2 of Schedule 6 to be given in respect of the donor of a recordable donation.

(2) If a registered party receives a donation which it is prohibited from accepting by virtue of section 54(1), or which it is decided that the party should for any other reason refuse, then—

(a) unless the donation falls within section 54(1)(b), the donation, or a payment of an equivalent amount, must be sent back to the person who made the donation or any person appearing to be acting on his behalf,

(b) if the donation falls within that provision, the required steps (as defined by section 57(1)) must be taken in relation to the donation,

within the period of 30 days beginning with the date when the donation is received by the party.

(3) Where—

(a) subsection (2)(a) applies in relation to a donation, and
(b) the donation is not dealt with in accordance with that provision,

the party and the treasurer of the party are each guilty of an offence.

(4) Where—

(a) subsection (2)(b) applies in relation to a donation, and
(b) the donation is not dealt with in accordance with that provision,

the treasurer of the party is guilty of an offence.

(5) For the purposes of this Part a donation received by a registered party shall be taken to have been accepted by the party unless—

(a) the steps mentioned in paragraph (a) or (b) of subsection (2) are taken in relation to the donation within the period of 30 days mentioned in that subsection; and
(b) a record can be produced of the receipt of the donation and—

(i) of the return of the donation, or the equivalent amount, as mentioned in subsection (2)(a), or
(ii) of the required steps being taken in relation to the donation as mentioned in subsection (2)(b),

as the case may be.

(6) Where a donation is received by a registered party in the form of an amount paid into any account held by the party with a financial institution, it shall be taken for the purposes of this Part to have been received by the party at the time when the party is notified in the usual way of the payment into the account.

Return of donations where donor unidentifiable

114–010   57.—(1) For the purposes of section 56(2)(b) the required steps are as follows—

(a) if the donation mentioned in that provision was transmitted by a person other than the donor, and the identity of that person is apparent, to return the donation to that person;
(b) if paragraph (a) does not apply but it is apparent that the donor has, in connection with the donation, used any facility provided by an identifiable financial institution, to return the donation to that institution; and
(c) in any other case, to send the donation to the Commission.

(2) In subsection (1) any reference to returning or sending a donation to any person or body includes a reference to sending a payment of an equivalent amount to that person or body.

(3) Any amount sent to the Commission in pursuance of subsection (1)(c) shall be paid by them into the Consolidated Fund.

Forfeiture of certain donations

Forfeiture of donations made by impermissible or unidentifiable donors

58.—(1) This section applies to any donation received by a registered party—   **114–011**

    (a) which, by virtue of section 54(1)(a) or (b), the party are prohibited from accepting, but

    (b) which has been accepted by the party.

(2) The court may, on an application made by the Commission, order the forfeiture by the party of an amount equal to the value of the donation.

(3) The standard of proof in proceedings on an application under this section shall be that applicable to civil proceedings.

(4) An order may be made under this section whether or not proceedings are brought against any person for an offence connected with the donation.

(5) In this section "the court" means—

    (a) in relation to England and Wales, a magistrates' court;

    (b) in relation to Scotland, the sheriff; and

    (c) in relation to Northern Ireland, a court of summary jurisdiction;

and proceedings on an application under this section to the sheriff shall be civil proceedings.

. . . . . .

PART VII

REFERENDUMS

CHAPTER I

PRELIMINARY

Referendums to which this Part applies

Referendums to which this Part applies

101.—(1) Subject to the following provisions of this section, this Part applies   **114–012**
to any referendum held throughout—

    (a) the United Kingdom;

    (b) one or more of England, Scotland, Wales and Northern Ireland; or

    (c) any region in England specified in Schedule 1 to the Regional Development Agencies Act 1998.

(2) In this Part—

    (a) "referendum" means a referendum or other poll held, in pursuance of any provision made by or under an Act of Parliament, on one or more questions specified in or in accordance with any such provision;

    (b) "question" includes proposition (and "answer" accordingly includes response).

(3) A poll held under section 36 of the Government of Wales Act 1998 is not, however, to be taken to be a referendum falling within subsection (2).

(4) If the Secretary of State by order so provides—

(a) subsection (2) shall apply to any specified Bill which has been introduced into Parliament before the making of the order as if it were an
Act; and
(b) any specified provisions of this Part shall apply, subject to any specified
modifications, in relation to any specified referendum for which provision is made by the Bill.

(5) In subsection (4) "specified" means specified in the order under that subsection.

. . . . . .

Referendum questions

114–013   **104.**—(1) Subsection (2) applies where a Bill is introduced into Parliament
which—

(a) provides for the holding of a poll that would be a referendum to which
this Part applies, and
(b) specifies the wording of the referendum question.

(2) The Commission shall consider the wording of the referendum question,
and shall publish a statement of any views of the Commission as to the intelligibility of that question—

(a) as soon as reasonably practicable after the Bill is introduced, and
(b) in such manner as they may determine.

(3) Subsections (4) and (5) apply where the wording of the referendum question in the case of any poll that would be a referendum to which this Part
applies falls to be specified in subordinate legislation within the meaning of the
Interpretation Act 1978.
(4) If a draft of the instrument in question is to be laid before Parliament for
approval by each House, the Secretary of State—

(a) shall consult the Commission on the wording of the referendum question before any such draft is so laid, and
(b) shall, at the time when any such draft is so laid, lay before each House
a report stating any views as to the intelligibility of that question which
the Commission have expressed in response to that consultation.

(5) If the instrument in question is to be subject to annulment in pursuance
of a resolution of either House of Parliament, the Secretary of State—

(a) shall consult the Commission on the wording of the referendum question before making the instrument; and
(b) shall, at the time when the instrument is laid before Parliament, lay
before each House a report stating any views as to the intelligibility of
that question which the Commission have expressed in response to that
consultation.

(6) Where any Bill, draft instrument or instrument to which subsection (2),
(4) or (5) applies specifies not only the referendum question but also any statement which is to precede that question on the ballot paper at the referendum,

any reference in that subsection to the referendum question shall be read as a reference to that question and that statement taken together.

(7) In this section "the referendum question" means the question or questions to be included in the ballot paper at the referendum.

Permitted participants

Permitted participants

105.—(1) In this Part "permitted participant", in relation to a particular refer- **114–014** endum to which this Part applies, means—

    (a) a registered party by whom a declaration has been made under section 106 in relation to the referendum; or

    (b) any of the following by whom a notification has been given under section 106 in relation to the referendum, namely—

        (i) any individual resident in the United Kingdom or registered in an electoral register (as defined by section 54(8)), or

        (ii) any body falling within any of paragraphs (b) and (d) to (h) of section 54(2).

(2) In this Part "responsible person" means—

    (a) if the permitted participant is a registered party—

        (i) the treasurer of the party, or

        (ii) in the case of a minor party, the person for the time being notified to the Commission by the party in accordance with section 106(2)(b);

    (b) if the permitted participant is an individual, that individual; and

    (c) otherwise, the person or officer for the time being notified to the Commission by the permitted participant in accordance with section 106(4)(b)(ii).

Declarations and notifications for purposes of section 105

106.—(1) For the purposes of section 105(1) a registered party makes a **114–015** declaration to the Commission under this section if the party makes a declaration to the Commission which identifies—

    (a) the referendum to which it relates, and

    (b) the outcome or outcomes for which the party proposes to campaign.

(2) A declaration under this section—

    (a) must be signed by the responsible officers of the party (within the meaning of section 64); and

    (b) if made by a minor party, must be accompanied by a notification which states the name of the person who will be responsible for compliance on the part of the party with the provisions of Chapter II.

(3) For the purposes of section 105(1) an individual or body gives a notification to the Commission under this section if he or it gives the Commission a notification which identifies—

    (a) the referendum to which it relates, and

    (b) the outcome or outcomes for which the giver of the notification proposes to campaign.

  (4) A notification under this section must—

    (a) if given by an individual, state—

       (i) his full name, and
      (ii) his home address in the United Kingdom, or (if he has no such address in the United Kingdom) his home address elsewhere,

    and be signed by him;

    (b) if given by a body falling within any of paragraphs (b) and (d) to (h) of section 54(2), state—

       (i) all such details in respect of the body as are required by virtue of any of sub-paragraphs (4) and (6) to (10) of paragraph 2 of Schedule 6 to be given in respect of such a body as the donor of a recordable donation, and
      (ii) the name of the person or officer who will be responsible for compliance on the part of the body with the provisions of Chapter II,

    and be signed by the body's secretary or a person who acts in a similar capacity in relation to the body.

  (5) If at any time before the end of the compliance period any of the statements which, in accordance with any provision of subsection (4), are contained in a notification under this section (as it has effect for the time being) ceases to be accurate, the permitted participant by whom the notification was given shall give the Commission a notification ("a notification of alteration") indicating that that statement is replaced by some other statement—

    (a) contained in the notification of alteration, and
    (b) conforming with that provision of subsection (4).

  (6) For the purposes of subsection (5)—

    (a) "the compliance period" is the period during which any provisions of Chapter II remain to be complied with on the part of the permitted participant; and
    (b) any reference to subsection (4) shall be read, in relation to a notification under subsection (2), as a reference to subsection (2).

  (7) In this section and sections 108 and 109 "outcome", in the case of a referendum, means a particular outcome in relation to any question asked in the referendum.

Register of declarations and notifications for purposes of section 105

114–016   **107.**—(1) The Commission shall maintain a register of—

    (a) all declarations made to them under section 106; and
    (b) all notifications given to them under that section.

  (2) The register shall be maintained by the Commission in such form as they may determine and shall contain, in the case of each such declaration or

notification, all of the information supplied to the Commission in connection with it in pursuance of section 106.

(3) Where any declaration or notification is made or given to the Commission under section 106, they shall cause—

(a) the information mentioned in subsection (2) to be entered in the register, or

(b) in the case of a notification under section 106(5), any change required as a consequence of the notification to be made in the register,

as soon as is reasonably practicable.

(4) The information to be entered in the register in respect of a permitted participant who is an individual shall, however, not include his home address.

Assistance for designated organisations

Designation of organisations to whom assistance is available

108.—(1) The Commission may, in respect of any referendum to which this **114–017** Part applies, designate permitted participants as organisations to whom assistance is available in accordance with section 110.

(2) Where there are only two possible outcomes in the case of a referendum to which this Part applies, the Commission—

(a) may, in relation to each of those outcomes, designate one permitted participant as representing those campaigning for the outcome in question; but

(b) otherwise shall not make any designation in respect of the referendum.

(3) Where there are more than two possible outcomes in the case of a referendum to which this Part applies, the Secretary of State may, after consulting the Commission, by order specify the possible outcomes in relation to which permitted participants may be designated in accordance with subsection (4).

(4) In such a case the Commission—

(a) may, in relation to each of two or more outcomes specified in any such order, designate one permitted participant as representing those campaigning for the outcome in question; but

(b) otherwise shall not make any designation in respect of the referendum.

Assistance available to designated organisations

110.—(1) Where the Commission have made any designations under section **114–018** 108 in respect of a referendum, assistance shall be available to the designated organisations in accordance with this section.

(2) The Commission shall make to each designated organisation a grant of the same amount, which shall be an amount not exceeding £600,000 determined by the Commission.

(3) A grant under subsection (2) may be made subject to such conditions as the Commission consider appropriate.

(4) Each designated organisation (or, as the case may be, persons authorised by the organisation) shall have the rights conferred by or by virtue of Schedule 12, which makes provision as to—

    (a) the sending of referendum addresses free of charge;
    (b) the use of rooms free of charge for holding public meetings; and
    (c) referendum campaign broadcasts.

(5) In this section and Schedule 12 "designated organisation", in relation to a referendum, means a person or body designated by the Commission under section 108 in respect of that referendum.

. . . . . .

CHAPTER III

CONTROLS ON PUBLICATIONS

Referendum campaign broadcasts

114–019   **127.**—(1) A broadcaster shall not include in its broadcasting services any referendum campaign broadcast made on behalf of any person or body other than one designated in respect of the referendum in question under section 108.
    (2) In this section "referendum campaign broadcast" means any broadcast whose purpose (or main purpose) is or may reasonably be assumed to be—

    (a) to further any campaign conducted with a view to promoting or procuring a particular outcome in relation to any question asked in a referendum to which this Part applies, or
    (b) otherwise to promote or procure any such outcome.

. . . . . .

Public Finance and Accountability (Scotland) Act 2000

(2001, asp1)

115–001 *An Act of the Scottish Parliament to make provision about public resources and finances and, for the purposes of section 70 of the Scotland Act 1998, about accountability for their use; and for connected purposes. The Bill for this Act of the Scottish Parliament was passed by the Parliament on 1st December 1999 and received Royal Assent on 17th January 2000*

PART 1

PUBLIC RESOURCES AND FINANCES

Use of resources

Use of resources

115–002   **1.**—(1) The use of resources by—

    (a) the Scottish Administration, and
    (b) each body or office-holder (other than an office-holder in the Scottish Administration) whose expenditure is payable out of the Scottish Consolidated Fund ("the Fund") under any enactment,

for any purpose in any financial year must be authorised for that year by Budget Act and must not exceed any amount so authorised in relation to that purpose.

(2) The use of resources accruing to the Scottish Administration or any such body or office-holder in a financial year ("accruing resources") for any purpose in that financial year must be so authorised separately from the use of other resources.

(3) In this Act a reference to the use of resources is a reference to their expenditure, consumption or reduction in value.

Emergency arrangements

2.—(1) This section applies where, at the beginning of any financial year **115–003** ("the current financial year"), the use of resources mentioned in section 1(1) has not been authorised for that year by Budget Act.

(2) Until there is in force a Budget Act authorising that use of resources for the current financial year—

    (a) any purpose for which the use of resources was authorised for the previous financial year by Budget Act shall be taken to be a purpose for which the use of resources is authorised for the current financial year, and

    (b) the use of resources for any purpose for each calendar month of the current financial year must not exceed whichever is the greater of—

        (i) one-twelfth of any amount authorised in relation to that purpose by Budget Act for the previous financial year, and

        (ii) the amount of resources used for that purpose in the corresponding calendar month of the previous financial year;

and section 1 has effect accordingly.

(3) Subsection (2) is subject to any provision made by Budget Act for the current financial year.

Contingencies

3. (1) This section applies where it is proposed that resources be used for **115–004** any purpose in any financial year by the Scottish Administration or a body or office-holder referred to in section 1(1)(b) other than in accordance with that section (whether or not as modified by section 2).

(2) The resources may be so used only with the authority of the Scottish Ministers.

(3) The Scottish Ministers may authorise the use of resources only if they consider that—

    (a) the use is necessarily required in the public interest, and

    (b) it is not reasonably practicable, for reasons of urgency, for the requirements of section 1 in relation to the use to be satisfied by a Budget Act.

(4) The aggregate amount of the resources which the Scottish Ministers may authorise to be used under this section in any financial year must not exceed 0.5% of the aggregate amount of the resources which, at the beginning of that year, were authorised to be used in that year by virtue of section 1.

(5) Where the Scottish Ministers authorise the use of resources under this section they must, as soon as possible, lay before the Parliament a report setting out the circumstances of the authorisation and why they considered it to be necessary.

Regulation of Investigatory Powers Act 2000

(2000, c. 23)

116–001 *An Act to make provision for and about the interception of communications, the acquisition and disclosure of data relating to communications, the carrying out of surveillance, the use of covert human intelligence sources and the acquisition of the means by which electronic data protected by encryption or passwords may be decrypted or accessed; to provide for Commissioners and a tribunal with functions and jurisdiction in relation to those matters, to entries on and interferences with property or with wireless telegraphy and to the carrying out of their functions by the Security Service, the Secret Intelligence Service and the Government Communications Headquarters; and for connected purposes.* [28th July 2000]

PART I

COMMUNICATIONS

CHAPTER I

INTERCEPTION

Unlawful and authorised interception

Unlawful interception

116–002   **1.**—(1) It shall be an offence for a person intentionally and without lawful authority to intercept, at any place in the United Kingdom, any communication in the course of its transmission by means of—

(a) a public postal service; or
(b) a public telecommunication system.

(2) It shall be an offence for a person—

(a) intentionally and without lawful authority, and
(b) otherwise than in circumstances in which his conduct is excluded by subsection (6) from criminal liability under this subsection,

to intercept, at any place in the United Kingdom, any communication in the course of its transmission by means of a private telecommunication system.

(3) Any interception of a communication which is carried out at any place in the United Kingdom by, or with the express or implied consent of, a person having the right to control the operation or the use of a private telecommunication system shall be actionable at the suit or instance of the sender or recipient, or intended recipient, of the communication if it is without lawful authority and is either—

    (a) an interception of that communication in the course of its transmission by means of that private system; or

    (b) an interception of that communication in the course of its transmission, by means of a public telecommunication system, to or from apparatus comprised in that private telecommunication system.

(4) Where the United Kingdom is a party to an international agreement which—

    (a) relates to the provision of mutual assistance in connection with, or in the form of, the interception of communications,

    (b) requires the issue of a warrant, order or equivalent instrument in cases in which assistance is given, and

    (c) is designated for the purposes of this subsection by an order made by the Secretary of State,

it shall be the duty of the Secretary of State to secure that no request for assistance in accordance with the agreement is made on behalf of a person in the United Kingdom to the competent authorities of a country or territory outside the United Kingdom except with lawful authority.

(5) Conduct has lawful authority for the purposes of this section if, and only if—

    (a) it is authorised by or under section 3 or 4;

    (b) it takes place in accordance with a warrant under section 5 ("an interception warrant"); or

    (c) it is in exercise, in relation to any stored communication, of any statutory power that is exercised (apart from this section) for the purpose of obtaining information or of taking possession of any document or other property;

and conduct (whether or not prohibited by this section) which has lawful authority for the purposes of this section by virtue of paragraph (a) or (b) shall also be taken to be lawful for all other purposes.

(6) The circumstances in which a person makes an interception of a communication in the course of its transmission by means of a private telecommunication system are such that his conduct is excluded from criminal liability under subsection (2) if—

    (a) he is a person with a right to control the operation or the use of the system; or

    (b) he has the express or implied consent of such a person to make the interception.

(7) A person who is guilty of an offence under subsection (1) or (2) shall be liable—

    (a) on conviction on indictment, to imprisonment for a term not exceeding two years or to a fine, or to both;

    (b) on summary conviction, to a fine not exceeding the statutory maximum.

(8) No proceedings for any offence which is an offence by virtue of this section shall be instituted—

    (a) in England and Wales, except by or with the consent of the Director of Public Prosecutions;

(b) in Northern Ireland, except by or with the consent of the Director of Public Prosecutions for Northern Ireland.

Meaning and location of "interception" etc.

116–003   2.—(1) In this Act—

"postal service" means any service which—

(a) consists in the following, or in any one or more of them, namely, the collection, sorting, conveyance, distribution and delivery (whether in the United Kingdom or elsewhere) of postal items; and

(b) is offered or provided as a service the main purpose of which, or one of the main purposes of which, is to make available, or to facilitate, a means of transmission from place to place of postal items containing communications;

"private telecommunication system" means any telecommunication system which, without itself being a public telecommunication system, is a system in relation to which the following conditions are satisfied—

(a) it is attached, directly or indirectly and whether or not for the purposes of the communication in question, to a public telecommunication system; and

(b) there is apparatus comprised in the system which is both located in the United Kingdom and used (with or without other apparatus) for making the attachment to the public telecommunication system;

"public postal service" means any postal service which is offered or provided to, or to a substantial section of, the public in any one or more parts of the United Kingdom;

"public telecommunications service" means any telecommunications service which is offered or provided to, or to a substantial section of, the public in any one or more parts of the United Kingdom;

"public telecommunication system" means any such parts of a telecommunication system by means of which any public telecommunications service is provided as are located in the United Kingdom;

"telecommunications service" means any service that consists in the provision of access to, and of facilities for making use of, any telecommunication system (whether or not one provided by the person providing the service); and

"telecommunication system" means any system (including the apparatus comprised in it) which exists (whether wholly or partly in the United Kingdom or elsewhere) for the purpose of facilitating the transmission of communications by any means involving the use of electrical or electro-magnetic energy.

(2) For the purposes of this Act, but subject to the following provisions of this section, a person intercepts a communication in the course of its transmission by means of a telecommunication system if, and only if, he—

(a) so modifies or interferes with the system, or its operation,

(b) so monitors transmissions made by means of the system, or

(c) so monitors transmissions made by wireless telegraphy to or from apparatus comprised in the system, as to make some or all of the contents of the communication available, while being transmitted, to a person other than the sender or intended recipient of the communication.

(3) References in this Act to the interception of a communication do not include references to the interception of any communication broadcast for general reception.

(4) For the purposes of this Act the interception of a communication takes place in the United Kingdom if, and only if, the modification, interference or monitoring or, in the case of a postal item, the interception is effected by conduct within the United Kingdom and the communication is either—

(a) intercepted in the course of its transmission by means of a public postal service or public telecommunication system; or

(b) intercepted in the course of its transmission by means of a private telecommunication system in a case in which the sender or intended recipient of the communication is in the United Kingdom.

(5) References in this Act to the interception of a communication in the course of its transmission by means of a postal service or telecommunication system do not include references to—

(a) any conduct that takes place in relation only to so much of the communication as consists in any traffic data comprised in or attached to a communication (whether by the sender or otherwise) for the purposes of any postal service or telecommunication system by means of which it is being or may be transmitted; or

(b) any such conduct, in connection with conduct falling within paragraph (a), as gives a person who is neither the sender nor the intended recipient only so much access to a communication as is necessary for the purpose of identifying traffic data so comprised or attached.

(6) For the purposes of this section references to the modification of a telecommunication system include references to the attachment of any apparatus to, or other modification of or interference with—

(a) any part of the system; or

(b) any wireless telegraphy apparatus used for making transmissions to or from apparatus comprised in the system.

(7) For the purposes of this section the times while a communication is being transmitted by means of a telecommunication system shall be taken to include any time when the system by means of which the communication is being, or has been, transmitted is used for storing it in a manner that enables the intended recipient to collect it or otherwise to have access to it.

(8) For the purposes of this section the cases in which any contents of a communication are to be taken to be made available to a person while being transmitted shall include any case in which any of the contents of the communication, while being transmitted, are diverted or recorded so as to be available to a person subsequently.

(9) In this section "traffic data", in relation to any communication, means—

(a) any data identifying, or purporting to identify, any person, apparatus or location to or from which the communication is or may be transmitted,

(b) any data identifying or selecting, or purporting to identify or select, apparatus through which, or by means of which, the communication is or may be transmitted,

(c) any data comprising signals for the actuation of apparatus used for the purposes of a telecommunication system for effecting (in whole or in part) the transmission of any communication, and

(d) any data identifying the data or other data as data comprised in or attached to a particular communication, but that expression includes data identifying a computer file or computer program access to which is obtained, or which is run, by means of the communication to the extent only that the file or program is identified by reference to the apparatus in which it is stored.

(10) In this section—

(a) references, in relation to traffic data comprising signals for the actuation of apparatus, to a telecommunication system by means of which a communication is being or may be transmitted include references to any telecommunication system in which that apparatus is comprised; and

(b) references to traffic data being attached to a communication include references to the data and the communication being logically associated with each other;

and in this section "data", in relation to a postal item, means anything written on the outside of the item.

(11) In this section "postal item" means any letter, postcard or other such thing in writing as may be used by the sender for imparting information to the recipient, or any packet or parcel.

Lawful interception without an interception warrant

116–004   3.—(1) Conduct by any person consisting in the interception of a communication is authorised by this section if the communication is one which, or which that person has reasonable grounds for believing, is both—

(a) a communication sent by a person who has consented to the interception; and

(b) a communication the intended recipient of which has so consented.

(2) Conduct by any person consisting in the interception of a communication is authorised by this section if—

(a) the communication is one sent by, or intended for, a person who has consented to the interception; and

(b) surveillance by means of that interception has been authorised under Part II.

(3) Conduct consisting in the interception of a communication is authorised by this section if—

(a) it is conduct by or on behalf of a person who provides a postal service or a telecommunications service; and

(b) it takes place for purposes connected with the provision or operation of that service or with the enforcement, in relation to that service, of any enactment relating to the use of postal services or telecommunications services.

(4) Conduct by any person consisting in the interception of a communication in the course of its transmission by means of wireless telegraphy is authorised by this section if it takes place—

(a) with the authority of a designated person under section 5 of the Wireless Telegraphy Act 1949 (misleading messages and interception and disclosure of wireless telegraphy messages); and

(b) for purposes connected with anything falling within subsection (5).

(5) Each of the following falls within this subsection—

(a) the issue of licences under the Wireless Telegraphy Act 1949;

(b) the prevention or detection of anything which constitutes interference with wireless telegraphy; and

(c) the enforcement of any enactment contained in that Act or of any enactment not so contained that relates to such interference.

Power to provide for lawful interception

4.—(1) Conduct by any person ("the interceptor") consisting in the interception of a communication in the course of its transmission by means of a telecommunication system is authorised by this section if— **116–005**

(a) the interception is carried out for the purpose of obtaining information about the communications of a person who, or who the interceptor has reasonable grounds for believing, is in a country or territory outside the United Kingdom;

(b) the interception relates to the use of a telecommunications service provided to persons in that country or territory which is either—

(i) a public telecommunications service; or

(ii) a telecommunications service that would be a public telecommunications service if the persons to whom it is offered or provided were members of the public in a part of the United Kingdom;

(c) the person who provides that service (whether the interceptor or another person) is required by the law of that country or territory to carry out, secure or facilitate the interception in question;

(d) the situation is one in relation to which such further conditions as may be prescribed by regulations made by the Secretary of State are required to be satisfied before conduct may be treated as authorised by virtue of this subsection; and

(e) the conditions so prescribed are satisfied in relation to that situation.

(2) Subject to subsection (3), the Secretary of State may by regulations authorise any such conduct described in the regulations as appears to him to constitute a legitimate practice reasonably required for the purpose, in connection with the carrying on of any business, of monitoring or keeping a record of—

(a) communications by means of which transactions are entered into in the course of that business; or

(b) other communications relating to that business or taking place in the course of its being carried on.

(3) Nothing in any regulations under subsection (2) shall authorise the interception of any communication except in the course of its transmission using apparatus or services provided by or to the person carrying on the business for use wholly or partly in connection with that business.

(4) conduct taking place in a prison is authorised by this section if it is conduct in exercise of any power conferred by or under any rules made under section

47 of the Prison Act 1952, section 39 of the Prisons (Scotland) Act 1989 or section 13 of the Prison Act (Northern Ireland) 1953 (prison rules).

(5) Conduct taking place in any hospital premises where high security psychiatric services are provided is authorised by this section if it is conduct in pursuance of, and in accordance with, any direction given under section 17 of the National Health Service Act 1977 (directions as to the carrying out of their functions by health bodies) to the body providing those services at those premises.

(6) Conduct taking place in a state hospital is authorised by this section if it is conduct in pursuance of, and in accordance with, any direction given to the State Hospitals Board for Scotland under section 2(5) of the National Health Service (Scotland) Act 1978 (regulations and directions as to the exercise of their functions by health boards) as applied by Article 5(1) of and the Schedule to The State Hospitals Board for Scotland Order 1995 (which applies certain provisions of that Act of 1978 to the State Hospitals Board).

(7) In this section references to a business include references to any activities of a government department, of any public authority or of any person or office holder on whom functions are conferred by or under any enactment.

(8) In this section—

"government department" includes any part of the Scottish Administration, a Northern Ireland department and the National Assembly for Wales;
"high security psychiatric services" has the same meaning as in the National Health Service Act 1977;
"hospital premises" has the same meaning as in section 4(3) of that Act; and
"state hospital" has the same meaning as in the National Health Service (Scotland) Act 1978.

(9) In this section "prison" means—

(a) any prison, young offender institution, young offenders centre or remand centre which is under the general superintendence of, or is provided by, the Secretary of State under the Prison Act 1952 or the Prison Act (Northern Ireland) 1953, or

(b) any prison, young offenders institution or remand centre which is under the general superintendence of the Scottish Ministers under the Prisons (Scotland) Act 1989, and includes any contracted out prison, within the meaning of Part IV of the Criminal Justice Act 1991 or section 106(4) of the Criminal Justice and Public Order Act 1994, and any legalised police cells within the meaning of section 14 of the Prisons (Scotland) Act 1989.

Interception with a warrant

116–006   **5.**—(1) Subject to the following provisions of this Chapter, the Secretary of State may issue a warrant authorising or requiring the person to whom it is addressed, by any such conduct as may be described in the warrant, to secure any one or more of the following—

(a) the interception in the course of their transmission by means of a postal service or telecommunication system of the communications described in the warrant;

(b) the making, in accordance with an international mutual assistance agreement, of a request for the provision of such assistance in connection with, or in the form of, an interception of communications as may be so described;

(c) the provision, in accordance with an international mutual assistance agreement, to the competent authorities of a country or territory outside the United Kingdom of any such assistance in connection with, or in the form of, an interception of communications as may be so described;

(d) the disclosure, in such manner as may be so described, of intercepted material obtained by any interception authorised or required by the warrant, and of related communications data.

(2) The Secretary of State shall not issue an interception warrant unless he believes—

(a) that the warrant is necessary on grounds falling within subsection (3); and

(b) that the conduct authorised by the warrant is proportionate to what is sought to be achieved by that conduct.

(3) Subject to the following provisions of this section, a warrant is necessary on grounds falling within this subsection if it is necessary—

(a) in the interests of national security;

(b) for the purpose of preventing or detecting serious crime;

(c) for the purpose of safeguarding the economic well-being of the United Kingdom; or

(d) for the purpose, in circumstances appearing to the Secretary of State to be equivalent to those in which he would issue a warrant by virtue of paragraph (b), of giving effect to the provisions of any international mutual assistance agreement.

(4) The matters to be taken into account in considering whether the requirements of subsection (2) are satisfied in the case of any warrant shall include whether the information which it is thought necessary to obtain under the warrant could reasonably be obtained by other means.

(5) A warrant shall not be considered necessary on the ground falling within subsection (3)(c) unless the information which it is thought necessary to obtain is information relating to the acts or intentions of persons outside the British Islands.

(6) The conduct authorised by an interception warrant shall be taken to include—

(a) all such conduct (including the interception of communications not identified by the warrant) as it is necessary to undertake in order to do what is expressly authorised or required by the warrant;

(b) conduct for obtaining related communications data; and

(c) conduct by any person which is conduct in pursuance of a requirement imposed by or on behalf of the person to whom the warrant is addressed to be provided with assistance with giving effect to the warrant.

Application for issue of an interception warrant

6.—(1) An interception warrant shall not be issued except on an application **116–007** made by or on behalf of a person specified in subsection (2).

(2) Those persons are—

(a) the Director-General of the Security Service;

(b) the Chief of the Secret Intelligence Service;

(c) the Director of GCHQ;

(d) the Director General of the National Criminal Intelligence Service;
(e) the Commissioner of Police of the Metropolis;
(f) the Chief Constable of the Royal Ulster Constabulary;
(g) the chief constable of any police force maintained under or by virtue of section 1 of the Police (Scotland) Act 1967;
(h) the Commissioners of Customs and Excise;
(i) the Chief of Defence Intelligence;
(j) a person who, for the purposes of any international mutual assistance agreement, is the competent authority of a country or territory outside the United Kingdom.

(3) An application for the issue of an interception warrant shall not be made on behalf of a person specified in subsection (2) except by a person holding office under the Crown.

Issue of warrants

116–008　7.—(1) An interception warrant shall not be issued except—

(a) under the hand of the Secretary of State or, in the case of a warrant issued by the Scottish Ministers (by virtue of provision made under section 63 of the Scotland Act 1998), a member of the Scottish Executive; or
(b) in a case falling within subsection (2) (a) or (b), under the hand of a senior official; or
(c) in a case falling within subsection (2)(aa), under the hand of a member of the staff of the Scottish Administration who is a member of the Senior Civil Service and who is designated by the Scottish Ministers as a person under whose hand a warrant may be issued in such a case.

(2) Those cases are—

(a) an urgent case in which the Secretary of State has himself expressly authorised the issue of the warrant in that case; and
[(b) an urgent case in which the Scottish Ministers have themselves (by virtue of provision made under section 63 of the Scotland Act 1998) expressly authorised the use of the warrant in that case and a statement of that fact is endorsed on the warrant; and]
(c) a case in which the warrant is for the purposes of a request for assistance made under an international mutual assistance agreement by the competent authorities of a country or territory outside the United Kingdom and either—

　(i) it appears that the interception subject is outside the United Kingdom; or
　(ii) the interception to which the warrant relates is to take place in relation only to premises outside the United Kingdom.

(3) An interception warrant—

(a) must be addressed to the person falling within section 6 (2) by whom, or on whose behalf, the application for the warrant was made; and
(b) in the case of a warrant issued under the hand of a senior official, must contain, according to whatever is applicable—

　(i) one of the statements set out in subsection (4); and
　(ii) if it contains the statement set out in subsection (4)(b), one of the statements set out in subsection (5).

(4) The statements referred to in subsection (3)(b)(i) are—

    (a) a statement that the case is an urgent case in which the Secretary of State has himself expressly authorised the issue of the warrant;

    (b) a statement that the warrant is issued for the purposes of a request for assistance made under an international mutual assistance agreement by the competent authorities of a country or territory outside the United Kingdom.

(5) The statements referred to in subsection (3)(b)(ii) are—

    (a) a statement that the interception subject appears to be outside the United Kingdom;

    (b) a statement that the interception to which the warrant relates is to take place in relation only to premises outside the United Kingdom.

Contents of warrants

8.—(1) An interception warrant must name or describe either—   **116–009**

    (a) one person as the interception subject; or

    (b) a single set of premises as the premises in relation to which the interception to which the warrant relates is to take place.

(2) The provisions of an interception warrant describing communications the interception of which is authorised or required by the warrant must comprise one or more schedules setting out the addresses, numbers, apparatus or other factors, or combination of factors, that are to be used for identifying the communications that may be or are to be intercepted.

(3) Any factor or combination of factors set out in accordance with subsection (2) must be one that identifies communications which are likely to be or to include—

    (a) communications from, or intended for, the person named or described in the warrant in accordance with subsection (1); or

    (b) communications originating on, or intended for transmission to, the premises so named or described.

(4) Subsections (1) and (2) shall not apply to an interception warrant if—

    (a) the description of communications to which the warrant relates confines the conduct authorised or required by the warrant to conduct falling within subsection (5); and

    (b) at the time of the issue of the warrant, a certificate applicable to the warrant has been issued by the Secretary of State certifying—

        (i) the descriptions of intercepted material the examination of which he considers necessary; and

        (ii) that he considers the examination of material of those descriptions necessary as mentioned in section 5(3)(a), (b) or (c).

(5) Conduct falls within this subsection if it consists in—

    (a) the interception of external communications in the course of their transmission by means of a telecommunication system; and

    (b) any conduct authorised in relation to any such interception by section 5(6).

(6) A certificate for the purposes of subsection (4) shall not be issued except under the hand of the Secretary of State.

Duration, cancellation and renewal of warrants

116–010   9.—(1) An interception warrant—

(a) shall cease to have effect at the end of the relevant period; but

(b) may be renewed, at any time before the end of that period, by an instrument under the hand of the Secretary of State[or, in the case of a warrant issued by the Scottish Ministers (by virtue of provision made under section 63 of the Scotland Act 1998), a member of the Scottish Executive] or, in a case falling within section 7(2)(b), under the hand of a senior official.

(2) An interception warrant shall not be renewed under subsection (1) unless the Secretary of State believes that the warrant continues to be necessary on grounds falling within section 5(3).

(3) The Secretary of State shall cancel an interception warrant if he is satisfied that the warrant is no longer necessary on grounds falling within section 5(3).

(4) The Secretary of State shall cancel an interception warrant if, at any time before the end of the relevant period, he is satisfied in a case in which—

(a) the warrant is one which was issued containing the statement set out in section 7(5)(a) or has been renewed by an instrument containing the statement set out in subsection (5)(b)(i) of this section, and

(b) the latest renewal (if any) of the warrant is not a renewal by an instrument under the hand of the Secretary of State,

that the person named or described in the warrant as the interception subject is in the United Kingdom.

(5) An instrument under the hand of a senior official that renews an interception warrant must contain—

(a) a statement that the renewal is for the purposes of a request for assistance made under an international mutual assistance agreement by the competent authorities of a country or territory outside the United Kingdom; and

(b) whichever of the following statements is applicable—

(i) a statement that the interception subject appears to be outside the United Kingdom;

(ii) a statement that the interception to which the warrant relates is to take place in relation only to premises outside the United Kingdom.

(6) In this section "the relevant period"—

(a) in relation to an unrenewed warrant issued in a case falling within section 7(2)(a) under the hand of a senior official, means the period ending with the fifth working day following the day of the warrant's issue;

(b) in relation to a renewed warrant the latest renewal of which was by an instrument endorsed under the hand of the Secretary of State with a statement that the renewal is believed to be necessary on grounds falling within section 5(3)(a) or (c), means the period of six months beginning with the day of the warrant's renewal; and

    (c) in all other cases, means the period of three months beginning with the day of the warrant's issue or, in the case of a warrant that has been renewed, of its latest renewal.

. . . . . .

Restrictions on use of intercepted material etc.

General safeguards

    15.—(1) Subject to subsection (6), it shall be the duty of the Secretary of **116–011** State to ensure, in relation to all interception warrants, that such arrangements are in force as he considers necessary for securing—

    (a) that the requirements of subsections (2) and (3) are satisfied in relation to the intercepted material and any related communications data; and
    (b) in the case of warrants in relation to which there are section 8(4) certificates, that the requirements of section 16 are also satisfied.

    (2) The requirements of this subsection are satisfied in relation to the intercepted material and any related communications data if each of the following—

    (a) the number of persons to whom any of the material or data is disclosed or otherwise made available,
    (b) the extent to which any of the material or data is disclosed or otherwise made available,
    (c) the extent to which any of the material or data is copied, and
    (d) the number of copies that are made,

is limited to the minimum that is necessary for the authorised purposes.

    (3) The requirements of this subsection are satisfied in relation to the intercepted material and any related communications data if each copy made of any of the material or data (if not destroyed earlier) is destroyed as soon as there are no longer any grounds for retaining it as necessary for any of the authorised purposes.

    (4) For the purposes of this section something is necessary for the authorised purposes if, and only if—

    (a) it continues to be, or is likely to become, necessary as mentioned in section 5(3);
    (b) it is necessary for facilitating the carrying out of any of the functions under this Chapter of the Secretary of State;
    (c) it is necessary for facilitating the carrying out of any functions in relation to this Part of the Interception of Communications Commissioner or of the Tribunal;
    (d) it is necessary to ensure that a person conducting a criminal prosecution has the information he needs to determine what is required of him by his duty to secure the fairness of the prosecution; or
    (e) it is necessary for the performance of any duty imposed on any person by the Public Records Act 1958 or the Public Records Act (Northern Ireland) 1923.

    (5) The arrangements for the time being in force under this section for securing that the requirements of subsection (2) are satisfied in relation to the intercepted material or any related communications data must include such

arrangements as the Secretary of State considers necessary for securing that every copy of the material or data that is made is stored, for so long as it is retained, in a secure manner.

(6) Arrangements in relation to interception warrants which are made for the purposes of subsection (1)—

    (a) shall not be required to secure that the requirements of subsections (2) and (3) are satisfied in so far as they relate to any of the intercepted material or related communications data, or any copy of any such material or data, possession of which has been surrendered to any authorities of a country or territory outside the United Kingdom; but

    (b) shall be required to secure, in the case of every such warrant, that possession of the intercepted material and data and of copies of the material or data is surrendered to authorities of a country or territory outside the United Kingdom only if the requirements of subsection (7) are satisfied.

(7) The requirements of this subsection are satisfied in the case of a warrant if it appears to the Secretary of State—

    (a) that requirements corresponding to those of subsections (2) and (3) will apply, to such extent (if any) as the Secretary of State thinks fit, in relation to any of the intercepted material or related communications data possession of which, or of any copy of which, is surrendered to the authorities in question; and

    (b) that restrictions are in force which would prevent, to such extent (if any) as the Secretary of State thinks fit, the doing of anything in, for the purposes of or in connection with any proceedings outside the United Kingdom which would result in such a disclosure as, by virtue of section 17, could not be made in the United Kingdom.

(8) In this section "copy", in relation to intercepted material or related communications data, means any of the following (whether or not in documentary form)—

    (a) any copy, extract or summary of the material or data which identifies itself as the product of an interception, and

    (b) any record referring to an interception which is a record of the identities of the persons to or by whom the intercepted material was sent, or to whom the communications data relates,

and "copied" shall be construed accordingly.

. . . . . .

Exclusion of matters from legal proceedings

116–012   **17.**—(1) Subject to section 18, no evidence shall be adduced, question asked, assertion or disclosure made or other thing done in, for the purposes of or in connection with any legal proceedings which (in any manner)—

    (a) discloses, in circumstances from which its origin in anything falling within subsection (2) may be inferred, any of the contents of an intercepted communication or any related communications data; or

    (b) tends (apart from any such disclosure) to suggest that anything falling within subsection (2) has or may have occurred or be going to occur.

(2) The following fall within this subsection—

    (a) conduct by a person falling within subsection (3) that was or would be an offence under section 1(1) or (2) of this Act or under section 1 of the Interception of Communications Act 1985;

    (b) a breach by the Secretary of State of his duty under section 1(4) of this Act;

    (c) the issue of an interception warrant or of a warrant under the Interception of Communications Act 1985;

    (d) the making of an application by any person for an interception warrant, or for a warrant under that Act;

    (e) the imposition of any requirement on any person to provide assistance with giving effect to an interception warrant.

(3) The persons referred to in subsection (2)(a) are—

    (a) any person to whom a warrant under this Chapter may be addressed;

    (b) any person holding office under the Crown;

    (c) any member of the National Criminal Intelligence Service;

    (d) any member of the National Crime Squad;

    (e) any person employed by or for the purposes of a police force;

    (f) any person providing a postal service or employed for the purposes of any business of providing such a service; and

    (g) any person providing a public telecommunications service or employed for the purposes of any business of providing such a service.

(4) In this section "intercepted communication" means any communication intercepted in the course of its transmission by means of a postal service or telecommunication system.

. . . . . .

Part II

Surveillance and Covert Human Intelligence Sources

Introductory

Conduct to which Part II applies

26.—(1) This Part applies to the following conduct—   **116–013**

    (a) directed surveillance;

    (b) intrusive surveillance; and

    (c) the conduct and use of covert human intelligence sources.

(2) Subject to subsection (6), surveillance is directed for the purposes of this Part if it is covert but not intrusive and is undertaken—

    (a) for the purposes of a specific investigation or a specific operation;

    (b) in such a manner as is likely to result in the obtaining of private information about a person (whether or not one specifically identified for the purposes of the investigation or operation); and

    (c) otherwise than by way of an immediate response to events or circumstances the nature of which is such that it would not be reasonably practicable for an authorisation under this Part to be sought for the carrying out of the surveillance.

(3) Subject to subsections (4) to (6), surveillance is intrusive for the purposes of this Part if, and only if, it is covert surveillance that—

    (a) is carried out in relation to anything taking place on any residential premises or in any private vehicle; and

    (b) involves the presence of an individual on the premises or in the vehicle or is carried out by means of a surveillance device.

(4) For the purposes of this Part surveillance is not intrusive to the extent that—

    (a) it is carried out by means only of a surveillance device designed or adapted principally for the purpose of providing information about the location of a vehicle; or

    (b) it is surveillance consisting in any such interception of a communication as falls within section 48(4).

(5) For the purposes of this Part surveillance which—

    (a) is carried out by means of a surveillance device in relation to anything taking place on any residential premises or in any private vehicle, but

    (b) is carried out without that device being present on the premises or in the vehicle,

is not intrusive unless the device is such that it consistently provides information of the same quality and detail as might be expected to be obtained from a device actually present on the premises or in the vehicle.

(6) For the purposes of this Part surveillance which—

    (a) is carried out by means of apparatus designed or adapted for the purpose of detecting the installation or use in any residential or other premises of a television receiver (within the meaning of section 1 of the Wireless Telegraphy Act 1949), and

    (b) is carried out from outside those premises exclusively for that purpose,

is neither directed nor intrusive.

(7) In this Part—

    (a) references to the conduct of a covert human intelligence source are references to any conduct of such a source which falls within any of paragraphs (a) to (c) of subsection (8), or is incidental to anything falling within any of those paragraphs; and

    (b) references to the use of a covert human intelligence source are references to inducing, asking or assisting a person to engage in the conduct of such a source, or to obtain information by means of the conduct of such a source.

(8) For the purposes of this Part a person is a covert human intelligence source if—

    (a) he establishes or maintains a personal or other relationship with a person for the covert purpose of facilitating the doing of anything falling within paragraph (b) or (c);

    (b) he covertly uses such a relationship to obtain information or to provide access to any information to another person; or

    (c) he covertly discloses information obtained by the use of such a relationship, or as a consequence of the existence of such a relationship.

(9) For the purposes of this section—

    (a) surveillance is covert if, and only if, it is carried out in a manner that is calculated to ensure that persons who are subject to the surveillance are unaware that it is or may be taking place;

    (b) a purpose is covert, in relation to the establishment or maintenance of a personal or other relationship, if and only if the relationship is conducted in a manner that is calculated to ensure that one of the parties to the relationship is unaware of the purpose; and

    (c) a relationship is used covertly, and information obtained as mentioned in subsection (8)(c) is disclosed covertly, if and only if it is used or, as the case may be, disclosed in a manner that is calculated to ensure that one of the parties to the relationship is unaware of the use or disclosure in question.

(10) In this section "private information", in relation to a person, includes any information relating to his private or family life.

(11) References in this section, in relation to a vehicle, to the presence of a surveillance device in the vehicle include references to its being located on or under the vehicle and also include references to its being attached to it.

Authorisation of surveillance and human intelligence sources

Lawful surveillance etc.

    27.—(1) Conduct to which this Part applies shall be lawful for all purposes **116–014** if—

    (a) an authorisation under this Part confers an entitlement to engage in that conduct on the person whose conduct it is; and

    (b) his conduct is in accordance with the authorisation.

    (2) A person shall not be subject to any civil liability in respect of any conduct of his which—

    (a) is incidental to any conduct that is lawful by virtue of subsection (1); and

    (b) is not itself conduct an authorisation or warrant for which is capable of being granted under a relevant enactment and might reasonably have been expected to have been sought in the case in question.

    (3) The conduct that may be authorised under this Part includes conduct outside the United Kingdom.

    (4) In this section "relevant enactment" means—

    (a) an enactment contained in this Act;

    (b) section 5 of the Intelligence Services Act 1994 (warrants for the intelligence services); or

    (c) an enactment contained in Part III of the Police Act 1997 (powers of the police and of customs officers).

Authorisation of directed surveillance

116–015   28.—(1) Subject to the following provisions of this Part, the persons designated for the purposes of this section shall each have power to grant authorisations for the carrying out of directed surveillance.

(2) A person shall not grant an authorisation for the carrying out of directed surveillance unless he believes—

(a) that the authorisation is necessary on grounds falling within subsection (3); and
(b) that the authorised surveillance is proportionate to what is sought to be achieved by carrying it out.

(3) An authorisation is necessary on grounds falling within this subsection if it is necessary—

(a) in the interests of national security;
(b) for the purpose of preventing or detecting crime or of preventing disorder;
(c) in the interests of the economic well-being of the United Kingdom;
(d) in the interests of public safety;
(e) for the purpose of protecting public health;
(f) for the purpose of assessing or collecting any tax, duty, levy or other imposition, contribution or charge payable to a government department; or
(g) for any purpose (not falling within paragraphs (a) to (f)) which is specified for the purposes of this subsection by an order made by the Secretary of State.

(4) The conduct that is authorised by an authorisation for the carrying out of directed surveillance is any conduct that—

(a) consists in the carrying out of directed surveillance of any such description as is specified in the authorisation; and
(b) is carried out in the circumstances described in the authorisation and for the purposes of the investigation or operation specified or described in the authorisation.

(5) The Secretary of State shall not make an order under subsection (3)(g) unless a draft of the order has been laid before Parliament and approved by a resolution of each House.[1]

[1] In relation to the detection of television receivers: s.28 is repealed.

Authorisation of covert human intelligence sources

116–016   29.—(1) Subject to the following provisions of this Part, the persons designated for the purposes of this section shall each have power to grant authorisations for the conduct or the use of a covert human intelligence source.

(2) A person shall not grant an authorisation for the conduct or the use of a covert human intelligence source unless he believes—

(a) that the authorisation is necessary on grounds falling within subsection (3);
(b) that the authorised conduct or use is proportionate to what is sought to be achieved by that conduct or use; and
(c) that arrangements exist for the source's case that satisfy the

requirements of subsection (5) and such other requirements as may be imposed by order made by the Secretary of State.

(3) An authorisation is necessary on grounds falling within this subsection if it is necessary—

(a) in the interests of national security;

(b) for the purpose of preventing or detecting crime or of preventing disorder;

(c) in the interests of the economic well-being of the United Kingdom;

(d) in the interests of public safety;

(e) for the purpose of protecting public health;

(f) for the purpose of assessing or collecting any tax, duty, levy or other imposition, contribution or charge payable to a government department; or

(g) for any purpose (not falling within paragraphs (a) to (f)) which is specified for the purposes of this subsection by an order made by the Secretary of State.

(4) The conduct that is authorised by an authorisation for the conduct or the use of a covert human intelligence source is any conduct that—

(a) is comprised in any such activities involving conduct of a covert human intelligence source, or the use of a covert human intelligence source, as are specified or described in the authorisation;

(b) consists in conduct by or in relation to the person who is so specified or described as the person to whose actions as a covert human intelligence source the authorisation relates; and

(c) is carried out for the purposes of, or in connection with, the investigation or operation so specified or described.

(5) For the purposes of this Part there are arrangements for the source's case that satisfy the requirements of this subsection if such arrangements are in force as are necessary for ensuring—

(a) that there will at all times be a person holding an office, rank or position with the relevant investigating authority who will have day-to-day responsibility for dealing with the source on behalf of that authority, and for the source's security and welfare;

(b) that there will at all times be another person holding an office, rank or position with the relevant investigating authority who will have general oversight of the use made of the source;

(c) that there will at all times be a person holding an office, rank or position with the relevant investigating authority who will have responsibility for maintaining a record of the use made of the source;

(d) that the records relating to the source that are maintained by the relevant investigating authority will always contain particulars of all such matters (if any) as may be specified for the purposes of this paragraph in regulations made by the Secretary of State; and

(e) that records maintained by the relevant investigating authority that disclose the identity of the source will not be available to persons except to the extent that there is a need for access to them to be made available to those persons.

(6) The Secretary of State shall not make an order under subsection (3)(g) unless a draft of the order has been laid before Parliament and approved by a resolution of each House.

(7) The Secretary of State may by order—

    (a) prohibit the authorisation under this section of any such conduct or uses of covert human intelligence sources as may be described in the order; and

    (b) impose requirements, in addition to those provided for by subsection (2), that must be satisfied before an authorisation is granted under this section for any such conduct or uses of covert human intelligence sources as may be so described.

(8) In this section "relevant investigating authority", in relation to an authorisation for the conduct or the use of an individual as a covert human intelligence source, means (subject to subsection (9)) the public authority for whose benefit the activities of that individual as such a source are to take place.

(9) In the case of any authorisation for the conduct or the use of a covert human intelligence source whose activities are to be for the benefit of more than one public authority, the references in subsection (5) to the relevant investigating authority are references to one of them (whether or not the same one in the case of each reference).[1]

---

[1] In relation to the detection of television receivers: s.29 is repealed.

Persons entitled to grant authorisations under ss. 28 and 29

116–017   **30.**—(1) Subject to subsection (3), the persons designated for the purposes of section 28 and 29 are the individuals holding such offices, ranks or positions with relevant public authorities as are prescribed for the purposes of this subsection by an order under this section.

(2) For the purposes of the grant of an authorisation that combines—

    (a) an authorisation under section 28 or 29, and

    (b) an authorisation by the Secretary of State for the carrying out of intrusive surveillance,

the Secretary of State himself shall be a person designated for the purposes of that section.

(3) An order under this section may impose restrictions—

    (a) on the authorisations under sections 28 and 29 that may be granted by any individual holding an office, rank or position with a specified public authority; and

    (b) on the circumstances in which, or the purposes for which, such authorisations may be granted by any such individual.

(4) A public authority is a relevant public authority for the purposes of this section—

    (a) in relation to section 28 if it is specified in Part I or II of Schedule 1; and

    (b) in relation to section 29 if it is specified in Part I of that Schedule.

(5) An order under this section may amend Schedule 1 by—

    (a) adding a public authority to Part I or II of that Schedule;

    (b) removing a public authority from that Schedule;

    (c) moving a public authority from one Part of that Schedule to the other;

(d) making any change consequential on any change in the name of a public authority specified in that Schedule.

(6) Without prejudice to section 31, the power to make an order under this section shall be exercisable by the Secretary of State.

(7) The Secretary of State shall not make an order under subsection (5) containing any provision for—

(a) adding any public authority to Part I or II of that Schedule, or
(b) moving any public authority from Part II to Part I of that Schedule,

unless a draft of the order has been laid before Parliament and approved by a resolution of each House.[¹]

¹ In relation to the detection of television receivers: s.30 is repealed.

Orders under s. 30 for Northern Ireland

31.—(1) Subject to subsections (2) and (3), the power to make an order under **116–018** section 30 for the purposes of the grant of authorisations for conduct in Northern Ireland shall be exercisable by the Office of the First Minister and deputy First Minister in Northern Ireland (concurrently with being exercisable by the Secretary of State).

(2) The power of the Office of the First Minister and deputy First Minister to make an order under section 30 by virtue of subsection (1) or (3) of that section shall not be exercisable in relation to any public authority other than—

(a) the Food Standards Agency;
(c) an authority added to Schedule 1 by an order made by that Office;
(d) an authority added to that Schedule by an order made by the Secretary of State which it would (apart from that order) have been within the powers of that Office to add to that Schedule for the purposes mentioned in subsection (1) of this section.

(3) The power of the Office of the First Minister and deputy First Minister to make an order under section 30—

(a) shall not include power to make any provision dealing with an excepted matter;
    . . .
(b) shall not include power, except with the consent of the Secretary of State, to make any provision dealing with a reserved matter.

(4) The power of the Office of the First Minister and deputy First Minister to make an order under section 30 shall be exercisable by statutory rule for the purposes of the Statutory Rules (Northern Ireland) Order 1979.

(5) A statutory rule containing an order under section 30 which makes provision by virtue of subsection (5) of that section for—

(a) adding any public authority to Part I or II of Schedule 1, or
(b) moving any public authority from Part II to Part I of that Schedule,

shall be subject to affirmative resolution (within the meaning of section 41(4) of the Interpretation Act (Northern Ireland) 1954).

(6) A statutory rule containing an order under section 30 (other than one to which subsection (5) of this section applies) shall be subject to negative resolu-

tion (within the meaning of section 41(6) of the Interpretation Act (Northern Ireland) 1954).

(7) An order under section 30 made by the Office of the First Minister and deputy First Minister may—

(a) make different provision for different cases;
(b) contain such incidental, supplemental, consequential and transitional provision as that Office thinks fit.

(8) The reference in subsection (2) to an addition to Schedule 1 being within the powers of the Office of the First Minister and deputy First Minister includes a reference to its being within the powers exercisable by that Office with the consent for the purposes of subsection (3)(b) of the Secretary of State.

(9) In this section "excepted matter" and "reserved matter" have the same meanings as in the Northern Ireland Act 1998; and, in relation to those matters, section 98(2) of that Act (meaning of "deals with") applies for the purposes of this section as it applies for the purposes of that Act. [¹]

¹ In relation to the detection of television receivers: s.31 is repealed.

Authorisation of intrusive surveillance

116–019 **32.**—(1) Subject to the following provisions of this Part, the Secretary of State and each of the senior authorising officers shall have power to grant authorisations for the carrying out of intrusive surveillance.

(2) Neither the Secretary of State nor any senior authorising officer shall grant an authorisation for the carrying out of intrusive surveillance unless he believes—

(a) that the authorisation is necessary on grounds falling within subsection (3); and
(b) that the authorised surveillance is proportionate to what is sought to be achieved by carrying it out.

(3) Subject to the following provisions of this section, an authorisation is necessary on grounds falling within this subsection if it is necessary—

(a) in the interests of national security;
(b) for the purpose of preventing or detecting serious crime; or
(c) in the interests of the economic well-being of the United Kingdom.

(4) The matters to be taken into account in considering whether the requirements of subsection (2) are satisfied in the case of any authorisation shall include whether the information which it is thought necessary to obtain by the authorised conduct could reasonably be obtained by other means.

(5) The conduct that is authorised by an authorisation for the carrying out of intrusive surveillance is any conduct that—

(a) consists in the carrying out of intrusive surveillance of any such description as is specified in the authorisation;
(b) is carried out in relation to the residential premises specified or described in the authorisation or in relation to the private vehicle so specified or described; and
(c) is carried out for the purposes of, or in connection with, the investigation or operation so specified or described.

(6) For the purposes of this section the senior authorising officers are—

(a) the chief constable of every police force maintained under section 2 of the Police Act 1996 (police forces in England and Wales outside London);

(b) the Commissioner of Police of the Metropolis and every Assistant Commissioner of Police of the Metropolis;

(c) the Commissioner of Police for the City of London;

(d) the chief constable of every police force maintained under or by virtue of section 1 of the Police (Scotland) Act 1967 (police forces for areas in Scotland);

(e) the Chief Constable of the Royal Ulster Constabulary and the Deputy Chief Constable of the Royal Ulster Constabulary;

(f) the Chief Constable of the Ministry of Defence Police;

(g) the Provost Marshal of the Royal Navy Regulating Branch;

(h) the Provost Marshal of the Royal Military Police;

(i) the Provost Marshal of the Royal Air Force Police;

(j) the Chief Constable of the British Transport Police;

(k) the Director General of the National Criminal Intelligence Service;

(l) the Director General of the National Crime Squad and any person holding the rank of assistant chief constable in that Squad who is designated for the purposes of this paragraph by that Director General; and

(m) any customs officer designated for the purposes of this paragraph by the Commissioners of Customs and Excise.[1]

---

[1] In relation to the detection of television receivers: s.32 is repealed.

Police and customs authorisations

Rules for grant of authorisations

33.—(1) A person who is a designated person for the purposes of section 28 **116–020** or 29 by reference to his office, rank or position with a police force, the National Criminal Intelligence Service or the National Crime Squad shall not grant an authorisation under that section except on an application made by a member of the same force, Service or Squad.

(2) A person who is designated for the purposes of section 28 or 29 by reference to his office, rank or position with the Commissioners of Customs and Excise shall not grant an authorisation under that section except on an application made by a customs officer.

(3) A person who is a senior authorising officer by reference to a police force, the National Criminal Intelligence Service or the National Crime Squad shall not grant an authorisation for the carrying out of intrusive surveillance except—

(a) on an application made by a member of the same force, Service or Squad; and

(b) in the case of an authorisation for the carrying out of intrusive surveillance in relation to any residential premises, where those premises are in the area of operation of that force, Service or Squad.

(4) A person who is a senior authorising officer by virtue of a designation by the Commissioners of Customs and Excise shall not grant an authorisation for the carrying out of intrusive surveillance except on an application made by a customs officer.

(5) A single authorisation may combine both—

(a) an authorisation granted under this Part by, or on the application of, an individual who is a member of a police force, the National Criminal

Intelligence Service or the National Crime Squad, or who is a customs officer; and

(b) an authorisation given by, or on the application of, that individual under Part III of the Police Act 1997;

but the provisions of this Act or that Act that are applicable in the case of each of the authorisations shall apply separately in relation to the part of the combined authorisation to which they are applicable.

(6) For the purposes of this section—

(a) the area of operation of a police force maintained under section 2 of the Police Act 1996, of the metropolitan police force, of the City of London police force or of a police force maintained under or by virtue of section 1 of the Police (Scotland) Act 1967 is the area for which that force is maintained;

(b) the area of operation of the Royal Ulster Constabulary is Northern Ireland;

(c) residential premises are in the area of operation of the Ministry of Defence Police if they are premises where the members of that police force, under section 2 of the Ministry of Defence Police Act 1987, have the powers and privileges of a constable;

(d) residential premises are in the area of operation of the Royal Navy Regulating Branch, the Royal Military Police or the Royal Air Force Police if they are premises owned or occupied by, or used for residential purposes by, a person subject to service discipline;

(e) the area of operation of the British Transport Police and also of the National Criminal Intelligence Service is the United Kingdom;

(f) the area of operation of the National Crime Squad is England and Wales;

and references in this section to the United Kingdom or to any part or area of the United Kingdom include any adjacent waters within the seaward limits of the territorial waters of the United Kingdom.

(7) For the purposes of this section a person is subject to service discipline—

(a) in relation to the Royal Navy Regulating Branch, if he is subject to the Naval Discipline Act 1957 or is a civilian to whom Parts I and II of that Act for the time being apply by virtue of section 118 of that Act;

(b) in relation to the Royal Military Police, if he is subject to military law or is a civilian to whom Part II of the Army Act 1955 for the time being applies by virtue of section 209 of that Act; and

(c) in relation to the Royal Air Force Police, if he is subject to air-force law or is a civilian to whom Part II of the Air Force Act 1955 for the time being applies by virtue of section 209 of that Act.[1]

[1] In relation to the detection of television receivers: s.33 is repealed.

Grant of authorisations in the senior officer's absence

116–021 34.—(1) This section applies in the case of an application for an authorisation for the carrying out of intrusive surveillance where—

(a) the application is one made by a member of a police force, of the National Criminal Intelligence Service or of the National Crime Squad or by a customs officer; and

(b) the case is urgent.

(2) If—

(a) it is not reasonably practicable, having regard to the urgency of the case, for the application to be considered by any person who is a senior authorising officer by reference to the force, Service or Squad in question or, as the case may be, by virtue of a designation by the Commissioners of Customs and Excise, and

(b) it also not reasonably practicable, having regard to the urgency of the case, for the application to be considered by a person (if there is one) who is entitled, as a designated deputy of a senior authorising officer, to exercise the functions in relation to that application of such an officer,

the application may be made to and considered by any person who is entitled under subsection (4) to act for any senior authorising officer who would have been entitled to consider the application.

(3) A person who considers an application under subsection (1) shall have the same power to grant an authorisation as the person for whom he is entitled to act.

(4) For the purposes of this section—

(a) a person is entitled to act for the chief constable of a police force maintained under section 2 of the Police Act 1996 if he holds the rank of assistant chief constable in that force;

(b) a person is entitled to act for the Commissioner of Police of the Metropolis, or for an Assistant Commissioner of Police of the Metropolis, if he holds the rank of commander in the metropolitan police force;

(c) a person is entitled to act for the Commissioner of Police for the City of London if he holds the rank of commander in the City of London police force;

(d) a person is entitled to act for the chief constable of a police force maintained under or by virtue of section 1 of the Police (Scotland) Act 1967 if he holds the rank of assistant chief constable in that force;

(e) a person is entitled to act for the Chief Constable of the Royal Ulster Constabulary, or for the Deputy Chief Constable of the Royal Ulster Constabulary, if he holds the rank of assistant chief constable in the Royal Ulster Constabulary;

(f) a person is entitled to act for the Chief Constable of the Ministry of Defence Police if he holds the rank of deputy or assistant chief constable in that force;

(g) a person is entitled to act for the Provost Marshal of the Royal Navy Regulating Branch if he holds the position of assistant Provost Marshal in that Branch;

(h) a person is entitled to act for the Provost Marshal of the Royal Military Police or the Provost Marshal of the Royal Air Force Police if he holds the position of deputy Provost Marshal in the police force in question;

(i) a person is entitled to act for the Chief Constable of the British Transport Police if he holds the rank of deputy or assistant chief constable in that force;

(j) a person is entitled to act for the Director General of the National Criminal Intelligence Service if he is a person designated for the purposes of this paragraph by that Director General;

(k) a person is entitled to act for the Director General of the National Crime Squad if he is designated for the purposes of this paragraph by that Director General as a person entitled so to act in an urgent case;

(l) a person is entitled to act for a person who is a senior authorising officer by virtue of a designation by the Commissioners of Customs and Excise, if he is designated for the purposes of this paragraph by those Commissioners as a person entitled so to act in an urgent case.

(5) A police member of the National Criminal Intelligence Service or the National Crime Squad appointed under section 9(1)(b) or 55(1)(b) of the Police Act 1997 (police members) may not be designated under subsection (4)(j) or (k) unless he holds the rank of assistant chief constable in that Service or Squad.

(6) In this section "designated deputy"—

(a) in relation to a chief constable, means a person holding the rank of assistant chief constable who is designated to act under section 12(4) of the Police Act 1996 or section 5(4) of the Police (Scotland) Act 1967;

(b) in relation to the Commissioner of Police for the City of London, means a person authorised to act under section 25 of the City of London Police Act 1839;

(c) in relation to the Director General of the National Criminal Intelligence Service or the Director General of the National Crime Squad, means a person designated to act under section 8 or, as the case may be, section 54 of the Police Act 1997.[1]

[1] In relation to the detection of television receivers: s.34 is repealed.

Notification of authorisations for intrusive surveillance

116–022   **35.**—(1) Where a person grants or cancels a police or customs authorisation for the carrying out of intrusive surveillance, he shall give notice that he has done so to an ordinary Surveillance Commissioner.

(2) A notice given for the purposes of subsection (1)—

(a) must be given in writing as soon as reasonably practicable after the grant or, as the case may be, cancellation of the authorisation to which it relates;

(b) must be given in accordance with any such arrangements made for the purposes of this paragraph by the Chief Surveillance Commissioner as are for the time being in force; and

(c) must specify such matters as the Secretary of State may by order prescribe.

(3) A notice under this section of the grant of an authorisation shall, as the case may be, either—

(a) state that the approval of a Surveillance Commissioner is required by section 36 before the grant of the authorisation will take effect; or

(b) state that the case is one of urgency and set out the grounds on which the case is believed to be one of urgency.

(4) Where a notice for the purposes of subsection (1) of the grant of an authorisation has been received by an ordinary Surveillance Commissioner, he shall, as soon as practicable—

(a) scrutinise the authorisation; and

(b) in a case where notice has been given in accordance with subsection (3)(a), decide whether or not to approve the authorisation.

(5) Subject to subsection (6), the Secretary of State shall not make an order under subsection (2)(c) unless a draft of the order has been laid before Parliament and approved by a resolution of each House.

(6) Subsection (5) does not apply in the case of the order made on the first occasion on which the Secretary of State exercises his power to make an order under subsection (2)(c).

(7) The order made on that occasion shall cease to have effect at the end of the period of forty days beginning with the day on which it was made unless, before the end of that period, it has been approved by a resolution of each House of Parliament.

(8) For the purposes of subsection (7)—

  (a) the order's ceasing to have effect shall be without prejudice to anything previously done or to the making of a new order; and
  (b) in reckoning the period of forty days no account shall be taken of any period during which Parliament is dissolved or prorogued or during which both Houses are adjourned for more than four days.

(9) Any notice that is required by any provision of this section to be given in writing may be given, instead, by being transmitted by electronic means.

(10) In this section references to a police or customs authorisation are references to an authorisation granted by—

  (a) a person who is a senior authorising officer by reference to a police force, the National Criminal Intelligence Service or the National Crime Squad;
  (b) a person who is a senior authorising officer by virtue of a designation by the Commissioners of Customs and Excise; or
  (c) a person who for the purposes of section 34 is entitled to act for a person falling within paragraph (a) or for a person falling within paragraph (b).[¹]

¹ In relation to the detection of television receivers: s.35 is repealed.

Approval required for authorisations to take effect

36.—(1) This section applies where an authorisation for the carrying out of **116–023** intrusive surveillance has been granted on the application of—

  (a) a member of a police force;
  (b) a member of the National Criminal Intelligence Service;
  (c) a member of the National Crime Squad; or
  (d) a customs officer.

(2) Subject to subsection (3), the authorisation shall not take effect until such time (if any) as—

  (a) the grant of the authorisation has been approved by an ordinary Surveillance Commissioner; and
  (b) written notice of the Commissioner's decision to approve the grant of the authorisation has been given, in accordance with subsection (4), to the person who granted the authorisation.

(3) Where the person who grants the authorisation—

  (a) believes that the case is one of urgency, and
  (b) gives notice in accordance with section 35(3)(b),

subsection (2) shall not apply to the authorisation, and the authorisation shall have effect from the time of its grant.

(4) Where subsection (2) applies to the authorisation—

  (a) a Surveillance Commissioner shall give his approval under this section to the authorisation if, and only if, he is satisfied that there are reasonable grounds for believing that the requirements of section 32(2)(a) and (b) are satisfied in the case of the authorisation; and

(b) a Surveillance Commissioner who makes a decision as to whether or not the authorisation should be approved shall, as soon as reasonably practicable after making that decision, give written notice of his decision to the person who granted the authorisation.

(5) If an ordinary Surveillance Commissioner decides not to approve an authorisation to which subsection (2) applies, he shall make a report of his findings to the most senior relevant person.

(6) In this section "the most senior relevant person" means—

(a) where the authorisation was granted by the senior authorising officer with any police force who is not someone's deputy, that senior authorising officer;

(b) where the authorisation was granted by the Director General of the National Criminal Intelligence Service or the Director General of the National Crime Squad, that Director General;

(c) where the authorisation was granted by a senior authorising officer with a police force who is someone's deputy, the senior authorising officer whose deputy granted the authorisation;

(d) where the authorisation was granted by the designated deputy of the Director General of the National Criminal Intelligence Service or a person entitled to act for him by virtue of section 34(4)(j), that Director General;

(e) where the authorisation was granted by the designated deputy of the Director General of the National Crime Squad or by a person designated by that Director General for the purposes of section 32(6)(1) or 34(4)(k), that Director General;

(f) where the authorisation was granted by a person entitled to act for a senior authorising officer under section 34(4)(a) to (i), the senior authorising officer in the force in question who is not someone's deputy; and

(g) where the authorisation was granted by a customs officer, the customs officer for the time being designated for the purposes of this paragraph by a written notice given to the Chief Surveillance Commissioner by the Commissioners of Customs and Excise.

(7) The references in subsection (6) to a person's deputy are references to the following—

(a) in relation to—

(i) a chief constable of a police force maintained under section 2 of the Police Act 1996,

(ii) the Commissioner of Police for the City of London, or

(iii) a chief constable of a police force maintained under or by virtue of section 1 of the Police (Scotland) Act 1967,

to his designated deputy;

(b) in relation to the Commissioner of Police of the Metropolis, to an Assistant Commissioner of Police of the Metropolis; and

(c) in relation to the Chief Constable of the Royal Ulster Constabulary, to the Deputy Chief Constable of the Royal Ulster Constabulary;

and in this subsection and that subsection "designated deputy" has the same meaning as in section 34.

(8) Any notice that is required by any provision of this section to be given in writing may be given, instead, by being transmitted by electronic means.[¹]

¹ In relation to the detection of television receivers: s.36 is repealed.

Quashing of police and customs authorisations etc.

37.—(1) This section applies where an authorisation for the carrying out of **116–024** intrusive surveillance has been granted on the application of—

(a) a member of a police force;
(b) a member of the National Criminal Intelligence Service;
(c) a member of the National Crime Squad; or
(d) a customs officer.

(2) Where an ordinary Surveillance Commissioner is at any time satisfied that, at the time when the authorisation was granted or at any time when it was renewed, there were no reasonable grounds for believing that the requirements of section 32(2)(a) and (b) were satisfied, he may quash the authorisation with effect, as he thinks fit, from the time of the grant of the authorisation or from the time of any renewal of the authorisation.

(3) If an ordinary Surveillance Commissioner is satisfied at any time while the authorisation is in force that there are no longer any reasonable grounds for believing that the requirements of section 32(2)(a) and (b) are satisfied in relation to the authorisation, he may cancel the authorisation with effect from such time as appears to him to be the time from which those requirements ceased to be so satisfied.

(4) Where, in the case of any authorisation of which notice has been given in accordance with section 35(3)(b), an ordinary Surveillance Commissioner is at any time satisfied that, at the time of the grant or renewal of the authorisation to which that notice related, there were no reasonable grounds for believing that the case was one of urgency, he may quash the authorisation with effect, as he thinks fit, from the time of the grant of the authorisation or from the time of any renewal of the authorisation.

(5) Subject to subsection (7), where an ordinary Surveillance Commissioner quashes an authorisation under this section, he may order the destruction of any records relating wholly or partly to information obtained by the authorised conduct after the time from which his decision takes effect.

(6) Subject to subsection (7), where—

(a) an authorisation has ceased to have effect (otherwise than by virtue of subsection (2) or (4)), and
(b) an ordinary Surveillance Commissioner is satisfied that there was a time while the authorisation was in force when there were no reasonable grounds for believing that the requirements of section 32(2)(a) and (b) continued to be satisfied in relation to the authorisation,

he may order the destruction of any records relating, wholly or partly, to information obtained at such a time by the authorised conduct.

(7) No order shall be made under this section for the destruction of any records required for pending criminal or civil proceedings.

(8) Where an ordinary Surveillance Commissioner exercises a power conferred by this section, he shall, as soon as reasonably practicable, make a report of his exercise of that power, and of his reasons for doing so—

(a) to the most senior relevant person (within the meaning of section 36); and

(b) to the Chief Surveillance Commissioner.

(9) Where an order for the destruction of records is made under this section, the order shall not become operative until such time (if any) as—

(a) the period for appealing against the decision to make the order has expired; and
(b) any appeal brought within that period has been dismissed by the Chief Surveillance Commissioner.

(10) No notice shall be required to be given under section 35 (1) in the case of a cancellation under subsection (3) of this section.[1]

[1] In relation to the detection of television receivers: s.37 is repealed.

Appeals against decisions by Surveillance Commissioners

116–025   38.—(1) Any senior authorising officer may appeal to the Chief Surveillance Commissioner against any of the following—

(a) any refusal of an ordinary Surveillance Commissioner to approve an authorisation for the carrying out of intrusive surveillance;
(b) any decision of such a Commissioner to quash or cancel such an authorisation;
(c) any decision of such a Commissioner to make an order under section 37 for the destruction of records.

(2) In the case of an authorisation granted by the designated deputy of a senior authorising office or by a person who for the purposes of section 34 is entitled to act for a senior authorising officer, that designated deputy or person shall also be entitled to appeal under this section.
(3) An appeal under this section must be brought within the period of seven days beginning with the day on which the refusal or decision appealed against is reported to the appellant.
(4) Subject to subsection (5), the Chief Surveillance Commissioner, on an appeal under this section, shall allow the appeal if—

(a) he is satisfied that there were reasonable grounds for believing that the requirements of section 32(2)(a) and (b) were satisfied in relation to the authorisation at the time in question; and
(b) he is not satisfied that the authorisation is one of which notice was given in accordance with section 35(3)(b) without there being any reasonable grounds for believing that the case was one of urgency.

(5) If, on an appeal falling within subsection (1)(b), the Chief Surveillance Commissioner—

(a) is satisfied that grounds exist which justify the quashing or cancellation under section 37 of the authorisation in question, but
(b) considers that the authorisation should have been quashed or cancelled from a different time from that from which it was quashed or cancelled by the ordinary Surveillance Commissioner against whose decision the appeal is brought,

he may modify that Commissioner's decision to quash or cancel the authorisation, and any related decision for the destruction of records, so as to give effect to the decision under section 37 that he considers should have been made.

(6) Where, on an appeal under this section against a decision to quash or cancel an authorisation, the Chief Surveillance Commissioner allows the appeal he shall also quash any related order for the destruction of records relating to information obtained by the authorised conduct.

(7) In this section "designated deputy" has the same meaning as in section 34.[¹]

¹ In relation to the detection of television receivers: s.38 is repealed.

Appeals to the Chief Surveillance Commissioner: supplementary

39.—(1) Where the Chief Surveillance Commissioner has determined an **116–026** appeal under section 38, he shall give notice of his determination to both—

(a) the person by whom the appeal was brought; and
(b) the ordinary Surveillance Commissioner whose decision was appealed against.

(2) Where the determination of the Chief Surveillance Commissioner on an appeal under section 38 is a determination to dismiss the appeal, the Chief Surveillance Commissioner shall make a report of his findings—

(a) to the persons mentioned in subsection (1); and
(b) to the Prime Minister.

(3) Subsections (3) and (4) of section 107 of the Police Act 1997 (reports to be laid before Parliament and exclusion of matters from the report) apply in relation to any report to the Prime Minister under subsection (2) of this section as they apply in relation to any report under subsection (2) of that section.

(4) Subject to subsection (2) of this section, the Chief Surveillance Commissioner shall not give any reasons for any determination of his on an appeal under section 38.[¹]

¹ In relation to the detection of television receivers: s.39 is repealed.

Information to be provided to Surveillance Commissioners

40.—It shall be the duty of—   **116–027**

(a) every member of a police force,
(b) every member of the National Criminal Intelligence Service,
(c) every member of the National Crime Squad, and
(d) every customs officer,

to comply with any request of a Surveillance Commissioner for documents or information required by that Commissioner for the purpose of enabling him to carry out the functions of such a Commissioner under sections 35 to 39.[¹]

¹ In relation to the detection of television receivers: s.40 is repealed.

Other authorisations

Secretary of State authorisations

41.—(1) The Secretary of State shall not grant an authorisation for the carry- **116–028** ing out of intrusive surveillance except on an application made by—

(a) a member of any of the intelligence services;

(b) an official of the Ministry of Defence;

(c) a member of Her Majesty's forces;

(d) an individual holding an office, rank or position with any such public authority as may be designated for the purposes of this section as an authority whose activities may require the carrying out of intrusive surveillance.

(2) Section 32 shall have effect in relation to the grant of an authorisation by the Secretary of State on the application of an official of the Ministry of Defence, or of a member of Her Majesty's forces, as if the only matters mentioned in subsection (3) of that section were—

(a) the interests of national security; and

(b) the purpose of preventing or detecting serious crime.

(3) The designation of any public authority for the purposes of this section shall be by order made by the Secretary of State.

(4) The Secretary of State may by order provide, in relation to any public authority, that an application for an authorisation for the carrying out of intrusive surveillance may be made by an individual holding an office, rank or position with that authority only where his office, rank or position is one prescribed by the order.

(5) The Secretary of State may by order impose restrictions—

(a) on the authorisations for the carrying out of intrusive surveillance that may be granted on the application of an individual holding an office, rank or position with any public authority designated for the purposes of this section; and

(b) on the circumstances in which, or the purposes for which, such authorisations may be granted on such an application.

(6) The Secretary of State shall not make a designation under subsection (3) unless a draft of the order containing the designation has been laid before Parliament and approved by a resolution of each House.

(7) References in this section to a member of Her Majesty's forces do not include references to any member of Her Majesty's forces who is a member of a police force by virtue of his service with the Royal Navy Regulating Branch, the Royal Military Police or the Royal Air Force Police.[1]

[1] In relation to the detection of television receivers: s.41 is repealed.

Intelligence services authorisations

116–029   42.—(1) The grant by the Secretary of State or, the Scottish Ministers (by virtue of provision under section 63 of the Scotland Act 1998) on the application of a member of one of the intelligence services of any authorisation under this Part must be made by the issue of a warrant.

(2) A single warrant issued by the Secretary of State or, the Scottish Ministers (by virtue of provision under section 63 of the Scotland Act 1998) may combine both—

(a) an authorisation under this Part; and

(b) an intelligence services warrant;

but the provisions of this Act or the Intelligence Services Act 1994 that are applicable in the case of the authorisation under this Part or the intelligence services warrant shall apply separately in relation to the part of the combined warrant to which they are applicable.

(3) Intrusive surveillance in relation to any premises or vehicle in the British Islands shall be capable of being authorised by a warrant issued under this Part on the application of a member of the Secret Intelligence Service or GCHQ only if the authorisation contained in the warrant is one satisfying the requirements of section 32(2)(a) otherwise than in connection with any functions of that intelligence service in support of the prevention or detection of serious crime.

(4) Subject to subsection (5), the functions of the Security Service shall include acting on behalf of the Secret Intelligence Service or GCHQ in relation to—

(a) the application for and grant of any authorisation under this Part in connection with any matter within the functions of the Secret Intelligence Service or GCHQ; and

(b) the carrying out, in connection with any such matter, of any conduct authorised by such an authorisation.

(5) Nothing in subsection (4) shall authorise the doing of anything by one intelligence service on behalf of another unless—

(a) it is something which either the other service or a member of the other service has power to do; and

(b) it is done otherwise than in connection with functions of the other service in support of the prevention or detection of serious crime.

(6) In this section "intelligence services warrant" means a warrant under section 5 of the Intelligence Services Act 1994.[1]

[1] In relation to the detection of television receivers: s.42 is repealed.

Grant, renewal and duration of authorisations

General rules about grant, renewal and duration

43.—(1) An authorisation under this Part—   **116–030**

(a) may be granted or renewed orally in any urgent case in which the entitlement to act of the person granting or renewing it is not confined to urgent cases; and

(b) in any other case, must be in writing.

(2) A single authorisation may combine two or more different authorisations under this Part; but the provisions of this Act that are applicable in the case of each of the authorisations shall apply separately in relation to the part of the combined authorisation to which they are applicable.

(3) Subject to subsections (4) and (8), an authorisation under this Part shall cease to have effect at the end of the following period—

(a) in the case of an authorisation which—

(i) has not been renewed and was granted either orally or by a person whose entitlement to act is confined to urgent cases, or

(ii) was last renewed either orally or by such a person,

the period of seventy-two hours beginning with the time when the grant of the authorisation or, as the case may be, its latest renewal takes effect;

    (b) in a case not falling within paragraph (a) in which the authorisation is for the conduct or the use of a covert human intelligence source, the period of twelve months beginning with the day on which the grant of the authorisation or, as the case may be, its latest renewal takes effect; and

    (c) in any case not falling within paragraph (a) or (b), the period of three months beginning with the day on which the grant of the authorisation or, as the case may be, its latest renewal takes effect.

(4) Subject to subsection (6), an authorisation under this Part may be renewed, at any time before the time at which it ceases to have effect, by any person who would be entitled to grant a new authorisation in the same terms.

(5) Sections 28 to 41 shall have effect in relation to the renewal of an authorisation under this Part as if references to the grant of an authorisation included references to its renewal.

(6) A person shall not renew an authorisation for the conduct or the use of a covert human intelligence source, unless he—

    (a) is satisfied that a review has been carried out of the matters mentioned in subsection (7); and

    (b) has, for the purpose of deciding whether he should renew the authorisation, considered the results of that review.

(7) The matters mentioned in subsection (6) are—

    (a) the use made of the source in the period since the grant or, as the case may be, latest renewal of the authorisation; and

    (b) the tasks given to the source during that period and the information obtained from the conduct or the use of the source.

(8) The Secretary of State may by order provide in relation to authorisations of such descriptions as may be specified in the order that subsection (3) is to have effect as if the period at the end of which an authorisation of a description so specified is to cease to have effect were such period shorter than that provided for by that subsection as may be fixed by or determined in accordance with that order.

(9) References in this section to the time at which, or the day on which, the grant or renewal of an authorisation takes effect are references—

    (a) in the case of the grant of an authorisation to which paragraph (c) does not apply, to the time at which or, as the case may be, day on which the authorisation is granted;

    (b) in the case of the renewal of an authorisation to which paragraph (c) does not apply, to the time at which or, as the case may be, day on which the authorisation would have ceased to have effect but for the renewal; and

    (c) in the case of any grant or renewal that takes effect under subsection (2) of section 36 at a time or on a day later than that given by paragraph (a) or (b), to the time at which or, as the case may be, day on which the grant or renewal takes effect in accordance with that subsection.

(10) In relation to any authorisation granted by a member of any of the intelligence services, and in relation to any authorisation contained in a warrant issued by the Secretary of State on the application of a member of any of the intelligence services, this section has effect subject to the provisions of section 44. [1]

---

[1] In relation to the detection of television receivers: s.43 is repealed.

General rules about grant, renewal and duration

43.—(1) An authorisation under this Part must be in writing.

(3) Subject to subsection (4), an authorisation under this Part shall cease to have effect—

(a) in the case of an authorisation which has not been renewed and in which is specified a period of less than eight weeks beginning with the day on which the grant of the authorisation takes effect, at the end of that period;

(b) in the case of an authorisation which has not been renewed and to which paragraph (a) does not apply, at the end of the period of eight weeks beginning with the day on which the grant of the authorisation takes effect;

(c) in the case of an authorisation which has been renewed, and in which is specified a period of less than eight weeks beginning with the day on which the grant of the authorisation takes effect, at the end of a period of the same length beginning with the day on which the latest renewal takes effect;

(d) in the case of an authorisation which has been renewed, and to which paragraph (c) does not apply, at the end of the period of eight weeks beginning with the day on which the latest renewal takes effect.

(4) [An] authorisation under this Part may be renewed, at any time before the time at which it ceases to have effect, by any person who would be entitled to grant a new authorisation in the same terms.

(5) Section 27A shall have effect in relation to the renewal of an authorisation under this Part as if references to the grant of an authorisation included references to its renewal.

(9) References in this section to the time at which, or the day on which, the grant or renewal of an authorisation takes effect are references—

(a) in the case of the grant of an authorisation, to the time at which or, as the case may be, day on which the authorisation is granted;

(b) in the case of the renewal of an authorisation, to the time at which or, as the case may be, day on which the authorisation would have ceased to have effect but for the renewal.

Special rules for intelligence services authorisations

44.—(1) Subject to subsection (2), a warrant containing an authorisation for **116–031** the carrying out of intrusive surveillance—

(a) shall not be issued on the application of a member of any of the intelligence services, and

(b) if so issued shall not be renewed,

except under the hand of the Secretary of State or, in the case of a warrant issued by the Scottish Ministers (by virtue of provision made under section 63 of the Scotland Act 1998), a member of the Scottish Executive.

(2) In an urgent case in which—

(a) an application for a warrant containing an authorisation for the carrying out of intrusive surveillance has been made by a member of any of the intelligence services, and

(b) the Secretary of State has himself or the Scottish Ministers (by virtue of provision made under section 63 of the Scotland Act 1998) have themselves expressly authorised the issue of the warrant in that case or, as the case may be, a member of the staff of the Scottish Administration who is a member of the Senior Civil Service and is designated by the Scottish Ministers as a person under whose hand a warrant may be issued in such a case (in this section referred to as "a designated official"),

the warrant may be issued (but not renewed) under the hand of a senior official.

(3) Subject to subsection (6), a warrant containing an authorisation for the carrying out of intrusive surveillance which—

(a) was issued, on the application of a member of any of the intelligence services, under the hand of a senior official or, as the case may be, a designated official, and

(b) has not been renewed under the hand of the Secretary of State or, in the case of a warrant issued by the Scottish Ministers (by virtue of provision made under section 63 of the Scotland Act 1998), a member of the Scottish Executive,

shall cease to have effect at the end of the second working day following the day of the issue of the warrant, instead of at the time provided for by section 43(3).

(4) Subject to subsections (3) and (6), where any warrant for the carrying out of intrusive surveillance which is issued or was last renewed on the application of a member of any of the intelligence services, the warrant (unless renewed or, as the case may be, renewed again) shall cease to have effect at the following time, instead of at the time provided for by section 43(3), namely—

(a) in the case of a warrant that has not been renewed, at the end of the period of six months beginning with the day on which it was issued; and

(b) in any other case, at the end of the period of six months beginning with the day on which it would have ceased to have effect if not renewed again.

(5) Subject to subsection (6), where—

(a) an authorisation for the carrying out of directed surveillance is granted by a member of any of the intelligence services, and

(b) the authorisation is renewed by an instrument endorsed under the hand of the person renewing the authorisation with a statement that the renewal is believed to be necessary on grounds falling within section 32(3)(a) or (c),

the authorisation (unless renewed again) shall cease to have effect at the end of the period of six months beginning with the day on which it would have ceased to have effect but for the renewal, instead of at the time provided for by section 43(3).

(6) The Secretary of State may by order provide in relation to authorisations of such descriptions as may be specified in the order that subsection (3), (4) or (5) is to have effect as if the period at the end of which an authorisation of a description so specified is to cease to have effect were such period shorter than that provided for by that subsection as may be fixed by or determined in accordance with that order.

(7) Notwithstanding anything in section 43(2), in a case in which there is a combined warrant containing both—

(a) an authorisation for the carrying out of intrusive surveillance, and

(b) an authorisation for the carrying out of directed surveillance,

the reference in subsection (4) of this section to a warrant for the carrying out of intrusive surveillance is a reference to the warrant so far as it confers both authorisations.[1]

---

[1] In relation to the detection of television receivers: s.44 is repealed.

. . . . . .

Supplemental Provision for Part II

Interpretation of Part II

48.—(1) In this Part— 116–032

"covert human intelligence source" shall be construed in accordance with
 section 26(8);
"directed" and "intrusive", in relation to surveillance, shall be construed
 in accordance with section 26(2) to (6);
"private vehicle" means (subject to subsection (7)(a)) any vehicle which is
 used primarily for the private purposes of the person who owns it or
 of a person otherwise having the right to use it;
"residential premises" means (subject to subsection (7)(b)) so much of any
 premises as is for the time being occupied or used by any person,
 however temporarily, for residential purposes or otherwise as living
 accommodation (including hotel or prison accommodation that is so
 occupied or used);
"senior authorising officer" means a person who by virtue of subsection
 (6) of section 32 is a senior authorising officer for the purposes of that
 section;
"surveillance" shall be construed in accordance with subsections (2) to (4);
"surveillance device" means any apparatus designed or adapted for use in
 surveillance.

(2) Subject to subsection (3), in this Part "surveillance" includes—

(a) monitoring, observing or listening to persons, their movements, their
 conversations or their other activities or communications;
(b) recording anything monitored, observed or listened to in the course of
 surveillance; and
(c) surveillance by or with the assistance of a surveillance device.

(3) References in this Part to surveillance do not include references to—

(a) any conduct of a covert human intelligence source for obtaining or
 recording (whether or not using a surveillance device) any information
 which is disclosed in the presence of the source;
(b) the use of a covert human intelligence source for so obtaining or
 recording information; or
(c) any such entry on or interference with property or with wireless telegraphy as would be unlawful unless authorised under—

  (i) section 5 of the Intelligence Services Act 1994 (warrants for the
   intelligence services); or
  (ii) Part III of the Police Act 1997 (powers of the police and of customs officers).

(4) References in this Part to surveillance include references to the interception of a communication in the course of its transmission by means of a postal
service or telecommunication system if, and only if—

(a) the communication is one sent by or intended for a person who has
 consented to the interception of communications sent by or to him; and
(b) there is no interception warrant authorising the interception.

(5) References in this Part to an individual holding an office or position with

a public authority include references to any member, official or employee of that authority.

(6) For the purposes of this Part the activities of a covert human intelligence source which are to be taken as activities for the benefit of a particular public authority include any conduct of his as such a source which is in response to inducements or requests made by or on behalf of that authority.

(7) In subsection (1)—

    (a) the reference to a person having the right to use a vehicle does not, in relation to a motor vehicle, include a reference to a person whose right to use the vehicle derives only from his having paid, or undertaken to pay, for the use of the vehicle and its driver for a particular journey; and

    (b) the reference to premises occupied or used by any person for residential purposes or otherwise as living accommodation does not include a reference to so much of any premises as constitutes any common area to which he has or is allowed access in connection with his use or occupation of any accommodation.

(8) In this section—

    "premises" includes any vehicle or moveable structure and any other place whatever, whether or not occupied as land;
    "vehicle" includes any vessel, aircraft or hovercraft.

PART III

INVESTIGATION OF ELECTRONIC DATA PROTECTED BY ENCRYPTION ETC.

Power to require disclosure

Notices requiring disclosure

116–033   **49.**—(1) This section applies where any protected information—

    (a) has come into the possession of any person by means of the exercise of a statutory power to seize, detain, inspect, search or otherwise to interfere with documents or other property, or is likely to do so;

    (b) has come into the possession of any person by means of the exercise of any statutory power to intercept communications, or is likely to do so;

    (c) has come into the possession of any person by means of the exercise of any power conferred by an authorisation under section 22(3) or under Part II, or as a result of the giving of a notice under section 22(4), or is likely to do so;

    (d) has come into the possession of any person as a result of having been provided or disclosed in pursuance of any statutory duty (whether or not one arising as a result of a request for information), or is likely to do so; or

    (e) has, by any other lawful means not involving the exercise of statutory powers, come into the possession of any of the intelligence services, the police or the customs and excise, or is likely so to come into the possession of any of those services, the police or the customs and excise.

(2) If any person with the appropriate permission under Schedule 2 believes, on reasonable grounds—

(a) that a key to the protected information is in the possession of any person,

(b) that the imposition of a disclosure requirement in respect of the protected information is—

    (i) necessary on grounds falling within subsection (3), or

    (ii) necessary for the purpose of securing the effective exercise or proper performance by any public authority of any statutory power or statutory duty,

(c) that the imposition of such a requirement is proportionate to what is sought to be achieved by its imposition, and

(d) that it is not reasonably practicable for the person with the appropriate permission to obtain possession of the protected information in an intelligible form without the giving of a notice under this section,

the person with that permission may, by notice to the person whom he believes to have possession of the key, impose a disclosure requirement in respect of the protected information.

(3) A disclosure requirement in respect of any protected information is necessary on grounds falling within this subsection if it is necessary—

(a) in the interests of national security;

(b) for the purpose of preventing or detecting crime; or

(c) in the interests of the economic well-being of the United Kingdom.

(4) A notice under this section imposing a disclosure requirement in respect of any protected information—

(a) must be given in writing or (if not in writing) must be given in a manner that produces a record of its having been given;

(b) must describe the protected information to which the notice relates;

(c) must specify the matters falling within subsection (2)(b) (i) or (ii) by reference to which the notice is given;

(d) must specify the office, rank or position held by the person giving it;

(e) must specify the office, rank or position of the person who for the purposes of Schedule 2 granted permission for the giving of the notice or (if the person giving the notice was entitled to give it without another person's permission) must set out the circumstances in which that entitlement arose;

(f) must specify the time by which the notice is to be complied with; and

(g) must set out the disclosure that is required by the notice and the form and manner in which it is to be made;

and the time specified for the purposes of paragraph (f) must allow a period for compliance which is reasonable in all the circumstances.

(5) Where it appears to a person with the appropriate permission-

(a) that more than one person is in possession of the key to any protected information,

(b) that any of those persons is in possession of that key in his capacity as an officer or employee of any body corporate, and

(c) that another of those persons is the body corporate itself or another officer or employee of the body corporate,

a notice under this section shall not be given, by reference to his possession of the key, to any officer or employee of the body corporate unless he is a senior officer of the body corporate or it appears to the person giving the notice that there is no senior officer of the body corporate and (in the case of an employee) no more senior employee of the body corporate to whom it is reasonably practicable to give the notice.

(6) Where it appears to a person with the appropriate permission—

    (a) that more than one person is in possession of the key to any protected information,

    (b) that any of those persons is in possession of that key in his capacity as an employee of a firm, and

    (c) that another of those persons is the firm itself or a partner of the firm,

a notice under this section shall not be given, by reference to his possession of the key, to any employee of the firm unless it appears to the person giving the notice that there is neither a partner of the firm nor a more senior employee of the firm to whom it is reasonably practicable to give the notice.

(7) Subsections (5) and (6) shall not apply to the extent that there are special circumstances of the case that mean that the purposes for which the notice is given would be defeated, in whole or in part, if the notice were given to the person to whom it would otherwise be required to be given by those subsections.

(8) A notice under this section shall not require the making of any disclosure to any person other than—

    (a) the person giving the notice; or

    (b) such other person as may be specified in or otherwise identified by, or in accordance with, the provisions of the notice.

(9) A notice under this section shall not require the disclosure of any key which—

    (a) is intended to be used for the purpose only of generating electronic signatures; and

    (b) has not in fact been used for any other purpose.

(10) In this section "senior officer", in relation to a body corporate, means a director, manager, secretary or other similar officer of the body corporate; and for this purpose "director", in relation to a body corporate whose affairs are managed by its members, means a member of the body corporate.

(11) Schedule 2 (definition of the appropriate permission) shall have effect.

. . . . . .

Part IV

Scrutiny etc. of Investigatory Powers and of the Functions of the Intelligence Services

Commissioners

Intelligence Services Commissioner

116–034   **59.**—(1) The Prime Minister shall appoint a Commissioner to be known as the Intelligence Services Commissioner.

(2) Subject to subsection (4), the Intelligence Services Commissioner shall keep under review, so far as they are not required to be kept under review by the Interception of Communications Commissioner—

[(a) the exercise by the Secretary of State of his powers under sections 5 to 7 of, or the Scottish Ministers (by virtue of provision made under section 63 of the Scotland Act 1998) of their powers under sections 5 and 6(3) and (4) of, the Intelligence Services Act 1994 (warrants for interference with wireless telegraphy, entry and interference with property etc.);]

(b) the exercise and performance by the Secretary of State, [or the Scottish Ministers (by virtue of provision made under section 63 of the Scotland Act 1998)], in connection with or in relation to—

  (i) the activities of the intelligence services, and

  (ii) the activities in places other than Northern Ireland of the officials of the Ministry of Defence and of members of Her Majesty's forces,

of the powers and duties conferred or imposed on him by Parts II and III of this Act [or on them by Part II of this Act];

(c) the exercise and performance by members of the intelligence services of the powers and duties conferred or imposed on them by or under Parts II and III of this Act;

(d) the exercise and performance in places other than Northern Ireland, by officials of the Ministry of Defence and by members of Her Majesty's forces, of the powers and duties conferred or imposed on such officials or members of Her Majesty's forces by or under Parts II and III; and

(e) the adequacy of the arrangements by virtue of which the duty imposed by section 55 is sought to be discharged—

  (i) in relation to the members of the intelligence services; and

  (ii) in connection with any of their activities in places other than Northern Ireland, in relation to officials of the Ministry of Defence and members of Her Majesty's forces.

(3) The Intelligence Services Commissioner shall give the Tribunal all such assistance (including his opinion as to any issue falling to be determined by the Tribunal) as the Tribunal may require—

(a) in connection with the investigation of any matter by the Tribunal; or

(b) otherwise for the purposes of the Tribunal's consideration or determination of any matter.

(4) It shall not be the function of the Intelligence Services Commissioner to keep under review the exercise of any power of the Secretary of State to make, amend or revoke any subordinate legislation.

(5) A person shall not be appointed under this section as the Intelligence Services Commissioner unless he holds or has held a high judicial office (within the meaning of the Appellate Jurisdiction Act 1876).

(6) The Intelligence Services Commissioner shall hold office in accordance with the terms of his appointment; and there shall be paid to him out of money provided by Parliament such allowances as the Treasury may determine.

(7) The Secretary of State shall, after consultation with the Intelligence Services Commissioner and subject to the approval of the Treasury as to numbers, provide him with such staff as the Secretary of State considers necessary for the carrying out of the Commissioner's functions.

(8) Section 4 of the Security Service Act 1989 and section 8 of the Intelligence Services Act 1994 (Commissioners for the purposes of those Acts) shall cease to have effect.

(9) On the coming into force of this section the Commissioner holding office as the Commissioner under section 8 of the Intelligence Services Act 1994 shall

take and hold office as the Intelligence Services Commissioner as if appointed under this Act—

(a) for the unexpired period of his term of office under that Act; and
(b) otherwise, on the terms of his appointment under that Act.

(10) Subsection (7) of section 41 shall apply for the purposes of this section as it applies for the purposes of that section.

Co-operation with and reports by s. 59 Commissioner

116–035   60.—(1) It shall be the duty of—

(a) every member of an intelligence service,
(b) every official of the department of the Secretary of State [and every member of staff of the Scottish Administration (by virtue of provision under section 63 of the Scotland Act 1998)], and
(c) every member of Her Majesty's forces,

to disclose or provide to the Intelligence Services Commissioner all such documents and information as he may require for the purpose of enabling him to carry out his functions under section 59.

(2) As soon as practicable after the end of each calendar year, the Intelligence Services Commissioner shall make a report to the Prime Minister with respect to the carrying out of that Commissioner's functions.

(3) The Intelligence Services Commissioner may also, at any time, make any such other report to the Prime Minister on any matter relating to the carrying out of the Commissioner's functions as the Commissioner thinks fit.

[(3A) The Intelligence Services Commissioner may also, at any time, make any such other report to the First Minister on any matter relating to the carrying out of the Commissioner's functions so far as they relate to the exercise by the Scottish Ministers (by virtue of provision made under section 63 of the Scotland Act 1998) of their powers under sections 5 and 6(3) and (4) of the Intelligence Services Act 1994 or under Parts I and II of this Act, as the Commissioner thinks fit.]

(4) The Prime Minister shall lay before each House of Parliament a copy of every annual report made by the Intelligence Services Commissioner under subsection (2), together with a statement as to whether any matter has been excluded from that copy in pursuance of subsection (5).

[(4A) The Prime Minister shall send a copy of every annual report made by the Intelligence Services Commissioner under subsection (2) which he lays in terms of subsection (4), together with a copy of the statement referred to in subsection (4), to the First Minister who shall forthwith lay that copy report and statement before the Scottish Parliament.]

(5) If it appears to the Prime Minister, after consultation with the Intelligence Services Commissioner[and, if it appears relevant to do so, with the First Minister], that the publication of any matter in an annual report would be contrary to the public interest or prejudicial to—

(a) national security,
(b) the prevention or detection of serious crime,
(c) the economic well-being of the United Kingdom, or
(d) the continued discharge of the functions of any public authority whose activities include activities that are subject to review by that Commissioner,

the Prime Minister may exclude that matter from the copy of the report as laid before each House of Parliament.

(6) Subsection (7) of section 41 shall apply for the purposes of this section as it applies for the purposes of that section.

. . . . . .

The Tribunal

The Tribunal

65.—(1) There shall, for the purpose of exercising the jurisdiction conferred **116–036** on them by this section, be a tribunal consisting of such number of members as Her Majesty may by Letters Patent appoint.

(2) The jurisdiction of the Tribunal shall be—

  (a) to be the only appropriate tribunal for the purposes of section 7 of the Human Rights Act 1998 in relation to any proceedings under subsection (1)(a) of that section (proceedings for actions incompatible with Convention rights) which fall within subsection (3) of this section;

  (b) to consider and determine any complaints made to them which, in accordance with subsection (4), are complaints for which the Tribunal is the appropriate forum;

  (c) to consider and determine any reference to them by any person that he has suffered detriment as a consequence of any prohibition or restriction, by virtue of section 17, on his relying in, or for the purposes of, any civil proceedings on any matter; and

  (d) to hear and determine any other such proceedings falling within subsection (3) as may be allocated to them in accordance with provision made by the Secretary of State by order.

(3) Proceedings fall within this subsection if—

  (a) they are proceedings against any of the intelligence services;

  (b) they are proceedings against any other person in respect of any conduct, or proposed conduct, by or on behalf of any of those services;

  (c) they are proceedings brought by virtue of section 55(4); or

  (d) they are proceedings relating to the taking place in any challengeable circumstances of any conduct falling within subsection (5).

(4) The Tribunal is the appropriate forum for any complaint if it is a complaint by a person who is aggrieved by any conduct falling within subsection (5) which he believes—

  (a) to have taken place in relation to him, to any of his property, to any communications sent by or to him, or intended for him, or to his use of any postal service, telecommunications service or telecommunication system; and

  (b) to have taken place in challengeable circumstances or to have been carried out by or on behalf of any of the intelligence services.

(5) Subject to subsection (6), conduct falls within this subsection if (whenever it occurred) it is—

  (a) conduct by or on behalf of any of the intelligence services;

  (b) conduct for or in connection with the interception of communications in the course of their transmission by means of a postal service or telecommunication system;

(c) conduct to which Chapter II of Part I applies;

(d) conduct to which Part II applies;

(e) the giving of a notice under section 49 or any disclosure or use of a key to protected information;

(f) any entry on or interference with property or any interference with wireless telegraphy.

(6) For the purposes only of subsection (3), nothing mentioned in paragraph (d) or (f) of subsection (5) shall be treated as falling within that subsection unless it is conduct by or on behalf of a person holding any office, rank or position with—

(a) any of the intelligence services;

(b) any of Her Majesty's forces;

(c) any police force;

(d) the National Criminal Intelligence Service;

(e) the National Crime Squad; or

(f) the Commissioners of Customs and Excise;

and section 48(5) applies for the purposes of this subsection as it applies for the purposes of Part II.

(7) For the purposes of this section conduct takes place in challengeable circumstances if—

(a) it takes place with the authority, or purported authority, of anything falling within subsection (8); or

(b) the circumstances are such that (whether or not there is such authority) it would not have been appropriate for the conduct to take place without it, or at least without proper consideration having been given to whether such authority should be sought;

but conduct does not take place in challengeable circumstances to the extent that it is authorised by, or takes place with the permission of, a judicial authority.

(8) The following fall within this subsection—

(a) an interception warrant or a warrant under the Interception of Communications Act 1985;

(b) an authorisation or notice under Chapter II of Part I of this Act;

(c) an authorisation under Part II of this Act or under any enactment contained in or made under an Act of the Scottish Parliament which makes provision equivalent to that made by that Part;

(d) a permission for the purposes of Schedule 2 to this Act;

(e) a notice under section 49 of this Act; or

(f) an authorisation under section 93 of the Police Act 1997.

(9) Schedule 3 (which makes further provision in relation to the Tribunal) shall have effect.

(10) In this section—

(a) references to a key and to protected information shall be construed in accordance with section 56;

(b) references to the disclosure or use of a key to protected information taking place in relation to a person are references to such a disclosure or use taking place in a case in which that person has had possession of the key or of the protected information; and

(c) references to the disclosure of a key to protected information include references to the making of any disclosure in an intelligible form (within the meaning of section 56) of protected information by a person who is or has been in possession of the key to that information;

and the reference in paragraph (b) to a person's having possession of a key or of protected information shall be construed in accordance with section 56.

(11) In this section "judicial authority" means—

(a) any judge of the High Court or of the Crown Court or any Circuit Judge;

(b) any judge of the High Court of Justiciary or any sheriff;

(c) any justice of the peace;

(d) any county court judge or resident magistrate in Northern Ireland;

(e) any person holding any such judicial office as entitles him to exercise the jurisdiction of a judge of the Crown Court or of a justice of the peace.

. . . . . .

Exercise of the Tribunal's jurisdiction

67.—(1) Subject to subsections (4) and (5), it shall be the duty of the Tribunal— **116–037**

(a) to hear and determine any proceedings brought before them by virtue of section 65(2)(a) or (d); and

(b) to consider and determine any complaint or reference made to them by virtue of section 65(2)(b) or (c).

(2) Where the Tribunal hear any proceedings by virtue of section 65(2)(a), they shall apply the same principles for making their determination in those proceedings as would be applied by a court on an application for judicial review.

(3) Where the Tribunal consider a complaint made to them by virtue of section 65(2)(b), it shall be the duty of the Tribunal—

(a) to investigate whether the persons against whom any allegations are made in the complaint have engaged in relation to—

(i) the complainant,

(ii) any of his property,

(iii) any communications sent by or to him, or intended for him, or

(iv) his use of any postal service, telecommunications service or telecommunication system, in any conduct falling within section 65(5);

(b) to investigate the authority (if any) for any conduct falling within section 65(5) which they find has been so engaged in; and

(c) in relation to the Tribunal's findings from their investigations, to determine the complaint by applying the same principles as would be applied by a court on an application for judicial review.

(4) The Tribunal shall not be under any duty to hear, consider or determine any proceedings, complaint or reference if it appears to them that the bringing of the proceedings or the making of the complaint or reference is frivolous or vexatious.

(5) Except where the Tribunal, having regard to all the circumstances, are

satisfied that it is equitable to do so, they shall not consider or determine any complaint made by virtue of section 65(2)(b) if it is made more than one year after the taking place of the conduct to which it relates.

(6) Subject to any provision made by rules under section 69, where any proceedings have been brought before the Tribunal or any reference made to the Tribunal, they shall have power to make such interim orders, pending their final determination, as they think fit.

(7) Subject to any provision made by rules under section 69, the Tribunal on determining any proceedings, complaint or reference shall have power to make any such award of compensation or other order as they think fit; and, without prejudice to the power to make rules under section 69(2)(h), the other orders that may be made by the Tribunal include—

    (a) an order quashing or cancelling any warrant or authorisation; and
    (b) an order requiring the destruction of any records of information which—

        (i) has been obtained in exercise of any power conferred by a warrant or authorisation; or
        (ii) is held by any public authority in relation to any person.

(8) Except to such extent as the Secretary of State may by order otherwise provide, determinations, awards, orders and other decisions of the Tribunal (including decisions as to whether they have jurisdiction) shall not be subject to appeal or be liable to be questioned in any court.

(9) It shall be the duty of the Secretary of State to secure that there is at all times an order under subsection (8) in force allowing for an appeal to a court against any exercise by the Tribunal of their jurisdiction under section 65(2)(c) or (d).

(10) The provision that may be contained in an order under subsection (8) may include—

    (a) provision for the establishment and membership of a tribunal or body to hear appeals;
    (b) the appointment of persons to that tribunal or body and provision about the remuneration and allowances to be payable to such persons and the expenses of the tribunal;
    (c) the conferring of jurisdiction to hear appeals on any existing court or tribunal; and
    (d) any such provision in relation to an appeal under the order as corresponds to provision that may be made by rules under section 69 in relation to proceedings before the Tribunal, or to complaints or references made to the Tribunal.

(11) The Secretary of State shall not make an order under subsection (8) unless a draft of the order has been laid before Parliament and approved by a resolution of each House.

(12) The Secretary of State shall consult the Scottish Ministers before making any order under subsection (8); and any such order shall be laid before the Scottish Parliament.

. . . . . .

Tribunal rules

69.—(1) The Secretary of State may make rules regulating—　　　**116–038**

    (a) the exercise by the Tribunal of the jurisdiction conferred on them by or under section 65; and

    (b) any matters preliminary or incidental to, or arising out of, the hearing or consideration of any proceedings, complaint or reference brought before or made to the Tribunal.

(2) Without prejudice to the generality of subsection (1), rules under this section may—

    (a) enable the jurisdiction of the Tribunal to be exercised at any place in the United Kingdom by any two or more members of the Tribunal designated for the purpose by the President of the Tribunal;

    (b) enable different members of the Tribunal to carry out functions in relation to different complaints at the same time;

    (c) prescribe the form and manner in which proceedings are to be brought before the Tribunal or a complaint or reference is to be made to the Tribunal;

    (d) require persons bringing proceedings or making complaints or references to take such preliminary steps, and to make such disclosures, as may be specified in the rules for the purpose of facilitating a determination of whether—

        (i) the bringing of the proceedings, or

        (ii) the making of the complaint or reference,

    is frivolous or vexatious;

    (e) make provision about the determination of any question as to whether a person by whom—

        (i) any proceedings have been brought before the Tribunal, or

        (ii) any complaint or reference has been made to the Tribunal,

    is a person with a right to bring those proceedings or make that complaint or reference;

    (f) prescribe the forms of hearing or consideration to be adopted by the Tribunal in relation to particular proceedings, complaints or references (including a form that requires any proceedings brought before the Tribunal to be disposed of as if they were a complaint or reference made to the Tribunal);

    (g) prescribe the practice and procedure to be followed on, or in connection with, the hearing or consideration of any proceedings, complaint or reference (including, where applicable, the mode and burden of proof and the admissibility of evidence);

    (h) prescribe orders that may be made by the Tribunal under section 67(6) or (7);

    (i) require information about any determination, award, order or other decision made by the Tribunal in relation to any proceedings, complaint or reference to be provided (in addition to any statement under section 68(4)) to the person who brought the proceedings or made the complaint or reference, or to the person representing his interests.

(3) Rules under this section in relation to the hearing or consideration of any matter by the Tribunal may provide—

    (a) for a person who has brought any proceedings before or made any complaint or reference to the Tribunal to have the right to be legally represented;

(b) for the manner in which the interests of a person who has brought any proceedings before or made any complaint or reference to the Tribunal are otherwise to be represented;

(c) for the appointment in accordance with the rules, by such person as may be determined in accordance with the rules, of a person to represent those interests in the case of any proceedings, complaint or reference.

(4) The power to make rules under this section includes power to make rules—

(a) enabling or requiring the Tribunal to hear or consider any proceedings, complaint or reference without the person who brought the proceedings or made the complaint or reference having been given full particulars of the reasons for any conduct which is the subject of the proceedings, complaint or reference;

(b) enabling or requiring the Tribunal to take any steps in exercise of their jurisdiction in the absence of any person (including the person bringing the proceedings or making the complaint or reference and any legal representative of his);

(c) enabling or requiring the Tribunal to give a summary of any evidence taken in his absence to the person by whom the proceedings were brought or, as the case may be, to the person who made the complaint or reference;

(d) enabling or requiring the Tribunal to exercise their jurisdiction, and to exercise and perform the powers and duties conferred or imposed on them (including, in particular, in relation to the giving of reasons), in such manner provided for in the rules as prevents or limits the disclosure of particular matters.

(5) Rules under this section may also include provision—

(a) enabling powers or duties of the Tribunal that relate to matters preliminary or incidental to the hearing or consideration of any proceedings, complaint or reference to be exercised or performed by a single member of the Tribunal; and

(b) conferring on the Tribunal such ancillary powers as the Secretary of State thinks necessary for the purposes of, or in connection with, the exercise of the Tribunal's jurisdiction, or the exercise or performance of any power or duty conferred or imposed on them.

(6) In making rules under this section the Secretary of State shall have regard, in particular, to—

(a) the need to secure that matters which are the subject of proceedings, complaints or references brought before or made to the Tribunal are properly heard and considered; and

(b) the need to secure that information is not disclosed to an extent, or in a manner, that is contrary to the public interest or prejudicial to national security, the prevention or detection of serious crime, the economic well-being of the United Kingdom or the continued discharge of the functions of any of the intelligence services.

(7) Rules under this section may make provision by the application, with or

without modification, of the provision from time to time contained in specified rules of court.

(8) Subject to subsection (9), no rules shall be made under this section unless a draft of them has first been laid before Parliament and approved by a resolution of each House.

(9) Subsection (8) does not apply in the case of the rules made on the first occasion on which the Secretary of State exercises his power to make rules under this section.

(10) The rules made on that occasion shall cease to have effect at the end of the period of forty days beginning with the day on which they were made unless, before the end of that period, they have been approved by a resolution of each House of Parliament.

(11) For the purposes of subsection (10)—

(a) the rules' ceasing to have effect shall be without prejudice to anything previously done or to the making of new rules; and
(b) in reckoning the period of forty days no account shall be taken of any period during which Parliament is dissolved or prorogued or during which both Houses are adjourned for more than four days.

(12) The Secretary of State shall consult the Scottish Ministers before making any rules under this section; and any rules so made shall be laid before the Scottish Parliament.

Terrorism Act 2000

(2000, c. 11)

An Act to make provision about terrorism; and to make temporary provision for **117–001**
Northern Ireland about the prosecution and punishment of certain offences,
the preservation of peace and the maintenance of order. [20th July 2000]

PART I

INTRODUCTORY

Terrorism: interpretation

1.—(1) In this Act "terrorism" means the use or threat of action where—   **117–002**

(a) the action falls within subsection (2),
(b) the use or threat is designed to influence the government or to intimidate the public or a section of the public, and
(c) the use or threat is made for the purpose of advancing a political, religious or ideological cause.

(2) Action falls within this subsection if it—

(a) involves serious violence against a person,
(b) involves serious damage to property,
(c) endangers a person's life, other than that of the person committing the action,

(d) creates a serious risk to the health or safety of the public or a section of the public, or

(e) is designed seriously to interfere with or seriously to disrupt an electronic system.

(3) The use or threat of action falling within subsection (2) which involves the use of firearms or explosives is terrorism whether or not subsection (1)(b) is satisfied.

(4) In this section—

(a) "action" includes action outside the United Kingdom,

(b) a reference to any person or to property is a reference to any person, or to property, wherever situated,

(c) a reference to the public includes a reference to the public of a country other than the United Kingdom, and

(d) "the government" means the government of the United Kingdom, of a Part of the United Kingdom or of a country other than the United Kingdom.

(5) In this Act a reference to action taken for the purposes of terrorism includes a reference to action taken for the benefit of a proscribed organisation.

Temporary legislation

117–003   2.—(1) The following shall cease to have effect—

(a) the Prevention of Terrorism (Temporary Provisions) Act 1989, and

(b) the Northern Ireland (Emergency Provisions) Act 1996.

(2) Schedule 1 (which preserves certain provisions of the 1996 Act, in some cases with amendment, for a transitional period) shall have effect.

PART II

PROSCRIBED ORGANISATIONS

Procedure

Proscription

117–004   3.—(1) For the purposes of this Act an organisation is proscribed if—

(a) it is listed in Schedule 2, or

(b) it operates under the same name as an organisation listed in that Schedule.

(2) Subsection (1)(b) shall not apply in relation to an organisation listed in Schedule 2 if its entry is the subject of a note in that Schedule.

(3) The Secretary of State may be order—

(a) add an organisation to Schedule 2;

(b) remove an organisation from that Schedule;

(c) amend that Schedule in some other way.

(4) The Secretary of State may exercise his power under subsection (3)(a) in respect of an organisation only if he believes that it is concerned in terrorism.

(5) For the purposes of subsection (4) an organisation is concerned in terrorism if it—

(a) commits or participates in acts of terrorism,
(b) prepares for terrorism,
(c) promotes or encourages terrorism, or
(d) is otherwise concerned in terrorism.

Deproscription: application

4.—(1) An application may be made to the Secretary of State for the exercise **117–005**
of his power under section 3(3)(b) to remove an organisation from Schedule 2.

(2) An application may be made by—

(a) the organisation, or
(b) any person affected by the organisation's proscription.

(3) The Secretary of State shall make regulations prescribing the procedure for applications under this section.

(4) The regulations shall, in particular—

(a) require the Secretary of State to determine an application within a specified period of time, and
(b) require an application to state the grounds on which it is made.

Deproscription: appeal

5.—(1) There shall be a commission, to be known as the Proscribed Organisa- **117–006**
tions Appeal Commission.

(2) Where an application under section 4 has been refused, the applicant may appeal to the Commission.

(3) The Commission shall allow an appeal against a refusal to deproscribe an organisation if it considers that the decision to refuse was flawed when considered in the light of the principles applicable on an application for judicial review.

(4) Where the Commission allows an appeal under this section by or in respect of an organisation, it may make an order under this subsection.

(5) Where an order is made under subsection (4) the Secretary of State shall as soon as is reasonably practicable—

(a) lay before Parliament, in accordance with section 123(4), the draft of an order under section 3(3)(b) removing the organisation from the list in Schedule 2, or
(b) make an order removing the organisation from the list in Schedule 2 in pursuance of section 123(5).

(6) Schedule 3 (constitution of the Commission and procedure) shall have effect.

Further appeal

6.—(1) A party to an appeal under section 5 which the Proscribed Organisa- **117–007**
tions Appeal Commission has determined may bring a further appeal on a question of law to—

(a) the Court of Appeal, if the first appeal was heard in England and Wales,
(b) the Court of Session, if the first appeal was heard in Scotland, or

    (c) the Court of Appeal in Northern Ireland, if the first appeal was heard in Northern Ireland.

(2) An appeal under subsection (1) may be brought only with the permission—

    (a) of the Commission, or
    (b) where the Commission refuses permission, of the court to which the appeal would be brought.

(3) An order under section 5(4) shall not require the Secretary of State to take any action until the final determination or disposal of an appeal under this section (including any appeal to the House of Lords).

Appeal: effect on conviction, etc.

117–008   7.—(1) This section applies where—

    (a) an appeal under section 5 has been allowed in respect of an organisation,
    (b) an order has been made under section 3(3)(b) in respect of the organisation in accordance with an order of the Commission under section 5(4) (and, if the order was made in reliance on section 123(5), a resolution has been passed by each House of Parliament under section 123(5)(b)),
    (c) a person has been convicted of an offence in respect of the organisation under any of sections 11 to 13, 15 to 19 and 56, and
    (d) the activity to which the charge referred took place on or after the date of the refusal to deproscribe against which the appeal under section 5 was brought.

(2) If the person mentioned in subsection (1)(c) was convicted on indictment—

    (a) he may appeal against the conviction to the Court of Appeal, and
    (b) the Court of Appeal shall allow the appeal.

(3) A person may appeal against a conviction by virtue of subsection (2) whether or not has already appealed against the conviction.
(4) An appeal by virtue of subsection (2)—

    (a) must be brought within the period of 28 days beginning with the date on which the order mentioned in subsection (1)(b) comes into force, and
    (b) shall be treated as an appeal under section 1 of the Criminal Appeal Act 1968 (but does not require leave).

(5) If the person mentioned in subsection (1)(c) was convicted by a magistrates' court—

    (a) he may appeal against the conviction to the Crown Court, and
    (b) the Crown Court shall allow the appeal.

(6) A person may appeal against a conviction by virtue of subsection (5)—

    (a) whether or not he pleaded guilty,
    (b) whether or not he has already appealed against the conviction, and

(c) whether or not he has made an application in respect of the conviction under section 111 of the Magistrates' Courts Act 1980 (case stated).

(7) An appeal by virtue of subsection (5)—

(a) must be brought within the period of 21 days beginning with the date on which the order mentioned in subsection (1)(b) comes into force, and

(b) shall be treated as an appeal under section 108(1)(b) of the Magistrates' Courts Act 1980.

. . . . . .

Section 7: Scotland and Northern Ireland

8.—(1) In the application of section 7 to Scotland—   **117–009**

(a) for every reference to the Court of Appeal or the Crown Court substitute a reference to the High Court of Justiciary,

(b) in subsection (2)(b), at the end insert "and quash the conviction",

(c) in subsection (4)—

(i) in paragraph (a), for "28 days" substitute "two weeks", and

(ii) in paragraph (b), for "section 1 of the Criminal Appeal Act 1968" substitute "section 106 of the Criminal Procedure (Scotland) Act 1995",

(d) in subsection (5)—

(i) for "by a magistrates' court" substitute "in summary proceedings", and

(ii) in paragraph (b), at the end insert "and quash the conviction",

(e) in subsection (6), paragraph (c) is omitted, and

(f) in subsection (7)—

(i) in paragraph (a) for "21 days" substitute "two weeks", and

(ii) for paragraph (b) substitute—

"(b) shall be by note of appeal, which shall state the ground of appeal,

(c) shall not require leave under any provision of Part X of the Criminal Procedure (Scotland) Act 1995, and

(d) shall be in accordance with such procedure as the High Court of Justiciary may, by Act of Adjournal, determine.".

(2) In the application of section 7 to Northern Ireland—

(a) the reference in subsection (4) to section 1 of the Criminal Appeal Act 1968 shall be taken as a reference to section 1 of the Criminal Appeal (Northern Ireland) Act 1980,

(b) references in subsection (5) to the Crown Court shall be taken as references to the county court,

(c) the reference in subsection (6) to section 111 of the Magistrates' Courts Act 1980 shall be taken as a reference to Article 146 of the Magistrates' Courts (Northern Ireland) Order 1981, and

(d) the reference in subsection (7) to section 108(1)(b) of the Magistrates' Courts Act 1980 shall be taken as a reference to Article 140(1)(b) of the Magistrates' Courts (Northern Ireland) Order 1981.

Human Rights Act 1998

117–010 **9.**—(1) This section applies where rules (within the meaning of section 7 of the Human Rights Act 1998 (jurisdiction)) provide for proceedings under section 7(1) of that Act to be brought before the Proscribed Organisations Appeal Commission.

(2) The following provisions of this Act shall apply in relation to proceedings under section 7(1) of that Act as they apply to appeals under section 5 of this Act—

    (a) section 5(4) and (5),
    (b) section 6,
    (c) section 7, and
    (d) [paragraphs 4 to 7 of Schedule 3][1].

(3) The Commission shall decide proceedings in accordance with the principles applicable on an application for judicial review.

(4) In the application of the provisions mentioned in subsection (2)—

    (a) a reference to the Commission allowing an appeal shall be taken as a reference to the Commission determining that an action of the Secretary of State is incompatible with a Convention right, and
    (b) a reference to the refusal to deproscribe against which an appeal was brought shall be taken as a reference to the action of the Secretary of State which is found to be incompatible with a Convention right.

[1] Word substituted by Regulation of Investigatory Powers Act 2000 (c.23), Sched. 4, para. 12(1).

Immunity

117–011 **10.**—(1) The following shall not be admissible as evidence in proceedings for an offence under any of sections 11 to 13, 15 to 19 and 56—

    (a) evidence of anything done in relation to an application to the Secretary of State under section 4,
    (b) evidence of anything done in relation to proceedings before the Proscribed Organisations Appeal Commission under section 5 above or section 7(1) of the Human Rights Act 1998,
    (c) evidence of anything done in relation to proceedings under section 6 (including that section as applied by section 9(2)), and
    (d) any document submitted for the purposes of proceedings mentioned in any of paragraphs (a) to (c).

(2) But subsection (1) does not prevent evidence from being adduced on behalf of the accused.

Offences

Membership

117–012 **11.**—(1) A person commits an offence if he belongs or professes to belong to a proscribed organisation.

(2) It is a defence for a person charged with an offence under subsection (1) to prove—

    (a) that the organisation was not proscribed on the last (or only) occasion on which he became a member or began to profess to be a member, and

(b) that he has not taken part in the activities of the organisation at any time while it was proscribed.

(3) A person guilty of an offence under this section shall be liable—

(a) on conviction on indictment, to imprisonment for a term not exceeding ten years, to a fine or to both, or

(b) on summary conviction, to imprisonment for a term not exceeding six months, to a fine not exceeding the statutory maximum or to both.

(4) In subsection (2) "proscribed" means proscribed for the purposes of any of the following—

(a) this Act;
(b) the Northern Ireland (Emergency Provisions) Act 1996;
(c) the Northern Ireland (Emergency Provisions) Act 1991;
(d) the Prevention of Terrorism (Temporary Provisions) Act 1989;
(e) the Prevention of Terrorism (Temporary Provisions) Act 1984;
(f) the Northern Ireland (Emergency Provisions) Act 1978;
(g) the Prevention of Terrorism (Temporary Provisions) Act 1976;
(h) the Prevention of Terrorism (Temporary Provisions) Act 1974;
(i) the Northern Ireland (Emergency Provisions) Act 1973.

Support

12.—(1) A person commits an offence if—   **117–013**

(a) he invites support for a proscribed organisation, and
(b) the support is not, or is not restricted to, the provision of money or other property (within the meaning of section 15).

(2) A person commits an offence if he arranges, manages or assists in arranging or managing a meeting which he knows is—

(a) to support a proscribed organisation,
(b) to further the activities of a proscribed organisation, or
(c) to be addressed by a person who belongs or professes to belong to a proscribed organisation.

(3) A person commits an offence if he addresses a meeting and the purpose of his address is to encourage support for a proscribed organisation or to further its activities.

(4) Where a person is charged with an offence under subsection (2)(c) in respect of a private meeting it is a defence for him to prove that he had no reasonable cause to believe that the address mentioned in subsection (2)(c) would support a proscribed organisation or further its activities.

(5) In subsections (2) to (4)—

(a) "meeting" means a meeting of three or more persons, whether or not the public are admitted, and
(b) a meeting is private if the public are not admitted.

(6) A person guilty of an offence under this section shall be liable—

(a) on conviction on indictment, to imprisonment for a term not exceeding ten years, to a fine or to both, or

(b) on summary conviction, to imprisonment for a term not exceeding six months, to a fine not exceeding the statutory maximum or to both.

Uniform

117–014   **13.**—(1) A person in a public place commits an offence if he—

(a) wears an item of clothing, or
(b) wears, carries or displays an article,

in such a way or in such circumstances as to arouse reasonable suspicion that he is a member or supporter of a proscribed organisation.

(2) A constable in Scotland may arrest a person without a warrant if he has reasonable grounds to suspect that the person is guilty of an offence under this section.

(3) A person guilty of an offence under this section shall be liable on summary conviction to—

(a) imprisonment for a term not exceeding six months,
(b) a fine not exceeding level 5 on the standard scale, or
(c) both.

PART III

TERRORIST PROPERTY

Interpretation

Terrorist property

117–015   **14.**—(1) In this Act "terrorist property" means—

(a) money or other property which is likely to be used for the purposes of terrorism (including any resources of a proscribed organisation),
(b) proceeds of the commission of acts of terrorism, and
(c) proceeds of acts carried out for the purposes of terrorism.

(2) In subsection (1)—

(a) a reference to proceeds of an act includes a reference to any property which wholly or partly, and directly or indirectly, represents the proceeds of the act (including payments or other rewards in connection with its commission), and
(b) the reference to an organisation's resources includes a reference to any money or other property which is applied or made available, or is to be applied or made available, for use by the organisation.

Offences

Fund-raising

117–016   **15.**—(1) A person commits an offence if he—

(a) invites another to provide money or other property, and
(b) intends that it should be used, or has reasonable cause to suspect that it may be used, for the purposes of terrorism.

(2) A person commits an offence if he—

    (a) receives money or other property, and

    (b) intends that it should be used, or has reasonable cause to suspect that it may be used, for the purposes of terrorism.

(3) A person commits an offence if he—

    (a) provides money or other property, and

    (b) knows or has reasonable cause to suspect that it will or may be used for the purposes of terrorism.

(4) In this section a reference to the provision of money or other property is a reference to its being given, lent or otherwise made available, whether or not for consideration.

Use and possession

16.—(1) A person commits an offence if he uses money or other property for **117–017** the purposes of terrorism.

(2) A person commits an offence if he—

    (a) possesses money or other property, and

    (b) intends that it should be used, or has reasonable cause to suspect that it may be used, for the purposes of terrorism.

Funding arrangements

17. A person commits an offence if— **117–018**

    (a) he enters into or becomes concerned in an arrangement as a result of which money or other property is made available or is to be made available to another, and

    (b) he knows or has reasonable cause to suspect that it will or may be used for the purposes of terrorism.

Money laundering

18.—(1) A person commits an offence if he enters into or becomes concerned **117–019** in an arrangement which facilitates the retention or control by or on behalf of another person of terrorist property—

    (a) by concealment,

    (b) by removal from the jurisdiction,

    (c) by transfer to nominees, or

    (d) in any other way.

(2) It is a defence for a person charged with an offence under subsection (1) to prove that he did not know and had no reasonable cause to suspect that the arrangement related to terrorist property.

Disclosure of information: duty

117–020   19.—(1) This section applies where a person—

(a) believes or suspects that another person has committed an offence under any of sections 15 to 18, and
(b) bases his belief or suspicion on information which comes to his attention in the course of a trade, profession, business or employment.

[(1A) But this section does not apply if the information came to the person in the course of a business in the regulated sector.]¹
(2) The person commits an offence if he does not disclose to a constable as soon as is reasonably practicable—

(a) his belief or suspicion, and
(b) the information on which it is based.

(3) It is a defence for a person charged with an offence under subsection (2) to prove that he had a reasonable excuse for not making the disclosure.
(4) Where—

(a) a person is in employment,
(b) his employer has established a procedure for the making of disclosures of the matters specified in subsection (2), and
(c) he is charged with an offence under that subsection,

it is a defence for him to prove that he disclosed the matters specified in that subsection in accordance with the procedure.
(5) Subsection (2) does not require disclosure by a professional legal adviser of—

(a) information which he obtains in privileged circumstances, or
(b) a belief or suspicion based on information which he obtains in privileged circumstances.

(6) For the purpose of subsection (5) information is obtained by an adviser in privileged circumstances if it comes to him, otherwise than with a view to furthering a criminal purpose—

(a) from a client or a client's representative, in connection with the provision of legal advice by the adviser to the client,
(b) from a person seeking legal advice from the adviser, or from the person's representative, or
(c) from any person, for the purpose of actual or contemplated legal proceedings.

(7) For the purposes of subsection (1)(a) a person shall be treated as having committed an offence under one of sections 15 to 18 if—

(a) he has taken an action or been in possession of a thing, and
(b) he would have committed an offence under one of those sections if he had been in the United Kingdom at the time when he took the action or was in possession of the thing.

[(7A) The reference to a business in the regulated sector must be construed in accordance with Schedule 3A.
(7B) The reference to a constable includes a reference to a person authorised

for the purposes of this section by the Director General of the National Criminal Intelligence Service.][2]

(8) A person guilty of an offence under this section shall be liable—

(a) on conviction on indictment, to imprisonment for a term not exceeding five years, to a fine or to both, or

(b) on summary conviction, to imprisonment for a term not exceeding six months, or to a fine not exceeding the statutory maximum or to both.

[1] Added by Anti-terrorism, Crime and Security Act 2001 (c.24), Sched. 2(3), para. 5(3).
[2] Added by Anti-terrorism, Crime and Security Act 2001 (c.24), Sched. 2(3), para. 5(4).

Disclosure of information: permission

20.—(1) A person may disclose to a constable—   **117–021**

(a) a suspicion or belief that any money or other property is terrorist property or is derived from terrorist property;

(b) any matter on which the suspicion or belief is based.

(2) A person may make a disclosure to a constable in the circumstances mentioned in section 19(1) and (2).

(3) Subsections (1) and (2) shall have effect notwithstanding any restriction on the disclosure of information imposed by statute or otherwise.

(4) Where—

(a) a person is in employment, and

(b) his employer has established a procedure for the making of disclosures of the kinds mentioned in subsection (1) and section 19(2),

subsections (1) and (2) shall have effect in relation to that person as if any reference to disclosure to a constable included a reference to disclosure in accordance with the procedure.

[(5) References to a constable include references to a person authorised for the purposes of this section by the Director General of the National Criminal Intelligence Service.][1]

[1] Added by Anti-terrorism, Crime and Security Act 2001 (c.24), Sched. 2(3), para. 5(5).

Cooperation with police

21.—(1) A person does not commit an offence under any of sections 15 to **117–022** 18 if he is acting with the express consent of a constable.

(2) Subject to subsections (3) and (4), a person does not commit an offence under any of sections 15 to 18 by involvement in a transaction or arrangement relating to money or other property if he discloses to a constable—

(a) his suspicion or belief that the money or other property is terrorist property, and

(b) the information on which his suspicion or belief is based.

(3) Subsection (2) applies only where a person makes a disclosure—

(a) after he becomes concerned in the transaction concerned,

(b) on his own initiative, and

(c) as soon as is reasonably practicable.

(4) Subsection (2) does not apply to a person if—

(a) a constable forbids him to continue his involvement in the transaction or arrangement to which the disclosure relates, and

(b) he continues his involvement.

(5) It is a defence for a person charged with an offence under any of sections 15(2) and (3) and 16 to 18 to prove that—

(a) he intended to make a disclosure of the kind mentioned in subsections (2) and (3), and

(b) there is reasonable excuse for his failure to do so.

(6) Where—

(a) a person is in employment, and

(b) his employer has established a procedure for the making of disclosures of the same kind as may be made to a constable under subsection (2),

this section shall have effect in relation to that person as if any reference to disclosure to a constable included a reference to disclosure in accordance with the procedure.

(7) A reference in this section to a transaction or arrangement relating to money or other property includes a reference to use or possession.

[Failure to disclose: regulated sector

117–023   21A—(1) A person commits an offence if each of the following three conditions is satisfied.

(2) The first condition is that he—

(a) knows or suspects, or

(b) has reasonable grounds for knowing or suspecting,

that another person has committed an offence under any of sections 15 to 18.

(3) The second condition is that the information or other matter—

(a) on which his knowledge or suspicion is based, or

(b) which gives reasonable grounds for such knowledge or suspicion,

came to him in the course of a business in the regulated sector.

(4) The third condition is that he does not disclose the information or other matter to a constable or a nominated officer as soon as is practicable after it comes to him.

(5) But a person does not commit an offence under this section if—

(a) he has a reasonable excuse for not disclosing the information or other matter;

(b) he is a professional legal adviser and the information or other matter came to him in privileged circumstances.

(6) In deciding whether a person committed an offence under this section the court must consider whether he followed any relevant guidance which was at the time concerned—

(a) issued by a supervisory authority or any other appropriate body,

(b) approved by the Treasury, and

(c) published in a manner it approved as appropriate in its opinion to bring the guidance to the attention of persons likely to be affected by it.

(7) A disclosure to a nominated officer is a disclosure which—

(a) is made to a person nominated by the alleged offender's employer to receive disclosures under this section, and
(b) is made in the course of the alleged offender's employment and in accordance with the procedure established by the employer for the purpose.

(8) Information or other matter comes to a professional legal adviser in privileged circumstances if it is communicated or given to him—

(a) by (or by a representative of) a client of his in connection with the giving by the adviser of legal advice to the client,
(b) by (or by a representative of) a person seeking legal advice from the adviser, or
(c) by a person in connection with legal proceedings or contemplated legal proceedings.

(9) But subsection (8) does not apply to information or other matter which is communicated or given with a view to furthering a criminal purpose.

(10) Schedule 3A has effect for the purpose of determining what is—

(a) a business in the regulated sector;
(b) a supervisory authority.

(11) For the purposes of subsection (2) a person is to be taken to have committed an offence there mentioned if—

(a) he has taken an action or been in possession of a thing and
(b) he would have committed the offence if he had been in the United Kingdom at the time when he took the action or was in possession of the thing.

(12) A person guilty of an offence under this section is liable—

(a) on conviction on indictment, to imprisonment for a term not exceeding five years or to a fine or to both;
(b) on summary conviction, to imprisonment for a term not exceeding six months or to a fine not exceeding the statutory maximum or to both.

(13) An appropriate body is any body which regulates or is representative of any trade, profession, business or employment carried on by the alleged offender.

(14) The reference to a constable includes a reference to a person authorised for the purposes of this section by the Director General of the National Criminal Intelligence Service.]¹

¹ Added by Anti-terrorism, Crime and Security Act 2001 (c.24), Sched. 2(3), para. 5(2).

[Protected disclosures

21B—(1) A disclosure which satisfies the following three conditions is not to be taken to breach any restriction on the disclosure of information (however imposed). **117–024**

(2) The first condition is that the information or other matter disclosed came to the person making the disclosure (the discloser) in the course of a business in the regulated sector.

(3) The second condition is that the information or other matter—

    (a) causes the discloser to know or suspect, or
    (b) gives him reasonable grounds for knowing or suspecting,

that another person has committed an offence under any of sections 15 to 18.

(4) The third condition is that the disclosure is made to a constable or a nominated officer as soon as is practicable after the information or other matter comes to the discloser.

(5) A disclosure to a nominated officer is a disclosure which—

    (a) is made to a person nominated by the discloser's employer to receive disclosures under this section, and
    (b) is made in the course of the discloser's employment and in accordance with the procedure established by the employer for the purpose.

(6) The reference to a business in the regulated sector must be construed in accordance with Schedule 3A.

(7) The reference to a constable includes a reference to a person authorised for the purposes of this section by the Director General of the National Criminal Intelligence Service.]¹

¹ Added by Anti-terrorism, Crime and Security Act 2001 (c.24), Sched. 2(3), para. 5(2).

Penalties

117–025 22. A person guilty of an offence under any of sections 15 to 18 shall be liable—

    (a) on conviction on indictment, to imprisonment for a term not exceeding 14 years, to a fine or to both, or
    (b) on summary conviction, to imprisonment for a term not exceeding six months, to a fine not exceeding the statutory maximum or to both.

Forfeiture

117–026 23.—(1) The court by or before which a person is convicted of an offence under any of sections 15 to 18 may make a forfeiture order in accordance with the provisions of this section.

(2) Where a person is convicted of an offence under section 15(1) or (2) or 16 the court may order the forfeiture of any money or other property—

    (a) which, at the time of the offence, he had in his possession or under his control, and
    (b) which, at that time, he intended should be used, or had reasonable cause to suspect might be used, for the purposes of terrorism.

(3) Where a person is convicted of an offence under section 15(3) the court may order the forfeiture of any money or other property—

    (a) which, at the time of the offence, he had in his possession or under his control, and
    (b) which, at that time, he knew or had reasonable cause to suspect would or might be used for the purposes of terrorism.

(4) Where a person is convicted of an offence under section 17 the court may order the forfeiture of the money or other property—

(a) to which the arrangement in question related, and

(b) which, at the time of the offence, he knew or had reasonable cause to suspect would or might be used for the purposes of terrorism.

(5) Where a person is convicted of an offence under section 18 the court may order the forfeiture of the money or other property to which the arrangement in question related.

(6) Where a person is convicted of an offence under any of sections 15 to 18, the court may order the forfeiture of any money or other property which wholly or partly, and directly or indirectly, is received by any person as a payment or other reward in connection with the commission of the offence.

(7) Where a person other than the convicted person claims to be the owner of or otherwise interested in anything which can be forfeited by an order under this section, the court shall give him an opportunity to be heard before making an order.

(8) A court in Scotland shall not make an order under this section except on the application of the prosecutor—

(a) in proceedings on indictment, when he moves for sentence, and

(b) in summary proceedings, before the court convicts the accused,

and for the purposes of any appeal or review, an order under this section made by a court in Scotland is a sentence.

(9) Schedule 4 (which makes further provision in relation to forfeiture orders under this section) shall have effect.

. . . . . .

Part IV

Terrorist Investigations

Interpretation

Terrorist investigation

32. In this Act "terrorist investigation" means an investigation of— **117–027**

(a) the commission, preparation or instigation of acts of terrorism,

(b) an act which appears to have been done for the purposes of terrorism,

(c) the resources of a proscribed organisation,

(d) the possibility of making an order under section 3(3), or

(e) the commission, preparation or instigation of an offence under this Act.

Cordons

Cordoned areas

33.—(1) An area is a cordoned area for the purposes of this Act if it is **117–028** designated under this section.

(2) A designation may be made only if the person making it considers it expedient for the purposes of a terrorist investigation.

(3) If a designation is made orally, the person making it shall confirm it in writing as soon as is reasonably practicable.

(4) The person making a designation shall arrange for the demarcation of the cordoned area, so far as is reasonably practicable—

    (a) by means of tape marked with the word "police", or
    (b) in such other manner as a constable considers appropriate.

Power to designate

117–029   **34.**—(1) Subject to [subsections (1A), (1B) and (2)]¹, a designation under section 33 may only be made—

    (a) where the area is outside Northern Ireland and is wholly or partly within a police area, by an officer for the police area who is of at least the rank of superintendent, and
    (b) where the area is in Northern Ireland, by a member of the Royal Ulster Constabulary who is of at least the rank of superintendent.

[(1A) A designation under section 33 may be made in relation to an area (outside Northern Ireland) which is in, on or in the vicinity of any policed premises by a member of the British Transport Police Force who is of at least the rank of superintendent.

(1B) A designation under section 33 may be made by a member of the Ministry of Defence Police who is of at least the rank of superintendent in relation to an area outside or in Northern Ireland—

    (a) if it is a place to which subsection (2) of section 2 of the Ministry of Defence Police Act 1987 (c. 4) applies,
    (b) if a request has been made under paragraph (a), (b) or (d) of subsection (3A) of that section in relation to a terrorist investigation and it is a place where he has the powers and privileges of a constable by virtue of that subsection as a result of the request, or
    (c) if a request has been made under paragraph (c) of that subsection in relation to a terrorist investigation and it is a place in, on or in the vicinity of policed premises.

(1C) But a designation under section 33 may not be made by—

    (a) a member of the British Transport Police Force, or
    (b) a member of the Ministry of Defence Police,

in any other case.]²
(2) A constable who is not of the rank required by subsection (1) may make a designation if he considers it necessary by reason of urgency.
(3) Where a constable makes a designation in reliance on subsection (2) he shall as soon as is reasonably practicable—

    (a) make a written record of the time at which the designation was made, and
    (b) ensure that a police officer of at least the rank of superintendent is informed.

(4) An officer who is informed of a designation in accordance with subsection (3)(b)—

    (a) shall confirm the designation or cancel it with effect from such time as he may direct, and

   (b) shall, if he cancels the designation, make a written record of the cancellation and the reason for it.

[1] Words substituted by Anti-terrorism, Crime and Security Act 2001 (c.24), Sched. 7, para. 30(2).
[2] Added by Anti-terrorism, Crime and Security Act 2001 (c.24), Sched. 7, para. 30(3).

Duration

   35.—(1) A designation under section 33 has effect, subject to subsections (2) **117–030**
to (5), during the period—

   (a) beginning at the time when it is made, and
   (b) ending with a date or at a time specified in the designation.

   (2) The date or time specified under subsection (1)(b) must not occur after the end of the period of 14 days beginning with the day on which the designation is made.
   (3) The period during which a designation has effect may be extended in writing from time to time by—

   (a) the person who made it, or
   (b) a person who could have made it (otherwise than by virtue of section 34(2)).

   (4) An extension shall specify the additional period during which the designation is to have effect.
   (5) A designation shall not have effect after the end of the period of 28 days beginning with the day on which it is made.

Police powers

   36.—(1) A constable in uniform may—   **117–031**

   (a) order a person in a cordoned area to leave it immediately;
   (b) order a person immediately to leave premises which are wholly or partly in or adjacent to a cordoned area;
   (c) order the driver or person in charge of a vehicle in a cordoned area to move it from the area immediately;
   (d) arrange for the removal of a vehicle from a cordoned area;
   (e) arrange for the movement of a vehicle within a cordoned area;
   (f) prohibit or restrict access to a cordoned area by pedestrians or vehicles.

   (2) A person commits an offence if he fails to comply with an order, prohibition or restriction imposed by virtue of subsection (1).
   (3) It is a defence for a person charged with an offence under subsection (2) to prove that he had a reasonable excuse for his failure.
   (4) A person guilty of an offence under subsection (2) shall be liable on summary conviction to—

   (a) imprisonment for a term not exceeding three months,
   (b) a fine not exceeding level 4 on the standard scale, or
   (c) both.

Information and evidence

Powers

117–032   37. Schedule 5 (power to obtain information, &c.) shall have effect.

. . . . . .

Part V

Counter-Terrorist Powers

Suspected terrorists

Terrorist: interpretation

117–033   40.—(1) In this Part "terrorist" means a person who—

    (a) has committed an offence under any of sections 11, 12, 15 to 18, 54 and 56 to 63, or

    (b) is or has been concerned in the commission, preparation or instigation of acts of terrorism.

(2) The reference in subsection (1)(b) to a person who has been concerned in the commission, preparation or instigation of acts of terrorism includes a reference to a person who has been, whether before or after the passing of this Act, concerned in the commission, preparation or instigation of acts of terrorism within the meaning given by section 1.

Arrest without warrant

117–034   41.—(1) A constable may arrest without a warrant a person whom he reasonably suspects to be a terrorist.

(2) Where a person is arrested under this section the provisions of Schedule 8 (detention: treatment, review and extension) shall apply.

(3) Subject to subsections (4) to (7), a person detained under this section shall (unless detained under any other power) be released not later than the end of the period of 48 hours beginning—

    (a) with the time of his arrest under this section, or

    (b) if he was being detained under Schedule 7 when he was arrested under this section, with the time when his examination under that Schedule began.

(4) If on a review of a person's detention under Part II of Schedule 8 the review officer does not authorise continued detention, the person shall (unless detained in accordance with subsection (5) or (6) or under any other power) be released.

(5) Where a police officer intends to make an application for a warrant under paragraph 29 of Schedule 8 extending a person's detention, the person may be detained pending the making of the application.

(6) Where an application has been made under paragraph 29 or 36 of Schedule 8 in respect of a person's detention, he may be detained pending the conclusion of proceedings on the application.

(7) Where an application under paragraph 29 or 36 of Schedule 8 is granted

in respect of a person's detention, he may be detained, subject to paragraph 37 of that Schedule, during the period specified in the warrant.

(8) The refusal of an application in respect of a person's detention under paragraph 29 or 36 of Schedule 8 shall not prevent his continued detention in accordance with this section.

(9) A person who has the powers of a constable in one Part of the United Kingdom may exercise the power under subsection (1) in any Part of the United Kingdom.

Search of premises

42.—(1) A justice of the peace may on the application of a constable issue a **117–035** warrant in relation to specified premises if he is satisfied that there are reasonable grounds for suspecting that a person whom the constable reasonably suspects to be a person falling within section 40(1)(b) is to be found there.

(2) A warrant under this section shall authorise any constable to enter and search the specified premises for the purpose of arresting the person referred to in subsection (1) under section 41.

(3) In the application of subsection (1) to Scotland—

(a) "justice of the peace" includes the sheriff, and
(b) the justice of the peace or sheriff can be satisfied as mentioned in that subsection only by having heard evidence on oath.

Search of persons

43.—(1) A constable may stop and search a person whom he reasonably **117–036** suspects to be a terrorist to discover whether he has in his possession anything which may constitute evidence that he is a terrorist.

(2) A constable may search a person arrested under section 41 to discover whether he has in his possession anything which may constitute evidence that he is a terrorist.

(3) A search of a person under this section must be carried out by someone of the same sex.

(4) A constable may seize and retain anything which he discovers in the course of a search of a person under subsection (1) or (2) and which he reasonably suspects may constitute evidence that the person is a terrorist.

(5) A person who has the powers of a constable in one Part of the United Kingdom may exercise a power under this section in any Part of the United Kingdom.

Power to stop and search

Authorisations

44.—(1) An authorisation under this subsection authorises any constable in **117–037** uniform to stop a vehicle in an area or at a place specified in the authorisation and to search—

(a) the vehicle;
(b) the driver of the vehicle;
(c) a passenger in the vehicle;
(d) anything in or on the vehicle or carried by the driver or a passenger.

(2) An authorisation under this subsection authorises any constable in uniform to stop a pedestrian in an area or at a place specified in the authorisation and to search—

(a) the pedestrian;

(b) anything carried by him.

(3) An authorisation under subsection (1) or (2) may be given only if the person giving it considers it expedient for the prevention of acts of terrorism.

(4) An authorisation may be given—

(a) where the specified area or place is the whole or part of a police area outside Northern Ireland other than one mentioned in paragraph (b) or (c), by a police officer for the area who is of at least the rank of assistant chief constable;

(b) where the specified area or place is the whole or part of the metropolitan police district, by a police officer for the district who is of at least the rank of commander of the metropolitan police;

(c) where the specified area or place is the whole or part of the City of London, by a police officer for the City who is of at least the rank of commander in the City of London police force;

(d) where the specified area or place is the whole or part of Northern Ireland, by a member of the Royal Ulster Constabulary who is of at least the rank of assistant chief constable.

[(4A) In a case (within subsection (4)(a), (b) or (c)) in which the specified area or place is in, on or in the vicinity of policed premises, an authorisation may also be given by a member of the British Transport Police Force who is of at least the rank of assistant chief constable.

(4B) In a case in which the specified area or place is a place to which section 2(2) of the Ministry of Defence Police Act 1987 applies, an authorisation may also be given by a member of the Ministry of Defence Police who is of at least the rank of assistant chief constable.

(4C) But an authorisation may not be given by—

(a) a member of the British Transport Police Force, or

(b) a member of the Ministry of Defence Police,

in any other case.][1]

(5) If an authorisation is given orally, the person giving it shall confirm it in writing as soon as is reasonably practicable.

[1] Added by Anti-terrorism, Crime and Security Act 2001 (c.24), Sched. 7, para. 31.

Exercise of power

117–038   45.—(1) The power conferred by an authorisation under section 44(1) or (2)—

(a) may be exercised only for the purpose of searching for articles of a kind which could be used in connection with terrorism, and

(b) may be exercised whether or not the constable has grounds for suspecting the presence of articles of that kind.

(2) A constable may seize and retain an article which he discovers in the course of a search by virtue of section 44(1) or (2) and which he reasonably suspects is intended to be used in connection with terrorism.

(3) A constable exercising the power conferred by an authorisation may not require a person to remove any clothing in public except for headgear, footwear, an outer coat, a jacket or gloves.

(4) Where a constable proposes to search a person or vehicle by virtue of section 44(1) or (2) he may detain the person or vehicle for such time as is

reasonably required to permit the search to be carried out at or near the place where the person or vehicle is stopped.

(5) Where—

(a) a vehicle or pedestrian is stopped by virtue of section 44(1) or (2), and
(b) the driver of the vehicle or the pedestrian applies for a written statement that the vehicle was stopped, or that he was stopped, by virtue of section 44(1) or (2),

the written statement shall be provided.

(6) An application under subsection (5) must be made within the period of 12 months beginning with the date on which the vehicle or pedestrian was stopped.

Duration of authorisation

46.—(1) An authorisation under section 44 has effect, subject to subsections **117–039** (2) to (7), during the period—

(a) beginning at the time when the authorisation is given, and
(b) ending with a date or at a time specified in the authorisation.

(2) The date or time specified under subsection (1)(b) must not occur after the end of the period of 28 days beginning with the day on which the authorisation is given.

(3) The person who gives an authorisation shall inform the Secretary of State as soon as is reasonably practicable.

(4) If an authorisation is not confirmed by the Secretary of State before the end of the period of 48 hours beginning with the time when it is given—

(a) it shall cease to have effect at the end of that period, but
(b) its ceasing to have effect shall not affect the lawfulness of anything done in reliance on it before the end of that period.

(5) Where the Secretary of State confirms an authorisation he may substitute an earlier date or time for the date or time specified under subsection (1)(b).

(6) The Secretary of State may cancel an authorisation with effect from a specified time.

(7) An authorisation may be renewed in writing by the person who gave it or by a person who could have given it; and subsections (1) to (6) shall apply as if a new authorisation were given on each occasion on which the authorisation is renewed.

Offences

47.—(1) A person commits an offence if he— **117–040**

(a) fails to stop a vehicle when required to do so by a constable in the exercise of the power conferred by an authorisation under section 44(1);
(b) fails to stop when required to do so by a constable in the exercise of the power conferred by an authorisation under section 44(2);
(c) wilfully obstructs a constable in the exercise of the power conferred by an authorisation under section 44(1) or (2).

(2) A person guilty of an offence under this section shall be liable on summary conviction to—

(a) imprisonment for a term not exceeding six months,
(b) a fine not exceeding level 5 on the standard scale, or
(c) both.

Parking

Authorisations

117–041 **48.**—(1) An authorisation under this section authorises any constable in uniform to prohibit or restrict the parking of vehicles on a road specified in the authorisation.

(2) An authorisation may be given only if the person giving it considers it expedient for the prevention of acts of terrorism.

(3) An authorisation may be given—

    (a) where the road specified is outside Northern Ireland and is wholly or partly within a police area other than one mentioned in paragraphs (b) or (c), by a police officer for the area who is of at least the rank of assistant chief constable;

    (b) where the road specified is wholly or partly in the metropolitan police district, by a police officer for the district who is of at least the rank of commander of the metropolitan police;

    (c) where the road specified is wholly or partly in the City of London, by a police officer for the City who is of at least the rank of commander in the City of London police force;

    (d) where the road specified is in Northern Ireland, by a member of the Royal Ulster Constabulary who is of at least the rank of assistant chief constable.

(4) If an authorisation is given orally, the person giving it shall confirm it in writing as soon as is reasonably practicable.

Exercise of power

117–042 **49.**—(1) The power conferred by an authorisation under section 48 shall be exercised by placing a traffic sign on the road concerned.

(2) A constable exercising the power conferred by an authorisation under section 48 may suspend a parking place.

(3) Where a parking place is suspended under subsection (2), the suspension shall be treated as a restriction imposed by virtue of section 48—

    (a) for the purposes of section 99 of the Road Traffic Regulation Act 1984 (removal of vehicles illegally parked, &c.) and of any regulations in force under that section, and

    (b) for the purposes of Articles 47 and 48 of the Road Traffic Regulation (Northern Ireland) Order 1997 (in relation to Northern Ireland).

Duration of authorisation

117–043 **50.**—(1) An authorisation under section 48 has effect, subject to subsections (2) and (3), during the period specified in the authorisation.

(2) The period specified shall not exceed 28 days.

(3) An authorisation may be renewed in writing by the person who gave it or by a person who could have given it; and subsections (1) and (2) shall apply as if a new authorisation were given on each occasion on which the authorisation is renewed.

Offences

51.—(1) A person commits an offence if he parks a vehicle in contravention **117–044** of a prohibition or restriction imposed by virtue of section 48.

(2) A person commits an offence if—

(a) he is the driver or other person in charge of a vehicle which has been permitted to remain at rest in contravention of any prohibition or restriction imposed by virtue of section 48, and

(b) he fails to move the vehicle when ordered to do so by a constable in uniform.

(3) It is a defence for a person charged with an offence under this section to prove that he had a reasonable excuse for the act or omission in question.

(4) Possession of a current disabled person's badge shall not itself constitute a reasonable excuse for the purposes of subsection (3).

(5) A person guilty of an offence under subsection (1) shall be liable on summary conviction to a fine not exceeding level 4 on the standard scale.

(6) A person guilty of an offence under subsection (2) shall be liable on summary conviction to—

(a) imprisonment for a term not exceeding three months,

(b) a fine not exceeding level 4 on the standard scale, or

(c) both.

Interpretation

52. In sections 48 to 51—   **117–045**

"disabled person's badge" means a badge issued, or having effect as if issued, under any regulations for the time being in force under section 21 of the Chronically Sick and Disabled Persons Act 1970 (in relation to England and Wales and Scotland) or section 14 of the Chronically Sick and Disabled Persons (Northern Ireland) Act 1978 (in relation to Northern Ireland);

"driver" means, in relation to a vehicle which has been left on any road, the person who was driving it when it was left there;

"parking" means leaving a vehicle or permitting it to remain at rest;

"traffic sign" has the meaning given in section 142(1) of the Road Traffic Regulation Act 1984 (in relation to England and Wales and Scotland) and in Article 28 of the Road Traffic Regulation (Northern Ireland) Order 1997 (in relation to Northern Ireland);

"vehicle" has the same meaning as in section 99(5) of the Road Traffic Regulation Act 1984 (in relation to England and Wales and Scotland) and Article 47(4) of the Road Traffic Regulation (Northern Ireland) Order 1997 (in relation to Northern Ireland).

Port and border controls

Port and border controls

53.—(1) Schedule 7 (port and border controls) shall have effect.   **117–046**

(2) The Secretary of State may by order repeal paragraph 16 of Schedule 7.

(3) The powers conferred by Schedule 7 shall be exercisable notwithstanding the rights conferred by section 1 of the Immigration Act 1971 (general principles regulating entry into and staying in the United Kingdom).

PART VI

MISCELLANEOUS

Terrorist offences

Weapons training

117–047   **54.**—(1) A person commits an offence if he provides instruction or training in the making or use of—

(a) firearms,

[(aa) radioactive material or weapons designed or adapted for the discharge of any radioactive material,][1]

(b) explosives, or

(c) chemical, biological or nuclear weapons.

(2) A person commits an offence if he receives instruction or training in the making or use of—

(a) firearms,

[(aa) radioactive material or weapons designed or adapted for the discharge of any radioactive material,][2]

(b) explosives, or

(c) chemical, biological or nuclear weapons.

(3) A person commits an offence if he invites another to receive instruction or training and the receipt—

(a) would constitute an offence under subsection (2), or

(b) would constitute an offence under subsection (2) but for the fact that it is to take place outside the United Kingdom.

(4) For the purpose of subsections (1) and (3)—

(a) a reference to the provision of instruction includes a reference to making it available either generally or to one or more specific persons, and

(b) an invitation to receive instruction or training may be either general or addressed to one or more specific persons.

(5) It is a defence for a person charged with an offence under this section in relation to instruction or training to prove that his action or involvement was wholly for a purpose other than assisting, preparing for or participating in terrorism.

(6) A person guilty of an offence under this section shall be liable—

(a) on conviction on indictment, to imprisonment for a term not exceeding ten years, to a fine or to both, or

(b) on summary conviction, to imprisonment for a term not exceeding six months, to a fine not exceeding the statutory maximum or to both.

(7) A court by or before which a person is convicted of an offence under this section may order the forfeiture of anything which the court considers to have been in the person's possession for purposes connected with the offence.

(8) Before making an order under subsection (7) a court must give an opportunity to be heard to any person, other than the convicted person, who claims

to be the owner of or otherwise interested in anything which can be forfeited under that subsection.

(9) An order under subsection (7) shall not come into force until there is no further possibility of it being varied, or set aside, on appeal (disregarding any power of a court to grant leave to appeal out of time).

¹ Added by Anti-terrorism, Crime and Security Act 2001 (c.24), Pt 13, s. 120(1).
² *ibid.*

Weapons training: interpretation

55. In section 54—   **117–048**

["biological weapon" means a biological agent or toxin (within the meaning of the Biological Weapons Act 1974) in a form capable of use
for hostile purposes or anything to which section 1(1)(b) of that Act
applies,]¹
"chemical weapon" has the meaning given by section 1 of the Chemical
Weapons Act 1996[, and]²
["radioactive material" means radioactive material capable of endangering
life or causing harm to human health.]³
[. . .]⁴

¹ Definition substituted by Anti-terrorism, Crime and Security Act 2001 (c.24), Pt 13, s. 120(2)(a).
² Definition inserted by Anti-terrorism, Crime and Security Act 2001 (c.24), Pt 13, s. 120(2)(b).
³ *ibid.*
⁴ Definition repealed by Anti-terrorism, Crime and Security Act 2001 (c.24), Sched. 8(7), para. 1.

Directing terrorist organisation

56.—(1) A person commits an offence if he directs, at any level, the activities **117–049**
of an organisation which is concerned in the commission of acts of terrorism.

(2) A person guilty of an offence under this section is liable on conviction on
indictment to imprisonment for life.

Possession for terrorist purposes

57.—(1) A person commits an offence if he possesses an article in circum- **117–050**
stances which give rise to a reasonable suspicion that his possession is for a
purpose connected with the commission, preparation or instigation of an act of
terrorism.

(2) It is a defence for a person charged with an offence under this section to
prove that his possession of the article was not for a purpose connected with the
commission, preparation or instigation of an act of terrorism.

(3) In proceedings for an offence under this section, if it is proved that an
article—

(a) was on any premises at the same time as the accused, or
(b) was on premises of which the accused was the occupier or which he
habitually used otherwise than as a member of the public,

the court may assume that the accused possessed the article, unless he proves
that he did not know of its presence on the premises or that he had no control
over it.

(4) A person guilty of an offence under this section shall be liable—

(a) on conviction on indictment, to imprisonment for a term not exceeding
10 years, to a fine or to both, or

(b) on summary conviction, to imprisonment for a term not exceeding six
    months, to a fine not exceeding the statutory maximum or to both.

Collection of information

117–051   58.—(1) A person commits an offence if—

(a) he collects or makes a record of information of a kind likely to be
    useful to a person committing or preparing an act of terrorism, or
(b) he possesses a document or record containing information of that kind.

(2) In this section "record" includes a photographic or electronic record.

(3) It is a defence for a person charged with an offence under this section to
prove that he had a reasonable excuse for his action or possession.

(4) A person guilty of an offence under this section shall be liable—

(a) on conviction on indictment, to imprisonment for a term not exceeding
    10 years, to a fine or to both, or
(b) on summary conviction, to imprisonment for a term not exceeding six
    months, to a fine not exceeding the statutory maximum or to both.

(5) A court by or before which a person is convicted of an offence under this
section may order the forfeiture of any document or record containing information of the kind mentioned in subsection (1)(a).

(6) Before making an order under subsection (5) a court must give an opportunity to be heard to any person, other than the convicted person, who claims
to be the owner of or otherwise interested in anything which can be forfeited
under that subsection.

(7) An order under subsection (5) shall not come into force until there is no
further possibility of it being varied, or set aside, on appeal (disregarding any
power of a court to grant leave to appeal out of time).

Inciting terrorism overseas

England and Wales

117–052   59.—(1) A person commits an offence if—

(a) he incites another person to commit an act of terrorism wholly or partly
    outside the United Kingdom, and
(b) the act would, if committed in England and Wales, constitute one of
    the offences listed in subsection (2).

(2) Those offences are—

(a) murder,
(b) an offence under section 18 of the Offences against the Person Act
    1861 (wounding with intent),
(c) an offence under section 23 or 24 of that Act (poison),
(d) an offence under section 28 or 29 of that Act (explosions), and
(e) an offence under section 1(2) of the Criminal Damage Act 1971
    (endangering life by damaging property).

(3) A person guilty of an offence under this section shall be liable to any
penalty to which he would be liable on conviction of the offence listed in subsection (2) which corresponds to the act which he incites.

(4) For the purposes of subsection (1) it is immaterial whether or not the person incited is in the United Kingdom at the time of the incitement.

(5) Nothing in this section imposes criminal liability on any person acting on behalf of, or holding office under, the Crown.

Northern Ireland

60.—(1) A person commits an offence if—   **117–053**

    (a) he incites another person to commit an act of terrorism wholly or partly outside the United Kingdom, and

    (b) the act would, if committed in Northern Ireland, constitute one of the offences listed in subsection (2).

(2) Those offences are—

    (a) murder,

    (b) an offence under section 18 of the Offences against the Person Act 1861 (wounding with intent),

    (c) an offence under section 23 or 24 of that Act (poison),

    (d) an offence under section 28 or 29 of that Act (explosions), and

    (e) an offence under Article 3(2) of the Criminal Damage (Northern Ireland) Order 1977 (endangering life by damaging property).

(3) A person guilty of an offence under this section shall be liable to any penalty to which he would be liable on conviction of the offence listed in subsection (2) which corresponds to the act which he incites.

(4) For the purposes of subsection (1) it is immaterial whether or not the person incited is in the United Kingdom at the time of the incitement.

(5) Nothing in this section imposes criminal liability on any person acting on behalf of, or holding office under, the Crown.

Scotland

61.—(1) A person commits an offence if—   **117–054**

    (a) he incites another person to commit an act of terrorism wholly or partly outside the United Kingdom, and

    (b) the act would, if committed in Scotland, constitute one of the offences listed in subsection (2).

(2) Those offences are—

    (a) murder,

    (b) assault to severe injury, and

    (c) reckless conduct which causes actual injury.

(3) A person guilty of an offence under this section shall be liable to any penalty to which he would be liable on conviction of the offence listed in subsection (2) which corresponds to the act which he incites.

(4) For the purposes of subsection (1) it is immaterial whether or not the person incited is in the United Kingdom at the time of the incitement.

(5) Nothing in this section imposes criminal liability on any person acting on behalf of, or holding office under, the Crown.

Terrorist bombing and finance offences

Terrorist bombing: jurisdiction

117–055 62.—(1) If—

    (a) a person does anything outside the United Kingdom as an act of terrorism or for the purposes of terrorism, and

    (b) his action would have constituted the commission of one of the offences listed in subsection (2) if it had been done in the United Kingdom,

he shall be guilty of the offence.

(2) The offences referred to in subsection (1)(b) are—

    (a) an offence under section 2, 3 or 5 of the Explosive Substances Act 1883 (causing explosions, &c.),

    (b) an offence under section 1 of the Biological Weapons Act 1974 (biological weapons), and

    (c) an offence under section 2 of the Chemical Weapons Act 1996 (chemical weapons).

Terrorist finance: jurisdiction

117–056 63.—(1) If—

    (a) a person does anything outside the United Kingdom, and

    (b) his action would have constituted the commission of an offence under any of sections 15 to 18 if it had been done in the United Kingdom,

he shall be guilty of the offence.

(2) For the purposes of subsection (1)(b), section 18(1)(b) shall be read as if for "the jurisdiction" there were substituted "a jurisdiction".

. . . . . .

PART VIII

GENERAL

Police powers

117–057 114.—(1) A power conferred by virtue of this Act on a constable—

    (a) is additional to powers which he has at common law or by virtue of any other enactment, and

    (b) shall not be taken to affect those powers.

(2) A constable may if necessary use reasonable force for the purpose of exercising a power conferred on him by virtue of this Act (apart from paragraphs 2 and 3 of Schedule 7).

(3) Where anything is seized by a constable under a power conferred by virtue of this Act, it may (unless the contrary intention appears) be retained for so long as is necessary in all the circumstances.

. . . . . .

Powers to stop and search

116.—(1) A power to search premises conferred by virtue of this Act shall **117–058**
be taken to include power to search a container.

(2) A power conferred by virtue of this Act to stop a person includes power
to stop a vehicle (other than an aircraft which is airborne).

(3) A person commits an offence if he fails to stop a vehicle when required
to do so by virtue of this section.

(4) A person guilty of an offence under subsection (3) shall be liable on
summary conviction to—

    (a) imprisonment for a term not exceeding six months,
    (b) a fine not exceeding level 5 on the standard scale, or
    (c) both.

. . . . . .

SCHEDULE 2

PROSCRIBED ORGANISATIONS

117–059

The Irish Republican Army.
Cumann na mBan.
Fianna na hEireann.
The Red Hand Commando.
Saor Eire.
The Ulster Freedom Fighters.
The Ulster Volunteer Force.
The Irish National Liberation Army.
The Irish People's Liberation Organisation.
The Ulster Defence Association.
The Loyalist Volunteer Force.
The Continuity Army Council.
The Orange Volunteers.
The Red Hand Defenders.
The entry for The Orange Volunteers refers to the organisation which uses that name and in the
name of which a statement described as a press release was published on 14th October 1998.
[Al-Qa'ida
Egyptian Islamic Jihad
Al-Gama'at al-Islamiya
Armed Islamic Group (Groupe Islamique Armée) (GIA)
Salafist Group for Call and Combat (Groupe Salafiste pour la Prédication et le Combat) (GSPC)
Babbar Khalsa
International Sikh Youth Federation
Harakat Mujahideen
Jaish e Mohammed
Lashkar e Tayyaba
Liberation Tigers of Tamil Eelam (LTTE)
Hizballah External Security Organisation
Hamas-Izz al-Din al-Qassem Brigades
Palestinian Islamic Jihad - Shaqaqi
Abu Nidal Organisation
Islamic Army of Aden
Mujaheddin e Khalq
Kurdistan Workers' Party (Partiya Karkeren Kurdistan) (PKK)
Revolutionary Peoples' Liberation Party-Front (Devrimci Halk Kurtulus Partisi- Cephesi) (DHKP-C)
Basque Homeland and Liberty (Euskadi ta Askatasuna) (ETA)
17 November Revolutionary Organisation (N17)][1]

---

[1] Entries inserted by S.I. 2001 No. 1261 (Terrorism Act 2000 (Proscribed Organisations)
(Amendment) Order), Art. 2.

SCHEDULE 3

THE PROSCRIBED ORGANISATIONS APPEAL COMMISSION

Constitution and administration

117–060   1.—(1) The Commission shall consist of members appointed by the Lord Chancellor.
(2) The Lord Chancellor shall appoint one of the members as chairman.
(3) A member shall hold and vacate office in accordance with the terms of his appointment.
(4) A member may resign at any time by notice in writing to the Lord Chancellor.

117–061   2. The Lord Chancellor may appoint officers and servants for the Commission.

117–062   3. The Lord Chancellor—

    (a) may pay sums by way of remuneration, allowances, pensions and gratuities to or in respect of members, officers and servants,
    (b) may pay compensation to a person who ceases to be a member of the Commission if the Lord Chancellor thinks it appropriate because of special circumstances, and
    (c) may pay sums in respect of expenses of the Commission.

Commission procedure

117–063   4.—(1) The Commission shall sit at such times and in such places as the Lord Chancellor may direct.
(2) The Commission may sit in two or more divisions.
(3) At each sitting of the Commission—

    (a) three members shall attend,
    (b) one of the members shall be a person who holds or has held high judicial office (within the meaning of the Appellate Jurisdiction Act 1876), and
    (c) the chairman or another member nominated by him shall preside and report the Commission's decision.

117–064   5.—(1) The Lord Chancellor may make rules—

    (a) regulating the exercise of the right of appeal to the Commission;
    (b) prescribing practice and procedure to be followed in relation to proceedings before the Commission;
    (c) providing for proceedings before the Commission to be determined without an oral hearing in specified circumstances;
    (d) making provision about evidence in proceedings before the Commission (including provision about the burden of proof and admissibility of evidence);
    (e) making provision about proof of the Commission's decisions.

(2) In making the rules the Lord Chancellor shall, in particular, have regard to the need to secure—

    (a) that decisions which are the subject of appeals are properly reviewed, and
    (b) that information is not disclosed contrary to the public interest.

(3) The rules shall make provision permitting organisations to be legally represented in proceedings before the Commission.
(4) The rules may, in particular—

    (a) provide for full particulars of the reasons for proscription or refusal to deproscribe to be withheld from the organisation or applicant concerned and from any person representing it or him;
    (b) enable the Commission to exclude persons (including representatives) from all or part of proceedings;
    (c) enable the Commission to provide a summary of evidence taken in the absence of a person excluded by virtue of paragraph (b);
    (d) permit preliminary or incidental functions to be discharged by a single member;
    (e) permit proceedings for permission to appeal under section 6 to be determined by a single member;
    (f) make provision about the functions of persons appointed under paragraph 7;
    (g) make different provision for different parties or descriptions of party.

(5) Rules under this paragraph—

    (a) shall be made by statutory instrument, and

(b) shall not be made unless a draft has been laid before and approved by resolution of each House of Parliament.

(6) In this paragraph a reference to proceedings before the Commission includes a reference to proceedings arising out of proceedings before the Commission.

6.—(1) This paragraph applies to— **117–065**

(a) proceedings brought by an organisation before the Commission, and
(b) proceedings arising out of proceedings to which paragraph (a) applies.

(2) Proceedings shall be conducted on behalf of the organisation by a person designated by the Commission (with such legal representation as he may choose to obtain).
(3) In [paragraph 5] [¹] of this Schedule a reference to an organisation includes a reference to a person designated under this paragraph.

¹ Words substituted by Regulation of Investigatory Powers Act 2000 (c.23), Sched. 4, para. 12(2).

7.—(1) The relevant law officer may appoint a person to represent the interests of an organisation **117–066** or other applicant in proceedings in relation to which an order has been made by virtue of paragraph 5(4)(b).
(2) The relevant law officer is—

(a) in relation to proceedings in England and Wales, the Attorney General,
(b) in relation to proceedings in Scotland, the Advocate General for Scotland, and
(c) in relation to proceedings in Northern Ireland, the Attorney General for Northern Ireland.

(3) A person appointed under this paragraph must—

(a) have a general qualification for the purposes of section 71 of the Courts and Legal Services Act 1990 (qualification for legal appointments),
(b) be an advocate or a solicitor who has rights of audience in the Court of Session or the High Court of Justiciary by virtue of section 25A of the Solicitors (Scotland) Act 1980, or
(c) be a member of the Bar of Northern Ireland.

(4) A person appointed under this paragraph shall not be responsible to the organisation or other applicant whose interests he is appointed to represent.
(5) In [paragraph 5] [¹] of this Schedule a reference to a representative does not include a reference to a person appointed under this paragraph.

¹ Words substituted by Regulation of Investigatory Powers Act 2000 (c.23), Sched. 4, para. 12(2).

. . . . . .

SCHEDULE 6

FINANCIAL INFORMATION

Orders

1.—(1) Where an order has been made under this paragraph in relation to a terrorist investigation, **117–067** a constable named in the order may require a financial institution to which the order applies to provide customer information for the purposes of the investigation.
[(1A) The order may provide that it applies to—

(a) all financial institutions,
(b) a particular description, or particular descriptions, of financial institutions, or
(c) a particular financial institution or particular financial institutions.] [¹]

(2) The information shall be provided—

(a) in such manner and within such time as the constable may specify, and
(b) notwithstanding any restriction on the disclosure of information imposed by statute or otherwise.

(3) An institution which fails to comply with a requirement under this paragraph shall be guilty of an offence.
(4) It is a defence for an institution charged with an offence under sub- paragraph (3) to prove—

(a) that the information required was not in the institution's possession, or
(b) that it was not reasonably practicable for the institution to comply with the requirement.

(5) An institution guilty of an offence under sub-paragraph (3) shall be liable on summary conviction to a fine not exceeding level 5 on the standard scale.

[1] Added by Anti-terrorism, Crime and Security Act 2001 (c.24), Sched. 2(4), para. 6(3).

Procedure

117–068 **2.** An order under paragraph 1 may be made only on the application of—

(a) in England and Wales or Northern Ireland, a police officer of at least the rank of superintendent, or
(b) in Scotland, the procurator fiscal.

117–069 **3.** An order under paragraph 1 may be made only by—

(a) in England and Wales, a Circuit judge,
(b) in Scotland, the sheriff, or
(c) in Northern Ireland, a county court judge.

117–070 **4.**—(1) Crown Court Rules may make provision about the procedure for an application under paragraph 1.
(2) The High Court of Justiciary may, by Act of Adjournal, make provision about the procedure for an application under paragraph 1.

Criteria for making order

117–071 **5.** An order under paragraph 1 may be made only if the person making it is satisfied that—

(a) the order is sought for the purposes of a terrorist investigation,
(b) the tracing of terrorist property is desirable for the purposes of the investigation, and
(c) the order will enhance the effectiveness of the investigation.

Financial institution

117–072 **6.**—(1) In this Schedule "financial institution" means—

(a) a person who has permission under Part 4 of the Financial Services and Markets Act 2000 to accept deposits,
(b) a building society (within the meaning of the Building Societies Act 1986),
(c) a credit union (within the meaning of the Credit Unions Act 1979 or the Credit Unions (Northern Ireland) Order 1985),
(d) a person carrying on a relevant regulated activity,
(e) the National Savings Bank,
(f) a person who carries out an activity for the purposes of raising money authorised to be raised under the National Loans Act 1968 under the auspices of the Director of National Savings,
(g) a European institution carrying on a home regulated activity (within the meaning of Directive 2000/12/EC of the European Parliament and of the Council relating to the taking up and pursuit of the business of credit institutions),
(h) a person carrying out an activity specified in any of points 1 to 12 and 14 of Annex 1 to that Directive, and
(i) a person who carries on an insurance business in accordance with an authorisation pursuant to Article 6 or 27 of the First Council Directive on the coordination of laws, regulations and administrative provisions relating to the taking up and pursuit of the business of direct life assurance.

[(1A) For the purposes of sub-paragraph (1)(d), a relevant regulated activity means—

(a) dealing in investments as principal or as agent,
(b) arranging deals in investments,
(c) managing investments,
(d) safeguarding and administering investments,
(e) sending dematerialised instructions,
(f) establishing etc. collective investment schemes,
(g) advising on investments.

(1B) Sub-paragraphs (1)(a) and (1A) must be read with—

(a) section 22 of the Financial Services and Markets Act 2000;
(b) any relevant order under that section; and
(c) Schedule 2 to that Act.] [¹]

(2) The Secretary of State may by order provide for a class of person—

(a) to be a financial institution for the purposes of this Schedule, or
(b) to cease to be a financial institution for the purposes of this Schedule.

(3) An institution which ceases to be a financial institution for the purposes of this Schedule (whether by virtue of sub-paragraph (2)(b) or otherwise) shall continue to be treated as a financial institution for the purposes of any requirement under paragraph 1 to provide customer information which relates to a time when the institution was a financial institution.

¹ Added by S.I. 2001 No. 3649 (Financial Services and Markets Act 2000 (Consequential Amendments and Repeals) Order), Pt 8, Art. 361(3).

Customer information

7.—(1) In this Schedule "customer information" means (subject to sub-paragraph (3))— **117–073**

(a) information whether a business relationship exists or existed between a financial institution and a particular person ("a customer"),
(b) a customer's account number,
(c) a customer's full name,
(d) a customer's date of birth,
(e) a customer's address or former address,
(f) the date on which a business relationship between a financial institution and a customer begins or ends,
(g) any evidence of a customer's identity obtained by a financial institution in pursuance of or for the purposes of any legislation relating to money laundering, and
(h) the identity of a person sharing an account with a customer.

(2) For the purposes of this Schedule there is a business relationship between a financial institution and a person if (and only if)—

(a) there is an arrangement between them designed to facilitate the carrying out of frequent or regular transactions between them, and
(b) the total amount of payments to be made in the course of the arrangement is neither known nor capable of being ascertained when the arrangement is made.

(3) The Secretary of State may by order provide for a class of information—

(a) to be customer information for the purposes of this Schedule, or
(b) to cease to be customer information for the purposes of this Schedule.

Offence by body corporate, &c

8.—(1) This paragraph applies where an offence under paragraph 1(3) is committed by an institu- **117–074**
tion and it is proved that the offence—

(a) was committed with the consent or connivance of an officer of the institution, or
(b) was attributable to neglect on the part of an officer of the institution.

(2) The officer, as well as the institution, shall be guilty of the offence.
(3) Where an individual is convicted of an offence under paragraph 1(3) by virtue of this paragraph, he shall be liable on summary conviction to—

(a) imprisonment for a term not exceeding six months,
(b) a fine not exceeding level 5 on the standard scale, or
(c) both.

(4) In the case of an institution which is a body corporate, in this paragraph "officer" includes—

(a) a director, manager or secretary,
(b) a person purporting to act as a director, manager or secretary, and
(c) if the affairs of the body are managed by its members, a member.

(5) In the case of an institution which is a partnership, in this paragraph "officer" means a partner.
(6) In the case of an institution which is an unincorporated association (other than a partnership),

in this paragraph "officer" means a person concerned in the management or control of the association.

Self-incrimination

117–075   9.—(1) Customer information provided by a financial institution under this Schedule shall not be admissible in evidence in criminal proceedings against the institution or any of its officers or employees.

(2) Sub-paragraph (1) shall not apply in relation to proceedings for an offence under paragraph 1(3) (including proceedings brought by virtue of paragraph 8).

SCHEDULE 7

PORT AND BORDER CONTROLS

INTERPRETATION

117–076   1.—(1) In this Schedule "examining officer" means any of the following—

    (a) a constable,
    (b) an immigration officer, and
    (c) a customs officer who is designated for the purpose of this Schedule by the Secretary of State and the Commissioners of Customs and Excise.

(2) In this Schedule—

    "the border area" has the meaning given by paragraph 4,
    "captain" means master of a ship or commander of an aircraft,
    "port" includes an airport and a hoverport,
    "ship" includes a hovercraft, and
    "vehicle" includes a train.

(3) A place shall be treated as a port for the purposes of this Schedule in relation to a person if an examining officer believes that the person—

    (a) has gone there for the purpose of embarking on a ship or aircraft, or
    (b) has arrived there on disembarking from a ship or aircraft.[1]

[1] In relation to the aspects of the channel tunnel system specified in S.I. 1993 No. 1813, Art.7(1):

    1.—(1) In this Schedule "examining officer" means any of the following—

    (a) a constable,
    (b) an immigration officer, and
    (c) a customs officer who is designated for the purpose of this Schedule by the Secretary of State and the Commissioners of Customs and Excise.

    (2) In this Schedule—

        "port" includes a railway station or other place where—

    (a) persons embark or disembark, or
    (b) goods are loaded or unloaded,
        on or from a through train or shuttle train, as the case may be.

    (3) A place shall be treated as a port for the purposes of this Schedule in relation to a person if an examining officer believes that the person—

    (a) has gone there for the purpose of embarking on a through train or shuttle train, or
    (b) has arrived there on disembarking from a through train or shuttle train.

Power to stop, question and detain

117–077   2.—(1) An examining officer may question a person to whom this paragraph applies for the purpose of determining whether he appears to be a person falling within section 40(1)(b).

(2) This paragraph applies to a person if—

(a) he is at a port or in the border area, and
(b) the examining officer believes that the person's presence at the port or in the area is connected with his entering or leaving Great Britain or Northern Ireland, or his travelling by air within Great Britain or within Northern Ireland.

(3) This paragraph also applies to a person on a ship or aircraft which has arrived [at any place in Great Britain or Northern Ireland (whether from within or outside Great Britain or Northern Ireland).] [¹]
(4) An examining officer may exercise his powers under this paragraph whether or not he has grounds for suspecting that a person falls within section 40(1)(b). [²]

¹ Words substituted by Anti-terrorism, Crime and Security Act 2001 (c.24), Pt 13, s. 118(3).
² In relation to the aspects of the Channel Tunnel system specified in S.I. 1993 No. 1813 Art.7(1):

2.—(1) An examining officer may question a person to whom this paragraph applies for the purpose of determining whether he appears to be a person falling within section 40(1)(b).
(2) This paragraph applies to a person if—

(a) he is at a port, and
(b) the examining officer believes that the person's presence at the port is connected with his entering or leaving Great Britain.

(3) This paragraph also applies to a person on a through train or shuttle train which has arrived in Great Britain.
(3A) An examination under sub-paragraph (1) may be commenced in a train during the period when it is a control area.
(4) An examining officer may exercise his powers under this paragraph whether or not he has grounds for suspecting that a person falls within section 40(1)(b).

3. An examining officer may question a person who is in the border area for the purpose of **117–078** determining whether his presence in the area is connected with his entering or leaving Northern Ireland.[¹]

¹ In relation to the aspects of the Channel Tunnel system specified in S.I. 1993 No. 1813 Art.7(1): Sched.7 para. 3 is repealed.

4.—(1) A place in Northern Ireland is within the border area for the purposes of paragraphs 2 **117–079** and 3 if it is no more than one mile from the border between Northern Ireland and the Republic of Ireland.
(2) If a train goes from the Republic of Ireland to Northern Ireland, the first place in Northern Ireland at which it stops for the purpose of allowing passengers to leave is within the border area for the purposes of paragraphs 2 and 3.[¹]

¹ In relation to the aspects of the Channel Tunnel system specified in S.I. 1993 No. 1813 Art.7(1): Sched.7 para. 4 is repealed.
5. A person who is questioned under paragraph 2 or 3 must— **117–080**

(a) give the examining officer any information in his possession which the officer requests;
(b) give the examining officer on request either a valid passport which includes a photograph or another document which establishes his identity;
(c) declare whether he has with him documents of a kind specified by the examining officer;
(d) give the examining officer on request any document which he has with him and which is of a kind specified by the officer.[¹]

¹ In relation to the aspects of the Channel Tunnel system specified in S.I. 1993 No. 1813 Art.7(1):

5. A person who is questioned under paragraph 2 must—

(a) give the examining officer any information in his possession which the officer requests;
(b) give the examining officer on request either a valid passport which includes a photograph or another document which establishes his identity;
(c) declare whether he has with him documents of a kind specified by the examining officer;
(d) give the examining officer on request any document which he has with him and which is of a kind specified by the officer.

6.—(1) For the purposes of exercising a power under paragraph 2 or 3 an examining officer **117–081** may—

(a) stop a person or vehicle;
(b) detain a person.

(2) For the purpose of detaining a person under this paragraph, an examining officer may authorise the person's removal from a ship, aircraft or vehicle.

(3) Where a person is detained under this paragraph the provisions of Part I of Schedule 8 (treatment) shall apply.

(4) A person detained under this paragraph shall (unless detained under any other power) be released not later than the end of the period of nine hours beginning with the time when his examination begins [1]

[1] In relation to the aspects of the Channel Tunnel system specified in S.I. 1993 No. 1813 Art.7(1):

6.—(1) For the purposes of exercising a power under paragraph 2 or 3 an examining officer may—

(a) stop a person or through train or shuttle train;
(b) detain a person.

(2) For the purpose of detaining a person under this paragraph, an examining officer may authorise the person's removal from a through train or shuttle train.

(3) Where a person is detained under this paragraph the provisions of Part I of Schedule 8 (treatment) shall apply.

(4) A person detained under this paragraph shall (unless detained under any other power) be released not later than the end of the period of nine hours beginning with the time when his examination begins.

Searches

117–082 **7.** For the purpose of satisfying himself whether there are any persons whom he may wish to question under paragraph 2 an examining officer may—

(a) search a ship or aircraft;
(b) search anything on a ship or aircraft;
(c) search anything which he reasonably believes has been, or is about to be, on a ship or aircraft.[1]

[1] In relation to the aspects of the Channel Tunnel system specified in S.I. 1993 No. 1813 Art.7(1):

7. For the purpose of satisfying himself whether there are any persons whom he may wish to question under paragraph 2 an examining officer may—

(a) search a through train or shuttle train;
(b) search anything on a through train or shuttle train;
(c) search anything which he reasonably believes has been, or is about to be, on a through train or shuttle train.

117–083 **8.**—(1) An examining officer who questions a person under paragraph 2 may, for the purpose of determining whether he falls within section 40(1)(b)—

(a) search the person;
(b) search anything which he has with him, or which belongs to him, and which is on a ship or aircraft;
(c) search anything which he has with him, or which belongs to him, and which the examining officer reasonably believes has been, or is about to be, on a ship or aircraft;
(d) search a ship or aircraft for anything falling within paragraph (b).

(2) Where an examining officer questions a person in the border area under paragraph 2 he may (in addition to the matters specified in sub-paragraph (1)), for the purpose of determining whether the person falls within section 40(1)(b)—

(a) search a vehicle;
(b) search anything in or on a vehicle;
(c) search anything which he reasonably believes has been, or is about to be, in or on a vehicle.

(3) A search of a person under this paragraph must be carried out by someone of the same sex.[1]

[1] In relation to the aspects of the Channel Tunnel system specified in S.I. 1993 No. 1813 Art.7(1):

8.—(1) An examining officer who questions a person under paragraph 2 may, for the purpose of determining whether he falls within section 40(1)(b)—

(a) search the person;
(b) search anything which he has with him, or which belongs to him, and which is on a through train or shuttle train;
(c) search anything which he has with him, or which belongs to him, and which the examining officer reasonably believes has been, or is about to be, on a through train or shuttle train;
(d) search a through train or shuttle train for anything falling within paragraph (b).

(3) A search of a person under this paragraph must be carried out by someone of the same sex.

9.—(1) An examining officer may examine goods to which this paragraph applies for the purpose of determining whether they have been used in the commission, preparation or instigation of acts of terrorism.   **117–084**

[(2) This paragraph applies to—

(a) goods which have arrived in or are about to leave Great Britain or Northern Ireland on a ship or vehicle, and
(b) goods which have arrived at or are about to leave any place in Great Britain or Northern Ireland on an aircraft (whether the place they have come from or are going to is within or outside Great Britain or Northern Ireland).]

(3) In this paragraph "goods" includes—

(a) property of any description, and
(b) containers.

(4) An examining officer may board a ship or aircraft or enter a vehicle for the purpose of determining whether to exercise his power under this paragraph. [¹]

¹ In relation to the aspects of the Channel Tunnel system specified in S.I. 1993 No. 1813 Art.7(1):

9.—(1) An examining officer may examine goods to which this paragraph applies for the purpose of determining whether they have been used in the commission, preparation or instigation of acts of terrorism.

(2) This paragraph applies to goods which have arrived in or are about to leave Great Britain on a through train or shuttle train.

(3) In this paragraph "goods" includes—

(a) property of any description, and
(b) containers.

(4) An examining officer may board a through train or shuttle train for the purpose of determining whether to exercise his power under this paragraph.

Detention of property

10.—(1) An examining officer may authorise a person to carry out on his behalf a search or examination under any of paragraphs 7 to 9.   **117–085**

(2) A person authorised under this paragraph shall be treated as an examining officer for the purposes of—

(a) paragraphs 9(4) and 11 of this Schedule, and
(b) paragraphs 2 and 3 of Schedule 14.

11.—(1) This paragraph applies to anything which—   **117–086**

(a) is given to an examining officer in accordance with paragraph 5(d),
(b) is searched or found on a search under paragraph 8, or
(c) is examined under paragraph 9.

(2) An examining officer may detain the thing—

(a) for the purpose of examination, for a period not exceeding seven days beginning with the day on which the detention commences,
(b) while he believes that it may be needed for use as evidence in criminal proceedings, or
(c) while he believes that it may be needed in connection with a decision by the Secretary of State whether to make a deportation order under the Immigration Act 1971.

Designated ports

12.—(1) This paragraph applies to a journey—   **117–087**

(a) to Great Britain from the Republic of Ireland, Northern Ireland or any of the Islands,

(b) from Great Britain to any of those places,
(c) to Northern Ireland from Great Britain, the Republic of Ireland or any of the Islands, or
(d) from Northern Ireland to any of those places.

(2) Where a ship or aircraft is employed to carry passengers for reward on a journey to which this paragraph applies the owners or agents of the ship or aircraft shall not arrange for it to call at a port in Great Britain or Northern Ireland for the purpose of disembarking or embarking passengers unless—

(a) the port is a designated port, or
(b) an examining officer approves the arrangement.

(3) Where an aircraft is employed on a journey to which this paragraph applies otherwise than to carry passengers for reward, the captain of the aircraft shall not permit it to call at or leave a port in Great Britain or Northern Ireland unless—

(a) the port is a designated port, or
(b) he gives at least 12 hours' notice in writing to a constable for the police area in which the port is situated (or, where the port is in Northern Ireland, to a member of the Royal Ulster Constabulary).

(4) A designated port is a port which appears in the Table at the end of this Schedule.
(5) The Secretary of State may by order—

(a) add an entry to the Table;
(b) remove an entry from the Table.[¹]

¹ In relation to the aspects of the Channel Tunnel system specified in S.I. 1993 No. 1813 Art.7(1): Sched.7 para.12 is repealed.

Embarkation and disembarkation

117–088 **13.**—(1) The Secretary of State may by notice in writing to the owners or agents of ships or aircraft—

(a) designate control areas in any port in the United Kingdom;
(b) specify conditions for or restrictions on the embarkation or disembarkation of passengers in a control area.

(2) Where owners or agents of a ship or aircraft receive notice under sub-paragraph (1) in relation to a port they shall take all reasonable steps to ensure, in respect of the ship or aircraft—

(a) that passengers do not embark or disembark at the port outside a control area, and
(b) that any specified conditions are met and any specified restrictions are complied with.[¹]

¹ In relation to the aspects of the Channel Tunnel system specified in S.I. 1993 No. 1813 Art.7(1):

13.—(1) The Secretary of State may by notice in writing to the owners or agents of a through train or shuttle train—

(a) designate control areas in any port in the Tunnel System;
(b) specify conditions for or restrictions on the embarkation or disembarkation of passengers in a control area.

(2) Where owners or agents of a through train or shuttle train receive notice under sub-paragraph (1) in relation to a port they shall take all reasonable steps to ensure, in respect of the a through train or shuttle train—

(a) that passengers do not embark or disembark at the port outside a control area, and
(b) that any specified conditions are met and any specified restrictions are complied with.

117–089 **14.**—(1) The Secretary of State may by notice in writing to persons concerned with the management of a port in the United Kingdom ("the port managers")—

(a) designate control areas in the port;
(b) require the port managers to provide at their own expense specified facilities in a control area for the purposes of the embarkation or disembarkation of passengers or their examination under this Schedule;
(c) require conditions to be met and restrictions to be complied with in relation to the embarkation or disembarkation of passengers in a control area;

(d) require the port managers to display, in specified locations in control areas, notices containing specified information about the provisions of this Schedule in such form as may be specified.

(2) Where port managers receive notice under sub-paragraph (1) they shall take all reasonable steps to comply with any requirement set out in the notice. [1]

[1] In relation to the aspects of the Channel Tunnel system specified in S.I. 1993 No. 1813 Art.7(1):

14.—(1) The Secretary of State may from time to time give written notice to persons operating international services designating all or any through trains as control areas while they are within any area in the UK specified in the notice or while they constitute a control zone.

(2) The Secretary of State may from time to time give written notice designating a control area—

(i) to the Concessionaires as respects any part of the tunnel system in the UK or of a control zone within the tunnel system in France or Belgium, or
(ii) to any occupier or person concerned with the management of a terminal control point in the UK.

(3) A notice under sub-paragraph (1) or (2) above may specify facilities to be provided and conditions and restrictions to be observed in a control area, and any persons to whom such a notice is given shall take all reasonable steps to secure that any such facilities, conditions or restrictions are provided or observed.

15.—(1) This paragraph applies to a ship employed to carry passengers for reward, or an aircraft, **117–090** which—

(a) arrives in Great Britain from the Republic of Ireland, Northern Ireland or any of the Islands,
(b) arrives in Northern Ireland from Great Britain, the Republic of Ireland or any of the Islands,
(c) leaves Great Britain for the Republic of Ireland, Northern Ireland or any of the Islands, or
(d) leaves Northern Ireland for Great Britain, the Republic of Ireland or any of the Islands.

(2) The captain shall ensure—

(a) that passengers and members of the crew do not disembark at a port in Great Britain or Northern Ireland unless either they have been examined by an examining officer or they disembark in accordance with arrangements approved by an examining officer;
(b) that passengers and members of the crew do not embark at a port in Great Britain or Northern Ireland except in accordance with arrangements approved by an examining officer;
(c) where a person is to be examined under this Schedule on board the ship or aircraft, that he is presented for examination in an orderly manner.

(3) Where paragraph 27 of Schedule 2 to the Immigration Act 1971 (disembarkation requirements on arrival in the United Kingdom) applies, the requirements of sub-paragraph (2)(a) above are in addition to the requirements of paragraph 27 of that Schedule.[1]

[1] In relation to the aspects of the Channel Tunnel system specified in S.I. 1993 No. 1813 Art.7(1): Sched.7 para.15 is repealed.

Carding

16.—(1) The Secretary of State may by order make provision requiring a person to whom this **117–091** paragraph applies, if required to do so by an examining officer, to complete and produce to the officer a card containing such information in such form as the order may specify.
(2) An order under this paragraph may require the owners or agents of a ship or aircraft employed to carry passengers for reward to supply their passengers with cards in the form required by virtue of sub-paragraph (1).
(3) This paragraph applies to a person—

(a) who disembarks in Great Britain from a ship or aircraft which has come from the Republic of Ireland, Northern Ireland or any of the Islands,
(b) who disembarks in Northern Ireland from a ship or aircraft which has come from Great Britain, the Republic of Ireland, or any of the Islands,
(c) who embarks in Great Britain on a ship or aircraft which is going to the Republic of Ireland, Northern Ireland or any of the Islands, or
(d) who embarks in Northern Ireland on a ship or aircraft which is going to Great Britain, the Republic of Ireland, or any of the Islands.[1]

[1] In relation to the aspects of the Channel Tunnel system specified in S.I. 1993 No. 1813 Art.7(1): Sched.7 para.16 is repealed.

Provision of passenger information

117–092 17.—(1) This paragraph applies to a ship or aircraft which—

    (a) arrives or is expected to arrive in any place in the United Kingdom (whether from another place in the United Kingdom or from outside the United Kingdom), or
    (b) leaves or is expected to leave the United Kingdom.

(2) If an examining officer gives the owners or agents of a ship or aircraft to which this paragraph applies a written request to provide specified information, the owners or agents shall comply with the request as soon as is reasonably practicable.
    (3) A request to an owner or agent may relate—

    (a) to a particular ship or aircraft,
    (b) to all ships or aircraft of the owner or agent to which this paragraph applies, or
    (c) to specified ships or aircraft.

(4) Information may be specified in a request only if it is of a kind which is prescribed by order of the Secretary of State and which relates—

    (a) to passengers,
    (b) to crew,[. . .] [¹]
    (c) to vehicles belonging to passengers or crew[, or] [²]
    [(d) to goods.] [³]

(5) A passenger or member of the crew on a ship or aircraft shall give the captain any information required for the purpose of enabling the owners or agents to comply with a request under this paragraph.
    (6) Sub-paragraphs (2) and (5) shall not require the provision of information which is required to be provided under or by virtue of paragraph 27(2) or 27B of Schedule 2 to the Immigration Act 1971. [⁴]

¹ Added by Anti-terrorism, Crime and Security Act 2001 (c.24), Pt 13, s. 119 (3)
² *ibid.*
³ *ibid.*
⁴ In relation to the aspects of the Channel Tunnel system specified in S.I. 1993 No. 1813 Art.7(1): Sched.7 para.17 is repealed.

Offences

117–093 18.—(1) [¹] A person commits an offence if he—

    (a) wilfully fails to comply with a duty imposed under or by virtue of this Schedule,
    (b) wilfully contravenes a prohibition imposed under or by virtue of this Schedule, or
    (c) wilfully obstructs, or seeks to frustrate, a search or examination under or by virtue of this Schedule.

(2) A person guilty of an offence under this paragraph shall be liable on summary conviction to—

    (a) imprisonment for a term not exceeding three months,
    (b) a fine not exceeding level 4 on the standard scale, or
    (c) both.

¹ In relation to the aspects of the Channel Tunnel system specified in S.I. 1993 No. 1813 Art.7(1):

18.—(1) A person commits an offence if he—

    (a) wilfully fails to comply with a duty imposed under or by virtue of this Schedule,
    (b) wilfully contravenes a prohibition imposed under or by virtue of this Schedule, or
    (c) wilfully obstructs, or seeks to frustrate, a search or examination under or by virtue of this Schedule.

(2) A person guilty of an offence under this paragraph shall be liable on summary conviction to—

    (a) imprisonment for a term not exceeding three months,
    (b) a fine not exceeding level 4 on the standard scale, or
    (c) both.

SCHEDULE 8

DETENTION

SCHEDULE PART I

TREATMENT OF PERSONS DETAINED UNDER SECTION 41 OR SCHEDULE 7

Place of detention
1. (1) The Secretary of State shall designate places at which persons may be detained under **117–094**
Schedule 7 or section 41.

(2) In this Schedule a reference to a police station includes a reference to any place which the Secretary of State has designated under sub-paragraph (1) as a place where a person may be detained under section 41.

(3) Where a person is detained under Schedule 7, he may be taken in the custody of an examining officer or of a person acting under an examining officer's authority to and from any place where his attendance is required for the purpose of—

(a) his examination under that Schedule,
(b) establishing his nationality or citizenship, or
(c) making arrangements for his admission to a country or territory outside the United Kingdom.

(4) A constable who arrests a person under section 41 shall take him as soon as is reasonably practicable to the police station which the constable considers the most appropriate.

(5) In this paragraph "examining officer" has the meaning given in Schedule 7.

(6) Where a person is arrested in one Part of the United Kingdom and all or part of his detention takes place in another Part, the provisions of this Schedule which apply to detention in a particular Part of the United Kingdom apply in relation to him while he is detained in that Part.

Identification
2. (1) An authorised person may take any steps which are reasonably necessary for— **117–095**

(a) photographing the detained person,
(b) measuring him, or
(c) identifying him.

(2) In sub-paragraph (1) "authorised person" means any of the following—

(a) a constable,
(b) a prison officer,
(c) a person authorised by the Secretary of State, and
(d) in the case of a person detained under Schedule 7, an examining officer (within the meaning of that Schedule).

(3) This paragraph does not confer the power to take—

(a) fingerprints, non-intimate samples or intimate samples (within the meaning given by paragraph 15 below), or
(b) relevant physical data or samples as mentioned in section 18 of the Criminal Procedure (Scotland) Act 1995 as applied by paragraph 20 below.

Audio and video recording of interviews

3.—(1) The Secretary of State shall— **117–096**

(a) issue a code of practice about the audio recording of interviews to which this paragraph applies, and
(b) make an order requiring the audio recording of interviews to which this paragraph applies in accordance with any relevant code of practice under paragraph (a).

(2) The Secretary of State may make an order requiring the video recording of—

(a) interviews to which this paragraph applies;
(b) interviews to which this paragraph applies which take place in a particular Part of the United Kingdom.

(3) An order under sub-paragraph (2) shall specify whether the video recording which it requires is to be silent or with sound.

(4) Where an order is made under sub-paragraph (2)—

(a) the Secretary of State shall issue a code of practice about the video recording of interviews to which the order applies, and

(b) the order shall require the interviews to be video recorded in accordance with any relevant code of practice under paragraph (a).

(5) Where the Secretary of State has made an order under sub-paragraph (2) requiring certain interviews to be video recorded with sound—

(a) he need not make an order under sub-paragraph (1)(b) in relation to those interviews, but

(b) he may do so.

(6) This paragraph applies to any interview by a constable of a person detained under Schedule 7 or section 41 if the interview takes place in a police station.

(7) A code of practice under this paragraph—

(a) may make provision in relation to a particular Part of the United Kingdom;

(b) may make different provision for different Parts of the United Kingdom.

117–097   **4.**—(1) This paragraph applies to a code of practice under paragraph 3.

(2) Where the Secretary of State proposes to issue a code of practice he shall—

(a) publish a draft,

(b) consider any representations made to him about the draft, and

(c) if he thinks it appropriate, modify the draft in the light of any representations made to him.

(3) The Secretary of State shall lay a draft of the code before Parliament.

(4) When the Secretary of State has laid a draft code before Parliament he may bring it into operation by order.

(5) The Secretary of State may revise a code and issue the revised code; and sub-paragraphs (2) to (4) shall apply to a revised code as they apply to an original code.

(6) The failure by a constable to observe a provision of a code shall not of itself make him liable to criminal or civil proceedings.

(7) A code—

(a) shall be admissible in evidence in criminal and civil proceedings, and

(b) shall be taken into account by a court or tribunal in any case in which it appears to the court or tribunal to be relevant.

Status

117–098   **5.** A detained person shall be deemed to be in legal custody throughout the period of his detention.

Rights: England, Wales and Northern Ireland

117–099   **6.**—(1) Subject to paragraph 8, a person detained under Schedule 7 or section 41 at a police station in England, Wales or Northern Ireland shall be entitled, if he so requests, to have one named person informed as soon as is reasonably practicable that he is being detained there.

(2) The person named must be—

(a) a friend of the detained person,

(b) a relative, or

(c) a person who is known to the detained person or who is likely to take an interest in his welfare.

(3) Where a detained person is transferred from one police station to another, he shall be entitled to exercise the right under this paragraph in respect of the police station to which he is transferred.

117–100   **7.**—(1) Subject to paragraphs 8 and 9, a person detained under Schedule 7 or section 41 at a police station in England, Wales or Northern Ireland shall be entitled, if he so requests, to consult a solicitor as soon as is reasonably practicable, privately and at any time.

(2) Where a request is made under sub-paragraph (1), the request and the time at which it was made shall be recorded.

117–101   **8.**—(1) Subject to sub-paragraph (2), an officer of at least the rank of superintendent may authorise a delay—

(a) in informing the person named by a detained person under paragraph 6;

(b) in permitting a detained person to consult a solicitor under paragraph 7.

(2) But where a person is detained under section 41 he must be permitted to exercise his rights under paragraphs 6 and 7 before the end of the period mentioned in subsection (3) of that section.

(3) Subject to sub-paragraph (5), an officer may give an authorisation under sub-paragraph (1) only if he has reasonable grounds for believing—

    (a) in the case of an authorisation under sub-paragraph (1)(a), that informing the named person of the detained person's detention will have any of the consequences specified in sub-paragraph (4), or

    (b) in the case of an authorisation under sub-paragraph (1)(b), that the exercise of the right under paragraph 7 at the time when the detained person desires to exercise it will have any of the consequences specified in sub-paragraph (4).

(4) Those consequences are—

    (a) interference with or harm to evidence of a serious arrestable offence,

    (b) interference with or physical injury to any person,

    (c) the alerting of persons who are suspected of having committed a serious arrestable offence but who have not been arrested for it,

    (d) the hindering of the recovery of property obtained as a result of a serious arrestable offence or in respect of which a forfeiture order could be made under section 23,

    (e) interference with the gathering of information about the commission, preparation or instigation of acts of terrorism,

    (f) the alerting of a person and thereby making it more difficult to prevent an act of terrorism, and

    (g) the alerting of a person and thereby making it more difficult to secure a person's apprehension, prosecution or conviction in connection with the commission, preparation or instigation of an act of terrorism.

(5) An officer may also give an authorisation under sub-paragraph (1) if he has reasonable grounds for believing that—

    (a) the detained person has committed an offence to which Part VI of the Criminal Justice Act 1988, Part I of the Proceeds of Crime (Scotland) Act 1995, or the Proceeds of Crime (Northern Ireland) Order 1996 (confiscation of the proceeds of an offence) applies,

    (b) the detained person has benefited from the offence within the meaning of that Part or Order, and

    (c) by informing the named person of the detained person's detention (in the case of an authorisation under sub-paragraph (1)(a)), or by the exercise of the right under paragraph 7 (in the case of an authorisation under sub-paragraph (1)(b)), the recovery of the value of that benefit will be hindered.

(6) If an authorisation under sub-paragraph (1) is given orally, the person giving it shall confirm it in writing as soon as is reasonably practicable.

(7) Where an authorisation under sub-paragraph (1) is given—

    (a) the detained person shall be told the reason for the delay as soon as is reasonably practicable, and

    (b) the reason shall be recorded as soon as is reasonably practicable.

(8) Where the reason for authorising delay ceases to subsist there may be no further delay in permitting the exercise of the right in the absence of a further authorisation under sub-paragraph (1).

(9) In this paragraph "serious arrestable offence" has the meaning given by section 116 of the Police and Criminal Evidence Act 1984 (in relation to England and Wales) and by Article 87 of the Police and Criminal Evidence (Northern Ireland) Order 1989 (in relation to Northern Ireland); but it also includes—

    (a) an offence under any of the provisions mentioned in section 40(1)(a) of this Act, and

    (b) an attempt or conspiracy to commit an offence under any of the provisions mentioned in section 40(1)(a).

9.—(1) A direction under this paragraph may provide that a detained person who wishes to **117–102** exercise the right under paragraph 7 may consult a solicitor only in the sight and hearing of a qualified officer.

(2) A direction under this paragraph may be given—

    (a) where the person is detained at a police station in England or Wales, by an officer of at least the rank of Commander or Assistant Chief Constable, or

    (b) where the person is detained at a police station in Northern Ireland, by an officer of at least the rank of Assistant Chief Constable.

(3) A direction under this paragraph may be given only if the officer giving it has reasonable grounds for believing that, unless the direction is given, the exercise of the right by the detained person will have any of the consequences specified in paragraph 8(4) or the consequence specified in paragraph 8(5)(c).

(4) In this paragraph "a qualified officer" means a police officer who—

(a) is of at least the rank of inspector,
(b) is of the uniformed branch of the force of which the officer giving the direction is a member, and
(c) in the opinion of the officer giving the direction, has no connection with the detained person's case.

(5) A direction under this paragraph shall cease to have effect once the reason for giving it ceases to subsist.

117–103   **10.**—(1) This paragraph applies where a person is detained in England, Wales or Northern Ireland under Schedule 7 or section 41.

(2) Fingerprints may be taken from the detained person only if they are taken by a constable—

(a) with the appropriate consent given in writing, or
(b) without that consent under sub-paragraph (4).

(3) A non-intimate sample may be taken from the detained person only if it is taken by a constable—

(a) with the appropriate consent given in writing, or
(b) without that consent under sub-paragraph (4).

(4) Fingerprints or a non-intimate sample may be taken from the detained person without the appropriate consent only if—

(a) he is detained at a police station and a police officer of at least the rank of superintendent authorises the fingerprints or sample to be taken, or
(b) he has been convicted of a recordable offence and, where a non-intimate sample is to be taken, he was convicted of the offence on or after 10th April 1995 (or 29th July 1996 where the non-intimate sample is to be taken in Northern Ireland).

(5) An intimate sample may be taken from the detained person only if—

(a) he is detained at a police station,
(b) the appropriate consent is given in writing,
(c) a police officer of at least the rank of superintendent authorises the sample to be taken, and
(d) subject to paragraph 13(2) and (3), the sample is taken by a constable.

(6) Subject to sub-paragraph (6A) an officer may give an authorisation under sub-paragraph (4)(a) or (5)(c) only if—

(a) in the case of a person detained under section 41, the officer reasonably suspects that the person has been involved in an offence under any of the provisions mentioned in section 40(1)(a), and the officer reasonably believes that the fingerprints or sample will tend to confirm or disprove his involvement, or
(b) in any case, the officer is satisfied that the taking of the fingerprints or sample from the person is necessary in order to assist in determining whether he falls within section 40(1)(b).

[(6A) An officer may also give an authorisation under sub-paragraph (4)(a) for the taking of fingerprints if—

(a) he is satisfied that the fingerprints of the detained person will facilitate the ascertainment of that person's identity; and
(b) that person has refused to identify himself or the officer has reasonable grounds for suspecting that that person is not who he claims to be.] [¹]

(7) If an authorisation under sub-paragraph (4)(a) or (5)(c) is given orally, the person giving it shall confirm it in writing as soon as is reasonably practicable.

¹ Added by Anti-terrorism, Crime and Security Act 2001 (c.24), Pt 10, s. 89(2).

117–104   **11.**—(1) Before fingerprints or a sample are taken from a person under paragraph 10, he shall be informed—

(a) that the fingerprints or sample may be used for the purposes of paragraph 14(4), section 63A(1) of the Police and Criminal Evidence Act 1984 and Article 63A(1) of the Police and Criminal Evidence (Northern Ireland) Order 1989 (checking of fingerprints and samples), and

(b) where the fingerprints or sample are to be taken under paragraph 10(2)(a), (3)(a) or (4)(b), of the reason for taking the fingerprints or sample.

(2) Before fingerprints or a sample are taken from a person upon an authorisation given under paragraph 10(4)(a) or (5)(c), he shall be informed—

(a) that the authorisation has been given,
(b) of the grounds upon which it has been given, and
(c) where relevant, of the nature of the offence in which it is suspected that he has been involved.

(3) After fingerprints or a sample are taken under paragraph 10, there shall be recorded as soon as is reasonably practicable any of the following which apply—

(a) the fact that the person has been informed in accordance with sub- paragraphs (1) and (2),
(b) the reason referred to in sub-paragraph (1)(b),
(c) the authorisation given under paragraph 10(4)(a) or (5)(c),
(d) the grounds upon which that authorisation has been given, and
(e) the fact that the appropriate consent has been given.

12.—(1) This paragraph applies where—   **117–105**

(a) two or more non-intimate samples suitable for the same means of analysis have been taken from a person under paragraph 10,
(b) those samples have proved insufficient, and
(c) the person has been released from detention.

(2) An intimate sample may be taken from the person if—

(a) the appropriate consent is given in writing,
(b) a police officer of at least the rank of superintendent authorises the sample to be taken, and
(c) subject to paragraph 13(2) and (3), the sample is taken by a constable.

(3) Paragraphs 10(6) and (7) and 11 shall apply in relation to the taking of an intimate sample under this paragraph; and a reference to a person detained under section 41 shall be taken as a reference to a person who was detained under section 41 when the non-intimate samples mentioned in sub-paragraph (1)(a) were taken.

13.—(1) Where appropriate written consent to the taking of an intimate sample from a person **117–106** under paragraph 10 or 12 is refused without good cause, in any proceedings against that person for an offence—

(a) the court, in determining whether to commit him for trial or whether there is a case to answer, may draw such inferences from the refusal as appear proper, and
(b) the court or jury, in determining whether that person is guilty of the offence charged, may draw such inferences from the refusal as appear proper.

(2) An intimate sample other than a sample of urine or a dental impression may be taken under paragraph 10 or 12 only by a registered medical practitioner acting on the authority of a constable.

(3) An intimate sample which is a dental impression may be taken under paragraph 10 or 12 only by a registered dentist acting on the authority of a constable.

(4) Where a sample of hair other than pubic hair is to be taken under paragraph 10 the sample may be taken either by cutting hairs or by plucking hairs with their roots so long as no more are plucked than the person taking the sample reasonably considers to be necessary for a sufficient sample.

14.—(1) This paragraph applies to—   **117–107**

(a) fingerprints or samples taken under paragraph 10 or 12, and
(b) information derived from those samples.

(2) The fingerprints and samples may be retained but shall not be used by any person except for the purposes of a terrorist investigation or for purposes related to the prevention or detection of crime, the investigation of an offence or the conduct of a prosecution.

(3) In particular, a check may not be made against them under—

(a) section 63A(1) of the Police and Criminal Evidence Act 1984 (checking of fingerprints and samples), or
(b) Article 63A(1) of the Police and Criminal Evidence (Northern Ireland) Order 1989 (checking of fingerprints and samples),

except for the purpose of a terrorist investigation or for purposes related to the prevention or detection of crime, the investigation of an offence or the conduct of a prosecution.

(4) The fingerprints, samples or information may be checked, subject to sub-paragraph (2), against—

(a) other fingerprints or samples taken under paragraph 10 or 12 or information derived from those samples,
(b) relevant physical data or samples taken by virtue of paragraph 20,
(c) any of the fingerprints, samples and information mentioned in section 63A(1)(a) and (b) of the Police and Criminal Evidence Act 1984 (checking of fingerprints and samples),
(d) any of the fingerprints, samples and information mentioned in Article 63A(1)(a) and (b) of the Police and Criminal Evidence (Northern Ireland) Order 1989 (checking of fingerprints and samples), and
(e) fingerprints or samples taken under section 15(9) of, or paragraph 7(5) of Schedule 5 to, the Prevention of Terrorism (Temporary Provisions) Act 1989 or information derived from those samples.

[(4A) In this paragraph—

(a) a reference to crime includes a reference to any conduct which—

(i) constitutes one or more criminal offences (whether under the law of a part of the United Kingdom or of a country or territory outside the United Kingdom); or
(ii) is, or corresponds to, any conduct which, if it all took place in any one part of the United Kingdom, would constitute one or more criminal offences;

and

(b) the references to an investigation and to a prosecution include references, respectively, to any investigation outside the United Kingdom of any crime or suspected crime and to a prosecution brought in respect of any crime in a country or territory outside the United Kingdom.] [¹]

(5) This paragraph (other than sub-paragraph (4)) shall apply to fingerprints or samples taken under section 15(9) of, or paragraph 7(5) of Schedule 5 to, the Prevention of Terrorism (Temporary Provisions) Act 1989 and information derived from those samples as it applies to fingerprints or samples taken under paragraph 10 or 12 and the information derived from those samples.

¹ Added by Criminal Justice and Police Act 2001 (c.16), Pt 3, s. 84(4).

117–108   15.—(1) In the application of paragraphs 10 to 14 in relation to a person detained in England or Wales the following expressions shall have the meaning given by section 65 of the Police and Criminal Evidence Act 1984 (Part V definitions)—

(a) "appropriate consent",
(b) "fingerprints",
(c) "insufficient",
(d) "intimate sample",
(e) "non-intimate sample",
(f) "registered dentist", and
(g) "sufficient".

(2) In the application of paragraphs 10 to 14 in relation to a person detained in Northern Ireland the expressions listed in sub-paragraph (1) shall have the meaning given by Article 53 of the Police and Criminal Evidence (Northern Ireland) Order 1989 (definitions).

(3) In paragraph 10 "recordable offence" shall have—

(a) in relation to a person detained in England or Wales, the meaning given by section 118(1) of the Police and Criminal Evidence Act 1984 (general interpretation), and
(b) in relation to a person detained in Northern Ireland, the meaning given by Article 2(2) of the Police and Criminal Evidence (Northern Ireland) Order 1989 (definitions).

Rights: Scotland

117–109   16.—(1) A person detained under Schedule 7 or section 41 at a police station in Scotland shall be entitled to have intimation of his detention and of the place where he is being detained sent without delay to a solicitor and to another person named by him.

(2) The person named must be—

(a) a friend of the detained person,
(b) a relative, or

(c) a person who is known to the detained person or who is likely to take an interest in his welfare.

(3) Where a detained person is transferred from one police station to another, he shall be entitled to exercise the right under sub-paragraph (1) in respect of the police station to which he is transferred.

(4) A police officer not below the rank of superintendent may authorise a delay in making intimation where, in his view, the delay is necessary on one of the grounds mentioned in paragraph 17(3) or where paragraph 17(4) applies.

(5) Where a detained person requests that the intimation be made, there shall be recorded the time when the request is—

(a) made, and
(b) complied with.

(6) A person detained shall be entitled to consult a solicitor at any time, without delay.

(7) A police officer not below the rank of superintendent may authorise a delay in holding the consultation where, in his view, the delay is necessary on one of the grounds mentioned in paragraph 17(3) or where paragraph 17(4) applies.

(8) Subject to paragraph 17, the consultation shall be private.

(9) Where a person is detained under section 41 he must be permitted to exercise his rights under this paragraph before the end of the period mentioned in subsection (3) of that section.

17.—(1) An officer not below the rank of Assistant Chief Constable may direct that the consulta- **117–110** tion mentioned in paragraph 16(6) shall be in the presence of a uniformed officer not below the rank of inspector if it appears to the officer giving the direction to be necessary on one of the grounds mentioned in sub-paragraph (3).

(2) A uniformed officer directed to be present during a consultation shall be an officer who, in the opinion of the officer giving the direction, has no connection with the case.

(3) The grounds mentioned in paragraph 16(4) and (7) and in sub-paragraph (1) are—

(a) that it is in the interests of the investigation or prevention of crime;
(b) that it is in the interests of the apprehension, prosecution or conviction of offenders;
(c) that it will further the recovery of property obtained as a result of the commission of an offence or in respect of which a forfeiture order could be made under section 23;
(d) that it will further the operation of Part VI of the Criminal Justice Act 1988, Part I of the Proceeds of Crime (Scotland) Act 1995 or the Proceeds of Crime (Northern Ireland) Order 1996 (confiscation of the proceeds of an offence).

(4) This sub-paragraph applies where an officer mentioned in paragraph 16(4) or (7) has reasonable grounds for believing that—

(a) the detained person has committed an offence to which Part VI of the Criminal Justice Act 1988, Part I of the Proceeds of Crime (Scotland) Act 1995 or the Proceeds of Crime (Northern Ireland) Order 1996 (confiscation of the proceeds of an offence) applies,
(b) the detained person has benefited from the offence within the meaning of that Part or Order, and
(c) by informing the named person of the detained person's detention (in the case of an authorisation under paragraph 16(4)) or by the exercise of the entitlement under paragraph 16(6) (in the case of an authorisation under paragraph 16(7)) the recovery of the value of that benefit will be hindered.

(5) Where delay is authorised in the exercising of any of the rights mentioned in paragraph 16(1) and (6)—

(a) if the authorisation is given orally, the person giving it shall confirm it in writing as soon as is reasonably practicable,
(b) the detained person shall be told the reason for the delay as soon as is reasonably practicable, and
(c) the reason shall be recorded as soon as is reasonably practicable.

18.—(1) Paragraphs 16 and 17 shall have effect, in relation to a person detained under section **117–111** 41 or Schedule 7, in place of any enactment or rule of law under or by virtue of which a person arrested or detained may be entitled to communicate or consult with any other person.

(2) But, where a person detained under Schedule 7 or section 41 at a police station in Scotland appears to a constable to be a child—

(a) the other person named by the person detained in pursuance of paragraph 16(1) shall be that person's parent, and
(b) section 15(4) of the Criminal Procedure (Scotland) Act 1995 shall apply to the person detained as it applies to a person who appears to a constable to be a child who is being detained as mentioned in paragraph (b) of section 15(1) of that Act,

and in this sub-paragraph "child" and "parent" have the same meaning as in section 15(4) of that Act.

117–112   **19.** The Secretary of State shall, by order, make provision to require that—

(a) except in such circumstances, and
(b) subject to such conditions,

as may be specified in the order, where a person detained has been permitted to consult a solicitor, the solicitor shall be allowed to be present at any interview carried out in connection with a terrorist investigation or for the purposes of Schedule 7.

117–113   **20.**—(1) Subject to the modifications specified in sub-paragraphs (2) and (3), section 18 of the Criminal Procedure (Scotland) Act 1995 (procedure for taking certain prints and samples) shall apply to a person detained under Schedule 7 or section 41 at a police station in Scotland as it applies to a person arrested or a person detained under section 14 of that Act.

(2) Subject to subsection (2A), a constable may take from a detained person or require a detained person to provide relevant physical data only if—

(a) in the case of a person detained under section 41 of the Terrorism Act 2000, he reasonably suspects that the person has been involved in an offence under any of the provisions mentioned in section 40(1)(a) of that Act and he reasonably believes that the relevant physical data will tend to confirm or disprove his involvement; or
(b) in any case, he is satisfied that it is necessary to do so in order to assist in determining whether the person falls within section 40(1)(b).

(2A) A constable may also take fingerprints from a detained person or require him to provide them if—

(a) he is satisfied that the fingerprints of that person will facilitate the ascertainment of that person's identity; and
(b) that person has refused to identify himself or the constable has reasonable grounds for suspecting that that person is not who he claims to be.

(2B) In this section references to ascertaining a person's identity include references to showing that he is not a particular person.

[(3) Subsections (3) to (5) shall not apply, but any relevant physical data or sample taken in pursuance of section 18 as applied by this paragraph may be retained but shall not be used by any person except for the purposes of a terrorist investigation or for purposes related to the prevention or detection of crime, the investigation of an offence or the conduct of a prosecution.

(4) In this paragraph—

(a) a reference to crime includes a reference to any conduct which—

(i) constitutes one or more criminal offences (whether under the law of a part of the United Kingdom or of a country or territory outside the United Kingdom); or
(ii) is, or corresponds to, any conduct which, if it all took place in any one part of the United Kingdom, would constitute one or more criminal offences; and

(b) the references to an investigation and to a prosecution include references, respectively, to any investigation outside the United Kingdom of any crime or suspected crime and to a prosecution brought in respect of any crime in a country or territory outside the United Kingdom.] [¹]

---

¹ Substituted by Anti-terrorism, Crime and Security Act 2001 (c.24), Pt 10, s. 89(4).

Anti-Terrorism, Crime And Security Act 2001

(2001, c. 24)

PART 1

TERRORIST PROPERTY

Forfeiture of terrorist cash

1.—(1) Schedule 1 (which makes provision for enabling cash which—   **118–001**

(a) is intended to be used for the purposes of terrorism,
(b) consists of resources of an organisation which is a proscribed organisation, or
(c) is, or represents, property obtained through terrorism,

to be forfeited in civil proceedings before a magistrates' court or (in Scotland)
the sheriff) is to have effect.

(2) The powers conferred by Schedule 1 are exercisable in relation to any
cash whether or not any proceedings have been brought for an offence in connection with the cash.

(3) Expressions used in this section have the same meaning as in Schedule 1.

(4) Sections 24 to 31 of the Terrorism Act 2000 (c. 11) (seizure of terrorist
cash) are to cease to have effect.

(5) An order under section 127 bringing Schedule 1 into force may make any
modifications of any code of practice then in operation under Schedule 14 to
the Terrorism Act 2000 (exercise of officers' powers) which the Secretary of
State thinks necessary or expedient.

. . . . . .

PART 2

FREEZING ORDERS

Orders

Power to make order

4.—(1) The Treasury may make a freezing order if the following two condi- **118–002**
tions are satisfied.

(2) The first condition is that the Treasury reasonably believe that—

(a) action to the detriment of the United Kingdom's economy (or part of
it) has been or is likely to be taken by a person or persons, or
(b) action constituting a threat to the life or property of one or more
nationals of the United Kingdom or residents of the United Kingdom
has been or is likely to be taken by a person or persons.

(3) If one person is believed to have taken or to be likely to take the action
the second condition is that the person is—

(a) the government of a country or territory outside the United Kingdom,
or
(b) a resident of a country or territory outside the United Kingdom.

(4) If two or more persons are believed to have taken or to be likely to take the action the second condition is that each of them falls within paragraph (a) or (b) of subsection (3); and different persons may fall within different paragraphs.

Contents of order

118–003   **5.**—(1) A freezing order is an order which prohibits persons from making funds available to or for the benefit of a person or persons specified in the order.

(2) The order must provide that these are the persons who are prohibited—

    (a) all persons in the United Kingdom, and

    (b) all persons elsewhere who are nationals of the United Kingdom or are bodies incorporated under the law of any part of the United Kingdom or are Scottish partnerships.

(3) The order may specify the following (and only the following) as the person or persons to whom or for whose benefit funds are not to be made available—

    (a) the person or persons reasonably believed by the Treasury to have taken or to be likely to take the action referred to in section 4;

    (b) any person the Treasury reasonably believe has provided or is likely to provide assistance (directly or indirectly) to that person or any of those persons.

(4) A person may be specified under subsection (3) by—

    (a) being named in the order, or

    (b) falling within a description of persons set out in the order.

(5) The description must be such that a reasonable person would know whether he fell within it.

(6) Funds are financial assets and economic benefits of any kind.

. . . . . .

PART 3

DISCLOSURE OF INFORMATION

Restriction on disclosure of information for overseas purposes

118–004   **18.**—(1) Subject to subsections (2) and (3), the Secretary of State may give a direction which—

    (a) specifies any overseas proceedings or any description of overseas proceedings; and

    (b) prohibits the making of any relevant disclosure for the purposes of those proceedings or, as the case may be, of proceedings of that description.

(2) In subsection (1) the reference, in relation to a direction, to a relevant disclosure is a reference to a disclosure authorised by any of the provisions to which section 17 applies which—

    (a) is made for a purpose mentioned in subsection (2)(a) to (d) of that section; and

(b) is a disclosure of any such information as is described in the direction.

(3) The Secretary of State shall not give a direction under this section unless it appears to him that the overseas proceedings in question, or that overseas proceedings of the description in question, relate or would relate—

(a) to a matter in respect of which it would be more appropriate for any jurisdiction or investigation to be exercised or carried out by a court or other authority of the United Kingdom, or of a particular part of the United Kingdom;

(b) to a matter in respect of which it would be more appropriate for any jurisdiction or investigation to be exercised or carried out by a court or other authority of a third country; or

(c) to a matter that would fall within paragraph (a) or (b)—

   (i) if it were appropriate for there to be any exercise of jurisdiction or investigation at all; and

   (ii) if (where one does not exist) a court or other authority with the necessary jurisdiction or functions existed in the United Kingdom, in the part of the United Kingdom in question or, as the case may be, in the third country in question.

(4) A direction under this section shall not have the effect of prohibiting—

(a) the making of any disclosure by a Minister of the Crown or by the Treasury; or

(b) the making of any disclosure in pursuance of a Community obligation.

(5) A direction under this section—

(a) may prohibit the making of disclosures absolutely or in such cases, or subject to such conditions as to consent or otherwise, as may be specified in it; and

(b) must be published or otherwise issued by the Secretary of State in such manner as he considers appropriate for bringing it to the attention of persons likely to be affected by it.

(6) A person who, knowing of any direction under this section, discloses any information in contravention of that direction shall be guilty of an offence and liable—

(a) on conviction on indictment, to imprisonment for a term not exceeding two years or to a fine or to both;

(b) on summary conviction, to imprisonment for a term not exceeding three months or to a fine not exceeding the statutory maximum or to both.

(7) The following are overseas proceedings for the purposes of this section—

(a) criminal proceedings which are taking place, or will or may take place, in a country or territory outside the United Kingdom;

(b) a criminal investigation which is being, or will or may be, conducted by an authority of any such country or territory.

(8) References in this section, in relation to any proceedings or investigation, to a third country are references to any country or territory outside the United Kingdom which is not the country or territory where the proceedings are taking place, or will or may take place or, as the case may be, is not the country or

territory of the authority which is conducting the investigation, or which will or may conduct it.

(9) In this section "court" includes a tribunal of any description.

Disclosure of information held by revenue departments

118–005 **19.**—(1) This section applies to information which is held by or on behalf of the Commissioners of Inland Revenue or by or on behalf of the Commissioners of Customs and Excise, including information obtained before the coming into force of this section.

(2) No obligation of secrecy imposed by statute or otherwise prevents the disclosure, in accordance with the following provisions of this section, of information to which this section applies if the disclosure is made—

    (a) for the purpose of facilitating the carrying out by any of the intelligence services of any of that service's functions;

    (b) for the purposes of any criminal investigation whatever which is being or may be carried out, whether in the United Kingdom or elsewhere;

    (c) for the purposes of any criminal proceedings whatever which have been or may be initiated, whether in the United Kingdom or elsewhere;

    (d) for the purposes of the initiation or bringing to an end of any such investigation or proceedings; or

    (e) for the purpose of facilitating a determination of whether any such investigation or proceedings should be initiated or brought to an end.

(3) No disclosure of information to which this section applies shall be made by virtue of this section unless the person by whom the disclosure is made is satisfied that the making of the disclosure is proportionate to what is sought to be achieved by it.

(4) Information to which this section applies shall not be disclosed by virtue of this section except by the Commissioners by or on whose behalf it is held or with their authority.

(5) Information obtained by means of a disclosure authorised by subsection (2) shall not be further disclosed except—

    (a) for a purpose mentioned in that subsection; and

    (b) with the consent of the Commissioners by whom or with whose authority it was initially disclosed;

and information so obtained otherwise than by or on behalf of any of the intelligence services shall not be further disclosed (with or without such consent) to any of those services, or to any person acting on behalf of any of those services, except for a purpose mentioned in paragraphs (b) to (e) of that subsection.

(6) A consent for the purposes of subsection (5) may be given either in relation to a particular disclosure or in relation to disclosures made in such circumstances as may be specified or described in the consent.

(7) Nothing in this section authorises the making of any disclosure which is prohibited by any provision of the Data Protection Act 1998 (c. 29).

(8) References in this section to information which is held on behalf of the Commissioners of Inland Revenue or of the Commissioners of Customs and Excise include references to information which—

    (a) is held by a person who provides services to the Commissioners of Inland Revenue or, as the case may be, to the Commissioners of Customs and Excise; and

    (b) is held by that person in connection with the provision of those services.

(9) In this section "intelligence service" has the same meaning as in the Regulation of Investigatory Powers Act 2000 (c. 23).

(10) Nothing in this section shall be taken to prejudice any power to disclose information which exists apart from this section.

. . . . . .

PART 4

IMMIGRATION AND ASYLUM

Suspected international terrorists

Suspected international terrorist: certification

21.—(1) The Secretary of State may issue a certificate under this section in **118–006** respect of a person if the Secretary of State reasonably—

(a) believes that the person's presence in the United Kingdom is a risk to national security, and
(b) suspects that the person is a terrorist.

(2) In subsection (1)(b) "terrorist" means a person who—

(a) is or has been concerned in the commission, preparation or instigation of acts of international terrorism,
(b) is a member of or belongs to an international terrorist group, or
(c) has links with an international terrorist group.

(3) A group is an international terrorist group for the purposes of subsection (2)(b) and (c) if—

(a) it is subject to the control or influence of persons outside the United Kingdom, and
(b) the Secretary of State suspects that it is concerned in the commission, preparation or instigation of acts of international terrorism.

(4) For the purposes of subsection (2)(c) a person has links with an international terrorist group only if he supports or assists it.

(5) In this Part—

"terrorism" has the meaning given by section 1 of the Terrorism Act 2000 (c. 11), and
"suspected international terrorist" means a person certified under subsection (1).

(6) Where the Secretary of State issues a certificate under subsection (1) he shall as soon as is reasonably practicable—

(a) take reasonable steps to notify the person certified, and
(b) send a copy of the certificate to the Special Immigration Appeals Commission.

(7) The Secretary of State may revoke a certificate issued under subsection (1).

(8) A decision of the Secretary of State in connection with certification under

this section may be questioned in legal proceedings only under section 25 or 26.

(9) An action of the Secretary of State taken wholly or partly in reliance on a certificate under this section may be questioned in legal proceedings only by or in the course of proceedings under—

(a) section 25 or 26, or
(b) section 2 of the Special Immigration Appeals Commission Act 1997 (c. 68) (appeal).

Deportation, removal, etc.

118–007 22.—(1) An action of a kind specified in subsection (2) may be taken in respect of a suspected international terrorist despite the fact that (whether temporarily or indefinitely) the action cannot result in his removal from the United Kingdom because of—

(a) a point of law which wholly or partly relates to an international agreement, or
(b) a practical consideration.

(2) The actions mentioned in subsection (1) are—

(a) refusing leave to enter or remain in the United Kingdom in accordance with provision made by or by virtue of any of sections 3 to 3B of the Immigration Act 1971 (c. 77) (control of entry to United Kingdom),
(b) varying a limited leave to enter or remain in the United Kingdom in accordance with provision made by or by virtue of any of those sections,
(c) recommending deportation in accordance with section 3(6) of that Act (recommendation by court),
(d) taking a decision to make a deportation order under section 5(1) of that Act (deportation by Secretary of State),
(e) making a deportation order under section 5(1) of that Act,
(f) refusing to revoke a deportation order,
(g) cancelling leave to enter the United Kingdom in accordance with paragraph 2A of Schedule 2 to that Act (person arriving with continuous leave),
(h) giving directions for a person's removal from the United Kingdom under any of paragraphs 8 to 10 or 12 to 14 of Schedule 2 to that Act (control of entry to United Kingdom),
(i) giving directions for a person's removal from the United Kingdom under section 10 of the Immigration and Asylum Act 1999 (c. 33) (person unlawfully in United Kingdom), and
(j) giving notice to a person in accordance with regulations under paragraph 1 of Schedule 4 to that Act of a decision to make a deportation order against him.

(3) Action of a kind specified in subsection (2) which has effect in respect of a suspected international terrorist at the time of his certification under section 21 shall be treated as taken again (in reliance on subsection (1) above) immediately after certification.

Detention

23.—(1) A suspected international terrorist may be detained under a provision **118–008** specified in subsection (2) despite the fact that his removal or departure from the United Kingdom is prevented (whether temporarily or indefinitely) by—

    (a) a point of law which wholly or partly relates to an international agreement, or

    (b) a practical consideration.

(2) The provisions mentioned in subsection (1) are—

    (a) paragraph 16 of Schedule 2 to the Immigration Act 1971 (c. 77) (detention of persons liable to examination or removal), and

    (b) paragraph 2 of Schedule 3 to that Act (detention pending deportation).

Bail

24.—(1) A suspected international terrorist who is detained under a provision **118–009** of the Immigration Act 1971 may be released on bail.

(2) For the purpose of subsection (1) the following provisions of Schedule 2 to the Immigration Act 1971 (control on entry) shall apply with the modifications specified in Schedule 3 to the Special Immigration Appeals Commission Act 1997 (c. 68) (bail to be determined by Special Immigration Appeals Commission) and with any other necessary modifications—

    (a) paragraph 22(1A), (2) and (3) (release),

    (b) paragraph 23 (forfeiture),

    (c) paragraph 24 (arrest), and

    (d) paragraph 30(1) (requirement of Secretary of State's consent).

(3) Rules of procedure under the Special Immigration Appeals Commission Act 1997 (c. 68)—

    (a) may make provision in relation to release on bail by virtue of this section, and

    (b) subject to provision made by virtue of paragraph (a), shall apply in relation to release on bail by virtue of this section as they apply in relation to release on bail by virtue of that Act subject to any modification which the Commission considers necessary.

Certification: appeal

25.—(1) A suspected international terrorist may appeal to the Special Immig- **118–010** ration Appeals Commission against his certification under section 21.

(2) On an appeal the Commission must cancel the certificate if—

    (a) it considers that there are no reasonable grounds for a belief or suspicion of the kind referred to in section 21(1)(a) or (b), or

    (b) it considers that for some other reason the certificate should not have been issued.

(3) If the Commission determines not to cancel a certificate it must dismiss the appeal.

(4) Where a certificate is cancelled under subsection (2) it shall be treated as never having been issued.

(5) An appeal against certification may be commenced only—

> (a) within the period of three months beginning with the date on which the certificate is issued, or
>
> (b) with the leave of the Commission, after the end of that period but before the commencement of the first review under section 26.

Certification: review

118–011   26.—(1) The Special Immigration Appeals Commission must hold a first review of each certificate issued under section 21 as soon as is reasonably practicable after the expiry of the period of six months beginning with the date on which the certificate is issued.

(2) But—

> (a) in a case where before the first review would fall to be held in accordance with subsection (1) an appeal under section 25 is commenced (whether or not it is finally determined before that time) or leave to appeal is given under section 25(5)(b), the first review shall be held as soon as is reasonably practicable after the expiry of the period of six months beginning with the date on which the appeal is finally determined, and
>
> (b) in a case where an application for leave under section 25(5)(b) has been commenced but not determined at the time when the first review would fall to be held in accordance with subsection (1), if leave is granted the first review shall be held as soon as is reasonably practicable after the expiry of the period of six months beginning with the date on which the appeal is finally determined.

(3) The Commission must review each certificate issued under section 21 as soon as is reasonably practicable after the expiry of the period of three months beginning with the date on which the first review or a review under this subsection is finally determined.

(4) The Commission may review a certificate during a period mentioned in subsection (1), (2) or (3) if—

> (a) the person certified applies for a review, and
>
> (b) the Commission considers that a review should be held because of a change in circumstance.

(5) On a review the Commission—

> (a) must cancel the certificate if it considers that there are no reasonable grounds for a belief or suspicion of the kind referred to in section 21(1)(a) or (b), and
>
> (b) otherwise, may not make any order (save as to leave to appeal).

(6) A certificate cancelled by order of the Commission under subsection (5) ceases to have effect at the end of the day on which the order is made.

(7) Where the Commission reviews a certificate under subsection (4), the period for determining the next review of the certificate under subsection (3) shall begin with the date of the final determination of the review under subsection (4).

. . . . . .

PART 6

WEAPONS OF MASS DESTRUCTION

Nuclear weapons

Use etc. of nuclear weapons

47.—(1) A person who—   **118–012**

(a) knowingly causes a nuclear weapon explosion;
(b) develops or produces, or participates in the development or production of, a nuclear weapon;
(c) has a nuclear weapon in his possession;
(d) participates in the transfer of a nuclear weapon; or
(e) engages in military preparations, or in preparations of a military nature, intending to use, or threaten to use, a nuclear weapon, is guilty of an offence.

(2) Subsection (1) has effect subject to the exceptions and defences in sections 48 and 49.

(3) For the purposes of subsection (1)(b) a person participates in the development or production of a nuclear weapon if he does any act which—

(a) facilitates the development by another of the capability to produce or use a nuclear weapon, or
(b) facilitates the making by another of a nuclear weapon,

knowing or having reason to believe that his act has (or will have) that effect.

(4) For the purposes of subsection (1)(d) a person participates in the transfer of a nuclear weapon if—

(a) he buys or otherwise acquires it or agrees with another to do so;
(b) he sells or otherwise disposes of it or agrees with another to do so; or
(c) he makes arrangements under which another person either acquires or disposes of it or agrees with a third person to do so.

(5) A person guilty of an offence under this section is liable on conviction on indictment to imprisonment for life.

(6) In this section "nuclear weapon" includes a nuclear explosive device that is not intended for use as a weapon.

(7) This section applies to acts done outside the United Kingdom, but only if they are done by a United Kingdom person.

(8) Nothing in subsection (7) affects any criminal liability arising otherwise than under that subsection.

(9) Paragraph (a) of subsection (1) shall cease to have effect on the coming into force of the Nuclear Explosions (Prohibition and Inspections) Act 1998 (c. 7).

Exceptions

48.—(1) Nothing in section 47 applies—   **118–013**

(a) to an act which is authorised under subsection (2); or
(b) to an act done in the course of an armed conflict.

(2) The Secretary of State may—

(a) authorise any act which would otherwise contravene section 47 in such manner and on such terms as he thinks fit; and

(b) withdraw or vary any authorisation given under this subsection.

(3) Any question arising in proceedings for an offence under section 47 as to whether anything was done in the course of an armed conflict shall be determined by the Secretary of State.

(4) A certificate purporting to set out any such determination and to be signed by the Secretary of State shall be received in evidence in any such proceedings and shall be presumed to be so signed unless the contrary is shown.

Defences

118–014 **49.**—(1) In proceedings for an offence under section 47(1)(c) or (d) relating to an object it is a defence for the accused to show that he did not know and had no reason to believe that the object was a nuclear weapon.

(2) But he shall be taken to have shown that fact if—

(a) sufficient evidence is adduced to raise an issue with respect to it; and

(b) the contrary is not proved by the prosecution beyond reasonable doubt.

(3) In proceedings for such an offence it is also a defence for the accused to show that he knew or believed that the object was a nuclear weapon but, as soon as reasonably practicable after he first knew or believed that fact, he took all reasonable steps to inform the Secretary of State or a constable of his knowledge or belief.

Assisting or inducing weapons-related acts overseas

Assisting or inducing certain weapons-related acts overseas

118–015 **50.**—(1) A person who aids, abets, counsels or procures, or incites, a person who is not a United Kingdom person to do a relevant act outside the United Kingdom is guilty of an offence.

(2) For this purpose a relevant act is an act that, if done by a United Kingdom person, would contravene any of the following provisions—

(a) section 1 of the Biological Weapons Act 1974 (offences relating to biological agents and toxins);

(b) section 2 of the Chemical Weapons Act 1996 (offences relating to chemical weapons); or

(c) section 47 above (offences relating to nuclear weapons).

(3) Nothing in this section applies to an act mentioned in subsection (1) which—

(a) relates to a relevant act which would contravene section 47; and

(b) is authorised by the Secretary of State;

and section 48(2) applies for the purpose of authorising acts that would otherwise constitute an offence under this section.

(4) A person accused of an offence under this section in relation to a relevant act which would contravene a provision mentioned in subsection (2) may raise any defence which would be open to a person accused of the corresponding offence ancillary to an offence under that provision.

(5) A person convicted of an offence under this section is liable on conviction on indictment to imprisonment for life.

(6) This section applies to acts done outside the United Kingdom, but only if they are done by a United Kingdom person.

(7) Nothing in this section prejudices any criminal liability existing apart from this section.

. . . . . .

PART 8

SECURITY OF NUCLEAR INDUSTRY

Prohibition of disclosures relating to nuclear security

79.—(1) A person is guilty of an offence if he discloses any information or **118–016** thing the disclosure of which might prejudice the security of any nuclear site or of any nuclear material—

(a) with the intention of prejudicing that security; or
(b) being reckless as to whether the disclosure might prejudice that security.

(2) The reference in subsection (1) to nuclear material is a reference to—

(a) nuclear material which is being held on any nuclear site, or
(b) nuclear material anywhere in the world which is being transported to or from a nuclear site or carried on board a British ship,

(including nuclear material which is expected to be so held, transported or carried).

(3) A person guilty of an offence under subsection (1) is liable—

(a) on conviction on indictment, to imprisonment for a term not exceeding seven years or a fine (or both); and
(b) on summary conviction, to imprisonment for a term not exceeding six months or a fine not exceeding the statutory maximum (or both).

(4) In this section—

"British ship" means a ship (including a ship belonging to Her Majesty) which is registered in the United Kingdom;
"disclose" and "disclosure", in relation to a thing, include parting with possession of it;
"nuclear material" has the same meaning as in section 76; and
"nuclear site" means a site in the United Kingdom (including a site occupied by or on behalf of the Crown) which is (or is expected to be) used for any purpose mentioned in section 1(1) of the Nuclear Installations Act 1965 (c. 57).

(5) This section applies to acts done outside the United Kingdom, but only if they are done by a United Kingdom person.

(6) Proceedings for an offence committed outside the United Kingdom may be taken, and the offence may for incidental purposes be treated as having been committed, in any place in the United Kingdom.

(7) Nothing in subsection (5) affects any criminal liability arising otherwise than under that subsection.

Prohibition of disclosures of uranium enrichment technology

118–017   80.—(1) This section applies to—

(a) any information about the enrichment of uranium; or
(b) any information or thing which is, or is likely to be, used in connection with the enrichment of uranium;

and for this purpose "the enrichment of uranium" means any treatment of uranium that increases the proportion of the isotope 235 contained in the uranium.

(2) The Secretary of State may make regulations prohibiting the disclosure of information or things to which this section applies.

(3) A person who contravenes a prohibition is guilty of an offence and liable—

(a) on conviction on indictment, to imprisonment for a term not exceeding seven years or a fine (or both); and
(b) on summary conviction, to imprisonment for a term not exceeding six months or a fine not exceeding the statutory maximum (or both).

(4) The regulations may, in particular, provide for—

(a) a prohibition to apply, or not to apply—

(i) to such information or things; and
(ii) in such cases or circumstances,

as may be prescribed;
(b) the authorisation by the Secretary of State of disclosures that would otherwise be prohibited; and
(c) defences to an offence under subsection (3) relating to any prohibition.

(5) The regulations may—

(a) provide for any prohibition to apply to acts done outside the United Kingdom by United Kingdom persons;
(b) make different provision for different purposes; and
(c) make such incidental, supplementary and transitional provision as the Secretary of State thinks fit.

(6) The power to make the regulations is exercisable by statutory instrument.

(7) The regulations shall not be made unless a draft of the regulations has been laid before and approved by each House of Parliament.

(8) In this section—

"disclosure", in relation to a thing, includes parting with possession of it;
"information" includes software; and
"prescribed" means specified or described in the regulations.

. . . . . .

PART 11

RETENTION OF COMMUNICATIONS DATA

Codes and agreements about the retention of communications data

102.—(1) The Secretary of State shall issue, and may from time to time **118–018** revise, a code of practice relating to the retention by communications providers of communications data obtained by or held by them.

(2) The Secretary of State may enter into such agreements as he considers appropriate with any communications provider about the practice to be followed by that provider in relation to the retention of communications data obtained by or held by that provider.

(3) A code of practice or agreement under this section may contain any such provision as appears to the Secretary of State to be necessary—

    (a) for the purpose of safeguarding national security; or

    (b) for the purposes of prevention or detection of crime or the prosecution of offenders which may relate directly or indirectly to national security.

(4) A failure by any person to comply with a code of practice or agreement under this section which is for the time being in force shall not of itself render him liable to any criminal or civil proceedings.

(5) A code of practice or agreement under this section which is for the time being in force shall be admissible in evidence in any legal proceedings in which the question arises whether or not the retention of any communications data is justified on the grounds that a failure to retain the data would be likely to prejudice national security, the prevention or detection of crime or the prosecution of offenders.

Criminal Justice and Police Act 2001

(2001, c. 16)

An Act to make provision for combatting crime and disorder; to make provision **119–001** *about the disclosure of information relating to criminal matters and about powers of search and seizure; to amend the Police and Criminal Evidence Act 1984, the Police and Criminal Evidence (Northern Ireland) Order 1989 and the Terrorism Act 2000; to make provision about the police, the National Criminal Intelligence Service and the National Crime Squad; to make provision about the powers of the courts in relation to criminal matters; and for connected purposes.*   [11th May 2001]

PART 1

PROVISIONS FOR COMBATTING CRIME AND DISORDER

CHAPTER 1

ON THE SPOT PENALTIES FOR DISORDERLY BEHAVIOUR

Offences to which this Chapter applies

Offences leading to penalties on the spot

1.—(1) For the purposes of this Chapter "penalty offence" means an offence **119–002**

committed under any of the provisions mentioned in the first column of the following Table and described, in general terms, in the second column:

Offence creating provision	*Description of offence*
Section 12 of the Licensing Act 1872 (*c.* 94)	Being drunk in a highway, other public place or licensed premises
Section 80 of the Explosives Act 1875 (*c.* 17)	Throwing fireworks in a thoroughfare
Section 31 of the Fire Service Act 1947 (*c.* 41)	Knowingly giving a false alarm to a fire brigade
Section 55 of the British Transport Commission Act 1949 (*c.* xxix)	Trespassing on a railway
Section 56 of the British Transport Commission Act 1949 (*c.* xxix)	Throwing stones etc. at trains or other things on railways
Section 169C(3) of the Licensing Act 1964 (*c.* 26)	Buying or attempting to buy alcohol for consumption in a bar in licensed premises by a peron under 18
Section 91 of the Criminal Justice Act 1967 (*c.* 80)	Disorderly behaviour while drunk in a public place
Section 5(2) of the Criminal Law Act 1967 (*c.* 58)	Wasting police time or giving false report
Section 43(1)(b) of the Telecommunications Act 1984 (*c.* 12)	Using public telecommunications system for sending message known to be false in order to cause annoyance
Section 12 of this Act	Consumption of alcohol in designated public place

(2) The Secretary of State may by order amend an entry in the Table or add or remove an entry.

(3) An order under subsection (2) may make such amendment of any provision of this Chapter as the Secretary of State considers appropriate in consequence of any change in the Table made by the order.

(4) The power conferred by subsection (2) is exercisable by statutory instrument.

(5) No order shall be made under subsection (2) unless a draft of the order has been laid before and approved by a resolution of each House of Parliament.

Penalty notices and penalties

Penalty notices

119–003   2.—(1) A constable who has reason to believe that a person aged 18 or over has committed a penalty offence may give him a penalty notice in respect of the offence.

(2) Unless the notice is given in a police station, the constable giving it must be in uniform.

(3) At a police station, a penalty notice may be given only by an authorised constable.

(4) In this Chapter "penalty notice" means a notice offering the opportunity, by paying a penalty in accordance with this Chapter, to discharge any liability to be convicted of the offence to which the notice relates.

(5) "Authorised constable" means a constable authorised, on behalf of the chief officer of police for the area in which the police station is situated, to give penalty notices.

Amount of penalty and form of penalty notice

3.—(1) The penalty payable in respect of a penalty offence is such amount **119–004**
as the Secretary of State may specify by order.

(2) But the Secretary of State may not specify an amount which is more than
a quarter of the amount of the maximum fine for which a person is liable on
conviction of the offence.

(3) A penalty notice must—

    (a) be in the prescribed form;

    (b) state the alleged offence;

    (c) give such particulars of the circumstances alleged to constitute the
offence as are necessary to provide reasonable information about it;

    (d) specify the suspended enforcement period (as to which see section 5)
and explain its effect;

    (e) state the amount of the penalty;

    (f) state the justices' chief executive to whom, and the address at which,
the penalty may be paid; and

    (g) inform the person to whom it is given of his right to ask to be tried for
the alleged offence and explain how that right may be exercised.

(4) "Prescribed" means prescribed by regulations made by the Secretary of
State.

(5) The power to make regulations or an order conferred by this section is
exercisable by statutory instrument.

(6) Such an instrument shall be subject to annulment in pursuance of a resolution of either House of Parliament.

Effect of penalty notice

4.—(1) This section applies if a penalty notice is given to a person ("A") **119–005**
under section 2.

(2) If A asks to be tried for the alleged offence, proceedings may be brought
against him.

(3) Such a request must be made by a notice given by A—

    (a) in the manner specified in the penalty notice; and

    (b) before the end of the period of suspended enforcement (as to which
see section 5).

(4) A request which is made in accordance with subsection (3) is referred to
in this Chapter as a "request to be tried".

(5) If, by the end of the suspended enforcement period—

    (a) the penalty has not been paid in accordance with this Chapter, and

    (b) A has not made a request to be tried,

a sum equal to one and a half times the amount of the penalty may be registered
under section 8 for enforcement against A as a fine.

General restriction on proceedings

5.—(1) Proceedings for the offence to which a penalty notice relates may not **119–006**
be brought until the end of the period of 21 days beginning with the date on
which the notice was given ("the suspended enforcement period").

(2) If the penalty is paid before the end of the suspended enforcement period,
no proceedings may be brought for the offence.

(3) Subsection (1) does not apply if the person to whom the penalty notice was given has made a request to be tried.

Secretary of State's guidance

119–007   **6.** The Secretary of State may issue guidance—

(a) about the exercise of the discretion given to constables by this Chapter;
(b) about the issuing of penalty notices;
(c) with a view to encouraging good practice in connection with the operation of provisions of this Chapter.

. . . . . .

CHAPTER 2

PROVISIONS FOR COMBATTING ALCOHOL-RELATED DISORDER

Alcohol consumption in designated public places

Alcohol consumption in designated public places

119–008   **12.**—(1) Subsection (2) applies if a constable reasonably believes that a person is, or has been, consuming intoxicating liquor in a designated public place or intends to consume intoxicating liquor in such a place.
(2) The constable may require the person concerned—

(a) not to consume in that place anything which is, or which the constable reasonably believes to be, intoxicating liquor;
(b) to surrender anything in his possession which is, or which the constable reasonably believes to be, intoxicating liquor or a container for such liquor (other than a sealed container).

(3) A constable may dispose of anything surrendered to him under subsection (2) in such manner as he considers appropriate.
(4) A person who fails without reasonable excuse to comply with a requirement imposed on him under subsection (2) commits an offence and is liable on summary conviction to a fine not exceeding level 2 on the standard scale.
(5) A constable who imposes a requirement on a person under subsection (2) shall inform the person concerned that failing without reasonable excuse to comply with the requirement is an offence.
(6) In section 24(2) of the 1984 Act (offences to which powers of arrest without warrant apply), after paragraph (q) there shall be inserted—

"(qa) an offence under section 12(4) of the Criminal Justice and Police Act 2001."

. . . . . .

CHAPTER 3

OTHER PROVISIONS FOR COMBATTING CRIME AND DISORDER

Intimidating, harming and threatening witnesses etc.

Intimidation of witnesses

39.—(1) A person commits an offence if— **119–009**

(a) he does an act which intimidates, and is intended to intimidate, another person ("the victim");

(b) he does the act—

(i) knowing or believing that the victim is or may be a witness in any relevant proceedings; and

(ii) intending, by his act, to cause the course of justice to be obstructed, perverted or interfered with; and

(c) the act is done after the commencement of those proceedings.

(2) For the purposes of subsection (1) it is immaterial—

(a) whether or not the act that is done is done in the presence of the victim;

(b) whether that act is done to the victim himself or to another person; and

(c) whether or not the intention to cause the course of justice to be obstructed, perverted or interfered with is the predominating intention of the person doing the act in question.

(3) If, in proceedings against a person for an offence under this section, it is proved—

(a) that he did any act that intimidated, and was intended to intimidate, another person, and

(b) that he did that act knowing or believing that that other person was or might be a witness in any relevant proceedings that had already commenced,

he shall be presumed, unless the contrary is shown, to have done the act with the intention of causing the course of justice to be obstructed, perverted or interfered with.

(4) A person guilty of an offence under this section shall be liable—

(a) on conviction on indictment, to imprisonment for a term not exceeding five years or to a fine, or to both;

(b) on summary conviction, to imprisonment for a term not exceeding six months or to a fine not exceeding the statutory maximum, or to both.

(5) References in this section to a witness, in relation to any proceedings, include references to a person who provides, or is able to provide, any information or any document or other thing which might be used as evidence in those proceedings or which (whether or not admissible as evidence in those proceedings)—

(a) might tend to confirm evidence which will be or might be admitted in those proceedings;

(b) might be referred to in evidence given in those proceedings by another witness; or

(c) might be used as the basis for any cross examination in the course of those proceedings.

(6) References in this section to doing an act include references to issuing any threat (whether against a person or his finances or property or otherwise), or making any other statement.

(7) This section is in addition to, and not in derogation of, any offence subsisting at common law.

Harming witnesses etc.

119–010
   40.—(1) A person commits an offence if, in circumstances falling within subsection (2)—

   (a) he does an act which harms, and is intended to harm, another person; or
   (b) intending to cause another person to fear harm, he threatens to do an act which would harm that other person.

(2) The circumstances fall within this subsection if—

   (a) the person doing or threatening to do the act does so knowing or believing that some person (whether or not the person harmed or threatened or the person against whom harm is threatened) has been a witness in relevant proceedings; and
   (b) he does or threatens to do that act because of that knowledge or belief.

(3) If, in proceedings against a person for an offence under this section, it is proved that, within the relevant period—

   (a) he did an act which harmed, and was intended to harm, another person, or
   (b) intending to cause another person to fear harm, he threatened to do an act which would harm that other person,

and that he did the act, or (as the case may be) threatened to do the act, with the knowledge or belief required by paragraph (a) of subsection (2), he shall be presumed, unless the contrary is shown, to have done the act, or (as the case may be) threatened to do the act, because of that knowledge or belief.

(4) For the purposes of this section it is immaterial—

   (a) whether or not the act that is done or threatened, or the threat that is made, is or would be done or is made in the presence of the person who is or would be harmed or of the person who is threatened;
   (b) whether or not the motive mentioned in subsection (2)(b) is the predominating motive for the act or threat; and
   (c) whether the harm that is done or threatened is physical or financial or is harm to a person or to his property.

(5) A person guilty of an offence under this section shall be liable—

   (a) on conviction on indictment, to imprisonment for a term not exceeding five years or to a fine, or to both;
   (b) on summary conviction, to imprisonment for a term not exceeding six months or to a fine not exceeding the statutory maximum, or to both.

(6) In this section "the relevant period", in relation to an act done, or threat made, with the knowledge or belief that a person has been a witness in any

relevant proceedings, means the period that begins with the commencement of those proceedings and ends one year after they are finally concluded.

(7) References in this section to a witness, in relation to any proceedings, include references to a person who has provided any information or any document or other thing which was or might have been used as evidence in those proceedings or which (whether or not it was admissible as evidence in those proceedings)—

(a) tended to confirm or might have tended to confirm any evidence which was or could have been given in those proceedings;
(b) was or might have been referred to in evidence given in those proceedings by another witness; or
(c) was or might have been used as the basis for any cross examination in the course of those proceedings.

(8) This section is in addition to, and not in derogation of, any offence subsisting at common law.

Relevant proceedings

41.—(1) A reference in section 39 or 40 to relevant proceedings is a reference **119–011** to any proceedings in or before the Court of Appeal, the High Court, the Crown Court or any county court or magistrates' court which—

(a) are not proceedings for an offence; and
(b) were commenced after the coming into force of that section.

(2) For the purposes of any reference in section 39 or 40 or this section to the commencement of any proceedings relevant proceedings are commenced (subject to subsection (5)) at the earliest time at which one of the following occurs—

(a) an information is laid or application, claim form, complaint, petition, summons or other process made or issued for the purpose of commencing the proceedings;
(b) any other step is taken by means of which the subject matter of the proceedings is brought for the first time (whether as part of the proceedings or in anticipation of them) before the court.

(3) For the purposes of any reference in section 39 or 40 to the time when any proceedings are finally concluded, relevant proceedings are finally concluded (subject to subsection (4))—

(a) if proceedings for an appeal against, or an application for a review of, those proceedings or of any decision taken in those proceedings are brought or is made, at the time when proceedings on that appeal or application are finally concluded;
(b) if the proceedings are withdrawn or discontinued, at the time when they are withdrawn or discontinued; and
(c) in any other case, when the court in or before which the proceedings are brought finally disposes of all the matters arising in those proceedings.

(4) Relevant proceedings shall not be taken to be finally concluded by virtue of subsection (3)(a) where—

(a) the matters to which the appeal or application relate are such that the proceedings in respect of which it is brought or made continue or

resume after the making of any determination on that appeal or application; or

  (b) a determination made on that appeal or application requires those pro-
      ceedings to continue or to be resumed.

(5) Where, after having appeared to be finally concluded, any relevant proceedings continue by reason of—

  (a) the giving of permission to bring an appeal after a fixed time for
      appealing has expired,
  (b) the lifting of any stay in the proceedings,
  (c) the setting aside, without an appeal, of any judgment or order, or
  (d) the revival of any discontinued proceedings,

section 39 and 40 and this section shall have effect as if the proceedings had
concluded when they appeared to, but as if the giving of permission, the lifting
of the stay, the setting aside of the judgment or order or, as the case may be,
the revival of the discontinued proceedings were the commencement of new
relevant proceedings.

Further provision about intimidation etc.

Police directions stopping the harassment etc of a person in his home

119–012   42.—(1) Subject to the following provisions of this section, a constable who
is at the scene may give a direction under this section to any person if—

  (a) that person is present outside or in the vicinity of any premises that are
      used by any individual ("the resident") as his dwelling;
  (b) that constable believes, on reasonable grounds, that that person is pre-
      sent there for the purpose (by his presence or otherwise) of representing
      to the resident or another individual (whether or not one who uses the
      premises as his dwelling), or of persuading the resident or such another
      individual—

      (i) that he should not do something that he is entitled or required to
          do; or
      (ii) that he should do something that he is not under any obligation to
           do; and

  (c) that constable also believes, on reasonable grounds, that the presence
      of that person (either alone or together with that of any other persons
      who are also present)—

      (i) amounts to, or is likely to result in, the harassment of the resid-
          ent; or
      (ii) is likely to cause alarm or distress to the resident.

(2) A direction under this section is a direction requiring the person to whom
it is given to do all such things as the constable giving it may specify as the
things he considers necessary to prevent one or both of the following—

  (a) the harassment of the resident; or
  (b) the causing of any alarm or distress to the resident.

(3) A direction under this section may be given orally; and where a constable
is entitled to give a direction under this section to each of several persons outside, or in the vicinity of, any premises, he may give that direction to those

persons by notifying them of his requirements either individually or all together.

(4) The requirements that may be imposed by a direction under this section include a requirement to leave the vicinity of the premises in question (either immediately or after a specified period of time).

(5) A direction under this section may make exceptions to any requirement imposed by the direction, and may make any such exception subject to such conditions as the constable giving the direction thinks fit; and those conditions may include—

(a) conditions as to the distance from the premises in question at which, or otherwise as to the location where, persons who do not leave their vicinity must remain; and

(b) conditions as to the number or identity of the persons who are authorised by the exception to remain in the vicinity of those premises.

(6) The power of a constable to give a direction under this section shall not include—

(a) any power to give a direction at any time when there is a more senior-ranking police officer at the scene; or

(b) any power to direct a person to refrain from conduct that is lawful under section 220 of the Trade Union and Labour Relations (Consolidation) Act 1992 (c. 52) (right peacefully to picket a work place);

but it shall include power to vary or withdraw a direction previously given under this section.

(7) Any person who knowingly contravenes a direction given to him under this section shall be guilty of an offence and liable, on summary conviction, to imprisonment for a term not exceeding three months or to a fine not exceeding level 4 on the standard scale, or to both.

(8) A constable in uniform may arrest without warrant any person he reasonably suspects is committing an offence under this section.

(9) In this section "dwelling" has the same meaning as in Part 1 of the Public Order Act 1986 (c. 64).

. . . . . .

PART 2

POWERS OF SEIZURE

Additional powers of seizure

Additional powers of seizure from premises

50.—(1) Where— **119–013**

(a) a person who is lawfully on any premises finds anything on those premises that he has reasonable grounds for believing may be or may contain something for which he is authorised to search on those premises,

(b) a power of seizure to which this section applies or the power conferred by subsection (2) would entitle him, if he found it, to seize whatever it is that he has grounds for believing that thing to be or to contain, and

    (c) in all the circumstances, it is not reasonably practicable for it to be determined, on those premises—

        (i) whether what he has found is something that he is entitled to seize, or
        (ii) the extent to which what he has found contains something that he is entitled to seize,

that person's powers of seizure shall include power under this section to seize so much of what he has found as it is necessary to remove from the premises to enable that to be determined.

    (2) Where—

    (a) a person who is lawfully on any premises finds anything on those premises ("the seizable property") which he would be entitled to seize but for its being comprised in something else that he has (apart from this subsection) no power to seize,
    (b) the power under which that person would have power to seize the seizable property is a power to which this section applies, and
    (c) in all the circumstances it is not reasonably practicable for the seizable property to be separated, on those premises, from that in which it is comprised,

that person's powers of seizure shall include power under this section to seize both the seizable property and that from which it is not reasonably practicable to separate it.

    (3) The factors to be taken into account in considering, for the purposes of this section, whether or not it is reasonably practicable on particular premises for something to be determined, or for something to be separated from something else, shall be confined to the following—

    (a) how long it would take to carry out the determination or separation on those premises;
    (b) the number of persons that would be required to carry out that determination or separation on those premises within a reasonable period;
    (c) whether the determination or separation would (or would if carried out on those premises) involve damage to property;
    (d) the apparatus or equipment that it would be necessary or appropriate to use for the carrying out of the determination or separation; and
    (e) in the case of separation, whether the separation—

        (i) would be likely, or
        (ii) if carried out by the only means that are reasonably practicable on those premises, would be likely,

to prejudice the use of some or all of the separated seizable property for a purpose for which something seized under the power in question is capable of being used.

    (4) Section 19(6) of the 1984 Act and Article 21(6) of the Police and Criminal Evidence (Northern Ireland) Order 1989 (S.I. 1989/1341 (N.I. 12)) (powers of seizure not to include power to seize anything that a person has reasonable grounds for believing is legally privileged) shall not apply to the power of seizure conferred by subsection (2).

    (5) This section applies to each of the powers of seizure specified in Part 1 of Schedule 1.

    (6) Without prejudice to any power conferred by this section to take a copy of any document, nothing in this section, so far as it has effect by reference to

the power to take copies of documents under section 28(2)(b) of the Competition Act 1998 (c. 41), shall be taken to confer any power to seize any document.

Additional powers of seizure from the person

51.—(1) Where—

119–014

    (a) a person carrying out a lawful search of any person finds something that he has reasonable grounds for believing may be or may contain something for which he is authorised to search,

    (b) a power of seizure to which this section applies or the power conferred by subsection (2) would entitle him, if he found it, to seize whatever it is that he has grounds for believing that thing to be or to contain, and

    (c) in all the circumstances it is not reasonably practicable for it to be determined, at the time and place of the search—

        (i) whether what he has found is something that he is entitled to seize, or

        (ii) the extent to which what he has found contains something that he is entitled to seize,

that person's powers of seizure shall include power under this section to seize so much of what he has found as it is necessary to remove from that place to enable that to be determined.

(2) Where—

    (a) a person carrying out a lawful search of any person finds something ("the seizable property") which he would be entitled to seize but for its being comprised in something else that he has (apart from this subsection) no power to seize,

    (b) the power under which that person would have power to seize the seizable property is a power to which this section applies, and

    (c) in all the circumstances it is not reasonably practicable for the seizable property to be separated, at the time and place of the search, from that in which it is comprised,

that person's powers of seizure shall include power under this section to seize both the seizable property and that from which it is not reasonably practicable to separate it.

(3) The factors to be taken into account in considering, for the purposes of this section, whether or not it is reasonably practicable, at the time and place of a search, for something to be determined, or for something to be separated from something else, shall be confined to the following—

    (a) how long it would take to carry out the determination or separation at that time and place;

    (b) the number of persons that would be required to carry out that determination or separation at that time and place within a reasonable period;

    (c) whether the determination or separation would (or would if carried out at that time and place) involve damage to property;

    (d) the apparatus or equipment that it would be necessary or appropriate to use for the carrying out of the determination or separation; and

    (e) in the case of separation, whether the separation—

        (i) would be likely, or

(ii) if carried out by the only means that are reasonably practicable at that time and place, would be likely,

to prejudice the use of some or all of the separated seizable property for a purpose for which something seized under the power in question is capable of being used.

(4) Section 19(6) of the 1984 Act and Article 21(6) of the Police and Criminal Evidence (Northern Ireland) Order 1989 (S.I. 1989/1341 (N.I. 12)) (powers of seizure not to include power to seize anything a person has reasonable grounds for believing is legally privileged) shall not apply to the power of seizure conferred by subsection (2).

(5) This section applies to each of the powers of seizure specified in Part 2 of Schedule 1.

. . . . . .

Obligation to return items subject to legal privilege

119–015   **54.**—(1) If, at any time after a seizure of anything has been made in exercise of a power of seizure to which this section applies—

(a) it appears to the person for the time being having possession of the seized property in consequence of the seizure that the property—

(i) is an item subject to legal privilege, or
(ii) has such an item comprised in it, and

(b) in a case where the item is comprised in something else which has been lawfully seized, it is not comprised in property falling within subsection (2),

it shall be the duty of that person to secure that the item is returned as soon as reasonably practicable after the seizure.

(2) Property in which an item subject to legal privilege is comprised falls within this subsection if—

(a) the whole or a part of the rest of the property is property falling within subsection (3) or property the retention of which is authorised by section 56; and

(b) in all the circumstances, it is not reasonably practicable for that item to be separated from the rest of that property (or, as the case may be, from that part of it) without prejudicing the use of the rest of that property, or that part of it, for purposes for which (disregarding that item) its use, if retained, would be lawful.

(3) Property falls within this subsection to the extent that it is property for which the person seizing it had power to search when he made the seizure, but is not property which is required to be returned under this section or section 55.

(4) This section applies—

(a) to the powers of seizure conferred by sections 50 and 51;
(b) to each of the powers of seizure specified in Parts 1 and 2 of Schedule 1; and
(c) to any power of seizure (not falling within paragraph (a) or (b)) con-

ferred on a constable by or under any enactment, including an enactment passed after this Act.

. . . . . .

Remedies and safeguards

Application to the appropriate judicial authority

59.—(1) This section applies where anything has been seized in exercise, or **119–016**
purported exercise, of a relevant power of seizure.

(2) Any person with a relevant interest in the seized property may apply to
the appropriate judicial authority, on one or more of the grounds mentioned in
subsection (3), for the return of the whole or a part of the seized property.

(3) Those grounds are—

(a) that there was no power to make the seizure;
(b) that the seized property is or contains an item subject to legal privilege
that is not comprised in property falling within section 54(2);
(c) that the seized property is or contains any excluded material or special
procedure material which—

(i) has been seized under a power to which section 55 applies;
(ii) is not comprised in property falling within section 55(2) or (3);
and
(iii) is not property the retention of which is authorised by section 56;

(d) that the seized property is or contains something seized under section
50 or 51 which does not fall within section 53(3);

and subsections (5) and (6) of section 55 shall apply for the purposes of paragraph (c) as they apply for the purposes of that section.

(4) Subject to subsection (6), the appropriate judicial authority, on an application under subsection (2), shall—

(a) if satisfied as to any of the matters mentioned in subsection (3), order
the return of so much of the seized property as is property in relation
to which the authority is so satisfied; and
(b) to the extent that that authority is not so satisfied, dismiss the application.

(5) The appropriate judicial authority—

(a) on an application under subsection (2),
(b) on an application made by the person for the time being having possession of anything in consequence of its seizure under a relevant power
of seizure, or
(c) on an application made—

(i) by a person with a relevant interest in anything seized under section 50 or 51, and
(ii) on the grounds that the requirements of section 53(2) have not
been or are not being complied with,

may give such directions as the authority thinks fit as to the examination, retention, separation or return of the whole or any part of the
seized property.

(6) On any application under this section, the appropriate judicial authority may authorise the retention of any property which—

(a) has been seized in exercise, or purported exercise, of a relevant power of seizure, and
(b) would otherwise fall to be returned,

if that authority is satisfied that the retention of the property is justified on grounds falling within subsection (7).

(7) Those grounds are that (if the property were returned) it would immediately become appropriate—

(a) to issue, on the application of the person who is in possession of the property at the time of the application under this section, a warrant in pursuance of which, or of the exercise of which, it would be lawful to seize the property; or
(b) to make an order under—

(i) paragraph 4 of Schedule 1 to the 1984 Act,
(ii) paragraph 4 of Schedule 1 to the Police and Criminal Evidence (Northern Ireland) Order 1989 (S.I. 1989/1341 (N.I. 12)),
(iii) section 20BA of the Taxes Management Act 1970 (c. 9), or
(iv) paragraph 5 of Schedule 5 to the Terrorism Act 2000 (c. 11),

under which the property would fall to be delivered up or produced to the person mentioned in paragraph (a).

(8) Where any property which has been seized in exercise, or purported exercise, of a relevant power of seizure has parts ("part A" and "part B") comprised in it such that—

(a) it would be inappropriate, if the property were returned, to take any action such as is mentioned in subsection (7) in relation to part A,
(b) it would (or would but for the facts mentioned in paragraph (a)) be appropriate, if the property were returned, to take such action in relation to part B, and
(c) in all the circumstances, it is not reasonably practicable to separate part A from part B without prejudicing the use of part B for purposes for which it is lawful to use property seized under the power in question,

the facts mentioned in paragraph (a) shall not be taken into account by the appropriate judicial authority in deciding whether the retention of the property is justified on grounds falling within subsection (7).

(9) If a person fails to comply with any order or direction made or given by a judge of the Crown Court in exercise of any jurisdiction under this section—

(a) the authority may deal with him as if he had committed a contempt of the Crown Court; and
(b) any enactment relating to contempt of the Crown Court shall have effect in relation to the failure as if it were such a contempt.

(10) The relevant powers of seizure for the purposes of this section are—

(a) the powers of seizure conferred by sections 50 and 51;
(b) each of the powers of seizure specified in Parts 1 and 2 of Schedule 1; and
(c) any power of seizure (not falling within paragraph (a) or (b)) conferred

on a constable by or under any enactment, including an enactment passed after this Act.

(11) References in this section to a person with a relevant interest in seized property are references to—

(a) the person from whom it was seized;
(b) any person with an interest in the property; or
(c) any person, not falling within paragraph (a) or (b), who had custody or control of the property immediately before the seizure.

(12) For the purposes of subsection (11)(b), the persons who have an interest in seized property shall, in the case of property which is or contains an item subject to legal privilege, be taken to include the person in whose favour that privilege is conferred.

. . . . . .

Construction of Part 2

Meaning of "appropriate judicial authority"

64.—(1) Subject to subsection (2), in this Part "appropriate judicial authority" **119–017** means—

(a) in relation to England and Wales and Northern Ireland, a judge of the Crown Court;
(b) in relation to Scotland, a sheriff.

(2) In this Part "appropriate judicial authority", in relation to the seizure of items under any power mentioned in subsection (3) and in relation to items seized under any such power, means—

(a) in relation to England and Wales and Northern Ireland, the High Court;
(b) in relation to Scotland, the Court of Session.

(3) Those powers are—

(a) the powers of seizure conferred by—

(i) section 448(3) of the Companies Act 1985 (c. 6);
(ii) Article 441(3) of the Companies (Northern Ireland) Order 1986 (S.I. 1986/1032 (N.I. 6)); and
(iii) section 28(2) of the Competition Act 1998; and

(b) any power of seizure conferred by section 50, so far as that power is exercisable by reference to any power mentioned in paragraph (a).

International Criminal Court Act 2001

(2001, c. 17)

120–001 *An Act to give effect to the Statute of the International Criminal Court; to provide for offences under the law of England and Wales and Northern Ireland corresponding to offences within the jurisdiction of that Court; and for connected purposes.* [11th May 2001]

PART 1

THE INTERNATIONAL CRIMINAL COURT

The ICC and the ICC Statute

120–002   1.—(1) In this Act—

"the ICC" means the International Criminal Court established by the Statute of the International Criminal Court, done at Rome on 17th July 1998;

"the ICC Statute" means that Statute; and

"ICC crime" means a crime (other than the crime of aggression) over which the ICC has jurisdiction in accordance with the ICC Statute.

(2) References in this Act to articles are, unless otherwise indicated, to articles of the ICC Statute.

(3) Schedule 1 to this Act contains supplementary provisions relating to the ICC.

PART 2

ARREST AND DELIVERY OF PERSONS

Proceedings on request

Request for arrest and surrender

120–003   2.—(1) Where the Secretary of State receives a request from the ICC for the arrest and surrender of a person alleged to have committed an ICC crime, or to have been convicted by the ICC, he shall transmit the request and the documents accompanying it to an appropriate judicial officer.

(2) If it appears to the Secretary of State that the request should be considered by an appropriate judicial officer in Scotland, he shall transmit the request and the documents accompanying it to the Scottish Ministers who shall transmit them to an appropriate judicial officer.

(3) If the request is accompanied by a warrant of arrest and the appropriate judicial officer is satisfied that the warrant appears to have been issued by the ICC, he shall endorse the warrant for execution in the United Kingdom.

(4) If in the case of a person convicted by the ICC the request is not accompanied by a warrant of arrest, but is accompanied by—

(a) a copy of the judgment of conviction,

(b) information to demonstrate that the person sought is the one referred to in the judgment of conviction, and

(c) where the person sought has been sentenced, a copy of the sentence imposed and a statement of any time already served and the time remaining to be served, the officer shall issue a warrant for the arrest of the person to whom the request relates.

(5) In this Part a warrant endorsed or issued under this section is referred to as a "section 2 warrant".

Request for provisional arrest

3.—(1) This section applies where the Secretary of State receives from the **120–004** ICC a request for the provisional arrest of a person alleged to have committed an ICC crime or to have been convicted by the ICC.

(2) If it appears to the Secretary of State that application for a warrant should be made in England and Wales—

    (a) he shall transmit the request to a constable and direct the constable to apply for a warrant for the arrest of that person, and

    (b) on an application by a constable stating on oath that he has reason to believe—

        (i) that a request has been made on grounds of urgency by the ICC for the arrest of a person, and

        (ii) that the person is in, or on his way to, the United Kingdom,

an appropriate judicial officer shall issue a warrant for the arrest of that person.

(3) If it appears to the Secretary of State that application for a warrant should be made in Scotland—

    (a) he shall transmit the request to the Scottish Ministers who shall instruct the procurator fiscal to apply for a warrant for the arrest of that person, and

    (b) on the application by the procurator fiscal, which shall state—

        (i) that a request has been made on grounds of urgency by the ICC for the arrest of a person, and

        (ii) that the person is in, or on his way to, Scotland,

an appropriate judicial officer shall issue a warrant for the arrest of that person.

(4) Where an appropriate judicial officer issues a warrant under this section, he shall notify the Secretary of State and, where the proceedings are in Scotland, the Scottish Ministers that he has done so.

(5) In this Part a warrant issued under this section is referred to as a "provisional warrant".

Dealing with person arrested under provisional warrant

4.—(1) A person arrested under a provisional warrant shall be brought before **120–005** a competent court as soon as is practicable.

(2) If there is produced to the court a section 2 warrant in respect of that person, the court shall proceed as if he had been arrested under that warrant.

(3) If no such warrant is produced, the court shall remand him pending the production of such a warrant.

(4) Provision shall be made by Order in Council under paragraph 3 of Schedule 1 (power to make provision to give effect to Rules of Evidence and Procedure) specifying—

(a) the period for which a person may be so remanded at any time, and

(b) the total period for which a person may be so remanded,

having regard to the time limits specified in Rules of Evidence and Procedure for the purposes of article 92.3.

(5) If at any time when the person is so remanded there is produced to the court a section 2 warrant in respect of him—

(a) the court shall terminate the period of remand, and

(b) he shall be treated as if arrested under that warrant—

(i) if he was remanded in custody, at the time the warrant was produced to the court;

(ii) if he was remanded on bail, when he surrenders to his bail.

(6) If no such warrant is produced to the court before the end of the period of the remand (including any extension of that period), the court shall discharge him.

(7) The fact that a person has been discharged under this section does not prevent his subsequent arrest under a section 2 warrant.

Proceedings for delivery order

120–006 **5.**—(1) A person arrested under a section 2 warrant shall be brought before a competent court as soon as is practicable.

(2) If the competent court is satisfied—

(a) that the warrant—

(i) is a warrant of the ICC and has been duly endorsed under section 2(3), or

(ii) has been duly issued under section 2(4), and

(b) that the person brought before the court is the person named or described in the warrant,

it shall make a delivery order.

(3) A "delivery order" is an order that the person be delivered up—

(a) into the custody of the ICC, or

(b) if the ICC so directs in the case of a person convicted by the ICC, into the custody of the state of enforcement,

in accordance with arrangements made by the Secretary of State.

(4) In the case of a person alleged to have committed an ICC crime, the competent court may adjourn the proceedings pending the outcome of any challenge before the ICC to the admissibility of the case or to the jurisdiction of the ICC.

(5) In deciding whether to make a delivery order the court is not concerned to enquire—

(a) whether any warrant issued by the ICC was duly issued, or

(b) in the case of a person alleged to have committed an ICC crime, whether there is evidence to justify his trial for the offence he is alleged to have committed.

(6) Whether or not it makes a delivery order, the competent court may of its own motion, and shall on the application of the person arrested, determine—

(a) whether the person was lawfully arrested in pursuance of the warrant, and

(b) whether his rights have been respected.

(7) In making a determination under subsection (6) the court shall apply the principles which would be applied on an application for judicial review.

(8) If the court determines—

(a) that the person has not been lawfully arrested in pursuance of the warrant, or

(b) that the person's rights have not been respected,

it shall make a declaration or declarator to that effect, but may not grant any other relief.

(9) The court shall notify the Secretary of State (and, where the proceedings are in Scotland, the Scottish Ministers) of any declaration or declarator under subsection (8) and the Secretary of State shall transmit that notification to the ICC.

. . . . . .

Supplementary provisions

Provisions as to state or diplomatic immunity

23.—(1) Any state or diplomatic immunity attaching to a person by reason **120–007** of a connection with a state party to the ICC Statute does not prevent proceedings under this Part in relation to that person.

(2) Where—

(a) state or diplomatic immunity attaches to a person by reason of a connection with a state other than a state party to the ICC Statute, and

(b) waiver of that immunity is obtained by the ICC in relation to a request for that person's surrender,

the waiver shall be treated as extending to proceedings under this Part in connection with that request.

(3) A certificate by the Secretary of State—

(a) that a state is or is not a party to the ICC Statute, or

(b) that there has been such a waiver as is mentioned in subsection (2),

is conclusive evidence of that fact for the purposes of this Part.

(4) The Secretary of State may in any particular case, after consultation with the ICC and the state concerned, direct that proceedings (or further proceedings) under this Part which, but for subsection (1) or (2), would be prevented by state or diplomatic immunity attaching to a person shall not be taken against that person.

(5) The power conferred by section 1 of the United Nations Act 1946 (c. 45) (power to give effect by Order in Council to measures not involving the use of armed force) includes power to make in relation to any proceedings such provision corresponding to the provision made by this section in relation to the proceedings, but with the omission—

(a) in subsection (1), of the words "by reason of a connection with a state party to the ICC Statute", and

(b) of subsections (2) and (3),

as appears to Her Majesty to be necessary or expedient in consequence of such a referral as is mentioned in article 13(b) (referral by the United Nations Security Council).

(6) In this section "state or diplomatic immunity" means any privilege or immunity attaching to a person, by reason of the status of that person or another as head of state, or as representative, official or agent of a state, under—

  (a) the Diplomatic Privileges Act 1964 (c. 81), the Consular Relations Act 1968 (c. 18), the International Organisations Act 1968 (c.48) or the State Immunity Act 1978 (c.33),

  (b) any other legislative provision made for the purpose of implementing an international obligation, or

  (c) any rule of law derived from customary international law.

. . . . . .

PART 3

OTHER FORMS OF ASSISTANCE

Forms of assistance

Questioning

120–008 **28.**—(1) This section applies where the Secretary of State receives a request from the ICC for assistance in questioning a person being investigated or prosecuted.

(2) The person concerned shall not be questioned in pursuance of the request unless—

  (a) he has been informed of his rights under article 55, and

  (b) he consents to be interviewed.

(3) The provisions of article 55 are set out in Schedule 3 to this Act.

(4) Consent for the purposes of subsection (2)(b) may be given—

  (a) by the person himself, or

  (b) in circumstances in which it is inappropriate for the person to act for himself, by reason of his physical or mental condition or his youth, by an appropriate person acting on his behalf.

(5) Such consent may be given orally or in writing, but if given orally it shall be recorded in writing as soon as is reasonably practicable.

. . . . . .

PART 5

OFFENCES UNDER DOMESTIC LAW

England and Wales

Genocide, crimes against humanity and war crimes

120–009 **51.**—(1) It is an offence against the law of England and Wales for a person to commit genocide, a crime against humanity or a war crime.

(2) This section applies to acts committed—

(a) in England or Wales, or
(b) outside the United Kingdom by a United Kingdom national, a United Kingdom resident or a person subject to UK service jurisdiction.

. . . . . .

SCHEDULE 3

RIGHTS OF PERSONS DURING INVESTIGATION: ARTICLE 55

Article 55

Rights of persons during an investigation

1. In respect of an investigation under this Statute, a person: **120–010**

(a) Shall not be compelled to incriminate himself or herself or to confess guilt;
(b) Shall not be subjected to any form of coercion, duress or threat, to torture or to any other form of cruel, inhuman or degrading treatment or punishment;
(c) Shall, if questioned in a language other than a language the person fully understands and speaks, have, free of any cost, the assistance of a competent interpreter and such translations as are necessary to meet the requirements of fairness; and
(d) Shall not be subjected to arbitrary arrest or detention, and shall not be deprived of his or her liberty except on such grounds and in accordance with such procedures as are established in this Statute.

2. Where there are grounds to believe that a person has committed a crime within the jurisdiction of the Court and that person is about to be questioned either by the Prosecutor, or by national authorities pursuant to a request made under Part 9, that person shall also have the following rights of which he or she shall be informed prior to being questioned:

(a) To be informed, prior to being questioned, that there are grounds to believe that he or she has committed a crime within the jurisdiction of the Court;
(b) To remain silent, without such silence being a consideration in the determination of guilt or innocence;
(c) To have legal assistance of the person's choosing, or, if the person does not have legal assistance, to have legal assistance assigned to him or her, in any case where the interests of justice so require, and without payment by the person in any such case if the person does not have sufficient means to pay for it; and
(d) To be questioned in the presence of counsel unless the person has voluntarily waived his or her right to counsel.

Office of Communications Act 2002

(2002, c. 11)

An Act to establish a body corporate to be known as the Office of Communica- **121–001**
tions; and to confer functions in relation to proposals about the regulation
of communications on that body, on certain existing regulators and on the
Secretary of State. [March 19, 2002]

The Office of Communications

1.—(1) There shall be a body corporate to be known as the Office of Com- **121–002**
munications (in this Act referred to as "OFCOM").

(2) OFCOM shall consist of such number of members as the Secretary of State may determine; but he shall not determine a membership for OFCOM of less than three or more than six.

(3) The membership of OFCOM shall comprise—

(a) a chairman appointed by the Secretary of State;
(b) such number of other members appointed by the Secretary of State as he may determine; and
(c) the executive members.

(4) The executive members of OFCOM shall comprise—

(a) the chief executive of OFCOM; and
(b) such other persons (if any) as may be appointed to membership of OFCOM from amongst their employees.

(5) It shall be for the members of OFCOM mentioned in subsection (3)(a) and (b), after consulting the chief executive of OFCOM—

(a) to determine whether there should be any executive members falling within subsection (4)(b) and (subject to subsections (2) and (6)(a)) how many; and
(b) to make any appointments of executive members required for the purposes of any such determination.

(6) The Secretary of State—

(a) may, by a direction to OFCOM, set a maximum and a minimum number for the executive members of OFCOM; and
(b) shall exercise his powers under this section to secure that the number of executive members of OFCOM is, so far as practicable, at all times less than the number of other members.

(7) The Secretary of State may be order made by statutory instrument modify the numbers for the time being specified in subsection (2) as the maximum and minimum membership for OFCOM.

(8) A statutory instrument containing an order under subsection (7) shall be subject to annulment in pursuance of a resolution of either House of Parliament; and the power to make such an order shall include power to make such incidental, supplemental, consequential and transitional provision as the Secretary of State thinks fit.

(9) OFCOM shall not be treated for any purposes as a body exercising functions on behalf of the Crown; and, accordingly, no person shall be treated as a servant of the Crown by reason only of his membership of, or employment by, OFCOM.

(10) The Schedule (which makes provision in relation to OFCOM) shall have effect.

Initial function of OFCOM

121–003 2.—(1) It shall be the function of OFCOM (subject to subsection (5)) to do such things as they consider appropriate for facilitating the implementation of, or for securing the modification of, any relevant proposals about the regulation of communications.

(2) It shall be the duty of OFCOM to carry out their function under subsection (1) in such manner as—

   (a) appears to them to ensure, so far as they are facilitating the implementation of any such proposals, that there is effective co-operation in relation to the implementation of the proposals between themselves and both the existing regulators and the Secretary of State; and

   (b) does not interfere—

      (i) with the effective carrying out by the existing regulators of the functions conferred on them otherwise than by this Act; or

      (ii) with the effective carrying out by the Secretary of State of his functions relating to wireless telegraphy.

(3) In this Act references to relevant proposals about the regulation of communications are references to the following proposals (whether or not Parliament has given any approval on which the implementation of the proposals depends)—

   (a) any proposals by the Secretary of State for the conferring on OFCOM (whether by transfers from the existing regulators or otherwise) of any functions relating to telecommunications, wireless telegraphy, broadcasting, radio and television services or other activities connected with the communications industry; and

   (b) any other proposals by the Secretary of State made in association with any proposals falling within paragraph (a) and relating to the subject-matter of those proposals, to any matters that are incidental or supplemental to those proposals or to any consequential or transitional matters.

(4) Subject to subsections (5) and (6), OFCOM shall have power, for the purpose of carrying out their function under subsection (1), to do such things as appear to them to be incidental or conducive to the carrying out of that function.

(5) Nothing in this section shall be taken, in relation to proposals that have not yet been approved by Parliament—

   (a) as dispensing with the need for any Parliamentary approval otherwise required for the implementation of the proposals; or

   (b) as authorising OFCOM, before any such approval is given, to engage in any activities other than activities which are connected with, or consist in, either—

      (i) the formulation of the proposals; or

      (ii) the taking of preparatory steps towards their implementation when approved.

(6) OFCOM shall not have any power, for the purposes of or in connection with their function under this section, to borrow money from any person other than the Secretary of State.

. . . . . .

OTHER MATERIALS

The Constitution of the United States of America

We the people of the United States, in order to form a more perfect union, **122–001** establish justice, insure domestic tranquility, provide for the common defense, promote the general welfare, and secure the blessings of liberty to ourselves and our posterity, do ordain and establish this Constitution for the United States of America.

Article I

Section 1.

All legislative powers herein granted shall be vested in a Congress of the **122–002** United States, which shall consist of a Senate and House of Representatives.

Section 2.

The House of Representatives shall be composed of members chosen every **122–003** second year by the people of the several states, and the electors in each state shall have the qualifications requisite for electors of the most numerous branch of the state legislature.

No person shall be a Representative who shall not have attained to the age of twenty five years, and been seven years a citizen of the United States, and who shall not, when elected, be an inhabitant of that state in which he shall be chosen.

Representatives and direct taxes shall be apportioned among the several states which may be included within this union, according to their respective numbers, which shall be determined by adding to the whole number of free persons, including those bound to service for a term of years, and excluding Indians not taxed, three fifths of all other Persons. The actual Enumeration shall be made within three years after the first meeting of the Congress of the United States, and within every subsequent term of ten years, in such manner as they shall by law direct. The number of Representatives shall not exceed one for every thirty thousand, but each state shall have at least one Representative; and until such enumeration shall be made, the state of New Hampshire shall be entitled to choose three, Massachusetts eight, Rhode Island and Providence Plantations one, Connecticut five, New York six, New Jersey four, Pennsylvania eight, Delaware one, Maryland six, Virginia ten, North Carolina five, South Carolina five, and Georgia three.

When vacancies happen in the Representation from any state, the executive authority thereof shall issue writs of election to fill such vacancies.

The House of Representatives shall choose their speaker and other officers; and shall have the sole power of impeachment.

Section 3.

The Senate of the United States shall be composed of two Senators from each **122–004** state, chosen by the legislature thereof, for six years; and each Senator shall have one vote.

Immediately after they shall be assembled in consequence of the first election, they shall be divided as equally as may be into three classes. The seats of the Senators of the first class shall be vacated at the expiration of the second year, of the second class at the expiration of the fourth year, and the third class at the expiration of the sixth year, so that one third may be chosen every second year; and if vacancies happen by resignation, or otherwise, during the recess of the legislature of any state, the executive thereof may make temporary appointments until the next meeting of the legislature, which shall then fill such vacancies.

No person shall be a Senator who shall not have attained to the age of thirty years, and been nine years a citizen of the United States and who shall not, when elected, be an inhabitant of that state for which he shall be chosen.

The Vice President of the United States shall be President of the Senate, but shall have no vote, unless they be equally divided.

The Senate shall choose their other officers, and also a President pro tempore, in the absence of the Vice President, or when he shall exercise the office of President of the United States.

The Senate shall have the sole power to try all impeachments. When sitting for that purpose, they shall be on oath or affirmation. When the President of the United States is tried, the Chief Justice shall preside: And no person shall be convicted without the concurrence of two thirds of the members present.

Judgment in cases of impeachment shall not extend further than to removal from office, and disqualification to hold and enjoy any office of honor, trust or profit under the United States: but the party convicted shall nevertheless be liable and subject to indictment, trial, judgment and punishment, according to law.

Section 4.

122–005 The times, places and manner of holding elections for Senators and Representatives, shall be prescribed in each state by the legislature thereof; but the Congress may at any time by law make or alter such regulations, except as to the places of choosing Senators.

The Congress shall assemble at least once in every year, and such meeting shall be on the first Monday in December, unless they shall by law appoint a different day.

Section 5.

122–006 Each House shall be the judge of the elections, returns and qualifications of its own members, and a majority of each shall constitute a quorum to do business; but a smaller number may adjourn from day to day, and may be authorized to compel the attendance of absent members, in such manner, and under such penalties as each House may provide.

Each House may determine the rules of its proceedings, punish its members for disorderly behavior, and, with the concurrence of two thirds, expel a member.

Each House shall keep a journal of its proceedings, and from time to time publish the same, excepting such parts as may in their judgment require secrecy; and the yeas and nays of the members of either House on any question shall, at the desire of one fifth of those present, be entered on the journal.

Neither House, during the session of Congress, shall, without the consent of the other, adjourn for more than three days, nor to any other place than that in which the two Houses shall be sitting.

Section 6.

122–007 The Senators and Representatives shall receive a compensation for their services, to be ascertained by law, and paid out of the treasury of the United

States. They shall in all cases, except treason, felony and breach of the peace, be privileged from arrest during their attendance at the session of their respective Houses, and in going to and returning from the same; and for any speech or debate in either House, they shall not be questioned in any other place.

No Senator or Representative shall, during the time for which he was elected, be appointed to any civil office under the authority of the United States, which shall have been created, or the emoluments whereof shall have been increased during such time: and no person holding any office under the United States, shall be a member of either House during his continuance in office.

Section 7.

All bills for raising revenue shall originate in the House of Representatives; **122–008** but the Senate may propose or concur with amendments as on other Bills.

Every bill which shall have passed the House of Representatives and the Senate, shall, before it become a law, be presented to the President of the United States; if he approve he shall sign it, but if not he shall return it, with his objections to that House in which it shall have originated, who shall enter the objections at large on their journal, and proceed to reconsider it. If after such reconsideration two thirds of that House shall agree to pass the bill, it shall be sent, together with the objections, to the other House, by which it shall likewise be reconsidered, and if approved by two thirds of that House, it shall become a law. But in all such cases the votes of both Houses shall be determined by yeas and nays, and the names of the persons voting for and against the bill shall be entered on the journal of each House respectively. If any bill shall not be returned by the President within ten days (Sundays excepted) after it shall have been presented to him, the same shall be a law, in like manner as if he had signed it, unless the Congress by their adjournment prevent its return, in which case it shall not be a law.

Every order, resolution, or vote to which the concurrence of the Senate and House of Representatives may be necessary (except on a question of adjournment) shall be presented to the President of the United States; and before the same shall take effect, shall be approved by him, or being disapproved by him, shall be repassed by two thirds of the Senate and House of Representatives, according to the rules and limitations prescribed in the case of a bill.

Section 8.

The Congress shall have power to lay and collect taxes, duties, imposts and **122–009** excises, to pay the debts and provide for the common defense and general welfare of the United States; but all duties, imposts and excises shall be uniform throughout the United States;

To borrow money on the credit of the United States;

To regulate commerce with foreign nations, and among the several states, and with the Indian tribes;

To establish a uniform rule of naturalization, and uniform laws on the subject of bankruptcies throughout the United States;

To coin money, regulate the value thereof, and of foreign coin, and fix the standard of weights and measures;

To provide for the punishment of counterfeiting the securities and current coin of the United States;

To establish post offices and post roads;

To promote the progress of science and useful arts, by securing for limited times to authors and inventors the exclusive right to their respective writings and discoveries;

To constitute tribunals inferior to the Supreme Court;

To define and punish piracies and felonies committed on the high seas, and offenses against the law of nations;

To declare war, grant letters of marque and reprisal, and make rules concerning captures on land and water;

To raise and support armies, but no appropriation of money to that use shall be for a longer term than two years;

To provide and maintain a navy;

To make rules for the government and regulation of the land and naval forces;

To provide for calling forth the militia to execute the laws of the union, suppress insurrections and repel invasions;

To provide for organizing, arming, and disciplining, the militia, and for governing such part of them as may be employed in the service of the United States, reserving to the states respectively, the appointment of the officers, and the authority of training the militia according to the discipline prescribed by Congress;

To exercise exclusive legislation in all cases whatsoever, over such District (not exceeding ten miles square) as may, by cession of particular states, and the acceptance of Congress, become the seat of the government of the United States, and to exercise like authority over all places purchased by the consent of the legislature of the state in which the same shall be, for the erection of forts, magazines, arsenals, dockyards, and other needful buildings;—And

To make all laws which shall be necessary and proper for carrying into execution the foregoing powers, and all other powers vested by this Constitution in the government of the United States, or in any department or officer thereof.

Section 9.

122–010 The migration or importation of such persons as any of the states now existing shall think proper to admit, shall not be prohibited by the Congress prior to the year one thousand eight hundred and eight, but a tax or duty may be imposed on such importation, not exceeding ten dollars for each person.

The privilege of the writ of habeas corpus shall not be suspended, unless when in cases of rebellion or invasion the public safety may require it.

No bill of attainder or ex post facto Law shall be passed.

No capitation, or other direct, tax shall be laid, unless in proportion to the census or enumeration herein before directed to be taken.

No tax or duty shall be laid on articles exported from any state.

No preference shall be given by any regulation of commerce or revenue to the ports of one state over those of another: nor shall vessels bound to, or from, one state, be obliged to enter, clear or pay duties in another.

No money shall be drawn from the treasury, but in consequence of appropriations made by law; and a regular statement and account of receipts and expenditures of all public money shall be published from time to time.

No title of nobility shall be granted by the United States: and no person holding any office of profit or trust under them, shall, without the consent of the Congress, accept of any present, emolument, office, or title, of any kind whatever, from any king, prince, or foreign state.

Section 10.

122–011 No state shall enter into any treaty, alliance, or confederation; grant letters of marque and reprisal; coin money; emit bills of credit; make anything but gold and silver coin a tender in payment of debts; pass any bill of attainder, ex post facto law, or law impairing the obligation of contracts, or grant any title of nobility.

No state shall, without the consent of the Congress, lay any imposts or duties on imports or exports, except what may be absolutely necessary for executing it's inspection laws: and the net produce of all duties and imposts, laid by any state on imports or exports, shall be for the use of the treasury of the United States; and all such laws shall be subject to the revision and control of the Congress.

No state shall, without the consent of Congress, lay any duty of tonnage, keep troops, or ships of war in time of peace, enter into any agreement or compact with another state, or with a foreign power, or engage in war, unless actually invaded, or in such imminent danger as will not admit of delay.

Article II

Section 1.

The executive power shall be vested in a President of the United States of **122–012** America. He shall hold his office during the term of four years, and, together with the Vice President, chosen for the same term, be elected, as follows:

Each state shall appoint, in such manner as the Legislature thereof may direct, a number of electors, equal to the whole number of Senators and Representatives to which the State may be entitled in the Congress: but no Senator or Representative, or person holding an office of trust or profit under the United States, shall be appointed an elector.

The electors shall meet in their respective states, and vote by ballot for two persons, of whom one at least shall not be an inhabitant of the same state with themselves. And they shall make a list of all the persons voted for, and of the number of votes for each; which list they shall sign and certify, and transmit sealed to the seat of the government of the United States, directed to the President of the Senate. The President of the Senate shall, in the presence of the Senate and House of Representatives, open all the certificates, and the votes shall then be counted. The person having the greatest number of votes shall be the President, if such number be a majority of the whole number of electors appointed; and if there be more than one who have such majority, and have an equal number of votes, then the House of Representatives shall immediately choose by ballot one of them for President; and if no person have a majority, then from the five highest on the list the said House shall in like manner choose the President. But in choosing the President, the votes shall be taken by states, the representation from each state having one vote; A quorum for this purpose shall consist of a member or members from two thirds of the states, and a majority of all the states shall be necessary to a choice. In every case, after the choice of the President, the person having the greatest number of votes of the electors shall be the Vice President. But if there should remain two or more who have equal votes, the Senate shall choose from them by ballot the Vice President.

The Congress may determine the time of choosing the electors, and the day on which they shall give their votes; which day shall be the same throughout the United States. No person except a natural born citizen, or a citizen of the United States, at the time of the adoption of this Constitution, shall be eligible to the office of President; neither shall any person be eligible to that office who shall not have attained to the age of thirty five years, and been fourteen Years a resident within the United States.

In case of the removal of the President from office, or of his death, resignation, or inability to discharge the powers and duties of the said office, the same shall devolve on the Vice President, and the Congress may by law provide for the case of removal, death, resignation or inability, both of the President and Vice President, declaring what officer shall then act as President, and such officer shall act accordingly, until the disability be removed, or a President shall be elected.

The President shall, at stated times, receive for his services, a compensation, which shall neither be increased nor diminished during the period for which he shall have been elected, and he shall not receive within that period any other emolument from the United States, or any of them.

Before he enter on the execution of his office, he shall take the following oath or affirmation:—"I do solemnly swear (or affirm) that I will faithfully execute the office of President of the United States, and will to the best of my ability, preserve, protect and defend the Constitution of the United States."

Section 2.

122–013   The President shall be commander in chief of the Army and Navy of the United States, and of the militia of the several states, when called into the actual service of the United States; he may require the opinion, in writing, of the principal officer in each of the executive departments, upon any subject relating to the duties of their respective offices, and he shall have power to grant reprieves and pardons for offenses against the United States, except in cases of impeachment.

He shall have power, by and with the advice and consent of the Senate, to make treaties, provided two thirds of the Senators present concur; and he shall nominate, and by and with the advice and consent of the Senate, shall appoint ambassadors, other public ministers and consuls, judges of the Supreme Court, and all other officers of the United States, whose appointments are not herein otherwise provided for, and which shall be established by law: but the Congress may by law vest the appointment of such inferior officers, as they think proper, in the President alone, in the courts of law, or in the heads of departments.

The President shall have power to fill up all vacancies that may happen during the recess of the Senate, by granting commissions which shall expire at the end of their next session.

Section 3.

122–014   He shall from time to time give to the Congress information of the state of the union, and recommend to their consideration such measures as he shall judge necessary and expedient; he may, on extraordinary occasions, convene both Houses, or either of them, and in case of disagreement between them, with respect to the time of adjournment, he may adjourn them to such time as he shall think proper; he shall receive ambassadors and other public ministers; he shall take care that the laws be faithfully executed, and shall commission all the officers of the United States.

Section 4.

122–015   The President, Vice President and all civil officers of the United States, shall be removed from office on impeachment for, and conviction of, treason, bribery, or other high crimes and misdemeanors.

Article III

Section 1.

122–016   The judicial power of the United States, shall be vested in one Supreme Court, and in such inferior courts as the Congress may from time to time ordain and establish. The judges, both of the supreme and inferior courts, shall hold their offices during good behaviour, and shall, at stated times, receive for their services, a compensation, which shall not be diminished during their continuance in office.

Section 2.

The judicial power shall extend to all cases, in law and equity, arising under **122–017** this Constitution, the laws of the United States, and treaties made, or which shall be made, under their authority;—to all cases affecting ambassadors, other public ministers and consuls;—to all cases of admiralty and maritime jurisdiction;—to controversies to which the United States shall be a party;—to controversies between two or more states;—between a state and citizens of another state;—between citizens of different states;—between citizens of the same state claiming lands under grants of different states, and between a state, or the citizens thereof, and foreign states, citizens or subjects.

In all cases affecting ambassadors, other public ministers and consuls, and those in which a state shall be party, the Supreme Court shall have original jurisdiction. In all the other cases before mentioned, the Supreme Court shall have appellate jurisdiction, both as to law and fact, with such exceptions, and under such regulations as the Congress shall make.

The trial of all crimes, except in cases of impeachment, shall be by jury; and such trial shall be held in the state where the said crimes shall have been committed; but when not committed within any state, the trial shall be at such place or places as the Congress may by law have directed.

Section 3.

Treason against the United States, shall consist only in levying war against **122–018** them, or in adhering to their enemies, giving them aid and comfort. No person shall be convicted of treason unless on the testimony of two witnesses to the same overt act, or on confession in open court.

The Congress shall have power to declare the punishment of treason, but no attainder of treason shall work corruption of blood, or forfeiture except during the life of the person attainted.

Article IV

Section 1.

Full faith and credit shall be given in each state to the public acts, records, **122–019** and judicial proceedings of every other state. And the Congress may by general laws prescribe the manner in which such acts, records, and proceedings shall be proved, and the effect thereof.

Section 2.

The citizens of each state shall be entitled to all privileges and immunities of **122–020** citizens in the several states.

A person charged in any state with treason, felony, or other crime, who shall flee from justice, and be found in another state, shall on demand of the executive authority of the state from which he fled, be delivered up, to be removed to the state having jurisdiction of the crime.

No person held to service or labor in one state, under the laws thereof, escaping into another, shall, in consequence of any law or regulation therein, be discharged from such service or labor, but shall be delivered up on claim of the party to whom such service or labor may be due.

Section 3.

122–021   New states may be admitted by the Congress into this union; but no new states shall be formed or erected within the jurisdiction of any other state; nor any state be formed by the junction of two or more states, or parts of states, without the consent of the legislatures of the states concerned as well as of the Congress.

Congress.
The Congress shall have power to dispose of and make all needful rules and regulations respecting the territory or other property belonging to the United States; and nothing in this Constitution shall be so construed as to prejudice any claims of the United States, or of any particular state.

Section 4.

122–022   The United States shall guarantee to every state in this union a republican form of government, and shall protect each of them against invasion; and on application of the legislature, or of the executive (when the legislature cannot be convened) against domestic violence.

Article V

122–023   The Congress, whenever two thirds of both houses shall deem it necessary, shall propose amendments to this Constitution, or, on the application of the legislatures of two thirds of the several states, shall call a convention for proposing amendments, which, in either case, shall be valid to all intents and purposes, as part of this Constitution, when ratified by the legislatures of three fourths of the several states, or by conventions in three fourths thereof, as the one or the other mode of ratification may be proposed by the Congress; provided that no amendment which may be made prior to the year one thousand eight hundred and eight shall in any manner affect the first and fourth clauses in the ninth section of the first article; and that no state, without its consent, shall be deprived of its equal suffrage in the Senate.

Article VI

122–024   All debts contracted and engagements entered into, before the adoption of this Constitution, shall be as valid against the United States under this Constitution, as under the Confederation.

This Constitution, and the laws of the United States which shall be made in pursuance thereof; and all treaties made, or which shall be made, under the authority of the United States, shall be the supreme law of the land; and the judges in every state shall be bound thereby, anything in the Constitution or laws of any State to the contrary notwithstanding.

The Senators and Representatives before mentioned, and the members of the several state legislatures, and all executive and judicial officers, both of the United States and of the several states, shall be bound by oath or affirmation, to support this Constitution; but no religious test shall ever be required as a qualification to any office or public trust under the United States.

Article VII

122–025   The ratification of the conventions of nine states, shall be sufficient for the establishment of this Constitution between the states so ratifying the same.

Amendment I

Congress shall make no law respecting an establishment of religion, or prohib- **122–026**
iting the free exercise thereof; or abridging the freedom of speech, or of the
press; or the right of the people peaceably to assemble, and to petition the
government for a redress of grievances.

Amendment II

A well regulated militia, being necessary to the security of a free state, the **122–027**
right of the people to keep and bear arms, shall not be infringed.

Amendment III

No soldier shall, in time of peace be quartered in any house, without the **122–028**
consent of the owner, nor in time of war, but in a manner to be prescribed by
law.

Amendment IV

The right of the people to be secure in their persons, houses, papers, and **122–029**
effects, against unreasonable searches and seizures, shall not be violated, and
no warrants shall issue, but upon probable cause, supported by oath or affirmation, and particularly describing the place to be searched, and the persons or
things to be seized.

Amendment V

No person shall be held to answer for a capital, or otherwise infamous crime, **122–030**
unless on a presentment or indictment of a grand jury, except in cases arising
in the land or naval forces, or in the militia, when in actual service in time of
war or public danger; nor shall any person be subject for the same offense to be
twice put in jeopardy of life or limb; nor shall be compelled in any criminal
case to be a witness against himself, nor be deprived of life, liberty, or property,
without due process of law; nor shall private property be taken for public use,
without just compensation.

Amendment VI

In all criminal prosecutions, the accused shall enjoy the right to a speedy and **122–031**
public trial, by an impartial jury of the state and district wherein the crime shall
have been committed, which district shall have been previously ascertained by
law, and to be informed of the nature and cause of the accusation; to be confronted with the witnesses against him; to have compulsory process for obtaining
witnesses in his favor, and to have the assistance of counsel for his defense.

Amendment VII

In suits at common law, where the value in controversy shall exceed twenty **122–032**
dollars, the right of trial by jury shall be preserved, and no fact tried by a jury,
shall be otherwise reexamined in any court of the United States, than according
to the rules of the common law.

Amendment VIII

Excessive bail shall not be required, nor excessive fines imposed, nor cruel **122–033**
and unusual punishments inflicted.

Amendment IX

122–034   The enumeration in the Constitution, of certain rights, shall not be construed to deny or disparage others retained by the people.

Amendment X

122–035   The powers not delegated to the United States by the Constitution, nor prohibited by it to the states, are reserved to the states respectively, or to the people.

. . . . . .

Amendment XIV

Section 1.

122–036   All persons born or naturalized in the United States, and subject to the jurisdiction thereof, are citizens of the United States and of the state wherein they reside. No state shall make or enforce any law which shall abridge the privileges or immunities of citizens of the United States; nor shall any state deprive any person of life, liberty, or property, without due process of law; nor deny to any person within its jurisdiction the equal protection of the laws.

Section 2.

122–037   Representatives shall be apportioned among the several states according to their respective numbers, counting the whole number of persons in each state, excluding Indians not taxed. But when the right to vote at any election for the choice of electors for President and Vice President of the United States, Representatives in Congress, the executive and judicial officers of a state, or the members of the legislature thereof, is denied to any of the male inhabitants of such state, being twenty-one years of age, and citizens of the United States, or in any way abridged, except for participation in rebellion, or other crime, the basis of representation therein shall be reduced in the proportion which the number of such male citizens shall bear to the whole number of male citizens twenty-one years of age in such state.

Section 3.

122–038   No person shall be a Senator or Representative in Congress, or elector of President and Vice President, or hold any office, civil or military, under the United States, or under any state, who, having previously taken an oath, as a member of Congress, or as an officer of the United States, or as a member of any state legislature, or as an executive or judicial officer of any state, to support the Constitution of the United States, shall have engaged in insurrection or rebellion against the same, or given aid or comfort to the enemies thereof. But Congress may by a vote of two-thirds of each House, remove such disability.

Section 4.

122–039   The validity of the public debt of the United States, authorized by law, including debts incurred for payment of pensions and bounties for services in suppressing insurrection or rebellion, shall not be questioned. But neither the United States nor any state shall assume or pay any debt or obligation incurred in aid of insurrection or rebellion against the United States, or any claim for the loss or emancipation of any slave; but all such debts, obligations and claims shall be held illegal and void.

Section 5.

The Congress shall have power to enforce, by appropriate legislation, the **122–040** provisions of this article.

Convention for the Protection of Human Rights and Fundamental Freedoms as amended by Protocol No. 11 with Protocol Nos. 1, 4, 6 and 7

The governments signatory hereto, being members of the Council of Europe, **123–001**
Considering the Universal Declaration of Human Rights proclaimed by the General Assembly of the United Nations on 10th December 1948;

Considering that this Declaration aims at securing the universal and effective recognition and observance of the Rights therein declared;

Considering that the aim of the Council of Europe is the achievement of greater unity between its members and that one of the methods by which that aim is to be pursued is the maintenance and further realisation of human rights and fundamental freedoms;

Reaffirming their profound belief in those fundamental freedoms which are the foundation of justice and peace in the world and are best maintained on the one hand by an effective political democracy and on the other by a common understanding and observance of the human rights upon which they depend;

Being resolved, as the governments of European countries which are like-minded and have a common heritage of political traditions, ideals, freedom and the rule of law, to take the first steps for the collective enforcement of certain of the rights stated in the Universal Declaration,

Have agreed as follows:

Article 1

Obligation to respect human rights

The High Contracting Parties shall secure to everyone within their jurisdiction **123–002** the rights and freedoms defined in Section I of this Convention.

SECTION I

RIGHTS AND FREEDOMS

Article 2

Right to life

1. Everyone's right to life shall be protected by law. No one shall be deprived **123–003** of his life intentionally save in the execution of a sentence of a court following his conviction of a crime for which this penalty is provided by law.

2. Deprivation of life shall not be regarded as inflicted in contravention of this article when it results from the use of force which is no more than absolutely necessary:

    (a) in defence of any person from unlawful violence;

    (b) in order to effect a lawful arrest or to prevent the escape of a person lawfully detained;

    (c) in action lawfully taken for the purpose of quelling a riot or insurrection.

Article 3

Prohibition of torture

123–004   No one shall be subjected to torture or to inhuman or degrading treatment or punishment.

Article 4

Prohibition of slavery and forced labour

123–005   1. No one shall be held in slavery or servitude.

    2. No one shall be required to perform forced or compulsory labour.

    3. For the purpose of this article the term "forced or compulsory labour" shall not include:

    (a) any work required to be done in the ordinary course of detention imposed according to the provisions of Article 5 of this Convention or during conditional release from such detention;

    (b) any service of a military character or, in case of conscientious objectors in countries where they are recognised, service exacted instead of compulsory military service;

    (c) any service exacted in case of an emergency or calamity threatening the life or well-being of the community;

    (d) any work or service which forms part of normal civic obligations.

Article 5

Right to liberty and security

123–006   1. Everyone has the right to liberty and security of person. No one shall be deprived of his liberty save in the following cases and in accordance with a procedure prescribed by law:

    (a) the lawful detention of a person after conviction by a competent court;

    (b) the lawful arrest or detention of a person for non-compliance with the lawful order of a court or in order to secure the fulfilment of any obligation prescribed by law;

    (c) the lawful arrest or detention of a person effected for the purpose of bringing him before the competent legal authority on reasonable suspicion of having committed an offence or when it is reasonably considered necessary to prevent his committing an offence or fleeing after having done so;

    (d) the detention of a minor by lawful order for the purpose of educational supervision or his lawful detention for the purpose of bringing him before the competent legal authority;

    (e) the lawful detention of persons for the prevention of the spreading of infectious diseases, of persons of unsound mind, alcoholics or drug addicts or vagrants;

    (f) the lawful arrest or detention of a person to prevent his effecting an unauthorised entry into the country or of a person against whom action is being taken with a view to deportation or extradition.

2. Everyone who is arrested shall be informed promptly, in a language which he understands, of the reasons for his arrest and of any charge against him.

3. Everyone arrested or detained in accordance with the provisions of paragraph 1.(c) of this article shall be brought promptly before a judge or other officer authorised by law to exercise judicial power and shall be entitled to trial within a reasonable time or to release pending trial. Release may be conditioned by guarantees to appear for trial.

4. Everyone who is deprived of his liberty by arrest or detention shall be entitled to take proceedings by which the lawfulness of his detention shall be decided speedily by a court and his release ordered if the detention is not lawful.

5. Everyone who has been the victim of arrest or detention in contravention of the provisions of this article shall have an enforceable right to compensation.

Article 6

Right to a fair trial

1. In the determination of his civil rights and obligations or of any criminal **123–007** charge against him, everyone is entitled to a fair and public hearing within a reasonable time by an independent and impartial tribunal established by law. Judgment shall be pronounced publicly but the press and public may be excluded from all or part of the trial in the interests of morals, public order or national security in a democratic society, where the interests of juveniles or the protection of the private life of the parties so require, or to the extent strictly necessary in the opinion of the court in special circumstances where publicity would prejudice the interests of justice.

2. Everyone charged with a criminal offence shall be presumed innocent until proved guilty according to law.

3. Everyone charged with a criminal offence has the following minimum rights:

(a) to be informed promptly, in a language which he understands and in detail, of the nature and cause of the accusation against him;

(b) to have adequate time and facilities for the preparation of his defence;

(c) to defend himself in person or through legal assistance of his own choosing or, if he has not sufficient means to pay for legal assistance, to be given it free when the interests of justice so require;

(d) to examine or have examined witnesses against him and to obtain the attendance and examination of witnesses on his behalf under the same conditions as witnesses against him;

(e) to have the free assistance of an interpreter if he cannot understand or speak the language used in court.

Article 7

No punishment without law

1. No one shall be held guilty of any criminal offence on account of any **123–008** act or omission which did not constitute a criminal offence under national or international law at the time when it was committed. Nor shall a heavier penalty be imposed than the one that was applicable at the time the criminal offence was committed.

2. This article shall not prejudice the trial and punishment of any person for any act or omission which, at the time when it was committed, was criminal according to the general principles of law recognised by civilised nations.

Article 8

Right to respect for private and family life

123–009 1. Everyone has the right to respect for his private and family life, his home and his correspondence.

2. There shall be no interference by a public authority with the exercise of this right except such as is in accordance with the law and is necessary in a democratic society in the interests of national security, public safety or the economic well-being of the country, for the prevention of disorder or crime, for the protection of health or morals, or for the protection of the rights and freedoms of others.

Article 9

Freedom of thought, conscience and religion

123–010 1. Everyone has the right to freedom of thought, conscience and religion; this right includes freedom to change his religion or belief and freedom, either alone or in community with others and in public or private, to manifest his religion or belief, in worship, teaching, practice and observance.

2. Freedom to manifest one's religion or beliefs shall be subject only to such limitations as are prescribed by law and are necessary in a democratic society in the interests of public safety, for the protection of public order, health or morals, or for the protection of the rights and freedoms of others.

Article 10

Freedom of expression

123–011 1. Everyone has the right to freedom of expression. This right shall include freedom to hold opinions and to receive and impart information and ideas without interference by public authority and regardless of frontiers. This article shall not prevent States from requiring the licensing of broadcasting, television or cinema enterprises.

2. The exercise of these freedoms, since it carries with it duties and responsibilities, may be subject to such formalities, conditions, restrictions or penalties as are prescribed by law and are necessary in a democratic society, in the interests of national security, territorial integrity or public safety, for the prevention of disorder or crime, for the protection of health or morals, for the protection of the reputation or rights of others, for preventing the disclosure of information received in confidence, or for maintaining the authority and impartiality of the judiciary.

Article 11

Freedom of assembly and association

123–012 1. Everyone has the right to freedom of peaceful assembly and to freedom of association with others, including the right to form and to join trade unions for the protection of his interests.

2. No restrictions shall be placed on the exercise of these rights other than such as are prescribed by law and are necessary in a democratic society in the interests of national security or public safety, for the prevention of disorder or crime, for the protection of health or morals or for the protection of the rights and freedoms of others. This article shall not prevent the imposition of lawful

restrictions on the exercise of these rights by members of the armed forces, of the police or of the administration of the State.

Article 12

Right to marry

Men and women of marriageable age have the right to marry and to found a family, according to the national laws governing the exercise of this right.   **123–013**

Article 13

Right to an effective remedy

Everyone whose rights and freedoms as set forth in this Convention are viol- **123–014** ated shall have an effective remedy before a national authority notwithstanding that the violation has been committed by persons acting in an official capacity.

Article 14

Prohibition of discrimination

The enjoyment of the rights and freedoms set forth in this Convention shall **123–015** be secured without discrimination on any ground such as sex, race, colour, language, religion, political or other opinion, national or social origin, association with a national minority, property, birth or other status.

Article 15

Derogation in time of emergency

1. In time of war or other public emergency threatening the life of the nation **123–016** any High Contracting Party may take measures derogating from its obligations under this Convention to the extent strictly required by the exigencies of the situation, provided that such measures are not inconsistent with its other obligations under international law.

2. No derogation from Article 2, except in respect of deaths resulting from lawful acts of war, or from Articles 3, 4 (paragraph 1) and 7 shall be made under this provision.

3. Any High Contracting Party availing itself of this right of derogation shall keep the Secretary General of the Council of Europe fully informed of the measures which it has taken and the reasons therefor. It shall also inform the Secretary General of the Council of Europe when such measures have ceased to operate and the provisions of the Convention are again being fully executed.

Article 16

Restrictions on political activity of aliens

Nothing in Articles 10, 11 and 14 shall be regarded as preventing the High **123–017** Contracting Parties from imposing restrictions on the political activity of aliens.

Article 17

Prohibition of abuse of rights

Nothing in this Convention may be interpreted as implying for any State, **123–018** group or person any right to engage in any activity or perform any act aimed at the destruction of any of the rights and freedoms set forth herein or at their limitation to a greater extent than is provided for in the Convention.

Article 18

Limitation on use of restrictions on rights

123–019   The restrictions permitted under this Convention to the said rights and freedoms shall not be applied for any purpose other than those for which they have been prescribed.

SECTION II

EUROPEAN COURT OF HUMAN RIGHTS

Article 19

Establishment of the Court

123–020   To ensure the observance of the engagements undertaken by the High Contracting Parties in the Convention and the Protocols thereto, there shall be set up a European Court of Human Rights, hereinafter referred to as "the Court". It shall function on a permanent basis.

Article 20

Number of judges

123–021   The Court shall consist of a number of judges equal to that of the High Contracting Parties.

Article 21

Criteria for office

123–022   1. The judges shall be of high moral character and must either possess the qualifications required for appointment to high judicial office or be jurisconsults of recognised competence.
2. The judges shall sit on the Court in their individual capacity.
3. During their term of office the judges shall not engage in any activity which is incompatible with their independence, impartiality or with the demands of a full-time office; all questions arising from the application of this paragraph shall be decided by the Court.

Article 22

Election of judges

123–023   1. The judges shall be elected by the Parliamentary Assembly with respect to each High Contracting Party by a majority of votes cast from a list of three candidates nominated by the High Contracting Party.
2. The same procedure shall be followed to complete the Court in the event of the accession of new High Contracting Parties and in filling casual vacancies.

Article 23

Terms of office

1. The judges shall be elected for a period of six years. They may be re-elected. However, the terms of office of one-half of the judges elected at the first election shall expire at the end of three years.

2. The judges whose terms of office are to expire at the end of the initial period of three years shall be chosen by lot by the Secretary General of the Council of Europe immediately after their election.

3. In order to ensure that, as far as possible, the terms of office of one-half of the judges are renewed every three years, the Parliamentary Assembly may decide, before proceeding to any subsequent election, that the term or terms of office of one or more judges to be elected shall be for a period other than six years but not more than nine and not less than three years.

4. In cases where more than one term of office is involved and where the Parliamentary Assembly applies the preceding paragraph, the allocation of the terms of office shall be effected by a drawing of lots by the Secretary General of the Council of Europe immediately after the election.

5. A judge elected to replace a judge whose term of office has not expired shall hold office for the remainder of his predecessor's term.

6. The terms of office of judges shall expire when they reach the age of 70.

7. The judges shall hold office until replaced. They shall, however, continue to deal with such cases as they already have under consideration.

Article 24

Dismissal

No judge may be dismissed from his office unless the other judges decide by **123–024** a majority of two-thirds that he has ceased to fulfil the required conditions.

Article 25

Registry and legal secretaries

The Court shall have a registry, the functions and organisation of which shall **123–025** be laid down in the rules of the Court. The Court shall be assisted by legal secretaries.

Article 26

Plenary Court

The plenary Court shall **123–026**

    (a) elect its President and one or two Vice-Presidents for a period of three years; they may be re-elected;

    (b) set up Chambers, constituted for a fixed period of time;

    (c) elect the Presidents of the Chambers of the Court; they may be re-elected;

    (d) adopt the rules of the Court, and

    (e) elect the Registrar and one or more Deputy Registrars.

Article 27

Committees, Chambers and Grand Chamber

123–027 1. To consider cases brought before it, the Court shall sit in committees of three judges, in Chambers of seven judges and in a Grand Chamber of seventeen judges. The Court's Chambers shall set up committees for a fixed period of time.

2. There shall sit as an ex officio member of the Chamber and the Grand Chamber the judge elected in respect of the State Party concerned or, if there is none or if he is unable to sit, a person of its choice who shall sit in the capacity of judge.

3. The Grand Chamber shall also include the President of the Court, the Vice-Presidents, the Presidents of the Chambers and other judges chosen in accordance with the rules of the Court. When a case is referred to the Grand Chamber under Article 43, no judge from the Chamber which rendered the judgment shall sit in the Grand Chamber, with the exception of the President of the Chamber and the judge who sat in respect of the State Party concerned.

Article 28

Declarations of inadmissibility by committees

123–028 A committee may, by a unanimous vote, declare inadmissible or strike out of its list of cases an application submitted under Article 34 where such a decision can be taken without further examination. The decision shall be final.

Article 29

Decisions by Chambers on admissibility and merits

123–029 1. If no decision is taken under Article 28, a Chamber shall decide on the admissibility and merits of individual applications submitted under Article 34.

2. A Chamber shall decide on the admissibility and merits of inter-State applications submitted under Article 33.

3. The decision on admissibility shall be taken separately unless the Court, in exceptional cases, decides otherwise.

Article 30

Relinquishment of jurisdiction to the Grand Chamber

123–030 Where a case pending before a Chamber raises a serious question affecting the interpretation of the Convention or the protocols thereto, or where the resolution of a question before the Chamber might have a result inconsistent with a judgment previously delivered by the Court, the Chamber may, at any time before it has rendered its judgment, relinquish jurisdiction in favour of the Grand Chamber, unless one of the parties to the case objects.

Article 31

Powers of the Grand Chamber

123–031 The Grand Chamber shall (a) determine applications submitted either under Article 33 or Article 34 when a Chamber has relinquished jurisdiction under Article 30 or when the case has been referred to it under Article 43; and (b) consider requests for advisory opinions submitted under Article 47.

Article 32

Jurisdiction of the Court

1. The jurisdiction of the Court shall extend to all matters concerning the **123–032** interpretation and application of the Convention and the protocols thereto which are referred to it as provided in Articles 33, 34 and 47.

2. In the event of dispute as to whether the Court has jurisdiction, the Court shall decide.

Article 33

Inter-State cases

Any High Contracting Party may refer to the Court any alleged breach of the **123–033** provisions of the Convention and the protocols thereto by another High Contracting Party.

Article 34

Individual applications

The Court may receive applications from any person, non-governmental **123–034** organisation or group of individuals claiming to be the victim of a violation by one of the High Contracting Parties of the rights set forth in the Convention or the protocols thereto. The High Contracting Parties undertake not to hinder in any way the effective exercise of this right.

Article 35

Admissibility criteria

1. The Court may only deal with the matter after all domestic remedies have **123–035** been exhausted, according to the generally recognised rules of international law, and within a period of six months from the date on which the final decision was taken.

2. The Court shall not deal with any application submitted under Article 34 that

    (a) is anonymous; or
    (b) is substantially the same as a matter that has already been examined by the Court or has already been submitted to another procedure of international investigation or settlement and contains no relevant new information.

3. The Court shall declare inadmissible any individual application submitted under Article 34 which it considers incompatible with the provisions of the Convention or the protocols thereto, manifestly ill-founded, or an abuse of the right of application.

4. The Court shall reject any application which it considers inadmissible under this Article. It may do so at any stage of the proceedings.

Article 36

Third party intervention

123–036   1. In all cases before a Chamber or the Grand Chamber, a High Contracting Party one of whose nationals is an applicant shall have the right to submit written comments and to take part in hearings.

2. The President of the Court may, in the interest of the proper administration of justice, invite any High Contracting Party which is not a party to the proceedings or any person concerned who is not the applicant to submit written comments or take part in hearings.

Article 37

Striking out applications

123–037   1. The Court may at any stage of the proceedings decide to strike an application out of its list of cases where the circumstances lead to the conclusion that

(a) the applicant does not intend to pursue his application; or
(b) the matter has been resolved; or
(c) for any other reason established by the Court, it is no longer justified to continue the examination of the application. However, the Court shall continue the examination of the application if respect for human rights as defined in the Convention and the protocols thereto so requires.

2. The Court may decide to restore an application to its list of cases if it considers that the circumstances justify such a course.

Article 38

Examination of the case and friendly settlement proceedings

123–038   1. If the Court declares the application admissible, it shall

(a) pursue the examination of the case, together with the representatives of the parties, and if need be, undertake an investigation, for the effective conduct of which the States concerned shall furnish all necessary facilities;
(b) place itself at the disposal of the parties concerned with a view to securing a friendly settlement of the matter on the basis of respect for human rights as defined in the Convention and the protocols thereto.

2. Proceedings conducted under paragraph 1.b shall be confidential.

Article 39

Finding of a friendly settlement

123–039   If a friendly settlement is effected, the Court shall strike the case out of its list by means of a decision which shall be confined to a brief statement of the facts and of the solution reached.

Article 40

Public hearings and access to documents

1. Hearings shall be in public unless the Court in exceptional circumstances **123–040** decides otherwise.

2. Documents deposited with the Registrar shall be accessible to the public unless the President of the Court decides otherwise.

Article 41

Just satisfaction

If the Court finds that there has been a violation of the Convention or the **123–041** protocols thereto, and if the internal law of the High Contracting Party concerned allows only partial reparation to be made, the Court shall, if necessary, afford just satisfaction to the injured party.

Article 42

Judgments of Chambers

Judgments of Chambers shall become final in accordance with the provisions **123–042** of Article 44, paragraph 2.

Article 43

Referral to the Grand Chamber

1. Within a period of three months from the date of the judgment of the **123–043** Chamber, any party to the case may, in exceptional cases, request that the case be referred to the Grand Chamber.

2. A panel of five judges of the Grand Chamber shall accept the request if the case raises a serious question affecting the interpretation or application of the Convention or the protocols thereto, or a serious issue of general importance.

3. If the panel accepts the request, the Grand Chamber shall decide the case by means of a judgment.

Article 44

Final judgments

1. The judgment of the Grand Chamber shall be final. **123–044**

2. The judgment of a Chamber shall become final

   (a) when the parties declare that they will not request that the case be referred to the Grand Chamber; or
   (b) three months after the date of the judgment, if reference of the case to the Grand Chamber has not been requested; or
   (c) when the panel of the Grand Chamber rejects the request to refer under Article 43.

3. The final judgment shall be published.

Article 45

Reasons for judgments and decisions

123–045   1. Reasons shall be given for judgments as well as for decisions declaring applications admissible or inadmissible.

2. If a judgment does not represent, in whole or in part, the unanimous opinion of the judges, any judge shall be entitled to deliver a separate opinion.

Article 46

Binding force and execution of judgments

123–046   1. The High Contracting Parties undertake to abide by the final judgment of the Court in any case to which they are parties.

2. The final judgment of the Court shall be transmitted to the Committee of Ministers, which shall supervise its execution.

Article 47

Advisory opinions

123–047   1. The Court may, at the request of the Committee of Ministers, give advisory opinions on legal questions concerning the interpretation of the Convention and the protocols thereto.

2. Such opinions shall not deal with any question relating to the content or scope of the rights or freedoms defined in Section I of the Convention and the protocols thereto, or with any other question which the Court or the Committee of Ministers might have to consider in consequence of any such proceedings as could be instituted in accordance with the Convention.

3. Decisions of the Committee of Ministers to request an advisory opinion of the Court shall require a majority vote of the representatives entitled to sit on the Committee.

Article 48

Advisory jurisdiction of the Court

123–048   The Court shall decide whether a request for an advisory opinion submitted by the Committee of Ministers is within its competence as defined in Article 47.

Article 49

Reasons for advisory opinions

123–049   1. Reasons shall be given for advisory opinions of the Court.

2. If the advisory opinion does not represent, in whole or in part, the unanimous opinion of the judges, any judge shall be entitled to deliver a separate opinion.

3. Advisory opinions of the Court shall be communicated to the Committee of Ministers.

Article 50

Expenditure on the Court

The expenditure on the Court shall be borne by the Council of Europe. **123–050**

Article 51

Privileges and immunities of judges

The judges shall be entitled, during the exercise of their functions, to the **123–051** privileges and immunities provided for in Article 40 of the Statute of the Council of Europe and in the agreements made thereunder.

SECTION III

MISCELLANEOUS PROVISIONS

Article 52

Inquiries by the Secretary General

On receipt of a request from the Secretary General of the Council of Europe **123–052** any High Contracting Party shall furnish an explanation of the manner in which its internal law ensures the effective implementation of any of the provisions of the Convention.

Article 53

Safeguard for existing human rights

Nothing in this Convention shall be construed as limiting or derogating from **123–053** any of the human rights and fundamental freedoms which may be ensured under the laws of any High Contracting Party or under any other agreement to which it is a Party.

Article 54

Powers of the Committee of Ministers

Nothing in this Convention shall prejudice the powers conferred on the Com- **123–054** mittee of Ministers by the Statute of the Council of Europe.

Article 55

Exclusion of other means of dispute settlement

The High Contracting Parties agree that, except by special agreement, they **123–055** will not avail themselves of treaties, conventions or declarations in force between them for the purpose of submitting, by way of petition, a dispute arising out of the interpretation or application of this Convention to a means of settlement other than those provided for in this Convention.

Article 56

Territorial application

123–056   1. Any State may at the time of its ratification or at any time thereafter declare by notification addressed to the Secretary General of the Council of Europe that the present Convention shall, subject to paragraph 4 of this Article, extend to all or any of the territories for whose international relations it is responsible.

2. The Convention shall extend to the territory or territories named in the notification as from the thirtieth day after the receipt of this notification by the Secretary General of the Council of Europe.

3. The provisions of this Convention shall be applied in such territories with due regard, however, to local requirements.

4. Any State which has made a declaration in accordance with paragraph 1 of this article may at any time thereafter declare on behalf of one or more of the territories to which the declaration relates that it accepts the competence of the Court to receive applications from individuals, non-governmental organisations or groups of individuals as provided by Article 34 of the Convention.

Article 57

Reservations

123–057   1. Any State may, when signing this Convention or when depositing its instrument of ratification, make a reservation in respect of any particular provision of the Convention to the extent that any law then in force in its territory is not in conformity with the provision. Reservations of a general character shall not be permitted under this article.

2. Any reservation made under this article shall contain a brief statement of the law concerned.

Article 58

Denunciation

123–058   1. A High Contracting Party may denounce the present Convention only after the expiry of five years from the date on which it became a party to it and after six months' notice contained in a notification addressed to the Secretary General of the Council of Europe, who shall inform the other High Contracting Parties.

2. Such a denunciation shall not have the effect of releasing the High Contracting Party concerned from its obligations under this Convention in respect of any act which, being capable of constituting a violation of such obligations, may have been performed by it before the date at which the denunciation became effective.

3. Any High Contracting Party which shall cease to be a member of the Council of Europe shall cease to be a Party to this Convention under the same conditions.

4. The Convention may be denounced in accordance with the provisions of the preceding paragraphs in respect of any territory to which it has been declared to extend under the terms of Article 56.

Article 59

Signature and ratification

123–059   1. This Convention shall be open to the signature of the members of the Council of Europe. It shall be ratified. Ratifications shall be deposited with the Secretary General of the Council of Europe.

2. The present Convention shall come into force after the deposit of ten instruments of ratification.

3. As regards any signatory ratifying subsequently, the Convention shall come into force at the date of the deposit of its instrument of ratification.

4. The Secretary General of the Council of Europe shall notify all the members of the Council of Europe of the entry into force of the Convention, the names of the High Contracting Parties who have ratified it, and the deposit of all instruments of ratification which may be effected subsequently.

Protocol to the Convention for the Protection of Human Rights and Fundamental Freedoms

The governments signatory hereto, being members of the Council of Europe, **123–060**
Being resolved to take steps to ensure the collective enforcement of certain rights and freedoms other than those already included in Section I of the Convention for the Protection of Human Rights and Fundamental Freedoms signed at Rome on 4th November 1950 (hereinafter referred to as "the Convention"),
Have agreed as follows:

Article 1

Protection of property

Every natural or legal person is entitled to the peaceful enjoyment of his **123–061**
possessions. No one shall be deprived of his possessions except in the public interest and subject to the conditions provided for by law and by the general principles of international law. The preceding provisions shall not, however, in any way impair the right of a State to enforce such laws as it deems necessary to control the use of property in accordance with the general interest or to secure the payment of taxes or other contributions or penalties.

Article 2

Right to education

No person shall be denied the right to education. In the exercise of any func- **123–062**
tions which it assumes in relation to education and to teaching, the State shall respect the right of parents to ensure such education and teaching in conformity with their own religious and philosophical convictions.

Article 3

Right to free elections

The High Contracting Parties undertake to hold free elections at reasonable **123–063**
intervals by secret ballot, under conditions which will ensure the free expression of the opinion of the people in the choice of the legislature.

Article 4

Territorial application

Any High Contracting Party may at the time of signature or ratification or at **123–064**
any time thereafter communicate to the Secretary General of the Council of

Europe a declaration stating the extent to which it undertakes that the provisions of the present Protocol shall apply to such of the territories for the international relations of which it is responsible as are named therein. Any High Contracting Party which has communicated a declaration in virtue of the preceding paragraph may from time to time communicate a further declaration modifying the terms of any former declaration or terminating the application of the provisions of this Protocol in respect of any territory. A declaration made in accordance with this article shall be deemed to have been made in accordance with paragraph 1 of Article 56 of the Convention.

Article 5

Relationship to the Convention

123–065   As between the High Contracting Parties the provisions of Articles 1, 2, 3 and 4 of this Protocol shall be regarded as additional articles to the Convention and all the provisions of the Convention shall apply accordingly.

Article 6

Signature and ratification

123–066   This Protocol shall be open for signature by the members of the Council of Europe, who are the signatories of the Convention; it shall be ratified at the same time as or after the ratification of the Convention. It shall enter into force after the deposit of ten instruments of ratification. As regards any signatory ratifying subsequently, the Protocol shall enter into force at the date of the deposit of its instrument of ratification.

Protocol No. 4 to the Convention for the Protection of Human Rights and Fundamental Freedoms securing certain rights and freedoms other than those already included in the Convention and in the first Protocol thereto

123–067   The governments signatory hereto, being members of the Council of Europe, Being resolved to take steps to ensure the collective enforcement of certain rights and freedoms other than those already included in Section 1 of the Convention for the Protection of Human Rights and Fundamental Freedoms signed at Rome on 4th November 1950 (hereinafter referred to as the "Convention") and in Articles 1 to 3 of the First Protocol to the Convention, signed at Paris on 20th March 1952,

Have agreed as follows:

Article 1

Prohibition of imprisonment for debt

123–068   No one shall be deprived of his liberty merely on the ground of inability to fulfil a contractual obligation.

Article 2

Freedom of movement

1. Everyone lawfully within the territory of a State shall, within that territory, **123–069**
have the right to liberty of movement and freedom to choose his residence.

2. Everyone shall be free to leave any country, including his own.

3. No restrictions shall be placed on the exercise of these rights other than
such as are in accordance with law and are necessary in a democratic society in
the interests of national security or public safety, for the maintenance of public
order, for the prevention of crime, for the protection of health or morals, or for
the protection of the rights and freedoms of others.

4. The rights set forth in paragraph 1 may also be subject, in particular areas,
to restrictions imposed in accordance with law and justified by the public interest
in a democratic society.

Article 3

Prohibition of expulsion of nationals

1. No one shall be expelled, by means either of an individual or of a collective **123–070**
measure, from the territory of the State of which he is a national.

2. No one shall be deprived of the right to enter the territory of the state of
which he is a national.

Article 4

Prohibition of collective expulsion of aliens

Collective expulsion of aliens is prohibited. **123–071**

Article 5

Territorial application

1. Any High Contracting Party may, at the time of signature or ratification of **123–072**
this Protocol, or at any time thereafter, communicate to the Secretary General
of the Council of Europe a declaration stating the extent to which it undertakes
that the provisions of this Protocol shall apply to such of the territories for the
international relations of which it is responsible as are named therein.

2. Any High Contracting Party which has communicated a declaration in
virtue of the preceding paragraph may, from time to time, communicate a further
declaration modifying the terms of any former declaration or terminating the
application of the provisions of this Protocol in respect of any territory.

3. A declaration made in accordance with this article shall be deemed to have
been made in accordance with paragraph 1 of Article 56 of the Convention.

4. The territory of any State to which this Protocol applies by virtue of ratification or acceptance by that State, and each territory to which this Protocol is
applied by virtue of a declaration by that State under this article, shall be treated
as separate territories for the purpose of the references in Articles 2 and 3 to the
territory of a State.

5. Any State which has made a declaration in accordance with paragraph 1
or 2 of this Article may at any time thereafter declare on behalf of one or more
of the territories to which the declaration relates that it accepts the competence
of the Court to receive applications from individuals, non-governmental organisations or groups of individuals as provided in Article 34 of the Convention in
respect of all or any of Articles 1 to 4 of this Protocol.

Article 6

Relationship to the Convention

123–073   As between the High Contracting Parties the provisions of Articles 1 to 5 of this Protocol shall be regarded as additional Articles to the Convention, and all the provisions of the Convention shall apply accordingly.

Article 7

Signature and ratification

123–074   1. This Protocol shall be open for signature by the members of the Council of Europe who are the signatories of the Convention; it shall be ratified at the same time as or after the ratification of the Convention. It shall enter into force after the deposit of five instruments of ratification. As regards any signatory ratifying subsequently, the Protocol shall enter into force at the date of the deposit of its instrument of ratification.

2. The instruments of ratification shall be deposited with the Secretary General of the Council of Europe, who will notify all members of the names of those who have ratified.

Protocol No. 6 to the Convention for the Protection of Human Rights and Fundamental Freedoms concerning the abolition of the death penalty

123–075   The member States of the Council of Europe, signatory to this Protocol to the Convention for the Protection of Human Rights and Fundamental Freedoms, signed at Rome on 4th November 1950 (hereinafter referred to as "the Convention"),

Considering that the evolution that has occurred in several member States of the Council of Europe expresses a general tendency in favour of abolition of the death penalty;

Have agreed as follows:

Article 1

Abolition of the death penalty

123–076   The death penalty shall be abolished. No-one shall be condemned to such penalty or executed.

Article 2

Death penalty in time of war

123–077   A State may make provision in its law for the death penalty in respect of acts committed in time of war or of imminent threat of war; such penalty shall be applied only in the instances laid down in the law and in accordance with its provisions. The State shall communicate to the Secretary General of the Council of Europe the relevant provisions of that law.

Article 3

Prohibition of derogations

No derogation from the provisions of this Protocol shall be made under Article 15 of the Convention. **123–078**

Article 4

Prohibition of reservations

No reservation may be made under Article 57 of the Convention in respect of the provisions of this Protocol.

Article 5

Territorial application

1. Any State may at the time of signature or when depositing its instrument **123–079** of ratification, acceptance or approval, specify the territory or territories to which this Protocol shall apply.

2. Any State may at any later date, by a declaration addressed to the Secretary General of the Council of Europe, extend the application of this Protocol to any other territory specified in the declaration. In respect of such territory the Protocol shall enter into force on the first day of the month following the date of receipt of such declaration by the Secretary General.

3. Any declaration made under the two preceding paragraphs may, in respect of any territory specified in such declaration, be withdrawn by a notification addressed to the Secretary General. The withdrawal shall become effective on the first day of the month following the date of receipt of such notification by the Secretary General.

Article 6

Relationship to the Convention

As between the States Parties the provisions of Articles 1 and 5 of this Protocol shall be regarded as additional articles to the Convention and all the provisions of the Convention shall apply accordingly. **123–080**

Article 7

Signature and ratification

The Protocol shall be open for signature by the member States of the Council **123–081** of Europe, signatories to the Convention. It shall be subject to ratification, acceptance or approval. A member State of the Council of Europe may not ratify, accept or approve this Protocol unless it has, simultaneously or previously, ratified the Convention. Instruments of ratification, acceptance or approval shall be deposited with the Secretary General of the Council of Europe.

Article 8

Entry into force

1. This Protocol shall enter into force on the first day of the month following **123–082** the date on which five member States of the Council of Europe have expressed

their consent to be bound by the Protocol in accordance with the provisions of Article 7.

2. In respect of any member State which subsequently expresses its consent to be bound by it, the Protocol shall enter into force on the first day of the month following the date of the deposit of the instrument of ratification, acceptance or approval.

Article 9

Depositary functions

123–083   The Secretary General of the Council of Europe shall notify the member States of the Council of:

(a) any signature;
(b) the deposit of any instrument of ratification, acceptance or approval;
(c) any date of entry into force of this Protocol in accordance with articles 5 and 8;
(d) any other act, notification or communication relating to this Protocol.

Protocol No. 7 to the Convention for the protection of human rights and fundamental freedoms

123–084   The member States of the Council of Europe signatory hereto,
Being resolved to take further steps to ensure the collective enforcement of certain rights and freedoms by means of the Convention for the Protection of Human Rights and Fundamental Freedoms signed at Rome on 4th November 1950 (hereinafter referred to as "the Convention"),
Have agreed as follows:

Article 1

Procedural safeguards relating to expulsion of aliens

123–085   1. An alien lawfully resident in the territory of a State shall not be expelled therefrom except in pursuance of a decision reached in accordance with law and shall be allowed:

(a) to submit reasons against his expulsion,
(b) to have his case reviewed, and
(c) to be represented for these purposes before the competent authority or a person or persons designated by that authority.

2. An alien may be expelled before the exercise of his rights under paragraph 1.(a), (b) and (c) of this Article, when such expulsion is necessary in the interests of public order or is grounded on reasons of national security.

Article 2

Right of appeal in criminal matters

123–086   1. Everyone convicted of a criminal offence by a tribunal shall have the right to have his conviction or sentence reviewed by a higher tribunal. The exercise of this right, including the grounds on which it may be exercised, shall be governed by law.

2. This right may be subject to exceptions in regard to offences of a minor character, as prescribed by law, or in cases in which the person concerned was tried in the first instance by the highest tribunal or was convicted following an appeal against acquittal.

Article 3

Compensation for wrongful conviction

When a person has by a final decision been convicted of a criminal offence **123–087** and when subsequently his conviction has been reversed, or he has been pardoned, on the ground that a new or newly discovered fact shows conclusively that there has been a miscarriage of justice, the person who has suffered punishment as a result of such conviction shall be compensated according to the law or the practice of the State concerned, unless it is proved that the non-disclosure of the unknown fact in time is wholly or partly attributable to him.

Article 4

Right not to be tried or punished twice

1. No one shall be liable to be tried or punished again in criminal proceedings **123–088** under the jurisdiction of the same State for an offence for which he has already been finally acquitted or convicted in accordance with the law and penal procedure of that State.

2. The provisions of the preceding paragraph shall not prevent the reopening of the case in accordance with the law and penal procedure of the State concerned, if there is evidence of new or newly discovered facts, or if there has been a fundamental defect in the previous proceedings, which could affect the outcome of the case.

3. No derogation from this Article shall be made under Article 15 of the Convention.

Article 5

Equality between spouses

Spouses shall enjoy equality of rights and responsibilities of a private law **123–089** character between them, and in their relations with their children, as to marriage, during marriage and in the event of its dissolution. This Article shall not prevent States from taking such measures as are necessary in the interests of the children.

Article 6

Territorial application

1. Any State may at the time of signature or when depositing its instrument **123–090** of ratification, acceptance or approval, specify the territory or territories to which the Protocol shall apply and state the extent to which it undertakes that the provisions of this Protocol shall apply to such territory or territories.

2. Any State may at any later date, by a declaration addressed to the Secretary General of the Council of Europe, extend the application of this Protocol to any other territory specified in the declaration. In respect of such territory the Protocol shall enter into force on the first day of the month following the expiration

of a period of two months after the date of receipt by the Secretary General of such declaration.

3. Any declaration made under the two preceding paragraphs may, in respect of any territory specified in such declaration, be withdrawn or modified by a notification addressed to the Secretary General. The withdrawal or modification shall become effective on the first day of the month following the expiration of a period of two months after the date of receipt of such notification by the Secretary General.

4. A declaration made in accordance with this Article shall be deemed to have been made in accordance with paragraph 1 of Article 56 of the Convention.

5. The territory of any State to which this Protocol applies by virtue of ratification, acceptance or approval by that State, and each territory to which this Protocol is applied by virtue of a declaration by that State under this Article, may be treated as separate territories for the purpose of the reference in Article 1 to the territory of a State.

6. Any State which has made a declaration in accordance with paragraph 1 or 2 of this Article may at any time thereafter declare on behalf of one or more of the territories to which the declaration relates that it accepts the competence of the Court to receive applications from individuals, non-governmental organisations or groups of individuals as provided in Article 34 of the Convention in respect of Articles 1 to 5 of this Protocol.

Article 7

Relationship to the Convention

123–091   As between the States Parties, the provisions of Article 1 to 6 of this Protocol shall be regarded as additional Articles to the Convention, and all the provisions of the Convention shall apply accordingly.

Article 8

Signature and ratification

123–092   This Protocol shall be open for signature by member States of the Council of Europe which have signed the Convention. It is subject to ratification, acceptance or approval. A member State of the Council of Europe may not ratify, accept or approve this Protocol without previously or simultaneously ratifying the Convention. Instruments of ratification, acceptance or approval shall be deposited with the Secretary General of the Council of Europe.

Article 9

Entry into force

123–093   1. This Protocol shall enter into force on the first day of the month following the expiration of a period of two months after the date on which seven member States of the Council of Europe have expressed their consent to be bound by the Protocol in accordance with the provisions of Article 8.

2. In respect of any member State which subsequently expresses its consent to be bound by it, the Protocol shall enter into force on the first day of the month following the expiration of a period of two months after the date of the deposit of the instrument of ratification, acceptance or approval.

Article 10

Depositary functions

The Secretary General of the Council of Europe shall notify all the member **123–094** States of the Council of Europe of:

(a) any signature;
(b) the deposit of any instrument of ratification, acceptance or approval;
(c) any date of entry into force of this Protocol in accordance with Articles 6 and 9;
(d) any other act, notification or declaration relating to this Protocol.

Treaty Establishing the European Community (Treaty of Rome) 1957 (Amsterdam Version)

PART ONE

PRINCIPLES

Article 1

By this Treaty, the HIGH CONTRACTING PARTIES establish among them- **124–001** selves a EUROPEAN COMMUNITY.

Article 2

The Community shall have as its task, by establishing a common market and **124–002** an economic and monetary union and by implementing common policies or activities referred to in Articles 3 and 4, to promote throughout the Community a harmonious, balanced and sustainable development of economic activities, a high level of employment and of social protection, equality between men and women, sustainable and non-inflationary growth, a high degree of competit-iveness and convergence of economic performance, a high level of protection and improvement of the quality of the environment, the raising of the standard of living and quality of life, and economic and social cohesion and solidarity among Member States.

Article 3

1. For the purposes set out in Article 2, the activities of the Community shall **124–003** include, as provided in this Treaty and in accordance with the timetable set out therein:

(a) the prohibition, as between Member States, of customs duties and quantitative restrictions on the import and export of goods, and of all other measures having equivalent effect;
(b) a common commercial policy;
(c) an internal market characterised by the abolition, as between Member States, of obstacles to the free movement of goods, persons, services and capital;
(d) measures concerning the entry and movement of persons as provided for in Title IV;

(e) a common policy in the sphere of agriculture and fisheries;

(f) a common policy in the sphere of transport;

(g) a system ensuring that competition in the internal market is not distorted;

(h) the approximation of the laws of Member States to the extent required for the functioning of the common market;

(i) the promotion of coordination between employment policies of the Member States with a view to enhancing their effectiveness by developing a coordinated strategy for employment;

(j) a policy in the social sphere comprising a European Social Fund;

(k) the strengthening of economic and social cohesion;

(l) a policy in the sphere of the environment;

(m) the strengthening of the competitiveness of Community industry;

(n) the promotion of research and technological development;

(o) encouragement for the establishment and development of trans-European networks;

(p) a contribution to the attainment of a high level of health protection;

(q) a contribution to education and training of quality and to the flowering of the cultures of the Member States;

(r) a policy in the sphere of development cooperation;

(s) the association of the overseas countries and territories in order to increase trade and promote jointly economic and social development;

(t) a contribution to the strengthening of consumer protection;

(u) measures in the spheres of energy, civil protection and tourism.

2. In all the activities referred to in this Article, the Community shall aim to eliminate inequalities, and to promote equality, between men and women.

Article 4

124–004   1. For the purposes set out in Article 2, the activities of the Member States and the Community shall include, as provided in this Treaty and in accordance with the timetable set out therein, the adoption of an economic policy which is based on the close coordination of Member States' economic policies, on the internal market and on the definition of common objectives, and conducted in accordance with the principle of an open market economy with free competition.

2. Concurrently with the foregoing, and as provided in this Treaty and in accordance with the timetable and the procedures set out therein, these activities shall include the irrevocable fixing of exchange rates leading to the introduction of a single currency, the ECU, and the definition and conduct of a single monetary policy and exchange-rate policy the primary objective of both of which shall be to maintain price stability and, without prejudice to this objective, to support the general economic policies in the Community, in accordance with the principle of an open market economy with free competition.

3. These activities of the Member States and the Community shall entail compliance with the following guiding principles: stable prices, sound public finances and monetary conditions and a sustainable balance of payments.

Article 5

124–005   The Community shall act within the limits of the powers conferred upon it by this Treaty and of the objectives assigned to it therein.

In areas which do not fall within its exclusive competence, the Community shall take action, in accordance with the principle of subsidiarity, only if and insofar as the objectives of the proposed action cannot be sufficiently achieved by the Member States and can therefore, by reason of the scale or effects of the proposed action, be better achieved by the Community.

Any action by the Community shall not go beyond what is necessary to achieve the objectives of this Treaty.

Article 6

Environmental protection requirements must be integrated into the definition **124–006** and implementation of the Community policies and activities referred to in Article 3, in particular with a view to promoting sustainable development.

Article 7

1. The tasks entrusted to the Community shall be carried out by the following **124–007** institutions:

— a EUROPEAN PARLIAMENT,
— a COUNCIL,
— a COMMISSION,
— a COURT OF JUSTICE,
— a COURT OF AUDITORS.

Each institution shall act within the limits of the powers conferred upon it by this Treaty.
2. The Council and the Commission shall be assisted by an Economic and Social Committee and a Committee of the Regions acting in an advisory capacity.

Article 8

A European System of Central Banks (hereinafter referred to as 'ESCB') and **124–008** a European Central Bank (hereinafter referred to as 'ECB') shall be established in accordance with the procedures laid down in this Treaty; they shall act within the limits of the powers conferred upon them by this Treaty and by the Statute of the ESCB and of the ECB (hereinafter referred to as 'Statute of the ESCB') annexed thereto.

Article 9

A European Investment Bank is hereby established, which shall act within **124–009** the limits of the powers conferred upon it by this Treaty and the Statute annexed thereto.

Article 10

Member States shall take all appropriate measures, whether general or particu- **124–010** lar, to ensure fulfilment of the obligations arising out of this Treaty or resulting from action taken by the institutions of the Community. They shall facilitate the achievement of the Community's tasks.

They shall abstain from any measure which could jeopardise the attainment of the objectives of this Treaty.

Article 11

1. Member States which intend to establish closer cooperation between them- **124–011** selves may be authorised, subject to Articles 43 and 44 of the Treaty on European Union, to make use of the institutions, procedures and mechanisms laid down by this Treaty, provided that the cooperation proposed:

(a) does not concern areas which fall within the exclusive competence of the Community;

(b) does not affect Community policies, actions or programmes;

(c) does not concern the citizenship of the Union or discriminate between nationals of Member States;

(d) remains within the limits of the powers conferred upon the Community by this Treaty; and

(e) does not constitute a discrimination or a restriction of trade between Member States and does not distort the conditions of competition between the latter.

2. The authorisation referred to in paragraph 1 shall be granted by the Council, acting by a qualified majority on a proposal from the Commission and after consulting the European Parliament.

If a member of the Council declares that, for important and stated reasons of national policy, it intends to oppose the granting of an authorisation by qualified majority, a vote shall not be taken. The Council may, acting by a qualified majority, request that the matter be referred to the Council, meeting in the composition of the Heads of State or Government, for decision by unanimity.

Member States which intend to establish closer cooperation as referred to in paragraph 1 may address a request to the Commission, which may submit a proposal to the Council to that effect. In the event of the Commission not submitting a proposal, it shall inform the Member States concerned of the reasons for not doing so.

3. Any Member State which wishes to become a party to cooperation set up in accordance with this Article shall notify its intention to the Council and to the Commission, which shall give an opinion to the Council within three months of receipt of that notification. Within four months of the date of that notification, the Commission shall decide on it and on such specific arrangements as it may deem necessary.

4. The acts and decisions necessary for the implementation of cooperation activities shall be subject to all the relevant provisions of this Treaty, save as otherwise provided for in this Article and in Articles 43 and 44 of the Treaty on European Union.

5. This Article is without prejudice to the provisions of the Protocol integrating the Schengen acquis into the framework of the European Union.

Article 12

124–012   Within the scope of application of this Treaty, and without prejudice to any special provisions contained therein, any discrimination on grounds of nationality shall be prohibited.

The Council, acting in accordance with the procedure referred to in Article 251, may adopt rules designed to prohibit such discrimination.

Article 13

124–013   Without prejudice to the other provisions of this Treaty and within the limits of the powers conferred by it upon the Community, the Council, acting unanimously on a proposal from the Commission and after consulting the European Parliament, may take appropriate action to combat discrimination based on sex, racial or ethnic origin, religion or belief, disability, age or sexual orientation.

Article 14

124–014   1. The Community shall adopt measures with the aim of progressively establishing the internal market over a period expiring on 31 December 1992, in accordance with the provisions of this Article and of Articles 15, 26, 47(2), 49, 80, 93 and 95 and without prejudice to the other provisions of this Treaty.

2. The internal market shall comprise an area without internal frontiers in which the free movement of goods, persons, services and capital is ensured in accordance with the provisions of this Treaty.

3. The Council, acting by a qualified majority on a proposal from the Commission, shall determine the guidelines and conditions necessary to ensure balanced progress in all the sectors concerned.

Article 15

When drawing up its proposals with a view to achieving the objectives set **124–015** out in Article 14, the Commission shall take into account the extent of the effort that certain economies showing differences in development will have to sustain during the period of establishment of the internal market and it may propose appropriate provisions.

If these provisions take the form of derogations, they must be of a temporary nature and must cause the least possible disturbance to the functioning of the common market.

Article 16

Without prejudice to Articles 73, 86 and 87, and given the place occupied by **124–016** services of general economic interest in the shared values of the Union as well as their role in promoting social and territorial cohesion, the Community and the Member States, each within their respective powers and within the scope of application of this Treaty, shall take care that such services operate on the basis of principles and conditions which enable them to fulfil their missions.

PART TWO

CITIZENSHIP OF THE UNION

Article 17

1. Citizenship of the Union is hereby established. Every person holding the **124–017** nationality of a Member State shall be a citizen of the Union. Citizenship of the Union shall complement and not replace national citizenship.

2. Citizens of the Union shall enjoy the rights conferred by this Treaty and shall be subject to the duties imposed thereby.

. . . . . .

CHAPTER 2

PROHIBITION OF QUANTITATIVE RESTRICTIONS BETWEEN MEMBER STATES

Article 28

Quantitative restrictions on imports and all measures having equivalent effect **124–018** shall be prohibited between Member States.

. . . . . .

Article 30

The provisions of Articles 28 and 29 shall not preclude prohibitions or restric- **124–019** tions on imports, exports or goods in transit justified on grounds of public morality, public policy or public security; the protection of health and life of humans, animals or plants; the protection of national treasures possessing artistic, historic or archaeological value; or the protection of industrial and commercial property. Such prohibitions or restrictions shall not, however, constitute a means of arbitrary discrimination or a disguised restriction on trade between Member States.

. . . . . .

TITLE III

FREE MOVEMENT OF PERSONS, SERVICES AND CAPITAL

CHAPTER 1

WORKERS

Article 39

124–020 1. Freedom of movement for workers shall be secured within the Community.
2. Such freedom of movement shall entail the abolition of any discrimination based on nationality between workers of the Member States as regards employment, remuneration and other conditions of work and employment.
3. It shall entail the right, subject to limitations justified on grounds of public policy, public security or public health:

(a) to accept offers of employment actually made;
(b) to move freely within the territory of Member States for this purpose;
(c) to stay in a Member State for the purpose of employment in accordance with the provisions governing the employment of nationals of that State laid down by law, regulation or administrative action;
(d) to remain in the territory of a Member State after having been employed in that State, subject to conditions which shall be embodied in implementing regulations to be drawn up by the Commission.

4. The provisions of this Article shall not apply to employment in the public service.

. . . . . .

Article 48

124–021 Companies or firms formed in accordance with the law of a Member State and having their registered office, central administration or principal place of business within the Community shall, for the purposes of this Chapter, be treated in the same way as natural persons who are nationals of Member States.
"Companies or firms" means companies or firms constituted under civil or commercial law, including cooperative societies, and other legal persons governed by public or private law, save for those which are non-profit-making.

CHAPTER 3

SERVICES

Article 49

124–022 Within the framework of the provisions set out below, restrictions on freedom to provide services within the Community shall be prohibited in respect of nationals of Member States who are established in a State of the Community other than that of the person for whom the services are intended.

The Council may, acting by a qualified majority on a proposal from the Commission, extend the provisions of the Chapter to nationals of a third country who provide services and who are established within the Community.

Article 50

Services shall be considered to be "services" within the meaning of this **124–023** Treaty where they are normally provided for remuneration, insofar as they are not governed by the provisions relating to freedom of movement for goods, capital and persons.

"Services" shall in particular include:

(a) activities of an industrial character;
(b) activities of a commercial character;
(c) activities of craftsmen;
(d) activities of the professions.

Without prejudice to the provisions of the Chapter relating to the right of establishment, the person providing a service may, in order to do so, temporarily pursue his activity in the State where the service is provided, under the same conditions as are imposed by that State on its own nationals.

Article 51

1. Freedom to provide services in the field of transport shall be governed by **124–024** the provisions of the Title relating to transport.

2. The liberalisation of banking and insurance services connected with movements of capital shall be effected in step with the liberalisation of movement of capital.

. . . . . .

TITLE VI

COMMON RULES ON COMPETITION, TAXATION AND APPROXIMATION OF LAWS

CHAPTER 1

RULES ON COMPETITION

SECTION 1

RULES APPLYING TO UNDERTAKINGS

Article 81

1. The following shall be prohibited as incompatible with the common market: **124–025** all agreements between undertakings, decisions by associations of undertakings and concerted practices which may affect trade between Member States and which have as their object or effect the prevention, restriction or distortion of competition within the common market, and in particular those which:

(a) directly or indirectly fix purchase or selling prices or any other trading conditions;

(b) limit or control production, markets, technical development, or investment;
(c) share markets or sources of supply;
(d) apply dissimilar conditions to equivalent transactions with other trading parties, thereby placing them at a competitive disadvantage;
(e) make the conclusion of contracts subject to acceptance by the other parties of supplementary obligations which, by their nature or according to commercial usage, have no connection with the subject of such contracts.

2. Any agreements or decisions prohibited pursuant to this Article shall be automatically void.

3. The provisions of paragraph 1 may, however, be declared inapplicable in the case of:

— any agreement or category of agreements between undertakings;
— any decision or category of decisions by associations of undertakings;
— any concerted practice or category of concerted practices,

which contributes to improving the production or distribution of goods or to promoting technical or economic progress, while allowing consumers a fair share of the resulting benefit, and which does not:

(a) impose on the undertakings concerned restrictions which are not indispensable to the attainment of these objectives;
(b) afford such undertakings the possibility of eliminating competition in respect of a substantial part of the products in question.

Article 82

124–026   Any abuse by one or more undertakings of a dominant position within the common market or in a substantial part of it shall be prohibited as incompatible with the common market insofar as it may affect trade between Member States.
Such abuse may, in particular, consist in:

(a) directly or indirectly imposing unfair purchase or selling prices or other unfair trading conditions;
(b) limiting production, markets or technical development to the prejudice of consumers;
(c) applying dissimilar conditions to equivalent transactions with other trading parties, thereby placing them at a competitive disadvantage;
(d) making the conclusion of contracts subject to acceptance by the other parties of supplementary obligations which, by their nature or according to commercial usage, have no connection with the subject of such contracts.

. . . . . .

CHAPTER 3

APPROXIMATION OF LAWS

Article 94

124–027   The Council shall, acting unanimously on a proposal from the Commission and after consulting the European Parliament and the Economic and Social Committee, issue directives for the approximation of such laws, regulations or administrative provisions of the Member States as directly affect the establishment or functioning of the common market.

Article 95

1. By way of derogation from Article 94 and save where otherwise provided **124–028** in this Treaty, the following provisions shall apply for the achievement of the objectives set out in Article 14. The Council shall, acting in accordance with the procedure referred to in Article 251 and after consulting the Economic and Social Committee, adopt the measures for the approximation of the provisions laid down by law, regulation or administrative action in Member States which have as their object the establishment and functioning of the internal market.

2. Paragraph 1 shall not apply to fiscal provisions, to those relating to the free movement of persons nor to those relating to the rights and interests of employed persons.

3. The Commission, in its proposals envisaged in paragraph 1 concerning health, safety, environmental protection and consumer protection, will take as a base a high level of protection, taking account in particular of any new development based on scientific facts. Within their respective powers, the European Parliament and the Council will also seek to achieve this objective.

4. If, after the adoption by the Council or by the Commission of a harmonisation measure, a Member State deems it necessary to maintain national provisions on grounds of major needs referred to in Article 30, or relating to the protection of the environment or the working environment, it shall notify the Commission of these provisions as well as the grounds for maintaining them.

5. Moreover, without prejudice to paragraph 4, if, after the adoption by the Council or by the Commission of a harmonisation measure, a Member State deems it necessary to introduce national provisions based on new scientific evidence relating to the protection of the environment or the working environment on grounds of a problem specific to that Member State arising after the adoption of the harmonisation measure, it shall notify the Commission of the envisaged provisions as well as the grounds for introducing them.

6. The Commission shall, within six months of the notifications as referred to in paragraphs 4 and 5, approve or reject the national provisions involved after having verified whether or not they are a means of arbitrary discrimination or a disguised restriction on trade between Member States and whether or not they shall constitute an obstacle to the functioning of the internal market.

In the absence of a decision by the Commission within this period the national provisions referred to in paragraphs 4 and 5 shall be deemed to have been approved.

When justified by the complexity of the matter and in the absence of danger for human health, the Commission may notify the Member State concerned that the period referred to in this paragraph may be extended for a further period of up to six months.

7. When, pursuant to paragraph 6, a Member State is authorised to maintain or introduce national provisions derogating from a harmonisation measure, the Commission shall immediately examine whether to propose an adaptation to that measure.

8. When a Member State raises a specific problem on public health in a field which has been the subject of prior harmonisation measures, it shall bring it to the attention of the Commission which shall immediately examine whether to propose appropriate measures to the Council.

9. By way of derogation from the procedure laid down in Articles 226 and 227, the Commission and any Member State may bring the matter directly before the Court of Justice if it considers that another Member State is making improper use of the powers provided for in this Article.

10. The harmonisation measures referred to above shall, in appropriate cases,

include a safeguard clause authorising the Member States to take, for one or more of the non-economic reasons referred to in Article 30, provisional measures subject to a Community control procedure.

. . . . . .

TITLE XI

SOCIAL POLICY, EDUCATION, VOCATIONAL TRAINING AND YOUTH

CHAPTER 1

SOCIAL PROVISIONS

Article 136

124–029   The Community and the Member States, having in mind fundamental social rights such as those set out in the European Social Charter signed at Turin on 18 October 1961 and in the 1989 Community Charter of the Fundamental Social Rights of Workers, shall have as their objectives the promotion of employment, improved living and working conditions, so as to make possible their harmonisation while the improvement is being maintained, proper social protection, dialogue between management and labour, the development of human resources with a view to lasting high employment and the combating of exclusion.

To this end the Community and the Member States shall implement measures which take account of the diverse forms of national practices, in particular in the field of contractual relations, and the need to maintain the competitiveness of the Community economy.

They believe that such a development will ensue not only from the functioning of the common market, which will favour the harmonisation of social systems, but also from the procedures provided for in this Treaty and from the approximation of provisions laid down by law, regulation or administrative action.

Article 137

124–030   1. With a view to achieving the objectives of Article 136, the Community shall support and complement the activities of the Member States in the following fields:

— improvement in particular of the working environment to protect workers' health and safety;
— working conditions;
— the information and consultation of workers;
— the integration of persons excluded from the labour market, without prejudice to Article 150;
— equality between men and women with regard to labour market opportunities and treatment at work.

2. To this end, the Council may adopt, by means of directives, minimum requirements for gradual implementation, having regard to the conditions and technical rules obtaining in each of the Member States. Such directives shall avoid imposing administrative, financial and legal constraints in a way which would hold back the creation and development of small and medium-sized undertakings.

The Council shall act in accordance with the procedure referred to in Article

251 after consulting the Economic and Social Committee and the Committee of the Regions.

The Council, acting in accordance with the same procedure, may adopt measures designed to encourage cooperation between Member States through initiatives aimed at improving knowledge, developing exchanges of information and best practices, promoting innovative approaches and evaluating experiences in order to combat social exclusion.

3. However, the Council shall act unanimously on a proposal from the Commission, after consulting the European Parliament, the Economic and Social Committee and the Committee of the Regions in the following areas:

— social security and social protection of workers;
— protection of workers where their employment contract is terminated;
— representation and collective defence of the interests of workers and employers, including co-determination, subject to paragraph 6;
— conditions of employment for third-country nationals legally residing in Community territory;
— financial contributions for promotion of employment and job-creation, without prejudice to the provisions relating to the Social Fund.

4. A Member State may entrust management and labour, at their joint request, with the implementation of directives adopted pursuant to paragraphs 2 and 3.

In this case, it shall ensure that, no later than the date on which a directive must be transposed in accordance with Article 249, management and labour have introduced the necessary measures by agreement, the Member State concerned being required to take any necessary measure enabling it at any time to be in a position to guarantee the results imposed by that directive.

5. The provisions adopted pursuant to this Article shall not prevent any Member State from maintaining or introducing more stringent protective measures compatible with this Treaty.

6. The provisions of this Article shall not apply to pay, the right of association, the right to strike or the right to impose lock-outs.

Article 138

1. The Commission shall have the task of promoting the consultation of man- **124–031** agement and labour at Community level and shall take any relevant measure to facilitate their dialogue by ensuring balanced support for the parties.

2. To this end, before submitting proposals in the social policy field, the Commission shall consult management and labour on the possible direction of Community action.

3. If, after such consultation, the Commission considers Community action advisable, it shall consult management and labour on the content of the envisaged proposal. Management and labour shall forward to the Commission an opinion or, where appropriate, a recommendation.

4. On the occasion of such consultation, management and labour may inform the Commission of their wish to initiate the process provided for in Article 139. The duration of the procedure shall not exceed nine months, unless the management and labour concerned and the Commission decide jointly to extend it.

Article 139

1. Should management and labour so desire, the dialogue between them at **124–032** Community level may lead to contractual relations, including agreements.

2. Agreements concluded at Community level shall be implemented either in accordance with the procedures and practices specific to management and labour and the Member States or, in matters covered by Article 137, at the joint request

of the signatory parties, by a Council decision on a proposal from the Commission.

The Council shall act by qualified majority, except where the agreement in question contains one or more provisions relating to one of the areas referred to in Article 137(3), in which case it shall act unanimously.

Article 140

124–033 With a view to achieving the objectives of Article 136 and without prejudice to the other provisions of this Treaty, the Commission shall encourage cooperation between the Member States and facilitate the coordination of their action in all social policy fields under this chapter, particularly in matters relating to:

— employment;
— labour law and working conditions;
— basic and advanced vocational training;
— social security;
— prevention of occupational accidents and diseases;
— occupational hygiene;
— the right of association and collective bargaining between employers and workers.

To this end, the Commission shall act in close contact with Member States by making studies, delivering opinions and arranging consultations both on problems arising at national level and on those of concern to international organisations.

Before delivering the opinions provided for in this Article, the Commission shall consult the Economic and Social Committee.

Article 141

124–034 1. Each Member State shall ensure that the principle of equal pay for male and female workers for equal work or work of equal value is applied.

2. For the purpose of this Article, 'pay' means the ordinary basic or minimum wage or salary and any other consideration, whether in cash or in kind, which the worker receives directly or indirectly, in respect of his employment, from his employer.

Equal pay without discrimination based on sex means:

(a) that pay for the same work at piece rates shall be calculated on the basis of the same unit of measurement;
(b) that pay for work at time rates shall be the same for the same job.

3. The Council, acting in accordance with the procedure referred to in Article 251, and after consulting the Economic and Social Committee, shall adopt measures to ensure the application of the principle of equal opportunities and equal treatment of men and women in matters of employment and occupation, including the principle of equal pay for equal work or work of equal value.

4. With a view to ensuring full equality in practice between men and women in working life, the principle of equal treatment shall not prevent any Member State from maintaining or adopting measures providing for specific advantages in order to make it easier for the under-represented sex to pursue a vocational activity or to prevent or compensate for disadvantages in professional careers.

. . . . . .

TITLE XVI

INDUSTRY

Article 157

1. The Community and the Member States shall ensure that the conditions **124–035**
necessary for the competitiveness of the Community's industry exist.

For that purpose, in accordance with a system of open and competitive markets, their action shall be aimed at:

— speeding up the adjustment of industry to structural changes;
— encouraging an environment favourable to initiative and to the development of undertakings throughout the Community, particularly small and medium-sized undertakings;
— encouraging an environment favourable to cooperation between undertakings;
— fostering better exploitation of the industrial potential of policies of innovation, research and technological development.

2. The Member States shall consult each other in liaison with the Commission and, where necessary, shall coordinate their action. The Commission may take any useful initiative to promote such coordination.

3. The Community shall contribute to the achievement of the objectives set out in paragraph 1 through the policies and activities it pursues under other provisions of this Treaty. The Council, acting unanimously on a proposal from the Commission, after consulting the European Parliament and the Economic and Social Committee, may decide on specific measures in support of action taken in the Member States to achieve the objectives set out in paragraph 1.

This Title shall not provide a basis for the introduction by the Community of any measure which could lead to a distortion of competition.

. . . . . .

PART FIVE

INSTITUTIONS OF THE COMMUNITY

TITLE I

PROVISIONS GOVERNING THE INSTITUTIONS

CHAPTER 1

THE INSTITUTIONS

SECTION 1

THE EUROPEAN PARLIAMENT

Article 189

The European Parliament, which shall consist of representatives of the **124–036**
peoples of the States brought together in the Community, shall exercise the powers conferred upon it by this Treaty.

The number of Members of the European Parliament shall not exceed seven hundred.

Article 190

124–037   1. The representatives in the European Parliament of the peoples of the States brought together in the Community shall be elected by direct universal suffrage.

2. The number of representatives elected in each Member State shall be as follows:

Belgium	25
Denmark	16
Germany	99
Greece	25
Spain	64
France	87
Ireland	15
Italy	87
Luxembourg	6
Netherlands	31
Austria	21
Portugal	25
Finland	16
Sweden	22
United Kingdom	87

In the event of amendments to this paragraph, the number of representatives elected in each Member State must ensure appropriate representation of the peoples of the States brought together in the Community.

3. Representatives shall be elected for a term of five years.

4. The European Parliament shall draw up a proposal for elections by direct universal suffrage in accordance with a uniform procedure in all Member States or in accordance with principles common to all Member States.

The Council shall, acting unanimously after obtaining the assent of the European Parliament, which shall act by a majority of its component members, lay down the appropriate provisions, which it shall recommend to Member States for adoption in accordance with their respective constitutional requirements.

5. The European Parliament shall, after seeking an opinion from the Commission and with the approval of the Council acting unanimously, lay down the regulations and general conditions governing the performance of the duties of its Members.

Article 191

124–038   Political parties at European level are important as a factor for integration within the Union. They contribute to forming a European awareness and to expressing the political will of the citizens of the Union.

Article 192

124–039   Insofar as provided in this Treaty, the European Parliament shall participate in the process leading up to the adoption of Community acts by exercising its powers under the procedures laid down in Articles 251 and 252 and by giving its assent or delivering advisory opinions.

The European Parliament may, acting by a majority of its Members, request the Commission to submit any appropriate proposal on matters on which it considers that a Community act is required for the purpose of implementing this Treaty.

Article 193

In the course of its duties, the European Parliament may, at the request of a **124–040** quarter of its Members, set up a temporary Committee of Inquiry to investigate, without prejudice to the powers conferred by this Treaty on other institutions or bodies, alleged contraventions or maladministration in the implementation of Community law, except where the alleged facts are being examined before a court and while the case is still subject to legal proceedings.

The temporary Committee of Inquiry shall cease to exist on the submission of its report.

The detailed provisions governing the exercise of the right of inquiry shall be determined by common accord of the European Parliament, the Council and the Commission.

Article 194

Any citizen of the Union, and any natural or legal person residing or having **124–041** its registered office in a Member State, shall have the right to address, individually or in association with other citizens or persons, a petition to the European Parliament on a matter which comes within the Community's fields of activity and which affects him, her or it directly.

Article 195

1. The European Parliament shall appoint an Ombudsman empowered to **124–042** receive complaints from any citizen of the Union or any natural or legal person residing or having its registered office in a Member State concerning instances of maladministration in the activities of the Community institutions or bodies, with the exception of the Court of Justice and the Court of First Instance acting in their judicial role.

In accordance with his duties, the Ombudsman shall conduct inquiries for which he finds grounds, either on his own initiative or on the basis of complaints submitted to him direct or through a Member of the European Parliament, except where the alleged facts are or have been the subject of legal proceedings. Where the Ombudsman establishes an instance of maladministration, he shall refer the matter to the institution concerned, which shall have a period of three months in which to inform him of its views. The Ombudsman shall then forward a report to the European Parliament and the institution concerned. The person lodging the complaint shall be informed of the outcome of such inquiries.

The Ombudsman shall submit an annual report to the European Parliament on the outcome of his inquiries.

2. The Ombudsman shall be appointed after each election of the European Parliament for the duration of its term of office. The Ombudsman shall be eligible for reappointment.

The Ombudsman may be dismissed by the Court of Justice at the request of the European Parliament if he no longer fulfils the conditions required for the performance of his duties or if he is guilty of serious misconduct.

3. The Ombudsman shall be completely independent in the performance of his duties. In the performance of those duties he shall neither seek nor take instructions from any body. The Ombudsman may not, during his term of office, engage in any other occupation, whether gainful or not.

4. The European Parliament shall, after seeking an opinion from the Commission and with the approval of the Council acting by a qualified majority, lay down the regulations and general conditions governing the performance of the Ombudsman's duties.

Article 196

124–043   The European Parliament shall hold an annual session. It shall meet, without requiring to be convened, on the second Tuesday in March.

The European Parliament may meet in extraordinary session at the request of a majority of its Members or at the request of the Council or of the Commission.

Article 197

124–044   The European Parliament shall elect its President and its officers from among its Members.

Members of the Commission may attend all meetings and shall, at their request, be heard on behalf of the Commission.

The Commission shall reply orally or in writing to questions put to it by the European Parliament or by its Members.

The Council shall be heard by the European Parliament in accordance with the conditions laid down by the Council in its Rules of Procedure.

Article 198

124–045   Save as otherwise provided in this Treaty, the European Parliament shall act by an absolute majority of the votes cast.

The Rules of Procedure shall determine the quorum.

Article 199

124–046   The European Parliament shall adopt its Rules of Procedure, acting by a majority of its Members.

The proceedings of the European Parliament shall be published in the manner laid down in its Rules of Procedure.

Article 200

124–047   The European Parliament shall discuss in open session the annual general report submitted to it by the Commission.

Article 201

124–048   If a motion of censure on the activities of the Commission is tabled before it, the European Parliament shall not vote thereon until at least three days after the motion has been tabled and only by open vote.

If the motion of censure is carried by a two-thirds majority of the votes cast, representing a majority of the Members of the European Parliament, the Members of the Commission shall resign as a body. They shall continue to deal with current business until they are replaced in accordance with Article 214. In this case, the term of office of the Members of the Commission appointed to replace them shall expire on the date on which the term of office of the Members of the Commission obliged to resign as a body would have expired.

SECTION 2

THE COUNCIL

Article 202

124–049   To ensure that the objectives set out in this Treaty are attained the Council shall, in accordance with the provisions of this Treaty:

— ensure coordination of the general economic policies of the Member States;
— have power to take decisions;
— confer on the Commission, in the acts which the Council adopts, powers for the implementation of the rules which the Council lays down. The Council may impose certain requirements in respect of the exercise of these powers. The Council may also reserve the right, in specific cases, to exercise directly implementing powers itself. The procedures referred to above must be consonant with principles and rules to be laid down in advance by the Council, acting unanimously on a proposal from the Commission and after obtaining the Opinion of the European Parliament.

. . . . . .

Article 205

1. Save as otherwise provided in this Treaty, the Council shall act by a majority of its members. **124–050**
2. Where the Council is required to act by a qualified majority, the votes of its members shall be weighted as follows:

Belgium	5
Denmark	3
Germany	10
Greece	5
Spain	8
France	10
Ireland	3
Italy	10
Luxembourg	2
Netherlands	5
Austria	4
Portugal	5
Finland	3
Sweden	4
United Kingdom	10

For their adoption, acts of the Council shall require at least:

— 62 votes in favour where this Treaty requires them to be adopted on a proposal from the Commission,
— 62 votes in favour, cast by at least 10 members, in other cases.

3. Abstentions by members present in person or represented shall not prevent the adoption by the Council of acts which require unanimity.

. . . . . .

SECTION 3

THE COMMISSION

Article 211

In order to ensure the proper functioning and development of the common market, the Commission shall: **124–051**

— ensure that the provisions of this Treaty and the measures taken by the institutions pursuant thereto are applied;

— formulate recommendations or deliver opinions on matters dealt with in this Treaty, if it expressly so provides or if the Commission considers it necessary;

— have its own power of decision and participate in the shaping of measures taken by the Council and by the European Parliament in the manner provided for in this Treaty;

— exercise the powers conferred on it by the Council for the implementation of the rules laid down by the latter.

. . . . . .

SECTION 4

THE COURT OF JUSTICE

Article 220

124–052   The Court of Justice shall ensure that in the interpretation and application of this Treaty the law is observed.

Article 221

124–053   The Court of Justice shall consist of 15 Judges.

The Court of Justice shall sit in plenary session. It may, however, form chambers, each consisting of three, five or seven Judges, either to undertake certain preparatory inquiries or to adjudicate on particular categories of cases in accordance with rules laid down for these purposes.

The Court of Justice shall sit in plenary session when a Member State or a Community institution that is a party to the proceedings so requests.

Should the Court of Justice so request, the Council may, acting unanimously, increase the number of Judges and make the necessary adjustments to the second and third paragraphs of this Article and to the second paragraph of Article 223.

Article 222

124–054   The Court of Justice shall be assisted by eight Advocates-General. However, a ninth Advocate-General shall be appointed as from 1 January 1995 until 6 October 2000.

It shall be the duty of the Advocate-General, acting with complete impartiality and independence, to make, in open court, reasoned submissions on cases brought before the Court of Justice, in order to assist the Court in the performance of the task assigned to it in Article 220.

Should the Court of Justice so request, the Council may, acting unanimously, increase the number of Advocates-General and make the necessary adjustments to the third paragraph of Article 223.

Article 223

124–055   The Judges and Advocates-General shall be chosen from persons whose independence is beyond doubt and who possess the qualifications required for appointment to the highest judicial offices in their respective countries or who are jurisconsults of recognised competence; they shall be appointed by common accord of the governments of the Member States for a term of six years.

Every three years there shall be a partial replacement of the Judges. Eight and seven Judges shall be replaced alternately.

Every three years there shall be a partial replacement of the Advocates-General. Four Advocates-General shall be replaced on each occasion.

Retiring Judges and Advocates-General shall be eligible for reappointment.

The Judges shall elect the President of the Court of Justice from among their number for a term of three years. He may be re-elected.

Article 224

The Court of Justice shall appoint its Registrar and lay down the rules governing his service. **124–056**

Article 225

1. A Court of First Instance shall be attached to the Court of Justice with **124–057** jurisdiction to hear and determine at first instance, subject to a right of appeal to the Court of Justice on points of law only and in accordance with the conditions laid down by the Statute, certain classes of action or proceeding defined in accordance with the conditions laid down in paragraph 2. The Court of First Instance shall not be competent to hear and determine questions referred for a preliminary ruling under Article 234.

2. At the request of the Court of Justice and after consulting the European Parliament and the Commission, the Council, acting unanimously, shall determine the classes of action or proceeding referred to in paragraph 1 and the composition of the Court of First Instance and shall adopt the necessary adjustments and additional provisions to the Statute of the Court of Justice. Unless the Council decides otherwise, the provisions of this Treaty relating to the Court of Justice, in particular the provisions of the Protocol on the Statute of the Court of Justice, shall apply to the Court of First Instance.

3. The members of the Court of First Instance shall be chosen from persons whose independence is beyond doubt and who possess the ability required for appointment to judicial office; they shall be appointed by common accord of the governments of the Member States for a term of six years. The membership shall be partially renewed every three years. Retiring members shall be eligible for reappointment.

4. The Court of First Instance shall establish its Rules of Procedure in agreement with the Court of Justice. Those rules shall require the unanimous approval of the Council.

Article 226

If the Commission considers that a Member State has failed to fulfil an obliga- **124–058** tion under this Treaty, it shall deliver a reasoned opinion on the matter after giving the State concerned the opportunity to submit its observations.

If the State concerned does not comply with the opinion within the period laid down by the Commission, the latter may bring the matter before the Court of Justice.

Article 227

A Member State which considers that another Member State has failed to **124–059** fulfil an obligation under this Treaty may bring the matter before the Court of Justice.

Before a Member State brings an action against another Member State for an alleged infringement of an obligation under this Treaty, it shall bring the matter before the Commission.

The Commission shall deliver a reasoned opinion after each of the States concerned has been given the opportunity to submit its own case and its observations on the other party's case both orally and in writing.

If the Commission has not delivered an opinion within three months of the date on which the matter was brought before it, the absence of such opinion shall not prevent the matter from being brought before the Court of Justice.

Article 228

124–060   1. If the Court of Justice finds that a Member State has failed to fulfil an obligation under this Treaty, the State shall be required to take the necessary measures to comply with the judgment of the Court of Justice.

2. If the Commission considers that the Member State concerned has not taken such measures it shall, after giving that State the opportunity to submit its observations, issue a reasoned opinion specifying the points on which the Member State concerned has not complied with the judgment of the Court of Justice.

If the Member State concerned fails to take the necessary measures to comply with the Court's judgment within the time-limit laid down by the Commission, the latter may bring the case before the Court of Justice. In so doing it shall specify the amount of the lump sum or penalty payment to be paid by the Member State concerned which it considers appropriate in the circumstances.

If the Court of Justice finds that the Member State concerned has not complied with its judgment it may impose a lump sum or penalty payment on it.

This procedure shall be without prejudice to Article 227.

Article 229

124–061   Regulations adopted jointly by the European Parliament and the Council, and by the Council, pursuant to the provisions of this Treaty, may give the Court of Justice unlimited jurisdiction with regard to the penalties provided for in such regulations.

Article 230

124–062   The Court of Justice shall review the legality of acts adopted jointly by the European Parliament and the Council, of acts of the Council, of the Commission and of the ECB, other than recommendations and opinions, and of acts of the European Parliament intended to produce legal effects vis-à-vis third parties.

It shall for this purpose have jurisdiction in actions brought by a Member State, the Council or the Commission on grounds of lack of competence, infringement of an essential procedural requirement, infringement of this Treaty or of any rule of law relating to its application, or misuse of powers.

The Court of Justice shall have jurisdiction under the same conditions in actions brought by the European Parliament, by the Court of Auditors and by the ECB for the purpose of protecting their prerogatives.

Any natural or legal person may, under the same conditions, institute proceedings against a decision addressed to that person or against a decision which, although in the form of a regulation or a decision addressed to another person, is of direct and individual concern to the former.

The proceedings provided for in this Article shall be instituted within two months of the publication of the measure, or of its notification to the plaintiff, or, in the absence thereof, of the day on which it came to the knowledge of the latter, as the case may be.

Article 231

If the action is well founded, the Court of Justice shall declare the act con- **124–063** cerned to be void.

In the case of a regulation, however, the Court of Justice shall, if it considers this necessary, state which of the effects of the regulation which it has declared void shall be considered as definitive.

. . . . . .

Article 234

The Court of Justice shall have jurisdiction to give preliminary rulings con- **124–064** cerning:

(a) the interpretation of this Treaty;
(b) the validity and interpretation of acts of the institutions of the Community and of the ECB;
(c) the interpretation of the statutes of bodies established by an act of the Council, where those statutes so provide.

Where such a question is raised before any court or tribunal of a Member State, that court or tribunal may, if it considers that a decision on the question is necessary to enable it to give judgment, request the Court of Justice to give a ruling thereon.

. . . . . .

CHAPTER 2

PROVISIONS COMMON TO SEVERAL INSTITUTIONS

Article 249

In order to carry out their task and in accordance with the provisions of this **124–065** Treaty, the European Parliament acting jointly with the Council, the Council and the Commission shall make regulations and issue directives, take decisions, make recommendations or deliver opinions.

A regulation shall have general application. It shall be binding in its entirety and directly applicable in all Member States.

A directive shall be binding, as to the result to be achieved, upon each Member State to which it is addressed, but shall leave to the national authorities the choice of form and methods.

A decision shall be binding in its entirety upon those to whom it is addressed.

Recommendations and opinions shall have no binding force.

Article 250

1. Where, in pursuance of this Treaty, the Council acts on a proposal from **124–066** the Commission, unanimity shall be required for an act constituting an amendment to that proposal, subject to Article 251(4) and (5).

2. As long as the Council has not acted, the Commission may alter its proposal at any time during the procedures leading to the adoption of a Community act.

Article 251

1. Where reference is made in this Treaty to this Article for the adoption of **124–067** an act, the following procedure shall apply.

2. The Commission shall submit a proposal to the European Parliament and the Council.

The Council, acting by a qualified majority after obtaining the opinion of the European Parliament,

— if it approves all the amendments contained in the European Parliament's opinion, may adopt the proposed act thus amended;

— if the European Parliament does not propose any amendments, may adopt the proposed act;

— shall otherwise adopt a common position and communicate it to the European Parliament. The Council shall inform the European Parliament fully of the reasons which led it to adopt its common position. The Commission shall inform the European Parliament fully of its position.

If, within three months of such communication, the European Parliament:

(a) approves the common position or has not taken a decision, the act in question shall be deemed to have been adopted in accordance with that common position;

(b) rejects, by an absolute majority of its component members, the common position, the proposed act shall be deemed not to have been adopted;

(c) proposes amendments to the common position by an absolute majority of its component members, the amended text shall be forwarded to the Council and to the Commission, which shall deliver an opinion on those amendments.

3. If, within three months of the matter being referred to it, the Council, acting by a qualified majority, approves all the amendments of the European Parliament, the act in question shall be deemed to have been adopted in the form of the common position thus amended; however, the Council shall act unanimously on the amendments on which the Commission has delivered a negative opinion. If the Council does not approve all the amendments, the President of the Council, in agreement with the President of the European Parliament, shall within six weeks convene a meeting of the Conciliation Committee.

4. The Conciliation Committee, which shall be composed of the members of the Council or their representatives and an equal number of representatives of the European Parliament, shall have the task of reaching agreement on a joint text, by a qualified majority of the members of the Council or their representatives and by a majority of the representatives of the European Parliament. The Commission shall take part in the Conciliation Committee's proceedings and shall take all the necessary initiatives with a view to reconciling the positions of the European Parliament and the Council. In fulfilling this task, the Conciliation Committee shall address the common position on the basis of the amendments proposed by the European Parliament.

5. If, within six weeks of its being convened, the Conciliation Committee approves a joint text, the European Parliament, acting by an absolute majority of the votes cast, and the Council, acting by a qualified majority, shall each have a period of six weeks from that approval in which to adopt the act in question in accordance with the joint text. If either of the two institutions fails to approve the proposed act within that period, it shall be deemed not to have been adopted.

6. Where the Conciliation Committee does not approve a joint text, the proposed act shall be deemed not to have been adopted.

7. The periods of three months and six weeks referred to in this Article shall be extended by a maximum of one month and two weeks respectively at the initiative of the European Parliament or the Council.

Article 252

Where reference is made in this Treaty to this Article for the adoption of an **124–068** act, the following procedure shall apply:

(a) The Council, acting by a qualified majority on a proposal from the Commission and after obtaining the opinion of the European Parliament, shall adopt a common position.

(b) The Council's common position shall be communicated to the European Parliament. The Council and the Commission shall inform the European Parliament fully of the reasons which led the Council to adopt its common position and also of the Commission's position.

If, within three months of such communication, the European Parliament approves this common position or has not taken a decision within that period, the Council shall definitively adopt the act in question in accordance with the common position.

(c) The European Parliament may, within the period of three months referred to in point (b), by an absolute majority of its component Members, propose amendments to the Council's common position. The European Parliament may also, by the same majority, reject the Council's common position. The result of the proceedings shall be transmitted to the Council and the Commission.

If the European Parliament has rejected the Council's common position, unanimity shall be required for the Council to act on a second reading.

(d) The Commission shall, within a period of one month, re-examine the proposal on the basis of which the Council adopted its common position, by taking into account the amendments proposed by the European Parliament.

The Commission shall forward to the Council, at the same time as its re-examined proposal, the amendments of the European Parliament which it has not accepted, and shall express its opinion on them. The Council may adopt these amendments unanimously.

(e) The Council, acting by a qualified majority, shall adopt the proposal as re-examined by the Commission.

Unanimity shall be required for the Council to amend the proposal as re-examined by the Commission.

(f) In the cases referred to in points (c), (d) and (e), the Council shall be required to act within a period of three months. If no decision is taken within this period, the Commission proposal shall be deemed not to have been adopted.

(g) The periods referred to in points (b) and (f) may be extended by a maximum of one month by common accord between the Council and the European Parliament.

. . . . . .

CHAPTER 3

THE ECONOMIC AND SOCIAL COMMITTEE

Article 257

An Economic and Social Committee is hereby established. It shall have advis- **124–069** ory status.

The Committee shall consist of representatives of the various categories of economic and social activity, in particular, representatives of producers, farmers, carriers, workers, dealers, craftsmen, professional occupations and representatives of the general public.

Article 258

124–070   The number of members of the Economic and Social Committee shall be as follows:

Belgium	12
Denmark	9
Germany	24
Greece	12
Spain	21
France	24
Ireland	9
Italy	24
Luxembourg	6
Netherlands	12
Austria	12
Portugal	12
Finland	9
Sweden	12
United Kingdom	24

The members of the Committee shall be appointed by the Council, acting unanimously, for four years. Their appointments shall be renewable.

The members of the Committee may not be bound by any mandatory instructions. They shall be completely independent in the performance of their duties, in the general interest of the Community.

The Council, acting by a qualified majority, shall determine the allowances of members of the Committee.

. . . . . .

Article 308

124–071   If action by the Community should prove necessary to attain, in the course of the operation of the common market, one of the objectives of the Community and this Treaty has not provided the necessary powers, the Council shall, acting unanimously on a proposal from the Commission and after consulting the European Parliament, take the appropriate measures.

. . . . . .

Article 311

124–072   The protocols annexed to this Treaty by common accord of the Member States shall form an integral part thereof.

Article 312

124–073   This Treaty is concluded for an unlimited period.

Treaty on European Union

Title I

Common Provisions

Article 1

By this Treaty, the High Contracting Parties establish among themselves a **125–01**
European Union, hereinafter called "the Union".

This Treaty marks a new stage in the process of creating an ever closer union
among the peoples of Europe, in which decisions are taken as closely as possible
to the citizen.

The Union shall be founded on the European Communities, supplemented by
the policies and forms of cooperation established by this Treaty. Its task shall
be to organize, in a manner demonstrating consistency and solidarity, relations
between the Member States and between their peoples.

Article 2

The Union shall set itself the following objectives: **125–02**

- to promote economic and social progress which is balanced and sustainable, in particular through the creation of an area without internal
  frontiers, through the strengthening of economic and social cohesion
  and through the establishment of economic and monetary union, ultimately including a single currency in accordance with the provisions
  of this Treaty;
- to assert its identity on the international scene, in particular through
  the implementation of a common foreign and security policy including
  the eventual framing of a common defence policy, which might in time
  lead to a common defence;
- to strengthen the protection of the rights and interests of the nationals
  of its Member States through the introduction of a citizenship of the
  Union;
- to develop close cooperation on justice and home affairs;
- to maintain in full the "acquis communautaire" and build on it with a
  view to considering, through the procedure referred to in Article N(2),
  to what extent the policies and forms of cooperation introduced by this
  Treaty may need to be revised with the aim of ensuring the effectiveness of the mechanisms and the institutions of the Community.

The objectives of the Union shall be achieved as provided in this Treaty and
in accordance with the condition and the timetable set out therein while respecting the principle of subsidiarity as defined in Article 3b of the Treaty establishing the European Community.

Article 3

The Union shall be served by a single institutional framework which shall **125–03**
ensure the consistency and the continuity of the activities carried out in order to
attain its objectives while respecting and building upon the "acquis communautaire".

The Union shall in particular ensure the consistency of its external activities as a whole in the context of its external relations, security, economic and development policies. The Council and the Commission shall be responsible for ensuring such consistency. They shall ensure the implementation of these policies, each in accordance with its respective powers.

Article 4

125–04　　The European Council shall provide the Union with the necessary impetus for its development and shall define the general political guidelines thereof. The European Council shall bring together the Heads of State or of Government of the Member States and the President of the Commission. They shall be assisted by the Ministers for Foreign Affairs of the Member States and by a Member of the Commission. The European Council shall meet at least twice a year, under the chairmanship of the Head of State or of Government of the Member State which holds the Presidency of the Council.

The European Council shall submit to the European Parliament a report after each of its meetings and a yearly written report on the progress achieved by the Union.

Article 5

125–05　　The European Parliament, the Council, the Commission and the Court of Justice shall exercise their powers under the conditions and for the purposes provided for, on the one hand, by the provisions of the Treaties establishing the European Communities and of the subsequent Treaties and Acts modifying and supplementing them and, on the other hand, by the other provisions of this Treaty.

Article 6

125–06　　1. The Union shall respect the national identities of its Member States, whose systems of government are founded on the principles of democracy.

2. The Union shall respect fundamental rights, as guaranteed by the European Convention for the Protection of Human Rights and Fundamental Freedoms signed in Rome on 4 November 1950 and as they result from the constitutional traditions common to the Member States, as general principles of Community law.

3. The Union shall provide itself with the means necessary to attain its objectives and carry through its policies.

. . . . . .

TITLE VI

PROVISIONS ON POLICE AND JUDICIAL COOPERATION IN CRIMINAL MATTERS

Article 29

125–07　　Without prejudice to the powers of the European Community, the Union's objective shall be to provide citizens with a high level of safety within an area of freedom, security and justice by developing common action among the Member States in the fields of police and judicial cooperation in criminal matters and by preventing and combating racism and xenophobia.

That objective shall be achieved by preventing and combating crime, organised or otherwise, in particular terrorism, trafficking in persons and offences against children, illicit drug trafficking and illicit arms trafficking, corruption and fraud, through:

— closer cooperation between police forces, customs authorities and other competent authorities in the Member States, both directly and through the European Police Office (Europol), in accordance with the provisions of Articles 30 and 32;
— closer cooperation between judicial and other competent authorities of the Member States in accordance with the provisions of Articles 31(a) to (d) and 32;
— approximation, where necessary, of rules on criminal matters in the Member States, in accordance with the provisions of Article 31(e).

Article 30

1. Common action in the field of police cooperation shall include: **125–08**

(a) operational cooperation between the competent authorities, including the police, customs and other specialised law enforcement services of the Member States in relation to the prevention, detection and investigation of criminal offences;
(b) the collection, storage, processing, analysis and exchange of relevant information, including information held by law enforcement services on reports on suspicious financial transactions, in particular through Europol, subject to appropriate provisions on the protection of personal data;
(c) cooperation and joint initiatives in training, the exchange of liaison officers, secondments, the use of equipment, and forensic research;
(d) the common evaluation of particular investigative techniques in relation to the detection of serious forms of organised crime.

2. The Council shall promote cooperation through Europol and shall in particular, within a period of five years after the date of entry into force of the Treaty of Amsterdam:

(a) enable Europol to facilitate and support the preparation, and to encourage the coordination and carrying out, of specific investigative actions by the competent authorities of the Member States, including operational actions of joint teams comprising representatives of Europol in a support capacity;
(b) adopt measures allowing Europol to ask the competent authorities of the Member States to conduct and coordinate their investigations in specific cases and to develop specific expertise which may be put at the disposal of Member States to assist them in investigating cases of organised crime;
(c) promote liaison arrangements between prosecuting/investigating officials specialising in the fight against organised crime in close cooperation with Europol;
(d) establish a research, documentation and statistical network on cross-border crime.

Police and Criminal Evidence Act 1984 — Code A
Code of Practice for the exercise by police officers of statutory powers of
stop and search and recording of police/public encounters

CONSULTATION DRAFT

MARCH 2002

1. Principles Governing Stop and Search

126–001   **1.1** Powers to stop and search must be used fairly, responsibly, with respect for people being searched and without unlawful discrimination. The Race Relations (Amendment) Act 2000 makes it unlawful for police officers to discriminate on the grounds of race, colour, or ethnic origin when using their powers.

1.2 The intrusion on the liberty of the person stopped or searched must be brief and detention for the purposes of a search must take place at or near the location of the stop.

1.3 If these fundamental principles are not observed the use of powers to stop and search may be drawn into question. Failure to use the powers in the proper manner reduces their effectiveness. Stop and search can play an important role in the detection and prevention of crime, and using the powers fairly makes them more effective.

1.4 The primary purpose of stop and search powers is to enable officers to allay or confirm suspicions about individuals without exercising their power of arrest. Officers may be required to justify the use or authorisation of such powers, in relation both to individual searches and the overall pattern of their activity in this regard, to their supervisory officers or in court. Any misuse of the powers is likely to be harmful to policing and lead to mistrust of the police. Officers must also be able to explain their actions to the member of the public searched. The misuse of these powers can lead to disciplinary action.

1.5 An officer must not search a person, even with his or her consent, where no power to search is applicable. Even where a person is prepared to submit to a search voluntarily, the person must not be searched unless the necessary legal power exists, and the search must be in accordance with the relevant power and the provisions of this Code. The only exception, where an officer does not require a specific power, applies to searches of persons entering sports grounds or other premises carried out with their consent given as a condition of entry.

2. Explanation of Powers to Stop and Search

126–002   **2.1** This code applies to powers of stop and search as follows:

    (a) powers which require reasonable grounds for suspicion, before they may be exercised, that articles unlawfully obtained or possessed are being carried, or under Section 43 of the Terrorism Act 2000 that a person is a terrorist;

    (b) authorised under section 60 of the Criminal Justice and Public Order Act 1994, based upon a reasonable belief that incidents involving serious violence may take place or that people are carrying dangerous instruments or offensive weapons within any locality in the police area;

    (c) authorised under section 44(1) and (2) of the Terrorism Act 2000 based upon a consideration that the exercise of one or both powers is expedient for the prevention of acts of terrorism;

    (d) powers to search a person who has not been arrested in the exercise of a power to search premises (see Code B paragraph 2.4).

Searches requiring reasonable grounds for suspicion

2.2 Reasonable grounds for suspicion depend on the circumstances in each **126–003** case. There must be an objective basis for that suspicion based on facts, information, and/or intelligence which are relevant to the likelihood of finding an article of a certain kind or, in the case of searches under section 43 of the Terrorism Act 2000, to the likelihood that the person is a terrorist. Reasonable suspicion can never be supported on the basis of personal factors alone without reliable supporting intelligence or information or some specific behaviour by the person concerned. For example, a person's race, age, appearance, or the fact that the person is known to have a previous conviction, cannot be used alone or in combination with each other as the reason for searching that person. Reasonable suspicion cannot be based on generalisations or stereotypical images of certain groups or categories of people as more likely to be involved in criminal activity.

2.3 Reasonable suspicion can sometimes exist without specific information or intelligence and on the basis of some level of generalisation stemming from the behaviour of a person. For example, if an officer encounters someone on the street at night who is acting warily or obviously trying to hide something, the officer may (depending on the other surrounding circumstances) base such suspicion on the fact that this kind of behaviour is often linked to stolen or prohibited articles being carried. Similarly, for the purposes of section 43 of the Terrorism Act 2000, suspicion that a person is a terrorist may arise from the person's behaviour at or near a location which has been identified as a potential target for terrorists.

2.4 However, reasonable suspicion should normally be linked to accurate and current intelligence or information, such as information describing an article being carried, a suspected offender, or a person who has been seen carrying a type of article known to have been stolen recently from premises in the area. Searches based on accurate and current intelligence or information are more likely to be effective. Targeting searches in a particular area at specified crime problems increases their effectiveness and minimises inconvenience to law-abiding members of the public. It also helps in justifying the use of searches both to those who are searched and to the general public. This does not however prevent stop and search powers being exercised in other locations where such powers may be exercised and reasonable suspicion exists.

2.5 Searches are more likely to be effective, legitimate, and secure public confidence when reasonable suspicion is based on a range of factors. The overall use of these powers is more likely to be effective when up to date and accurate intelligence or information is communicated to officers and they are well-informed about local crime patterns.

2.6 Where there is reliable information or intelligence that members of a group or gang habitually carry knives unlawfully or weapons or controlled drugs, and wear a distinctive item of clothing or other means of identification to indicate their membership of the group or gang, that distinctive item of clothing or other means of identification may provide reasonable grounds to stop and search a person.

2.7 A police officer may have reasonable grounds to suspect that a person is in innocent possession of a stolen or prohibited article or other item for which he is empowered to search. In that case the officer may stop and search the person even though there would be no power of arrest.

2.8 Under section 43(1) of the Terrorism Act 2000 a constable may stop and search a person whom the officer reasonably suspects to be a terrorist to discover whether the person is in possession of anything which may constitute evidence that the person is a terrorist. These searches may only be carried out by an officer of the same sex as the person searched.

2.9 An officer who has reasonable grounds for suspicion may detain the person concerned in order to carry out a search. Before carrying out a search the officer may ask questions about the person's behaviour or presence in circumstances which gave rise to the suspicion. As a result of questioning the detained person, the reasonable grounds for suspicion necessary to detain that person may be confirmed or, because of a satisfactory explanation, be eliminated. Questioning may also reveal reasonable grounds to suspect the possession of a different kind of unlawful article from that originally suspected. Reasonable grounds for suspicion however cannot be provided retrospectively by such questioning during a person's detention or by refusal to answer any questions put.

2.10 If, as a result of questioning before a search, or other circumstances which come to the attention of the officer, there cease to be reasonable grounds for suspecting that an article is being carried of a kind for which there is a power to stop and search, no search may take place. In the absence of any other lawful power to detain, the person is free to leave at will and must be so informed.

2.11 There is no power to stop or detain a person in order to find grounds for a search. Police officers have many encounters with members of the public which do not involve detaining people against their will. If reasonable grounds for suspicion emerge during such an encounter, the officer may search the person, even though no grounds existed when the encounter began. If an officer is detaining someone for the purpose of a search, he should inform the person as soon as detention begins.

Searches authorised under section 60 of the Criminal Justice and Public Order Act 1994

126–004   **2.12** Authority for a constable in uniform to stop and search under section 60 of the Criminal Justice and Public Order Act 1994 may be given if the authorising officer reasonably believes:

    (a) that incidents involving serious violence may take place in any locality in the officer's police area, and it is expedient to use these powers to prevent their occurrence, or

    (b) that persons are carrying dangerous instruments or offensive weapons without good reason in any locality in the officer's police area.

2.13 An authorisation under section 60 may only be given by an officer of the rank of inspector or above, in writing, specifying the grounds on which it was given, the locality in which the powers may be exercised and the period of time for which they are in force. The period authorised shall be no longer than appears reasonably necessary to prevent, or seek to prevent incidents of serious violence, or to deal with the problem of carrying dangerous instruments or offensive weapons. It may not exceed 24 hours.

2.14 If an inspector gives an authorisation, he or she must, as soon as practicable, inform an officer of or above the rank of superintendent. This officer may direct that the authorisation shall be extended for a further 24 hours, if violence or the carrying of dangerous instruments or offensive weapons has occurred, or is suspected to have occurred, and the continued use of the powers is considered necessary to prevent or deal with further such activity. That direction must also be given in writing at the time or as soon as practicable afterwards.

Powers to require removal of face coverings

126–005   **2.15** Section 60AA also provides a power to demand the removal of face coverings. The officer exercising the power must reasonably believe that someone is wearing the face covering wholly or mainly for the purpose of concealing identity. There is also a power to seize face coverings where the officer believes that a person intends to wear them for this purpose. There is no power to stop and search for face coverings. An officer may seize any face covering which is discovered when exercising a power of search for something else, or which is being carried, and which the officer reasonably believes is intended to be used for concealing anyone's identity. This power can only be used if an authorisation under section 60 or an authorisation under section 60AA is in force.

2.16 Authority for a constable in uniform to require the removal of face coverings and to seize them under section 60AA of the Criminal Justice and Public Order Act 1994 may be given if the authorising officer reasonably believes that activities may take place in any locality in the officer's police area that are likely to involve the commission of offences and it is expedient to use these powers to prevent or control these activities.

2.17 An authorisation under section 60AA may only be given by an officer of the rank of inspector or above, in writing, specifying the grounds on which it was given, the locality in which the powers may be exercised and the period of time for which they are in force. The period authorised shall be no longer than appears reasonably necessary to prevent, or seek to prevent the commission of offences. It may not exceed 24 hours.

2.18 If an inspector gives an authorisation, he must, as soon as practicable, inform an officer of or above the rank of superintendent. This officer may direct that the authorisation shall be extended for a further 24 hours, if crimes have been committed, or suspected to have been committed, and the continued use of the powers is considered necessary to prevent or deal with further such activity. This direction must also be given in writing at the time or as soon as practicable afterwards.

Searches authorised under section 44 of the Terrorism Act 2000

2.19 An officer of the rank of assistant chief constable (or equivalent) or **126–006** above, may give authority for the following powers of stop and search under section 44 of the Terrorism Act 2000 to be exercised in the whole or part of his or her police area if the officer considers it is expedient for the prevention of acts of terrorism;

    (a) under section 44(1) of the Terrorism Act 2000, to give a constable in uniform power to stop and search any vehicle, its driver, any passenger in the vehicle and anything in or on the vehicle or carried by the driver or any passenger; and

    (b) under section 44(2) of the Terrorism Act 2000, to give a constable in uniform power to stop and search any pedestrian and anything carried by the pedestrian.

An authorisation under section 44(1) may be combined with one under section 44(2).

2.20 If an authorisation is given orally at first, it must be confirmed in writing by the officer who gave it as soon as reasonably practicable.

2.21 When giving an authorisation, the officer must specify the geographical area in which the power may be used, and the time and date that the authorisation ends (up to a maximum of 28 days from the time the authorisation was given).

2.22 The officer giving an authorisation under section 44(1) or (2) must cause the Secretary of State to be informed, as soon as reasonably practicable, that such an authorisation has been given. An authorisation which is not confirmed by the Secretary of State within 48 hours of its having been given, shall have effect up until the end of that 48 hour period or the end of the period specified in the authorisation (whichever is the earlier).

2.23 Following notification of the authorisation, the Secretary of State may:

  (i) cancel the authorisation with immediate effect or with effect from such other time as he or she may direct;
 (ii) confirm it but for a shorter period than that specified in the authoris-ation; or
(iii) confirm the authorisation as given.

2.24 When an authorisation under section 44 is given, a constable in uniform may exercise the powers;

  (a) only for the purpose of searching for articles of a kind which could be used in connection with terrorism *(see paragraph 2.25)*;
  (b) whether or not there are any grounds for suspecting the presence of such articles.

2.25 The selection of persons stopped under section 44 of Terrorism Act 2000 should reflect an objective assessment of the threat posed by the various terrorist groups active in Great Britain. The powers must not be used to stop and search for reasons unconnected with terrorism. Officers must take particular care not to discriminate against members of minority ethnic groups in the exercise of these powers. There may be circumstances, however, where it is appropriate for officers to take account of a person's ethnic origin in selecting persons to be stopped in response to a specific terrorist threat (for example, some international terrorist groups are associated with particular ethnic identities).

2.26 The powers under sections 43 and 44 of the Terrorism Act 2000 allow a constable to search only for articles which could be used for terrorist purposes. However, this would not prevent a search being carried out under other powers if, in the course of exercising these powers, the officer formed reasonable grounds for suspicion.

Powers to search in the exercise of a power to search premises

126–007   **2.27** The following powers to search premises also authorise the search of a person, not under arrest, who is found on the premises during the course of the search:

  (a) section 139B of the Criminal Justice Act 1988 under which a constable may enter school premises and search the premises and any person on those premises for any bladed or pointed article or offensive weapon; and
  (b) under a warrant issued under section s.23(3) of the Misuse of Drugs Act 1971 to search premises for drugs or documents but only if the warrant specifically authorises the search of persons found on the pre-mises.

2.28 The powers in paragraph 2.27(a) or (b) do not require prior specific grounds to suspect that the person to be searched is in possession of an item for which there is an existing power to search. However, it is still necessary to ensure that the selection and treatment of those searched under these powers is based upon objective factors connected with the search of the premises, and not upon personal prejudice.

2.29 Before the power under section 139B of the Criminal Justice Act 1988 may be exercised, the constable must have reasonable grounds to believe that an offence under section 139A of the Criminal Justice Act 1988 (having a bladed or pointed article or offensive weapon on school premises) has been or is being committed. A warrant to search premises and persons found therein may be issued under section s.23(3) of the Misuse of Drugs Act 1971 if there are reasonable grounds to suspect that controlled drugs or certain documents are in the possession of a person on the premises.

3. Conduct of Searches

3.1 All stops and searches must be carried out with courtesy, consideration **126–008** and respect for the person concerned. This has a significant impact on public confidence in the police. Every reasonable effort must be made to minimise the embarrassment that a person being searched may experience.

3.2 The co-operation of the person to be searched must be sought in every case, even if the person initially objects to the search. A forcible search may be made only if it has been established that the person is unwilling to co-operate. Reasonable force may be used as a last resort if necessary to conduct a search or to detain a person or vehicle for the purposes of a search.

3.3 The length of time for which a person or vehicle may be detained must be reasonable and kept to a minimum. Where the exercise of the power requires reasonable suspicion, the thoroughness and extent of a search must depend on what is suspected of being carried, and by whom. If the suspicion relates to a particular article which is seen to be slipped into a person's pocket, then, in the absence of other grounds for suspicion or an opportunity for the article to be moved elsewhere, the search must be confined to that pocket. In the case of a small article which can readily be concealed, such as a drug, and which might be concealed anywhere on the person, a more extensive search may be necessary. In the case of searches mentioned in paragraph 2.1(b), (c), and (d), which do not require reasonable grounds for suspicion, officers may make any reasonable search to look for items for which they are empowered to search.

3.4 The search must be carried out at or near the place where the person or vehicle was first detained.

3.5 There is no power to require a person to remove any clothing in public other than an outer coat, jacket or gloves except under section 45(3) of the Terrorism Act 2000 (which empowers a constable conducting a search under section 44(1) or 44(2) of that Act to require a person to remove headgear and footwear in public) and under section 60AA of the Criminal Justice and Public Order Act 1994 (which empowers a constable to require a person to remove any item worn to conceal identity). A search in public of a person's clothing which has not been removed must be restricted to superficial examination of outer garments. This does not, however, prevent an officer from placing his or her hand inside the pockets of the outer clothing, or feeling round the inside of collars, socks and shoes if this is reasonably necessary in the circumstances to look for the object of the search or to remove and examine any item reasonably suspected to be the object of the search. For the same reasons, subject to the restrictions on the removal of headgear, a person's hair may also be searched in public *(see paragraphs 3.1 and 3.3)*.

3.6 Where on reasonable grounds it is considered necessary to conduct a more thorough search (e.g. by requiring a person to take off a T-shirt), this must be done out of public view, for example, in a police van unless paragraph 3.7 applies, or police station if there is one nearby. Any search involving the removal of more than an outer coat, jacket, gloves, headgear or footwear, or any other item concealing identity, may only be made by an officer of the same sex as the person searched and may not be made in the presence of anyone of the opposite sex unless the person being searched specifically requests it.

3.7 Searches involving exposure of intimate parts of the body must not be conducted as a routine extension of a less thorough search, simply because nothing is found in the course of the initial search. Searches involving exposure of intimate parts of the body may be carried out only at a nearby police station or other nearby location which is out of public view (but not a police van). These searches must be conducted in accordance with paragraph 11 of Annex

A to Code C except that an intimate search mentioned in paragraph 11(f) of Annex A to Code C may not be authorised or carried out under any stop and search powers. The other provisions of Code C do not apply to the conduct and recording of searches of persons detained at police stations in the exercise of stop and search powers.

Steps to be taken prior to a search

126–009   **3.8** Before any search of a detained person or attended vehicle takes place the officer must take reasonable steps to give the person to be searched or in charge of the vehicle the following information:

   (a) the officer's name (except in the case of enquiries linked to the investigation of terrorism, or otherwise where the officer reasonably believes that giving his or her name might put him or her in danger, in which case a warrant or other identification number shall be given) and the name of the police station to which the officer is attached;
   (b) the legal search power which is being exercised; and
   (c) a clear explanation of:

      (i) the purpose of the search in terms of the article or articles for which there is a power to search; and
      (ii) in the case of powers requiring reasonable suspicion *(see paragraph 2.1(a))*, the grounds for that suspicion; or
      (iii) in the case of powers which do not require reasonable suspicion *(see paragraph 2.1(b), and (c))*, the nature of the power and of any necessary authorisation and the fact that it has been given.

3.9 Officers not in uniform must show their warrant cards. Stops and searches under the powers mentioned in paragraphs 2.1(b), and (c) may be undertaken only by a constable in uniform.

3.10 Before the search takes place the officer must inform the person (or the owner or person in charge of the vehicle that is to be searched) of his entitlement to a copy of the record of the search, including his entitlement to a record of the search if an application is made within 12 months, if it is wholly impracticable to make a record at the time. If a record is not made at the time the person should also be told how a copy can be obtained *(see section 4)*. The person should also be given information about police powers to stop and search and the individual's rights in these circumstances.

3.11 If the person to be searched, or in charge of a vehicle to be searched, does not appear to understand what is being said, or there is any doubt about the person's ability to understand English, the officer must take reasonable steps to bring information regarding the person's rights and any relevant provisions of this Code to his or her attention. If the person is deaf or cannot understand English and is accompanied by someone, then the officer must try to establish whether that person can interpret or otherwise help the officer to give the required information.

4. Recording Requirements

126–010   **4.1** An officer who has carried out a search in the exercise of any power to which this Code applies, must make a written record of it at the time, unless there are exceptional circumstances which would make this wholly impracticable (e.g. in situations involving public disorder or when the officer's presence is urgently required elsewhere). If a record is not made at the time, the officer must do so as soon as practicable afterwards. There may be situations in which it is not practicable to obtain the information necessary to complete a record, but the officer should make every reasonable effort to do so.

4.2 A copy of a record made at the time must be given immediately to the person who has been searched. The officer must ask for the name, address and date of birth of the person searched, but there is no obligation on a person to provide these details and no power of detention if the person is unwilling to do so.

4.3 The following information must always be included in the record of a search even if the person does not wish to provide any personal details:

(i) the name of the person searched, or (if it is withheld) a description;
(ii) a note of the person's self-defined ethnic background or (if it is withheld) a description;
(iii) when a vehicle is searched, its registration number;
(iv) the date, time, and place that the person or vehicle was first detained;
(v) the date, time and place the person or vehicle was searched (if different from (iv));
(vi) the purpose of the search;
(vii) the grounds for making it, or in the case of those searches mentioned in paragraph 2.1(b) and (c), the nature of the power and of any necessary authorisation and the fact that it has been given;
(viii) its outcome (e.g. arrest or no further action);
(ix) a note of any injury or damage to property resulting from it;
(x) subject to paragraph 3.8(a), the identity of the officer making the search.

4.4 Nothing in paragraph 4.3 (x) requires the names of police officers to be shown on the search record or any other record required to be made under this Code in the case of enquiries linked to the investigation of terrorism or otherwise where an officer reasonably believes that recording names might endanger the officers. In such cases the record must show the officers' warrant or other identification number and duty station.

4.5 A record is required for each person and each vehicle searched. However, if a person is in a vehicle and both are searched, and the object and grounds of the search are the same, only one record need be completed. If more than one person in a vehicle is searched, separate records for each search of a person must be made. If only a vehicle is searched, the name of the driver and his self-defined ethnic background must be recorded, unless the vehicle is unattended.

4.6 The record of the grounds for making a search must, briefly but informatively, explain the reason for suspecting the person concerned, by reference to the person's behaviour and/or other circumstances.

4.7 Where officers detain an individual with a view to performing a search, but the search is not carried out due to the grounds for suspicion being eliminated as a result of questioning the person detained, a record must still be made in accordance with the procedure outlined above.

4.8 After searching an unattended vehicle, or anything in or on it, an officer must leave a notice in it (or on it, if things on it have been searched without opening it) recording the fact that it has been searched.

4.9 The notice must include the name of the police station to which the officer concerned is attached and state where a copy of the record of the search may be obtained and where any application for compensation should be directed.

4.10 The vehicle must if practicable be left secure.

Recording of encounters not governed by statutory powers

4.11 When an officer requests a person in a public place to account for themselves, i.e. their actions, behaviour, presence in an area or possession of anything, a record of the encounter must be completed at the time and a copy given to the person who has been questioned. This does not apply under the exceptional circumstances outlined in 4.1.

126–011

4.12 This requirement does not apply to general conversations such as when giving directions to a place, or when seeking witnesses. It also does not include occasions on which an officer is seeking general information or questioning people to establish background to incidents which have required officers to intervene to keep the peace or resolve a dispute.

4.13 When stopping a person in a vehicle, a separate record need not be completed when an HORT/1 form, a Vehicle Defect Rectification Scheme Notice, or an Endorsable Fixed Penalty ticket is issued. It also does not apply when a specimen of breath is required under Section 6 of the Road Traffic Act 1988.

4.14 Officers must inform the person of their entitlement to a copy of a record of the encounter.

4.15 The provisions of 4.4 apply equally when the encounters described in 4.11 and 4.12 are recorded.

4.16 The following information must be included in the record

(i) the name of the person, or (if it is withheld) a description;
(ii) the date, time and place of the encounter;
(iii) if the person is in a vehicle, the registration number;
(iv) a note of the person's self-defined ethnic background or (if it is withheld) a description;
(v) the reason why the officer questioned that person;
(vi) the outcome of the encounter.

4.17 If the person questioned does not wish to provide personal details, there is no power to require him or her to do so. In these instances a form must still be completed.

4.18 A record of an encounter must always be made when a person requests it, regardless of whether the officer considers that the criteria set out in 4.11 have been met. If the form was requested when the officer does not believe the criteria were met, this should be recorded on the form.

5. Monitoring and Supervising the Use of Stop and Search Powers

126–012 **5.1** Supervising officers must monitor the use of stop and search powers and should consider in particular whether there is any evidence that they are being exercised on the basis of stereotyped images or inappropriate generalisations. Supervising officers should satisfy themselves that the practice of supervised officers in stopping, searching and recording is fully in accordance with this code. Supervisors must also examine whether the records reveal any trends or patterns which give cause for concern, and if so take appropriate action to address this. This should include trends and patterns related to the encounters described in 4.11 and 4.12.

5.2 Senior officers with area or force-wide responsibilities must also monitor the broader use of stop and search powers and, where necessary, take action at the relevant level.

5.3 Supervision and monitoring must be supported by the compilation of comprehensive statistical records of stops and searches at force, area and local level. Any apparently disproportionate use of the powers by particular officers or groups of officers or in relation to specific sections of the community should be identified and investigated.

5.4 In order to promote public confidence in the use of the powers, forces must make arrangements for the records to be scrutinised by representatives of the community, and to explain the use of the powers at a local level.

Police and Criminal Evidence Act 1984 — Code B
Code of Practice for the searching of premises by police officers and the seizure of property found by police officers on persons or premises

CONSULTATION DRAFT

JUNE 2002

1. Introduction

1.1 This Code deals with police powers to search premises and to seize and **127–001** retain property found on premises and persons. These powers may be used to find property and material relating to a crime as well as wanted persons and children who have absconded from care.

1.2 Powers of entry search and seizure may be granted under a search warrant issued by a justice of the peace. Examples include warrants to search for stolen property, drugs and firearms and for evidence of serious offences. Police also have powers which do not require a search warrant. The main ones are provided by the Police and Criminal Evidence Act 1984 and include powers to search premises in order to make an arrest and to search after a person has been arrested.

1.3 The right to privacy and respect for personal property are key principles of the Human Rights Act 1998. Powers of entry, search and seizure may involve significant interference with privacy of those whose premises are searched and therefore need to be fully and clearly justified before they are used. In particular, police officers should consider at every stage whether the necessary objectives can be achieved by less intrusive means.

1.4 In all cases, police should exercise their powers courteously and with respect for the persons and property of those concerned and only use reasonable force where this is considered necessary and proportionate in all circumstances.

1.5 If the provisions of the Police and Criminal Evidence Act 1984 and this Code are not observed, evidence obtained from a search may be drawn into question.

2. General

2.1 This Code of Practice must be readily available at all police stations for **127–002** consultation by police officers, detained persons and members of the public.

2.2 The Notes for Guidance included are not provisions of this Code, but are guidance to police officers and others about its application and interpretation.

2.3 This Code applies to searches of premises:

(a) undertaken for the purposes of an investigation into an alleged offence, with the occupier's consent, other than searches made in the following circumstances:

— routine scenes of crime searches
— calls to a fire or a burglary made by or on behalf of an occupier or searches following the activation of fire or burglar alarms or discovery of insecure premises
— searches to which paragraph 5.4 applies
— bomb threat calls;

(b) under powers conferred by sections 17, 18 and 32 of the Police and Criminal Evidence Act 1984;

(c) undertaken in pursuance of a search warrant, the issue and execution of which are subject to sections 15 and 16 of the Police and Criminal Evidence Act 1984;

(d) subject to paragraph 2.5, under any other power given to police to enter premises with or without a search warrant for any purpose connected with the investigation into an alleged or suspected offence.

For the purpose of this Code "premises" is defined in section 23 of the Police and Criminal Evidence Act 1984. It includes any place and, in particular, any vehicle, vessel, aircraft, hovercraft, tent or movable structure. It also includes any offshore installation as defined in section 1 of the Mineral Workings (Offshore Installations) Act 1971.

2.4 Any search of a person who has not been arrested which is carried out during a search of premises shall be carried out in accordance with Code A.

2.5 This Code does not apply to the exercise of a statutory power to enter premises or to inspect goods, equipment or procedures if the exercise of that power is not dependent on the existence of grounds for suspecting that an offence may have been committed and the person exercising the power has no reasonable grounds for such suspicion. Where a search warrant or order which may be lawfully executed in England or Wales requires any items or evidence seized under that warrant or order to be handed over to a police force, court, tribunal, or other authority outside England or Wales, the provisions of this Code shall apply only to the extent that they do not interfere with the directions and requirements of such warrants or orders. Examples include warrants and orders issued in Scotland or Northern Ireland and search warrants issued under section 7 of the Criminal Justice (International Co-operation) Act 1990 (Search etc. for material relevant to overseas investigation).

2.6 Where this Code requires the prior authority or agreement of an officer of the rank of at least inspector or superintendent, that authority may be given by a sergeant or chief inspector who has been authorised to perform the functions of the respective higher rank by virtue of section 107 of the Police and Criminal Evidence Act 1984.

2.7 Written records required to be made under this Code which are not made in the search shall, unless otherwise specified, be made in the pocket book of the officer responsible for making the record or on forms provided for the purpose. References to "pocket book" in this Code include any official report book issued to police officers.

2.8 Nothing in this Code requires the identity of an officer to be recorded or disclosed in the case of enquiries linked to the investigation of terrorism, or otherwise where the officer reasonably believes that recording or disclosing their name might put them in danger. In these cases the officer shall use his or her warrant or other identification number and the name of the police station to which he or she is attached.

2.9 In this Code, the "officer in charge of the search" means the police officer to whom the provisions of this Code assign specific duties and responsibilities. Whenever a search of premises to which this Code applies takes place one officer must act as the officer in charge of the search.

3. Search Warrants and Production Orders

(a) Action to be taken before an application is made

127–003　**3.1** Where information is received which appears to justify an application, the officer concerned must take reasonable steps to check that the information is accurate, recent and has not been provided maliciously or irresponsibly. An application may not be made on the basis of information from an anonymous source where corroboration has not been sought.

3.2 The officer shall ascertain as specifically as is possible in the circumstances the nature of the articles concerned and their location.

3.3 The officer shall also make reasonable enquiries to establish what, if anything, is known about the likely occupier of the premises and the nature of the premises themselves; and whether they have been previously searched and if so how recently; and to obtain any other information relevant to the application.

3.4 No application to a justice of the peace for a search warrant or to a circuit judge under Schedule 1 to the Police and Criminal Evidence Act 1984 for a production order or a search warrant may be made without the signed written authority of an officer of at least the rank of inspector. In the case of an urgent application to a justice of the peace and an inspector or above is not readily available, the next most senior officer on duty may give the authority. No application to a circuit judge under Schedule 5 to the Terrorism Act 2000 for a production order or warrant, or for an order requiring an explanation of material seized or produced under a Schedule 5 warrant or production order, may be made without the signed written authority of an officer of at least the rank of superintendent.

3.5 Except in a case of urgency, if there is reason to believe that a search might have an adverse effect on relations between the police and the community then the local police/community liaison officer shall be consulted before it takes place. In urgent cases, the local police/community liaison officer shall be informed of the search as soon as practicable after it has been made.

(b) Making an application

3.6 An application for a search warrant must be supported in writing, specifying the following information: **127–004**

(a) the enactment under which the application is made;
(b) the premises to be searched and the object of the search; and
(c) the grounds on which the application is made (including, where the purpose of the proposed search is to find evidence of an alleged offence, an indication of how the evidence relates to the investigation);
(d) that there are no reasonable grounds to believe that the material to be sought and retained;

    (i) when making application to a justice of the peace or a circuit judge, consists of or includes items subject to legal privilege; and
    (ii) when making application to a justice of the peace, consists of or includes excluded material or special procedure material,

(this does not affect the additional powers of seizure in Part 2 of the Criminal Justice and Police Act 2001 mentioned under paragraph 7.7); and
(e) if applicable, a request for the warrant to authorise a person to accompany the officer who executes the warrant.

3.7 An application for a search warrant under paragraph 12(a) of Schedule 1 to the Police and Criminal Evidence Act 1984 shall also, where appropriate, indicate why it is believed that service of notice of an application for a production order may seriously prejudice the investigation. Applications for search warrants under paragraph 11 of Schedule 5 to the Terrorism Act 2000 must indicate why a production order would not be appropriate.

3.8 If an application for a search warrant is refused, no further application may be made for a warrant to search those premises unless supported by additional grounds.

4. Entry without Warrant—Particular Powers

(a) Making an arrest etc.

127–005   **4.1** The conditions under which an officer may enter and search premises without a warrant are set out in section 17 of the Police and Criminal Evidence Act 1984. It should be noted that section 17 of the Police and Criminal Evidence Act 1984 does not create or confer any powers of arrest.

(b) Search after arrest of premises in which arrest takes place or in which the arrested person was present immediately prior to arrest

127–006   **4.2** The powers of an officer to search premises in which that officer has arrested a person or where the person was immediately before being arrested are set out in section 32 of the Police and Criminal Evidence Act 1984.

(c) Search after arrest of premises occupied or controlled by the arrested person

127–007   **4.3** The specific powers of an officer to search premises occupied or controlled by a person who has been arrested for an arrestable offence are set out in section 18 of the Police and Criminal Evidence Act 1984. They may not (unless subsection (5) of section 18 applies) be exercised unless an officer of the rank of inspector or above has given authority in writing. That authority should only be given where the authorising officer is satisfied that the necessary grounds exist. The authority shall (unless wholly impracticable) be given on the Notice of Powers and Rights (see paragraph 6.7(i)) and (subject to paragraph 2.8) signed by the authorising officer. The record of the grounds for the search and the nature of the evidence sought as required by section 18(7) of the Act shall be made in the custody record, where there is one.

5. Search with Consent

127–008   **5.1** Subject to paragraph 5.4 below, if it is proposed to search premises with the consent of a person entitled to grant entry to the premises the consent must, if practicable, be given in writing on the Notice of Powers and Rights before the search takes place. The officer must make any necessary enquiries in order to be satisfied that the person is in a position to give such consent. [See paragraph 6.7 (i)]

5.2 Before seeking consent the officer in charge of the search shall state the purpose of the proposed search and its extent. This information must be as specific as possible, particularly in relation to the articles or persons to be sought and the parts of the premises it is proposed to search. The person concerned must be clearly informed that they are not obliged to consent and that anything seized may be produced in evidence. If at the time the person is not suspected of an offence, the officer shall say this when stating the purpose of the search.

5.3 An officer cannot enter and search premises or continue to search premises under 5.1 above if the consent has been given under duress or is withdrawn before the search is completed.

5.4 It is unnecessary to seek consent under paragraphs 5.1 and 5.2 above where in the circumstances this would cause disproportionate inconvenience to the person concerned.

6. Searching of Premises: General Considerations

(a) Time of searches

6.1 Searches made under warrant must be made within one calendar month **127–009** from the date of issue of the warrant.

6.2 Searches must be made at a reasonable hour unless this might frustrate the purpose of the search.

6.3 A warrant authorises an entry on one occasion only. Where the extent or complexity of a search mean that it is likely to take a long time to complete, the officer in charge of the search may wish to consider whether the seize and sift powers referred to in section 7 of this Code can appropriately be used.

(b) Entry other than with consent

6.4 The officer in charge of the search shall first attempt to communicate with **127–010** the occupier, or any other person entitled to grant access to the premises, by explaining the authority under which entry is sought to the premises and ask the occupier to allow entry, unless:

   (i) the premises to be searched are known to be unoccupied;
  (ii) the occupier and any other person entitled to grant access are known to be absent; or
 (iii) there are reasonable grounds for believing that to alert the occupier or any other person entitled to grant access by attempting to communicate with them would frustrate the object of the search or endanger the officers concerned or other people.

6.5 Where the premises are occupied the officer shall (subject to paragraph 2.8) identify themselves and, if not in uniform, show their warrant card; and state the purpose of the search and the grounds for undertaking it, before a search begins, unless sub-paragraph 6.4(iii) applies.

6.6 Reasonable and proportionate force may be used if necessary to enter premises if the officer in charge of the search is satisfied that the premises are those specified in any warrant, or in exercise of the powers described in 4.1 to 4.3 above, and where:

   (i) the occupier or any other person entitled to grant access has refused a request to allow entry to the premises;
  (ii) it is impossible to communicate with the occupier or any other person entitled to grant access; or
 (iii) any of the provisions of 6.4(i) to (iii) apply.

(c) Notice of Powers and Rights

6.7 If an officer conducts a search to which this Code applies the officer shall, **127–011** unless it is impracticable to do so, provide the occupier with a copy of a Notice in a standard format:

   (i) specifying whether the search is made under warrant, or with consent, or in the exercise of the powers described in 4.1 to 4.3 above (the format of the notice shall provide for authority or consent to be indicated where appropriate—see 4.3 and 5.1 above);
  (ii) summarising the extent of the powers of search and seizure conferred in the Act;
 (iii) explaining the rights of the occupier, and of the owner of the property

seized in accordance with paragraphs 6.11, and 7.1 to 7.5 below, set out in the Act and in this Code;

(iv) explaining that compensation may be payable in appropriate cases for damages caused in entering and searching premises, and giving the address to which an application for compensation should be directed;

(v) stating that a copy of this Code is available to be consulted at any police station.

6.8 If the occupier is present, copies of the Notice mentioned above, and of the warrant (if the search is made under warrant) shall, if practicable, be given to the occupier before the search begins, unless the officer in charge of the search reasonably believes that to do so would frustrate the object of the search or endanger the officers concerned or other people. If the occupier is not present, copies of the Notice, and of the warrant where appropriate, shall be left in a prominent place on the premises or appropriate part of the premises and endorsed (subject to paragraph 2.8) with the name of the officer in charge of the search. The warrant itself shall be endorsed to show that this has been done.

(d) Conduct of searches

127–012   **6.9** Premises may be searched only to the extent necessary to achieve the object of the search, having regard to the size and nature of whatever is sought. A search under warrant may not continue under the authority of that warrant once all the things specified in the warrant have been found. Similarly, a search under any other power may not continue once the object of that particular search has been found. No search may continue once the officer in charge of the search is satisfied that whatever is being sought is not on the premises. This does not prevent a further search of the same premises if additional grounds come to light which support a further application for a search warrant (see paragraph 3.8) or exercise or further exercise of another power. Examples would be when as a result of new information, it is believed that articles previously not found or additional articles are on the premises.

6.10 Searches must be conducted with due consideration for the property and privacy of the occupier of the premises searched, and with no more disturbance than necessary. Reasonable force may be used only where this is necessary and proportionate because the co-operation of the occupier cannot be obtained or is insufficient for the purpose.

6.11 The occupier shall be asked whether they wish a friend, neighbour or other person to witness the search. That person must be allowed to do so unless the officer in charge of the search has reasonable grounds for believing that the presence of the person asked for would seriously hinder the investigation or endanger the officers concerned or other people. A search need not be unreasonably delayed for this purpose. A record of the action taken under this paragraph, including the grounds for refusing a request from the occupier, shall be made on the premises search record.

6.12 A person is not required to be cautioned prior to being asked questions that are solely necessary for the purpose of furthering the proper and effective conduct of a search (see paragraph 10.1(c) of Code C). Examples would include questions to discover who is the occupier of specified premises, to find a key to open a locked drawer or cupboard or to otherwise seek co-operation during the search or to determine whether a particular item is liable to be seized. If, in a particular case, questioning goes beyond what is necessary for the purpose of the exemption in Code C, the exchange is likely to constitute an interview as defined by paragraph 11.1A of Code C and would require the associated safeguards included in section 10 of Code C.

(e) Leaving premises

6.13 If premises have been entered by force the officer in charge of the search **127–013** shall, before leaving them, be satisfied that they are secure either by arranging for the occupier or the occupier's agent to be present or by any other appropriate means.

(f) Search under Schedule 1 to the Police and Criminal Evidence Act 1984 or Schedule 5 to the Terrorism Act 2000

6.14 An officer of the rank of inspector or above shall take charge of and be **127–014** present at any search made under a warrant issued under Schedule 1 to the Police and Criminal Evidence Act 1984 or under Schedule 5 to the Terrorism Act 2000. This officer is responsible for ensuring that the search is conducted with discretion and in such a manner as to cause the least possible disruption to any business or other activities carried on in the premises.

6.15 Once satisfied that material may not be taken from the premises without his or her knowledge, the officer in charge of the search shall ask for the documents or other records concerned to be produced. The officer in charge of the search may also, if necessary, ask to see the index to files held on the premises, if there is one; and the officers conducting the search may inspect any files which, according to the index, appear to contain any of the material sought. A more extensive search of the premises may be made only if the person responsible for them refuses to produce the material sought, or to allow access to the index; if it appears that the index is inaccurate or incomplete; or if for any other reason the officer in charge of the search has reasonable grounds for believing that such a search is necessary in order to find the material sought.

7. Seizure and Retention of Property

(a) Seizure

7.1 Subject to paragraph 7.2 below, an officer who is searching any person **127–015** or premises under any statutory power or with the consent of the occupier may seize:

(a) anything covered by a warrant; and
(b) anything which the officer has reasonable grounds for believing is evidence of an offence or has been obtained in consequence of the commission of an offence; and
(c) anything covered by the powers in Part 2 of the Criminal Justice and Police Act 2001 which allow an officer to seize property from persons or premises and retain it for sifting or examination in secure conditions elsewhere.

Items under (b) may only be seized where this is necessary to prevent them being concealed, lost, disposed of, altered, damaged, destroyed or tampered with.

7.2 No item may be seized which an officer has reasonable grounds for believing to be subject to legal privilege (as defined in section 10 of the Police and Criminal Evidence Act 1984), other than under Part 2 of the Criminal Justice and Police Act 2001.

7.3 Officers must be aware of the provisions in section 59 of the Criminal Justice and Police Act 2001 which allow for applications to a judicial authority for the return of property which has been seized and the subsequent duty to secure in section 60 (see paragraph 7.12(iii)).

7.4 An officer may decide that it is not appropriate to seize property because of an explanation given by the person holding it but may nevertheless have reasonable grounds for believing that it has been obtained in consequence of the commission of an offence by some person. In these circumstances, the officer shall identify the property to the holder, inform the holder of their suspicions and explain that, if the holder disposes of, alters or destroys the property, he or she may be liable to civil or criminal proceedings.

7.5 An officer may photograph, image or copy, or have photographed, copied or imaged, any document or other article which the officer has power to seize in accordance with paragraph 7.1 above. This is subject to the specific restrictions on the examination, imaging or copying of certain property seized under Part 2 of the Criminal Justice and Police Act 2001. An officer must have regard to his or her statutory obligation to retain an original document or other article only when a photograph or copy would not be sufficient.

7.6 Where an officer considers that information which is stored in any electronic form could be used in evidence, the officer may require the information to be produced in a form which can be taken away and in which it is visible and legible or from which it can readily be produced in a visible and legible form.

(b) Specific procedures for seize and sift powers

127–016 **7.7** Part 2 of the Criminal Justice and Police Act 2001 provides officers with limited powers to seize property from premises or persons so that they can sift through it or otherwise examine it elsewhere. Officers must be careful that they only exercise these powers where it is essential to do so and that they do not remove any more material than is absolutely necessary. The removal of large volumes of material, much of which may not ultimately be retainable, may have serious implications for the owners, particularly where they are involved in business or in activities such as journalism or the provision of medical services. Officers must always give careful consideration to whether removing copies or images of relevant material or data would be a satisfactory alternative to removing the originals. Where originals are taken, officers must always be prepared to facilitate the provision of copies or images for the owners where that is reasonably practicable.

7.8 Property seized under sections 50 (from premises) or 51 (from persons) of the Criminal Justice and Police Act 2001 must be kept securely and separately from any other material seized under other powers. An examination under section 53 to determine which elements may be retained in accordance with the legislation must be carried out at the earliest practicable time, having due regard to the desirability of allowing the person from whom the property was seized, or a person with an interest in the property, an opportunity of being present or (if the person chooses) being represented at the examination.

7.9 It is the responsibility of the officer in charge of the investigation to ensure that, where appropriate, property is returned in accordance with sections 53 to 55. Material which is not retainable must be separated from the rest of the seized property and returned as soon as reasonably practicable after the examination of all the seized property has been completed. Delay is only warranted if very clear and compelling reasons exist. For example, the unavailability of the person to whom the material is to be returned or the need to agree a convenient time to return a very large volume of material. Legally privileged, excluded or special procedure material which cannot be retained must be returned as soon as reasonably practicable and without waiting for the whole examination to be completed. As set out in section 58, material must be returned to the person from whom it was seized, except where it is clear that some other person has a better right to it.

7.10 Where an officer involved in the investigation has reasonable grounds to believe that a person with a relevant interest in property seized under section 50 or 51 intends to make an application under section 59 for the return of any legally privileged, special procedure or excluded material, the officer in charge of the investigation must be informed and the material seized must be kept secure in accordance with section 61.

7.11 The responsibility for ensuring property is properly secured rests with the officer in charge of the investigation. Securing involves making sure that the property is not examined, copied, imaged or put to any other use except at the request of or with the consent of the applicant or in accordance with the directions of the appropriate judicial authority. Any such request, consent or directions must be recorded in writing and signed by both the initiator and the officer in charge of the investigation.

7.12 Where an officer exercises a power of seizure conferred by sections 50 or 51 that officer shall at the earliest opportunity and unless it is impracticable to do so, provide the occupier of the premises or the person from whom the property was seized with a written notice:

   (i) specifying what has been seized in reliance on the powers conferred by that section;
  (ii) specifying the grounds on which those powers have been exercised;
 (iii) setting out the effect of sections 59 to 61 which cover the grounds on which a person with a relevant interest in seized property may apply to a judicial authority for its return and the duty of officers to secure property in certain circumstance where such an application is made;
 (iv) specifying the name and address of the person to whom notice of an application to the appropriate judicial authority in respect of any of the seized property must be given; and
  (v) specifying the name and address of the person to whom an application may be made to be allowed to attend the initial examination of the property.

7.13 If the occupier is not present but there is some other person there who is in charge of the premises, the notice shall be given to that person. If there is no one on the premises to whom the notice may appropriately be given, it should either be left in a prominent place on the premises or attached to the exterior of the premises so that it will easily be found.

(c) Retention

7.14 Subject to paragraph 7.15 below, anything which has been seized in **127–017** accordance with the above provisions may be retained only for as long as is necessary in the circumstances. It may be retained, among other purposes:

   (i) for use as evidence at a trial for an offence;
  (ii) to facilitate the use in evidence of anything to which it is inextricably linked;
 (iii) for forensic examination or for other investigation in connection with an offence; or
 (iv) in order to establish its lawful owner in cases where there are reasonable grounds for believing that it has been stolen or obtained by the commission of an offence.

7.15 Property shall not be retained in accordance with 7.14(i), (ii) or (iii) if a copy or image would suffice for the purposes.

(d) Rights of owners etc.

127–018   **7.16** If property is retained, the person who had custody or control of it immediately prior to its seizure must on request be provided with a list or description of the property within a reasonable time.

7.17 That person or their representative must be allowed supervised access to the property to examine it or have it photographed or copied, or must be provided with a photograph or copy, in either case within a reasonable time of any request and at their own expense, unless the officer in charge of an investigation has reasonable grounds for believing that this would;

(i) prejudice the investigation of any offence or any criminal proceedings; or

(ii) lead to the commission of an offence by providing access to unlawful material such as pornography.

A record of the grounds must be made in any case where access is denied.

8. Action to Be Taken After Searches

127–019   **8.1** Where premises have been searched in circumstances to which this Code applies, other than in the circumstances covered by the exceptions to paragraph 2.3(a), the officer in charge of the search shall, on arrival at a police station, make or have made a record of the search. The record shall include:

(i) the address of the premises searched;

(ii) the date, time and duration of the search;

(iii) the authority under which the search was made. Where the search was made in the exercise of a statutory power to search premises without warrant, the record shall include the power under which the search was made; and where the search was made under warrant, or with written consent, a copy of the warrant and the written authority to apply for it (see paragraph 3.4) or consent shall be appended to the record or kept in a place identified in the record;

(iv) Subject to paragraph 2.8, the name of the officer in charge of the search and the names of all other officers who conducted the search;

(v) the names of any people on the premises if they are known;

(vi) any grounds for refusing the occupier's request to have someone present during the search (see paragraph 6.11);

(vii) either a list of any articles seized or a note of where such a list is kept and, if not covered by a warrant, the grounds for their seizure;

(viii) whether force was used, and, if so, the reason why it was used;

(ix) details of any damage caused during the search, and the circumstances in which it was caused.

8.2 Where premises have been searched under warrant, the warrant shall be endorsed to show:

(i) whether any articles specified in the warrant were found;

(ii) whether any other articles were seized;

(iii) the date and time at which it was executed;

(iv) Subject to paragraph 2.8, the names of the officers who executed it;

(v) whether a copy, together with a copy of the Notice of Powers and Rights was handed to the occupier; or whether it was endorsed as required by paragraph 6.8, and left on the premises together with the copy notice and, if so, where.

8.3 Any warrant which has been executed or which has not been executed within one calendar month of its issue shall be returned, if it was issued by a justice of the peace, to the clerk to the justices for the petty sessions area concerned or, if issued by a judge, to the appropriate officer of the court concerned.

9. Search Registers

9.1 A search register shall be maintained at each sub-divisional or equivalent **127–020** police station. All search records which are required to be made in accordance with paragraph 8.1 shall be made, copied, or referred to in the register.

Police and Criminal Evidence Act 1984—Code C
Code of Practice for the detention, treatment and questioning of persons by Police Officers

CONSULTATION DRAFT

JUNE 2002

1. General

1.1 All persons in custody must be dealt with expeditiously, and released as **128–001** soon as the need for detention has ceased to apply.

1.1A A custody officer is required to perform the functions specified in this Code as soon as is practicable. A custody officer shall not be in breach of this Code in the event of delay provided that the delay is justifiable and that every reasonable step is taken to prevent unnecessary delay. The custody record shall indicate where a delay has occurred and the reason why.

1.2 This Code of Practice must be readily available at all police stations for consultation by police officers, detained persons and members of the public.

1.3 The Notes for Guidance included are not provisions of this Code, but are guidance to police officers and others about its application and interpretation. Provisions in the Annexes to this Code are provisions of this Code.

1.4 If an officer has any suspicion, or is told in good faith, that a person of any age may be mentally disordered or otherwise mentally vulnerable then, in the absence of clear evidence which dispels any such suspicion, that person shall be treated as such a person for the purposes of this Code and an appropriate adult must be called.

1.5 If anyone appears to be under the age of 17 then he shall be treated as a juvenile for the purposes of this Code in the absence of clear evidence to show that he is older.

1.6 If a person appears to be blind or seriously visually impaired, deaf, unable to read, unable to speak or has difficulty orally because of a speech impediment, he shall be treated as such for the purposes of this Code in the absence of clear evidence to the contrary.

1.7 In this Code "the appropriate adult" means:

    (a) in the case of a juvenile:

        (i) the parent or guardian (or, if the juvenile is in care, the care authority or voluntary organisation. The term "in care" is used in this Code to cover all cases in which a juvenile is "looked after" by a local authority under the terms of the Children Act 1989);

        (ii) a social worker or a member of a local youth offending team;

(iii) failing either of the above, another responsible adult aged 18 or over who is not a police officer or employed by the police.

(b) in the case of a person who is mentally disordered or otherwise mentally vulnerable:

(i) a relative, guardian or other person responsible for their care or custody;

(ii) someone who has experience of dealing with mentally disordered or mentally vulnerable people but who is not a police officer or employed by the police (such as an approved social worker as defined by the Mental Health Act 1983, a specialist social worker or a community psychiatric nurse); or

(iii) failing either of the above, some other responsible adult aged 18 or over who is not a police officer or employed by the police.

1.8 Whenever this Code requires a person to be given certain information he does not have to be given it if he is incapable at the time of understanding what is said to him or is violent or likely to become violent or is in urgent need of medical attention, but he must be given it as soon as practicable.

1.9 Any reference to a custody officer in this Code includes an officer who is performing the functions of a custody officer.

1.10 Subject to paragraph 1.12, this Code applies to people who are in custody at police stations in England and Wales whether or not they have been arrested for an offence and to those who have been removed to a police station as a place of safety under sections 135 and 136 of the Mental Health Act 1983. Section 15 (Reviews and extensions of detention) however applies solely to people in police detention, for example those who have been brought to a police station under arrest for an offence or have been arrested at a police station for an offence after attending there voluntarily.

1.11 People in police custody include anyone detained under the powers conferred by section 41 of, and Schedule 8 to, the Terrorism Act 2000 having been taken to a police station after being arrested under section 41 of the Terrorism Act 2000 and in these cases, any reference to an offence in this Code shall include the commission, preparation and instigation of acts of terrorism.

1.12 The provisions of this Code do not apply to the following groups of people in custody:

(i) people who have been arrested on warrants issued in Scotland by police officers exercising powers under section 136(2) of the Criminal Justice and Public Order Act 1994, or who have been arrested or detained without warrant by officers from a police force in Scotland exercising their powers of arrest or detention under section 137(2) of the Criminal Justice and Public Order Act 1994 (Cross border powers of arrest etc.). In these cases, police powers and duties and the person's rights and entitlements whilst at a police station in England or Wales are the same as if the person had been arrested in Scotland by a Scottish police officer;

(ii) people arrested under section 142(3) of the Immigration and Asylum Act 1999 for the purpose of having their fingerprints taken;

(iii) people whose detention has been authorised by an immigration officer in accordance with the detention powers conferred on immigration officers under the Immigration Act 1971;

(iv) convicted or remanded prisoners held in police cells on behalf of the Prison Service under the Imprisonment (Temporary Provisions) Act 1980;

(v) persons detained for the purposes of examination under Schedule 7 to the Terrorism Act 2000 and to whom the Code of Practice issued under paragraph 6 of Schedule 14 to the Terrorism Act 2000 applies;

(vi) persons detained for the purposes of searches under stop and search powers except as required by Code A.

The provisions on conditions of detention and treatment in sections 8 and 9 of this Code must however be considered as the minimum standards of treatment for such detainees.

1.13 Unless otherwise specified, the custody officer (or investigating officer who is given custody of the detained person by the custody officer) may allow an "approved person" to carry out individual procedures or tasks at the police station where the law allows this, but the officer remains responsible for ensuring they are carried out correctly in accordance with this and any other Code of Practice. Approved persons are engaged to carry out duties or procedures as allowed under this Code and are:

(i) appointed by the Chief Officer of a police force and under the control and direction of that Chief Officer; and

(ii) employed by the police authority maintaining that force.

2. Custody Records

2.1 A separate custody record must be opened as soon as practicable for each **128–002** person who is brought to a police station under arrest or is arrested at the police station having attended there voluntarily. All information which has to be recorded under this Code must be recorded as soon as practicable in the custody record unless otherwise specified. Any audio or video recording made in the custody area is not part of the custody record.

2.2 In the case of any action requiring the authority of an officer of a specified rank, his name and rank must be noted in the custody record. The recording of names does not apply to officers dealing with people detained under the Terrorism Act 2000 or otherwise where an officer reasonably believes that recording names might endanger the officers. Instead the record shall state the warrant or other identification number and duty station of such officers.

2.3 The custody officer is responsible for the accuracy and completeness of the custody record and for ensuring that the record or a copy of the record accompanies a detained person if he is transferred to another police station. The record shall show the time of and reason for transfer and the time a person is released from detention.

2.4 A solicitor or appropriate adult must be permitted to consult the custody record of a person detained as soon as practicable after their arrival at the police station. When a person leaves police detention or is taken before a court, he or his legal representative or his appropriate adult shall be supplied on request with a copy of the custody record as soon as practicable. This entitlement lasts for 12 months after his release.

2.5 The person who has been detained, the appropriate adult, or the legal representative shall be permitted to inspect the original custody record after the person has left police detention provided they give reasonable notice of their request. A note of any such inspection shall be made in the custody record.

2.6 All entries in custody records must be timed and signed by the maker. In the case of a record entered on a computer this shall be timed and contain the operator's identification. Warrant or other identification numbers shall be used rather than names in the case of detention under the Terrorism Act 2000 or where the officer or approved person reasonably believes that giving his or her name might put him or her in danger.

2.7 The fact and time of any refusal by a person to sign a custody record when asked to do so in accordance with the provisions of this Code must itself be recorded.

3. Initial Action

(a) Detained persons: normal procedure

128–003   **3.1** When a person is brought to a police station under arrest or is arrested at the police station having attended there voluntarily, the custody officer must tell him clearly of the following rights and of the fact that they are continuing rights which may be exercised at any stage during the period in custody.

  (i) the right to have someone informed of his arrest in accordance with section 5 below;
  (ii) the right to consult privately with a solicitor and the fact that independent legal advice is available free of charge; and
  (iii) the right to consult these Codes of Practice.

3.2 In addition the custody officer must give the person a written notice setting out the above three rights, the right to a copy of the custody record in accordance with paragraph 2.4 above and the caution in the terms prescribed in section 10 below. The notice must also explain the arrangements for obtaining legal advice. The custody officer must also give the person an additional written notice briefly setting out his entitlements while in custody. The custody officer shall ask the person to sign the custody record to acknowledge receipt of these notices and any refusal to sign must be recorded on the custody record.

3.3 A citizen of an independent Commonwealth country or a national of a foreign country (including the Republic of Ireland) must be informed as soon as practicable of his rights of communication with his High Commission, Embassy or Consulate. [See section 7]

3.4 The custody officer shall note on the custody record any comment the person may make in relation to the arresting officer's account but shall not invite comment. If the custody officer authorises a person's detention he must inform him of the grounds as soon as practicable and in any case before that person is then questioned about any offence. The custody officer shall note any comment the person may make in respect of the decision to detain him but, again, shall not invite comment. The custody officer shall not put specific questions to the person regarding his involvement in any offence, nor in respect of any comments he may make in response to the arresting officer's account or the decision to place him in detention. Such an exchange is likely to constitute an interview as defined by paragraph 11.1A and would require the associated safeguards included in section 11. [See also paragraph 11.13 in respect of unsolicited comments.]

3.5 The custody officer shall ask the detained person whether at this time he would like legal advice (see paragraph 6.5). The person shall be asked to sign the custody record to confirm his decision. The custody officer is responsible for ensuring that in confirming any decision the person signs in the correct place.

3.5A If video cameras are installed in the custody area, notices which indicate that cameras are in use shall be prominently displayed. Any request by a detained person or other person to have video cameras switched off shall be refused.

(b) Detained persons: special groups

128–004   **3.6** If the person appears to be deaf or there is doubt about his hearing or speaking ability or ability to understand English, and the custody officer cannot establish effective communication, the custody officer must as soon as practicable call an interpreter and ask him to provide the information required above.

3.7 If the person is a juvenile, the custody officer must, if it is practicable, ascertain the identity of a person responsible for his welfare. That person may be his parent or guardian (or, if he is in care, the care authority or voluntary organisation) or any other person who has, for the time being, assumed responsibility for his welfare. That person must be informed as soon as practicable that the juvenile has been arrested, why he has been arrested and where he is detained. This right is in addition to the juvenile's right in section 5 of the Code not to be held incommunicado.

3.8 In the case of a juvenile who is known to be subject to a supervision order, action plan order, reparation order, curfew order or community part of a detention and training order, reasonable steps must also be taken to notify the person supervising him (the "responsible officer"). The responsible officer will normally be a member of a Youth Offending Team, unless the curfew order involves electronic monitoring in which case the contractor providing the monitoring will normally be the responsible officer.

3.9 If the person is a juvenile, is mentally disordered or otherwise mentally vulnerable, then the custody officer must, as soon as practicable, inform the appropriate adult (who in the case of a juvenile may or may not be a person responsible for his welfare, in accordance with paragraph 3.7 above) of the grounds for his detention and his whereabouts and ask the adult to come to the police station to see the person.

3.10 It is imperative that a mentally disordered or otherwise mentally vulnerable person who has been detained under section 136 of the Mental Health Act 1983 shall be assessed as soon as possible. If that assessment is to take place at the police station, an approved social worker and a registered medical practitioner shall be called to the police station as soon as possible in order to interview and examine the person. Once the person has been interviewed and examined and suitable arrangements have been made for his treatment or care, he can no longer be detained under section 136. The person should not be released until he has been seen by both the approved social worker and the registered medical practitioner.

3.11 If the appropriate adult is already at the police station, then the provisions of paragraphs 3.1 to 3.5 above must be complied with in his presence. If the appropriate adult is not at the police station when the provisions of paragraphs 3.1 to 3.5 above are complied with, then these provisions must be complied with again in the presence of the appropriate adult once that person arrives.

3.12 The person shall be advised by the custody officer that the appropriate adult (where applicable) is there to assist and advise him and that he can consult privately with the appropriate adult at any time.

3.13 If, having been informed of the right to legal advice under paragraph 3.11 above, either the appropriate adult or the person detained wishes legal advice to be taken, then the provisions of section 6 of this Code apply.

3.14 If the person is blind or seriously visually impaired or is unable to read, the custody officer shall ensure that his solicitor, relative, the appropriate adult or some other person likely to take an interest in him (and not involved in the investigation) is available to help in checking any documentation. Where this Code requires written consent or signification then the person who is assisting may be asked to sign instead if the detained person so wishes.

(c) Persons attending a police station voluntarily

3.15 Any person attending a police station voluntarily for the purpose of assisting with an investigation may leave at will unless placed under arrest. If it is decided that he should not be allowed to leave then he must be informed at once that he is under arrest and brought before the custody officer, who is responsible for ensuring that he is notified of his rights in the same way as other **128–005**

detained persons. If he is not placed under arrest but is cautioned in accordance with section 10 below, the officer who gives the caution must at the same time inform him that he is not under arrest, that he is not obliged to remain at the police station but if he remains at the police station he may obtain free and independent legal advice if he wishes. The officer shall point out that the right to legal advice includes the right to speak with a solicitor on the telephone and ask him if he wishes to do so.

3.16 If a person who is attending the police station voluntarily (in accordance with paragraph 3.15) asks about his entitlement to legal advice, he shall be given a copy of the notice explaining the arrangements for obtaining legal advice. [See paragraph 3.2]

(d) Documentation

128–006 **3.17** The grounds for a person's detention shall be recorded, in his presence if practicable.

3.18 Action taken under paragraphs 3.6 to 3.14 shall be recorded.

4. Detained Person's Property

(a) Action

128–007 **4.1** The custody officer is responsible for:

  (a) ascertaining:

    (i) what property a detained person has with him when he comes to the police station (whether on arrest, re-detention on answering to bail, commitment to prison custody on the order or sentence of a court, lodgement at the police station with a view to his production in court from such custody, arrival at a police station on transfer from detention at another police station or from hospital or on detention under section 135 or 136 of the Mental Health Act 1983);

    (ii) what property he might have acquired for an unlawful or harmful purpose while in custody;

  (b) the safekeeping of any property which is taken from him and which remains at the police station.

To these ends the custody officer may search him or authorise his being searched to the extent that he considers necessary (provided that a search of intimate parts of the body or involving the removal of more than outer clothing may be made only in accordance with Annex A to this Code). A search may be only carried out by an officer of the same sex as the person searched.

4.2 A detained person may retain clothing and personal effects at his own risk unless the custody officer considers that he may use them to cause harm to himself or others, interfere with evidence, damage property or effect an escape or they are needed as evidence. In this event the custody officer may withhold such articles as he considers necessary. If he does so he must tell the person why.

4.3 Personal effects are those items which a person may lawfully need or use or refer to while in detention but do not include cash and other items of value.

(b) Documentation

128–008 **4.4** The custody officer is responsible for recording all property brought to the police station which a detained person had with him, or had taken from him on arrest. The detained person shall be allowed to check and sign the record of property as correct. Any refusal to sign shall be recorded.

4.5 If a detained person is not allowed to keep any article of clothing or personal effects the reason must be recorded.

5. *Right Not to Be Held Incommunicado*

(a) Action

5.1 Any person arrested and held in custody at a police station or other pre- **128–009** mises may on request have one person known to him or who is likely to take an interest in his welfare informed at public expense of his whereabouts as soon as practicable. If the person cannot be contacted the person who has made the request may choose up to two alternatives. If they too cannot be contacted the person in charge of detention or of the investigation has discretion to allow further attempts until the information has been conveyed.

5.2 The exercise of the above right in respect of each of the persons nominated may be delayed only in accordance with Annex B to this Code.

5.3 The above right may be exercised on each occasion that a person is taken to another police station.

5.4 The person may receive visits at the custody officer's discretion.

5.5 Where an enquiry as to the whereabouts of the person is made by a friend, relative or person with an interest in his welfare, this information shall be given, if he agrees and if Annex B does not apply.

5.6 Subject to the following condition, the person shall be supplied with writing materials on request and allowed to speak on the telephone for a reasonable time to one person. Where an officer of the rank of inspector or above considers that the sending of a letter or the making of a telephone call may result in:

(a) any of the consequences set out in the first and second paragraphs of Annex B and the person is detained in connection with an arrestable or a serious arrestable offence, for which purpose, any reference to a serious arrestable offence in Annex B includes an arrestable offence; or

(b) either of the consequences set out in paragraphs 8 and 9 of Annex B and the person is detained under section 41 of, or Schedule 7 to, the Terrorism Act 2000 for which purpose any reference to a serious arrestable offence in Annex B includes an arrestable offence;

that officer can deny or delay the exercise of either or both these privileges. However, nothing in this section permits the restriction or denial of the rights set out in paragraphs 5.1 and 6.1.

5.7 Before any letter or message is sent, or telephone call made, the person shall be informed that what he says in any letter, call or message (other than in the case of a communication to a solicitor) may be read or listened to as appropriate and may be given in evidence. A telephone call may be terminated if it is being abused. The costs can be at public expense at the discretion of the custody officer.

(b) Documentation

5.8 A record must be kept of: **128–010**

(a) any request made under this section and the action taken on it;

(b) any letters, messages or telephone calls made or received or visit received; and

(c) any refusal on the part of the person to have information about himself or his whereabouts given to an outside enquirer. The person must be asked to countersign the record accordingly and any refusal to sign shall be recorded.

6. *Right to Legal Advice*

(a) Action

128–011   **6.1** Subject to the provisos in Annex B all people in police detention must be informed that they may at any time consult and communicate privately, whether in person, in writing or by telephone with a solicitor, and that independent legal advice is available free of charge from the duty solicitor. [See paragraph 3.1]

. . . . . .

6.3 A poster advertising the right to have legal advice must be prominently displayed in the charging area of every police station.

6.4 No police officer shall at any time do or say anything with the intention of dissuading a person in detention from obtaining legal advice.

6.5 The exercise of the right of access to legal advice may be delayed only in accordance with Annex B to this Code. Whenever legal advice is requested (and unless Annex B applies) the custody officer must act without delay to secure the provision of such advice to the person concerned. If, on being informed or reminded of the right to legal advice, the person declines to speak to a solicitor in person, the officer shall point out that the right to legal advice includes the right to speak with a solicitor on the telephone and ask him if he wishes to do so. If the person continues to waive his right to legal advice the officer shall ask him the reasons for doing so, and any reasons shall be recorded on the custody record or the interview record as appropriate. Reminders of the right to legal advice must be given in accordance with paragraphs 3.5, 11.2, 15.3, 16.4 and 16.5 of this Code and paragraphs 3.20(ii) and 6.3 of Code D. Once it is clear that a person neither wishes to speak to a solicitor in person nor by telephone he should cease to be asked his reasons.

6.6 A person who wants legal advice may not be interviewed or continue to be interviewed until they have received such advice unless:

- (a) Annex B applies, in which case the restriction on drawing adverse inferences from silence (paragraph 10.4) will apply because the person is not allowed an opportunity to consult a solicitor; or
- (b) an officer of the rank of superintendent or above has reasonable grounds for believing that:
    - (i) the consequent delay would be likely to lead to interference with or harm to evidence connected with an offence; or interference with or physical harm to other people; or serious loss of, or damage to, property; or lead to the alerting of other people suspected of having committed an offence but not yet arrested for it; or hinder the recovery of property obtained in consequence of the commission of an offence;
    - (ii) where a solicitor, including a duty solicitor, has been contacted and has agreed to attend, awaiting their arrival would cause unreasonable delay to the process of investigation;

    and in these cases the restriction on drawing adverse inferences from silence (paragraph 10.4) will apply because the person is not allowed an opportunity to consult a solicitor;
- (c) the solicitor the person has nominated or selected from a list:
    - (i) cannot be contacted; or

    (ii) has previously indicated that they do not wish to be contacted; or

    (iii) having been contacted, has declined to attend;

and the person has been advised of the Duty Solicitor Scheme but has declined to ask for the duty solicitor. In these circumstances the interview may be started or continued without further delay provided that an officer of the rank of inspector or above has given agreement for the interview to proceed in those circumstances. In these circumstances the restriction on drawing adverse inferences from silence (paragraph 10.4) will not apply because the person is allowed an opportunity to consult the duty solicitor.

(d) the person who wanted legal advice changes their mind, in which case the restriction on drawing adverse inferences from silence (paragraph 10.4) will not apply because the person is allowed an opportunity to consult the duty solicitor.

In these circumstances the interview may be started or continued without further delay provided that the person has given their agreement in writing or on tape to being interviewed without receiving legal advice and that an officer of the rank of inspector or above has inquired into the person's reasons for the change of mind and has given authority for the interview to proceed. Confirmation of the person's agreement, their change of mind, the reasons for it where given and (subject to paragraph 2.2) the name of the authorising officer shall be recorded in the taped or written interview record at the beginning or re-commencement of interview.

6.7 Where 6.6(b)(i) applies, once sufficient information to avert the risk has been obtained, questioning must cease until the person has received legal advice unless 6.6(a), (b)(ii), (c) or (d) apply.

6.8 Where a person has been permitted to consult a solicitor and the solicitor is available (i.e. present at the station or on his way to the station or easily contactable by telephone) at the time the interview begins or is in progress, the solicitor must be allowed to be present while he is interviewed.

6.9 The solicitor may only be required to leave the interview if his conduct is such that the investigating officer is unable properly to put questions to the suspect.

6.10 If the investigating officer considers that a solicitor is acting in such a way, he will stop the interview and consult an officer not below the rank of superintendent, if one is readily available, and otherwise an officer not below the rank of inspector who is not connected with the investigation. After speaking to the solicitor, the officer who has been consulted will decide whether or not the interview should continue in the presence of that solicitor. If he decides that it should not, the suspect will be given the opportunity to consult another solicitor before the interview continues and that solicitor will be given an opportunity to be present at the interview.

6.11 The removal of a solicitor from an interview is a serious step and, if it occurs, the officer of superintendent rank or above who took the decision will consider whether the incident should be reported to the Law Society. If the decision to remove the solicitor has been taken by an officer below the rank of superintendent, the facts must be reported to an officer of superintendent rank or above who will similarly consider whether a report to the Law Society would be appropriate. Where the solicitor concerned is a duty solicitor, the report should be both to the Law Society and to the Legal Services Commission.

6.12 In Codes of Practice issued under the Police and Criminal Evidence Act 1984, "solicitor" means a solicitor who holds a current practising certificate, a trainee solicitor, a duty solicitor representative or an accredited representative included on the register of representatives maintained by the Legal Services Commission. If a solicitor wishes to send a non-accredited or probationary representative to provide advice on his behalf, then that person shall be admitted to the police station for this purpose unless an officer of the rank of inspector or above considers that such a visit will hinder the investigation of crime and directs otherwise. (Hindering the investigation of crime does not include giving proper legal advice to a detained person in accordance with *Note 6D* [*not reproduced*].) Once admitted to the police station, the provisions of paragraphs 6.6 to 6.10 apply.

6.13 In exercising his discretion under paragraph 6.12, the officer should take into account in particular whether the identity and status of the non-accredited or probationary representative have been satisfactorily established; whether he is of suitable character to provide legal advice (a person with a criminal record is unlikely to be suitable unless the conviction was for a minor offence and is not of recent date); and any other matters in any written letter of authorisation provided by the solicitor on whose behalf the person is attending the police station.

6.14 If the inspector refuses access to a non-accredited or probationary representative or a decision is taken that such a person should not be permitted to remain at an interview, he must forthwith notify a solicitor on whose behalf the non-accredited or probationary representative was to have acted or was acting, and give him an opportunity to make alternative arrangements. The detained person must also be informed and the custody record noted.

6.15 If a solicitor arrives at the station to see a particular person, that person must (unless Annex B applies) be informed of the solicitor's arrival whether or not he is being interviewed and asked whether he would like to see him. This applies even if the person concerned has already declined legal advice or having requested it, subsequently agreed to be interviewed without having received advice. The solicitor's attendance and the detained person's decision must be noted in the custody record.

(b) Documentation

128–012　**6.16** Any request for legal advice and the action taken on it shall be recorded.

6.17 If a person has asked for legal advice and an interview is begun in the absence of a solicitor or his representative (or the solicitor or his representative has been required to leave an interview), a record shall be made in the interview record.

7. Citizens of Independent Commonwealth Countries or Foreign Nationals

(a) Action

128–013　**7.1** Any citizen of an independent Commonwealth country or a national of a foreign country (including the Republic or Ireland) may communicate at any time with his High Commission, Embassy or Consulate. He must be informed of this right as soon as practicable. He must also be informed as soon as practicable of his right, upon request to have his High Commission, Embassy or Consulate told of his whereabouts and the grounds for his detention. Such a request should be acted upon as soon as practicable.

7.2 If a person is detained who is a citizen of an independent Commonwealth or foreign country with which a bilateral consular convention or agreement is in force requiring notification of arrest, the appropriate High Commission, Embassy or Consulate shall be informed as soon as practicable, subject to paragraph 7.4 below. The countries to which this applies as at 1 January 1995 are listed in Annex F.

7.3 Consular officers may visit one of their nationals who is in police detention to talk to him and, if required, to arrange for legal advice. Such visits shall take place out of the hearing of a police officer.

7.4 Notwithstanding the provisions of consular conventions, where the person is a political refugee (whether for reasons of race, nationality, political opinion or religion) or is seeking political asylum, a consular officer shall not be informed of the arrest of one of his nationals or given access or information about him except at the person's express request.

(b) Documentation

7.5 A record shall be made when a person is informed of his rights under **128–014** this section and of any communications with a High Commission, Embassy or Consulate.

8. Conditions of Detention

(a) Action

8.1 So far as it is practicable, not more than one person shall be detained in **128–015** each cell.

8.2 Cells in use must be adequately heated, cleaned and ventilated. They must be adequately lit, subject to such dimming as is compatible with safety and security to allow people detained overnight to sleep. No additional restraints shall be used within a locked cell unless absolutely necessary, and then only suitable handcuffs. In the case of a mentally disordered or otherwise mentally vulnerable person, particular care must be taken when deciding whether to use handcuffs.

8.3 Blankets, mattresses, pillows and other bedding supplied shall be of a reasonable standard and in a clean and sanitary condition.

8.4 Access to toilet and washing facilities must be provided.

8.5 If it is necessary to remove a person's clothes for the purposes of investigation, for hygiene or health reasons or for cleaning, replacement clothing of a reasonable standard of comfort and cleanliness shall be provided. A person may not be interviewed unless adequate clothing has been offered to him.

8.6 At least two light meals and one main meal shall be offered in any period of 24 hours. Drinks should be provided at meal times and upon reasonable request between meal times. Whenever necessary, advice shall be sought from the police surgeon on medical and dietary matters. As far as practicable, meals provided shall offer a varied diet and meet any specific dietary needs or religious beliefs that the person may have; he may also have meals supplied by his family or friends at his or their own expense.

8.7 Brief outdoor exercise shall be offered daily if practicable.

8.8 A juvenile shall not be placed in a police cell unless no other secure accommodation is available and the custody officer considers that it is not practicable to supervise him if he is not placed in a cell or the custody officer considers that a cell provides more comfortable accommodation than other secure accommodation in the police station. He may not be placed in a cell with a detained adult.

8.9 Reasonable force may be used if necessary for the following purposes:

(i) to secure compliance with reasonable instructions, including instructions given in pursuance of the provisions of a Code of Practice; or
(ii) to prevent escape, injury, damage to property or the destruction of evidence.

8.10 People detained shall be visited every hour, and those who are drunk, at least every half hour. A person who is drunk shall be roused and spoken to on each visit. Should the custody officer feel in any way concerned about the person's condition, for example because he fails to respond adequately when roused, then the officer shall arrange for medical treatment in accordance with paragraph 9.2 of this Code.

(b) Documentation

128–016   **8.11** A record must be kept of replacement clothing and meals offered.
8.12 If a juvenile is placed in a cell, the reason must be recorded.

9. Treatment of Detained Persons

(a) General

128–017   **9.1** If a complaint is made by or on behalf of a detained person about his treatment since his arrest, or it comes to the notice of any officer that he may have been treated improperly, a report must be made as soon as practicable to an officer of the rank of inspector or above who is not connected with the investigation. If the matter concerns a possible assault or the possibility of the unnecessary or unreasonable use of force then the police surgeon must also be called as soon as practicable.

(b) Medical Treatment

128–018   **9.2** The custody officer must immediately call the police surgeon (or, in urgent cases, — for example, where a person does not show signs or sensibility or awareness, — must send the person to hospital or call the nearest available medical practitioner) if a person brought to a police station or already detained there:

    (a) appears to be suffering from physical illness or a mental disorder; or
    (b) is injured; or
    (c) [Not Used]
    (d) fails to response normally to questions or conversation (other than through drunkenness alone); or
    (e) otherwise appears to need medical attention.

This applies even if the person makes no request for medical attention and whether or not he has already had medical treatment elsewhere (unless brought to the police station direct from hospital). It is not intended that the contents of this paragraph should delay the transfer of a person to a place of safety under section 136 of the Mental Health Act 1983 where that is applicable. Where an assessment under that Act is to take place at the police station, the custody officer has discretion not to call the police surgeon so long as he believes that the assessment by a registered medical practitioner can be undertaken without undue delay.

9.3 If it appears to the custody officer, or he is told, that a person brought to the police station under arrest may be suffering from an infectious disease of any significance he must take steps to isolate the person and his property until he has obtained medical directions as to where the person should be taken, whether fumigation should take place and what precautions should be taken by officers who have been or will be in contact with him.

9.4 If a detained person requests a medical examination the police surgeon must be called as soon as practicable. He may in addition be examined by a medical practitioner of his own choice at his own expense.

9.5 If a person is required to take or apply any medication in compliance with medical directions, but prescribed before the person's detention, the custody officer should consult the police surgeon prior to the use of the medication. The custody officer is responsible for the safekeeping of any medication and for ensuring that the person is given the opportunity to take or apply medication which the police surgeon has approved. However no police officer may administer medicines which are also controlled drugs subject to the Misuse of Drugs Act 1971 for this purpose. A person may administer a controlled drug to himself only under the personal supervision of the police surgeon. The requirement for personal supervision will have been satisfied if the custody officer consults the police surgeon (this may be done by telephone) and both the police surgeon and the custody officer are satisfied that, in all the circumstances, self administration of the controlled drug will not expose the detained person, police officers or anyone to the risk of harm or injury. If so satisfied, the police surgeon may authorise the custody officer to permit the detained person to administer the controlled drug. If the custody officer is in any doubt, the police surgeon should be asked to attend. Such consultation should be noted in the custody record.

9.6 If a detained person has in his possession or claims to need medication relating to a heart condition, diabetes, epilepsy or a condition of comparable potential seriousness then, even though paragraph 9.2 may not apply, the advice of the police surgeon must be obtained.

(c) Documentation

9.7 A record must be made of any arrangements made for an examination by **128–019** a police surgeon under paragraph 9.1 above and of any complaint reported under that paragraph together with any relevant remarks by the custody officer.

9.8 A record must be kept of any request for a medical examination under paragraph 9.4, of the arrangements for any examinations made, and of any medical directions to the police.

9.9 Subject to the requirements of section 4 above the custody record shall include not only a record of all medication that a detained person has in his possession on arrival at the police station but also a note of any such medication he claims he needs but does not have with him.

10. Cautions

(a) When a caution must be given

10.1 A person whom there are grounds to suspect of an offence must be **128–020** cautioned before any questions about it (or further questions if it is the answers to previous questions which provide the grounds for suspicion) are put to them if either the person's answers or silence (i.e. failure or refusal to answer a question or to answer satisfactorily) may be given in evidence to a court in a prosecution. A person therefore need not be cautioned if questions are put for other necessary purposes, for example:

(a) solely to establish their identity or ownership of any vehicle;
(b) to obtain information in accordance with any relevant statutory requirement (see paragraph 10.10);
(c) in furtherance of the proper and effective conduct of a search (for example, to determine the need to search in the exercise of powers of stop and search or to seek co-operation while carrying out a search);
(e) to seek verification of a written record in accordance with paragraph 11.14;
(f) when examining a person in accordance with Schedule 7 to the Terrorism Act 2000 and the Code of Practice for Examining Officers issued under paragraph 6 of Schedule 14 to that Act.

10.2 Whenever a person who is not under arrest is initially cautioned, or is reminded that they are under caution (see paragraph 10.9), that person must at the same time be told that they are not under arrest and are free to leave if they wish to do so.

10.3 A person who is arrested or further arrested:

(a) must be informed:

(i) that they are under arrest; and
(ii) of the grounds for their arrest,

at the time of the arrest (or further arrest) or as soon as is practicable thereafter; and

(b) upon arrest (or further arrest) for an offence, they must also be cautioned unless:

(i) it is impracticable to do so by reason of their condition or behaviour at the time; or
(ii) they have already been cautioned immediately prior to arrest in accordance with paragraph 10.1 above.

(b) Inferences from silence

128–021   **10.4** Sections 34, 36 and 37 of the Criminal Justice and Public Order Act 1994 (as amended by section 58 of the Youth Justice and Criminal Evidence Act 1999) describe the conditions under which adverse inferences may be drawn from a person's failure or refusal to say anything about their involvement in the offence when interviewed or after being charged or informed they may be prosecuted. These provisions are however subject to an overriding restriction which means that a court or jury is not allowed to draw adverse inferences from a person's silence. This restriction applies:

(a) to a person detained at a police station who, before being interviewed (see section 11) or (as the case may be) being charged or informed they may be prosecuted (see section 16):

(i) has asked for legal advice (see paragraph 6.1);
(ii) has not been allowed an opportunity to consult a solicitor, including the duty solicitor, in accordance with this Code; and
(iii) has not changed their mind about wanting legal advice (see paragraph 6.6(d)).
The condition in paragraph (ii) will apply when a detained person who has asked for legal advice is interviewed before speaking to a solicitor in accordance with paragraph 6.6(a) or (b) above. It will not apply if the detained person declines to ask for the duty solicitor (see paragraphs 6.6(c) and (d)); or

(b) to a person charged with, or informed they may be prosecuted for, an offence who:

(i) has brought to their notice a written statement made by another person or the content of an interview with another person which relates to that offence (see paragraph 16.4);
(ii) is interviewed about that offence (see paragraph 16.5); or
(iii) makes a written statement about that offence (see Annex D paragraphs 4 and 9).

(c) Terms of the caution

128–022   **10.5** The caution which must be given:

(a) on arrest (see paragraph 10.3(b)); and

(b) on all other occasions before a person is charged or informed they may be prosecuted (see section 16) unless the restriction on drawing adverse inferences from silence (paragraph 10.4) applies,

shall be in the following terms:

"You do not have to say anything. But it may harm your defence if you do not mention when questioned something which you later rely on in Court. Anything you do say may be given in evidence."

10.6 Whenever a requirement to administer a caution arises and at the time it is given, the restriction on drawing adverse inferences from silence (paragraph 10.4) applies, the caution shall be in the following terms:

"You do not have to say anything, but anything you do say may be given in evidence."

10.7 Whenever the restriction on drawing adverse inferences from silence (paragraph 10.4) either begins to apply or ceases to apply after a caution has already been given, the person shall be re-cautioned in the appropriate terms. The changed position on drawing inferences and the fact that the previous caution no longer applies shall also be explained to him in ordinary language.

10.8 Minor deviations from the words of the caution do not constitute a breach of this Code provided that the sense of the relevant caution is preserved.

10.9 When there is a break in questioning under caution the interviewer must ensure that the person being questioned is aware that they remain under caution. If there is any doubt the relevant caution shall be given again in full when the interview resumes.

10.10 Where, despite the fact that a person has been cautioned, failure to co-operate or to answer particular questions may have an effect on their immediate treatment, the person should be informed of any relevant consequences and that they are not affected by the caution. Examples are when a person's refusal to provide their name and address when charged may make them liable to detention, or when their refusal to provide particulars and information in accordance with a statutory requirement, for example, under the Road Traffic Act 1988, may amount to an offence or may make the person liable to a further arrest.

(d) Special warnings under sections 36 and 37 of the Criminal Justice and Public Order Act 1994

10.11 When a suspect who is interviewed at a police station or authorised **128–023** place of detention after arrest fails or refuses to answer certain questions, or to answer them satisfactorily, after due warning a court or jury may draw such inferences as appear proper under sections 36 and 37 of the Criminal Justice and Public Order Act 1994. This applies only when the restriction on drawing adverse inferences from silence (paragraph 10.4) does not apply and:

(a) the suspect is arrested by a constable and there is found on the suspect's person, or in or on their clothing or footwear, or otherwise in their possession, or in the place where they were arrested, any objects, marks or substances, or marks on such objects, and the person fails or refuses to account for the objects, marks or substances found; or

(b) the arrested person was found by a constable at a place at or about the time the offence for which they were arrested is alleged to have been committed, and the person fails or refuses to account for their presence at that place.

When the restriction on drawing adverse inferences from silence (paragraph 10.4) applies, the suspect may still be asked to account for any of the matters in (a) or (b) but the special warning described in paragraph 10.12 of this Code will not apply and must not be given.

10.12 For an inference to be drawn when a suspect, to whom the restriction on drawing adverse inferences from silence (paragraph 10.4) does not apply, fails or refuses to answer a question about one of these matters or fails or refuses to answer it satisfactorily, the interviewing officer must first tell the suspect in ordinary language:

(a) what offence is being investigated;
(b) what fact the suspect is being asked to account for;
(c) that this fact may be due to the suspect's taking part in the commission of the offence in question;
(d) that a court may draw a proper inference if the suspect fails or refuses to account for this fact;
(e) that a record is being made of the interview and that it may be given in evidence if the suspect is brought to trial.

(e) Juveniles and persons who are mentally disordered or otherwise mentally vulnerable

128–024   **10.13** If a juvenile or a person who is mentally disordered or otherwise mentally vulnerable is cautioned in the absence of the appropriate adult, the caution must be repeated in the adult's presence.

(f) Documentation

128–025   **10.14** A record shall be made when a caution is given under this section, either in the officer's pocket book or in the interview record as appropriate.

11. Interviews: General

(a) Action

128–026   **11.1A** An interview is the questioning of a person regarding their involvement or suspected involvement in a criminal offence or offences which, by virtue of paragraph 10.1 of this Code, is required to be carried out under caution. Whenever a person is interviewed they must be informed of the nature of the offence, or further offence, concerned. Procedures undertaken under section 7 of the Road Traffic Act 1988 or section 31 of the Transport and Works Act 1992 therefore do not constitute interviewing for the purpose of this Code.

11.1 Following a decision to arrest a suspect they must not be interviewed about the relevant offence except at a police station or other authorised place of detention unless the consequent delay would be likely:

(a) to lead to interference with, or harm to, evidence connected with an offence; or interference with, or physical harm to, other people; or serious loss of, or damage to, property; or
(b) to lead to the alerting of other people suspected of having committed an offence but not yet arrested for it; or
(c) to hinder the recovery of property obtained in consequence of the commission of an offence.

Interviewing in any of these circumstances shall cease once the relevant risk has been averted or the necessary questions have been put in order to attempt to avert that risk.

11.2 Immediately prior to the commencement or re-commencement of any interview at a police station or other authorised place of detention the interviewer shall remind the suspect of their entitlement to free legal advice and that the interview can be delayed for legal advice to be obtained (unless one of the exceptions in paragraph 6.6 applies). It is the responsibility of the interviewer to ensure that all such reminders are recorded in the record of the interview.

11.3 [Not Used]

11.4 At the beginning of an interview carried out in a police station or other authorised place of detention, the interviewer, after cautioning the suspect (see section 10), shall put to them any significant statement or silence which occurred in the presence and hearing of a police officer or approved person before the start of the interview and which have not been put to the suspect in the course of a previous interview. The interviewer shall ask the suspect whether they confirm or deny that earlier statement or silence and whether they wish to add anything. A "significant" statement is one which appears capable of being used in evidence against the suspect, in particular a direct admission of guilt. A significant silence is a failure or refusal to answer a question or to answer it satisfactorily when under caution, which might, allowing for the restriction on drawing adverse inferences from silence (paragraph 10.4), give rise to an inference under Part III of the Criminal Justice and Public Order Act 1994.

11.5 No interviewer may try to obtain answers to questions or to elicit a statement by the use of oppression. Except as provided for in paragraph 10.10, no interviewer shall indicate, except in answer to a direct question, what action will be taken on the part of the police if the person being interviewed answers questions, makes a statement or refuses to do either. If the person asks directly what action will be taken in the event of their answering questions, making a statement or refusing to do either, then the interviewer may inform the person what action the police propose to take in that event provided that action is itself proper and warranted.

11.6 The interview or further interview of a person about an offence with which that person has not been charged or for which they have not been informed they may be prosecuted, must cease when the officer in charge of the investigation:

    (a) is satisfied that all the questions that officer considers relevant to obtaining accurate and reliable information from the suspect about the offence being investigated have been put to the suspect (this includes allowing the person an opportunity to give an innocent explanation and asking questions to test whether such an explanation is accurate and reliable, for example, to clear up ambiguities or otherwise clarify what the person has said);

    (b) has taken account of any other evidence which is available; and as a result,

the officer in charge of the investigation, or, in the case of a detained suspect, the custody officer (see paragraph 16.1), reasonably believes that there is sufficient evidence to provide a realistic prospect of conviction for that offence if the person was prosecuted for it.

This paragraph should not, however, be taken to prevent officers in revenue cases or acting under the confiscation provisions of the Criminal Justice Act 1988 or the Drug Trafficking Act 1994 from inviting suspects to complete a formal question and answer record after the interview is concluded.

(b) Interview records

11.7   **128–027**

    (a) An accurate record must be made of each interview with a person, whether or not the interview takes place at a police station.

(b) The record must state the place of the interview, the time it begins and ends, the time the record is made (if different), any breaks in the interview and, subject to paragraph 2.6, the names of all those present; and must be made on the forms provided for this purpose or in the interviewer's pocket book or in accordance with the Code of Practice for the tape recording or visual recording of police interviews with suspects.

(c) The record must be made during the course of the interview, unless this would not be practicable or would interfere with the conduct of the interview, and must constitute either a verbatim record of what has been said or, failing this, an account of the interview which adequately and accurately summarises it.

11.8 If an interview record is not made during the course of the interview it must be made as soon as practicable after its completion.

11.9 Written interview records must be timed and signed by the maker.

11.10 If an interview record is not completed in the course of the interview the reason must be recorded in the interview record.

11.11 Unless it is impracticable, the person interviewed shall be given the opportunity to read the interview record and to sign it as correct or to indicate the respects in which that person considers it inaccurate. If the interview is tape-recorded the arrangements set out in Code E apply. If the person concerned cannot read or refuses to read the record or to sign it, the senior interviewer present shall read it to the person and ask whether the person would like to sign it as correct (or make their mark) or to indicate the respects in which they consider it inaccurate. The interviewer shall then certify on the interview record itself what has occurred.

11.12 If the appropriate adult or the person's solicitor is present during the interview, they shall also be given an opportunity to read and sign the interview record (or any written statement taken down in the course of the interview).

11.13 A written record shall also be made of any comments made by a suspected person in the presence and hearing of a police officer or approved person, including unsolicited comments, which are outside the context of an interview but which might be relevant to the offence. Any such record must be timed and signed by the maker. Where practicable the person shall be given the opportunity to read that record and to sign it as correct or to indicate the respects in which they consider it inaccurate. Any refusal to sign shall be recorded.

11.14 Any refusal by a person to sign an interview record when asked to do so in accordance with the provisions of this Code must itself be recorded.

(c) Juveniles and mentally disordered or otherwise mentally vulnerable people

128–028   **11.15** A juvenile or a person who is mentally disordered or otherwise mentally vulnerable must not be interviewed or asked to provide or sign a written statement under caution or record of interview in the absence of the appropriate adult unless paragraph 11.1 or paragraphs 11.18 to 11.20 apply.

11.16 Juveniles may only be interviewed at their places of education in exceptional circumstances and then only where the principal or the principal's nominee agrees. Every effort should be made to notify both the parent(s) or other person responsible for the juvenile's welfare and the appropriate adult (if this is a different person) that the police want to interview the juvenile and reasonable time should be allowed to enable the appropriate adult to be present at the interview. Where awaiting the appropriate adult would cause unreasonable delay, and unless the interviewee is suspected of an offence against the educational establishment, the principal or their nominee can act as the appropriate adult for the purposes of the interview.

11.17 Where the appropriate adult is present at an interview, they shall be informed that they are not expected to act simply as an observer, and that the purposes of their presence are, first, to advise the person being questioned and to observe whether or not the interview is being conducted properly and fairly, and secondly, to facilitate communication with the person being interviewed.

(d) Vulnerable suspects: urgent interviews at police stations

11.18 An interview of the following persons may not take place in a police **128–029** station or other authorised place of detention unless an officer of the rank of superintendent or above considers that delay will lead to the consequences set out in paragraph 11.1(a) to (c) of this Code:

- (a) anyone other than in (b) below who at the time of the interview appears to be unable to appreciate the significance of questions put to them and their answers or to understand what is happening because of the effects of drink or drugs or any illness, ailment or condition;
- (b) a juvenile or a person who is mentally disordered or otherwise mentally vulnerable if at the time of the interview the appropriate adult is not present;
- (c) a person who has difficulty in understanding English or who has a hearing disability if at the time of the interview an interpreter is not present;

and the authorising officer is satisfied that the interview would not significantly harm their physical or mental state.

11.19 Interviewing in these circumstances may not continue once sufficient information to avert the consequences set out in paragraph 11.1(a) to (c) of this Code has been obtained.

11.20 A record shall be made of the grounds for any decision to interview a person under paragraph 11.18 above.

12. Interviews in Police Stations

(a) Action

12.1 If a police officer wishes to interview, or conduct enquiries which require **128–030** the presence of a detained person, the custody officer is responsible for deciding whether to deliver the detained person into the custody of the police officer concerned.

12.2 Except as provided for below, in any period of 24 hours a detained person must be allowed a continuous period of at least 8 hours for rest, free from questioning, travel or any interruption in connection with the investigation concerned. This period should normally be at night or other appropriate time which takes account of when the person concerned last slept or rested but it does depend on whether the person sleeps. If a person is arrested at a police station after going there voluntarily, the period of 24 hours runs from the time of their arrest and not the time of arrival at the police station. The period may not be interrupted or delayed, except:

- (a) where there are reasonable grounds for believing that not delaying or interrupting the period would:
  - (i) involve a risk of harm to people or serious loss of, or damage to, property; or
  - (ii) delay unnecessarily the person's release from custody; or
  - (iii) otherwise prejudice the outcome of the investigation.

(b) at the request of the person, their appropriate adult or their legal representative.

(c) when a delay or interruption is necessary in order to;

(i) comply with the legal obligations and duties arising under section 15 (Reviews and extensions of detention); or

(ii) to take action which is required under section 9 of this Code (Treatment of Detained Persons) or in accordance with medical advice.

If the period is interrupted in accordance with paragraph (a), a fresh period must be allowed. Interruptions under paragraphs (b) and (c), do not require a fresh period to be allowed.

12.3 When it is proposed to interview a detained person, the custody officer, in consultation with the officer in charge of the investigation and appropriate health care professionals as necessary, shall assess whether the person is fit enough to be interviewed. This means determining and considering the risks which the person's physical and mental state might present if the interview took place and determining what safeguards are needed in order to allow the interview to take place. (See Annex G which deals with the assessment of a person's fitness to be interviewed.) The custody officer shall not allow a detained person to be interviewed at a time when the custody officer considers that it would cause significant harm to the person's physical or mental state. In all other cases for the purposes of this Code, the following shall be treated as always being at some risk during an interview;

(a) anyone other than in (b) below who at the time of the interview appears to be unable to appreciate the significance of questions put to them and their answers or to understand what is happening because of the effects of drink or drugs or any illness, ailment or condition.

(b) a juvenile or a person who is mentally disordered or otherwise mentally vulnerable if at the time of the interview the appropriate adult is not present.

(c) a person who has difficulty in understanding English or who has a hearing disability if at the time of the interview an interpreter is not present. and these persons may not be interviewed except in accordance with paragraphs 11.18 to 11.20.

12.4 As far as practicable interviews shall take place in interview rooms which must be adequately heated, lit and ventilated.

12.5 A suspect whose detention without charge has been authorised under the Police and Criminal Evidence Act 1984, because the detention is necessary to interview them to obtain evidence of the offence for which they have been arrested, may choose not to answer any questions but police do not require the suspect's consent or agreement to interview them for this purpose. If a suspect takes steps to prevent him or herself from being questioned or further questioned, for example, by refusing to leave their cell to go into a suitable interview room, or by trying to leave the interview room, they shall be so advised that their consent or agreement to interview is not required. The suspect shall then be cautioned in accordance with section 10 of this Code, and informed that if they fail or refuse to co-operate, the interview may take place in the cell and that their failure or refusal to co-operate may be given in evidence. The suspect shall then be invited to co-operate and go into the interview room.

12.6 People being questioned or making statements shall not be required to stand.

12.7 Before the commencement of an interview each interviewer shall, subject to paragraph 2.6 identify him or herself and any other persons present to the person being interviewed.

12.8 Breaks from interviewing shall be made at recognised meal times. Short breaks for refreshment shall also be provided at intervals of approximately two hours, subject to the interviewer's discretion to delay a break if there are reasonable grounds for believing that it would:

- (i) involve a risk of harm to people or serious loss of, or damage to property;
- (ii) delay unnecessarily the person's release from custody; or
- (iii) otherwise prejudice the outcome of the investigation.

12.9 If in the course of the interview a complaint is made by the person being questioned, or a complaint is made on their behalf, concerning the provisions of this Code then the interviewer shall:

- (i) record it in the interview record; and
- (ii) inform the custody officer, who is then responsible for dealing with it in accordance with section 9 of this Code.

(b) Documentation

12.10 A record must be made of the time at which a detained person is not **128–031** in the custody of the custody officer, and why; and of the reason for any refusal to deliver him out of that custody.

12.11 The reasons why it was not practicable for an interview to take place in an interview room and any action taken in accordance with paragraph 12.5 shall be recorded. The record shall be made on the custody record and, if the action is taken whilst an interview record is being kept, in the interview record in which case the custody record may comprise a brief note which refers to the interview record.

12.12 Any decision to delay a break in an interview must be recorded, with grounds, in the interview record.

12.13 All written statements made at police stations under caution shall be written on the forms provided for the purpose.

12.14 All written statements made under caution shall be taken in accordance with Annex D to this Code. Before a person makes a written statement under caution at a police station they shall be reminded of the right to legal advice.

13. Interpreters

(a) General

13.1 Information on obtaining the services of a suitably qualified interpreter **128–032** for the deaf or for people who do not understand English is given in *Note for Guidance 3D* [*not reproduced*].

(b) Foreign languages

13.2 Except in accordance with paragraph 11.1 or unless paragraphs 11.18 to **128–033** 11.20 apply, a person must not be interviewed in the absence of a person capable of acting as interpreter if:

- (a) he has difficulty in understanding English;
- (b) the interviewing officer cannot speak the person's own language; and
- (c) the person wishes an interpreter to be present.

13.3 The interviewing officer shall ensure that the interpreter makes a note of the interview at the time in the language of the person being interviewed for use in the event of his being called to give evidence, and certifies its accuracy. He shall allow sufficient time for the interpreter to make a note of each question and answer after each has been put or given and interpreted. The person shall be given an opportunity to read it or have it read to him and sign it as correct or to indicate the respects in which he considers it inaccurate. If the interview is tape-recorded the arrangements set out in Code E apply.

13.4 In the case of a person making a statement in a language other than English:

    (a) the interpreter shall take down the statement in the language in which it is made;

    (b) the person making the statement shall be invited to sign it; and

    (c) an official English translation shall be made in due course.

(c) Deaf people and people with speech difficulties

128–034   **13.5** If a person appears to be deaf or there is doubt about his hearing or speaking ability, he must not be interviewed in the absence of an interpreter unless he agrees in writing to be interviewed without one or paragraph 11.1 or paragraphs 11.18 to 11.20 apply.

13.6 An interpreter shall also be called if a juvenile is interviewed and the parent or guardian present as the appropriate adult appears to be deaf or there is doubt about his hearing or speaking ability, unless he agrees in writing that the interview should proceed without one or paragraph 11.1 or paragraphs 11.18 to 11.20 apply.

13.7 The interviewing officer shall ensure that the interpreter is given an opportunity to read the record of the interview and to certify its accuracy in the event of his being called to give evidence.

(d) Additional rules for detained persons

128–035   **13.8** All reasonable attempts should be made to make clear to the detained person that interpreters will be provided at public expense.

13.9 Where paragraph 6.1 applies and the person concerned cannot communicate with the solicitor, whether because of language, hearing or speech difficulties, an interpreter must be called. The interpreter may not be a police officer when interpretation is needed for the purposes of obtaining legal advice. In all other cases a police officer may only interpret if he first obtains the detained person's (or the appropriate adult's) agreement in writing or if the interview is tape-recorded or visually recorded in accordance with Code E or F as applicable.

13.10 When a person is charged with an offence who appears to be deaf or there is doubt about his hearing or speaking ability or ability to understand English, and the custody officer cannot establish effective communication, arrangements must be made for an interpreter to explain as soon as practicable the offence concerned and any other information given by the custody officer.

(e) Documentation

128–036   **13.11** Action taken to call an interpreter under this section and any agreement to be interviewed in the absence of an interpreter must be recorded.

14. Questioning: Special Restrictions

128–037   **14.1** If a person has been arrested by one police force on behalf of another and the lawful period of detention in respect of that offence has not yet commenced in accordance with section 41 of the Police and Criminal Evidence Act 1984 no questions may be put to him about the offence while he is in transit between the forces except in order to clarify any voluntary statement made by him.

14.2 If a person is in police detention at a hospital he may not be questioned without the agreement of a responsible doctor.

15. Reviews and Extensions of Detention

(a) Action

15.1 The review officer is responsible under section 40 of the Police and **128–038** Criminal Evidence Act 1984 (or under Part II of Schedule 8 to the Terrorism Act 2000 in terrorism cases) for periodically determining whether or not a person's detention (before or after charge) continues to be necessary. The requirement for these reviews continues throughout the period the person is in police detention and except as described in paragraph 15.6, the review officer must be present at the police station where the person is detained.

15.2 In reaching a decision on whether detention continues to be necessary, the review officer shall provide an opportunity to the detained person to make representations (unless the person concerned is unfit to do so because of their condition or behaviour) or to the person's solicitor or to the appropriate adult if available at the time. Other people having an interest in the person's welfare may make representations at the review officer's discretion.

15.3 Before conducting a review or determining whether to extend the maximum period of detention without charge, the officer responsible must ensure that the detained person is reminded of their entitlement to free legal advice.

15.3A Under section 42 of the Police and Criminal Evidence Act 1984, an officer of the rank of superintendent or above who is responsible for the station where the person is detained may give authority any time after the second review to extend the maximum period for which a person may be kept in police detention without charge by up to 12 hours. The same people mentioned in paragraph 15.2 may make representations to that officer.

15.4 If after considering any representations made as above the officer decides to keep the person in detention or to extend the maximum period for which they may be detained without charge, any comment made by the person shall be recorded by the officer to whom it is made. If applicable, the officer making the record shall inform the officer responsible for making the decision of the comment as soon as practicable. [See also paragraphs 11.4 and 11.13]

15.5 No officer shall put specific questions to the suspect regarding their involvement in any offence, nor in respect of any comments they may make when given the opportunity to make representations or in response to a decision to keep them in detention or to extend the maximum period of detention. Such an exchange is likely to constitute an interview as defined by paragraph 11.1A and would be subject to the associated safeguards included in section 11 and, in respect of a person who has been charged, paragraph 16.5.

(b) Review of detention by telephone

15.6 Section 40A of the Police and Criminal Evidence Act 1984 provides that **128–039** the review officer responsible under section 40 for reviewing the detention of a person who has not been charged, need not attend the police station where the person is detained and may carry out the review by telephone if:

(a) it is not reasonably practicable for the officer to be present at that station;

(b) section 45A of the Police and Criminal Evidence Act 1984 (when in force), in respect of the use of video conferencing facilities, does not apply or it is not reasonably practicable in the circumstances to use such facilities; and

(c) the officer is able to communicate by telephone with persons who are present at that station.

15.7 When a review is carried out by telephone:

(a) any obligation of the review officer under section 40 or this Code to make any record in the person's custody record in connection with the review shall have effect as an obligation to require the record to be made by another officer at the station where the person is detained;

(b) any requirement under section 40 or this Code for the record in (a) to be made in the presence of the detained person shall apply to the making of that record by that other officer; and

(c) where the review officer is required under section 40 or this Code to give the detained person information, that information may also be given by that other officer.

15.8 When a review is carried out by telephone, the requirement to give the persons mentioned in paragraph 15.2 an opportunity to make representations (whether orally or in writing), to the review officer will be satisfied:

(a) where facilities exist for the immediate transmission of written representations to the review officer (for example, via a fax or email message), by giving the person an opportunity to make representations to the review officer:

(i) orally by telephone; or
(ii) in writing by means of those facilities; and

(b) in all other cases, by giving the person an opportunity to make representations orally by telephone to the review officer.

(c) Documentation

128–040   **15.9** It is the responsibility of the review officer to ensure that all reminders given in accordance with paragraph 15.3 are noted in the custody record.

15.10 The grounds for and extent of any delay in conducting a review shall be recorded.

15.11 When a review is carried out by telephone, a record shall be made of:

(a) the reason why the review officer did not attend the station where the person was detained;

(b) the place where the review officer was; and

(c) the method by which representations (oral or written) were made to the review officer (see paragraph 15.8).

15.12 Any written representations shall be retained.

15.13 A record shall be made as soon as practicable of the outcome of each review or determination whether to extend the maximum period of detention without charge and application for a warrant of further detention or its extension. If an authorisation is given under section 42 of the Police and Criminal Evidence Act 1984, the record shall state the number of hours and minutes (as applicable) by which the period of detention without charge is extended or further extended. If a warrant of further detention, or an extension thereof, is granted under section 43 or 44, the record shall state the period of detention which is authorised by the warrant and the date and time it was granted.

16. Charging of Detained Persons

(a) Action

16.1 When the officer in charge of the investigation reasonably believes that **128–041** there is sufficient evidence to provide a realistic prospect of the detained person's conviction for an offence if the person was prosecuted for it, (see paragraph 11.6), that officer shall without delay (and subject to the following qualification) inform the custody officer who shall then be responsible for considering whether or not the detained person should be charged. When a person is detained in respect of more than one offence it is permissible to delay informing the custody officer until the above conditions are satisfied in respect of all the offences (but see paragraph 11.6). Any resulting action shall be taken in the presence of the appropriate adult if the person is a juvenile or mentally disordered or otherwise mentally vulnerable.

16.2 When a detained person is charged with or informed that they may be prosecuted for an offence at a time;

(a) when the restriction on drawing adverse inferences from silence (paragraph 10.4) does not apply, they shall be cautioned in the manner described in paragraph 10.5 in the following terms;

> *"You do not have to say anything. But it may harm your defence if you do not mention now something which you later rely on in court. Anything you do say may be given in evidence."*

(b) when the restriction on drawing adverse inferences from silence (paragraph 10.4) applies, they shall be cautioned in the manner described in paragraph 10.6 in the following terms

> *"You do not have to say anything, but anything you do say may be given in evidence."*

16.3 When a person is charged they shall be given a written notice showing particulars of the offence with which they are charged and, subject to paragraph 2.6, the name of the officer in the case and the reference number for the case. So far as possible the particulars of the charge shall be stated in simple terms, but they shall also show the precise offence in law with which the person is charged. The notice shall begin with the following words:

> *"You are charged with the offence(s) shown below."* These words shall be followed by the words of the caution given in accordance with paragraph 16.2.

If the person is a juvenile or is mentally disordered or otherwise mentally vulnerable the notice shall be given to the appropriate adult.

16.4 If, at any time after a person has been charged with, or informed that they may be prosecuted for, an offence, a police officer or approved person wishes to bring to the notice of that person any written statement made by another person or the content of an interview with another person which relates to such an offence, the officer or approved person shall hand to that person a true copy of any such written statement or bring to their attention the content of the interview record, but shall say or do nothing to invite any reply or comment save to:

(a) caution the person in the following terms;

> *"You do not have to say anything unless you wish to do so, but what you say may be given in evidence." ;* and

(b) remind the person of their right to legal advice.

If the person cannot read then the officer or approved person may read it to them. If the person is a juvenile or mentally disordered or otherwise mentally vulnerable the copy shall also be given to, or the interview record brought to the attention of, the appropriate adult.

16.5 A person may not be interviewed about an offence after they have been charged with that offence, or informed that they may be prosecuted for it, unless the interview is necessary for the purpose of preventing or minimising harm or loss to some other person, or to the public, or for clearing up an ambiguity in a previous answer or statement, or where it is in the interests of justice that the person should have put to them, and have an opportunity to comment on, information concerning the offence which has come to light since they were charged or informed that they might be prosecuted. Before any such interview, the interviewer shall;

(a) caution the person in the following terms;

> *"You do not have to say anything unless you wish to do so, but what you say may be given in evidence." ;* and

(b) remind the person of their right to legal advice.

16.6 If the appropriate adult is already at the police station, then the provisions of paragraphs 16.2 to 16.5 as applicable must be complied with in the adult's presence. If the appropriate adult is not at the police station when these provisions are complied with, then these provisions must be complied with again in the presence of the appropriate adult when the adult arrives unless the person has been released from the station.

16.7 Where a juvenile is charged with an offence and the custody officer authorises their continued detention after charge, the custody officer must try to make arrangements for the juvenile to be taken into the care of a local authority and to be detained pending appearance in court, unless the custody officer certifies that it is impracticable to do so or, in the case of a juvenile of at least 12 years of age, no secure accommodation is available and there is a risk to the public of serious harm from that juvenile, in accordance with section 38(6) of the Police and Criminal Evidence Act 1984.

(b) Documentation

128–042 **16.8** A record shall be made of anything a detained person says when charged.

16.9 Any questions put in an interview after charge and answers given relating to the offence shall be contemporaneously recorded in full on forms provided for the purpose and the record signed by that person or, if they refuse, by the interviewer and any third parties present. If the questions are tape recorded the arrangements set out in Code E apply.

16.10 If it is not practicable to make arrangements for the transfer of a juvenile into local authority care in accordance with paragraph 16.7 above the custody officer must record the reasons and make out a certificate to be produced before the court together with the juvenile.

ANNEX A
INTIMATE AND STRIP SEARCHES [see Paragraph 4.1]

A. Intimate Search

1. An "intimate search" is a search which consists of the physical examination **128–043**
of a person's body orifices other than the mouth. The intrusive nature of such
searches means that the actual and potential risks associated with intimate
searches must never be underestimated.

(a) Action

2. Body orifices other than the mouth may be searched only if an officer of **128–044**
the rank of inspector or above has reasonable grounds for believing that the
person may have concealed on them:

(a) anything which they could and might use to cause physical injury to
him or herself or to others at the police station; or
(b) a Class A drug which they intended to supply to another or to export;
and that in either case the authorising officer has reasonable grounds
to believe that an intimate search is the only means of removing it.

The reasons why an intimate search is considered necessary shall be explained
to the person before the search takes place.
3. An intimate search may only be carried out by a registered medical practitioner or registered nurse, unless an officer of at least the rank of inspector
considers that this is not practicable and the search is to take place under subparagraph 2(a) above, in which case a police officer may carry out the search. Any
proposal for a search under subparagraph 2(a) to be carried out by someone
other than a registered medical practitioner or registered nurse should only be
considered as a last resort and when the authorising officer is satisfied that the
risks associated with allowing the item to remain with the person outweigh the
risks associated with removing it.
4. An intimate search under sub-paragraph 2(a) above may take place only at
a hospital, surgery, other medical premises or police station. A search under
sub-paragraph 2(b) may take place only at a hospital, surgery or other medical
premises and must be carried out by a registered medical practitioner or a registered nurse.
5. An intimate search at a police station of a juvenile or a mentally disordered
or otherwise mentally vulnerable person may take place only in the presence of
an appropriate adult of the same sex (unless the person specifically requests the
presence of a particular adult of the opposite sex who is readily available). In
the case of a juvenile the search may take place in the absence of the appropriate
adult only if the juvenile signifies in the presence of the appropriate adult that
they do not wish the adult to be present during the search and the adult agrees.
A record shall be made of the juvenile's decision and signed by the appropriate
adult.
6. Where an intimate search under sub-paragraph 2(a) above is carried out by
a police officer, the officer must be of the same sex as the person searched. A
minimum of two people, other than the person searched, must be present during
the search. Subject to paragraph 5 above, no person of the opposite sex who is
not a medical practitioner or nurse shall be present, nor shall anyone whose
presence is unnecessary. The search shall be conducted with proper regard to
the sensitivity and vulnerability of the person in these circumstances.

(b) Documentation

128–045   7. In the case of an intimate search the custody officer shall as soon as practicable record which parts of the person's body were searched, who carried out the search, who was present, the reasons for the search including the reasons to believe the article could not otherwise be removed, and the result.

8. If an intimate search is carried out by a police officer, the reason why it was impracticable for a suitably qualified person to conduct it must be recorded.

B. Strip Search

128–046   9. A strip search is a search involving the removal of more than outer clothing. For the purposes of this Code, outer clothing includes shoes and socks.

(a) Action

128–047   10. A strip search may take place only if it is considered necessary to remove an article which a person would not be allowed to keep, and the officer reasonably considers that the person might have concealed such an article. Strip searches shall not be routinely carried out where there is no reason to consider that articles have been concealed.

The conduct of strip searches
128–048   11. The following procedures shall be observed when strip searches are conducted:

    (a) a police officer carrying out a strip search must be of the same sex as the person searched;

    (b) the search shall take place in an area where the person being searched cannot be seen by anyone who does not need to be present, nor by a member of the opposite sex (except an appropriate adult who has been specifically requested by the person being searched);

    (c) except in cases of urgency, where there is a risk of serious harm to the person detained or to others, whenever a strip search involves exposure of intimate parts of the body, there must be at least two people present other than the person searched, and if the search is of a juvenile or a mentally disordered or otherwise mentally vulnerable person, one of the people must be the appropriate adult. Except in urgent cases as above, a search of a juvenile may take place in the absence of the appropriate adult only if the juvenile signifies in the presence of the appropriate adult that they do not wish the adult to be present during the search and the adult agrees. A record shall be made of the juvenile's decision and signed by the appropriate adult. The presence of more than two people, other than an appropriate adult, shall be permitted only in the most exceptional circumstances.

    (d) the search shall be conducted with proper regard to the sensitivity and vulnerability of the person in these circumstances and every reasonable effort shall be made to secure the person's co-operation and minimise embarrassment. People who are searched should not normally be required to have all their clothes removed at the same time, for example, a man shall be allowed to put on his shirt before removing his trousers, and a woman shall be allowed to put on her blouse and upper garments before further clothing is removed;

    (e) where necessary to assist the search, the person may be required to hold his or her arms in the air or to stand with his or her legs apart and to bend forward so that a visual examination may be made of the genital and anal areas provided that no physical contact is made with any body orifice;

(f) if, during a search, articles are found, the person shall be asked to hand them over. If articles are found within any body orifice other than the mouth, and the person refuses to hand them over, their removal would constitute an intimate search, which must be carried out in accordance with the provisions of Part A of this Annex;

(g) a strip search shall be conducted as quickly as possible, and the person searched allowed to dress as soon as the procedure is complete.

(b) Documentation

12. A record shall be made on the custody record of a strip search including **128–049** the reason it was considered necessary to undertake it, those present and any result.

ANNEX B
DELAY IN NOTIFYING ARREST OR ALLOWING ACCESS TO LEGAL ADVICE

A. Persons detained under the Police and Criminal Evidence Act 1984

1. The exercise of the rights in Section 5 (Right not to be held **128–050** incommunicado) or Section 6 (Right to legal advice) of this Code, or both, may be delayed if the person is in police detention (as defined in section 118(2) of the Police and Criminal Evidence Act 1984) in connection with a serious arrestable offence, has not yet been charged with an offence and an officer of the rank of superintendent or above (or inspector or above in respect of the rights in Section 5) has reasonable grounds for believing that the exercise of either right:

(i) will lead to interference with, or harm to, evidence connected with a serious arrestable offence or interference with, or physical injury to, other people; or

(ii) will lead to the alerting of other people suspected of having committed such an offence but not yet arrested for it; or

(iii) will hinder the recovery of property obtained as a result of such an offence.

2. These rights may also be delayed where the serious arrestable offence is either:

(i) a drug trafficking offence and the officer has reasonable grounds for believing that the detained person has benefited from drug trafficking, and that the recovery of the value of that person's proceeds of drug trafficking will be hindered by the exercise of either right or;

(ii) an offence to which Part VI of the Criminal Justice Act 1988 (covering confiscation orders) applies and the officer has reasonable grounds for believing that the detained person has benefited from the offence, and that the recovery of the value of the property obtained by that person from or in connection with the offence, or the pecuniary advantage derived by that person from or in connection with it, will be hindered by the exercise of either right.

3. Authority to delay a detained person's right to consult privately with a solicitor may be given only if the authorising officer has reasonable grounds to believe that the solicitor who the person wishes to consult will, inadvertently or otherwise, pass on a message from the detained person or act in some other way

which will have any of the consequences specified under paragraph 1. In these circumstances the detained person must be allowed to choose another solicitor.

4. Access to a solicitor may not be delayed on the grounds that the solicitor might advise the person not to answer any questions or that the solicitor was initially asked to attend the police station by someone else, provided that the person then wishes to see that solicitor. In the latter case the detained person must be told that the solicitor has come to the police station at another person's request, and must be asked to sign the custody record to signify whether or not they wish to see the solicitor.

5. The fact that the grounds for delaying notification of arrest may be satisfied does not automatically mean that the grounds for delaying access to legal advice will also be satisfied.

6. These rights may be delayed only for as long as is necessary and in no case beyond 36 hours after the relevant time as defined in section 41 of the Police and Criminal Evidence Act 1984. If the above grounds cease to apply within this time, the person must as soon as practicable be asked if they wish to exercise either right, the custody record must be noted accordingly, and action must be taken in accordance with the relevant section of the Code.

7. A detained person must be permitted to consult a solicitor for a reasonable time before any court hearing.

B. Persons detained under the Terrorism Act 2000

128–051　　8. The rights set out in sections 5 or 6 of this Code, or both, may be delayed if the person is detained under section 41 of, or Schedule 7 to, the Terrorism Act 2000, has not yet been charged with an offence and an officer of the rank of superintendent or above has reasonable grounds for believing that the exercise of either right:

(i) will lead to interference with or harm to evidence connected with a serious arrestable offence or interference with or physical injury to other people; or

(ii) will lead to the alerting of other people suspected of having committed such an offence but not yet arrested for it; or

(iii) will hinder the recovery of property obtained as a result of such an offence or in respect of which a forfeiture order could be made under section 23 of the Terrorism Act 2000.

(iv) will lead to interference with the gathering of information about the commission, preparation or instigation of acts of terrorism; or

(v) will, by alerting any person, make it more difficult to prevent an act of terrorism or to secure the apprehension, prosecution or conviction of any person in connection with the commission, preparation or instigation of an act of terrorism.

9. These rights may also be delayed if the officer has reasonable grounds for believing that the detained person;

(i) has committed an offence to which Part VI of the Criminal Justice Act 1988 (covering confiscation orders) applies,

(ii) has benefited from the offence, and

(iii) the exercise of either right will hinder the recovery of the value of that benefit.

10. Paragraphs 3, 4 and 5 above apply.

11. These rights may be delayed only for as long as is necessary and in no case beyond 48 hours from the time of arrest if arrested under section 41, or if detained under Schedule 7 to the Terrorism Act 2000 when arrested under sec-

tion 41, from the beginning of their examination. If the above grounds cease to apply within this time, the person must as soon as practicable be asked if they wish to exercise either right, the custody record must be noted accordingly, and action must be taken in accordance with the relevant section of this Code.

12. Paragraph 7 above applies.

C. Documentation

13. The grounds for action under this Annex shall be recorded and the person **128–052** informed of them as soon as practicable.

14. Any reply given by a person under paragraphs 6 or 11 above must be recorded and the person asked to endorse the record in relation to whether they wish to receive legal advice at this point.

D. Cautions and special warnings

15. When a suspect detained at a police station is interviewed during any **128–053** period for which access to legal advice has been delayed under this Annex, the court or jury may not draw adverse inferences from their silence.

ANNEX C
NOT USED

ANNEX D
WRITTEN STATEMENTS UNDER CAUTION (See paragraph 12.14)

(a) Written by a person under caution

1. A person shall always be invited to write down what they want to say. **128–054**

2. A person who has not been charged with, or informed that they may be prosecuted for, any offence to which the statement they wish to write relates, shall;

  (a) if the statement is made at a time when the restriction on drawing adverse inferences from silence (paragraph 10.4) does not apply, be asked to write out and sign the following before writing what they want to say;

  "I make this statement of my own free will. I understand that I do not have to say anything but that it may harm my defence if I do not mention when questioned something which I later rely on in court. This statement may be given in evidence."; or

  (b) if the statement is made at a time when the restriction on drawing adverse inferences from silence (paragraph 10.4) applies, be asked to write out and sign the following before writing what they want to say;

  "I make this statement of my own free will. I understand that I do not have to say anything. This statement may be given in evidence."

3. When a person, on the occasion of being charged with or informed that they may be prosecuted for any offence, asks to make a statement which relates to any such offence and wishes to write it they shall;

  (a) if the restriction on drawing adverse inferences from silence (paragraph 10.4) did not apply when they were so charged or informed they may be prosecuted, be asked to write out and sign the following before writing what they want to say;

"I make this statement of my own free will. I understand that I do not have to say anything but that it may harm my defence if I do not mention when questioned something which I later rely on in court. This statement may be given in evidence."; or

(b) if the restriction on drawing adverse inferences from silence (paragraph 10.4) applied when they were so charged or informed they may be prosecuted, be asked to write out and sign the following before writing what they want to say;

"I make this statement of my own free will. I understand that I do not have to say anything. This statement may be given in evidence."

4. When a person, who has already been charged with or informed that they may be prosecuted for any offence, asks to make a statement which relates to any such offence and wishes to write it they shall be asked to write out and sign the following before writing what they want to say;

"I make this statement of my own free will. I understand that I do not have to say anything. This statement may be given in evidence.";

5. Any person writing their own statement shall be allowed to do so without any prompting except that a police officer, or (if the statement is written during the course of an interview) the interviewer, may indicate to them which matters are material or question any ambiguity in the statement.

(b) Written by a police officer or approved person

128–055   6. If a person says that they would like someone to write the statement for them a police officer, or the approved person if appropriate (see paragraph 1.13 of this Code) shall write the statement.

7. If the person has not been charged with, or informed that they may be prosecuted for, any offence to which the statement they wish to make relates the interviewer shall before starting;

(a) if the statement is made at a time when the restriction on drawing adverse inferences from silence (paragraph 10.4) does not apply, ask the person to sign, or make their mark, to the following;

"I, ..., wish to make a statement. I want someone to write down what I say. I understand that I do not have to say anything but that it may harm my defence if I do not mention when questioned something which I later rely on in court. This statement may be given in evidence."; or

(b) if the statement is made at a time when the restriction on drawing adverse inferences from silence (paragraph 10.4) applies, ask the person to sign, or make their mark, to the following;

"I, ..., wish to make a statement. I want someone to write down what I say. This statement may be given in evidence.'

8. If, on the occasion of being charged with or informed that they may be prosecuted for any offence, the person asks to make a statement which relates to any such offence the interviewer shall before starting;

(a) if the restriction on drawing adverse inferences from silence (paragraph 10.4) did not apply when they were so charged or informed they may be prosecuted, ask the person to sign, or make their mark, to the following;

"I, ..., wish to make a statement. I want someone to write down what I say. I understand that I do not have to say anything but that it may harm my defence if I do not mention when questioned something which I later rely on in court. This statement may be given in evidence."; or

(b) if the restriction on drawing adverse inferences from silence (paragraph 10.4) applied when they were so charged or informed they may be prosecuted, ask the person to sign, or make their mark, to the following;

"I, ..., wish to make a statement. I want someone to write down what I say. This statement may be given in evidence."

9. If , having already been charged with or informed that they may be prosecuted for any offence, a person asks to make a statement which relates to any such offence the interviewer shall before starting ask the person to sign, or make their mark, to the following;

"I, ..., wish to make a statement. I want someone to write down what I say. This statement may be given in evidence.'

10. The interviewer who writes the statement must take down the exact words spoken by the person making it and must not edit or paraphrase it. Any questions that are necessary (e.g. to make it more intelligible) and the answers given must be recorded contemporaneously on the statement form.

11. When the writing of a statement is finished the person making it shall be asked to read it and to make any corrections, alterations or additions they wish. When they have finished reading it they shall be asked to write and sign or make their mark on the following certificate at the end of the statement:

"I have read the above statement, and I have been able to correct, alter or add anything I wish. This statement is true. I have made it of my own free will."

12. If the person making the statement cannot read, or refuses to read it, or to write the above mentioned certificate at the end of it or to sign it, the senior police officer or approved person present shall read it to them and ask them whether they would like to correct, alter or add anything and to put their signature or make their mark at the end. The police officer or approved person shall then certify on the statement itself what has occurred.

ANNEX E
SUMMARY OF PROVISIONS RELATING TO MENTALLY DISORDERED AND OTHERWISE MENTALLY VULNERABLE PEOPLE

1. If an officer has any suspicion, or is told in good faith, that a person of any **128–056** age may be mentally disordered or otherwise mentally vulnerable, or mentally incapable or understanding the significance of questions put to him or his replies, then that person shall be treated as mentally disordered or otherwise mentally vulnerable for the purposes of this Code. [See paragraph 1.4]

2. In the case of a person who is mentally disordered or otherwise mentally vulnerable, "the appropriate adult" means:

(a) a relative, guardian or some other person responsible for his care or custody;
(b) someone who has experience of dealing with mentally disordered or otherwise mentally vulnerable people but is not a police officer or employed by the police; or

(c) failing either of the above, some other responsible adult aged over 18 or over who is not a police officer or employed by the police. [See paragraph 1.7(b)]

3. If the custody officer authorises the detention of a person who is mentally vulnerable or appears to be suffering from a mental disorder he must as soon as practicable inform the appropriate adult of the grounds for the person's detention and his whereabouts, and ask the adult to come to the police station to see the person. If the appropriate adult is already at the police station when information is given as required in paragraphs 3.1 to 3.5 the information must be given to the detained person in the appropriate adult's presence. If the appropriate adult is not at the police station when the provisions of 3.1 to 3.5 are complied with then these provisions must be complied with again in the presence of the appropriate adult once that person arrives. [See paragraphs 3.9 to 3.11]

4. If the appropriate adult, having been informed of the right to legal advice, onsiders that legal advice should be taken, the provisions of section 6 of the Code apply as if the mentally disordered or otherwise mentally vulnerable person had requested access to legal advice. [See paragraph 3.13]

5. If a person brought to the police station appears to be suffering from mental disorder or is incoherent other than through drunkenness alone, or if a detained person subsequently appears to be mentally disordered, the custody officer must immediately call the police surgeon or, in urgent cases, send the person to hospital or call the nearest available medical practitioner. It is not intended that these provisions should delay the transfer of a person to a place of safety under section 136 of the Mental Health Act 1983 where that is applicable. Where an assessment under that Act is to take place at the police station, the custody officer has discretion not to call the police surgeon so long as he believes that the assessment by a registered medical practitioner can be undertaken without undue delay. [See paragraph 9.2]

6. It is imperative that a mentally disordered or otherwise mentally vulnerable person who has been detained under section 136 of the Mental Health Act 1983 should be assessed as soon as possible. If that assessment is to take place at the police station, an approved social worker and a registered medical practitioner shall be called to the police station as soon as possible in order to interview and examine the person. Once the person has been interviewed and examined and suitable arrangements have been made for his treatment or care, he can no longer be detained under section 136. The person shall not be released until he has been seen by both the approved social worker and the registered medical practitioner. [See paragraph 3.10]

7. If a mentally disordered or otherwise mentally vulnerable person is cautioned in the absence of the appropriate adult, the caution must be repeated in the appropriate adult's presence. [See paragraph 10.13]

8. A mentally disordered or otherwise mentally vulnerable person must not be interviewed or asked to provide or sign a written statement in the absence of the appropriate adult unless the provisions of paragraph 11.1 or paragraphs 11.18 to 11.20 of this Code apply. Questioning in these circumstances may not continue in the absence of the appropriate adult once sufficient information to avert the risk has been obtained. A record shall be made of the grounds for any decision to begin an interview in these circumstances. [See paragraphs 11.1 and 11.15 and 11.18 to 11.20]

9. Where the appropriate adult is present at an interview, he shall be informed that he is not expected to act simply as an observer; and also that the purposes of his presence are, first, to advise the person being interviewed and to observe whether or not the interview is being conducted properly and fairly, and, secondly, to facilitate communication with the person being interviewed. [See paragraph 11.17]

10. If the detention of a mentally disordered or otherwise mentally vulnerable

person is reviewed by a review officer or a superintendent, the appropriate adult must, if available at the time, be given an opportunity to make representations to the officer about the need for continuing detention. [See paragraphs 15.2 and 15.3A]

11. If the custody officer charges a mentally disordered or otherwise mentally vulnerable person with an offence or takes such other action as is appropriate when there is sufficient evidence for a prosecution this must be done in the presence of the appropriate adult. The written notice embodying any charge must be given to the appropriate adult. [See paragraph 16.1 to 16.3]

12. An intimate or strip search of a mentally disordered or otherwise mentally vulnerable person may take place only in the presence of the appropriate adult of the same sex, unless the person specifically requested the presence of a particular adult of the opposite sex. A strip search may take place in the absence of an appropriate adult only in cases of urgency where there is a risk of serious harm to the person detained or to others. [See Annex A, paragraphs 5 and 11(c)]

13. Particular care must be taken when deciding whether to use handcuffs to restrain a mentally disordered or otherwise mentally vulnerable person in a locked cell. [See paragraph 8.2]

ANNEX F
COUNTRIES WITH WHICH BILATERAL CONSULAR CONVENTIONS OR AGREEMENTS REQUIRING NOTIFICATION OF THE ARREST AND DETENTION OF THEIR NATIONALS ARE IN FORCE AS AT 1 JANUARY 1995

128–057

Armenia	Georgia
Austria	German Federal Republic
Azerbaijan	Greece
Balarus	Hungary
Belgium	Kazarkhstan
Kyrgystan	Norway
Macedonia	Poland
Mexico	Romania
Moldova	Russia
Mongolia	Slovak Republic
Code C	Slovenia
Bosnia-Hercegovina	Spain
Bulgaria	Sweden
China*	Tajikistan
Croatia	Turkmenistan
Cuba	Ukraine
Czech Republic	USA
Denmark	Uzbekistan
Egypt	Yugoslavia
France	

* *Police are required to inform Chinese officials of arrest/detention in the Manchester consular district only. This comprises Derbyshire, Durham, Greater Manchester, Lancashire, Merseyside, North South and West Yorkshire, and Tyne and Wear.*

TO BE UPDATED BEFORE NEW CODES ARE FINALISED
ANNEX G
FITNESS TO BE INTERVIEWED

1. This Annex contains general guidance to help police officers and health care professionals assess whether a detained person might be at risk in an interview. **128–058**

2. A detained person may be at risk in a interview if it is considered that;

(a) Conducting the interview could significantly harm the person's physical or mental state; or

(b) Anything the person says in the interview about their involvement or suspected involvement in the offence about which they are being interviewed **might** be considered unreliable in subsequent court proceedings because of their physical or mental state.

3. In assessing whether the person should be interviewed, the following must be considered;

(a) how the person's physical or mental state might affect their ability to understand the nature and purpose of the interview, to comprehend what is being asked and to appreciate the significance of any answers given and make rational decisions about whether they wish to say anything.

(b) the extent to which the detained person's replies may be affected by their physical or mental condition rather than representing a rational and accurate explanation of their involvement in the offence.

(c) how the nature of the interview, which could include particularly probing questions, might affect the detained person.

4. It is essential that health care professionals who are consulted consider the functional ability of the detained person rather than simply relying on a medical diagnosis. For example, it is possible for a person with severe mental illness to be fit for interview.

5. Health care professionals should advise on the need for an appropriate adult to be present, whether reassessment of the person's fitness for interview may be necessary if the interview lasts beyond a specified time, and whether a (further) specialist opinion may be required.

6. When health care professionals identify risks they should be asked to quantify the risks. They should inform the custody officer whether the person's condition is likely to improve, or require or be amenable to treatment ,and indicate how long it may take for such improvement to take effect.

7. The role of the health care professional is to consider the risks and advise the custody officer of the outcome of that consideration. The health care professional's determination and any advice or recommendations should be made in writing and form part of the custody record.

8. Once the health care professional has provided that information, it is a matter for the custody officer to decide whether or not to allow the interview to go ahead and if the interview is to proceed, to determine what safeguards are needed. Nothing prevents safeguards being provided in addition to those required under the Code. An example might be to have an appropriate health care professional present during the interview, in addition to an appropriate adult, in order constantly to monitor the person's condition and how it is being affected by the interview.

Criminal Procedure and Investigations Act 1996
Code of Practice Under Part II

Introduction

129–001   1.1 This code of practice is issued under Part II of the Criminal Procedure and Investigations Act 1996 ("the Act"). It applies in respect of criminal investigations conducted by police officers which begin on or after the day on which this code comes into effect. Persons other than police officers who are charged with the duty of conducting an investigation as defined in the Act are to have regard to the relevant provisions of the code, and should take these into account in applying their own operating procedures.

1.2 This code does not apply to persons who are not charged with the duty of conducting an investigation as defined in the Act.

1.3 Nothing in this code applies to material intercepted in obedience to a warrant issued under section 2 of the Interception of Communications Act 1985, or to any copy of that material as defined in section 10 of that Act.

1.4 This code extends only to England and Wales.

Definitions

2.1 In this code:

129–002

— a *criminal investigation* is an investigation conducted by police officers with a view to it being ascertained whether a person should be charged with an offence, or whether a person charged with an offence is guilty of it. This will include
  — investigations into crimes that have been committed;
  — investigations whose purpose is to ascertain whether a crime has been committed, with a view to the possible institution of criminal proceedings; and
  — investigations which begin in the belief that a crime may be committed, for example when the police keep premises or individuals under observation for a period of time, with a view to the possible institution of criminal proceedings;
— charging a person with an offence includes prosecution by way of summons;
— an *investigator* is any police officer involved in the conduct of a criminal investigation. All investigators have a responsibility for carrying out the duties imposed on them under this code, including in particular recording information, and retaining records of information and other material;
— the *officer in charge of an investigation* is the police officer responsible for directing a criminal investigation. He is also responsible for ensuring that proper procedures are in place for recording information, and retaining records of information and other material, in the investigation;
— the *disclosure officer* is the person responsible for examining material retained by the police during the investigation; revealing material to the prosecutor during the investigation and any criminal proceedings resulting from it, and certifying that he has done this; and disclosing material to the accused at the request of the prosecutor;
— the *prosecutor* is the authority responsible for the conduct of criminal proceedings on behalf of the Crown. Particular duties may in practice fall to individuals acting on behalf of the prosecuting authority;
— *material* is material of any kind, including information and objects, which is obtained in the course of a criminal investigation and which may be relevant to the investigation;
— material may be *relevant to an investigation* if it appears to an investigator, or to the officer in charge of an investigation, or to the disclosure officer, that it has some bearing on any offence under investigation or any person being investigated, or on the surrounding circumstances of the case, unless it is incapable of having any impact on the case;
— *sensitive material* is material which the disclosure officer believes, after

consulting the officer in charge of the investigation, it is not in the public interest to disclose;

— references to *primary prosecution disclosure* are to the duty of the prosecutor under section 3 of the Act to disclose material which is in his possession or which he has inspected in pursuance of this code, and which in his opinion might undermine the case against the accused;

— references to *secondary prosecution disclosure* are to the duty of the prosecutor under section 7 of the Act to disclose material which is in his possession or which he has inspected in pursuance of this code, and which might reasonably be expected to assist the defence disclosed by the accused in a defence statement given under the Act;

— references to the disclosure of material to a person accused of an offence include references to the disclosure of material to his legal representative;

— references to police officers and to the chief officer of police include those employed in a police force as defined in section 3(3) of the Prosecution of Offences Act 1985.

General responsibilities

129–003 3.1 The functions of the investigator, the officer in charge of an investigation and the disclosure officer are separate. Whether they are undertaken by one, two or more persons will depend on the complexity of the case and the administrative arrangements within each police force. Where they are undertaken by more than one person, close consultation between them is essential to the effective performance of the duties imposed by this code.

3.2 The chief officer of police for each police force is responsible for putting in place arrangements to ensure that in every investigation the identity of the officer in charge of an investigation and the disclosure officer is recorded.

3.3 The officer in charge of an investigation may delegate tasks to another investigator or to civilians employed by the police force, but he remains responsible for ensuring that these have been carried out and for accounting for any general policies followed in the investigation. In particular, it is an essential part of his duties to ensure that all material which may be relevant to an investigation is retained, and either made available to the disclosure officer or (in exceptional circumstances) revealed directly to the prosecutor.

3.4 In conducting an investigation, the investigator should pursue all reasonable lines of inquiry, whether these point towards or away from the suspect. What is reasonable in each case will depend on the particular circumstances.

3.5 If the officer in charge of an investigation believes that other persons may be in possession of material that may be relevant to the investigation, and if this has not been obtained under paragraph 3.4 above, he should ask the disclosure officer to inform them of the existence of the investigation and to invite them to retain the material in case they receive a request for its disclosure. The disclosure officer should inform the prosecutor that they may have such material. However, the officer in charge of an investigation is not required to make speculative enquires of other persons: there must be some reason to believe that they may have relevant material. That reason may come from information provided to the police by the accused or from other inquiries made or from some other source.

3.6 If, during a criminal investigation, the officer in charge of an investigation or disclosure officer for any reason no longer has responsibility for the functions falling to him, either his supervisor or the police officer in charge of criminal investigations for the police force concerned must assign someone else to assume that responsibility. That person's identity must be recorded, as with those initially responsible for these functions in each investigation.

Recording of information

4.1 If material which may be relevant to the investigation consists of informa- **129–004** tion which is not recorded in any form, the officer in charge of an investigation must ensure that it is recorded in a durable or retrievable form (whether in writing, on video or audio tape, or on computer disk).

4.2 Where it is not practicable to retain the initial record of information because it forms part of a larger record which is to be destroyed, its contents should be transferred as a true record to a durable and more easily-stored form before that happens.

4.3 Negative information is often relevant to an investigation. If it may be relevant it must be recorded. An example might be a number of people present in a particular place at a particular time who state that they saw nothing unusual.

4.4 Where information which may be relevant is obtained, it must be recorded at the time it is obtained or as soon as practicable after that time. This includes, for example, information obtained in house-to-house enquires, although the requirement to record information promptly does not require an investigator to take a statement from a potential witness where it would not otherwise be taken.

Retention of material

(a) Duty to retain material

5.1 The investigator must retain material obtained in a criminal investigation **129–005** which may be relevant to the investigation. This includes not only material coming into the possession of the investigator (such as documents seized in the course of searching premises) but also material generated by him (such as interview records). Material may be photographed, or retained in the form of a copy rather than the original, if the original is perishable, or was supplied to the investigator rather than generated by him and is to be returned to its owner.

5.2 Where material has been seized in the exercise of the powers of seizure conferred by the Police and Criminal Evidence Act 1984, the duty to retain it under this code is subject to the provisions on the retention of seized material in section 22 of that Act.

5.3 If the officer in charge of an investigation becomes aware as a result of developments in the case that material previously examined but not retained (because it was not thought to be relevant) may now be relevant to the investigation, he should, wherever practicable, take steps to obtain it or ensure that it is retained for further inspection or for production in court if required.

5.4 The duty to retain material includes in particular the duty to retain material falling into the following categories, where it may be relevant to the investigation:

— crime reports (including crime report forms, relevant parts of incident report books or police officers' notebooks);
— custody records;
— records which are derived from tapes of telephone messages (for example, 999 calls) containing descriptions of an alleged offence or offender;
— final versions of witness statements (and draft versions where their content differs from the final version), including any exhibits mentioned (unless these have been returned to their owner on the understanding that they will be produced in court if required);
— interview records (written records, or audio or video tapes, of interviews with actual or potential witnesses or suspects);
— communications between the police and experts such as forensic scientists, reports of work carried out by experts, and schedules of scientific

material prepared by the expert for the investigator, for the purposes of criminal proceedings;
— any material casting doubt on the reliability of a confession;
— any material casting doubt on the reliability of a witness;
— any other material which may fall within the test for primary prosecution disclosure in the Act.

5.5 The duty to retain material falling into these categories does not extend to items which are purely ancillary to such material and possess no independent significance (for example, duplicate copies of records or reports).

(b) Length of time for which material is to be retained

129–006   5.6 All material which may be relevant to the investigation must be retained until a decision is taken whether to institute proceedings against a person for an offence.
5.7 If a criminal investigation results in proceedings being instituted, all material which may be relevant must be retained at least until the accused is acquitted or convicted or the prosecutor decides not to proceed with the case.
5.8 Where the accused is convicted, all material which may be relevant must be retained at least until:

— the convicted person is released from custody, or discharged from hospital, in cases where the court imposes a custodial sentence or a hospital order;
— six months from the date of conviction, in all other cases.

If the court imposes a custodial sentence or hospital order and the convicted person is released from custody or discharged from hospital earlier than six months from the date of conviction, all material which may be relevant must be retained at least until six months from the date of conviction.
5.9 If an appeal against conviction is in progress when the release or discharge occurs, or at the end of the period of six months specified in paragraph 5.8, all material which may be relevant must be retained until the appeal is determined. Similarly, if the Criminal Cases Review Commission is considering an application at that point in time, all material which may be relevant must be retained at least until the Commission decides not to refer the case to the Court of Appeal, or until the Court determines the appeal resulting from the reference by the Commission.
5.10 Material need not be retained by the police as required in paragraph 5.8 if it was seized and is to be returned to its owner.

Preparation of material for prosecutor

(a) Introduction

129–007   6.1 The officer in charge of the investigation, the disclosure officer or an investigator may seek advice from the prosecutor about whether any particular item of material may be relevant to the investigation.
6.2 Material which may be relevant to an investigation, which has been retained in accordance with this code, and which the disclosure officer believes will not form part of the prosecution case, must be listed on a schedule.
6.3 Material which the disclosure officer does not believe is sensitive must be listed on a schedule of non-sensitive material. The schedule must include a statement that the disclosure officer does not believe the material is sensitive.
6.4 Any material which is believed to be sensitive must be either listed on a schedule of sensitive material or, in exceptional circumstances, revealed to the prosecutor separately.
6.5 Paragraphs 6.6 to 6.11 below apply to both sensitive and non-sensitive material. Paragraphs 6.12 to 6.14 apply to sensitive material only.

(b) Circumstances in which a schedule is to be prepared

6.6 The disclosure officer must ensure that a schedule is prepared in the fol- **129–008**
lowing circumstances:

— the accused is charged with an offence which is triable only on indictment;
— the accused is charged with an offence which is triable either way, and
it is considered either that the case is likely to be tried on indictment
or that the accused is likely to plead not guilty at a summary trial;
— the accused is charged with a summary offence, and it is considered
that he is likely to plead not guilty.

6.7 In respect of either way and summary offences, a schedule may not be
needed if a person has admitted the offence, or if a police officer witnessed the
offence and that person has not denied it.

6.8 If it is believed that the accused is likely to plead guilty at a summary
trial, it is not necessary to prepare a schedule in advance. If, contrary to this
belief, the accused pleads not guilty at a summary trial, or the offence is to be
tried on indictment, the disclosure officer must ensure that a schedule is prepared
as soon as is reasonably practicable after that happens.

(c) Way in which material is to be listed on schedule

6.9 The disclosure officer should ensure that each item of material is listed **129–009**
separately on the schedule, and is numbered consecutively. The description of
each item should make clear the nature of the item and should contain sufficient
detail to enable the prosecutor to decide whether he needs to inspect the material
before deciding whether or not it should be disclosed.

6.10 In some enquiries it may not be practicable to list each item of material
separately. For example, there may be many items of a similar or repetitive
nature. These may be listed in a block and described by quantity and generic
title.

6.11 Even if some material is listed in a block, the disclosure officer must
ensure that any items among that material which might meet the test for primary
prosecution disclosure are listed and described individually.

(d) Treatment of sensitive material

6.12 Subject to paragraph 6.13 below, the disclosure officer must list on a **129–010**
sensitive schedule any material which he believes it is not in the public interest
to disclose, and the reason for that belief. The schedule must include a statement
that the disclosure officer believes the material is sensitive. Depending on the
circumstances, examples of such material may include the following among
others:

— material relating to national security;
— material received from the intelligence and security agencies;
— material relating to intelligence from foreign sources which reveals
sensitive intelligence gathering methods;
— material given in confidence;
— material which relates to the use of a telephone system and which is
supplied to an investigator for intelligence purposes only;
— material relating to the identity or activities of informants, or under-
cover police officers, or other persons supplying information to the
police who may be in danger if their identities are revealed;
— material revealing the location of any premises or other place used for
police surveillance, or the identity of any person allowing a police
officer to use them for surveillance;
— material revealing, either directly or indirectly, techniques and methods

relied upon by a police officer in the course of a criminal investigation, for example covert surveillance techniques, or other methods of detecting crime;

— material whose disclosure might facilitate the commission of other offences or hinder the prevention and detection of crime;

— internal police communications such as management minutes;

— material upon the strength of which search warrants were obtained;

— material containing details of persons taking part in identification parades;

— material supplied to an investigator during a criminal investigation which has been generated by an official of a body concerned with the regulation or supervision of bodies corporate or of persons engaged in financial activities, or which has been generated by a person retained by such a body;

— material supplied to an investigator during a criminal investigation which relates to a child or young person and which has been generated by a local authority social services department, an Area Child Protection Committee or other party contacted by an investigator during the investigation.

6.13 In exceptional circumstances, where an investigator considers that material is so sensitive that its revelation to the prosecutor by means of an entry on the sensitive schedule is inappropriate, the existence of the material must be revealed to the prosecutor separately. This will apply where compromising the material would be likely to lead directly to the loss of life, or directly threaten national security.

6.14 In such circumstances, the responsibility for informing the prosecutor lies with the investigator who knows the detail of the sensitive material. The investigator should act as soon as is reasonably practicable after the file containing the prosecution case is sent to the prosecutor. The investigator must also ensure that the prosecutor is able to inspect the material so that he can assess whether it needs to be brought before a court for a ruling on disclosure.

Revelation of material to prosecutor

129–011   7.1 The disclosure officer must give the schedules to the prosecutor. Wherever practicable this should be at the same time as he gives him the file containing the material for the prosecution case (or as soon as is reasonably practicable after the decision on mode of trial or the plea, in cases to which paragraph 6.8 applies).

7.2 The disclosure officer should draw the attention of the prosecutor to any material an investigator has retained (whether or not listed on a schedule) which may fall within the test for primary prosecution disclosure in the Act, and should explain why he has come to that view.

7.3 At the same time as complying with the duties in paragraphs 7.1 and 7.2, the disclosure officer must give the prosecutor a copy of any material which falls into the following categories (unless such material has already been given to the prosecutor as part of the file containing the material for the prosecution case):

— records of the first description of a suspect given to the police by a potential witness, whether or not the description differs from that of the alleged offender;

— information provided by an accused person which indicates an explanation for the offence with which he has been charged;

— any material casting doubt on the reliability of a confession;

— any material casting doubt on the reliability of a witness;

— any other material which the investigator believes may fall within the test for primary prosecution disclosure in the Act.

7.4 If the prosecutor asks to inspect material which has not already been copied to him, the disclosure officer must allow him to inspect it. If the prosecutor asks for a copy of material which has not already been copied to him, the disclosure officer must give him a copy. However, this does not apply where the disclosure officer believes, having consulted the officer in charge of the investigation, that the material is too sensitive to be copied and can only be inspected.

7.5 If material consists of information which is recorded other than in writing, whether it should be given to the prosecutor in its original form as a whole, or by way of relevant extracts recorded in the same form, or in the form of a transcript, is a matter for agreement between the disclosure officer and the prosecutor.

Subsequent action by disclosure officer

8.1 At the time a schedule of non-sensitive material is prepared, the disclosure **129–012** officer may not know exactly what material will form the case against the accused, and the prosecutor may not have given advice about the likely relevance of particular items of material. Once these matters have been determined, the disclosure officer must give the prosecutor, where necessary, an amended schedule listing any additional material:

— which may be relevant to the investigation,
— which does not form part of the case against the accused,
— which is not already listed on the schedule, and
— which he believes is not sensitive,

unless he is informed in writing by the prosecutor that the prosecutor intends to disclose the material to the defence.

8.2 After a defence statement has been given, the disclosure officer must look again at the material which has been retained and must draw the attention of the prosecutor to any material which might reasonably be expected to assist the defence disclosed by the accused; and he must reveal it to him in accordance with paragraphs 7.4 and 7.5 above.

8.3 Section 9 of the Act imposes a continuing duty on the prosecutor, for the duration of criminal proceedings against the accused, to disclose material which meets the tests for disclosure (subject to public interest considerations). To enable him to do this, any new material coming to light should be treated in the same way as the earlier material.

Certification by disclosure officer

9.1 The disclosure officer must certify to the prosecutor that to the best of his **129–013** knowledge and belief, all material which has been retained and made available to him has been revealed to the prosecutor in accordance with this code. He must sign and date the certificate. It will be necessary to certify not only at the time when the schedule and accompanying material is submitted to the prosecutor, but also when material which has been retained is reconsidered after the accused has given a defence statement.

Disclosure of material to accused

10.1 If material has not already been copied to the prosecutor, and he requests **129–014** its disclosure to the accused on the ground that

— it falls within the test for primary or secondary prosecution disclosure, **or**

— the court has ordered its disclosure after considering an application from the accused,

the disclosure officer must disclose it to the accused.

10.2 If material has been copied to the prosecutor, and it is to be disclosed, whether it is disclosed by the prosecutor or the disclosure officer is a matter of agreement between the two of them.

10.3 The disclosure officer must disclose material to the accused either by giving him a copy or by allowing him to inspect it. If the accused person asks for a copy of any material which he has been allowed to inspect, the disclosure officer must give it to him, unless in the opinion of the disclosure officer that is either not practicable (for example because the material consists of an object which cannot be copied, or because the volume of material is so great), or not desirable (for example because the material is a statement by a child witness in relation to a sexual offence).

10.4 If material which the accused has been allowed to inspect consists of information which is recorded other than in writing, whether it should be given to the accused in its original form or in the form of a transcript is matter for the discretion of the disclosure officer. If the material is transcribed, the disclosure officer must ensure that the transcript is certified to the accused as a true record of the material which has been transcribed.

10.5 If a court concludes that it is in the public interest that an item of sensitive material must be disclosed to the accused, it will be necessary to disclose the material if the case is to proceed. This does not mean that sensitive documents must always be disclosed in their original form: for example, the court may agree that sensitive details still requiring protection should be blocked out, or that documents may be summarised, or that the prosecutor may make an admission about the substance of the material under section 10 of the Criminal Justice Act 1967.

Police and Criminal Evidence Act 1984
Code D
Code of Practice for the Identification of Persons by Police Officers

. . . . . .

2. Identification by Witnesses

Introduction

130–001   2.1 Identification by witnesses arises, for example, if the offender is seen committing the crime and a witness is given an opportunity to identify the suspect in a video identification, identification parade, or similar procedure. The procedures are designed to test the ability of the witness to identify the person they saw on a previous occasion and to provide safeguards against mistaken identification. Persons other than police officers, including "approved persons" (see paragraph 2.13), who are charged with the duty of investigating offences or charging offenders must, in the discharge of that duty, have regard to any relevant provision of this and any other Code.

Identification by witnesses

2.2 A record shall be made of the description of the suspect as first given by **130–002** a potential witness. This must be done before the witness takes part in the forms of identification under paragraphs 2.3 to 2.11 of this Code. The record may be made or kept in any form provided that details of the description as first given by the witness can accurately be produced from it in a written form which can be provided to the suspect or the suspect's solicitor in accordance with this Code. A copy shall be provided to the suspect or the suspect's solicitor before any procedures under paragraphs 2.3 to 2.11 of this Code are carried out.

(a) Cases where the suspect is known and available

2.3 In a case which involves disputed identification evidence, and where the **130–003** identity of the suspect is known to the police and he is available, (see paragraph 2.12) the following identification procedures may be used:

Video identification
2.4 A video identification is where the witness is shown images of a known **130–004** suspect together with images of other people who resemble the suspect.
2.5 Video identifications must be carried out in accordance with Annex A.

Identification parade
2.6 An identification parade is where the witness sees the suspect in a line of **130–005** other people who resemble the suspect.
2.7 Identification parades must be carried out in accordance with Annex B.

Group identification
2.8 A group identification is where the witness sees the suspect in an informal **130–006** group of people.
2.9 Group identifications must be carried out in accordance with Annex C.

Confrontation
2.10 A confrontation is where the suspect is directly confronted by the wit- **130–007** ness. This procedure may be used when it is not possible to arrange a video identification, identification parade, or group identification.
2.11 Confrontations must be carried out in accordance with Annex D.
2.12 References in this section to a suspect being "known" means there is sufficient information known to the police to justify the arrest of a particular person for suspected involvement in the offence. A suspect being "available" means that they are immediately available to take part in the procedure or will become available within a reasonably short time. A known suspect who fails or refuses to take part in any identification procedure which it is practicable to arrange, or takes steps to prevent themselves from being seen by a witness in such a procedure, may be treated as not being available for the purposes of this section.

Arranging identification procedures
2.13 Except as provided for in paragraph 2.23 below, the arrangements for, **130–008** and conduct of these types of identification procedures shall be the responsibility of an officer not below the rank of inspector who is not involved with the investigation ("the identification officer") other than for the purposes of these procedures. Unless otherwise specified, the identification officer may allow an "approved person" to make arrangements for, and to conduct any of the identification procedures in paragraphs 2.3 to 2.11. Approved persons are engaged to carry out specified duties or procedures as allowed under this Code and:

(i) appointed by the Chief Officer of any police force and under the control and direction of that Chief Officer; and

(ii) employed by the police authority maintaining that force.

No officer or any other person involved with the investigation of the case against the suspect beyond the extent required by these procedures may take any part in these procedures or act as the identification officer. This does not prevent the identification officer from consulting the officer in charge of the investigation in order to determine which procedure to use.

Circumstances in which an identification procedure must be held

130–009   2.14 Whenever a suspect disputes an identification made or purported to have been made by a witness, an identification procedure shall be held if practicable unless paragraph 2.15 applies. Such a procedure may also be held if the officer in charge of the investigation considers that it would be useful. When an identification procedure is required to be held, in the interests of fairness to suspects and witnesses, it must be held as soon as practicable.

2.15 An identification procedure need not be held if, in all the circumstances, it would serve no useful purpose in proving or disproving whether the suspect was involved in committing the offence. Examples would be where it is not in dispute that the suspect is already well known to the witness who saw the suspect commit the crime or where there is no reasonable possibility that a witness would be able to make an identification.

Selecting an identification procedure

130–010   2.16 If, as a consequence of paragraph 2.14, it is proposed to hold an identification procedure, the suspect shall initially be offered either a video identification or an identification parade unless paragraph 2.18 applies. The officer in charge of the case may choose freely between these two options to decide which is to be offered. The identification officer and the officer in charge of the investigation shall consult each other to determine which of these two options is the most suitable and practicable in the particular case. An identification parade may not be practicable because of factors relating to the witnesses such as their number, state of health, availability and travelling requirements. A video identification would normally be more suitable if, in a particular case, it could be arranged and completed sooner than an identification parade (see paragraph 2.14).

2.17 A suspect who refuses the identification procedure which is first offered shall be asked to state their reason for refusing and may obtain advice from their solicitor and appropriate adult if present. The suspect, solicitor and appropriate adult shall be allowed to make representations as to why another procedure should be used. A record shall be made of the reasons for the suspect's refusal and of any representations made. After considering any reasons given and representations made the identification officer shall, if appropriate, arrange for the suspect to be offered an alternative which the officer considers is suitable and practicable in that particular case. If the officer decides that it is not suitable and practicable to offer an alternative identification procedure, the reasons for that decision shall be recorded.

2.18 A group identification may initially be offered where the officer in charge of the investigation considers that in the particular circumstances it is more satisfactory than a video identification or an identification parade and the identification officer considers it is practicable to arrange.

2.19 If the suspect refuses or fails to take part in a video identification, an identification parade or a group identification, or refuses or fails to take part in the only practicable options from that list, the identification officer has discretion to make arrangements for a covert video identification or a covert group identification. In making arrangements for a covert video identification or other arrangements to test the ability of the witness to identify the person they saw on a previous occasion, the identification officer has discretion to use any suitable images of the suspect, whether moving or still, which are available or can be obtained.

2.20 If none of the options referred to above are practicable, the identification officer may arrange for the suspect to be confronted by the witness. A confrontation does not require the suspect's consent.

Notice to suspect
2.21 Unless paragraph 2.24 applies, before a video identification, an identification parade or group identification is arranged the following shall be explained to the suspect: **130–011**

(i) the purposes of the video identification or identification parade or group identification;
(ii) the suspect's entitlement to free legal advice;
(iii) the procedures for holding it (including the suspect's right to have a solicitor or friend present);
(iv) that the suspect does not have to take part in a video identification, identification parade or group identification;
(v) whether, for the purposes of the video identification procedure, images of the suspect have previously been obtained (see paragraph 2.24) and if so, that they may co-operate in providing further suitable images which shall be used in place of those previously taken;
(vi) where appropriate the special arrangements for juveniles;
(vii) where appropriate the special arrangements for mentally disordered or otherwise mentally vulnerable people;
(viii) that if the suspect does not consent to, and take part in, a video identification, identification parade or group identification, their refusal may be given in evidence in any subsequent trial and police may proceed covertly without their consent or make other arrangements to test whether a witness can identify them (see paragraph 2.19);
(ix) that if the suspect should significantly alter their appearance between being offered an identification procedure and any attempt to hold an identification procedure, this may be given in evidence if the case comes to trial, and the identification officer may then consider other forms of identification (see paragraph 2.19);
(x) that a video or photograph may be taken of the suspect when they attend for any identification procedure;
(xi) whether the witness has been shown photographs, a computerised or artist's composite likeness or similar likeness or picture by the police during the investigation before the identity of the suspect became known;
(xii) that if the suspect changes their appearance before a identification parade it may not be practicable to arrange one on the day in question or subsequently and, because of the change of appearance, the identification officer may then consider alternative methods of identification;
(xiii) that the suspect or their solicitor will be provided with details of the description of the suspect as first given by any witnesses who are to attend the video identification, identification parade, group identification or confrontation.

2.22 This information must also be contained in a written notice which must be handed to the suspect. The suspect must be given a reasonable opportunity to read the notice, after which they shall be asked to sign a second copy of the notice to indicate whether or not they are willing to co-operate with the making of a video or take part in the identification parade or group identification. The signed copy shall be retained by the identification officer.

2.23 The duties of the identification officer under paragraphs 2.21 and 2.22 may be performed by the custody officer or any other officer not involved in the investigation of the case against the suspect if;

(a) it is proposed to hold an identification procedure at a later date (for example if the suspect is to be bailed to attend an identification parade); and

(b) an inspector is not available to act as the identification officer (see paragraph 2.13) before the suspect leaves the station where they are detained.

The officer concerned shall inform the identification officer of the action taken and give them the signed copy of the notice.

2.24 If the identification officer and the officer in charge of the investigation have reasonable grounds to suspect that if the suspect was given the information and notice in accordance with paragraphs 2.21 and 2.22, they would thereafter take steps to avoid being seen by a witness in any identification procedure which it would otherwise be practicable to arrange, the identification officer has discretion to arrange for images of the suspect to be obtained for use in a video identification procedure before the information and notice in paragraphs 2.21 and 2.22 is given. If images of the suspect are obtained in these circumstances, the suspect may, for the purposes of a video identification procedure, co-operate in providing suitable images which shall be used in place of those previously taken (see paragraph 2.21 (v)).

(b) Cases where the suspect is known but is not available

130–012   2.25 Where a known suspect is not available or has ceased to be available for any reason (see paragraph 2.12), the identification officer has discretion to make arrangements for a video identification to be conducted. This must be done in accordance with the provisions applicable to covert video identification (see paragraph 2.19 and Annex A). However, any requirements of this section and Annex A for information in any form to be given to or sought from a suspect or for the suspect to be given an opportunity to view images before they are shown to a witness shall not apply if, at the time the requirement arises, the suspect is not available. For each such requirement, the record of the video identification shall indicate the reason why the suspect was not available. [See paragraph 2.31]

(c) Cases where the identity of the suspect is not known

130–013   2.26 A witness may be taken to a particular neighbourhood or place to see whether they can identify the person whom they saw on the relevant occasion. Although the number, age, sex, race and general description and style of clothing of other people present at the location and the way in which any identification is made cannot be controlled, the principles applicable to the formal procedures under paragraphs 2.3 to 2.11 shall be followed so far as is practicable in the circumstances. For example:

(a) Before asking the witness to make an identification, where practicable, a record shall be made of any description given by the witness of the suspect.

(b) Care should be taken not to direct the witness's attention to any individual unless, having regard to all the circumstances, this cannot be avoided. However, this does not prevent a witness being asked to look carefully at the people who are around at the time or to look towards a group or in a particular direction if this appears to be necessary to ensure that the witness does not overlook a possible suspect simply because the witness is looking in the opposite direction and also to enable the witness to make comparisons between any suspect and others who are in the area at the time.

(c) Where there is more than one witness, every effort should be made to keep them separate and where practicable, witnesses should be taken to see whether they can identify a person independently.

(d) Once there is sufficient information to justify the arrest of a particular individual for suspected involvement in the offence, for example after a witness makes a positive identification, formal identification procedures must be adopted for any other witnesses in relation to that individual.

(e) The officer or approved person accompanying the witness shall make a record in their pocket book of the action taken as soon as practicable and in as much detail as possible. The record should include: the date, time and place of the relevant occasion the witness claims to have previously seen the suspect; where any identification was made; how it was made and the conditions at the time (for example, the distance the witness was from the suspect, the weather and light); if the witness's attention was drawn to the suspect; the reason for this; and anything said by the witness or the suspect about the identification or the conduct of the procedure.

2.27 A witness must not be shown photographs, computerised or artist's composite likenesses or similar likenesses or pictures if the identity of the suspect is known to the police and the suspect is available to take part in a video identification, an identification parade or a group identification. If the identity of the suspect is not known, the showing of such pictures to a witness must be done in accordance with Annex E (see paragraphs 2.12, 2.21(xi) and 2.25).

(d) Documentation

2.28 A record shall be made of the video identification, identification parade, **130–014** group identification or confrontation on forms provided for the purpose.

2.29 If the identification officer considers that it is not practicable to hold a video identification or identification parade when either are requested by the suspect, the reasons shall be recorded and explained to the suspect.

2.30 A record shall be made of a person's failure or refusal to co-operate in a video identification, identification parade or group identification and, if applicable, of the grounds for obtaining images in accordance with paragraph 2.24.

(e) Showing films and photographs of incidents and information released to the media

2.31 Nothing in this Code inhibits the showing of videos or photographs to **130–015** the public at large through the national or local media, or to police officers for the purposes of recognition and tracing suspects. However, when such material is shown to potential witnesses (including police officers) for the purpose of obtaining identification evidence, it shall be shown on an individual basis so as to avoid any possibility of collusion, and the showing shall, as far as possible, follow the principles for video identification if the suspect is known (see paragraphs 2.12, 2.23 and Annex A) or identification by photographs if the suspect is not known (see paragraphs 2.12, 2.27 and Annex E) as appropriate.

2.32 Where a broadcast or publication is made, as in paragraph 2.31, a copy of the relevant material released by the police to the media for the purposes of recognising or tracing the suspect shall be kept and the suspect or their solicitor shall be allowed to view such material before any procedures under paragraphs 2.3 to 2.11 of this Code are carried out (see paragraph 2.12) provided it is practicable to do so and would not unreasonably delay the investigation. Each witness who is involved in the procedure shall be asked after they have taken part whether they have seen any broadcast or published films or photographs relating to the offence or seen any description of any person suspected of the offence and their replies shall be recorded. This paragraph does not affect any separate requirement under the Criminal Procedure and Investigations Act 1996 to retain material in connection with criminal investigations.

(f) Destruction and retention of photographs and images taken or used in identification procedures

130–016   2.33 Section 64A of the Police and Criminal Evidence Act 1984 provides powers to take photographs and images of suspects detained at police stations and allows the photographs and images so taken to be used or disclosed only for purposes related to the prevention or detection of crime, the investigation of offences or the conduct of prosecutions by or on behalf of police or other law enforcement and prosecuting authorities inside and outside the United Kingdom. After being so used or disclosed, they may be retained but must not be used or disclosed except for these purposes. Section 64A, therefore, allows photographs and images of suspects detained at police stations to be taken and used for the purposes of the identification procedures in paragraphs 2.3 to 2.11.

2.34 Subject to paragraph 2.36 the photographs and images (and the negatives and all copies thereof) of suspects who have not been detained which are taken for the purposes of, or in connection with, the identification procedures in paragraphs 2.3 to 2.11 must be destroyed unless the suspect;

    (a) is charged with, or informed they may be prosecuted for, a recordable offence;

    (b) is prosecuted for a recordable offence;

    (c) is cautioned for a recordable offence or given a warning or reprimand in accordance with the Crime and Disorder Act 1998 for a recordable offence; or

    (d) gives informed consent in writing for the photograph or image to be retained for purposes described in paragraph 2.33.

2.35 When paragraph 2.34 requires the destruction of any photograph or image the person must be given an opportunity to witness the destruction or to have a certificate confirming the destruction provided that they so request within five days of being informed that the destruction is required.

2.36 Nothing in paragraph 2.34 affects any separate requirement under the Criminal Procedure and Investigations Act 1996 to retain material in connection with criminal investigations.

ANNEX A
VIDEO IDENTIFICATION

(a) General

130–017   1. The arrangements for obtaining and ensuring the availability of a suitable set of images to be used in a video identification must be the responsibility of an identification officer or identification officers who have no direct involvement with the relevant case.

2. The set of images must include the suspect and at least eight other people who so far as possible resemble the suspect in age, height, general appearance

and position in life. Only one suspect shall appear in any set unless there are two suspects of roughly similar appearance in which case they may be shown together with at least twelve other people.

3. The images used to conduct a video identification shall, as far as possible, show the suspect and other people in the same positions or carrying out the same sequence of movements. They shall also show the suspect and other people under identical conditions unless the identification officer reasonably believes:

(a) that because of the suspect's failure or refusal to co-operate or other reasons, it is not practicable for the conditions to be identical; and

(b) that any difference in the conditions would not direct a witness's attention to any individual image.

4. The reasons why identical conditions are not practicable shall be recorded on forms provided for the purpose.

5. Provision must be made for each person shown to be identified by number.

6. If police officers are shown, any numerals or other identifying badges must be concealed. If a prison inmate is shown, either as a suspect or not, then either all or none of the people shown should be in prison clothing.

7. The suspect or their solicitor, friend, or appropriate adult must be given a reasonable opportunity to see the complete set of images before it is shown to any witness. If the suspect has a reasonable objection to the set of images or any of the participants the suspect shall be asked to state the reasons for the objection. Steps shall, if practicable, be taken to remove the grounds for objection. If this is not practicable the suspect and/or their representative shall be told why their objections cannot be met and the objection, the reason given for it and why it cannot be met shall be recorded on forms provided for the purpose.

8. Before the images are shown in accordance with paragraph 7 the suspect or their solicitor shall be provided with details of the first description of the suspect by any witnesses who are to attend the video identification. Where a broadcast or publication is made, as in paragraph 3.30, the suspect or their solicitor must also be allowed to view any material released to the media by the police for the purpose of recognising or tracing the suspect provided it is practicable to do so and would not unreasonably delay the investigation.

9. The suspect's solicitor, where practicable, shall be given reasonable notification of the time and place that it is intended to conduct the video identification in order that a representative may attend on behalf of the suspect. If a solicitor has not been instructed, then this information shall be given to the suspect. The suspect may not be present when the images are shown to the witness(es). In the absence of a person representing the suspect the viewing itself shall be recorded on video. No unauthorised people may be present.

(b) Conducting the video identification

10. The identification officer is responsible for making the appropriate **130–018** arrangements to ensure that, before they see the set of images, witnesses are not able to communicate with each other about the case or overhear a witness who has already seen the material. There must be no discussion with the witness about the composition of the set of images and they must not be told whether a previous witness has made any identification.

11. Only one witness may see the set of images at a time. Immediately before the images are shown the witness shall be told that the person they saw on an earlier relevant occasion may or may not appear in the images they are shown and that if they cannot make a positive identification they should say so. The witness shall be advised that at any point they may ask to see a particular part of the set of images or to have a particular image frozen for them to study. Furthermore, it should be pointed out to the witness that there is no limit on

how many times they can view the whole set of images or any part of them. However, they should be asked not to make any decision as to whether the person they saw is on the set of images until they have seen the whole set at least twice.

12. Once the witness has seen the whole set of images at least twice and has indicated that they do not want to view the images or any part of them again, the witness shall be asked to say whether the individual they saw in person on an earlier occasion has been shown and, if so, to identify him or her by number of the image. The witness will then be shown that image to confirm the identification (see paragraph 17).

13. Care must be taken not to direct the witness's attention to any one individual image or to give any indication to the suspect's identity. Where a witness has previously made an identification by photographs, or a computerised or artist's composite likeness or similar likeness, the witness must not be reminded of such a photograph or composite likeness once a suspect is available for identification by other means in accordance with this Code. Neither must the witness be reminded of any description of the suspect.

14. After the procedure each witness shall be asked whether they have seen any broadcast or published films or photographs or any descriptions of suspects relating to the offence and their reply shall be recorded.

(c) Image security and destruction

130–019

15. Arrangements shall be made for all relevant material containing sets of images used for specific identification procedures to be kept securely and their movements accounted for. In particular, no-one involved in the investigation against the suspect shall be permitted to view the material prior to it being shown to any witness.

16. Paragraph 3.32 of this Code (Destruction and retention of photographs and images taken or used in identification procedures) shall apply to a set of images obtained in respect of a detained suspect and paragraph 3.33 shall apply in respect of a suspect who has not been detained.

(d) Documentation

130–020

17. A record must be made of all those participating in or seeing the set of images whose names are known to the police.

18. A record of the conduct of the video identification must be made on forms provided for the purpose. This shall include anything said by the witness about any identifications or the conduct of the procedure and any reasons why it was not practicable to comply with any of the provisions of this Code governing the conduct of video identifications.

ANNEX B
IDENTIFICATION PARADES

(a) General

130–021

1. A suspect must be given a reasonable opportunity to have a solicitor or friend present, and the suspect shall be asked to indicate on a second copy of the notice whether or not they wish to do so.

2. A identification parade may take place either in a normal room or in one equipped with a screen permitting witnesses to see members of the identification parade without being seen. The procedures for the composition and conduct of the identification parade are the same in both cases, subject to paragraph 8 below (except that an identification parade involving a screen may take place only

when the suspect's solicitor, friend or appropriate adult is present or the identification parade is recorded on video).

3. Before the identification parade takes place the suspect or their solicitor shall be provided with details of the first description of the suspect by any witnesses who are to attend the identification parade. Where a broadcast or publication is made as in paragraph 3.30, the suspect or their solicitor should also be allowed to view any material released to the media by the police for the purpose of recognising or tracing the suspect, provided it is practicable to do so and would not unreasonably delay the investigation.

(b) Identification parades involving prison inmates

4. If a prison inmate is required for identification, and there are no security **130–022** problems about the person leaving the establishment, they may be asked to participate in an identification parade or video identification.

5. An identification parade may be held in a Prison Department establishment but shall be conducted as far as practicable under normal identification parade rules. Members of the public shall make up the identification parade unless there are serious security or control objections to their admission to the establishment. In such cases, or if a group or video identification is arranged within the establishment, other inmates may participate. If an inmate is the suspect, they shall not be required to wear prison clothing for the identification parade unless the other people taking part are other inmates in similar clothing or are members of the public who are prepared to wear prison clothing for the occasion.

(c) Conduct of the identification parade

6. Immediately before the identification parade the suspect must be reminded **130–023** of the procedures governing its conduct and cautioned in the terms of paragraphs 10.5 or 10.6, as appropriate, of Code C.

7. All unauthorised people must be excluded from the place where the identification parade is held.

8. Once the identification parade has been formed everything afterwards in respect of it shall take place in the presence and hearing of the suspect and of any interpreter, solicitor, friend or appropriate adult who is present (unless the identification parade involves a screen, in which case everything said to or by any witness at the place where the identification parade is held must be said in the hearing and presence of the suspect's solicitor, friend or appropriate adult or be recorded on video).

9. The identification parade shall consist of at least eight people (in addition to the suspect) who so far as possible resemble the suspect in age, height, general appearance and position in life. One suspect only shall be included in an identification parade unless there are two suspects of roughly similar appearance, in which case they may be paraded together with at least twelve other people. In no circumstances shall more than two suspects be included in one identification parade and where there are separate identification parades they shall be made up of different people.

10. Where the suspect has an unusual physical feature, for example, a facial scar or tattoo or distinctive hairstyle or hair colour which cannot be replicated on other members of the identification parade steps may be taken to conceal the location of that feature on the suspect and the other members of the identification parade if the suspect and their solicitor or appropriate adult agree. For example, by use of a plaster or a hat, so that all members of the identification parade resemble each other in general appearance.

11. Where all members of a similar group are possible suspects separate identification parades shall be held for each member of the group unless there are two suspects of similar appearance when they may appear on the same identi-

fication parade with at least twelve other members of the group who are not suspects. Where police officers in uniform form an identification parade any numerals or other identifying badges shall be concealed.

12. When the suspect is brought to the place where the identification parade is to be held they shall be asked whether they have any objection to the arrangements for the identification parade or to any of the other participants in it and to state the reasons for the objection. The suspect may obtain advice from their solicitor or friend, if present, before the identification parade proceeds. If the suspect has a reasonable objection to the arrangements or any of the
The Codes of Practice—Code D
participants steps shall, where practicable, be taken to remove the grounds for objection. Where it is not practicable to do so, the suspect shall be told why their objections cannot be met and the objection, the reason given for it and why it cannot be met shall be recorded on forms provided for the purpose.

13. The suspect may select their own position in the line, but may not otherwise interfere with the order of the people forming the line. Where there is more than one witness the suspect must be told, after each witness has left the room, that they can if they wish change position in the line. Each position in the line must be clearly numbered, whether by means of a numeral laid on the floor in front of each identification parade member or by other means.

14. Appropriate arrangements must be made to ensure that, before witnesses attend the identification parade, they are not able to:

(i)   communicate with each other about the case or overhear a witness who has already seen the identification parade;
(ii) see any member of the identification parade;
(iii) see or be reminded of any photograph or description of the suspect or be given any other indication to the suspect's identity; or
(iv) see the suspect either before or after the identification parade.

15. The person conducting a witness to an identification parade must not discuss with them the composition of the identification parade and, in particular, must not disclose whether a previous witness has made any identification.

16. Witnesses shall be brought in one at a time. Immediately before the witness inspects the identification parade, the witness shall be told that the person they saw on an earlier relevant occasion specified by the identification officer or approved person (see paragraph 1.7) conducting the procedure may or may not be on the identification parade and that if they cannot make a positive identification they should say so. The witness must also be told that they should not make any decision as to whether the person they saw is on the identification parade until they have looked at each member of the identification parade at least twice.

17. When the identification officer or approved person conducting the identification procedure is satisfied that the witness has properly looked at each member of the identification parade, they shall ask the witness whether the person they saw on an earlier relevant occasion is on the identification parade and, if so, to indicate the number of the person concerned (see paragraph 28).

18. If the witness wishes to hear any identification parade member speak, adopt any specified posture or see an identification parade member move, the witness shall first be asked whether they can identify any person(s) on the identification parade on the basis of appearance only. When the request is to hear members of the identification parade speak, the witness shall be reminded that the participants in the identification parade have been chosen on the basis of physical appearance only. Members of the identification parade may then be asked to comply with the witness's request to hear them speak, to see them move or to adopt any specified posture.

19. If the witness requests that the person they have indicated remove any-

thing used for the purposes of paragraph 10 to conceal the location of an unusual physical feature, that person may be asked to remove it.

20. If the witness makes an identification after the identification parade has ended the suspect and, if present, their solicitor, interpreter or friend shall be informed. Where this occurs consideration should be given to allowing the witness a second opportunity to identify the suspect.

21 After the procedure each witness shall be asked whether they have seen any broadcast or published films or photographs or any descriptions of suspects relating to the offence and their reply shall be recorded.

22. When the last witness has left the suspect shall be asked whether they wish to make any comments on the conduct of the identification parade.

(d) Documentation

23. A video recording must normally be taken of the identification parade. **130–024** Where that is impracticable a colour photograph must be taken. A copy of the video recording or photograph shall be supplied on request to the suspect or their solicitor within a reasonable time.

24. Paragraph 3.32 or 3.33, as appropriate, (Destruction and retention of photographs and images taken or used in identification procedures) shall apply to any photograph or video taken in accordance with paragraph 23 above.

25. If the identification officer or approved person asks any person to leave an identification parade because they are interfering with its conduct the circumstances shall be recorded.

26. A record must be made of all those present at an identification parade whose names are known to the police.

27. If prison inmates make up an identification parade the circumstances must be recorded.

28. A record of the conduct of any identification parade must be made on forms provided for the purpose. This shall include anything said by the witness or the suspect about any identifications or the conduct of the procedure, and any reasons why it was not practicable to comply with any of the provisions of this Code.

ANNEX C
GROUP IDENTIFICATION

(a) General

1. The purpose of the provisions of this Annex is to ensure that, as far as **130–025** possible, group identifications follow the principles and procedures for identification parades so that the conditions are fair to the suspect in the way they test the witness's ability to make an identification.

2. Group identifications may take place either with the suspect's consent and co-operation or covertly without their consent.

3. The location of the group identification is a matter for the identification officer, although the officer may take into account any representations made by the suspect, appropriate adult, their solicitor or friend.

4. The place where the group identification is held should be one where other people are either passing by or waiting around informally, in groups such that the suspect is able to join them and be capable of being seen by the witness at the same time as others in the group. Examples include people leaving an escalator, pedestrians walking through a shopping centre, passengers on railway and bus stations, waiting in queues or groups or where people are standing or sitting in groups in other public places.

5. If the group identification is to be held covertly the choice of locations will be limited by the places where the suspect can be found and the number of other

people present at that time. In these cases suitable locations might be along regular routes travelled by the suspect, including buses or trains or public places frequented by the suspect.

6. Although the number, age, sex, race and general description and style of clothing of other people present at the location cannot be controlled by the identification officer, in selecting the location the officer must consider the general appearance and numbers of people likely to be present. In particular, the officer must reasonably expect that over the period the witness observes the group, they will be able to see, from time to time, a number of others (in addition to the suspect) whose appearance is broadly similar to that of the suspect.

7. A group identification need not be held if the identification officer believes that because of the unusual appearance of the suspect none of the locations which it would be practicable to use satisfy the requirements of paragraph 5 necessary to make the identification fair.

8. Immediately after a group identification procedure has taken place (with or without the suspect's consent) a colour photograph or a video should be taken of the general scene, where this is practicable, so as to give a general impression of the scene and the number of people present. Alternatively, if it is practicable, the group identification may be video recorded.

9. If it is not practicable to take the photograph or video in accordance with paragraph 8 a photograph or film of the scene should be taken later at a time determined by the identification officer if the officer considers that it is practicable to do so.

10. An identification carried out in accordance with this Code remains a group identification notwithstanding that at the time of being seen by the witness the suspect was on their own rather than in a group.

11. Before the group identification takes place the suspect or their solicitor should be provided with details of the first description of the suspect by any witnesses who are to attend the identification. Where a broadcast or publication is made, as in paragraph 3.30, the suspect or their solicitor should also be allowed to view any material released by the police to the media for the purposes of recognising or tracing the suspect provided that it is practicable to do so and would not unreasonably delay the investigation.

12. After the procedure each witness shall be asked whether they have seen any broadcast or published films or photographs or any descriptions of suspects relating to the offence and their reply shall be recorded.

(b) Identification with the consent of the suspect

130–026   13. A suspect must be given a reasonable opportunity to have a solicitor or friend present. The suspect shall be asked to indicate on a second copy of the notice whether or not they wish to do so.

14. The witness, the person carrying out the procedure and suspect's solicitor, appropriate adult, friend or any interpreter for the witness may be concealed from the sight of the individuals in the group which they are observing if the person carrying out the procedure considers that this facilitates the conduct of the identification.

15. The person conducting a witness to a group identification must not discuss with the witness the forthcoming group identification and, in particular, must not disclose whether a previous witness has made any identification.

16. Anything said to or by the witness during the procedure regarding the identification should be said in the presence and hearing of those present at the procedure.

17. Appropriate arrangements must be made to ensure that, before witnesses attend the identification parade, they are not able to:

   (i)   communicate with each other about the case or overhear a witness who has already been given an opportunity to see the suspect in the group;

  (ii)   see the suspect; or

 (iii)   see or be reminded of any photographs or description of the suspect or be given any other indication of the suspect's identity.

18. Witnesses shall be brought to the place where they are to observe the group one at a time. Immediately before the witness is asked to look at the group the person conducting the procedure shall tell the witness that the person they saw may or may not be in the group and that if they cannot make a positive identification they should say so. The witness shall then be asked to observe the group in which the suspect is to appear. The way in which the witness should do this will depend on whether the group is moving or stationary.

Moving group

19. When the group in which the suspect is to appear is moving, for example **130–027** leaving an escalator, the provisions of paragraphs 20 to 24 below should be followed.

20. If two or more suspects consent to a group identification each should be the subject of separate identification procedures. These may however be conducted consecutively on the same occasion.

21. The person conducting the procedure shall tell the witness to observe the group and ask the witness to point out any person they think they saw on the earlier relevant occasion.

22. Once the witness has been informed in accordance with paragraph 21 the suspect should be allowed to take whatever position in the group that they wish.

23. When the witness points out a person in accordance with paragraph 21 the witness shall, if it is practicable, be asked to take a closer look at the person to confirm the identification. If this is not practicable, or the witness is unable to confirm the identification, the witness shall be asked how sure they are that the person they have indicated is the relevant person.

24. The witness should continue to observe the group for the period which the person conducting the procedure reasonably believes is necessary in the circumstances for the witness to be able to make comparisons between the suspect and other individuals of broadly similar appearance to the suspect in accordance with paragraph 5.

Stationary groups

25. When the group in which the suspect is to appear is stationary, for **130–028** example people waiting in a queue, the provisions of paragraphs 26 to 29 below should be followed.

26. If two or more suspects consent to a group identification each should be the subject of separate identification procedures unless they are of broadly similar appearance when they may appear in the same group. Where separate group identifications are held the groups must be made up of different persons.

27. The suspect may take whatever position in the group that they wish. Where there is more than one witness the suspect must be told, out of the sight and hearing of any witness, that they can, if they wish, change their position in the group.

28. The witness shall be asked to pass along or amongst the group and to look at each person in the group at least twice, taking as much care and time as is possible according to the circumstances, before making an identification. Once the witness has done this they shall be asked whether the person they saw on an earlier relevant occasion is in the group and to indicate any such person by whatever means the person conducting the procedure considers appropriate in

the circumstances. If this is not practicable the witness shall be asked to point out any person they think they saw on the earlier relevant occasion.

29. When the witness makes an indication in accordance with paragraph 28 arrangements shall be made, if it is practicable, for the witness to take a closer look at the person to confirm the identification. If this is not practicable, or the witness is unable to confirm the identification, the witness shall be asked how sure they are that the person they have indicated is the relevant person.

All cases

30. If the suspect unreasonably delays joining the group, or having joined the group, deliberately conceals him or herself from the sight of the witness, this may be treated as a refusal to co-operate in a group identification.

31. If the witness identifies a person other than the suspect that person should be informed what has happened and asked if they are prepared to give their name and address. There is no obligation upon any member of the public to give these details. There shall be no duty to record any details of any other member of the public present in the group or at the place where the procedure is conducted.

32. When the group identification has been completed the suspect shall be asked whether they wish to make any comments on the conduct of the procedure.

33. If the suspect has not been previously informed they shall be told of any identifications made by the witnesses.

(c) **Identification without suspect's consent**

130–029
34. Group identifications held covertly without the suspect's consent should, so far as is practicable, follow the rules for conduct of group identification by consent.

35. A suspect has no right to have a solicitor, appropriate adult or friend present as the identification will, of necessity, take place without the knowledge of the suspect.

36. Any number of suspects may be identified at the same time.

(d) **Identifications in police stations**

130–030
37. Group identifications should only take place in police stations for reasons of safety, security or because it is impracticable to hold them elsewhere.

38. The group identification may take place either in a room equipped with a screen permitting witnesses to see members of the group without being seen, or anywhere else in the police station that the identification officer considers appropriate.

39. Any of the additional safeguards applicable to identification parades should be followed if the identification officer considers it is practicable to do so in the circumstances.

(e) **Identifications involving prison inmates**

130–031
40. A group identification involving a prison inmate may only be arranged in the prison or at a police station.

41. Where a group identification takes place involving a prison inmate, whether in a prison or in a police station, the arrangements should follow those in paragraphs 37 to 39 of this Annex. If a group identification takes place within a prison other inmates may participate. If an inmate is the suspect they should not be required to wear prison clothing for the group identification unless the other persons taking part are wearing the same clothing.

(f) Documentation

42. Where a photograph or video is taken in accordance with paragraph 8 or **130–032** 9 a copy of the photograph or video shall be supplied on request to the suspect or their solicitor within a reasonable time.

43. Paragraph 3.32 or 3.33 of this Code, as appropriate, (Destruction and retention of photographs and images taken or used in identification procedures) shall apply where the photograph or film taken in accordance with paragraph 8 or 9 above includes the suspect.

44. A record of the conduct of any group identification must be made on forms provided for the purpose. This shall include anything said by the witness or the suspect about any identifications or the conduct of the procedure and any reasons why it was not practicable to comply with any of the provisions of this Code governing the conduct of group identifications.

ANNEX D
CONFRONTATION BY A WITNESS

1. Before the confrontation takes place the witness must be told that the **130–033** person they saw may or may not be the person they are to confront and that if he or she is not that person then the witness should say so.

2. Before the confrontation takes place the suspect or their solicitor shall be provided with details of the first description of the suspect given by any witness who is to attend the confrontation. Where a broadcast or publication is made, as in paragraph 3.30, the suspect or their solicitor should also be allowed to view any material released by the police to the media for the purposes of recognising or tracing the suspect provided that it is practicable to do so and would not unreasonably delay the investigation.

3. Force may not be used to make the face of the suspect visible to the witness.

4. Confrontation must take place in the presence of the suspect's solicitor, interpreter or friend unless this would cause unreasonable delay.

5. The suspect shall be confronted independently by each witness, who shall be asked 'Is this the person?'. If the witness identifies the person but is unable to confirm the identification, the witness shall be asked how sure they are that the person is the person they saw on the earlier relevant occasion.

6. The confrontation should normally take place in the police station, either in a normal room or in one equipped with a screen permitting a witness to see the suspect without being seen. In both cases the procedures are the same except that a room equipped with a screen may be used only when the suspect's solicitor, friend or appropriate adult is present or the confrontation is recorded on video.

7. After the procedure each witness shall be asked whether they have seen any broadcast or published films or photographs or any descriptions of suspects relating to the offence and their reply shall be recorded.

ANNEX E
SHOWING OF PHOTOGRAPHS

(a) Action

1. An officer of the rank of sergeant or above shall be responsible for super- **130–034** vising and directing the showing of photographs. The actual showing may be done by a constable or an approved person (see paragraph 1.7).

2. The supervising officer must confirm that the first description of the suspect given by the witness has been recorded before the witness is shown the photo-

graphs. If the supervising officer is unable to confirm that the description has been recorded the officer shall postpone the showing.

3. Only one witness shall be shown photographs at any one time. Each witness shall be given as much privacy as practicable and shall not be allowed to communicate with any other witness in the case.

4. The witness shall be shown not less than twelve photographs at a time, which shall, as far as possible, all be of a similar type.

5. When the witness is shown the photographs they shall be told that the photograph of the person they saw may or may not be amongst them and that if they cannot make a positive identification they should say so. The witness shall also be told that they should not make a decision until they have viewed at least twelve photographs. The witness shall not be prompted or guided in any way but shall be left to make any selection without help.

6. If a witness makes a positive identification from photographs then, unless the person identified is otherwise eliminated from enquiries or is not available, other witnesses shall not be shown photographs. But both they and the witness who has made the identification shall be asked to attend a video identification, an identification parade or group identification unless there is no dispute about the identification of the suspect.

7. If the witness makes a selection but is unable to confirm the identification, the person showing the photographs shall ask the witness how sure they are that the photograph they have indicated is the person that they saw on the earlier relevant occasion.

8. Where the use of a computerised or artist's composite likeness or similar likeness has led to there being a known suspect who can be asked to participate in a video identification, appear on an identification parade or participate in a group identification, that likeness shall not be shown to other potential witnesses.

9. Where a witness attending a video identification, an identification parade or group identification has previously been shown photographs or computerised or artist's composite likeness or similar likeness (and it is the responsibility of the officer in charge of the investigation to make the identification officer aware that this is the case), then the suspect and their solicitor must be informed of this fact before the video identification, identification parade, or group identification takes place.

10. None of the photographs shown shall be destroyed, whether or not an identification is made, since they may be required for production in court. The photographs shall be numbered and a separate photograph taken of the frame or part of the album from which the witness made an identification as an aid to reconstituting it.

(b) Documentation

130–035   11. Whether or not an identification is made, a record shall be kept of the showing of photographs on forms provided for the purpose. This shall include anything said by the witness about any identification or the conduct of the procedure, any reasons why it was not practicable to comply with any of the provisions of this Code governing the showing of photographs and the name and rank of the supervising officer.

12. The supervising officer shall inspect and sign the record as soon as practicable.

Civil Procedure Rules 1998

· · · · · ·

PART 54

JUDICIAL REVIEW

Scope and Interpretation

54—(1) This Part contains rules about judicial review.　　　　**131–001**
(2) In this Part—

  (a) a "claim for judicial review" means a claim to review the lawfulness
    of—

    (i) an enactment; or
    (ii) a decision, action or failure to act in relation to the exercise of a
       public function.

  (b) an order of mandamus is called a "mandatory order";
  (c) an order of prohibition is called a "prohibiting order";
  (d) an order of certiorari is called a "quashing order"
  (e) "the judicial review procedure" means the Part 8 procedure as modi-
    fied by this Part;
  (f) "interested party" means any person (other than the claimant and
    defendant) who is directly affected by the claim; and
  (g) "court" means the High Court, unless otherwise stated.

(Rule 8.1(6)(b) provides that a rule or practice direction may, in relation to a
specified type of proceedings, disapply or modify any of the rules set out in Part
8 as they apply to those proceedings)

When This Part Must Be Used

54.2 The judicial review procedure must be used in a claim for judicial review **131–002**
where the claimant is seeking—

  (a) a mandatory order;
  (b) a prohibiting order;
  (c) a quashing order; or
  (d) an injunction under section 30 of the Supreme Court Act 1981(1)
    (restraining a person from acting in any office in which he is not
    entitled to act).

When this Part May Be Used

54.3—(1) The judical review procedure may be used in a claim for judicial **131–003**
review where the claimant is seeking—

  (a) a declaration; or
  (b) an injunction.
    (Section 31(2) of the Supreme Court Act 1981 sets out the circum-
    stances in which the court may grant a declaration or injuction in a
    claim for judicial review).
      (Where the claimant is seeking a declaration of injunction in addition
    to one of the remedies listed in rule 54.2, the judicial review procedure
    must be used).

(2) A claim for judicial review may include a claim for damages but many not seek damages alone.

sectgion 31(4) of the Supreme Court Act 1981 sets out the circumstances in which the court may award damages on a claim for judicial review).

Permission Required

131–004 **54.4** The court's permission to proceed is required in a claim for judicial review whether started under this Part or transferred to the Administrative Court.

Time Limit for Filing Claim Form

131–005 **54.5**—(1) The claim form must be filed—

    (a) promptly; and
    (b) in any event not later than 3 months after the grounds to make the claim first arose.

(2) The time limit in this rule may not be extended by agreement between the parties.

(3) This rule does not apply when any other enactment specifies a shorter time limit for making the claim for judicial review.

Claim Form

131–006 **54.6**—(1) In addition to the matters set out in rule 8.2 (contents of the claim form) the claimant must also state—

    a. the name and address of any person he considers to be an interested party;
    b. that he is requesting permission to proceed with a claim for judicial review; and
    c. any remedy (including any interim remedy) he is claiming.

(Part 25 sets out how to apply for an interim remedy)

(2) The claim form must be accompanied by the documents required by the relevant practice direction.

Service of Claim Form

131–007 **54.7** The claim form must be served on—

    (a) the defendant; and
    (b) unless the court otherwise directs, any person the claimant considers to be an interested party,

within 7 days after the date of issue.

Acknowledgment of Service

131–008 **54.8**—(1) Any person served with the claim form who wishes to take part in the judicial review must file an acknowledgment of service in the relevant practice form in accordance with the following provisions of this rule.

(2) Any acknowledgment of service must be—

    (a) filed not more than 21 days after service of the claim form; and
    (b) served on—

(i) the claimant; and

(ii) subject to any direction under rule 54.7(b), any other person named in the claim form, as soon as practicable and, in any event, not later than 7 days after it is filed.

(3) The time limits under this rule may not be extended by agreement between the parties.

(4) The acknowledgment of service—

(a) must—

(i) where the person filing it intends to contest the claim, set out a summary of his grounds for doing so; and

(ii) state the name and address of any person the person filing it considers to be an interested party; and

(b) may include or be accompanied by an application for directions.

(5) Rule 10.3(2) does not apply.

Failure to file acknowledgent of service

54.9—(1) Where a person served with the claim form has failed to file an acknowledgment of service in accordance with rule 54.8, he— **131–009**

(a) may not take part in a hearing to decide whether permission should be given unless the court allows him to do so; but

(b) provided he complies with rule 54.14 or any other direction of the court regarding the filing and service of—

(i) detailed grounds for contesting the claim or supporting it on additional grounds; and

(ii) any written evidence,

may take part in the hearing of the judicial review.

(2) Where that person takes part in the hearing of the judicial review, the court may take his failure to file an acknowledgment of service into account when deciding what order to make about costs.

(3) Rule 8.4 does not apply.

Permission Given

54.10—(1) Where permission to proceed is given the court may also give directions **131–010**

(2) Directions under paragraph (1) may include a stay of proceedings to which the claim relates.

(Rule 3.7 provides a sanction for the non-payment of the fee payable when permission to proceed has been given).

Service of Order Giving or Refusing Permission

54.11 The court will serve— **131–011**

(a) the order giving or refusing permission; and

(b) any directions, on—

    (i) the claimant;
    (ii) the defendant; and
    (iii) any other person who filed an acknowledgment of service.

Permission Decision Without a Hearing

131–012   **54.12**—(1) This rule applies where the court, without a hearing—

(a) refuses permission to proceed; or
(b) gives permission to proceed—

    (i) subject to conditions; or
    (ii) on certain grounds only.

(2) The court will serve its reasons for making the decision when it serves the order giving or refusing permission in accordance with rule 54.11.

(3) The claimant may not appeal but may request the decision to be reconsidered at a hearing.

(4) A request under paragraph (3) must be filed within 7 days after service of the reasons under paragraph (2).

(5) The claimant, defendant and any other person who has filed an acknowledgment of service will be given at least 2 days' notice of the hearing date.

Defendant etc. May Not Apply to Set Aside

131–013   **54.13** Neither the defendant nor any other person served with the claim form may apply to set aside an order giving permission to proceed.

Response

131–014   **54.14**—(1) A defendant and any other person served with the claim form who wishes to contest the claim or support it on additional grounds must file and serve—

(a) detailed grounds for contesting the claim or supporting it on additional grounds; and
(b) any written evidence,
    within 35 days after service of the order giving permission.

(2) The following rules do not apply—

(a) rule 8.5 (3) and 8.5 (4)(defendant to file and serve written evidence at the same time as acknowledgment of service); and
(b) rule 8.5 (5) and 8.5(6) (claimant to file and serve any reply within 14 days).

Where Claimant Seeks to Rely on Additional Grounds

131–015   **54.15** The court's permission is required if a claimant seeks to rely on grounds other than those for which he has been given permission to proceed.

Evidence

131–016   **54.16**—(1) Rule 8.6 does not apply.
(2) No written evidence may be relied on unless—

(a) it has been served in accordance with any—

(i) rule under this Part; or
(ii) direction of the court; or

(b) the court gives permission.

Court's Powers to Hear Any Person

54.17—(1) Any person may apply for permission— **131–017**

(a) to file evidence; or
(b) make representations at the hearing of the judicial review.

(2) An application under paragraph (1) should be made promptly.

Judicial Review May be Decided Without a Hearing

54.18 The court may decide the claim for judicial review without a hearing **131–018**
where all the parties agree.

Court's Powers in Respect of Quashing Orders

54.19—(1) This rule applies where the court makes a quashing order in **131–019**
respect of the decision to which the claim relates.
(2) The court may—

(a) remit the matter to the decision-maker; and
(b) direct it to reconsider the matter and reach a decision in accordance
with the judgment of the court.

(3) Where the court considers that there is no purpose to be served in remitting
the matter to the decision-maker it may, subject to any statutory provision, take
the decision itself.
(Where a statutory power is given to a tribunal, person or other body it may
be the case that the court cannot take the decision itself).

Transfer

54.20 The court may **131–020**

a. order a claim to continue as if it had not been started under this Part;
and
b. where it does so, give directions about the future management of the
claim.

(Part 30 (transfer) applies to transfers to and from the Administrative Court).

INDEX